Volume III covers the period from 1798 to the end of 1801. The complete text, in five volumes of about 700 pages each, will take the correspondence up to 1810. A comprehensive subject index will be included in the final volume.

This is the third volume of the standard edition of the later correspondence of George III. The edition begins where Sir John Fortescue's edition of the earlier correspondence ended.

Each volume contains a general introduction to the period covered by the letters, and the letters themselves are annotated. They have been selected from a number of sources (including the private papers of the King, Queen Charlotte, and other members of the royal family). Professor Aspinall has permission to publish a number of key letters which are still in private hands, as well as many in public archives. All known surviving letters of any real importance, with the exception of some of those already in print, are included.

THE LATER
CORRESPONDENCE
OF
GEORGE III

IN FIVE VOLUMES

VOLUME III

THE LATER
CORRESPONDENCE
OF
GEORGE III

PUBLISHED BY AUTHORITY OF
HER MAJESTY QUEEN ELIZABETH II

EDITED BY
A. ASPINALL c.v.o.

Emeritus Professor of Modern History in the University of Reading

IN FIVE VOLUMES
VOLUME III
JANUARY 1798 TO DECEMBER 1801

CAMBRIDGE
AT THE UNIVERSITY PRESS
1967

Published by the Syndics of the Cambridge University Press
Bentley House, 200 Euston Road, London N.W.1
American Branch: 32 East 57th Street, New York, N.Y. 10022

© Cambridge University Press 1967

Library of Congress Catalogue Card Number: 62–52516

Printed in Great Britain
at the University Printing House, Cambridge
(Brooke Crutchley, University Printer)

PREFACE

THE publication of this volume, six years after the appearance of the first, enables me to refer to one or two of the more important points raised by reviewers. First, I should like to say that I regret as much as anyone the omission of practically all the King's letters that had already appeared in such volumes as Stanhope's *Pitt* and Holland Rose's *Pitt and Napoleon*. The cost of including them was deemed to add excessively to the cost of an already very expensive project. It has, however, been suggested that space could have been found for these important omitted letters by leaving out a considerable number of new ones of a trivial nature. The short answer, again, is that I was bound by my instructions to publish practically everything in the King's papers in the Royal Archives, and this, I am confident, is being done. Therefore, the suggestion that has been made, that a whole series of letters from the King to the Duke of York has been omitted, is fantastic. That the King did write to him, and write frequently, whilst he was abroad (and to his other sons and to the Princess Royal also) is clear enough—but these letters are not in the Royal Archives. They have long since been either destroyed or lost; from time to time some of them may reappear in sale-room catalogues.

In one trifling respect this volume differs from its predecessors. A very few letters to or from the Prince and Princess of Wales and others relating to their affairs, of themselves of small importance, have been omitted on the ground that they will be published in *The Correspondence of George, Prince of Wales* by Cassells. Hitherto this wasteful duplication was unavoidable.

A few British Museum letters which reached the printer too late for insertion in their proper places are printed on pages 642–3. References to some British Museum letters in footnotes in this and succeeding volumes may be incomplete or provisional: the folio numbers of some volumes recently acquired or made available to scholars may be changed.

On page 196 (note 1) the question is raised whether the King arranged his papers at a time when his sight was failing. It is worth noting that on Tuesday, 19 September 1809, when the King replied verbally, in a preliminary way, to the Cabinet's Minute of the previous day, Perceval having gone to see him at Windsor, 'he mentioned his having preserved every political paper that had come into his hands during his reign; that he had already arranged all of them from the time of Mr Pitt's first coming into office, so that he could lay his hand at once upon any one; and he was now employed in arranging all of the antecedent period; and that it was hard work, as he was obliged to stand by all the time, etc.' This is Speaker Abbot's account, as given him by Perceval (Colchester, *Diary and Correspondence*, II, 217, though the King's conversation is there attributed wrongly, to Monday the 18th). At the moment the King was particularly anxious to find Pitt's letter of 1801 in which, said the King, he had undertaken never again to bring forward the Catholic question during the King's reign. (Apparently he was looking for a letter

(v)

that did not exist, but it is just possible that he was thinking of a letter written in similar terms by George Rose at Pitt's suggestion, though this letter, too, is not in the Archives. See Rose, *Diaries and Correspondence*, I, 360.) Perceval, writing to Lord Liverpool on 19 September, 1809, after referring to this search, went on: 'The King...then digressed into an account of his papers. He was arranging them all regularly—that up to 1802 they were quite perfect—& from the commencement of the late Administration to August last, and that from that period he could turn to any paper in a minute—but he said he should find Mr Pitt's paper—it was an express assurance.' (Perceval MSS.)

Again it is my pleasant duty to express my thanks to Mr Mackworth-Young, M.V.O., Her Majesty's Librarian for the valuable assistance and advice which he has given me; also, to Miss Jane Langton, Registrar of the Archives, who has answered many queries most helpfully. The Rev. S.B.-R. Poole has been good enough to read the proofs of this volume and make many useful suggestions for footnotes. To the Staff of the British Museum and the Public Record Office, to mention only two great institutions, every scholar owes a debt of gratitude.

Finally, I again express thanks to all the owners of MSS. which are quoted in this volume, either in the text or in footnotes, for my indebtedness to them; and also to the Syndics and staff of the Cambridge University Press.

A. ASPINALL

Highlands,
Belle Vue,
Maughold,
Isle of Man

CONTENTS

CORRIGENDA AND ADDENDA
TO VOLUME II

Page 8, note 1, *for* 1796 *read* 1792.

Page 36, note 2 should read: 'Lieutenant-General Sir William Erskine (1728–95), who served in the army for about 53 years. Knighted, 1763; *cr.* Baronet, 28 July 1791.' Major-General Sir William Erskine was his son.

Page 56, line 2, *for* bets *read* begs.

Page 94, line 7, *read* the Dutch at Menin at which.

Page 94, line 10 should probably *read* 'with very visible mark[s]'. The Prince's 'hasty scawl' is hardly legible at times.

Page 137, note 1, and Index, *read* (1730–95).

Page 138, note 4, and Index, *read* (1739–1818).

Page 241, note. It is worth noting that the Calendars for 1804 mention for the first time the Rev. Wm. Harry Edward Bentinck as one of the four Chief Clerks of the Signet.

Page 277, note 1, line 4, *read* 1798–1801.

Page 286, note 2, line 2, *read* Treasurer.

Page 307, note 3, line 2. Full-stop after 1799.

Page 335, line 13, *read* degrees.

Page 410, note 1, line 3, *read* reversion.

Page 438, note 3, line 2, *for* 1815 *read* 1817.

Page 473, No. 1393. The MS. is not clear, but the date of the letter should be the 7th. *See The Corresp. of George, Prince of Wales*, III, 182 n.

Page 482, line 18, *read* to leave to chance that.

Page 484, line 7, *read* averr[*sic*].

Page 485, line 10, *read* jealousy

Page 508, note 1, line 2, *read* Bathurst.

Page 539, note 3, line 3, *read* by means.

Page 547, No. 1509, line 6, *read* Amendment.

Page 592, No. 1574, heading of the letter, *read* WURTEMBERG.

Page 653, line 17, *read* Brodrick.

Page 655, *read* Charles Francis Greville.

Garth, Thomas, *read* (1744–1829).
William, Duke of Clarence (1765–1837).

The dates of birth and death may usefully be added to the following:
Harcourt, Duc d' (1728–1802).
Jacobi, Constans Philipp Wilhelm, Baron von Klösst (1745–1817).
Lascelles, Francis (1744–99).
Münster, Count (1766–1839).
Nagel (1756–1851).
Panin (1771–1837).
Zeppelin (1767–1801).

Volume I has recently been reprinted with some minor corrections.

INTRODUCTION

THE present volume of the King's correspondence covers the last four years of the war against Revolutionary France and the first few months of the uneasy peace which began with the signing of the preliminary treaty in London on 1 October 1801. The year 1798 opened with the country in a dangerous, depressing and humiliating situation. The finances were in disarray, the Budget unbalanced, the currency depreciated, a mutinous spirit still pervading parts of the Channel Fleet. Ireland was on the brink of rebellion and ready to welcome an invading army. The First Coalition had collapsed, Prussia having made peace in 1795, and Austria in 1797 on terms which left France dominant in Italy and in possession of the left bank of the Rhine; and Pitt's peace overtures had been rejected, even though he had offered to recognise the Republic's continental conquests and to restore the French 'sugar' islands in the West Indies. Britain was carrying on the struggle virtually alone, and Dundas told Pitt, 'It is obvious that there is nothing to be done abroad to occupy any Office for a single hour of the day, and that the war...is almost exclusively a war for the defence of Great Britain and Ireland.'

The death of Frederick William II of Prussia on 16 November 1797, however, and the accession of his son as Frederick William III, seemed to open up possibilities of creating a new alliance against France. Pitt thought that if the remaining Sovereigns of Europe failed to lay aside their mutual jealousies, and to seize what was probably their last chance, their thrones would be taken from under them and they would fall a prey to the common enemy. 'If they are true to themselves,' he said, 'Europe will still be saved.' Success largely depended on the willingness of the new King to abandon his father's policy of neutrality and to dismiss Haugwitz, his chief Minister, who had been responsible for the Treaty of Basle in 1795. It was hoped in London that the Duke of Brunswick, whose influence over Frederick William was believed to be considerable, would go to Berlin and exert his influence to bring about the dismissal of Haugwitz and the negotiation of a Quadruple Alliance Treaty. As a preliminary step the British Government sent M. de Luc, a scholar of some repute whose family came from Geneva, and who had long been a member of the Royal Household as reader to Queen Charlotte, on a secret mission to Brunswick (though ostensibly to take up the post of Professor of Natural History in the University of Göttingen) with the idea of enlisting the Duke's support for this new diplomatic approach. De Luc and his friend General de Stamfort, who had served successively in the Prussian and Dutch armies before settling down in Brunswick as the Duke's confidential adviser, easily persuaded the Duke to go to Berlin. But the prerequisites of success were wanting. Prussia lacked the financial resources for another struggle; the peace party at Court, headed by Haugwitz and strongly supported by Prince Henry of Prussia, Frederick the Great's brother, was too powerful to be shaken: and, too, the traditional antagonism with Austria persisted. Subsequent Four-Power negotiations at Berlin came to nothing

(xi)

(financial arrangements with Austria presented one difficulty) but renewed aggressions by the Directory led to the formation of the Second Coalition—of Great Britain, Austria and Russia in 1799. The Tsar Paul was exasperated by French action in expelling from Malta the Knights of the Order of St John of Jerusalem, of which he was Grand Master, and Austria was again roused to arms by French interference in Switzerland, the dethronement of Charles Emmanuel of Savoy, and the conquest of Naples. On 25 March 1799 the Archduke Charles defeated Jourdan at Stockach in Swabia, drove the French back across the Rhine, and invaded, in order to liberate, Switzerland, whilst General Kray in Italy defeated General Schérer at Magnano. Then the Russians joined in, Suvoroff routing in quick succession three French armies under Moreau, McDonald and Joubert, and virtually expelling the enemy from Italy. But effective co-operation between the two continental allies was lacking, with the result that the French were soon able to retrieve the situation, Masséna and Soult routing the armies of Korsakow and Hotze respectively; and Suvoroff had to retreat from Switzerland. An Anglo-Russian force was sent to recover Holland, though Dundas doubted whether success was possible without Prussian co-operation, and this was not forthcoming. The capture of the Dutch fleet was the only real achievement. Thus were destroyed the high hopes entertained by Ministers at the beginning of the parliamentary session of 1799 that Europe's deliverance was at hand. Canning had echoed the opinions of many of his colleagues in expressing the belief that 'the accursed Republic' would be completely destroyed, leaving no trace but in the memory of its outrages and the example of its punishment.

Diplomatic activities by Lord Minto at Vienna (he having replaced the ineffective Sir Morton Eden) and by William Wickham in Switzerland and the South German States, including Wurtemberg; together with Lord Mulgrave's military mission to the Continent, failed to avert the collapse of the Second Coalition. Bonaparte escaped from Egypt, returned to France, overthrew the discredited Directory in November 1799, and made himself master of the country. His peace overtures to Britain in December were contemptuously rejected by Pitt and Grenville, and the King spoke with hatred and venom of the 'Corsican tyrant'. Bonaparte defeated the Austrians under Melas at Marengo in June 1800; in December the Archduke John was overwhelmed by Moreau at Hohenlinden, and the Emperor was compelled to make peace at Lunéville in February 1801. On the other hand, the Northern League which had been formed against England under the auspices of the Tsar in order to enforce their doctrine of the freedom of the seas as opposed to the traditional British doctrine of the right to search neutral ships for contraband of war, speedily collapsed after Nelson's victory over the Danish fleet at Copenhagen and the assassination of the lunatic Paul I.

Ministers had their hands full with pressing domestic problems too. The Duke of Portland, the Home Secretary, was preoccupied with the treasonable activities of the United Irishmen, the trials of O'Connor and his associates at Maidstone, the suppression of the Irish Rebellion, and the partial destruction of the violent and factious opposition in the Irish Parliament to the Union Bill. Cornwallis, who took over from Camden the Lord Lieutenancy of Ireland in 1798 in order to cope with the Rebellion, was almost as much disgusted at having to make use of corruption on a large scale to overcome the opposition of the politicians as he had been with the methods of terrorism employed to put down rebellion. He saw in the union of the two Legislatures the best hope for a contented and prosperous Ireland, especially if the Catholics could be conciliated by generous measures of concession in the matter of tithes, financial provision for the priesthood, and the removal of political disabilities. Opposition to such statesmanlike proposals, as he said, was contrary to common sense, 'but common sense is not in the habit of operating strongly upon people's minds on this side of St George's Channel, and when the interests of the country and private advantage take opposite sides, the latter is pretty sure of obtaining the victory'.

Finance gave Pitt less cause for anxiety than these other problems. The response of the nation to his appeal for voluntary contributions in 1798 was reasonably satisfactory; so were the terms on which he then raised a new loan of fifteen millions; and the sale of the land tax promised to reduce the burden of interest payments. The graduated income tax which he introduced in 1799 soon became the sheet-anchor of all war-time Budgets. By the end of April 1798 Pitt found the state of things greatly improved since the dark days of 1797. 'The spirit and courage of the country has risen so as to be fairly equal to the crisis.'

Pitt's parliamentary difficulties during these years were negligible. Fox admitted that the old Whig party was too much routed and dispersed to be rallied again. The 'old, worn-out jaded Opposition' ('the broken parts of a skeleton' was Addington's description) had to regain the confidence of the nation before anything substantial could be accomplished; and Fox's condemnation of the war, his rejoicings at French victories, his support of parliamentary reform and his advocacy of Catholic relief were not calculated to endear him to that part of public opinion which mattered. True, he regretted Bonaparte's manner of extinguishing the ancient Republic of Venice and his *coup d'état* of Brumaire (November 1799), but, he said, 'I have forgiven him and am willing to think him one of the best, as I am sure he is the greatest of men'. 'He certainly has surpassed...Alexander and Caesar, not to mention the great advantage he has over them in a cause he fights in.'

The Whig secession, of course, was never complete, though Tierney and William Smith were the only leading members of Opposition to attend the protracted debates on the Income Tax Bill. Sheridan appeared in the House on 20 April 1798 to oppose the suspension of the Habeas Corpus Act. Charles Grey too was present, but he neither spoke nor voted; and Fox declared, 'I mean to get quite rid of politics'. 'I see little prospect of good', said Lord John Russell (soon to become sixth Duke of Bedford). 'There is nothing cheering, nothing consolatory. Our horizon is dark and gloomy.' The secession he spoke of as 'rash, ill-judged, ill-advised and ever-to-be-lamented'. The point has sometimes been made that if the Whigs despaired of Parliament and thought that no good was to be done by attending the debates, they should have resigned their seats, since their absence meant the virtual disfranchisement of their constituents. On the other hand, many Whig members sat for nomination boroughs and were not troubled with an excessive number of constituents. Lord John Russell said that he had only one.

The feebleness of such opposition groups as still existed[1] accounts only partly for the strength of both Pitt and Addington. The support of the Crown was also of very great importance. Both Prime Ministers were the Ministers of the King's own choice, and, consequently, deserving of support in Parliament. The people were deeply attached to the Monarchy; republican feeling was insignificant, and their devotion to the King increased as they became painfully aware of his increasing disabilities. As Whitbread said later, in no times and in no circumstances had the people of any country been more loyal or more affectionately attached to their Sovereign than the people of this country over a long period of years. 'The King's Minister,' said Fox, after peace had been made at Amiens, 'be he who he may, is, in peace at least, all-powerful. Whether or not, in case of war, the universal apprehension of mischief from the weakness of these men, if such apprehension was supported by junctions of different parties, could do anything, may be more of a question, but even in that case...I think the Crown, in earnest, would beat all.' That the King ultimately failed (1804) to maintain in office his favourite Minister, was partly due to the fact that he himself had come to realise Addington's inadequacy as a War Minister. And such occasional weakness in numbers in the Commons as Addington was destined to experience, was partly due to doubts about the King's health—for a prolonged bout of insanity would mean, virtually, a change of Sovereign, a new reign.

Pitt had to encounter more difficulties in the Cabinet than in the House of Commons. His team was less united than it had been. Some of Dundas's colleagues, especially Windham, had no confidence in his capacity as Secretary of State for War to organise the country's defences against the probabilities of a French landing in Ireland during the early months of 1798. This particular threat, however, passed away as the Directory accepted Bonaparte's advice to conquer Egypt if not India too: a move countered by the Admiralty's bold decision, taken at a time when the destination of the Toulon fleet was unknown, to send a fleet again into the Mediterranean, and by Nelson's spectacular victory in Aboukir Bay. After the failure of the Helder expedition Dundas asked to be relieved of his office of Secretary of State and suggested that Pitt's brother Lord Chatham should succeed him: and, being dissatisfied with the Admiralty's arrangements for the despatch of that expedition, Dundas asked Pitt to remove Lord Spencer from the office of First Lord—as Canning later asked the Duke of Portland to remove Castlereagh from the War Department. It was with the greatest reluctance that Dundas in June 1800 acquiesced in the Cabinet's decision to send only a trifling reinforcement to General Abercromby in the Mediterranean: as many as 20,000 were to be diverted to an attack on Belle Isle to support the Royalists in western France. A few weeks later Dundas failed to get the support of the Cabinet for his suggested expedition against Cuba, Pitt apparently vetoing the proposal. Then, in September 1800 Dundas strongly disapproved the Cabinet's decision to negotiate a naval armistice with France whilst peace *pourparlers* were in progress, but terms could not be agreed upon and the project came to nothing. He had a hard struggle to overcome

---

[1] For an account of the parliamentary activities of the Carlton House members during these years, see the *Correspondence of George, Prince of Wales*, vol. IV.

opposition from both the King and some members of the Cabinet to his proposal to send an army to expel the French from Egypt, his view being that Britain would be severely handicapped in any peace negotiations if France were allowed to remain in undisturbed possession of that country. Windham, as usual, favoured the despatch of an expedition to the west coast of France to aid the Royalists. Grenville, too, expressed his dissent from the Cabinet Minute: he wanted an expedition to be sent to Italy. This sort of opposition embittered Dundas and made him increasingly anxious to resign his War Secretaryship, and it was with great difficulty that Pitt and the King persuaded him to stay. 'Most of you,' he wrote to Grenville on 25 July (1800), 'being of opinion that we ought not to send any force out of Europe (the reverse of which is my decided opinion), and the King and those in whose councils he confides being of opinion that our force is to go nowhere (which is the plain English of all this), my situation is become too ridiculous to be longer submitted to.' Amidst the jarring opinions prevailing in the Cabinet, he told Pitt, the essential interests of the country must daily suffer. Differences of opinion 'daily enter into every separate discussion which occurs on the subject of either peace or war'. He elaborated this point in a memorandum on the state of the Cabinet (22 September 1800): 'Some of us are of opinion that the repose of Europe and the security of Great Britain are only to be obtained by the restoration of the ancient royal family of France, and that every operation of war, and every step to negotiation which does not keep that object in view is mischievous and will ultimately prove to be illusory. Some of us are of opinion that although we ought not to consider the restoration of the ancient royal family as a *sine qua non*, we ought not to treat with a revolutionary Government, and that the present Government of France is of that description. Some of us are of opinion that whatever has been the foundation of the present Government, it has established within its power the whole authority, civil and military, of the country, and that we are not warranted to reject the negotiations with a Government so constituted and *de facto* existing. Some of us are of opinion that although we ought to negotiate with the present rulers of France, we ought only to do it in conjunction with our allies, particularly with the Emperor of Germany, it being the interest of this country closely to connect our interests with his. Some of us are of opinion that if ever it was practicable to influence by force of arms the interior Government of France, that time is past. That it is even problematical if the present revolutionary principles of that country are not maintained and supported in place of being weakened by the external pressure of its enemies.'

The King's own ideas were often sound enough. He had little belief that Prussia would re-enter the war against Revolutionary France; he knew that Austro-Prussian jealousy was too strong to be overcome when his Ministers were planning a new Quadruple Alliance. But he was wrong in believing that Bonaparte's *coup d'état* of Brumaire 1799 would facilitate at no distant date the restoration of the Monarchy. That his own ideas sometimes differed from those of the Cabinet is not surprising. In the summer of 1800 he opposed the plan to send an expedition to Ferrol and subsequently to Cadiz in order to destroy as much as possible of the enemy's naval force. Dundas felt it necessary to appeal to him not to withhold from his Ministers his confidence 'at a moment when it is so essentially necessary in every particular, and in none more than the conduct of the war'. The King complained that Dundas, as War Minister, should have discussed the matter with him personally before the Cabinet was invited to formulate policy. In reply to this criticism Dundas stoutly maintained the necessity of bringing matters of first-rate importance before the Cabinet, and repudiated the notion that he should act on his own judgment. 'The appropriation of the national force must in time of war, like every other resource of the Empire, be subject to the advice and responsibility of your Majesty's confidential servants.'

In June 1800 the King disapproved the Cabinet's decision to re-open peace negotiations. It would, he said, encourage Austria to treat with the enemy; and no confidence could be placed in the French Government. Soon afterwards he very reluctantly agreed to Dundas's plan to send an expedition to drive the French out of Egypt. It would prove to be another San Domingo business, he thought, and he feared that Abercromby's army was devoted to famine and destruction. He opposed so strongly the Cabinet's proposal to despatch an expedition to seize Ferrol, and then Cadiz and the Canary Islands, that Pitt, writing to Dundas, threatened to resign. Evidently the King would have changed his Ministry during the summer of 1800 had he felt confident of his ability to find other servants. In August the King, at Weymouth, commanded the attendance of Windham, the Secretary at War. Lord Malmesbury was later informed of its purpose by Pelham, who was soon to be in Addington's Cabinet. 'I was told,' wrote Malmesbury, that his Majesty had for a long time since been dissatisfied with Pitt's, and particularly with Lord Grenville's 'authoritative manners' towards him, and that an alteration in his Ministry had been often in his mind; that it was with this view he had sent for Windham and myself in August last to Weymouth; that he meant Windham should be his First Minister and I have the Seals for the Foreign Department; and although he never came to a direct explanation either with me, who stayed only three days at Weymouth, or with Windham, who stayed longer, yet my informant says he is sure of the fact.' Malmesbury believed that the disastrous outcome of the Austrian campaign in Italy, together with Pitt's peace proposals made though Otto, the French emissary in London who was charged with the arrangements for the exchange of prisoners of war, perplexed the King and diverted his attention from his purpose. 'Windham also,' he added, 'by his odd, absent and unacquiescent manner, did not encourage his Majesty in his views. I have now no doubt that it transpired somehow or other through the Chancellor.'

About the same time (8 February 1801) Canning told Malmesbury that for three years so many concessions had been made to the King and so many important measures overruled by him, that the Government had been weakened; and he thought that if Pitt had not made a stand on the Catholic question he would have remained in office with only nominal power. 'The real one would pass into the hands of those who influenced the King's mind and opinions out of sight.'

This further point, then, emerges: Pitt believed that the King was developing the habit of consulting persons other than himself and listening to advice which it was for his First Minister to give: especially on the Catholic question. As early as

March 1795 the Duke of Portland, the Home Secretary, had written to Thomas Pelham, then Secretary to Lord Westmorland, Lord Lieutenant of Ireland: 'I cannot but inform you for the purpose of putting you upon your guard, that we have heard from the most unquestionable authority that a correspondence has been carried on, or at least letters have been written by Lord Fitzgibbon [the Lord Chancellor of Ireland] to the King (to whom they have been delivered by Lord Westmorland) with a view and with more effect than could be wished, to prejudice his mind and *to alarm his conscience* against the concession to the Catholics. I don't know how *your friend* Pitt feels this, but if this is to be the practice, no Government can go on in Ireland, and I believe there are not two opinions in the *greater part* of the Cabinet respecting it.' Writing to the King on 31 January 1801 Pitt said that he had learnt of his hostility to a Catholic Relief Bill not merely from some of his colleagues, but also from 'other quarters'.

Sometime in 1798 (the letter is undated) Dundas wrote a warning to Pitt: 'I know not who he is, but I am positive there is somebody about him [the King] who does much mischief by agitating his mind and inflaming his prejudices' on the Catholic question. He added: 'Sooner or later he must make up his mind to the plainest of all political truths, that a country where a Parliament and a free Constitution is allowed to exist never can submit to the practice of three-fourths of the country being sacrificed to the whims, prejudices or opinions of the other fourth. This may be accomplished by annihilating their Parliament and subduing themselves, and having done that, begin on a new ground of governing them as a conquered country by a standing army of 50,000 men. Under the present frame of the Irish Government I positively pronounce the continuance of such a system to be impossible.'

Lord Malmesbury, though not in office, knew a good deal of what was going on behind the scenes: he referred to those who 'secretly and unknown to the Ministry, *practised* on the King's religion and disposed him to resist the intended measure of Catholic emancipation'. And Canning, who knew Pitt's mind, told Malmesbury that Pitt resigned in 1801, not on the Catholic question 'simply as a measure in which he had been opposed and to which, if he had assented, he would, as a Minister, have been on a footing totally different from what he had ever before been in the Cabinet. This obliged him to resign.' Malmesbury, who heard both sides in this controversy, emphasized that it was not on the Catholic question alone that people had sought to influence the King's mind in opposition to the views of his First Minister: 'The advocates for the Cabinet assert that of late there has been much opposition in the Closet to all measures proposed by them, that Government could no longer go on if the question as to their real power was not distinctly ascertained.' He went on: 'The advocates for the Closet say that for some time past it had been treated with disrespect and inattention, and that on this particular point it was requiring a violation of the coronation oath.'

This, then, with the King was a matter of conscience on which he was immoveable, and at the Levée on 28 January 1801 he is reported to have said, 'I shall reckon any man my personal enemy who proposes any such measure'. When Dundas tried to explain to him the distinction between his legislative and executive functions, he replied, 'None of your Scotch metaphysics!'

b (xvii)

Until the appointment of a new Archbishop of Canterbury in 1805 questions of patronage occasioned little difficulty between the King and his Ministers. The only serious one had arisen in the autumn of 1792 over the King's reluctance to nominate Dundas to a vacant Governorship of the Charterhouse, on the ground that men of rank had usually been honoured in that way. The Archbishop of Canterbury pointed out that it was customary for the Secretary of State to be appointed. Dundas was so indignant at the idea of his being passed over merely because he was a commoner that he threatened to resign: a point which seems to have escaped the notice of his biographers. Pitt wrote to him on 14 October 1792: 'You will, I am sure, easily believe that I have felt as strongly as you could do how different the King's conduct...has been from everything which you had a right to expect, and I certainly cannot help deeply regretting in my own mind what I must at least admit to be a mark of his not having those feelings of kindness and cordiality which, if they are to be earned by the steadiest and most honourable exertions in his service, are so much your due. But at the same time I feel with you how impossible it is either for you or me, circumstanced as we are, to indulge any sentiment of discontent; and I confess that besides this, I feel and believe you will agree with me that on occasions of this sort, it very seldom happens that the dignity of any man's official situation or personal character is affected in the public estimation unless he himself renders the subject of importance by complaining of the injury. I own, therefore, that whatever is the King's final decision, I believe the circumstance will be very little noticed or canvassed by the public.' He went on: 'I have not the most distant idea of the possibility of any impression arising which ought for a moment to lead to the idea which you point at of finding some other person for your situation, and I must add that one short and decisive answer on that point is that while Lord Cornwallis is abroad, there is no other person to be found.' Pitt wondered whether 'a previous impression' had been made on the King 'from other quarters', and he did not like the tone of the royal letters on this matter. In the end Dundas secured the nomination.

The King, not Pitt, nominated Dr Stuart as Primate of Ireland in 1800, but no controversy followed. Pitt evidently displayed little interest in this appointment. None of the English Bishops wanted to go to Armagh, and the King justifiably commented, 'I believe nothing but my own exertion on this occasion could have effected this right measure.' According to George Rose, who was in a position to know the facts, it was Addington, the Speaker, not Pitt who suggested to the King the appointment of Dr Huntingford as Bishop of St David's in succession to Dr Stuart. Addington, said Rose in February 1801, 'had for some time past had the most easy and constant access to the King at all hours, which gives additional sanction to the idea of his intriguing'. Rose, however, had a poor opinion of the Speaker and in this remark did him less than justice: Addington never intrigued for the Premiership, but accepted it as a duty he owed to his Sovereign who pressed it on him.

For the first time in English history an Irish question now destroyed a British Government. Pitt had convinced himself that the success of the Union depended on the possibility of ending the religious discords of Irishmen, first, by relieving

Catholics, who formed about three-quarters of the population, of their remaining disabilities, which could safely be done by a united Parliament in which they would command only a minority of the votes; and secondly, by giving the Irish Protestants ample security in an Imperial Parliament against the ultimate risk of being swamped by the rising tide of Irish nationalism. The Catholics had supported the Union in the confident hope that their grievances would be remedied, but Pitt was in no position to carry out a policy of conciliation: the Cabinet and both Houses of Parliament were deeply divided on the Catholic question, and the King was implacably hostile to any further substantial measure of relief. On 31 January Pitt informed the King that he should resign if he were not allowed to introduce a Relief Bill into Parliament 'with the whole weight of Government'. On 5 February the King reluctantly accepted his resignation and at once summoned the Speaker and commissioned him to form a Ministry. Pitt advised Addington to accept, promised him his cordial support, and urged his friends to remain in office. In favourable circumstances, then, the King still enjoyed and could exercise his constitutional right to dismiss as well as to nominate the Prime Minister, and no one questioned his action in February 1801.

Pitt was glad to be relieved of the burden of office: he could easily have supplanted Addington a week or two later when he made it known to the King and a few friends that he was prepared to waive the Catholic question for the duration of the reign in deference to the King's scruples about his coronation oath.[1] But though his virtual abandonment of the Catholic cause removed the only serious and pressing difference with the King and seemed to render his return to the Premiership a natural event, he preferred to abide by his promise of cordial support to Addington. Canning reported that Pitt was 'really as full of spirits in his new idleness as a boy just come home for the holidays'.

No informed person believes that, as was alleged by both British and French newspapers at the time, Pitt resigned because he felt incapable either of bringing the war to a successful conclusion or of making a satisfactory peace. Though there were others, as we have seen, the Catholic question was the principal and immediate cause of Pitt's virtual dismissal. Though the King had referred to the 'real affection' he had for Pitt and expressed genuine sorrow at what he chose to describe as 'the close' of his Minister's political life, he addressed him in a valedictory letter with unusual warmth and cordiality, 'My dear Pitt'. Yet their relations were less cordial than during the early years of the seventeen-year Administration.

At first sight it seems surprising that a man of middle class origin like Addington, who, though vain, never considered himself a genius, should have risen as high as

---

[1] The King told Perceval on 19 September 1809 that when he saw Pitt (? 14 March 1801) after receiving a written assurance that the Catholic question should never again be brought forward by Pitt during the remainder of the reign Pitt 'not only confirmed the assurance but added that he would not only not bring it forward, but that for private reasons of his own he would oppose it whoever brought it forward. This, he says, he voluntarily said to him; it was more than he expected, it surprised him, it appeared to be an expression of his own opinion, that he might have paid him (the King) the compliment of supposing that the determination was taken out of compliment to him, but he stated it to be for private reasons of his own.' (Perceval MSS. Perceval to Lord Liverpool, 19 Sept. 1809, reporting the King's statement to him at Windsor the same day.)

the Premiership. His career, like that of Canning, showed that, even in that aristocratic age, the highest offices in the State were within the reach of a man of ability who lacked the advantages both of family connection and of fortune. He owed his initial progress to the friendship of Pitt, who gave him the chance of developing into a highly successful Speaker of the House of Commons, in which capacity he made himself remarkably popular with that most influential body of opinion there, the independent country gentlemen. During the last decades of the unreformed House of Commons it was not unusual for the Sovereign to look with secret favour on the Speaker, who, being more or less dissociated from party strife and out of the immediate circle of party engagements, was well qualified by the prestige belonging to his position, to rally opinion in support of the Monarch when confronted with grave situations. In May 1832, for example, William IV tried to extricate himself from a sea of troubles arising out of his refusal to create enough Peers to ensure the passing of the Reform Bill, by asking Manners-Sutton to form a Government. In 1801 George III, confronted with Pitt's virtual ultimatum on the Catholic question, called on Addington to rescue him from an intolerable situation. Addington's anti-Catholic prejudices made him the obvious person on whom the King could fall back, and he was able to rally the independent part of the House of Commons which largely shared his 'Protestant' views.

As Speaker, then, Addington had been an outstanding success. 'No one', wrote the King, 'ever filled the Chair...more conspicuously.' He was a gentleman, and he looked like one. His deportment, in striking contrast with that of his successor, 'little Abbot', was impressive; his countenance dignified, his address affable. The unanimity which secured his re-election when the new Parliament met in 1796 testified to his continuing popularity. His situation brought him into close contact with the King, and Pitt, too, often consulted him on important matters of State.

The King's health was affected by the strain of the political crisis. The Catholic question had been agitating him for some weeks when on 28 January at the Levée Ministers saw symptoms of derangement. But it was not until about 19 February that he became unmistakably ill, and by that time his anxieties about the safety of the Protestant Constitution in Church and State should have been largely removed by Addington's nomination as Prime Minister. A Regency again became a possibility, and even a new reign, for his life was in danger for some days. It was not until 14 March that he was well enough to receive the seals from Pitt and hand them to Addington. During the preceding five weeks, though half the Cabinet Ministers had resigned, they continued to hold the seals of office. On the other hand, some of Addington's Cabinet colleagues had actually been sworn in at a meeting of the Privy Council, so that for several weeks there were in office the halves of two Administrations. One remarkable Cabinet meeting was held at which were present, in effect, two Prime Ministers, two Lord Chancellors and two Secretaries of State for War.

Lord Loughborough was not invited to remain Lord Chancellor, but it was not until 14 April that Eldon took his place. Even then, the Cabinet changes were not complete. Thomas Pelham was given to understand that he was to be Secretary of State for War and called up to the House of Lords to take the lead there, and on

13 February he left London to prepare the County (Sussex) for a by-election. Two days later, however, he received a letter from the Duke of Portland (not Addington), saying that this appointment could not after all be made, and asking him to accept the Board of Control instead—the Court of Directors disliking the idea of Lord Hobart being appointed to that office. Pelham, on his return to London, knowing nothing and caring less about Indian affairs, and feeling that the office was important only on account of its patronage, refused it, but offered to assist the Government in the House of Commons and sit in the Cabinet without a Department. Addington informed him that Hobart had to be appointed Secretary of State on account of the attitude of the India Directorate. Pelham and his friends felt that he had been 'tricked and jockeyed', as Malmesbury phrased it. Addington, realising that his Government needed additional strength in the Lords (Westmorland was of little use and Portland, always 'indolent and torpid', was in poor health and at best an indifferent speaker) then arranged that the Duke should be appointed Lord President of the Council and that Pelham should succeed him as Home Secretary and be called up to the House of Lords. But to everyone's astonishment the Duke kept on putting off his departure from the Home Office until in the end he had to confess, privately, to Pelham that it would be 'impracticable at present' to resign unless he could find about £30,000 of public money which he had evidently borrowed and which he was then unable to repay. It has long been known that the Duke was financially embarrassed, having entirely neglected his own affairs and being, said George Rose, 'in the hands of his servants and people about him', and the suggestion has sometimes been made that his financial situation made him cling to office in February 1801 when he should have resigned with Dundas, Grenville and Spencer; but the real reason for his extraordinary procrastination in the summer of 1801 only now emerges. Malmesbury, at a loss for an explanation of the mystery, wrote to his friend Pelham: 'The D. of P's conduct is really the most unaccountably weak of any I ever recollect to have seen or heard of, for it is the weakness of a child or a Miss to leave a Ball. He hurts his consequence and even character by it more than an eternal possession of the Seals could compensate. What does he expect to gain by the delay of ten days? Has he any *underplot* going forward, or does he think he can write or convey anything to the King which may make H.M. feel the importance of his remaining in his present office in preference to any other?...Is not the whole a womanish reluctance to quit an office he is grown *at once* so fond of, or can we think that the insisting to keep it over the 5th July (quarter day) enters into his mind as a reason for not remouncing it till after that period? Addington seems to have been doing what he ought, but not with the vigour and energy the case, I think required. It is a great satisfaction the being acquainted with the King's sentiments, and they seem so very clear that in that respect no doubt can remain...It is a matter of great concern to me that...our excellent friend the D. of P. should have contrived to injure his *fair fame* when he might have done himself so much credit.'

Pelham received the seals of office on 30 July, and he was at once informed by Addington that colonial affairs were henceforth to be the responsibility of the Secretary of State for War. 'This distribution was long since recommended and approved of, and has only waited (as you know) for the new arrangement to be carried into effect.' Pelham was annoyed that he had not been told of the change when he was given the Seals: the King was under the impression that Addington had informed him, and he said nothing. It is worth noting that although Pelham was a Cabinet Minister from 30 July, Addington suggested that he should not attend the Cabinet meeting that was to be held on 4 August on the subject of peace negotiations, on the ground that he had not been present at the earlier discussions.

Addington's first task was to negotiate peace, and on 19 March he informed the King of the Cabinet's decision to do so. In July 1800 the King had told Pitt that he would not consider any terms reasonable that did not secure to Britain the greater part of her conquests, 'particularly the Cape of Good Hope and the West India Islands'. He was so pleased with his new Minister that he apparently never registered a protest against the preliminary terms signed on 1 October 1801 whereby Britain handed back all her conquests except Ceylon and Trinidad, which had belonged not to France but to Holland and Spain respectively. The King tried to make the best of a poor situation, and, when conversing with his Ministers, emphasized the necessity of keeping the country in a state of preparedness for any emergency. Pitt described the terms as 'highly creditable, and on the whole very advantageous', though he regretted the retrocession of the Cape. Fox was delighted that the objects for which Britain had gone to war in 1793 had not been attained, and he told Grey, 'The triumph of the French Government over the English does in fact afford me a degree of pleasure which it is very difficult to disguise'. Dundas, Grenville and Spencer disapproved the restoration of the conquered colonies, but the two former were reluctant to oppose the King's Ministers. Canning, who would have done so from the beginning could he have borne to lose Pitt's friendship, privately described the peace as 'the most profligate and wasteful sacrifice of the honour and interests, and ultimately the essential safety of the country', but he had to admit that it had been received throughout the kingdom with the most unbounded joy and gratitude.

The King was in reasonably good health after his recovery in the spring. He continued to take an active part in discussing affairs of State with his Ministers, with whom the weight of his long experience counted for much. Though in Addington he had a Minister after his own heart he was not prepared to give him a free rein. He would not allow Addington to appoint anyone as Treasurer of the Navy in November 1801 after Ryder had resigned on account of ill health, until an offer had been made to Charles Yorke, whom he particularly respected.

The peace 'which every man ought to be glad of but no man can be proud of', as Sheridan put it, received overwhelming support from both Houses of Parliament. The minority in the Lords on 3 November 1801 was only ten; in the Commons on 14 May 1802 only twenty: most of them the friends either of Grenville or of Canning. Not until later did parties really 'assume a new face', as Charles Yorke said.

The King's five youngest sons were made Knights of the Garter in 1801, and the four youngest were given peerages: Ernest and Edward in 1799, Augustus and

Adolphus in 1801. Their Dukedoms of course entitled them to seats in the House of Lords and gave them opportunities of improving on the lamentable performances there of the Duke of Clarence on the Adultery Bill and the Slave Trade Bill. Arising out of the debates on the former, Pitt felt it necessary to ask the King to use his influence to prevent the Prince of Wales and the Dukes of Clarence and Cumberland from participating in a further debate in opposition to the line proposed to be taken by Ministers 'with the weight of Government'. The Duke of Clarence, in conjunction with a Cabinet Minister, Lord Westmorland (*le sot* [*sceau*] *privé*, as Canning contemptuously described him), put himself at the head of the opposition to the Slave Trade Bill, with the result that half the Peers who usually supported the Government, opposed Lord Grenville and his liberal colleagues, and, said Canning, Grenville would have been beaten four to one if he had risked a division on the Second Reading. Grenville hinted to him 'pretty strongly that Royal Dukes ought not to take part in contentious political discussions', and showed him that 'he put his father's Ministers in very awkward situations when he...took part against them'. 'The Duke of York,' Canning added, 'to his credit felt this so much that he refused his proxy to his brother. The Prince of Wales did not act so decorously. His proxy was given for the slave trade.' The Duke's 'outrageous conduct', said Canning, 'helped to convince Pitt that nothing was to be accomplished without making it in a great degree a Government question. The consequence of this conviction is a determination to bring on some Bill...to settle the question—not by total and immediate abolition (for against *that*, people have been suffered to pledge themselves too much) but for the next-best measure that can be devised, limitation and regulation of the trade in a way that will necessarily lead to its termination—and to bring this on either himself or Dundas, with *Government authority*!' But Pitt proved to be a broken reed, and what he was unable to accomplish was achieved triumphantly by his political opponents soon after his death.

The Duke of Clarence was now living with his family at Bushy Park, given him by the King, and Thomas Coutts had loaned him money to meet the cost of furnishing the house and equipping the farm. In 1800 and 1801 he was being hard pressed by creditors and had to ask Pitt for a loan of £15,000 to enable him to stave off the least accommodating: he was expecting a judgment to be laid on all his property at Bushy. One-third of this new loan was allotted to the floating debt, the rest for the liquidation of the bonded debt.

Prince Adolphus remained in Hanover until April 1801 when, the Prussians having occupied the Electorate, he returned home. He was raised to the rank of Lieutenant-General in 1798 and given an establishment, but was disappointed at not being allowed to take part in the Helder expedition and at not being given military employment in 1801 when he believed the country to be threatened with invasion. An affair of the heart, too, had an unfortunate ending. He had fallen in love with his cousin Princess Frederica of Mecklenburg-Strelitz who, at the age of eighteen, had lost her first husband, Prince Louis of Prussia. Prince Adolphus offered to marry her, and in January 1798 she accepted him. When, however, he sought the King's permission to marry, he was told that he would have to wait until the end of the war. The Princess was not prepared to remain a widow in-definitely, and she at once formed a connection with one of her friends, Prince Frederick of Solms-Braunfels, with the result that in the summer of 1798 she was expecting a child. A secret marriage took place some months later, and the child was born in March 1799. Prince Adolphus was miserable, but with his usual generosity he forgave her. Sixteen years later she became his sister-in-law when she married the Duke of Cumberland as her third husband. Remembering what had happened in 1798 Queen Charlotte refused to receive her at Court.

Prince Edward, injured by a fall from his horse in the summer of 1798, came home for more expert medical attention than Nova Scotia had to offer. The King would have liked to keep him in North America 'out of many difficulties' for the duration of the war, and but for this accident he might have succeeded in doing so. The Prince was happy to be home again: London had many attractions and he hated the severity of the long Canadian winters (his health had not been good: he complained of severe attacks of rheumatic fever). He was back in Halifax in September 1799, hoping, however, soon to be recalled and given employment either in the British Isles or in Hanover: unlike his brother Prince Ernest, he had no objection to serve under Wallmoden. But he made the unpleasant discovery that his connection with Mme de St Laurent disqualified him from high command in Britain, his brother the Commander-in-Chief informing him that there had been much talk of the way in which he had publicly associated himself with her every-where whilst in England. 'This,' said the Duke, 'may be done abroad . . . it cannot be done at home.' Ill health brought him home again in August 1800. He vainly asked the King for the office of Master-General of the Ordnance in February 1801 when Addington was planning his Government. He was never again employed.

The Duke of York's letters are mainly of a routine character: he was absorbed in his duties at the Horse Guards. In the summer of 1799, however, he was given the command of the joint Anglo-Russian expedition to the Helder, designed to recover Holland for the Orange family, but the capture of the Dutch fleet in the Texel was the only successful outcome. An attack on Bergen failed, and on 18 October the Duke made the unfortunate Convention of Alkmaar by which he agreed to evacuate Holland and surrender his prisoners, but retained the Dutch warships. His letter of 21 October shows that he signed the Convention before receiving the Cabinet's instructions of the 14th or thereabouts to withdraw the army. The expedition was badly planned and executed, and poorly supported by the Dutch people who for the most part seemed to prefer the continuance of the French occupation to the restoration of the House of Orange. This marked the end of British military intervention on the Continent until the beginning of the Peninsular War: the expedition to Ferrol in August 1800 was hardly much more than a reconnaissance in force.

The Duke played a minor part in the political crisis of 1801. In February he told the King that he would never abandon his opposition to Catholic emancipation and the repeal of the Test Act. When it became known (in March) that Pitt was willing to shelve the Catholic question for the rest of the reign, the Duke evinced anxiety to see him back in office, but Pelham, with whom he was very friendly, persuaded him not to try to influence the King's mind in favour of this solution, as his interference might create ill feeling towards him in the Prince of Wales. Pitt too advised him on no account of mix himself up with such matters, but to consider himself as belonging to the King and independent of all Ministers.

Prince Augustus was older than Prince Adolphus, the latter being given precedence with regard to a Dukedom partly because he was the King's favourite son, partly, no doubt, too, because Augustus, of all the King's sons, had incurred most severely his father's displeasure by going through a form of marriage in contravention of the Royal Marriages Act. It may be thought that the King treated him with excessive harshness by preventing Lady Augusta Murray and her child from joining him abroad, where he had to live partly for reasons of health (like his brother William he suffered severely from asthma), partly because the King would not have him at home. On the other hand the King would have had little objection to their living together unobtrusively if the Prince had been willing to treat her as a mistress rather than as a wife. One's sympathy for the Prince must in any case be affected by the fact that, even whilst he was persistently demanding recognition of his marriage (in other words, demanding that an Act of Parliament should be modified just to suit his convenience) he was unfaithful to Lady Augusta. Increased French naval activity in the Mediterranean in the early months of 1798 made it expedient for him to leave Naples, where he had been frequenting 'very improper society' and piling up debts to such an extent that the Government at home had to send money to save him from the disgrace of arrest and imprisonment. The King would not allow him to join his family in England, and he took refuge from the French invaders first in Vienna and then in Berlin. Whilst in Austria his attendant, Mr Livingston, an extraordinarily illiterate gentleman, heard that the Prince had been urged to offer himself as a candidate for Liverpool at the next election: Mr Livingston was evidently the victim of a little leg-pulling.

In the summer of 1799, whilst in Berlin, he was suddenly joined by Lady Augusta, who alleged that she had come to bid farewell to her husband who was reported to be dying. The King soon heard of 'Mrs Ford's' arrival in the Prussian capital, and threatened both her and her family with the weight of his displeasure unless she returned to England forthwith, along with her son whom Lady Dunmore, his grandmother, had sent to join his parents. The Prince sought to avert harsh consequences by threats of blackmail: he would publish 'for the amusement of the public' the entire correspondence on the subject of his marriage unless her debts were paid and an adequate income secured to her. The threat evidently sufficed.

In May 1800 Prince Augustus aggravated his errors by returning home without leave, but by that time he was ready to submit to the King's will and to accept the nullity of his marriage, being helped to arrive at this mortifying decision by the advice of the Prince of Wales and his lawyers, and by some disturbing and apparently unfounded rumours of improper conduct on the part of Lady Augusta. His departure for Lisbon in December, where he sought relief from his persistent complaint, at a time when she was pregnant (her daughter was born on 11 August 1801) probably made the separation easier. A year later he informed the King that, on account of Lady Augusta's 'imprudent conduct' he had decided that they should separate, and he asked that she should be given additional financial assistance to make her position less uncomfortable.

Prince Ernest, too, incurred his father's displeasure in 1798 by resigning his commission in the Hanoverian service, alleging that he could not serve under General Wallmoden, whose appointment as Commander-in-Chief in the Electorate in succession to old Field Marshal Freytag, was apparently imminent. It was not until he had threatened to enlist in the yeomanry in England as a private that the King offered him the rank of Lieutenant-General in the Hanoverian army, which, in view of the situation of affairs both at home and abroad, he reluctantly accepted. He was given the same rank in the British army a year later, and the colonelcy of one of the Light Dragoon Regiments in 1801.

He fully shared the King's prejudices against the Catholics and welcomed with immense satisfaction the formation of the Addington Ministry.

There are no copies of the Queen's letters to her continental relatives in the Archives,[1] but she evidently kept up a correspondence with them, and at the King's request in 1798 she wrote to her niece the Queen of Prussia 'to express the favourable opinions' held in London of her and and her husband, at a time when hopes were being entertained of drawing Prussia into a new alliance against France. At that time, too, she asked the King, in writing, to continue financial assistance to her brother, the Duke of Mecklenburg-Strelitz, impoverished by the war.

The Princess Royal's marriage was as unfruitful as the Queen's had been fruitful, but she soon recovered her health after the loss of her child. Her subsequent troubles sprang from the enemy occupation of Wurtemberg which inflicted untold hardships on the people. Urged on by her husband, to whom she seems to have been devoted in spite of his extraordinary appearance, she repeatedly appealed to the King for financial help for the Duchy, but Pitt's Government apparently ignored them.

[1] A microfilm of these letters has recently been acquired by the Archives, but arrived too late for the letters to be included in this volume.

THE CABINET, 1798–APRIL 1804

	Pitt	Addington				
	From 1798	*Feb.–April 1801*	*June–July 1801*	*Oct. 1802*	*17 Aug. 1803*	*Nov. 1803*
First Lord and the Treasury and Chancellor of the Exchequer	*Pitt*	*Addington* (14 March)	*Addington*	*Addington*	*Addington*	*Addington*
Lord Privy Seal[1]	Earl of Westmorland (14 Feb.)	Westmorland	Westmorland	Westmorland	Westmorland	Westmorland
Lord President of the Council	Earl of Chatham	Chatham	Portland (30 July)	Portland	Portland	Portland
Lord Chancellor	Lord Loughborough	Lord Eldon (14 April)	Eldon	Eldon	Eldon	Eldon
Home Secretary	Duke of Portland	Portland	Lord Pelham (30 July)	Pelham	*Charles Philip Yorke*	*Yorke*
Foreign Secretary	Lord Grenville	*Lord Hawkesbury* (20 Feb.)	*Hawkesbury*	*Hawkesbury*	*Hawkesbury*	*Hawkesbury*[2]
Secretary for War (and the Colonies, from July 1801)	*Henry Dundas*[3]	Lord Hobart (17 March)	Hobart	Hobart	Hobart	Hobart
First Lord of the Admiralty	Earl Spencer	Earl of St Vincent (19 Feb.)	St Vincent	St Vincent	St Vincent	St Vincent
President of the Board of Control				*Viscount Castereagh*[4]	*Castlereagh*	*Castlereagh*
Master-General of the Ordnance	Lord Cornwallis[5]		Earl of Chatham (27 June)	Chatham	Chatham	Chatham
Chancellor of the Duchy of Lancaster	Earl of Liverpool	Liverpool	Liverpoo	Liverpool	Liverpool[6]	Liverpool
President of the Board of Trade						
Secretary at War	*Wm. Windham*					
Minister without portfolio	Lord Camden (from June 1798)					

Members whose names are italicized sat in the Commons.

[1] In commission before Feb. 1798.

[2] Peerage, 15 Nov. 1803.

[3] Dundas was also Treasurer of the Navy (until May 1800) and President of the Board of Control.

[4] President of the Board of Control from 12 July, but not in the Cabinet until October.

[5] Not in the Cabinet as Lord Lieutenant of Ireland, June 1798–May 1801.

[6] Crippled with rheumatism, Liverpool probably never attended a Cabinet meeting whilst Addington was Prime Minister, but no evidence has come to light to suggest that he resigned his seat in the Cabinet, and there *is* evidence of his being sent Cabinet papers. He remained Chancellor of the Duchy of Lancaster until November 1803, and President of the Board of Trade until the Government resigned in 1804.

PITT'S MINISTRY, 1798–1801

Junior Lords of the Treasury	Hon. John Thomas Townshend, John Smyth, Sylvester Douglas, Charles Small Pybus
From July 1800	John Smyth, Sylvester Douglas, Pybus, Lord Granville Leveson-Gower
From Dec. 1800	John Smyth, Pybus, Lord Granville Leveson-Gower, John Hiley Addington
Joint Secretaries of the Treasury	George Rose, Charles Long
Junior Lords of the Admiralty	Lord Arden, Sir Phillip Stephens, James Gambier, Wm. Young, Thomas Wallace, Robert Man.
From July 1800	Lord Arden, Sir Philip Stephens, Gambier, Young, Man, Hon. William Eliot
Secretary of the Admiralty	Evan Nepean
Under-Secretaries of State	
Home Department	John King and William Wickham
Foreign Department	George Hammond and George Canning Hammond and John Hookham Frere (from 1 April 1799)
	Hammond and Edward Fisher (from 25 Sept. 1800)
War Department	William Huskisson
Commissioners of the Board of Control	Henry Dundas, Duke of Montrose, Viscount Belgrave, Earl Bathurst, Lord Hawkesbury, Sylvester Douglas, William Dundas
From 28 March 1799	Henry Dundas, Duke of Montrose, Viscount Belgrave, Earl Bathurst, Sylvester Douglas, Wm. Dundas, George Canning
From 28 May 1800	Henry Dundas, Duke of Montrose, Viscount Belgrave, Earl Bathurst, Sylvester Douglas,[1] Canning, Thomas Wallace, Earl Temple
Secretary to the Board of Control	Hon. William Brodrick
Master-General of the Ordnance	Marquess Cornwallis
Lieutenant-General of the Ordnance	Viscount Howe
Surveyor-General of the Ordnance	Major-General Alexander Ross

[1] Created Lord Glenbervie, 30 Nov. 1800.

Clerk of the Ordnance	John Sargent
Surveyor-General of Crown Lands	John Fordyce
Surveyor-General of Woods and Forests	John Robinson
Paymaster-General	Thomas Steele and Dudley Ryder
	Thomas Steele and George Canning (from 28 May 1800)
Treasurer of the Navy	Dudley Ryder (from 28 May 1800)
Postmaster-General	Earl of Leicester and Lord Auckland
	Lord Auckland and Lord Gower (from 22 Feb. 1799)
Master of the Mint	Sir George Yonge
	Lord Hawkesbury (from 6 March 1799)
Vice-President of the Board of Trade	Dudley Ryder
Judge Advocate-General	Sir Charles Morgan
Master of the Rolls	Sir Richard Pepper Arden
Attorney-General	Sir John Scott
	Sir John Mitford (from 17 July 1799)
Solicitor-General	Sir John Mitford
	Sir William Grant (from 17 July 1799)
Lord Advocate of Scotland	Robert Dundas of Arniston
Solicitor-General of Scotland	Robert Blair

THE IRISH GOVERNMENT

Lord Lieutenant	Marquess Cornwallis
Chief Secretary	Viscount Castlereagh
Lord Chancellor	Earl of Clare
Chancellor of the Exchequer	Sir John Parnell; Isaac Corry (from Jan. 1799)
Attorney-General	Arthur Wolfe; John Toler (from July 1798); John Stewart (from 23 Dec. 1800)
Solicitor-General	John Toler; John Stewart (from July 1798); William Cusack Smith (from Dec. 1800)
Under-Secretary of State	
Civil Department	Edward Cooke
Military Department[1]	William Elliot

[1] Sometimes referred to as the Secretaryship at War.

ADDINGTON'S MINISTRY, 1801–1804

Junior Lords of the Treasury	John Smyth, Charles Small Pybus, Lord George Thynne, Nathaniel Bond
From July 1802	Pybus, Lord George Thynne, Bond, John Hiley Addington
From Aug. 1803	Pybus, Lord George Thynne, Bond, William Brodrick
From Nov. 1803	Lord George Thynne, Bond, Brodrick, Edward Golding
Joint Secretaries of the Treasury	John Hiley Addington (from 24 March), and Nicholas Vansittart (from 9 April)
From 8 July 1802	Vansittart and John Sargent
Junior Lords of the Admiralty	Sir Philip Stephens, Hon. William Eliot, Sir Thomas Troubridge, James Adams, John Markham, William Garthshore
From 10 Jan. 1804	Stephens, Troubridge, Adams, Markham, John Lemon, Sir Harry Burrard Neale
Secretary of the Admiralty	Evan Nepean (Baronetcy, July 1802) William Marsden (from 21 Jan. 1804)
Under-Secretaries of State Home Department	John King and Edward Finch Hatton John King and Sir George Shee (from c. Aug. 1801) John King and Reginald Pole Carew (from 17 Aug. 1803)
Foreign Department	George Hammond and Lord Hervey George Hammond and Charles Arbuthnot (from c. Nov. 1803)
War [and the Colonies][1]	William Huskisson John Sullivan (from May 1801)
President of the Board of Control	Viscount Lewisham (Earl of Dartmouth, 15 July 1801) Viscount Castlereagh (from 12 July 1802) [in the Cabinet from Oct.]
Commissioner of the Board of Control	Viscount Lewisham (Earl of Dartmouth, 15 July 1801), Duke of Montrose, Earl Bathurst, Lord Glenbervie, Wm. Dundas, Thomas Wallace, Lord Aden, Thos. Pelham, Edward Golding

[1] From end July 1801.

From 6 July 1802	Viscount Castlereagh, Duke of Montrose, Lord Glenbervie, Wm. Dundas, Wallace, Lord Arden, Edward Golding
From Oct. 1803	Viscount Castlereagh, Lord Glenbervie, Wallace, Golding, Thomas Maitland
Secretary to the Board of Control	Hon. William Brodrick
	Benjamin Hobhouse (from Nov. 1803)
Secretary at War	Charles Yorke; Charles Bragge (from Aug. 1803)
Master-General of the Ordnance	Marquess Cornwallis (to June 1801)
Lieutenant-General of the Ordnance	Viscount Howe
Surveyor-General of the Ordnance	Major-General Alexander Ross
Clerk of the Ordnance	John Sargent; William Wellesley-Pole (from July 1802)
Surveyor-General of Woods and Forests	John Robinson; Lord Glenbervie (from 5 Jan. 1803)
Surveyor-General of Crown Lands	John Fordyce
Paymasters-General	Thomas Steele and Lord Glenbervie; Thomas Steele and John Hiley Addington (from 1 Jan. 1803)
Treasurer of the Navy	Dudley Ryder: Charles Bragge (from 17 Nov. 1801); George Tierney (from June 1803)
Postmasters-General	Lord Auckland and Lord Charles Spencer
Master of the Mint	Lord Arden; John Smyth (from 2 July 1802)
Vice-President of the Board of Trade	Dudley Ryder; Lord Glenbervie (from 17 Nov. 1801); Nathaniel Bond (from 8 Feb. 1804)
Chancellor of the Duchy of Lancaster	Lord Pelham (from 11 Nov. 1803)
Judge Advocate-General	Sir Charles Morgan
Master of the Rolls	Sir Richard Pepper Arden; Sir William Grant (from 21 May 1801)
Attorney-General	Sir Edward Law; Spencer Perceval (from 15 April 1802)
Solicitor-General	Spencer Perceval; Sir Thomas Manners-Sutton (from 11 May 1802)
Lord Advocate of Scotland	Charles Hope (from 12 May 1801)
Solicitor-General of Scotland	Robert Blair

THE IRISH GOVERNMENT

Lord Lieutenant	Earl of Hardwicke (appointed 27 April; sworn in, 25 May 1801)
Chief Secretary	Charles Abbot (from 25 May 1801); William Wickham (from 13 Feb. 1802); Sir Evan Nepean (from 6 Feb. 1804)
Lord Chancellor	Earl of Clare; Lord Redesdale (from 13 Feb. 1802)
Chancellor of the Exchequer	Isaac Corry
Attorney-General	Sir John Stewart; Standish O'Grady (from 28 May 1803)
Solicitor-General	William Cusack Smith; James McClelland (from 12 Jan. 1802); Wm. Conyngham Plunket (from 7 Nov. 1803)
Under-Secretaries of State	
Civil Department	Edward Cooke; Alexander Marsden (from Oct. 1801)
Military Department	Edward Baker Littlehales (from May 1801) [cr. Bart., 2 Sept. 1802]

THE KING'S HOUSEHOLD, 1798–APRIL 1804

Lord Steward	Duke of Dorset; Earl of Leicester (from 22 Feb. 1799); Earl of Dartmouth (from Aug. 1802)
Lord Chamberlain	Marquess of Salisbury
Treasurer	Viscount Stopford
Groom of the Stole	Duke of Roxburghe (d. 19 March 1804)
Master of the Horse	Earl of Westmorland; Earl of Chesterfield (from Feb. 1798); Viscount Falmouth
Captain of the Band of Gentlemen Pensioners	
Captain of the Yeomen of the Guard	Earl of Aylesford
Comptroller	Lord Charles Henry Somerset
Vice-Chamberlain	Charles Francis Greville
Master of the Buckhounds	Earl of Sandwich
Master of the Household	Henry Strachey (cr. Bart., 15 June 1801)

THE CORRESPONDENCE

1663 THE DUCHESS OF WURTEMBERG *to the* KING

[*Stutgard, 1 Jan. 1798.*] I look upon it as my first duty to write to your Majesty at the beginning of the year and hope that you will enjoy every blessing you so truly deserve and which it is my constant prayer to the Almighty to grant you. May I entreat of you to continue to me that goodness and protection which has ever been a source of happiness to me, as nobody can be more sincerely attached to your Majesty than I am?

It is not determined which day we are to take possession of our new habitation. I leave this house with regret as I have spent my time very agreably to myself here.

I am sure that it would give your Majesty pleasure to see the Duke's attentions to his mother and the respect he shews his father's memory.[1] He even intends with his sons and his brothers[2] to attend the great funeral, and went himself on Friday evening, when the body was removed for the private burial, to see that they might set out quietly and to prevent there being any noise which should shock the Dutchess who was kept ignorant of the body's being at Stutgard and to prevent her knowing it: the Duke had even a newspaper printed for her with the account of its arrival at Ludewigsbourg. The reason of this deception was the resolution she had formed to see her poor husband once before he was buried, and on the Duke's speaking to the physicians they assured him in her state of health that it would be death to her if they granted her request. Today I pity her very much as we have all put on our mourning and that we are obliged to dine with the States, which prevents any one of us being with her this morning. She feels very much the attentions of her son and expresses herself much pleased at my staying with her. (51453–4)

1664 WILLIAM PITT *to the* KING

[*Downing Street, 5 Jan. 1798, 5 a.m.*] Mr. Pitt humbly begs leave to acquaint your Majesty that on the adjourned debate on the Bill for the Assessed Taxes, the Bill was opposed by Mr. Hobhouse, Mr. Jekyll, Mr. Sheridan and Mr. Fox, and supported by Mr. Adams,[3] Mr. Lefevre,[4] Mr. Perceval (who distinguished himself by a most spirited and masterly speech), Mr. Dundas, Mr. Wilberforce and

---

[1] The Duchess Dowager of Wurtemberg (1736–98) died on 9 March.

[2] The Duke had six surviving brothers: Louis (1756–1817), Eugene (1758–1822), William (1761–1830), Ferdinand (1763–1834), Alexander (1771–1833), and Henry (1772–1833). He had two sons: William (1781–1864) who succeeded him in 1816; and Paul (1785–1852).

[3] There were then two M.P.s of that name, both supporting Ministers: first, James Adams (1752–1816), M.P. for West Looe, 1784–90; for Hindon, 1790–6; for Bramber, 1796–1802; for Harwich, 1803–6, 1807. The *Parl. Register* includes his name in the division list (XLIX, 637). In September 1796 he married a daughter of Leonard Hammond, of Cheam (Addington had married another in 1781). Second, William Adams (*c.* 1752–1811), M.P. for Plympton Erle, 1796–1801; for Totnes, 1801–11.

The speech is not even mentioned in *Parl. Hist.*, and in *Parl. Register*, XLIX, 557, is merely referred to, the Member's Christian name not being given.

[4] Charles Shaw-Lefevre (*c.* 1758–1823), a lawyer. M.P. for Newtown (Isle of Wight), 1796–1802; for Reading, 1802–20. His son Charles was afterwards Speaker of the House of Commons and was created Viscount Eversley.

Mr. Pitt. A Motion to postpone the third reading was negatived on a division by 204 to 75, and the Motion that it should be now read a third time was carried on a second division by 198 to 71. The farther consideration was deferred to this day (it being between four and five in the morning) in order to receive some trifling Amendments, but it was understood that no farther opposition will be made to the Bill's passing.[1] (8725)

1665 EARL SPENCER *to the* KING

[*Admiralty, 5 Jan. 1798.*] Earl Spencer has the honour of laying before your Majesty the Minutes of a court martial held on two seamen of your Majesty's ship the Tromp for mutiny, and is concerned to feel it his duty humbly to submit to your Majesty that the sentence should be carried into immediate execution, the case appearing a very strong one, & the President of the court martial having reported in a private letter that there were no alleviating circumstances belonging to it.[2] (8726)

1666 THE DUKE OF PORTLAND *to the* KING

[*Burlington House, Sunday night, 7 Jan. 1798.*] The Duke of Portland most humbly begs leave, in addition to the publick dispatches, to offer to your Majesty's consideration a private letter from the Lord Lieutenant of Ireland containing his reasons for presuming to submit to your Majesty an humble hope that your Majesty may be graciously pleased to confer the honor of a Baronetage of this kingdom upon Sir Charles Talbot,[3] whom your Majesty was pleased to raise to that dignity in your kingdom of Ireland in the year 1790, or to empower the Lord

---

[1] Fox spoke from 11.30 p.m. until 3 a.m., Pitt from 3 a.m. until 4 a.m. The numbers in both *Parl. Register* and *Parl. Hist.*, as well as in Charles Abbot's (Lord Colchester's) *Diary*, I, 132, are, accurately, given as 202 v 75, and 196 v 71. The King's reply, 8.32 a.m. on the 5th, expressing regret that these trifling Amendments had been accepted by the Government, is in Stanhope, III, Appendix, p. x. See *Correspondence of Lord Granville Leveson-Gower*, I, 193, and *Wellesley Papers*, I, 47.

Canning had expected a minority vote of between 70 and 80. 'But the clamour and the danger are at an end', he added. (Harewood MSS.) On the 17th he wrote: 'The Assessed Taxes gain ground everywhere. It remains only to hope that the Bill will be as productive as well as popular, when its principle and provisions are thoroughly understood' (*ibid.*). Pitt wrote to Mornington on the 26th: 'In spite of six weeks of more fatigue and anxiety than have attended almost any other Parliamentary campaign, I am greatly better than you left me, and I trust, equal to fighting the battle as long as may be necessary. Our great measure of the Assessed Taxes was for some time apparently in great danger of failing; less from any real difficulty or even general dislike to it than from the impression of local & partial clamour, and from the effect of a very great degree of panic which infected too many of those who are generally most free from it. It became necessary to shew that *at all risks* I was determined to persevere in it; and by those means alone I believe it was carried. Opposition I think added to the odium and disgrace of their secession by returning from it on this occasion, and by the whole of their conduct and language upon it. Our last debate (to my great joy) produced a speech from Perceval, which was in all respects one of the best I ever heard; and was an attack upon Fox pointed and galling enough to have drawn forth one of Grattan's warmest encomiums. It certainly sent him home very sick to his supper.' (Ann Arbor MSS.)

[2] The King's reply on the 6th (8.44 a.m.), lamenting that the spirit of mutiny in the Fleet had extended to 'every quarter of the globe', and approving the sentences, is in *Spencer Papers*, II, 173. Joseph Robinson and Charles Crawley were executed at Spithead on the 8th.

[3] Sir Charles Henry Talbot, of Belfast and of Mickleham, Surrey (1720–98), the son of Major-General Sherington Talbot, of Evesham, Worcestershire. Created an Irish Baronet, March 1790. He died on 10 June.

Lieutenant to signify to Sir Charles Talbot your Majesty's gracious intentions of including him in the first promotion of that description which your Majesty may think fit to make. The Duke of Portland will not incur the guilt of trespassing upon your Majesty by any attempt to support the Lord Lieutenant's representation to your Majesty, but the Duke of Portland with great humility conceives that your Majesty may not disapprove his taking the liberty of suggesting to your Majesty that resentment is but too obviously the motive of the Marchoness of Donegal's[1] conduct in the present instance. Her great object is to have her father recommended to your Majesty for a Bishoprick, in which, as he has now failed for the second time, & as, from the sense which, the Duke of Portland knows, the Lord Lieutenant entertains of his duty to your Majesty, it is very probable that she has received such an answer from the Lord Lieutenant as leaves her no hopes of success, it will not appear unreasonable to your Majesty to attribute her endeavours to the cause which the Duke of Portland has ventured to assign for it.

The Lord Lieutenant's anxiety for the event of a commission with which he charged Mr Pelham, prevails upon the Duke of Portland to take this opportunity of laying before your Majesty a most humble representation on the part of the Lord Lieutenant in favor of the gentleman who, in conformity to the practice of his ancestors, calls himself Lord Kenmare,[2] who, to all the loyalty & other publick & private virtues which eminently distinguished his father, adds great activity & energy & such unremitting attention to your Majesty's service as to have preserved the whole county of Kerry, one of the least civilized, & where the Roman Catholick religion predominates to as great a degree as in any part of that kingdom, from any taint of disaffection or symptom of disturbance. For this most meritorious & exemplary conduct of Lord Kenmare's, the Lord Lieutenant feels it a matter of duty to submit his humble opinion to your Majesty that it would tend most essentially to promote the interests of your Majesty's Government, & highly & equally gratify your Majesty's Protestant & Catholick subjects of that kingdom if your Majesty would be pleased to confer on Lord Kenmare the dignity of the peerage. At the same time however that the Lord Lieutenant presumes to state that he is induced to take this step by the high sense he has of the personal & hereditary claims of Ld. Kenmare to some mark of your Majesty's sanction & approbation, he feels that he is called upon in justice to Lord Kenmare to declare to your Majesty that this representation in his favor is not made at the instance of that gentleman, & would have been probably, though reluctantly, reserved for some other occasion, had he not been urged by the Earl of Westmorland to take your Majesty's commands for the accomplishment of an assurance of a peerage to Lady French[3] which that Earl considered himself empowered to give her in the

[1] Lord Donegall (1739–99) (Marquessate, [I.], 1791) married, as his third wife, in 1790, Barbara (c. 1768–1829), daughter of the Rev. Luke Godfrey, D.D., Rector of Midleton, Co. Cork.

[2] The Viscounty of Kenmare [I.] was one of the seven Irish peerages created by James II after his exclusion from the throne of England, but when possessed of his rights as King of Ireland (December 1688). Valentine Browne (1754–1812), succeeded his father (1726–95) as titular Viscount Kenmare. On 14 Feb. 1798 he was created Viscount Kenmare [I.], and on 2 Jan. 1801 Earl of Kenmare [I.].

[3] Rose Dillon (d. 1805), daughter of Patrick Dillon, of Killeen, Co. Roscommon, married (1761) Charles Ffrench (d. 1784), who was created an Irish Baronet in 1779. On 12 March 1798 she was created Baroness Ffrench [I.]. She was succeeded by her only son Thomas (c. 1765–1814), as 2nd Baron, who

course of his Administration in Ireland. And as that peerage, though given certainly in the first instance to a Protestant, was notoriously designed for the benefit & as a reward for a particular service which had been renderd by her son who was & is a Roman Catholick & who was to be the next in the limitation of the intended title, the Lord Lieutenant feels that in consideration of the many eminent & uniform services of Lord Kenmare & his father, he cannot, consistently with his duty to your Majesty, be the instrument of conveying such a mark of your Majesty's favor on a person of the Roman Catholick persuasion without laying this his most humble request in favor of Lord Kenmare at your Majesty's feet & representing with the utmost deference but with an earnestness which nothing but a sense of his duty could prompt him to express, that a peerage cannot be conferred upon a Roman Catholick & withheld from Lord Kenmare without material injury to your Majesty's service.

As the Duke of Portland conceives the case now submitted to your Majesty to be hitherto unprecedented, he is willing to flatter himself that it will appear to your Majesty that in laying it before your Majesty in writing he has adopted the mode which is most agreable to your Majesty & most consonant to the form which his duty to your Majesty required him to observe. (8727–31)

1667 THE KING *to* LORD LOUGHBOROUGH

[*Windsor, 9 Jan. 1798.*] The paper[1] drawn up on the 2d of this month by the Lord Chancellor so ably condences the unhappy subject of the Prince of Wales's dislike of the Princess of Wales, and his mode of putting forced constructions on ill-advised expressions she may have used, to ground the supposition that she is desirous of a separation, meets with my thorough approbation, and had I not previously thought him the most proper person to employ in this delicate business, I certainly should never have put it into his hands.

I therefore authorize the Lord Chancellor to express to the Prince of Wales the impossibility of my consenting to any public separation between him and the Princess of Wales, as incompatible with the religion, laws, and Government of my kingdom; secondly, to effect a reconciliation of the present difference between the Prince and Princess and persuade them to live on terms at least of reciprocal respect, however their intercourse may be unhappily limited, and thirdly, to establish rules which may prevent mutual irritation in future, and prevent the repetition of appeals to me. (8733)

founded a Bank at Tuam, but the troubles resulting from its failure about ten years later caused him to commit suicide. 'The grounds on which this old lady obtained a peerage are curious. Neither her husband nor her son nor any of her relatives appear to have been in Parliament, or to have done any political or other service, save that her son influenced, on behalf of the Government, certain members of the Roman Catholic Committee who were of his own faith. Accordingly he obtained a promise of a peerage, but such a grant to "a Papist" being obnoxious to the King, and in every way unpopular, the difficulty was solved by conferring it on the *Protestant* mother.' (G.E.C.). See also, Lecky, *Ireland in the Eighteenth Century*, IV, 182–5 (1913).

   [1] *Correspondence of George, Prince of Wales, 1770–1812*, III, 388, ed. A. Aspinall, no. 1314 (2 Jan. 1798).

[*Stutgard, 10 Jan. 1798.*] As Collonel Crawford has undertaken to convey this letter to your Majesty I must return you thanks for the one I had the honour to receive of the 20th of December. It gave me great pleasure to hear that the Thanksgiving at St. Paul's[1] went off to the satisfaction of every good Englishman. God grant that the sun which shone on that day may be an omen of the success your Majesty may meet with in all your undertakings to preserve your Kingdoms from mischief.

It is still quite uncertain when we shall get into the Castle as the workmen go on so dreadfully slow. They every day assure us that it will be ten days at least, which is uncomfortable as we all live now in the coach[house], and in one thing the Duke is very unlucky, as the only part of the house which was comfortably built as a double apartment was burnt down in the time of Duke Charles and only the walls rebuilt, which, as the Duke wishes to begin very prudently, prevents our being tolerably lodged for some years, as the expence would be immense were he to attempt at present to put that part to rights. Even Ludewigsbourg, which is a beautiful situation and an immense house, must have a good deal done to it that it may be comfortable. We both regret the quiet of dear little Scharnhausen and hope to contrive every now and then to spend a week there. Your Majesty who enjoys the being in the country will understand our feelings on that subject.

The Dutchess continues very indifferent, but through the attention of her children she meets with every comfort that her situation will admit of, and I flatter myself that I am of some use to her as I spend the chief part of the morning with her when the Duke's business prevents his being with her. (51457–8)

[*St. James, 10 Jan. 1798.*] I hope your Majesty will excuse my addressing you on a subject which 'till now I have postponed mentioning to you, but circumstances have occurred which render it absolutely necessary for me to address your Majesty. The news of the approaching death of Fieldmarshall Freytag being daily expected, and the command in consequence falling on General Walmoden, I wish to seize this opportunity of resigning my Regiment & quitting the Hannoverian Service, as I should be sorry to appear to do anything personal, and for many reasons I cannot possibly serve under General Walmoden. At the same time I threw [*sic*] myself on your Majesty's goodness, for having now served eight years, two of which were passed in very active campaigns, I should be loth to give up a profession I love. I shall therefore feel as grateful as I ought if your Majesty, reflecting on my situation, will, when an opportunity presents itself, give me some rank in the service of my own country. I will only take up your time with adding that I hope your Majesty will not misconceive or take ill my motive, or my manner

---

[1] On 19 Dec. 1797, celebrating the three great naval victories achieved by Lords Howe, St Vincent and Duncan over the French, Spanish and Dutch fleets. But Pitt, on his way to St Paul's, was hooted at and insulted by the mob, and he had to be escorted home by troops.

for thus addressing you, but do me justice for the gratitude, affection and duty with which I ever have been and shall be, Sir[1] [etc.] (47181)

1670   *Letters from* WILLIAM PITT *to the* KING, *with a reply*

[*Downing Street, Wednesday, 10 Jan. 1798, 10 p.m.*] Mr. Pitt humbly begs leave to submit the proposed Messages to the two Houses[2] and the accompanying warrants for your Majesty's Royal signature. (8736)

[*The King's reply, Windsor, 11 Jan., 9.25 a.m.*][3] At the same time that I return to Mr. Pitt the Messages to the two Houses of Parliament and the warrants which I have signed, I cannot help putting down a few hasty thoughts on the very judicious though most *tedious* letters of Monr. De Luc[4] to Lord Grenville and the secret paper transmitted by Lord Elgin. As I am overloaded with boxes I have not time [to] write to Lord Grenville and therefore desire Mr. Pitt will communicate this to him.

The little progress of explanation that has been gained through the channel of the Duke of Brunswick plainly shews that no rapid approach can be made at Berlin through him, but he has that kind of weight there that it would not be wise to let him feel that his personal timidity is known. I think it would be material therefore to keep up the correspondence with him through Monr. De Luc, which can be done by Lord Grenville's writing to Hannover instead of Brunswick, but to insist on Genl. Stampfort's[5] going to Berlin, who can certainly personally with the King of Prussia and through the Hereditary Prince of Orange advance things much more rapidly than any Minister, who must chiefly act through the medium of Count Haugwitz, whose conduct by no means obtains my esteem; at the same time on connecting the paper drawn up by that Count and the one sent by Lord Elgyn which manifestly comes either from the Austrian Minister at Berlin or from his Court, it seems that if a person was sent directly from hence to Berlin with a

---

[1] The Prince received no reply, and he wrote again to the King on 14 April. (No. 1718.) Freytag was already dead (*Gent. Mag.* 1798, 1, 86). As early as 24 Jan. the newspapers reported that Prince Ernest had resigned his Hanoverian command.

[2] A message presented to both Houses on the 11th providing for the calling out of the militia (augmented by an Act passed in the previous Session), in view of the invasion threat. See *Parl. Hist.* xxxiii, 1303.

[3] Endorsed by Pitt: 'Ansd. 3 p.m.'

[4] Jean André de Luc was the son of a well known citizen of Geneva. His defence of monarchy and revealed religion against the assaults of the Encyclopaedists had commended him to the King, who conferred on him the post of reader to Queen Charlotte after he had been resident in London for some time. He soon won the confidence of the royal family, and in November 1797 he was sent on a secret mission to Brunswick with the idea of inducing the Duke to support the scheme of a Second Coalition (of Russia, Austria, Britain and Prussia) against France. See *Dropmore Papers*, iv, 8, 26. The new King of Prussia, Frederick William III, would first have to be persuaded to dismiss his Minister Count de Haugwitz, who had been mainly responsible for the Treaty of Basle and Prussia's subsequent inglorious inaction.

[5] Lieutenant-General de Stamfort, apparently a Frenchman by birth. He had served in the Seven Years War under the Duke of Brunswick and subsequently in the Prussian army. After the death of Frederick the Great he entered the service of the Stadholder and took charge of the military education of the Orange Princes. He served in the 1793–4 campaigns in the Netherlands and subsequently became the confidential adviser of the Duke of Brunswick.

project of a quadruple alliance on the basis of preventing France from disturbing Germany and the north of Europe with an offer of money to Prussia if the services enjoined be performed, that person going forward to Petersburgh that the Russian Emperor may without loss of time be brought into the same alliance and that the two negociations may be communicated to Vienna by sending Lord Minto for that purpose, and England be with the consent of Prussia the kind of garantee of the sentiments of those Courts to each other; I think, though the task is arduous, the fate of every country depends so much on not an hour being lost, that I think it ought with vigour to be attempted. (Chatham Papers.)

[*Pitt's reply, Cleveland Square, Thursday, 11 Jan. 1798, 2.45 p.m.*] Mr. Pitt has been honored with your Majesty's commands, which he lost no time in communicating to Lord Grenville. They both concur in a clear opinion of the propriety of leaving nothing untried which can afford a prospect of improving the favorable disposition shewn at Berlin, and if possible of laying a foundation of a system which may comprehend the three Great Powers of the Continent jointly with Great Britain. A doubt however has occurred to them whether the negotiation may not be conducted with less observation and more effect thro the channel of the Hereditary Prince Frederic of Orange,[1] and by communications thro the means of Monsr de Luc with the Duke of Brunswick, than by any ostensible mission from hence, which might perhaps alarm the caution of those to whom it is addressed. This is however only submitted on the first view of the subject, to which they will not fail to give a more detailed consideration when the dispatches connected with it can be conveniently returned by your Majesty. Mr Pitt has no hesitation in the meantime in saying that the policy of engaging eventually to give a moderate subsidy to ensure the defense of the north of Germany appears to him unquestionable, and he trusts would be generally felt and admitted. (8737–8)

1671   LORD GRENVILLE *to the* KING

[*Cleveland Row, 11 Jan. 1798, 2.45 p.m.*] Lord Grenville has the honour humbly to acquaint your Majesty, that on conversing with Mr Pitt on the general outlines of the important subjects connected with the dispatches received yesterday and this morning from the Continent, it occurred to them that the objects in view might be in a great degree hazarded by the appearance of any ostensible mission from hence either to Berlin or Petersburgh, & still more to Vienna. As the great point of all is that no time should be lost, the best mode of communication would perhaps be that General Stamfort should be urged to go immediately to Berlin to convey your Majesty's answer to the suggestions received thro' the Duke of Brunswick, and to give eventual assurances of pecuniary assistance if the measures now adopted by the King of Prussia for defending the north of Germany should produce a renewal of the war with France. Prince Frederick of Orange might be desired to follow him as soon as it could be possible for him to reimbark for the

---

[1] His elder brother, William, was the Hereditary Prince.

Continent, and might be the best channel for conveying to the Court of Vienna the project of a Quadruple Alliance, supposing it agreed to at Berlin—and in this event any representations made on the subject at Petersburgh would perhaps be as effectually made by Sir Charles Whitworth as they could by any fresh person, especially as the Court of Berlin would probably send some person to Petersburgh for that purpose.

Lord Grenville thought that your Majesty would excuse his breaking in upon your Majesty with these general ideas, as it seems so very important that no time should be lost in preparing for their execution if approved by your Majesty; and it occurred to him that possibly your Majesty might chuse to see Prince Frederick, or might know how far circumstances (particularly that of his health,) would be likely to allow of his undertaking such a journey. The plans in view might be explained to Prince Frederick here in general terms only, as, if they are approved of at Berlin, the fullest communication could be made to him there by General Stamfort.

Lord Grenville has some doubts whether something might not be to be apprehended from too great eagerness & zeal on the part of Lord Minto, even supposing the objection to an ostensible mission to be less than it has struck him.

Lord Grenville takes the liberty to send to your Majesty the dispatches received this morning from Lord Elgin and Sir Morton Eden, as they are both in some degree material. (8739–40)

1672   EARL SPENCER *to the* KING, *and the reply*

[*Admiralty, 12 Jan. 1798.*] Earl Spencer is concerned to be under the necessity of laying before your Majesty the proceedings of a court martial held at Yarmouth on two seamen of the Adamant for a very heinous crime, and to submit to your Majesty the propriety of ordering the law to take its course on the man who has been found guilty by the Court, as there do not appear to be any circumstances which can recommend him to your Majesty's mercy. (8741)

[*The King's reply, Windsor, 13 Jan., 8.53 a.m.*] I have received this morning Earl Spencer's note accompanying the proceedings of a court martial on two seamen at Yarmouth belonging to the Adamant, for a most heinous crime. I cannot but feel the propriety of ordering the sentence to be put into execution. (Althorp MSS.)

1673   *Letters from* LORD GRENVILLE *to the* KING, *and the replies*

[*Downing Street, 13 Jan. 1798, 2.45 p.m.*] Lord Grenville has the honour to transmit to your Majesty the private letters for your Majesty, received from Wirtemberg, by the Comte d'Uxhall,[1] sent to announce to your Majesty the accession of the present Duke. (8742)

[*From Grenville, Cleveland Row, 13 Jan., 11 p.m.*] Lord Grenville has the honour humbly to submit to your Majesty his ideas of an answer to the paper from the

---

[1] Ukscull in 11, 646. The spelling of his name baffled English people, and there are many variations.

Court of Berlin, and of a letter to M. de Luc on the same subject. He hopes your Majesty will excuse the liberty he takes to send the latter in the original, in order to avoid extending the confidence of this transaction further than is absolutely necessary. Lord Grenville proposes with your Majesty's permission to send a messenger tomorrow with dispatches conformable to these ideas, to Lord Elgin & Sir Charles Whitworth, & he thinks the same messenger might without observation pass thro' Hanover, & leave this letter there for M. de Luc, under M. de Steinberg's cover.

Lord Grenville is to see Prince Frederic tomorrow morning, but he guesses from M. de Nagell's conversation that the former will think his own situation with the Court of Vienna too delicate to allow of his undertaking such a commission. (8743–4)

[*The King's reply, Windsor, 14 Jan., 8.56 a.m.*] The letter Lord Grenville has written to Monsieur de Luc contains everything that is proper, but I wish the answer to the paper from the Court of Berlin had been a little more pointed, and had stated the offer of some specific monthly sum if the King should be forced from the defensive measures he must take to change them to offensive measures against the French, as also an assurance that if Russia, England and Prussia cordially unite, no peace shall be made but with the mutual concurrence of the three Powers, and that Austria shall be invited to join this Alliance and become a principal in this measure.

Lord Grenville's proposal of having the letter left with Baron Steinberg[1] is very proper, as I suppose Lord Grenville will not send the messenger till the evening I will send a letter to Steinberg by the same messenger.

I have since writing this read the Memoire delivered by the Duke d'Harcourt,[2] it is impossible I can advise the Duke of Mecklenburg to let the French King settle in his Dutchy when the Duke of Brunswick is obliged to desire him to leave Blankenburg. (Fortescue MSS.)

[*From the King, Windsor, 14 Jan.*] As Lord Grenville proposes sending a messenger to the Continent this evening, I enclose a letter to be forwarded to Baron Steinberg. (Fortescue MSS.)

[*Lord Grenville's reply, Cleveland Row, 14 Jan. 1798, 11 p.m.*] Lord Grenville has been honoured with your Majesty's commands. He has in consequence of them made some alterations in the Memoire to be transmitted through the Duke of Brunswick, and in the dispatch to Lord Elgin he has stated the sum of one million as that which your Majesty's servants deemed admissible as the amount of subsidy supposing other points satisfactorily arranged. He was apprehensive that some inconvenience might arise from engaging immediately for that particular sum without some previous explanation on the points connected with the subject.

[1] The Hanoverian Minister. See *Dropmore Papers*, IV, *passim*.
[2] He was described as *Louis XVIII's* confidential Minister in England.

Lord Grenville will take care that your Majesty's letter to M. de Steinberg shall be sent by the messenger.

By a letter which Lord Grenville received this morning from M. de Nagell he perceives that Prince Frederick of Orange does not wish to undertake the business which had been proposed to him. (8745-6)

[*The King's reply, Windsor, 15 Jan., 8.50 a.m.*] I can scarcely find words suffici-ently expressive of my approbation of the various papers Lord Grenville has prepared on the plan of forming a Quadruple Alliance to combat the wicked and extravagant schemes of the French.

My reason for wishing the communication with Prussia might be more specific (which Lord Grenville has now very fully answered) arose from seeing that the forcing that Court forward is rather difficult, and suspecting that Count Haugwitz and Field Marshall Möllendorff will throw every possible difficulty in bringing the honorable sentiments of the King of Prussia into effect that consequently promises of assistance were required to be more specific than otherwise might, in the opening of a negociation, have been necessary.

I from the first doubted whether Prince Frederick of Orange could be brought to take any part in the negotiations now on foot, which was the cause of my directing Lord Grenville to sound Baron Nagell on the subject prior to my making any personal application which might have embarrassed the Prince. I see my suspicions were just by what Lord Grenville mentions in his note, and conse-quently no farther attempt ought to be made. (Fortescue MSS.)

1674 *Letters from* WILLIAM PITT *to the* KING

[*Hollwood, Monday, 22 Jan. 1798.*] Mr Pitt feels considerable reluctance in troubling your Majesty on a subject on which he is not sure that your Majesty will think him justified in doing so. But what he wishes humbly to submit to your Majesty appears to him in every view too important to withhold. The disposition at the present moment to great and vigorous exertion in the public defence is very prevalent, and nothing can be more essential to this object than the success of the measure of voluntary contribution, both as an important resource in itself and as most likely generally to reconcile men's minds to the measure lately adopted. On this idea many of your Majesty's servants and others zealous in the cause have thought it right to contribute a proportion of their income much beyond the amount of their proportion to the new assessment. It is however the universal opinion, as far as Mr Pitt has the means of judging, that the ardor and enthusiasm which would give this measure its full effect will not be produced unless your Majesty should condescend to let some example be set in your Majesty's name. To what amount your Majesty might think proper to carry the sum, if you should be graciously pleased to entertain the general idea, Mr Pitt cannot presume to guess. He ventures however to submit to your Majesty, and trusts he shall be forgiven for the freedom with which he does so, that the great object at such a moment must be to shew that your Majesty has *at least* as little hesitation as any of your subjects in making any pecuniary sacrifice in points connected with personal gratification or option. He is aware how small a proportion of your Majesty's Civil List revenue comes under this description, which in truth applies to no part of it but the *Privy Purse*. Whether there are any other means which your Majesty possesses or is at liberty to apply in the same manner your Majesty alone can judge. Mr Pitt only takes the liberty to add that an impression certainly prevails on this point, which if founded at all is probably greatly exaggerated, and which it might be highly material to remove by some proper mode of explanation. In offering this humble representation to your Majesty, Mr Pitt feels that his only apology is in the circumstances which lead to it, and in the view which he knows your Majesty forms of them. He is persuaded that your Majesty considers the issue of the present contest as the most important of all earthly objects. Penetrated with the same opinion, he cannot but see that the success of our exertion must chiefly depend on exerting the zeal of the public, and with this view he is persuaded that more rests on the *single point* which he now ventures to bring under your Majesty's consideration than on any other in the present state of the country.[1] (8747–50)

[*Hollwood, 23 Jan.*] Mr Pitt has been honored with your Majesty's gracious answer to the suggestion which he submitted to your Majesty yesterday. He feels very strongly the difficulties which the circumstances stated by your Majesty present to the adoption of those suggestions in as great an extent as might have been desireable, if practicable; and under such circumstances he cannot presume to submit to your Majesty, without further consideration, any specific opinion on so delicate a subject. But he will request your Majesty's permission to submit whatever may occur to him (on reflection in the interval) when he has the honor of attending your Majesty tomorrow. (8751)

1675　LORD GRENVILLE *to the* KING

[*Cleveland Row, 25 Jan. 1798.*] Lord Grenville has the honour humbly to return to your Majesty the copies of two letters from your Majesty to the King of Prussia,

---

[1] The King's reply on the 23rd, 8.25 a.m., is in Stanhope, III, Appendix, p. xi. There are two errors in the third line, which should read, 'brought before me by Mr. Pitt is entirely of that nature'. He undertook to subscribe £20,000 (one-third of his Privy Purse) although he owed his bankers money, borrowed chiefly in order to contribute to the Government's election fund. He explained that he had never drawn a shilling from his Hanoverian revenue. 'I am sorry to say the King of England is not so rich a man, and that every shilling taken from his Privy Purse must fall on the indigent; for if he has not the means, his workmen and the poor cannot but feel it to their sorrow.' See also *Colchester Diary*, I, 133.

Lord Camden, the Lord Lieutenant of Ireland, did not care to commit himself with regard to a voluntary subscription without knowing Pitt's feelings about it. Pitt wrote to him on the 31st: 'With respect to all those who are in marked public situations and have therefore been called upon to stand forward as supporters of the War, I have thought it right to recommend, wherever I have had any opportunity of giving my opinion, that the subscription should be not less than one-fifth of each man's whole annual income *computed on the largest scale*. Most of the Cabinet and almost all my immediate friends have acted on this principle.' In view of the fact that Camden and the Marquess of Buckingham held the enormously valuable sinecure offices of Tellers of the Exchequer (in war time, that is), and incurred much popular odium in consequence, Pitt suggested 'that neither of you will effectually consult your own credit, comfort or real interest by any measure short of subscribing annually as long as the War shall last the whole excess (whatever it may be) of your future profits in each year, beyond those which you received on the average of peace'. (Camden MSS.)

and to the Duke of Brunswick. The letters from M. de Luc he has given to Mr Hammond to remain with the dispatches in the Office, unless your Majesty should be pleased to give him any other orders on the subject.[1] (8752)

1676   THE DUKE OF PORTLAND *to the* KING

[*Burlington House, Saturday night, 27 Jan. 1798.*] Although the dispatches from the Lord Lieutenant of Ireland, which the Duke of Portland has now the honor of laying with all humility before your Majesty, do not appear to contain anything upon which it seems necessary for him to submit any observation to your Majesty, he cannot reconcile it to himself to offer to your Majesty a letter which appears to have been so long in his possession as that which contains the recommendation of Lord Dillon,[2] to your Majesty without in the first place imploring your Majesty's pardon for the neglect he must appear to have been guilty of, & humbly begging leave to represent to your Majesty that not having been in possession of that letter until after he had paid his duty to your Majesty at St James's, it did not appear to him of that importance that required him to lay it before your Majesty until he should have other papers to trouble your Majesty with.

The Duke of Portland is desired by the Marquiss of Bute to request your Majesty to permit the Marquiss to lay at your Majesty's feet a walking stick of cinnamon wood, the head of which is ornamented with specimens of all the precious stones which are to be found in the Island of Ceylon & which has been brought from thence by a person who is lately arrived, & that your Majesty will be graciously pleased to signify the time at which the Marquiss of Bute may present it to your Majesty.[3] (8753-4)

1677   EARL SPENCER *to the* KING, *and the reply*

[*Admiralty, 28 Jan. 1798.*] Earl Spencer has the honour to lay before your Majesty the proceedings of a general court martial held at Portsmouth on Major-

---

[1] The King wrote again to Pitt on the 25th at 5.58 p.m. from the Queen's House (Stanhope, III, Appendix, p. xii).

[2] Charles, 12th Viscount Dillon [I.] (1745–1813), succeeded to his father's peerage, 15 Sept. 1787; Constable of Athlone Castle, 1797–1813; K.P., 19 March 1798.

[3] Spain had joined France against England in 1796; Bute's diplomatic career then came to an end (Oct.), and, unsuccessfully, he sought office at home. He wrote to Pitt on 23 Feb. 1798: 'When I had the honor of seeing you on my return from Spain, you may possibly recollect, after rendering an account of the Embassy, my having mentioned that, although I should feel extremely gratified to be esteemed worthy of holding employment, I would not plague you with solicitation. Your answer was of course complimentary and general. Since the above period I have abstained from again making you a tender of my services, hoping the foreign line, so much suited to my disposition, might afford an opening. All likelihood, however, of such events appearing further removed than ever, permit me to express a wish of filling some situation at home. Permit me likewise to suggest a particular office—that of the Lord Steward—which from the Duke of Dorset's state of health may be looked upon as in fact vacant. Entertaining these views, and I trust, considering the important station lately committed to my care, they will not be deemed unreasonable, I was determined, without having recourse to other demands, to apply directly to yourself. You, as the King's First Minister, have, of right, the disposal of everything, and to you I shall be happy to owe the obligation. Flattering myself that you will favor me with a word of answer I have the honor [etc.].' (*Chatham Papers*, 118.) He wrote another appealing letter to Pitt on 7 July (*ibid.*).

General Wemyss[1] of the Marines for various irregularities with which he was charged by the officers of the Portsmouth division, and humbly submits to your Majesty the propriety of carrying the sentence into execution by causing General Wemyss to be placed on half pay, as it evidently appears that he is totally unfit to continue in the command of that division. (8755)

[*The King's reply, Windsor, 29 Jan., 8.15 a.m.*] The sentence of the court martial on Major Genl. Wemyss seems thoroughly grounded. I therefore approve of his being placed on half pay, which cannot but be advantageous to the discipline of the Portsmouth Division of Marines. (Althorp MSS.)

1678 *Letters from* WILLIAM PITT *to the* KING

[*Downing Street, 31 Jan. 1798, 1.30 p.m.*] Mr Pitt has the mortification of finding himself prevented by a slight indisposition from paying his duty to your Majesty today at St James's. He had meant to take the liberty of submitting humbly to your Majesty the expediency at the present moment of marking the sense entertained of the Duke of Norfolk's conduct in the meeting held last week at the Crown and Anchor, by dismissing him from the Lieutenancy of the West Riding of Yorkshire, and he has no doubt that such a measure is expected by all the zealous friends of the Constitution, and would give general satisfaction.[2] Mr Pitt

[1] Maurice Wemyss. Colonel, 1790; Major-General, Sept. 1794; Lieutenant-General, 1801.

[2] At this public dinner on the 24th (Fox's birthday) the Duke gave the toast, 'Our Sovereign, the Majesty of the People!' The inner history of the affair is given in a memorandum by the Duke's cousin, Henry Howard: '...It was expected that Mr. Gale Jones and some others who had the reputation of carrying their ideas on political subjects beyond the privilege which the Whig party entertained would be present at the meeting and this induced the Duke of Norfolk to send for the list of toasts which were proposed to be given at the dinner, that he might counteract any violence that might be deemed unconstitutional and give an improper colouring to the meeting. This list he revised and commented on in my presence the day before the meeting. I attended his Grace to it but found the principal room filled by persons who had taken their seats long before our arrival, so that all those who had come with his Grace and many others, among which were Lord Grey, Mr. Richard Wilson, &c. were obliged to leave the great room and dine below stairs. A report of the first toast which gave offence, comparing the situation of the friends of Mr. Fox to those of General Washington, was brought to us from above stairs, but was not with any one there present construed as alluding to physical force to be and in obtaining the reforms wished for, and the second toast given, which was "Constitutional Redress to *National Wrongs*," was sufficiently explanatory that there was no such meaning or intention. I went upstairs before the second toast which was objected to was given and certainly the Duke, I conceive unwarily and ad capeandum, gave it with additional words which gave some hold against him: the toast as given was *Our Sovereign, the Majesty of the People*, instead of the more usual words of the *Sovereignty of the People*, or the *Majesty of the People*, the Duke probably intending to combine the two modes of giving these toasts into one. I did not recollect that any very particular notice or sensation was caused by it at the meeting, and when we left the room and met some of the most moderate Whigs it did not appear to have made any particular impression or have caused any apprehension that it would be taken notice of, and all congratulated one another that the attempts and speeches made by some to provoke the stronger feelings of discontent had been successfully opposed and depressed.

'These toasts and the meeting became of course the subject of much comment, attack and defence in the papers, and it appears that the Duke prepared a paragraph to explain his intentions for one of the papers, but I did not hear him mention it at the time and do not believe it was sent to the press...The Duke of Norfolk was at that time in habits of great intimacy and frequent intercourse with the Duke of York. I was told that on the Duke's calling on his Royal Highness he received him very coolly, answered very short and bowed him out of the room. The Duke, to whom I mentioned this, stated that it might

cannot help also feeling a strong opinion (which is certainly not dictated by any personal partiality) that considering the circumstance of the Lieutenancy having been held by the late Lord Rockingham,[1] and the very zealous and proper conduct of Lord Fitzwilliam with respect to constitutional questions in this country, it might have a very useful effect if your Majesty should think it fit to allow him to succeed to the vacancy, if it should be found that he would receive the offer properly.[2] (8756–7)

[*Downing Street, Thursday, 1 Feb.*] Mr Pitt had intended, if he had not been prevented from attending your Majesty yesterday at St James's, to have submitted to your Majesty what occurs to him with respect to the manner of filling up the Privy Seal, which he is conscious has from different circumstances been too long delayed already, and which it seems now material to decide upon before the end of the present parliamentary recess. He therefore takes the liberty of laying his ideas before your Majesty in this mode, being anxious to know how far what he wishes to propose would meet with your Majesty's approbation, before he makes any general communication on the subject to your Majesty's confidential servants. It does not appear to Mr Pitt that there is any person now out of office, whose being added to the Cabinet would be attended with any very striking advantage; and of those who already hold offices, he sees no one who could be more properly selected than Lord Westmorland. In that event your Majesty might possibly not disapprove of Lord Chesterfield as Master of the Horse; and it would afford Mr Pitt great satisfaction if the opening in the Post Office could be supplied by the appointment of Lord Auckland, which would be attended with the convenience of relieving the Civil List from a contingent pension which he now enjoys.[3]

be so, but he had thought that the Duke of York was much occupied and therefore had only briefly mentioned some official business relating to the quarters of the Regiment.' (Arundel MSS.)

The official intimation of the dismissal arrived at Norfolk House whilst the Duke was entertaining the Prince of Wales. It was written by the Duke of Portland on the evening of Wednesday the 31st: 'I have the King's commands to signify to your Grace that his Majesty has no further occasion for your services in the capacity of Lord Lieutenant of the West Riding of the County of Yorkshire or as Colonel of the 1st West Riding Regiment of Militia.

'I am very sorry that my duty obliges me to acquaint your Grace with this determination on the part of his Majesty.' (Arundel MSS.)

[1] Charles, 2nd Marquess of Rockingham (1730–82), Prime Minister, 1765–66, and March–July 1782. On his death the vast Wentworth estates in Yorkshire and Wicklow passed to his nephew Lord Fitzwilliam. He had been dismissed from his Lieutenancy in December 1762 for disapproving the terms of the preliminaries of the Peace of Paris. Fitzwilliam succeeded the Duke of Norfolk (he also was dismissed from his Lord Lieutenancy in 1819 for his condemnation of the 'Peterloo massacre' and support of a Yorkshire protest meeting).

[2] The King's reply from the Queen's House, 1 Feb., 8.40 a.m., is in Stanhope, III, Appendix, p. xiii. 'The Earl of Chatham yesterday mentioned Mr. Pitt's idea of the propriety of removing the Duke of Norfolk...and had my permission, as he intimated Mr. Pitt's not being able to come out, to express my thorough concurrence in the proposed removal. The Chancellor, whom I had previously seen, was strong of the same opinion. I therefore authorized Lord Grenville to desire the Duke of Portland... to send the usual letter...to the Duke of Norfolk.'

[3] Lord Auckland wrote to his friend Lord Sheffield on the 8th: 'Some arrangement in my favour has long been in contemplation. It now seems likely to take place soon. The office to which I allude is not of the Cabinet, and its income, after deducting what I shall give up for it, will not materially help me. Still, however, it is as acceptable to me as any other would be under all existing circumstances.'

Portland wrote to Pitt on the 9th: 'I thank you for the communication of your intended arrangement

Mr Pitt did not fail to avail himself without delay of the authority which your Majesty had been graciously pleased to give him,[1] by announcing your Majesty's intention of applying twenty thousand pounds by quarterly installments to the public service. He confesses himself in some degree disappointed in having not yet been enabled to acquaint your Majesty that such effects had been produced from the example as might well be expected, but he has great reason to believe, notwithstanding the delay, that they will soon be seen in the more rapid encrease of the subscription.[2] (8758–60)

1679   THE DUKE OF PORTLAND *to the* KING

[*Burlington House, Thursday, 1 Feb. 1798, 10.25 p.m.*] The Duke of Portland most humbly begs leave to lay at your Majesty's feet the Duke of Norfolk's answer to the letter which the Duke of Portland wrote last night to him in obedience to your Majesty's commands to signify to him that your Majesty had no further occasion for his services as Lord Lieutenant of the West Riding of Yorkshire or as Colonel of the First West Riding Regiment of Militia. (8761)

1680   THE DUKE OF NORFOLK *to the* KING[3]

[*2 Feb.* [*sic*] *1798.*] To your Majesty's pleasure to remove me from the Lieutenancy of the West Riding of the county of York & command of a regiment, communicated to me by the Duke of Portland I implicitly bow, & do not obtrude myself to enquire the motive.

Conscious that I never was or can be capable of harbouring any sentiment but of strict loyalty to the Constitution, the Government & person of your Majesty, I disdain to notice idle rumours & mistatement of newspapers.

But least a misrepresentation of some unguarded expressions on a late occasion where nothing could be distinctly heard, should produce an unfavourable impression in the mind of my Sovereign towards me, I could not so far repress my feelings as to delay untill the first publick Levée declaring to your Majesty that my only meaning was to express a wish to support Mr Fox in his constitutional endeavours to obtain a reform in the representation of Parliament, a measure in my opinion favourable to the stability of the Constitution & your Majesty's Government.

Permit me therefore, Sir, to take this method of declaring, in the most dutifull & respectfull manner, that your Majesty has not in your dominions a person

in filling up the Privy Seal. As you seem to think it necessary and are of opinion that it will be agreeable to the King, I feel no disposition to object to it. But I cannot help saying that I still adhere to the opinion which I thought I held in common with all our colleagues in Administration at the time the Privy Seal was declined by the Duke of Devonshire and Lord Liverpool.' (Chatham Papers, 168.) It was in Sept. 1796 that Portland had said that the Duke of Devonshire might accept the Privy Seal (*Dropmore Papers*, III, 242).

[1] On the 25th, 5.58 p.m. (Stanhope, III, Appendix, p. xii.)

[2] The King's reply (12.05 a.m. on the 2nd, though dated by him the 1st, approving Pitt's suggestions, is in Stanhope, III, Appendix, p. xiii.

[3] The Prince of Wales sent for the Duke, and it was decided between them that the Duke should write this letter and take it himself to the King at Windsor.

more ready to sacrifice his life & fortune when required for your service than your Majesty's [etc.][1] (8762)

1681 WILLIAM PITT *to the* KING

[*Downing Street, 8 Feb. 1798.*] Mr. Pitt has the honor of submitting for your Majesty's signature Messages to the two Houses respecting the grant of the proposed annuity[2] to Lord Duncan, and also some Treasury warrants. (8765)

1682 LORD GRENVILLE *to the* KING, *and the reply*

[*Dropmore, 8 Feb. 1798.*] Lord Grenville has the honour humbly to submit to your Majesty that he has, under your Majesty's gracious approbation, settled with Mr. Talbot,[3] who was with Mr. Wickham as Secretary, that he should immediately return to the frontiers of Swisserland, to carry on such communications there as may be necessary, in the absence of your Majesty's Minister. But as Mr Talbot's residence in Swabia might under the present circumstances be insecure if the object of his journey should transpire here, Lord Grenville humbly recommends to your Majesty that he may be appointed your Majesty's Secretary of Legation at Petersburgh, which nomination will give a reason for his setting out immediately for the Continent, without any suspicion of a different purpose. (8763–4)

[*The King's reply, Queen's House, 9 Feb., 8.05 a.m.*] The appointment of Mr. Talbot as Secretary of Legation at Petersburgh seems the best means of covering his being employed on the frontiers of Switzerland. The sooner he returns to the Continent the better. (Fortescue MSS.)

1683 EARL SPENCER *to the* KING

[*Admiralty, 9 Feb. 1798.*] Earl Spencer has the honour to acquaint your Majesty that Sir James Marriott is now fully prepared to make his Report on the case of the prisoner convicted at the last Admiralty Sessions, and humbly proposes to your Majesty to receive his Report on Wednesday next at St. James's. (8766)

---

[1] The Duke was subsequently told (and he believed the information was accurate) that Pitt had proposed to the Cabinet that he should be proceeded against by law, but that Sir John Scott had said that in that case they must look for another Attorney-General. The proposal was dropped. The Duke's friendship with Lord Loughborough was never interrupted.

Pitt himself wrote to Mornington, saying that 'the two most distinguished traits' of the Fox birthday celebrations were 'a speech from the Duke of Norfolk, which I think even the Crown lawyers will hardly prove to be much short of treason, and a public profession from Horne Tooke of reconciliation and coalition with Fox, with which I think you will be delighted'.

[2] Of £2,000 a year net, payable to him and to the two next succeeding male heirs to whom the title of Viscount Duncan should descend. (*Parl. Register*, L, 293 [9 Feb.].)

[3] James Talbot, Chargé d'Affaires in Switzerland from William Wickham's departure on 7 Nov. 1797 until 20 Dec. 1797, when he notified the withdrawal of the special mission. Secretary of Legation and Chargé d'Affaires at Stockholm, 1799–1801. See *Dropmore Papers*, IV, *passim*.

Sir Charles Whitworth, the Minister to Russia, went on leave, presenting Justinian Casamajor, Secretary of Legation, as Chargé d'Affaires (June 1800), but the Tsar refused to receive Casamajor, and diplomatic relations were suspended until 1801.

[*Whitehall, Saturday, 10 Feb. 1798, 5.30 p.m.*] The Duke of Portland begs leave with great humility & satisfaction to lay before your Majesty a letter he has received from the Lord Lieutenant of Ireland by which it appears that by the exertions the Lord Lieutenant has made the attempt to raise a tax on the property of absentees will be completely defeated, & as for the disgust & ill humor which have been expressed upon the occasion, the Duke of Portland is willing to beleive that they cannot but subside upon reflection without the probability of their producing any ill consequences, & that the conduct of your Majesty's Government on the present occasion will be the most likely means that could be taken to prevent the revival of this attempt.

As the Duke of Portland understands that it is your Majesty's intention to confer the Order of the Bath on Vice-Admiral Colpoys, the Duke of Portland requests to know whether it is your Majesty's pleasure that the Officers of the Order should attend at St. James's on Wednesday next. (8767–8)

[*Bulstrode, Sunday, 11 Feb., 9.50 p.m.*] The Duke of Portland humbly legs leave to lay at your Majesty's feet a letter he has received this evening from the Lord Lieutenant of Ireland acquainting him with the death of the Earl of Clanbrassil[1] which happened on the 6th instant & expressing an anxious hope that your Majesty may condescend for the reasons assigned by the Lord Lieutenant to confer the Order of St. Patrick vacant by the Earl of Clanbrassil's death on the Earl of Ormonde.[2] (8769)

[*Bulstrode, Monday night, 12 Feb. 1798.*] The Duke of Portland has the honour of laying before your Majesty a dispatch which he has received this evening from the Lord Lieutenant of Ireland respecting the conduct which it may be adviseable for your Majesty's Government to pursue in that kingdom for the purpose of most effectually counteracting & defeating the traitorous designs of that desperate faction which wishes to separate the two Kingdoms & to form an alliance with the French republicans, of the expediency & necessity & urgency of which, although there cannot be any doubt, the Duke of Portland cannot but submit with all humility to your Majesty that the measure of arresting persons under a certainty of not being able to bring them to justice by trial is one which should require much more consideration than could be given to it in one meeting before it would be right to adopt it. The Duke of Portland ventures to add to the Lord Lieutenant's dispatch a letter written by his direction to Mr King which contains a short statement of the Irish Budget, & an intimation that Mr Latouche[3] will not bring forward his Motion for an absentee tax in an hostile manner, & that there is a possibility of his not moving it at all. (8770–1)

---

[1] James, Earl of Clanbrassill (1730–98) succeeded to his father's Irish peerage, 1758. K.P., March 1783 (one of the fifteen original Knights of the Order).

[2] K.P., 19 March 1798.

[3] There were five members of the Latouche family in the Irish House of Commons at this time: David and David, jun., who sat for Newcastle (Co. Dublin); John (Kildare Co.); Robert and John, jun., who sat for Harristown borough.

[*Downing Street, Monday, 12 Feb. 1798.*] Mr Pitt humbly begs leave to acquaint your Majesty that from a statement which he has recently received of the circumstances of Lord St Vincent (which he is convinced may be depended upon) he finds his income not more adequate to his rank than that of Lord Duncan. He therefore presumes that your Majesty will think him entitled to a similar provision, and he submits to your Majesty Messages for that purpose.[1] He also takes the liberty of sending for your Majesty's signature a warrant for a new appointment of Commissioners for the Tax Office which he flatters himself will place that Board in a situation of great efficiency and use, with scarce any additional expence to the public.[2] (8772)

Present Commissioners:

John Trenchard	Horace Hayes
George Blount	William Lowndes
Charles Dering	Barne Barne
John Farraby	Edward Medows
Barne Barne[3]	Horace Hayes
Edward Medows	and George Goodenough (8773)

[*The King's reply, Queen's House, 13 Feb., 10.20 a.m.*] As Mr. Pitt's information places the Earl of St. Vincent in point of circumstances in as scanty a situation as Viscount Duncan, I approve of the Message in his favour to both Houses of Parliament.

I am glad Mr. Pitt is enabled to render the Tax Office an efficient Board which, from the additional business now conferred to it, certainly requires men not inferior in tallents to those at the Boards of Custom and Excise. (Chatham Papers.)

1686   *Letters from the*   D U K E   O F   P O R T L A N D   *to the*   K I N G

[*Burlington House, Tuesday night, 13 Feb. 1798.*] The Duke of Portland most humbly begs leave to lay before your Majesty a draft of the official letter to the Earl Fitzwilliam acquainting him with your Majesty's gracious intention to appoint him your Majesty's Lieutenant of the West Riding of Yorkshire & the Earl's answer—& also a dispatch from the Lord Lieutenant of Ireland which only contains a more detailed account of the supply & ways & means proposed by the Chancellor of the Exchequer of Ireland[4] for the present year than that which the Duke of Portland had the honor of submitting to your Majesty this morning in the letter from Mr Yorke to Mr King.[5] (8774)

---

[1] See *Parl. Register*, L, 296 (13 Feb.).   [2] What now follows is in the King's hand.
[3] M.P. for Dunwich, 1777–91; Commissioner of Taxes, 1791–1820 (1754–1828).
[4] Sir John Parnell, 2nd Baronet (1744–1801). M.P. [I.] for Bangor, 1767–8; for Inistiogue, 1777–83, and for Queen's County, 1783–1800, and [U.K.] Jan.–Dec. 1801. Succeeded to the Baronetcy, 1782; Chancellor of the Exchequer [I.], 1785–99, being dismissed in Jan. for his opposition to the proposed Union.
[5] The following letters explain why the offer of the Lord Lieutenancy was not immediately accepted. First, Dr Laurence wrote to Fitzwilliam on the 7th: 'The note to which I alluded yesterday was from Mr. Windham. In the evening I received one from Mr. Pitt, wishing to see me this morning at half after

eleven. Before I went, I called on Mr. Windham to know how far I was at liberty to mention what had passed between him and me. He had no reserve on the subject. In the course of conversation he informed me that he had talked with the King relative to the appointment, who said that he believed "Lord Fitzwilliam to be a man who would feel it to be a point of honour at a moment like the present to do his duty, where he was called upon to shew himself." After stating the occasion of sending for me, Mr. Pitt expressed himself in very handsome terms of your Lordship's firm conduct in support of those principles in the *internal* politics of the kingdom which were so very essential at the present moment; professing at the same time to reserve his opinions on the grounds of former differences in another quarter. Under these circumstances he thought that any personal communication with him, even by letter, might not be agreeable to your Lordship's feelings. He wished it to be understood that he did not think it proper for him to offer, or your Lordship to accept, this or any appointment as a private favour. But from your estate, connection with the county, and your principles, he did not hold it consistent with his duty to look towards any other person than your Lordship as capable of equally serving your country in that station. The King, he said, considered the state of the country as imposing on every man a sort of military duty to be at his post; and he had it, in consequence, in command from his Majesty to signify his royal pleasure that your Lordship should take upon yourself the government of the West Riding of Yorkshire. This he desired me, and I consented, to communicate to your Lordship...' (Fitzwilliam MSS.)

On the 10th, Laurence wrote to Pitt: 'Dr. Laurence has the pleasure of informing Mr. Pitt that he had last night what he presumes will appear a very satisfactory conversation with Lord Fitzwilliam. His Lordship's wish is simply that the whole transaction on the face of it should be marked as a duty undertaken, not a favour accepted by him, and that his obedience should arise from the immediate commands of his Sovereign. Lord Fitzwilliam would certainly feel himself gratified by his Majesty's approbation of his former conduct in Ireland; and more so, if that approbation were considered not as a decision in his favour against his then colleagues, but as connected with a change of opinion in them from more reflection and experience, because though he is not very sanguine in expecting the same good effect now, as at an earlier period, he yet looks upon the adoption of other counsels than the present, as the only chance of ever settling that kingdom on any rational system of civil policy: his appointment to the Lieutenancy however has in his view of it no connexion whatever with that question. With regard to the second point intimated by Mr. Pitt, Lord Fitzwilliam does not desire the only mode of acceptance which he thinks consistent with his honour, to be understood as any disclaimer of Ministers on the part of his Majesty. He supposes them to be legally and constitutionally the advisers of, as they are responsible for, every public act of his Majesty's Government: but having no intercourse with them, his Lordship wishes, after receiving the regular official communication of his Majesty's pleasure, to take the King's commands from his own mouth. The mode which will ensure Lord Fitzwilliam's dutiful acceptance is shortly this. If the Secretary of State writes him an official letter, signifying that the Lieutenancy of the West Riding of Yorkshire being vacant, his Majesty thinks his Lordship the most proper person consistently with the good of his service to whom he can commit that important trust, and requiring his attendance at the next Levée, or to that effect, he will of course attend. He will then desire an audience, and if his Majesty will have the goodness to say that such are his royal sentiments and commands, Lord Fitzwilliam will instantly declare his obedience. Dr. Laurence is persuaded that in this decisive explanation of Lord Fitzwilliam's sentiments, Mr. Pitt will see nothing but that correct sense of honour and propriety which according to his Lordship's notions and principles has ever distinguished his political conduct...' (Fitzwilliam MSS.)

Portland wrote to Laurence on the 10th: 'Your letter to Mr. Pitt which he has just brought me, has most cruelly perplexed me, and stopped me in the middle of a letter I was actually writing to Lord Fitzwilliam to acquaint him that it was his Majesty's opinion that his service required that Lord Fitzwilliam should undertake the Lieutenancy of the West Riding. From the manner in which Lord Fitzwilliam's sentiments are stated it is impossible to determine whether Lord Fitzwilliam's acceptance is to depend upon what passes between his Majesty and him in the Closet; or whether he will take his Majesty's offer in the only constitutional way in which it can be made to him. I neither hope or imagine that Lord Fitzwilliam will accept any favour from those who compose his Majesty's Administration, but wishing as sincerely as I do for the public service that the Lieutenancy of the West Riding should be in the hands of a person who professes those sentiments in favour of the cause of government and good order by which Lord Fitzwilliam's conduct has always been actuated, I cannot notwithstanding commit the King and his Government by a deviation from what my duty and sense of the present state of things particularly require, and I am anxious to know without distinctions or differences, or references to matter wholly unconnected with this question, whether Lord Fitzwilliam will accept this employment as he accepted the Presidency of the Council in 1794, in doing which he certainly did not contract and was not understood to contract any obligation to the Ministers through whom the offer of that office

[*Whitehall, Friday, 16 Feb., 4.25 p.m.*] The Duke of Portland humbly begs leave to lay before your Majesty the warrant your Majesty was graciously pleased to sign for the creation of Sir John Shore[1] to be a Peer of Ireland. The Duke of Portland begs leave to represent to your Majesty that the warrant he returns herewith was settled & approved by your Majesty's Attorney General of this kingdom but that in consequence of the objections made to it by the Lord Chancellor & the Attorney-General of Ireland & still persisted in by them notwithstanding the reasons alledged in support of it by your Majesty's Law Officers here, the friends of Sir John Shore, at whose instance your Majesty condescended to confer the dignity of the peerage upon him, have been with the Duke of Portland to request him to express their most gratefull sense of your Majesty's goodness, & their humble hope that your Majesty will not refuse, in consideration of the objections which have been made in Ireland to the form of words in which the warrant is expressed, to suffer them to surrender it, & will graciously condescend to continue the favor your Majesty had intended to bestow on Sir John Shore by commanding a warrant to be prepared for that purpose in the usual form. The Duke of Portland therefore submits to your Majesty the original warrant to be cancelled in case your Majesty should be pleased to grant the petition of Sir John Shore's friends. (8775)

1687 THE QUEEN *to the* KING

[*Windsor, 18 Feb. 1798.*] Unhappy as it makes me to see your Majesty plagued, & the reluctance I feel to add at any time one moment's uneasiness to the various unpleasant affairs which constantly surround you, I feel myself, notwithstanding all the delicacy I possess, under the *necessity* to represent to you the truely miserable situation of my brother the Duke, caused by the death of Monsieur Schroeder, with whose life the Irish pension ceases. At the time Baron de Dewitz came over he brought me the account of the late Duke's[2] debts, amounting to 500,000 German crowns, & since all the public debts are collected, they are considerably above

was made to him, but might well consider himself as conferring a favour upon them. Your explanatory letter has made me quite unhappy.' (Fitzwilliam MSS.)

Pitt's letter to Laurence on the 11th concludes the correspondence: 'In order to prevent any misunderstanding Mr. Pitt begs to state to Dr. Laurence that the appointment of Lord Fitzwilliam to the vacant Lieutenancy has certainly no connexion whatever with any question respecting Ireland, and is not to be understood as implying any change of opinion in any quarter on that subject. With respect to the mode of appointment, Mr. Pitt hardly thinks it can be necessary to observe that the natural and regular mode of signifying the King's pleasure on such an occasion being by an official letter from the Secretary of State, it does not seem possible that such a letter should contain any direct or implied reference to any other mode of signifying it. But it would naturally announce that a Council would be held on Wednesday when Lord Ftzwilliam would have an opportunity of being sworn in, if he is willing to accept the office which his Majesty is disposed to confer on him. If in consequence of this communication Lord Fitzwilliam attends on that day, and wishes to have an audience of his Majesty previous to the Council, Mr. Pitt conceives there can be no difficulty in his obtaining it.' (Fitzwilliam MSS.)

[1] See No. 592 (the first reference to him in the Index to vol. 1 should be 592, not 590).

[2] Queen Charlotte's eldest brother, Adolphus Frederick (1738–94). Robert Fulke Greville said that the Baron de Witz arrived from Mecklenburg-Strelitz in Sept. 1794: 'Dress'd out in a full suit, bag, sword & broad yellow & Blue Ribbon with all the ceremony & pomp of a German little Court he contrasted srongly with *les conseilliers intimes* of our Weymouth Court.' (*Diaries of R. F. Greville*, p. 344 [18 Sept. 1794].) The Queen's letter explains No. 1137.

600,000 crowns. To this we must add a debt of 60,000 of my sisters, without any resource whatever to extricate the country out of this distress but by curtailing every article, & living as retired as possible. Everybody about Court with tolerable fortunes are retired, & those who would take half the salary remain. But there is in reality no Court, no more but one table for himself, his sons, their Governors, & his Gentlemen-in-waiting, & when strangers must be invited his table never exceeds the number of twelve including himself & family. In short, his Establishment is now that of a private gentleman. The Irish pension he employed partly *for the education of his sons*, & partly for paying off die Chatollen Schulden which are not included in the other debt, & though under promise not to reveal the sum, I will frankly own that they are very considerable. But as he was paid very regularly & thereby enabled to pay himself, the creditors have been kept quiet without molesting him, but should this fail he must fall not only under very great but extreme distress, which he desired me in his letter to represent to your Majesty, & his ardent wish is, that in case you would favor his request, to grant the pension to his son the Hereditary Prince. I received his letter a week ago & would not trouble your Majesty until I had seen *Best* to know whether Schroeder was really dead, & upon his confirming it & telling me that as yet he had not given in any information of his death, I could not with any propriety refuse my brother to make an application for the continuance of your bounty, particularly as it will not be a new grant. I well know the difficulties you have to grant new pensions, & the present times must increase them, but I also know your heart which is ever ready to give comfort when possible, & therefore I shall not trespass any longer upon your patience, being fully persuaded that you will do what can be done & what is right. (36489–90)

1688   THE DUKE OF PORTLAND *to the* KING

[*Burlington House, Sunday, 25 Feb. 1798, 3.55 p.m.*] The Duke of Portland most humbly begs leave to lay before your Majesty the dispatches which are just arrived from the Lord Lieutenant of Ireland, of which that marked (private) contains an account of the debate on the Earl of Moira's Motion—which, as the Duke of Portland supposes, your Majesty may have expected before this time, he only ventures to observe that three if not four of the Lords who divided with the Earl of Moira are connected with him by consanguinity or marriage.[1] (8776)

1689   LORD GRENVILLE *to the* KING, *and the reply*

[*Dropmore, 25 Feb. 1798.*] Lord Grenville has the honour to transmit to your Majesty two letters received from M. de Luc by the Hamburgh mail and also a private letter from Lord Elgin respecting the late communications between the Courts of Vienna and Berlin. (8777)

[1] Moira pleaded for a policy of conciliation and redress of grievances, advocating Catholic emancipation and parliamentary reform. He was answered by the Lord Chancellor, Lord Clare.

[*The King's reply, Queen's House, 26 Feb., 7.35 a.m.*] I return to Lord Grenville the letters he has received from Mr. de Luc as well as the secret one from the Earl of Elgin. The continual instances of the Duke of Brunswick's irresolution is [*sic*] lamentable. I am glad de Luc is gone to Berlin and think he has judged right in preceding Genl. Stampfort that their missions may not appear combined but their intercourse when the latter arrives the natural consequence of their former acquaintance.

Monr. de Luc did write a tedious letter on the 31st of Decr. wherein he suggested that perhaps the Queen of Prussia might be an useful channel. I am so fearful of causing any misunderstanding in conjugal felicity that I did not approve of the idea, but desired the Queen, whenever she wrote to her niece, to express the favourable opinions held here of the King of Prussia and her. This has been done in the letter carried by Count Tauenzien, but more I think might have been imprudent. I wrote no answer to Mr. de Luc, from a fixed opinion that double correspondence of[te]ner mars than assists public business, and that his correspondence having begun with Lord Grenville it was right for mine to cease. (Fortescue MSS.)

1690 THE DUCHESS OF WURTEMBERG *to the* KING

[*Stutgard, 27 Feb. 1798.*] Allow me to express to your Majesty the joy I experienced on Saturday in hearing from Mr. Arbuthnot[1] such good accounts of your health, a subject ever interesting to my heart, and in addition to which the satisfactory manner he speaks of the unanimity which reigns in all classes in England must give pleasure to all those who are not even so closely connected as I have the honour to be with your Majesty, but who have only the good of humanity at heart, and must rejoice to think that at least one part of Europe will escape the bad principles which too much pains are taken to spread throughout the world.

After near ten months being passed since I left England to speak to any person who within three weeks has seen all those so justly dear to me is easier felt than expressed, and I fear I shall at last grow quite troublesome to Mr. Arbuthnot by my making him repeat everything he knows about your Majesties and my sisters.

This evening I am to have an English card party. We are in hopes that many who have left Switzerland will settle here, at least till they see what turn affairs are likely to take. The lodgings at Stutgard being both difficult to find and very dear, some families I understand have taken houses at Ludewigsbourg.

I am today in a pretty state of confusion, for the Duke has begged me to remain upstairs till tomorrow, and every moment the people come in to move some

---

[1] Charles Arbuthnot (1767–1850), M.P. for East Looe, 1795–96; for Eye, 1809–12; for Orford, 1812–18; for St Germans, 1818–27; for St Ives, 1828–30; for Ashburton, 1830–1. Secretary of Legation (1795–99) and Chargé d'Affaires (1795–97) at Stockholm. Mission to Wurtemberg to congratulate Frederick II on his accession, Feb.–May 1798; Consul at Lisbon, Feb. 1799; Chargé d'Affaires at Lisbon, 1800–1; Envoy to Sweden, 1802–3; Ambassador to Turkey, 1805–7; Under-Secretary of State, Foreign Department, Nov. 1803–June 1804; Joint Secretary of the Treasury, April 1809–Feb. 1823; First Commissioner of Woods and Forests, Feb. 1823–April 1827, Feb.–June 1828; Chancellor of the Duchy of Lancaster June 1828–Nov. 1830. He left London for Stuttgart on 4 Feb.

of the furniture. My new apartment is both fine and convenient, as of one side
I have my private rooms and on the other those to receive company. Of course
the small head I have of your Majesty is to be hung in my favorite closset.

The Duke begs that I will present his humble duty to your Majesty, and I
entreat that you will be convinced of the respect and attachment with which I
am [etc.] (51459–60)

1691   *Letters from the* DUKE OF PORTLAND *to the* KING

[*Whitehall, Friday, 2 March 1798, 5.40 p.m.*] The Duke of Portland humbly
begs leave to acquaint your Majesty that no papers of any consequence have been
yet discovered in any of the boxes which belong to the persons who were brought
in yesterday from Margate, but as the boxes are uncommonly strong & thick it is
still possible that something may be found secreted when they come to be taken
to pieces. The only persons who have been yet examined are Binns,[1] who declined
answering any questions whatever, & O'Connor[2] who underwent a long examination, in the course of which he appeared at times very much embarassed & positively
denied his having had any intention of going to France. He pretended that Margate
was the place of his destination & that his intention was to have remained there &
at Lord Thanet's[3] & Lord Stanhope's,[4] to whose houses he had been invited, until
he could be informed of the time at which it would be necessary for him to return
to Ireland to save his bail—upwards of £900 in guineas & *louis d'Ors* were found
in two of the mahogany boxes which he in a manner acknowledged to be his
property & in one of the other two was a pair of double-barrelled pistols made by
Mantin & in the other a pair of common pistols which he said he had exchanged
with a friend. The prisoners are to be brought up again tomorrow morning at ten
for re-examination.[5] (8784–5)

[1] John Binns (1772–1860), journalist and politician; member of the London Corresponding Society,
and connected with the United Irishmen. See *Parl. Register*, XLIV, 2–9.
[2] Arthur O'Connor (1763–1852), the Irish rebel, brother of Roger O'Connor, another leading
United Irishman, and nephew of the Earl of Longueville. He had started a short-lived newspaper, the
Press, which, as an organ of the United Irishman, was suppressed by the Irish Government.
[3] Sackville, 9th Earl of Thanet (1769–1825), a Foxite Whig. He was convicted in the Court of King's
Bench on 25 April 1799 on a charge of attempting the rescue of O'Connor in the Court at Maidstone,
and was sentenced on 10 June to a year's imprisonment and a fine of £1,000. See Holland, *Memoirs of
the Whig Party*, I, 126. He lived very comfortably in the Tower in a private suite of rooms, and was
allowed to have his mistress with him. He was released from prison on 9 June 1800, and nine days later
he was presented to the King at the Levée.
[4] Charles, 3rd Earl Stanhope (1753–1816). See vol. I.
[5] O'Connor and the priest Quigley (or O'Coigly), the United Irishmen, and their servants or
associates John Binns, John Allen and Jeremiah Leary, were arrested at Margate whilst making preparations to sail to France. In the priest's pocket book was found an Address from the Secret Committee of
England to the Executive Directory of France, in which was expressed the hope that Bonaparte would
soon come to rescue them from the tyranny of the British Government. The treason trial at Maidstone
(21–2 May) resulted in the conviction of the priest (who was subsequently executed) and the acquittal
of the rest. Amongst those who testified to the good character of O'Connor, who was very lucky to be
acquitted (and the ministerial Press after the trial was for ever reminding its readers how these leading
Whigs had been duped)—were Fox, Sheridan, Grattan, Erskine, the Duke of Norfolk, Lord John
Russell and Whitbread. Charles Grey too was in Court, but was not called as a witness. Lord Holland
admitted that the trial exposed the Opposition to much calumny. 'Arthur O'Connor had, without

[*Whitehall, Saturday, 3 March, 3.45 p.m.*] The Duke of Portland most humbly begs leave to acquaint your Majesty that the other persons who were apprehended at Margate have been examined this morning; that Leary,[1] the boy, who is O'Connor's servant, pretended to be ignorant of everything, even of the manner in which he travelled from Whitstable to Margate, & would not answer any one question that was put to him except his being servant to O'Connor. Alley[2] very nearly observed the same course, admitting only that he had *passed* for a servant, but did not admit that he was in that capacity with any one of the persons who was at Margate. Fivey or Quigley, the priest, (Fivey being as he told us the English of Quigley or Coegley as it is written in Irish & in his Letters of Ordination which were found in his pocket book) declined answering many questions but yet he appears to have said enough to enable the proceeding to be traced out & to have given ground to prove the fact of their acting in concert & their intention of going to France for the purpose of inviting the French to invade this kingdom—or at least that of Ireland, & it is to be hoped that means may be found either here or in Ireland for supplying the defects which at present appear in the evidence & to render it sufficiently full & complete for their conviction. It was remarkable that almost all the persons whom Fivey acknowledges himself to be acquainted with are members of the London Corresponding Society. No papers have been found in any of the boxes or trunks. As some persons who were named by the prisoners have been sent for with a view to substantiate some parts of the evidence against them, they have been again remanded for farther examination, which is to take place on Monday, when it seems to be the opinion of your Majesty's law servants that they may be committed for high treason. Fivey, alias Quigley, was not less embarassed & alarmed in the course of his examination today than O'Connor was yesterday. (8786–7)

[*Whitehall, Monday, 5 March, 4.45 p.m.*] The Duke of Portland humbly begs leave to acquaint your Majesty that Fivey or Quigley, the priest, was brought up again today for examination, when he refused to answer any question that should be put to him, alledging that the treatment he had met with on *his way from Canterbury & the first night of his being in town* was such as to make it evident that his life was aimed at, & consequently that prudence forbad his saying anything, as it might be distorted to his prejudice. O'Connor refused also to answer any new questions but desired several alterations to be made in the copy of his examination which was read to him, & has since signed it. With this the business of the day ended, & the Council adjourned to eleven o'clock tomorrow morning for the purpose of examining several witnesses who are ordered to attend at that time, & who are summoned in consequence of information received last night of their having been privy or parties to so much of this conspiracy as there is reason to

scruple, summoned all his acquaintances in that party to speak of his character. From pardonable motives of humanity and friendship they endeavoured to give the most favourable colour they could, to his views and opinions about England, and they thereby exposed themselves to the imputation of being implicated in the plot.' (*Memoirs of the Whig Party*, I, 121.)

[1] Jeremiah Leary.
[2] He was charged under the name of John Allen.

imagine may by means of their evidence enable the charge of high treason to be brought home to the prisoners now in custody. *Maxwell*, whom your Majesty has mentioned as having been named to your Majesty as a person probably implicated in this traterous [*sic*] design, may possibly turn out to be O'Connor, as that is one of the many names which he has occasionally assumed. Sir Francis Burdett called yesterday twice upon O'Connor but, as your Majesty will judge, obtained no access whatever to him.

The Duke of Portland is under the necessity of requesting your Majesty's pardon for having presumed to say that O'Connor had signed his examination. It was writing out fair under O'Connor's direction when the Duke of Portland made the assertion which he is now obliged to retract, as O'Connor has at length refused to subscribe it. (8788–9)

1692   E. LIVINGSTON *to the* KING

[*Naples, 6 March 1798.*] I wrote my Lord Chancellor from Dresden, and Mr Dundas from Trieste, beging them to inform your Majesty of the difficultys I met with on my journey by bad roads and snow &c. I was twenty two days at sea from Trieste to Manfredonia; the situation of Rome and Cisalpine Republic render'd that sea voyage indispensable. I arrived here the 4th and had the honor yesterday to deliver to his Royal Highness Prince Augustus your Majesty's letter, the Queen's, and the Princesses, &c. The Prince had been ill, and I have now the satisfaction to inform your Majesty that he is in perfect health.

As your Majesty has been informed by Count Munster of the causes that desturb'd the harmony that ought to have subsisted between H.R.H. and these gentlemen, I shall only add with regret that they are on no better footing at present, and H.R.H. entirely in the hands of very improper society. However, in justice to the Prince, in a very long conversation I had with him this morning, I found H.R.H. very ready to adopt the plan [which] may be most agreeable to your Majesty, and has promised to write by this post to your Majesty and the Queen to that purpose.

The proximity of the French to this place, and the great number of ships of war they have at present in the Medeteranean and Adreatic seas, renders the Prince's leaving this extremely difficult, and his remaining here no less critical. Your Majesty may rest assured that I will act with all the prudence in my power for the Prince's safety, and hope soon may be able to fix on the most reasonable plan for his departure.

I am confidently informed that the Prince's personal debts far exceed the 2000 credit sent to Sir William Hamilton for the Prince's removing from Naples. The creditors having been informed that I was to bring money to pay all the debts, renders my situation very delicate, as the order to Sir William Hamilton is not to exceed 2000. I am promised a fair statement of the debts, when in my possession, [and] will send it to Mr Pitt by the first opportunity. Your Majesty will see the absolute necessity of some security being given the Prince's creditors before he can possibly leave this. The honor and dignity of the nation requires that his

Royal Highness leave Naples with the propriety beccoming a Prince of the Blood Royal of England. I flater myself the debts are not very considerable. In that event I will as far as my credit goes, answer for them, and I flater myself your Majesty will be graciously pleased to approve of my conduct.

I hope to be soon able to send your Majesty a full detail of the Prince's real situation. I found Mr Tatter[1] and Count Munster well informd and reasonable men. They have given me all the information in their power concerning the expences of the Prince's household, &c. (8790–3)

1693 *Letters from* LORD GRENVILLE *to the* KING, *and the replies*

[*Cleveland Row, 7 March 1798, 1 p.m.*] Lord Grenville has thought that he ought not to delay humbly submitting to your Majesty the dispatches received this morning from Lord Elgin & M. de Luc. He fears that your Majesty will find in them little more than an additional proof of the impossibility of placing any real confidence in the Court of Berlin under its present direction, or of getting that Government to attend to any objects of general concern or to any interests but those of the moment. In the state to which the business is now brought, Lord Grenville inclines to think, but subject to your Majesty's better judgment, that no advantage can arise from pursuing it any further thro' the channel of M. de Luc. (8796–7)

[*The King's reply, Queen's House, 7 March, 2.50 p.m.*] Having perused the despatches from the Earl of Elgin, the letter from Mr. de Luc, and the Memoire of Count Haugwitz in answer to the one sent by Lord Grenville, I entirely coincide in the opinion formed by Lord Grenville that there appears no hopes that the Court of Berlin will be roused to such exertions as the present critical situation of Europe requires. I therefore do not see that any farther advantage can arise from Mr. de Luc's returning to Berlin, but that the Earl of Elgin being now officially informed of the Memoire by Count Haugwitz, it is better to let the intercourse return to the natural channel, to authorize him to speak civilly, though one cannot but be intirely hurt that no good has arisen from the steps that have been taken; but to prevent mischief we must seem pleased, and the Earl of Elgin must keep a door open for further communications, should events make an appearance of success more probable than there is at present reason to suppose. (Fortescue MSS.)

[*From Lord Grenville, Cleveland Row, 7 March, 2.30 p.m.*] Lord Grenville has the honour to transmit to your Majesty a farther letter from M. de Luc, which he has just received thro' the German Office. (8794)

[*The King's reply, Queen's House, 7 March 1798, 4[?][2] p.m.*] I return to Lord Grenville the letter he has received from Mr. de Luc at Brunswick as well as the

---

[1] George Tatter had been tutor in history and geography to the King's sons whilst they were at the University of Göttingen. His father had been head gardener at Montbrillant.

[2] The minute figures are blotted out.

one written to me by the Duke of Brunswick. They certainly have not changed my opinion of wishing to put a stop to the secret negociation, and now having it brought into the regular channel of the Earl of Elgin; but I fear after the encouragement given from hence for Genl. Stampfort's going to Berlin, and who will be set out previous to any letter that can now reach Brunswick, we must let the business for a little longer remain in the mode it was, though with the avowed knowledge of Lord Elgin. I desire therefore Lord Grenville will draw up an answer to the Duke of Brunswick's letter, which ought to be very cordial, and perhaps in that there may be means to pave the throwing now the negociation into the regular channel. (Fortescue MSS.)

1694 THE DUKE OF PORTLAND *to the* KING

[*Whitehall, Wednesday, 7 March 1798, 12.35 a.m.*] The Duke of Portland most humbly begs leave to acquaint your Majesty that warrants have been this night issued for the commitment of O'Connor, Quigley the priest, Binns & Alley to the Tower on a charge of high treason, for which they will be brought to their trials in the county of Kent, & Leary, O'Connor's servant, who refused to answer any question whatever that was put to him, is order'd to be committed to the new goal in the Borough. (8795)

1695 E. LIVINGSTON *to the* KING

[*Naples, 8 March 1798.*] I had the honor to write your Majesty the 6th, which Count Munster sent in his packet. Having just learnd that a messenger sets out this afternoon for London, I think it my duty to inform your Majesty that Sir Wm. Hamilton has spoke to the Minister here to obtain a ship of war to carry H.R.H. to Trieste. That request was readily granted, but it is doubtful in the present critical situation of affairs how far the French may respect the Neapolitan flag. Before it is possible to arrange the Prince's afairs here, that business must be determined, and your Majesty may be assured I will act with all the prudence and precaution possible, and take nothing on myself without the best advice.

The Prince will have the honor to write your Majesty by the messenger. H.R.H. promises the most chearful obedience to your Majesty's Royal will and pleasure. If I am so fortunate as [to] get him out of this country I have no doubt but his R.H. will keep the promise he has made.

Any commands your Majesty is pleased to honor me with, be pleased to order them to be sent to Sir Morton Eden at Vienna. The Prince is in perfect health. (8798–9)

1696 PRINCE ADOLPHUS *to the* KING

[*Hannover, 10 March 1798.*] The messenger's arrival last Friday brought me your Majesty's very gracious letter, for which I return you my most humble thanks. The manner in which you have been pleased to express your approbation of the step I took of addressing myself directly to the King of Prussia on the appearance of a sudden attack of your Electoral dominions, has rendered me very happy, and I assure you that I shall always strive to act in a manner that may be pleasing to you. This has hitherto been and ever shall be the cheif aim of all my actions. I have rejoiced very much on seeing the fine spirit which is now prevailing in England, and without which undoubtedly no true check can be set to the French insolence. This is an experience which above half of Europe has made during the war, and though everybody owns that without energy nothing can be done, yet no steps are taken for to rouse this spirit. Unluckily the present constitution of Germany renders it very difficult to bring this about, for without concert and unity this spirit is of no use, and that is almost impossible in a country where there are such a number of Sovereigns who have all different views, and for this reason never act together. I spoke upon this subject to Mr. de Steinberg as your Majesty ordered me: he was quite of my opinion and said that as it was impossible to bring about a general spirit in Germany it would be disadvantageous for one country alone, for this would not be able to resist alone the French who, as soon as they remarcked it, would do all they could to crush it. This winter the troops have not been able to do much on account of the bad weather, but now the spring is coming on we shall soon begin to exercise: unluckily my Brigade is cantoned in so fertil[e] a country that it will be impossible to exercise with more than one Batallion together unless we encamp. I wish your Majesty could see your Hanno-verian troops, I am sure you would be pleased with them, for they certainly are now in very fine order. I dare not tresspass any longer on your patience. (48518)

1697　THE DUCHESS OF WURTEMBERG *to the* KING

[*Stutgard, 13 March 1798.*] As I know not how soon I may be prevented having the happiness to express my gratitude to your Majesty for your constant goodness to me, allow me to return you my most humble thanks for your gracious letter of the 27th of February, which, coming from you and containing such gracious and affectionate expressions, I can with truth say has served as a balm to my heart, which was still much affected with our recent melancholy events, and I can assure your Majesty that there does not exist a being more truly and gratefully attached to you than I am. Your picture is my constant companion and I trust the Almighty will long preserve your Majesty a blessing and a comfort to us all. The Duke is very much afflicted at the death of his mother and I fear it will be very long before he will be enabled to recover his spirits. However, I rejoice that it was in our power to be with her so much, for though at the time it makes us both feel the loss stronger, the thought of having contributed to ease her mind must ever be a comfort to us.

I am now very much taken up with Trinette,[1] who, unless she has lessons, never leaves me a moment. I hope by my care of her to try, though at a distance, to imitate the example our dear mother has set me, and though I cannot flatter

[1] The Duke's sole surviving daughter, Catherine (1783–1835), by his first wife, Princess Augusta of Brunswick-Wolfenbüttel (1764–88). On 22 Aug. 1807 she married Napoleon's brother Jerome, King of Westphalia (1784–1860).

myself to equal her trust, the Almighty will take the will for the deed and bless my attempts with success. One thing gives me great pleasure in the undertaking, that from the begining she took to me very much, and her age being the same as my dearest Amelia's makes her doubly interresting to me. Trinette's being constantly my companion makes it still more fortunate that the Duke has been so anxious to place Ladies of my own time [of] life with me, as it is more advantageous for her to have that society than that of girls. I ought to beg your Majesty's pardon to dwell so long on that subject but knowing your goodness to me, thought you would be anxious to know how I should be likely to fulfil this new duty, which I have most willingly undertaken, as I look upon it as the greatest proof of the Duke's confidence.

If I wrote anything incoherent in my letter on Friday I hope your Majesty will excuse it on account of the occasion.

It gives me great pleasure to hear that your Majesty has appointed Lord Chesterfield Master of the Horse, as I believe him to be personally attached to your Majesty and that one virtue will ever cover many foibles in my eyes. The Duke begs that I will present his humble duty, and I entreat that you will be convinced of the respect and attachment with which I am [etc.] (51461–2)

1698 LORD GRENVILLE *to the* KING, *and the reply*

[*Dropmore, 13 March 1798.*] Lord Grenville is extremely concerned that by a mistake, for which he humbly begs to apologize to your Majesty, this draft was not sent to your Majesty this morning; but with the present wind he imagines there is no doubt but that if your Majesty is graciously pleased to transcribe it tomorrow morning it will be in time to go by the mail. When it is returned to the Office, Lord Grenville will, with your Majesty's permission, direct it to be made up under cover to M. Steinberg, unless your Majesty pleases that it should be sent in any other manner. (8800)

[*The King's reply, Windsor, 14 March.*] I have lost no time in copying the draft to the Duke of Brunswick and therefore instantly return it by the messenger, that it may, agreable to Lord Grenville's intentions, be sent after the mail to Yarmouth. I think Baron Steinberg the best channel through which it may be forwarded. (Fortescue MSS.)

1699 EARL SPENCER *to the* KING, *and the reply*

[*Admiralty, 14 March 1798.*] Earl Spencer has the honour to lay before your Majesty the Minutes and sentence of a court martial held on three seamen of the Amelia frigate for mutiny, & humbly submits to your Majesty the propriety of orders being immediately issued for carrying the sentence into execution. (8801)

[*The King's reply, Queen's House, 14 March.*] I agree with Earl Spencer on the propriety of confirming the sentence of the court martial on three seamen of the Amelia frigate for mutiny, and on its being immediately put into execution. (Althorp MSS.)

[*Horse Guards, 17 March 1798.*] In obedience to your Majesty's commands of yesterday, I acquainted Sir William Fawcett with your pleasure that he should go to the Duke of Gloucester and explain to him fairly the difficulty that exists concerning the command of the Brigade of Guards and the necessary arrangements to be taken for the protection and police of London, and thinking that it would be more advisable that Sir William Fawcett should be exactly informed of what he was to say, I drew up the enclosed memorandum, which I trust contains as nearly as possible what your Majesty was pleased to express on the subject, desiring Sir William Fawcett to keep it for his own guidance but not to shew it to the Duke of Gloucester.

Sir William Fawcett having, however, informed me that the Duke of Gloucester would most probably, upon this occasion as upon any other, ask him whether he had received his orders immediately from your Majesty or from any other person, I trust that your Majesty will not be displeased with me for transmitting the memorandum to you, and if it meets with your Majesty's approbation, humbly begging your Majesty to give the orders yourself to Sir William Fawcett. (8802)

1701 *Letters from* THE DUKE OF PORTLAND *to the* KING

[*Burlington House, Saturday, 17 March 1798, 10 a.m.*] The Duke of Portland most humbly begs leave to lay before your Majesty the dispatches he has received this morning from the Lord Lieutenant, which he has the great satisfaction of observing to your Majesty contain an account of the success which has attended the measures which the Lord Lieutenant announced his intention & hope of effecting, & the consequent seizure of eighteen of the principal conspirators.

[*2.35 p.m.*] The importance of the accompanying papers having induced the Duke of Portland to direct, in case your Majesty had rode out when they arrived at the Queen's House, that they might be brought back to him for the purpose of being communicated to your Majestys [*sic*], now encourages [him] to venture to express an hope that they may be sent back to him as soon as suits your Majesty's convenience, that such of them may be laid before your Majesty's Law servants for their opinion upon the propriety of proceeding against Sir Francis Burdett or such other persons in this country as appear to be implicated in the transactions of the United Irishmen. (8803–4)

[*Burlington House, Monday, 19 March, 9.55 a.m.*] The Duke of Portland most humbly begs leave to lay before your Majesty the dispatches which are just arrived from the Lord Lieutenant, & to submit with great deference to your Majesty's superior wisdom the almost unavoidable necessity in which the Lord Lieutenant finds himself of offering Lord Castlereagh's[1] name to your Majesty's consideration as the proper person to supply the place of Mr. Pelham, of the state

---

[1] Castlereagh had been appointed Keeper of the Irish Privy Seal (24 July), and a Lord of the Irish Treasury (14 Oct.) in 1797. He was never Secretary of State (H. M. Hyde, *The Rise of Castlereagh*, p. 215 n.).

of whose health, although the accounts are not so unfavorable this morning, there is no ground to expect so speedy a re-establishment as to justify an hope of his being able in any reasonable time to resume the duties of his station.[1] With all the objections therefore which the Duke of Portland is aware the appointment of a person of the description of Lord Castlereagh is liable; considering the present state of Ireland, the extreme difficulty of finding any person in this country who is so qualified as to justify the proposing him for such an employment to your Majesty, the urgency of the case, the opinion which the Lord Lieutenant (& the Duke of Portland believes) very justly entertains of Lord Castlereagh, the respectability of Lord Castlereagh's character & the very high estimation in which he is held by the country as well as by the Lord Lieutenant & Mr Pelham, the Duke of Portland feels it his duty to submit it with all humility as his best opinion to your Majesty, under all the circumstances which he has presumed to state, that in desiring Lord Castlereagh's name to be offerd to your Majesty, the Lord Lieutenant has given the best testimony of his attention & judgement in furthering your Majesty's service, & the D. of P. cannot but hope that the appointment of Lord Castlereagh at least during Mr Pelham's illness may appear not unworthy of your Majesty's sanction.

The possibility of such a representation as the Lord Lieutenant has desired to be made to your Majesty in favor of Lord Castlereagh occurred so strongly yesterday to some of your Majesty's servants, that the opinion which the Duke of Portland has presumed to offer to your Majesty is not singly his own & will probably be submitted to your Majesty by Mr Pitt, with whom the Duke of Portland had some conversation yesterday upon this subject.[2] (8805–7)

1702 THE DUKE OF YORK *to the* KING

[*York House, 20 March 1798.*] I have the honor to acknowledge the receipt of your Majesty's most gracious letter, and feel myself highly gratified by the approbation you are pleased to express of my having hinted to your Majesty last night the application made to me by Mr Dundas in the name of your Cabinet.

[1] Pelham had contracted a severe fever, accompanied by an alarming 'spitting of blood', and for a time it was believed that he was dying.

[2] Camden further explained his views in a letter to Pitt on the 16th: 'Mr. Pelham is so ill that his recovery is hardly possible. At all events he will not be fit for many weeks, perhaps months. To be without a Secretary at this instant is impossible, to take time to look for one in England would be most inconvenient, & to have a person appointed to that situation at this moment unacquainted with the country would be most distressing & a measure to which I cannot give my assent. Under all the circumstances I have no hesitation in saying that the only person who can with effect be nominated Secretary is Lord Castlereagh. He unwillingly undertakes it, but he will do anything I wish, & what he considers to be his duty to the country. I beg therefore to receive by the return of the messenger the King's consent that he should be nominated Secretary to the Lord Lt. of Ireland. He will undertake it for a time if he or I or the King's Ministers wish hereafter for another arrangement. He is universally respected here & is considered as perfectly adequate to the situation, & I am confident he is so. The former objections to his being an Irishman cannot now be attended to; & under the present circumstances of the country & the unexampled difficulties of the moment from the rebellion which exists & the impression made by Sir Ralph Abercrombie's orders, I cannot really go on for the moment unless this measure takes place. I hope to receive the King's consent to it by the return of the messenger. I had thought of Elliot, but his health is not equal to it. (Camden MSS.)

I shall lose no time in drawing up the statement which your Majesty has ordered, and shall take care to lay it before your Majesty for your approbation before I transmit it to your Ministers. (8808)

1703   PRINCE ADOLPHUS *to the* KING

[*Hannover, 23 March 1798.*] Though I have lately done myself the honour of writing to your Majesty, yet I cannot refuse myself the pleasure of troubling you with a few lines by this opportunity of my friend General Don's[1] setting off for England. I am very sorry for myself to looze so good a friend, but on the other hand I rejoice very much that you have placed him on the Staff, as I am convinced he will acquit himself perfectly of whatever task that is given him. He is a very active and capable man, and, what is very seldom in these times, a perfect honest man. He has given himself great pains to acquire a just knowledge of this country, and I am sure that if ever troops should be ordered over to the Continent and he be sent with them he will be found very useful. Your Majesty will I hope forgive my having troubled you with these lines but I could not see my friend set off without writing in his favour, and I do assure you I have not written a word that I am not perfectly convinced of.

I dare not now importune you any longer. (48519)

1704   *Letters from* LORD GRENVILLE *to the* KING, *and a reply*

[*Cleveland Row, 29 March 1798.*] In consequence of your Majesty's most gracious permission Lord Grenville has the honour to transmit to your Majesty a printed copy of the report of his speech on the 22d inst. which, tho' far from accurate in point of expressions, contains he believes the substance of what he said.[2] (8810)

[*From Lord Grenville, Cleveland Row, 1 April 1798.*] Lord Grenville thinks it his duty to transmit to your Majesty a Minute of the very important communication this day made by Count Starhemberg. In the present state of the business he hardly ventures to form an opinion upon it, but he is very apprehensive that, even if in other respects the plan appeared to hold out any favourable prospects, the great jealousy & even animosity which appears to prevail respecting Prussia will prove a great obstacle to success, especially as there does not appear to be any probability of weakening those impressions so long as Count Haugwitz continues to be employed at Berlin. (8811)

[*The King's reply, Queen's House, 2 April, 7.20 a.m.*] I cannot return to Lord Grenville the Minute of the important communication he received yesterday from

---

[1] Sir George Don (1754–1832). Colonel, Feb. 1795; Major-General, Jan. 1797; Lieutenant-General, 1805; Lieutenant-Governor of Jersey, 1806; General, 1814, and Lieutenant-Governor of Gibraltar, 1814–31. G.C.H., 1816; G.C.B., 1820. He had been for about 62 years in active service without any intermission (a circumstance without parallel in the British army) when he died.

[2] The debate was on the Duke of Bedford's motion of censure, calling for a change of men and of measures. It was rejected by 113 to 13, including proxies (*Parl. Register*, L, 355–405).

Count Stahremberg without adding a few lines; the conduct of the Court of Berlin at Radstadt [*sic*] has been most unfair as it certainly has encouraged instead of checked the demand of France for the one side of the Rhine, that Prussia might obtain Secularizations on the other side as an indemnification for the loss of Cleves; but on the other hand Austria has uniformly refused to communicate the Secret Articles of her Peace at Campo Form[i]o to Prussia as she has also done to us. Whilst that is the case she has no right to lay the whole blame of want of concert on the Court of Berlin; and though I earnestly wish Britain, Austria, Russia and Berlin may unite to heartily withstand France, which has as yet in no degree been the case, an attack on Count Haugwitz I do not think the likely means of effecting this. If we do not get Prussia into the business, Russia will hold back and Austria as usual fail us when we may least expect it; if she is sincere she must communicate her Secret Articles; that is absolutely necessary to regain confidence. (Fortescue MSS.)

1705   THE DUKE OF PORTLAND *to the* KING

[*Burlington House, Sunday, 1 April 1798, 11.15 a.m.*] In laying the Lord Lieutenant's Dispatches which have been just received before your Majesty, the Duke of Portland begs leave with all humility to submit to your Majesty, that as your Majesty's servants are to have a meeting tomorrow morning to consider the destination of the military force of this kingdom, it might be usefull to their deliberations, if it should meet your Majesty's pleasure, to order the Lord Lieutenant's dispatches to be returned to the Duke of Portland, so that they might be communicated to your Majesty's servants previous to their intended meeting. (8812)

1706   THE DUCHESS OF WURTEMBERG *to the* KING

[*Stutgard, 5 April 1798.*] I cannot bear the thoughts of Monsieur de Reden bringing your Majesty the account of my confinement and not at least having the honour of sending you a few lines; but the Duke dreads so much that I might hurt myself that I have been obliged to give up the thoughts of writing for some time afterwards and as a compromise write now, as the physicians give me hopes that I shall be brought of bed by the end of this week [*sic*]. To my great comfort we have this morning taken the Sacrament, as the Duke was so good, wishing me to take it with him, to change his usual day, fearing that I might otherwise have been prevented and that I should be fatigued if there were too many communicants. Yesterday evening we attended the preparation, which pleased me very much. I own I felt a great deal of joy at being enabled to go to the Altar, as I think that when one has fulfilled that duty one's mind is better enabled to go through any undertaking in life: and God knows the present times are such that one feels doubly the necessity of putting one's whole trust in the Almighty, who alone can give us strength to support every trial. It is a very extraordinary thing that it is near a hundred years since a Duke and Dutchess have taken the Sacrament at Stutgard; ever since the year 1732 they have been of different religions.

I hope that your Majesty will have fine weather during the Easter week that you may enjoy the pleasure of being at Windsor. The instant my month is up we shall settle for six or seven months in the country, and as soon as the alterations are compleated at Ludewigsbourg I shall have the honour to send you the plan, but the Duke will not allow me to do it at present for fear your Majesty should take an unfavorable opinion of its beauty, of which we are very proud, and to the Duke's great joy I like it very much. It was a sad thing to see how everything had been allowed to go to ruin, as Duke Charles had the folly of constantly launching into the expence of building new Palaces and neglecting the old ones, instead of which the present intention is to make Stutgard and Ludewigsbourg comfortable and to attempt nothing more. As we are to have a menagerie in the country, will your Majesty forgive my entreating you to send us a pair of the congaroos [*sic*] which would be a great pleasure to us? I will now take up no more of your Majesty's time than to beg that you will be convinced of the respect and attachment with which [etc.] (51465–6)

1707   THE DUKE OF PORTLAND *to the* KING

[*Whitehall, Friday, 6 April 1798, 5.50 p.m.*] The Duke of Portland most humbly requests your Majesty's permission to represent to your Majesty that the inadvertence which the Lord Lieutenant charges him with & for which he takes shame to himself & humbly entreats your Majesty's pardon, was owing in a great measure to a supposition that your Majesty's consent to the sale of the quit rents in Ireland must have been obtained previously to its having been mentioned in the House of Commons by the Chancellor of the Exchequer of that kingdom, & that it must have been officially signified to the Lord Lieutenant by the Lords Commissioners of the Treasury of this kingdom in the manner in which all matters concerning your Majesty's revenue were heretofore notified, & in extenuation of this error of the Duke of Portland's he has now to observe to your Majesty that it is a point which cannot yet be ascertained in what manner the communication of your Majesty's pleasure upon this subject is to be made to the Lord Lieutenant. Considering the gracious manner in which your Majesty condescended to speak of Mr Pelham's recovery, the Duke of Portland presumes to think that your Majesty will not blame him for taking the liberty of acquainting your Majesty that it is the opinion of the physicians who attend Mr. Pelham that there is not now any objection to his indulging in a moderate degree the anxiety he feels to talk upon business, & that in a very short time he will be as well as he was before his late dangerous attack. (8813–4)

1708   *Letters from the* KING *to* WILLIAM PITT, *and the reply*

[*Queen's House, 8 April 1798.*] The accompanying letter,[1] written to me by the Queen in February, I should have then communicated to Mr. Pitt had I not thought it best to keep it back to these holydays when he might have time to communicate the Queen's wishes to the Lord Lieutenant of Ireland. I remember

[1] No. 1687.

perfectly mentioning the subject of this Irish pension to Mr. Pitt as well as to Lord Grenville on returning from Weymouth the year the late Duke of Mecklenburg-Strelitz died,[1] but as the pension was in the name of Schroeder who then still lived, it was thought best to make no alteration at that time. He died in September last. The Queen makes no objection to its standing in the name of her nephew, the Hereditary Prince of Mecklenburg-Strelitz.[2] I need not say that I am certain any Irish Parliament and Lord Lieutenant must be happy in having an opportunity of enabling me to fulfill the Queen's wishes. That Mr. Pitt may know the exact state of this pension I have on another paper stated it as nearly as I have been able to obtain the account from the German Chancery, who have ever had the receipt of it from the time it was granted by the late King. (Chatham Papers.)

[*From the King, 8 April 1798.*] A pension of £2,000 per annum was granted on the Irish revenue for the lives of Hoburgh and Schroeder, two of the late King's Pages of the Backstairs, but in reality for the sole use of Elizabeth Sophia, the widdow of [the] Duke of Brunswick.[3] On the death of Hoburgh in 1761, Ernst,[4] one of my Pages of the Back Stairs, was named in addition to Schroeder in the grant. In 1767 he also died and the pension remained only in the name of Schroeder.

The Dutchess died in 1764 [*sic*], from which time the late Duke of Mecklenburg-Strelitz received the pension, and since his death the present Duke, both brothers of the Queen, but it has ceased by the death of Schroeder and it is desired that after stating the above, the elapsed pension may now be granted with the consent of the Irish Parliament for the life of the Hereditary Prince of Mecklenburg, the Queen's nephew. (Chatham Papers.)

[*From the King, Queen's House, 8 April 1798.*] I understand there is an employment vacant that was held by the late Mr. Armstrong,[5] one of my Gentlemen Ushers, called the Husband of the $4\frac{1}{2}$ pr. cent Duty. It would be particularly agreable to me if Mr. Pitt would conferr it on John Chamberlain who has the care of my models and drawings. He has a large family and such an addition to his income would be very desirable at the present time.[6] (Chatham Papers.)

[1] 1794 (2 June).
[2] Prince George (1779–1860) was the Duke's sole surviving son by his first wife, Frederica (1752–82), daughter of George William, Landgrave of Hesse-Darmstadt. By his second wife, her sister Charlotte (1755–85) whom he married on 28 Sept. 1784, the Duke had one son, Prince Charles (1785–1837). Prince George succeeded his father as Grand Duke on 6 Nov. 1816.
[3] Presumably Augustus William (1662–1731), Duke of Brunswick-Wölfenbuttel, who married (1710), as his third wife, Elizabeth (1683–1767), daughter of Rudolph Frederick of Holstein-Norburg.
[4] George Ernst, a son of the Page who died in 1767, was one of the King's Pages at the time of the Regency crisis, and he was dismissed early in 1789 (*The Times*, 5 March 1789). There are in the Melville MSS. in the Scottish Record Office documents (G.D. 51/1/14/1–41) relating to Ernst's threat to make a public disclosure of events connected with the King's illness, 1788–9, and to his dismissal. He unsuccessfully petitioned for a pension and compensation, and for confirmation of a pension to Dorothy Ernst, his widowed mother.
[5] Edmund Armstrong, one of the Grooms of the Privy Chamber (*d.* Oct. 1797). He had held this sinecure since 1777.
[6] Still another letter from the King to Pitt, dated 8 April 1798, 8.48 a.m., is in Wheeler and Broadley, *Napoleon and the Invasion of England*, i, xvi.

[*Pitt' reply, Downing Street, Sunday, 8 April 1798, 5 p.m.*] Mr. Pitt is honored with your Majesty's gracious commands of this day, and will not fail immediately to apprize the Lord Lieutenant of the circumstances of the pension in question, and can have no doubt of his alacrity in doing whatever depends upon him to carry into effect the proposed arrangement.

Mr Pitt has the honor of enclosing herewith the letter from the Queen which your Majesty condescended to communicate to him.

It gives Mr Pitt peculiar satisfaction that the office of Husband of the $4\frac{1}{2}$ pr. cent is still vacant. He has given directions for Mr Chamberlain being immediately appointed to it. (8815–6)

1709 THE DUKE OF PORTLAND *to the* KING

[*Bulstrode, Monday, 9 April 1798, 11.35 p.m.*] The Duke of Portland humbly begs leave to lay before your Majesty the dispatches he has received this evening from the Lord Lieutenant. As the Duke of Portland has not the reports of the Committees of United Irishmen within his reach, & as he cannot recollect with sufficient accuracy the statement of the amount of the arms in the possession of the rebels in the counties named in the inclosed return, he will not presume to hazard any remark upon it, but upon the best consideration it is in his poor ability to give to the reasoning of the Lord Lieutenant upon the appointment of a Com-mander-in-Chief. The Duke of Portland cannot forbear representing with all deference to your Majesty his humble hope that if Sir Ralph Abercromby shall be successfull in subduing the rebels in the south, & shall appear to the Lord Lieuten-ant to have recover'd the confidence & conciliated the affections of your Majesty's loyal subjects of that kingdom in such a manner as to enable him to employ his professional talents in your Majesty's service to the best advantage, it may not be deemed by your Majesty an unbecoming act of condescension on the part of your Majesty to permit the Lord Lieutenant to demand of Sir Ralph Abercromby a continuance of his services in the capacity of Commander-in-Chief—& that if, on the contrary, the whole of this condition should not be realized, the Lord Lieutenant may be authorized to signify to Sir Ralph Abercromby your Majesty's permission that he may resign his command, & to direct Lieut.-Genl. Lake to take the command of your Majesty's forces in Ireland in such manner as may appear to the Lord Lieutenant to be most conducive to your Majesty's service. And the Duke of Portland ventures humbly to suggest that this liberty may be given to the Lord Lieutenant, because it is not of necessity that a Commander-in-Chief should be appointed, & because it may give time for forming some arrangement which may be better approved by your Majesty without necessarily wounding the professional feelings of Lt.-General Lake if it should be your Majesty's pleasure ultimately to appoint him to the station of Commander-in-Chief.[1] (8817–9)

---

[1] Abercromby, the Commander-in-Chief in Ireland, after vainly remonstrating against the excesses of the troops engaged in disarming the disloyal population, resigned his post, and was succeeded on 25 April by Lake, who had held the command in Ulster, and who was quickly called on to deal with the Rebellion and a French landing. On 26 Feb. Abercromby had stated, in a General Order, that 'the Irish army was only formidable to everybody but the enemy'. 'He has been exceedingly wrongheaded',

remarked Cornwallis (Ross, *Cornwallis Correspondence*, II, 335). Camden's views are set out at length in a letter to Pitt (26 March): 'I have communicated to the Duke of Portland that event which you will have been apprised by my letter of Saturday was likely to take place, & I cannot express the infinite concern I feel that the conduct which I thought it right to pursue towards Sir R. Abercromby has had the termination it so little deserved, & that he persists in his determination to resign the command. The correspondence I have held with Sir Ralph is enclosed in my dispatch to the Duke of Portland, & I trust will convince you that this determination has neither been forced by want of forbearance on the first issue of the order, or intemperance in the course of the transaction—but he appears to have determined from the first moment of that indiscreet order having been made public, neither to lend himself to the state of the country or to the well-being of the Government, but to have persisted in a line which would in the end enable him to withdraw himself from a scene which he contemplated with some dismay. He has done it in a manner to give the most severe wound which could have been inflicted on Government in Ireland, & I confess I shall conceive myself most sensibly hurt, if Sir Ralph is not made to feel, & the world to see, that his conduct is not considered as very culpable in Great Britain as well as Ireland. [*sic*] It is in vain to lament an event which human foresight could not have expected, but an instant remedy requires to be applied to it—& I must address you upon this subject with all the energy I am able as a public man as well as all the freedom which I am entitled to use from our old & intimate private friendship. Sir Ralph's military knowledge is undoubted. He has not said more (tho he has conveyed it almost in a criminal manner) than the relaxed state of military discipline requires, & it is therefore necessary that his successor should follow his steps in that part of his duty & not attempt to gain the confidence of the Army by indulging their want of care & attention. Sir Ralph's strictures will be interpreted by Opposition in the most invidious manner & therefore the appointment of a General as his successor of equal military merit appears to be absolutely necessary. On whom it is possible to fix I know not—Sir Wm. Howe, Sir Charles Gray, Lt-Gen. D. Dundas present themselves as military characters of the first importance. It is yet doubtful how far the two first can reconcile themselves to the sort of command which is presented to them in this kingdom & whether the services of Genl. D. Dundas can be spared from Great Britain, altho that ought not to be a question as the danger of this country is almost immediate. That a person totally unacquainted with the country should come into it is most inconvenient—that a person who does not heartily agree in the system adopted by Government should be appointed, is full of danger & we at present suffer under that calamity. Another suggestion occurs which might remedy some of the inconveniences to which we are at the moment liable, but it will not meet the exigencies of the case—I mean the appointment of Genl. Lake who is next in command: but I have not that opinion of his capacity as to think the complicated nature of the service in Ireland safe in his hands—at the same time he has shewed that his zeal is most useful & praiseworthy, & he has conducted a very unpleasant business in the North with great temper & ability. I merely throw out these suggestions for your consideration, & when you contemplate them I am convinced you will agree with me in opinion of the almost insuperable objections to them all, & that this Government is now become so intermixed with military measures, which military measures are so connected with the politics of the country, that the Lord Lieutt. ought to be a military man & really to command that army of which he is nominally at the head. This sort of appointment with a man of legal experience as his Secretary is the Government which ought to subsist in this kingdom at present. The situation of Com.-in-Chief here is one of little power, but of great responsibility. It will be difficult to find an officer of approved merit willing to undertake the task, & yet without such an aid I should be a very unworthy subject of the King's & a very dangerous friend of yours did I continue in the Government. When you first urged me to come to Ireland I stated my diffidence in myself. I was however commanded to come & I submitted. We are now involved in a rebellion within & are threatened by an invasion from France. Mr. Pelham, in whom both the English Ministers & myself have the greatest confidence, is so ill that I am convinced he will be long unfit for business, even if he is ever permitted to return to it & the Com.-in-Chief retires from his situation; can it be construed into an unfounded diffidence in myself that I should explicitly say that under such circumstances I feel his Majesty's interests in Ireland are not in the hands of a man of sufficient experience & ability to preserve them as they ought, & that some person ought to be sent hither who can command the Army with a Secretary who will have weight & authority with the Law servants of the Crown? These are my opinions delivered after the most mature deliberation & I am convinced it is a measure you are called upon to attempt to execute: in suggesting it I may be liable to the imputation of wishing to withdraw in time of danger. If I felt I had the necessary assistance, my own wishes must induce me to endeavour to overcome the difficulties which have occurred, & I conceive I am doing no more than my duty in stating these circumstances & in relieving you from any delicacy towards me. The appointment of Lord Cornwallis with Douglass as his Secretary might meet the difficulty in one way; that of Genl. Dundas or Sir Wm. Howe, if his health is fit for it, might enable the Government to go on as at present constituted, & lastly Genl. Lake is a resource to which it is possible

[*London, 9 April 1798.*] Soon after I returned from St James's yesterday Lord Uxbridge[1] called upon me, & wished to purchase the nine bay coach horses. I told him that the Marquess of Buckingham was through Mr Fremantle in treaty for them; this morning Lord Uxbridge sent for the horses, and enclosed a draft upon his banker for the amount (270 guineas). I immediately sent to Mr. Fremantle,[2] but finding that he had no authority from Lord Buckingham to conclude a purchase, and that he could do nothing untill he should receive an answer from Stowe, I thought it wiser to prefer a certainty to an uncertainty, and have therefore sold the horses to Lord Uxbridge, and paid the amount into Mr. Parker's[3] hands. The horses are to be delivered on Wednesday. I shall be very happy should your Majesty approve of what I have done. Mr. Parker & Morley are very thankfull for the value of one horse each, which I have given them from your Majesty. I have been some time this morning at the Mews, and find that by a little assistance from Clark & Frere, and occasionally by a pair of horses from Blumfield,[4] I shall be able without employing any of the horses necessary for your Majesty's own use & service, to wait untill Jacobs shall have furnished the nine horses which have been ordered from him, without putting your Majesty in the meantime to any extraordinary expence. There are at the Straw Yard three very good young horses which will be sent for tomorrow.

I beg pardon for having taken the liberty to trouble your Majesty with so long a detail, which I can only venture to have done, from the anxiety I must always feel, to be honoured by your approbation. (8820–1)

[*Chesterfield House, 10 April 1798.*] The very kind manner in which your Majesty graciously commanded me to acquaint you how Lady Chesterfield was after the operation, makes me take the liberty to write to your Majesty to say that it was performed at 12 o clock today. It produced rather a larger quantity of water. She appears very well and chearfull, and I hope will recover her strength very soon.[5] (8822)

to apply, but I cannot consider such an appointment as one which can be considered as a permanent one. Our difficulties encrease from the disturbances being more widely extended & the treason more deeply rooted than had been conceived. Sr. Ralph's orders have discouraged the military from acting with alertness, & the gentlemen have fled from the country for want of that protection they have been accustomed to. You cannot too soon apply yourself to consider the circumstances of this kingdom, & you will understand me to speak decisively as to my opinion of the necessity of the measure I recommend, but I will never hastily take a step which can be detrimental to those with whom I am acting. I now feel the evil of such conduct so sensibly that I cannot think myself from personal feelings entitled to adopt it.' (Camden MSS.)

[1] Henry Paget (1744–1812), the father of the 1st Marquess of Anglesey, succeeded his cousin as 10th Lord Paget, 1769; created Earl of Uxbridge, 19 May 1784.

[2] Sir William Henry Fremantle (1766–1850), M.P. for Enniskillen, 1806; for Harwich, 1806–7; for Saltash, 1807–8; for the Tain Burghs, 1808–12; for Buckingham, 1812–27. Private Secretary to the Lord Lieutenant of Ireland, 1782; Deputy Teller of the Exchequer, 1800–2; Joint Secretary of the Treasury, 1806–7; Commissioner of the Board of Control, 1822–6; Treasurer of the Household, April 1826–37. Deputy Ranger of Windsor Great Park, 1831–50. Knighted, 31 Oct. 1827.

[3] David Parker, Clerk of the Stables.   [4] James Blumfield, chaise man in the King's Stables.

[5] Lady Chesterfield (1759–98) died on 20 Oct. The Earl's date of birth (1755) is wrongly given in vol. I as 1744.

[*Bulstrode, Wednesday night, 11 April 1798.*] The Duke of Portland most humbly begs leave to lay before your Majesty the dispatches which have been this day received from the Lord Lieutenant of Ireland & to submit with all deference to your Majesty that the Duke of Portland humbly conceives, notwithstanding the Lord Lieutenant's apprehensions of exceeding his powers, have urged him upon reflection to signify your Majesty's permission to Sir Ralph Abercromby to resign his employment of Commander-in-Chief that the intentions your Majesty condescended to notify yesterday to the Duke of Portland upon the subject of that officer are not affected by the step which the Lord Lieutenant has taken & that [if] it still remains your Majesty's pleasure, in case a proper opportunity should offer itself for the Lord Lieutenant to require Sir Ralph Abercromby to resume his command, that the Lord Lieutenant should avail himself of it, & that if Sir Ralph persists in declining to undertake it, the Lord Lieutenant should then notify your Majesty's commands to Lieut.-General Lake, that he, in his capacity of Senior Lieutenant-General on the Irish Staff, is to take upon himself the command of your Majesty's forces in that kingdom until your Majesty's pleasure shall be farther made known respecting the appointment of a Commander-in-Chief. (8823–4)

1712   EARL SPENCER *to the* KING

[*Admiralty, 12 April 1798.*] Earl Spencer has the honour of laying before your Majesty some letters received yesterday from Sir Richard Strachan giving an account of a rencontre he has had with a party of the enemy's gunboats off Havre, together with a minute[1] of the orders which were issued in consequence. No further intelligence has been received this day on the subject, and Earl Spencer is inclined to hope that however trifling this check may be in itself, it may very probably have the good effect of discouraging the troops who were embarked on board this flotilla.[2] (8828)

[1] 'Ships and vessels ordered to reinforce the Squadron under Sir Richard Strachan on the coast of France.

10th April   Captain Barlow in the *Phoebe*, with the *Boston*, ordered to proceed from Plymouth to Guernsey & follow the orders of Sir Richard Strachan for the defence of that and the neighbouring islands.
Sir Peter Parker to send a frigate (sailed the same day) and a bomb off of Guernsey for the like purpose.
Sir Richard Strachan ordered, on the arrival of the former, to send the latter to Spithead, unless he should be of opinion that the bomb can be advantageously employed, in which case he is allowed to detain her for the present.
The *Arethusa* and *Eurydice* order'd to proceed to St Marcou for the protection of those islands and follow the orders of Sir Richard Strachan.

11th April   The *Ariadne, Strombolo* & *Vesuvius*, bombs, ordered to proceed off Havre in quest of Captain Sir Richd. Strachan, and to follow his orders.
Sir Richard Strachan to take them under his command and employ them for the more effectual destruction of any armament preparing in the enemy's ports within the limits of his station, keeping them with him 'til after the next spring tides.' (8829)

[2] The King's reply at 6.04 p.m. that day, commenting on the enclosed despatches, is in *Spencer Papers*, II, 315.

1713   GEORGE CANNING *to the* KING

[*Downing Street, 12 April 1798, 2 p.m.*] Mr Canning most humbly presumes, in the absence of Lord Grenville, to transmit to your Majesty the inclosed letters for her Majesty and the Princesses which came by the Hamburgh mail that arrived this morning—as also a letter for your Majesty, which has been sent to the Office by the Marquis de Circello[1] having been forwarded to that Minister by a courier from Naples, and another which has been received by the same courier from Sir William Hamilton. (8830)

1714   PRINCE ADOLPHUS *to the* KING

[*Hannover, 12 April 1798.*] It was my intention to inform your Majesty myself of the death of General Malortie, but I really was so affected at it that I could not write last post. The loss of a friend is always a sad thing, but particularly so in these times when there are so few people on whom one can depend. The late General was certainly a man whom one could relie on, and one of the uprightest and worthy characters I ever met with. He has left a sister, a Madame de Plate, a most excellent woman, who has lived with him for these last five years and who has attended him with the utmost love during his long illness. This poor woman loses very much by his death, being now obliged to live alone, which will be very difficult to her as she is in very bad circumstances. This consideration, joined to the many obligations I have to her late brother, have prompted me to write in her favour to your Majesty begging you to give her a small pension. The motive which has emboldened me to ask this favour will I trust serve as an excuse for my having troubled you; at least I should be very unhappy to incurr your displeasure by this request, as I have hitherto ever strived and ever shall endeavour to act in a manner pleasing to you.

   The weather being now very fine we have begun exercising the non-commissioned Officers and I hope in a fortnight to be able to exercise with Batallions.

   I dare not importune your Majesty any longer. (48520)

1715   HENRY DUNDAS *to the* KING, *and the reply*

[*Wimbledon, 12 April 1798, 8 a.m.*] Mr. Dundas takes the liberty humbly to inform your Majesty that on the receipt of your Majesty's note he wrote a private letter to Lord Spencer on several points and particularly on that adverted to by your Majesty, and Mr. Dundas conceives it may be satisfactory to your Majesty to peruse the answer, as it contains a succinct statement on several very material subjects connected with your Majesty's service. A copy of the letter is herewith sent.[2] (8825)

[*The King's reply, Windsor, 13 April, 8.55 a.m.*] I am pleased with Mr. Secretary Dundas's attention in transmitting a copy of the letter he has received from Earl

---

[1] The Neapolitan Minister in London.
[2] Spencer's letter of the 9th to Dundas is in *Spencer Papers*, II, 311.

Spencer on the subject of the intended invasion. The suggestion that the commanding Generals of the district should communicate to the Naval Commissioners of the Admiralty such proposals for co-operation on the coast as may make part of their measures of defence seems highly proper, for without previous communication it is impossible that in the moment of action ideas can be so judiciously formed as at a cooler period. (Add. MSS. 40100, f. 201.)

1716 THE DUCHESS OF WURTEMBERG *to the* KING

[*Stutgard, 13 April 1798.*] I shall find it very difficult to express to your Majesty the pleasure and happiness I had yesterday in receiving your gracious letter, which, with a heart and eyes overflowing with gratitude, I read over several times. I am perfectly convinced that the only true comfort in distress and the only real support through life is religion, and am thankful to your Majesty for the advice you so kindly give me to try by my example to imprint those principles on the mind of Trinette. The Duke had always insisted on her being brought up a Lutheran, and though she lived with her grandmother, was always instructed by a Lutheran clergyman who attends her daily. Therefore I trust that I shall succeed in my endeavours to make her as far as I can go through the same course of religion that mama made us read with Schrader.

This week the Hereditary Prince[1] was confirmed, but to my mortification the Duke thought that I might suffer by being so long at Church and I was the only person who did not attend that ceremony, which they all assure me he went through with great propriety, and on Sunday he is to take the Sacrament. The moment that the physicians will allow me after my confinement I shall go to Ludewigsbourg, and as it is so much after the time that we had reason to expect, I have entreated the Duke to go before me as his health suffers from the heat and the confinement of Stutgard. He will not hear of it till after the first ten days are over; and I have almost persuaded the wise people to promise if I am well that they will let me go at the end of the month, but it is the fashion here never to stir till after six weeks. However, I plead mama's example and then they must submit. Our weather is very fine but already much too hot, and if we have no cold afterwards, trust that our harvest is very promising and that we shall have no more misfortunes this year with the vines, which have been very bad these last three or four seasons.

I am very sorry to hear so indifferent an account of the dear little Dutchess of York and pity Frederick very much that he is so often exposed to anxiety on her account. I trust in God that she will get better as I think she would be a dreadful loss to him. The Duke begs that I will present his humble duty to your Majesty. (51467-8)

[1] He succeeded his father on 30 Oct. 1816 as William I, King of Wurtemberg (1781–1864). On 8 June 1808 he married Princess Charlotte of Bavaria (1792–1873).

[*Bulstrode, Friday, 12* [*13*] *April 1798, 1.14 p.m.*] In obedience to your Majesty's commands the Duke of Portland will immediately send a respite for Abraham Clark, who was left for execution by Mr Justice Buller, & will direct a conditional pardon to be prepared for your Majesty's royal signature. The applications which have been made on behalf of this unhappy convict have occasioned the Duke of Portland to make repeated inquiries respecting him, the results of all which the Duke of Portland is sorry to observe to your Majesty had been equally unfavourable, but whatever his character may be, as an accessory in the burglary only, your Majesty will condescend to consider him not unworthy of mercy.

The Duke of Portland most humbly begs leave to acquaint your Majesty that he has this moment received an answer from Maidstone, that the Grand Jury found the indictment against O'Connor, Quigley & Binns;[1] all the persons indicted for high treason under the Special Commission, without the least hesitation, though with an attention to the prisoners that does their feelings infinite credit. The Duke of Portland also begs leave to add that four persons out of thirteen, for whom warrants were issued by the Duke of Portland on suspicion of high treason for endeavouring to engage the soldiers to join the French in case of an invasion, & administring oaths to them for the purpose, have been apprehended at Manchester, where it is believed that the others, or at least the greater part of them, will also have been taken into custody by this time; & the four first are expected in town in the course of tomorrow, & will probably undergo their first examination on Saturday at the Secretary of State's Office, the result of which the Duke of Portland will consider it to be his duty to lay before your Majesty.

The Duke of Portland presumes to add that no dispatches or intelligence of any kind from Ireland have been received today. (8826–7)

[*Bulstrode, Friday, 13 April 1798, 10.30 p.m.*] The Duke of Portland, humbly conceiving that it will be a satisfaction to your Majesty to receive a proof of the loyalty & zeal of so populous a part of your Majesty's dominions as the town of Manchester & its neighbourhood, presumes to lay at your Majesty's feet the report of Mr Floud, one of the Police Magistrates who was sent to assist Mr Bayley of Manchester in taking up the persons who were charged with being guilty of treasonable practices, not one of whom your Majesty will be pleased to observe is likely to escape. The Duke of Portland begs leave to state that *Gray*, who is represented to have been in a state of great agitation, is the person who gave the first information to Mr Bayley which led to the discovery of these conspirators. The Duke of Portland requests your Majesty's permission to add that he has received today a private letter from Ireland, dated Waterford the 7th instt., by which he learns that the Assizes for that county had been attended by a greater number of gentlemen & well affected yeomen than had ever been remembered, that the Petty Juries had correctly fulfilled their duty, that nine United Irishmen had been convicted; one of whom, a leader of those deluded people & a Roman

---

[1] The Duke should also have added the names of John Allen and Jeremiah Leary. (*State Trials*, XXVI, 1197.)

Catholick, imagining that no persons of his own persuasion would convict him, challenged every Protestant on the pannel but three, but the other nine, who were all Papists, concurred without hesitation in the opinion of their three Protestant fellow jurors & found him guilty. The writer further assures the Duke of Portland that the city & county of Waterford are quite quiet & peaceable & that the spirited exertions of the Magistrates & Yeomanry there will be certain to establish the good order to which they are restored.

[P.S.] The Duke of Portland takes the liberty of acquainting your Majesty that the prisoners from Manchester are arrived in town & are lodged in the new House of Correction, as appears by a letter from Mr Wickham which the Duke of Portland has just this moment received & most humbly submits to your Majesty. (8831–2)

1718   PRINCE ERNEST *to the* KING

[*London, 14 April 1798.*] Allow me once more to address myself to your Majesty and threw [*sic*] myself on your goodness. Consider for one moment how great must be my anxiety to serve at this crisis, when the whole nation is arming, and even your Majesty in person intends to come forward, a time in which it behoves every man to assist in the defence of Great Britain. I have again offered my services to the Commander-in-Chief, who answer'd me by letter '*that it would do me more harm than good*, the mentioning the subject to you;' alluding to the step which I had taken in quitting the Hannoverian service. Y.M., highly tenacious of your own honor, if you reconsider this business, must feel that I should have forfeited *mine* had I continued in the Hannoverian service, contrary to my solemn and public declarations of never serving under Genl. Walmoden, who had personally ill treated me. It would be presumption in me to suppose that I have fewer enemies than other men, and there would not have been wanting those to have represented my conduct, if not in a dishonorable light, at least as inconsistent in making such declarations without foundation.[1]

My request to my brother the Duke of York was to have obtain'd me the Brevet rank of Lieutenant-General, and offering, when the 13th Light Dragoons arriv'd from the West Indies (if he could obtain me from Y.M. the being named Colonel Commandant) that I would superintend the reorganizing that Regiment, leaving all the emoluments naturally to Genl. Craiggs the Colonel (as he had said that at his time of life it would be a disagreeable task) and it would be my greatest ambition to gain Y.M. approbation by so doing. I named ye instance of the Prince of Wales, not meaning however to put myself upon a footing with him, yet trusting that as a son of your Majesty some indulgence or respect might be shewn, particularly in the present times, when in my humble opinion the honor of Y.M. & your descendants ought to be the more considered. Nevertheless, Sir, if it is your opinion that my application is improper, God forbid that one of your sons should be the person to give a bad example, & therefore if you should think

[1] There is an inaccurate version of this paragraph in G. M. Willis, *Ernest Augustus, Duke of Cumberland*, p. 54, and, incidentally, many other errors in his quotations from the Archives (but the Duke of Cumberland's letters are very difficult to decipher).

that what I have asked is detrimental to the service I have been too long a soldier to sollicit it, but will gladly accept any rank Y.M. thinks consistent with your dignity to grant, but should you be determin'd to refuse this humble request, I will then, Sir, go into the yeomanry as a private; by that means I shall shew my anxiety in a glorious cause in which I have already served, & by so doing shall prove my zeal & readiness to come forward in defence of my King & country. (47182–3)

1719   *Letters from the* KING *to* LORD GRENVILLE, *and the replies*

[*Windsor, 14 April 1798.*] Yesterday evening I saw Mr. de Luc who acquainted me with his having been with Lord Grenville in the forenoon at Dropmore, which renders it unnecessary for me to state what he mentioned of the reception he had met with from the King of Prussia. I forward the letter he had prepared at Cuxhaven and the Memoire, which I desire Lord Grenville after perusal will communicate to Mr. Pitt. I hope by what he has related and which is strongly confirmed by the despatches from Lord Elgin which I have read this morning, that a concert between the Courts of Vienna and Berlin may be effected.

I am certain the Prince of Orange will willingly consent to give up any territorial acquisition, provided the Courts of Vienna and Berlin will support him in his demands of compensation from the Dutch for his losses there, and some contribution to reinstate his finances in his German dominions which is also equitable to be supplied by the German Ecclesiastical Electors who have in former times made unjust [?demands][1] on the [?]domains[1] of his ancestors. (Fortescue MSS.)

[*Lord Grenville's reply, Dropmore, 14 April, 10.30 a.m.*] Lord Grenville is honoured with your Majesty's commands, which he will immediately execute. He had already written to Mr Pitt on the subject, and he will now send to him M. de Luc's memoire.

He humbly requests to receive tomorrow your Majesty's pleasure whether he should wait upon the Prince of Orange to make the proposal to him of authorizing M. de Stamfort to declare his readiness to renounce all pretensions to territorial indemnities, or whether your Majesty would take any other mode of sounding the Prince of Orange on the subject? (8833)

[*From the King, Windsor, 15 April, 10.26 a.m.*] In answer to Lord Grenville's note concerning the Prince of Orange, I have desired the Duke of York, with whom he dines this day, to acquaint him that I propose sending Lord Grenville to him to propose his giving a public declaration to the Courts of Vienna and Berlin of his readiness to renounce all pretensions to territorial indemnities in Germany, and trusting that they will acquire for him such pecuniary assistance as may enable him and his family to live at their ease in his German dominions.

I have received the enclosed papers from Mr. de Luc which will much encourage the necessity of taking this step. I desire these may also be communicated to Mr. Pitt. (Fortescue MSS.)

[1] Obscured by blots.

[*Lord Grenville's reply, Dropmore, 15 April.*] Lord Grenville is just honoured with your Majesty's commands, and in humble obedience to them he will write to the Prince of Orange to fix a time for Lord Grenville's waiting on him. He will not fail to communicate to Mr Pitt the papers received this morning from your Majesty, and he hopes to be enabled by Tuesday to write to Berlin on the subject. (8834)

1720 THE DUKE OF PORTLAND *to the* KING

[*Whitehall, Sunday night, 15 April 1798.*] The Duke of Portland most humbly begs leave to submit together with the Lord Lieutenant's dispatches which he has now the honor to lay before your Majesty, a letter which he received today from Sir Ralph Abercromby which was evidently written before the Lord Lieutenant had signified to him your Majesty's permission that he might resign, & which, the Duke of Portland fears, indicates a determination on the part of Sir Ralph Abercromby no longer susceptible of the impression which your Majesty's gracious condescension could not but have operated under any other circumstances.

The Duke of Portland most humbly acquaints your Majesty that the whole of this day has been employed in examining the persons who were apprehended at Manchester, from whom nothing has been obtained in the shape of information which is new—as the object of every one of them who has been examined has been to invalidate the testimony of the two informers, for which purpose it is evident they had concerted a plan which, by the inattention of the goaler who had suffer'd them to be together, they have had an opportunity of doing since their arrival in town, but of which the falsehood is too apparent not to make its success impossible. There does not remain above one or two at most of these traitors to be examined, & as your Majesty's Law Officers have only tomorrow to consider the evidence to be produced on the trials of O'Connor, &c (as the names of all the witnesses must be given to the prisoners on Tuesday) the examination of the one or two persons who have not yet been before the Council & the examination of the others is necessarily deferred 'till Tuesday. The circumstance of the trials at Maidstone obliged your Majesty's servants to employ this day in examining the persons who have been brought up from Manchester, as it was expected that important evidence might be obtained from them with regard to the prisoners now in Maidstone goal, but it is a matter of much doubt whether the Attorney-General will deem it safe to expose any of the Manchester witnesses to the test of a cross-examination. (8835–6)

1721 LORD GRENVILLE *to the* KING, *and the reply*

[*Cleveland Row, 18 April 1798, 11 p.m.*] Lord Grenville has the honour to transmit to your Majesty a letter which he has this night received from M. Fagel. Knowing as he does the favourable opinion which your Majesty is pleased to entertain of that worthy & excellent man, Lord Grenville is persuaded that he only anticipates your Majesty's commands in requesting your Majesty's permission to transmit to M. Fagel by tomorrow's mail assurances of your Majesty's gracious favour & protection, and to concert with Mr Pitt respecting the extent & mode of such provision as can be made for him. (8837)

[*The King's reply, Queen's House, 20 April, 8.10 a.m.*] Lord Grenville does but justice to my sentiments in favour of Mr. de Fagel in supposing I should favourably receive his application for pecuniary assistance; the conduct of his family for above a century, which he has by no means failed of pursueing, makes him highly deserving of every attention. I desire therefore Lord Grenville's answer may be full of assurances of good intentions and that he will lose no time in settling with Mr. Pitt the quantum of the pension on which he may depend.

I cannot lay down my pen without desiring Lord Grenville, previous to this day's debate, to guard Mr. Pitt against any too marked approbation of the line of conduct Mr. Sheridan means to hold, though I do not think at this hour anyone declaring hostility to France is to be rejected, yet any compliments would disgust friends, and certainly are not necessary; indeed, I should wish some intimation might be made that this change of language was very late. (Fortescue MSS.)

1722 *Letters from* WILLIAM PITT *to the* KING, *and a reply*

[*Downing Street, Friday, 20 April 1798, p.m.*] Mr Pitt humbly begs leave to acquaint your Majesty that on the Motion for the Address of Thanks for your Majesty's Message,[1] delivered to the House of Commons this day, Mr Sheridan made a speech in support of the Address, containing the strongest declarations of the necessity of exertion and unanimity in the present crisis. He at the same time made some protestations in favor of his former opinion, and introduced some invidious and unnecessary topics, but the general result of his speech was very useful. He concluded however with stating his opinion that it was not necessary to suspend the Habeas Corpus Act, but did not urge his objections with much vehemence or any effect. Mr Pitt in reply gave him the credit both due in itself and prudent to be given, to the general tenor of his declaration, but in such a manner as he trusts sufficiently upheld the tone and credit of those who have supported Government thro' all the preceding stages of the contest; and particularly insisted on the immediate necessity of suspending the Habeas Corpus Act. As soon as the Address had been agreed to, nemine contradicente, the Bill for the suspension was brought from the Lords. After a short conversation, the House divided on the second reading 183 to 5, and afterwards in the Committee, on a question of shortening the continuance of the Bill, the original date was carried by 113 to 15.[2] The Bill was then passed and ordered to be returned to the Lords.[3] (8838–9)

[1] Recommending further measures for the safety of the country in view of the invasion preparations of the enemy. (*Parl. Register*, LI, 4.)

[2] 113 to 14, according to *Parl. Register* and *Parl. Hist.* XXXIII, 1433; 109 to 13 according to Abbot (Colchester, I, 150).

[3] *Parl. Register*, LI, 4–27. Canning wrote on the 21st: 'S[heridan] did not quite do all that we had reason to expect. But he did enough to do a great deal of good, as much perhaps to the general cause, as if he had been less *qualified* in his support—though with not so much credit to himself. Fox must feel ashamed. And surely the country must feel ashamed of him...' (Harewood MSS.)

[The King's reply, Windsor, 21 April, 7.27 a.m.] I am much pleased with Mr. Pitt's account of the conduct of the House of Commons yesterday, and not less so that when Mr. Sheridan supported the Address of the necessity of exertion and unanimity at the present crisis, he so far threw off the mask as not to abandon his former opinions, and consequently greatly destroy any merit his present conduct might otherwise appear to deserve by also objecting to the suspension of the Habeas Corpus Act:[1] but what meets with my strongest approbation is Mr. Pitt's having in reply upheld the tone and credit of those who have supported Government through all the preceding stages of the contest, and the immediate necessity of suspending the Habeas Corpus Act, which on being brought from the House of Lords, instantly went through its various stages, and was returned to that House without any amendment, for the passing of which I have just signed a commission. (Chatham Papers.)

[From Pitt, Downing Street, 22 April.] Mr. Pitt humbly begs leave to submit to your Majesty the accompanying Messages to the two Houses, on which it is proposed to found a vote for including two millions at the charge of Ireland, in the approaching loan; which sum it is represented by the Lord Lieutenant to be of urgent necessity to provide here for the service of that kingdom.[2] (8840)

1723 PRINCE EDWARD *to the* KING

[Halifax, Nova-Scotia, 23 April 1798.] I was two days since honoured with your Majesty's very gracious and truly kind letter of the 11th of February, for which I beg leave to offer in the most dutiful manner my grateful and sincere thanks. I can only express the lively sense I entertain of the high favor you have conferred upon me in condescending to write, by saying that the moment when I first read the direction of your letter was one of the happiest of my life. It has long been the heigth of my ambition to learn from yourself that my conduct since you have been pleased to employ me actively in your several foreign possessions had met

[1] In a letter to Camden on the 21st Pitt commented on Sheridan's speech: 'You will see also the account of Sheridan's appearance in the House of Commons, which has certainly been upon the whole useful, has done him some credit and not too much; and added to the disgrace of his friends. The general zeal and spirit of the country is everything that we can wish.' (Camden MSS.)

[2] *H. of C. J.*, LIII, 494; *Parl. Register*, LI, 54. Pitt wrote to Camden on the 21st: 'I received yesterday morning your letter just before my first conference with our bidders for the Loan. I had hoped that with the sale of the quit-rents and the prospect of raising a million by Loan in Ireland, you would not have been obliged to call for so large a sum from hence. But in consequence of your letter I have not hesitated to add two millions on account of Ireland to fifteen which I must borrow on our own account, in consequence of the encreased expence attending our late military preparations. I am to settle the terms on Monday, and to bring it forward on Wednesday. If you still can make a million and an half sufficient, I am sure you will not be the less inclined to do so from my readiness to consult your wants. I must particularly beg you to consider of making some *very ample* and immediate provision for a Sinking Fund to pay off the capital created by this two millions in as short a time as possible. After the effort we have made to prevent the accumulation of permanent debt on our own account, it would be impossible for me to propose to Parliament to incur this charge on account of Ireland without some such provision. I reckon the interest of our Loan will be from $6\frac{1}{4}$ to $6\frac{1}{2}$ per cent, which is so much lower than the rate at which you would borrow without our guarantee, that you can the better afford a large Sinking Fund. Pray let me know how large you think you can make it. You will see that we have our share of traitors here, and I hope the steps we are taking against them will have their use in Ireland as well as here.' (Camden MSS.)

with your approbation, and as you have now been graciously pleased to assure me that this is the case, you will better conceive than I can describe the sentiments with which your most flattering letter has impressed me.

Your Majesty having been pleased to say that you did not see any place in which you could so usefully employ me while the war continued, as where I now am, it is my duty to obey your commands with the utmost cheerfulness, and believe me, Sir, your goodness in assuring me that when the war is over you would wish to see me, is not lost upon me, and I trust I feel it as I ought. I am fully sensible of the justice of what you are pleased to observe, that my absence from home on service has been the means of keeping me out of many difficulties, nor can I ever look back with regret upon the years that have been thus spent in your service and with your approbation, except when I reflect upon the length of my absence from your person.

When last I had the honor of addressing you, our winter was but just set in, and I had flattered myself that having been in perfect health throughout the summer, I should have escaped the severe attacks of rheumatic fever, bilious headach and sore throat from which I had at different times suffered the two preceding years, although I never ventured to make mention of this circumstance either to your Majesty or to any of my friends who had the honor of being more particularly about you. However, contrary to my expectations, this last winter, which was one of the most trying ever known in North America, brought on a return of the same complaints in a very increased proportion, and it becomes now a duty which I owe to myself to inform you that the most respectable medical gentleman of this country who has constantly attended me since my arrival from the West Indies has given it as his decided opinion that I ought on no account to risk another winter in this climate. Were it possible for any man on earth to say that the attacks I have experienced arose from intemperance or irregularity of any kind or description whatever, I should consider this representation as not having the most distant claim to any attention from your Majesty, but the whole of my conduct and mode of living must be so fully known to everyone, as being diametrically the reverse of anything tending even to a suspicion of that kind, that I feel confident they will bear the closest scrutiny. Not wishing to trespass on your indulgence with a detail of the sentiments of the phisician respecting my health, I have inclosed copies of that gentleman's opinion to two of my oldest and most esteemed friends, who I believe have often the honor of approaching your Majesty, (Major-General Goldsworthy, and Doctor Fisher) that, if you should condescend to devote a moment's attention to this subject, you may be enabled to satisfy yourself as to the truth of what I have presumed to represent, by commanding one of these gentlemen to lay the statement before you.

Should your Majesty in consequence be graciously pleased to allow me to quit this country before the winter I humbly sollicit that I may obtain your permission to embark early in October, when, from the situation of this province and the severity of the climate, no further apprehension can be entertained of the appearance of an enemy off the coast until the following spring, and the public works for the defence of the post will be approaching to a conclusion for the year.

The wish next my heart, if permitted to return to Europe, would certainly be that of being employed actively in the line of my profession in any part of Great Britain or Ireland, where, from being placed more immediately under your notice, I might have an opportunity of gaining to myself some credit by my punctuality and zeal in executing such service as might be committed to my care. At the same time I beg leave to assure your Majesty that in the event of your being pleased to admit of my serving in your dominions at home, I have not the most distant wish or idea of solliciting you either to confer upon me the high honor of Peerage or to augment my income, being firmly resolved to live in the most modest and œconomical manner possible, at whatever station I may be placed, where my pay as a General Officer, in addition to the allowance you grant me, will be amply sufficient to enable me to live both decently and respectably during the continuance of the war: but should your Majesty have reasons for not approving of my being thus employed at home, I beg leave to express my utmost willingness to repair directly from hence to your Electoral dominions, and to serve under General Walmoden with that part of your Hannoverian troops now stationed to form the Cordon, in any capacity or situation you may be pleased to point out, until such time as the happy moment shall arrive when you may wish to see me in England.

Permit me, Sir, now to conclude by solliciting your indulgence for the length and contents of this letter, with which I should not have presumed to trouble you had I not felt the urgent necessity of representing thus early the causes which have rendered it indispensable for me once more earnestly to apply to you for a removal from this station after the duties of the post for the season are completed, and before another winter sets in.

As I have done myself the honor of addressing the Queen by the present occasion, I have only to request that your Majesty will accept of the assurances of my most dutiful and devoted attachment, and that you will permit me to subscribe myself [etc.] (45934–7)

1724 WILLIAM PITT *to the* KING, *and the reply*

[*Downing Street, 23 April 1798, 10.30 p.m.*] Mr Pitt humbly begs leave to acquaint your Majesty that on the 2d reading this day of the Bill for the Sale of the Land Tax a Motion was made by Mr Jolliffe and seconded by Mr Pierrepoint,[1] to delay the 2d reading. The Amendment was supported by Lord Sheffield, Mr Hobhouse, Mr Bastard, Mr Hussey, and Mr Tierney, and opposed by Mr Dundas, Mr Buxton, the Solicitor General, Mr Simeon,[2] Col. Wood,[3] Mr Pitt and

---

[1] Evelyn Henry Frederick Pierrepont (1775–1801), eldest son of the 1st Earl Manvers. M.P. for Bossiney, 1796; for Nottinghamshire, 1796–1801, 'who', commented Lord Granville Leveson-Gower, 'for the new peerage conferred upon his father six months ago has thought proper to evince his gratitude to the King by declaring "that the Royal family not being taxed was quite *shocking*".' (*Corresp. of Lord G. Leveson-Gower*, I, 184.) He died, 22 Oct. 1801.

[2] Sir John Simeon (1756–1824), M.P. for Reading, 1797–1802, 1806–18. Created Baronet, 27 Dec. 1814. (Royal Kalendar, but on 22 May 1815 according to *Rider's British Merlin*.)

[3] Sir Mark Wood (c. 1747–1829), M.P. for Milborne Port, 1794–96; for Newark, 1796–1802, for Gatton, 1802–18. Created Baronet, 24 Sept. 1808. For him see *Farington Diary*, II, 94, and *Letters of George IV*, *passim*.

Mr. Wilberforce; and was rejected by 153 to 38; after which the Bill was read a second time and ordered to be committed. Mr Pitt has no doubt that this measure will be attended with the most salutary effect on public credit.[1] (8841)

[*The King's reply, Queen's House, 24 April 1798, 7.50 a.m.*] As Mr. Pitt is of opinion that the proposed sale of the Land Tax will be attended with the most salutary effect on public credit, I am happy to find that [on] the division on it yesterday the favourers were 153 to 38. (Chatham Papers.)

1725   *Letters from* LORD GRENVILLE *to the* KING, *and the replies*

[*Cleveland Row, 26 April 1798, 11 p.m.*] Lord Grenville has the honour most respectfully to submit to your Majesty the draft of an answer from your Majesty to the letter of the Count d'Artois containing the offer of the services of the émigrés for the defense of this country. If your Majesty should be graciously pleased to approve and to transcribe this answer, Lord Grenville will deliver it tomorrow to the Duc de Berri[2] whom he is to see by appointment on this subject. (8842)

[*The King's reply, Queen's House, 27 April, 8.58 a.m.*] The draft of an answer to the Count d'Artois' letter seems very proper. I have therefore transcribed it, that Lord Grenville may be enabled to deliver it this day to the Duc de Berri. (Fortescue MSS.)

[*From Lord Grenville, Cleveland Row, 27 April, 11.17 a.m.*] Lord Grenville has the honour to transmit to your Majesty the account of a tumult at Vienna, in which the French Ambassador's house has been attacked, & in consequence of which he was preparing to quit Vienna.

There are dispatches from Lord Elgin, but as they only contain further accounts of the correspondence between Vienna & Berlin Lord Grenville does not trouble your Majesty with them at this time, unless your Majesty should be pleased to direct them to be sent now. (8843)

[*The King's reply, Queen's House, 27 April, 11.25 a.m.*] I am sensible of Lord Grenville's attention in immediately communicating to me the account from Vienna which inevitably must occasion a change of conduct of that Court towards France, the insolence of whom has drawn on the tumult of Vienna. As Lord Grenville does not mention that anything material is contained in the letters from Berlin they need not be sent to me till tomorrow morning. (Fortescue MSS.)

[*From Lord Grenville, Cleveland Row, 27 April, 11 p.m.*] Lord Grenville has the honour humbly to acquaint your Majesty that he has this day seen the Duc de

---

[1] *Parl. Register*, LI, 28–42. Landowners were to redeem their land tax (four shillings in the pound), then producing about £2,000,000 a year, by purchasing Government Stock, at twenty years' purchase. The interest being paid on the Stock, which would thus be taken off the market, amounted to about £2,400,000, and so, Pitt calculated, the public would gain to the extent of about £400,000 a year.

[2] The Comte d'Artois's younger son (1778–1820). He was murdered.

Berri and delivered to him the letter from your Majesty to the Count d'Artois. The Duc de Harcourt had before the Duc de Berri's arrival in London asked Lord Grenville's opinion with respect to the line which the Duc de Berri ought to follow as to going to Court, and Lord Grenville took upon himself to say that it would be better to avoid it, in order to obviate some inconvenience that might possibly have arisen from it.

Today the Duc de Berri expressed in very strong terms, but at the same time with great propriety, his regret at not being allowed to pay his respects to your Majesty. Lord Grenville did not say anything to give him the least opening for any farther discussion of the subject, but it occurred to him that your Majesty might possibly have the goodness to allow the Duc de Berri to wait on your Majesty at the Queen's House some day next week for a few minutes, and that by this mode all appearance of harshness towards the Princes would be avoided, & none of the inconvenience incurred of a public reception at your Majesty's Levée, or in the Closet at St James's.

Lord Grenville thought it his duty humbly to submit this idea to your Majesty's consideration, but if your Majesty should not approve it, the business may rest as it is, and Lord Grenville is persuaded it will not be revived. (8844–5)

[*The King's reply, Windsor, 28 April, 8.30 a.m.*] I agree with Lord Grenville that my not seeing the Duc de Berri might have an appearance of harshness, but that his reception in public would be inconvenient. Certainly his coming to the Queen's House is the only proper mode; when I see Lord Grenville on Wednesday I will settle the day and time for this interview. (Fortescue MSS.)

[*From Lord Grenville, Cleveland Row, 28 April, 11 p.m.*] Lord Grenville has the honour to transmit to your Majesty a note[1] from Count Starhemberg containing a further account from Vienna by which it appears that General Bernadotte[2] has actually quitted that Court. In consequence of this intelligence and of the other considerations which apply to this subject, and which your Majesty spoke of to Lord Grenville when he had last the honour to pay his duty to your Majesty, your Majesty's servants this day agreed on the heads of an instruction to the Earl of St Vincent, directing him to send without delay a sufficient force into the Mediterranean to keep that of France in check: but as the keeping this resolution secret appeared of the utmost importance it was agreed that Lord Grenville should not make any communication of it to any of the Foreign Ministers here, but should immediately write to Vienna upon the subject, which he has accordingly done by the opportunity of Prince Frederick of Orange, who sets out early tomorrow morning. (8846–7)

[*The King's reply, Windsor, 29 April, 8.30 a.m.*] I am much pleased with Lord Grenville's attention in transmitting a copy of Count Starhemberg's note stating

---

[1] Folios 8848–9. Printed in *Dropmore Papers*, IV, 182.

[2] Bernadotte (1764–1844), who became one of Napoleon's Marshals, was elected heir to the throne of Sweden in 1810. The old King's health began to fail, and Bernadotte became the real ruler. He succeeded Charles XIII as King of Sweden and Norway in 1818.

that Bernadotte had actually quitted Vienna, and his unheard-of demands which are so curious that I have kept the paper.

Nothing can have been more judicious than Lord Grenville's so properly making use of the opinion I had communicated to him of attempting to prevent the French fleet sailing from Toulon, and that in consequence directions will be sent to the Earl of St. Vincent for that purpose; but I trust these orders will be accompanied by a speedy reinforcement to him of some ships from the North Sea and Channel squadrons. I have this morning seen a letter from Lisbon which states that he sailed on the fourth with all his ships to intercept the Spanish fleet who intend again coming from Cadiz to convoy for a certain distance three Spanish ships of 74 guns each with a considerable quantity of arms on board for the Spanish Colonies. If he succeeds in bringing them to action it will greatly assist the orders now going from hence, but which must be kept secret. (Fortescue MSS.)

1726   THE DUKE OF PORTLAND *to the* KING

[*Burlington House, Monday, 30 April 1798, 11.25 p.m.*] The Duke of Portland, humbly conceiving that it may be agreable to your Majesty to be informed of this day's proceedings at Maidstone on the arraignment of the prisoners under the Special Commission, takes the liberty of acquainting your Majesty that they have all been arraigned & have pleaded not guilty, & that the Court, on a strong affidavit of the absence of several material witnesses whom the prisoners have sent for from Ireland, & by consent of Mr Attorney-General, given upon the prisoners waving all objection to the jurisdiction &c &c & pleading not guilty to the indictment, has postponed the trial until the 21st of May. (8850)

1727   E. LIVINGSTON *to the* KING

[*Naples, 1 May 1798.*] The anxious situation I have been in since my arrival at Naples prevented my having the honor to adress your Majesty til I had it in my power to say something positive about Prince Augustus afairs. By my letters of the 6 and 8 March I had the honor to inform your Majesty that his Royal Highness enjoy'd good health, which he does at present. It gave me pain to see a total seperation of society betwixt the Prince, Count Munster and Mr. Tatter, which continued so til these gentlemen left Naples 16 April. Their acquaintance here esteem them much. I found them sensible and well inform'd, much attach'd to the honor and dignity of his Royal Highness: unfortunately the Prince for a long time has been entirely directed by a set of very improper society whose interest it was to keep up a division betwixt the Prince and his attendants, and I am sorry to say they were entirely master of all his actions and have been the cause of the Prince acting in public and private in a very improper manner.

Count Munster having told me that your Majesty has been amply inform'd of everything regarding the Prince before my arrival, I shall only add I found great disorder in his Royal Highnesses afairs within and without doors. On serious representations I got the Prince to give up the constant dinners and suppers with very bad society in his own appartment where it was impossible and would have been very improper for me to be present. I wish I could inform your Majesty that there was a total reform, but there is no chance of that in this country.

The moment the Prince's creditors heard of my arrival they became very pressing to be paid and even threaten'd to arrest his person. These demands was of so serious a nature that Sir William Hamilton was forced to authorize Mr. Gibbs, an English merchant here, to call in a list of the Prince's debts, and he, as your Majesty's Minister, engaged they should be all paid as soon as the proper arrangments could be taken in England. As the debts don't exceed 6,000 Ster. I am convinced your Majesty will approve Sir William's conduct. There was no alternative left; if Sir William had not become bound to see all the just debts paid, his Royal Highness must have remain'd here and run a great risk of falling ere long into the hands of an inveterate enemy that would have shewn him in triumph from this to Paris. The dignity of the Crown and honor of the nation also required that a Prince of the Blood Royal should not leave this country without satisfying his creditors. As soon as the Prince leaves this, Sir William Hamilton will inform Mr. Pitt and send an exact list of all the honorable debts he has engag'd to pay. Considering the Prince had 2,000 a year for his pocket money I cannot vindicate his having contracted debts, but when I reflect seriously on the number of years his Royal Highness has been in this imoral country, where nice feelings are not fashionable, it is not very surprizing the Prince follow'd the bad example he had constantly before him. To prevent the like conduct in future I take the liberty to give my opinion that your Majesty may be pleased to write the Prince in very strong terms concerning the propriety of genteel œconomy and of the absolute necessity of not contracting any more debts, and that he will incur your Royal disspleasure if he does not conform his expences exactly to the allowance you may be pleas'd to order for his Household and his pocket money, and I beg your Majesty may be graciously pleased to order very exact instructions to be sent me at Sir Morton Eden's, Vienna, on that subject. If I am not mistaken the Prince is of an indolent and easy temper, not nice in his society and an easy prey to designing men. Nothing can prove it so clearly as pensions he has given to people that never should have been admitted into his presence. All these dessagreeable afairs must end on our quiting Naples.

I hope your Majesty may not think it unreasonable that I wish for the assistance of another gentleman to attend the Prince. My health has suffer'd by the long winter journey. Should I be laid up with the gout the Prince would be without a single attendant. I wish that gentleman to be near the Prince's own age, of honorable sentiments and genteel behaviour. Doctor Domier remains with his Royal Highness; he is a very honest man and able physician and much attached to the Prince. Count Munster carry'd four servants with him; as the Prince leaves his cook here, his Household is allmost desolved at present. Count Munster sold before he left this the six horses belonging to your Majesty. The Prince also sold the horses that he had purchased himself. There was no possibility of sending them to Germany; neither is it possible for me at present to propose any reasonable plan to your Majesty for the Prince's future residence. I have not yet been admitted into the Prince's society of advisers. His pretended friends have keep'd me at as great a distance as possible. I have no doubt they do all they can to make the Prince beleive that he now is of an age to have the nomination of his attendants. His Royal Highness has allways been civil, and altho' he does not exactly follow the advice I have taken the liberty to offer, he allows I could not have acted otherways than I have done since I had the honor to attend him. I have also reason to beleive some of the Prince's correspondants at *home* have attempted to give him an unfavorable opinion of me. I know from undoubted authority they have put the Prince on his guard not *to trust* me in anything [that] concerns *them*. As my conduct shall on every occasion tend to his Royal Highness' honor and interest, I have no doubt when the Prince is better acquainted with me but he will do me the justice I deserve.

Sir William Hamilton on every occasion has shewn the most respectful friendship for the Prince. Count Munster told me Sir William had put himself to very great expence by the Balls and entertainments he had given to his Royal Highness, to this Court and nobility on the Prince's arrival, birthdays, &c.

I will have the honor to inform your Majesty as soon as the Prince gets on shore; for political reasons it is probable he may be landed in Dalmatia or Istrie.[1]
(16717–9)

[1] Livingston wrote to Pitt from Naples on 10 April: 'By his Majesty's commands I have the honor to inclose a State of his Royal Highness the Prince Augustus Household such as I found it the 4th March; by which you will see the annual expences since 1794 has not been less than 6000 sterling, including the 2000 sterling per annum ordered by the King for the Prince's pocket money.

At present I have not been able to procure an exact state of his Royal Highness's debts contracted in Italy. I believe they are not very considerable, but most certainly exceed the 2000 credit sent Sir William Hamilton by Lord Grenville. As the express terms of the credit does not allow Sir William to exceed the 2000 sterling, all the Prince's debts cannot be payd, and in this critical moment may render our departure precarious. I will be directed by the advice of Sir William, but I cannot hesitate to declare my own opinion that a Prince of the Blood Royal of England ought not to quit this country without paying his just debts; indeed, some of his creditors demand ready money, and threaten to arrest the Prince if not payd directly; that must be prevented if possible, and nothing shall be wanting on my part to satisfy his creditors.

If his Royal Highness is promised a safe conveyance from this, I foresee great difficultys, and considering the present critical state of afairs, it is impossible to leave this without some risk; at all events I flater myself no blame can be laid to my charge.

On leaving this we shall be very short of money. I beg, Sir, you may have the goodness to order a credit to be sent as soon as possible to Sir Morton Eden at Vienna, specifying the exact sum his Majesty may be pleased to order for the support of the Prince's Household, and for his Royal Highness's pocket money.

P.S. Since I finished my letter a state of the Prince's debts have been sent me from different quarters, I flater myself the whole cannot exceed 4000 sterling...' (W. Dacres Adams MSS.)
[Enclosure]

Extract from the Instructions given Count Munster before he left London with H.R.H. the Prince Augustus and signed by his Majesty at Windsor in January, 1794

	The King ordered 2000 sterling per annum for the Prince's pocket money; out of said sum H.R.H. was to pay every article belonging to his wardrobe, his Masters etc; in short, everything not included in the Establishment of H.R.H. Household, regulated by his Majesty['s] commands.
When Mr. Livingston arrived at Naples the 4th of March 1798 the Prince's Household was com-	The Count Munster Mr. Tatter

[*Stutgard, 4 May 1798.*] The first use that I make of the health & strength that it has pleased the Almighty to restore me is to address your Majesty to prove to you that nothing but illness can ever prevent my writing on all occasions to express to you my love and respect. Do not think me ungrateful to Providence for the many blessings with which I am surrounded when I say that the loss of my dear child has deeply afflicted me.[1] I trust that I feel this as a Christian and submit with resignation to the will of the Almighty, but nature must ever make me regret the loss of the little thing I had built such happiness on: when I do this I frequently blame myself as God [h]as made her happier than my warmest wishes could have done. On this subject I must stop to mention the blessing I enjoy in the affection and attentions of the Duke, who really is the best of husbands and who, God knows, has suffered cruelly from his anxiety of my subject [*sic*]. I am doubly sensible of this happiness as it falls to the lot of so few people in our situation of life, and therefore should be much more blameable if I did not submit chearfully to the will of God. I am also fortunate in having had Madame de Spiegel, whose conduct to me I shall never forget, as also my other two Ladies and Lady Stuart,[2] who have never left me.

I must also mention another subject that has vexed me. I pressed Mr Arbuthnot on his arrival here to stay till the Christening, as I had set my heart on yr. Majesty's being represented by your own Minister, and I then thought that I should have

posed of three gentlemen and nine servants; also a cook etc.

N.B. Count Munster, Mr. Tatter and four servants leave H.R.H. and return to Hanover.

The Doctor remains with H.R.H.

In the kitchen, in all, three men

In the stables five men

also a job coach, and coachman for the Prince and another for the gentlemen of his suite, the Prince's own coach and horses not going out but when H.R.H. was in full dress

N.B. The servants above nine, and horses above six, were to be payd out of the Prince's pocket money

Doctor Domier
a valet de chambre
a butler, and four footmen

The three servants belonging to the above gentlemen: as they were payd by the King, were also reckoned of the Prince's Household

a cook, and assistants

a coachman; a postilion and two grooms

four coach horses, and two saddle horses

To cover the expences of H.R.H. Household etc. Count Munster had a letter of credit from the House of Messrs Contard at Francfort, they by the King's commands to reimburse themselves from the Regency at Hanover.

By the extract given me and signed by Count Munster the expences of H.R.H.'s Household etc. including the 2000 sterling for the Prince's pocket money, since January 1794 has been 6000 sterling per annum.   (W. D. Adams MSS.)

---

[1] She had been delivered of a still-born daughter.

[2] She is referred to in Princess Augusta's letter to Lady Chatham, 2 April 1800: 'I have received the Queen's commands to inform you with her compliments, that a place in Scotland being become vacant by the death of Sir Charles Preston, her Majesty wishes you would be so good as to apply to Mr. Pitt that Sir *John Stuart*, now residing at *Stutgart*, might be appointed to succeed Sir Charles Preston. You will also confer great pleasure on your old friend the Dutchess of Wirtemberg by procuring this place for Sir John Stuart—and indeed Lady Stuart's conduct to my sister makes us all very anxious that he should be named one of the "*Officers of his Majesty's Revenues of Customs and Seizures.*" Mama begs you will be so good as to make this application as soon as possible.' (W. Dacres Adams MSS.)

been brought of bed [*sic*] early in March. He was so obliging as to stay, and from the death of the Dutchess and since that my unfortunate health at a time that Stutgard was uncommonly dull; but as the Huldigung was over and some pleasures allowed, he intended on the birth of my dear infant to have given a great Ball to the Duke. When he heard of my misfortune, the preparations being made, he wished to give it in honnour of my recovery but had the goodness to give it up when he heard how deeply I was afflicted at the knowledge of the death of my child, to spare my feelings, for which I shall ever be obliged to him, as for the interest he has shewn about me during my illness. However, I rejoice that he has been here as I shall see him again before he goes and that yr. Majesty will have it in your power to be perfectly satisfied of the care and attentions that the dear Duke has of me and which I can never be sufficiently grateful for. I can now only add that I am, Sir, [etc.] (51473–4)

[*Stutgard, 8 May 1798.*] I delayed writing to your Majesty till the last moment that you might see by the difference of my handwriting, and by that means be convinced how wonderfully I have already regained my health: indeed, I cannot be sufficiently grateful to Providence, as I am now better and stronger than most women are at the end of twelve days. I have regretted very much the uneasiness your Majesty has undergone when you received the first account, and hope that the second followed very soon that you might at least be spared the pain of suspence. I can with truth assure you that at the moment I felt the most deeply the loss of my little angel; my heart and thoughts were also much taken up with what my dear parents would feel about me. Thank God I am restored, and though I shall long silently mourn my child I am so convinced of the wisdom of the Almighty and of her happiness that were it in my power to recall her to life I would not do it. These times are not those to make one pity children it pleases God to save from the miseries of this life.

The physical people have advised the Duke to make me go to a famous water drinking place called Deinach where I am also to take the baths of Liebenzell which they assure [me] will perfectly cure me. This place is only at the distance of two hours drive from Wildbath where the Duke must go in June as his arm is in a sad state, and I am afraid he has hurt it by attempting to assist me too much during my illness, besides which the constant anxiety he has undergone these last four months has hurt his health, which I trust in God a quiet summer, exercise and the baths will cure. He has been obliged to go to Tubingen for two days for to settle some unpleasant things which had happened at the University, but which his presence will put an end to.

I am to see Mr. Arbuthnot to day that he may be enabled to give your Majesty an exact account of me. He has given here the greatest satisfaction by the propriety of his conduct, and Madame de Spiegel assures me she shall never forget the distress he was in while I was in danger, dreading the pain your Majesties would suffer on that occasion.

I will now take up no more of your Majesty's time than to beg that you will be convinced of the respect and attachment [&c]

[P.S.] The Duke begs that I will present his humble duty to your Majesty. I have taken the liberty to send you a letter I had written before, that you may see I was prepared for all events. (51478–9)

1729 WILLIAM PITT *to the* KING, *and the reply*

[*Downing Street, Tuesday, 8 May 1798, 8 p.m.*] Mr Pitt humbly begs leave to acquaint your Majesty that Mr Tierney this day made a Motion for a Committee, founded on a complaint of Lord Onslow's[1] conduct in rejecting a proposal for arming from an Association connected with Mr Tierney's friends in the Borough. The Motion was opposed with great force and much to the satisfaction of the House by Mr Secretary Dundas, and very ineffectually supported by Mr Sheridan, Lord William Russel, and Mr Tierney in reply, after which the Motion was rejected by 141 to 21.[2]

Mr Pitt takes the liberty also of intimating to your Majesty that, on consideration of the very inflammatory and almost undisguised language held by Mr Fox at the Whig Club last week (as reported by the Morning Post and Morning Chronicle, which account remains wholly uncontradicted) it seems to be the opinion of such of your Majesty's servants as Mr Pitt has as yet had an opportunity of consulting, that they ought humbly to submit to your Majesty the propriety of directing tomorrow that Mr Fox's name should be erased from the list of Privy Counsellors.[3] (8851–2)

[*The King's reply, Queen's House, 8 May, 11.10 p.m.*] I am glad to find by Mr. Pitt's note that Mr. Tierney's Motion has been rejected by so handsome a majority. I entirely coincide in the opinion of the propriety of my striking Mr. Fox's name out of the list of the Privy Counsellors, but prior notice should be given to the Lord President that the book may be brought to St. James's for that purpose, which intimation I desire Mr. Pitt will give to his brother. (Maggs Cat., 1942)

1730 THE ARCHBISHOP OF CANTERBURY (JOHN MOORE) *to the* MARQUESS OF SALISBURY

[*Lambeth House, 8 May 1798.*] Having been informed that a Grand Masquerade is intended to be given at the King's Theatre on the 17th of this month, (being Ascension-day, commonly called Holy Thursday) and the truth of the information being confirmed by advertisement in the public papers, I have thought it my duty to submit to his Majesty's consideration the great & manifest impropriety of such

---

[1] George, 4th Baron Onslow, and (1801) Earl of Onslow (1731–1814), son of Speaker Onslow. Succeeded his cousin, 1776. Comptroller of the Household, 1777–9; Treasurer of the Household, 1779–80; a Lord of the Bedchamber, 1780–1814. Colonel in the Army, 1794. Wilkins, *Mrs Fitzherbert and George IV*, I, 43, the *Complete Peerage*, and C. E. Vulliamy in *The Onslow Family* (1953), p. 175, erroneously state that it was he who was sent to Mrs Fitzherbert in 1784 to tell her that the life of the Prince of Wales was in danger. The reference should be to his son Thomas, who succeeded him as 2nd Earl. See *Corresp. of George, Prince of Wales, 1770–1812*, ed. A. Aspinall, I, 150. Lord Onslow had a secret pension of £600 a year in 1782.

[2] *Parl. Register*, LI, 104–30, where the numbers are correctly given as 141 to 22 (*H. of C. J.*, LIII, 552).

[3] Fox had repeated the Duke of Norfolk's toast—'the Sovereignty of the People'. Ministers considered a prosecution but feared an acquittal. (Stanhope, III, 127.)

a profanation of that Holy Festival, and his Majesty having been pleased to express his utter disapprobation of it, I am honoured with his Royal commands to assure your Lordship of his desire that it may be forbidden.[1] (8853)

1731   *Letters from* LORD GRENVILLE *to the* KING, *and the replies*

[*Cleveland Row, 8 May 1798, 11 p.m.*] Lord Grenville has the honour to acquaint your Majesty that M. Fagel is arrived, and will have the honour to pay his duty to your Majesty tomorrow. As Lord Grenville found on enquiry that M. Fagel has no children, he thought he should best execute your Majesty's gracious intentions towards M. Fagel's family by intimating to him that after his decease the pension will be continued in certain proportions to his brothers and sisters— and the grant will accordingly be prepared in this form if your Majesty shall be graciously pleased to approve of it.

Monsieur Fagel has desired Lord Grenville to lay at your Majesty's feet his grateful and dutiful acknowledgments for your Majesty's goodness towards him. (8854–5, and Fortescue MSS.)

[*The King's reply, Queen's House, 9 May, 8.05 a.m.*] I shall with pleasure see Monsieur Fagel this day at St. James's. Lord Grenville has very properly executed my intentions in favour of that gentleman, as he has no children, by intimating to him that after his decease, the pension shall be continued in certain fixed proportions to his brothers and sisters. (Fortescue MSS.)

[*From Lord Grenville, Cleveland Row, 9 May, 9.15 a.m.*] Lord Grenville has the honour to transmit to your Majesty the letters just arrived by a courier from Stutgard. He earnestly hopes from Mr Arbuthnot's account that all ground for uneasiness is past, and that your Majesty will continue to receive satisfactory accounts of her Royal Highness's health. Lord Grenville has taken the liberty to put into the box the letters for the Queen and the Princesses, conceiving that your Majesty would approve of it. (8856)

[*The King's reply, Queen's House, 9 May, 12.03 p.m.*] On returning from my ride, I have found Lord Grenville's box. We are all undoubtedly disappointed at the unfortunate delivery of the Dutchess of Wurtemberg, but feel highly thankful to Divine Providence for there being every reason to hope her health will not suffer from the sufferings she has had; indeed the account the Duke has sent is as favorable as could have been expected. (Fortescue MSS.)

1732   EARL SPENCER *to the* KING

[*Admiralty, 10 May 1798, 1.45 p.m.*] Earl Spencer has great satisfaction in laying before your Majesty the accompanying copy of a report[2] just received by

---

[1] It was forbidden, and the change of date from the 17th to the 21st was announced on the 11th.

[2] 'Orestes arrived. Marcoo was attacked on Monday by fifty two gun boats, which were beat off by the batteries, with the loss of seven. Particulars by post.' (8858)

the telegraph from Portsmouth, which he trusts is only a specimen of the manner in which the enemy will be received whenever they attempt to invade any part of your Majesty's dominions.[1] (8857)

1733   WILLIAM PITT *to the* KING

[*Downing Street, Saturday, 12 May 1798.*] Mr Pitt humbly begs leave to acquaint your Majesty, that in consequence of the vacancy in the Mastership of Trinity College occasioned by the death of Dr Postlethwayte,[2] he has made every inquiry in his power with respect to the qualifications of any persons who could be thought of to succeed to it. Upon the best consideration in his power he is strongly persuaded that no person can be found more fit to be selected for such an appointment than Dr Mansel,[3] a member of the College, who has for several years acquitted himself with great credit as Public Orator of the University. He is perfectly orthodox in his principles, has been very active in counteracting those of a contrary disposition, and of very conciliating manners, tho at the same time of a turn of mind likely to maintain the authority of the situation, and (what is much wanted) to improve the discipline of the College. On these grounds Mr Pitt ventures humbly to recommend him for your Majesty's approbation.[4] (8860–1)

1734   THE KING *to* LORD GRENVILLE, *and the reply*

[*Windsor, 12 May 1798, 7.25 a.m.*] That Lord Grenville may know what degree of credit he ought to give to any information from Mr. Ahrens[5] at Bremen, it happens to be in my power to give him some assistance on that head; Major-General Don on returning lately from Bremen mentioned him to me as a most zealous person in my Electoral service, and a man of considerable tallents who has warmly but with great propriety disputed there with Prince Lewis Ferdinand[6] of Prussia in favour of the true system against the French principles which that Prince has been attempting to propagate; I should think he may from his situation be able to give useful intelligence as to the demands of money by the French on that town and perhaps other transactions of that wicked nation perhaps with the dissaffected in Ireland. (Fortescue MSS.)

[1] The King's reply at 2.15 p.m. that day, commenting on the failure of the French attack on the island of St. Marcou off the French coast, near Cherbourg, the batteries and garrison under Lieutenant Price, R.N. beating off the enemy, is in Spencer Papers, II, 337. Unaware that Bonaparte had informed the Directory (23 Feb.) that an invasion of England was not then practicable, the British Government continued until the end of May to concentrate its attention on defensive preparations.

[2] Thomas Postlethwaite (1731–98), Master of Trinity College, Cambridge since 1789, died at Bath on 4 May.

[3] William Lort Mansel (1753–1820), Public Orator, 1788–98; Master of Trinity, 1798–1808; Vice-Chancellor, 1799–1800; Bishop of Bristol, 1808–20.

[4] The King's reply on the 13th, 7.30 a.m., approving Pitt's recommendation, is in Stanhope, III, Appendix, p. xiv. 'This appointment will restore discipline in that great seminary, and a more correct attachment to the Church of England and the British Constitution than the young men educated there for some time have been supposed to profess.'

[5] For him see *Dropmore Papers*, IV, 208, 215.

[6] The son of Frederick the Great's brother Ferdinand (1772–1806). Sir Herbert Taylor described him as 'a very fine young man of superior abilities, but a determined roué' (*Taylor Papers*, p. 22).

[*Lord Grenville's reply, Dropmore, 13 May.*] Lord Grenville is honoured with your Majesty's note respecting Mr Ahrens, & he will write to Sir James Craufurd in conformity to it by Tuesday's mail.[1] (8862)

1735 PRINCE ADOLPHUS *to the* KING

[*Monbrilliant, 13 May 1798.*] I cannot let Mr. Arbuthnot set off for London[2] without writing your Majesty a few lines to congratulate you on the very excellent accounts he has brought from Stuttgard. I have received by him a letter from my sister which mentions how much better she is and which is written, to my great joy, in very good spirits. She is so well that she is to go into the country at the beginning of next weeck.

I must now return your Majesty my most humble thancks for your very gracious letter which the quarterly messenger who arrived last Friday brought me. I rejoice in hearing of the fine spirit which has shewn itself in England of late, and I am convinced that should the French attempt an invasion, they will meet with such a reception as they deserve and will cure them of the insolent idea that they are to give laws to all Europe. The only thing I regret in case of an attack is my being deprived of the pleasure of seeing them treated according to their deserts. The late engagement between the Mars & the Hercules is one of the finest I ever heard of and does the highest credit to the English Navy.[3] May your Majesty's arms be always equally successful is the most sincere wish and most fervent prayer of [&c.] (48521)

1736 HENRY DUNDAS *to the* KING, *and the reply*

[*London, 14 May 1798, 1 p.m.*] Mr Dundas has the honour to convey to your Majesty the instructions and other papers relative to the secret expedition under the command of Major-General Cootte[4] and Captain Popham,[5] and he has the satisfaction to announce to your Majesty that the armament sailed last night, the secret having remained unknown to the end.[6] (8863)

[1] Grenville's letter to Craufurd, 18 May, is in *Dropmore Papers*, IV, 208.

[2] He left Stuttgart on or about the 10th.

[3] On 21 April *Mars* captured the French 74-gun *Hercule* off Brest.

[4] General Sir Eyre Coote (*c.* 1759–1823), nephew of the more famous General of the same name. Lieutenant-Colonel, 1788; Colonel, 1795; Major-General, 1797; Lieutenant-General, 1805; General 1814. M.P. for Queen's County, 1802–5; for Barnstaple, 1812–18. Lieutenant-Governor of Jamaica, 1805–7. K.B., 1802; G.C.B., 1815.

[5] Sir Home Riggs Popham (1760–1820). Lieutenant, 1783; Captain, 1795; Rear-Admiral, 1814. K.C.B., 1815; K.C.H., 1818. M.P. for Yarmouth (Isle of Wight), 1804–6; for Shaftesbury, 1806–7; for Ipswich, 1807–12.

[6] The object of the expedition was to destroy the gates of the canal at Ostend, and so to flood that part of the Netherlands then in the possession of the French. Protected by a cannonade of Popham's flotilla, Coote succeeded in landing over 1,000 men three miles east of Ostend on the 19th. The gates and sluices of the Bruges canal were destroyed, but a sudden deterioration of the weather prevented the troops from re-embarking. A concentration of enemy forces compelled the British troops to surrender, and Coote himself was wounded. See No. 1741.

The following note (8864) refers to the enclosures mentioned in Dundas's letter:

'1st Drafts to General Sir C. Grey & the Lords Commissioners of the Admiralty.

[*The King's reply, Queen's House, 14 May, 7.53 p.m.*] I have read the papers transmitted to me by Mr. Secy. Dundas relating to the expedition which was to sail the last evening under the commands of Major-General Coote and Captain Popham: I am sorry to be obliged to remark that two of the vessels intended for that service were not arrived. It is really unfortunate that the degree of exertion required can never be effect[ed] in that Department, and that no Board of Admiralty I ever remember seem to attend that the orders given be punctually obeyed.[1] (Add. MSS. 40100, f. 206.)

1737   *Letters from* PRINCE ERNEST *to the* KING

[*St. James, 14 May 1798.*] It is four weeks since I presumed to write to your Majesty entreating your acceptance of my services in any way that you might think consistent with your dignity to grant threwing myself entirely on your goodness, which, Sir, I again most humbly do, and again beg leave to state my willingness and anxiety to bear arms for the defence of my country *in any capacity*. Permit me, Sir, to repeat that I do not solicit Y.M. for any particular rank, but to be *employed* in any military situation whatever that meets with your approbation, which I pledge myself to fullfill, and if Y.M. determination should be that I should enter the service in a subordinate line, I shall be proud to do my duty & to give the example at such a moment of obeying as strictly as if I never had had a command. I should not have presumed to address Y.M. a second time upon the same subject, but as I have received no answer to my first letter, I have not thought it respectful to Y.M. to *act*, or to appear in your presence; for, Sir, believe me when I assure you upon my honor it is most painful to me to take any step contrary to your approbation, yet it is highly necessary that I should take some step for the sake of my character to prove my anxiety to assist in the defence of my country. Should Y.M. not be so gracious to employ me, in that case I have no step left, but to serve as a private in the yeomanry and thereby save my being looked upon as an enemy to my country in not sharing the impending danger thereof. (47184)

[*St. James, 16 May.*] I have received your Majesty's gracious letter, and with sorrow do I perceive that I have met with your disapprobation. I acted from a sense of honor in not wishing to bear any rank in a service which I was not particularly attached to. I knew from many circumstances (that cannot be related to your Majesty) that my presence there could be of little or no use. However, I entreat you to believe me that it was not either want of respect, affection, or duty that induced me to refuse that which at any other time I should have prided myself upon, the rank of a Lt. Genl. and command of a Light Dragoon Regiment the first in the world in point of men and discipline. But, Sir, the situation of affairs

2d Letter from General Sir Charles Grey to Mr Huskisson dated 10th inst. with a plan of the intended attack on Ostend.

3d Copy of a note from Lord Grenville referred to in the above-mentioned letter from Sir C. Grey.

4th Letters from General Sir C. Grey & Major General-Coote dated 13th inst.'

[1] Dundas himself complained to Spencer of the 'backwardness somewhere in somebody under you in expediting what they may not approve of or have not themselves suggested.' (*Spencer Papers*, II, 333.)

both here and all over the Continent is such that it becomes my duty to bury all *my private feelings*, and, *hard as my fate may be*, in compliance with Y.M. wishes and commands, with gratitude & respect to bow to your pleasure & to accept the rank of Lieutenant-General in your Electoral service, you have been graciously pleased to offer me, and I shall be happy, if by doing so, I may in time of danger be of use to *my own country here* for the defence of which I will *with readiness* sacrifice to the very last drop of my blood. (47185)

1738   THE DUCHESS OF WURTEMBERG *to the* KING

[*Stutgard, 19 May 1798.*] I had intended writing to your Majesty today to assure you that I continue gaining ground. I have been carried into the garden and the air has done me good, which makes me very anxious for Tuesday, as I shall then remove to Loudewigsbourg. But I have a double reason as I have this instant received a letter from Adolphus which has made me very happy, as he acquaints me that, thank God, your Majesty has been spared the anxiety of hearing the danger I have been in till the second account brought the news of my recovery. In all my distress for the loss of my child my mind was much taken up with the thoughts of what the uncertainty of my fate might make you suffer. I feel so thankful to God for this that I am much easier and feel more comforted than I have done since my misfortune, as I am by this still more than ever convinced that God will always stand by your Majesty.

The Duke begs that I will present his humble duty to your Majesty; he is very much taken up with making a large English garden, of which I shall attempt to give you a description as soon as I shall be strong enough to walk at that distance from the house. Our weather is very warm but most evenings we have thunderstorms which prevent my going out as much as the physicians wish.

If the wind is fair your Majesty will receive this on the fourth of June. I hope that you are too well convinced of my respect and sincere attachment for me to need repeating to you how fervently I entreat the Almighty to allow your Majesty long to be a blessing to your people and to your children who all feel how necessary your life is to the universal good and happiness. I will now take up no more of your Majesty's time than to entreat [&c.]. (51481–2)

1739   *Letters from* GEORGE CANNING *to the* KING

[*Downing Street, 20 May 1798, 12.45 p.m.*] Mr Canning most humbly thinks it his duty to transmit without delay to your Majesty the inclosed letter from Mr Arbuthnot, containing an account of her Royal Highness the Dutchess of Wurtemberg's improved state of health, together with the accompanying letters for her Majesty and the Princesses, which have been received by the mail just arrived from Hamburgh. (8872)

[*Downing Street, 20 May, 3 p.m.*] Mr Canning most humbly presumes to dispatch a second messenger to your Majesty, for the purpose of transmitting to your

Majesty a letter which has been received by a second Hamburgh mail, arrived since the former messenger was dispatched; and which, as he conceives it to relate to the subject of her Royal Highness the Dutchess of Wurtemberg's recovery, Mr Canning thinks it his duty to lose no time in forwarding. (8873)

1740 THE DUKE OF PORTLAND *to the* KING

[*Whitehall, Monday, 21 May 1798, 7.30 p.m.*] The Duke of Portland most humbly presumes to offer to your Majesty's perusal the inclosed letter from Mr King to Mr Wickham which is but just arrived, & which is the only account the Duke of Portland has received of the proceedings at Maidstone.[1] Mr Arthur Young's zeal has been sadly misplaced.[2] (8874)

1741 EARL SPENCER *to the* KING, *and the reply*

[*Admiralty, 22 May 1798.*] Earl Spencer has the honour of laying before your Majesty the dispatches[3] just arrived from Captain Popham off Ostend, and is much concerned that the success attending the undertaking in the first instance was by so unfortunate a change of wind at a most critical moment attended by the capture of so many officers & men, though considering the circumstances the loss in killed & wounded appears to have been very small.[4] Captain Winthorp[5] who brought the dispatches says that if the wind had not changed the object would have answered as completely as could have been desired.[6] (8875)

[*The King's reply, Bushy Park, 22 May, 4.25 p.m.*] Lord Spencer will find I am from home. I therefore just in pencil acknowledge the receipt of his note and of the dispatches. The object has succeeded of destroying the floodgates at Ostend, but I cannot but regret that the weather did not permit M. G. Coote to reimbark that day. I hope the men will be soon exchanged, though I doubt it.[7] (Althorp MSS.)

---

[1] The treason trials of O'Coigly and his associates opened at Maidstone as early as 7 a.m. on the 21st. Just before midnight the Court adjourned to 8 o'clock the next morning.

[2] The Rev. Arthur Young, of Bradfield, Surrey, had dined with three jurymen summoned to Maidstone, and he tried to impress on them a sense of the absolute necessity 'that the felons should swing'. 'I represented to them that the acquittal of Hardy and Co. laid the foundation of the present conspiracy ...These...arguments I pressed, with a view that they [the jurymen] should go into court avowedly determined in their verdict, no matter what the evidence.' Though apparently guilty of a gross contempt of court he could not then be punished because he failed to appear when summoned, and, said Mr. Justice Buller, 'Our commission is determinable before we can proceed to punishment.' Later he was arrested and put on trial at Maidstone Assizes (14 March 1799). The jury disagreed with the view of Mr. Justice Buller and accepted the defence that it was all 'a Cantab.'s joke upon Mr. Lloyd, an old politician' (*The Times*, 16 March 1799).

[3] See *Spencer Papers*, II, 349 (Home Popham to Spencer, 21 May).

[4] Less than sixty.

[5] Robert Winthorp, of H.M.'s ship *Circe*, of 28 guns. Lieutenant, 1790; Captain, 1796.

[6] The wind backed to the north, preventing the ships from taking off the 1,300 troops which had been disembarked to cut the sluices. Coote, who was severely wounded, was soon exchanged, and an exchange of his men, too, was eventually negotiated.

[7] The letter of 11 June 1798, 7.40 [? a.m.] from the King to Spencer, confirming court martial death sentences on two mutineers of the *Haughty* gun-vessel, is in *Spencer Papers*, II, 174.

[*Burlington House, Tuesday, 22 May 1798, 8.55 a.m.*] The Duke of Portland most dutifully submits to your Majesty farther accounts of the proceedings at Maidstone which he has just received from Mr Wickham, by which it appears that the Attorney-General closed his case last night, &, as it may be inferred, to his own satisfaction—& that the Court adjourned till eight o'clock this morning. The warrant repeatedly applied for for the detention of O'Connor[1] in case of his acquittal was sent to Mr White[2] at Maidstone yesterday evening by a messenger who waits to execute it should it be necessary. (8876)

[*Burlington House, Wednesday, 23 May, 8.10 a.m.*] The Duke of Portland most humbly begs leave to acquaint your Majesty that by accounts dated ½ past one this morning he learns that all the prisoners who were tried at Maidstone were acquitted except Quigley who was found guilty, & that the verdict appeared to be conformable to the opinion of the Court.[3] (8809)

1743   THE DUCHESS OF WURTEMBERG *to the* KING

[*Louisbourg, 23 May 1798.*] As your Majesty was graciously pleased to express a wish to hear from me after my arrival at Louisbourg, I delayed till today expressing my thanks and gratitude for your Majesty's letter, which is of the greatest use to me. Your goodness, on which my happiness so much depends, is doubly felt in moments of affliction and serves as a balm to my heart. I read your letter over and over again as it is a great comfort to me and always points out to me motives for resignation; indeed I am very grateful for it, it does me good and I should be very unworthy of the goodness of Providence if I did not submit quietly to his will. The Almighty has granted me blessings which he has refused to most women and still more to the greatest number of Princesses: parents that I so justly love and respect, to whom I owe the principles which at all times are the only real source of happiness and can in times of affliction be the only true comfort, and who have not only imprinted those principles on my mind, but shewn me an example which it is my duty to attempt to imitate: a husband whose affectionate tenderness has attached me to him in the strongest manner, sisters that I dearly love, and friends that are kind to me. Ought I then to repine or murmur when it pleases God to afflict me? Must I not share the misfortunes of other mortals or else I should be too much attached to life?

I certainly gain strength daily but am obliged to lay a good deal on the couch of an evening. Whenever the weather allows I am carried into the garden and here

---

[1] On a charge of high treason. As soon as he was acquitted he was re-arrested in Court (after a severe struggle). Some months later he confessed his guilt, but was allowed to retire to France. He entered the service of France, rose to the rank of Lieutenant-General, but was not employed after 1803, when he was to have commanded the army destined for the invasion of England.

[2] Joseph White was the Solicitor to the Treasury.

[3] Wickham, the Under-Secretary, declared that 'that unfortunate letter of Arthur Young's saved the lives of all the prisoners who escaped, and it was a miracle that it did not prove the salvation of Coigly'.

the Duke, to draw me more out, has made a flower garden out of my dressingroom, but today I cannot enjoy it as it [is] so cold the physicians will not hear of my going out.

The Duke begs that I will present his humble duty to you; he is very much taken up with his improvements.

I am very much distressed that I can get no other ink today than this sad pale stuff as I know your Majesty objects to it and shall take care for the future to have better, having sent to Stutgard for some. (51483–4)

1744   WILLIAM PITT *to the* KING, *and the reply*

[*Downing Street, 23 May 1798.*] Mr Pitt humbly presumes to transmit to your Majesty a letter which he received this day from Mr Livingston enclosing one addressed to your Majesty which Mr Pitt has thought it his duty to forward, and likewise another paper containing a statement of his Royal Highness's affairs. Mr Pitt trusts from these papers that the credit which he had previously received your Majesty's commands to authorize will be sufficient to prevent any embarrassment.

Mr Pitt also takes the liberty of submitting a warrant for carrying into execution your Majesty's gracious intentions in favor of the Greffier Fagel. (8877–8)

[*The King's reply, Queen's House, 24 May, 8.02 a.m.*] I have received the letter from my son Augustus and return the one Mr. Pitt has received from Mr. Livingston as well as the state of the annual expences of Augustus and the debts that must be paid before he can leave Naples.[1] I am glad to find the credit Mr. Pitt has sent, added to the one already in the hands of Sir William Hamilton, will satisfy those debts. Mr. Pitt will now give Mr. Livingston such instructions that the annual expences may be satisfied, but be strongly cautioned to keep those as moderate as decency will allow. [*sic*] (W. Dacres Adams MSS.)

1745   THE EARL OF CHATHAM *to* MAJOR-GENERAL FRANCIS EDWARD GWYNN

[*Hyde Park Corner, 27 May 1798.*] As I think it not improbable that before the King comes to town tomorrow some reports may reach Windsor of a transaction which took place today on the subject of which his Majesty's great goodness will, I know, lead him to feel not uninterested, and yet being at the same time sensible that it is of a nature that no direct report of what passed ought perhaps to be immediately made to his Majesty, I have been induced to trouble you with this to apprize you that my brother and Mr. Tierney, in consequence of a message from the latter, met today at three o'clock at Putney Heath, and after two fires from each party the business was satisfactorily adjusted by the interference of the Seconds. A statement of what passed has been agreed to by them tonight, conformably to what was settled before they left the ground, and which will be made

---

[1] See No. 1727 n.

publick tomorrow, a copy of which I enclose you that you may be enabled to give his Majesty any further information he may be pleased to ask on this subject.[1] (8879)

1746   *Letters from the* DUKE OF PORTLAND *to the* KING

[*Bulstrode, Sunday, 27 May 1798, 4 p.m.*] The Duke of Portland humbly begs leave to lay before your Majesty the dispatches from the Lord Lieutenant which he received this day at noon; to which he presumes to add a very short letter of Mr Cooke's to Mr Wickham, but which is sufficient to shew the temper & feelings of the House of Commons in the present crisis. The Duke of Portland also begs your Majesty's permission to add for your Majesty's farther information that he learns by the messenger, who was prevented upon account of the tide from embarking till *seven* o'clock on Friday morning, that the most perfect tranquillity had prevailed throughout the city of Dublin during the night, & that no accounts of any new acts of rebellion or outrage having been committed in the country had been received before the packet sailed. The messenger also says that the unanimous opinion of Dublin is for the necessity & certain success of coercive & active measures.[2]

The Duke of Portland most dutifully submits to your Majesty Mr. Justice Buller's report of Quigley's trial, which, when it has been before a Special Commission, it seems requires to be laid before your Majesty for the purpose of your Majesty's pleasure being taken respecting the manner in which the convict is to be disposed of, & also, at the suggestion of the Lord Chancellor, to ask your Majesty's commands whether your Majesty will please to be attended for that purpose on Wednesday next.[3]

The merits of the Attorney & Sollicitor-General of Ireland have been so conspicuous & the abilities & character of the former so universally acknowledged

[1] The hostile meeting took place in consequence of a brush between them in the House of Commons the previous Friday. Pitt was attended by Dudley Ryder, afterwards Earl of Harrowby, and Tierney by George Walpole. The King's criticism of the duellers, in a letter to Pitt on the 30th, 7.43 p.m., is in Stanhope, III, Appendix, p. xiv. See also, Holland, *Memoirs of the Whig Party*, I, 140–2. Pitt wrote to Camden on the 28th: 'The papers of today will give you a short account (but correct as far as it goes) of the result of a meeting which I found it necessary to have with Mr. Tierney yesterday, in consequence of some words which I used in a debate on Friday. It will I know be satisfactory to you to learn that the business passed and terminated exactly as I could wish. I adhered compleatly to the line which I had originally laid down to myself, and I am also very happy to say that I think he behaved with perfect propriety. I trust you are mastering successfully a great crisis. Cannot crushing the rebellion be followed by an Act appointing Commissioners to treat for an Union?' (Camden MSS.) Writing to Lord Mornington about the duel, Pitt said: 'I believe we parted better satisfied with each other than on any other occasion in our lives.'

[2] Castlereagh, who had just succeeded Pelham as Chief Secretary to the Lord Lieutenant, communicated to the Irish House of Commons a statement of the progress of the conspiracy against the Government, and asked for the speedy passage of emergency legislation. Martial law was proclaimed.

[3] O'Coigly was executed at Pennenden Heath on Thursday, 7 June. The last part of the sentence —the disembowelling and quartering—was graciously remitted by the King. Charles Grey, who was present at the trial, had to admit the fairness of the proceedings: 'There was no possibility of saving Quigley, and, to say the truth, he deserves his fate. It is a pity, for a more determined, undaunted spirit I never saw. He never changed countenance or shewed the least emotion either during the trial or upon his condemnation. At the latter I was not present, as I could not bear to hear the verdict delivered.' (Howick MSS.)

as rendering him a worthy object of your Majesty's condescension & favor, that the Duke of Portland ventures to express his humble hopes that your Majesty will be graciously pleased to assent to the prayer of the Lord Lieutenant on his behalf, & that your Majesty will not consider it to be improper, in that case, to direct Mr Wolfe to be raised to the dignity of the Peerage, which honor your Majesty was pleased to confer on his wife about three years since.[1] (8881–2)

[*Burlington House, Wednesday, 30 May 1798, 8.23 p.m.*] The Duke of Portland most humbly begs leave to lay before your Majesty the dispatches which are this moment arrived from the Lord Lieutenant. Success attends your Majesty's arms in every direction, but the influence of the horrid system which has occasioned this rebellion has spread itself so extensively and seems to require to be met in so many different directions that the Duke of Portland humbly hopes that your Majesty will approve the earnestness with which the Lord Lieutenant represents the necessity of being enabled by an increase of military force to crush it effectually.[2] (8883)

[*Burlington House, Saturday, 2 June 1798, 9.05 a.m.*] The Duke of Portland humbly begs leave to lay before your Majesty the dispatches he has received this morning from the Lord Lieutenant by which it appears that very considerable advantages have been gained over the rebels & that the communication with Cork & Limerick is again open. The Duke of Portland has to observe to your Majesty that the letter from Sir James Duff mentioned by the Lord Lieutenant to be inclosed, has been by some mistake omitted, & that the messenger left Dublin at twelve on Tuesday night.
[*9.40 a.m.*] The Duke of Portland has the satisfaction of adding the copy of Sir James Duff's report which is this moment brought by Mr. Wickham to whom it had been addressed. (8888–9)

1747 THE DUCHESS OF WURTEMBERG *to the* KING

[*Louisbourg, 2 June 1798.*] Knowing your Majesty's goodness to me I think that it will give you pleasure to hear that I am already much better for the air of Louisbourg, and though I cannot yet walk much, I am in the little garden most part of the day and drive out in an open carriage of an evening.

I have now seen the Duke's improvements which will add much to the beauty of this place; he is fortunate in the ground which allows of variety; the hill is planted and under it is a peice of water and a cascade which will have a good effect when compleated and the water will separate the menagerie from the garden. There was a very ugly wall which divided the pleasure ground from the woods; this is

---

[1] Anne (*d.* 1804), daughter of William Ruxton, of Ardee House, Co. Louth, married Wolfe in 1769. In September 1795, whilst he was Irish Attorney-General, she was created Baroness Kilwarden [I.] He was created Baron Kilwarden [I.] on 3 July 1798.

[2] Camden's reply to Pitt's letter of the 28th (No. 1745 n.) was non-committal on the question of a Legislative Union: '...The crisis to which you allude and which has arrived in this country is awful indeed—I can give you no answer to the point to which you think it possible it may lead and I have no object so much at heart at present, as crushing the Rebellion, although that may not be [the] readiest method of attaining the other object.' (W. D. Adams MSS.)

thrown down, the old and new plantations united and a sunk fence made to part the high road from the grounds. In front of the Castle there were planted fruit trees which quite blocked up the windows: they are all cut down and small shrubs and flowers are planted in their stead; beyond this is a large peice of ground which of late years has been let; this was in a dreadful state; now in the midst of it there is to be a peice of water and the rest is to be sown with trefoil as it is what answers best here. The orange trees which are very fine and [which] Duke Charles had removed to Hohenheim are brought back here. The woods had been much neglected and now to repair the mischief many trees have been planted.

I hope that your Majesty will not be displeased at not receiving a letter from the Duke to congratulate you on your birthday; he had intended writing this morning but knowing of old that those letters only torment your Majesty I entreated him to let it alone, which I, with some difficulty, obtained on condition that I would present his humble duty and take the blame of this apparent inattention on myself.

I must take the liberty to congratulate your Majesty on dear little Charlotte's recovery;[1] I trust that she will prove a great blessing. (51485–6)

1748   HENRY DUNDAS *to the* KING, *and the reply*

[*Wimbledon, 2 June 1798, 10 p.m.*] Mr Dundas humbly transmits for your Majesty's approbation the accompanying draft No. 1. together with the answer from his Royal Highness the Duke of York No. 2. and the proposed letter to the Duke of Portland No. 3.

It is with sincere reluctance Mr Dundas has been induced to consent to send so much of the small regular force in the country to Ireland, but considering the danger of the rebellion extending itself so far as to place the harbours of Cork & Waterford in the possession of the rebells, and consequently of France, Mr Dundas does not feel it possible *not* to advise your Majesty to concur in the measure as now proposed and arranged. (8884)

[*The King's reply, Windsor, 3 June, 7.59 a.m.*] I have received Mr. Secretary Dundas's note accompanying the draft of his letter to the Duke of York, its answer[2]

---

[1] From the effects of vaccination, on 15 April. She had been rather ill for some time.

[2] The Duke of York wrote to Dundas on 2 June: 'I take the earliest opportunity to acknowledge the receipt of your letter of this day's date, in which you convey to me the sentiments of his Majesty's servants respecting the request made by the Irish Government to obtain an immediate reinforcement for the service of that country and desire to be informed of the greatest disposable force of infantry which can be sent to Ireland.

In compliance with which I lost no time in acquainting you that the following are the only corps in Great Britain, Jersey and Guernsey which in my opinion can be sent at the present moment to that kingdom.

Viz.			
	2d or Queen's Regt		527
	29th	do	584
	100th	do	742
From Guernsey	{ Glengary Fencibles		454
	{ Nottingham	do	489
From Jersey	Cheshire	do	401
			3,197

and the subsequent draft to the Duke of Portland. I sincerely lament the necessity of sending this additional force to Ireland as it must be very likely that we shall have them returned in the course of the present season for active service, and that this must compleatly put an end to any measures of that kind during their absence. The draft Mr. Secretary Dundas has sent to the Duke of Portland ought to impress the Lord Lieutenant of Ireland with the necessity of not detaining them unnecessarily, but I trust, whilst there, that as the sword is drawn it [will] not be returned into the sheath untill the whole country has submitted without condition; the making any compromise would be perfect destruction. I wish there was more attention to the articles printed in the Gazette regarding to Ireland [sic], for I find many well disposed persons displeased as well as myself at there having been inserted a kind of well-intentioned paper from some of the principal Roman Catholicks of Ireland, but with adding the titular titles to the Irish Clergy that have signed it, which certainly is neither decorous nor strictly legal in a Government paper. (Chatham Papers.)

1749 PRINCE ADOLPHUS *to the* KING

[*Hannover, 4 June 1798.*] Though I have lately had the honour of writing to your Majesty, yet I cannot let this day pass without troubling you again with a few lines to present you my most humble congratulations and my sincerest and most ardent wishes that you may still see many and many very happy returns of it. It is impossible for me to express all I feel on this subject, but I trust and hope your Majesty is convinced of my unalterable attachment to your person and that therefore there is no happyness which you ever can enjoy that I do not wish you from the bottom of my heart. That the Almighty may still continue protecting

In order to explain to you exactly the reasons which induce me to state these corps as alone fit to be employed on that service, I think it right to lay before you the exact situation and composition of every other regiment in Great Britain, Jersey and Guernsey besides the Brigade of Guards.

The 8th, 10th, 23d, 49th, 58th, 81st, and 88th Regiments are almost entirely composed of Irish.

The 1st Battn of the Royals, 15th, 21st, 25th, & 79th regiments are raw recruits, though great care has been taken that no Irish should be inlisted into them.

The 16th, 22d, 34th and 65th Regiments are ordered to recruit none but boys.

The 5th, 9th, 20th, 31st, 35th, 44th, 46th, 48th, 55th, 62d and 85th Regiments are employed in recruiting from the Supplementary Militia, but I am sorry to say that their success has been so much short of what I had a right to expect, that by the return of last week, the whole of those corps together had only inlisted 1513 men, whom it is now intended to form into three battalions, and the 44th, 48th and 55th are the regiments proposed to receive them. It will however be near a month before the different detachments can be assembled and then the battalions must be allowed a certain time to be trained before they can be fit for any service.

The 61st Regiment is composed of the few quota men who were furnished by the parishes under the Act of the last Session of Parliament, and made up with deserters and Irish recruits.

In order to replace the battalions of Fencibles which are in Jersey and Guernsey and which have already received orders to be in readiness to imbark for Ireland, I propose that the 8th and 23rd Regiments should be sent to Guernsey and the 49th to Jersey, which corps with the recruits ordered to join them will fully replace in numbers those taken from those islands.

I think it right before I conclude to call your attention to the following circumstance, which is, that when the force proposed to be sent to Ireland is sailed and the reliefs have taken place in consequence in the islands of Jersey and Guernsey there will only remain the 10th Regiment in Great Britain in a state to be detached upon any immediate service.' (8885–7)

you and preserving you for your subjects and family is the most fervent prayer of [&c.].[1] (48522)

1750 E. LIVINGSTON *to the* KING

[*Vienna, 7 June 1798.*] Sir Morton Eden having informed me that a messenger sets out in an hour for London, I cannot refuse myself the satisfaction of congratulating your Majesty on the Prince Augustus geting safe out of Italy, and of his perfect recovery from the late very dangerous attack of asthma, which allarmd me very much.[2] Now, thank God, he is well and I flater myself by regular diet, exercise &c he may be keepd free of a relapse, at least during the warm weather; by the note from Doctor Domier[3] your Majesty will see that the Prince could not with safety live in any part of Germany. During this summer I hope a proper plan may be adopted to remove the Prince to some milder climate.

Your Majesty will be pleased to hear that his Royal Highness has met with the most cordial and friendly reception from the Emperor and every branch of the Imperial Family, and stil more so, when I assure your Majesty that the Prince's conduct at Vienna meets with the approbation of the whole Court and nobility of this place. Since we left Naples I have not had it in power to say that the Prince has once deviate from what is perfectly proper for a Prince of the Blood Royal of England, and I now flater myself he will continue to act in the same desirable manner. I will not trouble your Majesty with the many difficultys I had to remove before his Royal Highness left Naples. Sir William Hamilton having answerd to pay all the debts I could not pay out of the two thousand credit I had, have

[1] The King's letter to Pitt, 4 June, 7.50 a.m., urging him to go to Bath for a fortnight for the sake of his health, is in Stanhope, III, Appendix, p. xv. On 22 April Auckland had described Pitt as being 'particularly well' (*Wellesley Papers*, I, 55), but at the end of May he was 'in a most precarious state of health'. 'His powers of digestion were gone; he had a sort of habitual sickness and retching, and a loss of appetite.' 'He retired from parliamentary business, fixed himself to frequent light and regular nourishment, avoided all bustle, and by degrees is…much recovered' (*ibid.*, I, 60).

[2] The Prince travelled under the name of the Count of Diepholtz—a name derived from one of the counties in the Electorate of Hanover.

[3] Dr Domeier's note, dated Vienna, 4 June 1798, was as follows: 'I could not venture to say that the climate of Germany had produced the last dangerous fit of the asthma H.R.H. the Pr. A. suffered at his entrance in Germany, especially if I consider the irregular manner the Pr. lived in the last time at Naples. However it seems to me certain that the *cold & damp* season of this country will prove hurtful to H.R.H. health. Both the experience of nearly seven years & the theory about his constitution show to me equally clear the bad influence the autumn & winter will have in the Pr.'s constitution. For as often as the cutaneous perspiration is suppressed, this matter falls upon the lungs, & produces asthma, & nothing suppresses the perspiration easier than cold & damp weather, which is during six months the case in Germany. It is difficult for me to propose an abode for next winter, as political circumstances, of which I am not informed, have a great influence in this plan. Neither do I exactly know the degree of warmth & the quantity of rain in the southern part of England, to be able to propose this. Perhaps did Pisa or Lisbon answer best the purpose !—the first would be more advantageous on account of its vicinity. But should there be an absolute impossibility of leaving even Germany, I think Berlin would be a less hurtful place for the winter, on account of its sandy soil & consequently dryer atmosphere. I add to this, that a very regular & quiet life can make up some difficulties the climate opposes to the constitution of H.R.H. But as quietness & regularity are so necessary conditions for the Pr.'s good health, he should not remove from Vienna, as long as reasons for the preservation of his constitution can decide, till a proper plan is made out, where he could fix. Travelling must be avoided as much as possible, for it is impossible to keep to regular hours, though nothing is so necessary for the preservation of the Prince's good health.' (8890–1)

perfectly satisfied the creditors, the sum is only 2874 Ster. If your Majesty is graciously pleasd to approve my conduct in removing the Prince, I will be perfectly happy.

In justice to the King and Queen of Naples, when I mentioned the danger of the Prince going in a sloop of war, the French having given orders to two frigates to take the Prince at all risks, the King most generously orderd a 74 to be got ready with all possible expedition to carry the Prince to Trieste, which made the French frigates keep at a respectable distance. The King said he would rather risk his crown than the Prince Augustus not be protected, becomming a son of the King of England. When an opportunity offers I hope your Majesty may have the goodness to thank the King and Queen of Naples. Nothing could exceed the Queen's kindness to the Prince, and powerful protection to me.

I have sent Mr Pitt an exact state of the Prince's Household such as I found it on my arrival at Naples, and the annual amount of the expences, and begd of him to send a credit here for the support of the Prince: when the exact sum is fixed for his Household and his Royal Highness' pocket money, then I will act accordingly. I beg your Majesty may be graciously pleased to order proper instructions to be sent me and credit for the support of the Prince; at present I have not much money, and without, it is not easy to act with propriety.

I should fail in my duty if I did not inform your Majesty of the very respectful attention paid by Sir Morton to Prince Augustus. Nothing can exceed his anxiety to see the Prince appear as he ought in this country; his advice and example will be of great service. Every person in this country is inclined to shew the Prince every mark of respect, and they are all much pleased with his Royal Highness behaviour. Your Majesty may be assured of my earnest wish [which] is to merit your approbation. (8892–4)

1751 CABINET MINUTE, *8 June 1798.*

Present: Lord President, Lord Privy Seal, Duke of Portland, Earl Spencer, Lord Grenville, Mr Pitt, Mr Dundas.

His Majesty's confidential servants having taken under their most serious consideration the dispatches this day received from Ireland, and having maturely weighed the disastrous consequences which must follow, as well to the interests of Great Britain as to those of Ireland, if the rebellion in the latter kingdom is not speedily and effectually crushed, think it their indispensible duty to convey to his Majesty their united & decided opinion that a large additional reinforcement should be immediately sent to those parts of Ireland where the rebellion is most formidable; and with that view, they equally feel it to be their duty earnestly to submit to his Majesty to send immediately to Waterford a detachment of not less than two thousand Guards to act in conjunction with, and under the same limitation, as the reinforcement lately ordered to that port; and they conceive it necessary further to suggest to his Majesty the propriety of endeavouring to reconcile as many of the Fencible regiments of infantry now in Scotland as possible to extend their service to the north of Ireland, there to form together with the first battalion of the First Regiment of Foot, another Brigade of infantry to be kept collected & under the command of a General Officer, so as to be ready to return to their stations as soon as the rebellion shall be crushed. By this measure the Government of Ireland will be enabled to reinforce the troops acting in the south by withdrawing part of the force now stationed in the north of that kingdom. (8895–6)

1752 THE DUKE OF YORK'S MEMORANDUM

[*c. 8 June 1798.*] Three battalions of Guards to march (if possible) on Sunday morning next the 10th instant to Portsmouth, there to embark on board men of war for Ireland. Major-General Stanwix[1] to command this Brigade. The artillery men attached to the battalion guns of the Brigade to march with them.

Sir Ralph Abercromby to be desired to endeavour to engage the services of the Fencible regiments of infantry now in Scotland for Ireland and to immediately pass over to Donaghadee such of them as are disposed to go.[2] The corps most desirable to be engaged for this service are the Gordon Fencibles, the Sutherland and Sir James Grant's.[3] M.-General Campbell to take the command of such of the corps as go from Scotland. Upon their arrival in Ireland they are to be kept distinct from the Irish army, and are to be considered as still belonging to the British establishment.

The Brigade of Guards not to take their camp equipage but to be supplied with camp equipage at Portsmouth as well as with field pieces.

If the 1st battn. of the Royals have 300 men fit for service Sir Ralph Abercromby is to send them also to Ireland in addition to the Fencible regiments.

Lieut.-General Hulse to proceed to Ireland in command of the Brigade of Guards and the Brigade of the Line. (8897–8)

1753 THE DUKE OF PORTLAND *to the* KING

[*Burlington House, Friday, 8 June 1798, 8.17 a.m.*] The apparently defective state of the intelligence which the Duke of Portland has now the honor of laying before your Majesty makes him feel it incumbent upon him most humbly to acquaint your Majesty that the messenger has been very closely questioned whether he had not other letters from the Lord Lieutenant, & that he declares that he did not receive any other than those which are now submitted to your Majesty. (8899)

[1] Thomas Sloughter Stanwix. Colonel, April 1789, and A.D.C. to the King; Major-General, April, 1794; Lieutenant-General, June 1799; General, 1808 (*d.* 1815).

[2] After resigning his office of Commander-in-Chief in Ireland, Abercromby was given the military command in Scotland, Pitt taking the view that, in spite of his unjustifiable conduct in Ireland, his military services could not be spared. 'You know my opinion that he ought to be employed here', Pitt wrote to Dundas on 5 May. (Ann Arbor MSS.)

[3] Sir James Grant, 8th Bart. (1738–1811), M.P. for Elginshire, 1761–8; for Banffshire, 1790–5. Lord Lieutenant of Inverness, 1794–1809. Succeeded father, 1773. He raised the 1st Regt. of Fencible Infantry in 1793, and the 97th Regt. in 1794.

[*Windsor, 9 June 1798.*] I Understand that Mr. Vincent, who held the employment of my barber, is dead.[1] This employment has always been held by one of the pages in the reign of the late King. As his were all Germans, in the last vacancy in his reign, Mr. Ranby, his personal surgeon, lent his name whilst the profits went to Mr. Hoburgh, who died near the time of the King's demise. On my mounting the throne, the Duke of Devonshire[2] made out the warrant by my direction for Mr. Vincent, who was a musical servant of my late father, who paid a part to one of my pages. I desire therefore that the Marquess of Salisbury will now make out the appointment for Mr. Braun, one of my pages, as barber. (Hatfield MSS.)

[*Lord Salisbury's reply, 9 June, 5 p.m.*] Your Majesty's commands, have been this moment deliver'd to me here and your Majesty may be assur'd I shall pay every attention to them. I have sent directions to Mr. Hale[3] to prepare immediately the necessary documents. (8900)

1755 WILLIAM PITT *to the* KING

[*Downing Street, 9 June 1798.*] Mr Pitt humbly begs leave to submit to your Majesty a Message to Parliament for a Vote of Credit, which, tho' it may not be necessary to make use of, appears adviseable with a view to possible events; and which, if it receives your Majesty's approbation, may be delivered on Monday.[4] (8901)

[1] T. Vincent, the King's principal barber, had a salary of £170 a year.

[2] William, 4th Duke of Devonshire (1720–64). Master of the Horse, 1751–5; Lord Lieutenant of Ireland, 1755–6; First Lord of the Treasury, Nov. 1756–June 1757; Lord Chamberlain of the Household, 1757–62.

[3] John Hale was one of the Gentlemen Ushers of the Privy Chamber.

[4] The King's reply on the 10th, 7.43 a.m., is in Stanhope, III, Appendix, p. xv. He urged that Cornwallis should at once be sent to Ireland to replace the 'too much agitated' Camden, and that Pelham should accompany him as his Secretary.

As early as 26 March Camden had suggested to Pitt the appointment of Cornwallis as Lord Lieutenant and Commander-in-Chief. See No. 1709 n. But Pitt had then rejected the idea. Replying to Camden's letter, he had written (31 March): 'My first inclination on reading your letter was to have yielded so far to your suggestion, as to state all you had said to me, to Lord Cornwallis, and to learn whether he was willing to undertake the conduct of affairs in Ireland, after a full explanation of the principles by which at this moment they must be directed. I own to you, however, that with all the esteem, affection, and (as to many points) admiration, which I bear to Lord Cornwallis, I have great doubts whether his temper of mind and prejudices on Irish subjects make him qualified for the task. I am also, on a little farther reflection, perfectly satisfied in my own mind that *nothing* could compensate in this moment for your quitting your situation. Your doing so at any time before the present crisis is fully decided would I fear produce the worst consequences, and if it could be coupled with Abercromby's resignation, it would I think be *fatal*. It would leave it a doubt whether we supported *you* or *him*, and would I think at once disband the supporters of Government, and deliver over the country to the conspirators. Feeling this so strongly I have determined to take no steps with respect to Lord Cornwallis, at least till I can hear from you again. And I think the same sentiments which I feel on public grounds ought to influence me equally as your personal friend, looking to your reputation and credit. Of all the alternatives which present themselves in fixing on a Commander-in-Chief, I see none so good on the whole as the appointment of General Lake, or at least the letting the command devolve upon him, till we can consult farther. He is brave, active, and I believe popular, and his being put forward would be the most ready and immediate antidote to Abercromby's late measures. A new appointment would require an interval which the present state of things would not admit; and at the end of the interval I see no one to send. I doubt whether Sir W. Howe, Sir C. Grey or Genl. D. Dundas, would, any of them, now go, but by com-

[*Downing Street, Sat., 9 June, 1.30 p.m.* [*1798*].] Mr Canning most humbly presumes to transmit without delay to your Majesty several letters from Stutgard, received by the mail, which is arrived this morning.

Mr Canning at the same time humbly begs permission to submit to your Majesty, that having, in obedience to the commands which her Majesty was graciously pleased to signify to him on Monday last, made enquiry as to the best method of conveying letters to Stutgard, Mr Canning finds reason to believe that letters arrive more speedily at their destination if sent by the post and directed at once to Stutgard than if inclosed in the first instance to Hamburgh, to be forwarded by your Majesty's Minister at that place. But Mr Canning presumes most humbly to suggest for your Majesty's consideration whether, in order to avoid the risques to which letters addressed immediately to the Duke or Dutchess of Würtemberg might be subject in this mode of conveyance, it might not be expedient that her Royal Highness should name some person at the Court, or perhaps some banker or mercantile house in the town of Stutgard, under whose cover the letters might be sent, free from any suspicion. (8902–3)

1757 *Letters from the* DUKE OF PORTLAND *to the* KING

[*Burlington House, Sunday, 10 June 1798, 11.40 p.m.*] The Duke of Portland most humbly hopes for your Majesty's forgiveness for having so long detained the dispatches from the Lord Lieutenant of Ireland, but having been informed that a mail had arrived from Waterford he waited in expectation of being able to

pulsion, and I think, if they would, there are great objections to all but the first for this particular situation.

If a foreign enemy should come *in any force* to Ireland (which I believe impossible) I think we could send any General whom we before agree upon, probably any of these three or Lord Cornwallis. I rather think Genl. Dundas would not from health and habits of life answer the purpose. At present vigor, good will, and ordinary good sense and professional knowledge, with a cordial disposition to co-operate with your Government and with the sound part of the country, seem to be the chief qualities necessary for the command of the Army. The nature of the service required at this moment does not admit of all the regular and strict discipline that is to be wished. It certainly ought to be inculcated and enforced as far as possible, consistent with the prompt execution of the service, and with maintaining the spirit of the Army in the hour of trial. But the great object for the salvation of Ireland is, as it seems to me, to make a speedy and (as far as circumstances will admit) a well concerted effort for crushing the Rebellion, by the most vigorous military exertions, in all the disturbed provinces. The gentlemen unquestionably must be expected to aid the military by their own exertions, in the moment and by encouraging the Volunteer Force to come forward to the utmost; and I think they ought to understand that after a certain period, to that Force and to their own exertions their internal protection must be trusted, when the Army may necessarily be withdrawn to act in a body against any attempt of the enemy. The chief points to be settled for such a plan at this moment are more political than military. The general outlines must be fixed by yourself with the advice of those whom you consult confidentially, on the best local information. The execution rests on no peculiar exertion of professional skill, but requires great attention, diligence and steadiness as well as zeal in the officers employed. These qualities I trust and I believe, many of those whom you can employ are not without, and I should hope Genl. Lake will be fully equal to the general military superintendence, and certainly so to any operations of this sort in which he may be immediately engaged. With respect to yourself, what I have already said will I hope convince you (for I do not like to use many words on that part of the subject) that *all* you have done in the critical situation in which you are placed, is felt by every one here as a proof that you are better able than any other man to do *all* that is now so necessary for the safety of the country...' (Camden MSS.)

lay before your Majesty a confirmation of the very favorable reports which had been circulated yesterday, or at least a circumstantial account of the events which were said to have taken place in the county of Wexford in the course of the 5th & 6th instant. But after waiting to this late hour & having had a report made to him of the contents of all the letters which have been brought by the Waterford mail, he has it only in his power to acquaint your Majesty, that they all agree that the rebels have been defeated before New Ross, but are full of dismay as well on account of the obstinacy with which the rebels fought as because they appear to be neither dispersed nor discouraged. (8904–5)

[*Burlington House, Monday, 11 June 1798, 8 a.m.*] The Duke of Portland has great satisfaction in laying before your Majesty the dispatches which are just arrived from the Lord Lieutenant, & which, he humbly conceives, justify very sanguine expectations to be entertained of the decisive effects which will be produced by the reinforcements which your Majesty has been graciously pleased to order to be sent to Ireland.[1] (8906)

1758 THE KING *to* LORD GRENVILLE

[*Windsor, 11 June 1798, 10.55 p.m.*] Lord Grenville has judged very properly in forwarding the letter for me. I have detached it from that for Mr. Secretary Dundas which I return in the box, and have contrived not to tear the cover. (Fortescue MSS.)

1759 *Letters from* WILLIAM PITT *to the* KING

[*Downing Street, Monday, 11 June 1798, 3.30 p.m.*] At the same moment at which Mr Pitt was yesterday honored with your Majesty's letter,[2] he also received a most private and confidential one from the Lord Lieutenant which he ventures to submit to your Majesty's perusal. He thought it best immediately on receiving it to send it to Mr Dundas in order that he might communicate it to Lord Cornwallis whom he understood to be at Wimbledon. Mr Pitt has since his return to town this morning had a most satisfactory conversation with Lord Cornwallis and is happy to acquaint your Majesty that his zeal for the public service will induce him without hesitation to accept the arduous situation of Lord Lieutenant and to repair to Ireland without delay. He seems most anxiously to wish Mr Pelham for his

[1] Portland evidently regretted the impending change in Ireland. He wrote to Pitt on the 12th: 'We can have but one wish with respect to Ireland. I therefore will say nothing more about the Lord Lieutenant, than that there never was or will be a better than Lord Camden. On the receipt of your note I directed Lord Cornwallis's Patent to be made out immediately—I am told from a quarter that may be depended upon that Sheridan does not attempt to conceal that his object in making the Motion he has announced for Thursday is to do all the mischief he possibly can, and assigns your treatment of him as the cause and as a full justification of this act of resentment. The desponding language held by some of the General Officers on the Irish Staff is insufferable. General Lake himself calls them tremendous times and a General Goldie in a letter to a *Custom House* officer at Port Patrick stiles them terrible times, and sends a boy over to Scotland whom he recommends to the Revenue Officer's care because the times are too *terrible*. If military men talk such stuff, the consequences must be too obvious, and the business of the rebels is more than half done for them...' (W. D. Adams MSS.)

[2] See No. 1755 n.

Secretary, if his health will admit of it. If not, Mr Pitt is not without hopes that Mr T. Grenville would at such a moment not decline that office, and his appointment would in all views be highly satisfactory.[1] (8907–8)

[*Downing Street, 12 June 1798.*] Mr Pitt is happy to have it in his power to acquaint your Majesty that he finds Mr Pelham extremely ready to return to his situation in Ireland as soon as his health will permit; and in the interim Mr Pitt trusts Lord Cornwallis will find no difficulty in conducting the business thro Lord Castlereagh. Mr Pitt wrote to Lord Camden last night to apprize him of the intended arrangement;[2] and if Lord Cornwallis's appointment is declared in Council tomorrow, there seems nothing to prevent his setting out on Saturday at latest.[3] Mr Pitt takes this opportunity of submitting to your Majesty a warrant which he is sorry to find he inadvertently omitted when he had intended it to accompany a former note, and likewise another for an appointment to a small office which is vacant.[4] (8909–10)

[1] The King's reply on the 11th, 6.30 p.m., is in Stanhope, III, Appendix, p. xv. 'Lord Cornwallis,' he said, 'must clearly understand that no indulgence can be granted to the Catholics farther than has been, I am afraid unadvisedly, done, in former Sessions.'

[2] 'On the best consideration I could give to the repeated representation of your secret letters of the 6th & 7th (the latter of which I received this morning) it is impossible for me not to be convinced (tho' I own most reluctantly) of the absolute necessity of an immediate new arrangement of the military command; and I still more reluctantly own that I see no way in which that can be effected so as compleatly to answer the purpose intended but by the union of the two characters of Commander-in-Chief and Lord Lieutenant in the person of Lord Cornwallis. Your last letters to me and that to my brother are so decisive as to your personal sentiments, that I have had no scruple in opening myself confidentially to Lord Cornwallis, and I find him perfectly ready to undertake the task, and with sentiments, I believe, perfectly congenial to your own, and perfectly adapted to the crisis. I confess, however great the burden from which you are relieved, I know not how to help feeling regret that you should not have the satisfaction of yourself compleating the work, in which you have laboured so honourably and effectually thro unparalleled difficulties. I believe, however, that you have formed on the whole the right judgment, and I feel it impossible not to act upon it. I have therefore written to the King, giving him an account of my conversation with Lord Cornwallis, and as the best way of putting him in possession of the whole subject, I have ventured to send him your private letter to me of the 6th, which I am sure will make its just impression on his mind. I have thought it right to lose no time in apprising you of what has passed, because I conclude you will at all events think it right that the new arrangement should take place with the least possible delay, and you ought at the same time to have the opportunity of preparing the minds of your friends for it, in whatever way you think best, before it is publicly known. I shall think it right to state here the arrangement as arising from your urgent representation of the advantage likely to arise at the present moment from uniting the functions of Lord Lieutenant and Commander-in-Chief in some distinguished military character. The wind is I trust most favorable for the conveyance of our reinforcements, and I flatter myself you will have no reason to complain of the time taken in complying with your last requisition. Lord Cornwallis will I am sure carry with him the fullest determination to employ the utmost vigor and energy in speedily crushing the Rebellion; tho' he must certainly feel a wish in common with yourself and with us all, not to preclude the hopes of clemency towards those who may submit, and must ultimately and as soon as possible have in view some permanent settlement, which may provide for the internal peace of the country and secure its connection with Great Britain. This object I am more and more convinced can be attained only by an Union.' (Camden MSS.)

[3] Cornwallis arrived in Dublin on the 20th. Next day General Lake defeated the main rebel force at Vinegar Hill near Wexford, and the back of the Rebellion was broken. Within a fortnight of his arrival Cornwallis was declaring, 'The life of a Lord Lieutenant of Ireland comes up to my idea of perfect misery, but if I can accomplish the great object of consolidating the British Empire, I shall be sufficiently repaid' (*Cornwallis Corresp.*, II, 358).

[4] The King's reply on the 13th, 7.36 a.m., is in Rose, *Pitt and Napoleon*, p. 243. 'No farther indulgences must be granted to the Roman Catholics, as no country can be governed where there is more than one established religion.'

[*12 June 1798.*] The report of Mr Macpherson[1] having been considered by Lord Spencer & others of his Majesty's Ministers as very interesting, the outline is submitted with the profoundest reverence & duty to his Majesty.

As the name & conduct of the French Commissary *Petiton* should remain as secret as possible, Sir John Hippisley has taken the liberty to transmit the enclosed account, sealed, to his Majesty. (8911)

[*Enclosed Memorandum*]

After the confiscation of the property of the British & Irish Colleges in Rome, Mr Macpherson (who had the superintendance of the Scotch College) departed from Rome with the charge of *twenty* British & Irish students, to whom the French Commissaries had given 200 crowns each for their journey. They landed at *Genoa*, & from thence proceeded to *Nice, Marseilles, Lyons, Paris*, to *Gravelines*.

An embargo continuing 17 days at *Gravelines*, Mr M. procured a passport from the French Commissary, (whom he represents to be extremely well affected to the good cause) to visit the ports of *Boulogne, Calais* & *Dunkirk*, leaving the students at Gravelines. He states that there were only 4 gunboats at *Boulogne*— 5 at *Calais*—11 at *Dunkirk*—5 at *Gravelines*—& 3 at *St. Omers*: that many of these were not finished—that they were about 60 feet in length, but were not so substantial as a Thames wherry (each made for 2 guns, one before, the other aft) & appeared rather to be constructed for the amusement of the people than for any real service. At *Calais* there were *1000* infantry—at *Gravelines 800*—at *Dunkirk* between *4 & 500*—at *Boulogne* fewer. He saw no cavalry in the northern provinces.

He travelled in company with a merchant of *Brest* going to Holland, who said that it was with the extremest difficulty that the seamen could be prevailed on to work at all, being extremely dispirited, & exclaiming '*we are sure to be taken prisoners by the English the moment we are out of port*'. It did not appear that any project of a descent on our coasts was in contemplation from the northern parts of France, & most with whom he communicated were of opinion that the Toulon equipment was destined for the coast of *Spain* & to cross over to Portugal from Malaga.

The transports which he saw taken up at *Civita Vecchia—Genoa—*& *Marseilles*—were so slight & ill equipped that he could not imagine they were destined for any service out of the Mediterrean [*sic*].

He represents the country to be *generally*, but extremely *ill* cultivated—principally by old men, women & children—& says that the produce of a British acre of good cultivation would exceed *20* of the best French acres that he saw from the south to the north of France. The inhabitants in general scrupled not to declaim violently against the existing Government. The streets of *Lyons* & *Marseilles* were deserted, it was rare to find a whole pane of glass on the best houses in those towns—the roads in the worst state. He met with the extremest civility

---

[1] Paul Macpherson (1756–1846), Agent of the Scottish clergy at Rome, 1793–8, and 1800–11; first Scottish Rector of the Scots College in Rome, 1820–6, and 1834–46.

in every part of France, except at *Aire en Artois* which appeared to be the only *Jacobin town* he had seen.

Sir J. Hippisley introduced Mr Macpherson to Lord Spencer, the Speaker, Mr Windham, &c to whom he produced his general passports & *the particular order of the French Commissary at Gravelines* by which he was authorised to make the detour by *Boulogne, Calais & Dunkirk*. The Commissary assured him that it would take *40 millions of livres* to repair the damage at *Ostende* & he doubted whether it would ever be repaired under the present Government. 'Would to God (exclaimed the Commissary) that 40,000 of your troops instead of 2 or 3000 had made a descent on our coasts; it would have given confidence to our oppressed people & you would have seen our nation generally in arms to support them'. The name of the Commissary is *Petiton*. His Majesty's Ministers with whom Mr Macpherson communicated were naturally anxious to conceal M. Petiton's friendly conduct. (8912–3)

1761   THE DUKE OF PORTLAND *to the* KING

[*Whitehall, Tuesday, 12 June 1798, 1 p.m.*] It is with extreme concern that the Duke of Portland lays before your Majesty the dispatches which have been received this morning from the Lord Lieutenant of Ireland which contain the account of the insurrection which has taken place in the county of Antrim, although he hopes from the very great force which is quartered in that part of Ireland & the confidence with which M. General Nugent[1] speaks of the support he looks to & the disposition of the loyal part of the inhabitants that this appearance of rebellion will be speedily & effectually subdued. The Duke of Portland humbly begs to observe to your Majesty that he has presumed to withhold the extracts of all those letters mentioned for publication by the Lord Lieutenant of which the originals are submitted to your Majesty, & that the list of persons apprehended in the north by M. General Nugent's orders & referred to in his letter to Lord Castlereagh was omitted to be inclosed in that dispatch. (8914–5)

1762   LORD GRENVILLE *to the* KING

[*Cleveland Row, 14 June 1798, 6 p.m.*] Lord Grenville has the honour to forward to your Majesty a letter to your Majesty from his Royal Highness Prince Augustus which Lord Grenville has this moment received under cover to him from Sir Morton Eden. The seal having melted into that of another letter inclosed in the same cover Lord Grenville has sent them both for fear of tearing the cover in endeavouring to separate them.

As far as Lord Grenville has yet seen it does not appear that this mail brings anything new. (8916)

---

[1] Sir George Nugent (1757–1849). Colonel, Sept. 1794; Major-General, May 1796; Adjutant-General in Ireland, 1799; Lieutenant-General, 1803; General, 1813; Field Marshal, 1846. M.P. for Buckingham, 1790–1802, 1818–32; for Aylesbury, 1806–12. Lieutenant-Governor of Jamaica, 1801–6; Commander-in-Chief in India, 1812–13. Baronetcy, November 1806; K.B., 1813; G.C.B., 1815.

[*Louisbourg, 15 June 1798.*] How shall I find words to express the joy and gratitude I felt in receiving your Majesty's gracious letter of the 22nd of May? I can assure you that both the letters you have done me the honour of writing to me since my confinement have done me a great deal of good. I read them over frequently and always thank God for having given me such good parents who constantly remind me of my duties, and I may say their goodness and affection will ever be a motive for me to try to make myself worthy of them.

I continue so well that I am in great hopes that the physicians will agree to my remaining at Louisbourg as they wish me now to drink either the Schwalbach or Pyrmont waters as they are stronger than those of Deinach. The baths I can equally take here; as they must have had the water brought to Deinach the trouble will not be much greater. It would otherwise be very difficult for me to act about Trinette; to leave her alone would be awkward, and if I took her she must lose her masters and as I must, while I take the waters, walk a great deal, I could not give her up sufficient time to make up for that loss. Besides which, as the Duke must go to the Wildbath, it would be awkward for me without an absolute necessity to be at a public water drinking place without him, which has made me very desirous of this alteration which I trust your Majesty will approve of. On Sunday I went to church for the first time; there was a public thanksgiving for my recovery which was very awful.

I follow your Majesty's advice very exactly about taking exercise, going out regularly twice a day and spending the whole evening in the air. (51488–9)

1764 WILLIAM PITT *to the* KING

[*Hollwood,*[1] *Saturday, 16 June 1798.*] Mr Pitt humbly begs leave to acquaint your Majesty that in consequence of the spirited offers received from different regiments of militia, and the necessity of providing means to strengthen, if circumstances should require it, the reinforcements already sent to Ireland, it has appeared to your Majesty's servants to be essential to obtain an Act before the end of the Session to empower your Majesty to avail yourself of the voluntary offers of a certain proportion of the militia for service in Ireland during the present crisis. With this view Mr Pitt humbly submits to your Majesty the Mes-

[1] Pitt had not been in the House of Commons since 25 May when the storm blew up which led to the duel with Tierney, and the House never saw him again, apparently, that Session—which came to an end on 29 June. Pitt was ill, but on 15 June Canning said he was getting well again. 'I passed the day before yesterday with him at Hollwood, and found him both in health and spirits in a more promising way than I have seen him for many weeks past' (Harewood MSS.). Lord Minto, who saw him at Hollwood on 17 July, wrote on the 16th: 'I cannot tell whether there is any mystery or not in Pitt's illness or retirement. Some people think he stayed away from the House of Commons on account of the sort of difference with the Speaker in Tierney's business. The Speaker thought some apology due from Mr. Pitt to the House, and Pitt would not make one but got into one of his arrogant ways. The fact is that he has never been in the House since the duel. I can hardly think him so mad, however, as to quit the House of Commons in such times and in his situation for so nonsensical a reason, and I take it for granted it is only one of the foolish conjectures of coffee house politicians' (Minto MSS.). 'Pitt's health', wrote Addington on 8 Dec., 'which had long been in a precarious state, appears to be perfectly re-established' (Add. MSS. 37416, f. 31).

sages[1] which have been prepared to both Houses, and which, if your Majesty approves of them, may be presented on Monday, and an Act founded upon them may pass with the utmost expedition. Mr Pitt is persuaded that the impression alone of this measure will produce the most salutary effect in Ireland, both in the present moment and in future. (8917–8)

1765   THE DUKE OF YORK *to the* KING

[*Oatlands, 17 June 1798.*] I have the honor to acknowledge the receipt of your Majesty's most gracious letter, and beg leave to return your Majesty my most humble thanks for your gracious inquiries after my health. I am now in a manner well, though still exceedingly weak, Doctor Pitcairne[2] says, that I have had St Anthony's Fire in my throat.

I am thoroughly sensible of the necessity which your Majesty mentions of sending proper Major-Generals with the different corps of English Militia, which it may be thought expedient to send to Ireland, and which I understand from Mr Dundas (who arrived here soon after I received your Majesty's letter) is intended to be limited to 10,000 men. We have agreed if it meets with your Majesty's approbation, that in order to avoid all the difficulties which might arise with regard to the Colonels of Militia and the Brigadeers now serving in Ireland, that the Brigades of English Militia which are to go there are to be considered upon the English establishment, in the same manner as the two Brigades of the Guards and the Line already there, so as to be kept entirely distinct from the Irish army.

I beg leave to propose to your Majesty that Major-General Hunter[3] should be ordered to take the command of the Brigade of Militia consisting of the Buckinghamshire and Warwick, as I understand that the Colonels of both these regiments, having known him in the Eastern District, will be very happy to serve under him; and that Major-General Sir James Pulteney[4] should be appointed to the Brigade at Waterford in the place of Major-General Hunter.

In consequence of the additional number of Major-Generals which these new arrangements will require to be placed upon this as well as upon the Irish Staff, and which it is now impossible to supply, I find myself under the necessity, though with great reluctance, to propose to your Majesty a partial promotion of Colonels to Major-Generals down to Colonel Wemys[5] inclusive, of which I trust that your Majesty will see the necessity. As there has been already this year a large promotion in every other rank, and as this is merely a measure of necessity, I shall not recommend it to your Majesty to extend it any further.

I am sorry to be under the necessity of reporting to your Majesty the death of Major-General William Crosbie[6] who made away with himself at Portsmouth

---

[1] *Parl. Register*, LI, 403 (18 June). The House of Commons was recommended to make such provision as might be necessary to enable the King to avail himself of the services of part of the militia.

[2] David Pitcairn, M.D. (1749–1809), physician to St Bartholomew's Hospital, 1780–93.

[3] Peter Hunter, Lieutenant-Colonel, 1782; Colonel, 1793; Major-General, 1795.

[4] See No. 1459. He had been promoted to the rank of Major-General in April 1794.

[5] David Douglas Wemyss (1760–1839). Captain, 1783; Major, 1791; Lieutenant-Colonel, 1793; Major-General, 1802; Lieutenant-General, 1808; General, 1819.

[6] He was Lieutenant-Governor of Portsmouth. Lieutenant-Colonel, 1780; Colonel, 1790; Major-General, 1794.

yesterday. He had appeared very low and unwell for some time, and was un-doubtedly under the influence of mental derangement.

The senior general officers without regiments who have the strongest claims to your Majesty's favor are Major-Generals Johnstone[1] and Sir James Duff. General Johnstone's conduct at the last affair at New Ross is spoken of by all the officers who were present as most exemplary. Perhaps your Majesty may approve of removing some general officer who has already a young regiment to the 22d and of appointing Major-General Johnstone to succeed in the first instance to a young regiment; in that case I beg leave to mention the names of Major-Generals Simcoe,[2] Hunter and Morshead.[3] (8919–20)

1766   THE KING *to* LORD GRENVILLE

[*Windsor, 17 June 1798, 7.58 a.m.*] I never concurred more heartily in a measure than in the Messages to Parliament to empower me to avail myself of the very loyal and voluntary offers of the Militia for service in Ireland during the present crisis; indeed, on the offers of the Buckinghamshire and Warwickshire I desired Lord Grenville without loss of time to communicate my sentiments on the subject to Mr. Pitt.[4] (Fortescue MSS.)

1767   E. LIVINGSTON *to the* KING

[*Vienna, 20 June 1798.*] I had the honor to write to your Majesty the 1st June by Sir Morton Eden's last messenger. In case he may have been taken in crossing the sea, I take the liberty to trouble your Majesty with this letter by another messenger that sets out today for London. In my last I had the honor to inform you that his Royal Highness Prince Augustus was perfectly recoverd, and that his conduct met the approbation of every person here. I have now the satisfaction to be able to confirm that agreeable intelligence to your Majesty; his health at present is excellent, and it is impossible to behave better than his Royal Highness does. I begd in my last letter that your Majesty would be graciously pleased to order a credit to be sent me as soon as possible, and that I may know your Royal pleasure concerning the exact sum your Majesty may be pleased to order for the support

[1] Major-General, afterwards General Sir Henry Johnson, Bart. (*c.* 1748–1835). Colonel, 1783; Major-General, April 1794; Lieutenant-General, 1799; General, 1808; created Baronet, 1818; G.C.B., 1820. He commanded at the battle of New Ross, where he had two horses shot under him. 'Johnson, Gardiner and Eustace are all put off the Staff,' wrote Cornwallis on 15 July. 'It was a delicate business to make the selection, and after losing ten thousand of our best troops there was no good pretext for increasing our number of Lieut.-Generals. Johnson, although a wrong-headed blockhead, is adored for his defence at New Ross and considered as the saviour of the south.' (*Cornwallis Corresp.*, III, 116.) He was now appointed Colonel of the 81st Foot after having been Lieutenant-Colonel of the 17th Foot.

[2] John Graves Simcoe (1752–1806), who had been Governor of Upper Canada, 1793–4, and Governor of San Domingo, 1796–7 (see No. 705) now succeeded Crosbie as Colonel of the 22nd Foot. He became a Lieutenant-General in 1801. He had been M.P. for St Mawes, 1790–2.

[3] William Morshead. Lieutenant-Colonel, 2nd Foot Guards, 1783; Colonel, 1793 (not 1795, as in I, 317 n.); Major-General, 51st Foot, 1795; Lieutenant-General, 1802; General, 1812 (*d.* 1822).

[4] Copies of letters from the Marquess of Buckingham, Major Hawkins, of the Buckinghamshire and Warwickshire Militia respectively, and from the commanding officers of other militia regiments, are in *Parl. Register*, LI, 467–85.

of the Prince's Household; and for his Royal Highness pocket money. When I have your Majesty's express command, and a proper credit sent me, then I will be able to form a reasonable plan; without such instructions it is impossible.

I take the liberty to inclose for your Majesty's perusal a short extract from the account given me by Count Munster: and I beg your Majesty may be graciously pleased to send me your orders concerning the manner Doctor Domier is to receive his annual allowance which Count Munster told me is only 600 German dollars, 100 ster. The Doctor is esteemed by professional men as a very able physician, and by his affectionate attention to the Prince's health I think him deserving of your Majesty's protection. The Doctor stil persists in his opinion that no part of Germany will do for the Prince in autumn or winter; he beleives the climate in the west of England would be salutary for his Royal Highness.

The Prince past a very pleasant day last week with the six Archdukes in the country. I never saw greater attention than they all paid to his Royal Highness: part of the desert represented a troop of English Light Dragoons.

The Prince received some days ago a letter from her Royal Highness the Dutchess of Wurtemberg with a very kind invitation to the Court of Stutgard. If that invitation is repeated, is it your Majesty's pleasure the Prince may accept it?

[P.S.] Since I finished my letter, Doctor Domier has been with me, and desires me to inform your Majesty, if any solid reasons may prevent the Prince passing the winter in Devonshire, and political reasons prevent H.R.H. being at Lisbon; the Doctor thinks the climate of Gibraltar the very best for the Prince's complaints: Count Munster and Mr Tatter were of the same opinion. (8922–3)

1768   THE KING *to* HENRY DUNDAS

[*Queen's House, 21 June 1798.*] I have received Mr. Secretary Dundas's letter accompanied by the two he has received from Mr. Levingstone, the one of May 1st from Naples, the second of June 2d. from Vienna. His account of the company Augustus has kept and his consequent conduct is lamentable. Sir Wm. Hamilton has acted most zealously in stepping forward on the difficulty of debts, and I trust the credit that Lord Grenville told me Mr. Pitt had directed to be sent will now have eased that transaction. I desire Mr. Secretary Dundas will shew these letters to Mr. Pitt and if they do not satisfy the whole, that a further credit may be given to Mr. Livingston on account so that he may send over the expenditure and vouchers.

I wish a proper person could be pointed out to assist Mr. Livingston, but Lieut. Col. Anstruther's[1] military service makes it impossible to spare him for this commission.[2] I shall certainly by Tuesday's post write both to Augustus and to Mr. Livingston. I desire Mr. Secy. Dundas will write by tomorrow's post and

[1] Robert Anstruther (1768–1809). See No. 1443. Lieutenant-Colonel in the 3rd Foot Guards, 1797; Colonel, 1805; Quartermaster-General to Sir Ralph Abercromby in the Mediterranean, 1800; Brigadier-General in Portugal, 1807. Fought at Vimeiro and in the retreat of Moore's army; died the day before the battle of Corunna.

[2] Early in July Anstruther was appointed Baggage Master and Inspector of the Roads in North Britain, *vice* Sir Charles Preston.

press Mr. Livingston to point out any good climate for the winter; but this island must not be thought of, and indeed our damps would render it probably more fatal than any other were there not weighty reasons to render the idea otherwise highly improper.[1] (Chatham Papers.)

1769 THE DUKE OF YORK *to the* KING

[*Oatlands, 24 June 1798.*] I trust that your Majesty will pardon my intruding upon you with this letter, but as the time of the camp in Windsor Forest being assembled is drawing near, it is necessary that the General Officers who are to be employed there should be acquainted with it as soon as possible.

I beg leave therefore to recommend to your Majesty that as the camp is to be composed totally of cavalry, Lieutenant-General Sir Robert Laurie[2] should be ordered there instead of Lieutenant-General Stevens.[3]

As by that means there would be no General Officer of cavalry in the Southern District, that Major-General Lord Pembroke[4] should be ordered to his first destination at Canterbury, and that Major-General Staveley[5] should take the command of the Brigade intended for Lord Pembroke.

And as a Major-General is necessary to be posted at Dorchester, that Major-General Lord Charles Somerset[6] should be put upon the Staff and stationed there till such time as Major-General Garth can resume his post, when Lord Charles Somerset may be otherwise disposed of. (8921)

1770 WILLIAM PITT *to the* KING

[*Hollwood, Monday, 25 June 1798.*] Mr Pitt humbly begs leave to submit for your Majesty's consideration, a draft of the Speech for the conclusion of the Session, which will probably require revision, but which contains the principal topics which the present circumstances appear to him to suggest. Mr Pitt trusts there is nothing likely to prevent the prorogation on Friday, if that day is perfectly convenient to your Majesty.[7] (8924)

[1] The King clearly intended to keep Prince Augustus away from Lady Augusta Murray and her son.

[2] Sir Robert Laurie; succeeded his father as 5th Bart., 1779; M.P. for Dumfriesshire, 1774–1804; Colonel, 1782; Major-General, 1793; Lieutenant-General, 1798; General, 1803. He was Colonel of the 28th Light Dragoons. Died, 10 Sept. 1804.

[3] Edmund Stevens (*d.* 1825). Equerry to the Prince of Wales, 1780; Groom of the Bedchamber to the Prince, 1784; Colonel, Nov. 1782; Major-General, Nov. 1793; Lieutenant-General, Jan. 1798; General, 1803.

[4] Lord Pembroke entered the army, 1775; Colonel, 1793; Major-General, 1795; Colonel of the 6th Dragoons, 1797 until his death, 1827; Lieutenant-General, 1802.

[5] Major-General Miles Staveley (*d.* 1814). Colonel of the 28th Dragoons. Colonel, 1795; Major-General, 23 June 1798; Lieutenant-General, 1805.

[6] Lord Charles Henry Somerset (1767–1831), 2nd son of the 5th Duke of Beaufort. M.P. for Scarborough, 1796–1802; for Monmouth, 1802–13. Governor of the Cape of Good Hope, 1813–28. Lieutenant-Colonel, 1791; Major-General, 1798; Lieutenant-General, 1803; General, 1814. Comptroller of the King's Household, April 1797–May 1804; Joint Paymaster-General, July 1804–Jan. 1806, and 1807–13.

[7] The King's reply on the 26th, 7.35 a.m., approving the draft, and insisting on Pitt's having treatment for the gout at Cheltenham and Bath, is in Stanhope, III, Appendix, p. xvi. The Speech is in *Parl. Register*, LI, 496 (29 June).

[*Somerset Place, 25 June, 3 p.m.* [*1798*].] Mr Dundas humbly begs leave to inform your Majesty that he has communicated to Mr Pitt the letters from Mr Livingstone as directed by your Majesty, and Mr Pitt will without delay execute your Majesty's commands. Mr Dundas has taken the liberty of returning to your Majesty's perusal the first letter from Mr Livingstone, in order that your Majesty's pleasure may be taken how far any enquiry should be made respecting Captain Arbuthnot mentioned by Mr Livingstone. (8925)

[*The King's reply, Windsor, 26 June, 7.45 a.m.*] I am quite ignorant who the Capt. Anstruther is that Mr. Livingston alludes to, but if Mr. Secy. Dundas knows who it is and can sound whether he is willing to come forward I shall certainly be desirous of Mr. Livingston's having an assistant, which I proposed originally to him through the Lord Chancellor, but which he on the whole thought it best to have defferred till he had seen my son, and that he by experience should judge whether such an appointment would be expedient. I desire Mr. Secy. Dundas will acquaint Mr. Livingston that with my approbation he is taking the steps he has wished and that though I have been prevented from writing this day that I shall without fail write on Friday. (Add. MSS. 40100, f. 208.)

1772   *Letters from the* DUKE OF PORTLAND *to the* KING

[*Burlington House, Tuesday, 26 June 1798, 1.45 p.m.*] The Duke of Portland most humbly requests your Majesty's permission to express the extreme satisfaction with which he lays at your Majesty's feet the dispatches which have been this morning received from the Lord Lieutenant of Ireland[1] & which contain an account of the complete success which has attended your Majesty's arms under the conduct of Lieutt. General Lake, & the prospect which is thereby afforded of the speedy & intire extinction of the rebellion in that kingdom.[2] The Duke of Portland has presumed to retain the Lord Lieutenant's letter which was marked *official* & such of its inclosures as were only copies or extracts of the papers which are submitted herewith to your Majesty, a circumstance which he felt it incumbent upon him to take notice of as the letters from Sr. Charles Asgill[3] & Sir Hugh O'Reilly[4] made a part of those inclosures & might therefore lead your Majesty to imagine that the others had been omitted by mistake. (8926)

[1] Cornwallis: he had been sworn in on the 20th. Camden was back in London on the 27th, on which day Pitt wrote to him from Downing Street: '...On every account we all unanimously wish that you should immediately become a member of the Cabinet, and that this should be publicly known without delay. I only regret that I see no opening for any office to accompany it, but from what I know of your sentiments, I trust that will appear to you a less material object. The King has expressed his warm approbation of what I propose.' (Camden MSS.)

[2] See No. 1759 n. 2.

[3] See No. 384 n. 4 (I, 317) where the date should be August 1787, not March 1788. Asgill was now a Major-General (since January 1797) and was active in suppressing the Rebellion. Lieutenant-General, 1805; General, 1814; succeeded his father as 2nd Baronet, Sept. 1788.

[4] Sir Hugh O'Reilly, whose dates are unknown, and who was created a Baronet in 1795, was Lieutenant-Colonel of the Westmeath County Militia.

[*Whitehall, Thursday, 28 June 1798, 3 p.m.*] The Duke of Portland begs leave with all humility to lay before your Majesty the drafts of your Majesty's proposed Speech as it will stand if the alterations which it has occurred to your Majesty's confidential servants to be adviseable to submit to your Majesty should be so fortunate as to receive your Majesty's sanction. The Duke of Portland also humbly requests to have your Majesty's commands signified to him with respect to the hour at which your Majesty will please to be attended to have the Speech read, & whether it is your Majesty's pleasure that the Earl Camden should be order'd to attend your Majesty at that time with the rest of your Majesty's confidential servants, to whom the Duke of Portland has had the pleasure of being informed by Mr Pitt your Majesty has been graciously pleased to add Lord Camden's assistance.[1] (8927–8)

1773 WILLIAM PITT *to the* KING

[*Hollwood, Friday, 29 June 1798.*] Mr. Pitt humbly presumes to submit the accompanying warrant for your Majesty's signature which has been prepared in consequence of a report on the case from the Solicitor to the Board of Treasury.[2] He also takes the liberty of enclosing a letter which he received yesterday from Lord Auckland respecting a packet at Falmouth.[3] (8929)

[1] Camden explained his own views about his future situation in a letter to Pitt next day: 'The only object I could have in being created a Marquis, was to give an unequivocal proof to the world that I returned from Ireland with the full approbation of the King and his Ministers. If that mark of distinction clearly shewed that approbation I should certainly not wave the claim I conceive I have to be so considered, but as I think the receiving that rank might be misconstrued and that it might be considered the King was gratifying my vanity instead of rewarding my services, I have determined not to request you to mention this object to the King as one which would be desirable for me to accept, but I think it would be advantageous that it should be understood it had been proposed to me and that I had declined it, and that I might say so, if I was to converse upon the subject. To be desired to attend the Cabinet meetings and to be really consulted and to engage in those affairs in which every man must be so peculiarly interested is certainly flattering to me, but I know enough of public business to be aware that without an efficient office I cannot be very useful to you or to the country, and I therefore hope you will look to some arrangement which may introduce me into that sort of business to which I aspire. I shall, however, accept with satisfaction that mark of distinction which I conceive myself as receiving by being called in the manner I now am called to attend the Cabinet Councils here. I am perfectly satisfied with what you say about the Garter and I think Lord Spencer has a claim to be considered before me in the disposition of that distinction and I am completely satisfied with being considered as entitled to it—after Lord Spencer.' (W. Dacres Adams MSS.)

Pitt wrote to Camden the same day: 'I have stated my sentiments to you so freely, that I need not say how much I rejoice in your determination. There can, I conceive, be no doubt, that the King would most readily have given the Marquisate on knowing that you wished it, but as I had no actual authority to make the offer, some explanation must take place with the King, which can hardly be before Wednesday. I own I doubt whether it is worth while, but will of course be guided by what you wish. With respect to office I most ardently wish I saw the way of your being placed at once in one of the most efficient, and certainly (as far as depends on me) I shall avail myself most eagerly of the first practicable opening, but till something fresh arises to lead to it, I know not how to create one...' (Camden MSS.)

[2] Joseph White.

[3] The King did not reply until 1 July, from Windsor: 'I have this morning received Mr. Pitt's note enclosing the letter to him from Ld. Auckland with the information of that Lord having appointed Mr. Stevens to the command of the Prince Edward packet boat; I am certain the duty will be ably and honestly performed and will be an advantageous appointment for the public service. The warrant, which was also in the box, seems on perusal very proper.' (Chatham Papers.)

1774 THE DUKE OF YORK *to the* KING

[*Horse Guards, 29 June 1798.*] At my return from attending your Majesty at the House of Lords, Sir William Faucett brought me Mr. Coleman's report of the state of the horses of the different Regiments of Dragoons proposed to encamp in Windsor Forest, which I lose no time in laying before your Majesty, and beg to receive your Majesty's orders whether in consequence of the suggestion contained in it your Majesty would approve of the camp being delayed for a fortnight. (8930)

1775 E. LIVINGSTON *to the* KING

[*Vienna, 30 June 1798.*] I have the honor to inform your Majesty that Sir Morton Eden has received an order from Lord Grenville to furnish me a credit to the amount of 4000 ster. for the use of his Royal Highness Prince Augustus; your Majesty may depend that every possible attention will be paid to proper œconomy in the Prince's family and to every branch of expence in my department. If your Majesty will be graciously pleased to order that I may be informed of the exact sum alloted for his Royal Highness pocket money and for the support of his household, then I will be able to form a proper plan for the expence of the Prince's family, &c. Without a positive order from your Majesty I forsee it may prove difficult for me to manage matters with propriety.

The Prince is at present in perfect health, but Doctor Domier continues to think that his Royal Highness cannot with a degree of safety, remain the winter or late in the autumn in any part of Germany. The Doctor thinks Lisbon, Devonshire or Gibraltar may be favorable for the Prince's complaints; to the last, I have reason to beleive, unless his Royal Highness had a military rank there, it would be difficult to get his consent to pass a winter in that garrison.

I took the liberty to mention Doctor Domier's annual allowance from Hanover. I beg your Majesty may be graciously pleased to send me your commands in what manner the Doctor is to receive his salary. (8931–2)

1776 *Letters from the* DUKE OF PORTLAND *to the* KING

[*Burlington House, Sunday, 1 July 1798, 3.55 p.m.*] The Duke of Portland most humbly begs leave to lay before your Majesty a dispatch received this morning from the Lord Lieutenant of Ireland containing a report of a very decisive advantage gained over the rebels in the neighbourhood of Gores Bridge by Sir Charles Asgill. The Duke of Portland also begs leave to acquaint your Majesty that the Bill for the government of the English Militia in Ireland is arrived, & is now before your Majesty's Law servants, who will have prepared their report upon it in the course of this afternoon, but unfortunately not at so early an hour as to make it possible to have it submitted to your Majesty in the course of this evening, but considering the great importance of this Bill's being passed into a law with all the dispatch which is consistent with your Majesty's convenience, the Duke of

Portland presumes to request your Majesty's permission for the Council to attend your Majesty tomorrow at Windsor at as early an hour as your Majesty will please to command. (8933–4)

[*Bulstrode, Monday, 2 July, 4 p.m.*] The Duke of Portland most humbly begs leave to add to the publick dispatches from the Lord Lieutenant of Ireland which are herewith submitted to your Majesty a private letter from him which in as far as it intimates his intention of trying the effect of a Proclamation of pardon with certain exceptions[1] & of endeavouring to correct the ideas & language of those who are far too much disposed to give this rebellion the colour of a war of religion has anticipated the purport of a dispatch of which the Duke of Portland had prepared a draft before he left town to be laid before your Majesty. The Duke of Portland begs leave also to acquaint your Majesty that he has the satisfaction to find by a private letter he has received from Major-General Loftus dated Wexford the 27th June, that Lt. Genl. Lake had got possession of almost every one of the chiefs of the rebellion in that county without any compromise or condition whatever, that the distress of the rebels is very great, that from his own observation & all the information which can be procured it is evident that they have very little ammunition, & that he looks upon the business as entirely settled in that part of the country. M. Genl. Loftus concludes his letter by saying that he is going with Lt. Genl. Lake to Dublin. (8935–6)

1777 LORD GRENVILLE *to the* KING, *and the reply*

[*Downing Street, 5 July 1798.*] Your Majesty will receive with this box a despatch from Sir W. Hamilton notifying the recall of M. de Circello,[2] and the appointment of the Prince de Belmonte to reside here as Minister from the Court of Naples. M. de Circello made this morning a similar communication to Lord Grenville, but shewed him at the same time a cyphered despatch in which M. de Gallo[3] acquaints him that there are circumstances which will in the present moment prevent the Prince de Belmonte from setting out for England, and that M. de Circello is therefore to continue to exercise his functions as before, and to be guided by his former orders.

In this state of uncertainty and contradiction Lord Grenville has advised M. de Circello to keep his recall secret for the present, and has promised to do so likewise. (8937–8)

[*The King's reply, Kew, 6 July, 8.20 a.m.*] M. Circello seems to have conducted himself so properly whilst employed here that I cannot approve the idea of his Court of recalling him unless it is for some promotion to his advantage at Naples; if it is done by the instigation of Monsieur de Gallo I should fear it does not bear a good aspect, but then Sir William Hamilton's recommendation of the Prince

---

[1] On 3 July a Proclamation was published in the *Dublin Gazette* authorising the King's Generals to give certificates for their protection to such rebels as surrendered themselves and their arms, and took the oath of allegiance. See *Cornwallis Corresp.*, II, 359.

[2] The Neapolitan Minister in London.   [3] The Neapolitan Minister at Vienna.

Belmonte has the appearance of that nobleman being educated with proper principles; at all events as his departure from Naples is not to be immediate, I think M. Circello's keeping the intention of his recall secret is very proper. (Fortescue MSS.)

1778   THE DUCHESS OF WURTEMBERG *to the* KING

[*Louisbourg, 6 July 1798.*] Fearing that it might be troublesome to your Majesty to receive letters whilst you had so much important busines to take up your time I withstood my inclination and abstained from writing last week, but fearing that a trifling accident which has just happened might be exagerated and alarm your Majesty, I take the liberty to write. Ever since twelve o'clock we have had a dreadful storm of thunder, lightning and rain. Whilst we were drinking coffee I heard a sad crash and could not help saying that I wished all those who chose to pretend being unbelievers might frequently meet with such storms, as I thought it must impress them not only with great awe but also with the conviction of their being a Supreme Being. This brought on a long conversation with some of the gentlemen who had been at sea in storms, and all agreed that religion alone prevented people from being too much alarmed, for all those they had met with who pretended to deny a Supreme Being had ever on those occasions shewn great fear. Owing to our talking a good while on this subject it was past three o'clock when I returned to my dressingroom and had but just began reading with Trinette when Princess Ferdinand[1] came into the room to assure me she was not hurt but that the lightning had struck in her apartment. I instantly went to the old part of the Castle where she lodges and found an old figure in the ceiling with its arm broke and below stairs a hole in the plaister and in the pavement. However, on several gentlemen examining the spot they assured us that it was only the violence of the shock, for at the same instant two men were thrown down. I cannot pretend to decide whether these things proceed from the lightning or the shock, but in either case they are very extraordinary.

Will your Majesty now allow me to offer my congratulations on the Almighty having again manifested how much he watches over the welfare of dear England and that that dreadful conspiracy was discovered in time? Thank God your arms are successful and I trust that they will continue so. It is in moments of danger that I most regret the being absent from your Majesty, as from my birth I have ever been with you at those times and though useless, could at least flatter myself that I could share the distress and shew the sincere attachment that I have for you. I must now take leave of your Majesty. (51490–1)

1779   EARL SPENCER *to the* KING, *and the reply*

[*Wimbledon Park, 8 July 1798.*] Earl Spencer has the honour of laying before your Majesty the proceedings of a court martial held on three seamen of the

---

[1] The wife of Prince Ferdinand (1763–1834), a younger brother of Frederick, Duke of Wurtemberg. She, who was the daughter of Christian of Schwarzburg-Sondershausen, was married, 18 March 1795. (1771–1829.)

Adamant for mutiny, and humbly submits to your Majesty the propriety of ordering the sentence of death to be carried into execution on Steevens and Mullins, but that Kelly, whom the Court have recommended to your Majesty's mercy, should in consideration of the circumstances stated by them obtain your Majesty's pardon. (8939)

[*The King's reply, Windsor, 9 July, 7.25 a.m.*] It grieves me to find that a spirit of mutiny still continues among some of the sailors, which certainly can only be quashed by rigorously executing the sentence of court martials. I therefore authorize Earl Spencer to let the law take its course on Steevens and Mullins, but that Kelly shall be pardoned. (Althorp MSS.)

1780   THE DUCHESS OF WURTEMBERG *to the* KING

[*Louisbourg, 9 July 1798.*] Your Majesty's constant kindness is too deeply impressed on my heart to find words which can sufficiently express the gratitude I feel at your being so gracious when your time is taken up with so much important business to bestow a thought on me. How little could I expect that I should have the joy of receiving a letter? Indeed I was overcome with this proof of your Majesty's goodness and I think it would have given you pleasure to see my happiness.

The Gazette of the 26th of June is just come and by its contents I trust that I shall soon be able to congratulate your Majesty on peace and quiet being again established in poor deluded Ireland. It makes me shudder when I reflect how nearly they might have executed their vile plans if Providence had not protected us and allowed their conspiracy to be annihilated. I offer up my most hearty prayers to God that he may ever equally protect your Majesty and our dear country.

By this time I hope that you have received my letter in which I mentioned to your Majesty a little change in our measures and my taking at Louisbourg the Schwalbach water and also bathing. These mineral waters agree perfectly with me and I am quite well notwithstanding our sad weather which I fear if it continues must hurt our harvest; till now everything is in a promising state, which would be a particular mercy as every necessary has been very dear for the last three or four years and prizes [*sic*] are beginning to lower.

The Duke begs that I will present his humble duty to your Majesty. I hear from him every day; he complains much of the pain in his arm and still more at his being parted from his family. The children are my constant companions and I have the pleasure to see that they are all anxious to be with me. Indeed in the present times it is doubly requisite for families to be united as the happiness one meets with at home can alone make one a little forget the sad state of the world. (51492–3)

1781   EARL SPENCER *to the* KING

[*Admiralty, 10 July 1798.*] It is with great concern that Earl Spencer finds himself under the necessity of so soon again laying before your Majesty a sentence on two seamen for mutiny, and of humbly submitting to your Majesty the propriety of its being carried into execution, but the present case is of so very atrocious a description that any relaxation from the utmost rigour of the law could not fail of being attended with dangerous consequences to your Majesty's service. (8941)

1782 LORD GRENVILLE *to the* KING, *and the reply*

[*Dropmore, 10 July 1798.*] Lord Grenville has the honour to transmit to your Majesty the private letters with their inclosures which he has received from Sir William Hamilton by the last mail. (8940)

[*The King's reply, Windsor, 11 July, 7.40 a.m.*] The note from the Queen of Naples shews that her sentiments are the same as previous to the Neapolitan Peace with France.

Sir William Hamilton has acted very properly for whoever [*sic*] my son Augustus is to be blamed for the debts he has incurred, it would have been highly disgraceful as well as hazardous if he had be[en] detained at Naples. I desire Lord Grenville will speak to Mr. Pitt that proper steps may be taken for satisfying the debts.[1] (Fortescue MSS.)

1783 GEORGE HAMMOND *to the* KING

[*Downing Street, 13 July, 1 a.m.*] Mr Hammond most humbly begs leave to represent to your Majesty that there are by the mail just arrived a dispatch from Mr Grenville, another from Sir Charles Whitworth, and a third from Lord Robert FitzGerald, in cypher; but as they will require some time to be decyphered, Mr Hammond has not thought it proper to detain, on account of them, the messenger for your Majesty beyond the usual hour. (8942)

1784 THOMAS KEATE *to* [   ]

[*Arlington Street, 15 July '98.*] Having received the inclosed letter & paper this morning from Mr Sharp at Fulham I think it is my duty to transmit both to you, and shall be obliged to you, if you see no objection, to lay them before the King. It is scarcely necessary for me to add that the paper, addressed to the King, contains my sentiments also, because I flatter myself his Majesty is already informed thereof. I beg leave to add one circumstance, that in case his Majesty should be pleased to inquire if I know of any situation possessing the requisites stated in Mr Sharp's paper, I should humbly submit to his Majesty the village of Worthing, between Little Hampton & Shoreham, on the Sussex coast. There are houses near the sea that have been built within these three or four years, with no road between them and the sea; the bathing very good, and the sands unequalled anywhere that I have ever seen. The village is retired, and there is not room for much company.

---

[1] On 7 March Sir William Hamilton had informed Grenville that the French would probably overrun Naples in due course, and that Prince Augustus had consented to leave Naples as soon as possible. (*Dropmore Papers*, IV, 121.)

I have been also informed since I received Mr Sharp's letter that three of the houses above-mentioned are at present unoccupied. Whether these would be adequate to her Royal Highness's accommodation is not for me to judge. They are at least clean, and the two rooms, fore & back, are laid together so as to produce a thorough air, when necessary. The descent to the sands is the easiest possible, & when on them a carriage may go for fourteen miles at the water edge without interruption.

Having been there with my children about three years since, I am enabled to give this particular account.

The river at Shoreham terminates the excursions upon the sands, so that there is no possibility of going further eastwards towards Brighton &c, but as far as Little Hampton westward.

Of Bognor I can say but little, having only seen it during a ride upon the sands from Worthing. There are however no sands, and the airings must be inland. I have heard that the place is more public but that it has good accommodation in houses.

Of Rottingdean I can only say that the houses are tolerable; there are no sands, and at certain times of tide no bathing; here also my children were three summers.

Of Eastbourne I need say nothing. I leave you to make what use you please of the above information. I can have no other view & no possible wish but upon all occasions to study their Majestie's pleasure, & to throw myself at their Majestie's feet. (8943–4)

Enclosure.

WILLIAM SHARP *to* THOMAS KEATE

[*Fulham, 15 July 1798.*] Having some doubts that I may not have explained myself properly to his Majesty after I had the honor of making my last visit to her Royal Highness the Princess Amelia, I am anxious to state my opinion in writing, desiring you to explain to his Majesty more clearly & fully, anything I may have omitted; & I am the rather inclined to represent this through yourself as the long conversations we had together enable you to know my sentiments perfectly. (8945)

Enclosure:

[*William Sharp to the King.*] Mr Sharp most humbly begs permission to lay before his Majesty those circumstances which occurred to him after the last visit he had the honor of paying to her Royal Highness the Princess Amelia, viz, that on making some trials of the ability of her Royal Highness to bear motion, he was much disappointed at finding that every motion produced some distress; also that it is clearly his opinion, that the sea air is highly necessary for the recovery of her Royal Highness.

Should his Majesty be pleased to wish to be informed of Mr Sharp's opinion in the present case of a journey to Weymouth, he begs leave humbly to represent that so long a journey cannot, with safety to her Royal Highness, be performed in one day; and it would be extremely hazardous to set out on a journey of more than one easy day both on account of the impossibility of beginning a second day's journey, whilst under the influence of additional pain, & the almost certainty of one day's journey, even a short one, producing some temporary distress.

Mr Sharp therefore begs leave, with the utmost defference, to recommend that the place to be wished for may be as near as possible to Windsor, where there is an open sea view, with the windows of the apartments looking upon the sea; good accommodations at all times of the tide for bathing & sands upon which a carriage may drive. (8946)

1785 THE EARL OF ST VINCENT *to the* KING

[*Ville de Paris before Cadiz, 17 July 1798.*] My labors and the last drop of my blood are devoted to the defence of your Majesty's sacred person and Government: should I survive this war, and your Majesty would be graciously pleasd to bestow the Rangership of Greenwich Park on me, the remainder of my days would be pleasingly pass'd amidst the scenes of my youth, for I was educated at Swinden's Academy[1] and near the asylum of those gallant seamen who have carried your Majesty's arms to a pitch of glory beyond that of any former reign.

Greenwich Park, from rights exercis'd by the people time immemorial, exhibits a scene of frolicksome gambol and indecorous passtime which renders it a very unfit residence for any branch of the Royal Family, or I should not have presum'd, after what I have heard, to have again thought of it. (8948)

1786 EARL SPENCER *to the* KING, *and the reply*

[*Admiralty, 17 July 1798.*] Earl Spencer has the honour to lay before your Majesty the proceedings of a court martial held at Portsmouth on two men belonging to the Pluto sloop; and humbly submits to your Majesty that it will be necessary to order the sentence of death passed on John Bryan to be carried into execution, as he appears to be a very fit object for an example. (8947)

[*The King's reply, Windsor, 18 July, 7.25 a.m.*] There cannot be any reason to doubt the propriety of the sentence of the court martial on John Bryan of the Plato sloop. I therefore desire Earl Spencer will direct the putting the above sentence into effect. (Althorp MSS.)

1787 E. LIVINGSTON *to the* KING

[*Vienna, 18 July 1798.*] I am honor'd with your Majesty's letter of 29 June, and made very happy by your gracious aprobation of my conduct. Your Majesty may depend on my making it my chief study to obey your commands, and to render every service in my power to the Prince Augustus, who's conduct since our arrival here has been very proper. At same time I cannot flatter myself that his

---

[1] *G.E.C.* merely says 'a private school in Greenwich'.

Royal Highness honors me with his confidence. I am afraid the advice the Prince got from England before my arrival has made a deep impression on his mind, and will not be easily removed; I will do everything possible to deserve his friendship, and to merit his esteem.

Lord Grenville sent last week an order to Sir Morton Eden to furnish me with a credit to the amount of 4000 Ster. which I will manage with proper œconomy, and Mr Pitt shall have very exact vouchers for every shilling spent for the Prince's service; I beg your Majesty may be graciously pleas'd to let me have your commands concerning the Prince's allowance for his pocket money, also, the exact sum for the support of his Royal Highness Household; til I have your Majesty's commands on that subject it is not easy for me to act with propriety. Hitherto the Prince's demmands for money have been moderate. His Royal Highness thinks it will be better for him and me that your Majesty fix the exact sum for his pocket money; since our arrival here I have paid all the Prince's personal bills every week, also that of his Household.

As Doctor Domier is stil of opinion that the Prince's constitution cannot stand the climate of Germany in winter or late in the autumn, it is necessary to think seriously of removing soon from Vienna. The Doctor says Portugal is preferable to every other climate, Italy excepted. To that country I never can advise his return, and since the French are in possession of Malta, all Italy is in a most critical situation. Doctor Domier says on reflection altho the climate of Gibraltar would be favorable to the Prince's health, that he is certain the style of living there would prove pernicious to his Royal Highness, and I have reason to beleive the Prince would not easily consent to be shut up there unless employd as an officer. The next climate the Doctor says is Devonshire, where he thinks the climate would agree with the Prince perfectly. Your Majesty's pleasure as to our removing and where to fix for the winter is very necessary, and the sooner you are graciously pleasd to order your commands to be sent me, the better: the Prince cannot bear the fatigue of traveling quick, and I wish to have his Royal Highness in winter quarters before the bad weather sets in. (8949–50)

1788   THE DUKE OF YORK *to the* KING

[? *19 July 1798*.] Having understood from the Prince of Wales that your Majesty had not been pleased to approve of his passing by at the head of the 10th Regiment of Light Dragoons which are to be reviewed by your Majesty tomorrow,[1] and having remarked that he appear'd a good deal hurt at the idea that Sir William Faucit had not sufficiently explained to your Majesty the manner in which this proposal took its rise, and the reasons which induced my brother to consent to its being laid before your Majesty I trust, Sir, that you will not be displeased with me if I take the liberty of mentioning them to your Majesty in order that you may not be displeased with him or be induced to think that it only originated with

[1] On Friday the 20th the King reviewed the Prince of Wales's Regiment at Wimbledon. *The Times* reported that on the previous Saturday the Regiment had a field day on Wimbledon Common (a long way from Blackheath)—but this part of the statement may not have been accurate. If it is, the date suggested is wrong.

him. We went down together last Saturday to Black Heath to be present at a Field Day of the Regiment. During the manoeuvres General Pitt expressed how happy it would make him and the whole Regiment if, as they bore the name of the Prince of Wales's Regiment, he would do them the honor of appearing at their head before your Majesty. At the same time it was hinted by other persons who were present that this would give a great relief to the whole army, at a moment when parties appeared so very desirous of lowering it in the eyes of the nation. These were the reasons which made my brother think this proposition would not meet with your Majesty's disapprobation, and therefore induced him to consent to its being laid before you. Permit me, Sir, to repeat again my hopes that your Majesty will not find fault with me for having tried to explain to you the reasons as it would give me the greatest pain to know your Majesty displeased with any part of your family, if it is any ways in my power to prevent it [*sic*]. (44147)

1789 PRINCE ADOLPHUS *to the* KING

[*Hannover, 20 July 1798.*] When the messenger left Hannover at the beginning of this month my intention was to trouble your Majesty with a letter, but as I was just returned from camp it was impossible to me; besides, having wrote to you last month and knowing how much you are now employed, I was afraid of being troublesome, not having anything of consequence to mention. Now, though as it is some time since I have had the honour of writing to you, I think it my duty to address you these lines to assure you that it is not out of negligence but merely out of discretion that I have not wrote. Our camp went off very well, and the Duke of Brunswick who reviewed us seemed very well contented. I am very happy to be able to assure you that your infantry is come on very much since the war and that it is at present in a very good and serviceable condition. We all of us wished very much to have been reviewed by your Majesty and I dare venture to say you would have been pleased.

I cannot express in words how much I rejoice at the good accounts we have received from Ireland, and I hope and trust that the rebels will soon be brought to proper obedience by the late measures that have been taken by Government. I have not offered your Majesty this year my services in that country as you refused them last summer; I trust, though, that you are convinced that you will always find me ready to obey your orders and that no one is readier to offer up the last drop of his blood for his country and Sovereign than [&c.]. (48523)

1790 THE DUKE OF PORTLAND *to the* KING

[*Bulstrode, Saturday night, 21 July 1798.*] The Duke of Portland most humbly begs leave to acquaint your Majesty that the Act of Grace, the preamble of which was sent over by the Lord Lieutenant of Ireland on Thursday, & which the Duke of Portland was commanded by your Majesty to refer to your Majesty's Law servants has been settled by them & will be ready to be laid before your Majesty at any time after one o clock tomorrow at which your Majesty will be pleased to signify your commands to the Duke of Portland that your Majesty will appoint to be attended by your Council for the purpose of declaring your royal pleasure to grant an Act of Grace & Pardon to your Majesty's subjects in Ireland & to sign the Bill to that effect.[1] The Lord Chancellor, who is with the Duke of Portland & Lord Grenville & Mr Ryder will be in readiness to attend your Majesty's commands. The Duke of Portland humbly begs leave to lay before your Majesty Mr Cooke's letter to Mr Wickham which contains the only account which has been transmitted today of the state of Ireland & is as far as it goes a confirmation of the alteration which appeared by the last letters to be happily taking place in the disposition & sentiments of the deluded people of that country. (8951-2)

1791 LORD GRENVILLE *to the* KING, *and the reply*

[*Dropmore, 23 July 1798.*] Lord Grenville has the honour to transmit to your Majesty a letter from Mr. Livingston respecting which he humbly begs to be honoured with your Majesty's commands. He has also the honour to submit to your Majesty two separate letters from Lord Elgin with the draft of the answer which, if your Majesty should be graciously pleased to approve it, he proposes sending by Lord Elgin's servant tomorrow. (8953)

[*The King's reply, Windsor, 24 July, 7.56 a.m.*] In answer to Lord Grenville's note concerning the letter he has received from Mr. Livingston, I chuse that Mr. Pitt should be consulted previous to any positive answer being given; but should he concurr with me, I should think the sum of 2000 as pocket money and 500 as the other travelling expences including the wages of servants, exclusive of the £1000 per annum for Mr. Livingston and the £500 for Mr. Arbuthnot as much as in the present state of the Civil List can be reasonably expected, which will make the whole amount £9000.

I cannot sufficiently approve of the answer Lord Grenville has prepared to the indiscreet, to call it not more, letter of Lord Elgin (for the second seems to be his own allowing it to be sent) and it is a real comfort to me that the pen that conveys directions to the British Ministers is in such safe hands who so justly views the impropriety of any secret treating with the French; but Lord Grenville's conduct deserves being fully informed of my sentiments. I certainly feel myself as warmly and zealously attached to my Electoral dominions as any Sovereign can be, and never will part with them but with my life. (Fortescue MSS.)

1792 THE KING *to* E. LIVINGSTON

[*Windsor, 24 July 1798.*] Mr. Livingston's letter of the 1st of May states this very commendable conduct of Sir William Hamilton on the dilemma concerning the debts of my son Augustus. Mr. Pitt has my directions to have that matter arranged, though they certainly greatly exceed my expectation and are an additional justification of Count Munster's conduct.

[1] The Act 38 George III, c. 55 gave legislative sanction to the Lord Lieutenant's Proclamation of 3 July.

7 (97)

I do not enter farther on the subject of money as I think it better that article should remain in the hands of Lord Grenville, Mr. Pitt and Mr. Dundas, who have my fullest instructions on that head and will write to you on that subject.

I shall certainly strongly, though affectionately, point out to Augustus the necessity of his keeping within such allowance as shall be made for him, and you shall by the Ministers be enjoined to keep within the sum they shall state to you.

It may not be improper to add here that I so fully feel the necessity of Mr. Livingston having a gentleman to assist him in the accompanying my son, that I had suggested it to the Lord Chancellor prior to Mr. Livingston's departure from hence, but I understood that upon the whole Mr. Livingston thought it better deferred till he should have by his own observation felt the propriety of such an appointment. I am very happy that by the means of Mr. Dundas I have got Mr. Arbuthnot, whom I understand is the person most wished for by Mr. Livingston.

That *persons* on this side of the water have tried to place Mr. Livingston in an unfavourable light in the eyes of my son because he had too much honour to be their instrument is not impossible, but I trust on farther acquaintance Augustus must see with more just eyes.

Mr. Livingston's letter of the 7th of June on the safe arrival at Vienna gave me heartfelt satisfaction, and enables me so early after placing him with my son cordially to thank him for having so successfully brought him from Naples; the conduct of both King and Queen of Naples deserve my warmest thanks.

In the letter of the 20th of June mention is made that the health of my son and his conduct at Vienna are as could be wished. I by no means can agree to his coming to England. Mr. Livingston's own good sense must point out various reasons. I therefore trust that he will find out some proper climate for the winter. I should not object to Gibraltar if I saw a safe mode of arriving there. Might not the southern dominions of Russia be suitable and desirous objects for a traveller? A journey to Wurtemberg seems to lye quite out [of] any tour at present, being too near the enemy to be visited without some degree of hazard.

Mr. Pitt has certainly sent a credit to Vienna which Mr. Livingston must have received before this time. As Dr. Domeyer is proposed to stay, his pay must be out of the allowance that will be made from hence for Augustus and whilst the journey continues may have such addition to what he before received as Mr. Livingston may think right.

Since writing so far I have received Mr. Livingston's letter of the 30th of June by which I see the credit is arrived; the subsequent directions will now soon follow, but I cannot help just writing that the moment military rank is expected if Gibraltar is fixed on for the winter residence, I must entirely forgoe that plan and desire that some moderate climate as Astracan or such other Russian Province as may be thought better may be fixed on.[1] (Add. Georgian 2/44.)

[1] Folio 8954 is a draft of the first three paragraphs of this letter.

[*Downing Street, Wednesday, 25 July 1798.*] Mr Pitt begs leave to make his humble excuses for not paying his duty at St James's today. He was prevented from coming at as early an hour as he had intended, and stopped afterwards on being informed (as he since finds, by mistake) that there was a Recorder's Report, till he was too late. He takes the liberty also, in consequence of the intimation which your Majesty has had the condescension and goodness to send by Mr Dundas, to submit to your Majesty that the two persons in the House of Commons, whom he should venture to recommend as the fittest objects of professional distinction, are Mr Perceval and Mr Bragge.[1] The office of Solicitor to the Queen might perhaps be more material on account of its rank to the latter than to Mr Perceval who has already a silk gown. But he is at the same time not certain without inquiry whether the nature of Mr Bragge's practice would render precedence advantageous to him. Your Majesty may perhaps have the goodness to permit Mr Pitt to ascertain privately this point from the Speaker, to whom it will be peculiarly gratifying to learn that Mr Bragge (who is his brother-in-law) has been in contemplation.

Mr Pitt submits some warrants for your Majesty's signature. (8955–6)

1794   EARL SPENCER *to the* KING

[*Admiralty, 25 July 1798.*] Earl Spencer having been informed that Captain Matthew Smith, late of your Majesty's ship the Diomede, intends to attend today at St James's in order to pay his duty to your Majesty, thinks it his duty to lay before your Majesty the accompanying copy of an order issued by your Majesty-in-Council for Captain Smith's remaining on the list of Captains notwithstanding the sentence of a court martial by which he was dismissed from your Majesty's service, lest the circumstances of his case should have escaped your Majesty's recollection. Your Majesty will observe that though by the opinion of the Attorney & Solicitor-General the sentence was reported to be irregular, the merits of the case do not appear to be at all affected by that determination. (8957)

1795   *Letters from* LORD GRENVILLE *to the* KING, *and the replies*

[*Cleveland Row, 26 July 1798, 4 p.m.*] Lord Grenville trusts that the great import-ance of the subject of the inclosed papers, to your Majesty's Government in Ireland, will plead his apology to your Majesty for breaking in upon your Majesty this evening, as it may be important that any orders which your Majesty may think proper to give on the subject to Baron Lenthe,[2] or to him, should be executed in

---

[1] Bragge, who was Addington's brother-in-law, was a practising barrister on the Oxford Circuit. Pitt wrote to Addington on the 27th: 'I cannot help enclosing a note I have just received which will tell its own story, when I have premised, that on the King's enquiring who ought to succeed Grant as Solicitor to the Queen, I mentioned Perceval and Bragge, but inclining for the latter, if I should find on inquiring from you that the precedence would be an advantage to him. I am afraid that is the whole question, as the office is only rank without emolument. Pray let me know, after consulting Bragge if necessary.' (Sidmouth MSS.)

[2] The Hanoverian Minister in London. The name is sometimes inaccurately spelt Lerthe and Lentha. Cf. No. 1489.

time for tomorrow's mail. Lord Grenville is perfectly sensible that the matter itself is in many respects a delicate one, and he presumes to say no more upon it than that, from the intelligence which has at different times been procured, this man appears to have been the principal channel of communication between the enemy and the Irish rebels; and therefore that his being sent to Ireland (if the thing is possible) would be a point of very great advantage. But your Majesty alone can judge how far this can be done.

Nothing else of importance is come by the mail. (8958–9)

[*The King's reply, Windsor, 26 July 1798, 7.21 p.m.*] I have just received the papers Lord Grenville has forwarded to me; the whole business seems so irregular and in its consequences so delicate that I do not think it is possible I can with any safety give the orders Mr Crauford[1] seems to wish. I have kept the papers for farther consideration. I will send for Baron Lenthe and tomorrow morning write more explicitly, though I do not think at present I can possibly consent to his taking a step which I fear is contrary to every idea of neutrality in Germany. (8960)

[*From Lord Grenville, Cleveland Row, 26 July, 11 p.m.*] Lord Grenville is just now honoured with your Majesty's commands. He takes the liberty to return the note, as other matter was written on the reverse of the sheet, & he thought your Majesty might possibly imagine it had been mislaid. (Add. Georgian 2/58.)

[*The King's reply, Windsor, 27 July, 8.35 a.m.*] On mature reflection I am confirmed in the opinion I loosely wrote to Lord Grenville the last evening (and with so much hurry that I did not perceive it was not on a fresh piece of paper) that without the grossest breach of the neutrality I cannot support the irregular conduct of Sir James Craufurd in having seized a suspicious character in my Electorate, and directing from hence that the said person shall be delivered into his hands to be sent here. What I can do is, if the man has not been released at Hannover (which I think very probable) to have his papers secretly examined and copies sent here, but totally without the knowledge of Sir James Craufurd; these directions I have given to Baron Lenthe.

I do not see that any other answer can be given to Sir James Craufurd than that I excuse on account of his zeal the irregular step he has taken, but can in no way as Elector direct Duckett's being delivered up to him or his papers publickly examined, particularly as the whole ground is placed on suspicion; had this man been an avowed rebel in arms, and escaped from Ireland, there might have been some grounds for such an application to me. (Fortescue MSS.)

1796   WILLIAM PITT *to the* KING

[*Downing Street, Friday, 27 July 1798.*] Mr Pitt begs your Majesty's permission to express how much he feels your Majesty's goodness in encouraging him to

---

[1] He had succeeded his father as 2nd Bart., 15 Dec. 1797. (1761–1839.)

make use of the present interval for his excursion to the sea coast,[1] and he means immediately to avail himself of your Majesty's gracious permission. He has written to the Speaker to make the inquiry which your Majesty has had the goodness to allow with respect to Mr Bragge.

The accompanying warrants are submitted for your Majesty's signature. (8961)

1797 THE DUKE OF PORTLAND *to the* KING

[*Bulstrode, Monday, 30 July 1798, 9.30 p.m.*] Your Majesty was pleased to signify upon the cap of the Recorder[2] of London's letter in which he acquainted the Duke of Portland that his Report of the convicts who were tried last Session at the Old Bailey was ready to be laid before your Majesty, that your Majesty would receive it either on last Wednesday or next Wednesday the first of August. The Duke of Portland most humbly requests to know whether it is your Majesty's pleasure that the Recorder should be orderd to attend your Majesty at St. James's at the usual hour after the Levée on Wednesday next. (8962)

1798 LORD GRENVILLE *to the* KING

[*Dropmore, 31 July 1798.*] Lord Grenville has the honour humbly to acquaint your Majesty that the Marquis de Spinola who long since received his letters of recall, is now returning to Genoa, and has applied to have the honour of an audience of leave. As M. de Spinola's principles are good, and as his personal conduct has always been unexceptionable, Lord Grenville judged that your Majesty would not refuse this request, and, has therefore appointed M. de Spinola for tomorrow unless he should receive any different orders from your Majesty. (8963)

1799 THE DUCHESS OF WURTEMBERG *to the* KING

[*Louisbourg, 1 Aug. 1798.*] Having been this last week much plagued by straining my wrist I delayed writing to your Majesty in hopes that I should in a few days recover my strength and my usual handwriting, but finding that not to be the case I will try to make these lines legible by writing very slow, that I may not appear to neglect recalling myself to your Majesty which I am ever both happy and anxious to do.

On the 25th of July to my great joy the Duke returned home from Wildbad. He looks, thank God, well but has not yet received the benefit I so anxiously wished from the waters. The physicians assure me that in a fortnight or three weeks he will begin to feel a considerable amendment.

Our weather has been very extraordinary this whole summer notwithstanding which we have thank God a plentiful harvest which I trust will lower the price of provisions, which are considerably encreased of late years in this part of Germany. I dread that the vintage will not be as good as we had reason to expect from the manner in which the vines flowered, as though we have had a great deal of

---

[1] To Walmer Castle, where he arrived on 1 August, and stayed about a fortnight.
[2] Sir John William Rose. He had been knighted on 24 November 1790.

rain it has been always with storms and has not sufficiently penetrated into the earth, which makes the grapes fall off before they are ripe. Had the ears of corn appeared to me fuller or larger than those in the Great Park I should not have failled sending some to your Majesty, but having walked a good deal in the fields I examined them closely and found no difference. The oats appear to me particularly fine but they are not yet quite ripe. They have here a great deal of what they call Türkischer Weizen with which they feed all the poultry and make flower, which is used more for soups than bread. It is cultivated in every small slip of land and very much amongst the vines. I wish that your Majesty could see this country as I think the cultivation would please you very much. One sad thing is that in the course of a few years wood will be very scarce as everybody tries to cultivate wheat as it bears so good a price and by degrees they neglect totally planting which is very necessary in a country where there are no coal mines. (51494–5)

1800   *Letters from the* DUKE OF PORTLAND *to the* KING

[*Bulstrode, Friday, 3 Aug. 1798, 5.50 p.m.*] The Duke of Portland most humbly begs leave to acquaint your Majesty that he has not yet received any dispatches from the Lord Lieutenant of Ireland. But as the accounts contained in Lord Castlereagh's letters to Mr Wickham are of unquestionable authenticity & as far as respects the Act of Pardon are strictly conformable to the wishes which were signified to the Lord Lieutenant upon that subject, & as it appears that every caution has been used in the communication to the Committees of Secrecy of the intelligence your Majesty permitted to be sent to the Lord Lieutenant, the Duke of Portland conceives that these letters of Lord Castlereagh's will be so satisfactory to your Majesty as to make it his duty to submit them to your Majesty without delay.[1] (8967)

[*Bulstrode, Saturday, 4 Aug. 1798, 11.45 p.m.*] The Duke of Portland most humbly begs leave to acquaint your Majesty that the Act of Grace is arrived & has been laid before the Lord Chancellor who has read it over & over again with the Attorney & Sollicitor-General & that by every one of them alterations have been suggested which are reducing into form; that the Lord Chancellor is very desirous of keeping it for the purpose of reconsidering it so as that it may be ready for your Majesty's royal signature on Wednesday next unless it should be your Majesty's pleasure that it should not be so long delayed.

The Duke of Portland humbly begs leave to add for your Majesty's information that he has received this evening an account from Mr Wickham of the apprehension of Crossfield, one of the most able & active members of the London Corresponding Society & who has for a long time had the dexterity to elude the vigilance of the persons employed to take him into custody.[2] (8968)

---

[1] The leading rebels then in prison, about 124 in number, were pardoned on condition that they quitted the Kingdom and retired to any country not at war with England. Among them were Emmett and Arthur O'Connor.

[2] A reward of £200 for his apprehension had been offered. After being charged at Worship-Street Public Office he was taken to the Home Office, there examined by Wickham and then committed to prison.

[*Worthing, ? 5 or 6 Aug. 1798.*¹] Not being able to express to you by word of mouth how grateful I am for your repeated goodness & affection to me, I have recourse to my pen & I am afraid I shall find the same fault with this as it is quite out of my power to express my gratitude & all I feel for the kindness I experience from you & dear mama.

I never knew anything so good as you were concerning my journey to this place; what I felt at leaving all those so dear to me cannot easily be described, & nothing but the great hopes of a perfect cure could lessen the regret I ever feel at being parted from you. Thank you, my dearest papa, again & again for letting me have G[enera]l Goldsworthy; he is a great addition to our party & nothing can be more pleasant & good natured than they all are. I can never tell you what excellent servants you have sent down with me; indeed I am quite sorry they cannot attend you at the same time. I bore the journey to Horsham better than I expected, but from there the pain in my face encreased; what I felt the last eight miles I shall never forget. I still feel it very much.

It is but justice to say how attentive Mr. Keate is; I have seen his nephew² who seems to be a very modest, civil young man & anxious to do what is right.

I sat out yesterday for above an hour in a little garden near the sea; this eveng. at five o'clock I am to go & set out on the sands. The chairmen were overturned on their road here just after changing horses at Horsham; everybody says it was the coachman's fault. All the passengers were hurt, some very badly; the chairmen were among the least hurt but could not carry me till today.

We had a very violent thunderstorm last night; it rained a good deal this morng. but it is now a fine day; however I fear the rain must have prevented your going to the Camp.

I will not trespass any longer on your time & will merely beg of you, my dearest papa, to be assured no one is more attached to you than your dutiful & affte. daughter.

[P.S.] George Augustus Curzon is now standing by me & desires me to give his compts. to the dear King & is very anxious to see him. I could not do otherwise than comply with his wish & I thought it might amuse you. (Add. Georgian 14/7.)

[*Worthing, 9 Aug. 1798.*] It is impossible for me to find words to express how thankful I am for your very kind letter I received from you this morng. I cannot express to you, my dearest papa, how attentive & anxious to do right Captain Cumberland³ is. He has managed his barge in such a way as to allow of my *sopha* being laid all along, & with the leave of Mr. Keate I went in the boat today. I liked it much & dare say I shall find the motion easier every time. It appears strange to say but no doubt it was warmer on the sea than on shore. I think the Captain very good humoured & sincerely anxious to make everything pleasant & convenient.

---

¹ Endorsed by the King, 'Recd. Augt. 7th, 1798. Answered the same day.'

² Robert Keate, surgeon (1777–1857), nephew of Thomas Keate, surgeon (1745–1821). For many years he attended the royal family.

³ He commanded the *Fly* sloop.

The people here & all about shewed every mark of respect they possibly could on Tuesday, for which I am truly obliged & wish much to shew them my gratitude.

Upon my honour, your letter has made me so happy I know not what to say, & the very kind expressions you make use of on my account make me very vain, though every hour I wish to merit them more, & every hour convinces me how far off I am from that happy moment.

Notwithstanding my great partiality to Weymouth, it is impossible for me to say I think I could have got there at this moment, for from what I felt on my journey of going up & down hills from Horsham & the last eight miles from Stenin [sic] convince me how impossible it would have been for me to have continued my route for some days. You cannot but agree, my dearest papa, that it would not have been agreable had I been obliged to stop for some days at an Inn.

I am glad the weather has never prevented your going to the camp. Several people in the neighbourhood as well as here have been kind enough to enquire after me, amongst others the Duke of Norfolk. I was much surprised when I heard it, but wonders never cease.

Knowing how good you are I cannot conclude without saying that I find my leg at present much the same, but certainly the vapour & warm sea bath are of use, & therefore I hope that I shall soon be able to assure you I am better. Dare I say God Almighty bless you, my dearest papa. (Add. Georgian 14/9.)

1802 THE DUKE OF PORTLAND *to the* KING

[*Bulstrode, Saturday night, 11 Aug. 1798.*] The Duke of Portland most humbly begs leave to lay at your Majesty's feet a dispatch from the Lord Lieutenant together with one from Lord Castlereagh to Mr Wickham containing a copy of the narrative which the prisoners proposed to give of the progress & state of the rebellion in which so much reserve has been used & so much arrogance & insolence have been manifested as appears to have satisfied the Lord Lieutenant that he is at liberty to take other methods of getting at the bottom of the rebellion & lead the Duke of Portland to hope that your Majesty will have the satisfaction of finding that the character of your Majesty's Government will be duly sustained & that your Majesty's lenity will not be ultimately misapplied. (8969)

1803 HENRY DUNDAS *to the* KING, *and the reply*

[*Parl[iamen]t Street, 13 Aug. 1798, 11 a.m.*] Mr. Dundas humbly submits to your Majesty's perusal a private letter he has received from Mr. Livingstone in case your Majesty should wish to give Mr. Dundas any commands on any part of the contents of it.

Mr. Dundas likewise takes the liberty of bringing under your Majesty's view a memorandum put into Mr. Dundas's hands, as, if the papers referred to could be obtained, Mr. Dundas would wish much to peruse them. (8970)

[*The King's reply, Windsor, 14 Aug. 1798, 7.20 a.m.*] This morning I have received Mr. Secretary Dundas's note transmitting the letter he has received from Mr. Livingston. I have wrote the letter of advice to my son Augustus, which that gentleman wished on the score of his want of oeconomy, and have fixed the sum of £2,000 as his pocket money, which is the same sum he had before, and considering the debts he had contracted and which now are to be paid, is as much as could be done. Lord Grenville has also acquainted Mr. Livingston of this and that seven thousand more will be allowed for the paying the other expences, so that the disposable sum for Mr. Livingston is now fixed. As this was settled with Mr. Pitt I thought it best that instruction should be sent through a ministerial, not my private channel. The only thing that Mr. Dundas has to inculcate is the impropriety of attempting a journey either to Lisbon or this island: I have suggested the visiting the warmer provinces of the Russian Empire which was Mr. Livinston's owne idea before he proceeded to Italy, and indeed in the present disturbed state of Europe that seems the most eligible plan, besides travelling gently in good climates at the time that it must afford amusement must be conducive to health.

I will send a memorandum to Hannover that the deposit of papers may be examined to find if there is any plan as stated in the memorandum Mr. Secy. Dundas has sent to me for an attack on Egypt. (Add. MSS. 40100, f. 210.)

Enclosure. E. LIVINGSTON *to* HENRY DUNDAS

(*Private and Confidential*)

[*Vienna, 1 Aug. 1798.*] I only got by last post the honor of your letter of 29 June, and I refer you to mine of 18 July. I have not yet got his Majesty's instructions and commands for the allowance to be made for the annual expences of the Prince's Household, H.R.H. pocket money &c. The King's instructions becomes every day more necessary: the Prince tels his friends 'I have never seen the King's orders to make any reform in my Household, or Mr Livingston's authority to keep back any part of the 2000 per annum his Majesty allow'd for my pocket money.'

In the many conversations I have had with the Prince, concerning genteel œconomy and proper reforms in his Household, & personal expences, H.R.H. has allways agreed I was perfectly right, and that he was determined to follow my advice, at [the] same time I know he blames me for the reforms made in his family, he says the King writes in an affectionate manner to him; and concludes his Majesty is pleased with his conduct. You must see the absolute necessity of my receiving the King's positive commands; without such an authority it will be impossible to prevent many unnecessary expences.

I have sent his Majesty Doctor Domier's opinion about the best climates for the Prince. The Doctor says Italy is the most salutary, Portugal the next, and then Devonshire. The last is out of the question; you must know how far the political state of Portugal will permit of the Prince passing the winter there with safety. I can speak freely about Italy, I do declare to you if the Prince was my only son, and heir to the first estate in Europe I rather would see him dead than surrounded by such society as he lived with at Naples; if he returns to Italy (allowing the political state of that country permitted it) I am certain the worst part of that horrid society would join him directly.

I must now mention a plan going forward, which I have discovered within these two days; I am assured H.R.H. has been advised from England to offer himself a candidate for Liverpool. There is now here two gentlemen from that city that the Prince pays great attention to; consulting with them about the best manner of canvassing &c &c and with strict injunctions to keep everything a profound secret from me; I am told these gentlemen laugh at the Prince's plan; I think it my duty to let you know, he has such a mad project in contemplation. It was necessary to let the King know, that the Prince does not honor me with his confidence. The letters he received from London before my arrival at Naples have had the desired effect. He read an article of a letter to Sir Wm. Hamilton, where the lady says, Mr Livingston is to be soon with you, dont trust him with anything, he is not *our* friend, and he is a d—— Government man, &c. The Prince I am afraid is weak enough to pay attention to such nonsense; prudence required that the King should know the Prince does not honor me with his confidence; as he may do many things in a clandestine manner, which is impossible for me to prevent, such as borrowing money &c. I know from experience he is not delicate on that subject: I also know that few men will refuse to lend a Prince of England, or give him credit, as they think all his debts will honorably be paid: these things I cannot mention to the King; in justice to myself it is proper you be informed of part of the difficultys I have to struggle with: I will be answerable for everything that is done above board, and allways give the best advice, and example in my power.

In one of my letters to the King I mentioned Gibraltar as a fine climate, but there I beleive H.R.H. will not go, unless he gets a suitable commission in the Army; from the military ardour the Prince sometimes shows, I am convinced if his Majesty writes him a kind letter, showing the situation of the country demmands the service of the Princes of the Blood Royal, and promising him preferment as far as the custom of the Army permits, if these steps are taken I have little doubt but the Prince may be engaged to go to Gibraltar: from every observation I have been able to make I realy think it would be the *safest*, and *best place* for H.R.H. to pass a year or two; there the climate is excellent and I presume *good* and *exact* discipline in the garison; the King giving his commands to the Governr. concerning œconomy &c; at least one half of the money may be saved; that must be spent on the continent. I have taken the liberty to write you freely; your good understanding will shew you what use to make of my letter, particularly in regard to Gibraltar; I think that part of it deserves your serious consideration: *perhaps* if the Prince is informed that I have suggested this plan, it probably may occasion a seperation directly. H.R.H. has many correspondants at present in England, and he is informed of most things going on in the capital.

If we remain on the continent and it suit Capt. Arbuthnot to join H.R.H. I will be very glad to have him for an assisstant: it may be necessary that the King take the trouble to inform the Prince that he intends to let him have another gentleman.

Some time ago I begd H.R.H. to let me know if there was any particular gentleman he wished to have about his person, and I would take the liberty to mention
his name to his Majesty; he answered no: to others I know he says it is hard he has
not the nomination of his own Household.

I have taken the liberty to inclose a letter for Lord Morton and beg you may
have the goodness to order it to be sent to the Post Office. (8964–6)

1804   PRINCESS AMELIA *to the* KING

[*Worthing, 19 Aug. 1798.*] I cannot defer any longer troubling you with a letter
to return you many thanks for a very kind one you wrote me a few days ago &
which as usual made me extreemly happy. I can never forget dear Lady Belgrave's[1]
kindness in coming to see me; you were quite right in saying you knew how happy
it would make me, for indeed it did please me very much & I was very sorry when
she left us. It gives me great pleasure to know you approve of her so much. I
heard from her today & she tells me that Lord Grey[2] is coming over to see me
tomorrow & remains till Wednesday.

Since I had last the pleasure of writing to you, my dearest papa, I have again
been on the sea & into the sloop.[3] It was vastly well contrived & nothing can be
more anxious & attentive than Captain Cumberland.[4] The sloop appears to be a
very nice vessel & was very clean.

I like Mr. & Mrs. Ellis[5] & Miss Parker; they seem good humour'd & they have
offered us their house which is a little distance from ours & have been exceedingly
obliging in the offer of making any alterations that might suit my particular
convenience & which we have of course declined. I must say they loose no
opportunity of shewing us every civility in their power. One cannot help being
prejudiced in their favour as Mr. Ellis was nephew to Lady Effingham[6] & related
to dear Ly. Fanny.

Dear General Goldsworthy is very charming & really very well. I cannot
conclude without giving you some little account of myself. I still feel a great deal
of pain in my knee & in short no alteration as to my own feeling since I wrote you
last, but as I am assured that these complaints generally take time I do not allow
myself to be disheartned that I do not find the part affected as yet materially better.

Pray my dear papa give my duty to mama. Gl. Goldsworthy presents his most
humble duty. (Add. Georgian 14/10.)

[1] Lord Belgrave (1767–1845), later, Earl Grosvenor and Marquess of Westminster, married (1794)
Eleanor (1770–1846) only daughter of Thomas, 1st Earl of Wilton.
[2] Lord Grey de Wilton.
[3] The *Fly.*
[4] William Cumberland (*c.* 1765–1832). Lieutenant, 1790; Commander, 1795; Captain, 8 Nov.
1798; Rear-Admiral, 1825. He was a son of Richard Cumberland, the dramatist.
[5] Charles Rose Ellis's brother John (*d.* 1832) married Antoinette Parker, daughter of Sir Peter
Parker, Bart., in 1795. His cousin George Ellis (1753–1815)—they were the grandsons of George
Ellis, Chief Justice of Jamaica—married Antoinette's sister Anne ('Miss Parker') in 1801 (not 1800
as in *D.N.B*).
[6] The 2nd Earl of Effingham (*d.* 1763) married Elizabeth Beckford (*d.* 1791) in 1745 (her sister
Anne married the Chief Justice of Jamaica), and in 1776 she married, as her second husband, Field
Marshal Sir George Howard (*c.* 1720–96); Lady Frances [Howard] was the Earl's daughter.

[*Admiralty, 25 Aug. 1798.*] Your Majesty having been pleased to signify your intention of seeing the gun and colours lately brought from the Mediterranean at the Admiralty on Wednesday next, Earl Spencer humbly requests your Majesty's orders at what hour the Admiralty will be honoured with your presence, that he may be perfectly ready to attend on your Majesty; and he further presumes to suggest that if your Majesty will deign to do him the honour of alighting at his house by the door that opens on the Parade, it will be the readiest entrance and less liable than any other to inconvenience or obstruction from a crowd of people.[1] (8971)

[*The King's reply, Windsor, 25 Aug., 8.10 a.m.*] I shall certainly alight at the Earl Spencer's house on the parade of St. James's Park by one quarter before twelve on Wednesday. I am glad he has desired me to fix the time; the place I had naturally supposed would be the most convenient. (Althorp MSS.)

[*From Lord Spencer, Admiralty, 25 Aug. 1798.*] Earl Spencer has the honour to lay before your Majesty the sentence of a court martial lately held at Plymouth on several seamen & marines of the Cæsar for being concerned in a very dangerous mutiny on board of that ship, whereby six of them are condemned to death, and Earl Spencer is under the disagreable necessity from the very daring and atrocious nature of the case humbly to recommend to your Majesty that the above sentence may be carried into execution as speedily as possible, as the most effectual means of checking a new species of mutiny which has of late unfortunately made its appearance in some of the ships of the Channel Fleet, & which seems to be in some degree connected with the rebellion in Ireland. (8972)

[*The King's reply, Windsor, 25 Aug., 8.10 a.m.*] It is most unpleasant that the spirit of mutiny cannot be thoroughly eradicated in the fleet, and that severe execution of the sentence of court martials seems indispensible. I so fully concurr in that opinion that I instantly empower Earl Spencer to direct the six men convicted that belonged to the Caesar to suffer death. I trust the Captains of all the ships of the Navy will very carefully attend to any suspicious correspondence that may be carried on, for though I trust the open rebellion in Ireland is greatly checked, it cannot be supposed that the embers of it will not long subsist and be ready to blaze out on the first more favorable opportunity. (Althorp MSS.)

1806   THE DUKE OF ROXBURGHE *to the* KING

[*Fleurs, 26 Aug. 1798.*] The death of Mr. Isaac Walton, one of your Majesty's Pages of the Bedchamber, having been notified to me, I hope to receive the honor of your Majesty's commands respecting his successor.

---

[1] On Wednesday the 29th the King inspected the cannon, the flags, the silver boat and other trophies taken by the *Sea Horse* in the French frigate sailing home from Malta.

If your Majesty has no person in view to succeed to the late Mr. Walton, and in that case only, I beg leave most humbly to recommend Mr. Thomas Coles,[1] who has been twenty years in my service. (8973)

1807 PRINCESS AMELIA *to the* KING

[*Worthing, 26 Aug. 1798.*] It is quite out of my power to defer any longer returning you my thanks for the very kind letter you were so good to write me. The very affectionate manner that you express yourself on my not going with you to Weymouth gave me the greatest pleasure. I was very glad when mama informed me of your going, for I know how much you like it & how much good it always does you. It is impossible for me to deny but that I am very sorry not to be of the party, but everything is for the best & I content myself with thinking that next year I shall be able to go with you & the idea that remaining here will entirely restore my health is a great blessing indeed. Now I will tell you that I am quite sorry that we cannot sometimes meet on the sea; how pleasant would that have been, but Weymouth is an hundred miles from here by water. However, as I said before, everything is for the best.

Certainly this place is as pleasant as it can be without any of my dear family, owing to the great kindness everyone shews me; indeed I meet with so much from all quarters I know not what to say & only wish I did deserve it. Lord Grey de Wilton came over to see us last Monday & left us again on Wednesday; he told me his Regiment was ordered to the Isle of Wight.

You will have heard everything concerning me from Mr. Keate, therefore I have nothing new to say about myself from that time as no material alteration can have taken place.

For this last week I have not been upon the water: the next time I go I am to be in a cot which is a very clever invention as it will prevent my feeling a great deal of the motion. I shall now take my leave as I am sure my dear papa must be tired with reading this letter, but I could not resist returning you as soon as possible my grateful thanks for your dear letter & believe me [&c.]. (Add. Georgian 14/11.)

1808 *Letters from the* DUKE OF PORTLAND *to the* KING

[*Bulstrode, Sunday, 26 Aug. 1798, 11 p.m.*] The Duke of Portland most humbly begs leave to lay at your Majesty's feet the draft of the intended Report of the Committee of Secrecy of the House of Commons of Ireland & the evidence of four of the prisoners of State which was taken on oath before the Committee of Secrecy of the Lords of that Kingdom, & also a letter from Lord Castlereagh to Mr Wickham by which it appears that the principal object of the Report is to justify the measures which have been pursued by your Majesty's Government by stating the progress of the treason & the successive efforts which have been made to counteract it with reference to each other in doing which it appears that the attention of the Committee has been particularly pointed to the selection of such

[1] He was appointed: salary, £80 a year.

of the most striking features of the conspiracy as they thought would be most likely to enable the publick to peruse the documents intended to be given in the Appendix, with a reference to the succession of events. The Duke of Portland farther presumes to acquaint your Majesty that it appears by a letter Mr Wickham has received today from Lord Castlereagh that the Report of the Secret Committee of the Commons was presented to the House on last Tuesday night, & that in the Committee on the Bill of Attainder Lord Edward FitzGerald's guilt was so fully proved that the Council on the part of the executors declined calling any evidence to controvert it, & that the vote for retaining his name in the Bill passed unanimously. The Duke of Portland is extremely sorry to inform your Majesty that the same letter from Lord Castlereagh, which is dated the 22d instt. mentions that accounts had been received of some farther appearances of disturbance in the west & particularly in the county of Tipperary, but whether they were connected with any intimation of succours from France or to what other cause they were to be attributed he (Ld. Castlereagh) could not take upon him to ascertain. (8974–5)

[*Bulstrode, Monday, 27 Aug. 1798, 6.30 p.m.*] The Duke of Portland most humbly lays before your Majesty the dispatches which arrived this morning from the Lord Lieutenant of Ireland, which the Duke of Portland is very sorry to acquaint your Majesty contain an account of the French having landed in Killalla Bay in the county of Sligo about 900 men on the evening of the 22d. instt.,[1] but as it seems that the number above mentioned comprises their whole force & that they have no transports with them, it is to be hoped that the expedition may terminate in the same manner as that which took place in Wales. The Duke of Portland is extremely concerned that his absence from home has prevented his receiving & consequently laying the above-mentioned information before your Majesty at an earlier hour. (8976)

1809 THE DUCHESS OF WURTEMBERG *to the* KING

[*Louisbourg, 28 Aug. 1798.*] I had just begun writing yesterday to your Majesty when the Duke came to propose to me a hunting party. We had a beautiful drive of five and thirty English miles to Reichenberg Forrest at the skirts of which the toils were erected into which the game was driven, the Duke shot the greatest part of it. It is a fine sight for those who have never met with anything of the sort before and must always appear chearful from the number of people.

The difference of climate is strongly seen as near Louisbourg the harvest is almost over and in that part of the country not begun.

I have been sadly mortified by the fine reports which had been spread through Italy and by Vienna turning out false. At this moment it is a sad thing but one does not dare to give credit to any news that comes, as there are undoubtedly

[1] Commanded by Humbert, who won an initial success in an action (known as the Castlebar Races) against several regiments of Irish militia, whom Sir Ralph Abercromby described as being formidable only to their friends. They ran away almost without firing a shot, some from panic, others from disaffection (several hundreds at once joined the French). Humbert's small force was soon rounded up and the survivors surrendered at Ballynamuck.

people who from hidden motives wish to discover the effect that reports have on the minds of everybody, and therefore publish things to obtain that knowledge which on investigation are totally invented; but with so many circumstances that at first one cannot be aware of their falsity and too often one is led to express joy or sorrow when it would be more prudent to keep it to oneself.

As your Majesty is always so gracious as to interest yourself about my taking exercise, I must mention that I walk a great deal, generally two hours a day and near five or six English miles in the woods and often in the fields. I am afraid that my pace is sometimes a little irksome to the other Ladies but having now obtained that they divide themselves and that some walk in the morning and the others in the evening I go on my old way, as I find it agrees very much with me, as notwithstanding all this exercise I continue very fat, without it I should be a perfect sight. (51496–7)

1810   PRINCE ADOLPHUS *to the* KING

[*Monbrilliant, 29 Aug. 1798.*] I cannot find words to express what I feel at this new marck of your Majesty's graciousness in advancing me out of my turn to the ranck of Lieutenant-General. I certainly never shall forget this fresh prooff of your affection and shall always endeavour to shew you my gratitude for it by applying myself as much as I can to my duty. God knows this has been my constant endeavour ever since I have begun to act in the world and I do assure you it shall ever remain it as long as I live.

I must also return your Majesty my most humble thancks for your graciousness in giving me an Establishment, which Mr. de Lenthe wrote me word of last post, as also for the very flattering manner in which you have been pleased to order me to fix the sum necessary for to defray the expenses of it. Your Majesty may be assured that I shall not abuse of your goodness and will not asck a farthing more than is necessary. A plan is now making, which, as soon as it is finished, I shall send to Mr. de Lenthe to present to you and I trust it will meet with your approbation. I am perfectly convinced of the necessity of economy at all times and much more so at the present so that you may be sure I shall not abuse of your generosity.

I have now nothing more to add than the assurance of my ever remaining [etc.]. (48525)

1811   SIR WILLIAM HOWE *to the* KING

[*Office of Ordnance, 29 Aug. 1798.*] Lieutenant Robison [*sic*] of the Royal Regiment of Artillery having, from the effect of a scrophulous complaint in his face, been unfortunately so disfigured as to be rendered totally incapable of appearing in public; either in the exercise of his duty as an officer, or in that of any other profession or pursuit, by which he may obtain a livelihood, the Lieutenant-General of the Ordnance begs leave to submit this case to his Majesty, and to propose, that his Majesty may be graciously pleased to approve of Lieutenant Robison being allowed a pension, equal to four shillings a day, to be paid from the Department of the Ordnance. (8978)

1812   THE DUKE OF PORTLAND *to the* KING

[*Burlington House, Wednesday, 29 Aug. 1798, 6.30 p.m.*] The Duke of Portland begs leave in consequence of the Duke of Roxburghe's particular request most humbly to lay before your Majesty the enclosed letter[1] addressed to your Majesty.

The Duke of Portland feels that he must not omit this opportunity of requesting your Majesty's indulgence for permitting him to absent himself from his attendance on your Majesty for the space of three weeks or a month which he understands will be the time requisite for his recovery from the fracture of a rib which he was so unlucky as to experience yesterday & which prevented his paying his duty to your Majesty today at St James's.[2] (8979)

1813   HENRY DUNDAS *to the* KING

[*Edinburgh,*[3] *29 Aug. 1798.*] Mr Dundas takes the liberty of conveying to your Majesty a letter he has received from Mr Livingstone, as the only means of bringing under your Majesty's view the particulars it contains.

Mr Dundas cannot omit taking this opportunity of giving to your Majesty the satisfaction of knowing that the change on the dispositions and feelings of the people in this part of the kingdom is scarcely to be conceived. There is a universal sentiment of zeal and loyalty, and a growing aversion to everything connected with the revolutionary principles and practices of France. Mr Dundas would not speak so decisively from his own observation of only two days he has been here, but from the many persons of different descriptions with whom he has conversed he has no doubt of the justice and truth of his representation. (8980–1)

1814   LORD GRENVILLE *to the* KING, *and the reply*

[*Cleveland Row, 29 Aug. 1798.*] Lord Grenville omitted to mention to your Majesty today the letters which he received this morning by direction of poor Baron de Kutzleben who died last night. (8977)

[*The King's reply, Windsor, 30 Aug. 1798, 6.25 a.m.*] The two letters Lord Grenville has transmitted to me from the late Baron Kurtzleben [*sic*] are in German, the first dated Oct. 21st 1797, wherein he mentions that he feels his distresses of mind will soon end his days, and recommending his three children to my protection and charity. In the second dated Augt. 18th 1798 he explains himself more clearly by imploring a pension for the support of his three children, and that his two sons may be educated at the Charterhouse or any other school I may approve of; that the one is inclined to be employed hereafter in the line of foreign affairs, and the other to be placed in the Church. I leave it to Lord Grenville when he has informed himself of the case and spoke to Mr. Pitt to make such proposition as the case may require to me. (Chatham Papers.)

[1] No. 1806.

[2] On his way to town from Bulstrode the Duke fell from his horse near Hounslow Barracks. He was carried in a post-chaise to Burlington House.

[3] Dundas was on holiday, his first long one for some years.

[*Worthing, 30 Aug. 1798.*] This letter will find you at Weymouth I hope safe & well after your journey.[1] I wish I could fly over to see you & to content myself in being sure you are well. My thoughts are always at Windsor & beleive me they will never quit you on Saturday nor during the whole of your stay at Weymouth. I confess I wish very sincerely I was with you. Every mile you go you are further from me, but, my dearest papa, everything is for the best & the being deprived this year of enjoying these six weeks & all the time I have been separated from you will make me feel the blessing the more of being again amongst you & on my *two* legs doing like the rest of the family. God knows how thankful I am for the kindness I meet with. Indeed the goodness & affection I have experienced from you & dear mama I shall ever feel most grateful for & do my utmost to deserve it. I always knew how much you loved me but your kindness to me is much beyond what I deserve or what I ever could have expected from you, my dear papa.

What pleasure shall I have to receive my letters from Weymouth. It is very odd that though the distance from hence is so much further than it is from Worthing to Windsor, yet the letters are the same time on the road. It is a great comfort to think they are no longer coming for I should be very sorry to be more than two days without hearing from those I love so dearly.

Not being a surjeon I can only judge by my own feelings how my knee is still the same. I must say however Mr. Keate may find things going on better though my pain is still in the same state: yes, indeed I shall be too happy to send you word that I have walked across our little room & with little or no pain.

I shall now take my leave, beging you, my dearest papa, to beleive no one can be more grateful or love you more than [&c.]. (Add. Georgian 14/12.)

1816   *Letters from the* DUKE OF PORTLAND *to the* KING

[*Burlington House, Thursday, 30 Aug. 1798, 11 a.m.*] The Duke of Portland has great satisfaction in humbly laying before your Majesty the dispatches from Ireland which arrived this morning. He has presumed to withhold the Bill to prevent rebels returning from transportation which is mentioned in different passages of Lord Castlereagh's letter to Mr Wickham, for the purpose of laying it without loss of time before your Majesty's Law servants in order to fulfill the very reasonable & just wishes of the Lord Lieutenant to be enabled to put as early a period to the Session as the actual circumstances of the country will permit. (8982)

[*Burlington House, Friday, 31 Aug., 1.50 p.m.*] The Duke of Portland has received so satisfactory an account of the state of the north of Ireland from a very intelligent well informed & zealous individual that although he has not received any official communication from that kingdom by this day's mail, he humbly conceives it to

---

[1] On Saturday, 1 September, their Majesties and the Princesses left Windsor at 5 a.m., breakfasted at Hartford Bridge, were entertained at the Bishop's Palace, Salisbury, and arrived at Gloucester Lodge soon after 5 p.m. Stationed there for their protection were two 64-gun ships, *Dictator* and *Diadem*, and the *Blonde* frigate of 32 guns.

be his duty to acquaint your Majesty that on the arrival of the news of the French having landed in the west, the yeomanry who had been discontinued for some time past, immediately reassembled in the neighbourhood of Belfast, & are now doing the garrison duty of that town, & as a proof of the loyalty & good order of that part of the country M. Genl. Nugent has sent the Fifeshire Fencibles towards Connaught. By various persons who had arrived at Belfast on that day (which was the 26th instt.) from different parts of the counties of Down & Antrim it appears that no symptom whatever of dissaffection had manifested itself in either of these counties, or in any other part of the province of Ulster. The Duke of Portland however cannot but venture with all humility to express his anxious hope that your Majesty may graciously condescend to reconsider the opinion your Majesty was pleased to signify this morning to the Duke of Portland, & in consequence of the effect which might be produced by countermanding the three regiments of Militia which the Duke of Portland thought himself authorized to notify to the Lord Lieutenant were ordered to embark for Ireland may still permit them to proceed according to that destination which from what appeared by the dispatches of yesterday would not be likely to detain them out of this kingdom for many days.

The Duke of Portland humbly requests your Majesty's permission to lay his most dutifull & gratefull thanks at your Majesty's feet for the most gracious manner in which your Majesty has condescended to express yourself upon the subject of his accident. (8983–4)

[*Burlington House, Saturday, 1 Sept., 3.40 p.m.*] It is with extreme concern that the Duke of Portland lays before your Majesty the dispatches which have arrived this morning from Ireland giving an account of another advantage which has been gained over your Majesty's troops under the command of Lt.-General Lake,[1] & of the enemy having taken possession of Tuam. With a view however to counteract as speedily as possible the bad effects of these events, such of your Majesty's confidential servants as are in town are humbly of opinion to recommend with all deference to your Majesty that such a number of Militia regiments as will amount with those already in Ireland to 12000 men, the number which your Majesty was empower'd by the Act of last Session to send to that kingdom, should be orderd to prepare themselves to embark for it without loss of time, & the pressure of the occasion appeared to be so urgent that your Majesty's servants have felt it to be their indispensable duty to presume to give such directions as are necessary for the immediate conveyance of that number of your Majesty's Militia forces from those ports which consistently with their present stations are most commodious for their arriving at the different places of destination specified in the Lord Lieutenant's dispatch from Kilbeggan. (8989–90)

---

[1] This was the action known as the 'Castlebar Races', the Galway Volunteers and the Kilkenny and Longford Militia running away on the appearance of the French. As Edward Cooke said, there was disaffection in these Regiments, and there were many United Irishmen among them. (*Cornwallis Corresp.*, II, 394–5.)

[*Vienna, 1 Sept. 1798.*] I have received by Mr Arbuthnot the honor of your Majesty's most gracious letter; by the long acquaintance I have had of that gentle-man I have no doubt of his Royal Highness Prince Augustus having made a valuable acquisition.

I want words to express my respectful gratitude to your Majesty for having been graciously pleased to have sent me Mr Arbuthnot for an assistant. I have also received by Mr Arbuthnot a letter from Lord Grenville informing me that he had got your Majesty's commands to let me know that you had been graciously pleased to fix the different sums for the Prince's pocket money, for his Royal Highness attendants, and for the support of his Household; your Majesty has made so ample an allowance, I think it impossible any more debts can be contracted, the Prince has assured me in a very sober manner that he is determined to regulate his conduct to your Majesty's satisfaction: in my department your Majesty may depend on the greatest attention being paid to genteel œconomy and regularity in the management of the Prince's Household.

As your Majesty has been graciously pleased to command me to augment Doctor Domier's allowance, as he sits at his Royal Highness table, and allways admitted into the Prince's society he must be genteely dress'd, and by his constant attendance on the Prince and careful attention to his health, he cannot have much practice without doors, therefore if your Majesty approves it, I propose giving him 300 a year, but shall not mention it to the Doctor til I receive your Majesty's commands.

I had yesterday the honor of a long conversation with the Prince on the subject of your Majesty's letter to me, and on your paternal affection in wishing to have his Royal Highness removed before winter to as mild a climate as the critical state of Europe may permit with safety, and that your Majesty had mentioned Astracan, or some other of the southern provinces of Russia. I have taken the liberty to propose to the Prince to leave Vienna as soon as the carriages can be put in good repair for a long journey, to go from this to Dresden, to remain there as long as necessary to see everything worth the attention of a traveller, and to pay our respects to the Elector &c. Then to proceed to Berlin; after a short stay there, his Royal Highness and the Doctor will be able to determine how far it may be prudent, or the Prince's health permit our undertaking in October and Novr. the journey to Petersburg: if his Royal Highness health dont permit travelling so far at that season, we may proceed to Breslau in Silesia, or to Warsaw, both large citys, and very good society, where the Prince may stop for a few months, in winter, and proceed early in the spring to Petersburg. So far as I have been able to judge after so short a tryal, I think keeping the Prince moving, and not allowing his Royal Highness to remain very long in the same place may be of great service, and wear off habits contracted in Italy, I wish the Prince at a very great distance from that country, and as much as possible to give up all correspondence with the society he left in that country, that can only be done by carrying him at a very great distance; the journey proposed may be very interesting, and give the Prince a just notion of the Courts and constitution of the northern countrys. I intend writing to your Majesty's Minister at Petersburg to send me the Emperor's passports for his Royal Highness and his attendants, without them no foreigner can enter the Russian dominions. It also may be necessary that your Majesty give your orders to Lord Grenville to inform Sir Charles Whitworth that you intend that Prince Augustus shall be some time in Russia and he will take the proper method to inform the Emperor. I will take all the necessary precaution that the Prince be received in the different countrys we may go to, with the attention and respect due to his high rank.

I have the satisfaction to assure your Majesty that the Prince is at present in good health and I hope with prudence may continue so. As his Royal Highness will be near Brunswick when at Berlin he certainly will be invited to visit his aunt. When I had the honor to pay my respects there, her Royal Highness and the Duke express'd a great desire to see the Prince Augustus. If your Majesty allows his Royal Highness to go to Brunswick for a short time, I hope you may be graciously pleased to allow Prince Adolphus to come for a few days to see his brother; he will give Prince Augustus good advice. His letters to his brother are admirable and full of fine and delicate sentiments.

Prince Frederick of Orange is now here. I have done everything in my power to have him as much as possible with Prince Augustus. He is a charming young man, modest, brave and generous, an excellent officer, very much respected and in very high estimation with the Emperor and the whole army. If he lives he certainly will be soon at the head of his profession.

I beg your Majesty may be graciously pleased to order your commands for me to be sent to Berlin. (8985–8)

1818 PRINCE EDWARD *to the* KING

[*Halifax, Nova Scotia, 1 Sept. 1798.*] With humble submission I beg leave to trespass upon your Majesty's indulgence for a few moments, although, not having as yet been honoured with your commands in consequence of the application I took the liberty of laying before you in my letter of the 23d of April last, I perhaps ought not so soon again to trouble you respecting myself. But my present situation compels me to it, and when you have perused these lines, I flatter myself you will consider them as a sufficient excuse for this intrusion. On the 8th of last month, when returning on horseback to a house of Sir John Wentworth[1] in the country, where I reside during the summer months after having completed the duties of the day, my horse unfortunately broke through a small wooden bridge which covered one of the drains in the town, and we fell together with extreme violence, owing to the speed with which I was then going. I found myself completely under the animal, his whole weight resting upon my left thigh, and pressing it upon a heap of stones, that were piled up in a dry ditch into which he had rolled with me. Providentially I had no bones broke, and notwithstanding the violence of the pain I felt from the contusion occasioned by this accident, being unwilling to give way to it, I treated it at first with no more attention than is generally given to a common

---

[1] Lieutenant-Governor of Nova Scotia, 1792–1808. Baronetcy, 1795. (1737?–1820.)

bruise, and although rendered very lame and stiff I exerted myself so far as to neglect no part of my duty until the 13th. After that, however, finding that although the blackness of the bruises wore off, the numbness and swelling of the thigh still continued, I thought it necessary to take the advice of a surgeon. He recommended strongly rest, and the use of some medicinal applications usual in those cases. Notwithstanding my repugnance to a life of inactivity, I submitted to his injunction of remaining within doors for several days, when, after fair trial given, finding not the least alteration for the better, at the advice of the Governor and my friends in general, Mr. Halliburton, Surgeon to the Naval Hospital, who is considered by far the best and first man of that profession here, was called in, and by his direction for five successive days I suffered my thigh to be bound up with a very strong charge of wormwood, vinegar, and other powerful drugs, which however failed also of the desired effect, having only caused extreme inflammation, and excoriation without affording the least relief. On seeing this, Mr. Halliburton judged from the appearance of the limb at that time, that it was probable a considerable period would elapse before the injury could be removed, and intimating, should an operation eventually become necessary, he should be backward to perform it in this country, he gave it as his decided opinion that as the first advice could only be procured in England, I ought immediately to make application to Admiral Vandeput[1] for one of your Majesty's ships to convey me home. But the fear of incurring your displeasure by taking this step without first procuring your approbation, added to the apprehension that, if I recovered the free use of my limb on the passage, (which the surgeons thought, would, from the rest and quiet in which passengers on board of ship generally remain, be more likely to take place under those circumstances than in any other situation) it might be suggested that I was endeavouring to impose upon you, and, if I may presume to say so, the distant hope that the July mail would have brought me your gracious permission to visit England, made me at once determine not to follow that counsel, however good it might be, until a more distant period. The Packet arrived on the 24th ultimo, but no commands from you being communicated by it, the stiffness, and swelling of my thigh still continuing stationary, and the surgeon pressing me not to defer following his advice until it might perhaps be too late to counteract a confirmed blemish for life, I have at length determined, (twenty four days having now elapsed since the accident happened,) to make one effort more before I would comply with his repeated counsel, by endeavouring to obtain the best advice that can be procured in your Majesty's dominions in North America, and therefore to send to Quebec to sollicit General Prescott[2] to permit Doctor Nooth, the Inspector-General of Hospitals, who is considered as the most respectable medical man on this Continent, to come immediately to me from thence. For this purpose Captain Hale, one of the Gentlemen of my family, sails this day for that place, and I flatter myself within four weeks, I shall be acquainted with the Doctor's opinion

[1] George Vandeput (d. 1800). Lieutenant, 1759; Captain, 1765; Rear-Admiral, 1793; Vice-Admiral 1794; Admiral, 1799.
[2] Robert Prescott (d. 1815). Major-General, 1781; Lieutenant-General, 1793; General, 1798. Governor of Martinique, 1794; Governor of Canada, 1796–9.

upon my case, when, if *he* coincides in the sentiments of Mr. Halliburton, I trust your Majesty will have the goodness, and the indulgence to approve of my *then* taking advantage of General Prescott's permission, (which I have sollicited) to give up my command into the hands of Brigadier-General Murray,[1] and to proceed to England. But you may rest assured, that, *in that event only*, shall I presume to take the liberty of approaching you, until it is by your own command. The anxiety I have shewn to leave nothing untried before I take the step which is so strongly pressed by Mr. Halliburton, and of which, everyone who knows me here, can bear testimony, will, I hope, justify me, in your Majesty's opinion, should I find myself at length obliged to adopt it.

Least you should form an opinion of my state different from what it exactly is, I beg leave further to state, that the pain I at present suffer, is inconsiderable, nor does it arise, except when I am obliged to exert the limb to its utmost, or when I move from a posture in which I have remained for some time. I *can* walk without the assistance of a stick, but with great stiffness and weakness in the limb, and though I am able, if I force myself to it, to bring the heel to the ground, I feel an unaccountable repugnance to do so, when I move naturally, without paying particular attention to the motion of my leg. The upper part of the thigh still continues in the same condition as to swelling and numbness in which it was the third day. I do not myself apprehend so much a confirmed lameness, as that the limb will retain for a length of time, even if the tumor should dissipate shortly, a considerable degree of weakness, which will render it subject to be constantly affected with rheumatism, a complaint almost universal in this province, from the very sudden changes of climate.

I must now again sollicit your Majesty's utmost indulgence for having so long trespassed on your patience to speak only of myself; but conscious that I have no object on earth so much at heart as that my conduct should appear to you clear and correct, I feel the utmost anxiety that you should be convinced of it, and I humbly hope that the statement I have made of my situation will insure me your forgiveness should I be compelled to go home on account of my lameness; or should I so far recover as to render that step unnecessary, that my conduct on this occasion will impress your mind with the conviction that to obey your will, however painful it may be in some cases to my own feelings, will ever be the first study of my life. (45940–3)

1819   THE DUKE OF YORK *to the* KING

[*Horse Guards*, 2 *Sept. 1798.*] I have the honor to report to your Majesty that in consequence of the very unpleasant accounts which were received yesterday from Ireland, I was sent for to town, where I found an official letter in your Majesty's name from the Duke of Portland which probably has been transmitted to your Majesty, but if by mistake it has not, I have the honor to subjoin a copy, directing a very considerable reinforcement to be sent without loss of time to Ireland, in

---

[1] Major-General Thomas Murray was appointed Lieutenant-Governor of Portsmouth in Feb. 1799; *vice* Lieutenant-General Cuyler, resigned.

obedience to which arrangements have been made conformable to the inclosed memorandum, which I trust will meet with your Majesty's approbation.

As there are a sufficient number of regiments of Militia under orders for Ireland to form four brigades, I have directed Major-Generals Graham and Loftus in addition to Major-General Morshead to proceed there immediately to take the command of two of them, and I beg leave to recommend to your Majesty that Major General Wemys, who is still in Ireland, may be placed upon the British Staff and ordered to take the command of the fourth Brigade.

As it will be necessary for the regiments going to Ireland to take their flank companies with them which will be infinitely too great a diminution of the force at Weymouth, I humbly propose to your Majesty that the Chester Militia which consist of above one thousand rank and file, may be ordered to Weymouth, and that the flank companies of the regiments remaining in Sir William Pitt's district may upon their arrival be ordered to join their respective batallions. (8991)

1820   THE DUKE OF PORTLAND *to the* KING

[*Burlington House, Tuesday, 4 Sept. 1798, 3 p.m.*] The Duke of Portland has the honor to lay before your Majesty the letters which arrived this morning from Ireland & a letter from Lord Castlereagh received after the departure of the mail inclosing the minute of a conversation which passed between Mr Marsden,[1] a person confidentially employed in the Chief Secretary's Office in Ireland, & the three prisoners of state who subscribed the advertisement which has so deservedly incurred your Majesty's indignation. The Duke of Portland fears your Majesty will not be more satisfied with this than with the former proceedings respecting those traitors to which the Lord Lieutenant seems to have been induced to give way from the difficulties which it had been represented to him would attend their conviction, & the great desire of restoring quiet to the country, possibly among other views with that of re-establishing the discipline of that part of your Majesty's army which is composed of the Irish Militia, whose enormous irregularities surpass all imagination. The Duke of Portland humbly ventures to acquaint your Majesty that he has had the satisfaction of seeing a letter from the north of Ireland dated the 30th of August in the evening from a very accurate & impartial observer which states that the most perfect tranquillity & good order prevail in that part of the kingdom.

As in case of any accident happening to Lord Cornwallis which should deprive him of the power of administring the Government of Ireland, its powers would cease & be suspended until your Majesty's pleasure could be signified, or, as some are disposed to imagine, if the appointment of a new Chief Governor by your Majesty should not be notified in 8 days after the decease or other cessation of the Lord Lieutenant's functions, the Privy Council would have the choice of a temporary Governor until they received the notification of your Majesty's com-

---

[1] William Marsden, Second Secretary of the Admiralty, March 1795 (an appointment he owed to Lord Spencer). Spencer, on his own resignation in 1801, advised him to remain in office. He was promoted to First Secretary, Jan. 1804, in succession to Nepean. (*d.* 6 Oct. 1836.)

mands. Your Majesty's servants, deeply impressed with the sense of the dangers of that country's falling into such a position at such a crisis as the present, consider it their duty most humbly to submit this representation to your Majesty, & with the most dutifull & respectfull deference to suggest to your Majesty as an expedient the ordering a provisional appointment of a Lord Deputy to be made out in case of any of the events which may occasion a vacancy. The peculiar circumstances of the times induce them to offer it as their most humble opinion to your Majesty that it may be more conducive to your Majesty's service that the powers of Government should be placed in one or two hands at most than in a greater number, & that confining it to one or two persons at most would be more likely to prevent such an eventual appointment, should your Majesty think proper to make it, from being unnecessarily known & speculated upon. With this view also it is farther submitted to your Majesty that Mr Pelham, whose health it is hoped is sufficiently restored to enable him to resume the duties of his employment in Ireland & respecting which the Duke of Portland has taken the means of informing himself, appears to such of your Majesty's servants as are in town to be the most worthy of being singly intrusted with so important a charge, or jointly with the Lord Chancellor of Ireland, or in case Mr Pelham should not be able to return immediately to Ireland, that the Lord Chancellor alone is well qualified to fill that station & would be better able to discharge the duties of it by himself than in conjunction with any of his countrymen.[1] (8992–4)

1821   THE DUKE OF YORK *to the* KING

[*Oatlands, 5 Sept. 1798.*] I have the honor to acknowledge the receipt of your Majesty's two most generous letters of the 2d and 3d instant, and am rejoiced to hear that your Majesties arrived safely at Weymouth.

I am very happy that your Majesty is pleased to approve of the different arrangements which have been made for sending the reinforcement to Ireland. I trust, however, that in consequence of the last intelligence from the Lord Lieutenant, it will not be judged necessary to send the whole force now under orders, at least till some account is received of the event of the attack intended to be made by Lord Cornwallis.

Directions shall be sent in obedience to your Majesty's orders to assemble all the men belonging to the corps of Sir William Pitt's district, who have not volunteered going to Ireland, at Poole Barracks, which certainly is the fittest place for them.

I have the honor to transmit the different weekly states and returns, as likewise the recommendations for vacant commissions, for your Majesty's approbation. (8995)

---

[1] On 2 Nov. 1798 Thomas Pelham informed Castlereagh that on account of the 'critical state' of his health he had declined returning to Ireland. 'I have long foreseen my inability to resume the labour.' (Castlereagh Corresp., I, 419.) Portland explained the proposal to Pelham in a letter dated the 7th (Add. MSS. 33106, f. 70.)

[*Louisbourg, 8 Sept. 1798.*] My first employment this morning must be to recall myself to your Majesty and the Queen, a day so dear and interesting to us all cannot be passed over in silence by me. I trust the Almighty will allow you to see many returns of it and that you will be convinced that none of your children can more sincerely form wishes for your Majesties health and happiness than myself, who am attached to you by every tie of duty and affection. I rejoice at the hearing that Ireland is quiet. I trust that the misfortunes of that unhappy Kingdom will open the eyes of many and make them perceive that they ought to prefer their duty to their pleasure, and reside more on their estates, which I believe would in great measure keep the minds of the lower class in order and prevent the discontent of seeing the money which they acquire with pain and trouble squandered in London. I offer your Majesty my humble congratulations at your being now easy on that subject, and hope that on the whole it will have warned the English and shew them the necessity of unanimity.

I trust that Weymouth and the sea bathing will do your Majesty good. I trembled least the multiplicity of unpleasant business would have made the boil give you some trouble, and am delighted that your Majesty has found means to go to the sea which will brace you for the winter, and enable you to go through those fatigues attached to your high situation.

I have been very uneasy about dear Amelia but think that as she can begin to get into the air she will soon mend. I am sure she is much mortified at being prevented accompanying your Majesty however from the moment she cannot enter into the life lead at Weymouth or at Windsor during the Camp, she appears to me happier at a distance as she is not then daily tantalized with hearing of parties she cannot partake off [*sic*].

Our weather is extraordinary and I believe unwholesome as one day it is quite cold and rainy and the next a burning heat; we are all very anxious for rain for the grapes which, if the weather is favourable, will be very profitable this year. (51498–9)

1823   PRINCESS AMELIA *to the* KING

[*Worthing, 8 Sept. 1798.*] As my pen is the only method I have at present of conveying my congratulations to you, my dearest papa, I must have recourse to it on this day to assure you of my sincere attachment & my fervent prayers which I trust will be heard that you & my dear mama may live to see many happy returns of the 8th. God grant every one may prove more happy & that next year I may be able to express all my best & most affte. wishes by word of mouth. My first thoughts this morng. when I woke was you & mama, but that I may say is always the case. I wished I could fly to see you today, but saying my attachment is stronger one day than another is impossible, for be assured no one can possibly love you, my dear papa, better than I do, or feel more grateful for having such a father than myself. Indeed it is in vain my attempting to describe what my feelings are on this subject & were I to say ever so much it could never express all my heart could wish to say.

Your kind letter, my dearest papa, made me truly happy, & I am very grateful for the affte. expressions you make use of about me, & you may imagine your kindness does not make me a little happy. You are very good in saying you want me at Weymouth. I should be truly happy to be amongst you but I look for better times & comfort myself with the thoughts that when we next meet I shall be well & the blessing of being recovered & once more with you will amply reward me for my long confinement.

Though I do not feel any material amendment in my knee, Mr. Keate's finding it going on well, affords me great comfort. He left us yesterday to go to poor Lady Chesterfield: his nephew, who is very gentle, attends me you know. He seems very desirous of doing everything that is proper & will write every day to his uncle.

I go into a warm sea bath every other night, which seems to agree very well.

I can assure you that General Goldsworthy is very well; he appears to be made extremely happy in the continuance of Mrs. Buxton's[1] recollection. I am ashamed of having trespassed so long on your time but trust on your usual goodness to forgive it as the intercoursing with you, though it is but with my pen, gives me great & real satisfaction. I shall now take my leave, beging [sic] of you, my dearest papa, to be convinced of the eternal & unalterable attachment of your dutiful & affte. child. (Add. Georgian 14/14.)

1824   THE DUKE OF PORTLAND *to the* KING

[*Burlington House, Sunday, 9 Sept. 1798, 3 p.m.*] The Duke of Portland most humbly begs leave to acquaint your Majesty, in addition to the dispatches which he now most dutifully submits to your Majesty, that he has signified your Majesty's gracious intentions to Mr Pelham, & is desired by him to lay him most humbly at your Majesty's feet, to assure your Majesty of his implicit obedience to the commands your Majesty has been pleased to lay upon him, & to express to your Majesty his most gratefull sense of this distinguished mark of your Majesty's approbation & favor. The Duke of Portland has therefore directed the Commission to be prepared by which the Earl of Clare & Mr Pelham are to be provisionally appointed Lords Deputies, & it is now under the consideration of the Sollicitor-General, who will have it prepared with all the dispatch which the secrecy he has been instructed to observe will permit.[2]

The Duke of Portland presumes to lay before your Majesty a copy of the Report from the Committee of Secrecy of the House of Lords of Ireland which is alluded to in Lord Castlereagh's dispatch private, & which is now officially transmitted for the first time. (8996–7)

[1] Perhaps the Mrs Buxton whom the Queen and Princesses visited whilst at Weymouth on 6 September. Belle Vue was her seat.
[2] By the beginning of October Pelham's long illness seemed to have run its course, and he announced his intention of returning to Ireland as Chief Secretary. He suggested that Castlereagh, who had been deputising for him, should be appointed Irish Chancellor of the Exchequer, but William Elliot told Pelham on 4 Oct. that Castlereagh 'feels considerable reluctance to the arrangement from personal feelings towards Parnell' (Sir John Parnell was then the holder of that office). [Add. MSS. 33106, f. 94.) Parnell was to be compensated with Castlereagh's office of Keeper of the Signet and also a peerage.

[*Horse Guards, 12 Sept. 1798.*] I have the honor to lay before your Majesty for your approbation the recommendations for the vacant commissions which have been received this week, as likewise the weekly states and returns.

I also add a return of the effective strength of such of the regiments of Militia and Fencibles as are embarked for Ireland and who have sent up their returns together with the number of men of each regiment who have refused to go. Nothing can have exceeded the spirit and loyalty which has been shewn by every one of them, except the East Suffolk Militia and the West Lowland Fencibles; only one hunderd and twenty three men of the East Suffolk turned out to go to Ireland though the whole regiment had upon the former occasion volunteered their services. I therefore thought it right to countermand their march immediately, which I trust will meet with your Majesty's approbation. Not above forty men of the West Lowland Fencibles also offered to go to Ireland, in spite of every effort of Lord Eglintoun[1] their Colonel. Sir Ralph Abercrombie has therefore immediately ordered the regiment from Glasgow to Edinburgh in order to have them under his own eye as he says that he can have no confidence in them.

The Duke of Portland has communicated to me a dispatch from the Lord Lieutenant of Ireland proposing to augment the English Fencible Cavalry in Ireland to fifty five rank and file pr troop, and desiring that they may be allowed to recruit for this augmentation in Great Britain, as these corps have been raised in Great Britain, and as it is of the most essential consequence that these corps should not be polluted, I should humbly suppose that your Majesty will be graciously pleased to consent to the Lord Lieutenant's request.

Understanding that it will be necessary for your Majesty to hold a Council about the latter end of next week to pass the Irish Bills, and that there is a difficulty in finding Councillors, I will beg leave to pay my duty to your Majesty at that time at Weymouth for a few days.

I cannot conclude without congratulating your Majesty most sincerely upon the accounts received this day of everything being happily terminated in Ireland. I confess I am particularly happy that it is to Lieutenant-General Lake that the enemy has surrendered. (8998–9)

1826   WILLIAM PITT *to the* KING

[*Downing Street, Thursday, 13 Sept. 1798.*] Mr. Pitt humbly begs leave to submit to your Majesty a warrant for the appointment of Mr. Hunt to the Transport Office in order to bring Mr. Marsh,[2] whom he succeeds, to the Victualling Office, where his services are thought likely to be particularly useful; also another warrant for an advance to Genl. Gardner (to be hereafter gradually repaid out of his pension) to enable him to quit Warsaw, and some other Treasury warrants in the usual course. (9002)

[1] Hugh, 12th Earl of Eglintoun (1739–1819), a Scottish Representative Peer, 1798–1806. Created Baron Ardrossan [U.K.], 15 Feb. 1806.

[2] John Marsh, a Commissioner of the Transport Office (salary, £1,000 a year).

[*Cleveland Row, 13 Sept. 1798.*] Lord Grenville having seen in Mr Shepherd's[1] dispatches the account of Count Rumford's[2] nomination to reside in this kingdom, with the character of Minister from the Elector of Bavaria[3] to your Majesty, and of his having actually set out to take upon him this Mission, humbly begs leave to submit to your Majesty whether under all the circumstances of Count Rumford's character, it may not be proper that Mr Paget should be instructed to inform the Elector that this nomination is not agreable to your Majesty. Lord Grenville thinks that this may be put simply on the ground of Count Rumford being your Majesty's subject, & in that respect not proper to be accredited to your Majesty as a foreign Minister, without entering into any further particulars.

If your Majesty should approve this idea, instructions might be sent to Sir James Craufurd to signify to Count Rumford on his arrival at Hamburgh, that a notification to this effect is to be made at Munich, and that he should therefore not proceed to London to take upon him a character in which he cannot be received. (9000–1)

[*The King's reply, Weymouth, 14 Sept., 4 p.m.*] On reading Mr. Shepherd's dispatch on the nomination of Count Rumford to reside here as Minister from the Elector of Bavaria, I should have expressed the propriety of refusing the receiving him as such, had I not been certain that Lord Grenville would see it in the same light and consequently suggest the proper mode of having this nomination recalled; I think the method proposed highly proper but in addition to his having been a British subject till the separation from America, may be added his having been Under-Secretary in the American Office. (Fortescue MSS.)

1828   THE DUKE OF PORTLAND *to the* KING

[*Burlington House, Friday, 14 Sept. 1798.*] The Duke of Portland has the satisfaction of laying with all humility before your Majesty the details of the action which he trusts have not only annihilated but will prevent any future attempt at an invasion of your Majesty's kingdom of Ireland.[4] He also begs leave with the utmost deference to your Majesty's superior wisdom to submit to your Majesty the propriety of ordering the Lord Lieutenant to strike out of the list of the Privy Councillors of that kingdom the name of Mr Grattan in case he shall not within a reasonable time take some means of exculpating himself from the charge of misprision of treason[5] in which it appears by the evidence of Neilson[6] & Hughes,

[1] Richard Shepherd. In charge of affairs at Munich, 1794–8, during the absence of Thomas Walpole, the Minister.

[2] Sir Benjamin Thompson, Count von Rumford (1753–1814). Born in Massachusetts. Under-Secretary of State for the Colonies, 1780. In the service of the Elector of Bavaria, 1784–95; made Count von Rumford, and knighted, 1784.

[3] Charles Theodore (1724–99), Elector Palatine, 1742, Elector of Bavaria, 1777.

[4] Writing from his camp near St Johnstown on 8 Sept., Cornwallis informed the Duke that the French had surrendered. (*Cornwallis Corresp.*, II, 402–3.)   [5] That is, concealment of treason.

[6] Samuel Neilson (1761–1803), the son of a Belfast Presbyterian Minister. As a United Irishman he had been in prison before the rebellion, and had been released on bail early in 1798, but in violation of his promise never again to join in treasonable activities he connected himself with Lord Edward Fitzgerald, with the result that he was again arrested and arraigned. He died in America.

given upon oath to the Committee of Secrecy of the House of Lords, that he is so deeply implicated.[1] The Duke of Portland does not mean in submitting this proposal to your Majesty to prevent a prosecution being instituted against Mr Grattan for this crime if it shall appear to your Majesty's Law servants in that country that there is sufficient evidence to convict him of it in a course [*sic*] of law,[2] & still less to prejudice him in the opinion of a jury by removing him from the Privy Council if there is ground to proceed against him by the usual forms of law—but as your Majesty's servants here entertain strong doubts of the probability of ground being found for such a proceeding & are yet not less satisfied of the reality & extent of Mr Grattan's guilt, the Duke of Portland feels it to be his duty to represent the case to your Majesty & humbly to request your Majesty's commands respecting it. (9003–4)

1829 LORD CHARLES HENRY SOMERSET *to the* KING

[*Weymouth, Sunday, 16 Sept. 1798.*] Having nothing to offer to your Majesty in excuse, I shall not attempt to apologize for this intrusion, but trust to your Majesty's well known goodness to forgive it.

Some (*very kind*) words which your Majesty condescended to say to me, 'That you hoped Lord Botetourt's estate was not entailed further than on my father'[3] could not fail to make a deep impression on one whose wife and family[4] are so totally unprovided for as to be reduc'd to *beggary* in the event of his death, and those words could not also fail to impress with greater force as they came from one whom I am bound by nature to revere as my Sovereign, and by every tie that can bind the human mind to adore as an example to mankind, in virtue and excellence, as a husband, father, friend and as my own patron in particular. Having said that this kind expression made this impression on my mind, I now venture to say to your Majesty that it is in your power and in yours alone, to effect this kind wish, and at the same time that you bestow a lasting blessing on me and my poor children, I will venture to affirm that you will add also an obligation on my father that he will consider greater than any that can be conferr'd on him. I dare not proceed; I fear I have already undone myself with your Majesty for my presumption and insolence. Ah, give it not, my gracious Liege, such harsh epithets; think that a father pleads for four unprovided children and forgive my boldness.

[1] An informer named John Hughes told the Secret Committee of the Irish House of Lords which was investigating the activities of the rebels that Grattan had been sworn in as a United Irishman by Neilson. This was untrue.
[2] The Irish Law Officers decided that a prosecution would fail. 'No jury would convict him on the evidence of Hughes, contradicted as he already has been in parts of his evidence by Neilson.' So Cornwallis reported to Portland on 24 Sept. But the publication of Hughes's evidence, and the admitted fact that some leading United Irishmen had visited Grattan at his home, convinced many Irishmen that the allegations were true. The King ordered the Lord Lieutenant to strike Grattan's name from the list of Irish Privy Councillors, and this was done on 6 Oct. (*Cornwallis Corresp.*, II, 417.)
[3] Lord Charles Somerset's father was the 5th Duke of Beaufort (1744–1803), who married, 2 April 1766, Elizabeth (1747–1828), sister of the 3rd Viscount Falmouth. On 4 June 1803 the Duke obtained, by patent, a declaration of the termination in his favour of the abeyance of the Barony of Botetourt, to which, *jure matris*, he was one of the co-heirs. See Nos. 1831, 2489.
[4] Lord Charles married, June 1788, Elizabeth (*d.* 1815), daughter of William, 2nd Viscount Courtenay, by whom he had three sons and three daughters. Two of the three sons were born after the date of this letter.

When I am assur'd your Majesty has forgiven (which I humbly implore) my having gone thus far, and when I have your free permission (which I scarcely dare hope) to explain how it is in your Majesty's power so effectually to serve me and mine, I will explain it: till then permit me to acknowledge myself with the sincerest gratitude most truly thankful for the many great favors I have already experienc'd from your Majesty and to subscribe myself [&c.]. (9005–6)

1830 CAPTAIN C. BASSETT JONES[1] *to the* KING, *with an enclosure*

[*Beaver, off St. Albans, 16 Sept. 1798.*] Hearing your Majesty was at Weymouth by Lieutenant Shepherd of the Pigmy cutter, and judging that it might be interesting, I have just time to enclose your Majesty a copy of a letter I wrote this morning to my Lords Commissioners of the Admiralty, which I conceive it my duty to inform my Leige.

General Pichegreu[2] and six exiled members are on board Captain Lobb[3] of his Majesty's ship L'Amiable. Having a valuable convoy, I trust your Majesty will excuse my haste. (9007)

[*Enclosure*]:

CAPTAIN C. BASSETT JONES *to the* ADMIRALTY (*Copy*)

[*His Majesty's Sloop Beaver, 16 Sept. 1798.*] I have the honor to inform you for their Lordships' information of the safe arrival of his Majesty's Sloop Beaver under

---

[1] Christopher Bassett Jones. Lieutenant, 1783; Commander, 27 June 1798. He signed himself as Commander of H.M.'s sloop *Beaver*.

[2] Charles Pichegru (1761–1804), the French General, who was arrested in Sept. 1797 for his Bourbon intrigues, and deported to Cayenne. He contrived to escape and was captured at sea by the *John Bull* and brought to England. Canning dined with him shortly afterwards. 'I like him of all conquerors that I ever saw by far the best. Simple, modest, wholly unlike a Frenchman, talking in a quiet, narrative style. And then, poor fellow, he had an ague upon him, and when one thought of him entering Holland in triumph, when one thought of his campaigns on the Rhine and of his election to the Presidency of the Councils some fifteen months ago by the unanimous voice of all France, and of the hopes which that election had raised of a speedy overthrow of the Directory, and then saw him after a ten months' sojourn at Cayenne, chattering his teeth with a shivering ague-fit by Wickham's fire in his little room in Duke Street, Westminster, it gave one a sort of sensation such as one had never experienced in reality before ...He is so much the greatest man that their Revolution has produced! His *victories* are of themselves *something*. But then recollect his refusal to execute the Decree against the British and Hanoverian prisoners—his respect for private property, and his protection of persons in Holland—recollect the single act of throwing into the fire all the covers of a bag full of letters which were seized upon a messenger coming from England to The Hague, and thereby saving all the persons to whom they were addressed from confiscation and death—recollect too that he did not make one farthing, whereas every other General employed in the Revolution has amassed enormous wealth—that while his subaltern Generals were living in splendour on requisitions throughout the conquered countries, he was always to be found in the smallest house or in the meanest room with his one or two Aide-de-camps and the dinner of the mess—it was impossible not to recollect all this and to wish that we may treat him well. There are shabbinesses about that would fain prevent it...He is going into the country to a quiet little town, and I hope Wickham will let nobody know where, and then he cannot be molested, and if forgotten, so much the better for the present, tho' the time may come when he may be a great card in our hands.' (Harewood MSS.) Finally, Canning wrote on 7 May 1800: 'What should you have said in the year '94 or 5, when Pichegru was conquering Holland, if anyone had prophesy'd that in the year 1800 I should receive a letter from him congratulating me on my marriage?' (Harewood MSS.)

[3] William Granville Lobb. Lieutenant, 1777; Captain, 1795.

my command with part of the Leeward Island convoy which sailed from Tortola on the 31st of July under the charge of Captain Lobb of his Majesty's Ship L'Aimaible, from whom we parted company on the 25th of last month in latitude 39° 05 N., longitude 39° 4 W., having been ordered by him to attend his Majesty's armed storeship L'Etrusco (at that period in the utmost distress) distant from the convoy about six leagues SW at sunsett that evening. I have the satisfaction to inform their Lordships that during a short interval between two violent gales I had just time to save the lives of all the officers and crew of the said ship, the further particulars of which I must refer their Lordships to Captain Reynolds' letter of this day's date.

Having made sail to join the convoy on the 28th of August, being moderate in latitude 41° 00 N., longitude 31° 54 W. I lay too all day to collect such of them as were near me, which amounted to the number as pr. enclosed list.

On the 11th instant, being in latitude 49° 20 N., longitude 14° 00 W. I spoke the whole of them and order'd the ships bound up the North Channel not to part, that I should see them safe into Falmouth w[h]were they would get a coasting convoy, but a gale at NW. came on early on that evening and they all hauled up W by N, disobeying my signals, and we parted company. I am sorry to add that it is very probably some of the convoy were totally lost in the second gale; several of them were in great distress and the weather too bad to afford them assistance. His Majesty's sloop, although not a fast sailer, proves uncommonly easy and a good sea boat. The enclosed lists I have the honor to send for their Lordship's inspection. (9008)

1831 LORD CHARLES HENRY SOMERSET *to the* KING

[*Weymouth, Monday, 17 Sept. 1798.*] That your Majesty should receive my letter without displeasure was all I could hope, but that you should add to my most sanguine hopes the kind expressions you condescended to use towards me fills me with a gratitude I am totally unable to express. Receive, Sire, I beg, the humble, the unfeigned thanks of an heart overcome by your goodness, overwhelm'd by your bounty.

Still dare I scarcely explain what I have requested your Majesty's leave to do, but encouraged by your all-prevailing goodness, I venture to say that the only method by which I can succeed to what your Majesty so kindly hinted to me, is that my grandmother's[1] Barony (of Bottetourt) should descend to me at her death.

I scarcely know what to add. After the kindness with which your Majesty treated my letter yesterday I ought not to dread your displeasure, and yet, when I reflect on my own unworthiness and the little claim I have to your Majesty's favor, I can hardly hope for forgiveness for such presumption. I should be tempted to offer to your Majesty some assurances of my attachment, but that the blackest ingratitude must characterize me did I not already feel myself bound to sacrifice not only life but everything more dear for my Sovereign's welfare. (9009)

[1] The 4th Duke of Beaufort (1709–56) married, 1 May 1740, Elizabeth, sister and heiress of Norborne, Lord Botetourt (*d.* 1770). She died, 8 April 1799, aged 80.

[*Burlington House, Wednesday, 19 Sept. 1798.*] The Duke of Portland most humbly begs leave to acquaint your Majesty that twenty two Bills have been transmitted from Ireland for your Majesty's signature & are now before the Attorney-General, but as the Lord Lieutenant informs the Duke of Portland that the remainder of those which are intended to pass this Session will be ready in a few days, the Duke of Portland humbly presumes that your Majesty will prefer being attended with them all at the same time & that they may be ready in the course of next week if it shall be your Majesty's pleasure to order a Council to be held at Weymouth for the purpose of signing them. (9010)

1833   THE DUKE OF YORK *to the* KING

[*Horse Guards, 19 Sept. 1798.*] I beg to return your Majesty my most humble thanks for your gracious permission to pay my duty to your Majesty at Weymouth and mean to have that honor next Monday.

I accept with many thanks of Mrs Stuart's obliging offer to lodge at her house[1] as I did during the lifetime of her late husband.

I am exceedingly happy to hear that your Majesty is pleased with the appearance of the 3d Dragoon Guards. I have always thought Colonel Payne one of our most promising officers of Cavalry and had no doubt of his bringing that regiment into order.

In obedience to your Majesty's orders contained in your letter of last week, I sent directions to Major-General Nicolls[2] at Liverpool to stop the sailing till further orders of such of the regiments of Militia as had not as yet proceeded to Ireland, but every one of them had already sailed.

I have the honor to transmit the weekly states and returns, as likewise the recommendations for the vacant Commissions, for your Majesty's approbation. (9011)

1834   EARL SPENCER *to the* KING

[*N[orth] Creek, 20 Sept. 1798.*] Earl Spencer has the honour of laying before your Majesty the proceedings and sentence of a court martial on 25 men belonging to the Defiance for a traitorous & mutinous conspiracy to murder their officers & carry the ship over to the enemy. Earl Spencer is much concerned to be obliged to state to your Majesty that on an attentive perusal of the Minutes he cannot see any ground for extending the recommendation to your Majesty's mercy farther than the Court have done in their sentence; and he therefore humbly submits to your Majesty that the eleven men following, viz: John Brady, William Lindsay, David Reed, Thomas Darbyshire, Nicholas Ryan, Cornelius Callaghan, Richard Kennedy, Thomas Laffin, Edward Swinney, Michael Kelly and Edward Mac-

---

[1] At Weymouth. Steward is the correct spelling.
[2] Oliver Nicolls (*c.* 1742–1829). Lieutenant, 1760; Major, 1781; Lieutenant-Colonel, 1787; Colonel, 1794; Major-General, 1796; Lieutenant-General, 1803; General, 1813.

laughlin should be ordered for execution; and that the eight following, viz: John Hopkins, Christopher Mabane, Terence Dunn, Thomas Jourdain, James Cannon, Patrick Devay, Peter McGuire and John Hoare should receive your Majesty's most gracious pardon on condition of their being transported for life to Botany Bay.

Your Majesty will perceive by the date of this note that Earl Spencer has availed himself of your Majesty's permission to reside for a few days in the country; but as all the necessary arrangements had been settled previous to his departure, he trusts that your Majesty's service will not suffer by his absence.[1] (9013–4)

1835   THE DUCHESS OF WURTEMBERG *to the* KING

[*Louisbourg, 21 Sept. 1798.*] I have many thanks to return your Majesty for your gracious letter of the 4 of September. I rejoice very much at your being at Weymouth and hope the bathing will have its usual good effect. After all the fatigues your Majesty has undergone this summer I should think it doubly necessary as a preparation for the winter. Ours will now begin very soon as about the 15th of October we shall return to Stutgard, which is very necessary on account of the fires, as having several additional people with us in the country who do not reside in the Palace in town, the expence would be much encreased were we to remain here longer. This is very right, as in times like the present one cannot be sufficiently careful of all one's actions. I shall however leave the country with great regret as I lead a most comfortable quiet life and have the opportunity of taking beautiful walks. I have done wonders as I have taught all the ladies to walk four or five miles at a time. At Stutgard I shall keep up my exercise, though not so pleasantly, as there is only three walks which it is possible to take near the town, and if it rains two are impassable. I hope that early in the spring we shall come back to Louisbourg.

Your Majesty is very gracious to mention dear little Lady Mary Paulet. She must be much improved since I had the pleasure of seeing her and I am very much pleased that she has not forgotten me.

I have taken the liberty to send your Majesty a print painted in oils which was brought me the other day by a great print seller from Manheim. He had many to dispose of, but this being the best in my opinion I bought it, flattering myself that you would do me the honour to accept of it and place it in your collection.

The Duke begs that I will present his humble duty to your Majesty. Now that hunting has begun he takes an amazing deal of exercise, but his arm continues pretty much the same. (51500–1)

1836   THE DUKE OF PORTLAND *to the* KING

[*Burlington House, Friday, 21 Sept. 1798, 3 p.m.*] In obedience to your Majesty's commands the Duke of Portland most humbly begs leave to submit to your Majesty that as there is the best reason to beleive from the postscript of a private

---

[1] Lord Spencer had gone to Norfolk on a shooting excursion. Lady Spencer went to Brighton during his absence. See No. 1838 for the reply.

letter from Lord Castlereagh to Mr Wickham that the rest of the Bills to be passed this Session will be transmitted from Dublin in the course of this day & that they may be ready for your Majesty's royal signature on Friday next, it is the intention of the Lord Chancellor & the Duke of Portland to be at Weymouth on that day time enough to attend your Majesty if it shall be your Majesty's pleasure to receive the Report of the Council any time in the course of it. The Duke of Portland will lose no time in obeying your Majesty's commands respecting the attendance of another Privy Councillor. (9015–6)

1837 THE DUKE OF YORK *to the* KING

[*Oatlands, 22 Sept. 1798.*] I have the honor to return your Majesty my most humble thanks for your very gracious letter, as well as for your great condescention in acquainting me with your having appointed the Council to meet at Weymouth only at the end of next week. I shall, therefore, with your Majesty's permission pay my duty to you on Wednesday next instead of Monday, having some particular business which I wish to finish.

I beg leave to congratulate your Majesty upon the intelligence received yesterday by the French papers of the total destruction of the French Fleet in the Mediterranean.[1] Though in general little confidence can be placed in what is found in those papers, yet it is hardly possible to imagine that such intelligence which if true must be so detrimental to all the French projects in Europe, would have been allowed to be published if it had not been so well ascertained that it could not be either concealed or denied. (9017)

1838 THE KING *to* EARL SPENCER, *and a reply*

[*Weymouth, 23 Sept. 1798, 4 p.m.*] I am sorry to find myself obliged to coincide entirely with Earl Spencer's opinion as to the necessity of ordering the sentence of the court martial on the 25 men belonging to the Defiance to be exactly executed, consequently that the eleven shall be hanged, and eight transported for life to Botany Bay.

In the box that brought the minutes of this court martial dispatches were communicated from Capt. Keats[2] of the Boadicea containing information of the sailing of a fleet from Brest undoubtedly for Ireland; the enemy has taken occasion of Lord Bridport's being driven into port by the equinoxious [*sic*] winds to venture out, but I hope both he and the squadron in Plymouth will have made every exertion to get out and perhaps frustrate this fresh attempt on Ireland.[3]

[1] The Battle of the Nile, 1 August.

[2] Sir Richard Goodwin Keats (1757–1834). Lieutenant, 1777; Commander, 1782; Captain, 1789; Rear-Admiral, 1807; Vice-Admiral, 1811; Admiral, 1825. K.B., 1808; G.C.B., 1815. Governor of Newfoundland, 1813–15.

[3] Keats's message was to the effect that one French ship of the line, the *Hoche*, and eight frigates, with troops on board, had sailed from Brest on the 16th. Lord Bridport at once put to sea from Torbay, but it was not until 11 October that, in bad weather, the enemy was sighted. The action took place on the 12th; the *Hoche* struck her flag, three of the frigates surrendered, and three others were soon afterwards picked up, but not before they and the other two had landed some 2,000 troops in Killala Bay. The frigates hurriedly put to sea when they sighted a British squadron making for the Bay.

I am happy to find Earl Spencer is shooting in Norfolk; if the weather is as favorable there as it is here he cannot fail of having good sport. (Althorp MSS.)

[*From Earl Spencer, Admiralty, 24 Sept.*] Your Majesty having expressed a wish that the St Fiorenzo frigate could have been ordered to attend upon your Majesty at Weymouth, which from her being in dock at the time, was impossible to be effected when your Majesty went there, Earl Spencer has now the honour of acquainting your Majesty that the St Fiorenzo has been ordered to proceed to Weymouth Roads as soon as she is ready for sea which will probably be in a very few days, and he hopes that the other ships already there, though they are not likely to sail as well as the St Fiorenzo, will however be equal to attend upon your Majesty in any excursion which you may be pleased to make.[1] (9018)

1839 THE DUKE OF PORTLAND *to the* KING

[*Bulstrode, Monday, 24 Sept. 1798.*] The Duke of Portland most humbly begs leave, in consequence of the Lord Lieutenant's request to submit to your Majesty the usual instrument for the signification of your Majesty's permission to the Lord Chancellor of Ireland to absent himself from that kingdom, & for the appointment of Commissioners of the Great Seal during his absence.[2] The Duke of Portland is not yet informed that the remainder of the Bills are yet arrived, but from the urgency with which it is pressed that the Lord Lieutenant's request for the Lord Chancellor's leave of absence should be laid before your Majesty, & the hope which is entertained by them that a period may be put to the Session on the 6th of October, the Duke of Portland flatters himself that all the Bills will be ready to be reported to your Majesty on Friday.

The Duke of Portland most humbly begs leave to offer his most anxious & earnest wishes that the expectation your Majesty condescended to express in your note of last Saturday may be fulfilled to its utmost extent. (9019–20)

1840 PRINCE EDWARD *to the* KING

[*Halifax, 26 Sept. 1798.*] Having, in my letter of the 1st of this month, intimated to your Majesty my apprehension that it was possible I should be under the necessity of proceeding home to obtain relief for the hurt I met with from a fall with my horse on the 8th of August, without having it in my power first to await your sanction, I have now the honor to inclose the certificate of Doctor Nooth, by whose advice and opinion I expressed my intention of being entirely and implicitly governed. Your Majesty will see by this that he is very pointed in his recommendation that I ought to have early recourse to the hot pump at Bath to insure a speedy and a certain cure, and above all particularly to avoid the winter of Nova Scotia. I have therefore applied to Vice-Admiral Vandeput for one of the

---

[1] The frigate, commanded by Sir Harry Burrard Neale, arrived at Weymouth on the 28th.

[2] Lord Clare sailed for England on 8 Oct. to have conversations with the Government in London about a Union of the two countries. He was convinced that only a Union would ensure the continued connection between them.

frigates of his Squadron to convey me to England, and the Topaze having been appointed by him for the purpose, it is my intention to embark about the 12th of next month, by which time I shall be able to complete all the public business in my department for the season, and to make Brigadier-General Murray fully acquainted with every detail relative to the District.

Trusting in your Majesty's justice and paternal goodness that from the peculiar circumstances under which I find myself obliged to take this step, you will not disapprove of it, I shall not presume to trespass any longer upon your indulgence at present, than humbly to intreat that you will graciously accept of those assurances of my most respectful, and dutiful attachment. (45951)

1841 LORD GRENVILLE *to the* KING, *and the reply*

[*Cleveland Row, 26 Sept. 1798, 3 p.m.*] Lord Grenville cannot transmit to your Majesty the inclosed dispatches from Sir Morton Eden & Mr Smith,[1] which seem to put the defeat of the French Fleet near Alexandria beyond all doubt, without humbly offering to your Majesty his dutiful and respectful congratulations on the fresh lustre given by this happy event to the brilliant successes of your Majesty's Navy in the course of this war.

Lord Grenville has consulted with such of your Majesty's servants as are in town, who have agreed with him in the propriety of submitting to your Majesty their humble advice in favour of the acceptance of proposals of alliance such as have been made from Naples and the Porte; and he is preparing the necessary papers to that effect, which he hopes, with your Majesty's permission, to be enabled to dispatch by Tuesday's mail. (9021–2)

[*The King's reply, Weymouth, 27 Sept., 4 p.m.*] I am very sensible of the congratulations of Lord Grenville on the news transmitted from Sir Morton Eden and Mr. Smith which seem fully to confirm the defeat of the French fleet near Alexandria, an event not only adding additional lustre to the British Navy but highly essential to the safety of the Neapolitan dominions.

The proposal of alliance with Naples and the Porte meets with my fullest concurrence. I shall therefore receive the paper Lord Grenville is preparing with great pleasure. (Fortescue MSS.)

1842 THE DUCHESS OF WURTEMBERG *to the* KING

[*Louisbourg, 27 Sept. 1798.*] I am delighted to have it in my power to offer your Majesty my humble congratulations on the noble victory of Admiral Nelson,[2]

---

[1] John Spencer Smith (1769–1845). Secretary in charge of affairs at Constantinople, 1795–8; Secretary of Legation, April 1798; given full power, jointly with his brother Sir Sidney Smith, to treat with Turkey, Sept. 1798; Secretary of Embassy at Constantinople, 1798–1801; Minister Plenipotentiary *ad int.*, 1798–1801. Special Mission to Wurtemberg, 1804. M.P. for Dover, 1802–6.

Eden was still Envoy at Vienna.

[2] Prince Adolphus's undated letter to the King probably referred to the battle in Aboukir Bay, and if this is so, the letter may well have been written towards the end of September: 'I cannot refuse myself the pleasure of profiting of this opportunity of the quarterly messenger leaving Hanover of troubling your Majesty with a few lines to present you my most humble congratulations on the late glorious

we had so often been deceived by false news that till I received the confirmation from Augustus last night from Vienna, I would not allow myself to credit what I anxiously wished to be true, I think that we cannot be sufficiently grateful to the Almighty for granting your Fleets such constant success. May your Majesty ever meet with the same signal protection you have so wonderfully had this summer in quelling the Rebellion in Ireland, taking the French troops which had landed, and destroying this immense Fleet. I wish that the example of the great mercies shewn to the English might awaken in other nations a stronger regard to their religious duties, as I am thoroughly convinced that it is owing to the sad loss of principles that we have all suffered so cruelly, and shall ever look on the odious philosophers as the beings through whom these misfortunes originated. God grant they may soon be put an end to, and that we might return to the ignorance of former centuries that we might regain our old principles.

I believe that Admiral Nelson has taken the greatest number of ships of the line ever heard of. I am sorry that this brave man is wounded and hope that his life will be spared to be of further use to his country.

The Duke begs that I will present his humble duty to your Majesty; at the beginning of next month he is going into Upper Swabia to shoot about ten days.

I will now take up no more of your Majesty's time than to assure you [etc.]. (51502–3)

1843   LORD GRENVILLE *to the* KING, *and the reply*

[*Cleveland Row, 28 Sept, 1798.*] Lord Grenville has the honour most respectfully to submit to your Majesty the minute of instructions to be given to your Majesty's Minister at Constantinople, together with the draft of the projet to which it refers, and the instrument of your Majesty's full powers authorizing him to sign the Alliance in this shape, either jointly or in conjunction with his brother Sir Sidney Smith if he should arrive in time, which is doubtful, it having on the whole appeared better that he should proceed there in his ship, rather than overland as had at first been intended.

On a full discussion with M. de Circello yesterday Lord Grenville found that altho' furnished with full powers for the purpose, he was afraid to take upon him to sign the Alliance in the uncertainty which still prevails respecting the conduct of the Court of Vienna. Lord Grenville judged that it was by no means proper that this matter should appear to be pressed on your Majesty's part, and therefore

victory your Navy has gained over the French. Certainly a more important event has not taken place during the whole war and I believe never in the annals of history, and I trust that every Englishman will glory at it. The joy this has spread on the Continent is very great indeed and I only wish that it would have the good effect to rouse the different Sovereigns out of the lethargy into which they are fallen. If these would but shew but a little energy I am convinced matters would soon change, and the French give up the insolence with which they treat almost all the nations on the Continent. Since a weeck we have received orders to call back all our men that are on furlow so that in a very few days all the Battallions will be compleat. As yet no new dislocation has taken place, so that it seems the Regiments will keep their cantonments this winter. We are however all ready to march at the first winck, but should this be the case I hope our campaign will be successful and that we shall be able to shew our ennemies that there are still some troops on the Continent who are not afraid of them. That your Majesty's Navy and Army may always be equally successful is the most fervent prayer of' [&c.]. (48524)

proposed that the whole negotiation should be referred to Naples to be treated there by the means of full powers to be sent to your Majesty's Minister at that Court.[1] M. de Circello readily agreed to this, and his messenger will set off on Tuesday for Naples, with the account of what has passed.

Lord Grenville does not think that any difficulty can arise with respect to the Articles of the Treaty, if the resolution were once definitely taken at Naples to meet the danger of war, as being less than that of such a peace as they now enjoy. The point of subsidy was much pressed, but Lord Grenville felt himself obliged to answer that your Majesty's actual engagements of that nature were so extensive as not to admit of any addition. (9023–4)

[*The King's reply, Weymouth, 29 Sept. 1798, 4 p.m.*] The Minute of instructions for the Minister at Constantinople is drawn up with the clearness that constantly attends Lord Grenville's pen; it is highly proper that the instrument authorizing the signing the Alliance should be in the shape proposed, as it may be uncertain how soon Sir Sidney Smith may arrive at Constantinople, as he goes in the ship he commands.

Lord Grenville seems to have made the best arrangement concerning the Neapolitan treaty, as the strange conduct of Austria certainly to a degree has palzied that of Naples. (Fortescue MSS.)

1844   *Letters from* EARL SPENCER *to the* KING, *and the replies*

[*Admiralty, 2 Oct. 1798.*] It is impossible for words to express the satisfaction with which Earl Spencer has the honour of laying before your Majesty the accompanying letters from Sir Horatio Nelson, giving an account of a most signal & brilliant victory obtained under the blessing of Almighty God by your Majesty's Fleet on the coast of Egypt. The circumstance of not one British ship having been lost in a conflict of so arduous a nature adds very considerably to the pleasure that must be derived from the event, which Earl Spencer cannot but flatter himself will produce the most important consequences.

Earl Spencer trusts that your Majesty will pardon him for not waiting upon your Majesty himself with the dispatches, as the distance of Weymouth might draw him too long from his publick duty at the Admiralty at this moment, but he thought it necessary to send a messenger with the news in hope that it might reach your Majesty before night. (9025)

[*The King's reply, Weymouth, 3 Oct.*] Having seen the propriety and elegance of the shortness with which Sir Horatio Nelson has stated this glorious of action [*sic*] of the 1st of August, I shall certainly so far copy him as not to pretend to express to Earl Spencer the degree of joy I have felt on the occasion. The beating and destroying the Brest fleet would be highly glorious and advantageous to this kingdom, but the success of this brave Admiral is of more utility to the cause we are engaged in; if it electrifies Austria and Naples it may save Italy.

[1] Sir William Hamilton.

Sir Horatio Nelson is not rich and therefore declined being created a Baronet. This puts his getting a peerage quite out of the question,[1] but is a reason that he should have a handsome pension settled on him.

Lord Spencer has judged quite right in not coming himself. The messenger rode the 131 miles in 9 hours and ¼. I thought therefore he ought to have a night's rest, and now re-dispatch him after having seen the feue de joie of the ships and troops that are here. The St. Fiorenzo sails as well as I believe any frigate can. (Althorp MSS.)

[*From Earl Spencer, Admiralty, 4 Oct.*] Earl Spencer was preparing, when he had the honour of receiving your Majesty's note of the 3d instant, humbly to submit to your Majesty the propriety of distinguishing Sir Horatio Nelson by conferring on him a Barony of Gt. Britain, the honour which on consulting with Mr Pitt yesterday evening they both agreed would be the most suitable on the present occasion, which Earl Spencer humbly hopes your Majesty will approve on the consideration that an honorary as well as a pecuniary reward will naturally & earnestly be looked for by the publick on an atchievement of a magnitude like the present. A handsome pension should certainly accompany it; and with your Majesty's approbation Earl Spencer proposes to make the promotions of the First Lieutenants belonging to the ships in action on the same principle as has lately been adopted in general actions. Earl Spencer also humbly submits to your Majesty that gold medals should also be given to Sir Horatio Nelson & the Captains as in the three former general actions in the course of this war. If your Majesty should approve of the Peerage, it may be inserted in Saturday's Gazette, and his own name seems to be the properest title. (9026)

[*The King's reply, Weymouth, 5 Oct. 1798, 10.25 p.m.*] I have this instant received Earl Spencer's two notes. I entirely approve of Sir Horatio Nelson being created a Baron of Great Britain by the title of Lord Nelson, on condition that a suitable [pension] be joined to the peerage, without which it would be disadvantageous to his family;[2] also that medals be prepared for him and his captains as on the former great actions; and I am pleased the 1st Lieutenants of the ships have been promoted.[3] (Althorp MSS.)

[1] In view of the magnitude of this victory it seems odd that the King had to be reminded by his Ministers that nothing short of a peerage would satisfy public opinion. Indeed there was some public criticism that a higher dignity than a Barony was not conferred upon him. Sir John Jervis had been made an Earl and Admiral Duncan a Viscount as a reward for the battles of St Vincent and Camperdown, neither of which was comparable in any way with Nelson's achievement. Lord Spencer explained to him that 'it is the highest honour that has ever been conferred on an officer of your standing in the Service and who was not a Commander-in-Chief'. (Nicolas, *Despatches and Letters of Lord Nelson*, III, 75.)

[2] For the annuity see No. 1881.

[3] Writing to Pitt that day Portland congratulated him 'on Nelson's stupendous victory, which as much exceeds all expectation as it surpassed in point of achievement and may surpass in its effect and consequences the most gallant and important event of our naval annals; because it is certainly within possibility that it may be the death's blow of that tremendous monster, the present French Government, and become the instrument of the restoration of the tranquillity and security of the world'. (W. Dacres Adams MSS.)

[*Weymouth, 5 Oct. 1798, 4 p.m.*] The dispatches I have read this day from Petersburgh and those from Vienna are so diametrically opposite that it is difficult for me to conceive the tenour of Count Staremberg's conversation with Lord Grenville. I am perfectly satisfied in the justice of our cause, in the present unhappy difference with his Court; but I think the fate of Europe so entirely depends upon the line of conduct we may take on the present occasion that should the Count not be enabled to act as we had reason to expect, I should think the victory at the mouth of the Nyle so thoroughly changes the aspect of affairs, that we ought not to let Austria remain quiet, for a mere point of honour, as we must all feel that any real payment of money cannot be expected from Vienna at the present moment; why therefore may we not be explicit that they must acknowledge their debt and no payment be called for from them at present, but that of attention to the general cause in which we are gloriously engaged, that we will engage to pay a monthly sum of money provided Austria will in the first place send such a corps of troops as shall be proposed from hence to Switzerland to be commanded by General Holtze[1] who is already there? I am certain this would be so popular a measure here that no difficulty will be found in furnishing money from this country for so desirable an event. The Emperor of Russia will also feel that his interposition has effected this measure. This will strengthen his ardour in the cause he is now for the first time going to embrace, and by the letter from Berlin I do not despair Prussia may yet also be brought again into action.

I desire Lord Grenville will communicate this letter to Mr. Pitt, and that as the question is undoubtedly of the greatest magnitude, that he will not give a decisive answer till he has called a Cabinet meeting, for indeed on our present decision depends, if Austria is sincere, the fate of Italy and indeed the rest of Europe. It therefore deserves the most mature deliberation. (Fortescue MSS.)

[*Lord Grenville's reply, Dropmore, 6 Oct., 9.15 a.m.*] Lord Grenville is this moment honoured with your Majesty's letter, and will lose no time in obeying the commands therein contained. He expects to see Count Woronzow in the course of this morning, and to learn from him the general nature of Count Starhemberg's instructions, and he will not fail to apprize your Majesty either by the mail of today or tomorrow of what he may collect on the subject. Lord Grenville has no doubt that if anything can be done, the mode pointed out by your Majesty, that of combining the measure with the steps to be taken for the recovery of Swisserland, is infinitely the best, both in its impression here, and in its real effects.[2] (9029–30)

1846   *Letters from* EARL SPENCER *to the* KING, *with a reply*

[*Admiralty, 5 Oct. 1798, 11.15 a.m.*] The box having by a mistake been omitted to be sent to your Majesty by the mail coach of yesterday, Earl Spencer, in order

---

[1] David van Hotze, the Austrian General. In September 1799 his corps was decisively defeated by Soult on the river Linth, and its remnants were driven out of Switzerland.
[2] For Pitt's comments on the King's letter, see *Dropmore Papers*, IV, 337.

not to lose the opportunity of the Gazette of tomorrow night, in case your Majesty should be pleased to approve of the distinction proposed to be conferred on Sir Horatio Nelson, has taken the liberty of forwarding it by a messenger. (9027)

[*From Lord Spencer, Admiralty, 6 Oct.*] Earl Spencer is extremely happy to find that your Majesty has been graciously pleased to approve of his proposal respecting the dignity to be conferred on Sir Horatio Nelson; and he humbly trusts your Majesty will not disapprove his being styled Baron Nelson of the Nile, as it appears on reference to several titles bestowed on similar occasions, that some such indication of the service for which they were granted has generally accompanied them, as in the cases of Lord Clive, Lord Heathfield & Lord Duncan.[1] (9028)

[*The King's reply, Weymouth, 7 Oct., 4 p.m.*] As the new Peer has unfortunately no estate, he could not with much propriety to the title of Nelson add so proper an appendix as of the Nile, and it having been done in the cases of Lords Clive, Heathfield and Duncan, makes the proposal of Earl Spencer highly proper. (Althorp MSS.)

1847   DR MOORE *to the* KING

[*Clandon House, 6 Oct. 1798.*] The Archbishop of Canterbury humbly begs permission to present his dutiful congratulation to your Majesty on the great & glorious victory obtained by your Majesty's Fleet under the command of Admiral Sir Horatio Nelson.

He presumes also respectfully to submit to your Majesty's consideration the great propriety & duty of appointing a day of General Thanksgiving to Almighty God on an event so important, & which excites universal joy, & the most devout gratitude to His Divine Providence.[2] (9031)

1848   E. LIVINGSTON *to the* KING

[*Dresden, 7 Oct. 1798.*] In the letter[3] I had the honor to write your Majesty the 1st September I mentioned that his Royal Highness the Prince intended to leave Vienna as soon as the travelling carriages could be put in repair for a long journey. From the situation of the Prince Augustus health, and other circumstances we did not set out til the 28 September. At that period his Royal Highness was not well, but the doctor gave it as his opinion that the Prince might go as far as Berlin without any risk of danger. I am sorry to inform your Majesty that his Royal Highness has been very ill and sufferd so much from the jolting of the carriage on excessive bad roads, that he has not been able to go to bed since we left Vienna, or since our arrival here the 5th. The Prince is so much exausted by this very

[1] Clive had been created Baron Clive of Plassey (March 1762). The defender of Gibraltar had been created Baron Heathfield of Gibraltar (July 1787). Admiral Duncan became Viscount Duncan of Camperdown (Oct. 1797). Lord Spencer might also have referred to Amherst of Montreal (1788) and Admiral Sir John Jervis's title of Earl of St Vincent.
[2] See No. 1851 for the reply.   [3] No. 1817.

violent fit of asthma, we must remain here til his Royal Highness gets better, and recover strength to proceed to Berlin. The Elector[1] having been informed by Mr Elliot[2] that the Prince was to arrive here, orders were given to receive his Royal Highness with every possible mark of distinction; one of the Elector's Gentlemen of the Bedchamber and a page were appointed to attend the Prince, and one of his Serene Highness' coaches: from the state of his Royal Highness' health I begd Mr Elliot to decline all these honors: and I am to have the honor tomorrow of an audience of his Electoral Highness to express the Prince's regret of not being able to thank him in person. Your Majesty will see by the doctor's bulletin I have the honor to inclose that there can be no further question this autumn or winter of his Royal Highness undertaking a long journey by land. The Prince's sufferings, which have lasted eight days, are far beyond any I have ever seen, and I have reason to thank God that I suggested this short journey for a tryal before we undertook that for Russia. I would have been miserable had the Prince been taken ill in the remote parts of Poland or Russia, where it would have been impossible to have procured comfortable lodgings or the common conveniencys suitable to his present state of health.

By Mr Dundas letter of 14 August he informs me that your Majesty does not wish the Prince to go to Lisbon. Perhaps the late glorious success of your Majesty's Fleet may alter the political situation of that country; at all events the Prince must remain very quiet at Berlin at least one month. There I hope to receive your Majesty's commands where you wish the Prince to pass this winter. His Royal Highness does not like Gibraltar, and many weighty reasons render Italy improper.

In Lord Elgin's absence I have wrote to Mr Garlike, your Majesty's *Chargé d'Affaire* at Berlin, to let him know that Prince Augustus intends being soon there, and have desired him to intimate it in the proper manner to his Prussian Majesty's Minister. I cannot doubt of the King giving the Prince a hearty wellcome, but I have begd of Mr Garlike to take every proper precaution on that subject before he hires lodgings for the Prince and his attendants. In case Mr Garlike finds they are not cordially inclined towards the Prince making a long stay at Berlin, I intreat your Majesty may be graciously pleased to honor me with your commands and advice where to fix for the winter, for I now am convinced that the Prince cannot bear the fatigue of a long journey by land without eminent danger, and if it is your Majesty's pleasure the Prince proceeds to Russia it must be by sea.

I flatter myself the Prince's acquaintance at Vienna will regret his absence, and I am certain every bill was paid before we left it.

I presume his Royal Highness has informed your Majesty that Count Sauran[3], the Emperor's Minister of Finance, sent the Prince two very ellegant déjeunées of Vienna china with his Royal Highness cipher. I have reason to beleive the china was made by the Emperor's orders for the Prince, but in the letter the Count Sauran wrote me when he sent the déjeunées he did not mention his Imperial Majesty.

[1] Frederick Augustus (1750–1827), Elector (1763) and King (1806) of Saxony. He owed his crown to Napoleon.
[2] Hugh Elliot (1752–1830) was Minister to Saxony, 1792–1802.   [3] Saurau.

Prince Augustus took leave of the Emperor and the Empress[1] before the asthma began, but his Royal Highness was obliged to send me to express his regret of not being able to take leave of the Archeducs,[2] the Archeduchesse Amelie[3] and the Princess of France.[4] They all expressd very great concern to hear the Prince was indisposed and sent their Grand Maitres next day to enquire after his Royal Highness health and to wish the Prince a good journey.

Some time before the Prince left Vienna his Royal Highness gave by my advice a very genteel ball and supper to one hundred and forty ladys and gentlemen. I was told it was one of the best conducted fêtes ever given in that country; by the proper arrangments taken it only cost 96 pound sterling. I thought it the best mode of returning the civilitys the Prince had received at Vienna.

Sir Morton Eden continued without intermission his respectful attention and hospitality to the Prince and his attendants.

The doctor has just informed me that he finds his Royal Highness much better this morning and allmost free of fever, and assures me that I may congratulate your Majesty on the Prince being out of all danger. (9032–5)

[*Dr. William Domeier's Bulletin, Dresden, 6 Oct. 1798.*] His R.H. Prince Augustus has been affected with complaints in his breast before he left Vienna, and during the whole of the journey from that place, he has been so very ill as not to be able to lye down upon a bed, but was forced to remain all the night in an arm chair.

Travelling always disagreed with his constitution and increases the paroxyms of his disorder, and as this is the first season for many years that he has passed the autumn or winter in a cold climate, there is great reason to fear that the attacks may be more severe. H.R.H. never failed to suffer upon a journey, even when going from the north to the south, and I should be wanting to the duty I owe to the Prince, if I did not mention the danger to which he would be exposed if he were to continue to travel at this advanced season of the year in a northern climate.

It is absolutely necessary for the health of H.R.H. that he should remain for some length of time in the same place, and in as warm a climate as the circumstances of the times will admit. A voyage by sea would be attended with less risk than a long journey by land. The experience I have now had for seven years of the nature of the Prince's disease has convinced me that irregularities of every kind are the greatest enemies to his health, and when travelling it is impossible, even with the greatest care and precaution, to avoid irregularities. The roads in some countries of Germany are extremely bad, and the inns in small towns are not calculated to afford to H.R.H. the comforts and conveniencies which the nature of his case requires. (9036–7)

[1] The Emperor Francis II married (1790) as his second wife, Maria Theresa (1772–1807), daughter of Ferdinand I, King of the Two Sicilies.
[2] The Emperor's brothers.
[3] The Emperor's sister (1780–98), who died on Christmas Day.
[4] Louis XVI's daughter Maria Theresa (1778–1851) who married (1799) her cousin Louis, Duc d'Angoulême (1775–1844), the elder son of 'Monsieur', afterwards Charles X.

[*Taunton, 8 Oct. 1798.*] Your Lordship's attention to my late husband and your kind offer of rendering him any further service has made me presume to address you and I trust my distresses and your known benevolence will plead my excuse for the liberty I take in solliciting your interest in promoting the success of the inclosed Memorial.

My situation I should hope might entitle me to some claim on his Majesty's compassion, as, added to the loss of the best of husbands, and a son (from whose promising worth I had every expectation, who both fell victims to climate in the service of their country) I am left with eight children under great pecuniary embarrassments, as my husband's fortune was spent in the purchase of his own and his son's Commissions.

There are likewise some peculiar hard circumstances attending my situation which I beg leave to state to your Lordship. While Lord Amherst was Commander-in-Chief my husband, in consideration to his family, wished to resign, as he had a most favorable opportunity of disposing of his Commission and settling himself to advantage, but Lord Amherst requested he would not quit the Service and he should have no reason to complain; unfortunately Lord A. retired soon after.[1] Again, at his return from the West Indies, as his health was visibly declining, he had permission to retire from the Service and had five thousand guineas lodged for his Commission, when it was stopped by the Major's Father saying he would give the regulation. These are facts well known. I presented a Memorial to the Secretary at War, who returned for answer that he sincerely regretted that the Lieutenant Colonelcy being permitted to be sold, prevented *his Department* from affording me that assistance my situation claimed—but, alas, my Lord, the sale of my husband's Commission, after settling money raised for his son's purchases, and the expences incurred in the Services he was imployed in, and his long illness, leaves little to support a numerous family. My boys I mean at a proper age to dedicate to the service of their country, but to educate them properly must be attended with greater expence than the most eoconomical plan I can follow will allow.

If I have been too prolix in stating my situation, I hope my anxiety for my children will plead my excuse, and induce your Lordship to afford me your assistance. (9038)

1850   Lord Grenville *to the* King

[*Dropmore, 8 Oct. 1798.*] Lord Grenville has the honour to acquaint your Majesty that he has been disappointed of seeing Count Woronzow here as he had expected, but he has appointed to see him tomorrow morning. In the meantime he has the honour to transmit to your Majesty the copy (with the original written in a hand

---

[1] In Feb. 1795. See No. 829 n. In August and September of the following year Ministers were hoping that he would accept the Governorship of Jamaica. Canning in particular hoped that he would, 'because I am persuaded that no essential good can be done in the slave trade business without a Governor of Jamaica favourable to the measure himself, and qualified by his temper and abilities to conciliate those with whom he has to deal in the island. Amherst strikes me as exactly the person best calculated for the purpose' (Saltram MSS.).

almost illegible) of a letter to him from Count Starhemberg, by which your Majesty will see that Sir Charles Whitworth has been misinformed with respect to the nature of M. de Cobenzl's[1] instructions to Count Starhemberg.

Your Majesty's servants will meet on this subject tomorrow, and Lord Grenville does not therefore presume to submit to your Majesty anything like a fixed opinion respecting it, though he has great apprehensions of the effect of entering into any fresh pecuniary arrangements for the support of the Court of Vienna, while those made so long since remain not only unexecuted, but even not ratified by that Court, notwithstanding it has received the full benefit of them. (9039–40)

1851 THE KING *to the* ARCHBISHOP OF CANTERBURY

[*Weymouth, 9 Oct. 1798.*] My good Lord, I have just received your letter of congratulations on the signal success of the Fleet under the command of Lord Nelson which deserves the most marked tribute of thanks from myself and all my subjects to the Almighty. This can only be done with proper solemnity during the sitting of Parliament. The proper day cannot therefore be fixed till it is known when the Parliament will actually assemble, it being much doubted whether it will not be postponed till late in November.[2] I therefore think the [*sic*] your Grace[3] had best in my name direct a short Prayer of Thanksgiving for the first Sunday possible in London and in the rest of the kingdom on the first Sunday after its being received; and to have it understood that one General Thanksgiving day will be fixed for a future day.

P.S. Your letter was delivered since the departure of the post, therefore this cannot be sent till tomorrow. (9041)

1852 THE DUKE OF YORK *to the* KING

[*Horse Guards, 10 Oct. 1798.*] I have the honor to transmit to your Majesty the weekly returns and states, as likewise the recommendations for vacant Commissions for your Majesty's approbation. Among these your Majesty will find one which has been received this morning from Lieutenant-General Stuart of Colonel Leighton[4] of the 46th Regiment to be appointed a Brigadeer-General in Portugal.

The General was to leave Lisbon on the 29th of September to proceed to join Lord St. Vincent's Fleet. He takes with him upon his expedition besides his own Staff, Major-General Sir James St. Clair,[5] and Brigadier-General Stuart, and had

[1] The Imperial Foreign Minister.

[2] Parliament met again on 20 Nov. The 29th was fixed as the Thanksgiving Day, and Dr Rennell preached a sermon to the Members (about 40 out of 558) at St Margaret's, Westminster.

[3] 'Your Grace' is written over 'Archbishop'.

[4] Baldwin Leighton (1747–1828). Colonel, 1798; Major-General, 1803; Lieutenant-General, 1809; General, 1819. Governor of Carrickfergus, 1817. Succeeded to the Baronetcy, 1819.

[5] Sir James St Clair-Erskine, 2nd Earl of Rosslyn (1762–1837), nephew of Lord Loughborough, the Lord Chancellor, who was created Earl of Rosslyn, April 1801. Succeeded his father, Lieutenant-General Sir Henry Erskine, as 6th Baronet, 1765. Lieutenant-Colonel, 1792; A.D.C. to the King, 1792; Colonel, 1795; Brigadier-General in Portugal, 1796; Major-General, Jan. 1798; Lieutenant-General, 1805. M.P. for Castle Rising, 1782–4; for Morpeth, 1784–96; for Kirkcaldy Burghs, 1796–1805. Lord Privy Seal, 1829–30; Lord President of the Council, 1834–5.

promised Major General Villettes[1] that he should be allowed to return to England by the next packet. The troops in Portugal will therefore remain under the command of Major-General Fraser,[2] with Brigadeer-General Wauchope[3] and Brigadeer-General Leighton, if your Majesty is pleased to approve of his appointment.

I have likewise the honor to report to your Majesty that I received last week from the Lord Lieutenant of Ireland a letter inclosing a Memorial from the Deputy-Adjutant[4] and Deputy Quarter-Master-Generals[5] on that Staff, stating the inefficiency of their pay and allowances, and begging for an increase. Having referred this to the Secretary at War for his opinion I find that the Deputy-Adjutant and Quarter-Master-Generals both of Great Britain and Ireland receive only ten shillings pr day, together with a contingent allowance of one hunderd and seventy five pounds a year, in lieu of travelling expences and other casualties, which the Secretary at War thoroughly agrees with me in opinion is very inadequate to the extraordinary expences to which they are liable. It is therefore humbly submitted to your Majesty that the pay of those Staff Officers, who are permanent, may be increased to twenty shillings pr day and that their contingent allowance should be continued to them as at present, but that no alteration should be made to the pay of officers filling similar situations in detached parts of the Army.

Understanding from Mr Pitt that there is no intention of withdrawing any part of the troops which have been lent to Ireland by this country during the winter, and that therefore the General Officers sent with them must remain, I shall have the honor to lay before your Majesty a new arrangement of the Generals in the different districts for your approbation. (9042–3)

1853 PRINCE AUGUSTUS *to the* KING

[*Dresden, 10 Oct. 1798.*] Before your Majesty will receive this letter you will most probably know the unfortunate state of my health. Had attention been pay'd to my former letters this would not have happen'd, for you must recollect, Sir, I foretold the event. However, as my conduct ever 'till now has been that of wishing to obey your royal commands when the plan was proposed to me for going to Russia and mention'd as your Majesty's wish, I immediately agreed to it, for at least I thought time would prove to your Majesty whether my complaints were imaginary or not. I confess when the first proposal was made me I was not a little surprised, for when I recollected Germany was too cold for me, that travelling was found equally pernicious to my health, that on that very account after having spent four winters in a warm climate I was fix'd for six more in Italy without ever removing even the summer, it seem'd to me inexplicable how I was to risk all these former dangers which were already known to be so pernicious to me, and

[1] William Anne Villettes (1754–1808). Major, 1787; Lieutenant-Colonel, 1791; Major-General, June 1798; Lieutenant-General, 1805; Governor of Malta, 1801–7; Governor of Jamaica, 1807–8, and died there.
[2] Simon Fraser (1738–1813). Colonel, 1794; Major-General, 1796; Lieutenant-General, 1803.
[3] Patrick Wauchope (*d.* 1807). Major-General, 1803.
[4] Lieutenant-Colonel L. Walpole.
[5] Major-General C. Eustace and Lieutenant-Colonel Handfield.

with every new difficulty that could be thought of. I was to go to a colder climate than Germany though Germany was found too severe for my breast, I was to begin travelling there, though time had shewn the bad effect it had upon me, and all this undertaken in a winter season which was the time I had always been sent to a warm climate. Your Majesty's idea this could never be. It must have been the plan of someone who wish'd to get rid of your son, and I make no doubt that if I remain in this country the end will be most amply obtain'd. How much your Majesty will be surprised on such an occasion I can easily conceive, but had you believed my former letters, Sir, you would have known the event for I foretold it you though I wrote it with as much delicacy at the time as possible. Your Majesty will find my expressions strong, but put yourself in my situation and who would not speak so? I am now twenty six years old, of an age to know what is good and bad for me, and instead of being left to my own plans I am to be drawn about, contrary to my own will and pleasure, without any hope of improvement and with bad effects to my health, and of course to my happiness. If your Majesty will please to consider that between Trieste and Vienna, and Vienna and this place I have not been one single night in bed, nor able to eat a mouthful quietly; today is already a fortnight that I have left Vienna and not been once in bed; only conceive, Sir, my unhappy situation. I trust therefore your Majesty will give up any further plans of my travelling, for with all dutiful respect I cannot and must not do it. I must take care of my own health; it is a duty incumbent on me for more reasons than one. Your Majesty will not find it amiss, therefore, I hope, if I firmly but dutifully represent to you the total impossibility in which I am of being able to travel any more. The present situation of Europe renders it almost impossible to find out a warm climate for my residence. If, therefore, your Majesty would be graciously pleased to give me some employment in the West Indies I shall readily and thankfully accept it. The idea of leaving Europe causes me a sincere pain but if I can get employed and settle myself in a comfortable and quiet way I shall have gain'd a great point. However, if I am not fit for any employment of this sort I cannot think of leaving Europe on any account whatsoever. If I was to have a desire I should like to go to Jamaica or, if more agreable, even to the Cape of Good Hope, but I shall leave this entirely to your Majesty's own feelings. All that I beg is that if this can be settled, your Majesty will be so good as to make it out with me and not introduce a third person; it would render me so much more happy. Why should anyone mix in a father and son's affairs? Believe me, Sir, there are always invidious people in the world who find it their interest in keeping us asunder; this ought not to be and especially must not be the case in the present situation of affairs. Trusting to have a favourable answer and begging pardon for a sick man's scrawl I have the honor [etc.]. (48131–2)

1854   *Letters from* LORD GRENVILLE *to the* KING, *and a reply*

[*Cleveland Row, 10 Oct. 1798, 3 p.m.*] Lord Grenville has the honour humbly to acquaint your Majesty that he has seen Count Woronzow, and that he had the mortification to learn from him that the instructions sent by Monsieur de Cobenzl to Count Starhemberg are very little more than a repetition of what has been so often written from Vienna, and that they do not, in Count Woronzow's opinion, afford the least opening for any amicable arrangement of the point in dispute. Lord Grenville has not yet received M. de Starhemberg's memorial, but he concludes that he may expect it today or tomorrow.

On consulting yesterday with such of your Majesty's confidential servants as are in town or in the neighbourhood, Lord Grenville found that they all agreed in the opinion, which has strongly impressed his mind, that as the sums which may eventually be paid to Continental powers already amount to two millions sterling, namely twelve hundred thousand pounds to Russia, (exclusive of what will remain as debt to be provided for after the Peace) three hundred thousand pounds to Portugal, and five hundred thousand for the formation of a Swiss army and for its maintenance, your Majesty's servants could not in any case venture to advise the going beyond that amount. That the last of these sums, that appropriated to Swisserland, might indeed possibly be so combined with the Austrian operations in that quarter, as to be made of material benefit to them. But that in bringing forward to Parliament any proposal of that nature, or any plan of pecuniary aid to Austria, it would be indispensable that the former Convention should be ratified, as the continuance of a refusal in this respect must throw an unsurmountable discredit on the public faith of that Government. And that it can hardly be supposed that the Court of Vienna, if really desirous to renew the war, would hesitate to fulfill this engagement, which need not be considered as obliging them to any present payment.

Count Woronzow in his conversation with Lord Grenville suggested an idea which appears to Mr Pitt & him to merit great consideration. It is, that application should be made on your Majesty's part to the Emperor of Russia, to declare himself a principal in the war, and having done so, to claim the cooperation of Austria, offering on one hand the assistance of the sixty thousand men, under the terms of the proposed Convention with your Majesty, but on condition of the ratification of the former Convention, but intimating on the other hand that in case of a refusal or delay a similar proposition will be made to Prussia.

Lord Grenville is preparing to put his ideas on this subject into the form of a draft, which he will have the honour to submit to your Majesty for your Majesty's commands. (9044–6)

[*The King's reply, Weymouth, 11 Oct. 1798.*] Lord Grenville's letter has really mortified me, as I had flattered myself that Sir Charles Whitworth could not have been so totally misinformed as to have given so contrary a colour to the letter from Count Cobentzel, as Count Woronzow's language gives reason to suppose the Memorial of Count Starhemberg will authorize. The conduct of the Court of Vienna is so perfectly unfair that I cannot but suppose it is occasioned by some private understanding with the enemy. I from this opinion am clearly of opinion that the suggestion of Count Woronzow is not only worthy of consideration but ought to be instantly adopted, namely, the applying in my name to the Emperor of Russia that he may declare himself a principal in the war, and to call on Austria for co-operation, and at the same time to state that if either delay or refusal is made, a similar proposition will be made to Prussia.

If we can get the Swiss to act and get the Russians to send the 60,000 to co-operate with them, as much as I wish to prevent additional expence to this country, I should feel much inclined to add some specific sum to Russia if they would by sea send 15,000 men in the spring to take possession of Holland; this would be a diversion that would greatly assist the operations in Swisserland; though these are but hastily put on paper they are the result of much consideration; as such I desire this may be communicated to Mr. Pitt. (Fortescue MSS.)

[*From Lord Grenville, Wotton,*[1] *13 Oct. 1798, 8 a.m.*] Lord Grenville has this morning been honoured with your Majesty's commands which he will not fail to execute without delay. He had arranged with Count Woronzow that the Russian messenger should return on Friday next, & he imagines that Count Woronzow will hardly be ready before that day. (9048)

1855   THE DUKE OF PORTLAND *to the* KING

[*Bulstrode, Saturday, 13 Oct. 1798.*] The Duke of Portland most humbly represents to your Majesty that he has been requested by the Sheriffs of London to acquaint your Majesty that the Corporation has unanimously voted an Address to your Majesty on Lord Nelson's glorious victory & to receive your Majesty's commands respecting the time at which your Majesty will be graciously pleased to permit the Sheriffs to attend your Majesty in order to know at what time & place your Majesty will please to be attended with the Address.

The anxiety & impatience of the Lord Mayor,[2] who privately called at the Duke of Portland's Office, to obtain information upon these two points, that the attendance on your Majesty may be as numerous as possible, induced the D. of Portland to say that he thought it probable that your Majesty would appoint the Sheriffs to be at Windsor on Tuesday the 23d instant between two & three o clock in the afternoon, & would be attended by the Corporation at St. James on the following day at two o' clock. (9047)

1856   DR. MOORE *to the* KING

[*Lambeth House, 13 Oct. 1798.*] The Archbishop has the honour to acknowledge with all duty and thankfulness the receipt of your Majesty's commands from Weymouth,[3] but at the same time he is obliged to add, with much concern, that the Prayer of Thanksgiving is prevented from being issued in time for London on Sunday, by an accident. He is sorry to add that it was in consequence of a mistake of his own, which he hopes that your Majesty, with your usual goodness to him, will pardon. The Prayer will now be dispersed through its whole extent in time for Sunday the twenty-first.

[1] The Marquess of Buckingham's country seat, in Bucks.
[2] Sir John William Anderson (1736?–1813), Lord Mayor, 1797–8. Baronetcy, 14 May 1798.
[3] No. 1851.

P.S. One consequence of the mistake has been a shaking hand, which would not admit of the Archbishop's writing to your Majesty sooner his dutiful acknowledgments of the honour of your Majesty's commands. (9049)

1857   THE DUKE OF YORK *to the* KING

[*Horse Guards, 17 Oct. 1798.*] I have the honor to transmit to your Majesty the weekly states and returns, as likewise to lay before your Majesty for your approbation the recommendations for vacant Commissions. Among these your Majesty will remark the exchange between Lieutenant-Colonel Slade[1] and Lieutenant Colonel Kinsey. As Colonel Slade called upon me yesterday I took the oportunity to signify to him your Majesty's intentions with regard to the dispute which has subsisted between him and Colonel Cartwright,[2] and he assured me that he had given up all thoughts of taking any more notice of it.

Your Majesty will likewise receive a list of General Officers whom it is humbly proposed to your Majesty to place upon the Staff to supply the different vacancies which have happened in the districts which I trust will meet with your Majesty's approbation. The necessary orders have been given in obedience to your Majesty's commands to the different Regiments to furnish the detachments upon the road from Weymouth to Windsor on Monday next.[3] (9050)

1858   PRINCESS AMELIA *to the* KING

[*Worthing, 18 Oct. 1798.*] Thank you very much for your last kind letter & the affectionate expressions you make use of on my account. You have heard of the spasms I have had in my knee. They are now less: however, they still give me a great deal of pain *but* it is a great comfort to think that notwithstanding I find them at present very disagreable, that in the end they may be of infinite use. I am very happy you & dear mama do not think it necessary for me to see a phygician [*sic*]: I own I should have been sorry had you wished it, as I am certain Mr. Keate does everything he possibly can & that in time his exertions will answer & I shall be quite well. No one can do more than he does.

The dear Duke & Dss. of York have been to see me; how very good of them to come. It is a great comfort to me in this long confinement to find how many kind friends I have; indeed, my dear papa, yours & everybody's kindness to me is beyond what I can ever describe.

I am very glad the St. Fiorenzo is at Weymouth as I know how much you all like sailing in her. I shall ever look back with pleasure to those happy hours I have passed on board. I know how happy Sir Harry[4] is to be on that station.

---

[1] Sir John Slade (1762–1859). Lieutenant-Colonel, April 1795; Colonel, 1802; Major-General, 1809; Lieutenant-General, 1814; General, 1837. Cr. Baronet, 1831. Equerry to the Duke of Cumberland, March 1801.

[2] William Cartwright (*c.* 1753–1827). Lieutenant, 1775; Major, 1786; Lieutenant-Colonel, 1793; Colonel, Sept. 1796; Major-General, 1802; Lieutenant-General, 1808; General, 1819.

[3] On Monday the 22nd the royal family returned to the Queen's Lodge, Windsor, from Weymouth, arriving at 6.15 p.m.

[4] Sir Harry Burrard Neale, who commanded the *St Fiorenzo*, of 42 guns.

I must, my dearest papa, return you my thanks for the bed & chair you have so kindly allowed me to have. As to my saying what my heart dictates for all yours & dear mama's goodness, volumes will not contain, therefore I shall only beg of you to believe that I am very grateful & most thankful for having such parents. Every day I find reason to be more so.

I shall now conclude, beging you to excuse this long & stupid letter & will only add that no one can love you more than your dutiful & affte. child. (Add. Georgian 14/17.)

1859   EARL SPENCER *to the* KING, *and replies*

[*Admiralty, 18 Oct. 1798.*] Earl Spencer has the honour to acquaint your Majesty that Sir James Marriott having found himself from his infirmities unable to attend to the duties of his office of Judge of the Court of Admiralty, has been induced, in consideration of a pension of £2000 a year being settled upon him, to resign his office; and Earl Spencer humbly hopes that your Majesty will be pleased to approve of the appointment of Sir William Scott to succeed him, who in every point of view seems to be the most proper person to fill that office.

The accounts received this morning from Dublin leave very little room to doubt but that Earl Spencer will be enabled very shortly to offer his congratulations to your Majesty on the defeat of the French squadron which lately sailed for the purpose of invading that country. (9051)

[*The King's reply, Weymouth, 19 Oct. 1798.*] The retiring of Sir James Marriott and Sir William Scott being his successor are events highly advantageous to the credit of the Court of Admiralty, and I very willingly give my consent to Earl Spencer's proposals on this business.

I have read the accounts received by the Home Department, which clearly shews the French squadron on the coast of Ireland was defeated on the 14th. I therefore flatter myself by the mail coach tomorrow to receive a circumstantial account, which cannot but be highly creditable to the officers who have been partakers of this victory.

The letters from the Earl of St. Vincent give too much reason to suppose that the Leander has been taken, and that he approves of Lord Nelson's having destroyed the Guerrier, Heureuse and Hercule. I am certain Earl Spencer will coincide with me that as they were taken in so glorious an action, the officers and men of the victorious British fleet must not be loosers[1] by this necessary determination of the brave Commander. (Althorp MSS.)

[*From the King, Weymouth, 20 Oct. 1798, 4 p.m.*] The conduct of the Irishmen on board of the Glory[2] has been so atrocious that I cannot but see the propriety of letting the sentence of the court martial be put into execution, and I trust this second strong act of rigour will serve as an example to the rest of those men both on board the Glory and serving in the rest of the fleet. (Althorp MSS.)

[1] Of prize money.   [2] A 98-gun line of battle ship, commander, Captain James Brine.

[*Stutgard, 20 Oct. 1798.*] We have been here about a week but I have been so unwell with a rash that I could not sooner have the honour of writing to your Majesty. I left Louisbourg with regret, our weather being delightful till the last morning, and have been much amused with going out of an evening to catch larks. We spared many of their lives to the great delight of Paul and Trinette, who are my constant companions during the Duke's absence. He returned yesterday from his hunting party to my great joy. I know that his travelling about the Dutchy is a very necessary thing and has been neglected for many years by all the late Dukes. However, I always rejoice when he comes home and I must say he appears on every occasion to have the same sentiments, which makes me truly happy.

I hope that your Majesties bathing will have strengthened you for the winter and I think Admiral Nelson will prove a most efficatious remedy against the bile.

I am very grateful to the Almighty for the succes your Majesties arms have again met with in Ireland. I trust that there will be no more attempts at mischief. I feel easy about everything which regards your Kingdoms as I am convinced that God will never abandon your Majesty, who have ever put your trust in him alone.

I am very uneasy about Amelia, poor dear little angel. She has suffered sadly and I fear when once she begins to move, will find herself much weaked by her tedious confinement.

The Duke presents his humble duty to your Majesty. (51504–5)

1861 THE DUKE OF PORTLAND *to the* KING

[*Bulstrode, Sunday, 21 Oct. 1798, 8 a.m.*] The Duke of Portland most humbly begs leave to offer to your Majesty a dispatch from Lord Castlereagh which was received at an early hour this morning by Mr Wickham & to lay his most dutifull congratulations at your Majesty's feet on this farther success with which it has pleased the divine Providence to bless your Majesty's arms.

The Duke of Portland ventures to hope that this event (which he trusts is decisive of all farther attempts of the enemy upon your Majesty's kingdom of Ireland) will appear of sufficient importance to dispose your Majesty to pardon his disobedience of your Majesty's orders in sending this intelligence to your Majesty on this day. (9052)

1862 EARL SPENCER *to the* KING, *and the reply*

[*Wimbledon Park, 21 Oct. 1798, 1.15 a.m.*] Earl Spencer has the honour of congratulating your Majesty on the event of the action with the French squadron on the N.W. coast of Ireland, described in the accompanying letter from Sir John Warren, and flatters himself that when further particulars arrive, it will prove a most compleat defeat of this attempt to invade your Majesty's dominions. (9053)

[*The King's reply, Weymouth, 21 Oct., 8.08 p.m.*] It is with the utmost thankfulness to the Allmighty that I am enabled to express my joy to Earl Spencer for the good news he has just sent me of Sir John Borlace Warren's success, and having taken the Hoche of 84 guns and three frigates, and the letter that accompanies this charming news mentions the Melampus having brought in a fourth. I trust that from the disabled state of the rest of that squadron that we shall still find them brought into some British port. (Althorp MSS.)

1863   E. LIVINGSTON *to the* KING

[*Berlin, 23 Oct. 1798.*] On our arrival yesterday at Berlin I received the honor of your Majesty's gracious letter of 7 October covering one for his Royal Highness Prince Augustus. I had the honor to write your Majesty of 7 October[1] when I took the liberty to mention that I saw the danger of the Prince attempting a long journey by land this winter. The further tryal of the short journey from Dresden here convinces me that his Royal Highness cannot without iminent danger proceed further north til some happy alteration takes place in his constitution. The Prince has not been once in bed since we left Vienna 28 September, or able to lay down his head to rest. I never saw any person suffer more, or bear his sufferings with more patience than the Prince has done during a tedious and painful illness. I have the honor to inclose Doctor Domier's opinion of the late and present state of the Prince's health; and, as his Royal Highness is to write your Majesty by this post, I refer to what the Prince may say on that subject.

Mr Garlike, your Majesty's Chargé d'Affaire[s] at this Court, wrote me to Dresden that he was charged by Comtes Finkensteen[2] and Haugwitz[3] to inform me that they had his Prussian Majesty's commands to order appartments to be prepared for the Prince Augustus at the King's Pallace, and that every honor should be paid to his Royal Highness due to a Prince of England. I sent a messenger to Mr Garlike to desire he would wait on the Prussian Minister, and to beg they would inform the King that Prince Augustus was extremely flattered with his Majesty's intentions, but on account of his bad state of health, which required his Royal Highness living very retired for some time, he hoped the King would excuse his not accepting his Majesty's gracious offer, and I hope your Majesty may approve what I did, by Prince Augustus' consent.

By the manner the King of Prussia and his Minister have mentioned his Royal Highness since his visit here was announced by your Majesty's chargé d'affaire, I have no doubt of the Prince meeting a very gracious reception when he is able to go to Court &c. Therefore if it meets your Majesty's approbation the Prince intends remaining quietly here til your Majesty's further commands is known. For the present, altho the Prince is not in any danger, it would be very imprudent to remove his Royal Highness til a happy change takes place. The Prince wishes very much to see his brother Prince Adolphus, but I do not think he can for some time pay his respects at Brunswick or Strelitz.

Your Majesty may depend on my paying the greatest attention to proper oeconomy in every branch of the Prince's Household. It is my intention and my

[1] No. 1848.   [2] Count Finckenstein, the Prussian Minister of State
[3] The Prussian Foreign Minister.

duty to bring the expences into as narrow bounds as possible, and as the high rank of the Prince will permit. According to your Majesty's commands the Prince is allways announced as Comte Diepholtz, nevertheless it is impossible to prevent his Royal Highness being treat as a Prince of the Blood Royal of England and a[s] such we cannot prevent considerable expence; but the sum your Majesty has been graciously pleased to allow is perfectly sufficient, and I have no doubt of keeping the whole expences within bounds.

I am glad your Majesty has been graciously pleased to approve what I proposed for Doctor Domier; he is a very deserving good man, and most affectionately attached to the Prince, tender, and careful in his attendance on his Royal Highness. My reason for proposing the 300 a year proceeded from my knowing that the Doctor had refused a very respectable situation for life, and 300 year appointments, which the Doctor refused in a very delicate manner, assuring me he never would quit your Majesty's service while you was graciously pleased to employ him. I will have the honor to write your Majesty when I have seen Comtes Finkensteen & Haugwitz or when I may be permitted to pay my respects to the King of Prussia and the Royal Family. The King and Court are now at Potsdam.

The Prince continues to be much pleased with Mr Arbuthnot which gives me great satisfaction. Nothing could exceed the kind attention of the whole Electoral family of Saxony during the Prince's stay at Dresden. (9055–7)

DR. WILLIAM DOMEIER'S *Memorandum*

[*Berlin, 23 Oct. 1798.*] (*Enclosure.*) H.R.H. the Prince Augustus left Dresden as soon as his health allowed him to travel without danger to his life. The journey produced the effect it always has done of bringing on repeated and violent attacks of the asthma, so that he was not able to lie down upon a bed, but was forced to sleep in an arm chair. Neither has he eat nor drunk anything, except such remedies and diluting liquors, which served to keep off imminent danger, and afford temporary relief.

If the Prince's health is the criterion by which he is to be guided, and in my situation, as H.R.H. physician, I can have no other principle to act upon, it is impossible for him to travel any more during the course of this winter. To undertake a fresh journey would not only shorten the Prince's life, but it would be impossible to answer for what might happen on the road. As H.R.H. pays the greatest attention at present to regimen, diet, and everything in which his health is concerned, and enjoys now repose in airy comfortable appartments, I am flattered with the hope that the violent paroxism which has continued from his first leaving Vienna untill his arrival at Berlin will soon cease, and that by unremitting care and attention he may pass the winter as well as can be expected in a cold climate, which is always hurtful to breast complaints of all kinds, but particularly so to those under which H.R.H. labours. (9058–9)

1864 EARL SPENCER *to the* KING

[*Admiralty, 23 Oct. 1798.*] Earl Spencer has the honour of laying before your Majesty some further letters which have been received relative to the proceedings of the squadron on the N.W. coast of Ireland. No accounts have reached the Admiralty this day from that quarter. (9060)

1865 PRINCESS AMELIA *to the* KING

[*Worthing, 25 Oct. 1798.*] It is quite out of my power to resist writing you on this day to offer my congratulations & to assure you no one feels more thankful than I do for your accession to the throne. I feel the more thankful every day as every hour convinces me more of the real attachment with which you are beloved, & nothing can be so gratifying to a child as seeing their father so loved & respected. I cannot but say how much I wish I could have seen you today & tried, though in vain, to express what my heart feels.

I am most grateful for your kindness to me. Mr. Keate's arrival has made me very happy as he gave me so good an account of all those I love so dearly. I am ready to stay here as long as it is thought necessary. I am sorry not to see & be with you, but regaining my health will repay me for being deprived of the pleasure of being with you at this minute. The kindness & affection you shew me affords me many pleasant & happy moments in the day. As to thanking you or saying what my heart dictates is impossible therefore I must have recourse to your usual goodness to be convinced of my gratitude & beg of you, my dearest papa, to be assured of the affection with which I remain your dutiful & grateful child. (Add. Georgian 14/18.)

1866 PRINCE ADOLPHUS *to the* KING

[*Hannover, 28 Oct, 1798.*] Your Majesty's very gracious letter of the 15th of this month which I received last Tuesday has rendered me infinitely happy, and I return you my most humble thanks for it. I rejoice infinitely to hear that Weymouth agrees so well with your Majesty, and I offer up my most sincere prayers to the Almighty that you may long continue enjoying such good health, and also that you may always receive such good accounts of the success of your arms.

Last Thursday the great news arrived here of the transports which had conveyed the French troops to Egipt being all burned to the number of *361*, and two Venetian men of war; and that Buonaparte has been forced to retreat from Cairo to Rosette. I hope in a very short time we shall have the account of this General being taken with all his men, and then this expedition will have ended in a glorious manner for us. All this advantage is owing to the fine victory gained by your Navy, and may this ever be the case, and all the French expeditions fail in the same manner.

I am very much obliged to your Majesty for the permission you have given me to meet my brother at Brunswick; my intention was to have met him there in case he took that road, but as I did not know that for certain I thought it better not to trouble you on this subject. I received yesterday a letter from him mentioning his being so very unwell as to be incapable of continuing his journey to Russia; and that he would probably be obliged to remain the winter in Germany. Should this be the case, and that he should not come to Brunswick, I hope your Majesty will allow me to go over and see him. I might be perhaps of some use to him and after so long an absence I should be very glad to see him again. I have now nothing more to add. (48526)

1867   E. LIVINGSTON *to the* KING

[*Berlin, 3 Nov, 1798.*] I had the honor to write your Majesty the 7 October from Dresden and the 23 from Berlin, when I inclosed Doctor Domier opinion of his Royal Highness Prince Augustus' health. I have now the satisfaction to inform your Majesty that his Royal Highness is very much better, and I now flatter myself that the violence of the fit of asthma is drawing towards an end; at same time Doctor Domier is decidedly of opinion that the Prince must remain some time very quiet and must be on his guard against geting cold. The doctor says he is certain his Royal Highness cannot with any degree of safety proceed any further north this winter, and from long experience, he sees with regret the Prince's complaints augments to a very allarming degree by travelling, even in the best season of the year.

His Royal Highness has not been able to pay his respects to his Prussian Majesty and the Royal Family; the Prince sent me last Wednesday to Potsdam to make his excuses to the King and Queen and to express his regret at not being able to wait on them in person; also to assure their Majestys of his gratitude for the flatering attention payd him since his arrival at Berlin. I was received most graciously by their Majestys and had the honor to dine at the King's table with all the Royal Family. The King of Prussia express'd himself in very high terms of esteem for your Majesty and in a very friendly manner for the happyness of your Family and the prosperity of your Kingdoms and said many very handsome things of your Majesty brave Admirals and invincible Fleets, and assured me it gave him great pleasure to have it in his power to shew his wish to be of service to Prince Augustus and that your Majesty may depend on his making Berlin as agreeable as possible to the Prince. The Queen was also very gracious and made very exact enquireys about the Prince's health, offering earnest wishes for his speedy and perfect recovery, as did every one of the Royal Family. I can assure your Majesty it is impossible the King and his Ministers could have shewn more flattering attention than they have done for his Royal Highness since our arrival, and I have no doubt the same attentions will be continued for the Prince during his stay at Berlin.

His Royal Highness is extremly well lodged, the rooms are lofty and well air'd, the Prince says he has not breath'd so freely in any lodging since he left Naples. Doctor Domier wishes that the Prince may be removed to some warm climate, at same time he thinks the very short journey from this to Cuxhaven would be very severe on his Royal Highness at this advanced season of the year. So far as I am able to learn I believe the Prince wishes to stay here the winter;

at [the] same time I dare say he will be ready to obey your Majesty's commands if you wish him to pass the winter in some other country. His Royal Highness sufferings were so great from Vienna here and even on the journey from Trieste to Vienna, I tremble at the thoughts of the Prince undertaking a long journey by land. (16720–1)

1868 THE DUKE OF PORTLAND *to the* KING

[*Bulstrode, Saturday night, 3 Nov. 1798.*] The Duke of Portland most humbly conceives it to be his duty in laying the Lord Lieutenant's dispatch before your Majesty to observe to your Majesty that it is written in consequence of a representation from the American Minister[1] on the behalf of his Government of the dangerous consequences which he apprehended would arise from suffering the Irish traitors to reside or even to remain in America for ever so short a time, which the Duke of Portland transmitted the substance of to the Lord Lieutenant, as also the opinions of your Majesty's Law servants that no Power had a right to transport its convicts into the territories of a State with which it was in amity without having previously obtained the consent of such State; which was communicated to the Lord Lieutenant at the same time.[2]

Considering that by the ordinary course of the post the signification of your Majesty's pleasure respecting the attendance of the University of Cambridge cannot be made to the Vice-Chancellor[3] earlier than Tuesday, the Duke of Portland submits with all humility to your Majesty whether your Majesty will please to command them to attend at St James's sooner than the week after next.

The Duke of Portland humbly begs leave to observe to your Majesty that no dispatches or accounts of any sort from Ireland have been received today excepting that of the Lord Lieutenant which is herewith submitted to your Majesty.[4] (9061–2)

[1] Rufus King (?1754–1827). Minister in England, 1796–1803.

[2] Rufus King told Wickham that the President of the U.S.A. (John Adams) 'would not suffer any of the traitors from Ireland to land in America, and that if they set foot on shore he would instantly have them sent back to Europe'. 'There were', said Cornwallis, 'about eighty of the prisoners who signed their acquiescence in perpetual banishment...but there are not more than fifteen of that number who are men of sufficient talents and consequence to render the place of their exile a matter of any material importance, and I much doubt whether the fifteen principal traitors will not be able to do as much mischief during their imprisonment in Ireland as they could effect by their intrigues in any part of Germany.' (Ross, *Cornwallis Corresp.*, II, 427–8.) The prisoners were eventually allowed to enter the Prussian service.

[3] Dr Robert Towerson Cory (*c.* 1759–1835). Master of Emmanuel, 1797–1835; Vice-Chancellor, 1797–8, and 1813–14; Professor of Moral Philosophy, 1809–13. He was presented at Court on 7 Nov., when the King received the congratulatory Address from the University.

[4] There is no reference in Portland's correspondence with the King of the decision, called for by Cornwallis, to appoint Castlereagh Irish Secretary, Pelham having finally decided that his health was not sufficiently re-established to enable him to return to Ireland. The King's consent was given verbally on 31 Oct. Next day Portland wrote to Pelham: 'Had other more urgent occupations permitted me I should have told you yesterday that I performed the sad task of acquainting the King with your finding it necessary to decline returning to Ireland—upon which he expressed his sincere concern, and observed that you were too much a man of honour for him to urge you to do what, he was sure, your want of health alone would have suffered you to decline, & again repeated that *he was most extremely sorry for it.* After some time he resumed the subject, & added "*with the views you (meaning myself) know I had, & in the present circumstances it is the greatest loss & the greatest disappointment I could have experienced*".

1869   EARL SPENCER *to the* KING, *and the reply*

[*Admiralty, 6 Nov. 1798, 2 p.m.*] Earl Spencer has the honour to lay before your Majesty the proceedings of a court martial held on two marines of the Diomede, one of whom is sentenced to death, and as there are no circumstances of alleviation in his case Earl Spencer feels it his duty to submit to your Majesty that the sentence should be carried into execution.

Earl Spencer also has the honour of laying before your Majesty letters that have been received this morning from Lord Duncan and from Ireland. (9063)

[*The King's reply, Windsor, 6 Nov., 6.33 p.m.*] I see the propriety of the court martial having sentenced one of the marines of the Diomede to be hanged, and therefore direct that it shall be enforced.

By the letter which accompanied it I find the two captures made by Captain King[1] is confirmed, and trust that the two letters from Dublin also transmitted to me by Earl Spencer are the forerunners of the captures of the French frigates seen in Killala Bay. (Althorp MSS.)

1870   *The* REV. HENRY LLOYD'S[2] *Petition to the* KING

[*Cambridge, 6 Nov. 1798.*] The very humble Petition of Henry Lloyd, A.M., late Fellow of Trinity College, and at this time Regius Professor of Hebrew at Cambridge, sheweth,

That if ever it was particularly necessary for the sacred light of Scripture to shine before men, with full and unclouded splendour, it is so, in this age of irreligion and infidelity.

That with an earnest wish to counteract the baneful effects of some modern publications, the petitioner has given public lectures explaining the Scriptures in their original language, to a respectable audience in the University of Cambridge, where sacred studies would easily be revived were the Hebrew Professor encouraged to give *gratuitous* instruction.

That the petitioner's first ambition is to be able to persevere, with effect, in the discharge of this most important duty.

I thought in justice to H.M. & to you I ought to make this report to you of what passed in the Closet relative to yourself, & I certainly have not added one though I may have omitted many words expressive of the same sentiments.' (Add. MSS. 33106, f. 120.)

The King was strongly prejudiced against the appointment of an Irishman as Chief Secretary; for one thing, it was a departure from precedent. Portland too had his doubts. He referred (in a letter to Pelham, 4 Oct.) to 'the jealousy of an Irish Secretary of which (notwithstanding all the merit which I am most ready to allow, and which you first taught me to believe was possessed by Lord Castlereagh) I cannot be surprised or can regret the difficulty and unwillingness H.M. feels in divesting himself' (Add. MSS. 33106, f. 98). And see *Cornwallis Corresp.*, II, 430, 441. 'He is so very unlike an Irishman.'

[1] Sir Richard King (1774–1834). Lieutenant, 1791; Captain, 1794; Rear-Admiral, 1812; K.C.B., 1815; Commander-in-Chief in the East Indies, 1816–20; Vice-Admiral, 1821; Commander-in-Chief at the Nore, 1833–4. Succeeded his father as 2nd Baronet, 27 Nov. 1806. In 1798 he commanded the *Sirius*, of 36 guns. The two Dutch frigates which he captured off the Texel were the *Waakzaamheid*, of 26 guns, and the *Furie*, of 36 guns, each with French troops on board.

[2] Regius Professor of Hebrew, 1795–1831; Vicar of Babraham, Cambs., 1798–1831. Died 23 Jan. 1831, aged 67.

That, notwithstanding the plain intention of the Royal Founder,[1] King Henry 8th, and the subsequent express desire of King James 1st that some high ecclesiastical dignity should be annexed to the Hebrew Professorship, (as is actually the case in the sister University)[2] no addition whatever has been made to the original £40 a year: a scanty provision for a Royal Professor with a wife and an increasing family!

That the petitioner being likely to derive no solid advantage from his high academical honours, or the friendly disposition shewn him by some exalted characters among whom he may reckon his Grace the Archbishop of Canterbury, the Bishops of Ely[3] & Landaff;[4] the Vice Chancellor, and Masters of Colleges at Cambridge, real necessity induces him to sollicit, what it shall be the study of his whole life to merit, from a monarch, never indifferent to the interests of religion, some assistance to his endeavours in the revival of sacred literature, among those who are to be teachers of it, and stewards of the mysteries of God!

And the petitioner shall ever pray,[5] [&c]. (9064–5)

1871 SIR WILLIAM HOWE to the KING

(*Copy*)[6]

[*7 Nov. 1798.*] Captain Godfrey of the Royal Artillery, having from the peculiar and distressing situation of his family considered himself obliged to make every sacrifice rather than hazard a seperation from them by embarking to join his command in the West Indies, has with the most poignant regret humbly requested his Majesty's permission to resign his Company in the Artillery.

Captain Godfrey, feeling every zeal for his Majesty's service and extreme distress of mind in taking a measure in time of war which nothing but necessity has driven him to, most humbly beseeches his Majesty in consequence of nineteen years faithful service and being wounded at the seige of Gibraltar, to be permitted to hold his present rank and pay, and serve in Great Britain as an Artillery Officer during the war. (9067)

1872 THE DUKE OF PORTLAND to the KING

[*Burlington House, Wednesday, 7 Nov. 1798, 12.55 p.m.*] The Duke of Portland most humbly requests your Majesty's permission to use this method of laying

---

[1] Of the Chair of Hebrew (1540).

[2] Benjamin Blayney (1728–1801), Professor of Hebrew at Oxford since 1787, was also Canon of Christ Church.

[3] James Yorke (d. 1808), Bishop of St David's, 1774; of Gloucester, 1779; of Ely, 1781–1808.

[4] Richard Watson (1737–1816), Bishop of Llandaff, 1782–1816.

[5] Writing to Pitt on 9 June 1801 the Professor admitted that he had been troublesome to him during the last four years of his Administration on account of his repeated applications. He said, 'The income of the Hebrew Professor in the sister University has actually been raised from the original £40 to more than £1000 per annum, which accounts for the greater proficiency in *sacred literature* in *that* University. I may add that to your bounty several Cambridge Professors (whose lectures are *surely* of less importance than such as would promote a study of the scriptures in their original language—a study at no period so loudly called for as at the present) are actually indebted for augmentation of income.' He concluded, on a very pathetic note: 'I will give a brief account of my sufferings by saying that I have been *for four months*, after a painful struggle and without any extravagant, much less vicious propensities, a prisoner in the Fleet!' (*Chatham Papers*, 152.)   [6] Signed by Howe.

before your Majesty the fair copy of the answer to the Address of the University of Cambridge which your Majesty has been pleased to approve, & begs leave at the same time to submit to your Majesty a drawing which Garter[1] has sent of the form in which he would propose to carry your Majesty's commands into effect respecting the augmentation to the arms & supporters of Lord Nelson & his additional crest.

The Duke of Portland humbly hopes your Majesty will condescend to pardon the Duke of Portland's absenting himself today from his duty on your Majesty in consideration of an eresipylus which has appeared on one of his legs & entirely disables him from walking. (9068–9)

1873   THE DUCHESS OF WURTEMBERG *to the* KING

[*Stutgard, 9 Nov. 1798.*] I had just taken up my pen to congratulate your Majesty on Sr John Warren's having anew saved Ireland by his having beat the Brest Fleet, when I was honoured with your gracious letter of ye 7th of October which made me very happy, as it brings me so good an account of your health.

I regret that my dear sisters Sophia and Amelia are not yet quite recovered. Sophia's nerves I fear will never be as strong as we could wish. They are all five so amiable that it is a pity when there is anything to give them pain. The more I see of other people the more attached I feel to my sisters, as I believe it seldom happens to find so many equally good in their different ways, which makes them the pleasanter to live with. My poor little Amelia is a constant grief to me. I pity her sadly at her age to be deprived of every sort of exercise and amusement. However, I flatter myself, severe as this complaint has been, it will be of use to her through life, as by her letters it appears to have given her a serious pious turn, which she most likely would never have had to the same degree at her time of life without this illness which has opened her mind.

Your Majesty is very good to enquire about the Duke's arm, I am very uneasy about it and fear I must look on it as a lost case. The fracture was very well cured but the contusion will never be got the better of. He begs me to present his humble duty to your Majesty.

Our weather continues very fine. I go out almost every day in an open carriage. On Wednesday I was at the Opera which is a new peice, a translation of the Tempest and set to music by Zumsteeg; the connoisseurs look on it as very fine. They wanted to have performed it on Monday which was the Duke's birthday, but he would not allow any notice to be taken of the day, and spent it with me and the children at Luisbourg. We supt at Count Zeppeline's who inhabits a building adjoining to the Castle.

My walking is a little prevented by the great damp of the Plannis which is something in the style of the middle walk in the Park, which makes me much regret Louisbourg. I believe however it would have been almost impossible to have remained there any longer as like most old houses neither the doors nor windows shut sufficiently to keep out the cold. (51506–8)

[1] Sir Isaac Heard (1730–1822), Garter King-of-Arms since 1784. Knighted, 1786.

1874 HENRY DUNDAS *to the* KING

[*Wimbledon, 9 Nov. 1798.*] Mr Dundas humbly transmits for your Majesty's information a precis of the interesting paper which your Majesty was pleased to procure for Mr Dundas from the Library at Hanover. It is perfectly obvious that upon this document are founded all the ideas which have been floating in France for near a century past respecting the conquest of Egypt. (9070)

1875 PRINCESS AMELIA *to the* KING

[*Worthing, 13 Nov. 1798.*] I cannot resist again trespassing on your time, though I troubled you so very lately with one of my letters, to thank you for the very kind one I received from you this morning, & likewise to tell you myself of the improvements that have taken place in my knee. Sr. Lucas[1] & Mr. Keate returned on Saturday morng.; they desired me to keep my leg down & no longer lay it up upon a sopha. This I have done notwithstanding the very severe pain it makes me suffer, as you may immagine, as it is four months since I have let it hang, & therefore of course it hurts me very much, but my dear papa, I am more certain than ever that I cannot recover without going through a great deal of pain & exerting very much, which I am ready to do how much soever it makes me suffer at the time if it in the end cures me & enables me to be amongst the rest of my family.

Sunday I went out of airing & on Monday I drove in the carriage as far as the *Downs* where no one could see me & tried a horse of Gl. Goldsworthy's. The motion naturally was painful but Mr. Keate assures me it is entirely owing to the joint at this moment being so unaccustomed to any exercise & that though the real disorder is so much better I shall for some time feel the same pain, therefore what I suffer at this moment need not alarm me. Certainly I am better from all I have now told you, & be assured, my dearest papa, of my willingness to undergo any pain to get well. Nothing ever was so goodnatured as Gl. Goldsworthy; the horse he is so good as to lend me is *Frolick*. I tried him again today. He says you know him very well.

Now, my dearest papa, allow me to thank you for the kind things you say in your letter. In the midst of my sufferings nothing can be so comfortable as being assured of your affection & of yours & mama's approbation. I perfectly agree with you in thinking it would be a great pity to remove me from hence till it is certain it can be done without any chance of its hurting me.

I am ashamed of having written you so long an epistle, but knowing your dear good heart would rejoice at hearing of my improvements I could not resist the temptation they gave me of writing, as I never feel so happy as when conversing with you & dear mama, even in this manner, & be assured of the unalterable attachment with which I remain [&c.]

[P.S.] Might I beg of you to give my most affte. duty to dear mama & I will write to her tomorrow. (Add. Georgian 14/20.)

---

[1] Sir Lucas Pepys (1742–1830), the King's physician; created Baronet, 22 Jan. 1784. President of the College of Physicians, 1804–10.

1876   THE BISHOP OF WORCESTER (RICHARD HURD) *to the* KING

[*Hartlebury, 14 Nov. 1798.*] I am unable to express the sense I have of your Majesty's goodness in honouring me with the gracious letter of the 11th from Windsor, this moment received. It is full of that unaffected piety & generous concern for the good of your people, & indeed of all Europe, which has distinguished your Majesty's reign, so replete with extraordinary events. It pleases God to discipline your virtues by unusual trials, &, I hope, to lead us all to repentance and reformation by your means. Accept, Sir, my warmest congratulations on the striking success of your Fleets, & courage as well as conduct of your seamen in a part of the globe whence your Majesty's glory will spread itself to the utmost bounds of it; while we at home are also rejoicing at the blessing wch. God has given to your arms & endeavours to protect your dominions from the most malignant enemy that has appeared in the world. May we profit, as we should do, by so signal an instance of divine favour!

It is with infinite pleasure we understand that your Majesty and the Queen & the Royal Family have returned in good health from Weymouth. Princess Amelia's complaint is of that sort, & her R. Highness so young, that a speedy & perfect recovery may, we hope, be expected.

Your Majesty is pleased to take notice of some late exertions in my office. I wish they were in all parts of it such as they ought to be. But age and the infirmities of age forbid this, but will never I think lessen the veneration & duty, with which I am [etc.]

P.S. Your Majesty will be pleased to accept my best thanks for your condescension in forwarding the Gottingen exercises to me. I suppose they now lie at Worcester, to wch. place I will send for them. I shall not be able to read them with any attention. But I hope your University continues to deserve your royal favour & protection in spreading good principles in religion & government all around them. (9071-2)

1877   WILLIAM PITT *to the* KING

[*Downing Street, Friday, 16 Nov. 1798.*] Mr Pitt humbly begs leave to submit to your Majesty the draft of the Speech for opening the Session, which he hopes will meet with your Majesty's approbation.

It has been thought on consideration that it may be more prudent to omit any reference to the intended measure of an Union with Ireland, as so long an interval must elapse before any communication on the subject can be made to the Irish Parliament, and as it might not be advantageous to announce the intention publicly till further prepararatory [*sic*] measures have been taken for preventing an hasty opposition arising in Ireland.[1] (9077)

1878   THE DUKE OF PORTLAND *to the* KING

[*Burlington House, Saturday night, 17 Nov. 1798.*] The Duke of Portland humbly begs leave to acquaint your Majesty that he has received this evening a letter from

---

[1] The King's reply from Windsor on the 17th, 8.25 a.m., is in Stanhope, III, Appendix, p. xvii. He approved the suggestion about the proposed Union.

the Recorder to inform him that he (the Recorder) is so severly attacked by the gout in his feet as not to be capable of attending your Majesty with his Report on Monday, but that if it should be your Majesty's pleasure to have the Report made on that day the Common Serjeant[1] will be ready to supply the Recorder's place. The Duke of Portland therefore humbly requests your Majesty's commands whether the Report is to be postponed or the Common Serjeant ordered to attend with it in the place of the Recorder. (9076)

1879 *Letters from* LORD GRENVILLE *to the* KING, *and the reply*

[*Cleveland Row, 17 Nov. 1798.*] Lord Grenville begs leave to inform your Majesty that Lord Buckingham has sent to Dropmore (to be forwarded from thence to your Majesty) one ram & ten ewes of the Irish breed, which Lord Grenville has directed to be sent to your Majesty's farm at Windsor. (9073)

[*From Lord Grenville, Cleveland Row, 17 Nov.*] Lord Grenville has the honour to transmit to your Majesty the drafts of the dispatches which were sent last night by messenger to Sir Charles Whitworth. The leading ideas which they contain were discussed in the morning at the meeting of your Majesty's confidential servants, and being generally approved there, Lord Grenville thought they were so conformable to the general system which your Majesty has been pleased to approve, that your Majesty would not be displeased at their being executed without any loss of time.

Lord Grenville begs leave humbly to acquaint your Majesty that his brother Mr Grenville has undertaken to proceed on a special Mission to Berlin and Vienna to carry these ideas into execution, if your Majesty should graciously approve of it. Under these circumstances Lord Grenville humbly submits to your Majesty that it may be better for the present to postpone the appointment of any successor to Lord Elgin. (9074-5)

[*The King's reply, Windsor, 18 Nov., 10.25 a.m.*] The dispatches for the direction of Sir Charles Whitworth are so conformable to the sentiments I have constantly expressed to Lord Grenville that he has judged very properly in not delaying the messenger till they had been laid before me.

I am happy to find he has at length persuaded his brother Mr. Grenville to proceed on a special commission to Berlin and Vienna to attempt to carry into execution the ideas that have been now transmitted to Petersburgh; this fortunate appointment undoubtedly makes it elligible not to name a successor to the Earl of Elgin at Berlin till this great plan has been brought to maturity.[2]

I desire Lord Grenville will return my thanks to the Marquiss of Buckingham for the Irish ram and ten ewes now at Dropmore. I desire Lord Grenville will

[1] John Silvester (1745–1822). He attended at the Queen's House on the 19th. Common Serjeant of the City of London, 1790; Recorder, 1803–22. Created Baronet, 27 Dec. 1814.
[2] Thomas Grenville was given full power to treat with Austria, Prussia and Russia. He arrived in Berlin on 17 Feb. 1799, and was there until the end of August. He did not proceed to Vienna.

either order them to be sent to the Home Park at Windsor or I will order that they may be sent for from Dropmore whichever is most convenient to Lord Grenville. (Fortescue MSS.)

1880   THE DUKE OF YORK *to the* KING

[*Oatlands, 18 Nov. 1798.*] I have the honor to report to your Majesty that I met Mr Pitt this morning by appointment at Mr Dundas's, when he mentioned to me that accounts had been received from Holland which could be relied upon that the French troops have been for the most part moved out of Holland into Brabant on account of the insurrection, and that the Dutch are so exceedingly discontented with the French that if a body of troops could be sent there, it would be easy to sieze upon Flushing. He added that it was intended to run as little risk as possible at that therefore [*sic*] a confidential person had been sent over to Holland and that nothing was to be undertaken till his return, but that if his report was as favourable as there was every reason to suppose, that it would be necessary for the troops to be almost instantaneously embarked and that therefore every preparation must be secretly made without loss of time, and that being aware that there was not a sufficient body of infantry in Great Britain to form such a corps particularly at so very short a notice he anxiously wished that your Majesty would allow a detachment of Foot Guards to be employed upon this service. I answered Mr Pitt that I certainly would lay his request before your Majesty, and I thought it my duty to trouble your Majesty with this letter, as I understand that Mr Dundas means to pay his duty to your Majesty tomorrow and lay before you the whole plan proposed and the intelligence upon which it is founded. (9078–9)

1881   *Letters from* WILLIAM PITT *to the* KING

[*Downing Street, Tuesday, 20 Nov. 1798, 6 p.m.*] Mr Pitt humbly begs leave to acquaint your Majesty that the Address this day was moved and seconded with great propriety by Lord Granville-Leveson, and Sir H. Mildmay,[1] and after a few desultory observations from Sir John Sinclair and Sir Francis Burdett, was unanimously agreed to.[2] (9080)

[1] Sir Henry Paulet St John-Mildmay (1764–1808), M.P. for Westbury, 1796–1802; for Winchester, 1802–7; for Hampshire, 1807–8. Succeeded his father as 3rd Baronet, 8 Aug. 1784. By his wife Jane (c. 1764–1857), daughter of Carew Mildmay, he had three daughters and eleven sons, and she survived him almost fifty years.

[2] *Parl. Register*, LII, 34–50; *Colchester Diary*, I, 163. Canning wrote to his uncle, the Rev. William Leigh, on the 21st: 'All the plagues of party squabble, & hopeless expectation, light on Opposition, for not moving an Amendment yesterday to the Address! Sir John Sinclair & Sir F. Burdett did their best to be sure—but they afforded no reasonable excuse for any human being on our side saying anything. It would have looked too like a determination of speech-making to have got up after their nonsense, at which the House only laughed; & so we were up at ½ p. 5. And here am I with a speech in pocket (not *literally* so) for the first opportunity. And that cannot occur in less than a fortnight or three weeks.

But Granville Leveson!—It was gratification enough for one day to hear *him*! Next to speaking very well one's self, which is a strong *sensual* pleasure—is the delight of hearing any one about whom one is interested acquit himself to admiration. And never since Charles's [i.e. Ellis's] first speech was I so highly satisfied as yesterday. It was much in Charles's manner—& I think as good as his was—modest—

[*Downing Street, Thursday, 22 Oct.* [*Nov.*].] Mr Pitt humbly begs leave to submit to your Majesty's consideration the answer to the Address of the House of Commons, and also a Message recommending a provision for Lord Nelson similar to what has been made on other occasions, which if it receives your Majesty's approbation may be presented to the House either today or tomorrow.[1] (9054)

1882   THE DUKE OF PORTLAND *to the* KING

[*Burlington House, Sunday, 25 Nov. 1798.*] Your Majesty has been pleased to intimate at different times to the Duke of Portland a desire that a plan should be formed for the settlement of the Charaib land in the island of St. Vincent; the Duke of Portland therefore most humbly begs leave to submit to your Majesty a plan by which he presumes to think that object might be speedily and effectually attained, and with that view he has communicated it to the Board of Treasury, his correspondence with which Board and Mr. Secretary Dundas upon that subject he lays with all humility at your Majesty's feet. (9081)

1883   LORD GRENVILLE *to the* KING, *and the reply*

[*Cleveland Row, 26 Nov. 1798.*] Lord Grenville has the honour to transmit to your Majesty a private letter which he has received from Mr. Garlike, and he proposes with your Majesty's permission, to authorise Mr. Garlike to pay to General Stamfort his expences at the sum there fixed. Lord Grenville has also received from the Prince of Orange an application on this subject. (9082)

[*The King's reply, Windsor, 27 Nov., 9.03 a.m.*] Lord Grenville is very right in directing that Genl. Stamfort shall be paid the monthly fixed sum, which is certainly very moderate, but all that gentleman seems to wish. (Fortescue MSS.)

1884   PRINCE ADOLPHUS *to the* KING

[*Hannover, 28 Nov. 1798.*] I have just received from Mr. de Lenthe the agreeable news of your Majesty's having purchased Mr. Eckhart's house and of your having approved of the plan which I sent him over for your perusal. I cannot refuse myself the pleasure of returning you by this post my most humble thanks for the very gracious and generous manner in which you have been pleased to settle everything and I begg you to be assured that I shall strive as long as I live to

temperate—manly—embarrassed now & then, but never perplexed—& full of good sense & good taste throughout. I believe there never was an Address better moved—and it was admirably *seconded* too...Sir Harry did wonders...' (Harewood MSS.)

[1] The King's Message was presented by Pitt on 22 Nov. It proposed to give Nelson and the two next successors, being his male heirs, an annuity of £2,000 for and during their lives. 'But H.M. not having it in his power to grant an annuity to that amount, or to extend the effect of the said grant beyond the term of his own life, recommends it to his faithful Commons to consider of a proper method of enabling H.M. to grant the same' and to settle it on Nelson 'and the two next persons on whom the title of Baron Nelson of the Nile...shall descend...' (*Parl. Register*, LII, 61). The East India Company gave him £10,000.

render myself worthy of this new proof of your favour.[1] It is impossible for me to find words to express how happy this new change in my situation makes me and particularly the very advantageous and flattering manner for me everything has been arranged. I can only say that my constant endeavours shall be to prove to you by my behavior the gratitude I feel for your goodness. I cannot conclude without presenting your Majesty my most humble and sincere congratulations on Edward's safe arrival, on whose account I own I had been alarmed, and may you enjoy still many as glorious and happy years as this has been hitherto is the most fervent prayer of [&c.]. (48527)

1885   *Letters from* WILLIAM PITT *to the* KING

[*Downing Street, 3 Dec. 1798, 8.30 p.m.*] Mr Pitt humbly begs leave to acquaint your Majesty that in the Committee of Ways and Means this day, he opened the plan for substituting a tax of 10 prct. on all income[2] (the produce of which he estimates at £10,000,000 within the year) in lieu of the assessment imposed last Session; and the Resolutions for that purpose, after some opposition from Mr Tierney and a few words from Sir John Sinclair, were agreed to without a division, and with great appearance of cordial concurrence in the principle of the plan.[3] (9083)

[*Downing Street, Wednesday, 5 Dec.*] Mr Pitt humbly begs leave to offer his excuses for not having attended your Majesty at St James's today, having thought it prudent to stay one day at home, in order to get rid of a cold and hoarseness, the continuance of which would just at present be very inconvenient. He also takes this mode of requesting your Majesty's permission to recommend Mr Weston,[4]

---

[1] He also became Lieutenant-General in the Hanoverian army in 1798.

[2] That is, exceeding £60 per year, and the tax to be graduated on incomes between £60 and £200 (from less than $\frac{1}{2}\%$ on incomes between £60 and £65 to just under 10% on incomes between £195 and £200. He estimated the national income, allowing for 'the necessary deductions', at something like £102,000,000:

	Millions
Rent on land possessed by landlords	20
Land in the hands of tenants	5
Tithes	4
Mines, and shares in canals, timber &c	3
Rent of houses	6
Income arising from professions	2
Income on the above article in Scotland	5
Income of Irish absentees	1
Income from West Indies	4
Interest of the Funds	12
Profit on foreign trade	12
Profit on home trade	28
	102

(*Parl. Register*, LII, 94–125. See also Colchester, *Diary and Corresp.*, I, 164.)

[3] Fox wrote to his friend O'Bryen: '...I have not read nor shall I read the new Income Tax Act, but I hear it is very oppressive upon the commercial men, and the more it is so, the better will it please me.' (Add. MSS. 47560, f. (?)43.)

[4] Samuel Ryder Weston (*c.* 1748–1821) was a Canon Residentiary of St Paul's, 15 Dec. 1798–1821. He was Rector of St Leonard's, Exeter, 1778–80; Rector of Marwood, Devon, 1782–1804; Rector of Little Hempston, 1784–1821; Rector of Kelshall, Herts., 1805–21; Rector of Therfield, 1812–21.

now Prebendary of Canterbury, to succeed to the vacant Residentiaryship of St. Paul's, and Mr Norris[1] to succeed Mr Weston at Canterbury. Lord Hardwicke has long anxiously interested himself for the former, and Lord Spencer for the latter, who was his tutor at Cambridge; and they will both be much gratified should this arrangement meet your Majesty's approbation. (9086–7)

1886 LORD GRENVILLE *to the* KING, *and the reply*

[*Cleveland Row, 5 Dec. 1798, 11 a.m.*] Lord Grenville humbly hopes that that [*sic*] your Majesty will be graciously pleased to excuse his attendance on your Majesty today, he being confined with a severe cold. Mr Grenville will have the honour, with your Majesty's permission, to take leave of your Majesty today, & will set out on Monday or Tuesday next.

Lord Grenville will trouble your Majesty tomorrow morning with his credentials & powers for your Majesty's royal signature, and also with the warrant for his appointments at the same rate as those of your Majesty's Minister at Vienna,[2] which he hopes your Majesty will not disapprove.

Lord Grenville's indisposition has prevented his getting as forward as he had wished with the drafts, but he has no doubt of having them finished in time to submit them to your Majesty previous to Mr Grenville's departure. (9084–5)

[*The King's reply, Queen's House, 6 Dec., 7.15 p.m.*] I am sorry to find Lord Grenville's absence yesterday was occasioned by a severe cold. I should hope a little attention to it will be a perfect cure. I was much pleased with Mr. Grenville's language; he assured me that if he receives his instructions he will set out on Monday; his having appointments as the Minister at Vienna seems highly just. (Fortescue MSS.)

1887 THE DUCHESS OF WURTEMBERG *to the* KING

[*Stutgardt, 7 Dec. 1798.*] The gracious manner in which your Majesty is always so good as to interest yourself about the Duke and me, makes me look on it as my duty with my husband's leave to acquaint you of a most vexatious event which has taken place here within these few days. The Duke has discovered that a set of wicked intriguing men had got hold of the Hereditary Prince and availing themselves of his youth drawn him into taking inconsiderate steps which had his father not instantly put a stop to, must hereafter have made the young man very unhappy. The Duke feels doubly wretched at being obliged to have some people who were concerned in this cruel business taken up, as he fears he shall be necessitated to punish one or two of them.

Your Majesty I am sure will pity us, and as a father feel how miserable the Duke is at seeing this business made public. He is very fond of all his children but

[1] The Rev. Charles Norris (*c.* 1743–1833) was appointed a Prebendary of Canterbury, also on 15 Dec. Vicar of Shudy Camps, Cambs., 1780; Rector of Fakenham, Norfolk, 1790–1833; Rector of Wolterton with Wickmere, 1791–1800. He was a Prebendary until his death.
[2] Sir Morton Frederick Eden.

particularly so of this son, and is wounded to the soul at his being drawn into mischief. I am worked to death out of love to the Duke and to his children which I look on as my own. I have been doubly uneasy as at first I had great reason to tremble for the effect it would have on my husband's health. Thank God he is now better, though I fear he will be very long recovering this severe blow. I am very anxious by every attention in my power to ease his mind and shew him the affection I so strongly feel for him.

I must however intreat your Majesty not on this one imprudence to form a bad opinion of our son, whose heart I believe to be very good, but from that very cause is the more open to be drawn into mischief when hid under the cloak of friendship.

The world is very bad and what I think most horrid is that people are not satisfied with being wicked themselves but they wont allow anybody else to be good and try to undermine and destroy the principles of youth. (51509–10)

1888   E. LIVINGSTON *to the* KING

[*Berlin, 9 Dec. 1798.*] I had the honor to write your Majesty the 3d November. The King arrived at Berlin from Potsdam the 13th; since that period nothing exceeds the very kind attention shewn Prince Augustus by everyone of the Royal Family. His Royal Highness dines with the King very frequently, and every time I have the honor to meet their Majestys they express their wish to render Berlin as agreeable to the Prince as possible and never fail making the most affectionate enquireys after your Majesty, the Queen and all the Royal Family. The nobility and Ministers of State are also extremly attentive and hospitable to the Prince. Hitherto his Royal Highness, from his precarious state of health, has been under the necessity of refusing most of the invitations to dine or sup abroad.

Since we left Vienna the 28 Septr. the Prince has suffer'd exceedingly and has not been in bed above six nights. Your Majesty will see by the note[1] I have the honor to inclose from Doctor Domeier that there can be no question of proceeding to Russia this winter. The Doctor assures me that the Prince's constitution cannot stand the severity of the winters in Germany or Russia, and by remaining long in either, the consequences would be fatal. Hitherto the Prince has been very careful in his diet &c. and I hope may continue so during the winter. I observe the least cold never fails bringing on a severe fit of asthma. The Prince bears the very frequent and severe attacks of asthma with more patience than I ever saw. As there can be no question of returning to Italy in these critical moments, and the climates of all the northern countrys on the continent being hurtful to the Prince's

[1] Dated 8 December: 'Since the arrival at Berlin H.R.H. the Prince Augustus has, upon the whole, enjoyed a better state of health than travelling. However, the cold climate shows evidently its hurtful influence, for the paroxysms of the indisposition have since six years not been so frequent than this winter. Both the expectoration of the matter & the difficulty in breathing leaves H.R.H. only for short intervals and soon after a new paroxysm comes on again. Altogether the present state of health of the Prince is such that it seems not to allow any thought of removing from this town during the winter or early in the spring from here, without throwing the patient's life in danger. I thank it to H.R.H.'s constancy in taking remedies and to his prudence in the diet that at present he breathes free, and that the expectoration of matter has much diminished, so that he has been out, but he has not been able to sleep in the bed, but only in an arm chair.' (16726)

constitution, I cannot take on me to give any opinion and will wait your Majesty's commands on that subject.

I think it my duty to inform your Majesty that I have the Prince's commands to remit 500 per annum to Mr. Coutts the banker. I understand that money is to be employ'd for the education of his son, which does honor to the Prince's feelings, and I dare say will meet your Majesty's approbation.

I take the liberty to inclose for your Majesty's perusal a letter I received from Sir Charles Whitworth, which will explain Sir Charles' sentiments better than any extract I could make from his letter.

These three last days his Royal Highness has been freer of asthma than at any period since our arrival at Berlin. (16722–3)

SIR CHARLES WHITWORTH *to* E. LIVINGSTON

[*St. Petersburg, 20 Nov. 1798.*] (*Enclosure.*) I have the honor to acknowledge the favor of your letter and to express the sincere pleasure I feel at the hope of seeing his Royal Highness Prince Augustus in this country. I perceive however with regret that we are not likely, on account of the continuance of his Royal Highness indisposition, to be gratified with his visit untill the spring.

I shall expect his Royal Highness's further orders, and in the meantime I can venture to engage that his Royal Highness will be receiv'd by his Imperial Majesty with every mark of distinction and friendship which can be expected from the friendly sentiments which subsist between his Majesty and the Emperor of Russia, as well as from those amiable qualities by which his Royal Highness has endear'd himself in every country which he has visited.

I beg, Sir, that you will have the goodness to assure his Royal Highness of my most sincere devotion & of the zeal with which I shall endeavour to render his stay in this country as satisfactory as possible. I have an appartment in my own house in which I flatter myself I shall be able to accomodate his Royal Highness and his suite, and I can only say that the gratification which I should feel at being able to contribute personally to his Royal Highness's comfort would infinitely overbalance every other consideration which his Royal Highness might, in his goodness, urge in opposition to my sincere wishes.

I wait his Royal Highness's further orders for everything relating to passports, &c. (16724–5)

1889   THE DUKE OF PORTLAND *to the* KING

[*Burlington House, Monday night, 10 Dec. 1798.*] The Duke of Portland most humbly begs leave, for the reasons assigned in the last paragraph but one of Lord Grenville's letter, to lay at your Majesty's feet in addition to the dispatches which have been this day received from Ireland, which contain such farther accounts of the dispositions of the English Militia Regiments as, the Duke of Portland hopes, will appear to your Majesty to leave little doubt of the offer of their services being renewed by them all; & of the progress which the Lord Lieutenant has made in sounding the opinions of the principal persons in Ireland upon the subject of an Union, the success of which measure, considering the quarter from whence it is to meet with the greatest resistance; the Duke of Portland presumes to think your Majesty may be of opinion that a proper degree of firmness & liberality may effectually secure. Your Majesty will probably not be displeased to know that Mr Foster, the Speaker of the Irish House of Commons, & Sir John Parnell have been prevailed upon to wait for Lord Castlereagh's arrival, & that *that* may be expected in the course of tomorrow or Wednesday at farthest.

The motives which have suggested to Lord Grenville the propriety of writing the letter which is herewith most humbly submitted to your Majesty, are so obvious, that the Duke of Portland cannot but think that it would be a very unbecoming presumption in him to offer any observations upon it to your Majesty. He confines himself therefore to the mere statement of the purport of his answer to Lord Grenville, by which he promised Lord Grenville to lay his letter at your Majesty's feet & afterwards to communicate it to such of your Majesty's confidential servants as are intitled to have access to the official correspondence; & he concluded his note with assurances to Lord Grenville that he should be most ready to cooperate with the common friends of the Lord Lieutenant & of the Marquiss of Buckingham in restoring them to those habits of intercourse & confidence which had heretofore prevailed between them & which were so desireable for the interest of your Majesty's service. With this view therefore, unless your Majesty should order it otherwise, it is the Duke of Portland's intention to withhold from the Lord Lieutenant the communication of Lord Grenville's letter, which would almost necessarily call for a reply on the part of the Lord Lieutenant & provoke an explanation which might increase the difficulty of beleiving that the difference which has unhappily arisen between the Lord Lieutenand & the Marquiss of Buckingham is attributable only to those causes to which Lord Grenville seems desirous to ascribe it.[1] (9088–90)

1890   LORD GRENVILLE *to the* KING

[*Cleveland Row, 10 Dec. 1798, 11 p.m.*] Lord Grenville has the honour humbly to submit to your Majesty the drafts of instructions to Mr. Grenville, who is now quite ready to set out as soon as there shall be any appearance or probability of a change of wind. Lord Grenville is concerned to say that his hopes of success are much diminished by the last letters both from Berlin & Vienna. (9091)

1891   THE DUKE OF NORTHUMBERLAND *to the* KING

[*Syon, 11 Dec. 1798.*] With every sentiment of respect and reverence to your royal Government and person, I humbly beg leave to approach your Majesty, and intreat your Majesty to accept this declaration of my feelings, not as the ordinary

---

[1] A bitter quarrel had broken out between Cornwallis and the Marquess of Buckingham on the question whether the Lord Lieutenant had the right to prevent him from taking his militia regiment back to England, now that the rebellion had been suppressed. Buckingham described the Lord Lieutenant as 'the most contemptible personage' he knew. (*Dropmore Papers*, IV, 412.)

language of ceremony or etiquette, but as the deep and sincere effusions of a mind attached from well considered devotion to that system of government of which your Majesty is happily the presiding principle, and if I might venture to say so, of affectionate attachment and regard to your royal person and family.

I should not, Sire, have ventured to have obtruded upon your Majesty these, I hope, almost unnecessary declarations, but that I feel myself called upon to make a solemn appeal to your Majesty on a subject which bears upon my feelings and honour as a man and as a person of some rank and station in the country.

Your Majesty, descended from a long line of glorious and illustrious ancestry, will not be offended that another man of comparatively plain and humble pretensions, should partake in a small degree in the feelings of his Royal master; nor be much surprised that a Duke of Northumberland should entertain some dissatisfaction at being exposed to the delays, uncertainty, coldness, and indignity of office.

I will not venture, Sire, to obtrude upon your Majesty any further preface. I complain of the conduct of your Majesty's Secretary of State for the Home Department, and know not where to look for redress but in the justice and condescension of your Majesty.

In consequence of a resolution which had been come to on the 25th of April 1798 by the Lieutenancy of the county of Northumberland, I did myself the honour of writing to the Duke of Portland on the 1st of May last, requesting your Majesty's permission to resign the situation of your Majesty's Lieutenant for that county, and on the 3d of the same month, his Grace returned an answer signifying your Majesty's assent to my request.

For the particulars contained in these several papers I must beg leave to refer your Majesty to the copy of the correspondence, which accompanies this.

Your Majesty will be pleased to take into your gracious consideration the situation in which I have been placed from the date of the letter above alluded to, up to the present moment. I was aware, Sire, that there was neither obedience to your Majesty, nor duty to the Constitution under which I live, to continue to be the ostensible holder of an important office from which your Majesty had accepted my removal, and for the discharge of the duties of which, I had of course ceased to be legally responsible. Under these feelings and impressions, I have repeatedly written to the Duke of Portland, as your Majesty's proper officer in this Department, but have had the ill fortune to receive no distinct answer to any of my applications, and to many of my letters no answer whatever.

Permit me therefore to implore your Majesty to release me from my present ambiguous situation, of equal contradiction I am certain to your royal wishes and the intentions of the Constitution. I have no desire upon the subject but a direct and specific understanding of its issue. I can resist no command, no wish of my Sovereign; but as my health forbids me to pursue any object of very active business, so my honour demands of me to acquiesce in no indignity of office; more particularly in a case where I conscientiously meant to have deserved well of my King and my country.

I have thought it right, Sire, to lay before your Majesty the whole of the correspondence[1] between the Duke of Portland and myself on this subject, which accompanies this humble representation, in order that your Majesty may in your gracious wisdom observe whether any exaggeration has obtained in this paper respecting it. (9092–3)

1892 EARL SPENCER *to the* KING, *and the reply*

[*Admiralty, 11 Dec. 1798.*] Earl Spencer proposes to have the honour of presenting Captain Berry[2] to your Majesty at St James's tomorrow, & presumes to submit to your Majesty the propriety of conferring the honour of knighthood on that officer, which would have been conferred on him had he arrived with Lord Nelson's dispatches, and has only been prevented by the unfortunate capture of the Leander, on which occasion great praise is due to all those concerned, and therefore it ought not to be the cause of their losing any mark of your Majesty's approbation to which they might otherwise have been entitled. (9094)

[*The King's reply, Windsor, 12 Dec., 7.40 a.m.*] There cannot be a doubt of the propriety of Captain Berry being knighted this day, which honour would have been conferred on him had he arrived with the news of Ld. Nelson's success, from which he was prevented by the capture of the Leander on board of which he was a passenger, and where he as well as those belonging to the ship behaved in a manner to deserve great praise. (Althorp MSS.)

1893 WILLIAM PITT *to the* KING

[*Downing Street, Tuesday, 11 Dec. 1798, 9 p.m.*] Mr Pitt humbly begs leave to acquaint your Majesty that a Motion was made this day by Mr Tierney declaring the opinion of the House against forming any fresh engagements on the Continent; which was objected to in a speech of peculiar eloquence and force by Mr Canning, and after a few observations in its support by Mr Jekyll, and against it by Mr W. Dickenson,[3] was negatived without a division.[4] (9095)

1894 THE KING *to* LORD GRENVILLE, *and the reply*

[*Windsor, 11 Dec. 1798, 9.25 a.m.*] The drafts of Instructions to Mr. Grenville seem very well calculated for the arduous task he has to attempt, and though the

---

[1] Folios 9101–15.

[2] Sir Edward Berry (1768–1831), Lieutenant, 1794; Captain, 1797; Nelson's flag captain at the battle of the Nile; knighted, 12 Dec. 1798; created Baronet, 1806; K.C.B., 1815; Rear-Admiral, 1821. Captain Berry, who was sent to England in the *Leander* with Nelson's dispatches was captured off Candia on 18 Aug., and Captain Capel proceeded with duplicates, overland, *via* Naples.

[3] William Dickinson (1771–1837), M.P. for Ilchester, 1796–1802; for Lostwithiel, 1802–6; for Somerset, 1806–31. A Lord of the Admiralty in Pitt's last Ministry, 1804–6. His father, also named William, was in Parliament with him.

[4] *Parl. Register*, LII, 158–211. The King's reply from Windsor on the 12th, 7.55 a.m., is in Stanhope, III, Appendix, p. xvii. Canning's speech, said Lord Minto, 'was one of those great performances which establishes him in a very high rank of parliamentary ability and makes him for a very rising as well as aspiring person in England' (Minto MSS.).

letters from Vienna are far from encouraging, yet as Berlin is better in the last than the former post, I trust that the negociation may at length succeed.

I am surprised by a correspondence in the box which has been without authority carried on by Mr. Mitchell[1] with P[rince] Charles of Hesse;[2] this may clogg the interview with Lieut. Col. Anstruther; I owne I love plain dealing, and ever dread the interference of intriguers. (Fortescue MSS.)

[*Lord Grenville's reply, Cleveland Row, 11 Dec.*] Lord Grenville has been honoured with your Majesty's commands of this morning. He begs leave to express to your Majesty his dutiful acknowledgements for the approbation which your Majesty has been graciously pleased to signify of the drafts to Mr. Grenville.

Lord Grenville was as much surprised as your Majesty expresses yourself to be at the letter from Mr. Mitchell. He had on the receipt of it immediately directed Mr. Hammond to write to that gentleman to discontinue these intrigues, and a letter to that effect will go by tonight's mail. (Fortescue MSS.)

1895 PRINCE EDWARD *to the* KING

[*Windsor Castle, 13 Dec. 1798.*] With humble submission I beg leave to intrude upon your Majesty for a few moments to report that, as the period for which the house in St. James's Street was engaged, will expire on the 20th instant, it is my intention to move on that day into Kensington Palace, and to make shift, with the apartments that were late Mrs Crofton's, until the upper ones can be got ready for me. Permit me, Sir, therefore to hope you will condescend to grant me the same indulgences, when resident at that Palace, which my brother Ernest enjoys at St. James's: these are the breakfast, fuel, candles, and household linen, together with the necessary attendance of maid servants to keep the apartments in order, and a porter to wait at the door. These, though in themselves trifling, will be of great consequence to me, and I flatter myself your Majesty will not think me too presuming in troubling you respecting them, a liberty I should not have taken, had I not found that it was expected I should pay for the fuel and candles that have been provided for the house in St. James's Street, as well as for the wages and board of the maid servant who was hired to take care of the house.

As I have not the opportunity of addressing your Majesty personally respecting my own concerns, and if even such were afforded me, as I should probably feel too apprehensive of offending or being troublesome to venture speaking as fully as I should wish, perhaps you will condescend to admit of my taking this mode to sollicit of your bounty, that some arrangements may be adopted for my table and equipage. However limited your Majesty may be pleased to make the establishment of the former, if it were furnished from the Board of Green Cloth, in the manner the Duke of Clarence's is, the advantage, and personal comfort to myself would be infinitely greater, than were I to receive an allowance in money far more considerable than the expence it would so cost, as the necessity of providing

---

[1] Mitchell is not mentioned in the *Dropmore Papers*, and Anstruther very obscurely.

[2] Prince Charles (1744–1836) was the brother of William, Landgrave of Hesse-Cassel (1743–1821).

myself at first with every requisite for housekeeping, together with the wages of the different servants whom I should be obliged to employ to conduct such an establishment, would fall very heavy upon me, notwithstanding an allowance ever so liberal were granted me for that purpose. At the same time I request your Majesty will understand I only hope for this indulgence while resident at the Palace or in any other place to which I may be sent by your express commands; but if at any time I am absent on my own pleasure I must of course expect that the expence of my living, while away, must fall entirely upon myself.

With respect to equipage, as my first, and principal object must ever be that of being as much about your Majesty's person as possible, without running the risk of appearing officious or intrusive, I sollicit your gracious assistance to keep up only such an establishment of horses as may be found absolutely necessary to enable me to do this, expecting that any additional ones I may keep for my own private amusement or satisfaction must be out of my own pocket. I have therefore taken the liberty of inclosing herewith a statement of what appears to me to come under the description of horses of indispensible necessity which is humbly submitted to your Majesty. As I flatter myself you will be graciously pleased to permit my horses to stand in the Royal stables at Kensington, I shall beg leave to observe that if your Majesty condescends to acquiesce with my sollicitations on this head, the expence will be rendered far less to you, and the benefit to be derived by me infinitely enhanced, if the forage for my stable is supplied from the Department of the Master of the Horse in kind, instead of being left to me to provide from a pecuniary allowance to be made for that purpose; for where so large a proportion of provender is laid in as is requisite for your Majesty's Establishment, the comparative very small addition that would be wanted for mine will scarcely be felt; but if I should be obliged to lay it in myself, the same quantity would occasion to me a very heavy expence.

Humbly hoping that your Majesty will condescend to take the requests I have thus preferred into your gracious consideration, I beg leave to assure you of my firm and decided intention to use every endeavour to live within the bounds of such income, and to confine myself in the purchase of appointments of every description to the limits of such sum (destined for me to equip myself on my first setting out), as you may be pleased hereafter to allot, and that my conduct in every respect shall be guided by that one object which I shall ever hold foremost in view; the desire of giving you satisfaction and of meriting your good will.

Should anything in this letter, in the most distant manner give your Majesty displeasure, I humbly sollicit your pardon for it, as nothing is further from my intentions, and the only motive which has induced me to address you on the several subjects it contains, is to prevent my incurring debts which it would hereafter fall very heavy on me to discharge. (45955–6)

[*Enclosure.*]

Statement of the number of horses which I humbly conceive to be indispensibly necessary to enable me to attend upon his Majesty at such times as he shall be pleased to permit, submitted with the utmost deference to the King's consideration.

Saddle horses	{	2 chargers 4 hacks for the road 4 inferior hacks for the groom to follow upon.
Coach horses	{	10, including a relay to take the postchaise between Kensington and Windsor 4 to remain at Kensington for to be in readiness to take me to the Queen's House, St. James's or the theatres, when the others have been out
Footmen's hacks	{	4, including a relay for the footmen to use, when in attendance on the post chaise between Kensington and Windsor

It may not be improper to observe that twelve carriage and ten saddle horses, including the grooms hacks, was the establishment fixed by his Majesty for me at Luneburg, and that afterwards on my removal to Hannover stable room and forage was found by the Master of the Horse for six of my own in addition to this number, which makes up precisely the same establishment that is now submitted to the King. (45955–6)

1896 *Letters from the* DUKE OF PORTLAND *to the* KING

[*Burlington House, Thursday night, 13 Dec. 1798.*] The Duke of Portland most humbly begs leave to lay his most dutifull & gratefull acknowledgements at your Majesty's feet for your Majesty's most gracious condescension in letting him know what passed in the Audience your Majesty was pleased to give yesterday to the Earl of Moira. The Earl appears to have been sensible that the Duke of Northumberland had not borne himself in such a manner as to prove that he was impressed with a proper sense of your Majesty's great indulgence to him, & with that view the Earl of Moira seems to have submitted to your Majesty the only circumstance which could justify the impatience which the Duke of Northumberland has so repeatedly & unreservedly expressed, & possibly in the hope of disposing your Majesty to listen with favor to the Duke of Northumberland should he presume to request your Majesty to consider him as devoted to your Majesty's service as his infirmities will permit.

The Duke of Portland begs leave with all humility to acquaint your Majesty that he has seen Lord Castlereagh who arrived this afternoon, & has learnt from him that all the great personal interests in Ireland are disposed in favor of the Union, that the Bar will probably be so divided upon it as to prevent any serious consequences from the violence with which it was first apprehended that their resistance to it would be carried on, & that if Mr Foster the Speaker can be induced to refrain from taking an active part against it, which Lord Castlereagh cannot bring himself to think impracticable, the Opposition will not have any rallying point, & will be likely to produce little more than the clamour which cannot but be expected to arise out of the apprehensions which such a measure must naturally create in the proprietors of land & houses in Dublin & the traders & shopkeepers of that city. No clear opinion has yet been able to be formed of the part which the inhabitants of the northern part of Ireland will take on this subject, but Lord Castlereagh is confident that no hostile declaration to it had been made by the linen manufacturers at the time he left Ireland, that there was some occasion to beleive that the old advocates for parliamentary reform might not be disinclined to consider the incorporation of their House of Commons into the Legislature of Great Britain as having a tendency to ameliorate the state of their representation; that from the aspect which the Rebellion had wore in the south they might be disposed to look to a Union as a necessary safeguard against the power of the Catholicks (the better sort of whom seem inclined to consider it no less an instrument of protection to them) & that the treatment which the Americans, with whom the people of Ulster are very intimately connected, have received from the French, & the total inability of that Power to give the Irish any assistance in their schemes of separating themselves from this country, together with the flourishing state of their trade & manufactures, have softened in a considerable degree their prejudices against the Government of this country, & brought them at least to hear an Union mentioned without resentment or emotion. It was Lord Castlereagh's opinion that there was no part of Ireland, not even of Dublin itself, where the question of Union would be now considered as such a violation of the Constitution as not to be fit to be entertained or where the merits of it would not be discussed, & that being the case the Duke of Portland hopes your Majesty will not deem him too sanguine in his expectations of its being perfected in the course of the present Session. (9096–9)

[*Burlington House, Friday night, 14 Dec.*] The Duke of Portland humbly begs leave to acknowledge the receipt of your Majesty's commands respecting the Lieutenancy of Northumberland, & to express his most gratefull sense of the sanction which your Majesty has most graciously condescended to bestow on his conduct in that unpleasant business. (9100)

1897 WILLIAM PITT *to the* KING

[*Downing Street, Friday, 14 Dec. 1798, 11.45 p.m.*] Mr Pitt humbly begs leave to acquaint your Majesty that the Income Bill was opposed on the Report this day by Mr Taylor, Sir John Sinclair, Sir Francis Baring and Mr W. Smith and supported by Mr Simeon, the Solicitor-General, Sir W. Young, Mr Dundas and Mr Pitt. The numbers in favor of the Bill were 183, and against it, 17.[1] The House afterwards went into the Committee, and after reporting a progress, fixed Monday for resuming the Committee. (9116)

[1] The number is wrongly given as 23 in *Parl. Register*, LII, 276, but 17 names, excluding the Tellers, are given. On the 18th *The Times* declared: 'Upon inquiry we find that the minority in the House of Commons on Friday night was 17 and not 23. It was misstated in all the papers, and the report in the House was generally such as was first stated.' See also Colchester, *Diary and Corresp.*, I, 165–6.

[*Cleveland Row, 14 Dec. 1798, 10.45 p.m.*] Lord Grenville having just received the inclosed, loses not a moment in forwarding it to your Majesty. He has not yet received anything from Mr. Smith or from the India House, but if anything material should arrive he will have the honour to transmit it to your Majesty by another messenger.[1] (9117)

[*The King's reply, Windsor, 14 Dec. 1798, 2.05 p.m.*] I am infinitely pleased with Lord Grenville's attention in having, immediately on the receipt of Sir Moreton Eden's dispatch, communicated it to me. So strange an end of Bonaparte's life and that of his army must in the opinion of every religious mind appear the interposition of Divine Providence against that wicked nation, and ought to rouze every European Power to step forth in defence of everything that is dear to man. Should any further accounts arrive I trusted [*sic*] they will be also forwarded to me. (Fortescue MSS.)

[*From Lord Grenville, Cleveland Row, 16 Dec.*] Lord Grenville humbly begs leave to submit to your Majesty the draft of a letter to the Duke of Brunswic which would be very useful to Mr Grenville, and which if your Majesty should be graciously pleased to transcribe it, would still be in time to overtake him at Yarmouth. He set off this morning. (9118)

[*The King's reply, Windsor, 17 Dec., 9.20 a.m.*] I forward to Lord Grenville the letter for the D. of Brunswick which I have transcribed, as also one for my sister, both of which I desire may be sent to Mr. Grenville. I think the news brought on Friday by Sir Moreton Eden's servant must have great effect when known in France, and if the Neapolitans take possession of the Ecclesiastical State a general rising in Italy will probably attend it, which must place so clear a game before the Court of Vienna that unless some very unfair underhand negociation has been carried on, she cannot but avail herself of so fortunate an event. (Fortescue MSS.)

1899   The Duke of Portland *to the* King

[*Burlington House, Monday night, 17 Dec. 1798.*] In obedience to your Majesty's commands the Duke of Portland has consulted with Mr Pitt on the subject of the Duke of Northumberland's letter to your Majesty, & upon the fullest consideration they are satisfied that it is their duty to submit, with all deference to your Majesty's superior wisdom, their humble opinion that the Duke of Northumberland does

---

[1] Early in the morning of the 14th a King's messenger arrived at the Foreign Office with despatches from Sir Morton Eden, the British Envoy at Vienna, with the information that at a Council of War in Egypt, which was attended by some Egyptians who professed to be friendly, a man from Tripoli shot Bonaparte dead and the native officers at once fell on the French officers and killed them all. This was followed, it was said, by a general massacre of the French who were in Cairo. This was believed to be the result of a bold conspiracy to get Bonaparte and his superior officers together, and, having dispatched them, to produce a general rising against the French troops dispersed over the great city of Cairo. This information came to Vienna from Constantinople. He had to admit (5 Dec.) that the news was at least premature, 'and that there has only been an insurrection at Cairo in which, indeed, many French were slain'. (*Paget Papers,* I, 141.)

not express the desire which, your Majesty is pleased to observe, he feels to retain the Lieutenancy of the county of Northumberland in that explicit & dutifull manner in which, independently of the great indulgence your Majesty has condescended to shew him, it would have become him to have testified his readiness to obey your Majesty's commands, & that it is not for the interest of your Majesty's service, or indeed in their power, consistently with what your Majesty's dignity appears to them to require, to offer to your Majesty's consideration any means which have not been already employed to bring the Duke of Northumberland to a more correct sense of his duty to your Majesty. They therefore feel it incumbent upon them most humbly to recommend it to your Majesty not to suffer a longer time to intervene on the appointment of Commissioners to execute the office of Lieutenant of Northumberland than is necessary for your Majesty to make choice of proper persons for that service, & as soon as your Majesty shall have satisfied yourself in that respect, that your Majesty should order the Duke of Portland to signify to the Duke of Northumberland that your Majesty has released him from the Lieutenancy of that county, & has appointed the persons whom your Majesty will by that time have fixed upon, to execute that office.

The Duke of Portland humbly begs leave to acquaint your Majesty that he has been informed today by Mr Steele that Sir Thomas Liddel[1] is ready to obey any commands your Majesty may be pleased to lay upon him, & the Duke of Portland has no doubt but that when he pays his duty to your Majesty on Wednesday he shall be able to submit to your Majesty the names of a sufficient number of other gentlemen to afford your Majesty a choice of fit & respectable persons able & willing to execute the commission of Lieutenancy of your Majesty's county of Northumberland. (9120–1)

1900   THE KING *to* HENRY DUNDAS, *and the reply*

[*Windsor, 22 Dec. 1798, 6.30 p.m.*] I sincerely congratulate Mr. Dundas on the very suitable connection that is going to take place in his family by the proposed marriage of his youngest daughter[2] with the eldest son of Sir Ralph Abercromby, and perfectly coincide with him in opinion that every good quality is more affected by blood than many persons choose to allow and were this not the case, why are there some families noted for valor, others for generosity; whilst some for cruelty and others for avarice, and I am certain Sir Ralph Abercromby must be highly delighted also at this event. His old father will also rejoice, and I could have wished it had been one year sooner, when a most respectable woman,[3] now at rest, would have been a partaker of the happiness of her relations. (Melville MSS. Scottish Record Office.)

[1] Sir Thomas Henry Liddell, Lord Ravensworth (1775–1855). M.P. for Durham, 1806–7. Succeeded his father as 6th Baronet, 1791; Sheriff of Northumberland, 1804; peerage, 1821.

[2] Montague Dundas (1772–1837) married, 20 Jan. 1799, George Abercromby (1770–1843), who succeeded his mother (the wife of General Sir Ralph Abercromby) as 2nd Baron Abercromby, on 11 Feb. 1821. She was given a peerage, 28 May 1801 in reward for her late husband's gallantry. George Abercromby was M.P. for Edinburgh, 1805–6; for Co. Clackmannan, 1806–7, and 1812–15.

[3] Dundas's mother, Anne, daughter of Sir William Gordon, 1st Baronet of Invergordon, married Robert Dundas, of Arniston (d. 1753), as his second wife, in June 1734. She died, 19 March 1798, aged 92.

[*Dundas's reply, Downing Street, 22 Dec., 3 p.m.*] Your Majesty's very condescending goodness to Mr. Dundas respecting his domestick feelings at a late interview with which he was honoured, can alone plead his apology for presuming to ask your Majesty to read the enclosed letter from his daughter now at Edinburgh, to which is subjoined Mr. Dundas's answer. (9122)

1901 EARL SPENCER *to the* KING, *and the reply*

[*Admiralty, 23 Dec. 1798.*] Earl Spencer has the honour of congratulating your Majesty on the complete success of the expedition against the Island of Minorca, an account of which is contained in the accompanying dispatches from the Earl of St Vincent, and it is a great additional ground of satisfaction that this important acquisition has been made without any loss on the part of your Majesty's forces. (9123)

[*The King's reply, Windsor, 24 Dec., 9.18 a.m.*] It is impossible to have read with more pleasure the matter of Captain Duckworth's[1] dispatches, though the style is not the most correct. The expedition to Minorca has that most agreable circumstance, that the success has been attained without any loss.

Earl Spencer probably expected that the Earl of St. Vincent would feel the rebuke he has, I think, justly received. I trust it will make him a little more civil to those under his command. (Althorp MSS.)

1902 THE DUCHESS OF WURTEMBERG *to the* KING

[*Stutgard, 1 Jan. 1799.*] Though it will be out of my power to finish my letter today I cannot at this early hour deny myself the pleasure of recalling to your Majesty a daughter who has been taken up in entreating the Almighty to continue to you the marked protection which on every occasion he has so strongly evinced, and that your life may long be granted for the comfort and happiness of your subjects and family. I hope your Majesty is convinced that amongst them all none is more attached to you by every tie of respect and affection than myself.

This week has been very fatiguing to me who am now used to the quietest of all lives. Tuesday was a continual hurry as it is the only great Gala throughout the year, and Wednesday we had a very fine traineau party consisting of two and thirty sledges; the sight is beautiful and the motion very pleasant. At our return home the Duke gave a Ball and I did not get to bed till one o'clock which is very late for this house as I believe there is not a candle burning in general at half past ten o'clock. On Thursday, to add to the fatigues, they unfortunately gave the Tragedy of Fiesco which lasted without end, and is like most modern pieces full of nonsense and much better not to be acted. Indeed much mischief is done at present by the Theatre, as Kotzebue,[2] who is the favorite author of the public

---

[1] Sir John Thomas Duckworth (1748–1817). Captain, 1780; Rear-Admiral, 1799; Vice-Admiral, 1804; Admiral, 1810; K.B., 1801; G.C.B., 1815; Commander-in-Chief at Jamaica, 1803–5; Governor and Commander-in-Chief of Newfoundland, 1810–13; created Baronet, 1813.

[2] August Friedrich Ferdinand von Kotzebue (1761–1819), the German dramatist; a prolific writer of plays, historical works, &c. He was assassinated by Karl Sand, a Jena student, for ridiculing the *Burchenschaft* movement.

tries to render vice plausible and virtue insignificant, in addition to which he weakens every principle. I regret very much to see by the papers that many of his plays are translated into English but trust their total mischievous tendency may when acted offend a British audience and compleatly prevent any body encouraging them. There is an Englishman here of the name of Laurence who is so much vexed at some of the things that having been translated have appeared at Drury Lane that he is employing his leisure time in making a literal translation of some good peices, and I hope will send them to Covent Garden.

I am now almost totally confined to the house, as our weather has been dreadfully severe. I hope that in England it is not equally so or your Majesty will be prevented hunting. The cold being very unusual here, has done much harm in the vineyards and everybody thinks they will be three years before they can recover.

On Monday the Hereditary Prince went to the University at Tubingen where he is to study some time and has expressed great regret for the errors he was drawn into.

The Duke begs that I will present his humble duty to your Majesty. I know your dislike to unnecessary letters and have therefore undertaken to present his good wishes with my own for the New Year. I will now intrude no longer on your Majesty than to assure that I am [etc.]. (51511–3).

1903   WILLIAM PITT *to the* KING, *and the reply*

[?*3 Jan. 1799.*] Mr Pitt entreats your Majesty's permission humbly to acquaint your Majesty that Mr Dundas has stated to him on the part of his Under-Secretary Mr Huskisson an anxious wish (in consequence of his having formed an engagement to marry) to obtain from your Majesty's favor a floating pension for himself (in the event of his quitting his present office without any other provision) and the settlement of a part to his wife in case she should survive him.[1] From the arrangements which your Majesty has been pleased to approve of in similar instances with respect to persons holding the same description of office, Mr Pitt trusts the request may not appear unreasonable; and takes the liberty also to submit whether £1000 pr annm. (as a floating pension) to Mr Huskisson, with £600 pr annm. continued to his wife, may not be a proper allowance.[2] (9193–4)

[*The King's reply, Windsor, 4 Jan. 1799, 8.30 a.m.*] I do not mean to object to the floating pension in favour of Mr. Huskisson, though I cannot but remark that these kind of provisions for Under-Secretaries are quite novel, for they were not known in the reign of my late grandfather and seem now claimed as matters of course, which cannot but be the more felt when I am hourly applied to by persons of quality for very necessitous relations who I cannot in the least assist, and I cannot, when the thought occurrs, but feel the very dreadful situation in

[1] Huskisson married (6 April 1799) Elizabeth Emily (*d.* 1856), daughter of Admiral Mark Milbanke. He remained Under-Secretary of State for War until March 1801. *The Times* published an accurate report of the matter on the 15th.

[2] Docketed by the King: 'Mr. Pitt. Not dated'—which would seem to indicate that the King's docket was added at a later date.

which my younger children will be left should it please Heaven to put a period to my life. (W. D. Adams MSS.)

1904 THE DUKE OF PORTLAND *to the* KING

[*Burlington House, Monday night, 7 Jan. 1799.*] The Duke of Portland most humbly entreats your Majesty's forgiveness for his having omitted to lay the enclosed dispatches from the Lord Lieutenant at your Majesty's feet this morning. By the mistake of the messenger who carried them yesterday afternoon to Mr Pitt they were returned to the Duke of Portland's Office instead of being brought to him or to Mr Wickham & were by that means not discovered till this morning, when to the Duke of Portland's great mortification he found that his directions had not been observed, for which act of inadvertence he again with all humility implores your Majesty's pardon.

The sanction which your Majesty has been pleased to give to the means which your confidential servants have submitted to your Majesty as necessary to be taken by the Lord Lieutenant for insuring the success of the Union, incline them to beleive it to be their duty most humbly to recommend it to your Majesty to order the Duke of Portland to signify your Majesty's commands to the Lord Lieutenant to withdraw without further delay from Mr Saurin[1] those distinctions which have been conferred upon him & which the D. of Portland understands to be a Patent of Precedence which gives that gentleman a professional rank immediately after your Majesty's Attorney General; the very conspicuous situation in which Mr Saurin stands both as a man of character & of abilities & knowledge in his profession makes the violence of his conduct with respect to the Union & particularly the last attempt he is stated to have made, which is little short of an act of mutiny, appear to your Majesty's servants to be of so dangerous a tendency & so subversive of all order & authority that they feel it their indispensable duty to lay this humble representation before your Majesty, & also in consequence of the Lord Lieutenant's report of the dangerous & disloyal conduct of the non-commissioned officers & privates of the Royal Irish Regiment of Dragoons they beg leave with all humility to submit to your Majesty's superior wisdom their dutifull representations that the case is too flagrant to admit of the delicacy which the Lord Lieutenant has felt upon the occasion & that an immediate reduction of the Regiment is as expedient as the other modes of proceeding upon which he has desired to receive your Majesty's commands.[2] (9126–8)

[1] William Saurin (?1757–1839), M.P. [I.] for Blessington, 1799–1800, and an opponent of the Union, but subsequently a placeman as Attorney-General [I.], 1807–22.

[2] Cornwallis wrote to Portland on the 2nd: 'I understand Mr. Saurin was this day employed in soliciting the Officers of the different corps of yeomanry in Dublin, to sign a paper stating their determination to lay down their arms in case the measure of Union was brought forward...I much fear Mr. Saurin's conduct will render it necessary for me to submit, through your Grace, to his Majesty, the indispensable necessity of withdrawing from him those professional distinctions of which his former conduct has rendered him so deserving.' Portland drafted a reply, stating: 'I am ordered to desire your Excellency to inform him that the King has no further occasion for his services. It is to be distinctly understood that it is because Mr. Saurin mixed up military and civil proceedings.' Before the letter was sent to Dublin, Portland received one from Castlereagh, dated the 7th, in which he said: 'Mr. Saurin

[*Hannover, 9 Jan. 1799.*] The messenger's setting off for England procures me an opportunity which I cannot refuse myself the pleasure of profiting of, that of presenting to your Majesty my most humble congratulations on the beginning of this new year; that you may see many very happy returns of it, and that it may turn out as glorious for your arms as the last was. This wish is and must be the sincere one of every honest man, particularly at the present moment when the superiority of your arms over those of the ennemy can alone rouse the Sovereigns of Europe out of the phlegmatic state into which they are fallen. It seems unluckily that Austria is not to be roused; at least it is inconceivable how it can leave the King of Naples so long in the lurch: if the Austrians would advance I am convinced that the French would soon be obliged to leave the greatest part of Italy, all the Ecclesiastical territory, as they would risk to have their retreat cut off; but now that the Emperor has not done anything the French have fallen with all their forces on the Napolitans and I am very much afraid they will soon ruin their Army. General Mack has certainly done all in his power to make his Army act well, but with troops which have not served in almost half a century, and which are very ill officered it is almost impossible to expect that much can be done, espeacially when they have been twice or thrice beat: I am doubly sorry for the King of Naples, as he is the only Sovereign on the Continent who has played a noble part and tryed to resist the French.

I have the honor of sending your Majesty by the messenger two packets I received some weecks ago from Stuttgard, which I have had no opportunity of forwarding before. My sister mentions in all her letters how happy she is, and everybody who comes from Stuttgard assures me the same. My house has employed me a good deal of late: the worckmen have worcked very hard to get my rooms ready but they have been very much stopped by the cold weather. I hope it will be finished in a fortnight and then I shall remove into it immediately. I cannot express in words to your Majesty how much I feel for this new proof of your goodness, and I certainly shall endeavour all my life to render myself worthy of your favor, which I value above everything, and the preservation of which will ever be the cheif aim of [etc.]. (48528-9)

[*Hannover, 12 Jan.*] I am very sorry to be obliged to importune your Majesty so soon again with a letter, but the importance of the subject will I trust excuse me. The very gracious manner in which you were pleased to express yourself to Mr. Dundas on his mentioning to your Majesty my desire of marrying my cousin Princess Louis of Prussia,[1] has been always deeply impressed in my heart, and

called on me today. I had a very long conversation with him. I am inclined to think he will not persevere in his intention of laying down his arms.' Consequently, Portland informed the Lord Lieutenant that 'the execution of the above orders may be suspended'. (*Cornwallis Corresp.*, III, 29, 39; *Castlereagh Corresp.*, II, 84.)

[1] Frederick William III's brother Louis (1773–96) had married Princess Frederica (1778–1841), daughter of Queen Charlotte's brother Charles, Duke of Mecklenburg-Strelitz, on 26 Dec. 1793. He had died on 28 Dec. 1796. On 7 Jan. 1799 (or possibly on 10 Dec. 1798—the authorities differ) she married Prince Frederick of Solms-Braunfels (1770–1814), long after she had become pregnant by him. As her third husband, she married the Duke of Cumberland on 29 May 1815. Sir Herbert Taylor

nothing but the express order never to touch this subject to you, could have prevented expressing to you, my humble gratitude for it. Since that time I have not taken any further step in this affair, having resolved never to do anything without your approbation; I only kept up a correspondence with the Princess who seemed very happy with the hopes that the matter would in time be settled. This correspondence has continued till about five months ago when I remarked a great relap[se] on her side, and since that time I have heard but very seldom from her: all this made me conclude that she had altered her affection for me, and yesterday I received the account of her having secretly marryed a Prince of Solms Braunfels. This fatal event has certainly made me very miserable, but I do not murmur at my fate, having the comfort of having acted as an honest man in this whole affair, which the Queen of Prussia has acknowledged in the kindest manner. It is this disagreeable news which I thought it my duty to inform your Majesty of, and I hasten to write it by this post for fear it should come to your ear by another channel. I hope you are persuaded I should never have disobeyed your orders in mentioning to you this subject before the Peace was made, as long as I had hopes that the match could have taken place; but now that all these are over, I thought it would be a want of confidence from a son who loves his father as I do, to conceal from him an event which sooner or later he must be informed of. I begg your Majesty to excuse the incoherence of this letter, but I own I am too much moved to be able to write better. That you may continue long enjoying the most perfect health is the sincerest wish, and most ardent prayer of [etc.]. (48530–1)

1906   THE DUCHESS OF WURTEMBERG *to the* KING

[*Stutgard, 16 Jan. 1799.*] I have in my life never met with anything like the severity of the cold; the thermometer has been at twenty three degrees and a half below the freezing point and I fear much the mischief this weather will do in the country. About nine or ten years ago there was a winter of the same sort, though they say the cold was not then above twenty degrees; the greatest part of the fruit trees were destroyed, which is a shocking loss as great part of the income depends on the sail of the fruit. Some people pretend that many trees will be saved if the proprietors will have the courage to cut them down as far as the frost has attacked them.

I have been three times in a sledge and am much pleased with the motion. The day after New Year's Day was a great party, but the other times I have only been with the Duke. I should enjoy this amusement much oftener if the severity of the cold had not froze the ears of several people, amongst whom our cousin the younger Prince of Taxis[1] has been a sufferer. The worst, I think of the weather is the difficulty to keep the rooms temperate; they are either too cold or so hot that it quite stupefies me.

I have been quite shocked this morning by reading in the Stutgard newspaper

described Princess Frederica and her sister Louise (who married the Prince Royal, later, Frederick William III of Prussia, and who was Prince Louis's brother) as being, in 1793, 'beautiful girls' (*Taylor Papers*, p. 22).
[1] Princess Therese (1773–1839), daughter of Charles, Duke of Mecklenburg-Strelitz, married (1789) Charles Alexander, Prince of Thurn and Taxis (1770–1827).

the account of Prince Frederick of Orange's death.[1] How I pity his poor parents: it is doubly cruel for them in their situation to have additional misfortunes.[2] The greatest comfort they can meet with will be your Majesty's goodness. Their eldest son being with them at present I am glad of as it will a little draw their minds to think of their other children.

I hope that the weather does not prevent your Majesty's hunting as I know how fond you ever were of that amusement. (51514–5)

1907 CABINET MINUTE

[*Whitehall, Thursday, 17 Jan. 1799.*]

Present: The Lord Chancellor, The Duke of Portland, The Earl Camden, The Earl of Liverpool, Mr Chancellor of the Exchequer, Mr Secretary Dundas, Mr Secretary at War.

The Lords of his Majesty's Privy Council who have assisted at the examinations or have perused all the papers relative to the transaction in which Lord Camelford has been concerned & upon account of which he has been brought before them are unanimously of opinion that it should be humbly recommended to his Majesty to grant Lord Camelford a free pardon; but on a review of all the circumstances of the case, they think it their duty at the same time most humbly to submit to his Majesty that it is not adviseable that Lord Camelford should be intrusted with the command of any ship or vessel in his Majesty's service.[3] (9134)

1908 *Letters from* LORD GRENVILLE *to the* KING, *and the replies*

[*Cleveland Row, 19 Jan. 1799, 4 p.m.*] Lord Grenville has the honour to acquaint your Majesty that by a dispatch received from Sir Charles Whitworth it appears that the Emperor had proposed the furnishing a body of forty five thousand men, in consideration of a subsidy from your Majesty.

[1] He died at Venice of a contagious fever on 6 Jan., whilst in the service of the Emperor.

[2] The Stadholder and his wife remained in exile (they were still in residence at Hampton Court) until the end of the Napoleonic War. Their surviving family now consisted only of the Hereditary Prince and a married daughter.

[3] Lord Camelford (1775–1804), Lord Grenville's brother-in-law, had been a Lieutenant and Commander in the Royal Navy since 1797, and an uncertified lunatic. On Saturday the 12th he arrived at Dover in a coach, and asked a boatman to carry him to Deal, saying that he wanted to be landed at Calais in order to dispose of some watches and muslins in France. The man agreed to take him for twelve guineas, but deemed it prudent to inform the authorities of the affair, who arranged for Lord Camelford's arrest as soon as he stepped into the boat. On his person were discovered a brace of pistols and a dagger. He was taken to London and examined by the Privy Council. He could have been imprisoned for contravening an Act of 1798 which rendered the mere act of embarking for France illegal but as it appeared that his motives were not criminal he was given a free pardon for the breach of the Statute. (See *Life and Letters of Lord Minto*, III, 45.) On Tuesday, 28 May, *The Times* reported that Lord Camelford embarked the previous Sunday at Yarmouth for the Continent. He passed most of his time whilst abroad, in Zurich. It was said that he offered to serve as a volunteer in the Archduke Charles's army, but that the offer was declined. Subsequently he went to the headquarters of Marshal Suvoroff in Italy. He returned to England in October 1799 in the *Isis* frigate. He died on 10 March 1804 from the effects of a duel fought with Captain Thomas Best three days earlier.

Evidently the Cabinet Minute was not sent to the King until the 20th. See No. 1909. It will be noticed that Lord Grenville was not present. Lady Grenville was Lord Camelford's sister.

Lord Grenville apprehends that the details of this proposal are sent to Count Woronzow whom he has not yet seen, but is in hourly expectation of seeing. Lord Grenville has not yet found anything else material in the mails. All the nine are arrived. (9136)

[*The King's reply, Queen's House, 19 Jan., 6.20 p.m.*] The Emperor of Russia applying for a subsidy on proposing to furnish a body of forty-five thousand men, as stated in Lord Grenville's note, is the most convincing proof of his coming forward; though the Courts of Vienna and Berlin should remain in their present equivocal situations, it certainly deserves examination and acceptance if the sum required is agreable to what has been paid for a similar number. (Fortescue MSS.)

[*From the King, Queen's House, 19 Jan., 8.15 p.m.*] The information I have just received from the P. of Orange is so material that I have retired to my room just to communicate to Lord Grenville that he has received a letter from Mr. Stampfort at Berlin of the 3d. of Jany. which states that C[oun]t Haugwitz has assured him that the King is desirous of joining with England and Russia in any hostile measures against France, though Austria should hang back; this probably is the cause of the Prussian messenger's arrival the last evening, and I hope most sincerely that we may still be able to bring both Russia and Prussia forward. (Fortescue MSS.)

[*From Lord Grenville, Cleveland Row, 19 Jan. 1799, 10 p.m.*] Lord Grenville feels himself under the highest obligations for your Majesty's great goodness in communicating to him the information received by your Majesty from the Prince of Orange: which was the more acceptable to him on account of the severe mortification he has experienced in receiving from Sir Charles Whitworth the copy of the extravagant & dishonourable Convention which Sir Charles has, without the smallest authority, taken upon him to sign with Count Cobenzel.

The proposed engagements with Russia, supposing them to be framed, as Lord Grenville trusts they will be, on the ground of the instructions which your Majesty was pleased to authorize him to send on that subject, will, as he hopes, be highly advantageous to your Majesty's interests; but those which Sir Charles Whitworth has thought proper to enter into, in your Majesty's name, with the Court of Vienna, are of such a nature that Lord Grenville thinks it his duty humbly to submit to your Majesty that, as it appears to him, no time should be lost in transmitting to Petersburgh a complete disavowal of that most extraordinary transaction, with an order to Sir Charles Whitworth to abstain from all further discussions on the subject with Count Cobenzel, & to leave your Majesty's affairs with the Court of Vienna to be transacted through their proper channels. (9137–8)

[*The King's reply, Queen's House, 20 Jan., 11.46 a.m.*] Though in some degree prepared by Lord Grenville's note I read with astonishment the Convention Sir Charles Whitworth has without the smallest authority signed with Count Cobenzel, and highly approve of Lord Grenville's not losing a moment in transmitting to Petersburgh a complete disavowal of the whole transaction, and in the most *positive* and *strong* manner forbidding Sir Charles to interfere any more in the concerns of this country with the Court of Vienna; so improper do I view his conduct that if the prudential reflection that he is well seen at Petersburgh had not restrained me I would have proposed his immediate recall, but I think from adverse to the Court at which he resides, his vanity has been so far cajoled that he seems to think England must not set bounds to any absurd views of the Russian Emperor, which appears in certainly encouraging the idea that a large sum will be given from hence for re-establishing the Order of Malta.[1] (Fortescue MSS.)

[*From Lord Grenville, Cleveland Row, 20 Jan. 1799, 3.15 p.m.*] Upon discussing the subject with Mr Pitt & afterwards with the rest of your Majesty's servants Lord Grenville finds that they all concur in the opinion which has suggested itself to your Majesty, that Sir Charles Whitworth's recall is a measure adviseable, & indeed they think indispensably necessary. Lord Grenville is decidedly impressed with the same opinion, and had only delayed submitting it to your Majesty, in order that he might give himself some little time for reflection, and not act in a business of that nature on the impression of his first disappointment & indignation at reading the paper transmitted by Sir Charles Whitworth.

Lord Grenville would propose with your Majesty's permission to offer this situation, first to Lord Bathurst, and in the event of his declining it, to Lord Hobart.[2] In the meantime as the immediate presence of a Minister at Petersburgh may be of the greatest importance, Mr Grenville has offered to proceed thither from Berlin, where his stay, according to the plan humbly submitted to your Majesty in the Minute herewith transmitted, would probably be very short, at least in the first instance.

Lord Grenville only delays framing the instructions till he is apprized of your Majesty's pleasure on the outlines of this plan, and till he receives from the Prince of Orange General Stamfort's letter, which he imagines his Serene Highness will probably send to him in the course of today or tomorrow.

Lord Grenville hopes that the importance of these subjects will excuse his breaking in upon your Majesty.[3] (9139–40)

---

[1] Lord Grenville wrote to Lord Bathurst on 20 Jan.: 'I think I could convince you that no one would be so fit to replace him [Whitworth] as yourself, and that you ought not to decline going there for a year or two to keep my friend Paul steady to his traces.' (Bathurst MSS.)

[2] Lord Hobart had been unemployed since his return to England in 1798, after being Governor of Madras. He had intimated to Dundas his anxiety for an official situation at home. 'I accepted the Government of Madras,' he wrote (20 Aug. 1799), 'upon the express condition of succeeding to the Supreme Government, and embarked for a distant country and fatal climate in a perfect reliance on that condition being fulfilled.' But Lord Mornington had been appointed Governor-General, and Hobart felt that his supersession had injured his character. (W. Dacres Adams MSS.)

[3] Grenville wrote again to Lord Bathurst on the 21st: 'Since I saw you Woronzov has been with me. He has this moment left me and he has urged so very strongly the inconvenience which would result just now from Whitworth's recall, that this point must at least become matter of a little fresh consideration. I owed it to you not to lose a moment in mentioning this to you.' (Bathurst MSS.) Whitworth left Petersburg in June 1800, and diplomatic relations between the two Courts were suspended until 1801.

[*The King's reply, Queen's House, 20 Jan. 1799, 3.52 p.m.*] The opinion of the Cabinet both on the making an explicit proposal to the King of Prussia, and of recalling Sir Charles Whitworth meet so fully with my approbation that I instantly communicate it to Lord Grenville. I highly approve of his proposing to Earl Bathurst the mission of Petersburgh and if he declines it, Lord Hobart, and I am much pleased that Mr. Grenville is inclined on concluding his proposal at Berlin to go for a time to Russia.

P.S. I desire Lord Grenville will return to me the inclosed Minute of Cabinet which I only send least he has not kept a copy of it. (Fortescue MSS.)

[*Cabinet Minute, 20 Jan. (Enclosure.[1])*]

Present: Lord Chancellor, Lord President, Lord Privy Seal, Duke of Portland, Earl Spencer, Earl Camden, Earl of Liverpool, Mr. Pitt, Mr. Secretary Dundas, Lord Grenville.

It was agreed humbly to submit to his Majesty that instructions should immediately be sent to Petersburgh & to Vienna, to disavow the whole of the negotiation entered into by Sir Charles Whitworth with Count Cobenzel, and to declare his Majesty's adherence to his former resolutions on that subject.

That Sir Charles Whitworth should be recalled, but that the most explicit assurances should be given both at Petersburgh and through Count Woronzow, that supposing the intended Convention with Russia should be framed on grounds consistent with the overtures already made there in his Majesty's name, his Majesty will with great pleasure enter into such arrangements with that Court.

That Mr Grenville should forthwith proceed to Berlin, and should be charged with a distinct overture to that Court, that if the King of Prussia will now declare himself, and will join with his Majesty & the Emperor of Russia in a plan for hostile measures against France, & particularly for the restoration of the independence of Holland, his Majesty will, for that object, furnish to his Prussian Majesty or to the support of a Dutch Army a sum of one million sterling in addition to the subsidy to be agreed upon between his Majesty and the Emperor of Russia. (9142–3)

1909   THE DUKE OF PORTLAND *to the* KING

[*Burlington House, Sunday, 20 Jan. 1799.*] The Duke of Portland begs leave with all deference to submit to your Majesty the humble opinion of such of your

---

[1] In Lord Grenville's hand, as one would expect, but, curiously, docketed by the Duke of Portland, 'Minute of Cabinet most humbly submitted to his Majesty'. Grenville's letter to Windham, 26 Aug. 1799, illustrates Cabinet practice with regard to Cabinet Minutes: 'With respect to the Cabinet decisions, there is no very precise rule that has either in our time, or, as far as I can learn, in times before us, been adopted on the subject. There is nowhere any record of those decisions. Sometimes, on points that have been considered as important in the conduct of foreign business, I have, as you know, brought them distinctly and in writing before the Cabinet, and have made written minutes of the opinion then agreed to. These minutes have in that case invariably been read to the persons present, or afterwards transmitted to the King, but no Office copy is ever kept of them. Of these I have copies for my own satisfaction and private use, and I have always considered them as implying the consent or acquiescence of those persons only who were present, and who did not desire their dissent to be expressed.' (Add. MSS. 37846, f. 146.)

Majesty's servants as assisted at the investigation of Lord Camelford's late conduct in attempting to go over to France, or who perused all the examinations & depositions which were taken in the course of it. The Duke of Portland also requests your Majesty's permission to lay before your Majesty the draft of the Message which your Majesty's servants humbly offer to your Majesty's consideration for the purpose of bringing the measure of an Union with Ireland before the Parliament of this kingdom; which, if fortunate enough to receive your Majesty's sanction, the Duke of Portland will hope to receive your Majesty's orders to have prepared for your Majesty's signature in order that it may be sent to both Houses on Tuesday next.[1] (9144–5)

1910   THE DUKE OF YORK *to the* KING

[*York House, 22 Jan. 1799.*] I trust that your Majesty will be graciously pleased to pardon this intrusion, but having spoken to Mr Pitt and Mr Dundas in consequence of your Majesty's gracious acquiescense in Sir William Faucett's humble request to appoint him one of your Majesty's Privy Council, I am desired by them to beg your Majesty as there is to be a Privy Council tomorrow, to signify your pleasure to the Lord President time enough that he may be sworn in, as his anxiety to receive this honor is so great that he can neither eat nor sleep.[2] (9146)

1911   WILLIAM PITT *to the* KING

[*Downing Street, Wednesday, 23 Jan. 1799, 9 p.m.*] Mr Pitt humbly begs leave to acquaint your Majesty that on the delivery of your Majesty's Message this day respecting an Union, an Address of Thanks was moved by Mr Dundas, to which an Amendment was proposed by Mr Sheridan objecting to the agitation of the question at this time. The Amendment was supported by Mr Tyrwhitt Jones, and objected to by Mr Canning and Mr Pitt. It was rejected without a division, after which the original Address was agreed to, and the further consideration of the Message fixed for tomorrow sennight.[3] (9147)

[1] 'His Majesty is persuaded that the unremitting industry with which our enemies persevere in their avowed design of effecting the separation of Ireland from this Kingdom, cannot fail to engage the particular attention of Parliament, and his Majesty recommends it to this House to consider of the most effectual means of counteracting and finally defeating this design; and he trusts that a review of all the circumstances which have recently occurred (joined to the sentiment of mutual affection and common interest) will dispose the Parliaments of both Kingdoms to provide, in the manner which they shall judge most expedient, for settling such a complete and final adjustment as may best tend to improve and perpetuate a connection essential for their common security, and to augment and consolidate the strength, power and resources of the British Empire.' (*H. of C. J.*, LIV, 146.)

[2] Docketed by the King: 'Yorke [*sic*] House, Jany. 22, 1799. Immediately answered and Sir Wm. Faucett directed to attend tomorrow at St James.' Fawcett had just resigned his office of Adjutant-General of the Forces, retiring to his Government of Chelsea Hospital, and being succeeded by his Deputy, Col. Calvert. Col. Wynyard was appointed Deputy Adjutant-General.

[3] *Parl. Register*, LII, 579–625. *Colchester Diary*, I, 169–71.
The King's reply on the 24th, 8.56 a.m., is in Stanhope, III, Appendix, p. xviii. In line 5, for 'observes', read 'deserves'. He expressed his strong disapproval of a proposal put forward by Castlereagh that the Catholic clergy in Ireland should be paid by the State. It would 'give real offence to the Established Church in Ireland as well as to the true friends of our Constitution; for it is certainly creating a second

[*Cleveland Row, 25 Jan. 1799.*] Lord Grenville has the honour, in humble obedience to your Majesty's commands, to return your Majesty the Minute of Cabinet of the 20th instant.

Mr Grenville's instructions being sent down to him tonight, Lord Grenville trusts he will sail tomorrow.[1] (9141)

1913 *Letters from the* DUKE OF PORTLAND *to the* KING

[*Whitehall, Saturday, 26 Jan. 1799, 12.40 p.m.*] The Duke of Portland humbly conceives that your Majesty will expect to receive the earliest possible notice of the result of the debate on the Lord Lieutenant's Speech at the opening of the Irish Parliament, & therefore lays before your Majesty without loss of time the dispatches which have been brought to town this morning by Capt Tayler,[2] by which the Duke of Portland has the mortification to think that your Majesty will find the Address was only carried in the House of Commons by a majority of *one* vote which the Duke of Portland therefore fears must check the progress of the measure of Union for some time if not for the remainder of the present Session.[3] The D. of Portland learns from Captain Tayler that the violence & indecent language of the Opposition in the House of Commons exceeded all imagination, & that it was equalled by the partiality & gross disregard of order on the part of the Speaker, who when the House rose was drawn hence by the mob, that Lord Ely went behind the Throne to avoid voting when the question was put upon the Address in the House of Lords, & that none of his or Lord Downshire's members voted in the House of Commons.[4]

The city of Dublin remained perfectly quiet, nor was any insult offered to the Lord Lieutenant on his way either to or from the House. (9148–9)

Church establishment, which could not but be highly injurious. The tollerating Dissenters is fair, but the trying to perpetuate a separation in religious opinions by providing for the support of their clergy as an establishment is certainly going far beyond the bounds of justice or policy'.

[1] Thick fog together with contrary winds prevented Thomas Grenville from sailing from Yarmouth until the 28th in the frigate *Proserpine*, which was wrecked off the mouth of the Elbe. He and most of the crew were able to reach the shore by crossing the ice on foot. He lost all his clothes but saved most of his papers.

[2] Afterwards Sir Herbert Taylor. He had been private secretary to Cornwallis, and was just leaving Dublin to take up his appointment as private secretary to the Duke of York, the Commander-in-Chief. Cornwallis was very sorry to lose him, and told the Duke, 'Captain Taylor, with great readiness and quickness of parts, is most indefatigable in business; and in honesty, fidelity and goodness of heart he has no superior' (*Taylor Papers*, p. 56).

[3] Cornwallis's despatch to Portland, dated the 23rd, is in Ross, *Cornwallis Corresp.*, III, 40. The Opposition's Amendment was defeated by 106 to 105, and the Address carried by 107 to 105. Fox wrote on 2 Feb.: 'I am heartily glad the Union is defeated, for all circumstances considered it would have been to my judgement the most unequivocal instance of despotism that we have yet seen, and that is saying a great deal; not to mention that Pitt's arguments if they are rightly given go against the very principle of all free government.'

[4] Lord Ely, 'relying on the favour of the Crown in an object personal to himself' (that is, a Marquessate), had promised, in November 1798, to support the Union. In any case he was a placeman— Joint Postmaster-General [I.]. Early in January his opinions were reported to be 'unsettled', but Cornwallis declared that he would not be allowed to 'shuffle'. On the 28th Castlereagh wrote to Portland saying that 'instead of bringing forward eighteen members, as these Noble Lords [Downshire and Ely]

[*Burlington House, Wednesday night, 30 Jan.*] The Duke of Portland begs leave with all humility to submit to your Majesty the opinion of your Majesty's confidential servants on the subject of the Lord Lieutenant's letters secret & confidential which the Duke of Portland had the honor of laying before your Majesty this afternoon, & at the same time with all deference to your Majesty's superior wisdom to request the signification of your Majesty's pleasure to prepare an instruction conformable to the inclosed Minute of Cabinet[1] to be forthwith sent to the Lord Lieutenant.[2] (9150)

1914   WILLIAM PITT *to the* KING

[*Downing Street, Thursday night, 31 Jan. 1799.*] Mr Pitt humbly begs leave to acquaint your Majesty that he this day moved that the House should resolve itself into a Committee to consider of your Majesty's Message respecting Ireland, and opened fully the Resolutions which he should propose. This Motion was objected to by Mr Sheridan and Dr Lawrence[3] and supported by Lord Hawkesbury, and was carried by 140 to 15. The House then went into the Committee, when the Resolutions[4] were (according to the notice previously given) laid upon the table for further consideration, and the proceeding upon them was adjourned till this day sennight.[5] (9151)

might have done, but five appeared, and one of Lord Downshire's, my colleague, Mr. Savage, voted against us the second night. I could neither be prepared for nor guard against this misfortune by any previous communication, as Lord Downshire was absent, and Lord Ely did not land till the Lord Lieutenant was at the House delivering his Speech' (Ross, *Cornwallis Corresp.*, II, 452; III, 34, 36, 41, 43, 47; *Castlereagh Corresp.*, II, 143).

Lord Ely returned six members to the Irish House of Commons—for the boroughs of Bannow, Clonmines and Fethard, in the County of Wexford (all being disfranchised at the Union); and influenced the return of the members for Co. Wexford and Wexford City (one each).

The Marquess of Downshire returned seven members to the Irish Parliament for constituencies which disappeared at the Union: Blessington, Fore, Hillsborough, and Carlingford (one seat only). He also returned one, if not two, members for Co. Down.

Cornwallis wrote to Dundas on 8 Feb.: 'The speech which Mr. Pitt made on Thursday last, the 31st, arrived yesterday, and will I trust at a future period produce much good, but at the present moment we are steeled by passion and prejudice against all the powers of reason and eloquence. Lord Ely promises general support, and resistance to any propositions to pledge the House against all Union, but he is so weak and corrupt that I do not place much confidence in him. I have heard nothing lately of Lord Downshire, but from what I saw of him when he was last in Ireland, I should suspect that he will always be very troublesome and impracticable...' (Melville MSS.)

See also *Castlereagh Corresp.*, II, 241.

[1] Missing.

[2] Docketed by the King: 'Answered Jany 31st 32m pt 8. a.m. Approving the Lord Lieut. of Ireland's being directed to use the greatest efforts to prevent an emancipation of the Roman Catholics and declaring that though a strong friend to the Union of the two kingdoms, I should become an enemy to the measure if I thought a change of the situation of the Roman Catholics would attend this Measure.'

[3] French Laurence (1757–1809), M.P. for Peterborough, 1796–1809; Burke's intimate friend.

[4] Resolutions laying down the general principles to be embodied in the scheme of Union. They occupy nearly three pages of the *Parl. Register* (LII, 657–60).

[5] *Parl. Register*, LII, 626–79. Auckland said that Pitt's speech 'surpassed even the most sanguine expectation of his friends, and, perhaps, even any former exhibition of parliamentary eloquence'. He and Charles Long made special efforts 'to have the best possible notes' of the speech taken, so that it might be correctly printed and forwarded to Dublin Castle 'for the fullest and most extensive circulation in Ireland' (*Auckland Corresp.*, IV, 87). Canning wrote on 2 Feb.: 'Pitt's speech on Thursday will, I hope, set our countrymen on the other side of the Channel right. They have been going terribly astray

1915 HENRY DUNDAS *to the* KING

[*Whitehall, 31 Jan.* [?*1799*], *12.30.*] Mr. Dundas takes the first moment humbly to inform his Majesty that the Government dispatches by the Swallow are arrived. Mr. Dundas is endeavouring to read them before the House of Commons meets, but in the meantime thinks it is duty to communicate to his Majesty that he has read enough already to perceive that everything is as comfortable as possible.[1]
(9133)

1916 THE DUKE OF PORTLAND *to the* KING

[*Burlington House, Friday night, 1 Feb. 1799.*] The Duke of Portland most humbly begs leave to lay before your Majesty two dispatches from Ireland which were brought to him this afternoon by Mr Elliot,[2] whom the Lord Lieutenant has sent over for the purpose of obtaining distinct & positive instructions for his conduct upon several subjects which it is supposed the Opposition in the House of Commons of Ireland may bring into discussion; upon some of the most important of which, such as the Catholick question, the Union of the two kingdoms, & the treatment of persons in office who have opposed the measures of his government his inquiries have been anticipated, & the others are of a nature which the Duke of Portland conceives it will not be difficult to satisfy, so that if your Majesty shall please, Mr Elliot may be enabled to return to Ireland on Sunday evening or at latest on Monday morning. The Duke of Portland has the satisfaction to acquaint your Majesty that Mr Elliot's report of the state of Ireland & even of Dublin itself is by no means alarming, & that there is no reason to apprehend that the generality of those who opposed the paragraph of the Address which implied an engagement to consider the measure of Union, will consider themselves pledged to resist the discussion of it at a future time or will be at all likely to join in an opposition to the general measures of your Majesty's Government.

In submitting to your Majesty the Lord Lieutenant's letter which accompanies a list of successions proposed for your Majesty's army in Ireland, the Duke of Portland presumes in consequence of an observation transmitted to him by the orders of his Royal Highness the Duke of York to represent with all humility to your Majesty that in the succession in the 54th Foot the Captain Lieutenant

in their notions. Sheridan's *complimentary abuse* of me was very well done with great good taste, & good nature.' (Harewood MSS.) And he wrote to his mother on the 1st: 'It is too true that the Irish Ho. of Coms. have been mistaken & frantic enough to negative the measure of the Union for the present. It will be all the same this time twelvemonth. You will see that we go on here to shew them what we meant for their good. Mr. Pitt's speech of last night must carry conviction to everything but faction & prejudice. It is so complete that you will not wonder to see few speakers on the same side after him...' (Harewood MSS.)

[1] The year is by no means certain, but in any case the reference seems to be to the arrival of the despatches from India. The Mysore war was still in progress in 1799, and Tipu's capital, Seringapatam, was captured only in May.

[2] William Elliot (1766–1818), M.P. for St Cannice [I.], 1796–7, and 1798–1800; for Portarlington, 1801–2; for Peterborough, 1802–18. Under-Secretary of State, Military Department [I.], 1797–1801; Irish Secretary, March 1806–April 1807. He was thought of for the Irish Secretaryship as early as 1795 when Camden succeeded Cornwallis as Lord Lieutenant. See *Castlereagh Corresp.*, I, 421; II, 10, 29. He was well known when first in Ireland by the sobriquet of the *Castle Spectre*, and on his return in 1806 was called *Le Revenant*. See No. 1701 n.

is brought forward in preference to two or three Captains who belong to the Regiment & have been seconded & who are ready & anxious to be restored to your Majesty's service.

The Duke of Portland humbly requests your Majesty's pardon for having omitted to pay his duty to your Majesty today at St James's, & hopes your Majesty will graciously condescend to forgive him in consideration of Mr Elliot's arrival almost at the moment he was setting out to attend your Majesty. (9152–4)

1917   LORD GRENVILLE *to the* KING

[*Cleveland Row, 1 Feb. 1799, 4.10 p.m.*] Lord Grenville has just received from Mr Dundas's Office a French paper which speaks of the death of Prince Frederick of Orange as a thing known & certain. Lord Grenville has the honour to transmit it to your Majesty, & humbly solicits your Majesty's commands as to the manner of breaking this melancholy account to the Prince & Princess of Orange. Lord Grenville has enquired & finds that their S. & R.H.H.[1] are both in town, but that there is nobody with them. He had thought of sending to Mr Fagel who is at Wimbledon, but judged it best to wait your Majesty's commands, especially as, from the state of the weather, it seems hardly possible to bring Mr Fagel up this evening.

There are letters from Sir William Hamilton with an account of the arrival of the King & Queen of Naples at Palermo the 25th of December.

Lord Grenville understands that Lord St Helens is in town. Perhaps your Majesty would approve of his being desired to go to the Prince of Orange. (9155–6)

1918   THE MARQUESS OF BUTE *to the* KING

[*Hill Street, 3 Feb. 1799.*] Presuming on the custom which has usually prevailed as well in this country as in all others of decorating with the Order those persons of high rank who have filled without reproach great foreign employment, and your Majesty having esteemed me worthy to be placed in that situation, may I be permitted to lay with all humility at your Majesty's feet my ambitious desire to succeed to the vacant Blue Ribband? and if not in the present moment, to express an hope that your Majesty would be graciously pleased to honor me with the distinction on a future vacancy. When I compare my own birth and position with some who possibly aim at receiving this gratification I am encouraged to believe your Majesty will more readily pardon my thus boldly bringing forward my pretensions. Upon whomever the dignity may devolve, your Majesty in bestowing the Garter certainly bestows the first honor in the universe. It differs also from political arrangements in as much as, whilst these are negotiated through Ministers, the Garter flows absolutely and solely from your Majesty's Royal person. At the same time I humbly beg leave to assure your Majesty that no new instance of goodness and protection is necessary to make me continue to reflect with the

---

[1] Serene and Royal Highnesses.

most lively sentiments of gratitude on the multiplicity of bountiful favors heaped upon my late father, of which his descendants partake, and of which the deepest sense can never be eradicated from my breast.[1] (9159–60)

1919   THE KING to LORD GRENVILLE

[*Queen's House, 4 Feb. 1799, 6.55 p.m.*] The Princess of Orange was here at the time I received Lord Grenville's note enclosing the French newspaper. I knew the Prince of Orange was to dine at the Earl of Chesterfield's. I therefore sent for the Duke of York who was also to be there, and sent him to communicate the disagreable information to the Prince and to conduct him to his lodging, from whence he is returned, and has taken the Princess to Pall Mall. She was much affected when I took the task of breaking the sad report to her; she was fully sensible of Lord Grenville's attention in wishing to convey the intelligence in the least abrupt manner; till some farther account comes I pity the parents as they must remain under a cruel suspence; but I do not see that anything further can be done. (Fortescue MSS.)

1920   E. LIVINGSTON to the KING

[*Berlin, 5 Feb. 1799.*] I had the honor to write your Majesty the 9 Decr. Since that period, in spite of the severest winter known in Germany for many years, his Royal Highness has continued to recover his health and on the whole has been much better than I have seen him since I have had the honor to attend his Royal Highness; nevertheless he has not yet ventured to go to bed. I presume from experience that may be judged a necessary precaution. The Prince sleeps tolerably well in an arm chair made here for that purpose.

On the 18 Janry. we had the honor to celebrate her Majesty's birthday. As the Prince has no cook at present I order'd the dinner at Lord Elgin's house;[2] all the English and some foreigners had the honor to dine at the Prince's table. The dinner &ce. was genteel and everything as it should be on that happy day.

The 27 Janry. his Prussian Majesty made Prince Augustus a visit, and in honor of the Prince's birthday gave a dinner to 60 ladys and gentlemen; most of the English had the honor to dine at the King's table. During the dinner the King proposed your Majesty's health, the Queen's and all the Royal Family of England. As soon as that toast was drunk, a very fine band of music the King had order'd from Potsdam playd God Save the King and Rule Britannia. In the evening the Queen gave a very great supper and Ball to all the nobility; the Ball lasted til near six in the morning. The invitations to the dinner, supper and Ball was to celebrate the birthday of his Royal Highness Prince Augustus of England.

I have the honor to assure your Majesty that it is impossible to exceed the

[1] Bute, who had been given a Marquessate in March 1796, was disappointed in his hope of getting the Garter. It was given to Lord Spencer.

[2] Presumably the residence of the Minister. Lord Elgin, the Minister Plenipotentiary, had been recalled on 25 Jan., though the original recall was lost in the shipwreck of the *Proserpine* frigate in the Elbe estuary. Elgin left Berlin on leave 13 Aug. 1798 and did not return.

flatering and hospitable attention paid the Prince by the King, the Queen, the Queen Mother[1] and all the Royal Family, and all the nobility of Berlin.

The present deplorable situation of Italy puts it out of the power of the warmest partizans of that climate to think of returning there, and it's difficult to guess what may be ere long the situation of the German Empire. I am now pretty clear that climate has not great influence on the Prince's complaints, but I cannot inform your Majesty what are the Prince's own wish or the country he prefers to fix in. I have heard his Royal Highness express a disslike to long journeys and particularly to Russia, which proceeds from the accounts given him by young men lately return'd from that country. As things appear to me on the continent at present I cannot pretend to offer any opinion and must wait your Majesty's commands, which I will communicate to the Prince when you honor me with them.

I have suffered very much with rheumatism this cold winter but I have stil been able to do my duty. I am fortunate in my assistant Mr. Arbuthnot; he is a sensible, well inform'd, honorable man and his Royal Highness appears fond of him. (16727–8)

1921   THE DUCHESS OF WURTEMBERG *to the* KING

[*Stutgard, 5 Feb. 1799.*] I have this instant had the happiness to receive your Majesty's letter of the 22d January and am very unhappy to find that several letters are missing which I have had the honour of writing to you since, which must make me appear very negligent and disrespectful. There is such an irregularity in the posts that plagues me very much; this morning I have received letters of the 3d. of December.

I am truly sensible of your Majesty's goodness to me about the Hereditary Prince who I understand is going on well at Tubingen; God grant that this unfortunate business may serve him as a lesson through life to be on his guard against intriguing people. The Duke begs of me to present his humble duty to your Majesty and express his gratitude for the gracious message you have sent him.

Your Majesty's letter has been a very great comfort to me as I am too happy to find that my thoughts perfectly coincide with your opinion which must ever be gratifying to me: my greatest distress was the effect this miserable history had on the Duke's health. Thank God he is better, but I believe he will not get quite well while this uncertain weather continues as we never have two days that are alike, which is very trying to the constitution.

I rejoice very much at the great amendment of dear Amelia; poor thing, she has been sadly plagued for six months, but her now taking the courage to undergo everything proposed will I trust abridge her confinement and restore her strength.

This last week has been here gay; we have had two Balls on the Monday and Tuesday to conclude the Carneval to the great delight of Paul and Trinette; the Duke gave them the first, the second was at the house of the Imperial Minister,

[1] Frederick William II of Prussia had married (1769) as his second wife, Frederica (1751–1805), daughter of the Landgrave Louis of Hesse-Darmstadt.

and I feel today much fatigued with having set up till near one o'clock, which, as I am quite out of that custom, appears to me very unpleasant. (51516–7)

1922 WILLIAM PITT *to the* KING

[*Downing Street, Friday, 8 Jan.* [*Feb.*] *1798* [*1799*].] Mr. Pitt humbly begs leave to acquaint your Majesty that on the Motion for the House to go into the Committee for the farther consideration of your Majesty's Message it was opposed again on the same grounds as before by Mr. Grey, Mr. Sheridan, Mr. Tierney and Mr. W. Smith, and supported by Mr. Dundas, Mr. Windham and Mr. Grant. The Motion was carried for the Speaker's leaving the Chair by 149 to 24, but at so late an hour as to make it necessary to report a progress, after which the farther proceeding was fixed for Monday.[1] (8732)

1923 LORD GRENVILLE *to the* KING, *and the reply*

[*Cleveland Row, 11 Feb. 1799.*] In obedience to your Majesty's commands Lord Grenville has made enquiry respecting the value of the office now vacant in the Exchequer, and of that in the Customs held by Mr. Chamberlayne; the first is four hundred and fifty, and the latter one hundred and fifty pounds per annum.

Lord Grenville thought it his duty to mention this to your Majesty, and he begs to be permitted most humbly to assure your Majesty that no other disposition that he could by possibility make respecting the office in the Exchequer can afford him half the satisfaction that he should derive from obeying any command of your Majesty's respecting it. (9161)

[*The King's reply, Queen's House, 12 Feb.*] This morning I have received Lord Grenville's note respecting the vacant office under him in the Exchequer; though the difference between that and the employment held by Mr. Chamberlayne in the Customs is greater than I supposed, yet the very handsome manner in which Lord Grenville offers to appoint Mr. Chamberlayne, I cannot but accept as a fresh mark of that attention I have long experienced from Lord Grenville. (Fortescue MSS.)

1924 THE KING *to* EARL SPENCER

[*Queen's House, 13 Feb. 1799.*] The very gallant behaviour of Captain Thompson[2] in his unsuccessful action with the Genereux renders Earl Spencer's suggestion

---

[1] This letter is an interesting example of the vagaries of letter writers. Either Pitt was very tired after a protracted sitting of the House (until 2.30 a.m. on the 8th), or was very careless, or had drunk too much port; there is a mistake not merely in the year (common enough in a January letter) but even in the month. The paper is watermarked 1796. See *H. of C. J.*, LIV, 155; *Parl. Register*, LII, 743.

[2] Sir Thomas Boulden Thompson (1766–1828). Captain, 1790; Rear-Admiral, 1809; Vice-Admiral, 1814. Knighted, 13 Feb. 1799; created Baronet, Nov. 1806. M.P. for Rochester, 1807–16. On this day, the 13th, he was also given a medal for his meritorious conduct in the battle of the Nile, the medal bearing the inscription, 'In memory of the defeat of the French Fleet on the coast of Egypt'.

On 11 May 1800 Lord Spencer congratulated Lord St Vincent 'on the capture of the *Génereux*, which makes a good completion of the Nile squadron' (*Spencer Papers*, III, 330).

of the propriety of his receiving the honour of Knighthood when presented this day at St. James's highly proper. (Althorp MSS.)

1925 THE DUKE OF PORTLAND *to the* KING

[*Whitehall, Tuesday, 19 Feb. 1799, 3 p.m.*] The accounts contained in the dispatches which have been received this morning from Ireland appear to the Duke of Portland to be so satisfactory & so fatal to the future efforts of those who are combined in opposing the measures of your Majesty's Government in that kingdom, that the Duke of Portland humbly conceives it to be his duty to lose no time in laying them at your Majesty's feet.[1] (9162)

1926 WILLIAM PITT *to the* KING, *and the reply*

[*Downing Street, Thursday, 21 Feb. 1799.*] Mr Pitt humbly begs leave to acquaint your Majesty that he has found Lord Leicester particularly desirous of being honored with the office of Lord Steward, and making it his request that he might be appointed to it.[2] Mr Pitt begs to be honored with your Majesty's commands whether Lord Leicester may attend at St James's tomorrow to receive the Staff, and Lord Gower to kiss hands for the Post Office. As the latter office is not tenable with the House of Commons Mr Pitt ventures to presume that your Majesty will not object to Lord Gower's being called up to the House of Lords by writ for any of the Baronies in Lord Stafford's family. Such an arrangement being no permanent encrease to the Peerage seems preferable to leaving the office out of Parliament. (9163)

[*The King's reply, Queen's House, 22 Feb.*] I desire Mr. Pitt will acquaint the Earl of Leicester that if he is at the Levée at St. James's this day I shall in a private audience as [is] customary after the Levée conferr the Staff of Steward of the Household on him. Lord Gower may be presented at the Levée as one of the Joint Postmasters-General, and his being called up by writ to the House of Lords by the Barony of the Marquiss of Stafford is perfectly proper. (Chatham Papers.)

1927 *Letters from the* DUKE OF PORTLAND *to the* KING

[*Burlington House, Friday, 22 Feb., 10 p.m.*] Your Majesty's commands to acquaint the Bishop of Salisbury to summon a Chapter of the Garter for Friday March 1st.

---

[1] See *Cornwallis Corresp.*, III, 64, for Cornwallis's despatch of the 16th, in which he announced that in the Irish House of Commons the Government had a majority of 20 (123 *v.* 103) on Lord Corry's State of the Nation motion, the object of which was 'to league the country gentlemen who had voted against the measure of Union in a general opposition to Government'.

[2] He was even more desirous of a Marquessate, for which he applied at least twice—in 1794 and on 1 Jan. 1800. Pitt naturally thought that he was not entitled to ask for a second Marquessate in his family (his father, whom he succeeded in Sept. 1807, had been created Marquess Townshend on 31 Oct. 1786). Lord Leicester felt it was most inappropriate that he, holding the first Household office, should be merely an Earl, whilst Lord Salisbury, holding only the second Household office (that of Lord Chamberlain) should be a Marquess. In support of his plea he instanced his services to the Government and his long attachment to Pitt's Administration. (Chatham Papers, 151.)

at half past one, for filling up the vacant Stall in St. George's Chapel at Windsor have been received by the Duke of Portland & will be immediately obeyed.[1] (9164)

[*Burlington House, Sunday night, 24 Feb. 1799.*] The Duke of Portland humbly begs leave to lay before your Majesty a letter[2] from Lord Castlereagh to Mr Wickham which is the only account which has been received of the debate on the Bill brought in by your Majesty's Attorney General in Ireland[3]—a copy of which has been submitted to your Majesty & is now under the consideration of your Majesty's Law servants in this country who see no objection to the principle of the Bill in the actual state of Ireland, though they find great inaccuracies in the wording of it—which they will endeavour to remedy as soon as possible that it may be returned to Ireland, where the necessity of some such measure is but too obvious— as the Duke of Portland presumes it will appear to your Majesty when your Majesty is informed that on three farms only, belonging to a gentleman for whose veracity the Duke of Portland can answer, one thousand & fifty seven feeding sheep were hamstrung or stabbed with pikes in the course of one night.[4] (9165)

[*Bulstrode, Wednesday, 27 Feb., 10 a.m.*] As it appears by a diligent search throughout the books in the Secretary of State's Office that there is but one instance of a convict who had not been guilty of murder having been ordered by your Majesty or any of your Royal predecessors to be hung in chains, the Duke of Portland humbly conceives it to be his duty, in submitting to your Majesty an order for that punishment to be inflicted on John Haynes,[5] whose case was reported to your Majesty by Mr. Recorder on Friday last, to lay before your Majesty the circumstances he has presumed to state, & also to offer with all humility to your Majesty the reasons which induce him to move your Majesty to order this case to be distinguished by so exemplary a punishment. As soon as it was known that your Majesty had ordered that the law should take its course upon this convict, an unanimous representation was made to the Duke of Portland by the Bow Street Magistrates of the expediency of making such an example, & considering the spot where this crime was committed, & that it & its neighbour- hood have been much too long the scene of similar attempts & of every species of depredation; that in the case of Haynes the intent to murder was unquestionable; & that it may not be unreasonably presumed that the motive to that act was a knowledge or strong suspicion at least that the persons at whom he fired were Officers of Justice; the Duke of Portland thought himself called upon to consult your Majesty's Law servants respecting the exercise of your Majesty's prerogative

---

[1] The Chapter was held at the close of the Levée at St James's, and Earl Spencer was invested with the insignia of the Order. The Prince of Wales and the Royal Dukes were present.

[2] Not in *Castlereagh Correspondence* nor in *Cornwallis Correspondence*. [3] John Toler.

[4] 'The slaughter of sheep and black cattle was so great', wrote Cornwallis to Portland in a subsequent letter (23 Feb.) 'and the mischief was spreading itself so rapidly that the county of Galway has been placed under the provisions of the Insurrection Act, and I thought it right, on the 20th instant, to issue orders for executing martial law with vigour...I am to expect much opposition to the Bill for legalising the exercise of martial law' (*Cornwallis Corresp.*, III, 66).

[5] The highwayman. His name was sometimes spelt Haines.

in this case, & in consequence of their reporting to him that they did not see any objection to it, the Duke of Portland has taken upon himself to offer the necessary order for your Majesty's royal signature with the most perfect submission & deference to your Majesty's superior wisdom. (9166–7)

1928   THE DUCHESS OF WURTEMBERG *to the* KING

[*Louisbourg, 1 March 1799.*] On Tuesday we settled here for the summer and I hope in a few days the weather will sufficiently mend to enable me to re-begin my walks which this uncommon severe winter has totally stopt. We had three or four beautiful days before we left Stutgard and I made great use of them by going out in an open cariage.

Your Majesty would be much pleased could you see the apartment I now inhabit, which, being above stairs, is not exposed to damp and cold like the rooms I occupy in summer, and I should like very much to remain in these if the Duke did not find it very inconvenient to be always obliged to go upstairs, particularly as the staircases here are very steep. This apartment was the one originally intended for the Dutchess's but before it was finished the first wife[1] of Duke Charles returned to Barreuth and since that time it has been either given to company in part or the Duke's daughters have had it.

I hope that your Majesty has not by the severity of the weather been as totally prevented going on with your improvements in the park as we have here. Fortunately the trees have not suffered as much as we had reason to expect but everything else, and particularly the vines, are much injured. About ten years ago there was six weeks of violent cold and almost all the fruit trees were destroyed which was a dreadful loss and is not yet quite got the better of. (51518–9)

1929   WILLIAM PITT *to the* KING

[*Downing Street, Sunday, 3 March 1799.*] Mr Pitt ventures to hope your Majesty will not disapprove of his presuming to trouble your Majesty again with the Message to the House of Commons which your Majesty was pleased to sign on Wednesday, but in which accidentally the usual addition of your Majesty's initials at the end of the Message was omitted. If your Majesty has the goodness now to add them, the copy of the Message will be enter'd on the Journals in the same manner as if it had originally been so presented.[2] (9168)

---

[1] Charles, Duke of Wurtemberg (1728–93) married (1748) as his first wife, Frederica (1732–80)' daughter of Frederick, Margrave of Brandenburg-Bayreuth.

[2] On Friday, 1 March the following Message from the King was presented to the House by Pitt: 'His Majesty, being desirous of making competent provisions for the honourable support and maintenance of his dearly beloved sons, Prince Edward and Prince Ernest Augustus, which the monies applicable to the purposes of his Majesty's Civil Government would be insufficient to defray; and being also desirous of being enabled to extend to his beloved daughter, the Princess Amelia, the provision which he has been enabled to make out of the Hereditary Revenue for the other branches of his Royal Family, desires the assistance of Parliament...' (*H. of C. J.*, LIV, 255.) Princess Amelia's name was included in the Message because the last parliamentary grant for the support of the Princesses was made before her birth, consequently no provision had ever been made for her. All her sisters had £6,000 a year.

[*Cleveland Row, 3 March 1799.*] Lord Grenville has the inexpressible satisfaction of informing your Majesty that he has just seen Lord Auckland who has had the goodness to bring him the inclosed note with the account of Mr Grenville's having landed in safety on the first of February.[1] The great goodness with which your Majesty has been pleased to express your anxiety for Mr. Grenville's safety has induced Lord Grenville to trouble your Majesty with this note. He understands that the ice still continues to make it impossible for the mails to get out.

There are no certain accounts of the Prince Frederick of Orange but reports from the Hague which seem to make his death but too probable.[2] (9169)

[*The King's reply, St. James's, 3 March.*] No one more sincerely shares Lord Grenville's joy on the now certain account of Mr. Grenville's having safely landed on the first of February, nor is more sensible of the extreme danger that attended the situation in which the Proserpine was placed before that gentleman and the crew could get on shore; the hand of Providence has been manifestly shewn on this occasion, and I trust all those saved will duely feel so gracious an interposition in their favour. I cannot lay down my pen without again repeating my congratulations to Lord Grenville on the providential escape of his brother. (Fortescue MSS.)

1931 THE DUKE OF YORK *to the* KING

[*York House, 4 March 1799.*] I think it my duty to acquaint your Majesty that my brother Ernest has had the misfortune this afternoon to be thrown from his horse upon Kew Green and to be considerably hurt, though I trust not dangerously. Inclosed I have the honor to send your Majesty Dr. Pemberton's[3] and Mr Keate's report of him.

As far as I can understand of the accident from himself and his groom, his horse took fright, just as he was attempting to get upon him, at two Turks who were passing by, and plunged away with him before he could fling his leg over. He in vain struggled for some time to gain his seat and was at last flung off upon his shoulder and back. A Mr Nicolls, who was formerly a surgeon and lives at present upon Kew Green, was sent for and bled him plentifully upon the spot, after which he was put into a post chaise, and brought to London by Mr Aiton,[4] your Majesty's gardener, who appears to have taken the greatest care of him. (9170)

[1] See No. 1912 n.

[2] On Thursday the 7th the Lord Chamberlain published orders for the Court to go into mourning for Prince Frederick of Orange, from Sunday the 10th to the 21st.

[3] Christopher Robert Pemberton (1765–1822), physician.

[4] William Townsend Aiton (1766–1849), Keeper of Kew Gardens and one of the founders of the Royal Horticultural Society.

[*Downing Street, Tuesday, 5 March 1799.*][1] The proposed appointment of Sir George Yonge to the Government of the Cape[2] (which Mr Pitt understands Mr Dundas has mentioned to your Majesty) producing a vacancy in the Office of Master of the Mint, Mr Pitt humbly hopes that your Majesty will not disapprove of Lord Hawkesbury's succeeding to that situation,[3] and of Mr Canning's succeeding Lord Hawkesbury as a member of the India Board. If your Majesty should be graciously pleased to consent to this arrangement, it may be convenient that they should attend at St James's to kiss hands tomorrow,[3] by which means their writs may be moved, and the re-elections take place, before any further material business is likely to arise in the House of Commons.[4] Mr Pitt also presumes to

[1] Docketed by the King 'March 9th'. Did the King go over and arrange his papers at a later period when his sight was failing? A great many, however, were not docketed by him at all.

[2] Sir George Yonge's appointment was gazetted on 3 April. 'It seems to promise very ill', remarked Lord Bathurst (*Wellesley Papers*, I, 89). 'Lord Camelford has brought Sir George into Parliament. He could not before that go beyond the precincts of the Palace for fear of being arrested.'

Addington later remarked that Yonge's appointment was the most disgraceful that had ever been made. 'To think of sending out a man of *his* character to be the King's representative! At the time it was in agitation I did everything I could, and more perhaps than I was quite justified in doing, to prevent it, for I felt that it would be a perfect scandal to the country' (Sidmouth MSS.).

[3] Canning had written to Windham on 4 Feb.: 'Pitt is going to write to you about the Mint, which you may remember I mentioned to you some days ago as likely to be vacated by Sir George Yonge. I suppose you will not take it.' (*Windham Papers*, II, 92.) And he wrote on the 9th: 'Windham to have the Mint if he likes it (which, however, I do not think he will, though it has less trouble & more salary than the War Office, & what recommends it to him more, was once held by Sir Isaac Newton.' (Harewood MSS.) Lord Liverpool wrote to John Robinson on the 9th: 'It is true that Lord Hawkesbury is Master of the Mint. This office is certainly a sinecure, in general, but I do not think it will be so for some time in future, for much is to be done at the Mint, and many reforms are to be made there, in which I have been and shall be principally employed. Lord Hawkesbury is to have the Mint, not upon the ancient footing; he is not to have the profits of coinage, but a salary instead of them, which is not yet settled, but it will be handsome. His great object, however, was to have an office which will give him the rank of Privy Councillor, and he is to be put into all the official Committees of Council, so that he will be much more a man of business than he was before.' (Abergavenny MSS.) Hawkesbury, said Lord Bathurst, was to have a fixed salary of £3,000. 'It was to have been only £2,500, and as such was offered to Steele and Ryder, who both thought the difference not worth the trouble of changing. Lord Hawkesbury accepted it as such, and then old Liverpool showed him in every respect whatsoever it would be better to have it amount to £3,000...All this change, you will see, was made for Canning, who is gone to the India Board.' (*Wellesley Papers*, I, 90.)

According to *The Times* (14 March) it was not until Wednesday the 13th that Lord Hawkesbury was presented at the Levée by his father on being appointed Master of the Mint. After the Levée he was sworn in as a member of the Privy Council.

[4] The writ for Rye, Hawkesbury's constituency, was moved on the 6th, but that for Wendover, Canning's, only on the 20th. Canning wrote on 20 Feb.: 'The writs will not be moved till the Easter Recess. Windham will not take the Mint' (Harewood MSS.). And on 6 March: 'Hawkesbury kisses hands today for the Mint. I was to have done so too for the India Board, but the mails are likely to come tumbling in (15 of them at once) and I think it fair to get through all the work that they bring, before I quit my station. I shall probably continue Under-Secretary of State a week or fortnight longer' (*ibid.*). And on the 20th: 'I am just come from kissing the King's hand as Commissioner of the India Board, and by this time, probably, my writ is moved and I am no longer a member of the House of Commons. But I hope to be so again on Tuesday next when my election is fixed for Wendover. I do not mean to cease to be Under-Secretary till I am fairly in Parliament again, and gazetted for my new office' (*ibid.*). A further letter, on Sunday the 24th has an interesting reference to the bogus qualification with which his uncle, the Rev. William Leigh, provided him on this as on a former occasion, in order to comply with the Act of Queen Anne: 'I forgot to mention to you that I wanted £300 a year of you, which I must have by the day on which I take my seat—that is, by Monday sen'night. I returned my former qualification, did I not? You may send the deed inclosed to me by Friday's or Saturday's post' (*ibid.*).

take this opportunity of submitting to your Majesty the name of Dr Lukin,[1] one of the Prebendaries of Westminster, whom at the desire of Mr Windham (to whom Dr Lukin is half-brother), he would humbly recommend to succeed to the Deanery of Wells, and that of Mr Causton,[2] the Speaker's Chaplain in the last Parliament, to succeed to the Stall at Westminster. (9171–2)

[*The King's reply, Queen's House, 6 March 1799.*] On coming to town I have found Mr. Pitt's note. I desire Lord Hawkesbury and Mr. Canning may be presented this day for their new appointments and consent to Dr. Lukin's removal to the Deanery of Wells and Mr. Causton to the Prebendary of Westminster. (Chatham Papers.)

1933 *Letters from* LORD GRENVILLE *to the* KING, *and the reply*

[*Dropmore, 6 March 1799.*] As no mails are arrived, and as Lord Grenville has no business to trouble your Majesty with, he trusts your Majesty will excuse his taking the liberty to remain at this place a day or two longer. He cannot omit this opportunity of humbly offering to your Majesty his most dutiful acknowledgments for your Majesty's gracious expressions towards him in your Majesty's note[3] of Sunday last. (9173)

[*From Lord Grenville, Dropmore, 6 March, 11.15 a.m.*] Lord Grenville is concerned to acquaint your Majesty that he has received, (under a private cover) from Sir Morton Eden a dispatch, with a letter from the Aid de Camp of Prince Frederic of Orange, notifying to Mr. Larrey the melancholy event of the Prince's death. Lord Grenville has judged that your Majesty would approve of his transmitting both these to your Majesty without delay, but if your Majesty should be pleased to give him any other commands respecting them he will have the honour to execute them immediately. (9175)

[*From Lord Grenville, Dropmore, 6 March, 11 p.m.*] Although the accompanying letters from Mr Grenville are merely of a private nature and relate principally to the details of his providential escape, Lord Grenville has judged they might be in some degree interesting to your Majesty, and has therefore taken the liberty to transmit them with the dispatches. (9174)

[*The King's reply, Queen's House, 7 March.*] Lord Grenville's communicating to me the three letters he has received on his miraculous escape from the frigate to Newwork, the succeeding danger from thence to Cuxhaven, and his safe arrival at Berlin has given me much pleasure, and not less so than the impression it has had on Mr. Grenville whose manner of feeling the hand of Providence

---

[1] The Rev. George William Lukin (*c.* 1740–1812). Rector of Felbrigge and Aylmerton, Norfolk, 1763–1812; Prebendary of Westminster, 1797; Dean of Wells, 1799–1812.
[2] The Rev. Thomas Causton (*d.* 1842). Vicar of Turweston, Bucks., 1799–1842; Prebendary of Westminster, 1799–1842; Chaplain to the House of Commons. D.D., 1820.
[3] No. 1930.

during these trials shew that the religious principles of his father and mother[1] have properly prepared his mind to return thanks where it is most due. I desire Mr. Grenville will now express to all his family the just share I take in the joy they must feel at Mr. Grenville's most wonderful escape. (Fortescue MSS.)

1934   *Letters from the* DUCHESS OF WURTEMBERG *to the* KING

[*Louisbourg, 8 March 1799.*] Thinking your Majesty will be uneasy when you hear that my sister-in-law, Princess Ferdinand,[2] has left us and is gone to Hanover on hearing the report that the French intend marching through the Dutchy, I take up my pen to assure you that as far as human prudence can guide us, I am perfectly safe, her being the wife of an Austrian General alters the case and at a moment like this was I parted from my husband I should be wretched. He has, however, insisted on my promising him to be guided by his directions, and if he has the most distant idea of my being exposed to anything unpleasant, I am then to leave him, but we trust in God that I shall not have this misfortune. The Duke says he owes your Majesty as well as himself the taking every possible care of me. My agitation would be dreadful was I at a distance, but out of love to him I shall do everything to spare his feelings. I trust in God everything will turn out for the best. Some days ago I was low with the thoughts of what might happen, but now that the decisif moment approaches I am perfectly calm and rely that Providence will do whatever is right. I must own that in moments like the present I think it absolute duty to remain on the spot, and the attachment all ranks shew the Duke must ever attach me to this country. I believe that much mischief universally would have been prevented if everybody had remained till the last moment in the situation it had pleased God to place them in. My heart bleeds for this poor country which is so happy in itself and where I have met with so much affection.

The Duke begs that I will present his humble duty to yr. Majesty. I will write soon again. (51521)

[*Louisbourg, 8 March 1799.*] Being convinced your Majesty will wish to have further accounts how everything goes on in the Dutchy I think it my duty to acquaint you everything here continues quiet. The French troops entered the country on Monday and the Duke offered me again to go to Anspach if I had any fears, but I took the liberty to be very averse to the step and entreated to remain here as I should be miserable at a distance from him. He with some difficulty consented on condition that I would promise to go at a moment's warning if he had reason to think I should be exposed to anything unpleasant. As for himself he is determined to stay as long as possible, which he most certainly owes to his subjects, who have promised to undergo anything if he will not leave them, and in a body have declared they would let themselves be cut to peices for to ensure his safety.

[1] George Grenville, the Prime Minister (1712–70), married (1749) Elizabeth (*d.* 1769), daughter of Sir William Wyndham, Bart.

[2] Prince Ferdinand of Wurtemberg (1763–1834), married (1795) Albertine (1771–1829), daughter of Prince Christian of Schwarzburg-Sondershausen.

Even my staying I look upon as a great duty, as it prevents people of property leaving the country. They cannot for shame sake shew less courage than a woman. Had people of all classes remained quiet in the place Providence had placed them in, instead of flying at the first appearance of danger, half the mischief would have been avoided. All the well inclined out of fear leaving their homes only evil minded people remained, who gave up their country as a prey to destruction. It is from these principles that I act and therefore I hope your Majesty will approve of my conduct as I should think I did not fulfill my duty were I only ready to go through what is pleasant, and not share the trials which the Duke is called to go through.

The Duke begs me to present his humble duty to your Majesty and assure you that if he sees any necessity for my leaving this place in two hours I shall be in safety. I am not naturally fearful, and trust that Providence will put a stop to the rebeginning of a war which must otherwise ruin all Germany.

Our weather continues very uncertain, but I go out whenever it clears up a little. (51522-3)

1935   THE DUKE OF YORK *to the* KING

[*Oatlands, 10 March 1799.*] I have the honor to acquaint your Majesty that I received yesterday evening the account of General Christie's[1] death, by which the command of the 1st Batallion of the 60th Regiment is become vacant.

As your Majesty has already mentioned to me your intention of appointing Major-General Manners[2] to the command of the 54th Regiment, whenever the account shall be received of General Frederick's[3] death, I beg leave to lay before your Majesty the names of two or three officers whose rank and merit your Majesty may think particularly worthy of your consideration in the disposal of this batallion, which, though equally as advantageous in point of profit as any other regiment of Infantry in your Majesty's service, is not in general so much sought after.

The first is Major-General Gardiner,[4] whose situation and distresses are well known to your Majesty. He is just returned from the continent, and has been obliged to set off immediately for Ireland from Yarmouth, on account of his pecuniary embarassments.

The second is Major-General England[5] who, though he has no particular

---

[1] Gabriel Christie. He died at Montreal. Major-General, 1781; Lieutenant-General, 1793; General, 1798.

[2] See No. 158. (I, 117.) He had been a Major-General since May 1796. Lieutenant-General, 1803; General, 1813.

[3] Moriscoe Frederick. Lieutenant-General, 1777; General, 1793. (c. 1723-1801.)

[4] William Gardiner (1748-1806). Colonel, 1783; Major-General, 1794; Lieutenant-General, 1799. Cornwallis, under whom he had long served, wrote (20 March): 'Gardiner is come over, and looks well, but is much changed from what we remember him both in manners and in spirits...I mean to propose to recommend him to the Duke of York for the Staff in this country, and to place him next in command to Lake in the Province of Munster.' (*Cornwallis Corresp.*, III, 77.) And on 28 March: 'He does not open his mouth so much...He has lost all his teeth' (*ibid.*, III, 81). In 1801 Cornwallis thought he would make a good Commander-in-Chief in Ireland, although, 'to be sure, he takes...rather too much wine' (*ibid.*, III, 353).

[5] Richard England (*d.* 1812). Colonel, 1794; Major-General, 1796; Lieutenant-General, 1803. At the time of his death he was Lieutenant-Governor of Plymouth.

military merit to boast of, yet has certainly been very unfortunate in the service, and particularly in his last captivity in France.

The third is Major-General Fraser who is a very old and deserving officer and of whose conduct during the time he has been in the chief command in Portugal your Majesty has been graciously pleased to express your approbation.

There is a fourth officer whom I ought to have named who is Lieutenant-General Craig,[1] but being upon the Staff in Ireland possibly your Majesty may approve of his waiting till some regiment upon the Irish Establishment after the 54th becomes vacant. (9176)

1936   LORD GRENVILLE *to the* KING, *and the reply*

[*Cleveland Row, 12 March 1799, 5.20 p.m.*] The importance of the private letter from Mr. Grenville of the second of this month induces Lord Grenville to lose no time in forwarding to your Majesty the dispatches received today by messenger and by the post from Berlin.[2]

There is nothing of any importance from Vienna. (9177)

[*The King's reply, Windsor, 12 March, 10.40 p.m.*] I lose no time in acknowledging to Lord Grenville the receipt of his note accompanied by the dispatch from Mr. Grenville, a few minutes have been lost by the lock of the box not answering to my key, and the necessity therefore of sending for a locksmith to pick the lock, who says the wards do not in the least suit my key.

Nothing can be more judicious than Mr. Grenville's manner of judging of the state of the question entrusted to his management, and eager as I am for what I think the interest of every society demands, I cannot but grieve at seeing so little energy in the Court of Berlin to be equalled only by the appathy of that of Vienna; should the account from Radstadt of the 28th Feby., communicated in Mr. Grenville's private letter of the 2nd March, prove true, the Emperor must be anxious to effect a good understanding with this country, Russia and Prussia; and then the pushing on the latter will be the most essential point to render a general system useful. (Fortescue MSS.)

1937   EARL SPENCER *to the* KING

[*Admiralty, 13 March 1799.*] Earl Spencer has the honour of laying before your Majesty a parcel of letters & other papers transmitted to him by the Earl of St. Vincent,[3] which Earl Spencer, on receipt of them, thought it necessary to send to Lord Grenville that he might be apprized of their contents before he saw the Marquis de Circello;[4] Lord Grenville having only returned them this evening will account to your Majesty for the delay in their being submitted to your Majesty's perusal. (9178)

---

[1] Peter Craig. Colonel, 1782; Major-General, 1793; Lieutenant-General, 1798; General, 1803 (?1748–1810).
[2] There are Thomas Grenville's private letters of 28 Feb. and 4 March in *Dropmore Papers*, IV, 481, 485.   [3] See *Spencer Papers*, IV, 41–5.   [4] The Neapolitan Minister in London.

1938   LORD GRENVILLE *to the* KING, *and the reply*

[*Cleveland Row, 16 March 1799, 2.40 p.m.*] Lord Grenville has the honour to transmit to your Majesty the dispatch which he has this morning received from Berlin, with its inclosures, which put the fact of the renewal of the war between Austria and France out of all doubt. The papers sent by Mr. Grenville having been copied in a copying-press, Lord Grenville had transcripts of them made, which are now sent to your Majesty. He proposes with your Majesty's permission to send a messenger to Mr. Grenville tonight with fresh instructions to discourage all idea of measures of eventual defence, and to authorize Mr Grenville to declare that if the co-operation of Prussia in offensive measures cannot be obtained, that of Austria must be looked to.

   Lord Grenville also transmits to your Majesty the dispatches from Sir Morton Eden, judging that your Majesty would chuse to see them without delay though they contain so little. (9179–80)

[*The King's reply, Queen's House, 16 March, 3.42 p.m.*] The dispatch from Mr. Grenville which I return to Lord Grenville removes all doubt on the renewal of the war between Austria and France. The sending a messenger this night to Mr. Grenville is highly proper, with instructions discouraging all ideas of eventual measures of defence, and that none but of an offensive kind can be admitted.

   I am sorry to find by the dispatches from Vienna that as yet the same strange language on the Austrian Loan is held, and that obstinacy still prevails, to the detriment of the great cause of society.[1] (Fortescue MSS.)

1939   HENRY DUNDAS *to the* KING, *and the reply*

[*Downing Street, 19 March 1799, 11 a.m.*] Mr Dundas takes the liberty humbly to mention to your Majesty that Mr George Bolton[2] is going immediately to the West Indies and is advised by his friends that it would be of use to him in the line he is going, if your Majesty would be graciously pleased to confer upon him the honour of knighthood. (9181)

[*The King's reply, Windsor, 19 March 1799, 7 p.m.*] I have just received Mr. Dundas's note stating that Mr. George Bolton is desirous of receiving the honour of Knighthood prior to his embarking for the West Indies, to which I see no objection. (Add. MSS. 40100, f. 221.)

1940   THE DUKE OF PORTLAND *to the* KING

[*Burlington House, Tuesday night, 19 March 1799.*] The Duke of Portland begs leave most humbly to represent to your Majesty that the Martial Law Bill[3] &

---

[1] The King's letter to William Wickham, 18 March, is in *Wickham Corresp.* II, 96 [1870].

[2] For many years he was Preceptor to the younger Princesses in writing, geography and arithmetic. He was knighted, 3 April 1799.

[3] See No. 1927 and also *Cornwallis Corresp.* III, 74. The Bill had been amended, following the representations of the Law Officers of the Crown in England.

five other Bills arrived yesterday morning from Ireland & are now ready for your Majesty's signature, &, considering the anxiety which the Lord Lieutenant expresses for their return before the 25th. instt., the Duke of Portland presumes to submit to your Majesty that your Majesty would graciously condescend to allow the Privy Council to attend your Majesty tomorrow before the Levée, as it will be a saving of several hours in expediting the Bills. (9182)

1941 THE DUCHESS OF WURTEMBERG *to the* KING

[*Louisbourg, 22 March 1799.*] No material alteration has taken place here since I had last the honour of writing to your Majesty, but at about fifty miles distance I imagine there has, though we can obtain no information on the subject. The French, who on the 17th had almost left the Dutchy, on the 19th began to return; as yet we are all ignorant of the cause.

We have this morning taken the Sacrament, which is a great comfort in these times as it quiets the mind and makes it look up for protection from whence alone we can hope to receive support in every situation.

Our weather continues uncertain and a great many people are ill, being suddenly taken with very violent feverish colds which appear to me like the old influenza.

The Duke begs that I will present his humble duty to your Majesty.

I hope that the weather will be pleasant during the Easter Week, that your Majesty may enjoy the being ten days at Windsor. (51524-5)

1942 THE DUKE OF PORTLAND *to the* KING

[*Burlington House, Tuesday, 2 April 1799, 10.35 p.m.*] The Duke of Portland most humbly begs leave to submit to your Majesty the form of a Message from your Majesty to the two Houses of Parliament for the purpose of acquainting them with the orders which your Majesty has directed to be given for the removal of several of the State prisoners from Ireland into this kingdom, which, if approved by your Majesty, your Majesty's servants humbly hope may receive the sanction of your Majesty's royal signature. It is the Duke of Portland's duty to represent to your Majesty that the proposed communication to Parliament is deemed necessary as the basis of an Act to legalize the proceeding which your Majesty has ordered to be taken, & to enable your Majesty in future to order persons in the same predicament as the State prisoners to be removed for safe custody from Ireland to this kingdom.[1] (9189-90)

[1] Dundas presented the Royal Message to the House of Commons on the 3rd: 'His Majesty thinks it proper to acquaint the House of Commons that, in consequence of representations received from his Lord Lieutenant of Ireland, His Majesty has judged it important, for the peace and security of that Kingdom, to give directions that several persons who were in custody at Dublin and Belfast on account of the active part they took in the Rebellion, or for treasonable practices committed in promoting the same, should be immediately removed to some place of safe custody out of that Kingdom, and his Majesty has therefore ordered that they should be brought over to this country and should for the present be kept in custody in Fort George' (*H. of C. J.* LIV, 401).

[*Berlin, 3 April 1799.*] I had the honor to inform your Majesty the 5th Febry. that Prince Augustus then enjoy'd good health. Since that period his Royal Highness has had two very slight attacks of asthma which the doctor says were occasioned by the Prince overheating himself by dancing and not paying proper attention to his diet, &ce. On the whole his Royal Highness is so much recover'd it will be very fortunate if the present circumstances permit your Majesty employing the Prince in any of your armys. If he was placed under the direction of a sensible and steady General where his Royal Highness would have some sort of responsibility, it might wean him by degrees from that very indolent life he has led for many years, which is hurtful to his health and attended with many other inconveniencys. Portugal and Minorca are both excellent climates and I am told both are favorable for the Prince's complaint. His Royal Highness declares openly his dislike to go to any part of Russia. The very critical situation these countrys are in at present, and the dissjointed politics which prevail over all Germany, put it out of my power to recommend to your Majesty any place in preferance to another where his Royal Highness may fix with safety. If it is your Majesty's pleasure the Prince is to remain on the continent 'For the present', I know no place where he can be better than at Berlin. His Prussian Majesty, the Queen and all the Royal Family continue to treat his Royal Highness with flattering kindness. The Prince has got a kind invitation from the Duke of Brunswick and Landgrave of Hesse to meet the King and Queen of Prussia early in June; I beleive the Prince has accepted these invitations if agreeable to your Majesty.

I have the honor to inform your Majesty that I have closed the accounts of the Prince's Household from 1t. April 1798 to 1t. April 1799; after paying the doctor's salary, servants wages, traveling expences and every article connected with that Establishment, I have saved, out of the 5,500 allowed for the support of the Household, about 1,800. I have inform'd Mr. Long[1] of the Treasury that my accounts and vouchers are ready to be sent him.

As I found the Prince had neither plate, bed or table linen and wanted every necessary article to begin housekeeping, I resolved to lay down for the first year a steady plan of œconomy, and I further consider'd, if your Majesty is pleased that his Royal Highness makes a campaign or two, that a considerable sum will be wanted to provide horses, camp equipage, &ce. I now flatter myself whatever plan your Majesty may determine for the Prince, that the 1,800 not yet drawn for may prove sufficient to provide his Royal Highness in what may be necessary without puting your Majesty to any additional expence.

I have been confined to my room for a considerable time with very violent rheumatism and flying gout, which has tormented me more or less since my three weeks voyage in an open boat on the Adreatic. At present I am unfit to do my duty and not the least appearance of my getting better. In case I do not soon

---

[1] Charles Long, Lord Farnborough (1760–1838), M.P. for Rye, 1789–96; for Midhurst, 1796–1802; for Wendover, 1802–6; for Haslemere, 1806–26. Joint Secretary of the Treasury, 1791–1801; a Lord of the Treasury, 1804–6; Irish Secretary, 1805–6; Joint Paymaster-General, 1807–17, and (sole) Paymaster-General, 1817–26. G.C.B., May 1820; peerage, July 1826.

recover I must now, with infinite regret, implore your Majesty to be graciously pleased to allow me to return to try the Bath waters, which I am assured is the only remedy that has a chance to set me on my leges again. I have the honor to assure your Majesty that my absence will be no loss to the Prince or to your Majesty's interest. Captain Arbuthnot is a very sensible and honorable man and in every sense of the word very fit to conduct and manage the Prince's business. He is well known and much esteem'd on the continent and his Royal Highness is fond of him.[1]

I hope your Majesty may be graciously pleased to honor me with your commands or to order instructions to be sent me concerning your Royal pleasure about the Prince, and to authorise me, if I don't soon recover my health, to deliver up my charge to Captain Arbuthnot. (16729–30)

1944   PRINCE ADOLPHUS *to the* KING

[*Hannover, 3 April 1799.*] I seize this opportunity of the Quarterly messenger's departure for England, to inform your Majesty that I have lately received an invitation from the Landgrave of Hesse to come to Cassel to meet the King of Prussia there. I answered that I should be very happy to accept his invitation if unforeseen circumstances did not prevent me, and for this reason I take the liberty of addressing myself to your Majesty, begging you to grant me your permission to go to Cassel. I have very often been invited by the Landgrave, but have never accepted for various reasons, and I have never even ventured to ask your leave, knowing that you prefer I should remain at Hannover as long as I am on the Staff; but as the King goes to Cassel, where he is to review the Hessian troops, which is certainly an interesting sight for a soldier, I hope your Majesty will permit me to accept of the invitation.

I am very happy to be able to give you a good account of the operations of the Army under the Archduke. Yesterday we received the certain news of his having attacked General Jourdan's Army on the 21st of this last month, near Altshausen, a town in Suavia which is but a few leagues from the Lake of Constance; the French General retreated through Pfullendorf and Stockach to *Engen*, where he was again attacked on the 25th by the Archduke and compleatly beat; so that it is said the ennemy have lost 8000 men. In consequence of this victory the two French armies are seperated; General Jourdan has retreated towards Strasburg and by this time it is very probable that he has passed the Rhine. It is likewise said that the Austrians have occupied Schafhausen, and by this they have turned General Massena's[2] left wing, so that probably he will be forced to retire from Swisserland. I rejoice very much for my sister's sake, for she will now be able to remain for the present quiet at Louisburg. I received a letter from her of the 23rd of last month in which she mentions that she was very well and that as long as the ennemy did not come to Stuttgart she should remain in the country. The last accounts I received from Berlin mention that Augustus had had a return of his old complaint.

[1] On the contrary, the Prince detested Captain Arbuthnot. See No. 1945.
[2] The most famous of Napoleon's Marshals (1758–1817).

Upon the whole, he has borne the winter very well, and the Duke of Brunswick, who passed through Hannover yesterday, and who saw my brother lately at Berlin, assures me he loocks very healthy, and that he was very much liked by everybody there, but particularly by the King and Queen. I dare now not trespass any longer on your Majesty's patience than just to add the assurance of my ever remaining [etc.]. (48534-5)

1945   PRINCE AUGUSTUS *to the* KING

[*Berlin, 6 April 1799.*] It is a painful, very painful duty for me to complain to your Majesty, but when every possible attempt of mine to please seems to meet with no approbation whatsoever, the mind is naturally driven to despair. The letter your Majesty did me the honor of writing me at Vienna in date of the 24th of July afforded me hopes of some relief, and could it be otherwise, Sir, after these words?—'You seem to imagine all your brothers have Establishments; that is far from the case, only the three eldest have, and 'till Peace shall be restored it is impossible for me to do the same for Edward, Ernest, you, and Adolphus, for my income will not permit it and I must therefore have the assistance of Parliament, which cannot possibly be thought of till the return of Peace.' My conclusion naturally was that when my elder brothers would be provided for, my own person would also come into consideration with my brother Adolphus, as certainly it could not, neither ought, otherwise to have been but with them. Judge then, Sir, of my astonishment when informed by the newspapers of your Majesty's Message to Parliament for the provision of my brothers Ernest and Edward. That they have got it I most sincerely rejoice, but that I should be forgot seems to me rather unfortunate, after the hopes I conceived were held out to me. This has been the more painful to me as no letter has ever come in answer to those I had the honor of addressing your Majesty on my journey here in the midst of a very serious indisposition, and one even after my arrival at this place. From all this there is left me but one unfortunate and dreadful remark, which is that your Majesty must have banished me, or must have wished to have banished me from your thoughts—and this I am the more readily lead to conceive from the very unfortunate society your Majesty graciously pleased to send me. Neither of the persons were ever known to me before, and they were sent me without my having in any way been asked my consent, though a man at twenty six must have so much knowledge of the world as to know what is proper or right. The first of them, Mr. Livingston, is in *no way* calculated for me, by the indecency of his conduct always wishing to appear the travelling Governor and to have the superior command, which I cannot and will not allow. Secondly, he cannot be agreable to me after *his breaking his promise*, which was that your Majesty would pay *all* my debts, and the list of which I most religiously gave him. Either he had the power or he had not, in which case he equally told me a falsehood. As to the second gentleman[1] was it only for his impertinent curiosity, wishing to look into every paper, he must render himself *completely* obnoxious to me. Your Majesty sees I speak to

[1] Captain Robert Arbuthnot.

you fairly, for I know not deception, neither have I ever used any with you. Your Majesty may easily conceive the deep and cruel impression which such a conclusion must have necessarily made upon a heart that has already been but too frequently wounded by cares, and which is therefore the more susceptible of any blow of this sort.

It is therefore with a broken heart but with all dutiful respect that I inform your Majesty of my determination to adopt such measures as will render my person henceforth of no more encumbrance to your Majesty, and at the same time will in one way or another put an end to my unfortunate situation. It may appear to you, Sir, as difficult for me to execute such a resolution as to take it, but I can assure your Majesty that am I to die, my last moments will be perfectly calm, from the conviction of having honourably fulfilled the duties of an honest man, a faithful subject and a dutiful son. May God grant your Majesty long life and may you never feel, after I shall be no more, should such be the decrees of Providence, that those who have misrepresented me to my father are more your enemies than they were mine. Such are the prayers of him who has the honor of signing himself, with all dutiful respect [etc.]. (48136–8)

1946   THE DUCHESS OF WURTEMBERG *to the* KING

[*Louisbourg, 8 April 1799.*] I am very uneasy at being obliged every post to contradict the accounts I have had the honour of giving your Majesty the foregoing, the French are every moment changing their positions and are in two or three days in and out of the Dutchy before it is possible to have an idea of the alteration which has taken place. I believe they have for the present left us. God grant it may be for good, as they do sad mischief not only by eating up everything, but taking away horses, cattle &c. &c. Some of the Oberämter are so compleatly ruined that the peasants will not be able either to sow or till their fields. We all tremble that even with the greatest care a famine must ensue, as the Austrians make equal extravagant demands. I hope the Almighty will assist us. Providentially we were blest with an uncommon good harvest last year which has enabled these requisitions to be complied with; and the same hand which sent that will, I trust, have again mercy on us and prevent the calamity we are threatened with.

I hope your Majesty's weather during the Easter week allowed of your enjoying your hunting and your farm; ours is still very changeable and of course unwholesome. Some days it snows and others I am till near six o'clock in an open carriage.

In all distress there is some comfort and I think it my duty to tell your Majesty that on the first entry of troops into the Dutchy the Duke sent for his eldest son from Tubingen. I never in my life saw anybody in three months so much improved as he is, and it gives me great pleasure to see him and his father on a very comfortable, friendly footing. As I look upon a good understanding in one's family as the only real happiness, the seeing them so well together is a great joy to me. (51526–7)

[*Downing Street, 15 April 1799, 3 p.m.*] Mr. Dundas takes the liberty of transmitting to your Majesty a letter[1] addresst to your Majesty by Mr. Livingston, together with one to Mr. Dundas by which it was accompanyed. Mr. Dundas will wait your Majesty's commands before he writes an answer to Mr. Livingstone. (9191)

1948 THE DUCHESS OF WURTEMBERG *to the* KING

[*Louisbourg, 18 April 1799.*] Your Majesty's constant goodness to me makes me think you will be uneasy till you are certain that we are quite free from the French, and knowing the irregularity of the posts at present may keep your Majesty some time in suspence I send an express to Hanover to inform you we are, thank God, quit of them; they have done sad mischief and destroyed almost 13 Oberämter in the upper part of the country, but the people have most providentially behaved wonderfully well, universally hating the horrid monsters who have ruined them, and acknowledging they love their Sovereign and can rely on him as a just man giving them every assistance their situation requires. I shall in a few days have the honour to enter into greater details on all these subjects: as on the 7th the Duke received by a messenger a letter from his sister the Empress of Russia[2] according to her wishes he intends sending a confidential person to Vienna and at the same time to my *great comfort* has begged me to acquaint your Majesty with his humble duty; that he thinks himself bound to send to London a very sensible man as his Minister, who has been employed ever since Duke Charles's time at Berlin, Vienna and Petersburgh; the whole of the two or three last campaigns he was with the Archduke at Head Quarters, General Baron de Melius. He has been with us in the country ever since we left Stutgard, and knowing him by that means I am very glad the Duke's choice has fallen on him, looking on the General as fit for the situation. The Duke will have the honour of writing by him a long letter to your Majesty.

I write in a great hurry as I wish very much your Majesty to receive from nobody else the account that Citizen Trouvé,[3] the French Minister, left Stutgard the 16th accompanied by an Austrian Officer and a detachment. On the 15th the Duke received a very polite letter from the Archduke to say the Austrian armies would suffer if the Citizen was allowed to remain here and carry on quietly his correspondence with the Republic. He therefore desired that it might be intimated to him to leave Stutgard in 24 hours. On the whole Trouvé behaved better than could have been expected. He begged to take leave of the Duke and set out at five a clock on the 16. By travelling all night he was beyond the frontier yesterday morning.

---

[1] No. 1943.

[2] The Duke's sister Sophia (1759–1828) married (1776) the Tsar Paul (1754–1801), who succeeded his mother Catherine II in 1796.

[3] Thomas Grenville wrote from Berlin on 4 March: 'Trouvé was originally employed in England by Prussia, but proving himself, as Haugwitz told me, to be a very mischievous democrat, they sent for him here to shut him up, which he avoided by escaping to France, and has since become one of the most active agents for the revolutionizing of Germany' (*Dropmore Papers*, IV, 486).

Your Majesty cannot imagine the joy I feel at being able once again to write to you a letter I am certain will arrive safe. Had I followed my inclination I should long ago have sent off a messenger, but feeling ourselves surrounded by Republican Ministers and spies it was impossible for me to expose the Duke to the mischief which would have ensued had it only been surmized that I ventured to acquaint your Majesty with the many unpleasant transactions I have either known or been witness to. But our *all* was at stake, and silence was the wisest conduct till circumstances again gave me freedom.

Till last Sunday we had not seen any company from the moment we left Stutgard, but Count and Countess Metternich,[1] who have left Rastadt in their way to Ratisbonne, came here on that evening. She is a very pleasant woman and having seen much of the world has a great deal of conversation.

I will now take up no more of your Majesty's time than to beg of you to be convinced of the respect and attachment with which I have the honour [etc.]. (51528–30)

1949 PRINCE ADOLPHUS *to the* KING

[*Hannover, 20 April 1799.*] I was rendered very happy at the arrival of the Quarterly Messenger by your Majesty's very gracious letter, for which I return you my most humble thanks. I rejoiced very much to hear how well you are, and I most sincerely wish that you may continue enjoying such good health for many years still. The new house you have been so gracious to buy for me is now almost finished, and I cannot enough say how comfortable it is. The only thing I should wish still would be to have the honor of waiting upon your Majesty in it. I do not give up all hopes that this wish may once be fulfilled, for as the operations of the Austrians have been hitherto very successful, and it is to be hoped they will continue so, the French will soon alter their insolent tone and be forced to make a Peace, and then is the moment I trust we may see you here. The joy this would spread through the whole is undoubtedly very great, and I am sure your Majesty would not be displeased with your subjects here who, for the most part, are very loyal. Yesterday's post has brought us an account of a fresh victory gained by General Kray over the French Army under the command of General Scherer.[2] The Austrians attacked on the 5th inst. the ennemy near Verona, and after a very hot engagement compleatly defeated them; the loss is very considerable on both sides: 7000 prisoners, 11 Colours and 19 pieces of cannon have been taken. The Austrians compute their loss at 4000 men. This affair is of the utmost importance, the ennemy being now obliged to give up their plan of forcing a passage through Tirole; and should General Kray succeed in taking Peschiera, which is now blocked up, I trust matters will end very well in Italy, for the Austrians are then sure on one side. The French have according to the last accounts retreated to the left side of the Rhine, and General St. Cyr's Division is alone remained on this side for to

---

[1] The famous Austrian statesman (1773–1859). He was already in the Austrian diplomatic service, and he had represented the Empire at the Congress of Rastatt, 1797–8.

[2] Schérer, who had been appointed French Minister of War in 1797, was now commanding the French army in Italy.

cover Kehl. By this time Schaffhausen will probably be in the hands of the Austrians, and I trust that General Hotze will have advanced into Switzerland.[1] It is a great pity that no diversion is made in the north, for I am sure that if this was possible Holland would be soon in our hands. I dare now not trespass any longer on your patience but just to add the assurance that I shall ever remain [etc.]. (48536–7)

1950   WILLIAM PITT to the KING

[*Downing Street, 22 April 1799, 11.30 p.m.*] Mr Pitt humbly begs leave to acquaint your Majesty that the Address[2] to your Majesty on the subject of the Union, communicated from the Lords, was today agreed to in the House of Commons without a division.[3] It was opposed by Genl Fitzpatrick, Sir Francis Burdett, and Lord William Russell, and supported in a very sensible speech by Mr Douglas, and afterwards by Lord Sheffield, and with peculiar brilliancy and effect by Mr Canning.[4] (9192)

1951   THE DUCHESS OF WURTEMBERG to the KING

[*Louisbourg, 26 April 1799.*] I am all gratitude for your Majesty's most gracious letter of the 9th which I have just had the happiness to receive. My heart is deeply impressed with the gracious kind manner in which your Majesty mentions your anxiety about my wellfare. I entreat you to believe that in all situations your goodness is the greatest comfort to me, and the trying to deserve it will ever be the study of my life.

I enjoy very much the being in the country, and though our weather is still very changeable, contrive to get out some part of every day either on foot or in an open carriage. I amuse myself in watching the progress of the Spring in the little garden into which my room opens, and in drawing the flowers which blow there. The Duke continues the improvements which were begun last year, but thinks it prudent to begin nothing new till things have the appearance of being a little more settled. Only planting goes on which is highly necessary, as the country is in want of wood, the scarcity of which was dreadfully felt by the poor last Winter.

We lead even a quietter life than usual as we have had no company here except Count and Countess Metternich in their way to Vienna, and some of the Austrian Officers. Yesterday Count Colloredo[5] supt with us; he has been with the Archduke ever since the beginning of the campaign.

The Duke begs that I will present his humble duty to your Majesty. (51531–2)

---

[1] See No. 1845 n.

[2] The Address of the Lords in answer to the King's Message on the subject of the proposed Union, is in *H. of C.J.* LIV, 472–3.

[3] *Parl. Register*, LIII, 482–541.

[4] Canning, who dined with Pitt after the House rose, wrote, next day: 'They pretend it was the best speech that I ever made, but I do not think that. However, I am quite satisfied and happy in W.L. [his uncle] having been by' (Harewood MSS.).

[5] The Imperial Field-Marshal (1735–1815). Possibly Count Joseph Maria Colloredo.

[*Cleveland Row, 6 May 1799, 11 p.m.*] Lord Grenville has the honour humbly to submit to your Majesty that immediately on the receipt of the important dispatch from Mr Grenville he directed a meeting of your Majesty's confidential servants to be summoned for tomorrow, and if their opinion should coincide with the view he entertains of the subject, he humbly hopes your Majesty will not disapprove of his sending, with the least possible delay, instructions to Mr Grenville authorizing him to conclude a treaty on the footing stated in his dispatch.

As in that case Lord Grenville would necessarily be occupied the whole of tomorrow evening, he would take the liberty of humbly soliciting her Majesty's permission not to avail himself of the great honour conferred upon him by her Majesty's commands for tomorrow, unless your Majesty should please to direct his attendance in order to give him any orders on the subject. (9195–6)

[*The King's reply, Queen's House, 7 May, 8.03 a.m.*] I am highly pleased with the ability shewn by Mr. Grenville in availing himself of the change of system of the Court of Prussia, and I shall most certainly do justice to the decision he has so properly addopted on the occasion. There cannot be a doubt but the Cabinet must view the business in the same light I and Lord Grenville view it. I shall certainly make his excuse to the Queen for his not coming here this evening, and I trust that in the course of tomorrow or at farthest by Thursday he will forward the messenger with full instructions to Berlin for concluding the Subsidiary Treaty. (Fortescue MSS.)

[*From Lord Grenville, Cleveland Row, 8 May, 1 a.m.*] Lord Grenville has the honour humbly to acquaint your Majesty that in obedience to your Majesty's commands the dispatches have been completed, and will be forwarded with this night's mail. (9197)

[*The King's reply, Queen's House, 8 May, 8.06 a.m.*] I am happy to find Lord Grenville has compleated the dispatches for Berlin so as to dispatch the messenger with the mail of last night.

I return a box of the Northern Department which my key could not open, and on looking at the scutcheon I perceive there is a cross marked which I should suppose is a private mark, that all the keys do not pass easily. (Fortescue MSS.)

1953   THE DUCHESS OF WURTEMBERG *to the* KING

[*Louisbourg, 11 May 1799.*] I am very uneasy that your Majesty will not have received my letter of the 25th of last month, as I hear the French have seized on the posts for some days before it was known here, and now they are obliged to take a roundabout way that they may avoid falling into their hands.

Your Majesty's Minister, Monsieur de Reden, has been here some days, but he was to[o] ill to appear till the Sunday evening. She is a very chearful pleasant woman, very much delighted with the thoughts of returning to Hannover and shocked with the melancholy horrid history of Rastadt. Madame de Brie and her daughters were brought to her house and she spent a most dreadful night expecting Madame de Brie to be brought of bed [*sic*] every moment till she received the certain news of her husband's being alive and then her joy was almost as violent as her grief had been. God grant the authors of this sad useless murder may be discovered and that suspicions may not fall on innocent people.

Monsieur de Jacobi[1] and his daughter, Madame de Klost, dined with us last Friday; he has married a very young handsome woman, but she did not appear, as her situation does not admit of her undergoing the fatigue of dressing.

On Monday my sister-in-law, Princess Ferdinand, to my great joy, returned here. She is delighted with Hannover and assures me dear Adolphus is beloved by every class. He opened his house for the first time the evening before the Princess went away.

Our weather continues very changeable but I now begin to hope that the mischief done by the severity of the weather to the trees is a little exagerated; the leaves now begin to appear but still the vegetation is very backward. (51535–6)

1954 LORD GRENVILLE *to the* KING, *and the reply*

[*Cleveland Row, 17 May 1799.*] Lord Grenville has the honour to lay before your Majesty the copy of Memoranda delivered by Count Haugwitz to Mr Grenville, and which the latter has inclosed to Lord Grenville in a private letter, not thinking them of a nature to be sent in a public dispatch. The confused & envelopped stile in which they are written makes their meaning in many parts scarcely intelligible. Mr Grenville is of opinion that this is owing (in great degree) to the wavering state of Count Haugwitz's mind, and to his doubts respecting his own situation and influence. (9198)

[*The King's reply, Windsor, 18 May, 8.35 a.m.*] The opinion I form on the Memoranda delivered by Count Haugwitz to Mr. Grenville, and which Lord Grenville has this morning communicated to me, is certainly to be rather surprised that any Minister could have given himself the trouble of drawing up so confused and little pointed a paper; but I believe the truth is that the idea arose from wanting some fresh ground to rouse the King of Prussia to take a becoming part more than placing any confidence that this production could be of much weight here; the only conclusion I therefore draw from this is that it is melancholy that the King of Prussia does not view with energy the necessity of his stepping forward, and that at the moment when offensive measures are the sole object, he should be wasting his time in forming vague ideas on the kind of Peace that in the end is to be obtained. (Fortescue MSS.)

[1] *The Times* announced on 5 Nov. that Baron Jacobi, formerly Prussian Minister in London (see No. 802), was about to return in the same capacity.

[*Hannover, 18 May 1799.*] The very gracious manner in which your Majesty has been pleased to express yourself on my subject in your last letter of the 7th inst. has rendered me infinitely happy, and it is impossible for me to find words strong enough to describe what I felt in reading it. God knows that to deserve your approbation has been the constant aim of all my conduct, and there is nothing I would not do to prove the truth of this assurance. I am perfectly convinced of the justness of your Majesty's remarks on my late unlucky affair, and I cannot enough thank you for your delicacy in not touching this subject till time had made me reflect more coolly on what had passed. I certainly have suffered a great deal, but the conviction of having acted as an honest man in this whole busyness has helped to support well what I have gone through, and the assurance of your approbation is a comfort which I cannot express, for though I feel that I am happy in not having married a woman who has behaved in such a manner, yet I find it very difficult to forget a person to whom I have been most sincerely attached.[1]

Our accounts from Italy continue to be very good. The French have been beat everywhere, and the Austrian headquarters were at Milan, which town the ennemy has left in consequence of General Wukossowich[2] having surrounded a corps of three thousand men commanded by General Serrurier[3] and taken them all prisoners near Milan. This corps was posted at about four leagues from that town, and was intended to oppose any operations that could be made in consequence of the Austrians passing the Adda, but General Wukossowich took the resolution of attacking this Corps immediately after his having passed that river at Lecco, and his plan has perfectly succeeded. Poor General Hotze has made an unfortunate attack in Swisserland in trying to force the Pass of Lucie about four leagues from Coin; he has been repulsed with some loss, but I trust that this misfortune will soon be repaired. It is a great pity that the King of Prussia will not take an active part, for I am sure Holland would be soon in our hands. How happy should I be could I have the advantage of contributing somewhat with my Brigade to the glorious exploits that most probably we should make, were we to act.

I hope your Majesty will forgive thes[e] remarks of a young soldier who loves his profession and is sorry not to be employed at a moment when there is every probability of success, if a decisive step was taken.

I cannot conclude without repeating my thanks for your last very gracious letter, and I begg you to be assured that I ever shall [&c.]. (48538–9)

1956 THE DUCHESS OF WURTEMBERG *to the* KING

[*Louisbourg, 19 May 1799.*] Trusting that your Majesty will receive this on the 4th of June, allow me to express to you the warm wishes I make that you may long be allowed to continue a blessing to us all and may continue to enjoy that health

[1] See No. 1905 (12 Jan. 1799).
[2] Baron Joseph Philip von Vukăssovich, the Austrian commander, who in 1796, had won a small success against Bonaparte's Army of Italy.   [3] Sérurier [Serrurier], the French Marshal.

so necessary to your happiness. I pray the Almighty that he may through many succeeding years continue to bless your undertakings as he has done of late, and that your Majesty may be blest with the satisfaction of knowing that you have been his chosen instrument to re-establish religion and regularity in the world.

I cannot pass over in silence this day on whose return I congratulate your Majesty. God grant that many many years we may enjoy the happiness of celebrating two days which must be dear not only to your children but to all those who are blest with your protection.

As in a few days I shall have the honour of writing your Majesty a long letter I shall now only add the Duke's most humble duty. (51537–8)

1957   WILLIAM PITT *to the* KING

[*Downing Street, 20 May 1799.*] Mr Pitt trusts to your Majesty's indulgence to forgive his breaking in on your Majesty for a moment more respecting the Message in favor of Sir James Marriott, in which the initials of your Majesty's signature have not been added at the end of the Message, and which, from a scrupulous attention to regularity on the part of the Officers of the House, he has been desired to submit to your Majesty.[1] He also takes the liberty of submitting a warrant for a small pension (in the room of one which he would humbly propose to be cancelled) for the purpose of inserting words in the new warrant, which leave to the Trustee the discretion of distributing the pension in the manner thought most beneficial to the parties. (9199)

1958   THE DUKE OF PORTLAND *to the* KING

[*Whitehall, Monday, 20 May 1799, 5 p.m.*] The Duke of Portland humbly begs leave to lay before your Majesty some intelligence respecting the situation & course of the French Fleet on the 2d instt. which he has just received by the new mode of conveyance established between this & Dublin. (9200)

1959   *Letters from* LORD GRENVILLE *to the* KING, *and the replies*

[*Cleveland Row, 23 May 1799.*] Lord Grenville has the honour most respectfully to submit to your Majesty that on [*sic*] conversation with your Majesty's servants, it seemed to be their general opinion that if your Majesty were graciously pleased to receive the Count d'Artois, it would certainly be an honour highly gratifying to that Prince, & does not appear to be liable to inconvenience. As Lord Grenville understood from Mr Pitt that tomorrow was the day fixed by your Majesty for

---

[1] On the 8th Pitt presented the King's Message to the House of Commons: 'His Majesty, being desirous of conferring a mark of his Royal favour on Sir James Marriott, Knight, late Judge of the High Court of Admiralty, in consideration of his diligent and faithful services in the execution of that Office, recommends it to his faithful Commons to consider of enabling his Majesty to grant an annuity of two thousand pounds, clear of all deductions whatever, to the said Sir James Marriott, during the term of his natural life, to be paid out of the Consolidated Fund' (*H. of C.J.* LIV, 525).

that purpose, he begs leave to say that he will have the honour to bring the Comte d'Artois to the Queen's House at whatever hour your Majesty may be pleased to appoint. (9201)

[*The King's reply, Queen's House, 24 May, 8.05 a.m.*] In consequence of Lord Grenville's note I desire he will bring the Comte d'Artois at eleven this morning; so early an hour will less break into Lord Grenville's busy day, and at the same time be less remarked. (Fortescue MSS.)

[*From Lord Grenville, Cleveland Row, 25 May, 11.45 a.m.*] Lord Grenville has the happiness of transmitting to your Majesty without delay the account from Vienna of the taking of Peschiera, Novara, & Vercelli, and also of Modena.

The dispatch from Mr Grenville mentions that General Stamford proceeds immediately to Petersburgh with a hearty zeal to execute the commission with which your Majesty had been pleased to charge him. As a part of his dispatch seems to require immediate answer, Lord Grenville delays sending it to your Majesty till the usual time. (9202)

[*The King's reply, Windsor, 25 May, 3.44 p.m.*] I sincerely rejoice at the account I have just received from Lord Grenville of the account from Vienna of the farther success of Marechal Souvaroff[1] which I trust will soon change the face of things not only in Italy but if Genl. Hotze obtains the promised reinforcement will restore the Grisons and Switzerland. (Fortescue MSS.)

[*From Lord Grenville, Cleveland Row, 25 May, 11 p.m.*] In forwarding to your Majesty the dispatch received today from Berlin, Lord Grenville ventures to express his hope that your Majesty will not disapprove of his having without a moment's delay sent such instructions both to Sir Charles Whitworth and to Mr Grenville as will authorize each of them to pursue & conclude the negotiation with which he is charged, whether that of the other succeeds or not.

By this means Lord Grenville trusts that the body of forty-five thousand Russians to act by sea against Holland will be obtained, and if an army of sixty thousand Prussians should likewise be obtained Mr Pitt agrees with him in thinking that the additional expence will be amply compensated by the increased chance of speedy and complete success.

Lord Grenville troubles your Majesty with Mr Grenville's private letter, on account of the circumstance mentioned at the end of it, & which is not stated in the dispatch. (9203–4)

[*The King's reply, Windsor, 26 May, 9.12 a.m.*] I cannot take up my pen without highly approving of the step Lord Grenville has taken of not losing one moment in sending such instructions both to Sir Charles Whitworth and to Mr. Grenville

---

[1] Count Alexander Suvoroff (1729–1800), Russian Field Marshal. In 1799 he was sent into Italy to help the Austrians against the French. He defeated Moreau on the Adda, Macdonald at the Trebbia, and Joubert at Novi, but lack of concerted action from the other Allied forces ensured the failure of his campaign to liberate Switzerland.

as will authorize each of them to pursue and conclude the negociation with which he is charged, whether that of the other succeeds or not; as my sentiments are decidedly known that every expence should be risked that Mr. Pitt can think himself able to furnish the means to make the most effectual push now that I trust Divine Providence is turning the tide against the wicked foes of every religious and social tye; these exertions may in the end be the saving of expence and blood, as it will probably greatly shorten the conflict.

P.S. One of the persons I alluded to on Friday I find to be Beyme, Private Cabinet Counsellor and Private Secretary. (Fortescue MSS.)

1960   WILLIAM PITT *to the* KING

[*Wimbledon, Sunday, 27 [26] May 1799.*] Mr Pitt humbly begs leave to submit to your Majesty a Message to the House of Commons and a similar one for the House of Lords, which, if they receive your Majesty's approbation, may be delivered on Tuesday next together with copies of the Treaty concluded with the Emperor of Russia. Mr Pitt proposes afterwards in the Committee of Supply to move for the grant of a specific sum sufficient to discharge the engagements of the Treaty, which may amount for the present year to about eleven hundred thousand pounds, and for a farther sum in the shape of a Vote of Credit, not less than two millions and an half or three millions, in order to provide for any farther engagements which may be formed either with Russia or Prussia in addition to the aid destined to Switzerland and Portugal. Mr Pitt flatters himself your Majesty will approve the policy of incurring considerable additional expence, in order to make every effort for improving to the utmost the great advantages which the present moment seems peculiarly to offer.[1] (9205–6)

1961   THE DUCHESS OF WURTEMBERG *to the* KING

[*Louisbourg, 27 May 1799.*] I had the honour of mentioning to your Majesty about a month ago the Duke's intention of sending General Baron de Melius as Minister to your Majesty. At last, thank God, the many impediments which prevented this step are partly removed, and I now feel myself at liberty to lay before your Majesty many things which it has long been my wish you should be thoroughly acquainted with.

Your Majesty knows that the Peace which three years ago the late Duke was constrained to sign with the French when they had taken possession of this country, was always a great distress to my husband, who looked on a partial Peace as a source of great mischief, thinking it exposed the Dutchy to become the seat of war and that both armies drawing from thence their sustenance must totally ruin his subjects. However, when he came to the Dutchy he found himself

---

[1] Not until Thursday, 6 June, did Dundas present the King's Message to the House of Commons. The Message (*H. of C.J.* LIV, 603) informed the House that a Treaty of subsidiary alliance had been concluded with Russia whereby the Tsar was to be given £225,000 as 'preparation money'; a further payment of £75,000 a month, and another of £37,500 a month which was to date from the conclusion of a peace made by common consent.

in a very difficult situation, his country open on all sides to the enemy, without sufficient troops to stem the torrent and the States assembled too ready to join in every confusion. They have now been assembled above two years and have not found means to fix the taxes for to pay the expences incurred by the war, which was the only object they had to decide on, but have continually attempted to interfere in every branch of Government and delayed executing their promises. Many of their Members, as is customary in popular Assemblies, are weak and are lead by a few hot headed men who by having no property think they can gain by bringing on disturbances. When the Duke first came to the Dutchy he confirmed according to the Constitution their privileges, and a few months after, wishing by gentle means to bring them round, he yielded to them on many points, but unfortunately was not repaid by success. They have for many months continued to torment the Duke, who has bore it with great patience and always hoped they would at last fulfil their duty. When the French entered the Dutchy the States themselves entreated the Duke not to leave them, which he most willingly agreed to on condition they would agree to the leveying more troops. They apparently came into it, but ever since continue to throw every impediment they can think of in the way to prevent the recruiting. In this situation your Majesty will easily see that it was impossible to take an active part and that the most that could be obtained was to keep home quiet.

The country people are attached to the Duke, and to their credit, though 13 Oberämter are quite ruined, not a peasant has moved. They say their Sovereign is a just man and they are convinced will do everything in his power to assist them: the French even acknowledge that nobody in the country is ready to receive their Revolutionary principles, instead of which the Wirtembergers hate them.

I trembled at the begining of the war that the French should have their usual success, being convinced we should then be the first prey they would seize on, for if we did not remain, the peasants suffering from the absence of the Court would grow dissatisfied and by that means be drawn into Republicanising; they are now all pleased at the Duke's having staid, which is a great mercy.

On the 7th of April the Duke received a messenger from the Empress of Russia his sister. She pressed him in the Emperor's name to take an open and active part in the war, which, could he have followed his inclination, he would have done long ago, but situated as he is, could not venture on such a step without the protection and assistance of Great Powers. Since that he has received both from Russia and other places strong proofs that notwithstanding the declarations of the Directory the Generals had received orders underhand to make the Dutchy a Republic. It is therefore, Sire, at the moment we understand the extent of our danger, and are free from these monsters, that we entreat your Majesty to take us under your protection and be graciously pleased to take our situation into consideration and assist us by taking into your pay the troops which the Duke offers to raise, and to unite to the Archduke's Army to fight against the French, who have ever sought to destroy religion, government and happiness. The Duke is too happy to have it in his power to shew his attachment to your Majesty, and I hope you will forgive my anxiety on a subject on which I see totally depends the future existance of the Duke and our children. He is very much encouraged by the Russian Court and I flatter myself will also meet with approbation at Vienna, where Count Zeppeline is at present.

May I now recommend to your Majesty's protection General de Melius who, I flatter myself, you will be pleased with as he is a sensible man and has been now above thirty years employed by the different Dukes. His having been with us three months in the country enables him to give very exact accounts about me, which, knowing your Majesty's constant goodness to me, makes me hope will give you pleasure.

May I entreat your Majesty to accept of two breakfast cups which the Queen will be so good as to offer you in my name. I shall now only beg your Majesty to be convinced of the respect and attachment with which [etc.]. (51539–43)

1962   THE DUKE OF PORTLAND *to the* KING

[*Burlington House, Wednesday, 29 May 1799, 6.15 p.m.*] The Duke of Portland most humbly begs leave to lay before your Majesty the summary of the accounts which have been extracted from an imperfect set of French papers (of the arrival of which the Duke of Portland was ignorant when he was attending his duty upon your Majesty this morning), & which has been made in pursuance of your Majesty's commands.[1] (9207)

1963   EARL SPENCER *to the* KING

[*Admy., 30 May 1799.*] Earl Spencer has the honour to lay before your Majesty a private letter he has just received from Lord Nelson, giving an account of the successes of your Majesty's squadron under his command in the neighbourhood of Naples, by which it appears highly probable that the whole of that kingdom is by this time returned under the dominion of its lawful Sovereign.[2] (9208)

1964   LORD GRENVILLE *to the* KING, *and the reply*

[*Cleveland Row, 30 May 1799, 1.30 p.m.*] Lord Grenville has the satisfaction humbly to inform your Majesty that accounts are received from Sir Morton Eden & Lt.-Colonel Craufurd, the former as late as the 16th and the latter the 14th of this month, by which it appears that Pizzighitone had surrendered, that the Russians were in possession of the town of Tortona, the citadel of which was said to be defended only by a very feeble garrison, and that the Austrian light troops had pushed on to the environs of Turin, the whole of Piedmont being in insurrection against the French.

And that on the 14th of May General Hotze made a general attack on the French

[1] The King's letter to William Wickham, 29 May, 7.05 p.m., is in *Wickham Corresp.* II, 102.

[2] Writing to Lord Spencer from Palermo on 29 April, Nelson said, 'I think it very probable that in ten days their Sicilian Majesties may be again in Naples. These happy prospects have been brought about, first, by the war of the Emperor; secondly, by the wonderful loyalty of the lower order of the people; and lastly…by the conduct of the English' (Nicolas, *Despatches and Letters of Lord Nelson*, III, 340).

in the Grisons & dislodged them from all their posts in that country from Lucien-steig to Coire, both inclusive, having taken sixteen pieces of cannon and two thousand prisoners.

There are also accounts from Palermo which mention that the greatest part of the south of the Kingdom of Naples is in insurrection in favour of the King. (9209–10)

[*The King's reply, Oatlands, 30 May, 4.40 p.m.*] I have this instant received Lord Grenville's most favorable news. The tide seems completely turning, and I trust by this time but few French are left in Italy. Hotze's success in the Grisons is not less material. I take it for granted that Earl Spencer will have communicated to Lord Grenville the substance of his private letter from Lord Nelson by which there is every reason to suppose that on the 8th of this month the King of Naples and his family were safely returned to Naples. (Fortescue MSS.)

1965   EARL SPENCER *to the* KING

[*Admiralty, 31 May* [*1799*], *1 a.m.*] Earl Spencer has the honour to assure your Majesty that measures have already been taken for bringing the earliest intelligence of the sailing of the Dutch Fleet. Earl Spencer is not yet fully informed of the exact state of the ships under Admiral Duncan, several of them having come to the Nore today without orders as the Admiralty have learnt by telegraph; but he trusts that the rest will be able to give protection to their Royal & Serene Highnesses past the Texel, which service may otherwise be performed by some ships ordered round from Portsmouth.[1] (9211)

1966   THE DUKE OF PORTLAND *to the* KING

[*Burlington House, Saturday, 1 June 1799, 9.45 p.m.*] The Duke of Portland most humbly begs leave to represent to your Majesty, that having been induced by the novelty of the circumstance to read the warrant by which the Attorney-General was directed by your Majesty to enter a Noli prosequi in the cases of the Earl of Thanet[2] & Mr Fergusson,[3] there appeared to him such a misstatement in the recital as made him, notwithstanding he had countersigned it, think it advise-able to consult with the Lord Chancellor upon it before he sent it to the Attorney-General. The Duke of Portland therefore stated his objection to the Lord Chancellor, who, agreeing with him, suggested the correction in conformity to

[1] Admiral Duncan's squadron which was blockading the Texel frustrated the French plan to con-centrate the French, Spanish and Dutch fleets and then break the blockade of Alexandria, Malta and Corfu, thereby crushing the Kingdom of Naples and re-embarking the French army locked up in Egypt ever since the Battle of the Nile, and bringing it back to France.

[2] See No. 1691 n. When Lord Thanet and Robert Cutlar Fergusson were brought up for judgment into the Court of King's Bench on 10 June, the Attorney-General said that he had received the King's commands to enter a *nolle prosequi* with respect to the first three counts.

[3] Robert Cutlar Fergusson (1768?–1838), M.P. for Kirkcudbright, 1826–38. He had been one of the 'Friends of the People'. Like Thanet he was sent to prison for twelve months, but fined only £100. After his release he emigrated to Calcutta to practice at the Bar, returning home about twenty years later. He was Judge Advocate-General, July–Nov. 1834, and 1835–8.

which the new warrant has been prepared which the Duke of Portland ventures to lay before your Majesty for your royal signature, together with the warrant which your Majesty signed yesterday, in order that it may be cancelled by your Majesty if your Majesty shall so think fit.[1] (9212)

1967   PRINCE ADOLPHUS *to the* KING

[*Hannover, 4 June 1799.*] It is impossible for me to let pass this day without presenting your Majesty my most humble congratulations on it, and my most sincere wishes that you may see still many and many very happy returns of it. This is the sentiment which every honest subject has, and I am happy to say that this is the case with all the Hannoverians. I am sure that if ever your Majesty was to come over to this country you would be pleased with the loyalty of your Hannoverian subjects, for though they do not know you, yet they love you prodigeously, and I will answer for the military being ready to shed the last drops of their blood for your sake. Since my last letter I have been for some days at Minden to wait upon the King, and at the same time to see the Prussian troops. I should not have failed to have asked your Majesty's permission to go there, had I not been convinced that you would have no objection to this excursion. Minden being only 7 German miles from hence: the troops, particularly the infantry, are in the finest order, and it is a great pleasure to see them manouvre. The weather was very bad the first days, and the ground so swampy that the Cavalry could scarce exercise at all. However, the last four days the King was there the weather changed and everything succeeded perfectly; at least the King said he was very much pleased with his troops.

I hope your Majesty will excuse the liberty I have taken of troubling you with these lines, in favor of the motive that has prompted me to it; and that you do not doubt the assurance of my ever remaining [etc.]. (48540)

1968   THE LORD CHANCELLOR (LORD LOUGHBOROUGH) *to the* KING

[*8 June 1799.*] Your Majesty's great goodness & constant attention to the administration of justice have encouraged the Chancellor to commit an irregularity by transmitting two warrants for the call of Serjeants upon which he has not had the means of asking your Majesty's commands.

Since the appointment of Mr Justice Le Blanc[1] two gentlemen at the Bar have entertained the idea of being called to the degree of Serjeant. The Lord Chief Justice[2] having been obliged on account of his health to go into the country they have not had the opportunity of applying to him, but it is supposed by the other Judges of the Common Pleas whom the Chancellor has consulted, that the promotion of these gentlemen would be very agreeable to him & very beneficial to the publick. One of the two, Mr Lens,[3] assures me that the Lord Chief Justice did him the honour to express a desire to have him in the Court of Common Pleas,

---

[1] Sir Simon Le Blanc (*d.* 1816). Sergeant-at-law, 1787; Puisne Judge of the King's Bench, and knighted, 1799.   [2] Lord Kenyon.

[3] John Lens (1756–1825). Serjeant-at-law, 1799; King's Serjeant, 1806.

which I cannot doubt from my own knowledge of the character & abilities of Mr Lens, having invited him some years ago to take that situation. The other gentleman, Mr Baily,[1] I have had no opportunity of knowing personally, but I am assured by the concurrent opinion of all the Judges who for some time past have gone the Home Circuit that he is a very respectable man. The excuse for my presenting them irregularly & without the positive sanction of the Ch. Justice is that they cannot be admitted after Wednesday, which is the last day of the term, and I beg leave to add that if I have no assurance of the Ld. Chief Justice's approbation the warrants will remain in my custody without any effect, but to be cancelled.[2] (9213–14)

1969   *Letters from* WILLIAM PITT *to the* KING

[*Downing Street, 9 June 1799.*] Mr. Pitt humbly begs leave to submit the accompanying warrants for your Majesty's signature, one of which is for filling the vacancy which has just taken place at the Customs by the death of Mr. Bates,[3] and for which he requests your Majesty's permission to recommend the second son of Mr. Wilson,[4] the Canon of Windsor. (9215)

[*Wimbledon, 9 June 1799.*] Mr. Pitt has been honored with your Majesty's commands respecting the vacant office of Deputy Surveyor of the Woods, and will give immediate directions for the appointment of Mr. Wyatt which, he has no doubt, will be of great advantage in that Department. (9216)

1970   THE DUCHESS OF WURTEMBERG *to the* KING

[*Louisbourg, 10 June 1799.*] I trust that your Majesty at Windsor enjoys the same fine weather which within the last week has set in here.

Thank God, notwithstanding the great backwardness of the vegetation this Spring we have now the prospect of a good harvest, which is the greatest of all blessings. Indeed on every account we cannot be sufficiently grateful to Providence for the mercies he has shewn us, and I feel it very deeply when of an evening before supper we set [*sic*] with the Duke in the garden and reflect that had we not been wonderfully protected we should have been deprived of all the comforts we enjoy. Louisbourg is particularly dear to me as its fine old trees allow me every evening, even in the warmest weather, to take a long walk. My pace is much complained of by my Ladies, but fortunately my sister-in-law Princess Ferdinand having been used to walk with her father enjoys finding somebody who without grumbling is always ready to accompany her, and we are generally a quarter of an hour before the rest of the company. I also now frequently amuse myself in walking to a small farm the Duke has laid out quite in the English style. The house

[1] Sir John Bayley (1763–1841). Judge of the King's Bench, 1808; Judge of the Exchequer Court, 1830–4.
[2] John Vaughan, the Recorder of Leicester, was called to the degree of Serjeant-at-law before the end of the month.
[3] Joah Bates, a Commissioner of the Customs, and Director of Greenwich Hospital.
[4] The Rev. Edward Wilson.

and garden are very small but please me very much as they are very like home, and the Duke is quite as much delighted with the thoughts of having succeeded in surprizing me, as he would not agree to my seeing this little spot till it was compleatly finished. The cows are housed every night, but contrary to the custom in this country are taken into the air three or four times a day. They are very large and the breed is kept up at great expence as it is looked upon as advantageous to the country. I am very much accused of looking with an envious eye at a flock of Spanish sheep as I sometimes regret that a few of them are not at the Flemish Farm. I wish it was possible that your Majesty could ever see this place as I am sure its variety would please you, and still more according to Mr Brown's[1] phrase, its capabilities. It was in a sad state when the Duke first came here having been quite neglected but now it begins to lift up its head and I trust will continue to be attended to, as the Hereditary Prince takes very much to it. (51547–9)

1971 THE KING to HENRY DUNDAS

[*Windsor, 13 June 1799, 8.20 a.m.*] I return to Mr. Dundas the letter he received on the 14th of April from Mr. Livingston which I have had from misapprehension kept, thinking Mr. Dundas had answered it in consequence of the conversation I had with him on that subject, but finding yesterday that I was mistaken, I now forward it to him and desire he will by tomorrow's post write to Mr. Livingston the leave to come to Bath for the recovery of his health, but desire, as I am perfectly satisfied with his conduct, that he will not determine the not returning to my son Augustus till he finds what effect the Bath waters may have effected. He is to fully instruct Mr. Arbuthnot that the same line of conduct may be continued which he seems to think has been of use. As to any opportunity of my son's going to any of the armies I do not see any real end it would answer. I therefore think the remaining at Berlin the best arrangement, as my son objects so strongly to visiting the southern provinces of Russia. (Add. MSS. 40100, f. 223.)

1972 WILLIAM PITT to the KING

[*Downing Street, Thursday, 20 June 1799.*] Mr Pitt humbly begs leave to submit to your Majesty a Message to the House of Lords and one to the House of Commons, which are necessary to authorize the provisions for remitting to Ireland the proportion of the Loan raised for the service there.[2] (9217)

1973 *Letters from* LORD GRENVILLE *to the* KING, *and a reply*

[*Cleveland Row, 21 June 1799, 1 p.m.*] Lord Grenville humbly acquaints your Majesty that the two mails which were due arrived this morning. They bring

---

[1] Lancelot Brown ('Capability Brown'), the landscape gardener (1715–83).

[2] *H. of C.J.* LIV, 675 (21 June): 'His Majesty recommends it to the House of Commons to consider of enabling his Majesty to make remittances, from time to time, to be applied to his service in Ireland, in such manner as shall be approved by the Parliament of that Kingdom, to an amount not exceeding three millions, on provision being made by the Parliament of Ireland, for defraying the interest and charges of a loan to that amount.'

accounts of the Austrians being in possession of Zurich, Turin, and Alexandria, (the towns only but not the citadels of the two latter,) and of the fortresses of Ferrara, Valenza, & Ravenna. The French were concentrating their force at Coni, and Marshall Suvarow had begun the seige of the Castle of Turin.

Nothing was known at Berlin, so late as the 14th instant, respecting the King of Prussia's determination. Count Haugwitz was not to return till the 15th or even later. (9218)

[*The King's reply, Queen's House, 21 June, 5.20 p.m.*] On returning from the most loyal scene any Sovereign can boast of, I have found Lord Grenville's note, and I am fully sensible of his attention.[1] (Fortescue MSS.)

[*From Lord Grenville, Cleveland Row, 26 June, 10 a.m.*] Doctor Pegge,[2] a physician of eminence at Oxford, being to be presented today to your Majesty as one of the officers of the Oxford Volunteers, Lord Grenville begs leave to mention to your Majesty that it would he understands be highly agreable to Doctor Pegge if your Majesty were graciously pleased to confer on him the honour of Knighthood. (9219)

1974   LORD LOUGHBOROUGH *to the* KING

[*27 June 1799.*[3]] The Chancellor has the honour to transmit to your Majesty Mr Baron Perryn's letter requesting that you would be graciously pleased to accept of his resignation from bad health after 23 years service.

As the time for supplying the vacancy is extremely short, the Midland Circuit beginning on Tuesday next at Northampton, the Chancellor presumed to apply directly thro' the Lord Chief Baron[4] to Mr. Chambré,[5] who came to him this morning & expressed with great modesty his readiness to undertake the duty, if he should be thought by your Majesty not unworthy of receiving your commands to take upon him a political character. The Chancellor has also presumed to send such warrants as can at present be prepared. (9220)

1975   *Letters from the* DUKE OF PORTLAND *to the* KING

[*Bulstrode, Tuesday, 30 June 1799,*[6] *8 a.m.*] The Duke of Portland ventures with all humility to lay before your Majesty an account which has been transmitted him from Dover of an action which is said to have taken place in the Mediterranean

---

[1] Grenville endorsed the letter: 'Written the day the King inspected the Volunteer Corps of London and Westminster at their respective stations. I had sent his Majesty the account of the entry of the Austrians into Turin. G.'

[2] Sir Christopher Pegge (1765–1822). Regius Professor of Anatomy at Oxford, 1801–22; Knighted, 26 June 1799, being then described as Reader of Anatomy, and Major of the Oxford University Association.   [3] Wrongly endorsed the 29th.   [4] Sir Archibald Macdonald.

[5] Sir Alan Chambré (1739–1823). Baron of the Exchequer, 1799; Justice of the Common Pleas, 1800–15. Knighted, 6 Nov. 1799. W. A. Shaw (*Knights of England*) was unable to give the date.

[6] There is an error here: the 30th was a Sunday. *July* 30 was a Tuesday, but it is doubtful whether the Duke was at Bulstrode that day.

between your Majesty's Fleet & that of the French. Notwithstanding its defects in point of authenticity & detail the Duke of Portland humbly hopes that at such a moment your Majesty will condescend to hold this presumption upon such a subject not inexcusable, & will have the goodness not to disapprove the means which Mr King has taken to endeavour to ascertain the facts. (9221)

[*Bulstrode, Sunday, 30 June 1799, 10.50 p.m.*] The Duke of Portland feels it to be his duty in laying the Lord Lieutenant's dispatch before your Majesty to apprize your Majesty that the letter which your Majesty commanded the Duke of Portland to write to the Lord Lieutenant on the subject of the Provostship of Trinity College in Dublin could not have been received by him at the time of his writing the letter in which he desires the name of Dr Kearney,[1] the Vice Provost, to be submitted to your Majesty as a proper person to succeed the late Provost.[2] (9222)

1976 HENRY DUNDAS *to the* KING, *and the reply*

[*Downing Street, 5 July 1799, 4 p.m.*] Mr Dundas takes the liberty humbly to inform your Majesty that he has this day seen Lord Romney, and hopes your Majesty will permit Mr Dundas to attend your Majesty to-morrow at Windsor at any hour your Majesty may appoint, as Mr Dundas would wish personally to state to your Majesty what Lord Romney has represented to Mr Dundas on the subject of your Majesty's proposed visit to the county of Kent.[3] (9223)

[*The King's reply, Windsor, 5 July, 7.24 p.m.*] I shall be at home to receive Mr. Dundas at two tomorrow when I shall be glad to hear what he has to suggest in the name of Lord Romney concerning my either seeing the Kentish Corps in this month or not till in the middle of October. (Add. MSS. 40100, f. 225.)

1977 THE DUKE OF CUMBERLAND *to the* KING

[*St. James, 7 July 1799.*] Excuse my troubling your Majesty with a letter, but as I have not had a proper opportunity of speaking to you I take the liberty of addressing myself to you by letter and submitting to your Majesty my humble request of only granting me the rank of Lieutenant-General in the British service with the date of the commission I bear in the Hannoverian service.

I merely request *the rank*, for I am perfectly aware that there are many Officers in your service unprovided for who from their experience & services are infinitely more deserving than what my humble merits give me pretensions to.

---

[1] John Kearney (1741–1813), Provost of Trinity College, 1799–1806; Bishop of Ossory, 1806–13. The Provostship, said *The Times* (1 July) was worth £3,000. 'It is generally believed that Dr. Kearney will be nominated to it, as the Chancellor's interest is decidedly in his favour.'

[2] Dr Richard Murray. He died on 20 June.

[3] Lord Romney entertained the King and Queen and Princesses Elizabeth and Augusta at the Mote, his seat near Maidstone, on 1 August. Five thousand (not 500, as stated in *G.E.C.* XI, 86 n.) Kentish Volunteers were reviewed, and dinner was provided for more than 6,000 people, including all the Volunteers. Vast quantities of meat, fruit pies, port, ale, porter and beer were consumed. This was followed by a sumptuous banquet served up to the royal family and their party.

Should your Majesty be most graciously pleased to acquiesce in my humble request, you may depend upon your not having a more zealous Officer in your service.[1] (47186)

1978   THE DUKE OF PORTLAND *to the* KING

[*Burlington House, Wednesday, 10 July 1799, 11 p.m.*] It having been signified to the Duke of Portland by Lord Grenville that it was your Majesty's pleasure to be attended at St James's at half an hour after one o'clock for the purpose of having your Majesty's Speech read in Council by the Duke of Portland, he presumes, as Lord Grenville was not able to specify the day, that it is your Majesty's intention that it should be Friday next, & the notices to the members of the Privy Council who are permitted to attend your Majesty on such occasions,[2] will be prepared accordingly, unless the Duke of Portland receives your Majesty's commands to the contrary. (9925)

1979   *Letters from* HENRY DUNDAS *to the* KING

[*Downing Street, 10 July 1799, 1.15 p.m.*] Mr Dundas being prevented from waiting upon your Majesty in consequence of the pressing arrangements he has to settle with his Royal Highness the Duke of York, thinks it right humbly to inform your Majesty that by dispatches received from Captain Popham it appears that the Emperor of Russia has directed seventeen battalions of Infantry to be ready to embark at Revel, and that he has directed six ships of the Line, four frigates and two store ships to be prepared as troop ships under the direction of Captain Popham to aid in the embarkation of these troops. Captn. Popham reports that the ships will be ready by the 20th of this month.

The dispatches containing this pleasing intelligence will be forwarded to your Majesty as soon as Mr. Dundas returns from his Royal Highness the Duke of York.[3] (9227)

[*Downing Street, 10 July '99, 3 p.m.*] As Mr Dundas is to have the honour of seeing your Majesty tomorrow at Swinley,[4] it is unnecessary to enter at large upon

[1] The Duke's wishes were now gratified, his appointment being gazetted on the 13th, and dated 18 May 1798.

[2] That is, the members of the 'Grand Cabinet' (or Great Cabinet): the Cabinet Ministers, together with the great Household officials, the Lord Chief Justice, the Archbishop of Canterbury and the Speaker of the House of Commons. For the history of the Nominal Cabinet see A. Aspinall, *The Grand Cabinet, 1800–1837* (*Politica*, December 1938, pp. 324–44).

[3] See No. 1960 for the Anglo-Russian treaty which led to Russian participation in the expedition to Holland. Sir Ralph Abercromby agreed to command the force but to hand over the command to the Duke of York if it should be thought fit that he should do so. On 27 Aug. 12,000 British troops landed at the Helder, and, assisted by Dutch Royalists, gained possession of the Dutch fleet in the Texel. A Russian force under General Hermann arrived in September, but a joint attack on Bergen, on the 19th, failed. The outbreak of fever caused the British Government to recall its troops, and the Duke of York, who had taken the command a few weeks earlier, concluded a Convention with the French at Alkmaar (18 Oct.), by which he agreed to evacuate Holland, though he retained the Dutch fleet. This marked the end of British military intervention on the Continent until the beginning of the Peninsular War.

[4] Swinley Lodge, the Duke of York's house near Windsor. The Duke had the royal family and retinue to dinner.

the subject, but he takes the liberty to bring it under your view, for your Majesty's consideration, how far justice will be done to his Royal Highness the Duke of York, if the deliverance of Holland, and perhaps of the Netherlands, should be accomplished without the personal participation of the Duke of York. (9228)

1980 WILLIAM PITT *to the* KING

[*Downing Street, Thursday, 11 July 1799.*] Mr Pitt humbly begs leave to lay before your Majesty a rough draft of the Speech,[1] in which many corrections may be necessary, but of which the outline is, he trusts, conformable to the sentiments which your Majesty expressed yesterday. (9229)

1981 THE LORD CHANCELLOR (LORD LOUGHBOROUGH) *to the* KING

[*House of Lords, 11 July [1799], 12 p.m.*] The messenger who is said to have been dispatched about noon, not having yet returned with the Commission to pass Bills, that Commission could not now bear date till tomorrow, & it would be an erroneous proceeding that Bills should pass by Commission on the same day that your Majesty was present in Parliament, to pass other Bills & to prorogue.

The number of Bills included in the Commission is sixty three, those not included are twelve, & the time during which your Majesty would be detained in the House of Lords could not be less than one hour. The Chancellor & the Speaker have thought it their duty to represent to your Majesty the inconvenience to which your Majesty would be exposed by passing so great a number of Bills, & to state that there is no necessity for proroguing tomorrow & very little inconvenience to deferring it to a future day, when the great number of Bills may have been passed. If it should be your Majesty's pleasure to postpone it to Wednesday next, the two Houses, after passing the sixty three Bills tomorrow, could adjourn to that day. This is humbly suggested to prevent your Majesty's undergoing an unnecessary fatigue in consequence of the delay of the Commission, at the same time that everything will be in readiness to execute your Majesty's commands either for tomorrow or any subsequent day.[2] (9230–1)

1982 EARL SPENCER *to the* KING

[*Admiralty, 13 July 1799.*] Earl Spencer has the honour to lay before your Majesty the proceedings of a court martial held on five seamen of your Majesty's

[1] The Speech from the Throne, at the prorogation (12 July).
[2] 'The Duke of Portland is attacked in a morning paper of yesterday for having been the cause of the disappointment that occurred on Thursday evening in the two Houses of Parliament on account of some irregularity in signing the Commission...The business of laying Parliamentary Commissions before his Majesty for signature...[did not belong to the Duke's Department]. The error proceeded from his Majesty's having accidentally omitted to sign one of the sides of paper on which the Bills for the Royal Assent were described, and in consequence of this omission there was an irregularity which could not be got over, and a messenger was accordingly dispatched to Windsor. But the King being at dinner at Swinley Lodge, did not sign the new Commission till yesterday morning' (*The Times*, 13 July).

sloop the Dart for mutiny, one of whom is sentenced to death, and as the case appears one in which an example ought to be made, Earl Spencer humbly submits to your Majesty that it will be proper to order the law to take its course. (9232)

1983   HENRY COWPER[1] *to ? the* PRINCE OF WALES

(*Copy*)

[*Old Palace Yard, 14 July 1799.*] In obedience to your Royal Highness's commands, I humbly submit the enclosed to your Royal Highness's perusal.

The tellers, Lord Hay[2] and Lord Holland,[3] being unus'd to that office, may I apprehend have made some mistake. The proxies for the Bill[4] appear by the inclosed list to have been 37; but I thought it was mentioned that Lord Spencer did not give Lord Duncan's proxy. I know that Lord Chatham who held the Duke of Rutland's[5] proxy, as well as Lord Abercorn's, only gave Lord Abercorn's: but I am at a loss to know what became of Lord Stair[6] and Lord Grantley,[7] both of whom were present during the debate.

To judge of the comparitive strength of both parties it may be proper to add

[1] Clerk Assistant of the House of Lords. (1758–1840.)

[2] Robert Auriol, Baron Hay [G.B.] and 10th Earl of Kinnoull [S.] (1751–1804). P.C., 1796.

[3] Henry Richard, 3rd Lord Holland (1773–1840), nephew of Charles James Fox. Succeeded his father, 1774. Lord Privy Seal, Oct. 1806–March 1807; Chancellor of the Duchy of Lancaster, 1830–4, and 1835–40.

[4] A Bill 'to prohibit the trading for slaves on the coast of Africa within certain limits'. 'The question that was decided on Saturday morning in the House of Lords respecting the Slave Trade Limitation Bill, was canvassed in its progress with greater interest and zeal than any that has occurred since the Regency. The votes of the Peerage were solicited out of doors with as much spirit and perseverance as if it had been a Party question' (*The Times*, 8 July).

'The late conduct of Administration in the business of the slave trade is the fullest refutation of all those malicious censures to which they have frequently been exposed for not *pressing*, *insisting* and using the whole of their *influence* in its support. We this day lay before our readers the division in the House of Lords upon that question on Friday night, and they will perceive that no subject has been agitated with so much of zeal, sincerity and the *spirit of party* for a very considerable time indeed. Many expresses were sent and many proxies given and withdrawn, in a manner that will sufficiently prove in what light Government regarded this question' (*ibid.* 12 July).

As *The Times* list is not identical with the one here printed, the former is given:

For the Bill: Chatham, Grenville, Bayning, Boringdon, Carrington, Spencer, Montrose, Somerville, Fortescue, Digby, Holland, Amherst, Bathurst, Camden, Loughborough, Hampden, Macclesfield, Powis, Radnor, Rochester, Canterbury, London, Chichester, Carlisle. Total, 25 [*sic*].

Against the Bill: Cumberland, Clarence, Kent, Bradford, Boston, Walsingham, Ducie, Kinnoull, Liverpool, Westmorland, Lonsdale, Wentworth, Onslow, Leicester, Romney, Thurlow, Harborough, Northwick, Selsea, Powlett, Morton, Galloway, Somers, Winchilsea, Heathfield, Mansfield, Maynard, Craven, Abingdon, Portland, Carlisle, Sydney. Total, 32.

The Times added: 'The proxies on each side were 36. The Duke of Cumberland had the Prince of Wales's, which was against the Motion. The Bishops' proxies were all in favour of it. The Bishop of Bangor withdrew his during the debate, and his Lordship did not vote on either side.'

Lord Grenville moved the Order of the Day for the second reading of the Bill. It was read a second time (on the 5th) but it was not committed. (*H. of L.J.* XLII, 319.) The division list is not given there.

[5] John Henry, 5th Duke of Rutland (1778–1857); succeeded his father, 1787. A supporter of Pitt.

[6] John, 6th Earl of Stair [S.] (1749–1821). See No. 318.

[7] William, 2nd Lord Grantley (1742–1822), son of Fletcher Norton, the Speaker of the House of Commons, 1770–80. He sat in the Commons for various constituencies from 1768 to 1789, when he succeeded to his father's peerage (1 Jan.).

that the following proxies, besides those before stated, were not made use of, the Peers not attending:

Bp. of Exeter,[1] had the Proxy of	Bp. of Salisbury
Bp. of Lichfield[2]	Bp. of Bristol
Ld. Willoughby de Broke,[3] whose own proxy was given for the Bill	Ld. Wodehouse
Ld. Auckland (Quære, whether for or against)	{ Ld. Bolton { Ld. Perth[4]
E. of Elgin	Marq. of Tweeddale[5]
E. of Thanet	E. of Albermarle[6]
V. Hood	Lord Bridport
E. Fitzwilliam	Duke of Ancaster[7]
Bp. Bangor[8]	Bp. of Winchester[9,10]

(9233)

[1] Henry Reginald Courtenay (1741–1803), Bishop of Bristol, 1794; of Exeter, 1797–1803.

[2] James, 4th Earl Cornwallis (1743–1824), Bishop of Lichfield and Coventry, 1781–1824; succeeded his uncle in the peerage, 1823. He was the Governor-General's brother.

[3] John, 14th Lord Willoughby de Broke (1738–1816); a Lord of the Bedchamber.

[4] James Drummond, Lord Perth (1744–1800), who, in 1785, recovered the family estates, forfeited in 1745. Created Lord Perth, 1797.

[5] George, 7th Marquess of Tweeddale (1753–1804); Representative Peer [S.], 1796–1804.

[6] William Charles, 4th Earl of Albemarle (1772–1849). Master of the Buckhounds, 1806–7; Master of the Horse, 1830–4, and 1835–41.

[7] Brownlow, 5th Duke of Ancaster (1729–1809); succeeded his nephew, 1779.

[8] John Warren (1730–1800), Bishop of St David's, 1779; of Bangor, 1783–1800.

[9] Brownlow North (1741–1820), Bishop of Lichfield and Coventry, 1771; of Worcester, 1774; of Winchester, 1781–1820.

[10] The following division list is the enclosure:

For the Bill		Against the Bill	
Peers present	Proxies	Peers present	Proxies
1. Arch. Canterbury	Bp. St. Asaph	1. His Royal Highness the Duke of Clarence	{ Ld. Rawdon { Ld. Saltersford
2. Ld. Chancellor	{ E. of Doncaster { Ld. Napier	2. His Royal Highness the Duke of Kent	......
3. E. of Chatham	Mar. of Abercorn		
4. E. of Radnor	Ld. Lifford	3. His Royal Highness the Duke of Cumberland	{ His Royal Highness { the Prince of Wales
5. E. Spencer	{ E. of Harcourt { Vist. Duncan		
6. E. of Graham	{ E. of Elgin { Ld. Minto	4. E. of Westmorland	{ E. of Harborough { Ld. Dynevor
7. E. of Carlisle	Ld. Cawdor	5. Duke of Portland	{ E. of Dunfries { Ld. Mendip
8. E. Fortescue	......		
9. E. of Digby	{ E. of Exeter { Ld. Berwick	6. Marq. of Bute	......
10. E. Camden	{ E. of Clarendon { E. of Dartmouth	7. E. of Leicester	{ Ld. Audley { Ld. Say & Sele
11. E. Bathurst	Ld. Glastonbury	8. E. of Liverpool	{ E. of Effingham { Ld. Lyttelton
12. Vis. Hampden	Vis. Sackville		
13. Bp. of London	{ Bp. of Durham { Bp. of Landaff	9. E. of Mansfield	......
14. Bp. of Lincoln	{ Bp. of Carlisle { Bp. of Bath & Wells	10. E. of Winchilsea	{ E. of Buck-shire { V. Dudley & Ward
15. Bp. of Norwich	......	11. E. of Abingdon	......
		12. E. of Macclesfield	......

[*Whitehall, 16 July 1799.*] I trust your Majesty is persuaded that nothing but inability from age & infirmities has prevented my paying my duty to your Majesty during my stay in London.

I now presume to write this letter, impell'd by the anxiety I feel in common with many other relations & friends of Lord Thanet,[1] who by his imprudence has subjected himself to severe punishment, to solicit your Majesty in his behalf. I know Sir, that mercy & benevolence predominate in your mind, and that it is always your Majesty's inclination to extend it whenever it can be granted con-

16. Bp. of Rochester {	Bp. of St. Davids / Bp. of Peterborough	13. E. of Lonsdale	E. of Darlington
17. Bp. of Chichester {	Bp. Lichfield & Covy. / Bp. of Gloucester	14. E. Poulett	......
18. Ld. Grenville {	Ld. Bagot / Ld. Curzon	15. E. of Powis	......
		16. Vis. Wentworth	{ E. Fauconberg / Ld. Harewood
19. Ld. Bayning {	Mar. Townshend / E. of Guilford	17. Vis. Maynard	......
20. Ld. Holland {	E. of Oxford & Mortn. / E. of Thanet	18. Vis. Sydney	{ E. of Ailesbury / E. of Portsmouth
21. Ld. King	......	19. Ld. Hay	Ld. Strafford
22. Ld. Boringdon	Duke of Somerset	20. Ld. Stewart of Garlies	{ E. of Mount- Edgcumbe / V. Falmouth
23. Ld. Somerville {	E. of Norwich / E. of Essex	21. Ld. Walsingham	{ E. of Chesterfield / Ld. Cadogan
24. Ld. Carington {	Ld. Willoughby de Br. / Ld. Cemelford	22. Ld. Douglas of Lochleven	......
25. Ld. Amherst {	Ld. Malmsbury / Ld. Hobart	23. Ld. Bradford	{ E. of Stamford / V. Torrington
		24. Ld. Romney	{ Ld. Brownlow / Ld. Broderick
	Total 37	25. Ld. Yarborough	{ V. Newark / Ld. Dundas
		26. Ld. Somers	......
		27. Ld. Heathfield	{ E. of Shaftesbury / E. of Dorchester
		28. Ld. Selsey	{ E. of Cardigan / E. of Sandwich
		29. Ld. Boston	E. of Denbigh
		30. Ld. Craven	E. of Berkeley
		31. Ld. Onslow & Cranley	Ld. Rivers
		32. Ld. Northwic	......
		Total 36	

N.B. The following Peers were also present:

Ld. Ponsonby, who paired off with Lord Thurlow.

Lord Rodney, who left the House before the question was put & held the proxy of Lord Suffield.

The Earl of Stair & Ld. Grantley—Quære whether they staid the division?

The Earl of Carnarvon & the Earl Strange. Both left the House before the debate began (9234–5).

Canning discussed the attitude of the Prince of Wales and the Royal Dukes (9 July): 'Lord Grenville's treatment of the D. of Clarence...was intended to hint to him pretty strongly that Royal Dukes ought not to take any part in contentious political discussions, & to shew him that he put his father's Ministers in very awkward situations when he came down & took part against them. The Duke of York, to his credit, felt this so much that he refused his proxy to his brother. The P. of Wales did not act so decorously. His proxy was given for the slave trade.' (Harewood MSS.)

[1] Lord Thanet wrote a letter to the King, protesting his innocence (21 May 1799). It might well have been drafted by Philip Francis (Parkes and Merivale, *Memoirs of Sir Philip Francis*, II, 316).

sistantly with what is due to public justice and example. I will therefore only add my hope that your Majesty, with your accustom'd goodness, will excuse my troubling you with this petition, and allow me to subscribe myself with the highest loyalty & veneration [etc.] (9236)

1985   LORD GRENVILLE *to the* KING, *and the reply*

[*Cleveland Row, 20 July 1799, 6 p.m.*] Lord Grenville is much concerned that your Majesty did not receive the Berlin dispatches this morning. They had been sent by him last night to Mr Pitt with a request that the messenger might be directed to proceed with them so as to be at Windsor at the usual hour. But the messenger not arriving at Holwood till Mr Pitt was gone to bed this was not done, & Mr Pitt did not receive the box till this morning when he brought it back to town with him. (9237)

[*The King's reply, Windsor, 21 July, 7.50 a.m.*] I am happy to find by the dispatches arrived on Friday which Lord Grenville has transmitted to me and are arrived this morning that Mr. Grenville has been enabled by two mails to continue the prospect that though late, the King of Prussia will enter into that line of conduct which is more conformable to his dignity than the one he has as yet pursued, and that we may soon receive a project deserving of attention and that may with corrections be brought to some degree of precision. (Fortescue MSS.)

1986   THE KING *to* HENRY DUNDAS

[*Windsor, 24 July 1799, 8.43 p.m.*] Having this day heard that Mr. Secretary Dundas lyes at Staines, I have ordered the messenger to go there; I desire Mr. Livingston may be directed to be here tomorrow at three in the afternoon.

I have put answers to Lord Romney's questions on the opposite part of the page which will enable Mr. Dundas fully to satisfy them.[1] (Add. MSS. 40100, f. 227.)

1987   LORD GRENVILLE *to the* KING, *and the reply*

[*Dropmore, 26 July 1799.*] Lord Grenville humbly begs leave to submit to your Majesty that on the occasion of the ratification of the late Convention with Russia, it would be, he is sure, a mark of your Majesty's favour in the highest degree acceptable to Sir Charles Whitworth, & perhaps not wholly without its use at Petersburgh, if your Majesty were graciously pleased to confer the honour of an Irish Peerage on Sir Charles Whitworth. Lord Grenville has mentioned this idea to the Duke of Portland, and to Mr Pitt who both agree with him in humbly recommending it to your Majesty. (9238)

[1] See No. 1976.

[*The King's reply, Windsor, 26 July, 7.30 a.m.* [*sic*]] I do not in the least object to Lord Grenville's idea of conferring an Irish peerage on Sir Charles Whitworth as it may indulge the vanity of the Emperor of Russia.[1] (Fortescue MSS.)

1988   THE DUCHESS OF WURTEMBERG *to the* KING

[*Louisbourg, 29 July 1799.*] Ever happy when employed in writing to your Majesty I feel doubly so when I can do it with safety.

General de Melius having sent to the Duke for additional instructions, to avoid unnecessary writing the Duke has determined on sending Baron de Wimpfen, one of his Chamberlains, to the General with verbal instructions; he is to remain in England during the General's stay. Baron de Wimpfen has been frequently employed by the Duke and been very useful to him at different times. I take the liberty to recommend him to your Majesty; his having been constantly in the country with us, and being able to give very exact accounts of me, will I hope engage your Majesty to take some notice of him when he has the honour of being presented to you.

I hope soon to give your Majesty some account of the Russian troops who on the 4th are to be at Augsbourg where the Duke intends meeting them, and in a few days I shall join him at Hohentweil as part of the column is to pass near that fortress and we all wish very much to see them. I am delighted with the thoughts of seeing great part of the Dutchy, particularly as I am told the country between this and Hohentweil is very picturesque. I believe Switzerland is seen from the Castle.

The French will I believe be much alarmed at the approach of the Russians, as from the beginning of the campaign they expressed great curiosity to know whether they were likely to come into this part of Europe. How grateful must we be to providence if he enables them to free Germany from the yoke which has so cruelly oppressed us of late years.

One thing astonishes me very much, which is that the misfortunes which have befallen the nobility, instead of making them feel the necessity of attaching themselves stronger to their Sovereigns, has given them a spirit of independance which does great harm. I every day see the unpleasant effects of the principles they have imbibed, as everything like order and regularity in a Court is looked on as severity, and the system of equality is constantly attempted, which will make it difficult for me to find Ladies.

The Hereditary Prince continues to behave very well and seems very sensible of his father's goodness to him. Trinette every day more attached to me and I think very much improved since she has totally lived with us, and Paul, a most charming little pickle, who I regret cannot go to Eaton. (51550–2)

1989   PRINCE ADOLPHUS *to the* KING

[*Hannover, 31 July 1799.*] I take the liberty of writing your Majesty a few lines by this post to inform you that I returned last Wednesday from my military

---

[1] It was not until 4 April 1800 that Whitworth was created Baron Whitworth in the peerage of Ireland. Pitt told Grenville on 18 July that it had been 'fully earned' (*Dropmore Papers*, v, 153).

excursion. I am very happy to be able to assure you that I have found the Avant Corps in very good order, and I wish your Majesty could have seen them, as I am sure you would have been pleased with them. The men and horses are all in very good condition and perfectly fit for active service: indeed, I cannot denie that when I saw the troops I was sorry at the thought of their not being employed. The present unactive life we lead is undoubtedly a very disagreeable one for a soldier who likes his profession and who wishes to distinguish himself. We have one comfort, however, and that is that our inactivity is not our fault. I trust that a time will come soon when your Majesty's troops will be called upon to act, and I hope then that they will behave in such a manner as to meet with your approbation. The spirit in the troops is really very good, and their loyalty and attachment to their Sovereign very great. To keep up this will be the constant study and aim of him who has the honor to remain [&c.]. (48541)

1990   THE LORD CHANCELLOR (LORD LOUGHBOROUGH) *to the* KING

[*Canterbury, 1 Aug. 1799.*] The Prince of Wales being engaged yesterday at the camp & with Sir Charles Grey, the Chancellor was not able to see his Royal Highness till this morning. The letter received from your Majesty has given him very great satisfaction, and upon the perusal of the letter from Prince Augustus to your Majesty, H.R.H. immediately observed that the idea he had entertained of desiring his brother to return to England, was compleatly barred by the intimation in that letter of Lady Augusta Murray's intended return, tho he remarked the period for her departure was left in the utmost uncertainty by making it to depend upon her ability to undergo the fatigue of a journey which would be subject as much to her inclination to undertake it as the state of her health. It seemed therefore very necessary that Prince Augustus should be made sensible of the extreme impropriety of Lady Augusta Murray's residence with him & in his own house.

The Prince of Wales said he never had had any communication with his brother on the subject of Lady Augusta Murray untill he received the letter he had the honour to transmit to your Majesty, but he felt that upon this first address to him from Prince Augustus which seemed in some manner to sollicit his intervention, it was incumbent upon him to state to his brother his sentiments upon his situation & the conduct he ought [to] observe, which he meant to do immediately with kindness but at the same time with energy & in terms that he hoped would merit your Majesty's approbation. He supposed, (and upon a question put to me I said nothing that could affect that supposition) that your Majesty, whose pleasure Prince Augustus appears by his own letter to have perfectly understood, might not think fit to make any answer to that letter as relating to a subject on which all discussion was closed; and on this account the Prince of Wales thought it would be the more proper for him to enter upon a subject on which his brother had never occasion to have learnt his opinion.

The Prince of Wales adopts the idea of preventing the child[1] from being

---

[1] Augustus Frederick d'Esté. See No. 1009 n.

removed, & feels the mischievous tendency of that project, which he suggested different ways of defeating by the means which he in conjunction with the Duke of Cumberland could take, but the decision in what way it would be best to proceed was postponed to a further conversation, except so far that the Prince has written to the Duke of Cumberland to order Prince Augustus's servant, who is known to him, not to move from London till he receives the P. of Wales's permission & the dispatches which he is to carry from him.

Some hours after this conversation & after the Chancellor had written the account of it, the Prince of Wales told him he had a mind to go to Walmer to-morrow morning and talk over the subject with Mr. Pitt & Mr. Dundas, upon which the Chancellor thought it best to postpone sending this paper to your Majesty for one day. (48142–3)

1991   EARL SPENCER *to the* KING, *and the reply*

[*Admiralty, 5 Aug. 1799, 1 p.m.*] Earl Spencer has the honour to lay before your Majesty the dispatches received this morning from Captain Gore[1] of the Triton frigate which bring an account of the combined Fleets of France and Spain having sailed from Cadiz on the 21st ulto. Lord Keith had not passed the Straights on the 20th, but from the tenor of the dispatches Earl Spencer is still in hopes that he may be in time to come up with the enemy; in the event, however, of their proceeding to the northward unmolested, every possible measure is now taking for a collecting as strong a force in the Channel as can be got together without loss of time.

[*1.15 p.m.*] Earl Spencer is truly concerned to inform your Majesty that he has just heard of the death of Earl Howe which took place this morning in Grafton Street at ½ past nine o'clock. (9255)

[*The King's reply, Windsor, 5 Aug., 6.42 p.m.*] The hearing that the combined fleets of the enemy have sailed from Cadiz the 21st of the last month and that there is no account of Lord Keith later than the 8th of that month is certainly unpleasant, but I have that compleat trust in the protection of Divine Providence that I do not doubt we shall speedily hear of our fleet having passed the Streights of Gibraltar and giving such an account of the enemy as will set every person's mind at ease. The collecting as strong a force as possible in the Channel seems to be highly proper.

I am sorry to find that Earl Howe dyed this morning. His public services and private virtues makes him a serious loss. (Althorp MSS.)

1992   E. LIVINGSTON *to the* KING

[*Bath, 6 Aug. 1799.*] I have the honor to send your Majesty a letter I received by last post from his Royal Highness Prince Augustus. It will give your Majesty a truer notion of the Prince's wishes than I can do by any extract I could make from

---

[1] Sir John Gore (1772–1836). Captain, 1794; Rear-Admiral, 1813; Vice-Admiral, 1825; Knighted, 21 Feb. 1805; K.C.B., 1815; G.C.H., 1835.

it. Before I solicit to have Mr. Arbuthnot sent as my assistant, I took the liberty to say to his Royal Highness, 'if you have any person you prefer, I will mention that gentleman to his Majesty'. The Prince answerd, 'I have none'. I presume that has escaped his Royal Highness memory.

I have no dout, if his Royal Highness names gentlemen that has your Majesty's approbation but everything will go on more comfortable for the Prince. I beg your Majesty may be graciously pleased to honor me with your commands concerning the answer I may send his Royal Highness. (9259)

Enclosure

PRINCE AUGUSTUS *to* E. LIVINGSTON

[*Berlin, 21 July 1799.*] In consequence of the conversation we had together and of your promise to represent my ideas to his Majesty before your departure from hence, I send you the enclosed heads which you will be so good as to forward.

At the time of life I am arrived, and with the experience I certainly have, it is both just and proper that I should have my own affairs in my own hands. Without any personal reflection I am the first Prince of England who has been deprived of this privilege at my age; and why or wherefore I cannot conceive. The idea of minority which appears as wished to be observed with regard to me is as useless as it is improper. If I could from private considerations speak to his Majesty, I believe, without a very long conversation, that it would be in my power to prove to him in a satisfactory and not improper manner the cause of my former derangements, from very different motives than those he either conceives or has been taught to believe. However, as I never was asked, and as I neither wish to seek or demand favour, but am solely anxious of getting what [I] conceive with reason my own due, I never pushed the matter further. If the intention of my not having my money in my own hands arose from the idea that it would prevent my making debts, it is perfectly erroneous, for you must know as well as myself that did I not feel the impropriety of making debts, and deranging myself as [I] certainly do, nothing could prevent my making them even now. Had I the money in my own hands I could make my own plan of living, and when [I] wished to spend in one way, should curtail on another point of expense. I was taught to believe that my Establishment was to have been given me with my other brothers. It did not take place, and rather than accuse those of forgetfulness who ought to have had my welfare likewise at heart, I will endeavour to teach myself to believe that some circumstances unknown to me render'd the measure unpopular, or made it prudent not to bring it forward in this Session of Parliament. But if this is the real case, why at least deprive me of the disposal of that allowance which is given me? At my age there can be but one master in my house, and it cannot be another but myself. My time of travelling with a Governor is over, and could such an idea be believed by the public it is as injurious to his Majesty as to myself. The honor of both it is my duty and inclination to defend. Having evidently proved the necessity and I trust the justice of the first article I shall now touch upon another, which is more delicate but not less important for the happiness of my own interior,

I mean the choice of the gentleman about me which my rank must require. The idea of this person is to be my friend, but how can this be the case if I do not know him? It is not a sufficient reason for me to consider a person my friend because his Majesty sends him me. I may esteem such a person but for to consider him as a friend of mine he must be the choice of my own heart, he must have a certain similarity of age & manners. In short, to gain a man's confidence it requires more than a few days acquaintance. You must allow the manner in which you and Mr Arbuthnot were sent me must be equally disagreable to both parties. Private letters from my own friends anounced me the report of your coming else I should have been ignorant of your arrival till the moment you got out of your carriage at Naples. This circumstance would have actually taken place with Mr Arbuthnot had not the breaking down of his carriage at Prague giving him time to write to you a few lines which reached Vienna some hours before him. On the other hand you were both sent me without being the least acquainted with my person and consequently totally ignorant whether we should agree or not. To me, who am forced to be abroad on account of my health, such a matter becomes highly interesting. It is my intention therefore never to have anyone who might be disagreable to his Majesty, but on the other hand I have equally a right to pretend not to have any person who does not perfectly suit me. My own health and my own private affairs would not only render my stay in England prejudicial to me but even unpleasant, and therefore if the King fears my coming to England upon my getting my title and establishment he is perfectly mistaken. My own candour forces me to confess that for the advantage of my physical and moral feelings a stay in England could not be a desirable thing for me. I wish to be allowed my pension and have the choice to spend it where I like best, in which case I may flatter myself at last to have a dawn of happiness and of recovering in some measure my health. Your having promised and offer'd to lay my plans before his Majesty has engaged me to write to you with the sincerity I have done. You may make use of this letter consequently as you think most expedient. I have not wrote to his Majesty because I conceive my letters to be neither pleasant nor interesting, for I can only repeat what [I] have so often wrote, and consequently should fear to weary the King, which [I] confess would grieve me. Trusting you will favour me with a few lines in answer, I have the pleasure to sign myself with the highest esteem and consideration [etc.]. (9260–2)

1993   THE DUCHESS OF WURTEMBERG *to the* KING

[*Louisbourg, 8 Aug. 1799.*] Allow me to return your Majesty my most humble thanks for your gracious letter of July 23d which made me very happy, and to express my gratitude for the notice you have had the goodness to take of General Melius which is very flattering to me, and a proof of the continuance of the goodness and graciousness with which you ever honoured me, and which I set the highest value on.

The Duke returned yesterday from Augsburg quite delighted with the beauty and good conduct of the Russian troops. He assures me that though many of their

Regiments have marched nine months with only three days rest at a time during that period, their looks do not shew their having undergone any fatigue. The end of next week I shall go to Hohentweil and shall afterwards have the honour of writing to your Majesty.

The taking of Mantua puts everybody in good spirits and makes us all look forwards with anxiety to the next news from Italy, as we trust the addition of thirty thousand men which besieged it and are now at liberty to attack the French army, will strike Morreau with dismay and that he will be willing to evacuate all his posts. God grant General Corsakof[1] the same success in Switzerland. I am told he has said that he cannot be assured of victory crowning his arms but that he never will retire.

The King of Naples's return is also a great event, and I trust will only be the forerunner of things returning to their old courses. It gives me particular pleasure as it was Admiral Nelson who conveyed him, who I shall ever look on as the first cause of things taking a good turn by the victory of the Nile. (51555–6)

1994   HENRY DUNDAS to the KING

[*Walmer Castle, 9 Aug. 1799.*] Mr Dundas takes the liberty of conveying to your Majesty a letter which came under his cover this day from Mr Livingston. The purport of his Royal Highness Prince Augustus's letter to Mr. Livingstone has been communicated to Mr Dundas. It seems difficult for either Mr. Livingstone or Mr Arbuthnot to remain with his Royal Highness, as their company is so disagreeable to him, but his Royal Highness does not suggest any other person for your Majesty's approbation.

Mr Dundas has the honour to inform your Majesty that the embarkations of the troops for the expedition are so far advanced as to leave no reason to doubt its sailing on Sunday if the weather is favourable.

Mr Dundas humbly submits to your Majesty's perusal the precis of advices received this morning from India and Constantinople. (9263–4)

1995   LORD GRENVILLE to the KING, *and the reply*

[*Stowe, 11 Aug. 1799.*] Lord Grenville has the honour humbly to acquaint your Majesty that he has settled everything with the Count d'Artois for his setting out for the continent at the end of next week. The Count d'Artois is to be in town on Monday night, and he has expressed to Lord Grenville a strong wish that if your Majesty should not disapprove it he might be permitted to express to your Majesty and to the Queen (if her Majesty should be in town), his gratitude for your Majesty's great goodness towards him.[2] (9265)

---

[1] Alexander Korsakoff, the Russian General. He was defeated at Zurich by Oudinot and Masséna on 25 Sept., and both he and Suvoroff were recalled to Russia a month later, the Tsar having quarrelled with his ally the Emperor.

[2] The Comte left his apartments in Holyrood Palace, not intending to return, on 6 August. He arrived at Stowe, the Marquess of Buckingham's seat, two days later, and stayed there for a few days and subsequently in London until his intended departure for Cuxhaven, *via* Yarmouth, his ultimate

[*The King's reply, Windsor, 13 Aug. 1799, 7.33 a.m.*] The Queen will not be in town this week and I shall not arrive tomorrow but for my Levée at St. James's, therefore must decline the seeing the Count d'Artois; besides, I think it much more advantageous to his interest that he should without loss of time proceed to the Continent. (Fortescue MSS.)

1996   THE DUKE OF PORTLAND *to the* KING

[*Burlington House, Tuesday, 13 Aug. 1799, 11.10 p.m.*] The Duke of Portland humbly conceives that your Majesty will not be disposed to blame him for presuming to represent to your Majesty that it was the opinion of such of the Lords Commissioners of the Admiralty as Mr Nepean had communicated with, that the Fleet, which is stated in Lord Castlereagh's letter to have been seen on the 5th off Achil Head was a Swedish convoy going north about.[1] (9271)

1997   ROBERT ARBUTHNOT *to* E. LIVINGSTON

[*Berlin, 13 Aug. 1799.*] Many thanks to you, my dear Sir, for your kind & agreeable letter of the 1st which I received last Sunday in due course of post. I am extremely happy to hear of the good reception you met with from his Majesty, altho I had no reason to doubt of it, as it certainly is no more than what you are well intitled to, after so ably accomplishing the very difficult & disagreeable business of cleaning the Augean stable in which the Prince was immersed at Naples. I am rather surprized at your not having received a letter from me & one from the Prince of the 20th July as I gave them myself to Fisher & they were sent off by a messenger the following day. I have since written to you twice by conveyances of the same kind, one of the 27th July & one of the 6th August. As I am no stranger to the neglect of letters sent to the Secretary of State's Office, I shall in future write to you by the common post.

Since my last letter a circumstance has occurred which gives me a good deal of uneasiness. Lady Augusta Murray arrived here on Saturday under the borrowed name of Mrs Ford. She pretends that her motive for taking such an imprudent step was to see her husband for the last time, as she had heard from Lady Strafford[2]

destination being Switzerland. But on the 21st *The Times* announced that his departure had been postponed *sine die*. 'Illness has been assigned as the cause for delaying his journey, but there are probably other motives.' And it declared on 31 August: 'His departure for Switzerland...is adjourned *sine die*, upon political considerations arising in a certain Court, the conduct of which has already occasioned no trifling degree of disquietude...Monsieur has taken the house belonging to Major Cleves, in the neighbourhood of Guildford, to which he will remove on Monday, not from any dislike...to the amusements of the capital, but to escape from the absurdity and impatience of a host of emigrants who are daily besieging his doors.'

[1] John King, the Under-Secretary of State, wrote to Castlereagh from Whitehall on the 13th: 'I have forwarded your Lordship's letter, giving an account of the fleet seen off Achill Head to the Duke of Portland, who is at Bulstrode, and in my letter to Cooke have given the reasons why I conceive them to be only Swedes' (*Castlereagh Corresp.* II, 372).

[2] Frederick Thomas, 3rd Earl of Strafford (1742-99), who died suddenly on 6 August, married (1772) Elizabeth, daughter of Thomas Gould of Frome Billet, Dorset. She married, as his second wife, in 1803 William Churchill (*d.* July 1808), and she died in 1811. Churchill's first wife was Lady Louisa Greville, sister of George, 2nd Earl of Warwick, whom he married in 1770.

that he was dangerously ill & dying. I do not believe a word of this as I know that she had seen Brummel[1] in London who gave her letters for Mr Richard & who certainly must have told her that the Prince's health was by no means in a dangerous situation, & I have a strong idea that her plan is to fix herself with the Prince. I have done all in my power to endeavour to convince his R.H. how very essential it is for his future hopes & prospects that she should not remain here, & he has assured me that she will return to England in ten days or a fortnight. In the meantime, contrary to my opinion, she is lodged in the same hotel in the apartment occupied formerly by Graves & Brummel. The Prince at my earnest request has acquainted Mr Grenville[2] of Lady Augusta being here, & intends to write to the King & send him the first intelligence of it. He sends his own servant Ferdinand with the letter, which is so unnecessary a precaution that I have no doubt there is some private underhand plan in it, & should not be surprized if Ferdinand was to bring out his son to Berlin. The Prince only acquainted me yesterday of Lady Augusta being here, but he informed the King of Prussia of it the very day she came & begged of his Majesty to take her under his protection. What motive Lady Augusta could have to lose her own pension & risk the ruin of a man she pretends to be so strongly attached to, I cannot [paper torn] divine, but I beg you may write to me as soon as you receive this letter, & let me know how you think I should act. I shall write to the King & Mr Dundas by Ferdinand. Lady Augusta's visit here, however short it may [be], will be attended with considerable expence, & as I know for certain that the Prince is already several hundred pounds in debt, I wish you could procure me an ostensible letter recommending œconomy & declaring that my bills will not be answered if for a guinea above the allowance, &c.

It is thought here that the Emperor of Russia will turn away Mr de Graevner, the Prussian Minister at Petersburg, which may produce a war between the two countries; which I am afraid will hurt the common cause.

All your friends here are well & desire to be remembered to you. The weather continues cold & wet. (9269–70)

1998   ROBERT ARBUTHNOT *to the* KING

[*Berlin, 13 Aug. 1799.*] I should not have presumed to have written to your Majesty so soon after the departure of Mr. Livingston, if a circumstance had not occurred which gives me great uneasyness, & with which I think it my duty to acquaint your Majesty without loss of time.

Lady Augusta Murray arrived here last Saturday the 10th inst. under the borrowed name of Mrs. Ford, & since yesterday, contrary to my opinion, she is lodged in the same house with his Royal Highness Prince Augustus. I am perfectly convinced that the Prince was totally unacquainted with Lady Augusta's intention to leave England, & that he was compleatly surprised at her unexpected appearance. Her Ladyship assigns as a motive for this imprudent step her earnest &

---

[1] George Bryan Brummell (1778–1840), 'Beau' Brummell.

[2] Thomas Grenville, who was at Berlin, on his special Mission, until 1 Sept. (*Dropmore Papers*, v, 342).

anxious desire to see the Prince, who she had heard was in a most alarming state of health, & indeed just dying. It gives me infinite pleasure to say that altho' his Royal Highness has from time to time attacks of his old complaint the asthma, yet they are neither so long nor so violent as last year, & the physician assures me that they are not attended with danger. I have endeavoured by every argument in my power to convince the Prince how very essential it is that Lady Augusta should not remain here, & he has promised to me that she shall return in ten days or a fortnight to England. There are several circumstances, however, which make me doubt whether she will be prevailed upon to remove so soon unless your Majesty strongly expresses your displeasure at her remaining upon the Continent, which will certainly produce the desired effect.

Prince Augustus has many amiable & excelent qualities, & has conducted himself since his arrival at Berlin in such a manner as to conciliate the affection & esteem of the Royal Family & of all those who have had the honor of seeing him, but he has a facility of temper & disposition which makes him frequently be influenced by the opinion of others rather than by his own reason & judgement. Altho I cannot flatter myself with being honored with the confidence of his Royal Highness, yet I think myself under great obligation to him for the politeness & civility with which he has allways treated me. I am sure it is as much my inclination as my interest to secure his good opinion & to avoid doing anything which may incur his displeasure, but I owe a higher & more sacred duty to your Majesty, which, I trust, no consideration upon earth will ever induce me to violate. (48144–5)

1999   ROBERT ARBUTHNOT *to* HENRY DUNDAS

[*Berlin, 13 Aug. 1799.*] I did not think I should have had occasion to have troubled you with a letter about Prince Augustus's affairs so soon after Mr. Livingston's departure but a circumstance has just now occurred which gives me a good deal of uneasyness & which I hope will make you excuse the liberty I take in writing to you.

Lady Augusta Murray arrived here last Saturday under a borrowed name. She first stopped at the Hotel de Russie but is now, contrary to my advice & opinion, lodged in an apartment of the hotel, the rest of which is occupied by his Royal Highness. Her pretence for this imprudent step was, as she says, her eager desire to see her husband for the last time, having heard in England from Lady Catherine Murray, who had it from Lady Strafford, that he was dangerously ill & just dying, which I am happy to say is far from being the case. I have endeavoured to convince the Prince by every method in my power how very essential it is for his future hopes & prospects that her Ladyship should leave Berlin immediately, & he has assured me that it is her intention to return to England in ten days or a fortnight, but there are several circumstances which make me believe that she means to make a much longer stay, unless the King very strongly expresses his displeasure at her remaining upon the Continent. The Prince is to write to his Majesty what has happened, & sends his own valet de chambre with the letter, which appears to me so unnecessary an expence & precaution, as a messenger goes from Mr. Grenville's at the same time, that I am persuaded he is intrusted with some other comission, & I think it very probable that he goes to bring over the child whom Lady Augusta has left in London with Lady Dunmore. I take the liberty of inclosing a letter to his Majesty, to whom I thought it my duty to write upon this occasion. I shall wait for his Majesty's orders & conform to them in the strictest manner.

I beg ten thousand pardons for importuning you with all those details: you are the only Minister of State existing with whom one could venture to do so. I shall not incroach any more upon your goodness by lengthening this letter & only request you will present my respectful compts to Lady Jane. (48146–7)

2000 ROBERT ARBUTHNOT *to* E. LIVINGSTON

[*Berlin, 14 Aug. 1799.*] I had the honor of writing to you yesterday & inclosing a letter from the King to acquaint you of my embarassment & uneasiness occasioned by the arrival of Lady Augusta Murray at Berlin. I have this morning seen her Ladyship at her own desire & had a long conversation with her. I can easily perceive that she is very desirous of remaining here where she thinks she can live more comfortably than in London. I have made use of every argument in my power of honor, of duty & of regard to the interest of the Prince, to persuade her to return immediately, & she at last promised me that she would set out as soon as her health permits her to travel, which has suffered a good deal from the fatigues of her journey. If she keeps her word & goes quickly away from hence I really think she is intitled to some merit, which may perhaps induce his Majesty graciously to excuse the fault she has committed & not take away her pension, of which she is very much afraid. She looks upon her return as a great sacrifice, as Prince Augustus has told her that if she remains she will be acknowledged as his wife & received with the honors due to that rank; such indeed is the indulgence & laxity of this Court that I should not be exceedingly surprized if this were to be the case. The Prince acquainted the King of Prussia of her arrival the very day she came, before I knew anything of it. I own I shall entertain some doubt whether she will leave Berlin so soon as she says, & I shall wait with great anxiety untill I receive his Majesty's commands what steps I should take in case of her remaining.

Lady Augusta complained much of some debts she has contracted in England not having been paid as she had been taught to expect. She requests me very strongly to recommend her to your protection & is particularly very desirous of seeing you when she returns to London. I deliver her message as she desired me altho I can easily believe that you are not very anxious for such an interview. (9272–3)

2001 PRINCE ADOLPHUS *to the* KING

[*Hannover, 14 Aug. 1799.*] Your Majesty will allow me to trouble you with a few lines on a subject which I think when known to you will not meet with your disapprobation. It regards the humble request to be permitted to attend my brother[1]

[1] The Duke of York.

on the secret expedition. I own I have long had the intention of offering your Majesty my services, but the fear of being refused as long as none of the family were of the party, and the conviction that you know me always desirous to serve when called for, prevented me taking any step before: but now that I hear that my brothers are to be of the expedition I should be miserable to be left behind, and I trust your Majesty will not find this feell unnatural for a young soldier who wishes to be of some use to his country. The supposition that the Hannoverians are to remain at home is the reason of this request, as certainly in the contrary case I never could wish to leave them, and I do assure you that nothing but the desire to be of use and to lead an active life in my profession have prompted me to take this step; not in the least an idea to get into the British Service, for I wish nothing more than to remain in this country where I am perfectly happy and contented, and where I know your Majesty wishes I should stay. My humble request is therefore only to attend the expedition in case the Hannoverians should not be of it, and then to return immediately back. I trust your Majesty will not disapprove of the liberty I have taken of troubling you with this letter, and if you would be so gracious to grant my request you would render infinitely happy him who has the honour to remain [etc.]. (48542)

2002   PRINCE AUGUSTUS *to the* KING

[*Berlin, 15 Aug. 1799.*] A circumstance which must be interesting to your Majesty from all what has passed having taken place, I conceive it my duty to give you the earliest intelligence of it. The conviction that your Majesty should learn it from me is an encouragement for me to give you a fair statement of the matter.

My Augusta, having been violently alarmed by the reports she got relative to my health, and which she had reason to credit from the reputable quarter from which they came—determined to verify the truth of them herself; accordingly she left London without informing any one of her relations or servants, and arrived here two days ago. The motive which engaged her to this step, as also the proof of her affection towards me, are a cordial to my drooping heart, and I confess the moment I saw her was the first happy instant I have experienced since my departure from England.

In conformity to the line I have layed down for myself upon this business, and according to the dictates of my honor and conscience, I conceived myself authorized to receive her immediately in my own house, and treat her in the manner which she deserves, and as my duty and inclination prompted me. How far these sentiments may be opposite to your Majesty's I cannot say, but as my wish is to satisfy you to the utmost, as far as my duty will allow me, I have advised Augusta to return, which she has agreed to upon finding my health not quite so bad as she imagined; how soon this will take place God knows, as partly from the fatigue of the journey, partly from the weak state of her body, and partly from anxiety of mind, she is confined to her bed.

Trusting to your Majesty's goodness, as well as convinced of having acted right, I hope you will approve of my conduct and view hers in such a light as may ensure her no injury on her return home. In order that your Majesty may get earlier intelligence of the matter, I have sent one of my own servants who is to wait your Majesty's orders, and have the honor to sign myself [etc.]. (48148–9)

2003 THE KING *to* LORD GRENVILLE

[*Swinley, 16 Aug. 1799, 5.15 p.m.*] I am extremely happy to find by Lord Grenville's communication that the news brought by the Neapolitan messenger on Wednesday is confirmed.

The whole French and Spanish fleets being in Brest harbour is also most material. Lord Keith will soon give a good account of them; but Lord Bridport should without loss of time be ordered with all the ships assembled in Torbay to go in quest of them. (Fortescue MSS.)

2004 EARL SPENCER *to the* KING, *and the reply*

[*Admiralty, 17 Aug. 1799.*] Earl Spencer has the honour to lay before your Majesty the letters received from Lord Bridport & Lord Keith, as also copies of the orders that have been sent to these officers, which it was thought more adviseable to issue under the present circumstances of the Fleets, as it does not appear that the combined Fleet of the enemy can be prepared for any further movement, at least for a few days, and Lord Keith by forming a junction with Lord Bridport will enable us to form a fleet of large ships in good order equal to counteract anything which the enemy may wish to attempt, whereas by keeping the Fleet out, in which there are so many ships not in a very fit condition for sea, nothing could well be gained, and the safety of the remainder might be endangered unnecessarily. Earl Spencer is concerned to inform your Majesty that the St Fiorenzo has got on shore in her passage to Weymouth from Portsmouth and will therefore not be in the Roads at the time of your Majesty's arrival, but it is hoped she may be got off, & if she is able to proceed, Sir Harry Neale will of course lose no time in executing his orders. (9266–7)

[*The King's reply, Weymouth, 18 Aug. 1799.*] On arriving yesterday afternoon I had the pleasure of hearing that Lord Keith and his fleet were safely situated in Torbay, which, considering the gale of the last night, which has not yet subsided, was most fortunate.

I am happy Earl Spencer has sent the orders for Lord Bridport to sail as soon as the weather will permit with a sufficient force off of Brest [*sic*]. I desire a list may be sent to me of the ships he had in Torbay previous to his being joined by Lord Keith, of whose fleet I have taken a copy, as also of the French and Spanish ships.

The St. Fiorenzo cannot arrive till the wind shifts,[1] nor I suppose can the

[1] The *St Fiorenzo* frigate, commanded by Sir Harry Burrard Neale, arrived off Weymouth on the 20th.

expedition attempt landing till the wind has abated. I owne I put that trust in Divine Providence that I do not feel in the least anxious as to the speed with which the business may be effected. (Althorp MSS.)

2005   THE DUKE OF YORK *to the* KING

[*Horse Guards, 22 Aug. 1799.*] I have the honor to transmit to your Majesty the weekly states and returns, as likewise the recommendations for commissions which have been sent in this week.

Your Majesty will remark in the weekly states that the 35th Regiment has returned 667 men as discharged, which is owing to a mistake of the Commanding Officer, as these men have been placed in the Second Batallion. The 52d likewise appears to have discharged 77 men, which is caused by that regiment having been originally intended to have recruited boys, but having been afterwards named by your Majesty as one to receive volunteers from the Militia, they were directed to transfer all their boys to the 22d and 34th.

As the 9th Regiment has already four hunderd men above its establishment of two batallions, and expects still more volunteers to join it according to the plan which your Majesty was pleased to approve, a third batallion might be formed, and I beg leave to recommend to your Majesty Colonel Vereker, who is at present the 1st Lieutenant-Colonel, is a very old Officer, having served thirty eight years, and has been particularly instrumental in persuading the militiamen to volunteer for the ninth Regiment, to be appointed Colonel Commandant of it. I have the less difficulty in recommending this to your Majesty, which is particularly pressed by Mr Pitt, as there being two senior Colonels to the ninth Regiment, there is little chance of Colonel Vereker ever succeeding to the command of the original batallion.

The North Lowland Regiment of Fencible Infantry having become vacant by the death of Colonel Balfour,[1] I beg leave to recommend to your Majesty that Colonel John Hope,[2] who is now Lieutenant-Colonel of the 25th Regiment and Deputy Adjutant-General, with Sir Ralph Abercrombie may be appointed to the command of it. Colonel Hope is an exceeding good officer, and his promotion will enable your Majesty to appoint an effective Lieutenant-Colonel to the 25th Regiment.

A report has been received this morning from Sir Ralph Abercrombie dated the 18th, when the Fleet appeared to be tolerably together, and no accident of consequence had happened to any of the ships, in spite of the dreadful gales which they had met with. As the weather has been very mild since, it is to be hoped that

[1] Colonel Thomas Balfour (Colonel, 1794) died at Bath on 9 Aug.
[2] John Hope (1765–1823), who succeeded his half-brother as 4th Earl of Hopetoun [S.] and 2nd Baron Hopetoun [U.K.] in 1816, and who was created Baron Niddry on 17 May 1814. Entered the army, 1784; Colonel, May 1795; Major-General, 1802; Lieutenant-General, 1808; General, 1819. K.B., 1809; G.C.B., 1815. M.P. for Co. Linlithgow, 1790–1800. He was Dundas's brother-in-law, and was wounded during the Helder campaign (*Spencer Papers*, III, 178). Just as it was being announced that the Duke of York had negotiated the Convention of Alkmaar, Hope was appointed Adjutant-General to the Duke's Army (he had been Deputy Adjutant-General), and his brother, Lieutenant-Colonel Alexander Hope (1769–1837), the Assistant Adjutant-General, succeeded him as Deputy.

they have been able to proceed to their destination, particularly as they were only eighteen leagues from the Texel.

As long as the wind continues in the present quarter the Russians cannot be expected and therefore no time can be fixed for my departure. (9276–7)

2006 EARL SPENCER *to the* KING, *and the reply*

[*Admiralty, 22 Aug. 1799.*] Earl Spencer is very happy to inform your Majesty that the Fleet of transports &c under the orders of Admiral Mitchell[1] were safe on Sunday evening last at 7 o'clock notwithstanding the very uncommon gales which have prevailed, as will appear by the accompanying letter received from him this morning.

Earl Spencer proposes to make an excursion to see the Channel Fleet now assembled at Torbay, having several points on which he is desirous of holding some personal communication with Lord Bridport and some other Officers in the Fleet, who could not be allowed to quit their ships at this moment; for this purpose he means to set off so as to be in Torbay on Monday morning next, & having staid there a day or two, proposes doing himself the honour of paying his duty to your Majesty at Weymouth on his return, when he shall be able more fully to explain the cause of his having so suddenly determined to leave town. (9275)

[*The King's reply, Weymouth, 23 Aug.*] I am extremely happy to find that the Fleet under the command of V. Ad. Mitchell has so providentially weathered the severe and unusual gale that has prevailed. Though not apprised of the particular motive of Earl Spencer's sudden departure for Torbay, I cannot but look on it as highly proper; I shall be glad of seeing him here on his return. If the weather should prove favorable I strongly recommend his coming from Torbay by sea, as the passage will probably be very short. (Althorp MSS.)

2007 HENRY DUNDAS *to the* KING, *and a reply*

[*Downing Street, 26 Aug. '99, 2 p.m.*] Mr Dundas is much concerned to be obliged to intrude upon your Majesty with any unpleasant circumstances respecting any of your Majesty's family, but he does not conceive himself at liberty to lose a moment in transmitting the accompanying letter[2] to your Majesty. (9281)

[*The King's reply, Weymouth, 27 Aug., 4 p.m.*] I should have no difficulty in expressing to Mr. Secretary Dundas my consent to Capt. Popham's receiving the Order offered to him by the Emperor of Russia had not Lord Grenville in my name some months ago declined the same favour in the case of Sir Charles Whit-

---

[1] Sir Andrew Mitchell (1757–1806). Captain, 1778; Rear-Admiral, 1795; Vice-Admiral, 1799; Admiral, 1805; K.B., 1800; Commander-in-Chief on the North American Station, 1802. 'A very good humoured, shrewd Scotchman', Charles Grey described him, 'But I hear that the expedition to Holland has not raised his reputation in the Navy' (Howick MSS.).

[2] Probably No. 1999.

worth. I therefore desire Lord Grenville may be consulted previous to any answer being returned.[1] (Add. MSS. 40100, f. 229.)

2008 THE DUKE OF YORK *to the* KING

[*Horse Guards, 27 Aug. 1799.*] Having been engaged yesterday morning with Mr. Dundas, I did not receive your Majesty's gracious letter till after the departure of the Weymouth mail. I therefore beg leave to take the earliest opportunity to make my excuses to your Majesty for Colonel Manningham's[2] name having been laid before your Majesty by a mistake for the appointment of Brigadeer-General in Ireland.

Upon receiving the Lord Lieutenant's letter, in which he recommended different General Officers to be placed upon the Irish Staff and among the rest Colonel Maningham, I immediately said that personally there could not be the least objection to Colonel Maningham who is an excellent officer, but that I could not suppose that your Majesty would approve of his being placed upon the Irish Staff as you would require his attendance upon your own person, and I had intended in laying the recommendations before your Majesty to have mentioned the circumstance but unfortunately by some mistake the Memoranda was sent down to your Majesty while I was out of town.

I take this oportunity to report to your Majesty that Colonel Noel Edwards, of the Rutland Fencible Cavalry, finding himself for family reasons unable to join his regiment, begs leave to resign it. The four senior officers of Cavalry who have any pretentions to your Majesty's favor on this occasion are Major-General Churchill,[3] and Colonels Lord Paget,[4] Dunn,[5] and Crawford.[6] Major-General Churchill is in Jamaica, and I can hardly suppose that either Lord Paget or Colonel Dunn, both of whom are under orders and very anxious for service, would wish to accept of this corps, which would preclude their going. I therefore humbly beg leave to recommend Colonel Crawford to your Majesty to succeed Colonel Edwards; his services and wounds certainly give him claims to your Majesty's favor, and his promotion will give another effective Field Officer to the Queen's Dragoon Guards. Should your Majesty approve of this I beg leave to recommend Major Dupuis to succeed to the Second Lieutenant-Colonelcy of the Bays, and that a Major from another regiment may be brought in, as the Captains of the Queen's Dragoon Guards are not of sufficient standing in the army to be recommended for the majority. (9282–3)

[1] Not referred to in *Dropmore Papers*, v. See No. 2027, and No. 2012 for the King's reply to the letter of the 26th. Popham was made a Knight of Malta.

[2] Coote Manningham. Colonel, 1798; Major-General, 1805 (*d.* 1809).

[3] George Churchill. Major, 1781; Lieutenant-Colonel, 1790; Colonel, 1795; Major-General, 1798; Lieutenant-General, 1805 (*d.* 1808). Equerry to the Prince of Wales, 1784.

[4] Henry William Paget (1768–1854), styled Lord Paget, 1784–1812; succeeded his father as 2nd Earl of Uxbridge, 1812; created Marquess of Anglesey, 1815. M.P. for the Carnarvon Boroughs, 1790–6; for Milborne Port, 1796–1804, and 1806–10. Lieutenant-Colonel, 1793; Colonel, 1796; Major-General, 1802; Lieutenant-General, 1808; General, 1819. Commanded the cavalry at Waterloo. Master-General of the Ordnance, 1827–8, and 1846–52; Lord Lieutenant of Ireland, 1828–9, and 1830–3.

[5] Edward Dunne (*c.* 1762–1844). Colonel, 1797; Major-General, 1803; Lieutenant-General, 1810; General, 1821.   [6] Sir Charles Gregan-Craufurd. See No. 384.

2009 THE LORD CHANCELLOR (LORD LOUGHBOROUGH) *to the* KING, *and the reply*

[*27 Aug. 1799.*] When the Chancellor had the honour to attend the Prince of Wales, H.R.H. was pleased to inform him that from the account which Prince Augustus's servant had given to the Duke of Cumberland there was reason to believe that Lady Augusta Murray's arrival at Berlin was quite unexpected by the Prince, tho' he did not seem to be displeased with it.

The idea which had occurred to the Prince of Wales was, that if Prince Augustus were in England, it would not be difficult to make him perfectly sensible of his real situation, & to remove from his mind that species of attachment which he now seemed disposed to uphold, by shewing him how unfit it was in every point of view to form an object of serious concern to him. Pursuing the same idea, the Prince of Wales suggested that if the terms of Prince Augustus's letter to your Majesty did not make it absolutely necessary to take some notice of it, perhaps an intimation from the P. of Wales that it was your Majesty's pleasure Prince Augustus should return immediately to England would be the best return to the communication he had made.

The Chancellor thought it his duty to submit this for your Majesty's consideration, and has the pleasure to add that in the whole course of the discussion H.R.H. shewed the most anxious attention to consult your Majesty's repose & expressed the most proper sentiments upon every part of the subject, flowing from an earnest desire to extricate the Prince his brother from so improper & so dangerous a connection. (48151–2)

[*The King's reply, Weymouth, 28 Aug.*] I have this morning received the Lord Chancellor's note accompanying the Prince of Wales's letter transmitting the letter he has got from my son Augustus and the one for me.

I am happy to find by the Lord Chancellor's account that the Prince of Wales feels so properly on this very strange and improper meeting at Berlin.

I cannot see any advantage but much inconvenience in letting Augustus come to England; but that the Lord Chancellor may be fully apprized of the whole business I enclose for his perusal the letter I received yesterday from Mr. Dundas forwarding one from Mr. Arbuthnot, to both which I have as yet wrote no answer, meaning to have the Lord Chancellor's opinion before I take any step.

I have no doubt that, however adverse Lord Thurlow may be to my Ministers, any opinion he will give to Augustus will [be] that which his own character not his temper will dictate.

I shall only write a civil answer[1] to the Prince of Wales and refer him to the Lord Chancellor for further information. (48155)

2010 E. LIVINGSTON *to the* ARCHBISHOP OF CANTERBURY

[*Bath, 28 Aug. 1799.*] I have the honor to inform your Grace that I received a letter[2] yesterday from Mr. Arbuthnot to let me know Lady Augusta Murray was

---

[1] *The Correspondence of George, Prince of Wales*, No. 1475.   [2] No. 1997.

arrived at Berlin and lodged in the same house with H.R.H. Prince Augustus. I have sent Mr. Arbuthnot's letter to Mr. Dundas, and it is probable he may send it to the King. She arrived under the name of Mrs. Ford. She gives out that Lady Stafford[1] said the Prince was dying, which was the cause of that visit to her *husband*. The day of her arrival the Prince informed the King of Prussia, and begd. he might take her under his protection. The King is a moral man and certainly will not allow her to remain there if he is informed that it is not agreeable in this country. But it becomes a question of doubt with me whether or not Lady Augusta may not be a less dangerous and less expencive companion than La Grasini, who certainly was intended to meet his Royal Highness in Italy, where the Prince says he is to pass the winter. I know H.R.H. has kept up a constant correspondance with La Grasini since we left Naples, and has made her the most solemn promise to take her into his family. She is a most corrupted and dangerous woman. The Prince sent his own valet de chambre to London, for what purpose I am not certain; one of my letters says, to bring over his son; another letter says to make an apology to the King for Lady Augusta's visit, declaring his absolute ignorance of her coming to join him. Whatever may be the truth, she has done a rash and imprudent action, and I am afraid may not augment her favor with his Majesty or his Ministers. I most sincerely pity the King; after all he has done for the Prince his Majesty must feel hurt at the present untoward circumstance. If my Lord Chancellor is near your Grace I beg you may communicate the contents of this letter to his Lordship with my best wishes for the perfect recovery of his health.

It will give me great satisfaction to hear good accounts of your Grace and Mrs. Moore.[2] I beg leave to offer her my kind respects and best wishes to the young folks.

Everything goes well in Italy. God grant the same good success may attend our secret expedition; many circumstances makes me extremly anxious. Poor Lady Erroll[3] continues in a very dissagreeable state of health, and bears it with great patience. (48156–7)

2011   HENRY DUNDAS *to* WILLIAM PITT

[*Wimbledon, 28 Aug. 1799.*] In the course of the night I have been ruminating upon what directions it might be necessary to give before I leave London, and this has led me to consider of the disposal of our present force and the objects further to be pursued under the different contingencies which may happen. Perhaps the accounts which may arrive in the course of this day or tomorrow morning may supercede much of what has occurred to me, but that is only the trouble of writing a little more than may be useful, which is of no consequence, and if it should prove otherwise, a day may be gained.

Of course the deliverance of Holland is the primary object to which all our force, whether British or Russian, must be immediately appropriated. And if the

[1] *Sic.* Lady Strafford in Nos. 1997 & 1999.
[2] The Archbishop married (1770) as his second wife, Catherine, daughter of Sir Robert Eden, Bart.
[3] George, 16th Earl of Erroll [S.] (1767–98), who killed himself at Grenier's Hotel in Jermyn Street, married (1790) Elizabeth Jemima (*d.* 1831), daughter of Joseph Blake of Ardfry, Co. Galway, and sister of Lord Wallscourt. In 1816 she married Canning's friend, John Hookham Frere.

armament under Sir Ralph Abercromby is successful on making good its landing and establishing itself in the province of Holland, everything is then plain and simple, and the only order to give is, that as soon as the transports shall return and have received what additional water or other outfit they may be in need of, the troops at Barham Downs shall be ordered to march and embark without delay, and proceed to join the others in Holland. Our idea was that the Duke of York should sail as soon as the Russian troops arrived at Yarmouth. I am very clear this plan should be altered, and I shall immediately communicate to his Royal Highness my reasons, and I know he is ready to go on an hour's warning. Independent of the Russian troops we shall have in Holland an army of 24,000 British infantry, besides what cavalry it may be proper to send. This is certainly a command fit for the King's son, and I cannot help thinking that with a view to future connection it is desirable that a Prince of the Blood should have a chief part in the deliverance of Holland, and the re-establishment of the House of Orange. Besides his Royal Highness being on the spot, and having the influence which it is said he has with the Prince of Orange, may be of essential use in the future details we talked over the last time Lord Grenville you and I met together.

The next supposition is that Sir Ralph may not be able to execute his present plan, but obliged to yield to the weather and make for the Ems. If he goes there, I am not too sanguine in hoping, after all the information we have received, that the speedy deliverance of Groninguen and Friezeland will be the consequence, and that accomplished, five or six thousand troops is the utmost that, in conjunction with the force of the country, can be requisite to confirm what the success of our arms has atchieved. A General Officer (probably General Don, from the communications he has already had with the Prince of Orange's friends in those countries, may be thought the best) with a force to that amount being left, there will still remain about ten thousand. Those with General Abercromby and the other Officers under his command, should either return to the Downs, if they want any additional outfit for the ships & transport, or if they do not, should be ordered to repair to such rendezvous as may be concerted, and along with the troops at Barham Downs, to put themselves under the command of the Duke of York. The force will then amount to 18,000 British infantry and a proportion of cavalry, and with such a force I should hope, when the weather permits, there could be no difficulty of the Duke successfully undertaking what Sir Ralph Abercromby, from uncommonly boisterous weather, has been obliged to postpone. Even if the troops under Sir Ralph should not return to the Downs, where the Duke of York proposes to embark, still I would think it right to order Sir Ralph himself to come, in order that we may, before the Duke of York sails, lay before his Royal Highness in detail the plan by which, according to the concert between him and Lord Duncan and Admiral Mitchell, the attack on the Helder and Texel was proposed to be made. This would save a great deal of time, and to make it complete, either Lord Duncan, if he is returned, or Admiral Mitchell or both should be ordered likewise to attend the Duke of York before he sails. By such a previous well digested arrangement much time will be saved, and the armament, when it does sail, would be ready, if the weather allows, to go directly to the execution of its object. I mentioned to the Duke of York the idea of his coming to Walmer Castle before he sailed, and the previous arrangement, to which I have referred, could all be concerted there. I shall probably see his Royal Highness in the course of this day or tomorrow morning, and in suggesting the other particulars I have detailed to you, I shall at the same time mention to him that he may be probably called upon sooner than I once thought of. It will certainly occur to you that, in the execution of what I have mentioned, no preparation is requisite that can create any delay; for the transports that would return from the Ems would carry the troops at Barham Downs within two thousand, and if I recollect right, there are already prepared supernumerary transports to that amount; but if there is not, I shall give orders about it today.

I shall write to Lord Grenville today to communicate to him what I have wrote to you in case he has any suggestions to offer to me, and I shall not leave London till Friday in place of tomorrow, in order that I may receive your answer to this, and give any additional orders that may become necessary in consequence of the suggestions I may receive. I take it for granted it will be no inconvenience to you to take your ride over to Barham that you may convey to Sir Charles Grey and your brother some general idea of the time when the troops, now at Barham Downs, may be called upon to march and embark. (9286–9)

2012   HENRY DUNDAS *to the* KING, *and a reply*

[*Wimbledon, 28 Aug. 1799, 8 a.m.*] As the subject in its present state does not admit of Mr Dundas's laying anything officially before your Majesty, he has humbly presumed to send for your Majesty's perusal a copy of a letter he has this morning wrote to Mr Pitt, and, as it contains the outlines of what occurs to Mr Dundas to be the best plan of future operation, it will afford to your Majesty an opportunity of correcting any of Mr Dundas's ideas which may not meet your Majesty's concurrence. (9285)

[*From the King, Weymouth, 29 Aug.*] I have received this day Mr. Dundas's two letters,[1] the one which deserves more consideration before I return an opinion than I could with propriety return this day, the other enclosing the very proper letter from Mr. Livingston on the outrageous step Lady Augusta Murray has taken in going to Berlin. I shall certainly be glad to see Mr. Livingston previous to sending any directions to Berlin, but till I have heard fully from the Lord Chancellor, to whom I have written on the subject, I think it best to avoid any conversation on this most disagreable business. (Add. MSS. 40100, f. 231.)

2013   *Letters from the* DUKE OF YORK *to the* KING

[*Horse Guards, 29 Aug. 1799.*] I have the honor to transmit to your Majesty the weekly states and returns, as well as to lay before you the recommendations for Commissions for your Majesty's approbation.

---
[1] See No. 2007 for the other one.

I must also beg leave to propose to your Majesty that an eleventh company may be added to each batallion of infantry which is gone or may be ordered upon actual service. The strength of most of the batallions, particularly of those who have received volunteers from the militia being such as to demand the presence with them of their full complement of officers, and it being absolutely necessary that a proportion of officers should be left at home to carry on the recruiting service in order to keep up their establishment as much compleat as possible.

I have the honor to lay before your Majesty Sir Charles Morgan's[1] opinion upon the two courts martial transmitted from Dublin by the Lord Lieutenant of Ireland upon Lieutenant-Colonel Sir Thomas Chapman[2] of the 6th Dragoon Guards, and Mr Owen Wynne Gray, the Paymaster of the same regiment. I beg leave to say that I concur perfectly in Sir Charles Morgan's opinion upon both of them except in that part upon Sir Thomas Chapman in which he expresses a hope that your Majesty may consider a censure as a sufficient punishment for the charges proved against him.

Though I am willing to hope with the Judge Advocate that Sir Thomas Chapman had no interested or dishonourable intention in signing false returns, yet I suppose Sir Charles Morgan is not aware that this crime has of late not unfrequently occurred in Ireland, and, I am sorry to say, sometimes in Great Britain, particularly among the Fencibles, and I am very much affraid that if Sir Thomas Chapman is allowed to remain in your Majesty's service it will encourage others, whose principles of honor are not peculiarly nice, to consider his crime in a less serious point of view than they ought. I should therefore humbly recommend that after expressing your Majesty's high displeasure at Sir Thomas Chapman's conduct, he should be told that as your Majesty is willing to believe that he was not actuated by interested motives, you will graciously permit him to sell at the regulated price the commission which he bought.

As Mr Dundas acquainted me that he had informed your Majesty of the necessity of reinforcing Sir Ralph Abercrombie as expeditiously as possible with two Brigades, and that they had embarked last Sunday I did not chuse to trouble your Majesty with a report upon the subject, I have now however to state to your Majesty that in consequence of Sir Ralph Abercrombie's last letters in which he urges the necessity of a regiment of Light Dragoons being sent to him, whether he succeeds in his attack upon the Helder or whether he proceeds to the Ems, I was under the necessity of sending orders to the 11th Regiment of Light Dragoons at Canterbury to embark the moment the transports were reported to be ready, and I understand that it was hoped they would be embarked either yesterday evening or this morning. (9294–5)

[*Horse Guards, 29 Aug. 1799.*] I have the honor to acquaint your Majesty that in consequence of a letter which I received last Monday from Mr Dundas of which the inclosed is a copy, I took the earliest oportunity to see him in order to understand fully what Mr Pitt's views were by the proposed reduction of the Staff, when he informed me that as so considerable a diminution had taken place in the

---

[1] Judge Advocate General. See No. 173.   [2] Knighted, 1780. Lieutenant-Colonel, 1794.

defensive force of this country by the allowing the Militia to volunteer for the Regular service, and a still greater diminution was intended, Mr Pitt thought it of great consequence to reduce as far as possible every military expence not absolutely necessary, and particularly the Staff, which had already been animadverted upon during the last Session of Parliament. He at the same time asked me if I really thought the number of Generals, particularly those of the superior ranks, of essential consequence to be kept upon the Staff, to which I answered that I could not say that I did, but that from delicacy to the Duke of Gloucester, I felt an awkwardness in making any proposal; having, however, now received his opinion officially I could no longer delay laying it before your Majesty.

I should never have recommended to your Majesty a reduction of all the Generals upon the Staff if Mr Pitt had not laid a particular stress upon Sir Charles Gray remaining upon the Staff, whose services are certainly exceedingly usefull in the Southern District, which besides is the one of the most consequence. I therefore inclose for your Majesty's approbation an arrangement for the Staff, removing from it all those Generals who are senior to Sir Charles Gray.

As however by this arrangement Sir Charles Gray, finding himself at the head of the Staff during my absence, may possibly wish to assume to himself a greater degree of authority than your Majesty may think convenient to the service, I beg leave to mention whether your Majesty may not think right to order Sir William Faucett, who is senior to Sir Charles Gray, and is already paid upon the Staff, to receive and lay before your Majesty all reports. I should not have ventured to submit this proposal to your Majesty if I did not consider it as the only means to prevent your Majesty being troubled.

Having drawn up by the desire of your Majesty's Ministers a general statement of your Majesty's Infantry at the present moment, I have the honor to inclose a copy of it for your Majesty's use. (9290–1)

[*Enclosure*]

[*Henry Dundas to the Duke of York, Wimbledon, 25 Aug. (Copy).*] I have had lately a full conversation with Mr Pitt on the subject of our various military plans and arrangements, considered with a reference to the pecuniary demands which they will of necessity produce. At the present crisis & with the prospects before us, it is certainly our wish to make every possible exertion and to save no expence necessary for that purpose, but with that determination, your Royal Highness will feel how essential it is in calling upon the country to make great pecuniary exertions, to be able to satisfy it that we are attentive at the same time to curtail every unnecessary expence. In considering this subject it has forcibly struck Mr Pitt and myself that the present Establishment of the Staff of this kingdom will of course attract attention, and it will be felt that it was formed upon the scale it now is, at a time when the country was menaced with formadable invasion and when of course it behoved his Majesty's servants to advise his Majesty to put the country universally into a state of arrangement and preparation such as to qualify it for complete defence in every quarter. The great force which the voluntary portions of his Majesty's subjects have produced since the period to which I have referred, the renewal of the war on the continent, and the fortunate change in the situation and affairs of the enemy with which we are contending, have pointed out the propriety of conducting the war upon a different principle, and to employ a considerable proportion of our forces in operations of an offensive nature. These exertions must lead to very considerable addition of expences abroad, and make it highly desirable that every reduction, consistent with this new situation of affairs, should be made at home. I trouble your Royal Highness with this detail in order to suggest to you the propriety of taking under your consideration the whole of the military arrangements of every description as they now subsist at home, and to revise them with a view of curtailing every expence that may not be necessary in the present circumstances of the country.

Your Royal Highness will not from what I have stated conceive that it is the wish of his Majesty's servants upon any ideas of narrow or ill judged economy to curtail or to cut off any really useful or benificial establishment, but in the revisal of this extensive subject your Royal Highness will keep in view the variation of circumstances in the state of the country, to which I have alluded. (9292–3)

2014 THE LORD CHANCELLOR (LORD LOUGHBOROUGH) *to the* KING, *and the reply*

[*29 Aug. 1799.*] The Chancellor is persuaded that the Prince of Wales would not have entertained an idea of desiring Prince Augustus to return to England at this time, if the contents of the Prince's letter to your Majesty had been known to him, because such an intimation would have been construed into a permission to the lady to accompany him in his return.

Under the present circumstances it seems most desireable that Lady Augusta Murray should return soon, as the Prince expresses it to be his intention that she should, tho' he leaves the period of her return in too great a state of uncertainty.

The suspicion which Mr. Arbuthnot expresses that the messenger is entrusted with a commission to bring over the child seems to be very well founded, & as that event, besides other obvious mischiefs, would be the means of prolonging her Ladyship's stay, the Chancellor humbly thinks that the most immediate object of attention must be to disappoint that intention. This may be done by your Majesty's order, but not without some inconvenience. It might perhaps be done with less éclat by the P. of Wales, and as the measure must be speedily taken, the Chancellor proposes to follow H.R.H. to Canterbury where he now is, in full confidence that the Prince has no other wish upon the subject but to give such advice to Prince Augustus & to take such other steps as may be most agreable to your Majesty. (48159)

[*The King's reply, Weymouth, 30 Aug.*] I have this morning received the Lord Chancellor's note informing [me] of his intention to go to Canterbury, and through the channel of the Prince of Wales to prevent the child being carried abroad, which is a more preferable method than my name being in the smallest degree employed on this occasion.

That the Lord Chancellor may be fully informed of any farther information I may have obtained on this affair I transmit a letter from Mr. Livingston to Mr. Dundas enclosing the one he has got from Mr. Arbuthnot. The answer I sent to Mr. Dundas was that I chose to postpone seeing Mr. Livingston till I had fully heard from the Lord Chancellor, not chusing to employ too many engines in a business which I am convinced requires great discression rather than expedition. The public talk is occasioned by Lady Augusta Murray's arrival at Berlin, not the number of days or weeks she remains there. (48160)

2015 THE DUCHESS OF WURTEMBERG *to the* KING

[*Goeppingen, 31 Aug. 1799.*] I must acquaint your Majesty that we have again had a worse alarm from the French than in March, as they directed their march towards Louisbourg. The moment the Duke was apprised of the extent of our danger he sent me off at twelve o clock at night, on the 28th here, with directions to stop till he wrote to me, as if things got worse I should be within three hours at Ulm, and then proceed towards Augsbourg. But thanks to the Almighty who watched over us, the two Austrian Regiments of Cavalry and the Wurtzbourgers, who had been forced to retire on the 28th because they had no canon, were able to take a good post as the Duke sent some troops and eight canon to their assistance and the French remained in or near Hailbron the whole day—General Meerfeld[1] sent by General Starey has now come round by Rastadt and is at Dourlach with a considerable body of troops which obliges the French to retire and I trust in a few days I shall again join the Duke at Louisbourg. Though he had promised to follow me if he found it impossible to prevent the French advancing I cannot express to your Majesty what I felt at taking leave of him and thinking that most likely in a few hours our dear Louisbourg would be destroyed. I can never be sufficiently grateful to Providence who has protected us so wonderfully, and must acknowledge that being convinced He always acts for the best at all times submit quietly to His will.

I hope your Majesty will excuse this scrawl but I cannot get either better pens or paper here; the moment I get home I shall again have the honour of writing, and I hope that we shall now have sufficient troops: sent to cover the Rhine. (2015)

2016 *Letters from* EARL SPENCER *to the* KING

[*Admiralty, 31 Aug. 1799.*] Earl Spencer has the honour to send your Majesty the accompanying letter from Lord Duncan to Mr Nepean together with two private letters[2] addressed to himself, and humbly offers his very sincere congratulations on the brilliant success which has crowned the exertions of your Majesty's troops on this occasion; Earl Spencer hopes that in a very few days more he shall have the satisfaction of congratulating your Majesty on the surrender of the Dutch Fleet, which he understands from Lieutenant Clay[3] had moved higher up in the Zuyder See than their usual anchorage. (9298)

[1] Maximilian, Count von Merveldt, the Austrian General. [2] *Spencer Papers*, III, 178–80 (28 Aug.).
[3] Edward Sneyd Clay. Lieutenant, 1794; Commander, Dec. 1799; Captain, April 1802.

[*Admiralty, 1 Sept.*] Earl Spencer thinks it right to inform your Majesty that no further accounts have yet arrived either from Sir Ralph Abercromby or Admiral Mitchell, though from the present state of the wind they may be hourly expected, and when they do arrive your Majesty may depend on their being sent by a messenger.[1] (9299)

2017   LORD LOUGHBOROUGH *to the* KING

[*Walmer Castle, 1 Sept. 1799.*] The Chancellor had the honour of receiving your Majesty's most gracious letter this morning and is extremely happy that the measure he presumed to take, & which if right he felt would be more so when he could truely say it was not by your Majesty's order, & if not right he alone was committed by it, has been honoured with your approbation.

The Prince of Wales has been here this morning. He repeated to Mr. Pitt & Mr. Dundas the topics of the letter he meant to write to the Prince his brother, and they are both perfectly satisfied that such a letter may have a very good effect & will come with great propriety & force from the Prince.

The principal doubt with respect to the plan for preventing the child being carried abroad was wher. the Prince should take the child out of the care under which he is now placed, & acquaint his brother that he had done so, or first write to P. Augustus that he would take charge of the child & place him where he would be properly brought up, desiring that he would direct him to be put into his hands for that purpose. Tho' there is some risk in adopting the latter plan (which, however, may by some attention be diminished) lest the child may be conveyed away in the meantime, yet it seemed to be the most eligible, as it was likely to produce no talk & would not be irritating to Prince Augustus. If it should be opposed by Ly. Augusta Murray the Prince must be convinced that she regards herself more than her child or him.

This has always appeared to the Chancellor the only part of this unfortunate business that required any degree of expedition. Mr. Pitt & Mr. Dundas feel as strongly as he does the justice of your Majesty's observation that the number of days the business may continue in its present state at Berlin is of no consequence, & it is far from being impossible that these days may soon seem abundantly long to Prince Augustus, especially if during that time he is secluded from the usual intercourse & amusements he has found in that place.

Mr. Dundas has received by the mail a letter from Mr. Arbuthnot which mentions a new circumstance with a surmise of the possibility of Ly. Augusta Murray being received at Berlin. Tho' this is extremely unlikely, it may perhaps be fit that Mr. Grenville should be informed of it, & the letter is therefore sent to your Majesty.

The others papers are also returned, in case it should be your Majesty's opinion that it would be fit under the present circumstances to take any immediate notice

[1] The King's reply, 1 Sept., is in *Spencer Papers*, III, 182 (expressing satisfaction that the Dutch and French troops had been driven from the Helder). Since the enemy had shown more vigour than had been expected, 'the remaining force ought to wait for the Russian troops, that the next move may prove decisive'.

of the occurrence either by writing to Prince Augustus or by directing a letter to be written to Mr. Arbuthnot by Mr. Secry. Dundas, who has corresponded with him, or by Mr. Livingston.

It seems probable that your Majesty may think that there can be no harm in a delay till an answer may be received to the Prince of Wales' letter, and that no other inference can be drawn from your Majesty's silence but the just one that you are much displeased with the letters that have been sent.

The Chancellor will remain about town till he knows that the Prince of Wales has executed his intentions, or shall receive your Majesty's farther commands and shall then have the honour to be favoured with them at Weymouth, where he intended to be the end of this week. (48161–2)

2018 *Letters from* EARL SPENCER *to the* KING, *and the replies*

[*Admiralty, 2 Sept. 1799.*] Earl Spencer has great satisfaction in congratulating your Majesty on the total expulsion of the French from the kingdom of Naples by the surrender of Capua and Gaeta, the particulars of which are contained in the accompanying letters from Rear-Admiral Lord Nelson and Captain Troubridge;[1] Earl Spencer hopes for your Majesty's approbation of his notifying to the Duke of Portland your Majesty's gracious intention of conferring the dignity of a Baronet of Great Britain on Captain Troubridge as a reward for his distinguished services on this and former occasions. (9301)

[*Admiralty, 2 Sept., 5.15 p.m.*] Earl Spencer has the honour and satisfaction once more today to offer his congratulations to your Majesty on the very brilliant events the details of which are contained in the accompanying dispatches.[2] Nothing can be more satisfactory than the verbal account brought by Captains Hope[3] and Oughton[4] of the disposition of all those inhabitants with whom they have had any communication; they also add that the Texel Island had voluntarily surrendered, and that the squadron under Vice-Admiral Mitchell was standing into the anchorage of the Texel with a fair wind before they were out of sight. (9302)

[1] Sir Thomas Troubridge (1758?–1807). Captain, 1783; Rear-Admiral, 1804; created Baronet, 30 Nov. 1799. M.P. for Great Yarmouth, 1802–6. A Lord of the Admiralty, 1801–4. Nelson recommended him 'for some mark of his Majesty's favour', and described him as 'a first-rate general' (15 July 1799 [*Spencer Papers*, III, 90]). Troubridge's letter was published in the *London Gazette* on 3 Sept. The Articles for the surrender of Gaeta, dated 31 July, signed by Nelson and others, are in Nicolas, III, 428 n. 'You will rejoice with me on the entire liberation of the Kingdom of Naples from French robbers,' Nelson wrote to Rear-Admiral Duckworth on 1 Aug. (*ibid.* III, 429).
[2] Dated 29 Aug. and 1 Sept. and published in a *London Gazette Extraordinary* on the 2nd. They brought news of the capture of seven Dutch warships detached from the main Dutch fleet, and of thirteen merchantships and transports lying in the Nieu Diep.
[3] William Johnstone Hope, of the *Kent*. See Nos. 363, 419, where he is not identified. Lieutenant, 1782; Commander, 1791; Captain, 1794; Rear-Admiral, 1812. M.P. for the Dumfries Burghs, 1800–2; for Dumfries-shire, 1804–30. A Lord of the Admiralty, 1807–9, 1820–7; member of the Lord High Admiral's Council, May 1827–March 1828. K.C.B., 1815; G.C.B., 1825. (1766–1831.)
[4] James Oughton, of the *Isis*. Lieutenant, 1783; Captain, May 1799.

[*From the King, Weymouth, 2 Sept.*] I am sensible of Earl Spencer's attention in having communicated that no further intelligence is arrived from the Texel, but that when it comes it shall be immediately forwarded by a messenger.

From the Foreign Office I have just received the important news from the French papers of Genoa being in the possession of the Austrians and Russians after a severe conflict in which Genl. Joubert[1] was killed and most of the other Generals of the enemy wounded. This I trust will accellerate the motions of the Austrians and enable the Russians to have their winter quarters in France. (Althorp MSS.)

[*From the King, Weymouth, 3 Sept. 1799.*] This day I have had the great satisfaction of receiving Earl Spencer's two notes, the first on the total expulsion of the French from the kingdom of Naples, and the second on the full accomplishment of the attack on the Helder, which cannot but make a rapid effect on the Dutch, and will render our farther successes there not difficult.

I highly approve of Captain Trowbridge being created a baronet. (Althorp MSS.)

2019   MRS. CAROLINE HOWE *to the* KING[2]

[*Grafton Street, 3 Sept. 1799.*] Mrs. Howe can give no other answer to her most gracious Sovereign than tears of sensibility and gratitude; the constant approbation of your Majesty during his life is the highest eulogium that could be written upon Earl Howe's tomb, and his family must always feel comfort from that, and for the honor your Majesty is pleased to confer upon his memory.

His loss to his family is undoubtedly irraparable, but Mrs. Howe can truely say she should still more mourn his death had his health been such as to have given hope he could have continued to prove his duty to his King by further actions which might have been beneficial to his country.

Mrs. Howe rejoices in the mended health of the Princess Amelia; she prays that it may soon be perfected, and that every blessing which affection and duty can wish, may now and ever attend your Majesty and your august family. (9306)

2020   WILLIAM PITT *to the* KING

[*Barham Court, Tuesday, 3 Sept. 1799, 1 p.m.*] Mr Pitt has deferred troubling your Majesty with the suggestion which he wishes now to lay before your Majesty till he could learn the result of the first operations in Holland.

The accounts received today enable him humbly to offer to your Majesty his congratulations on the glorious success which has been obtained in the commencement of the enterprize. And he is persuaded your Majesty will think the moment a favorable one for making every exertion to procure such additional force as

---

[1] Joubert was defeated and killed at the battle of Novi on 15 Aug. by the Austrians under General Kray.

[2] For the King's letter dated Weymouth the 2nd, see Barrow's *Life of Howe*, p. 387.

may improve to the utmost these advantages and furnish the means of making an impression on the enemy during the remainder of the year in every vulnerable quarter. With this view Mr Dundas and Mr Pitt have conversed with Sir Charles Grey, whose accounts of the zeal of the militia in his district, added to the reports from all other quarters, satisfy them that under the present circumstances almost any additional number of volunteers may be procured within a very short time. The only difficulty likely to arise would be from the limitation of numbers in the Act passed in the last Session.[1] But as there could be no doubt of obtaining a short Act to enlarge the number, and as a Session of Parliament confined to that single object would certainly not require more than a very few days, Mr Dundas and Mr Pitt, as well as the Lord Chancellor, Lord Chatham and Lord Grenville (to whom they have had the opportunity of mentioning the idea) concur in thinking that it would be adviseable without loss of time to excercise the power of calling Parliament, on a notice of fourteen days, which is all the time that the Law now requires. Should your Majesty be graciously pleased to approve this idea, Mr Pitt is persuaded your Majesty will think it cannot be too speedily executed, as the success of the measure will be greatly aided by the impression made by the accounts now received. In that case your Majesty will probably approve of a Council being held on the earliest day possible for the purpose, and as the Chancellor will be in town on Thursday in his way to Weymouth, your Majesty will perhaps have the goodness (in order to save time) to signify your pleasure immediately to him. Mr Pitt or Mr Dundas would not have failed to have the honor of personally attending your Majesty, but they trust your Majesty will accept their excuse, on the account of the number of arrangements here which require dispatch.[2] (9307–8)

2021 EARL SPENCER *to the* KING

[*Admiralty, 3 Sept. 1799.*] Earl Spencer, with the most sincere pleasure, has the honour of congratulating your Majesty on the surrender of the whole Dutch Fleet in the Texel to your Majesty's arms. The dispatches from Vice-Admiral Mitchell will explain the particulars, and though the Vice-Admiral regrets that no resistance was made, it cannot but be an additional subject of satisfaction to your Majesty that this important blow was struck with so inconsiderable a loss.[3] (9303)

[1] An Act 'for the reduction of the Militia forces at the time, and in the manner, therein limited, for enabling his Majesty more effectually to increase his Regular forces for the vigorous prosecution of the war, and for amending the laws relating to the Militia'.

[2] The Speech from the Throne delivered at the opening of the special Autumn Session (24 Sept.) began thus: 'I have called you together at this unusual season in order to recommend it to you to consider the propriety of enabling me, without delay, to avail myself to a further extent of the voluntary services of the Militia, at a moment when an increase of our active force abroad may be productive of the most important and beneficial consequences.' (*H. of C.J.* LV, 3.)

[3] The King replied next day, from Weymouth (there is an inaccurate version in *Spencer Papers*, III, 182): 'I cannot return the Admiralty box to Earl Spencer without expressing the joy I feel at the surrender of the rest of the Dutch fleet. The having taken the ships by force of arms might have been more brilliant, but not so agreable to the upright plan of conduct followed alone by this nation: the restoring the established Governments of Europe, not a thirst for conquest and plunder.' (Althorp MSS.)

[*Horse Guards, 3 Sept. 1799.*] I am sure that your Majesty will be sorry to learn that General Lascelles[1] died yesterday. I understand that his death was occasioned by a complaint in his bowells which he neglected till it was too late.

As your Majesty was graciously pleased upon a former occasion to give Sir Charles Gray some hopes that you would promote him to the command of a regiment of Cavalry upon the British Establishment, your Majesty may perhaps approve of his succeeding General Lascelles in the King's Own.[2]

Should this be the case there are three different modes of disposing of the 8th Light Dragoons which I beg leave to lay before your Majesty for your commands. The one is to give it to Lord Rossmore,[3] who has received your Majesty's promise of a regiment when the 5th Dragoons were reduced, unless perhaps your Majesty may think it better for him to wait till a regiment of Dragoons upon the Irish Establishment becomes vacant.

The second is to promote Lieutenant-General Ralph Dundas[4] to the command of it, and the third is to remove Sir Robert Laurie[5] from the 28th Light Dragoons to it, which will enable your Majesty to give the young regiment either to Major-General Staveley, who called upon me the other day, and begged me to lay him at your Majesty's feet and to express to you, Sir, how sorry he was at having declined accepting your Majesty's gracious offer of the 22d Light Dragoons, as upon consideration, he thought that though for his own private interest he should prefer after the war retiring from the service, selling his Lieutenant-Colonelcy in the Blues, yet that it was an injustice to the officers of the regiment to stop their promotion and that therefore he should thankfully accept any regiment which your Majesty should be graciously pleased to appoint him to.

I shall have the honor to transmit to your Majesty tomorrow the memoranda papers and weekly states, and at the same time shall take leave of your Majesty as I have received this morning an intimation from your Majesty's Ministers that they wish me to embark as soon as possible. I mean therefore to leave London tomorrow evening for Walmer Castle and hope to go on board the frigate which is to convey me to Holland in the course of Thursday.

I beg leave to wish your Majesty most humbly joy of the excellent news from Sir Ralph Abercrombie; nothing can have exceeded the courage and conduct of the troops. (9304–5)

[*Horse Guards, 4 Sept. 1799.*] I have the honor to lay before your Majesty the weekly states and monthly return of quarters, as likewise the different recom-

---

[1] Colonel of the 3rd Dragoons, and Groom of the Bedchamber to the King. Colonel, 1777; Major-General, 1782; Lieutenant-General, 1793; General, Jan. 1799. See No. 1259 (II, 355).

[2] Grey did succeed to this command. He had previously commanded the 8th Dragoons.

[3] Robert Cuninghame (*c.* 1728–1801) was created Baron Rossmore [I.] in 1796. He was an Irish M.P., 1751–96, and M.P. for East Grinstead, 1788–9. Colonel, 1762; Major-General, 1772; Lieutenant-General, 1777; Commander-in-Chief in Ireland, May 1793–6; General, 1793. The 5th Royal Irish Dragoons were disbanded for insubordination in April 1799, but Rossmore was not held responsible.

[4] Colonel, 1782; Major-General, 1790; Lieutenant-General, 1797; General, 1802. He remained Colonel of the 8th Foot. (*d.* 1814.)

[5] See No. 1763. He now became Colonel of the 8th Dragoons.

mendations for the vacant Commissions which have been received during this week, upon which, however, I must humbly beg your Majesty to signify your orders to Sir William Faucitt, as I am to set out for Walmer this evening and hope either tomorrow afternoon or at latest on Friday morning to embark for Holland.

I will not tresspass upon your Majesty's time by high-flown declarations, being thoroughly persuaded that your Majesty is fully convinced of my dutifull and filial attachment to you, Sir, and of my anxious desire to forward to my utmost your Majesty's service and to endeavour to prove myself not undeserving of the important situation in which your Majesty's gracious and affectionate partiality towards me has induced you to place me. (9310)

2023   *Letters from the* KING *to* LORD LOUGHBOROUGH, *and a reply*

[*St. Fiorenzo,*[1] *4 Sept. 1799, 4.45 p.m.*] I desire the Lord Chancellor will make necessary preparations before he leaves town that a Privy Council may be held here for calling the Parliament that further powers may be given for obtaining a farther supply of men from the Militia to serve in the army in Europe. There is no other Privy Councillor here but Lord Cathcart;[2] it would be easy to persuade Lords Eldon and Walsingham to come on the occasion. I only suggest those names, but provided four come besides the Lord Chancellor it is quite immaterial who they are. I cannot suppose my attendance in London can be in the least necessary on the occasion of such an assembling of the Parliament. (9309)

[*Lord Loughborough's reply, Staines, 6 Sept., 10 p.m.*] The Chancellor flatters himself that your Majesty's commands have been executed for holding a Council on Monday. Lord Walsingham, Lord Eldon[3] & Sir William Wynn[4] will not fail to attend. Ld. Westmorland, by the account of his servants in town, must be at Weymouth by this time & certainly is in Dorsetshire. For greater precaution letters have also [been] written to Ld. Leicester & Mr Windham which were left in the charge of Mr Faukener[5] who, together with the Solcr-General,[6] will set out tomorrow after they have prepared the necessary papers. (9313)

[*From the King, Weymouth, 4 Sept. 1799.*] I should not have written to the Lord Chancellor on having recieved his two letters this day, the one from Canterbury, the other from Walmer Castle, as in the latter he mentions his intention of arriving here at the end of the week, but that I think it must give him satisfaction to know that I fully approve of every step proposed to be taken, and that I think it best I should remain perfectly silent till the effect of the Prince of Wales's letter to

[1] The royal family spent most of that day on board the frigate which was stationed at Weymouth during their visit.

[2] He was Colonel of the 2nd Regiment of Life Guards (Gold Stick), 1797–1843.

[3] Sir John Scott, the Attorney-General, had been appointed Lord Chief Justice of the Common Pleas in July 1799, and given a peerage. See Twiss, I, 331.

[4] Sir William Wynne (1728–1815), Dean of the Court of Arches, and Judge of the Prerogative Court of Canterbury (1788–1809), had been knighted in Sept. 1788 and made a Privy Councillor in 1789.

[5] Fawkener, the Clerk of the Privy Council.

[6] Sir William Grant had recently succeeded Sir John Mitford as Solicitor-General.

Augustus is known. I desire the Lord Chancellor will intimate this to Mr. Dundas and desire he will communicate this information to Mr. Arbuthnot, which will explain why no instructions are sent to him and at the same time put him on the watch, which may give rise to information that might not otherwise be got. The only difference I could have wished in the plan would have been the securing the child, but if others are of another opinion I am far from pressing it.[1] (48163)

[1] There are no further references to Prince Augustus in the King's correspondence during the year 1799, but the Prince was in correspondence with Dundas:

(1) *The Prince to Dundas, Berlin, 29 Sept.*
(*Copy*)

'Mr. Dundas will have seen by the letters I wrote Mr. Livingston, and which he has informed me had been shewn to you, my wish to get some sort of a settlement for myself which was at my own entire disposal, and my desire of seeing the partner of my misfortunes and our child, properly, comfortably and decently settled. All this I proposed when perfectly ignorant of Augusta's coming over and visiting me at Berlin, which she solely did inspired by the most disinterested and real affection. From motives of doing what I conceived agreeable to his Majesty I have now allowed her to return to England, and therefore I have the greater right to expect now that she will be allowed those comforts which she can enjoy far from me, and which will soften in some measure the rigour of our separation. If this is not the case I must come to England, for, paltry as my own allowance is and can be made by his Majesty at present, yet he cannot entirely deprive me of it as the King is allowed so much by the nation for the maintenance of his children, and is therefore by duty bound to give me wherewith to subsist, and will share that humble pittance with her who is my partner in every moral concern, and certainly even now, in every other place where the law of England does not reach. I trust his Majesty's principal Ministers who are those selected from the House of Commons, will, with that independent spirit which is the characteristic of the House of Commons, stand forth, and with a British spirit represent to his Majesty the impropriety of a person of Augusta's rank being treated in the indecent manner in which she has been till now. The world knows, or will know with time, the impossibility of my supporting her at present in a manner suitable to her rank and dignity, but it equally does, or will learn, that if those who have advised his Majesty in the whole of this transaction, had spoken with that freedom which their situation both required and ordered them to do, and which would have been becoming of men of honour, she would have been amply provided for. Perhaps time may disclose many truths, and though Lord Loughborough thinks that having got back his letter from Augusta through the means of Mr. Coutts, in which he promised her debts should be paid, and which were contracted by her having been left pennyless for three years, yet I would have his Lordship to know that an attested copy of that very letter is now in my possession, and will be even produced by me for the amusement of the public whenever such a measure for our mutual advantage will render it necessary. However handsome the allowance to Augusta may be made, it is not such a one as will ruin the nation, and I am sure that in the House of Commons, where the rusty books of the law do not blunt the nicer feelings of men of honour and probity, Ministers will never be called to account in such an instance for lavishing idly away the treasures of the State. It is for your interest, Mr. Dundas, and for that of Mr. Pitt, that I apply, in order that something comfortable may be done for Augusta, as I repeat that from delicacy towards his Majesty I have allowed her to return to England, which in my sickly situation is a very great sacrifice, as her presence is absolutely necessary for my comfort and happiness; and having shewn this respect to the King, have a right to expect a return which must consist in a proper provision for myself, her, and our child.' (Melville MSS., Scottish Record Office.)

(2) *Dundas to Prince Augustus, Wimbledon, 14 Nov. 1799.* 'Your Royal Highness's letter of the 29th September has reached me. The communications made to me by Mr. Livingston and likewise by Mr. Arbuthnot were duly laid before his Majesty, and his Majesty was pleased to put them into the hands of the Lord Chancellor, with whom alone it was his Majesty's pleasure to have any intercourse on the subject of those communications. I can therefore, consistently with my duty to his Majesty, do nothing more than put your Royal Highness's letter into the same channel, and which I am the more induced to do by observing that a material part of your Royal Highness's statement can only be known to him.

I cannot however close my letter without endeavoring to undeceive your Royal Highness upon a point which seems to be misunderstood by you. None of his Majesty's Ministers in either House of Parliament will think themselves at liberty to move any question respecting any of the Royal Family except in consequence of the express commands of his Majesty, and your Royal Highness will further forgive me if I humbly state to you that your Royal Highness is under a misapprehension when you

[*Admiralty, 5 Sept. 1799.*] Earl Spencer having found it impracticable to persuade Sir Alan Gardner to accept of the situation at Portsmouth which was offered to him, thinks it his duty to inform your Majesty that he proposes with your Majesty's approbation to yield to the great desire which Admiral Milbanke[1] entertains of commanding at that port, of which Earl Spencer had some years ago held out expectations to him, & which he in some degree feels himself bound to fulfil, as there does not appear to be any arrangement more desirable for the interest of your Majesty's service in the way of it; Earl Spencer proposes however on this occasion to revert to the appointment of a Rear-Admiral to assist in superintending the duties of the port, which, as there is now so large a Fleet at home, will possibly become rather too heavy for the Commander-in-Chief to execute with propriety, and Sir Richard Bickerton[2] will not be improper for that office till an opening presents itself for employing him more actively afloat. (9311)

[*The King's reply, Weymouth, 6 Sept.*] I am sorry to find by Earl Spencer's note that Sir Alan Gardner still persists in not accepting of the command at Portsmouth, which would have been an appointment highly pleasing to the officers of the Navy, and with his disinclination to command a fleet might on some occasion have taken him out of an unpleasant predicament. I therefore approve of Admiral Milbank's succeeding Sir Peter Parker,[3] and Sir Richard Bickerton being stationed at Portsmouth to assist in fitting out the ships for service. (Althorp MSS.)

2025   THE DUCHESS OF WURTEMBERG *to the* KING

[*Goeppingen, 6 Sept. 1799.*] I hope your Majesty will allow me to offer you my humble congratulations on the 8th of September. I trust the Almighty will grant us many happy returns of a day so justly dear to us all. I believe we shall still stay some days here as General Starey will not be able in less than three days to come near enough to the enemy to oblige them to retire. God grant the Austrian arms success and may we when once more freed from the fear of the French approaching, enjoy a little quiet.

On the 22d of August we returned from Hohentweil and I was delighted with my journey, having gone through a most beautiful cultivated country intermixed with woods, villages and mountains. Its appearance as comfortable and wealthy as England from every little spot of ground being employed. The situation of

suppose that any aid will be derived to any wishes of your Royal Highness in the House of Commons by bringing forward your name in connection with those whose interests seem to have been the peculiar inducement to your Royal Highness honouring me with your correspondence on the present occasion.' (Melville MSS., Scottish Record Office.)

[1] Mark Milbanke (?1725–1805). Lieutenant, 1744; Captain, 1748; Rear-Admiral, 1779; Vice-Admiral, 1780; Admiral, 1793. Commander-in-Chief at Portsmouth, 1799–1803.

[2] Sir Richard Hussey Bickerton (1759–1832), son of Admiral Sir Richard Bickerton. Lieutenant, 1777; Captain, 1781; Rear-Admiral, Feb. 1799; Vice-Admiral, 1805; Admiral, 1810. K.C.B., 1815.

[3] *The Times*, 5 Sept., wondered whether Parker's promotion to the rank of Admiral following Lord Howe's death, disqualified him from the post of Port Admiral which he had held with so much credit to himself and so much advantage to the nation.

Hohentweil is beautiful and very extraordinary as it is built on a steep rock which rises in the midst of a plain; the ascent is very difficult and unpleasant but when arrived the fine prospect fully makes up for the fatigue one has undergone. I should like very much to have spent some days in seeing the country round about, but providentially the Duke's business did not allow of it, and had we delayed our return three days, the French would have advanced unknown to us, and we must have lost everything, as no troops could otherwise have been assembled to stop their march. On the 20th we saw two Regiments of Russian Infantry and one of Cossacks; they are very fine troops, and I trust from the spirit and courage which leads them on will do wonders and meet with the same glorious successes their fellow soldiers have done in Italy. The Duke gave a breakfast to the whole division who were rejoiced at the seasonable relief offered them, as they had marched ever since two o'clock in the morning. They do not appear to have suffered from the fatigues they have undergone.

I offer up most hearty prayers that the troops your Majesty entrusts to Frederick may be blest with the protection of the Almighty and obtain those successes which will give universal joy to every British and well thinking heart.

The Duke begs that I will present his humble duty to your Majesty. I will now take up no more of your time than to entreat you to be convinced of the duty and affection with which [etc.]. (51559–61)

2026 GENERAL SIR WILLIAM FAWCETT *to the* KING

[*Horse Guards, 6 Sept. 1799.*] General Sir William Fawcett thinks it his duty to report to your Majesty his receipt by this morning's post from Weymouth of his Royal Highness the Commander-in-Chief's box with the note to himself, with which your Majesty has been graciously pleas'd to honor him, relative to the official papers therein contained, and he most humbly entreats your Majesty to pardon him for presuming to avail himself of this opportunity to throw himself at your Majesty's feet to express, as far as words can do it, that deep sense of gratitude which he feels for this new and distinguish'd mark of your Majesty's confidence and favor in placing him at the head of the Home Staff during the absence of his Royal Highness, the Commander-in-Chief, on foreign service, assuring your Majesty that no exertions whatever shall be wanting on his part to render himself, if possible, not unworthy of this important trust by discharging the duties of it as far as the extent of his abilities will permit, to your Majesty's satisfaction. (9312)

2027 *Letters from* HENRY DUNDAS *to the* KING, *and a reply*

[*Walmer Castle, 6 Sept. 1799, 2 p.m.*] Mr Dundas takes the liberty of submitting to your Majesty's perusal the only private letters he has received from Sir Ralph Abercrombie, and begs leave to call your Majesty's attention to the concluding part of the first of the two etters respecting Colonel Hay's family. He married the daughter of a very respectable family in the county of Perth. The connexion was more the dictates of attachment than of prudential considerations, and in addition to the six daughters mentioned in Sir Ralph Abercromby's letter a son has been born since Colonel Hay went abroad. Mr Pitt, with whom Mr Dundas has conversed on the subject, has suggested to him the propriety of mentioning a pension of five or six hundred per annum to the widow, with a survivance of one hundred of it to each of the daughters.[1]

His Royal Highness the Duke of York arrived here yesterday morning. All the business which his Royal Highness has to transact with Mr Dundas will be finished in the course of this day, when Mr Dundas will deliver to his Royal Highness his instructions, and he will embark so soon as the Cambrian frigate shall get round from Portsmouth.

The expected transports are not yet arrived from the Texel, but are *hourly* expected. The wind is now perfectly fair for the Russian troops. (9315–16)

[*From Dundas, Walmer Castle, 6 Sept. 1799.*] Mr Dundas humbly transmits for your Majesty's perusal the letter he has received from Lord Grenville on the subject of Captain Popham, and Mr Dundas presumes he will now be directed by your Majesty to intimate to Captain Popham your Majesty's acquiescence to his acceptance of the honour proposed to him by the Emperor of Russia.[2] (9317)

[*From Dundas, Walmer Castle, 8 Sept., 6 p.m.*] Mr Dundas has the honour to inform your Majesty that his Royal Highness the Duke of York embarked this evening on board the Amethiste at half-past five o'clock. The wind is high and adverse, but it may probably moderate in the course of the night, and if possible his Royal Highness will proceed in his voyage early in the morning.

The transports from the Texel anchored in the Downs this forenoon. They require some little refitting, but nothing to prevent the whole of the troops at Barham Downs from embarking one Brigade on Tuesday and the other on Wednesday morning.

The Brigade commanded by Lord Chatham embarked this morning. (9318–9)

[*The King's reply, Weymouth, 8 Sept.*] I have this morning received both Mr. Secretary Dundas's letters. I very fully enter into the situation of the late Colonel Hay's family and consent to his widdow having a pension with a survivance of one hundred each to the daughters.

I consent to Captain Popham's having leave to accept the Order offered him by the Emperor of Russia, but the permission must be drawn up in the established form. (Add. MSS. 40100, f. 233.)

2028   THE DUKE OF YORK *to the* KING

[*Walmer Castle, 8 Sept. 1799.*] I had not intended to have tresspassed upon your Majesty's leisure again before I left this country, but having been detained here

---

[1] Lieutenant-Colonel Hay, of the Royal Engineers, was killed on 27 Aug. during the first action after the landing at the Helder. He was about forty.   [2] See No. 2007.

two days longer than I expected by the wind being contrary, I had the honor to receive yesterday your Majesty's most gracious and affectionate letter, and cannot refrain from expressing to your Majesty how deeply sensible I am of everything you are so good as to say in it, and to assure your Majesty that it shall ever be my first endeavour to fullfill your Majesty's wishes, and to execute to your satisfaction the very important commission with which, through your Majesty's goodness and partiality, I have been entrusted.[1]

I did not receive back from Mr [?]Lewes[2] the papers which your Majesty directed me to communicate to him upon the accounts of the Life Guards, till the day before yesterday. I have now the honor to return them to your Majesty with Mr Lewes's remarks upon them, which I trust will meet with your Majesty's approbation.

I have likewise the honor to acquaint your Majesty that I had an oportunity yesterday of speaking to Mr Pitt upon the augmentation which your Majesty wished should be made to the Life Guards and Blues. At first he seemed very much averse to that of the Life Guards, on account of the expence, but upon representing to him that their strength was not sufficient to do the duty in London he agreed to a tenth troop being added to each regiment, but wished that no augmentation should be made to the strength of the troops, at least till it was seen whether the additional fifty men per regiment which the new troop would give, would be sufficient to do the duty. With regard to the Blues he made no objection to their establishment being put at eight troops of sixty four per troop, with the additional field officers. I have therefore sent the necessary papers to the War Office for the Blues.

If your Majesty approves of the proposed augmentation of the Life Guards, your Majesty will be graciously pleased to give your orders upon it.

The wind having borne more to the south I am this instant going to embark at Deal.

P.S. I beg leave to mention to your Majesty that having looked out among the Captains of Cavalry for a proper officer to be recommended to your Majesty for the Majority vacant in the Queen's Dragoon Guards by the promotion of Lieutenant-Colonel Dupuis, as the Captains in the Regiment are too young to succeed to it I have desired Sir William Faucitt to lay before your Majesty the name of Major Vickars[3] of the 2d Regiment of Life Guards for it. He is a very old and a very good officer and exceedingly anxious to be employed in a more active line than he is in at present. (9320–1)

2029   EARL SPENCER *to the* KING, *and the reply*

[*Admiralty, 9 Sept. 1799.*] Earl Spencer has the honour to acquaint your Majesty that his Royal Highness the Duke of York sailed this morning from the Downes

[1] On 7 Sept. it was announced that the Duke had been appointed Captain-General of the Land Forces in Great Britain, and of the Land Forces employed on the Continent in conjunction with the Allied Armies.

[2] Probably Lewis. There was a Mr. Lewis in the Office of the Commander-in-Chief, and Matthew Lewis was Deputy Secretary at War and First Clerk in the War Office.

[3] Edward Vicars. Major, 1796.

on board the Amethyst frigate; and Lord Chatham with his Brigade were preparing to sail when the telegraph message came away.

The second division of Russian troops were at Elsinore on the 1st instant, and are probably by this time well advanced on their way to Yarmouth, whither they will come unless they should meet with any of the vessels which have been sent to meet them & order them to the Texel. (9322)

[*The King's reply, Weymouth, 10 Sept.*] I am happy at finding by Earl Spencer's note that the D. of York sailed yesterday from the Downes. By a letter from Mr. Secretary Dundas I find the Earl of Chatham and his Brigade embarked yesterday, and that though some of the transports have suffered, that all of the troops of Barham Downes will embark tomorrow. (Althorp MSS.)

2030   *Letters from* HENRY DUNDAS *to the* KING

[*Walmer Castle, 9 Sept. 1799, 4 p.m.*] Mr Dundas has the honour to inform your Majesty that his Royal Highness the Duke of York sailed this morning early, but the vessell is still in sight and a dead calm, so that she can make very little if any progress. What wind there is occasionally blowing is south-east. The seafaring persons at Deal are of opinion from the appearance of the sky that the wind is veering round, and that probably at daylight tomorrow morning it will be in the southwest. (9323)

[*Walmer Castle, 10 Sept., 4 p.m.*] Mr Dundas has the honour to inform your Majesty that about 9 o clock last night the wind got to N.N.W. and continues so all this day, so that with so fair a wind it is to be hoped his Royal Highness the Duke of York is very far on his passage to the Texell.

Earl Chatham and Lt.-General Hulse sailed this morning in the Pomone frigate. (9324)

2031   THE KING *to* LORD GRENVILLE, *and the reply*

[*Weymouth, 10 Sept. 1799.*] The dispatch of Mr. Grenville from Klitz of the 3d[1] seems really to state so properly objections to his being sent to Petersburgh, and his being without doubt the most proper person to be employed in settling matters in Holland, as I am convinced that Lord Malmesbury's health cannot suit for the present so active a scene;[2] I therefore think it best not to lose a moment in communicating my sentiments on this head to Lord Grenville; the idea had suggested itself to me some days since, but Mr. Grenville's letter has much enforced it. (Fortescue MSS.)

[1] Thomas Grenville's private letter of the 3rd to his brother, written from Kleitz, is in *Dropmore Papers*, v, 351.
[2] Malmesbury, Glenbervie declared a little later, 'is lame, his deafness increased, and seemed to me to look very ill' (*Glenbervie Journals*, I, 176).

[Lord Grenville's reply, Dropmore, 11 Sept.] Lord Grenville has been honoured with your Majesty's note of this date,[1] and will not fail to take the proper measures in consequence.

In the event of Mr Grenville having gone to Petersburgh, Mr Pitt had thought that the settlement of affairs in Holland after the expulsion of the French might possibly be facilitated by Lord Grenville's obtaining your Majesty's permission to proceed for a month or six weeks to The Hague, and some conversation had passed between them on the subject. The commission would certainly not be an agreable one, as Lord Grenville has seen enough of that country to be satisfied that private interest will always be much more considered there than the public good, and that this circumstance will create an almost insurmountable obstacle in the way of any proper arrangement for giving efficiency to that weak and complicated Government. Lord Grenville however knows his duty too well to hesitate to engage in any service where your Majesty should think he can be useful. He is of opinion that much of the advantage which was expected from his going will be equally, and in some respects even better, obtained if your Majesty shall condescend to appoint Mr Grenville to be your Majesty's Ambassador there. But if, when the time arrives, it should appear that by a temporary residence there he could assist Mr Grenville, and promote the success of your Majesty's service without prejudice to his other duties, he would certainly hold himself bound to obey any orders he might receive from your Majesty on that as on every other subject. (9325–6)

2032 SIR RALPH ABERCROMBY *to* HENRY DUNDAS

(Copy, Private)

[Schagen, 11 Sept. 1799.] It is possible that my determination to remain on the defensive until reinforced may not meet with the approbation of his Majesty's Ministers or of professional men, yet I am certain that I have acted right. The difficulties of the country in a military point of view are such that to gain any advantage you must pay dear for it, and independent of that, the risk of a check appeared so hazardous and the hope of reinforcement so certain, that I trust my judgement is right. I believe I could not give a better proof of it than the business of yesterday. Although the enemy had long made preparation for an attack, although they knew every inch of the country, and although they behaved in general with uncommon spirit, yet they were soon and severely repulsed.

The enemy is certainly in great force; there could not have been less than 12,000 men in the field yesterday, probably more. The Dutch took every opportunity to desert, and in a short time near 300 made their escape. The troops behaved as well as I could wish; before the action was over they grew cool, reserving their fire, altho' full of ardor. The militia men are, I think, a superior race of men, and a great acquisition to the army at this time. I reckon that the troops I have with me are made for this campaign, and up to anything, if they do not receive an unforeseen check.

---

[1] The different dates will be noticed.

The Hereditary Prince of Orange arrived a few days ago. He has many projects to which I listen, but follow what to me appears for our interest. He has organized 2,500 sailors & deserters with which he wished to join this army & has solicited levy money and pay for them. My answer has been that they should be subsisted at the usual rate allowed to Dutch sailors and soldiers until I shall receive instructions from home. I have directed them to be sent to the Island of Texel, there either to be cantoned or encamped. They shall have some arms and they may either be employed on the armed vessels in the Zuyder Zee or on the coasts of Friezeland in promoting a revolution. I really imagine the Prince has been deceived in thinking he had more friends than enemies in this country. If we can advance, everyone will be on our side, but there are few who are willing to risk anything. I am very happy the Admiral[1] has been ordered to send to England all the Line of Battle ships—British as well as Dutch. It has been my constant advice to him, but without any effect. Captain Oughton, his Captain, has fortunately returned from England—he is a man of sense and alone can manage him.

Captain Halkett, who was my brother's[2] Aid-de-Camp and now mine, is an old officer. He received yeaterday a severe wound which broke his jaw bone; it would gratify my brother if he could get the Brevet of Major, to which he will be entitled in the first promotion. I shall ask this favor from the Duke of York, and I shall be much obliged to you if you would be so good as to mention him likewise to his Royal Highness. (9327-8)

2033   HENRY DUNDAS *to the* KING

[*Horse Guards, 12 Sept. 1799, 2 p.m.*] In transmitting to your Majesty the accompanying drafts Mr Dundas thinks it his duty humbly to state to your Majesty the grounds upon which he has thought it incumbent upon him to make so material a change in the distribution of the troops from what your Majesty would observe on the face of the drafts sent to your Majesty a few days ago. The substantial ground of difference arises from the recent dispatches from the continent. The pressure of the moment did not admit of delay, nor of the means of submitting the reasons of the change to your Majesty or to your Majesty's confidential servants, but Mr Dundas being satisfied of the impropriety of making at this critical moment so material a change of the regiments at present serving under his Royal Highness the Duke of York, that, after communicating with Mr Pitt, he decided to act on his own opinion and countermand the distribution which had been resolved. The points which now press most are the arrangements necessary to be made for strengthening the force in the West Indies, a measure which seems absolutely necessary for the security of your Majesty's valuable possessions in that quarter of the world, and therefore your Majesty may rest assured no exertion shall be omitted for effectuating that material object. If in any of his dispatches Mr Dundas shall appear to your Majesty to urge importunately the execution of the duties of any of the other departments, he trusts your Majesty will do him the justice to believe that he can have no other motive for doing so than a desire to do his

---

[1] Mitchell.   [2] Sir Robert Abercromby (1740–1827).

own duty, and a conviction that such urgency is essentially necessary for that purpose.

Mr Dundas transmits for your Majesty's use a copy of a letter he has received from Mr Wyndham which is connected with the subject of the first part of this letter.

Mr Dundas is sorry to inform your Majesty that Mr Nepean has been so seriously ill for this week past as to be totally disabled from business; he is as yet very little better but your Majesty may rest assured that however distressing the circumstance is, Mr Dundas shall take care care [*sic*] that your Majesty's service does not suffer from it. (9329–33)

2034 *Letters from the* KING *to* LORD GRENVILLE

[*Weymouth, 13 Sept. 1799.*] Nothing can be more handsome than Lord Grenville's willingness if my service shall require it to go to Holland, but as his presence is very necessary in his own Department, I shall not avail myself of this offer without the cause should seem to require it; and I trust Mr. Grenville will so fully answer every purpose of having a man in a civil capacity there that the public service will be well executed and the orders from hence be prepared by the present able hand. (Fortescue MSS.)

[*Weymouth, 14 Sept.*] Lord Grenville, not having here a key to the new locks, I am obliged to return that box unopened. (*Ibid.*)

2035 THE KING *to the* MARQUESS OF SALISBURY

[*Weymouth, 14 Sept. 1799.*] On Thursday I received the Marquess of Salisbury's letter. I desire he will remain at Aldeburgh, though the Parliament meets on the 24th, as a continuation of sea bathing is recommended to him. I shall certainly meet Parliament on the day that they are to assemble, shall receive the Address of the House of Lords the next day, and return here the moment I have got that of the House of Commons. This necessary call to London will make me on my return prolong my stay here one week longer than I had at first proposed. I have sent the necessary notice to Mr. Hale so that I doubt not the Gentlemen Ushers will have received notice for the attendance on the 24th. (Hatfield MSS.)

2036 THE DUKE OF KENT *to the* KING

[*Halifax, 16 Sept. 1799.*] Your Majesty's frigate the Arethusa being under orders to sail tomorrow on her voyage back to England, I have thought it my duty to report my arrival here on the 6th instant after a passage of forty three days. Permit me, Sir, to embrace this opportunity of again expressing my humble acknowledgments for the distinguished honor conferred on me, in my present appointment,[1] which is the more particularly flattering, as it conveys to the inhabi-

[1] In July the Duke, who had been given the rank of General in May, was appointed Commander-in-Chief of the Forces in North America.

tants of this Province and to the troops whom I lately commanded in this District, the most unequivocal proof of your Majesty's approbation of my conduct while I resided amongst them. I trust that my exertions, which shall be unremitting during my continuance in North America, will shew that I am not altogether undeserving of the confidence you have been pleased to repose in me. Your Majesty is not ignorant of the motives that induced me to make the sacrifice of once more absenting myself so far again from your person, at a time, too, when your very gracious conduct towards me had made me particularly happy in the idea of having regained your good opinion, and rendered those moments, when I was permitted to approach you, the happiest of my life. You will therefore easily believe that I felt it severely, but as you condescended to approve of the step, under the peculiar circumstances of my position, I left England with chearfulness, considering that in so doing I acted, as both my duty to you, and those principles of honor, from which, I trust, I shall never deviate, seemed to dictate. I flatter myself therefore, it will not be thought by you as indicating either caprice on my part or a foolish wish for change or novelty if I presume now to express the same hope I did, when last I had the honor of an audience at Windsor, that, should an opportunity offer at any time during my absence from home of placing me nearer your person in a situation of equal respectability with that I now hold, such as the Chief Command of your troops in Ireland or Scotland, your Majesty would condescend not to forget me. (45970–1)

2037   THE DUKE OF YORK *to the* KING

[*Schagen Bruck, 16 Sept. 1799.*] I should have done myself the honor of reporting my arrival at the Helder to your Majesty by the cutter which sailed the day before yesterday if I had not found myself under the necessity of setting out almost immediately for this place, which is the headquarters of the army, in order to obviate anything unpleasant which might have happened had the Russian General joined Sir Ralph Abercrombie's corps while I was not present.

I had a very tedious passage of five days, of which we were becalmed the three first, and afterwards experienced a severe gale of wind. Upon my arrival in the Texel I found the Second Division of Russians already disembarked, and they marched the same evening. The body of men are very fine and strong, though not remarkably tall; they are cloathed exactly in the style the Prussians were in the time of Frederick the 2d only that their cloathing is green instead of blue.

The first Division is likewise arrived from Yarmouth, as also all the British Infantry and the 7th Light Dragoons from Deal. I am anxiously waiting for their disembarkation and for their joining me here, when I mean to lose no time in moving forward, which I hope that I shall be able to do on the 18 or 19th instant at farthest.

I yesterday examined the whole of our position from Kallantsoog upon the German Ocean to Colhorn[1] upon the Zuyderzee. It is astonishingly strong. The Hereditary Prince of Orange accompanied me and I was rejoiced to see him so

[1] Kolhorn.

well received by the country people in all the villages through which we passed; it appeared to me really to come from the heart and not at all to be put on.

I am desired by Sir Ralph Abercrombie to lay him at your Majesty's feet, and to express to your Majesty his humble thanks for the gracious approbation which you have been pleased to express of his conduct, but above all things for your great munificence to the widow and children of poor Lieutenant-Colonel Hay, which he desired me to say that he feels more than any favor which could be conferred upon himself. When I told him of your Majesty's goodness he burst into tears.

I will not tresspass longer at present upon your Majesty's leisure.

P.S. I beg pardon for troubling your Majesty with this postscript but it slipped my memory to beg your Majesty to grant the local rank of General to Sir Ralph Abercrombie upon the continent of Europe, and if your Majesty is graciously pleased to approve of this suggestion and to order the commission to be dated on the day on which he sailed from England, I believe it would obviate all difficulties with the Russian General, who would find that Sir Ralph had the rank before he joined the army. (9334–5)

2038   THE DUKE OF PORTLAND *to the* KING

[*Bulstrode, Thursday Even., 19 Sept. 1799.*] The Duke of Portland humbly begs leave to acquaint your Majesty that the Sheriffs of London have desired him to request your Majesty's pleasure respecting the time at which they may be permitted to receive your Majesty's commands when your Majesty would please to be attended by the Corporation of London with the Address which they have voted to your Majesty on the glorious success of your Majesty's arms in Holland & the surrender of the Dutch Fleet. The Duke of Portland ventured to intimate to them the possibility of your Majesty's condescending to admit the Sheriffs on Tuesday next before your Majesty went to the House, & of your Majesty's appointing the Corporation to attend you with their Address on Wednesday after your Majesty has received the Address of the House of Lords.

The Bishop of Oxford,[1] who was consecrated the beginning of this month, has requested the Duke of Portland to signify to him your Majesty's commands as to the time at which your Majesty will permit him to do his homage. (9336–7)

2039   WILLIAM PITT *to the* KING

[*Downing Street, Sunday, 22 Sept. 1799.*] Mr Pitt humbly begs leave to submit to your Majesty the draft of your Majesty's Speech for opening the Session, which has been postponed till this time from the daily and almost hourly expectation of farther accounts from the Army in Holland. Should any of a decisive nature yet arrive before the meeting on Tuesday, some addition may probably still be necessary in the paragraph relative to that subject, but Mr Pitt has thought it best in the meantime to lay the draft before your Majesty, in case there should be any

[1] John Randolph (1749–1813), Regius Professor of Greek, 1782–3; of Divinity at Oxford, 1783–1807; Bishop of Oxford, 1799; of Bangor, 1807; of London, 1809–13.

part of it on which your Majesty may wish to honor him with your commands. It has been thought adviseable to recommend voting the annual duties substituted for the land tax, and the annual malt duty, as the forms necessary for that purpose will add at most but two or three days to the length of the present Session, and will render it wholly unnecessary to meet Parliament again till after the Christmas holidays.[1] (9338–9)

2040 HENRY DUNDAS *to the* KING

[*Downing Street, 24 Sept. 1799, 3 p.m.*] Mr Dundas begs leave humbly to state to your Majesty that he intends this evening to send of[f] a messenger to the Army in Holland, in order to convey to his Royal Highness the Duke of York the sentiments of your Majesty's servants, that his conduct and that of his army is entitled to every degree of approbation, and that the disappointment his Royal Highness has met with is solely to be attributed to one of those accidents to which such combined attacks are liable. From the spirits the troops are in, and the proofs of steadiness and valour they have given, Mr Dundas trusts your Majesty may soon expect accounts of a different nature. Mr Dundas wishes to be informed whether your Majesty has any intention of writing to his Royal Highness, that the messenger may be instructed accordingly. (9340–1)

2041 THE DUCHESS OF WURTEMBERG *to the* KING

[*Louisbourg, 24 Sept. 1799.*] I am happy to have it in my power to write to your Majesty by Collonel Crawford, who having dined here in his way to join Frederick has promised to send this over by the first good opportunity.

Allow me to congratulate your Majesty on the taking of Seringapatam[2] and the death of Tippo. I hope that this glorious news will have great effect in alarming the French, and occasion an encrease in the dissatisfaction which gains ground at Paris.

This morning I have seen seventeen hundred French prisoners which were taken at Manheim. About one-third were creditable looking and pretty well dressed in uniforms, but the other two-thirds were a set of banditti, many without

[1] The King's reply, on the 23rd, approving the draft of the Speech and Pitt's other proposals, is in Stanhope, III, Appendix, p. xix. 'It is generally understood', said *The Times* on Wednesday the 25th, 'that the reason of postponing the reading of the King's Speech at the Cockpit on Tuesday night was in consequence of the dispatch which had been received in the course of that afternoon from the Duke of York, in which our Government was informed of the intention of the allied armies to attack the enemy's entrenchments on the 10th inst. While the result was pending, and under the expectation of receiving it before the Speech should be delivered from the Throne, it was not thought prudent to hazard the publication of it unnecessarily. The reading of the Speech was accordingly postponed, and in consequence of the news received yesterday, we know that that paragraph of it which relates to the United Provinces underwent a revision.'

[2] A *London Gazette Extraordinary* published an extract of a letter from Lord Mornington to Dundas, dated Fort St George, 16 May, announcing that Tipu's capital had been stormed on 4 May. This marked the end of the second Mysore War. Much to his disgust and anguish of mind Mornington was rewarded only with an Irish Marquessate (his 'double-gilt potato'). See *Wellesley Papers*, I, 121. To the end of his days he hoped for a Dukedom.

shoes and in peasants cloaths. I felt very thankful to God as I saw them pass by, as these were the very men who a fortnight ago threatned to destroy Louisbourg. On Sunday the Officers went by in carts and I am told the Austrians had great difficulty to prevent the inhabitants of Heilbron from killing them.

It gave me infinite pleasure to hear of the surrender of the Dutch Fleet whose example I hope will be followed by the Army. Would it please the Almighty also to bless the Archduke's undertaking and now that he has taken Manheim enable him to take Mayence, I should then look on Germany as saved. For till some fortresses are in the hands of the Austrians the loss of one battle may destroy all our hopes, as they unfortunately always receive too soon the orders to retire. In the last fortnight had not the Duke's troops behaved most bravely we should all have been lost, as the Austrians on the first onset had orders to retire near Stutgard, which would have laid the whole country at the mercy of the enemy.

I hope the seabathing does your Majesty a great deal more good than ever as you have the comfort of seeing that all your enterprises are blest with success. (51562–3)

2042   *Letters from the* QUEEN *to the* KING

[*Weymouth, 24 Sept. 1799.*] Our little colonie & myself were made extreamly happy this morning by the arrival of the mail to hear that your journey as far as Salisbury had gone on without any accident, & I trust in God that the rest of the journey continued to do so. At least if my wishes & prayers have any effect you will never fail to be prosperous & happy.

All the Princesses bathed this morning. The first was little Charlotte, who of course I have not seen, but she has invited me for tea this evening & I understand by Elyzabeth that cards are sent out for the usual company to meet me there by eight a clock & that I am to pass the whole evening there. The weather is as fine as one could wish, a little windy but dry, & such here at least, that I fain hope you will meet the same at Kew as I know your Majesty will enjoy it much.

Mrs Damer[1] hath been with Elyza to invite for tomorrow to Cames[2] where she proposes to give us a dejeuné dinatoire at two a clock & as it was her own idea, & meant as an attention I excepted [*sic*] of the offer. We shall be back in time to dress for the Play, & I hope that the little Jewess will in the end have a good benefit.

Amelia desired Sophia not to go out this morning untill she had finished her breakfast, that she might ride with her; accordingly, the four ladies, attended by General Goldsworthy & Mr. Damer, are gone to enjoy this fine day by a long ride. This shews how dear Amelia's nerves are encreasing in strength which made me name it.

I have now related all I know to interest your Majesty & will only add that all

[1] Mrs Damer was the daughter of Sir Theodore Jansen, Chamberlain to the City of London, and she married Lionel Damer (1748–1807), the youngest son of Joseph, Lord Milton (1718–98), afterwards (May 1792) Earl of Dorchester. M.P. for Peterborough, 1786–1802.

[2] Came, near Dorchester, was the Damers' seat.

here but most myself long for Fryday to see you return in health & spirit & to assure you by word of mouth how truly I am [etc.].[1] (36516)

[*Weymouth, 25 Sept. 1799.*] I return you my sincerest thanks for the trouble you have taken amidst all your hurry to inform me yourself of your safe arrival at Kew. I do assure you this kindness is most gratefully felt by me & I trust I shall ever deserve the continuation of your goodness. I am sorry that the Duke of York's first letter is to anounce a reverse of fortune, but thank God he is well & safe, & I trust that with his zeal, added to that of the troops under his command, he may soon be enabled to make us forget this blow by sending us an account of a complete victory over the ennemy. This is at least the sincere wish of an anxious mother, & I am pritty certain of the whole nation.

Our party went off extreamly well last night. Little Charlotte did the honors of her house capitally well. At eight I saw her undressed & then we played at cards, & at ten we had a very elegant supper for all the ladies entirely directed & executed by her own woman cook, & we were at home by eleven. The weather continues very fine. I took a walk of three miles yesterday morning & intend doing the same today at Cames, to which place Sophia & Amelia are to go on horseback. We are to return by five to be ready for Quick's[2] entertainment, & as Mr. Hughes[3] insists upon the poor Penleys taking tomorrow for their Benefit, I have promised to go & make all the interest I can to make others do the same.

I have the satisfaction to say that everybody is well, & that every inhabitant wishes for your return. I think the house very dull without you, & enjoy the thoughts of seeing you on Fryday.

The dullness of this place will not permit me to relate any thing more worth your notice. I will therefore take my leave & subscribe myself [etc.]. (36517–18)

2043   QUEEN CHARLOTTE *to* HENRY DUNDAS

[*Weymouth, 25 Sept. 1799.*] I cannot think of going out this morning until I have returned you thanks for the attention of sending me an account of the news from Holland. Thank God the Duke is well & safe. I trust this little reverse will lead him to greater victory, of which we can hardly doubt when we consider the zeal & bravery of the troops he commands. That you may soon be enabled to confirm these sincere prayers of an anxious mother will, I am sure, give pleasure to yourself & happiness to the nation. (Melville MSS., Scottish Record Office.)

2044   THE BISHOP OF WORCESTER (RICHARD HURD) *to the* KING

[*Hartlebury, 29 Sept. 1799.*] I presume to trouble your Majesty with this letter, occasioned by one received from Sir Edward Littleton,[4] who informs me that, having been to attend your Majesty's Levée on Wednesday last the 25th inst.,

---

[1] The King left Weymouth on the night of the 23rd after visiting the Theatre, and travelled all night to Kew and London for the opening of the Session. His return journey was another all-night one, during a severe storm, and the lamps of his carriage were blown out, so that he arrived an hour late at Weymouth, at 7.30 a.m. on Friday the 27th.   [2] John Quick (1748–1831), the actor.
[3] The theatre manager in the West country.   [4] See No. 1463.

your Majesty had the goodness to inquire after me, & that your Majesty said you was sure *the B.W. was lazy, for that some time ago your Majesty had sent him a book with a letter inclosed in it, to wch your Majesty had received no answer of three months, & was sure he had never opened the book in all that time.* If this refers to a book sent to me by your Majesty's order within three or four months past, I certainly had not the honour of receiving any such, nor consequently the letter which your Majesty was pleased to inclose in it.

I am therefore very anxious to clear myself immediately from the imputation of *laziness*, or rather want of duty in not acknowledging so signal a mark of favour, and address the inclosed to your Majesty under cover to your Majesty's Equerry-in-Waiting at Weymouth, who is requested to deliver it to your Majesty without delay.

I am, Sir, an old man, under many infirmities, but the least degree of carelessness or inattention with regard to any favour wch your Majesty vouchsafes to confer upon me, cannot be one of them.

I thank God for His mercies of all sorts showered down upon your Majesty, & in particular for the continued health of your Majesties & the Royal Family, and am with all possible duty [etc.]. (9345)

2045   WILLIAM PITT *to the* KING

[*Downing Street, Monday, 30 Sept. 1799.*] Your Majesty having been graciously pleased to approve of the warrant which the Duke of Portland at Mr Pitt's desire laid before your Majesty, for paying to the Privy Purse the sum of £10,000 from the Regie Fund at Martinique, in order to apply it to some objects of Secret Service in Ireland, Mr Pitt takes the liberty of humbly requesting from your Majesty the necessary authority to Lord Cardigan[1] for carrying the arrangement into execution, for which purpose it seems most convenient that Lord Cardigan should give the proper receit for the money at the Treasury, and should receive your Majesty's directions to pay it over to Lord Castlereagh or anyone appointed to receive it on his account. (9347)

2046   EARL SPENCER *to the* KING, *and the reply*

[*Admiralty, 30 Sept. 1799, 4 p.m.*] Earl Spencer has the honour of acquainting your Majesty that a message is just come up by the telegraph by which it appears that the Harpy sloop was just arrived from the Texel, having left it on the 26th instant, at which date no action had taken place since that of the 19th but 3000 more Russians had arrived from the Baltick. (9346)

[*The King's reply, Weymouth, 1 Oct.*] I am sensible of Earl Spencer's attention in communicating the intelligence he has received by the telegraph from Deal. I trust that the activity of V.Ad. Mitchell on the Zuyder See will soon enable the troops to take possession of Amsterdam. The arrival of 3000 Russians will be a seasonable reinforcement. (Althorp MSS.)

[1] Keeper of the King's Privy Purse. See No. 51.

[*Hannover, 2 Oct. 1799.*] I cannot let the quarterly messenger leave Hannover without giving him a few lines for your Majesty to congratulate you on the glorious news from the East Indies,[1] and the different successes of your British troops in Holland. The strong resistance they have met with does them the highest credit, and I dare say that now a Corps has been detached into the province of Friesland, the ennemy will soon leave their position at Alkmaar, and retire to Amsterdam. Nothing could render me happier than to be ordered to join with the Hannoverians the Army in Holland, and I am sure the fine condition in which our troops at present are, would enable them to act in a manner that would merit your Majesty's approbation. We have not been able to exercise much the last six weecks, most of our men being on furlow to assist the peasants during the harvest time: but now that that is over the men are ordered in, and both batallions will exercise again on the 15th of this month. I hope the weather will be favourable about that time, for since a fortnight we have had very cold and windy weather, and three or four nights a very hard frost. The harvest has been very plentyful this year notwithstanding the cold summer we have had, and this is a great blessing for the poor people, for the corn was grown so very dear that the peasants have scarce been able to pay their bread. I hope the air of Weymouth has done your Majesty good, and that you may ever enjoy the most perfect health is the most fervent prayer of [etc.]. (48543)

[*Zyper Sluys, 4 Oct. 1799.*] I cannot let my Aid de Camp Captain Fitzgerald carry over to England the account of the success which your Majesty's arms have had on the 2d of this month without begging leave to express to your Majesty myself how much the conduct of your Majesty's troops is worthy of your Majesty's approbation. It is to their steadiness and gallantry alone that, through Divine Providence, the victory was gained. Their loss I am affraid is considerable, particularly in officers, as the chief part of the engagement was in the sandhills and brushwood above the village of Bergen. Too much praise cannot be given to Sir Ralph Abercrombie and Lieutenant-General Dundas for their exertions in leading their respective columns. I am sure that your Majesty will be pleased to hear that both Lord Chatham and Lord Paget distinguished themselves very much. Lord Huntley[2] and General Moore[3] are both wounded, but neither of them dangerously. Lord Cavan[4] had the misfortune just as Sir Ralph Abercrombie's

---

[1] See No. 2041.

[2] George, Marquess of Huntly, and (1827), 5th Duke of Gordon (1770–1836). Styled Marquess of Huntly till 1827, when he succeeded his father. Entered the Army, 1790; Major-General, 1801; Lieutenant-General, 1808; General, 1819. He was Colonel of the 92nd Foot (the Gordon Highlanders), 1796–1806. M.P. for Eye, 1806–7; summoned to Parliament v.p. as Lord Gordon (his father's Barony), 11 April 1807.

[3] Lieutenant-General Sir John Moore (1761–1809), who was killed at Corunna. Major-General, 1798; Lieutenant-General, 1805.

[4] Lord Cavan, who had entered the army in 1779, had been a Major-General since June 1798.

column began its march to be run over by an unruly dragoon horse, by which his right leg has been broke, and is otherwise very much hurt.

I cannot conclude without begging leave to return your Majesty my most humble thanks for the two very gracious letters which I received by the last messenger. They relieved my mind from an anxiety which I naturally felt lest your Majesty might impute the failure of the attack of the 19th to any fault of mine. I trust in God that the consequences of the victory which we have gained may be such as to answer fully your Majesty's expectations; at least your Majesty may be assured that no effort or no exertion shall be wanting on my part to fullfill your Majesty's intentions, and to bring to a prosperous conclusion the great and important cause in which we are engaged.[1] (9348–9)

2049 THE KING to LORD LOUGHBOROUGH, THE LORD CHANCELLOR

[*Weymouth, 7 Oct. 1799.*] This morning I have received the Commission for passing the Bill for accepting the services of an additional number of volunteers from the Militia which, having [been] signed, will I trust receive tomorrow the Assent. I perceive by the Minutes of the House of Commons that a Bill is coming forward enabling Parliament to be summoned during an Adjournment; this will certainly obviate difficulties which might at present arise.[2] If the business closes on Saturday, as the Lord Chancellor's note seems to expect, I hope he will not lose an hour in setting out for Bath, and that he will so dispose his business as to drink the waters a suitable time; his having an excuse for not attending Alderman Coombe's[3] dinner may be an additional reason for protracting his stay at that place. (9351)

2050 THE DUCHESS OF WURTEMBERG to the KING

[*Louisbourg, 7 Oct. 1799.*] Though I have made it a rule never to trouble your Majesty with any petitions and have invariably refused all those which I have been desired to present, I hope your Majesty will forgive my acting differently on this occasion and permit me to send you the enclosed paper from the Rheingrave of Salm who has so bravely defended Philipsbourg, which town has been totally destroyed by the French last month when they crossed the Rhine. A sub-

[1] Lord Spencer's letter to the King, 6 Oct. (9350), on the subject of the challenge sent to Lord St Vincent by Vice-Admiral Sir John Orde; and the King's reply on the 7th, are in *Spencer Papers*, III, 24–6. On page 25, line 12 should read, 'and on', and line 15 should read 'only effectual'.

[2] The Bill 'empowering his Majesty to shorten the time for the meeting of Parliament in cases of adjournment' was passed on the 12th and received the Royal Assent the same day. The House of Commons then adjourned until 21 Jan. 1800. (*H. of C.J.* LV, 49.)

[3] Harvey Christian Combe (c. 1752–1818), M.P. for London, 1796–1817. He was a brewer, and Lord Mayor of London in 1800. Though a Foxite Whig, Farington remarked that the City had confidence in him when business was to be transacted. At first the Court of Aldermen refused to return him on account of his allegedly violent politics—in direct opposition to the voice of the Livery of London, the voting (8 Oct.) being 12 to 6. A new election was therefore required; the second Alderman chosen refused to serve, and Combe therefore had to be accepted—after a stormy meeting of the Common Hall on the 22nd. 9 Nov. was Lord Mayor's Day, and Combe gave a splendid dinner at Guildhall. Fox and his Whig friends were prominent guests.

scription is set on foot in Germany to relieve the poor sufferers, and it would be very gracious if your Majesty would have the goodness to give something towards it. The Rheingrave not having the honour of being known to your Majesty would not trouble you with a letter, but has written to me and begged that I would lay the case before you and entreat your protection and assistance.

We have of late had frequent false alarms on account of the French, but thank God they have all turned out with little or no foundation. Even the check the Austrians and Russians met with last week I trust is quite repaired as Field-marschal Suvarrow is in Switzerland. The Austrian General Hotze who fell on 27th Sepbr is much regretted.

Our plans are all changed since Friday; the Duke had intended going a hunting for three weeks or a fortnight and I had desired to stay here during that time. But business preventing this scheme taking place on Wednesday we are obliged to settle at Stutgard which I acknowledge does not suit me very much, but it cannot be helped and therefore I am very much taken up in arranging my books, drawings and work for the Winter. (51564–5)

2051   HENRY DUNDAS *to the* KING, *and the reply*

[*Downing St., 7 Oct. 1799, 11 p.m.*] Mr Dundas thinks it his duty, altho the details are not yet arrived, to forward a messenger to inform your Majesty that your Majesty's arms under the command of his Royal Highness the Duke of York have gained a compleat victory over the enemy and are in possession of Alkmaar. The weather is extreamly bad, but the troops have not yet become sickly. It is impossible for Mr. Dundas in the first moment of receiving the dispatches to convey any particular suggestions to your Majesty or to conjecture what may be most expedient hereafter to pursue, but your Majesty may rest assured Mr. Dundas will take the first possible moment of transmitting to your Majesty every information in his power. At present he has it only in his power with much humility, but with heartfelt satisfaction to congratulate your Majesty on a brilliant success obtained under the auspices of his Royal Highness the Duke of York.

The only officers of rank wounded are General Moore and Lord Huntley, but neither of them dangerously. A good number of officers of inferior rank are killed and wounded, in all about 72 officers killed, wounded and missing, and about one thousand privates. The praise due to the British troops cannot be too greatly stated. Mr Dundas wishes he could say as much with regard to the Russians, but it is essential at the present moment that no idea of that kind should be uttered. Mr Dundas has instructed Capt. Fitzgerald accordingly. (9353–4)

[*The King's reply, Weymouth, 9 Oct.*] My mind is greatly releaved by the receipt the last evening of Mr. Secretary Dundas's letter, accompanied by the public letter he has received from the Duke of York. After this glorious success we must wait till we hear from him, for I look upon it that from home the duty is to consider how far the proposals from the Army can be fulfilled, not to plan the measures the General is [to] addopt, which is the fatal line of the Court of Vienna which has been the true cause of the Austrian Army's ill success after having by the gallantry of the Generals and troops given reason to form the most promising hopes of success which the directions from Court have ever thwarted. Indeed, it is impossible without being on the spot and seeing the face of the country that any well grounded directions can be given farther than pointing out what is the general object wished, but how to be effected or when must be left to those who are on the spot.

P.S. There being no vacant place in the mail coach I have ordered the messenger to go to Dorchester and if possible[?] go in the Exeter mail. (Add. MSS. 40100, f. 235.)

2052   THE KING to EARL SPENCER

[*Weymouth, 8 Oct. 1799.*] The note[1] enclosed by Earl Spencer received by the telegraph from Deal gives every reason to expect very good news from Holland, but it is impossible one's hopes should not be a little damped till certain that the success has not been attended with the loss of many officers and privates. (Althorp MSS.)

2053   SIR WILLIAM FAWCETT to the KING

[*Horse Guards, 9 Oct. 1799.*] Your Majesty's Ministers having taken into their consideration the expediency of reinforcing with as little delay as possible the army under the command of his Royal Highness the Captain General, now serving in Holland, with such part of the disposeable force as can be spared at present from this country, it is propos'd to appoint the Light Infantry Battn. of the Foot-Guards for this service, to be augmented to 800 rank & file from the other Battns., and the 11th Regt. of Foot, to be added to this Battn.

Genl. Sir Willm. Fawcett is directed by your Majesty's Ministers to lay this arrangement before your Majesty, & most humbly to sollicit the honor of your Majesty's commands thereupon for their information.

Genl. Sir Willm. Fawcett has the honor to send herewith to your Majesty the usual weekly states of the troops, together with a return of the General & Staff-Officers in the several districts in Great Britain. (9355)

2054   HENRY DUNDAS to the KING, *and the reply*

[*Downing Street, 10 Oct. 1799, 3 p.m.*] Mr Dundas humbly transmits to your Majesty the accompanying correspondence with his Royal Highness the Duke of York for your Majesty's perusal and consideration. Independant of his general feeling of duty as an officer and a good subject, Mr Dundas has personally reason to know that no reward he could ever receive, nor no distinction that could be conferred upon him would give Sir Ralph Abercrombie half the satisfaction he derives from every opportunity afforded to him of proving the high sense of gratitude he feels from the generous support your Majesty and the Duke of York

[1] A telegraphic message.

administered to him on his last return from Ireland, a time when every support was necessary to protect him from the unprincipled faction which was then combined against him. Mr Pitt has never said so to Mr Dundas, but he cannot help thinking that part of Mr Pitt's anxiety to mark Sir Ralph Abercromby on the present occasion may arise from his recollection of some circumstances that occurred at that time. (9356–7)

[*The King's reply, Weymouth, 11 Oct.*] I have not the smallest reluctance in instantly answering Mr. Secretary Dundas's letter, as I can equally commend my son the Duke of York, Mr. Secretary Dundas and above all Sir Ralph Abercrombie. The first was right in wishing a Peerage for Sir Ralph and he most judicious in declining it, and Mr. Dundas shews his solid sense in feeling the propriety of the General's motives.

I am clear a Peerage would be highly detrimental to the familly, but if any means of giving him an advantageous grant of lands formerly held by the Caribbes, I should think that a very honourable and just mark of favour, and he having commanded in the West Indies not unnatural.

I am not surprised Mr. Pitt feels that Sir Ralph was not *justly* treated in Ireland, but I know he has an heart, when he has had time to reflect, that ever inclines him to judge equitably.[1] (Melville MSS., Scottish Record Office.)

[1] The following are copies of the enclosures:

(a) *The Duke of York to Dundas, Zyper Sluys, 4 Oct.:* 'Thinking how anxious you must be to hear of our success, I lose no time in sending you Captain Fitzgerald my Aid-de-Camp, and you shall receive a messenger with the details of the action and the returns as soon as I can put them together. The affair has been a very severe one indeed, and nothing but the gallantry & steadiness of the *British* troops could have made us gain the day. Our loss is very considerable. I wish I could say as much of the Russians as I can of the British, but I will enter into that subject more fully in my next letter.

What I have very much at heart is that this opportunity should be taken of shewing some mark of his Majesty's approbation to our friend Sir Ralph. I know his delicacy about accepting a Peerage for himself as also on account of the pursuits of his eldest son. It is for you to consider how far his own feelings ought to be consulted when certainly it would be a compliment to the whole army. Possibly if the Peerage was conferred on Lady Abercromby, who I understand is a person likely to live many years, with a reversion to Sir Ralph's children, it might remove his scruples. The action was fought between Bergen and Egmont. Sir Ralph Abercromby himself was engaged at Egmont—that therefore would certainly be the title most complimentary to himself. Should, however, any difficulty arise on account of the Egmont family, may I say that I should consider it as a favour done to me, if he was to receive the title of Bergen.

May I beg my best respects to Lady Jane and Miss Alicia—Pray tell Lady Jane that I think it was her cockade which brought us good luck. (Melville MSS., Scottish Record Office.)

(b) *Henry Dundas to the Duke of York, Wimbledon, 10 Oct.* Your Royal Highness's two private letters of the 30th September only arrived yesterday, a day after the dispatches which gave an account of your successes on the 2nd. Perhaps I am not sorry they did not arrive sooner, for all the private letters of that date which I have seen gave rather an unpromising prospect of the attack which your Royal Highness has since made with such brilliant success.

The purpose of this letter is to answer the one I received from your Royal Highness on the subject of Sir Ralph Abercrombie of date the 4th. I shall certainly not feel myself at liberty to keep back from his Majesty the highly flattering sentiments your Royal Highness entertains of the services of that gallant officer and excellent man, and both on public and private accounts I feel truly happy in the opportunities he has had of signalising himself in the manner he has done in the course of this expedition. At the same time, however, that I transmit your Royal Highness's wishes to the King, it will be necessary for me to transmit to his Majesty a letter I lately received from Sir Ralph on the same subject as that which has occupied the attention of your Royal Highness. I send you a copy of the letter; it is wrote before the action of the 2nd.

At the time the news arrived of the success of the army at the Helder, and the subsequent capture of the Dutch fleet, Mr. Pitt observed to me that no such brilliant service had been performed during the war, or perhaps any war, without receiving a distinguished mark of his Majesty's approbation and favour, and he mentioned his wish of conveying to his Majesty his opinion that a Peerage should be conferred upon him, which he considered to be the more necessary as so many distinctions of that nature had been conferred on naval services, but none in the course of the war upon services by his Majesty's land forces. I could at that time speak only from general knowledge of Sir Ralph's turn of mind, having never certainly conversed upon such a topic with him. Judging, however, from that knowledge, I stated to Mr. Pitt my reason for thinking that Sir Ralph would not wish to remove his family from the respectable situation and rank it held in the country as a gentleman's family, in order to place it in a situation of honours beyond its fortune or its prospects. In general I knew that both himself and his eldest son were most desirous that the latter should follow out the profession in which he was embarked, and in which he is likely to rise to some of its highest situations. Upon this ground he had declined coming into Parliament when his father left it, and his uncle Sir Robert was chosen in his room. I, however, thought it right, after what Mr. Pitt had said, to report the conversation to Sir Ralph, which I did by a letter a few days after, and the letter, of which the enclosed is a copy, was the answer. I would not act with the candour I owe to your Royal Highness if I did not confess to you the answer was such as I expected, and met my perfect approbation.

I hope your Royal Highness will not suppose that there is anything in my disposition which would lead me to under-value the most substantial and exalted favour his Majesty has it in his power to bestow. I feel quite the reverse, and when a family can boast of an honour conferred on the score of great and meritorious services to its country, it is an honourable pride, and one that ought to animate every branch that may grow out of such a root. Even this, however, like every other proper feeling, ought to be regulated by judgement and sound sense, and above all, the substantial interests of a family ought not to be sacrificed to such a feeling. Sir Ralph Abercrombie will leave to his son a respectable gentleman's fortune, but it is not a fortune adequate to the rank of a Peerage, however much it may be sufficient for any gentleman who has it in his power to add to it the profits of any profession or line of life he may think proper to pursue amidst the range of pursuits which the happy Constitution of this country presents to the talents and industry of every individual. I admit that the expedient your Royal Highness suggests would obviate the difficulty which would occur in the immediate case of his eldest son because Lady Abercrombie is likely to live to a period when Mr. Abercrombie may be arrived at some high judicial situation which will not be injured by a title of honour devolving upon him. But this, with great submission, only removes the difficulty in the first instance, but it bars the descendants of his family in all time coming from following the same profession, and be the sons of the family as numerous as may be supposed, they have no option to operate upon but being either soldiers or sailors. Consider likewise, Sir, the situation of the ladies of such a family; any of them may probably remain unmarried (and they are more likely to do so from their advanced rank), and they are obliged to spend their lives with their blood ennobled and their habits of expense increased without any of the means of supporting it but that moderate pittance of fortune which a private gentleman is enabled to give to his daughter.

I have many apologies to make to your Royal Highness on this subject, but I wished to put you in possession of my sentiments upon it; they are not new to me, I have often reflected on the subject. It would be invidious to give illustrations but I confess to your Royal Highness it has often astonished me when I have seen persons of good understanding in other respects soliciting peerages on the most frivolous pretences, and sacrificing to a miserable and contemptible personal vanity the fortunes and pursuits of their family, both immediately and hereafter, so long as any part of it hangs together.

Your Royal Highness hints at the circumstances of the army being gratified at such a distinction being conferred on Sir Ralph Abercromby. That is a point which I confess myself unable to appreciate, but if any individual whatever can, by placing himself in any situation, truly contribute to the service of his country, I go the length of saying, without any reserve, that he has no title to consider it as a personal question but ought to submit to the commands of his Sovereign. That is a sacrifice every individual is bound to make without looking to consequences, but if your Royal Highness is induced by any observations I have submitted to you to view the subject in the light I have stated it, I am certain your Royal Highness's friendship and kind partiality to Sir Ralph Abercrombie will incline you to reconsider that opinion, and to allow the considerations personal to himself and family which I have detailed, to have their full weight. I have mentioned to your Royal Highness my intention of sending Sir Ralph's letter to the King, and I trust you will not conceive me to be acting with impropriety if I take the same means of conveying my own sentiments to his Majesty.

I only wait the arrival of your messenger in order to give any necessary orders which may be requisite and I then proceed to Walmer Castle where I shall convey to Lady Jane your kind recollection of her.

I mention my intention that your Royal Highness may resume your former practice of writing to me

2055   EARL SPENCER *to the* KING, *and the reply*

[*Admiralty, 10 Oct. 1799.*] Earl Spencer in obedience to your Majesty's commands has caused a letter to be written to the Earl of St. Vincent, of which the inclosed is a draft, and has also notified it to Sir John Orde by transmitting to him a copy of that letter. The draft of the letter to Sir John Orde is also sent herewith for your Majesty's information.[1] (9358)

[*The King's reply, Weymouth, 11 Oct.*] It is impossible to have written the letters to the Earl of St. Vincent and Sir John Orde more properly than those prepared by Mr. Nepean in consequence of my intimation to Earl Spencer. (Althorp MSS.)

2056   THE KING *to* LORD LOUGHBOROUGH

[*Weymouth, 11 Oct. 1799.*] I return to the Lord Chancellor the Commission for passing the Bills now finished for the Royal Assent, as also the Commission for Earl Gower as Lord Lieutenant of Staffordshire, having signed them.[2]

I am glad to find the Lord Chancellor proposes setting out in the course of tomorrow for Bath, as I trust the waters will be of essential use to his health. (9359)

2057   SIR WILLIAM FAWCETT *to the* KING

[*Horse Guards, 11 Oct. 1799.*] Your Majesty's approbation of the arrangement for the immediate departure of the Light Infantry Battn. of the Foot-Guards & of the 11th. Regt. of Foot to join the army under the command of his Royal Highness the Duke of York, Captn. General of your Majesty's land forces in Holland, as signified to Genl. Sir Wm. Fawcett in your Majesty's most gracious letter of yesterday's date, rendering it necessary to withdraw the 2d. Battn. of the 1st. Regt. of Foot Guards from the Tower, where it is now quarter'd, to assist in the performance of the ordinary duties at this end of the town, your Majesty's order, in the usual form, for quartering the said Battn. in the Borough of South-wark, is herewith enclos'd for your Majesty's signature.

In order to equalize the 8 companies of this Light Battn. of the Foot Guards with those now serving in Holland, they have been completed to 120 rank & file pr. company, amounting in the whole to 960, which it is humbly hoped your

there as often as you have occasion. I get my letters a day sooner in general, and I can always send a letter from the Downs with an answer. (Melville MSS., Scottish Record Office.)

[1] See p. 275, n. 1. The two parties to the dispute were bound over to keep the peace. 'This expedient', Spencer told the King, 'will, however only avail for a certain time, and, on consulting with Mr. Pitt and others of your Majesty's confidential servants, we have agreed, as the only effectual means of preventing further mischief, humbly to recommend to your Majesty to permit your Royal authority to be interposed, by signifying to me your pleasure that the Earl of St. Vincent should be commanded by the Board of Admiralty not to accept of a challenge...' (9350).

[2] Lord Gower had written to Pitt on 12 August: 'I know not how to apologize to your for not having answered your kind letter of the 4th before this time; the truth is that there are some circumstances which render my acceptance of the Lieutenantcy of Staffordshire not perfectly pleasant. I cannot however *but* accept it and I am as much obliged to you for this additional mark of your good will as if it had been the object of my wishes.' (W. Dacres Adam MSS.)

Majesty will be graciously pleas'd to approve. They are to assemble & march early tomorrow morning to Greenwich, to be there embark'd in vessels prepar'd to receive & convey them to the Nore, where ships are ready to take them on board. The 11th. Regt. of Foot now quarter'd at Chelmsford will be embark'd at Tilbury Fort on Sunday next, & proceed down the river to the Nore, to be there, in like manner put on board of transport-ships, in readiness to receive it, & to sail with the first fair wind afterwards to the place of its destination.

The 52d. Regt. has been order'd to furnish a sufficient detachment to replace the Battn. of the Guards in the Tower.

The official orders & instructions for carrying into effect the new Act of Parliament to enable your Majesty to accept the services of an additional number of volunteers from the Militia, being just put in circulation from this Office, Genl. Sir Willm. Fawcett most humbly presumes to transmit the enclos'd copies thereof for your Majesty's information. (9360)

2058   SIR HARRY BURRARD NEALE *to the* KING

[*St. Fiorenzo, Ports., 12 Oct.*] The many & repeated favors I have received from your Majesty induces me to take the liberty of begging you will bestow some Church preferment upon my brother.[1] He is at present without any, & all my efforts hitherto to serve him have proved ineffectual. From your Majesty's great condescension to me upon every occasion I cannot help applying to your Majesty as my only friend, to whom I already feel bound by every tie of gratitude & affection. (9361)

2059   PRINCE ADOLPHUS *to the* KING

[*Hannover, 12 Oct. 1799.*] I begg your Majesty to accept my most humble thanks for your very gracious letter of the 30th of last month which I received on Tuesday, together with the enclosed for my sister, which has been forwarded yesterday to Stuttgart. I rejoice in being able to congratulate you on the glorious affair of the 2d inst. in Holland, and I do most sincerely wish that the future operations of the Combined Army may be always crowned with the compleatest success. This great news arrived here from Holland some days ago; and though the account as stated in the Dutch Gazette is as little favourable to the British as possible, yet one can easily see that General Brune's army has been compleatly beat, at least the left wing of his troops consisting cheifly of French.

General Suvorow has forced the St. Gotthart, and had joined the Austrians under the command of General Auffenberg: he had intended to march to Lucern, and from thence push on to Berne. Should this plan succeed, the position the ennemy had on the Albis Mountains before they retook Zurig would be perfectly turned, and the French obliged to retire, and perhaps to leave Swisserland. The

---

[1] The Rev. Geo. Burrard (1769–1856), brother of Sir H. B. Neale, whom he succeeded as 3rd Baronet in 1840, was appointed Chaplain to the Prince of Wales in Nov. 1799, and became Rector of Yarmouth, I. of Wight (1801), Vicar of Middleton Tyas, Yorkshire, 1804–56, and Rector of Burton Coggles, Lincolnshire, 1822–56. He was Chaplain to four successive Sovereigns.

Corps of Hessians commanded by General Korsakow was advancing on the 30th of last month together with the Austrian Corps under General Petrorsch's orders, and it is to be hoped that a general attack will have taken place by this time, and I trust then that all the advantages the ennemy have had will be lost. I have not heard from my sister for this last fortnight, which I look upon as a sign that in Suavia everything is quiet, for else she would certainly have written. I dare now not trespass any longer on your Majesty's patience than just to add the assurance of my ever remaining [etc.]. (48544)

2060   *Letters from* HENRY DUNDAS *to the* KING, *and a reply*

[*Downing Street, 13 Oct. 1799.*] Mr Dundas has the honour humbly to inform your Majesty that the messenger is arrived from the army with the detail of the action of the 2d. and a very short account without details of another action on the 6th. Mr Dundas thinks it his duty to send this short account to your Majesty without any delay. The accompanying bulletin is the substance of the dispatches so far as yet received.[1] (9362)

[*The King's reply, Windsor, 14 Oct. 1799, 8.20 p.m.*] Though after the fatigue of a long journey[2] the instantly giving a decision on the continuance or close of a campain is not very pleasant, yet the present moment is so critical that I have waved deferring an answer till tomorrow. I feel so forcibly the exertions that have been used and still more the loss of officers and men that I cannot have the smallest doubt of the propriety, nay necessity of recalling the forces now in Holland. I trust that we shall learn experience from this severe lesson and not place so much confidence in the assertions of those who thought the Dutch would have on this occasioned [*sic*] acted more suitable to the assistance that has been afforded them.

I have wrote a few lines of comfort to my son which he most richly deserves. (Add. MSS. 40100, f. 237.)

[*From Dundas, Downing St., 14 Oct., 3 p.m.*] Mr Dundas has the honour to transmit to your Majesty, along with the dispatches publick and private, a Minute of Cabinet, and a proposed draft of a dispatch to his Royal Highness the Duke of York founded on the opinion of your Majesty's confidential servants. Mr Dundas at the same time takes the liberty of troubling your Majesty with a copy of the answer Mr Dundas means to return to the private letters he has had the honour of receiving from the Duke of York by Col Brownrigg.[3] It is Mr Dundas's intention to dispatch Colonel Brownrigg this evening or at a very early hour tomorrow morning. (9367)

---

[1] The later action involved heavy casualties and the loss of Alkmaar which had been captured on the 2nd.

[2] The royal family left Weymouth at 5 a.m. on the 14th, arriving at Windsor in the evening.

[3] Brownrigg (1759–1833) [see Nos. 1212, 1607] had become a Colonel in 1796. Major-General, 1802; Lieutenant-General, 1808; General, 1819; Governor of Ceylon, 1811–20; created Baronet, 1816. At this time he was Public Secretary to the Commander-in-Chief.

Cabinet Minute (*in Dundas's hand*)
Downing Street, 14 Oct. 1799, 2 p.m.
Present: Duke of Portland, Earl Spencer, Lord Grenville, Mr Pitt, Mr Wyndham, Mr Dundas

Humbly represent to your Majesty that having perused the dispatches formerly and now received from his Royal Highness the Duke of York, they are of opinion that everything has been done in the execution of your Majesty's instructions that military skill or valour could accomplish, and have a full confidence that if it was expedient to prosecute the campaign farther in the direction where the army now is, the same skill and valour would continue to be displayed. But from the losses the army has already sustained in the severe actions they have fought, from the additional means of reinforcements the enemy possess from late events on the continent, from the small progress your Majesty's army have been enabled to make owing to the unexampled inclemency of the weather, and from the late season of the year, which leaves no room to hope that at present these complicated difficulties can in any degree be removed, and therefore they humbly recommend to your Majesty that directions may be immediately given for withdrawing the Allied troops from Holland to be cantoned according to circumstances in Great Britain and Ireland and the Islands of Jersey and Guernsey.[1] (9368–9)

2061 GENERAL SIR WILLIAM FAWCETT *to the* KING

[*Horse Guards, 14 Oct. 1799.*] General Sir Willm. Fawcett most humbly presumes to inform your Majesty that by direction of your Majesty's Ministers, the embarkation of the 10th. (or Prince of Wales's) Regt. of Light Dragoons, of the Light Infantry Battalion of the Guards, & of the Eleventh Regt. of Foot, is countermanded, & that the two last are order'd to return to their former quarters. (9364)

2062 THE BISHOP OF WORCESTER (RICHARD HURD) *to the* KING

[*Hartlebury, 14 Oct. 1799.*] I had the honour of receiving your Majesty's most obliging letter from Weymouth of Octr 5th 1799, but have omitted to make my acknowledgment of it till this day, when I conclude your Majesty will be returned to Windsor.

Your Majesty makes me extremely happy in so readily accepting the vindication

---

[1] Lord Hawkesbury, the Master of the Mint, but not yet a Cabinet Minister, wrote to Addington on the 18th: 'I certainly was never friendly to the expedition, but it may have been a wise one; to avoid however feeling dismay at its failure is what I cannot conceive. If to have ruined for ever the Orange cause in Holland, if to have given confidence to the French Government, and to have convinced Europe that we were not invulnerable, if to have sacrificed 10,000 of the best troops in the world (after taking possession of the Helder and the fleet) for no purpose, and if the defence, the only defence, of all this *must* be that our troops were uniformly victorious, but that they had been sent into a country where it was impossible they could act. If all this is not ground of dismay I am at a loss to conceive what can be so. Let us be persevering, let us be bold, let us be intrepid, but in God's name let us feel what we have lost, and that the greatest part of what we have lost, we have lost for nothing.' (Sidmouth MSS.)

of myself from what your Majesty calls by the softest name, *laziness*, but wd. indeed have been an unpardonable fault if I had been capable of committing it. If two years ago I incurred the blame of any such charge, it must have been occasioned by the book's lying too long at Worcester.

No intelligence could be more welcome to me than that of your Majesty & the Royal Family having benefited by the fine air & sea-bathing of Weymouth: and the usual good effects I hope will follow, of your increased health & spirits. For these supports your Majesty's unwearied exertions for the general good of Europe, as well as of your own dominions, are likely to call for in no common measure. I judge so from your Majesty's late successes & efforts everywhere by sea & land, & particularly from the news just now received from Holland, & of the laurells wch his Royal Highness the Duke of York has acquired in a cause so just & important. I beg your Majesty will have the goodness to accept my sincerest congratulations.

Nothing can be juster than what your Majesty is pleased to intimate of your attention to ecclesiastical preferments, & of wch. your Majesty has given a recent proof in filling the See of Oxford.[1] I doubt not Cambridge will be able to furnish it's proportion of candidates for your Majesty's notice; tho', from my long absence from that place, & total unacquaintance with it's present members, I am unable to mention particular names. Of Dr Paley,[2] I know nothing but from his writings, wch. shew him to be a learned and ingenious man. And if in any of these he may have been somewhat biassed by his obligations to Bishop Law,[3] his riper age & experience must by this time, I suppose, have reformed his judgment. (9365–6)

2063   GENERAL SIR WILLIAM FAWCETT *to the* KING

[*Horse Guards, 18 Oct. 1799.*] In compliance with the desire of your Majesty's Ministers, General Sir Wm. Fawcett most humbly presumes to submit to your Majesty's consideration the expediency of your Majesty's being graciously pleas'd to grant to Captn. Fitzgerald of the 3d. Regt. of Foot-Guards, Aide-de-Camp to his Royal Highness the Captain-General, and to Captain Browne, Aide-de-Camp to Lieut. Genl. Trigge[4] & eldest Captn. in the 59th Regt., the Brevet rank of Majors in the Army, on account of the agreeable intelligence of the successful operations of your Majesty's forces on foreign service, which these Officers have respectively brought home for your Majesty's information. (9370)

[1] See No. 2038.

[2] William Paley (1743–1805), Archdeacon of Carlisle; author of *Principles of Morals and Political Philosophy* (1785), *Evidences of Christianity* (1794), and *Natural Theology* (1802).

[3] Edmund Law (1703–87), Bishop of Carlisle, 1769–87; author of *Essay on the Origin of Evil* (1731); *Enquiry into the Ideas of Space and Time* (1734); *Considerations on the State of the World with regard to the Theory of Religion* (1745), and *Considerations on the Propriety of requiring Subscription to Articles of Faith* (1774).

[4] Sir Thomas Trigge (*d.* 1814). Colonel, 1782; Major-General, 1793; Lieutenant-General, 1798; General, 1803. Lieutenant-Governor (later, Governor) of Gibraltar, 1796; Lieutenant-General of the Ordnance, 1804, and 1807–10. K.B., 1801.

[*Stutgard, 18 Oct. 1799.*] I have had the honour and happiness to receive your Majesty's gracious letter of the 30th of September. It could not have come more opportunely to keep up my spirits which are again very low with the French having crossed the Rhine and threatning us with another visit. Indeed I fear this will be the case the whole Winter unless the Archduke will leave two or three Regiments of Infantry near the Rhine, as the Heavy Dragoons make it a rule to fly the moment they are attacked. Indeed it is cruel to place them there, as the whole country is not made for them to act in. The receiving orders on every occasion to retire is enough to make these fine Regiments totally loose their courage.

At this moment I feel it quite a providential event that the Duke was prevented going on his hunting party, as it would have been above two days before he could have returned, or even his directions be received at Stutgard. I hate to spoil anything that can give him pleasure, as he has so many things to torment him, but I own that I suffered great apprehension at the thoughts of the events which might take place during his absence.

I rejoice very much at the benefit dear Amelia receives from the sea and hope that now she will get quite free from all complaint. I hear from everybody that she is very much improved, which gives me great pleasure. (51566–7)

2065 THE DUKE OF YORK *to the* KING

[*Schagen Bruck, 21 Oct. 1799.*] I beg leave to return your Majesty my most humble thanks for your most gracious letter of the 14th instant which was delivered to me by Colonel Brownrigg yesterday.

I want words to express to your Majesty how much I feel the paternal and affectionate expressions which you are pleased to make use of upon my conduct during the time I have been employed in this country. I can safely say that no officer ever was placed in the command of braver troops than those whom your Majesty has entrusted to me, and it has certainly not been from want of courage or resolution on their part that we have not fullfilled your Majesty's expectations.

Whether your Majesty will fully approve of the step which I have thought necessary to take of making a truce with the enemy to avoid the loss of many brave men on our embarkation, I cannot pretend to judge, but I must beg leave to say that knowing the loss which we must have sustained of most of our artillery and of the whole of our rearguard at the Helder and of all our horses, I thought myself in duty bound to sacrifice all personal and private feelings, which I cannot conceal from your Majesty were very tried, to what I judged the advantage of your Majesty's service and the saving of many valuable men's lives.

Every measure shall be taken for the immediate removal of your Majesty's troops from this country, and I hope that it will not be long before I shall have the happiness of paying my duty to your Majesty.[1] (9373)

[1] Canning wrote, on the 19th: 'The recall of our troops from Holland proceeds upon this simple and prudent calculation—that we had better have our army without Holland than Holland without our army—and it is plain that though we probably should have succeeded in forcing our way to Amster-

[*Wimbledon, 21 Oct.* [*1799*], *11 p.m.*] Mr Dundas has just learnt from Mr Huskisson that he has transmitted to your Majesty the letter this day received from the Duke of York addrest to Mr Dundas, but that in several particulars the information it contains was not compleat. It is probable the official accounts may arrive in the course of the night, but Mr Dundas thinks it his duty humbly to transmit for your Majesty's perusal all the private information of which he is possest. Mr Dundas from what he sees has no hesitation in submitting his opinion to your Majesty that the arrangement which is supposed to have been made is in every respect judicious. Mr Dundas has been informed that the prisoners to be released are about 8000 men. Without any stipulation it would be desirable to get rid of that number or even more. If by such a sacrifice we are relieved of all the difficulties attending such an embarkation, no person can hesitate in rejoicing in any arrangement which has been productive of such consequences. (9371–2)

[*The King's reply, Windsor, 22 Oct., 7.15 a.m.*] Mr. Secretary Dundas must do me the justice to remember I never was very sanguine as to the success of the attempt on Holland, and for some time have certainly felt that the earlier it was given up the better. Indeed, had the people of that country been hearty it might have ended better, but would ever have been most hazardous. I therefore approve of the suspension of hostilities even at the giving up 8000 prisoners of the French. I trust every exertion is using to send additional transports and provisions for bringing back the troops.[1] (Ann Arbor MSS.)

2067 SIR WILLIAM FAWCETT *to the* KING

[*Horse Guards, 22 Oct. 1799.*] The note with which your Majesty has been graciously pleas'd to honor General Sir Wm. Fawcett of yesterday's date has not less distress'd than surpriz'd him, fearing that your Majesty might think he had

dam, we should not have done so without many actions which would have cost many lives—and that when we had obtained our object, the change of affairs on the Continent has so increased the power of the French to send forces into Holland that we should have found it difficult to keep it through the winter. Our choice therefore was between an untenable conquest and a disposable army, and we have wisely chosen the latter. We receive our army back again not disgraced nor dispirited but proud of having measured themselves with an equal French force, and shewn that our militia conscripts can face and beat their veteran troops, and we receive them, applicable, I hope, to as brilliant and more successful undertakings hereafter.' (Harewood MSS.)

[1] The Duke of York arrived in London from Holland on 4 Nov. He wrote to his friend Charles Greenwood from Schagen Brug on 27 Oct.: 'Inclosed I send you a draft upon the Paymaster-General for two thousand seven hunderd and twenty pounds, at sixty day sight, which I desire that you will be so good as to receive and place to my account. It is my pay up to the 24 of December as likewise my table money up to the 28th of this month and my two hunderd days bat and forage money. I explain this to you lest you might imagine from its being so large a sum that I had made free with the publick purse.

We begin embarking a part of the troops tomorrow; as fast as transports arrive the rest will follow. I shall leave this place for the Helder to superintend the embarkation tomorrow. How soon however I shall be able to embark myself for England I cannot as yet say, as it must depend upon the means of getting everything off. I hope however that it will not be long.

Adieu. Remember me to all friends.' (Add. Georgian 38/13.)

been guilty of a neglectful omission in not having regularly reported to your Majesty the circumstances referr'd to by your Majesty respecting the forming a Battalion from the Volunteers of the Staffordshire Militia, to be added as a 2d Battn. to the 52d. Regt. & commanded by Lord Granville Leveson-Gower. But no official account of any such arrangement had arriv'd at his hands, nor had he receiv'd any authority from your Majesty's Ministers to take your Majesty's commands upon the subject till his arrival at the Horse Guards from Chelsea this morning, when, upon enquiry, he found that a letter had been receiv'd at the Office, from Mr. Secretary Dundas, the 18th inst., though it is dated the 10th., explaining the particulars relative to the formation of this Battn., but which it was thought unnecessary to communicate to Genl. Sir Willm. Fawcett untill his Royal Highness the Captn.-General's opinion upon it had been receiv'd, which Coll. Brownrigg (who, it seems, had been made acquainted, while he was lately here, with the whole business, at the Secretary of State's Office) promis'd to transmit for your Majesty's information as expeditiously as possible after his return to Holland, which however is not yet arriv'd. Genl. Sir Wm. Fawcett most humbly presumes, for your Majesty's farther satisfaction, to lay before your Majesty copy of a letter with its enclosures which he has this moment receiv'd from Mr. Dundas, relative to this transaction.

Having made enquiry at the Admiralty & the Transport Office concerning the insufficiency of tonnage, which your Majesty mentions, Sir Willm. Fawcett is inform'd that the former Board has sent over to the Texel in ships of the Line, armed transports, & other vessels, tonnage for about 24,000 men—& that at least 50,000 tons more have been sent from the Transport Office for the conveyance of cavalry, infantry & military stores of all kinds. It is therefore to be hoped that there will be tonnage sufficient in the Texel for the accommodation of the whole army. (9374)

2068   HENRY DUNDAS *to* SIR WILLIAM FAWCETT

(*Copy*)

[*Downing Street, 22 Oct. 1799.*] In consequence of some communication Mr Pitt and I had with Lord Granville Leveson-Gower before the late Act was passed, we formed an opinion that the number of men to be raised from the three Staffordshire Battalions under that Act, amounting to 854, would be much more likely to come forward if they could be formed into a Corps under his Lordship's command, and finding that his Lordship had no reluctance to such a command, it appeared to us that by recommending him to it with the temporary rank of Lieutenant-Colonel only, we were consulting the interests of his Majesty's service without interfering with the regulations of the army. On these grounds I addressed to you my letter of the 10th instant.[1]

A few days afterwards, in consequence of a letter from Lieutenant-Colonel Maddon of the 2nd Stafford, of which the enclosed is an extract, I desired, under

[1] 'Not received till the 18th.'

the pressure therein stated, that Major-General St. John[1] should be informed that a Corps of Staffordshire Volunteers was to be formed, and in order to give authority over them, I recommended a letter of service to be prepared.

I must observe that it was by no means the wish of Lord Granville Leveson-Gower that this Corps should be attached to the 52nd but that, on the contrary, this condition was impressed upon him for the advantage of the service, and for this reason, that the men belonging to that Regiment as a second Battalion might be turned over to the first, whenever it might please his Majesty to reduce the 2nd. but, should they form a different Corps of Staffordshire Volunteers (as was Lord Granville Leveson-Gower's wish) they must be dismissed and totally lost to the service, when reduced, as the power of drafting them into any other regiment is expressly prohibited by the Act of Parliament.

I lament that the urgency of the circumstances I have stated should have rendered it necessary to take any steps until you could hear from his Royal Highness, but I trust his Majesty will be satisfied that if erroneous, they had for motive to promote the success of the late important Act of Parliament, by procuring a body of men which could not otherwise have been formed.

Should it be his Majesty's pleasure, after this statement may have been submitted to him, that this Corps should be established distinct from the 52d. or that it should be dissolved altogether, I shall take measures with Lord Granville Leveson-Gower for executing his commands, but I must observe that, in the latter case, a valuable body of men would, I am afraid, be lost to his Majesty's service. (9375–6)

2069   THE BISHOP OF WORCESTER (RICHARD HURD) *to the* KING

[*Hartlebury, 25 Oct. 1799.*] I received yesterday the Gottingen Prize Dissertations for 1799, wch. your Majesty has had the goodness to send me, together with the honour of your Majesty's gracious letter of the 18th, & beg leave to make my humble acknowledgments for both these favours.

I cannot be enough sensible of your Majesty's condescending to take notice of my health and even to take an interest in it. I wish it wd. enable me to express my duty in any way that might be acceptable to your Majesty & agreable to my station, but I can only applaud the efforts of others among my brethren to oppose the incroaching impiety of the times and to supplicate the divine blessing upon them; and when I consider how much depends on your Majesty's zeal and endeavours to promote so good a cause and how uniformly they have been expressed thro' the whole course of your reign, I cannot but joyn my fellow subjects in the most heart-felt acknowledgments of these great & publick services, & particularly in the ardent prayers & good wishes wch. they are everywhere putting up to heaven for your Majesty's life, health and prosperity on this day. (9378)

[1] Frederick St John (1765–1844), brother of George Richard, 3rd Viscount Bolingbroke. Colonel, 1795; Major-General, 1798; Lieutenant-General, 1805; General, 1814. M.P. for Oxford, 1818–20.

[*Horse Guards, 26 Oct. 1799.*] The enclos'd copy of a letter[1] from Mr. Secretary Dundas which Genl. Sir Willm. Fawcett has the honor to transmit to your Majesty, though dated yesterday, was not deliver'd to him till this morning, having apparently been just brought from Wimbledon. Your Majesty will perceive from its contents that it is meant as a reply to the substance of your Majesty's commands regarding Lord G. L. Gower's propos'd new Battn. convey'd to Sir Willm. in the honor of your Majesty's gracious note of the 22d. inst. Mr. Dundas's receipt of your Majesty's further pleasure on the same subject, dated & receiv'd by Sir Willm. yesterday & dispatch'd to him without delay, has not yet been acknowledg'd, probably by reason of his remaining out of town the whole day. (9384)

[1] Dundas wrote to Sir William from Downing Street at 11 a.m. on the 25th: 'Mr. Huskisson has delivered to me your message on the subject of the Corps proposed to be raised from the volunteers of the Staffordshire Militia, and to be commanded by Lord Granville Leveson-Gower. If it is conceived that all the militia men to be disembodied will be speedily recruited into the regular Regiments of the Army, I am positive, and I have not hitherto been mistaken in any of my ideas on the subject, that this expectation will lead to disappointment. To prevent such disappointment and to accomplish my wish that not a man of them should be lost to the public service is the sole object of every clause in the Bill and of every measure I have suggested. If after disembodying them they do not recruit into the Army there is no means left but to have recourse to their former Officers or others animated by public zeal or a point of honour who from county influence or otherwise may have weight in bringing them into general service. If Corps formed upon this principle are attached as second or third Battalions to established Regiments with temporary rank to the Officers employed in raising them, they bring no ultimate additional expense on the country and it would be in his Majesty's power at any time, without any breach of faith to the privates, to draft them into the regular Regiments to which they might be attached as second or third Battalions. By raising them as separate Corps of Volunteers without being so attached they cannot, consistently with the Act of Parliament, be drafted into any other Corps whatever.

If however his Majesty has been pleased to decide that they are to be so raised without being attached, there cannot be a reason why the Corps under Lord Granville Leveson-Gower should not be called the *Loyal Staffordshire Volunteers*, or any other local name his Majesty pleases to direct, but his Majesty will probably not think it right to allow the word *Fencible* to be added to the designation because that word is generally given to Corps applicable *only* to home defence which I take it for granted is a limitation nobody can wish to countenance, nor would it be consistent with the terms of the Act to place any such Volunteers upon the Fencible establishment, though I am ready to admit (and to claim credit to the Officers for it) the terms for themselves are less advantageous than are allowed to Fencible Regiments which agree to serve beyond the limits of the Kingdom.

I have troubled you with this additional explanation, not from any personal anxiety, for I can have none on the subject, but because I am anxious to have it distinctly understood that if, at the distance of twelve months or any other period, his Majesty is deprived of the means of incorporating ten or fifteen thousand men into his regular Regiments, it may not be imputed to Mr. Pitt or to me that we had not afforded the means of suggesting to his Majesty in what manner that object might have been accomplished.' (9385–6)

Dundas wrote again to Sir William on the 26th: 'I have this morning received your letter of yesterday's date enclosing the communication made to me by his Majesty's orders, and I shall not delay to inform Lord Granville Leveson-Gower that his Majesty disapproves of my proposition contained in my letter to you of the 10th of October.

I shall privately communicate to Lord Granville Leveson-Gower the terms of his Majesty's orders, that he may feel that his Majesty's disapprobation of my proposition does not proceed from any personal disregard to him.

With regard to what his Majesty states respecting a Fencible Regiment to be raised by Lord Granville Leveson-Gower, I certainly know no reason why it would be right to do so, and after the full explanation of my sentiments in my letter of yesterday you will have no difficulty in perceiving it is a measure I cetainly could not recommend. If Lord Granville Leveson-Gower makes any proposition of the kind to me it will of course be my duty to transmit it to his Royal Highness, the Captain General, or to you for his Majesty's information.' (9387)

2071 EARL SPENCER *to the* KING, *and the reply*

[*Admiralty, 26 Oct. 1799.*] Earl Spencer has the honour to convey to your Majesty the accompanying letter from his Royal Highness the Duke of Kent, and is happy to inform your Majesty that his Royal Highness arrived safe at Halifax on the 6th of Sepr. last. (9379)

[*The King's reply, Windsor, 26 Oct.*] I have just received the letters which Earl Spencer has forwarded to me, and I am happy to find my son the Duke of Kent arrived safe at Halifax on the 6th of last month. (Althorp MSS.)

2072 LORD GRENVILLE *to the* KING, *and the reply*

[*Cleveland Row, 27 Oct. 1799.*] Lord Grenville has the honour to submit to your Majesty the Minute taken at the meeting of your Majesty's servants yesterday, and if your Majesty should be graciously pleased to approve it, the messenger might be dispatched to St. Petersburgh on Tuesday night.

In order to obviate the defects which Mr. Wickham and Lieutenant-Colonel Clinton[1] have pointed out in the composition of the Russian army in Swisserland, your Majesty's servants have thought that it might be useful to instruct the former to endeavour to obtain Marshal Suvarrow's co-operation in such representations as it will be necessary to make on that head at St. Petersburgh, and eventually to authorize Major-General Lord Mulgrave[2] to take upon him an active and efficient station on the Staff of that army. (9380–1)

[*Enclosure*]

Cabinet Minute, 26 Oct.[3]

Present: The Duke of Portland, Earl Spencer, Mr. Chancellor of the Exchequer, Mr. Secretary Dundas, Mr. Windham, Lord Grenville.

On consideration of the present state of the Allied Force, and of the prospect and means for pursuing the War with energy in the ensuing campaign, it is humbly represented to his Majesty,

That it may be proper to instruct his Majesty's Minister in Russia to propose to the Emperor the conclusion of a treaty of subsidy for next year, by which the Emperor shall engage to employ under Field Marshall Suvarow, in operations in Swisserland, and from thence in France, a force of not less than eighty or ninety thousand men, in addition to the troops to be furnished by the Elector of Bavaria.[4] And that Sir Charles Whitworth should be authorized to agree to the same terms as have been already given.

[1] Aide-de-Camp to the Duke of York, 1793. Entered the Army, 1787; Captain, 1791; Lieutenant-Colonel, 1795; Assistant Adjutant-General in Eastern District, June 1801; Colonel, 1803; Major-General, 1810; Lieutenant-General, 1814; K.B., 1813; G.C.B., 1815. M.P. for Boroughbridge, 1808–18.

[2] See No. 589 (I, 477). Note 1, line 3 on that page should read 'Master-General'. Mulgrave had been a Major-General since March 1794. He became a Lieutenant-General in 1801, and General in 1809.

[3] In Grenville's hand.

[4] Maximilian Joseph (1756–1825), succeeded Charles Theodore as Elector, 16 Feb. 1799. Created King by Napoleon, 1805.

That it should also be proposed to the Emperor of Russia to treat in concert with his Majesty at Vienna, for the co-operation of the Austrian army in the next campaign. And that his Majesty's readiness should be expressed to concur in such arrangements respecting Italy and the Netherlands as may best facilitate these objects without any infringement of those principles of justice on which his Majesty and the Emperor of Russia are acting—particularly by a just and equitable exchange, if it shall be necessary, of the King of Sardinia's[1] dominions in Piedmont for an adequate compensation in another part of Italy, and by making such a disposition of the Netherlands as may be subservient to this plan. (9382–3)

[*The King's reply, Windsor, 28 Oct., 7.58 a.m.*] The Minute of Cabinet which Lord Grenville has transmitted meets with my thorough approbation, and I desire no time may [be] lost in putting the matter of it in the proper shape for being sent to Russia.

The letter of the 9th from Lieut. Col. Clinton is so masterly that I wish Lord Grenville would avail himself of the substance to instruct Sir Charles Whitworth now that the army in the Grisons is proposed to be so materially augmented of the necessity of forming a commissariat and every other appendage of an independant army without loss of time as the steps necessary for forming magazines and procuring constantly supplies for the army are essential articles for restoring discipline in the troops, as well as being ready to advance with any degree of hopes of success in the Spring. (Fortescue MSS.)

2073 HENRY DUNDAS *to the* KING, *and the reply*

[*Wimbledon, 27 Oct. 1799, 11 p.m.*] Mr Dundas in transmitting the accompanying papers to your Majesty takes the liberty of humbly suggesting to your Majesty that if the draft of the dispatch proposed to be sent in approbation of the Armistice meets with your Majesty's concurrence, your Majesty will be pleased to signify that approbation on the back of the draft, which is the one intended to remain in the Office. (9388)

[*The King's reply, Windsor, 28 Oct., 8.36 a.m.*] In consequence of Mr. Secretary Dundas's note, I have on the back of the draft of his public dispatch to the D. of York put my approbation to the measure he has in my opinion most laudably addopted for the security of my troops now I trust embarking in Holland. (Add. MSS. 40100, f. 239.)

2074 *Letters from* GENERAL SIR WILLIAM FAWCETT *to the* KING

[*Horse Guards, 28 Oct. 1799.*] General Sir Willm. Fawcett has the honor to transmit herewith to your Majesty copy of a letter receiv'd yesterday evening from Mr. Secretary Dundas in reply to the communication which had been made to him of your Majesty's last commands on the subject of the propos'd new 2nd Battn. of the Staffordshire Volunteers, dated the 25th inst.

[1] Charles Emmanuel (1751–1819) succeeded his father Victor Amadeus as King on 16 Oct. 1796.

The usual daily return of Militia Volunteers and a general return of the Forces under the command of his Royal Highness, the Captn. General, are also enclos'd herewith for your Majesty's information. (9389)

[*Horse Guards, 1 Nov. 1799.*] General Sir Willm. Fawcett has the honor to enclose herewith for your Majesty's information copy of a letter written by the Adjutant-General[1] to Majr.-Genl. St. John, by the express direction of Mr. Pitt who also desir'd Sir Willm. to forward the same to your Majesty, and to acquaint your Majesty that he should do himself the honor of explaining the necessity of this proceeding by a letter to your Majesty from himself in the course of this evening.

Genl. Sir Wm. Fawcett was honor'd with your Majesty's most gracious note of this day's date & most humbly presumes to send herewith to your Majesty a memorandum of the arrivals of troops from Holland according to the latest reports receiv'd at this Office, together with the daily return of militia volunteers. (9396)

2075   THE DUCHESS OF WURTEMBERG *to the* KING

[*Stutgard, 1 Nov. 1799.*] Since I had last the honour of writing to your Majesty things continued pretty much in the same situation till yesterday when the French advanced to Knitlingen. At their approach the Austrians fled, and it is impossible to repeat the horrors which they committed during the short time they remained masters of the town, which this morning the Austrians had again taken possession of. The Duke has lost a great deal there as the French have plundered the place and carried of[f] everything belonging to him. What we have the most to dread is there making an inroad from Heilbron, as I believe this morning there were no troops on that side. I have been all day in hourly expectation of being obliged to fly, but as it is five o'clock and nothing new I hope they may be afraid and not advance towards here, as they know that there is infantry here who would prevent their doing all the mischief they intend. Louisbourg I always have apprehensions about, as the Duke's affection for it is known, and the prisoners who I saw go by after the taking of Manheim threatned very much to destroy it if they ever got into the Dutchy again.

I shall not fail to acquaint your Majesty with every change that takes place, and beg that you will be quite easy about me as at the least appearance of danger the Duke will send me off. (51568–9)

---

[1] Sir Harry Calvert (?1763–1826), Adjutant-General of the Forces, 1799–1818; Colonel, 1797; Major-General, 1803; G.C.B., 1815; G.C.H., 1817; created Baronet, 1818; General, 1821.

Calvert's letter is dated 1 November: 'I have General Sir William Fawcett's commands to inform you that some circumstances have occurred which induce him to desire you will suspend the further execution of the orders contained in my letter of the 30th of last month relative to the Second Battalion of Stafford Militia, and that in the meantime the Volunteers for the Regular Service from the three Battalions of Stafford Militia assembled at Winchester are to consider themselves under the command of those Officers who have voluntered to serve with Lord Granville Levison-Gower in the same manner and on the same footing as if such Orders had not been transmitted.' (9397)

[*Hartlebury, 1 Nov. 1799.*] I am extremely honoured by your Majesty's gracious letter of the 29th from Windsor, & for the small packet inclosing it, wch contains the *Prorector's Oration* on the Prize Essays of Gottingen, & *Dr Majendie's*[1] *Prayer.*[2] I beg leave to return my humble thanks to your Majesty for both these fresh instances of your condescending goodness to me.

The *Prorector's* Oration, wch I have hastily run over, seems well calculated to serve the true interests of learning & of your Majesty's University, & is a seasonable admonition to the learned of all places.

Dr Majendie's Prayer, being shorter, I have read with more care and think the title of *excellent*, wch your Majesty is pleased to give it, is most justly deserved. I hope these efforts of your clergy, which appear to have been general, will contribute to revive in that [*sic*] all sense of their religious & civil duties, wch it so much concerns them to have, and which your Majesty uses every means of recommending to them by your own example, & by the zeal you have ever expressed for the admirable Constitution it hath pleased God to bestow upon us both in Church & State. Your subjects, Sir, have only to pray to God that He will continue to bless your endeavours for the public good, & to make themselves truly sensible of the deep obligations they have to their Sovereign & of the duty they owe him. (9391)

2077 EARL SPENCER *to the* KING

[*Admiralty, 1 Nov. 1799.*] Earl Spencer has the honour to acquaint your Majesty that all the arrangements which are required at present both for the operations on the coast of Holland in embarking the troops[3] and for the present disposition of the Channel Fleet to the westward are completed; and as there does not appear any great probability of his attendance being much required in town, he humbly solicits your Majesty's permission to go into the country for a week or ten days; and should he obtain it, he proposes to set off tomorrow evening.[4] (9398)

[1] See No. 1617.

[2] Folios 9392–5 (printed by Charles Knight, of Windsor).

[3] This was the best executed part of the whole operation (like the withdrawal of the Army from Gallipoli in 1916). Some of the Russian troops were landed at Yarmouth in a pitiable condition. 'I... do not at all wonder at their having been beaten,' wrote Charles Grey from Yarmouth. 'My father cannot at all get over his astonishment at their appearance. They really are not human, and their filth is shocking to the greatest degree. Those that are landed to be carried to the Hospital are immediately washed from head to foot in a warm sea bath, their heads are shaved, and new clothes are given to them to prevent contagion. Such parts of their own clothes as can be rendered wholesome and useful by washing, are reserved for them, and the rest are burnt... The convicts in the galleys in France or in the hulks in England come the nearest to them in general resemblance and dress. Most of them are in rags, squalid and disgusting to the sight, or wrapped up in a large loose white greatcoat of a texture something between a blanket and cloth, which is tied by a string or dirty pocket handkerchief round the waist.' (Howick MSS.)

[4] The King's reply, approving the proposal, dated 2 Nov., is in *Spencer Papers*, III, 207.

The failure of the Helder expedition made Dundas anxious to be relieved of the responsibility of the War Department, and also to see Lord Spencer removed from the Admiralty. He wrote to Pitt on 4 November: 'I am really sorry my proposition strikes you in the light it does. I pondered well on every argument that I think can have occurred to you, but I satisfied myself thoroughly by a perfect conviction

[*Windsor, 2 Nov. 1799.*] When H.R. Highness the Duke of Kent was last in England he expressed both your Majesty's and his own sentiments towards me in a manner which H.R. Highness must have felt would be highly gratifying to me. The gracious reception, indeed, which I have uniformly experienced has long since induced me to cherish the hope that your Majesty was not wholly dissatisfied either with my past services or my present conduct.

Among various other marks of attention H.R. Highness then offer'd to make any application to your Majesty's Ministers on my behalf which I should think proper. If I had thought myself justified in accepting such an offer I should have told H.R. Highness that according to the common course of human events the Treasurership of the Ordnance would very soon become vacant; that in the present state of my family and circumstances the acquisition of it would be a considerable object to me, and that if H.R. Highness thought me worthy of the situation an application on that subject would entitle him to a due return of my grateful acknowledgments.

But if I had accepted any such mediation your Majesty well knows that I should have violated one of the most express conditions under which I originally entered into your Royal service, and that in every such case it was the line of my duty to make a direct application to your Majesty.

In having presumed to mention the above circumstances I repose myself on your Majesty's accustomed benevolence in the fullest assurance that after a period of twenty years the wish of a servant to receive some special mark of Royal

that every circumstance which occurred relative to your brother leaving the Admiralty would now ensure perfect activity and exertion in another arduous situation he might be called to. His talents for it are unquestionable and if I am right in my belief that no symptoms of it would now appear, I say it without affectation of disparaging myself, that he is under all circumstances better calculated for it than the person who now holds it. I need not however dwell upon the subject at present because I am free to confess to you that on receiving last night from Huskisson the deplorable state of our affairs on the Continent, I had determined when we met to state to you upon consideration *merely personal to myself* the necessity of having all thoughts of any arrangement which removed me from responsibility till Easter or perhaps the end of the Session.' (Chatham Papers, 157.)

Pitt refused to entertain the idea, replying, the same day: 'I need not say how far your wishes and opinions will always go in deciding mine, in any case that admits of it, but on the present occasion I should be wanting to the strongest obligations both of public duty and of personal friendship and affection if I did not say explicitly that it is impossible for any consideration to reconcile my mind to the measure you propose, either with a view to the public service at this difficult period, or to what is due to your own reputation, character and peace of mind. Whatever might in another moment be the comfort to you in being released from duties necessarily laborious and anxious and by recent circumstances rendered still more irksome and unpleasant, I am sure no consideration will induce you to decline going thro' with the task you have undertaken, without a motive of real necessity and a sufficient justification to the world and I must say that neither one nor the other seem to exist in the present case. I state this opinion on general grounds, because there is *no* mode of your quitting your situation under the present circumstances which would not in my opinion be injurious to your own credit, and produce irreparable public mischief. But in addition to this, the arrangement which you propose as a substitute, is in the very first article of it, liable to such insuperable objections, that the idea of it instead of furnishing an argument in favor of the measure would strengthen tenfold all the other arguments against it. You will believe I do not say this lightly, or without regret as to the grounds on which my opinion is founded, but you must I am sure upon reflection feel that they are just. Let me therefore entreat you for all our sakes, to abandon wholly this idea, and to reconcile yourself to a duty which, however difficult and painful, you are really at this moment not at liberty to relinquish.' (Ann Arbor MSS.)

[1] He had been one of Prince Edward's Preceptors.

approbation, originating with your Majesty, will be thought neither presumptuous nor obtrusive. (9399–400)

2079   WILLIAM PITT *to the* KING, *and the reply*

[*Downing Street, 2 Nov. 1799.*] Mr Pitt humbly hopes that your Majesty will not disapprove his having ventured to request Sir William Fawcett to delay executing the order respecting the Volunteers who had enlisted to serve under Lord Gran-ville-Leveson, that time might be given for bringing under your Majesty's con-sideration the circumstances which have occurred, and which seemed likely to be productive of unpleasant consequences which could not be intended to the individual concerned, as well as to impede materially the obtaining the full number of recruits for your Majesty's service. Either Mr Dundas or Mr Pitt will beg your Majesty's permission to lay the particulars before you when they have the honor of attending your Majesty on Wednesday. (9401)

[*The King's reply, Windsor, 4 Nov.*] Sir Wm. Fawcett communicated to me by letter his having directed the Adjutant Genl. to suspend the order for transferring the men from the Staffordshire Militia; I approved of the delay though I am thoroughly convinced of the propriety of my conduct and I must say in confidence to Mr Pitt of the great impropriety at least of that of Mr. Dundas from the begin-ning of the business.[1] I shall certainly, as I feel I am right, not object to hearing what Mr. Pitt may have to say on the subject when I see him on Wednesday, and as I am certain he is not fully apprised of the unaccountable steps that have been taken I will have the papers laid before him after that conversation, as I am certain, however he may feel for others, he would be much more mortified at my acting a part unbecoming of myself and open to real blame.[2] (9402)

[1] Lord Granville Leveson-Gower's letter to Pitt on 13 Nov. closes this correspondence, which had offended both the King and Dundas: 'As Mr. Dundas was naturally enough, unwilling to trouble himself further upon the subject of my annihilated regiment after the opposition its establishment had received from His Majesty, & as he threw upon your shoulders the discussion with the King upon it, you will I hope excuse my writing to you—it is not to plague you with my own regrets, which have not been a little encreased since my arrival here, by the disappointment the men have expressed at the command being taken from me, even though my removal has given them their free discharge, but it is to represent to you the hardship which the officers of the Staffordshire Militia sustain by the disbanding the Staffd. Volunteers—they are now deprived of an advantage which the last Act of Parliament has bestowed upon every other Militia Officer in the kingdom—I see no remedy to this grievance, but Govt. allowing them a bounty to induce the Stafford Volunteers to enlist into some regt. of the line, not one of the men will of course serve without a bounty.

I have written to Calvert desiring him to represent to the D. of York these circumstances, but if you wd. have the goodness to mention to his Royal Highness that you think these officers have some claim to his consideration something will of course be done—I cannot but feel anxious upon the subject, because they of course will look upon me as the cause of their being deprived of the benefit they wd. naturally have possessed, & because from their zeal & spirit they really are deserving of attention.' (Chatham Papers, 152.)

[2] According to the Ann Arbor typescript Pitt wrote again to the King on 4 Nov. 1799. The correct date is 4 Nov. 1787, and the letter is printed in vol. I, p. 350. Only a small quantity of this typescript has been seen, consequently the magnitude of the errors cannot be estimated.

[*Cleveland Row, 7 Nov. 1799, 11 p.m.*] Lord Grenville has the honour humbly to submit to your Majesty the Minute of Cabinet of this day. He hopes that if your Majesty should be pleased to approve of the suggestions there stated, the circumstances at Vienna stated in Lord Minto's[1] dispatches since received will considerably facilitate their execution, except in what relates to Lord Mulgrave, who appears by a private letter of Lord Minto's to be already on his way home[2]. (9403)

[*Enclosure*]

Cabinet Minute, Downing Street, 7 Nov.

Present: The Lord Chancellor, Lord President, Duke of Portland, Earl Camden, Earl of Liverpool, Mr. Chancellor of the Exchequer, Mr. Secretary Dundas, Mr. Windham, Lord Grenville.

Upon consideration of the last dispatches from Vienna and Swisserland, it is agreed humbly to submit to his Majesty that it may be proper so far to vary the last instructions as to authorize Lord Minto and Lord Mulgrave to represent to the Austrian Government that his Majesty is desirous of receiving a communication of the opinion of the Court of Vienna respecting the manner in which the combined efforts of the Allies may be employed in the next campaign most to the advantage of the common cause. And that if those ideas, being so communicated, should concur with those entertained by his Majesty, and already explained to his Majesty's Minister at Vienna, or should appear in general to be likely to promote the objects which his Majesty has in view, Lord Mulgrave should be instructed to proceed to Marshall Suvarrow's Headquarters and to endeavour to obtain his acquiescence in them, in order that they may then be jointly recommended to the Court of Petersburgh: it being always understood that the joining to the Russian army a large body of Austrian force, and the adoption of all the necessary measures for the supply of the army so formed, are indispensable conditions of his Majesty's concurrence in these plans, and that if these conditions are refused his Majesty is determined to recommend it to the Emperor of Russia to withdraw his troops entirely from all co-operation with those of Austria, and will himself withhold all further pecuniary aid for any such purpose.

But that if these conditions are complied with, and a proper plan in other respects duly arranged between the Allies in consequence of this overture, his Majesty would in that case agree to make pecuniary exertions for the reinforcement of the Russian army to the extent, and in the manner stated in the last instructions. (9404–6)

[*The King's reply. Queen's House, 10 Nov. 1799, 8.52 a.m.*] The Minute of Cabinet which I have received this morning in Lord Grenville's box accompanied with his note meets with my thorough approbation; the dispatches from Lord

---

[1] Minto had been sent to Vienna in July, along with William Wickham, to treat with the Emperor and some of the States of the Empire. He arrived on 1 Aug. 1799, presented his recalls on 16 Sept. 1801 and left Vienna soon afterwards.   [2] Mulgrave arrived in London from the Continent on 18 Nov.

Minto arrived yesterday certainly facilitate the execution of the measures proposed, if any confidence can be placed in the present appearance of the Court of Vienna. I am sorry to find Lord Mulgrave will return previous to his receiving the instructions, which I am certain he would have ably executed, but it is very fortunate that Mr. Wickham is fully capable of holding such conference with General Suvarow as this change will render necessary. (Fortescue MSS.)

2081 THE DUKE OF GLOUCESTER *to the* KING

[*15 Nov. 1799.*] I received last night a letter from the Duke of York to acquaint me your Majesty had graciously complied with my request and had given my son the rank of Lt. General. I feel it as an additional mark of your goodness to me, and my son is most sincerely grateful for your continual protection and graciousness to him. (54418)

2082 *Letters from* LORD GRENVILLE *to the* KING, *and the replies*

[*Dropmore, 19 Nov. 1799, 11 p.m.*] In transmitting to your Majesty the inclosed dispatches from Sir Charles Whitworth, Lord Grenville begs leave humbly to mention to your Majesty that Mr Pitt being here Lord Grenville has talked over the subject with him. They are persuaded that your Majesty will think that, notwithstanding this discouraging circumstance, every effort ought still to be made for carrying into execution the plans which were before in contemplation. With this view Lord Grenville would propose to dispatch Sr. Home Popham immediately to Petersburgh charged with such representations on your Majesty's part as may best tend to produce the desired effect.[1] And in order to save time Mr Pitt and Lord Grenville humbly request your Majesty's permission to remain here tomorrow, unless your Majesty should have any orders to give them at St James's. (9407–8)

[*The King's reply, Windsor, 20 Nov., 8.30 a.m.*] I thoroughly approve of Lord Grenville and Mr. Pitt remaining this day at Dropmore to forward the preparing the dispatches to be carried to Petersburgh by Captain Popham, as they are both entirely master of my sentiments on the present arduous occasion and of my thorough resolution to exert every nerf to carry on the war with effect, and if that cannot be effected from the shameless conduct of one Court and I now fear timidity of the other, then to keep our exertions within such bounds that we may

---

[1] Popham had already been sent to Russia, in July, to arrange for the embarkation of the Russian forces destined to co-operate with the Duke of York's Army in Holland, and the Tsar had presented him with a gold snuff box set with diamonds and constituted him a Knight of Malta. Popham wished to be sent back in November 'for the purpose of stating fully to the Emperor many important particulars of which he has been an eye-witness, and also of explaining confidentially the ideas entertained here on the late extraordinary events, and on the whole of the present situation of affairs' (*Dropmore Papers*, VI, 36). Pitt wrote to Dundas on 12 Nov.: 'I shall be very glad to do anything that on consideration seems reasonable for Sir Home Popham, but have not at present the smallest notion what is the sort of provision he looks to. His services may I think be invaluable, and his conversation is on the whole very encouraging.'

continue the war for many years and thus by time overcome the enemy, as the want of concert of others may prevent the more active line better suited to my inclination.

On the present violence of the Emperor of Russia towards that of the Romans,[1] for which there certainly is just ground, though I applaud the heart that dictates it, I cannot admire the judgement that has not repressed it. Little as I expect any real nobleness of mind or sound policy in the Court of Berlin, I could almost wish as a last attempt that Mr. Grenville could be persuaded to return to Berlin, his perfect knowledge of the great question, and he alone from his personal habits being able to correspond with Count Panin[2] might perhaps if the Court of Vienna should break off which I think most likely, raise that jealousy of Austria at Berlin that might bring to a considerable degree the King of Prussia into such a concert with this country and Russia as might greatly mend our prospect of success through the north of Germany to Holland and the Low Countries, and perhaps even to France itself; but then it must be by three concerting armies, not one combined, which from natural jealousies is ever liable to the greatest inconveniences, and by thus forcing the enemy to divide their force would make operations of attack more easy.

The recent Revolution at Paris[3] shews how very unstable the Republic was, and the present violent change cannot possibly hold long, but every revolution there is advantageous to the opinions of those who wish the restoration of Royalty.

P.S. I thought it best to return to Dropmore the Russian letters as they might be useful when preparing the drafts. (Fortescue MSS.)

[*From Lord Grenville, Dropmore, 23 Nov.*] Lord Grenville has the honour humbly to submit for your Majesty's consideration the draft of two dispatches to Sir Charles Whitworth, formed on such ideas as occurred to Mr Pitt and himself to be most practicable and adviseable under the circumstances stated in the last dispatches from the continent. He hopes that your Majesty will find the idea of renewing the intercourse between the Courts of Petersburgh and Berlin stated in such a manner as to meet the idea which your Majesty did Lord Grenville the honour of expressing to him. He is persuaded that Mr Grenville would not hesitate to obey any commands respecting the execution of which your Majesty might think that he could be useful, but he begs leave humbly to submit to your Majesty whether Mr Grenville's return to Berlin in the present moment might not give so much countenance to the reports of negotiations for peace as materially to injure your Majesty's service.

Lord Grenville thinks it his duty humbly to submit to your Majesty the inclosed copy of a letter which he has received from Sir John Hippisley. He has conversed with Mr Pitt on the subject of it, and Mr Pitt has authorized him to submit to your Majesty that if your Majesty's magnanimity and generosity should incline your

[1] The Emperor Francis II.

[2] The Russian Envoy to Berlin until August or thereabouts, when he was transferred to Vienna.

[3] On 9 Nov. Bonaparte, who had contrived to escape from Egypt, overthrew the discredited Directory and established the Consulate, with Sieyès and Ducos as his colleagues.

Majesty to extend your Majesty's goodness to the last remaining individual of a family once so distinguished in station, he thinks he could point out to your Majesty the means of doing it without inconvenience.[1] (9409–10)

[*The King's reply, Windsor, 24 Nov., 8.43 a.m.*] Lord Grenville's two able despatches to Petersburgh fully contain my sentiments on the present very embarrassed scene, not less occasioned by the profligacy of the political conduct of the Court of Vienna than by the violence of temper of the Emperor of Russia, and the timid nonentity of the Court of Berlin; but our contest with an impious enemy is too serious not to attempt if possible to keep those three Courts together and if possible bring them on this shameless revolution at Paris to act in concert, and then we may render that event advantageous by a vigorous campain to the restoration of a Government which may render the idea of peace less fatal than it would be at the present hour.

As much as I am anxious that if the Courts of Petersburgh and Berlin can be brought to act with more cordiality Mr. Grenville should return to the latter capital, I see very forcibly the objection of his going there at the present hour as it might give rise to there being an intention to receive overtures of peace, which of all evil steps I most cautiously would avoid; but as his future journey may become necessary for opposite views, those of forming fresh alliances for a vigorous campain, I should think it best that Mr. Arthur Paget should not be permitted for the present to go to his post, as it might in future embarass this transaction and would bear the same colour with regard to overtures of peace.

I have read Sir John Hippisley's communication; I trust Lord Grenville is too

---

[1] Pitt wrote to Dundas on 12 Nov.: 'The picture given of the Cardinal York's character and situation makes me very desirous of finding some means for his relief, but it is a point of some delicacy, especially from what passed, if I recollect right, on a former occasion.'

The King approved the draft of the following secret letter from Lord Grenville to Lord Minto on the 27th:

'My Lord,

A communication having been made to me from the Cardinal Borgia through the channel of Sir John Cox Hippisley, stating the distress and difficult situation to which His Eminence the Cardinal of York has found himself reduced, in consequence of the various exactions of the French, and the plunder and devastation committed upon his property, at the same time that the various sources of his annual revenue in France, Spain, and Italy, have been either entirely or in great part cut off, I have thought it my duty to submit the circumstances of the case to his Majesty's consideration; and I have it in command from his Majesty to direct you to find some proper channel for conveying to the Cardinal, the sum of two thousand pounds, as a present from his Majesty; with an intimation that a similar sum will be sent in the month of July next, if the situation of the Cardinal should be such as to require it.'

'Windsor. Nov. 27. 1799.

P.S. Your Lordship will draw for this sum upon Mr. Frere, sending at the same time a receipt for it as for Secret Service money, according to the article of your Instructions which relates to the form of accounting for Secret Service money. And you will do the same in June next.

His Majesty having been graciously pleased, on account of the particular circumstances attending this case, to grant to your Lordship his Majesty's warrant under his Royal Sign Manual, as a special authority to your Lordship for executing the directions contained in this despatch, I have the honour to enclose it to your Lordship, and to desire that your Lordship will be pleased to acknowledge the receipt of it.' (Fortescue MSS.)

(*Copy*)

'The delicacy of the subject of this letter seems to require a signed approval of this draft—I therefore sign this draft. George R.'

much acquainted with my sentiments to be surprised at my eagerly opening the door to any mode he may have of assisting the person alluded to that can be done without inconvenience. I cannot forget from whence that unfortunate man sprung, and have ever thought that grounding his origin on deception might answer a political intrigue, but never was putting the invitation of my family to mount the Throne on its true solid basis, namely, that it came to preserve the free Constitution of this Empire, both in Church and State, which compact I trust none of my successors will ever dare to depart from. (Fortescue MSS.)

[*From Lord Grenville, Dropmore, 25 Nov.*] Lord Grenville has the honour to transmit to your Majesty a letter from the Emperor of Russia to your Majesty which Count Woronzow received by this last courier, but which he omitted to deliver to Lord Grenville when he saw him at Dropmore last Friday, and did not send to the Office until the following day.

Lord Grenville also submits to your Majesty the draft of an answer to it. (Fortescue MSS.)

[*The King's reply, Windsor, 26 Nov., 7.05 a.m.*] The letter which the Emperor of Russia has written to the Emperor of the Romans, of which he has communicated to me a copy, so entirely shuts the door to any possible union between them, that I rather incline to wish that Lord Grenville would add to the draft of my answer some encouragement to the Emperor of Russia's attempting to awaken the King of Prussia, which his letter to me seems to indicate, and if he could be brought to sacrifice his just complaints against the Court of Vienna for the good of the great cause in which we are all engaged it would be highly desirable. (*Ibid.*)

[*From Lord Grenville, Dropmore, 26 Nov.*] In humble obedience to your Majesty's commands Lord Grenville has made such an addition to the draft of your Majesty's letter to the Emperor of Russia as he trusts will meet your Majesty's intentions. He takes the liberty to mention to your Majesty that the Emperor's letter appears to be written in his own hand-writing. (9413)

[*From Lord Grenville, Cleveland Row, 28 Nov.*] Lord Grenville begs leave humbly to submit to your Majesty two warrants which he has prepared for your Majesty's sign manual on the subject of the draft to Lord Minto which your Majesty had the goodness to approve. If your Majesty should see no objection to these he thinks they may make the transaction more strictly regular, though he has in truth no apprehension that any man will ever be found to impute to him as blame the honour of having received and executed your Majesty's commands, for this act of generosity and humanity.[1] (9414-15)

---

[1] The following is one of these warrants:

'GEORGE R.

WHEREAS WE are graciously pleased to extend Our Royal Bounty for the Relief and support of the Person commonly called the Cardinal of York, now in old age, and deprived of all Revenues and Means of Subsistence: We do therefore hereby authorise and command you, and Our Royal Will and Pleasure is, that you do take the necessary steps for remitting from time to time to the said Person, through the

2083   DAVID DUNDAS[1] to [   ]

[*Richmond, 29 Nov. 1799.*] I beg you will respectfully inform his Majesty that Lord Willoughby underwent the operation for the hydrocele last Monday sennt., that he has hitherto gone on uncommonly well, has had no fever & has been out of his room these last four days. (9416)

2084   *Letters from* MRS HOWE *to the* KING

[*Grafton Street, 30 Nov. 1799.*] Mrs. Howe has just received your Majesty's gracious commands & will hasten to execute them as far as is in her power. (9417)

[*Nov. 1799.*][2] When Mrs. Howe communicated to Lord Gower yesterday the hints she had received from your Majesty, she learnt that having thought it his duty, from the opinion he had formed of the spirit of the Act of Parliament, to offer to name to the supernumer[ar]y Lieutenant Colonelcy the two Colonels and the two Lieutt. Colonels of the disbanded Battalions, he had already proposed it to Lord Granville Leveson-Gower, and he having declined it, to Colonel Elliot, from him he has received as yet no answer. The Lieutt. Colls. know not of his intentions with respect to them. He also read her a letter he had received from Major Disbrowe[3] in answer to his last to him; a copy of these she encloses to your Majesty.

Lord Gower has been this morning with Mrs. Howe and informed her that from the consideration of what has passed (as she has had the honor to relate above) he has thought the certain way to further your Majesty's wishes with respect to this business would be to continue no longer in the situation of Lord Lieutenant of the county of Stafford, and has accordingly sent his resignation through the proper channel.

Channel of Our Envoy Extraordinary and Minister Plenipotentiary at the Court of Vienna, a sum or sums of money, not exceeding in the whole, in any one Year, the Sum of Four Thousand Pounds. The said Sum being to be applied for and received by you from Our Exchequer under the Head of Foreign Secret Service, in the usual Form of Monies so applied for and received by Our Principal Secretaries of State; and the same being to be accounted for by you as Secret Service Money in the manner prescribed by the Act of the Twenty Second Year of Our Reign entitled "an Act for enabling His Majesty to discharge the Debt contracted upon His Civil List Revenues, and for preventing the same from being in arrear for the future, by regulating the mode of Payments out of the said Revenues, and by suppressing or regulating certain Offices therein mentioned, which are now paid out of the Revenues of the Civil List."

And for so doing this shall be Your sufficient Warrant.—Given at Windsor this Twenty Eighth Day of November in the Fortieth Year of Our Reign, and in the Year of Our Lord, One Thousand Seven Hundred and Ninety nine.   G. R.'

To Our Right Trusty and
Well-beloved   Councillor
William Wyndham Baron
Grenville of Wotton, Our
Principal Secretary of State
for Foreign Affairs.
    (Fortescue MSS.)

---

[1] One of the King's surgeons.   [2] Endorsement.

[3] Edward Disbrowe (*c.* 1754–1818) who, in Feb. 1801 succeeded William Price as the Queen's Vice-Chamberlain. M.P. for Windsor, 1806–18. He died a few days after her. E. J. Littleton, M.P., wrote: 'He had been a rank democrat in his youth, but was won over by the King's attention to him. He was Lieutenant-Colonel in the King's Own Staffordshire Militia, and a most humorous, agreeable and gentlemanlike person'. (Hatherton MSS., Diary, Dec. 1818.)

Mrs. Howe takes the liberty to add that from the two conversations she has had with Lord Gower she is very much of opinion that he is not sorry to be released from a situation which must render him liable to frequent embarrassment. (9418–19)

[*Grafton Street, 2 Dec. 1799.*] Mrs. Howe has just received the enclosed from Lord Gower: she hopes your Majesty will not think she takes too great a liberty in sending the whole note instead of an extract from it. (9420)

[*Enclosure*]

[*Earl Gower to Mrs Howe, Monday morning* [*2 Dec.*]] I have just received a letter from Colonel Eliot by which I find that he accepts my nomination of him to the supernumerary Lieutenant Colonelcy; at the same time he confesses that he has some strong objections to it. The truth is that he is a gentleman of small fortune and burdened with a large family, and I am confident that if he could be otherwise provided for he would with pleasure decline it.

Would it not be proper that his Majesty should be informed of the circumstance of his acceptance? (9421)

2085   LORD AUCKLAND *to the* KING

[*Eden Farm, 2 Dec.* [*1799*].] Lord Auckland is most grateful to your Majesty on many accounts but on none more than when credit is given to him for a most earnest disposition to promote your Majesty's gracious wishes and to execute your commands. In the present instance that disposition has been exerted necessarily without effect.

Lord Auckland did not lose a moment in communicating with Lord Gower whose sentiments (he was sorry to learn) had a few hours before been submitted thro' Mrs. Howe to your Majesty, and the result had been the resignation of the Lieutenancy 'as the best means of promoting your Majesty's wishes'.

Lord Auckland has preserv'd the strictest secrecy on this occasion, upon the principle that if his intervention could not do good it should not at least occasion any possible misconception. The intimation was stated *most confidentially* to Lord Gower and was receiv'd by him as originating in a kind motive on the one hand to prevent some very unpleasant consequences if the proposed appointment had taken place, and in a most condescending delicacy on the part of your Majesty on the other hand to learn how far he might feel himself committed. In this latter case Lord Auckland had hoped that it might still have been discuss'd and consider'd whether, tho' Lord Gower might have precluded himself from any present nomination of Major Desbrowe to the new Lieutt. Colonelcy, still he might not under a fair construction of the Act & by postponing, or modelling, or qualifying the report on the new formation of the Battalions, have avoided the necessity of making any appointment whatever. (9423–4)

2086 EARL SPENCER *to the* KING, *and the reply*

[*Admiralty, 2 Dec. 1799.*] Earl Spencer has the honour of laying before your Majesty the proceedings and sentence of a court martial held at the Nore on a seaman belonging to the Pylades for endeavouring to excite the prisoners on board that sloop to rise and take possession of her for the enemy; and as the facts alledged appear to be very clearly proved, and the crime is one of a very dangerous tendency, Earl Spencer humbly submits to your Majesty the propriety of ordering the law to take its course. (9422)

[*The King's reply, Windsor, 3 Dec.*] There cannot be a more attrocious offence than the case of the prisoner now brought before me, namely, his exciting the Dutch prisoners on board of the Pylades to rise and take possession of that sloop for the enemy. As the fact is clearly proved there cannot be a doubt of the propriety of ordering the law to take its course. I therefore desire Earl Spencer will give the necessary orders for that purpose. (Althorp MSS.)

2087 HENRY DUNDAS *to the* KING, *and the reply*

[*Wimbledon, 8 Dec. 1799.*] Mr Dundas humbly requests your Majesty's permission to be absent from London a few weeks, wishing at present to spend a short time with that part of his family now in Scotland.

Mr Dundas begs leave to take this opportunity of humbly submitting to your Majesty's goodness his desire to be relieved from the situation he holds in the War Department. His sentiments on that subject remain the same as they were when, in obedience to your Majesty's special commands, he reluctantly remained in the exercise of a part of the duties usually performed by the Secretary of State for the Home Department. He has repeatedly stated those sentiments to Mr Pitt, and has recently urged him to some arrangement of your Majesty's business, which might confine Mr Dundas solely to the functions of the Indian Department. He has not hitherto been successfull in satisfying Mr Pitt upon that subject, and can therefore at present only state his humble hopes that your Majesty's goodness will, when convenient, condescend to take his earnest wishes under your Majesty's gracious consideration. Mr Dundas does not presume to press his own convenience or comfort in any manner which may on due reflexion be judged by others incompatible with the publick service; but a Commander-in-Chief being now established at the head of the army with authority and confidence adequate to the situation, all the important foreign possessions of your Majesty's enemies being now subdued, your Majesty's own distant and colonial possessions being now in a state of safety and tranquillity, the internal defence of the kingdom being amply provided for, and a large and efficient army being collected adequate to every exigency, there seems to remain very little use, if there ever was any before, for the continuance of a separate War Department in addition to the ordinary channels through which that part of the publick service has formerly been conducted. (9425–8)

[*The King's reply, Windsor, 9 Dec., 8.47 a.m.*] I have this morning received Mr. Secretary Dundas's letter. As his private affairs require his going to Scotland for a few weeks I cannot in the smallest degree object to it. As to his desire of relinquishing the War Department and only keeping that of the East Indies, he cannot be surprised that I cannot enter on that subject unless Mr. Secretary Dundas has obtained the full acquiescence of Mr. Pitt to such an idea, which I do not at present expect.[1] (Add. MSS. 40100, f. 243, and 9429.)

2088   THE DUCHESS OF WURTEMBERG *to the* KING

[*Stutgard, 10 Dec. 1799.*] Though I fear your Majesty will think me very little to be depended on after the different peices of false news which I have written, I think it my duty to acquaint you that the Archduke has refused accepting of the Armistice offered by the enemy. Manheim being now in the hands of the Austrians and the French not appearing to have any intention of advancing at present gives us hopes of a quiet Winter. God grant it that we may be able to recruit our spirits against the opening of the campaign in Spring. Indeed, could your Majesty form any idea of the constant anxiety we have undergone you would think a little quiet as necessary for our minds as for the health of the troops who have been harassed by their frequent marches and counter marches.

Sir, I hope your Majesty will allow me to present you from Stuhmsteg, the Duke's Chapel Master, his new Opera of Die Geister Insel which is dedicated to

---

[1] Dundas's views are given at length in a letter to Pitt, dated merely Wimbledon, Sunday morning: 'I entreat you not to lay aside the enclosed memorandum, but to give it the most serious consideration. Depend upon it the general sentiment of the publick, and the opinions of your most intimate and best friends will concur under the present circumstances of the country in reprobating the idea of Lord Chatham's going at present upon any foreign service, and the King will be under the necessity of interfering to prevent it. It may not always be so, and it would be cruel on Lord Chatham to oblige him totally to abandon a line of life which is congenial to his own wishes, and which there is no reason why he should abandon, although for substantial reasons he may be bound for a while to suspend the functions of it. By doing the duties of the situation which I have suggested he in truth connects himself more closely with military ideas and habits than in any other situation. His income will be adequate to the expences of his situation while the war continues, and as in the meantime he will be going forward in the profession of the Army, it is more probable than otherwise that before that time (Peace), his military emoluments will be superior to any he enjoys as President of the Council. You are certain that the arrangement will be highly acceptable to the King, and as he will have constant opportunities of private intercourse with his Majesty, many things disagreeable in the conduct of business will be prevented or immediately remedied. I know with certainty that the Duke of York and Lord Chatham will go on together with perfect cordiality and great efficiency in their respective departments, rendered to both of them highly comfortable by Mr. Steele being at the War Office. I should think Lord Chatham would judge well, if he kept about him Huskisson and those now in my Department, but he need not put himself to any inconvenience in that respect, because if he would wish to have William Broderick about him, I could easily arrange that by carrying Huskisson to the India Board in the room of Broderick. As to all the other parts of the arrangements, I think every one of them will be highly gratifying and convenient to you.

One word with regard to myself. Some recent circumstances have rendered the situation even less comfortable to me than it was. It never was very consonant either to my talents or my habits, and I can assure you most sincerely that I would receive it as an act of kindness and of friendship if you would relieve me from it. Let the very few years of talents and powers of business that remain to me be devoted to the service of India which is in truth my proper element, and let the remainder of my time be appropriated to domestick happiness and the enjoyment of a few select friends.' (W. Dacres Adams MSS., and Add. MSS., 40102, f. 36.)

you and he has had it bound at Leipzig that it might be more worth your Majesty's acceptance.

The Duke, who begs I will present his most humble duty to your Majesty, has taken advantage of the present quiet and intends this evening going for a few days a hunting. (51570-1)

2089 Cabinet Minute, Downing Street, 12 Dec. 1799

Present: The Lord Chancellor, Lord Privy Seal, Duke of Portland, Earl Spencer, Earl of Liverpool, Mr. Chancellor of the Exchequer, Mr. Windham, Lord Grenville. Upon consideration of the dispatches received from the Earl of Elgin it is agreed humbly to submit to his Majesty that it would be proper that instructions should be sent to the Earl of Elgin to decline all applications for any passports for the transport of the French army in Egypt from that country to France: and to state that the power of granting capitulations rests not with his Majesty's Ambassadors or Ministers at foreign Courts, but with the proper officers of his Majesty's Fleets and Armies. But to add that for the information of the Porte he is authorized to acquaint the Turkish Ministers that his Majesty's orders to the Commander-in-Chief of his forces in the Mediterranean, enjoin him not to consent to the return of the French army, or to their capitulating on any other terms than that of surrendering as prisoners of war to the Allied forces employed against them, and of giving up their arms, and also all their vessels of every description, to be divided amongst the Allies in proportion to the naval force which may at that time be employed in the blockade of Alexandria, or in other operations against that army.

That instructions should be sent to Lord Keith accordingly, and that he should be further instructed to order the Commanders of any of his Majesty's ships of war who may fall in with any vessels carrying any such troops, that they should disregard any such passports in case the same should have been granted, but that they should not in that case exercise any other act of hostility against the said ships than such as may be indispensably necessary in order to compell such ships to return to Alexandria.

And that Lord Keith should take the first opportunity to communicate these determinations by a flag of truce to the French army in Egypt.[1] (9430-1)

2090 THE KING *to* LORD GRENVILLE

[*Windsor, 13 Dec. 1799, 7.55 a.m.*] I have this morning received the Minute of Cabinet of yesterday which fully meets with my approbation. Lord Grenville will therefore prepare his directions to the Earl of Elgin in conformity to it, as also write the proper letter to the Lords Commissioners of the Admiralty informing them of the instructions they must send to Vice Admiral Lord Keith, agreable to the only proper line of conduct that can be suggested from hence. (Fortescue MSS.)

[1] See also Pitt's letter of the 12th to Dundas, who was in Scotland (Stanhope, III, 204).

2091   THE KING *to the* ARCHBISHOP OF CANTERBURY

[*Windsor, 18 Dec. 1799.*] My Lord, having already expressed the desire of my daughter Amelia that you would confirm her, I now desire that you will come here on Monday before four, as I am desirous you shall have some private conversation with her in the evening on the serious duty she is to perform on Tuesday, and on Wednesday the anniversary of the birth of Our Blessed Saviour I hope you will administer the Holy Communion to her and the rest of us here. The Bishop being confined with the gout at Bath, I have desired the Bishop of St. Davids[1] to preach the sermon. If he is as fortunate as in the three he has preached in his residence, I flatter myself he will meet with your approbation. (9432)

2092   THE KING *to the* MARQUESS OF SALISBURY

[*Queen's House, 20 Dec. 1799.*] Thinking it might be of utility that the Marquess of Salisbury should be exactly informed of the situation of the supposed dormant Patent belonging to Covent Garden Theatre, I can now from certain authority acquaint him that on the rebuilding Drury Lane Theatre, to satisfy those who are renters and the creditors of the House, Mr. Sheridan bought that patent of Mr. Harris as an apparent security for the property; that it cannot be used but by the joint consent of both houses; that it cannot be sold to the Opera House, and therefore in reality seems to have been rather a swindling transaction than of any real advantage to the Drury Lane creditors; by this the Lord Chamberlain may rest assured that Mr. Taylor's[2] alligation of having got that patent is perfectly a fiction. (Hatfield MSS.)

2093   THE KING *to* SIR JOSEPH BANKS

[*Windsor, 25 Dec. 1799.*] The King is thoroughly satisfied, from the very able report he has received from Sir Joseph Banks, that the sheep offered for sale to him by Mr. Olivier are by no means worth his notice. He is not in the least ambitious of acquiring any further sorts of foreign sheep, but by due attention to improve the natural sheep of this island, of which the Wiltshire, improved by rams of the best Somerset stocks, and the true Hereford Ryland sheep, are those he prefers. (Ann Arbor MSS.)

2094   *Letters from the* DUKE OF PORTLAND *to the* KING

[*Bulstrode, Wednesday, 25 Dec. 1799, 9.45 p.m.*] As it will appear to your Majesty by the Lord Lieutenant's dispatch that he will not consider it expedient to attempt to carry into effect the measure of recruiting from the Irish Militia until he is informed of the specifick Regiments to which the recruits are to be allotted &

---

[1] William Stuart. See No. 733. He was a Canon of Windsor.

[2] William Taylor (?1754–1825), 'Opera Taylor'. M.P. for Leominster, 1797–1802; for Barnstaple, 1806–12. 'Taylor of the Opera House, a Scotchman, came to London, was a clerk in Mayne's House— lent Sheridan £1,000—got connected with Opera—and into Parliament at recommendation of Prince of Wales. D. of Norfolk, who brought him in, now sorry—two Members were not easily found to present him to the Speaker.' (*Farington Diary*, 10 July 1797.)

until some part at least of the Regular troops which are destined to serve in Ireland are arrived there, the Duke of Portland humbly conceives your Majesty may not deem it improper in him to observe to your Majesty that he was enabled by his Royal Highness the Duke of York to transmit on the 12th of this month to the Lord Lieutenant a particular statement of the Regiments ordered on that service together with a note of those from which recruiting parties were to be sent, & to let him know at the same time that your Majesty's orders had been given to the Board of Admiralty to give the necessary directions for the embarkation of the troops & parties in question without loss of time.

Your Majesty having directed the petition of Ralph Smith, a sadler, to be appointed a pensioner on the Charter House Foundation, to be sent to the Duke of Portland, he begs leave with all humility to represent to your Majesty that nearly a twelvemonth ago he submitted, at the instance of Mr Alderman Hibbert,[1] who had then lately renderd material service to your Majesty's Government by the distinguished part he had taken at a meeting in the City on the subject of the income tax, the name of a person to your Majesty for this situation, who is in every respect qualified to fill it, & in consequence of your Majesty's gracious condescension the Duke of Portland gave the Alderman encouragement to hope that his wishes would be accomplished at no very distant period. The Duke of Portland therefore requests your Majesty's pleasure may be signified to him whether the appointment to the present vacancy is to be made out in favor of Smith or of the person for whom it was sollicited by Mr Alderman Hibbert. If your Majesty should prefer Smith, the person recommended by the Alderman will only wait till it comes to the Duke of Portland's turn to nominate a pensioner, & if on the contrary your Majesty should decide in favor of the Alderman's man & will condescend to permit the Duke of Portland to nominate Smith on his first vacancy, your Majesty's commands will be executed with as much zeal in one as in the other case. (9434–6)

[*Bulstrode, Saturday, 28 Dec., 9.10 p.m.*] The Duke of Portland humbly begs leave to lay before your Majesty a dispatch which he received this morning from the Lord Lieutenant of Ireland. As it appears to require as immediate an answer as the circumstances respecting it will admit, the Duke of Portland, conceiving that it may save your Majesty some trouble & prevent delay & suspense, has ventured with all humility to submit to your Majesty a draft of an answer which he has prepared to the Lord Lieutenant's letters which, from the state, as he is given to understand, of the cloathing of the regiments destined for Ireland, he cannot but feel to be dictated by necessity as well as by expediency, & considering the intention of adjourning the Irish Parliament immediately after the Address has been voted to your Majesty, for the purpose of filling up the unusually great number of vacancies which have been occasioned in the House of Commons,[2]

---

[1] George Hibbert (1757–1837), Alderman of Bridge Within Ward of the City of London, 1798–1803; M.P. for Seaford, 1806–12. A West India merchant.

[2] Castlereagh informed the Duke on 11 Dec. that there were then 22 seats vacant, 'which will be filled by our friends' (*Cornwallis Corresp.* III, 151). In view of the fact that the Irish Government had been defeated on the Union proposal, it was essential that the composition of the House of Commons should be changed. Between the prorogation of the Irish Parliament in 1799 and the renewed debates on the Union in 1800, as many as 63 seats fell vacant.

it may appear to your Majesty that the same cause may be assignable for acquiescing in the mode proposed by the Lord Lieutenant for introducing the measure into Parliament.[1] (9437–8)

2095   LORD GRENVILLE *to the* KING, *and the reply*

[*Dropmore, 31 Dec. 1799, 7.15 p.m.*] Lord Grenville has the honour to transmit to your Majesty the inclosed letters which he has just received from London.[2] They were brought by a messenger from Dover where, very properly, neither the courier nor the passengers were allowed to land.

Lord Grenville has taken measures for summoning without delay a meeting of your Majesty's servants to consider of these papers. He does not presume to anticipate the result of that discussion, but he cannot refrain from expressing to your Majesty the strong impressions of his mind that this overture should at all counts be declined, in such a way as may be most likely to satisfy the feelings of the public in this country. Lord Grenville is persuaded that the prevailing sentiment on the subject will be such as might be wished, provided proper care be taken to give a right tone in the first instance.[3] (9440–1)

[*The King's reply, Windsor, 1 Jan. 1800, 7.08 a.m.*] The last evening I received Lord Grenville's note forwarding the letter addressed to me by Bonaparte, and that to him from Talleyrand. I trust Lord Grenville is convinced that I am perfectly easy that every one of my Ministers must view this in the same light I and he do, namely, that it is impossible to treat with a new, impious, self-created aristocracy, and I have too good an opinion of my subjects at large to doubt that when properly stated, they must see it in the same light; therefore I am clearly of opinion that the only consideration is how to reject the proposal with that dignity and seriousness which must set this country in an high light with other European countries, and make Englishmen look with respect on their own situation. I do not enter on the want of common civility of the conclusion of the Corsican tyrant's letter, as it is much below my attention, and no other answer can be given than by a communication on paper, not a letter, from Lord Grenville to Talleyrand. (9441)

2096   THE DUCHESS OF WURTEMBERG *to the* KING

[*Stutgard, 1 Jan. 1800.*] I look on it as my duty to begin the year by writing to your Majesty and expressing the warm wishes I form for your happiness. May the Almighty hear my prayers and bless your Majesty's arms everywhere with success and give us hopes that religion and justice may again be established in Europe, which must give your Majesty double pleasure as you certainly feel that this is

---

[1] The King's letter to the Bishop of St David's, 29 Dec., is in Jesse, III, 231.

[2] First, a letter from Bonaparte, as First Consul, addressed to the King of Great Britain and Ireland; second, a covering letter from Talleyrand to Grenville; both dated 25 Dec. 1799. (*Annual Register*, 1800, pp. 54–5.)

[3] For Pitt's views, see his letter of the 31st to Dundas, who was still in Scotland (Stanhope, III, 206).

chiefly owing to your steady noble conduct which has been universally the same in these critical times.

I seize this opportunity to entreat the continuance of your Majesty's goodness and protection to myself and to the Duke.

The very severe frost which has begun above ten days will I hope prevent the French from making any attempt of being troublesome for some time.

Today being by an old established custom the one on which the Deputies of the States dine with the Duke, we are to have a sort of great dinner, though not the usual one as we have no plate, and no Ladies except those in attendance on me are to be invited. In the evening there is to be a great concert for the whole Court, the Duke being determined in these times to give no Balls or anything which illnatured people could call a Fête and then abuse us for spending money when the country has suffered so much.[1] (51572–3)

2097 LORD GRENVILLE *to the* KING, *and the reply*

[*Cleveland Row, 2 Jan. 1800.*] Lord Grenville has the honour to transmit for your Majesty's consideration the draft of the answer to the overture from France. It has not yet been finally adopted in its present state by your Majesty's servants, but from the unanimous opinions this day expressed, Lord Grenville has no doubt that, should it meet your Majesty's ideas, he may be enabled to re-dispatch the French messenger with it in the course of tomorrow: and this he thinks desirable as so speedy an answer will exclude all appearance of hesitation. (9454–5)

[*The King's reply, Windsor, 3 Jan., 7.50 a.m.*] Lord Grenville, I can with truth assert that I never read a paper which so exactly contained the sentiments of my heart as the draft of your declaration to Talleyrand,[2] and I cannot see the shaddow of reason for altering any expression it contains; when sent, I desire I may have a copy of it, as it is a paper I shall with pleasure refer to. I trust no time will be lost in communicating it to the Courts of Russia, Austria and Prussia, and indeed to all the other Courts of Europe, and I should wish to have it with a Message laid before both Houses of Parlt. on the day of their assembling. (9455)

2098 THE BISHOP OF WORCESTER (RICHARD HURD) *to the* KING

[*Hartlebury, 4 Jan. 1800.*] I am equally honoured & surprized with receiving this day your Majesty's most gracious remembrance of me on the beginning of the new year. I cannot express the sense I have of this favour.

The new year & century cannot open more auspiciously than I trust it does

[1] The King's letter to the Bishop of Worcester, 1 Jan., is in Jesse, *Memoirs of the Life and Reign of George III*, III, 229.

[2] 'The answer is this morning finally settled', wrote Grenville on the 3rd, 'and will be dispatched today. It is long, but states in substance that the King has had to defend himself against the system, &c.— that he yet sees no security for the abandonment of that system, and cannot therefore now treat—that the best pledge of that abandonment would be the restoration of the King, &c., but that this is not the only way to peace, and that whenever the King has sufficient security, &c., he will be ready to treat... The paper...I doubt not...will alarm some weak friends. From what I have heard here, the universal belief was that we should refuse to treat.' (Buckingham, *Court and Cabinets of George III*, III, 4.)

with your Majesty's perfect health, & that of the Queen and every part of the Royal Family. Princess Amelia's recovery & late Confirmation are subjects that require my sincere congratulation. Bred up in such a family, her Royal Highness cannot fail of entering the world with a serious sense of religion, & of desiring all the benefits that might be expected from the Abp.'s ministry. What your Majesty is pleased to add of the Bishop of St David's sermons is not only honourable to himself, but another good symptom of the times, when the industry & talents of the pastors of the Church are so commendably displayed, and accepted with so much distinction.

Political subjects are out of my sphere & beyond my comprehension. All I know of them is that they are directed by the Supreme Power at his good pleasure, & are always tending to some great & good end, let the means be ever so strange & unexpected. The portentous elevation of the adventurer[1] your Majesty glances at, may be seen in due time to justify this observation.

I must not conclude the trouble I am giving to your Majesty in this letter without acknowledging the honour his R.H. the Duke of York is pleased to do me in so kindly remembring his old friend & servant under the name of Bishop of Lichfield. In wishing the continuance of every blessing to your Majesty, I of course include my wishes for the long health & preservation of his Royal Highness.

Be pleased, Sir, to accept my sincere thanks for the many instances of your goodness I have had the honour to receive, & to believe me [etc.]. (9456–7)

2099   SIR WILLIAM HAMILTON'S *Memorandum for* LORD GRENVILLE

[*4 Jan. 1800.*] His Lordship will remember that Sir Wm. did not request his recall but a short leave of absence—that he obtained the King's leave to return home for a short time to look after his private concerns in Wales, which suffer'd from his long absence, above four years ago, but Sir Wm. finding that both the King's interest and that of his Sicilian Majesty wou'd be in danger of suffering greatly from his quitting Naples at the moment of a threaten'd French invasion, sacrificed every view of private interest in order to pursue what he thought his duty to his King and country, and for the advantage of their Sicilian Majesties. It is true that Sir Wm. in a private letter to Lord Grenville, dated from Naples the 18th of Octr. 1797, did say that if his Lordp. on his return home wou'd ensure to him for his retreat an annual net income of two thousand pounds, his Lordp. was at liberty to dispose of his post at Naples to which he had been appointed by his Lordship's father in the year 1764, and altho' when last in England Sir Wm. had been graciously assured by the King his Royal master, that he shou'd not be removed from the Court of Naples unless it shou'd be at his own request—Sir Wm.'s surprise when Mr Paget arrived at Palermo with his credential letters, as the King's Minister at the Court of the Two Sicilies, was great indeed![2] not having receiv'd the

Grenville's official reply to Talleyrand, the French Minister for Foreign Affairs, dated the 4th, is in *Annual Register*, 1800, p. 55.   [1] Bonaparte.

[2] 'I suppose it is a Cabinet job, wishing to provide for Paget', wrote Sir William in disgust. 'Poor Emma is in the greatest distress. But let me get home and settle my affairs, and she and the Queen may dispose of my old carcass as they please.' (Nicolas, Nelson *Dispatches and Letters*, IV, 186 n.)

smallest intimation of it from Ld. Grenville, but when he had received from Mr. Paget and read his Lordp.'s official letter of the 24th of Decr. 1799, No. 7 and a very friendly private letter also from his Lordship, in which he approves of Sir Wm.'s long and faithfull service and particularly of his conduct at the difficult close of it, which as his Lordp. was pleased to add, has unquestionably well entitled Sir Wm. to his Majesty's favor on his retreat, and that his Lordp. had his Majesty's gracious permission to assure Sir Wm. of it, he was much comforted, not doubting but that immediately on his arrival in England, after having received such gracious assurances from Lord Grenville, his retreat wou'd have been made both easy and honorable to him; untill that is done, Sir Wm. having been supplanted without his previous knowledge must appear to the Court of Naples as a sort of disgrace to him, and difficult to be accounted for after Sir Wm.'s diligent and faithfull services during the long term of 37 years. Sir Wm. has already taken the liberty of making known to Lord Grenville[1] the pecuniary distresses he suffer'd on his arrival here, and continues to suffer, having been obliged, in order to maintain his unsullied character, to pay off all his debts at once, both at Naples and Palermo, and which debts plainly appear to have been contracted within the last two years, and in consequence of the very heavy extraordinary expences and the severe losses occasioned by the French invasion of Naples. Sir Willm. is now *seventy years of age* and his health much impair'd; he has no time to lose, and he flatters himself that Lord Grenville will take all that he has said into his immediate and friendly consideration, having been more than two months at home without knowing more of his future destination than he did the first day of his arrival. He can expect to live but a very few years, and after having passed his whole life in the service of his King & country it is hard to find himself in his present forlorn situation, particularly as he can prove clearly that during his long Ministry at Naples, he has not only expended the income attached to his office, but the whole income from his estate in South Wales, and even incurred a considerable debt on that estate in order to support with honor the dignity of his foreign mission. (9458–9)

2100   *Letters from* LORD GRENVILLE *to the* KING, *and the reply*

[*Dropmore, 6 Jan. 1800.*] Lord Grenville has the honour humbly to apprize your Majesty that the letters for Paris were dispatched yesterday, the delay having arisen from some suggestions of verbal alterations which have, however, in no degree varied the sense of the papers. Nothing could have afforded to Lord Grenville a higher pleasure than the approbation which your Majesty was graciously pleased to express to him of the draft. He presumes to hope that your Majesty will think it improved by throwing the first paragraph into the form of a separate letter, as thereby the paper in which Lord Grenville has the honour to speak in your Majesty's name is confined to the declaration of your Majesty's sentiments on the point in question without any notice of the paper addressed to your Majesty in so unusual and unbecoming a shape.

---

[1] 'According to Ld. Grenville's instructions Sir Wm. waited upon Mr Chs. Long of the Treasury and has left with him the true state of his debts & pecuniary difficulties.'

In humble obedience to your Majesty's gracious commands, Lord Grenville has the honour to send copies for your Majesty's use, of the two papers in their present form. (9469)

[*Dropmore, 7 Jan.*][1] Lord Grenville had the mortification to receive the above letter this morning from the Office in his box, into which it had been put by mistake, instead of being forwarded to your Majesty. He now takes the liberty to transmit it to your Majesty in its original shape in order that your Majesty may not think him so remiss in his duty as to have neglected obeying your Majesty's commands; but as the papers are now printed he does not trouble your Majesty with written copies of them.

He ventures to solicit your Majesty's indulgence for his absence from town tomorrow, wishing to remain here a few days longer. (9469–71)

[*The King's reply, Windsor, 8 Jan., 7.20 a.m.*] I have this morning received Lord Grenville's two notes and think the excellent declaration he has sent to Paris fully entitles him to some days quiet at Dropmore (Fortescue MSS.)

2101   JOHN HOOKHAM FRERE[2] *to the* KING

[*7 Jan. 1800.*] Mr Frere begs leave most humbly to represent to your Majesty that the omission alluded to by Lord Grenville did not originate in any inattention on his part, but was occasioned by the neglect of one [of] the clerks, in consequence of which he did not receive the copies intended for your Majesty's use till this morning. Mr Frere thought it his duty to mention the subject to Lord Grenville and at the same time to return the letter, with a view to the explanation which his Lordship has subjoined. (9480–1)

2102   THE DUKE OF PORTLAND *to the* KING

[*Burlington House, Friday, 17 Jan. 1800, 10.20 p.m.*] The Duke of Portland begs leave with all humility to submit to your Majesty's superior wisdom that considering the sentiments & intentions which, it appears by his Royal Highness the Duke of Kent's letter (private) the Duke of Orleans[3] professed during the time he passed at Halifax, the purpose for which alone it may be presumed that he has determined to come himself & to bring both his brothers[4] to this kingdom

---

[1] On the same sheet as the above.

[2] Under-Secretary of State in the Foreign Department, April 1799–Sept. 1800; M.P. for West Looe, Nov. 1796–1802. Minister to Portugal, 1800–2; Envoy to Spain, 1802–4; Minister to Spain, 1808–9. P.C., 1805. One of Canning's intimate friends. (1769–1846.)

[3] Louis Philippe, Duke of Orleans, later (1830–48), King of the French (1773–1850), and son of Égalité, who was guillotined in 1793. He had fought on the Republic side but had deserted with Dumouriez. He was in America for some time after 1796, but came to England in 1800 and lived at Twickenham.

[4] Antoine Philippe, Duc de Montpensier (1775–1807); and Louis Charles, Count of Beaujolais (1779–1808). *The Times* declared on the 21st: 'About three weeks since, an application arrived in this country addressed to a very high quarter, from the three unhappy and highly culpable Princes of the House of Orleans. It is dated at the Bahamas, from whence they request permission and passports for their voyage to this country, where they implore the Royal pardon and protection. The memorial of these unfortunate

& the advantage which the Duke of Portland humbly conceives would be the probable result of an union of all the branches of the French Royal Family, your Majesty would graciously condescend to permit the Duke of Orleans & his brothers to come up to town in order to give them the most early & favorable opportunity of atoning for the part which, it may be hoped, they were compelled to take at their first entrance into life by a declaration of their allegiance & of their desire to exert themselves in support of the rights of their lawfull Sovereign & in re-establishing him upon his throne. This is stated in a private letter from Sir John Wentworth (your Majesty's Lieutenant-Governor of Nova Scotia) to Mr. King, to have been the object they publickly & unreservedly avowed while they resided at Halifax, where they brought, in dollars, the amount of about £1500 sterling which they have remitted to Mr. Coutts the banker in the Strand.

As there is no other official dispatch from Ireland than that which is herewith humbly submitted to your Majesty, the Duke of Portland considers it to be his duty to inform your Majesty of the vacancy of the Primacy as the event was communicated to him by the Bishop of Killalla,[1] who was brother-in-law to the late Primate,[2] who states that melancholy event to have taken place about eight o clock in the evening of last Saturday the 11th instant. (9485–6)

2103 LORD GRENVILLE *to the* KING, *and the reply*

[*Cleveland Row, 18 Jan. 1800, 10 a.m.*] Lord Grenville thinks it his duty to lose no time in transmitting to your Majesty the inclosed letter[3] from M. Talleyrand, which was brought to the Office at two o'clock this morning. (9487)

[*The King's reply, Queen's House, 18 Jan., 5 p.m.*] I lose no time in returning to Lord Grenville the paper he has received from Talleyrand; it in no degree destroys the solidity of the able declaration drawn up by Lord Grenville; and I should think requires no rejoinder, but should it be thought otherwise I trust the tone of the former declaration will be sustained and not the flimsy quibbles with which this French paper abounds.[4] (Fortescue MSS.)

persons states the sincerest conviction and contrition for their offences, and professes their desire to return to their duty to their lawful Sovereign, and to peace with their own consciences...

It has long been impossible to add anything to the merciful character of our Sovereign or to be surprised at any exercise of his Godlike prerogative. The Comte d'Artois was immediately waited on by Mr. Pitt, who, meeting with no difficulty on the part of H.R.H., has signified his Majesty's acquiescence in the solicitation of the French Princes, who will in consequence take up their abode in this country.'

[1] Joseph Stock (1740–1813), Bishop of Killala, 1798–1810; of Waterford and Lismore, 1810–13.

[2] William Newcome. His death, said Grenville, was embarrassing, 'from the difficulty of finding a good successor to him on either Bench'.

[3] See 9472–9. This correspondence, like that noted earlier (No. 2097 n.), was subsequently published. See *Annual Register*, 1800, pp. 58–61 (Talleyrand to Grenville, 14 Jan., and Grenville's reply on the 20th).

[4] The King saw the draft of Grenville's reply to Talleyrand dated the 20th, and endorsed it at 7.48 a.m. on the 21st: 'The enclosed declaration so correctly corresponds with the former declaration sent to France that it deserves my most entire approbation.' (Fortescue MSS.)

[*Burlington House, Sunday, 19 Jan. 1800, 11.35 p.m.*] The Duke of Portland has this moment received the dispatches from Ireland which he has the satisfaction of laying most humbly at your Majesty's feet, & which he only presumes to detain to observe to your Majesty that the seats for which writs will have been moved for, when filled will add at least twenty to the majority which decided the question on the Address.[1] He further begs leave to add that the Lord Lieutenant has sent several copies of the newspapers inclosed. (9488)

2105 EARL SPENCER *to the* KING, *and the reply*

[*Admiralty, 19 Jan. 1800.*] Earl Spencer has very particular satisfaction in laying before your Majesty the accompanying letter from Sir Hyde Parker[2] inclosing an account of the capture of the Hermione frigate by Captain Hamilton[3] of the Surprize in the boat of that frigate; the spirit & judgment with which this brilliant & useful service has been performed will, he has no doubt, meet with your Majesty's approbation, and he humbly suggests whether it might not be proper to confer the honour of knighthood on Captain Hamilton by patent on the occasion. (9489)

[*The King's reply, Queen's House, 19 Jan., 1.50 p.m.*] I am truly happy at the well planned and executed enterprize of Captain Hamilton of the Surprize by which the Hermione has been regained to the British list of ships. I perfectly approve of his being a Knight by patent, but think his conduct so deserving of reward that he ought to be allowed to add to his arms some memorial of this gallant action. (Althorp MSS.)

2106 THOMAS COUTTS *to the* KING

[*Bath, 26 Jan. 1800.*] Having formerly had the honour of showing to your Majesty some letters of the Duke of Orleans to whom from very intimate knowledge and acquaintance I felt a partiality in spite of his father's crimes, I take the liberty of laying before your Majesty a letter I received from him a few days ago, together with one from Mr de Grave,[4] a Frenchman long connected & much in

---

[1] See No. 2094 n. The last session of the Irish Parliament opened on 15 Jan., and after an eighteen-hour debate on the Union question, Government had a majority of 42, the numbers being 138 v 96. 'We had two locked out and three did not act as we expected, so that our majority ought to have been fifty', wrote Edward Cooke to Lord Auckland from Dublin on the 18th (Sneyd MSS.). During the first few days of the session as many as 39 writs were moved, and the great majority of the vacant seats had been secured by the Government.

[2] Admiral Sir Hyde Parker (1739–1807), second son of Vice-Admiral Sir Hyde Parker (1714–82). Lieutenant, 1758; Captain, 1763; Rear-Admiral, 1793; Vice-Admiral, 1794; Admiral, 1799. Knighted, 1779. He commanded at the battle of Copenhagen, 1801.

[3] Sir Edward Hamilton, 1st Baronet (1772–1851). Lieutenant, 1793; Captain, 1797; Rear-Admiral, 1821; Vice-Admiral, 1837; Admiral, 1846. Knighted, 1 Feb. 1800 for this exploit; created Baronet, 7 Dec. 1818.

[4] Cf. *The Times*, 3 Feb.: 'The three sons of the late Duke of Orleans are arrived at Guildford, where

the confidence of his family himself and his brothers who were mere boys when I was in Paris. Mr de Grave is gone to Falmouth to wait their arrival and I have always heard him spoken of as a man of character & blameless life, and I have been assured by several people at Kensington, where he has long resided, that his conduct there has been always very good and respectable. My reason for sending his letter is that in any communication I have the honour to make I may conceal nothing, but so far as I am informed or can judge, place the whole naked and unvarnished truth before your Majesty, for I have little to boast of but the purity and sincerity of my intentions, which I thank heaven has carried me creditably through life, and has been my comfort in a very dangerous illness from which I am but just recovering, tho' I hope it may not be long before I gain strength sufficient to return to London. I have been in that view for some time at an agreable residence of a kind friend at seven and twenty miles distance from Bath, and I am going there again tomorrow for a week: what has done me as much good as the friendly quiet of that retreat is a letter I received from Lord Bute[1] since he went to town in which he was so good to tell me your Majesty had had the condescension to mention to him my humble name and to enquire after me. I cannot attempt to express my feelings upon such a mark of favour, or on the happiness it gave me to hear of your Majesty's perfect health, and the happiness of all the Royal Family, to the promoting of which in every branch no poor endeavour of mine ever has or ever will be wanting—and under Heaven I have no doubt, with your Majesty's guidance, of Great Britain and Ireland, united, continuing more & more to flourish—and that it will get the better of all its enemies, foreign and domestic.

I should humbly express my wish at leisure time in no hurry to have back the Duke of Orleans's letter some part of it relating to money business.[2] (9490–1)

2107   LORD GRENVILLE *to the* KING, *and the reply*

[*Cleveland Row, 27 Jan. 1800, 11 p.m.*] Lord Grenville has directed that the Vienna dispatches, which appeared to him the most important of those received today, and also the last dispatches from Sir Charles Whitworth & Mr Garlike, should be sent to your Majesty tonight. The rest of the mail will, if your Majesty approves of it, be successively sent. (9492)

they will remain until they receive H.M.'s permission to proceed to London. The elder son travels under the title of Count de Commines, from an estate formerly possessed by his family in Flanders.

'As soon as these Princes had disembarked at Falmouth, a letter was despatched (rather inauspiciously) from M. de Montjoie, who enjoys the chief place in their confidence, to M. de Grave in London, requesting him to attend their Highnesses without delay upon the most important business. The latter of these gentlemen has been one of the Ministers in the service of the Republic, and is not distinguished since his emigration by any attachment or personal respect towards the cause, or the family of his lawful Sovereign. This urgent application therefore to him, unpreceded by any communication to Monsieur or to the British Ministers, has very justly given suspicion, though it cannot create uneasiness...The Princes received an order to wait H.M.'s commands at Guildford, and M. de Grave has been enjoined not to depart from London.'
   [1] The Earl of Bute (1744–1814) married, 17 Sept. 1800, Coutts's second daughter, Frances (1773–1832). His first wife died, 28 Jan. 1800.
   [2] Coutts wrote again to the King from Bath on 1 Feb.: 'Desirous that nothing may be ommitted in any communication I have the honour to make to your Majesty, I take the liberty again of inclosing a letter from the Duke of Orleans which, tho' of a prior date to the former, I received only this day.' (9494)

[*The King's reply, Queen's House, 28 Jan., 8.20 a.m.*] The mode directed by Lord Grenville for [s]electing that part of the correspondence arrived yesterday by the seven mails which should be in first place transmitted for my perusal is very satisfactory, as without such a selection in the first instance it would have been difficult to retain their contents.

The dispatches from Lord Minto are most interesting and not in the smallest degree prolix; they state the whole of the *wants* great indeed, but they also state what in my opinion gives the only true chance of the conflict ending successfull. These dispatches cannot therefore, when Lord Grenville and Mr. Pitt can fully discuss them and a proposition for the decision of Cabinet be put on paper, be too soon taken under consideration: there is no time for delay. (Fortescue MSS.)

2108 WILLIAM PITT *to the* KING

[*Downing Street, Tuesday, 4 Feb. 1800, 4.45 a.m.*] Mr. Pitt humbly begs leave to acquaint your Majesty that the Motion for an Address of thanks and approbation on the subject of the answers to the late overture was made by Mr. Secretary Dundas.[1] It was opposed by Mr. Whitbread and Mr. Erskine and supported by

[1] The original intention was that Pitt should move the Address, and that Dundas should reply to the first Opposition speaker (who would probably be Fox), but on the 3rd Canning reported that 'the order of battle' had been changed, 'which', he added, 'gives me a better chance of an opportunity, as Fox probably will not follow him as he would have followed Pitt, immediately. But I shall have many competitors for the Speaker's eye.' (Harewood MSS.)

Next day Canning wrote: 'Well. I "got spoke" last night (to use a significant expression of Dundas's). And everybody tells me I ought to be quite satisfied with what I did—& so I must be, I suppose, though I will own I did not quite do *all* that I intended.

'Our debate altogether was quite triumphant. Dundas did his part extraordinarily well—and Pitt's speech was one of the best that I ever heard from him. Fox, tho he had the last word, made less advantage of it than usual, & left but little impression. So all is, as it should be.' (Harewood MSS.)

Another letter, on the 5th, completes Canning's account of the debate: 'I told you yesterday that I was not quite satisfied myself with what I had done the night before: but that was only because I compared it in my own mind with what I *meant* to have done—and I had in point of fact—from apprehension of being too long (as Pitt & Fox were both to come after me) left out at least half of what I had to say. But I find I have no reason to be discontented—for I hear praises on all sides which are very comfortable to me. And Pitt is satisfied & happy in my success. The speech is nowhere well reported—as always is the case when Pitt & Fox speak. And so much of it arose out of reply, that I cannot (I am afraid) recollect it sufficiently to be able to make out a tolerably accurate report for Woodfall & Debrett—else I should certainly think it worth while to do so.

Fox does not mean to attend again. But all the rest do, so I trust we shall have a pretty active Session.' (*Ibid.*)

The Times' report of the debate occupies the whole paper except for six lines on the last page. The House adjourned at 4 a.m. Many members must have left the House before the division, for *The Times* declared on the 5th: 'We never recollect the benches of the House of Commons to have been more crowded than on Monday, nor the attention of the auditors to have been more rivetted to the eloquent speeches of Mr. Pitt and Mr. Fox.' It added: 'Mr Canning every day confirms the sanguine hope entertained of him. No man transfuses his character more naturally into his speeches. That of Monday was a just mixture of wit and argument, and a happy compound of information, modesty and good humour.' But Thomas Grenville, however, declared that Canning spoke 'with great indications of talents for speaking, but with a want of judgment and an affected vehemence which told more than one should expect against the merit of his arguments and of his language' (Buckingham, *Court and Cabinets*, III, 24).

At the Levée on the 5th the King, reported Canning, 'received me with the most marked kindness and talked to me a long time about the debate, and the negotiation, and about my cold, and exertions, &c. &c., all in a way much more flattering than I ever experienced from his Majesty before. Indeed, Pitt had told me some time ago that he had enquired about me, and spoke of me to him in the most comfortable manner' (Harewood MSS.).

Mr. Canning and Mr. Pitt, the latter of whom was replied to by Mr. Fox, after which the House divided and the original Address was carried by 265 to 64. The general impression in the House upon the whole question appeared to be highly favorable and satisfactory. (9495)

2109 THE DUKE OF PORTLAND *to the* KING

[*Burlington House, Sunday, 9 Feb. 1800, 4.45 p.m.*] The interruption which the communication with Ireland has suffer'd for some days by the contrariety of the wind induces the Duke of Portland to hope that your Majesty will not disapprove the liberty he takes of laying before your Majesty without delay the dispatches which have been received today from the Lord Lieutenant containing the result of the debate which took place upon the Message which the Lord Lieutenant was directed to send to the Irish Parliament respecting the Union in favor of which the numbers were 158 against 115 & on which occasion, though the majority was not so great as expected, the Duke of Portland hopes from the firmness & ability with which the measure is supported, will be found sufficient to secure its success in the course of the present Session.

The Duke of Portland is extremely sorry to add that he conceives that if, upon the investigation which it is the Lord Lieutenant's intention to make into the conduct of the Marquess of Downshire, it would appear that he has made use of the influence of his military situation to prevail upon the regiment of Militia which he commands to oppose the measure of Union, his removal from the command of that Regiment, as proposed by the Lord Lieutenant, will not be deemed by your Majesty a sufficient mark of your Majesty's displeasure for so improper an act of conduct, & that your Majesty will judge it expedient also to remove him from the Privy Council & the Government of the County of Down.[1] (9507–8)

2110 THE KING *to the* COUNTESS OF HOLDERNESSE[2]

[*Queen's House, 17 Feb. 1800.*] The King cannot but most sincerely congratulate Lady Holdernesse on the proposed marriage of Lord Francis Osborne[3] with Miss

---

[1] Lord Downshire was deemed guilty of a grave breach of military discipline in sending down a petition against the Union to his regiment of militia for signature, and on 12 Feb., by the King's command, Portland informed him that he was dismissed from his regiment (of which he was Colonel) and from his office of Governor of County Down, and that his name was to be struck out of the Privy Council. Cornwallis considered this step decisive as to the success of his Administration. (*Cornwallis Corresp.* III, 179, 188, 192, 197.) Downshire had already, before the 8th, been suspended from the command. 'He came to me to remonstrate', wrote Cornwallis that day, 'but I told him my mind in strong language, and he went away as meek as a lamb.' (Cornwallis MSS., Kent Record Office.) See also Buckingham, *Court and Cabinets*, III, 30, 38.

The King's letter to Pitt, 10 Feb., 8.05 a.m., is in Stanhope, III, Appendix, p. xix.

[2] The 4th Earl of Holdernesse (1718–78), who had been Governor to the Prince of Wales, 1771–6, married (1743) Mary (?1721–1801), daughter of Francis Doublet, of Groeneveldt, Member of the States of Holland.

[3] Lord Francis Godolphin Osborne (1777–1850), second son of the 5th Duke of Leeds. M.P. for Helston, 1799–1802; for Lewes, 1802–6; for Cambridgeshire, 1810–31; created Baron Godolphin, 14 May 1832. On 31 March 1800 he married Elizabeth Charlotte (1780–1847), third daughter of the 1st Lord Auckland. Lord Francis's mother, Amelia, Baroness Conyers (1754–84) was Lady Holdernesse's daughter.

Charlotte Eden, as he trusts from the good education she has received she will be deserving of Lady Holdernesse's protection. The King will rejoice when enabled to congratulate on a proper alliance for Lady Mary Osborne.[1] (Add. MSS. 33131, f. 79.)

2111 THE DUKE OF PORTLAND *to the* KING

[*Burlington House, Tuesday, 18 Feb. 1800, 9.20 a.m.*] The Duke of Portland humbly conceives that the contents of the dispatches which are just arrived from Ireland will appear too interesting & satisfactory to your Majesty for him to defer for an unnecessary moment to lay them before your Majesty.[2] (9511)

2112 HENRY DUNDAS *to the* KING, *and the reply*

[*Downing Street, 22 Feb. 1800, 3 p.m.*] Mr Dundas takes the liberty of humbly submitting to your Majesty a Minute[3] of a resolution of your Majesty's confidential servants, which they have directed him to transmit to your Majesty. (9513)

[*The King's reply, Windsor, 22 Feb., 7.58 p.m.*] I have just received the Minute of Cabinet forwarded by Mr. Secretary Dundas for collecting at Minorca a body of British troops to co-operate with the Austrians or Royalists in the South of France. No General in the service is more worthy of being entrusted with such a command than Sir Charles Stuart, but I must observe on this as I have on many former occasions that I trust attention will be had to the real state of our forces, not to falacious states on paper which always make a greater appearance than can be depended upon when the troops are collected, and consequently that we may not trust on having a larger force than can be effected. Those already sent to Ireland must greatly diminish the means of furnishing so large a force as 20,000 men.[4] (Add. MSS. 40100, f. 245.)

2113 THE DUKE OF YORK *to* HENRY DUNDAS

Secret (Copy)

[*Horse Guards, 28 Feb. 1800.*] I have to acknowledge the receipt of your letters of the 23d instant (one of them marked secret) conveying to me his Majesty's commands 'that a British army amounting, with the disposable force now in the

---

[1] Lady Mary Osborne (1776–1862), daughter of Francis, 5th Duke of Leeds by his 1st wife, Baroness Conyers, married (16 July 1801) Thomas Pelham (1756–1826), who became Lord Pelham in June 1801, and who succeeded his father in 1805 as 2nd Earl of Chichester.

[2] Cornwallis informed the Duke in a letter dated the 15th, that the Government had increased its majority in the Irish House of Commons, the numbers then being 157 v. 110 (*Cornwallis Corresp.* III, 194). A week earlier, the Lord Lieutenant had been less confident of success: 'Our situation is critical. Twelve of our supporters deserted to the enemy on the last division. One was bought during the debate —Jerusalem Whaley, the Chancellor's brother-in-law. The enemy, to my certain knowledge, offer £5,000 ready money for a vote. If we had the means and were disposed to make such vile use of them, we dare not trust the credit of Government in the hands of such rascals...How it will end God only knows. I think there are not more than four or five of our people that can be either bought off or intimidated, but there is no answering for the courage or integrity of our Senators.' (Cornwallis MSS., Kent Record Office.)   [3] Not in the Archives.

[4] The King's letter to Pitt, 20 Feb., 8.23 a.m., is in Rose, p. 244.

Mediterranean to at least 20,000 effective men should by every exertion be collected with all possible dispatch at Minorca, with a view to its being employed in that quarter under the command of Lieut.-General Sir Charles Stuart; and further that the proportion to be sent from this country (amounting as you conceive to at least 15,000 men) should be forthwith selected and should consist of whatever regiments most fit for immediate service.'

I shall not delay, in obedience to his Majesty's commands making the necessary arrangements for the effectual execution of the object in view, and no exertion shall be wanting on my part towards fulfilling in the utmost degree possible the expectations which his Majesty may have formed of an efficient, disposable force from the late augmentation which the Infantry of the army has received from the Militia of Great Britain and Ireland.

Coinciding most fully in the justness of his Majesty's observations, in regard to the fallacy in general of paper statements, upon which you remark that you can alone form your judgement: and being most truly desirous to furnish his Majesty's Ministers with every information in my power, of the actual state of that force to which his Majesty looks for the successful execution of any measure which may be now in contemplation, I shall proceed to make such representation as I think will best tend to give a clear conception of the condition of the troops from which the force required is to be taken.

In the first instance I shall advert to the regiments whose services, being confined to Europe, are those which I naturally conclude his Majesty would wish to employ in the Mediteranean in preference to such as from being unlimited in their services can alone be expected to answer any sudden call for reinforcements to his Majesty's possessions out of *Europe*, or for the execution of any hostile attempt which it may be thought exepedient to make on the distant possessions of the enemy.

The former are as stated in the margin. It is necessary to observe that the major part of these Battns. were those which were entirely composed of Volunteers from the English Militia under the first Act and, and which from the urgency of the moment were obliged to be hastily brought together, and sent on the Expedition to Holland, incomplete in cloathing, arms and appointments, and without having undergone that preparation which is absolutely necessary for troops previous to their proceeding on actual service.

			Effective Rank & File
4h Regiment	{	1t Battn.	886
		2d do.	892
		3d do.	905
5h do.	{	1 Battn.	640
		2d do.	635
9th Regiment	{	1t Battn.	738
		2d do.	733
		3d do.	731
15h do. Ireland	{	1t do.	834
		2d do.	897
16h do. Ireland			847
17h do.	{	1t do.	622
		2d do.	654
20h do. Ireland	{	1t do.	742
		2d do.	723

(319)

During any active campaign particularly during one so arduous as that sustained by the army in Holland it must be evident that it is impossible to exercise troops or to ground them in the first rudiments of their business; since the return of that army from Holland, the season has been so adverse to exercise in the field that little progress has been made in their advancement in discipline. No exertion however has been wanting to supply the deficiencies in arms, cloathing & appointments naturally occasioned by the severity of the service upon which they were employed.

		Effective Rank & File
31t do.		947
35h do.	1t do.	761
	2d do.	847
36h do. Ireland		1166
40h do.	1t do.	687
	2d do.	632
46h do. Ireland		1019
52d do.	1t do.	973
	2d do.	982
56h do. Ireland		875
62d do.	1t do.	373
	2d do. Ireland	800
63d do.		646
82d do. Ireland		792

Upon receiving his Majesty's commands to furnish a reinforcement for Ireland I thought it my duty as far as circumstances would admit to select the Regiments which were at this time considered as the most efficient in point of number, exclusive of sick, although in every other respect I was sensible that they were by no means in that state of discipline in which alone I should have recommended that troops should be sent upon service. Several of them had very lately been entirely formed of recruits from the Militia, others had received a considerable proportion of men in consequence of the last Act for reducing the Militia, in addition to those who volunteered in the first instance.

The Officers originally belonging to the Regiments could have no knowledge whatever of the men, and those who were necessarily received from the Militia were without experience. Under these material disadvantages, and until time could be allowed for making good the deficiencies in arms and cloathing sustained by some of the corps which had served in Holland, and for perfecting the whole in the most essential points of discipline they ought not (had not the exigency of circumstances required it) to have been sent out of the Kingdom. Ten battalions, however, proceeded, consisting in the whole of 8695 effective men.

The foregoing observations equally apply to the Regts. of the same description now in England. Their present inefficient state is not in any respect attributable to neglect or want of exertion on the part of those in command of them, but the manner in which so considerable a force has been collected has utterly precluded the possibility of their being at this time completely disciplined and appointed, in cloaths, arms and accoutrements.

It will therefore be evident that although the number of men required may be embarked, yet I must feel it a duty to give it as my decided opinion that there are not any of the corps mentioned in a state for actual service, and that unless they are allowed uninterruptedly to employ the ensuing two months in equipment, formation and instruction, little advantage is to be expected from their services against the enemy, however conducted. I shall therefore conclude my remarks on these corps by expressing an earnest hope that it may suit the arrangements in agitation, not to call upon them until the expiration of the period above mentioned, when, confiding in the zeal and ability of the Generals and other Officers in command of them, I think I may safely pronounce that they will be in a state to act as his Majesty may be pleased to direct.

The Regiments in Great Britain whose services are unlimited and whose numbers can in any degree be considered such as to warrant their being sent upon any service, are as stated in the margin. In these numbers also a considerable allowance must be made for sickness, and for recruits recently joined, particularly in the 23d, 27th and 85th Regts. which have each had a large encrease to their strength by volunteers from the Irish Militia, and which in consequence cannot at present be considered in a fit state to be sent upon foreign service, although they may become very efficient if a fair proportion of time is allowed to them for that purpose.

1t Regiment (2d Battn.)	124
2d or Queens	568
23d	600
25h	472
27h	1243
29h	566
49h	470
55h	460
60h (6h Battn.)	574
65h (Boys)	608
69h	560
79h	376
85h	1346
92d	706

Independent of being utterly deprived of the means of supplying the possessions out of Europe by sending upon the service in question these regiments, there are several arrangements now in their infancy to which in consequence an entire stop must be put: of these the formation of a Corps of Riflemen by detachments, to be returned to their Corps when properly instructed, and the exercising five Regts altogether as Light Corps, are two which must be dropped.

The six battalions expected from Ireland are very efficient in point of number, but in every other respect, from the nature of their formation, they must be considered altogether unfit for any service, and if hurried abroad in their present state, they will be sent without having afforded to them the means of deserving the most trifling degree of confidence.

1t Battn. Royals ...	883
13h Regiment	806
54 do.	1241
64 do.	913
68h (2 Battns.)	2013

Having thus made a fair representation of the state of what is considered to be the disposable force in Infantry of this kingdom (in which you will, however, observe I have not made any mention of the Foot Guards) amounting in the whole to 8180 rank and file), I shall proceed to state the means by which I propose to make up the number of men (15,000) required, which as you specify neither artillery, or cavalry, is, I conclude, intended to be composed altogether of regiments of infantry.

These regiments include all in Great Britain (except the 63d) which have been recruited from the English Militia, and whose services are limited.

Whenever it is thought expedient that this force should proceed by detachments, and they can until required for actual service be placed in a settled garrison, where time can be given for exercise and instruction, any five or six of the Battalions mentioned, may without material inconvenience to their progress in discipline embark as soon as arrangements for that purpose can be made.

I trust I shall have succeeded in laying before you, for his Majesty's information, a comprehensive detail of the force of infantry in Great Britain which can first be calculated upon for active operation.

Regts		Effective including sick
4th or King's Own		
1t Battn	909	
2d do.	891	
3d do.	926	
		2,726
9th Regiment		
1t Battn.	738	
2d do.	733	
3d do.	730	
		2,201
17th Regiment		
1t Battn.	622	
2d do.	654	
		1,276
35th Regiment		
1t Battn	761	
2d do.	849	
		1,610
40th Regiment		
1t Battn	685	
2d do.	669	
		1,354
52d Regiment		
1t Battn.	973	
2d do.	982	
		1,955
31t Regiment		947
5h Regiment		
1t Battn	640	
2d do.	635	
		1,275
Three Battalions from Ireland to be replaced by 2000 Guards—say		2,400
Total		15,744

The Regiments which I have not yet noticed and which may be called upon at a future period are

	Rank & file	
21t	246	} Recruiting in Scotland
71t	219	
72d	173	
32d	96	just returned from the Bahama Islands
38th Regiment	373	} expected from the West Indies
43d	251	
28th	660	do. from Gibraltar
24th	639	} do. from N. America
26th	616	

The three last mentioned Corps are completely formed and may on their arrival in England be considered as equal to any service required of them. (9515–22)

2114   THE KING to WILLIAM PITT

[*Queen's House, 1 March 1800, 7.30 [?a.m.]*] I am surprised that Mr. Tierney, who is supposed to be a man of some tallents, should not see the great impropriety of the Motion he made yesterday in the House of Commons and the fate it must evidently meet with—the calling forth many respectable persons to oppose it, and consequently pledge themselves farther to the support of the war, besides ensuring a very handsome majority authorizing the sentiments last entertained.[1]
P.S.

Mr. Pitt wished to know who was the last Primate [of] Ireland taken from the English Bench of Bishops. Hugh Boulter[2] was Bp. of Bristol and in 1726, when Achbp. of Armagh, appointed a Lord Justice in the absence of the Lord Lieutenant,[3] which he successively conducted on the like occasion till his death in 1742. The Bp. of Bath and Wells[4] has drawn up a short but very pointed paper on the Irish Church which I wish Mr. Pitt would get from the Duke of Portland, which seems to me to obviate all the difficulties in uniting it with that of England and to require much less to be done than by any of the other plans suggested. (Chatham Papers.)

2115   THE DUCHESS OF WURTEMBERG to the KING

[*Stutgard, 2 March, 1800.*] It is a great comfort to me that I can now speak openly to your Majesty on many subjects which prudence forbid my mentioning by the post.

---

[1] Tierney's Motion 'That it is the opinion of this House that it is both unjust and unnecessary to carry on the war for the purpose of restoring Monarchy in France' was defeated by 142 to 34. (*Parl. Register*, LV, 732–67.) Neither Grey nor Fox was present. On 20 Feb. Grey had written to General Fitzpatrick: 'I feel much inclined to attend Tierney's Motion...I feel a desire to enter my protest against the continuance of the war. I have not determined upon this, and have not said a word upon the subject to Tierney yet, but if I should attend, it would be a great gratification to me to see you and Hare in the House.' (Howick MSS.)

[2] Dr Hugh Boulter (1672–1742), Bishop of Bristol, 1719; Archbishop of Armagh, 1724–42.

[3] John, Lord Carteret (1690–1763), who was Chief Governor of Ireland as Lord Lieutenant, 1724–30.

[4] Charles Moss (1711–1802), Bishop of St David's, 1766–74; of Bath and Wells, 1774–1802.

The knowing the Duke is at last enabled to conclude the Treaty according to the plans sent him from England gives me great pleasure. I hope your Majesty is not displeased at the length of time elapsed since any steps were apparently taken on the subject, as the Duke's situation unfortunately deprives him frequently of acting according to his inclinations.

The States of the Dutchy, who ever since the Duke's reign have been a constant source of distress by opposing themselves to every step which the situation of the country requires, have at length two months ago by their bad conduct obliged the Duke to dissolve them. This was occasioned by the Emperor wishing Suabia to rise in a body, on which the Duke gave the necessary orders for settling the business and sent Commissioners for that purpose to the different Oberämter. The States, who have no right to interfere with the Executive Government, sent to stop the preparations for raising the men, and the gentlemen employed by the Duke were even ill used. On this the Emperor was applied to who sent a strong Rescript and ordered the States to submit. Two days afterwards the Duke dissolved the Assembly, notwithstanding which, they continued to meet, which is unlawful, and did not return to their duty till they were threatned with the military.

All the distress this has occasioned the Duke your Majesty will easily believe has given me great pain, which has been infinitely encreased by a most wretched conspiracy having been discovered by the Archduke Charles, who acquainted the Duke that the Dutchy of Württemberg was the seat of it, and that it extended through Suabia and the adjoining Circles. The Archduke gave the option whether he should in the Emperor's name have the suspicious persons arrested, or whether the Duke would have them taken up and tried. Of course the Duke chose the latter and it makes one tremble to see the danger we have all run and from which Providence alone has preserved us. Every day new horrors come to light, and the numbers of people mixed in the business are without end. I am sorry for human nature to be obliged to say that many of the prisoners are under great obligations to the Duke, as their whole families are dependant on his bounty. It is singular that it lays totally in the middling rank and that the peasant and lower class are quite free from these revolutionary principles.

The Duke is much affected by these events and I am sure nothing but his firm trust in God could enable him to undergo this constant fatigue of body and mind. The only time he can in the least forget himself is the few hours he can steal from his business to spend with me, and even that is continually interrupted. I am very eager to get him into the country where I hope he will be able to take a little more exercise, which I think very necessary for him. At present he is much taken up with the recruits which are to compleat his contingent. I believe they march next week and then if the snow does not continue I hope to settle at Louisbourg. I must now beg your Majesty to forgive my having taken up so much of your time.

I will now entreat your Majesty to be graciously pleased to send us the congarous [sic] I applied for two years ago. The Duke's Chasseur who is to return soon will take charge of them. A garden and house is making for them at Louisbourg, where I shall often visit them. (51574–6)

[*Wimbledon, 3 March 1800, 3 p.m.*] Mr Dundas humbly takes the liberty of mentioning to your Majesty that in consequence of the probability of General Lake going to India,[1] the Irish Staff became the subject of conversation at an interview here this morning at which his Royal Highness the Duke of York and Mr Pitt were present, and Mr. Dundas took the liberty of suggesting the propriety of Lord Chatham being appointed to succeed General Lake, which would of course put him next to Lord Cornwallis in the efficient command of the army in Ireland. Mr Dundas was induced to make this suggestion in consequence of the communication your Majesty was pleased to make to him of your Majesty's views respecting Lord Chatham. The more Mr Dundas has thought of it, the more he is satisfied in every point of view that no arrangement could be so beneficial for your Majesty's service. Both the Duke of York and Mr Pitt seemed to enter very strongly into the propriety of the suggestion made by Mr Dundas, and Mr Pitt proposed without delay to speak to his brother. Everything therefore seems to depend on Lord Chatham's own decision, but altho the Lord Lieutenancy of Ireland is no ways within the line of Mr Dundas's official arrangements, he thought it his duty to put your Majesty confidentially in possession of those particulars. (9523–4)

[*The King's reply, Windsor, 4 March, 8.15 a.m.*] I am sensible of Mr. Secretary Dundas's attention in communicating the idea that has occurred of placing the Earl of Chatham at the head of the Irish Staff on Lieut. General Lake's going to the East Indies. I should doubt whether the Earl would choose to accept a situation that has ever been held by an Officer of superior rank, and which must occasion the taking off of that Staff four Generals that are his seniors; this objection would not hold good as to his being Lord Lieutenant of Ireland, for that office superceeds all other appointments. Should this objection not occurr to the Earl of Chatham, I shall certainly not be the person to start it, but I thought it right to mention it in confidence. (Add. MSS. 40100, f. 247.)

[*From Dundas, Downing Street, 5 March 1800.*] Mr Dundas takes the liberty of sending to the Queen's House agreeable to your Majesty's direction the bird lately arrived from India, which formed part of the ornaments of Tippo Sultan's throne. The key of the box and the description of the throne accompanies this. (9525)

2117 LORD AUCKLAND *to the* KING

[*Palace Yard, 12 March 1800.*] Lord Auckland was honour'd some months ago by a gracious intimation of your Majesty's disposition to give a packet boat to a deserving officer of the Navy whose name, Lord Auckland thinks, was mention'd at the time. A vacancy is now made on the Falmouth Station by the sudden death

---

[1] Lake was Commander-in-Chief in India from July 1801 (appointed Aug. 1800), to July 1805, and from Oct. 1805 to 1807.

of Captain Dillon, and Lord Auckland will be most happy to make the nomination conformably to your Majesty's commands at any convenient interval of time.

The situation (which should be fill'd by an active & experienced seaman) produces at first only from 400£ to 800£ a year, but there is a gradual rise, and the five Senior Commanders do not gain less than from 1,000£ to 1,500£ per ann. (9528)

2118   PRINCE ADOLPHUS *to the* KING

[*Hannover, 16 March 1800.*] As the weather has a little changed these last three days and therefore there is some small hopes of the opening of the Elbe, I take the liberty of profiting of this first opportunity to return your Majesty my most humble thanks for your two last letters which I received at the end of January. The enclosed were immediately forwarded to Stuttgard and have safely arrived at the place of their destination to the infinite joy of my sister, who had been a long time without receiving any accounts from England owing to the irregularity of the posts. We are at present in a much worse predicament, twelve mails being at present due and the thirteenth due tomorrow, which is the greatest number I have ever known since I have been on the Continent. Luckily nothing of any great consequence has taken place between the two armies in Germany, the operations not having yet begun, most probably on account of the excessive cold weather. The Archduke had not yet quitted the Army when the last letters from thence arrived; he was, however, expected to set out for Prague in a very short time, to the great regret of the whole army, by whom he is adored. General Kray will by this time be arrived at Donoueschengen: he certainly is a very excellent Officer and has distinguished himself very much in the last campaign in Italy and I heartily wish he may have the same success this year. The Archduke has not given up entirely the command of the Army which makes me hope that should his health permit him, he will return. This is certainly an event which is very much to be wished for, as he enjoys the entire confidence of his troops and is very much beloved by all the inhabitants of that part of Germany where he has been and with such advantages he can do more than anybody else.

The cold weather has prevented our exercising as yet. All the Officers and uncommissioned have been ordered in since the 1st instant, and the 1st of next month a third of our privates that are on furlow are to come in likewise, so that about the end of next month the Batallions will be compleat and I hope then that the Brigades will be brought together this year. The first thing we must wish for now is a change of weather and this I do in a double sense, as I sincerely hope to hear by the arrival of the mails that your Majesty is in perfect health, for the conservation of which I offer up the most ardent prayers to the Almighty, and it is with this assurance that I have the honor to remain [etc.]. (48547–8)

[*Berlin, 19 March 1800.*] In compliance with the desire of Mr. Gentz[1] I have the honor to lay before your Majesty a copy of his work upon the Finances of Great Britain. This pamphlet originally appeared as fragments in a monthly Journal, which its author publishes in opposition to Revolutionary principles. The great success they met with upon the Continent has engaged Mr. Gentz to compile them and have them translated into French for the more general perusal of the curious. The very marked approbation the Emperor of Germany has signified to the author, though a Prussian, & the very high esteem he possesses in the political world are motives for my granting his request and for my taking the liberty of laying his book at your Majesty's feet. Trusting that it will meet with a favourable and gracious reception, and with the most ardent prayer for your Majesty's prosperity and that of your country I have the honor [etc.]. (48184)

2120   *Letters from* LORD GRENVILLE *to the* KING, *and the replies*

[*Cleveland Row, 24 March 1800, 11 p.m.*] Lord Grenville has the honour to submit to your Majesty a Minute of Cabinet on the point which appeared to be most pressing in Lord Minto's dispatches. (9529)

[*Cabinet Minute, Downing Street, 24 March.* (*Enclosure.*)] *Present*: The Lord Chancellor, Lord President, Lord Privy Seal, Duke of Portland, Earl Spencer, Earl Camden, Earl of Liverpool, Mr Chancellor of the Exchequer, Mr Windham, Lord Grenville.
It is agreed, upon the consideration of Lord Minto's dispatches, humbly to represent to his Majesty that it may be proper to authorize Lord Minto to enter into a reciprocal engagement, in his Majesty's name, with the Court of Vienna not to make any Peace or Armistice (of a general nature) with the enemy during the remainder of the present year except by common consent. (9530)

[*The King's reply, Windsor, 25 March, 8.15 a.m.*] The Minute of Cabinet transmitted this morning for my approbation by Lord Grenville meets with my fullest concurrence; indeed, had no declaration been made I should have thought it madness to enter during the campaign into any negociation. I consequently see the advantage of the present measure in binding the Court of Vienna to the proper line of conduct. (Fortescue MSS.)

[*From Lord Grenville, Cleveland Row, 27 March 1800.*] Lord Grenville has the honour humbly to submit to your Majesty the Minute[2] taken at the Cabinet this morning. He trusts that the length of the Minute, and the great pressure of the business occasioned by the arrival of so many mails at once will plead his excuse to your Majesty for not having transcribed it himself. (9531)

---

[1] Friedrich von Gentz (1764–1832), the most famous German publicist of the time, and a most persistent enemy of the Revolution.
[2] Not in the Archives.

[*The King's reply, Queen's House, 28 March, 8.30 a.m.*] I do not mean to refuse my acquiescence to the opinion proposed on the most unpleasant circumstance of the truce granted in Egypt with permission to the French to return to Europe, although Sir Sidney Smith has acted most improperly in making himself an adviser if not a party to this ill advised transaction; but had a contrary tone been adopted, the expressing a total disapprobation of Sir Sidney's conduct, and the instructing Lord Keith to seize any of the vessels bringing the troops from Egypt and such ships as may be going to assist in transporting them to Europe I fairly should not have had the smallest difficulty to have authorized the measure.[1]
(Fortescue MSS.)

2121   THE DUCHESS OF WURTEMBERG *to the* KING

[*Louisbourg, 30 March 1800.*] I am sure your Majesty is always so gracious to me that you will rejoice at my being settled in the country. Three weeks ago the Duke intended to return here but was constantly prevented by business. I cannot express to your Majesty the joy I felt at finding myself in my little garden and my gratitude to the Almighty who has preserved this place from our destructive enemies, who were so near us last winter. I hope the air of Louisbourg will do my health good, as I can here go out at all times without being seen. This morning the Duke has been giving orders to prepare a very pretty spot for the congaroos who I hope will be able to live in this climate. Great additions have been made to the gardens and to the English farm which I shall visit this evening; it is my favourite spot, as it is quite like a very neat English cottage and the garden corresponds perfectly with it.

I am very glad to hear from my sisters that your Majesty intends building at Kew, being convinced that it will amuse you very much, though my partiality for Windsor makes me fear that this new employment may take your Majesty much away from the Lodge.

Being called to church I must now take my leave of your Majesty. (51577–8)

2122   THE DUKE OF PORTLAND *to the* KING

[*Burlington House, Monday, 31 March 1800, 11.30 p.m.*] The Duke of Portland most humbly begs leave to lay before your Majesty a dispatch[2] which he has had the very great satisfaction of receiving this evening from the Lord Lieutenant containing an account of the Articles of Union having been agreed to by the two Houses of the Parliament of Ireland & having been communicated to him together with an Address to your Majesty with which, in pursuance of their desire, he has

---

[1] The Convention of El Arish (24 Jan. 1800), negotiated with the Turks by the French General in Egypt, Kléber, under the sanction of Sir Sidney Smith, allowed the French army to evacuate Egypt on condition of their not serving against Great Britain and Turkey for the rest of the war. In agreeing to this arrangement, Smith disregarded his instructions, and Keith in effect repudiated it by informing Kléber that his troops would not be allowed to leave Egypt unless they surrendered as prisoners of war with their ships and stores. Kléber then renewed hostilities.

[2] *Cornwallis Corresp.* III, 222 (28 March). The Union Resolutions were agreed to by the Lords 'by a majority of 50—the contents present being 48, the proxies 24; the non-contents present 16, proxies 6'.

transmitted them to be presented to your Majesty. But as neither the Resolutions nor the Address differ in any respect whatever from the drafts of them which have been submitted to your Majesty, the Duke of Portland ventures to hope that your Majesty will be so gracious as not to disapprove his presuming to retain them for the purpose of having copies made of them for the two Houses of your Majesty's Parliament of this Kingdom in order that they may be enabled to proceed in the business without any unnecessary delay as soon as it shall be communicated to them by your Majesty's order, with which view the draft of a Message is preparing to be submitted to your Majesty. (9534-5)

2123 LORD GRENVILLE *to the* KING, *and the reply*

[*Cleveland Row, 31 March 1800.*] Lord Grenville has the honour to lay before your Majesty the copy of a dispatch from the Emperor of Russia to Count Woronzow demanding the recall of Sir Charles Whitworth—and also the copy of a private letter from Count Rostopchin,[1] communicated to Lord Grenville by Count Woronzow in confidence. He imagines that your Majesty will think it right that under the present circumstances no time should be lost in fixing upon a proper person to succeed Sir Charles Whitworth, and as upon a former occasion your Majesty had approved of Earl Bathurst for that purpose Lord Grenville proposes to sound him upon it, though he fears it will be difficult to persuade him to undertake the Mission in the present state of affairs.

Lord Grenville also humbly submits to your Majesty some communications made by the Prince of Orange through M. Fagel, but on which it does not appear to Lord Grenville that any step can be taken. (9532-3)

[*The King's reply, Windsor, 1 April 1800, 7.58 a.m.*] As the Emperor of Russia in so explicit a manner requires the recall of Lord Whitworth it would be absurd not to effect it as soon as possible, though I am entirely ignorant of the imprudent language Count Rostopshin seems to allude to. No one would succeed better at Petersburgh than Earl Bathurst, but I have no idea he can be persuaded to go abroad, and much less so to so ficcle a Court as unhappily that one must with truth be called.[2]

I entirely agree with Lord Grenville that the communications he has received from M. Fagel and transmitted to me cannot at present in any way be acted upon. (Fortescue MSS.)

2124 THE DUKE OF PORTLAND *to the* KING

[*Burlington House, Tuesday, 1 April 1800, 10 p.m.*] The Duke of Portland humbly begs leave to offer to your Majesty the draft of a Message from your

---

[1] Count Rostopchin, the Russian Foreign Minister; later, Imperial Chancellor.

[2] The unstable Tsar was already contemplating an Armed Neutrality against Great Britain, and it materialised in the summer. On 27 Aug. he invited the Kings of Prussia, Denmark and Sweden to join with him in asserting and enforcing the principle of the freedom of the seas. Whitworth left Petersburg at the beginning of August, and diplomatic relations between the two Courts were suspended until the following spring; the lunatic Emperor was strangled after being forced to abdicate (24 March 1801).

Majesty to the two Houses of your Majesty's Parliament of this Kingdom to communicate to them the Address of the Parliament of Ireland together with the Articles of Union which have been transmitted by the Lord Lieutenant to be laid before your Majesty, which, if fortunate enough to receive your Majesty's approbation, is prepared in due form to receive your Majesty's royal signature & with that view the Duke of Portland has ventured to submit two copies of it to your Majesty.[1]

The Duke of Portland begs leave at the instance of the Duke of Atholl,[2] whose letter the Duke of Portland herewith submits to your Majesty, to acquaint your Majesty that the Duke of Atholl has received an account this evening of the death of his son-in-law Sir John Menzies,[3] & in consequence of it requests that your Majesty's further commands may be signified to him relative to your Majesty's gracious intention of investing him with the Order of St Andrew on Friday next. (9536–7)

2125   THE DUCHESS OF WURTEMBERG to the KING

[*Louisbourg, 4 April 1800.*] I ought to apologise to your Majesty for the liberty I am going to take, but hope that you will be graciously pleased to forgive me if my application is improper. A Baron de Wöllwarth whose estate is situated near Suabia has six daughters of which only the two eldest are provided for. The one being Maid of Honour to my sister-in-law, Princess Ferdinand, she wishes me very much to entreat your Majesty to place one of them in the Convent of Wunsdorf. I objected some time, thinking these places were only for the noblesse of the Electorate, but am assured many others have also been in these Convents. Should your Majesty grant this request I have enclosed the name of one of these young ladies and must again entreat your pardon if I have asked anything wrong.

Our weather is very uncertain; some days warm, others cold enough to snow; the vegetation is sadly backwards at present. I am very much pleased with the additions the Duke has made to his garden and think some spots would please your Majesty; indeed it is astonishing to see what has been done in two years after finding everything in a ruinous condition. The very ground before the house was let and everywhere the beauty was destroyed by parting with great part of the land which had either been sold or let on long leases. The Duke by degrees tries

[1] Cornwallis wrote to Pitt on 31 March: 'Our prospect of success on the question of Union is certainly favorable, but knowing as I do that a great number of our supporters act most unwillingly with us and omit no opportunity of doing us mischief when they can effect it without danger of being called to account, I confess that I shall not feel easy until the Act is finally passed. I think besides that the French have a more advantageous game to play in Ireland than in Portugal, and that if such a force has been embarked as the last reports mention, this island must be their object. Wolfe Tone, when he was recognized by Sir George Hill on board the Hoche, said, "Mr. Pitt is mad if he does not attempt an Union, and the French are mad if they do not attack Ireland before it can be effected".' (P.R.O., W. Dacres Adams MSS.)

[2] The Duke of Atholl (1755–1830), who had been Governor of the Isle of Man since Feb. 1793, became a K.T. on 4 April 1800.

[3] Sir John Menzies, 4th Bart. [S.] who married (4 March 1797) the Duke's daughter Charlotte, died on 26 March.

to recover these grounds and if God grants him life I am sure will make this the most beautiful place in Germany.

The Duke begs that I will present his humble duty to your Majesty and I will now take my leave entreating you to be convinced of the dutiful attachment [etc.]. (51579–80)

2126   THE DUKE OF PORTLAND *to the* KING

[*Burlington House, Saturday, 5 April 1800, 4.30 p.m.*] The Duke of Portland humbly begs leave to acquaint your Majesty that the Bills which arrived the day before yesterday from Ireland are ready to be laid before your Majesty in Council & that the Parliament of that Kingdom is adjourned to the 10th instant. The Duke of Portland therefore requests to have your Majesty's commands signified to him at what time your Majesty will please to be attended by your Privy Council in order that the Bills may be submitted to your Majesty for your royal signature. (9538)

2127   THE DUCHESS OF WURTEMBERG *to the* KING

[*Louisbourg, 6 April 1800.*] Having had the honour of writing to your Majesty last week I should not have troubled you again with a letter had the Duke not desired me to present his humble duty to your Majesty and to acquaint you that he hears his brother Prince Henry[1] intends going to England. The conduct of this Prince is so bad that his brother takes no notice of him and we entreat your Majesty not to receive him. Last year he quitted the King of Prussia's service and married an actrice, which he is trying to persuade the Emperor to create a Countess of the Empire, which the Duke has refused to consent to. As your Majesty will certainly see by this that this Prince is really a disgrace to the family, I flatter myself that you will grant our request.

The weather begins to be very sultry here, and I hope when your Majesty spends your next week at Windsor that you will be able to enjoy both your hunting and farming. The Duke is very much taken up with improving his grounds. Above two hundred of the seeds from Kew are come up and I hope will do very well. It is singular that though this country is more South than England, many plants which are out the whole winter at Kew are destroyed if we attempt to treat them in the same way. (51581–2)

2128   PRINCE ADOLPHUS *to the* KING

[*Hannover, 8 April 1800.*] Discretion alone has prevented my returning sooner to your Majesty my most humble thanks for your very gracious letter of the 18th Feby. which I received by the last quarterly messenger. Knowing that Uhle was

---

[1] Prince Henry of Wurtemberg (1772–1833) married Caroline Alexis (1779–1853), an *actrice* who had been his mistress. According to Von Isenburg (*Stammtafeln zur Geschichte der Europaischen Staaten*), this marriage took place in 1798 (no date specified), but, assuming the accuracy of the Duchess's statement, this must be an error. See No. 2127 and *Correspondence of George, Prince of Wales*, No. 1542.

to leave Hannover on the 9th I thought it would be better to write by him, and I hoped to be able to give you some interesting information of the operations of the Austrian Army; but hitherto nothing has been done, and each Army seems to be expecting the other should begin. The unlucky news of the Queen Charlotte having blown up near Leghorn has been confirmed, and only 150 of the crew have been saved. The letters from Italy also mention the arrival of the Genereux at Siracuse, and of the whole reinforcement that was sent to Malta being taken by Admiral Nelson except three corvettes that had escaped and made for France. The only ship now remaining of the Fleet that was beat at the battle of Aboukir is the William Tell, which is at Malta, and as there is great hopes that the fort of La Vallette will soon surrender, this ship will then also fall into our hands. God grant that your Majesty's arms may always be crowned with such success, and I am confident that then the ennemy will soon be forced to make such a peace as will be honorable for your Majesty and make them give up their infamous plans of overthrowing the different Governments of Europe.

The very fine weather that we have had for this last fortnight has favored very much our exercising, and we have been able to finish drilling the non-commissioned Officers and first men. As soon as the Easter holidays are over we begin exercising the men, and I trust I shall be able by the end of next month to bring my Brigade together. General Wallmoden has informed me that the troops should exercise till the end of June, when the privates are to be sent on furlough. It is then that I should wish to execute a plan which I have long had in view, but which different considerations prevented my mentioning sooner to your Majesty. The very long absence I have made from home has given me a desire to see my family again which, I trust, you will find natural. The situation in which this country has been for these last three years, ever since our troops have been on the Cordon, has made me give up all ideas that I had had of asking your Majesty's permission to come over to England; but after having waited so long, and seeing that there are no hopes of our being employed in an active way I cannot miss this opportunity of touching this subject to your Majesty, and I trust and hope you will not be offended at my humble request. I do assure you that nothing but the desire of seeing you and my family has prompted me to this step, as I wish nothing more than to remain settled in *this country* where I feel I can be of more use to you than in England. Should your Majesty be so gracious as to grant my request I begg you will fix the time of my stay, and you may depend on my not asking for a day's respite. I dare now not trouble you any longer, than just to add the assurance of my ever remaining [etc.]. (48549–50)

2129   MRS HOWE *to the* KING

[*From the Countess Howe's,*[1] *Grafton Street, 9 April 1800.*] Mrs. Howe is charged by the Countess Howe to express as strongly as is in her power her deep sence of

[1] Lord Howe, the Admiral, who died in Grafton Street on 5 Aug. 1799, married (1758) Mary, daughter of Chiverton Hartopp, of Leicestershire. She, who was born in 1732, died in Grafton Street on 9 Aug. 1800. Her second daughter, Lady Mary Howe (1765–1800), who, for some years after 1791 had been one of the Ladies of the Bedchamber to the Princesses, died on 9 April. It was incorrectly

your Majesty's gracious condescension, and oppressed as she is by most heavy grief, she can yet say she feels such goodness at her heart.

The Baroness Howe[1] desires her to add her most dutiful acknowledgements to your Majesty.

Mrs. Howe has so frequently experienced the gracious notice of her beloved Sovereign that she is not surprised, though most thoroughly flattered & penetrated by this late instance of your Majesty's great graciousness, and she can find no words adequate to express her gratitude.[2] (9539)

2130 THE DUCHESS OF WURTEMBERG *to the* KING

[*Louisbourg, 15 April 1800.*] It is with a very greatful heart that I take up my pen to express to your Majesty my thanks for sending Mr. Wickham here; the propriety of his conduct and his good sense must please every where.

The Duke begs me to present his humble duty to your Majesty and assure you that though at first a little vexed to find that he had lost the most advantageous moment to conclude the Treaty from others having prevented his following his own inclinations, still he felt thoroughly that the situation of affairs being altered from what they were last year, he readily accepts of the proposed terms, only wishes your Majesty, out of consideration for the state of the Dutchy, and the great expences as well as losses we have had owing to the war, would allow your Ministers to conclude this Treaty for six years instead of three. Mr. Wickham, finding the Duke very anxious on this head, told him he had no powers to lengthen the time, but hoped that it would not meet with much difficulty if a proper application was made to the Ministers: he also promised as far as it lay within his power to back this proposal.

I have reason to flatter myself that your Majesty will be satisfied with the troops, as the contingent has obtained much praise from the Austrians, and as I had the honour to mention in my letter of 18th March that those kept back for your Majesty's service are infinitely a finer body, the Duke has taken great pains to have good Officers and to equip the men thoroughly. The behaviour of these troops in September last and during the cruel winter campaign makes me hope they will continue to fulfil their duty and do us credit.

The Duke has also desired me in his name to present to your Majesty the History of the States. Last week the Rescript came from Vienna authorising the Duke to dissolve the two Committees of the Assembly which is an unheard of event, as those who form the Committees always remained members of the new

stated in the newspapers that on 2 March 1800 she married the Earl of Morton. They were only engaged; the marriage had been postponed on account of her illness, and was to have taken place a few days after 9 April. *The Times* declared (5 May): 'The Dowager Countess Howe has made a present of £20,000 sterling to the Earl of Morton. Lady Mary had made no will since her marriage was in contemplation, and the whole of her property (more than £100,000 sterling) is divided in comparatively small legacies amongst her friends and relations.'

[1] When in 1788 the Admiral was given an Earldom he was also created Baron Howe, with a special remainder of the Barony to his daughters, failing a male heir, consequently his daughter Sophia Charlotte (1762–1835) succeeded him in 1799 as Baroness Howe.

[2] The King's letter of the 9th to Mrs Howe is printed in Barrow's *Life of Howe*, p. 392.

Assembly; and the Committees only ceased on the opening of the Assembly when those who formed them laid down their places and were frequently re-elected. On the 29th the Duke has ordered the new Assembly to meet. God grant that more care may be taken in the elections and that the people may at last feel the blessings they enjoy.

I am very much pleased with having made Mrs Wickham's[1] acquaintance. She is a chearful unassuming woman and appears to like being here. They are lodged in the Grafen Haus and we do everything in our power to make their stay pleasant. Since yesterday the weather has mended, which enabled us to shew them some of the beauties of this place. Now the country grows every day pleasanter as every moment some fresh thing comes out.

Your Majesty will be a little surprized to hear that I am going to ride. My stomach, though better, has continued so long troublesome that the physicians declare that riding will be the best cure. The Duke is looking out for a horse but begs that I will be satisfied with its being safe and quiet.

Having now taken up a great deal of your Majesty's time I will only add that to my great joy the Hereditary Prince is in a few days to join the Austrian Army as a volunteer. I am in great hopes that this will cure him of his great shyness. (51583-5)

2131 THE DUKE OF PORTLAND to the KING

[*Bulstrode, Tuesday, 15 April 1800, 9.20 p.m.*] The Duke of Portland most humbly begs leave in addition to the dispatches from Ireland, which have been transmitted to him this evening by Mr Cooke, to submit for your Majesty's consideration the sketch of the Act for settling the representation of the Lords & Commons on the part of Ireland in the Parliament of the United Kingdom.[2] (9540)

2132 THE DUKE OF YORK to the KING

[*York House, 17 April 1800.*] Having at last obtained leave to make a little use of my right hand I beg leave to return your Majesty my most dutifull thanks for your very gracious letter, as well as for your affectionate solicitude about me. I am, thank God, dayly recovering, though still in much pain when I cough or make any exertion. However, the surgeons are anxious that I should go out of town as soon as possible for a week or ten days, and flatter me with the hopes of being able to bear the journey to Oatlands by next Saturday.[3]

I have the honor to transmit to your Majesty the weekly states and returns and the recommendations for commissions for your Majesty's approbation.

[1] Wickham, who had been sent to the Continent to treat with Austria and other German States, and who was at Munich in March, married Eleanor Magdelene (or Madeleine), daughter of Louis Bertrand, Professor of Mathematics at Geneva. She died in 1836.

[2] Lord Spencer's letter of the 15th to the King (9541) respecting Lord Bridport's resignation of the command of the Channel Fleet, and the King's reply next day agreeing that the Admiral should be advanced to the rank of Viscount, are in *Spencer Papers*, III, 325–6.

[3] George Rose wrote to Pitt on 8 April: 'The Duke of York has had a fall from his horse and it is feared he has broken one or two of his ribs.' (P.R.O., W. Dacres Adams MSS.)

I beg leave also to lay before your Majesty the draft of a letter from the Adjutant-General to the Secretary at War in your Majesty's name on the subject of the pay of officers returned absent without leave, as the willfull disobedience of orders to join is encreasing to a very unpleasant pitch.

In consequence of intelligence communicated by the Admiralty of the possibility of an attempt being made upon Plymouth in case the French Fleet should come out and escape the vigilance of your Majesty's Fleet, I have ordered the Queen's and Welsh Fuziliers to march into the south-west district, as well as the two Hampshire Regiments of Militia and the North Gloucester. Lieutenant-General Grenville[1] has also been directed to return to his command immediately, and as there is little cavalry in the west and no Major-General of Cavalry I have been under the necessity to order Major-General Garth[2] to return as expeditiously as possible to Weymouth and to be in readiness to move to the westward with the Royals and Greys in case he receives any application from Lieutenant-General Grenville.

The 79th and 92d Regiments have likewise been ordered to move from Chelmsford to Southampton and the Isle of Wight to occupy the quarters left by the two Hampshire Batallions. All of which arrangements I trust will meet with your Majesty's approbation. (9542–3)

2133   THE BISHOP OF WORCESTER (RICHARD HURD) *to the* KING

[*Hartlebury, 21 April 1800.*] The gracious letter I have this day the honour to receive from your Majesty affords me the highest possible satisfaction. After the good character I had always heared of Dr. Moss,[3] and the evidence he had given of his merits at Weymouth, I assured myself that his appointment to serve in your Clos[e]t, in the absence of your disabled clerk, would not be unacceptable to your Majesty. I was besides anxious to bring into that attendance on your Majesty a person that might be no unworthy successor to the new Bishop of Chester,[4] whose promotion is a fresh instance of your Majesty's care of us.

I was infinitely alarmed by an accident which lately happened, but hope the danger is over and that your Majesty & Royal Family are relieved from all apprehension on that subject.

What your Majesty hints in the close of your letter concerning the Westminster

[1] Richard Grenville had been a Lieutenant-General since May 1796, and he became a General in Jan. 1801.

[2] Thomas Garth (1744–1829). The following amplifies the note in vol. II, p. 591 and corrects the Index date (II, 664). General Garth was the son of John Garth (1701–64), M.P. for Devizes, 1740–64. He had two elder brothers: Charles Garth (*c.* 1734–84), M.P. for Devizes, 1765–80; and General George Garth (*d.* 1819). He entered the army as Cornet in the 1st Dragoons, 1762, and served in the Seven Years' War in Germany under Prince Ferdinand. Lieutenant, 1765; Captain, 1775; Lieutenant-Colonel, 1790; A.D.C. to the King, March 1795; served in the Flanders campaign, 1794; Major-General, 1797; Lieutenant-General, 1805; General, 1814. Colonel of the 1st or Royal Regiment of Dragoons, Jan. 1801, *vice* Philip Goldsworthy, *dec.* For his later career and attendance on Princess Charlotte of Wales, see *The Letters of Princess Charlotte, 1811–17*, ed. A. Aspinall, *passim.*

[3] Charles Moss (1763–1811), son of Charles Moss, Bishop of Bath and Wells (1711–1802). D.D., 1797; Bishop of Oxford, 1807–11.

[4] Henry William Majendie (1754–1830). See No. 194.

inscription is so flattering to the writer that he ought to make a particular acknowledgment of it, & yet his merit consists only in this, that he used but few words in giving the character of his friend, and those plain ones: but this is an instance, among many others, of your Majesty's accustomed indulgence and partiality to [etc.]. (9545)

2134   THE DUCHESS OF WURTEMBERG *to the* KING

[*Louisbourg, 22 April 1800.*] I had intended yesterday writing to your Majesty the moment the Treaty was signed, but the Duke acquainting me with Frederic's accident,[1] and Lady Mary Howe's death quite prevented my having that honour, as my spirits were very much shook by these events. But now that I am quite quiet I must return your Majesty my most grateful thanks for having sent Mr Wickham and express how happy I feel to see all parties satisfied. The Duke from the first was very much taken by Mr Wickham's sensible conversation, and the more he had to do with him the better he was pleased with his conduct. It also is very agreeable to me that both Mr and Mrs Wickham are very much satisfied with their stay here. I hope it is needless for me to say that it must ever give me great pleasure to have it in my power to testify my respect and attachment to your Majesty by shewing attentions to any of those who have the honour of belonging to you. Today Mr Wickham sets out for Headquarters and she goes to Canstadt to bathe. As she remains in our neighbourhood I hope to see her frequently. We all parted with regret yesterday evening.

Our weather continues wonderfully warm and the vegetation very quick, the apricots being not only set but nearly the size of a nut, and the grapes also beginning to shew themselves. I never saw in ten days so great a change in the look of the country. My pretty little flower garden improves every day and the Duke has been so good as to build me in it a small house covered with moss which adds much to its comfort.

I understand that a horse is already found but it will require some little time before it will be fit for me to ride. I shall begin to ride in the manage [*sic*] as the Duke is full of fears that I might meet with an accident unless I learn well from the begining. (51586–7)

2135   WILLIAM PITT *to the* KING, *and the reply*

[*Downing Street, Tuesday, 22 April 1800, 12.30 a.m.*] Mr Pitt humbly begs leave to acquaint your Majesty that after going into the Committee of the whole House to consider of your Majesty's Message, he moved a Resolution to agree to the first Article of Union as transmitted from Ireland. This Motion was opposed by Mr Grey who moved that the Chairman should leave the Chair, in which he was supported by Mr Sheridan and Mr Tierney. The supporters of the original Motion

---

[1] On the 8th. 'As H.R.H. was riding along the King's Road, a dog belonging to a drove of cattle crossed his horse, and the animal fell. The Duke's leg being entangled in the stirrup, he was dragged some distance, and two of his ribs were broken, besides his receiving a contusion in the face.' (*The Times*, 9 April.)

were Mr Johnstone[1] (a son of the late Govr. Johnstone[2]), Mr Nicholl,[3] Mr Secy. Dundas, General Loftus, Lord Carysfort and Lord Sheffield. Mr Grey's Motion was negatived on a division by 236 to 31, after which the three first Articles were agreed to without further debate, and it was fixed to proceed on the fifth and seventh Resolutions tomorrow, and on the fourth (that respecting the Parliament) on Thursday, on which latter day Mr Grey gave notice that he should move an instruction with a view to some alteration in the representation of Great Britain.[4] (9546–7)

[*The King's reply, Windsor, 22 April.*] It is with infinite satisfaction I learn from Mr. Pitt's note that the three first Articles of Union with Ireland was agreed to in a Committee on a division of 236 to 31, and from the House of Lords I understand an equal progress has been made and the division 82 to 3.[5] I therefore think the sense of Parliament now so clearly known that I hope no great trouble will arise in getting through this most salutary measure.

What measure Mr. Grey means to propose on Thursday I cannot well conceive from what is mentioned, but I trust any alteration in the representation of the present British House of Commons will not meet with much countenance in Parliament. (Chatham Papers.)

2136   THE DUKE OF YORK *to the* KING

[*Oatlands, 24 April 1800.*] I have the honor to lay before your Majesty for your approbation the recommend[at]ions for vacant commissions, and to transmit the weekly states, as likewise a report of the Judge Advocate-General upon a court martial held in Minorca upon a private of the 90th Regiment for the murder of a sergeant of the Regiment of Rolle and trust that your Majesty will be graciously pleased to approve of Sir Charles Morgan's recommendation to extend your mercy to the criminal.

Mr Dundas, whom I have seen this morning, has acquainted me that your Majesty has been pleased to accept of Sir Charles Stuart['s] resignation of the command in the Mediterranean. I cannot but say that I think it a measure absolutely necessary, and can only regret that Sir Charles Stuart's unfortunate jealousy of temper and impatience of controul from any superior authority preclude the possibility of taking advantage of his otherwise excellent talents.

The proposal of sending Sir Ralph Abercromby to Portugal, if he will accept

[1] George Johnstone (*c.* 1767–1813), a natural son of Capt. George Johnstone by Martha Ford. M.P. for Aldeburgh, 1800–2; for Hedon, 1802–13. A Commissioner for India, April 1807–July 1809. He had been in the service of the East India Company. He gave an independent support to most of the Governments of the day. This was his maiden speech.

[2] George Johnstone (1730–87), M.P. for Cockermouth, 1768–74; for Appleby, 1774–80; for Lostwithiel, 1780–4; for Ilchester, 1786–7; an East India Director, 1784–6. Lieutenant, R.N., 1755; Commander, 1760; Captain, 1762. Governor of West Florida, 1763–7. He is referred to in No. 386 but not there identified.

[3] John Nicholls, whose name Pitt spells wrongly in No. 1507.

[4] *Parl. Register*, LVI, 264–305 (21 April). The 31 in the minority included Grey as Teller.

[5] *Parl. Register*, LVI, 247–58. The first paragraph is given, inaccurately, in Rose, p. 244.

of it, and the employing Sir James Pulteney in the Mediterranean, subject to Sir Ralph's orders, will I trust meet with your Majesty's approbation.

In order to render the Regular Infantry in Great Britain fit for service as expeditiously as possible, I beg leave to propose to your Majesty that one Brigade shall be placed at Canterbury, that a second shall be encamped in the Isle of Wight and that the remainder shall be assembled in as large a camp as possible in Windsor Forest, which is the only ground in the south of England at your Majesty's disposal capable of containing and furnishing space for exercising a large body of troops. (9548–9)

2137   WILLIAM PITT *to the* KING

[*Downing Street, Friday, 25 April 1800, 10.45 p.m.*] Mr Pitt humbly begs leave to acquaint your Majesty that previous to going into the Committee of the Whole House this day, Mr Grey moved an instruction to provide for the independence of Parliament, which he professed to mean as introducing Parliamentary Reform. The Motion was very ably opposed by Lord Hawkesbury, and afterwards by Sir W. Young & Mr Hawkins Browne, and was supported by Mr Bouverie,[1] Mr Bankes, Mr Wilberforce (who however expressed himself very doubtfully) and Dr Lawrence. The sense of the House seemed decidedly against the Motion, and it was rejected by 176 to 34. The House then went thro' the fourth Article which, after a short discussion, was agreed to without a division.[2] (9550)

2138   THE KING *to the* LORD CHANCELLOR (LORD LOUGHBOROUGH)

[*Windsor, 26 April 1800.*] The accompanying paper, though not possessing much information, was delivered to me yesterday by Earl Berkeley after his having assured me he had now decided proofs of his first marriage,[3] and that he is authorised to say by Mr. Mansfield,[4] the Chief Justice of Chester. I should not have immediately troubled the Lord Chancellor on this subject had he not, as he was

---

[1] There were three Bouveries in Parliament at this time, and not precisely the three referred to in vol. II, p. 351, note. Whether accurately or not the *Parl. Register's* division list contains W. H. Bouverie's name. He (1752–1806), the second son of the 1st Earl of Radnor (by his second wife) was M.P. for Salisbury, 1776–1802.

[2] *Parl. Register*, LVI, 346–87 (25 April). The King's reply on the 26th, expressing satisfaction that the House had shown its wisdom 'on that fallacious subject'—parliamentary reform—is in Stanhope, III, Appendix, p. xix.

[3] The 5th Earl of Berkeley (1745–1810) claimed to have married Mary Cole (*c.* 1767–1844) daughter of a publican and butcher, on 30 March 1785, though the truth of the matter was that the marriage took place only on 16 May 1796, the bogus ceremony, invented by the Earl, being designed with the object of legitimating his children born before 1796. In July 1811 the House of Lords decided that the alleged marriage had not been proved, and the eldest son, William Fitz Hardinge Berkeley, who, from 1796 had been styled Lord Dursley, was not allowed to assume his father's title. Bragge Bathurst told Lord Glenbervie that Lady Berkeley had been a common prostitute at Worcester, and that he had often been, with several members of the Oxford Circuit, 'in the exercise of that profession, in houses of accommodation for such temporary amours'. The King refused to receive her at Court. (Glenbervie, *Journals*, I, 400.)

[4] Sir James Mansfield (1734–1821), M.P. for Cambridge University, 1779–84; Solicitor-General, 1780–2, and Nov.–Dec. 1783; Chief Justice of Chester, 1799–1804; Chief Justice of the Common Pleas, 1804–14. Knighted, May 1804.

retiring from his audience, dropped an intention of bringing Lady Berkeley to St. James's, on which I replied that I trusted he would not take such a step untill his first marriage be decidedly proved. He appeared to acquiesce, but as the good Lord is not remarkably correct, I think it best to trouble the Lord Chancellor as the business is of a legal not a Court etiquette, thinking him the proper channel to communicate to Earl Berkeley that after the kind of talk occasioned by what passed the last year in the House of Lords[1] it is impossible Lady Berkeley can be received at Court untill the first marriage be satisfactorily proved. (48187)

2139   THE DUCHESS OF WURTEMBERG *to the* KING

[*Louisbourg, 28 April 1800.*] I was made very happy on Saturday by being honoured with your Majesty's gracious letter of April 8th by which I am sorry to find that many of those I wrote during the winter are lost. The enemy having been so near us quite destroyed the post, but now I trust that the Austrians surround us, things will get into order.

Monsieur de Wimpfen gives me great comfort by the good account he gives of your Majesty's health which is equally essential to my happiness and the good of Europe.

When I first heard of Frederick's fall I was very much allarmed, but am now easy as I find no fever came on after the accident. The poor little Dutchess is much to be pitied as I fear her nerves will suffer from the fright and hope great care was taken in breaking the news to her. Amelia's recovering her health is great joy to me who love her dearly, and have gone through much uneasiness about her. I hear she is much improved in beauty since I saw her, and I am sure her understanding has gained by the sensible letters she indulges me with.

Your Majesty is very gracious in interesting yourself about our various vexations. Tomorrow the new Assembly of States open; God grant that a better spirit may reign amongst them than the last. I wish the next fortnight was over that we may judge a little on what ground they will act. The fate of the conspirators is not yet decided; as soon as it is I shall not fail to acquaint your Majesty.

The good news which continues to come from Italy gives everybody spirits; and though the enemy have crossed the Rhine I believe they only flatter themselves to make a faint attack, which, when they find they cannot succeed in, I do not doubt they will retire and attempt the same somewhere else in hopes to fatigue the Austrians.

Your Majesty is very gracious about the congaroos; the Duke begs me to present his humble duty and thanks for your goodness and condescention in taking so much trouble about them. A very pretty spot is laid out here for their reception, and Faber receiving directions how to feed them I hope they will be able to live here. (51588–9)

[1] The House of Lords sat as a Committee of Privileges on 3, 5, 6, 13 and 20 June 1799 (*Parl. Register*, LIII, 636, 642, 645; LIV, 12, 25). The proceedings ended inconclusively.

[*Queen's House, 2 May 1800, 10.40 a.m.*] I am very happy at finding by Mr. Pitt's note[1] that the seventh Article[2] of the Union was agreed to in the Committee[3] and that the Report of all the Resolutions will be considered this day, which I trust, if the Lords are as dilligent, will enable the joint Address[4] being either presented on Wednesday or at latest on Thursday. (Chatham Papers.)

[*From Pitt, Downing Street, Friday, 2 May, 11.30 p.m.*] Mr Pitt humbly begs leave to acquaint your Majesty that Dr Lawrence this day in a very long speech opposed bringing up the Report of the Resolutions passed in the Committee on the Union. He was answered by Mr Morritt[5] (who spoke for the first time and with great good sense) and more fully and with great effect by Mr Ryder, after which Mr Bankes spoke against the Resolutions, and Sir Richard Glynn, Sir William Young, Coll. Wood and Mr Nicholl[s] for them. The House divided in favor of the Resolution being read a second time, 208 to 26, and the three first Resolutions were agreed to without farther debate. The consideration of the remainder of the Report was deferred on account of the lateness of the hour till Monday. (9557)

[*The King's reply, Windsor, 3 May, 8.20 a.m.*] If Dr. Laurence chose to discuss the acceptation of the report of the Committee on the Irish Propositions, he could not divest of length and much heaviness [*sic*]. I hear with pleasure that Mr. Morritt answered him with great good sense, as that is certainly more useful and less common than sprightliness. The three first Resolutions having been agreed to by 208 to 26 I augur that the rest will meet with as favorable a reception. (Chatham Papers.)

[*From Pitt, Downing Street, Monday, 5 May, 9.30 p.m.*] Mr Pitt has great satisfaction in being enabled humbly to acquaint your Majesty that on the Report this day of the Resolutions containing the Articles of the proposed Union with Ireland, they were all agreed to by the House, and ordered to be communicated to the Lords together with an Address, laying them before your Majesty. Mr Grey moved some Amendments in the 4th Article conformable to the plan he had before stated respecting the representation, and Dr Lawrence also renewed his proposal on the same subject, but neither entered into any discussion or called for a division. Mr Tierney afterwards moved to recommit the Commercial Article with a view to propose a duty on the export of wool, which after a short conversation was negatived by 111 to 19. Some objection was also stated to moving the Address tonight, but was not pressed, and it was finally agreed to demand a conference for communicating the Resolutions and Address to the Lords, who

---

[1] Missing.

[2] Concerning the financial arrangements.

[3] *H. of C. J.* LV, 453 (Thursday, 1 May). A Motion was made '. . . that the Report be received tomorrow morning'.

[4] The King received the joint Address of both Houses of Parliament at St James's on Friday the 9th.

[5] John Bacon Sawrey Morritt (*c.* 1771–1843), M.P. for Beverley, 1799–1802; for Northallerton, 1814–18; for Shaftesbury, 1818–20; one of Sir Walter Scott's friends.

will probably take them into consideration on Wednesday. Mr Pitt therefore flatters himself that your Majesty may be attended with the Address on Thursday, or at latest on Friday.[1] (9559–60)

2141 PRINCE AUGUSTUS *to the* KING

[*Carleton House, 8 May 1800.*] The Prince of Wales having informed me your Majesty is apprized of my arrival here,[2] I venture most humbly to petition the long-wished for happiness of presenting myself before you. My view in coming at this moment to England was to enable me to make a longer stay in this country than [I] should else have done arriving at a later period, as my health is good at present, and I suffer generally in cold weather particularly travelling in the winter. My object was particularly to wait upon your Majesty and prove to you my readiness to comply with your wishes in everything that is in my power, which God knows has ever been my daily and most sincere desire. If I have err'd in the manner of executing this plan I trust your Majesty will attribute it more to an ignorance of the proper mode of so doing than to any wish of doing anything that can savour of want of duty. I trust your Majesty will therefore allow me to throw myself at your feet and place myself here where duty, inclination, nature, and my own personal interest shew me I ought to be. With every sincere wish for your Majesty's private and publick happiness I sign myself [etc.]. (48191)

2142 *Letters from* LORD GRENVILLE *to the* KING, *and the reply*

[*5 May 1800, 2 p.m.*] Lord Grenville has the honour to transmit to your Majesty the military intelligence brought by the mail today. The rest of the mail will be sent to your Majesty as usual, tomorrow morning. It does not contain anything of importance. (9561)

[*Cleveland Row, 8 May 1800.*] Lord Grenville has the honour to acquaint your Majesty that Count Woronzow has this day communicated to him in confidence an order from the Emperor of Russia allowing him to ask for his recall from this Mission. This order, couched in very dry & harsh terms, is grounded on some representations which Count Woronzow had made on the subject of some of the Emperor's late orders. He wishes that this should not be known, but allowed Lord Grenville to mention it to your Majesty. He also communicated to Lord Grenville some private letters which he has received giving the most terrible description of the state of affairs at Petersburgh.

Lord Grenville requested Earl Spencer, he being dressed for the Drawing Room, to lay before your Majesty the arrangement respecting the Address as Mr Pitt & he settled it this morning on finding that the last steps could not be taken in the House of Commons till tomorrow, and which Lord Grenville had hoped to

[1] *Parl. Register*, LVI, 507–18. The King's reply (6 May, 7 a.m.), expressing his satisfaction at the progress achieved, and the hope that the Union would prove to be one of the most useful measures effected during his reign, is in Stanhope, III, Appendix, p. xx. Grey told his wife, 'I feel, I believe, as eager to defeat the Union as if I were myself an Irishman' (Howick MSS.).
[2] Prince Augustus arrived from Cuxhaven in the *King George* packet on the 5th.

have been able to lay before your Majesty, for your Majesty's commands upon it, if the debate in the House of Lords had not been protracted till near four.

Lord Grenville presumes to transmit to your Majesty the answer to be given to the Address if your Majesty shall be pleased to approve of it.

Lord Grenville also humbly submits to your Majesty the Minute of today, & that of yesterday, which was by mistake omitted to be sent; and also the secret papers which he had the honour to mention to your Majesty yesterday. (9565–7)

[*The King's reply, Queen's House, 9 May 1800, 12.58 a.m.*] The directions now given to Count Woronzow to ask for his recall fully compleats the strange conduct held by the Emperor of Russia since the failure in Holland, and gives but too much reason to fear it is not the effect of passion but of more fatal distemper, which, if not soon changed, may occasion some horrid explosion in that country.

Earl Spencer acquainted me yesterday with the change proposed in receiving the Address in consequence of the delays which have arisen. I never saw much weight in its being brought by the two Houses unless very fully attended. The mode proposed will be more expeditious. I suppose it cannot be ready for delivering before tomorrow but that need not in the least delay the sending the Resolutions to Ireland the moment they have passed the two Houses and the joint Address ordered to be delivered to me.

I therefore authorize Lord Grenville to desire the Duke of Portland to send off the Articles of Union the moment they have been as corrected agreed to by the House of Commons to Ireland. The deputation from the two Houses cannot return the answer to the two Houses till they meet on Monday, therefore may come at any hour convenient to them tomorrow to Windsor. By this arrangement the business will not be delayed and I trust no one put to any unnecessary trouble.

The answer seems perfectly proper, a duplicate must be prepared to be given to the messengers from the House of Commons. (Fortescue MSS.)

2143 THE DUKE OF PORTLAND *to the* KING

[*Bulstrode, Friday, 9 May 1800, 10.35 p.m.*] The Duke of Portland most humbly begs leave to acquaint your Majesty at the instance of the Deputies who are expected to attend your Majesty with the joint Address of the two Houses of Parliament on the subject of an Union with Ireland, that it is their intention to be at Windsor tomorrow at three o'clock to wait your Majesty's commands respecting the time at which your Majesty will please to receive the Address. The Deputies on the part of the Lords are the Lord Steward & Lord Walsingham. Those on the part of the Commons are Lord Hawkesbury, Mr Ryder, Mr Secretary at War & Mr Sylvester Douglas. (9570)

2144 WILLIAM PITT *to the* KING, *and the reply*

[*Downing St., Friday, 9 May 1800.*] Mr. Pitt humbly begs leave to submit to your Majesty that Mr. Windham not wishing to exchange the office of Secretary at War for that of Treasurer of the Navy,[1] and Mr. Steele having no anxiety for any other office than that which he now holds, he sees no person who has better pretensions to be promoted to the Treasurership of the Navy than Mr. Ryder. As this arrangement would equally open the office of Joint Paymaster, he trusts your Majesty will continue to approve of Mr. Canning's succeeding to that office,[2] and as Mr. Smythe does not wish to quit the Treasury he would take the liberty of humbly proposing Mr. Wallace to fill the vacancy at the India Board. Should these different arrangements meet your Majesty's approbation, there may be an advantage in considering them as fixed, tho' it may possibly be desireable on account of some business depending in the House, to defer for a short time the moving of the writs.[3] (9568–9)

[*The King's reply, Windsor, 10 May 1800, 8.46 a.m.*] As neither Mr. Windham nor Mr. Steele are desirous of changing their present employments I approve of Mr. Ryder's intended appointment to the Treasurership of the Navy;[4] Mr. Canning to that of Joint Paymaster, and Mr. Wallace to the Indian Board, and think Mr. Pitt is quite right in having this arrangement now settled, though he thinks it more convenient to defer the making out the appointments for a short time.[5] (Chatham Papers.)

[1] Windham wrote to Pitt on 25th April: 'I lose no time in thanking you for the consideration, which has led to the offer contained in your letter. Though the situation would in many respects be more eligible than that which I now hold, yet, under all the circumstances, I cannot hesitate in declining it, including, certainly, as an insuperable objection, any condition that would seem to deliver the office to me in a state less complete and respectable than that in which it had been before held.' (W. Dacres Adams MSS.) Pitt had told him on the 24th: 'tho' it is probably not a very material point, I ought to add that, as it would be a considerable inconvenience to Mr. Dundas to remove from the house in Somerset Place, it is proposed that in future it should be considered as annexed to the office of First Commissioner of India instead of that of Treasurer of the Navy.' (*Windham Papers*, II, 152.)

[2] This office brought Canning into the Privy Council. 'I always determined to be a Privy Councillor *at thirty*', he wrote on 8 April (he was born on 11 April 1770). [Harewood MSS.]

[3] The writ for Tiverton (Ryder) was moved on 28 May; those for Wendover (Canning) and Penryn (Wallace) on the 30th. Wallace's Commissionership of the India Board was one of the paid ones. This promotion did something to remove Wallace's dissatisfaction with his own position. He had felt 'the *humiliation* of being neglected' at a time when he was still at the Admiralty and others were about to be moved up.

[4] 'Dundas', wrote Canning on the 15th: 'seems...quite reconciled to the arrangement...The King approved mightily of the whole arrangement...and I hope we shall all kiss hands next week' (Harewood MSS.). Canning had just become engaged (on the 10th) and, two days later he wrote: 'Our town house I hope will be the Pay Office—and it is an admirable one' (*Ibid.*).

[5] It was the death of James Stuart Mackenzie, Lord Bute's brother, on 6 April, which led to these ministerial changes. Dundas was as anxious as ever to resign the War Secretaryship, and his first intention (8 April) was to resign both that office and the Treasurership of the Navy, on 1 October, 'when the campaign [in the Mediterranean], or at least its preparations, are over'. 'The more maturely I consider the business', he wrote again to Pitt, on 10 April, 'the more I am satisfied I ought not to lose this opportunity of retiring *with credit*. My only difficulty arose from the consideration due to another, but on explaining every circumstance to her, she feels as I do on the subject.' (Add. MSS., 40102, ff. 44–5.) Lady Jane was sure he had been overworking, and she was concerned for his health. On the 14th he told her that he had promised not to give up the War Secretaryship whilst the war continued, but, he added, in a third letter to Pitt (14 April) 'all that could still be retracted, and...it was impossible for me to retain any situation whatever on any account that contributed in so material a degree to make her unhappy.' But she had to admit that he could not leave the War Department without great inconvenience to the public service and without loss of character; and that situation she could not face. So, whilst he reluctantly agreed to remain, he asked Pitt to move him to some other Department or allow him to

[*Windsor, 10 May 1800.*] The enclosed letters I received yesterday, and forward them for the information of the Lord Chancellor whom I am sorry to hear is now confined with the gout. It occurs to me that Augustus's letter, though declaring submission to me, certainly in no degree treats with the seriousness he ought the offence of coming over without having asked my permission or with that decency that should have attended the journey of a Prince of my House but more like that of a culprit, and on the unfortunate affair that has caused to me so much uneasiness, he does not give any explanation that I can think sufficiently explicit of his giving up the absurd ideas he has as yet adopted, to give me reason for admitting him into my presence. These are the thoughts that his letter[s] have occasioned. I freely communicate them to the Lord Chancellor, and desire to have his opinion on the subject. If he will send that in a letter for me to the Secretary of State's Office tomorrow evening, I shall receive it on Monday morning. (48192)

[*The Lord Chancellor's reply, 11 May, 2 p.m.*] His Royal Highness the Prince of Wales & Prince Augustus had the goodness to visit the Chancellor on Saturday at 3 p.m. The Prince of Wales chiefly spoke, but Prince Augustus followed up the subject of the unfortunate affair that has been the cause of so much uneasiness to your Majesty in a very explicit manner & with the greatest appearance of frankness. He ascribed his past conduct to a sentiment of a conscientious nature & an hope he had been induced to nourish that all relief from a situation which so much distressed him was not totally impossible. He said that he had now obtained every opinion which could assist him & was perfectly convinced that his former ideas were without foundation and that he must ever regret the uneasiness which his errors had occasioned to your Majesty.

It may possibly occur to your Majesty's recollection that in a few months after the Prince went abroad, the ideas to which the Prince now refers as the origin of his errors appeared to have been infused into his mind & particularly from letters

retire altogether, if the opportunity offered. He would have liked to retain his £4,000 a year sinecure of Treasurer of the Navy, but felt that retention would retard 'the natural progress and ambition of those behind' him. As he could not afford to sacrifice that income he would take Stuart Mackenzie's £3,000 a year office of Lord Privy Seal of Scotland—an office tenable for life. He wanted to retain the office of President of the Board of Control, but without the salary of £2,000 a year, and to create a new office, that of Vice-President, with the same salary, for Canning. But Canning disliked the idea: 'It would be a *new* place, created on purpose for me, which I should think would naturally give rise to some clamour... India is of all the Departments that for which I am *least* qualified...My objections to it are, I confess, so strong, that if it is ultimately proposed to me, I shall prefer taking *nothing* now, to taking it, and shall wait another turn.' (Harewood MSS.) On 13 April Canning communicated to Dundas his objections, whereupon Dundas suggested to Pitt (14 April) that Steele should be asked to take this new office 'in the event of his not going to the War Office, from the arrangement not taking place which we talked of yesterday'. 'He may rest assured that at the end of this Parliament the Treasurership of the Navy would to a certainty be opened to him, and events may happen to do it sooner; and I need not tell you that during the two next years, when he would be occupied in giving the finishing stroke to the settlement of our Indian Empire, there is no man breathing would be so pleasing to me to act with as Steele.' (Chatham Papers, 157.) It was owing, as Canning said, to 'the press of business in all Departments and in Parliament just now' that the final arrangements were delayed until May.

addressed to the Archbishop & the Chancellor, which seems to give the more solidity to his present declaration that he is convinced they were ill founded.

In the course of the evening Mr. Erskine came to the Chancellor, and informed him that he had attended the Prince by H.R.H. orders, that he had given him his opinion in point of law, that his supposed marriage or any other he might attempt to contract in any country upon earth otherwise than according to the Act of Parlt. for the Royal Marriages, was & must ever remain absolutely & indefeasibly null. The Prince then desired his advice what conduct he ought to pursue, to which Mr. Erskine declined answering but in the presence of Lady Augusta Murray & her brother,[1] & on their coming into the room, Mr. Erskine, after a good deal of discourse with all the partys, stated as his decided opinion that it was neither consistent with plain reason nor a real sense of honour to keep up any appearances of a condition so very opposite to the truth. Mr. Erskine added that the Prince seemed satisfied & certainly H.R.H.'s discourse in the morning very much supported that idea. He observed that in the letter he had desired to lay at your Majesty's feet, he would not presume to hint at any explanation of an error it was his hope to efface, & he had confined himself entirely to the one great object to his mind of obtaining your Majesty's pardon for his precipitate journey, & to be admitted into your presence when you should think fit.

The Chancr. cannot but flatter himself from all these circumstances that there is a fair ground to hope that the issue of so disagreable a subject may turn out more satisfactory to your Majesty than its commencement promised.

The Chancellor has this moment received the inclosed note from Mr. Livingstone, which he presumes to send. (48193–4)

[*Enclosure*]

[*E. Livingston to the Lord Chancellor, Sunday, 4 p.m.* [*11 May*].] I had the honor by his R.H. Prince Augustus desire to pay my respects to him at Carleton House. I remained about two hours with the Prince. He was pleased to enter into a very full explanations of all his afairs. He now says he is perfectly convinced it is impossible to make good his marriage, and that he has told so to Lady Augusta Murray, her brother Lord Fincastle &c. The Prince says he has done what he thought his duty to her Ladyship and the child, and he hopes the King may be graciously pleased to forgive the rash step he took in comming here without his Majesty's leave. H.R.Hss. assured me in the most positive terms that he was determined to obey his Majesty's commands in the most implicit manner and adopt without reserve the plan of life the King may be pleased to prescribe.

It gave me great satisfaction to find H.R.H. so very reasonable. (48195–6)

[1] Viscount Fincastle (1762–1836), so styled until 25 Feb. 1809 when he succeeded his father as 5th Earl of Dunmore. M.P. for Liskeard, 1800–2. Created Baron Dunmore [U.K.] 1831 (a Coronation peerage).

2146 THE DUKE OF PORTLAND *to the* KING

[*Bulstrode, Sunday, 11 May 1800, 11 p.m.*] The Duke of Portland, humbly conceiving that any circumstance which may tend to shew the disposition of your Majesty's Parliament of Ireland will not at this moment be uninteresting to your Majesty, ventures to hope that he shall not incur your Majesty's displeasure by laying before your Majesty a letter from Lord Castlereagh to Mr King which contains an account of the proceedings of the House of Commons on last Thursday on the motion for adjournment to the following Monday. (9571)

2147 THE DUCHESS OF WURTEMBERG *to the* KING

[*Dunkelspiel, 12 May 1800.*] Your Majesty's known goodness to me makes me take up my pen to acquaint you that we are on our flight, as the Austrians have been beat several times by the French since the 4th they retire sadly on all sides, and the enemy taking advantage of this have done us dreadful mischief. I left Louisbourg at 3 o'clock yesterday evening; the Duke is determined to stay as long as he can without great danger. Our situation is very cruel as all the efforts he has made have been in vain. He is quite broken hearted at the treachery of the Commandant of Hohentweil who in a most cowardly manner yielded up to the French. Whenever I shall have it in my power to write safely to your Majesty I shall give you some details on that head which will make you shudder. Indeed I dreaded on Monday last that this news would have been fatal to my dear Duke. Nothing but his firm trust in Providence can support him under so many trials. A party of four or five thousand French have carried off greatest part of his Stud at Urach and a great deal of property he had at Tuttlingen. I hope the Almighty will still have mercy on us and at least prevent our poor country being totally ruined. Our comfort we have in all our distress is that our eldest son has behaved very well at the Army. I hope tomorrow to go to Weiltingen and if I can without danger shall stay there; it is an old castle and is the last place in the Duke's dominions on the Prussian side. I know nothing since I left home yesterday, which I did with a most heavy heart. God grant that I may be able to return soon in safety.

Your Majesty will forgive this scrawl as I cannot get here either better pens or paper. I shall not fail to write every post till things are quiet. (51590–1)

2148 THE KING *to the* PRINCE OF WALES

[*Queen's House, 12 May 1800.*] I have received your letter enclosing the one written to you by Augustus, from which I learn that he is at length convinced of the invalidity of the unwise step he took some years past, and that I am to be no farther troubled on that subject. I therefore now authorize you to bring him here tomorrow at three. (48197)

[*Queen's House, 13 May 1800.*] I am desirous of acquainting Mr. Pitt that to my great surprize on Tuesday May 6th I received a packet from the Prince of Wales containing a note from Lady Augusta Murray to the Earl of Moyra desiring him to come to her, and a letter from him to the Prince of Wales stating that though not acquainted with the lady, he had gone to her and to his utmost astonishment found Augustus there, who desired him to acquaint the Prince of Wales with his arrival. I instantly sent back the papers and desired that the Lord Chancellor might be acquainted with the event. On returning from Kew the P. of Wales came and stated that it was by the Chancellor's advice he had forwarded the papers to me; that he thought it highly improper Augustus should remain in the house with Lady Augusta, and that he (the P. of Wales) would persuade him to remove to Carlton House if it met with my approbation. I encouraged this as I thought it highly indecent that in addition to the great impropriety of coming over in stealth it should bear the additional appearance of being in defiance of me by the quarters he had taken. When I saw the Chancellor I mentioned what had past, that he had my leave to visit Augustus when at Carlton House if it was desired, but that I could as yet have no directions to communicate; that I saw no objection to Augustus's seeing Lord Thurlow and Mr. Erskine, as they could not but convince him of the nullity of his marriage. He has seen them both and they have in the most decided manner held the language I expected. On Friday the P. of Wales wrote me the enclosed letter accompanied by one from Augustus. I forwarded them to the Chancellor with my opinion that Augustus's letter not stating his relinquishing the idea of his marriage, and no proper excuse for his sudden arrival, I did not think without farther explanation that I would receive him. Instead of giving any opinion the Chancellor wrote the enclosed letter, accompanied by the note to him from Mr. Livingston. On coming to town I found the P. of Wales, whom I informed that I was not satisfyed with Augustus's letter; that what he now said, and the Chancellor's letter, made me hope he saw the nullity of the marriage, but I was not personally informed of it; that I did not require a letter to that effect, as it would oblige me to write an answer, but that if Augustus would write to that effect to the P. of Wales and he send it to me for my information, I would certainly return it to him. In the course of the evening I got such a letter, but to clear up all farther doubts I wrote to the P. of Wales the note, of which the enclosed is a copy. I have just seen Augustus, and on that unpleasant business touched no farther than that understanding that a cloud was to be drawn over all passed unpleasant subjects, I should only look forward. (Chatham Papers.)

[*Pitt's reply, Downing Street, Tuesday, 13 May.*] Mr Pitt humbly begs leave to return the papers of which your Majesty has had the goodness to allow him the perusal. He rejoices to find from them that the line which your Majesty has thought proper to adopt, has not failed to produce, as far as can be judged at present, the effect which might be justly expected from it, and that your Majesty is likely to be relieved from any farther anxiety or trouble on so unpleasant a subject. (9572)

[*Queen's House, 14 May 1800.*] On Monday morning I received the Lord Chancellor's letter and on coming to town saw the Prince of Wales, to whom I expressed the same objections to the letter from Augustus I had stated to the Lord Chancellor, though accompanied with my belief from what he said and from what I had learnt, of Augustus's language to the Lord Chancellor that Augustus now felt the i[n]validity of the marriage, but that I could not think myself at liberty to admit him to my presence, as his letters had always borne another opinion, untill his present conviction was stated on paper. I did by no means wish that should be by letter to me, that his writing what he had already said to the Prince of Wales in a letter to him and sent for my information, I should certainly instantly return it. In the course of the evening I received the enclosed letter from the P. of Wales to which I wrote the accompanying answer, as I chose to put a final stop to any further discussion, and saw him yesterday. I trust now there is a final end of this most unpleasant business. (48199)

[*Lord Loughborough's reply, 14 May.*] Your Majesty's great goodness in acting immediately upon the first communication of Prince Augustus's alteration of opinion & without farther discussion cannot fail to make the deepest impression on the Prince's mind, & revive in it a due sense of those dutys from which by a fatal error he had been so long estranged.

The Chancellor's knowledge of your Majesty's most gracious disposition to forgive as soon as your *justice* will permit, had led him to express his hope that there might be a favourable issue found for this disagreable subject, and he most humbly thanks your Majesty for your condescension in communicating to him the mode your Majesty most wisely adopted to put an immediate & final end to a business that had been the cause of so much uneasiness. (48200)

[*Weiltingen, 14 May 1800.*] On Tuesday we arrived here and I had intended not troubling your Majesty with a letter till I could acquaint you with something positive as to our situation, but the Duke sending to Mr Wickham enables me to acquaint your Majesty with some particulars about Hohentweil I did not think prudent to send by the post. General Bielfinger the Commandant is seventy five years of age, and the Duke not wishing to hurt an old man, though he thought it dangerous to entrust him alone with the defence of Hohentweil, appointed Colonel Wolf vice Commandant in February 1799, with two secret orders, the one ordering him to supersed Bielfinger if he found him inclined to deliver up this place, and the other by which the Duke possitively forbids his ever yielding the fortress to the enemy, if even the Duke being in their hands might be forced to write such an order, unless it was accompanied by certain signs which the Duke was determined never to give, as he thought Hohentweil of too much consequence for his family. The fortress is built on a rock nine hundred feet high and so strong that by breaking down the drawbridge it was quite impossible for the enemy to do any mischief. It was victualed for three years and had not only every necessary provision but even luxuries. I cannot comprehend how this wretched man who always bore a good character could be so treacherous. Thank God he is taken and I trust will be severely punished. The loss of Hohentweil goes very hard with the Duke but he knows that this as well as all our other misfortunes comes from the Almighty and therefore bears them like a Christian. Since I left him on Sunday he has quelled a sad mob at Stutgard which was occasioned by the States wanting to send their money away secretly; he has now insisted that it shall go publicly. I believe the courage he shewed has at least made Stutgard remain quiet. I wish that town had the same good spirit which reigns in the rest of the country.

Today Kray I understand is to attack the French. God grant he may be successful as on this hangs our fate. I try to prepare my mind for all events and to bear with fortitude the misfortunes it may please God to send us. Should we be obliged to leave our country I wish much to go to some quiet place in the neighbourhood that we may be able to return as soon as the enemy has left it and by great oeconomy enable myself to assist the Duke's poor subjects who must become victims of the inhuman enemy. It is very cruel that the Austrians by taking all our troops with them have prevented our defending the Dutchy as we did last year, and notwithstanding all their Treaty's abandon the Empire to the mercy of the French. Could once a spirit of unity reign in their Army things would be very different, and I believe that nothing but having an Archduke at its head will ever make them do anything reasonable. The young Archduke Ferdinand[1] is quite a hero and has more than once saved the army and particularly on the 4th, Field Marshal Kray. Amongst all our misfortunes the conduct of our eldest son gives us great comfort. Poor dear boy, it is a dreadful beginning for him, but his prudence and good sense make it of advantage to his mind and he gains the good will of everybody. (51592–4)

2152 [THOMAS] KEATE to the KING

[*The Queen's House, 15 May 1800.*] Mr. Keate has the honor to represent for the information of the King that, in obedience to his Majesty's commands, he has seen Mr. Ongley,[2] who was wounded by a musket ball this morning in Hyde Park. It passed through both thighs, but happily in such direction as not to endanger his life, and only through fleshy parts. Every kind of assistance is rendered, and he is so near to York Hospital as to derive all manner of comfort and help from thence. Mr. Keate has seen Mr. Rush,[3] concerted proper measures of relief, and will meet him there at twelve tomorrow. (9574)

[1] The Emperor Francis II's brother (1769–1824). Grand Duke of Tuscany, 1790.

[2] On the 15th the King was attending the field exercises of the Grenadier Guards in Hyde Park when, during one of the volleys, a ball cartridge was fired by a soldier which struck William Ongley, a clerk in the Navy Pay Office, who was said to be standing only 23 feet away from the King. It passed through his thigh, but the wound was not fatal. Whether, as seems likely, this was an accident or whether it was intentional was never ascertained, as the man who fired the shot could not be discovered. That evening the King was shot at by the lunatic Hadfield at Drury Lane Theatre.

[3] John Rush, Inspector of Military Hospitals.

[*Burlington House, Thursday night, 15 May 1800.*] The Duke of Portland humbly requests your Majesty's leave to acquaint your Majesty that James Hadfield[1] the traitor who fired a pistol into your Majesty's box at the theatre this evening has after a long examination of himself & witnesses been fully committed to Newgate for high treason, & the Duke of Clarence has since condescended to inform the Duke of Portland that one of the slugs with which Hadfield confessed the pistol had been loaded, had penetrated the pillar of your Majesty's box which is the farthest from the stage, & had been found flattened on the floor. The evidence which was taken at the Secretary of State's Office will be transcribed fair tomorrow, & will be ready to be laid before your Majesty in the course of the morning.[2]
(9573)

[*Burlington House, Saturday, 17 May, 11 p.m.*] The Duke of Portland most humbly begs leave to lay before your Majesty the letters from Ireland which have been received this day by Mr. King, which the Duke of Portland presumes to hope your Majesty will find contain as favorable accounts of the progress which has been made by the House of Commons of that kingdom in the great work of Union as your Majesty had expected.[3]

The Duke of Portland also begs leave to acquaint your Majesty that the Corporation of the City of London having unanimously voted a dutifull & loyal Address to your Majesty on the subject of your Majesty's providential escape from the late atrocious attempt on your sacred person, the Sheriffs have expressed to the Duke of Portland great anxiety to be informed of the time & place at which your Majesty will permit them to take your commands respecting the time which your Majesty will appoint to be attended with the Address of the Corporation—and the motives of that anxiety being obvious to the Duke of Portland, & your Majesty

---

[1] Hadfield (*c.* 1772–1841) had served in the 15th Light Dragoons and had been one of the Duke of York's orderlies. He had been severely wounded in the head during the Flanders campaign and had had to be discharged from the army on the ground of insanity. He was tried on a charge of high treason before the Court of King's Bench on 26 June; his insanity was clearly proved, and on the Judges' direction the jury found him not guilty, being under the influence of insanity at the time the act was committed. He was sent to Bedlam, where he died. E. J. Littleton, M.P., saw him (and also Margaret Nicholson) there on 7 May 1818, and talked to him. Hadfield said that he 'much wished he had suffered at the time. The loss of liberty he said, was worse than death. But he appeared clearly mad.' Littleton added, 'All the maniacs talked of the loss of their liberty, but liked their present residence [the New Bedlam] better than the old one—because they could see out of the windows.' At *that* time Margaret Nicholson was not chained to the floor of her cell [see I, 240 n.], and Littleton said that he saw only one person out of 180 in a strait waistcoat. (Hatherton MSS., Diary.)

[2] At the conclusion of the Farce Sheridan's impromptu verses were added to *God save the King* and sung with enthusiastic applause:

> From every latent foe,
> From the assassin's blow,
>   God save the King.
> O'er him thine arm extend,
> For Britain's sake defend
> Our father, Prince, and friend.
>   God save the King.

[3] Cornwallis's official letter to the Duke, dated the 13th, giving an account of the debate in the Irish House of Commons on the 12th, in which the Government had a majority of 135 v. 80, is in *Cornwallis Corresp.* III, 232.

having condescended to intimate no disinclination to receive this Address after that of the two Houses of your Parliament had been presented to your Majesty, the Duke of Portland presumed to give it as his opinion to the Sheriffs that your Majesty might probably order them to attend your Majesty at the Queen's House on Monday between the hours of three & four, & might appoint the same or nearly the same time on the following Wednesday to receive the Address of the Corporation at St. James's. (9579–80)

[*Burlington House, Sunday, 18 May, 11 p.m.*] The Duke of Portland humbly begs leave to offer his most gratefull acknowledgements to your Majesty for your Majesty's great goodness & condescension in having marked, with pencil the fourth printed list inclosed in Lord Castlereagh's letter of the 10th instant to Mr. King for the reasons which your Majesty has been graciously pleased to mention. The Duke of Portland herewith submits to your Majesty a dispatch from the Lord Lieutenant of the 13th instant, which though of an older date than the letters from Lord Castlereagh & Mr. Cooke, which were laid yesterday before your Majesty, as it contains a copy of the Lord Lieutenant's Message to the Parliament of Ireland on his communicating to them, in pursuance of your Majesty's commands, the Articles of Union & the joint Address of the two Houses of Parliament of this kingdom to your Majesty on that occasion, together with a short statement of the proceedings of the Irish Parliament on the same subject, the Duke of Portland considered it to be his duty to lay at your Majesty's feet.

Copies of the further examinations which have been taken relative to Hadfield are also herewith most humbly submitted to your Majesty,[1] & as soon as those which have been taken or shall hereafter be taken can be transcribed fair, it is the Duke of Portland's intention to lay them from time to time before your Majesty unless your Majesty's pleasure shall be signified to him to the contrary.

As your Majesty did not intimate any disapprobation of the time or place at which the Duke of Portland had ventured to suppose it might be your Majesty's pleasure to see the Sheriffs tomorrow he has presumed to direct them to attend tomorrow at the Queen's House at three o'clock in the afternoon to receive your Majesty's commands respecting the time at which your Majesty will please to be attended with the Address of the Corporation. (9581–2)

[*Burlington House, Monday, 19 May, 4.05 p.m.*] Your Majesty's commands respecting the attendance of the Sheriffs of London were immediately obeyed. It is with great satisfaction the Duke of Portland lays before your Majesty the accounts of the farther progress of the Union which have been transmitted by Lord Castlereagh to Mr. King. The Duke of Portland humbly begs leave to apprize your Majesty that the University of Oxford has by this time resolved to present a dutifull Address to your Majesty on your Majesty's providential escape from the horrid attempt made on your Majesty's sacred life on last Thursday which they will be ready to lay at your Majesty's feet whenever your Majesty will condescend to appoint a time for that purpose. (9583)

[1] Folios 9596–644.

[*Hannover, 22 May 1800.*] No words can express what I felt today on receiving the account of your Majesty's providential escape. This fresh proof of the goodness of the Almighty in preserving your precious days for your nation and family is such that every honest subject must feel it and exult at it, and certainly no one more than myself. God knows how great my affection is for you. I am not able to express the sensations of my heart but I trust your Majesty will do me the justice not to doubt of them and that you are persuaded of the fervent prayers I offer up to the Almighty for your preservation.

I begg you will excuse the shortness of this letter, but I really am so overcome that I am not able to add more than the assurance of my ever [etc.]. (48551)

2155   THE DUKE OF KENT *to the* KING

[*Halifax, Nova Scotia, 22 May 1800.*] By this time your Majesty will probably have received from the Duke of York an application on my behalf for leave of absence for me to return to England, in consequence of the deranged state of my health. I should have done myself the honor of addressing myself directly to you in the first instance, had I not been apprehensive that, considering the official situation I hold here, the Duke of York might have been offended at my not preferring the request through him. To avoid the possibility of this, I therefore determined to let the opportunity, by which I wrote to him, pass without troubling your Majesty upon the subject. At present, however, as the matter will have been laid before you, if not already, at least long before this letter can reach England, I conceive it to be my duty most respectfully to state that since I wrote to the Duke of York, my health has continued to be to the full as indifferent as it was at that time. Scarce a day passes without my suffering severely from the effects of a bilious disorder, which is in my blood, notwithstanding the constant use of medicine and the most temperate mode of life it is possible to pursue. In addition to this my chest is grown so uncommonly weak that I am sensible nothing but your Majesty's permission to leave this country before the approach of the cold weather can secure me from the certain prospect of a severe attack the moment the inclemency of the season commences. The apprehension of trespassing upon your Majesty's patience prevents me from going on with the detail of my complaints, although with the strictest adherence to veracity I might add much more to what I have already stated. I shall therefore only say that I feel my state of health to be such that I am confident my return to my native climate is indispensable to effect my recovery, and as such, I humbly hope your Majesty will have condescended, on the Duke of York's application, to grant me your permission to embark towards the close of summer.

I trust the zeal and readiness which I have ever endeavoured to evince in the discharge of whatever duty has been intrusted to me, and of which you have at all times been pleased to signify your gracious approbation, render it needless for me to say that if I did not feel myself so seriously indisposed as I do, I should not presume to sollicit this indulgence, although it naturally must be the wish nearest my heart to enjoy the satisfaction of again approaching your person and living in the society of my family.

Anxious not to trouble your Majesty with a long letter or to trespass further upon your patience, I shall beg leave to conclude here,¹ (45985–6)

2156 THE ARCHBISHOP OF CANTERBURY *to the* KING

[?*Saturday, 24 May 1800.*] Having found it impossible yesterday, when I had the honor to pay my duty to your Majesty at St James's, to take your Majesty's commands respecting a Thanksgiving Prayer² to Almighty God for the merciful interposition of His good Providence in bringing to nought the late horrible attempt against your Majesty's person & life; it is my duty to inform your Majesty that I have presumed to print & to send forth a Prayer, which I trust will be read in all the Churches in the Metropolis & within the Bills of Mortality tomorrow, tho' I had no authority for so doing. I have done it, Sir, under a full confidence of your Majesty's approbation & that of the ardent desire of your subjects to express their thankfulness to God, the guardian of good & godly Kings. Copies of the Prayer will go by this evening's mail to Ireland. (9593)

2157 THE DUKE OF PORTLAND *to the* KING

[*Bulstrode, Sunday, 25 May 1800, 11.15 p.m.*] The Duke of Portland most humbly requests your Majesty's leave to express the very great satisfaction with which he lays before your Majesty the dispatch he has just received from the Lord Lieutenant by the express because the Duke of Portland most firmly beleives the

¹ The Duke had written to Pitt from Halifax on 23 April asking for the post of Commander-in-Chief in Ireland: 'Accounts having reached this from England as late as the 22nd of February, we are inclined from them to be confident that the measure of the Union is before this completed to your entire satisfaction.

My extreme anxiety not to be forgot in the arrangements that will take place upon this event, leads me to trouble you with these lines, although I am sensible you will not be able to find time to answer them. After the polite assurance you gave me when last we met in Downing Street, of your intention to support my views of serving in Ireland, my mind would be perfectly at ease, had I not received a communication from the Duke of York, that rather tended, though not to destroy, yet in some measure to damp my expectations. I write by the present opportunity to him, in a manner which I hope will amply do away any objections he might have had before to my being recommended to the King for the command of his forces in Ireland. But should I not have succeeded, I beg leave to say, that I place that reliance on your good will, as to trust *you* will not suffer any frivolous cause to be started, in order to prevent your kind intentions in my behalf from taking effect. My conduct when in England will I trust bear the closest investigation, and I believe you will be of opinion that in my political conduct I faithfully adhered to those principles, which I informed you were my creed, the first time I ever saw you. I believe few men of my rank in life, have been fifteen years away from their native country, or can boast of having served uninterruptedly for *ten* of that time in the most trying climates; when to this I add that my constitution has seriously suffered from this cause and that a longer residence in North America would be essentially injurious to my health, I flatter myself you will require no stronger inducement to engage you to be my friend on this occasion, which is one of the most interesting of my life: for I look forward to it as a provision which I hope I shall enjoy for years.

I shall now only add that you may rely upon my conduct being uniformly such as to prove that I am not unworthy of the trust reposed in me, and that it will be my greatest pride, not to discredit your friendship.' (W. Dacres Adams MSS.)

² Folio 9594. The Archbishop was at the Levée on Friday the 23rd.

sentiments professed by Sir Laurence Parsons[1] on your Majesty's late providential deliverance to be, with very few exceptions, universally & indelibly imprinted on the hearts of your Majesty's Irish as well as on those of your British subjects, & because he conceives himself authorized by the event of Wednesday's debate to offer his most dutifull congratulations to your Majesty on the certain & successfull issue of the great measure of Union, which considering the numbers & steadiness of its supporters & the temper, disposition & despondency which its opponents are no longer able to conceal, it is almost impossible not to suppose will be such as will be perfectly agreable to your Majesty.[2]

The other dispatches from the Lord Lieutenant contain only a petition from the person calling himself the Viscount Gormanston[3] for the Lord Lieutenant's favourable representation to your Majesty of his claim to a writ of summons to Parliament in consequence of the reversal of two outlawries against his ancestors & the reports of your Majesty's Law servants of Ireland in his behalf; & six petitions against the Union, which have been detained at the Office—& the last dispatch is merely an acknowledgement of the account which Mr Wickham had given of the actions at Engen & Moeskirk which the Duke of Portland had transmitted to the Lord Lieutenant.[4]

The Duke of Portland has received an application this evening from Aldermen Sir Watkin Lewes, Sir John Eamer & Mr Shaw[5] who together with Mr Smith their clerk have been deputed by the Commissioners of Lieutenancy for the City of London to attend your Majesty in order that they may receive, as they alledge conformably to ancient usage, your Majesty's pleasure respecting the time at which your Majesty will please to be attended with the Address of that body—& he accordingly most humbly requests that your Majesty will graciously condescend to signify to him your commands in that respect. (9588–9)

2158   SIR JOHN MITOFRD (ATTORNEY-GENERAL) *to* LEONARD SMITH

[*Adelphi, 27 May 1800, 12 p.m.*] I am this moment returned from the House of Commons, where I have been detained by the Committee on the Income Bill till this late hour. I am extremely sorry I had not the pleasure of seeing you when you

[1] Sir Lawrence Parsons (1758–1841), succeeded his uncle as 2nd Earl of Rosse [I.], 20 April 1807. M.P. for Dublin University, 1782–90; for King's County, 1791–1807. Succeeded to his father's Baronetcy, 1 May 1791. Though an uncompromising opponent of the Union, he was later in office as a Lord of the Treasury [I.], 1805–9, and as Joint Postmaster-General [I.], 1809–31. A Representative Peer, 1809–41. For Cornwallis's comments on his speech see *Cornwallis Corresp.* III, 238.

[2] On the 21st the Irish House of Commons gave leave for the introduction of the Union Bill by 160 votes to 100. It was brought in and read a first time. (Ross, *Cornwallis Corresp.* III, 238–9.)

[3] Jenico Preston (1775–1860), a Roman Catholic. At Easter 1800 the outlawries of his Jacobite ancestors, the 6th and 7th Viscounts Gormanston were pronounced by the Court of King's Bench in Ireland to be void, and on 2 August he had a writ of summons to take his seat in the Irish House of Lords; but owing to the prorogation of the House, which never again met because of the Union, he had no opportunity of taking his seat (in any case he could not have taken the required oaths).

[4] Moreau's army had crossed the Rhine to engage the Austrians under General Kray. There was a series of engagements at Engen and Stockach (3 May), at Moesskirch on the 5th and at Biberach on the 10th.

[5] Sir James Shaw (c. 1764–1843), M.P. for London, 1806–18; Lord Mayor of London, 1806; created Baronet, Sept. 1809.

did me the honour of calling, as I could better have explained the stile of the Bill to which you allude, perhaps, verbally, than I can do by this note. It has been the subject of very serious consideration of the Solicitor General & myself, with the assistance we could obtain, for a considerable time; & I *think* it is now completed. At the same time I am anxious to know what was done with respect to the will of his late Majesty King George the First, for which purpose I have obtained the Duke of Portland's order for inspection of some papers at the Paper Office. I am aware of nothing to prevent the Bill being early brought forward, but I was very anxious not to offer it to the consideration of Parliament without every previous consideration which the nature of the business would permit. I have given a general view of the necessity for the aid of Parliament, & the particular objects intended to be embraced by the Bill, to the Lord Chancellor & Mr. Pitt; but they have not seen it in detail. Lord Eldon has also been informed of the measure proposed. The state of anxiety in which Lord Kenyon has been with respect to his son,[1] & his unwillingness, at any time, to give attention to Parliamentary business, have induced me to forbear from troubling him. I could have wished to have talked to Lord Thurlow upon it; but I must confess I have not courage to struggle with the peculiarities of his mind in a private conversation upon it. You will judge of the difficulty of dealing with him on such a Bill when I tell you that about four years ago, being then Treasurer of the Inner Temple, I had to propose to his Lordship, as one of four surviving Trustees of the Temple estates, a conveyance to new Trustees in the form which has been pursued for several centuries. I called Lord Kenyon & Lord Eldon to my assistance but was not able to prevail on him to approve the draught of the deed; & four successive Treasurers have been equally unsuccessful. The thing is abandoned in despair. (9590–1)

2159   THE DUCHESS OF WURTEMBERG *to the* KING

[*Weiltingen, 29 May 1800.*] I am so overcome at the news of your Majesty's providential escape that I fear my pen will have great difficulty to do justice to the feelings of my heart. Your Majesty who knows my dutiful attachment will not be surprized when I assure you that I was more affected by the account of the danger you had been in than with our own misfortunes. The Duke begs me to present his humble duty to your Majesty and congratulations on your having been preserved in so wonderful a manner; he would have written himself had he not feared the being troublesome. He joins with me most heartily in thanking the Almighty for watching over your precious life and in praying God to grant that you may continue many many years a blessing to the world and doubly so to your children who owe you everything and are proud to look up to you as their parent and protector.

The situation here continues very uncertain: some days ago the French made a feint retreat and have taken up another position. They attacked Gunzbourg where the Bavarians and Wurttembergs are and were repulsed for the time; our men behaved very well and I trust will continue to give your Majesty satisfaction.

---

[1] Lord Kenyon's eldest son, Lloyd (1775–1800), died on 15 Sept. after a long illness.

I long to have a safe opportunity to write as I have many things to say which I cannot trust by the post. I must now take my leave with great respect [etc.]. (51596–7)

2160 THE BISHOP OF WORCESTER (RICHARD HURD) *to the* KING

[*Hartlebury, 31 May 1800.*] I thank God that, amidst so many & such perils, your Majesty's sacred person is still safe, but these gratulations being the subject of a publick Address from your faithful clergy of my Diocese on that most interesting occasion, & being, as I hoped, to be presented soon, I thought it would be too presuming in me to trouble your Majesty with a private letter on a subject wch. is not to be reflected on without horror. I find however that our Address cannot be carried through the usual & necessary forms yet of some time, so as that all the clergy may have an opportunity of subscribing it with hand & heart as they wish to do. Finding this delay therefore unavoidable, I can no longer repress the impatience I feel of expressing the sense I have of your Majesty's late wonderful deliverance, & of my thankfulness to Almighty God for his gracious interposition in a moment so full of terror to all your subjects. If you yourself, Sir, felt little of that terror, it is because your Majesty is not apt to be alarmed by sudden surprizes & because your Majesty has just reason to know that no Sovereign of this or any country had ever less to fear.

It is with infinite satisfaction I hear that the Queen & Royal Family are restored to their former health & spirits, and humbly begging your Majesty's pardon for the liberty of this short letter I am [etc.]. (9592)

2161 THE DUCHESS OF WURTEMBERG *to the* KING

[*Weiltingen, 4 June 1800.*] As I cannot have the happiness of offering your Majesty jointly with your other children my congratulations on this day so justly dear to us all, I hope you will permit me to express the ardent wishes I form that the Almighty may ever watch over your precious life, and grant you every happiness and blessing this world contains. The Duke begs me also to present his humble duty and congratulations. His fear of being troublesome prevents his expressing his feelings on this occasion himself.

I envy all those who will have the honour of being at the Breakfast and hope your Majesty is sufficiently convinced of my attachment to believe that none enjoy more than I do celebrating this day. The Duke has ordered the mourning to be put off, and though our situation does not allow of great doings, we shall do everything in our power to shew our respect and love for your Majesty in a quiet way.

Everything continues in the same state at Ulm; the enemy has taken Augsbourg and Friedberg. The Elector[1] has left Munich. Field Marshal Kray has detached General Mehrfeld towards Augsbourg but I fear too late. It is dreadful that since the 11th May no great trial has been made to stop the French, who always continue to advance and do mischief. Nothing but the hand of God can save us, for the enemy appears to have very deep laid plans. (51600–1)

[1] Maximilian Joseph, Elector of Bavaria.

[*Hannover, 4 June 1800.*] This day is much too interesting to me ever to let it pass without presenting your Majesty my most humble and sincere congratulations on it, and I offer up the most fervent prayers to the Almighty that he may continue preserving you for many years and that you may see many happy returns of this day. I am just going to fire a feu de joie in honour of the day and I will answer for all my Brigades doing it with great loyalty. Indeed I can with truth assure your Majesty that the joy that has been shewn here on your late providential escape has been universal, and that every class has behaved in a proper manner on this occasion. I am convinced it is impossible that a Sovereign can be more loved by his subjects than you are, and I rejoice in being able to say that they are worthy of your affection. How happy should we all be if ever you were to come here; you would then be able to convince yourself of the truth of my assurance.

Saturday next my Brigade marches to camp. We have been exercising for these four weeks past and I trust that we shall meet with the approbation of General Wallmoden. Should I be too much employed to write to you from camp I shall certainly not fail to do myself that honour as soon as I return.

I dare now not trespass any longer on your Majesty's patience than just to add the humble assurance of my ever remaining [etc.]. (48552)

2163 SIR JOSEPH BANKS *to the* KING

[*Soho Square, 5 June 1800.*] Sir Joseph Banks begs leave humbly to submit the enclos'd plan for the sale of rams & ewes out of your Majesties Spanish flock, hoping that it may be found conformable to the ideas on that subject which your Majesty did Sir Joseph the honor to approve last autumn.

If this plan is honord with your Majesties approbation, it may be publishd as an appendix to a pamphlet on wool which Ld. Sheffield will publish in a few days at the request of Mr Pitt, by which means it will be put into the hands of most of the woolen manufacturers at once, & it may also be circulated in a separate sheet, which Sr. Joseph Banks will have an opportunity of putting into the hands of most of the great sheep breeders, at the Duke of Bedford's sheep shearing which begins at Wooborn Abbey on the 16 of the present month. (9645)

2164 LORD AUCKLAND *to the* KING

[*Palace Yard, 7 June 1800.*] Lord Auckland hopes that in sending the inclosed small work he has not presumed too much on your Majesty's gracious goodness & favour. It was thought that this publication might have an useful effect in many points of view, both as serving to explain a question of serious importance to the public mind & morals, & as serving to convey some salutary intimations & truths to all of both sexes whom it may concern. As such Lord Auckland hopes that he has not done wrong in presuming humbly to lay it at your Majesty's feet. (9646)

[*Downing Street, Saturday, 7 June 1800.*] Mr Pitt is persuaded your Majesty will have the goodness not to disapprove his venturing humbly to submit to your Majesty's consideration a circumstance which appears in many views to be of great public importance.

Your Majesty is probably informed that Lord Carlisle has made a complaint to the House of Lords of a breach of privilege, founded on an account in a newspaper of a charge stated to be given by Lord Kenyon to a jury in a recent action on account of adultery; which charge Lord Carlisle considers as containing reflections on himself for his language in Parliament, and on those who voted against the Bill for the prevention of adultery, in the House of Lords. The complaint is in the first instance, in point of form against the printer, but is evidently aimed against Lord Kenyon, of whose personal merits Mr Pitt knows your Majesty's opinion, and whose station renders the support of his credit and authority a point of no small interest to the administration of justice and to the character of Government. On this account it appears to most of your Majesty's servants to be highly necessary to resist such a proceeding, for which (on its own merits) there seems to be no sufficient ground; as the charge refers not to any particular Peer or to the proceedings of the House of Lords, but to newspaper statements of sentiments said to be recently delivered, which the Chief Justice supposes, to have been untruly represented, and which he seems to have thought himself bound to counteract, lest they should have an undue influence on the minds of the jury. There would be probably little difficulty on the question, were it not that the heat which was raised on the Bill lately depending appears to extend to this question, and in particular that the Prince of Wales and the Dukes of Clarence and Cumberland are supposed to be taking a very active part in support of Lord Carlisle's complaint. The mischief which must arise from such an influence exerted on such an occasion, directed personally against Lord Kenyon and in opposition to the line which your Majesty's Ministers must feel themselves bound to support with the weight of Government, is but too obvious. And (if the subject appears to your Majesty in the light in which Mr Pitt has viewed it) your Majesty may possibly not be unwilling to convey such an intimation as may prevent the Princes from persisting in what is understood to be their present intention. Mr Pitt deeply regrets being under the necessity of intruding these considerations on your Majesty. He will only take the liberty of adding that the consideration of Lord Carlisle's complaint is fixed for Tuesday next.[1] (9648–50)

[*Hollwood, 8 June, 3 p.m.*] Mr. Pitt is this moment honored with your Majesty's commands of this morning,[2] and is deeply sensible of the condescending goodness with which your Majesty has been pleased to receive the suggestion which he ventured to offer. The draft of what your Majesty proposes to write appears to

---

[1] 'That puppy and adulterous profligate the Earl of Carlisle was to bring on his Motion...against me for breach of privilege in alluding to his infamous speech on the Bill against adultery, but he withdrew his Motion' (Lord Kenyon's Diary, 10 June 1800 [Kenyon MSS.]).

[2] The King's reply on the 8th to Pitt's letter of the 7th is in *Dropmore Papers*, VI, 246.

Mr Pitt so perfectly adapted to the occasion, that it is impossible for him to wish a single alteration in it.[1] (9654)

Letters from the DUKE OF PORTLAND *to the* KING

[*Bulstrode, Sunday, 8 June 1800, 8.50 p.m.*] The Duke of Portland is extremely concerned to find himself under the necessity of expressing a doubt of its being in his power to obey your Majesty's commands to attend your Majesty tomorrow at three o'clock. Your Majesty's orders reached him at this place, & on the breaking up of the meeting of your Majesty's servants yesterday he understood that it was Mr Pitt's intention to go to & remain at Hollwood till tomorrow morning. The Duke of Portland will be in town tomorrow by nine o'clock & he has sent to Mr Pitt to desire him to meet him, by which means the Duke of Portland hopes to be enabled to obey your Majesty's commands, but in case it should not be in his power to report to your Majesty the result of his conversation with Mr Pitt at the time your Majesty has been pleased to appoint, he most humbly begs leave to know at what other time it may be your Majesty's pleasure to be attended by the Duke of Portland for that purpose.[2] (9652–3)

[*Bulstrode, Monday, 9 June, 11.45 p.m.*] The Duke of Portland has the satisfaction to submit with all humility to your Majesty the dispatches from the Lord Lieutenant of Ireland which contain an account of the proceedings of the Opposition on the course of the progress of the Union Bill through the House of Commons, & of its having finally passed that House on last Saturday.[3] The Duke of Portland ventures to beleive that your Majesty will not be inclined to be of opinion that there is much cause of alarm either upon account of the measures which have been thrown out by the Opposition or of their secession. The D. of Portland is very sorry to acquaint your Majesty that the notification of the concurrence of the Irish Parliament in the countervailing duties proposed to be laid by the Parliament

---

[1] The draft letter from the King to the Prince of Wales and the Dukes of York, Clarence and Cumberland, dated the 8th, is as follows: 'On reading the Minutes of the House of Lords and the account in the newspapers of what passed on Friday concerning a complaint of the Earl of Carlisle which is to be taken into consideration on Tuesday, I should not do my duty if I did not point out what a very bad effect it would have in the world if you joined in supporting this complaint; for though it appears only as affecting the printer of a newspaper, it is certainly meant against the Lord Chief Justice of the King's Bench acting in his judicial capacity, and not mentioning any person, but if truly stated only condemning opinions, which whoever broached were those of men of loose principles, not those worthy of commendation or adoption. The majority of this country, however custom may have weakened the opinions of some men, view the conduct of the Lord Chief Justice in its true light as that of a worthy and upright man wishing to support the laws of religion and of this country, and consequently would feel particularly hurt as well as myself if any of my family could countenance this attack; I am certain it cannot be necessary for me to add more but that I wish you should ever hold that conduct which may make you respected.' (9651)

[2] The King was so pressing with his commands because of the long list of proposed Irish peerages and promotions which Cornwallis had sent from Dublin. The King was anxious to see 'how much those various lists can be curtailed', Portland informed Pitt on the 9th (Chatham Papers, 168). The list is in Ross, *Cornwallis Corresp.* III, 318.

[3] Cornwallis's despatch of the 7th is not in Ross, *Cornwallis Correspondence*, but Edward Cooke's letter to John King, describing the scene in the Irish House of Commons on the 7th, is in Ross, III, 250 'About two-thirds of Opposition left the House in a body.'

of this kingdom on all articles imported into it has not yet been transmitted, & he therefore fears that the Union Bill which was to have been introduced tomorrow must necessarily be deferred. (9655–6)

2167 THE DUKE OF CUMBERLAND *to the* KING

[*Kew Green, 9 June 1800.*] I am this moment honoured with your Majesty's gracious letter,[1] & you may depend upon it I never will in the whole course of my life take any step that may be disagreeable to your Majesty. I can assure you, Sir, upon the honor of a gentleman, that no later than yesterday evening I declared to Mr. Cookson who is here that I should certainly not attend the House of Lords next Tuesday, as I really had the greatest respect for Ld. Kenyon not only as a Judge but as a *man*, and as I feared his warmth of temper might have led him to say more than he meant I should not like to attend the discussion. But your Majesty may depend upon one thing, that I never *willingly* would act in anything contrary to your wishes. Believe, Sir, you have not a more dutiful nor devoted son than I am and ever shall be. (47187)

2168 THE BISHOP OF WORCESTER (RICHARD HURD) *to the* KING

[*Worcester, 10 June 1800.*] Coming hither yesterday evening after the post was gone, I found here your Majesty's most kind & gracious letter of the 7th from Windsor. I confess the sight of your Majesty's hand-writing, after what has happened, raised the greatest emotion in me; and I cannot but humbly request your pardon for the fresh trouble I give your Majesty, tho' it be but in one word of grateful acknowledgment for this & all other marks of grace with which your Majesty condescends to honor [etc.]. (9657)

2169 THE DUKE OF PORTLAND *to the* KING

[*Burlington House, Friday, 13 June 1800, 11.05 p.m.*] The Duke of Portland most humbly begs leave to lay before your Majesty a dispatch received this afternoon from Lord Castlereagh, by which your Majesty will see the progress which has been made towards the Compensation Bill, & the amount of the provision intended for the Speaker,[2] which, though very abundant, has been dictated by a spirit of liberality which, considering all the circumstances, the Duke of Portland presumes to hope that your Majesty will not disapprove in this instance.[3]

The Bishop of Chester[4] (elect) has applied this evening to the Duke of Portland to request to have your Majesty's pleasure signified to him with respect to the day on which your Majesty will give the Bishop leave to do his homage. (9658)

[1] No. 2165 n.

[2] John Foster.

[3] The long list of pensions granted as compensation for losses sustained as a result of the extinction of their offices following the extinction of the Irish Parliament, is in *Annual Register*, 1800, Appendix to Chronicle, pp. 208–9. The Speaker's pension amounted to £5,083 3s. 4d.

[4] Henry William Majendie.

2170 WILLIAM PITT *to the* KING, *and the reply*

[*Downing Street, Monday, 16 June 1800.*] Mr Pitt humbly begs leave to submit for your Majesty's signature the accompanying Message[1] to the two Houses of Parliament, which are thought necessary as the foundation of the Bill which the Attorney-General is to move, in pursuance of your Majesty's commands, to remove any doubts respecting the disposal of property vested in your Majesty. (9659)

[*The King's reply, Windsor, 17 June 1800, 7.15 a.m.*] I return to Mr. Pitt the Messages to the two Houses of Parliament concerning the Bill the Attorney-General has prepared for removing doubts respecting the property vested in me which at present stands on a most unclear and unfair footing, I being restrained by Queen Anne's Act, though I have given up for my life the land revenue of the Crown. (Chatham Papers.)

2171 HENRY DUNDAS *to the* KING

[*Downing Street, 16 June 1800, 5 p.m.*] Mr Dundas humbly transmits for your Majesty's perusal a memorandum circulated by him in concert with with [*sic*] Mr Pitt for the consideration of your Majesty's confidential servants. The difficulty stated by several of your Majesty's servants founded on supposed want of transports adequate to the service does not exist, and laying aside that objection, the generality of your Majesty's servants concur in the propriety of the measure.

The dispatches yesterday received from Brigadier-General Maitland have suggested an alteration in the mode of executing the measure. If the capture of the island of Belle Isle is considered as a measure of importance to be adhered to, it does not admit of the same pressure as that of sending the force to the Mediterranean, and upon that ground it is hoped the resolution Mr Pitt and Mr Dundas have taken of sending the accompanying instructions to Brigadier-General Maitland and General Sir Ralph Abercrombie will meet with your Majesty's approbation. The blockade of Belle Isle is at present perfectly compleat, and will in its effects of course facilitate any future operations. (9660-1)

[1] 'His Majesty being informed that doubts have arisen touching the powers vested in his Majesty to dispose of certain estates purchased by his Majesty and also concerning the powers of his Majesty and his successors to dispose of such real property as they may hereafter purchase or may become entitled to otherwise than by descent with the Crown, and also touching the application of and succession to such personal property as his Majesty and his successors may be entitled to at the time of his or their demise; and that doubts have also arisen touching the powers vested in the Queen to dispose of certain estates purchased by her Majesty, as well as the general powers of the Queen Consort to dispose of real and personal property; and his Majesty being also informed that by reason of the restrictions imposed on the alienation of the Crown lands, difficulties have arisen where lands escheated to his Majesty have been subject to trusts or charges, and that in other cases inconveniences may arise from such restrictions; his Majesty recommends to his faithful Commons to take these subjects into their consideration and to make such provisions concerning the same as may appear to them to be proper.' (*H. of C.J.* LV, 664.)

[*Weiltingen, 17 June 1800.*] Having this moment heard that Genoa is taken I cannot resist offering your Majesty my humble congratulations on the occasion. I trust that this news will have some effect on our sad enemy and make him retire.[1]

Yesterday we were much alarmed by the French having attacked Günzbourg and General Staray having left it in the night. Our troops have lost a great many men. They continue to behave very bravely and even the Austrians acknowledge it and employ them in all their most difficult posts.

Since Saturday we have every day dreaded the being obliged to leave this place but now I hope Kray will take courage and attempt to attack the enemy. (51602)

2173   JOHN HOOKHAM FRERE *to the* KING

[*Downing Street, 17 June 1800.*] Mr Frere begs leave most humbly to express to your Majesty his concern at discovering some inaccuracies in the copy of the letter to the Prince Regent of Portugal,[2] on account of which he finds himself under the necessity of requesting your Majesty's gracious permission to submit a second copy for your Majesty's signature.[3] (9664)

2174   WILLIAM PITT *to the* KING, *and the reply*

[*Downing Street, Tuesday, 17 June 1800.*] Mr Pitt thinks it his duty humbly to acquaint your Majesty that it is conceived to be necessary in point of form that the Queen's consent (as far as her Majesty is concerned) should be signified to the Bill to be moved tomorrow by the Attorney-General, in consequence of your Majesty's Message of this day. He takes the liberty of adding that Mr Perceval, as being Solicitor-General to her Majesty, has been suggested as a proper person to make this communication to the House, if her Majesty should be graciously pleased to give him authority for that purpose.

Mr Pitt also takes this opportunity of humbly submitting to your Majesty a Memorandum which has been given him by the Speaker, of a new arrangement which it is wished to form respecting the distribution of fees now payable to the Clerk and other Officers of the House of Commons, which he trusts will meet with your Majesty's approbation, to which in that case it will be necessary that Mr Pitt should signify your Majesty's consent. (9662–3)

[*The King's reply, Windsor, 18 June, 6.20 a.m.*] It is very proper that Mr Perceval as the Queen's Solicitor-General should give her consent to the Bill now before

---

[1] Genoa, where Masséna commanded one French division, was taken by the Austrians on 4 June, ten days before Bonaparte won the battle of Marengo.

[2] John (1767–1826), Regent, 1792, later (1816), King John VI.

[3] George Rose wrote to the Bishop of Lincoln on 30 July: 'It is true that Mr. Frere is to go Ambassador, rather Envoy Extraordinary to Portugal. The King told George that Lord Grenville had complained of Mr. Canning having placed an inefficient person under him, to whom he must make such an offer to be rid of him. This is the third gentleman who has had a large or a forced[?] provision for himself to induce him to give up the situation of Under-Secretary to his Lordship on account of insufficiency.' (Tomline MSS., Suffolk Record Office.)

the House of Commons freeing me from the purposes of Queen Anne's Act, as well as enabling a Queen Consort to leave her personal property by Will. Mr. Pitt is therefore authorized to give him this notice. As to the regulations proposed in the office of Clerks of the House of Commons, I fully authorize Mr. Pitt to give my consent to the Bill proposed, as it has the approbation of the worthy and excellent Speaker of the House, who would not countenance the measure if not advantageous to the public. (Chatham Papers.)

2175 HENRY DUNDAS *to the* KING

[*Wimbledon, 19 June* [*1800*], *6 p.m.*] Mr Dundas had the honour of receiving your Majesty's note on the subject of sending a large reinforcement to the Mediterranean. However impressed with an opinion that under many probable contingencies a large British force in that quarter would have been productive of very beneficial consequences, under the doubts stated by your Majesty and the division of opinion upon the subject amongst your Majesty's servants, Mr Dundas did not feel himself warranted to press his opinion, and the reinforcement to the Mediterranean is proposed to be confined to the two battalions originally required by General Sir Ralph Abercrombie.

Along with the consideration of this particular point your Majesty's confidential servants, taking under their mature consideration the present state of affairs on the continent, the state of your Majesty's forces at this time in Great Britain and Ireland, and the objects most likely to distract the enemy and strengthen your Majesty's allies and promote the common cause, came to the decisions contained in the accompanying Minute[1] which in compliance with their unanimous approbation Mr Dundas has the honour humbly to submit to your Majesty's consideration.[2] (9668–9)

[1] Missing from the Archives, but there is a copy in the British Museum Add. MSS.:

[2]   *Cabinet Minute, 19 June 1800* (*Copy*)
'That it is necessary in the present critical situation of affairs on the Continent to place the whole of the disposable force of this Kingdom in such situation as that it may most immediately produce an effect, either in the way of direct attack or of diversion, in order to counteract the operations of the enemy.

That a reinforcement of two strong battalions should be sent immediately to the army under the command of General Sir Ralph Abercromby.

That a force of not less than 6,000 effective men in addition to those now serving under Brigadier-General Maitland should be sent successively and as speedily as the means of their conveyance can be provided, to prosecute that expedition, and that the battering train and other necessaries for the siege (if that should become requisite) should be forwarded with all possible dispatch.

That a force of 4,000 men be reserved and placed in a proper situation, to co-operate with the Dutch troops in an attack against such point of the Dutch coast as shall be judged most expedient, with a view to create an effectual diversion and to place the troops in such a position where they may either remain in safety or be re-embarked without loss.

That General Maitland be instructed to apprize Genl. Georges of the intended attack upon Belle Isle. That he be informed that the view of this operation is to form a depot there, where a force of about 20,000 men may be assembled, and that the Commander-in-Chief of that army will be instructed to concert with Genl. Georges both during the siege & afterwards, all such operations as may according to the events of the campaign best tend to support the Royalists or to distract the operations and attention of the enemy, and that all the measures to be taken by Genl. Georges must be guided by a reference to these intentions.

That a similar communication should be made to Monsieur.

That as these operations will materially contribute to the security of Ireland, the Lord Lieutenant

[*Cleveland Row, 19 June 1800.*] Lord Grenville has the honour humbly to submit to your Majesty a Minute of the Cabinet held today respecting the instructions to be given on the subject of the French army in Egypt, and the answer to be returned to the application from the Swedish Chargé d'Affaires to be admitted to present his successor, notwithstanding what has lately passed at Stockholm. (9665)

[*Enclosure*]

[*Cabinet Minute, Downing Street, 19 June 1800.*]

Present: The Lord Chancellor, Lord Privy Seal, Duke of Portland, Earl Spencer, Earl Camden, Mr Chancellor of the Exchequer, Mr Secretary Dundas, Mr Windham, Lord Grenville.

It was agreed humbly to submit to his Majesty,

That it may be proper that instructions to the following effect should be sent to the Earl of Elgin and to Lord Keith:

That under all the circumstances which have arisen the opinion of his Majesty's servants is that if the French and Turks should agree for the re-establishment of the Convention of El Arish no obstacle should be given thereto on his Majesty's part; but the whole subject placed in the same state in which it would have stood according to the orders sent from this country in March last.

And that if any different arrangement should be proposed, or any unforeseen events arise, Lord Keith should as the Commander-in-Chief of his Majesty's naval forces on that station exercise his own discretion for the good of his Majesty's service, bearing in mind that the ultimate evacuation of Egypt by the French is considered as an object of the first importance to this country, although in the execution of this it would be wished to delay as long as possible the arrival of any reinforcements from Egypt to the French army in Italy or the south of France.

It was also agreed on consideration of Mr Talbot's dispatches, humbly to submit to his Majesty that the new Swedish Chargé d'Affaires should be informed that as soon as accounts shall be received that Mr Talbot is received and acknowledged in that quality at Stockholm there will be no difficulty in his being received and acknowledged in like manner here. (9666–7)

[*The King's reply, Windsor, 20 June 1800, 7.11 a.m.*] The very perplexed manner in which the affairs of Egypt is now placed, it seems to me that no other orders could have been given than those suggested by the Minute of Cabinet transmitted to me by Lord Grenville.

should be directed to hold in readiness a detachment of 4,000 men to be applied as may be judged best to these different services, so that by this arrangement 5,000 regular troops would still be left in Ireland.' (Add. 40102, ff. 46–7.)

There is no copy of the King's reply in the Archives, but Dundas wrote to Spencer on the 20th: 'I have an answer from the King, apparently with a very cordial approbation of the Minute of the Cabinet.' He added, 'I am, the more I think of it, the more dissatisfied with our decision in not sending a larger force to the Mediterranean' (*Spencer Papers*, IV, 285).

After the conduct held towards Mr. Talbot no other answer could with propriety be given to the Swedish Secretary than the one proposed. (Fortescue MSS.)

2177 THE DUCHESS OF WURTEMBERG *to the* KING

[*Anspach, 20 June 1800.*] I think it my duty to acquaint your Majesty that the French having crossed the Danube yesterday on many points and a column marching towards Nordlingen, it was unsafe for us to remain at Weiltingen, and we have taken refuge here for a few days till the Duke can get a house at Erlangen. I hope tomorrow he will get an answer having sent Monsieur de Görlitz off yesterday to find one. I hope that at last the Field Marshal will attack the enemy to free us from the constant anxiety and distress we exist in. I fear very much that if the French retreat they will again go through part of the Dutchy, which would be destruction to us.

It rains incessantly and I believe will do much harm to the harvest; the barley beginning to look quite yellow, which is looked on as a very bad sign here.

An Officer who is just come to the Duke from his troops brings the account of their having suffered dreadfully. They are so brave it makes one['s] heart bleed to see them sacrificed to so little purpose. (51603–4)

2178 HENRY DUNDAS *to the* KING

[*Holwood, 21 June 1800, 3 p.m.*] Mr Dundas has the honour humbly to transmit to your Majesty for your Majesty's approbation and signature the Message[1] preparatory to the Bill relative to the Dutch ships and troops. (9670)

2179 THE DUKE OF PORTLAND *to the* KING

[*Burlington House, Saturday, 21 June 1800, 4.50 p.m.*] It is with very serious concern that the Duke of Portland submits to your Majesty representations so feelingly urged against the opinions he was commanded to signify to the Lord Lieutenant as your Majesty will find in the dispatch of the 17th. instant[2] which

[1] 'His Majesty acquaints the House of Commons that Conventions have been entered into by his direction with the Hereditary Stadholder of the United Provinces, for placing at his Majesty's disposal certain ships of war and seamen, together with a body of land forces which, in consequence of their submitting to the authority vested in his Serene Highness as Captain-General and Admiral of the Union, had been passed over to this country...' (*H. of C.J.* LV, 697.)

[2] See *Cornwallis Corresp.* III, 262. The pressure which the King had brought to bear on his Ministers to cut down the number of new Irish peerages, meant, in effect, that the Government was repudiating obligations which Cornwallis had been empowered to incur. The Lord Lieutenant's indignation was shared by Castlereagh, the Chief Secretary, who declared: 'If the Irish Government is not enabled to keep faith with the various individuals who have acted upon a principle of confidence in their honour, it is morally impossible...that either Lord Cornwallis or I can remain in our present situations...It will remain a breach of faith as injurious to the character of Government as to our own, having given an assurance which we were not enabled to fulfil.' (*Castlereagh Corresp.* III, 327.) Cornwallis wrote to Pitt on 7 July: '...I am not naturally of a jealous or suspicious temper, and I have received too many proofs of your kindness, and am too sensible of the calls of your arduous occupations, to attribute your not writing to any unfriendly cause. In the case however of the Peerages, I was inclined to think from your silence that you did not see any great objection to what I proposed, and was encouraged therefore

is herewith most humbly laid before your Majesty, but the Lord Lieutenant's approved zeal in your Majesty's service & long tried attachment to your Majesty's royal person & Government may dispose your Majesty in your great goodness to admit the high sense of duty by which these representations have been dictated, & not to hold them unworthy of an indulgent consideration.

The subjects upon which the Lord Lieutenant desires in his dispatch of the 18th that your Majesty's pleasure may be taken are so conformable to the precedents in similar cases as to incline the Duke of Portland to hope that he may receive your Majesty's orders to acquaint the Lord Lieutenant that he may proceed without delay to make the communications to Parliament under your Majesty's authority which are usual upon such occasions. (9671–2)

2180 WILLIAM PITT *to the* KING

[*Hollwood, Monday, 23 June 1800.*] Mr Pitt humbly begs leave to acquaint your Majesty that Lord Temple, after farther consulting with his friends, is not desirous of a seat at the Admiralty, from an apprehension that it might be considered rather as an office of emolument than as an introduction to business;[1] but with the latter view he would be extremely gratified by being included in the Commission for the affairs of India, without salary.[2] As he would in this case be the junior member of the Board, it is by no means intended to propose that he should be a Privy Counsellor, but as there can be (by the Act) only two members who have not that rank, it would be necessary in order to make the vacancy to bring one of them to the Privy Council, and as Mr William Dundas is the senior of the two,[3] and of considerable standing in Parliament, Mr Pitt hopes your Majesty will not think there is any impropriety in selecting him for that purpose, or any material

to give stronger hopes than I might otherwise have done to the urgent candidates for the Representative Peerage.

It is unnecessary to say any more about the expressions of the Duke of Portland's first letter, as he has since written in the most proper manner; but I believe you will recollect that his style was not always gracious and pleasant before I came to Ireland.' (P.R.O., W. Dacres Adams MSS.)

[1] For Lord Grenville's views see Buckingham, *Court and Cabinets of George III*, III, 75. Cf. *The Times*, 28 June: 'We understand that in consequence of Lord Temple's having been advised by his friends that accepting the place of a Lord of the Admiralty, with a salary, might be thought inconsistent with his high birth and immense fortune, his Lordship has been nominated a Commissioner for the Affairs of India, without a salary.' He and Wallace kissed hands at the Levée for their respective offices on the 25th.

[2] Pitt's India Act of 1784 had established the Board of Control, consisting of six Privy Councillors. One of the two Secretaries of State was constituted President, and in his absence, the Chancellor of the Exchequer, and in the absence of both, the senior Commissioner was to preside. The Act of 1793 (33 George III, c. 52) reconstituted the Board. It was to consist of the two Secretaries of State and the Chancellor of the Exchequer and an unspecified number of other Privy Councillors, plus two other persons 'as his Majesty...shall think fit to be...Commissioners'. Their joint salaries were not to exceed £5,000 a year. The unsalaried members of the Board (i.e. those 'not having any special salary annexed to such appointment') were not required to resign their seats and seek re-election, on appointment (section viii).

[3] William Dundas was senior to Thomas Wallace and Lord Temple as the Board was constituted after this reshuffling. This letter, incidentally, makes clear the fact that Haydn's *Book of Dignities*, which is usually accurate, is in error in terminating William Dundas's India Commissionership at this time, and in reappointing him in May 1801. This necessitates a correction of the footnote referring to William Dundas in vol. II, p. 624: 1797–1800 should read 1797–1803.

objection to any part of this arrangement.[1] The circumstances respecting the county of Stafford, Mr Pitt finds, are such as to preclude Lord Granville Leveson from vacating his seat at this time,[2] and Mr Pitt would therefore humbly beg to submit to your Majesty Mr William Eliot for the seat at the Admiralty; as he is on many accounts very anxious for some situation at home, and as his obtaining it will be highly gratifying both to Lord Stafford and to Lord Eliot. (9673–4)

2181   *Letters from* LORD GRENVILLE *to the* KING, *and the replies*

[*Cleveland Row, 24 June 1800, 2 p.m.*] It is with very great concern that Lord Grenville transmits to your Majesty the inclosed account[3] just received from the Collector at Dover. The matter of the Capitulation is stated in a very confused way, but there seems no ground to hope that the fate of Italy has not been decided by this action. (9675)

[*The King's reply, Windsor, 24 June, 5.52 p.m.*] I am infinitely concerned at the information[3] just transmitted to me by Lord Grenville which I fear may [be] depended upon, and if so little good is to be expected from Austria. (Fortescue MSS.)

[*From Lord Grenville, Cleveland Row, 26 June, 11 p.m.*] Lord Grenville has the honour humbly to submit to your Majesty the Minute[4] of the meeting of Cabinet this day: and also the extract of a letter which he received this morning from Count Woronzow. The rest, being merely compliments to himself, he does not trouble your Majesty with it. (9676)

[1] William Dundas was sworn of the Privy Council on the 25th.

[2] Canning (who, incidentally, retained his seat at the India Board after being appointed Joint Paymaster) writing to his friend Granville Leveson on the 16th, after hearing from Pitt that the seat at the Admiralty Board was still to be had (Temple having declined it), referred to the re-election difficulty: '...I will not venture to advise in a case where the risk is so great—as that of a contest might be—but I cannot forbear suggesting to you, as Pitt has suggested to me, that the difference in point of emolument between the Admiralty and Treasury is now very little—the Admiralty being made £1000 real, the Treasury being nominally £1600—but in effect not more than between £1200 and £1300, and in point of consideration I really do not know that there is any great difference—and in most cases I think it is the person that gives the character to the office rather than the office to the person.

Undoubtedly if the Treasury were to fall a few months hence it would be provoking to have put yourself out of the way of taking it: but if, as is perhaps at least equally probable, no vacancy should happen there before the General Election, you will have gained near three years of office, and of official habits; which (considering what your habits now are) appears to me a circumstance of no small weight and importance.

Upon the whole, *if* there is no fear of a contest for the County, I am *clear* that you ought to accept.' (P.R.O., Granville MSS.)

Finally, Granville Leveson wrote to Canning on or about 21 June (the letter, undated, was forwarded to Pitt on the 22nd): '...I am glad W. Eliot has got the seat at the Admiralty Board. Has it been intimated to him that notwithstanding his priority to me in holding official situation, Pitt considers me to have the first claim to the Lordship of the Treasury. It would be well to have this thoroughly understood, if explained to him at present I am persuaded he would be very well satisfied, but if the explanation does not come till there may happen to be a vacancy at the Treasury he may feel uncomfortable, and Lord Eliot may be indignant at my stepping in before him...' (W. Dacres Adams MSS.)

[3] News of the Armistice at Alessandria, following the battle of Marengo.

[4] Missing.

[*The King's reply, Kew, 27 June, 7.30 a.m.*] Lord Grenville is too well apprized of my sentiments to be surprized at my reading with great sorrow the Minute of Cabinet he has transmitted to me; the Court of Vienna has on all occasions shewn such an inclination to treat with France that I fear the overture to be made will make all endeavours of exertion cease and the inclination to negociate be warmly adopted; whilst the war is continued, though expensive, we are safe, but whenever peace is obtained it can be nothing but an armed neutrality, which is a most hazardous situation. These are sentiments I can never change.

P.S. I trust Lord Grenville's answer to Count Woronzow will fully explain the regard I must ever have for him. (Fortescue MSS.)

[*From Lord Grenville, Cleveland Row, 27 June, 11 p.m.*] Lord Grenville has been honoured with your Majesty's commands of this morning's date. He begs leave humbly to assure your Majesty that as far as he can judge no one of your Majesty's servants entertains any other sentiment than that which your Majesty has done Lord Grenville the honour to express to him, both on the precariousness and instability of any peace which can be concluded with the present usurper in France, and on the great inconvenience of that state of uncertainty and of continual preparation for war, in which such a peace must consequently place this country.

But if the late events in Italy shall, as is too probable, drive the Court of Vienna to an immediate negotiation and treaty of peace, they are persuaded that in that case the offering to consent to moderate and reasonable terms of peace would be the only possible method of inducing Parliament and the country to concur in those measures which would be necessary, with a view to your Majesty's carrying on the war alone, if unreasonable terms should be demanded by the enemy. It is in this view alone, and by no means as being insensible to the difficulties and dangers of such a peace, that your Majesty's servants have brought themselves to advise your Majesty to offer to concur in the negotiations of the Court of Vienna if the determination to treat should be there adopted.

Your Majesty's gracious message to Count Woronzow was delivered by Lord Grenville. The Emperor of Russia has allowed Count Woronzow to quit the service and to remain in England. (9677–9)

[*The King's reply, Windsor, 28 June, 7.30 a.m.*] As I have no other view in life than to the best of my judgement to fulfill my duty, and that I am not actuated by the events of the day but look to the reality of a subject, I owne I cannot see the present intended measure of shewing an inclination to Austria of treating for a general peace on reasonable terms but as most hazardous, as that Court has destroyed every concert during the war by her constant inclination to that fatal step. Whilst French principles are victorious no peace can be safe; and the forming political measures on the sole foundation of the assertion of a French telegraph and without any knowledge of the extent of the mischief, I cannot think but premature. (Fortescue MSS.)

2182   WILLIAM PITT *to the* KING

[*Downing Street, Friday, 27 June 1800, 9 p.m.*] Mr Pitt humbly begs leave to acquaint your Majesty that a Motion was made today by Mr Sheridan for a Call of the House, grounded on the change of affairs in Italy.[1] The Motion was opposed by Mr Pitt as having a tendency to encourage the enemy and discourage your Majesty's Allies, and was negatived by 124 to 27.[2] (9680)

2183   THE DUKE OF PORTLAND *to the* KING

[*Whitehall, Tuesday, 1 July 1800, 5.30 p.m.*] The Duke of Portland most humbly begs leave to acquaint your Majesty that the Union Bill has now passed the two Houses & lays ready to receive the Royal Assent whenever it shall be your Majesty's pleasure to have it pronounced, & your Majesty's servants represent with all humility to your Majesty their hope that your Majesty will deem it proper to have that ceremony performed in your Royal presence.[3] The Duke of Portland is desired also to inform your Majesty that several Bills having passed yesterday by virtue of your Majesty's Commission, the Union Bill is the only one which is ready to receive your Majesty's Royal assent.

The Duke of Portland begs leave to acquaint your Majesty that the Sheriff of Caermarthenshire, who has been directed by the meeting of his county to present an Address to your Majesty on your Majesty's late providential deliverance, has expressed his humble hope that your Majesty would condescend to confer the honor of knighthood upon him, & from what the Duke of Portland can learn, Mr Powell,[4] the Sheriff, is not unworthy of that distinction if your Majesty shall think proper to bestow it upon him. (9681–2)

2184   HENRY DUNDAS *to the* KING, *and the reply*

[*Wimbledon, 1 July, 10 p.m.*] Mr Dundas humbly transmits for your Majesty's information a dispatch this day received from Brigadier-General Maitland. Mr Dundas is perfectly at a loss to understand by what accident the orders forbidding the troops to go to the Mediterranean had not reached Quiberon Bay before the 23d. Perhaps there may have been time, (if the orders at all arrived) to stop them before they reached Gibraltar. It is not, however, of very essential moment, as the two thousand men intended for the Mediterranian have been countermanded and destined for the Belle Isle service, so that there are only two thousand more have proceeded to the Mediterranian than were intended. Mr Dundas is to meet with the Duke of York and Mr Pitt tomorrow forenoon, when he wishes to submit several new ideas which have occurred to him in the present state of affairs, and if those ideas shall be ultimately advised by your Majesty's confidential

[1] *Parl. Register*, LVII, 189–208.
[2] The King's reply (6.20 a.m. on the 28th) is in Stanhope, III, Appendix, p. xxi. He approved of Pitt's reply to Sheridan, and for that reason disapproved of Thursday's Cabinet Minute.
[3] The King went to the House of Lords on the 2nd to give the Union Bill the royal assent.
[4] He was knighted at the Levée at St James's on the 2nd.

servants and adopted by your Majesty, it will be a fortunate circumstance if a considerable body of troops can be speedily assembled at Gibraltar. (9683–4)

[*The King's reply, Windsor, 2 July, 6.18 a.m.*] I am sorry to find Colonel Maitland has so expeditiously obeyed the orders sent him, as it is highly inconvenient that any forces should be sent at present to the Mediterranean and must lessen the forces supposed to have been collected for the expedition under Sir James Pulteney; indeed, orders and counter-orders are too frequently given which puzzle the services and creates much confusion. (Add. MSS. 40100, f. 249.)

2185   THE DUCHESS OF WURTEMBERG *to the* KING

[*Erlangen, 3 June* [?*July*] *1800.*] Having nothing new to acquaint your Majesty with I would not trouble you with a letter till I had been settled here some days, and could give some account of the country which I am sorry to say is neither beautiful or pleasant, a deep sand and few other trees but firs on all sides. At Anspach the Duke could find no house to suit us, as for one which could only contain us and Trinette they asked two hundred guineas a month. The one we inhabit here is neat but small and without any outlet, which is very unpleasant in so warm a summer. However, after the anxiety we have undergone for months we may rejoice to be in a quiet place. The news from the Army continues very vexatious and the unfortunate armistice concluded in Italy makes our situation very cruel as it destroys even the hopes of things taking a better turn. (51598–9)

2186   EARL SPENCER *to the* KING, *and the reply*

[*Admiralty, 5 July 1800.*] Earl Spencer has the honour to lay before your Majesty the minutes of a court martial on one of the mutineers of the Hermione who has been clearly convicted of being concerned in that horrible transaction; and as there appear no circumstances of mitigation in his case, Earl Spencer humbly submits to your Majesty the propriety of allowing the law to take its course. (9685)

[*The King's reply, Windsor, 6 July, 7.20 a.m.*] I have this instant received Earl Spencer's note on the court martial held the last week on another of the mutineers of the Hermione, whose guilt was clearly proved. I therefore approve of the law taking its course. (Althorp MSS.)

2187   *Letters from* WILLIAM PITT *to the* KING, *and a reply*

[*Downing Street, Monday, 7 July 1800.*] Mr. Pitt takes the liberty of humbly submitting to your Majesty a letter which he has this day received from the Attorney-General and which he trusts your Majesty will approve of his laying before you as the best mode of explaining the two points on which the Attorney-General is anxious to be honored with your Majesty's commands for his guidance in the conduct of the Bill now depending. (9686)

[From Pitt, Tuesday, 8 July.] Mr Pitt is extremely mortified to find that by an unfortunate mistake the accompanying papers which were intended to be sent to your Majesty last night have been overlooked till today. (9687)

[The King's reply, Windsor, 9 July, 6 a.m.] I have this instant received Mr. Pitt's box enclosing the letter he has got from the Attorney-General on Monday. The reason of naming a trustee in whom the copyhold and leasehold estates shall be vested arises from my not thinking it just that by any private purchase of mine the taxes should fall on the parishes in which these should lye, and at the same time not to give up the right of the Crown of being exempted from taxes. It seemed necessary for that purpose alone that some person should stand forth to pay those taxes: this seems to point out the Privy Purse for the time being as the proper person to be appointed as Trustee. I approve of the Attorney-General's suggestion that in default of disposition of my personal estate it shall go as the law would carry it if the Act had not been made. (Chatham Papers.)

2188 PRINCE ADOLPHUS *to the* KING

[Hannover, 9 July 1800.] I had intended doing myself the honour of writing to your Majesty by the messenger, but being still at camp I was prevented. I did not return here till Saturday last, four days after his departure, and I really was so tired the evening of my return that I could not write by Sunday's mail. The camp has succeeded very well, at least the Field Marschal seemed very well contented with us. He has employed the troops a great deal, and he has made us worck with system: nothing could have rendered me happier than to have shewn your Majesty my Division, and I believe you would not have been displeased with it. The different changes that we have made in our exercise we have found very good, and our principles of acting in a great line very just: in short, Sir, your Hannoverian infantry is certainly at present in such a condition that it can render great services whenever it is called for. The cavalry has always been very fine, and is undoubtedly still so, so that I can say but very little on that subject. The Field Marshall has made us manoeuvre together several times, first by Divisions, and afterwards the whole troops together: and he seemed to be contented with the troops. Could these have been in Italy on the 14th of last month,[1] I am sure General Melas would not have made such an ignominious Convention: at least I hope I should not have survived it. I never heard anything more shameful than the Articles of that Convention, and I cannot conceive how it is possible for a General to sign them. By this time the Austrians have abandoned all the fortresses they were to give up, and their Army is marched back to Mantua.

My sister is at present at Erlangen: the Duke has taken a house there, and he intends remaining there till he can return to his country. I dare not trespass any longer on your Majesty's patience, than just to add the humble assurance that [etc.]. (48553)

[1] At Marengo.

2189 WILLIAM PITT to the KING

[*Downing Street, Thursday, 10 July 1800, 2.30 a.m.*] Mr Pitt humbly begs leave to acquaint your Majesty that a Motion having been made by Mr Western for a Committee on the State of the Nation with a view to introduce some measure tending to peace, was opposed by Mr Wilberforce, Mr Windham, Mr Hawkins Browne, Mr Buxton, Mr Hiley Addington,[1] and the Solicitor General, and supported by Mr Martin, Mr Wm. Smith, Mr Nicholl,[2] Mr Hobhouse, Sir Francis Burdett, Mr Sheridan and Mr Tierney, and after a long debate was negatived by 148 to 26.[3] (9688)

2190 EARL SPENCER to the KING, *and the reply*

[*Admiralty, 11 July 1800.*] Earl Spencer has the honour of laying before your Majesty the sentence & proceedings of a court martial held in Yarmouth Roads, on a seaman of your Majesty's ship the Monarch, for using words tending to excite the ship's company to mutiny, whereby he has been sentenced to be hanged; and Earl Spencer humbly submits to your Majesty that as the circumstances of the case, though highly criminal, do not appear to have been attended with much intention on the part of the prisoner to stir up the crew to any act of mutiny, it may be proper that your Majesty's mercy should be extended to him on condition of his being transported to Botany Bay for life. (9689)

[*The King's reply, Windsor, 12 July, 7.10 a.m.*] As Earl Spencer thinks the mutation of the sentence of death in the case of a seaman tried in Yarmouth Road for words tending to excite mutiny, to transportation for life at Botany Bay, will not be detrimental to the discipline of the Navy, I consent to this alteration. (Althorp MSS.)

2191 THE KING to LADY CHARLOTTE FINCH

[*Windsor, 13 July 1800.*] An earnest desire of promoting the permanent happiness of my subjects actuates every desire of my heart, and I am certain this can in no

---

[1] Addington's brother Hiley was appointed a Lord of the Treasury in December, a step long in contemplation. Addington had written to Hiley on 27 June: 'I am this moment returned from a long ride with Mr. Pitt and I feel more pleasure than I can express in acquainting you that from this time to the general election you will have the offer of the first office that may become vacant, which you could supply.' (Sidmouth MSS.) Hiley wrote to Pitt on 5 October: '...In placing me in the precise situation which you have for some months past so kindly thought of for me, you are doing me as great a favor as it is well possible for one individual to confer on another. To be in the Department of that person under whose auspices I began public life, and under whose I mean to close it—what can I wish for more? I cannot help adding that the delay in this arrangement, which circumstances rendered unavoidable, has been attended with numberless conveniences to me on domestic accounts. It is impossible that any event, however personally gratifying, can add to the wish which has long been the uppermost in my heart, of rendering service to a Government with whose security that of the country appears to me to be inseparably connected, or to the regret I have so frequently felt in finding myself unable to act up to it, and which I am likely still to feel.' (W. Dacres Adams MSS.)

[2] John Nicholls. John Nicholl was not in Parliament until 1802.

[3] *Parl. Register*, LVII, 299–341. The numbers are there incorrectly given as 143 v. 27.

manner be more effectually attained than by the most careful attention in filling up the vacancies in the Church and more particularly in the more exalted situations. This has made me reflect much on the now vacant Archbishoprick of Armagh, and I am clearly of opinion that the tallents and zeal for religion, besides the being a man of noble family, points out the Bishop of St. David's as peculiarly suited for that preferment. Whilst he was out of health I deferred wishing to know his sentiments on this subject, as on those occasions men are not able to judge with firmness, but rather to view the difficulties that ever attend any change. I wish, therefore, Lady Charlotte Finch would, through the channel of Mrs Stuart,[1] apprize the Bishop of my earnest wish to place him where he can be of so much use, and that in point of emolument it is infinitely more lucrative than is in general supposed; I know that will not actuate him, but at the same time with an encreasing family it ought not to be disregarded. (9690)

2192   *Letters from* WILLIAM PITT *to the* KING

[*Wimbledon, Monday, 14 July 1800.*] In consequence of the note which he had the honor of receiving from your Majesty this morning, Mr Pitt has examined afresh the state of business in Parliament, and much fears that it will not be possible by any dispatch, consistent with the necessary forms, to bring it to a conclusion till Monday or Tuesday in the week after next, as the last Money Bills cannot be brought in till all the Votes of Supply have been compleated; and it was not thought prudent to name an earlier day than Friday next for voting the subsidy to Austria, which day had been accordingly fixed by a notice given in the House yesterday.

Mr Pitt humbly begs leave to take this opportunity of acquainting your Majesty that he finds Lord Stafford no longer feels any hesitation with respect to Lord Granville Leveson's vacating his seat for Staffordshire, and Mr Pitt presumes that your Majesty will not disapprove of Lord Granville being appointed to fill the vacancy in the Treasury.[2] With respect to the office of Chief Justice in Eyre, Mr Pitt finds that that appointment would be particularly agreeable to Mr Grenville, and conceives that his talents and services in the course of last year will appear to your Majesty to render him not unworthy of it. There is certainly no ground but that of your Majesty's favor and goodness on which it could be asked for him on the same tenure on which it was held by Lord Sydney and his predecessor,[3] but if your Majesty should think proper to extend so far your gracious indulgence, it would compleat the satisfaction of Mr Grenville and those immediately connected with him; and on that account, not being aware that it could be attended with any inconvenience, Mr Pitt ventures humbly to submit it to your Majesty's favorable consideration.[4] (9691–2)

[1] Lady Charlotte's aunt.   [2] See No. 2180.

[3] Thomas Grenville, writing on 7 July, referred to 'the last two instances, viz. to Lord Sydney and to Mr. Villiers.' (Buckingham, *Court and Cabinets*, III, 81.) J. C. Villiers was appointed in 1790; Sydney in 1789. Sydney died in June 1800. Speaker Cornwall was Chief Justice from 1780 until his death in 1789.

[4] Thomas Grenville and Lord Granville Leveson-Gower were presented to the King at the Levée on the 23rd on their appointment as Chief Justice in Eyre and a Lord of the Treasury respectively. Thomas

[*Downing Street, Monday, 14 July 1800.*] Mr Pitt trusts that your Majesty will approve of an immediate communication being made to Parliament of the Treaty signed with the Court of Vienna, in order to vote the subsidy without the delay which would arise from waiting for the ratification, and with that view he humbly begs leave to submit for your Majesty's signature, Messages to the two Houses which may, if your Majesty thinks proper, be delivered tomorrow.[1] (9693)

2193   LORD GRENVILLE *to the* KING, *and the reply*

[*Cleveland Row, 16 July 1800, 11 p.m.*] Lord Grenville has the honour to submit to your Majesty the Minute of the unanimous opinion of your Majesty's servants at the Cabinet today. In consequence of what fell from your Majesty this morning he thinks it due to his colleagues as well as to himself to assure your Majesty that he cannot see any ground for thinking that the exertions necessary for continuing the war unsupported by any Continental Power can be made in any other manner than by showing to Parliament and to the country a readiness to treat conjointly with Austria for a general peace on reasonable terms.

No one can lament more sincerely than himself the necessity of such negotiation. But it is his duty to submit to your Majesty with the same sincerity the full persuasion of his mind that it is rendered unavoidable by the determination of Austria to negotiate. And if this opinion be now acted upon he trusts it is in the power of your Majesty's Government to keep the business in their own hands, and to conduct it with dignity, with firmness, & with a due regard to your Majesty's

Grenville was too much of a scholar to be excessively concerned about political advancement, but in May he did seem slightly annoyed because there had evidently been little inclination to admit his claims, in spite of the 'great palaver' made to him in 1794 when the Portland Whigs joined the Government. He admitted that the Chief Justiceship became 'a considerable object' when he learnt that the grant could be for life, as 'in the last two instances, viz., to Lord Sydney and to Mr. Villiers.' 'I have heard today from Pelham', he wrote on the 9th, 'whose father held it, that the salary of this place is not more than £1300 per annum. To Lord Pelham it was made up £2000; to Lord Sydney, £3000'. On the 16th he wrote: 'Pitt has received a favourable answer from the King as to the *tenure* of the offices; with respect to the salary, Pitt will look into the matter'. Pitt had wondered whether the King would object to a life appointment as diminishing the influence of the Crown. (Buckingham, *Court and Cabinets*, III, 68, 79–83.)

   Lord Falmouth, Captain of the Band of Gentlemen Pensioners, in vain applied to Pitt on 3 July for the late Lord Sydney's office. He wrote: 'The vacancy that has lately happened in the office of Chief Justice in Eyre south of Trent, occasions my taking the liberty of troubling you at present, and of expressing that it would be extremely desireable to me to change the present situation I hold in his Majesty's Household, for the above-mentioned post. I beg leave to call to your remembrance that some years ago, I gave up an office of the same nature (though entirely suitable and satisfactory to me) in compliance with your desire to facilitate an arrangement of Government. This I hope may in your mind give me some claim to make the present application, and I have only to add, what I once before took an opportunity of expressing to you, that my state of health of late years, and my being subject to such frequent attacks of the gout, makes the change of situation which I sollicit, more particularly desireable to me. I presume my constant attachment to you is sufficiently known to make any repetitions of it unnecessary, as it will be to say how greatly I should feel your compliance with my present request, as an additional favor conferred on me. Should that not be entirely convenient however to the present views of Government, perhaps the changes that this vacancy may occasion, may enable you to make some arrangement that may be suitable to me.' (W. D. Adams MSS.) See No. 64 n. Lord Charles Spencer, too, would have liked the appointment (letter to Lord Spencer, 10 July, Althorp MSS.).

   [1] The Message to the Commons, and the copy of the Treaty, dated 20 June, are in *H. of C.J.* LV, 757–8 (15 July).

honour & to the interests of the country; whereas an effect precisely the contrary must result, as former experience has shewn, from any measure taken under the pressure of public opinion, or under the influence of a failure of support in Parliament.

So long as any Continental Power would continue the war for the purpose of rescuing the Continent from the overbearing influence of the arms & revolutionary principles of France, it was, & still is, Lord Grenville's decided opinion that this country ought to persevere, and could do so with reasonable hopes of success. But in a contest single-handed, although the means and resources of the country are abundantly sufficient to ensure the attainment of fit and honourable terms, Lord Grenville does not see the possibility of our compelling the enemy, by our separate exertions, either to destroy the present usurpation in France, or to restore tranquility and independance to the Continent of Europe.

It is with the most sincere distrust of his own judgment, even when confirmed by that of his colleagues, that Lord Grenville ventures to urge an opinion contrary to the impressions which seem to prevail in your Majesty's mind. To his own feelings it would unquestionably be far more gratifying to persevere to the very last extremity, and to take every possible chance of a change of fortune. But he cannot think that your Majesty's servants would be justified in grounding their advice to your Majesty on such feelings only; and entertaining that opinion he is sure your Majesty would be the last person to wish that he should conceal or disguise it, or even to approve of his doing so. (9697–9)

[*Enclosure*]
[*Cabinet Minute, Downing Street, 16 July 1800.*]
Present: The Lord Chancellor, Lord Privy Seal, Duke of Portland, Earl Spencer, Earl Camden, Earl of Liverpool, Mr Chancellor of the Exchequer, Mr Secretary Dundas, Lord Grenville.
It was agreed most humbly to advise his Majesty,

That instructions should be sent to Lord Minto to declare that under the present circumstances his Majesty will not oppose the Austrian Armistice, if judged absolutely necessary for the interests of the Court of Vienna, notwithstanding the right which arises to his Majesty under the late treaty: but Lord Minto is to declare, if any occasion should arise, that his Majesty does not judge it proper to agree to any armistice on his part.

That Lord Minto having already been instructed to apprize the Court of Vienna that if that Court should be compelled to treat with the enemy, his Majesty would not decline to take part in a negotiation entered into, in that case, for a general Peace, he should in any such event require that such negotiation should be carried on, not, as proposed by the enemy, in Italy, but in some proper town of Germany where a proper person would be sent on his Majesty's part.

That in such case his Majesty would certainly support such terms of Peace in Italy as the Court of Vienna would deem most advantageous to its own interests: and that his Majesty has in that view ratified the Secret Treaty, though the stipulations of it are now so inapplicable that it would be best not to exchange the ratifications: which, however, if desired, Lord Minto is at liberty to do.

But that the basis on which his Majesty proposes in such case to treat for peace, is that of an uti possidetis, from which he is not disposed to relax for the sake of any continental arrangements other than such as may relate to Holland and the Netherlands.

That the first payment of £666,000, under the late treaty, should immediately be made; but that the decision respecting the September payments must be deferred till his Majesty is enabled to judge of the course of events to which the present circumstances may give rise.

That Lord Minto should press for the immediate conclusion of the Treaty of Alliance, including in it the article respecting commerce and navigation. (9700–2)

[*The King's reply, Windsor, 17 July 1800, 6.41 a.m.*] I never put pen to paper without wishing to convey in the most explicit manner the sentiments of my heart, but I cannot find words adequate to the uneasiness I feel at the unanimous Minute of Cabinet. They are so contrary to what I should have hoped, but if anything could in the least alleviate my mind it is the very clear and explicit letter accompanying it written by Lord Grenville that holds out a gleam of hope to me that my opinion is not very different from those of my Cabinet as to the unpleasantness of the entering into a negociation, and I think I see from it a resolution not to accede to any but reasonable terms; how those are to be attained I do not well form any idea. This country has made great sacrifices, and consequently I shall not think any terms reasonable that do not secure the greatest part of our acquisitions, particularly the Cape of Good Hope and the West India Islands. I feel too much agitated to add more than that left alone in the opinion of prosecuting the war without continental assistance, I will not resist acquiescing to the instructions being drawn up agreable to the Minute of yesterday; but I trust Lord Grenville will strongly state to Lord Minto that we cannot accede to any but reasonable terms of peace of which this country can alone be the judge; for that no English mind can ever submit to make a bad peace with the Italian policy of meaning to break it: if peace is made it must be permanent. I cannot add more but that I never shall forget the kind manner in which Lord Grenville has communicated the most unpleasant of opinions.

P.S. I trust if a negociation shall become from the answer necessary that Mr. Thos. Grenville will be the person employed from hence. (Fortescue MSS.)

2194 MRS SOPHIE M. STUART *to* LADY CHARLOTTE FINCH

[*Ham, 16 July 1800.*] I inclose a letter from the Bishop which we should be obliged to you to deliver to his Majesty. It is impossible for me to express how much we are both penetrated with his Majesties constant attention & goodness to him— and the honor he has conferred on him in the *manner* in which the notification was delivered.

I shall make use, my dear Madam, of the stay you make in London to get a short sight of you & I hope of dear Matilda who I trust will be arrived by that time. (9703)

2195 THE BISHOP OF ST DAVID'S *to the* KING

[*Ham*,[1] *16 July 1800*.] Permit me to express the lively sense I entertain of your Majesties repeated favours, and particularly of your goodness in thinking of me for so high a station in the Church.

Nothing can be more flattering to me than such a mark of your Majesties approbation; but I should very ill deserve it were I not humbly to represent to your Majesty that my infirm state of health renders me little fitted for an office which requires unimpaired vigour both of body and mind.

The humid climate of Ireland would, probably, further enfeeble a very weak constitution; and (were not my life to be protracted for some years) the great expence of taking possession of Armagh would utterly ruin my children.

The same goodness which prompted your Majesty to write will, I trust, induce you to pardon the presumption with which I have now laid before you some of the reasons that would influence me to decline going to Ireland unless I received your Majesties command, or unless I were informed that my going thither might be of real service in supporting the cause of religion & virtue, which I well know to be an object nearest your Majesties heart.[2]

Your Majesties goodness will render me forward on all occasion to profess the inviolable attachment & gratitude with which I am, Sir, [etc.]. (9704)

2196 WILLIAM PITT *to the* KING, *and the reply*

[*Downing Street, Thursday, 17 July 1800*.] Mr Pitt humbly presumes to submit to your Majesty the accompanying Messages[3] which are necessary to be delivered in order to compleat the provision for the Supply of the year. Mr Pitt particularly entreats your Majesty's indulgence for sending them at an hour which he fears may be inconvenient, but they were unfortunately omitted by mistake to be sent yesterday and it is material that they should if possible be delivered today. (9706)

[*The King's reply, Windsor Great Lodge, 17 July 1800, 3.40 p.m.*] I have this instant received Mr. Pitt's note forwarding the Messages, I have instantly signed; if there has been any delay it does not arise from me.

I can now assure Mr. Pitt that the Bishop of St. David's will thankfully accept

---

[1] Possibly Ham House, near Richmond and Kingston. The Bishop was a Canon of Windsor.

[2] It was not until 16 Oct. that the Bishop finally agreed to go to Ireland (No. 2267).

[3] 'As the state of public business may soon enable his Majesty to put an end to the present Session, his Majesty thinks it proper to recommend it to the House of Commons to consider of making provision to enable his Majesty to defray such extraordinary expenses (in addition to those which will be incurred in fulfilling the specific engagements which his Majesty has already directed to be laid before Parliament) and to take such measures as the exigency of affairs may require.' (*H. of C.J.* LV, 766 [18 July].)

the Primacy of Ireland which will open the English Bishoprick for Dr. Hunting-ford[1] and the Canonry of Windsor for Dr. Heath. (Chatham Papers.)

2197 THE KING *to the* BISHOP OF ST DAVID'S, *and the reply*

[*Windsor, 18 July 1800, 12 a.m.*] Yesterday I received the Bishop of St David's letter. The diffidence he expressed as to his health I rather expected; though the Irish climate is certainly damp, it is uncommonly mild and therefore not void of real merit. I certainly had fully viewed the advantages that must arise to the cause of religion and virtue in Ireland by his promotion to the vacant Primacy of that part of the British Empire, that I should not fulfill my duty if I did not in the most explicit manner now call on him to accept of that eminent situation, nor do I think he would shew the zeal I know he possesses for those two great objects if he does not instantly yield to this fresh communication of my sentiments on this momentous subject.[2] (9705)

[*Dr Stuart's reply, Ham, Friday morning, [?18 July].*] Whatever reluctance I felt to go to Ireland, or however adverse I conceive the situation to be to my private happiness, I cannot delay an instant to assure your Majesty of my cheerful submission to your commands; & I trust I shall be ever forward to profess on all occasions the inviolable attachment & gratitude with which I am [etc.]. (9707)

2198 THE DUCHESS OF WURTEMBERG *to the* KING

[*Erlangen, 18 July 1800.*] I had just taken up my pen to write to your Majesty when the Duke received the sad news that an Armistice is concluded for Germany, by which means we shall be precluded returning home, as the French remain in possession of the greatest part of Bavaria and all Suabia. Our situation is most deplorable, as we now see our poor country exposed to every misery without the means of assisting it. I am sure your Majesty will feel for us who, notwithstanding all we have done, are quite abandoned. My only trust and hope is in you, who, I am sure, will never give up those who trust in you and have made very great sacrifices.

The Duke begs that I will present his humble duty to your Majesty and return you our joint thanks for the four congarous who arrived here in good health on Monday evening. The house being partly built round a Court, the Duke has found means to place them in it, and they appear to enjoy themselves very much. Several painters have attempted to take their pictures and I believe intend to engrave them. (51605-6)

[1] George Isaac Huntingford (1748–1832), Bishop of Gloucester, 1802–15; of Hereford, 1815–32. George Murray succeeded William Stuart as Bishop of St David's. *The Times* declared on the 26th that Dr Huntingfield was to be the new Bishop, and it said (accurately so far as the English Bishops were concerned) that the Primacy of Ireland had 'gone literally a-begging'. George Rose believed that Speaker Addington suggested this appointment to the King: 'The King told Mr. Pitt that Dr. Hunting-ford (Warden of Winchester) would be the best man who could be thought of to fill the see, for learning and every other quality; which his Majesty could have heard from no one but Mr. Addington, who then possessed the King's mind with the impression to carry his point, lest he should fail with Mr. Pitt.' (Rose, *Diaries & Corresp.* I, 318.)

[2] Printed in Jesse, III, 232, with variations, and there addressed to Lady Charlotte Finch.

[*Downing Street, Friday, 18 July 1800, 8 p.m.*] Mr Pitt humbly begs leave to acquaint your Majesty that he this day moved the subsidy[1] to the Emperor, and after some opposition from Mr Jones and Mr Tierney (the latter of whom was replied to with great effect by Mr Canning[2]) the vote was agreed to without a division.[3]

The Report is to be received tomorrow, and Mr Pitt has the satisfaction to add that unless in the event of the failure of a House in the course of next week (which every exertion will be used to avoid) there can be nothing to prevent the prorogation on Tuesday sen'night.

Mr Pitt presumes to take this opportunity of mentioning that in consequence of the intimation which your Majesty was graciously pleased to convey to him thro' Lord Grenville, he has spoken to Lord Sydney,[4] who will be much gratified if your Majesty has the goodness to appoint him to succeed to the vacancy in your Majesty's Bedchamber. (9708–9)

[*The King's reply, Windsor, 19 July, 6.46 a.m.*] I am glad to find by Mr. Pitt's note that the subsidy to the Emperor was agreed to yesterday without any division, and that the House of Commons sets [*sic*] this day to receive the Report. I am unacquainted with the supposed failure of an House in the next week, and trust it will be prevented without the interference of Parliament which is certainly not a good mode and of very late introduction and ought if possible to be avoided, and more particularly at the end of a Session of Parliament, and of so unprecedented a length.

In consequence of Mr. Pitt's information I shall give the necessary directions to the D. of Roxburgh concerning Lord Sydney. Since my note to Mr. Pitt from the Great Lodge, I have received from the Bp. of St. David's an explicit acceptance of the Primacy of Ireland, which I look upon as essential to the quiet of the Irish Established Church, and to the promoting religion and virtue in that island. I believe nothing but my own exertion on this occasion could have effected this right measure. (Chatham Papers.)

[1] Of £1,500,000.

[2] Canning wrote, the next day: 'You will see that I reached town yesterday just time enough to take my part in the last debate of the Session. I was very anxious to do so, as it was a sort of sequel to the *first* debate of the Session, in which I had taken part: & more particularly as I had been attacked, in my absence (by Tierney on the debate on Mr. Western's Motion) for having said what I thought of Bonaparte—and I was determined to assert myself, & my *principle* of "*speaking the* TRUTH, come what will". I did so...' (Harewood MSS.)

Canning thought so well of his speech that he revised it for publication in Woodfall's and Debrett's *Parl. Register*. He wrote, 1 Aug., 2.30 p.m., from Putney Hill: 'Very hard work it has been, I promise you, & very hard work poor dear little Joan [his newly-married wife] has had in copying it, & it is but just done, this bloody hot day—but just finished, though it was begun the day before yesterday. But it was rather material to have one's speech upon so important a close of a Session correctly recorded, especially as that at the beginning of the Session was so, and the topicks in both were necessarily for the most part the same. So I determined to do it—& Joan determined to help me; and the two corrected copies for Woodfall & Debrett are just finished, & sealed, & ready to set off for town at the same time with this letter...' (Harewood MSS.) [3] *Parl. Register*, LVII, 396–426.

[4] Lord Sydney (1764–1831), who had just succeeded his father, was presented to the King at the Levée on the 23rd, on his appointment as a Lord of the Bedchamber *vice* the Earl of Denbigh, *dec.* (14 July). He held that Household office until 1810.

[*Halifax, Nova Scotia, 22 July 1800.*] Having five days since received by the arrival of the June mail a letter from Lieutenant-Colonel Wetherall informing me of the very gracious manner in which your Majesty had been pleased to accede to my request of being permitted to return to England for the recovery of my health, I conceive it my duty to embrace the opportunity of a packet that has touched here in her way from New York to Falmouth to offer my humble and most grateful acknowledgments for this fresh mark of your favor, and affection. The Assistance of fifty guns commanded by Captain Hall,[1] that was under orders for England, is in consequence preparing for my reception, and I have hopes of being able to embark in the course of the first week in August. Should I not be disappointed in this, I shall flatter myself with having the happiness of paying my duty to your Majesty by the last of that month, or very early in September.[2] Since I had the honor of addressing you on the 22d of May, I have had one of the severest bilious attacks I ever yet experienced, and in the course of the last fortnight, a very violent rheumatism settled in my head for several days, from the consequence of which I am at this moment entirely deaf of one ear. However, the gentlemen of the Faculty give me reason to hope that the voyage home will not only be of infinite service to my health, but may also remove this inconvenience.

Should your Majesty be at Weymouth at the time of my arrival, which, if I calculate right, is likely to be the case, I shall intreat your permission to remain there for a short time, for the purpose of taking the benefit of sea bathing, which is very strongly recommended to me by Doctor Haliburton, the physician who attends me here.

Had the present occasion not presented itself of addressing your Majesty, I should have presumed to have written notwithstanding, to endeavour to express all I felt, when made acquainted with your late most providential escape. But I am sensible that any words I could make use of would be at the best totally inadequate to convey the sentiments with which I should wish you to believe I am impressed on the occasion. I will therefore only presume to say, that of all your children, none is more truly grateful to Divine Providence for the protecting hand extended over your life so invaluable to us all, and none more firmly or devotedly attached to your person than I am. I trust your Majesty will condescend to receive this assurance with your usual indulgence, and that, though not conveyed in florid language, you will not be the less convinced of my faithful attachment and dutiful respect. (45987–8)

2201 THE EARL OF CLARE *to* LORD AUCKLAND

[*24 July* [*1800*].] Many thanks for your last confidential communication, which I received with great pleasure and shall certainly not transpire from me. I do most sincerely believe that the King is one of the most right-headed men in his own

---

[1] Robert Hall. Lieutenant, 1782; Commander, 1796; Captain, 1799. Knighted, 15 July 1816.

[2] A remarkably accurate prediction: he landed at Plymouth on Sunday, 31 Aug., and set off to join the royal family at Weymouth.

dominions, and in this instance he has certainly evinced it strongly in not yielding to the recommendation of Doctor Cleaver,[1] who must appear, to every man accustomed to his violent and overbearing temper, most eminently disqualified for the situation to which he aspired. I find they have softened our little friend Cashel[2] and sure I am he will take care that he has full equivalents for his acquiescence in the promotion of any other man. What a blessing it is that we have succeeded so well in abolishing that system of universal jobbing and cabal to which every Government in this country has been so long forced to bend, and certainly there is no more perfect master of the art than the aforesaid little Prelate.

I mean to go down to Mount Shannon for the summer the day after the prorogation of our Parliamt. which will take place on the 2d of August. It is my intention to go to Bath for a month at Christmass and not to think of remaining in England after the first day of the ensuing term unless I am ordered so to do; and whenever you can ascertain whether my attendance will be required at London in the course of the next winter I shall thank you to let me know it, that I may arrange my affairs here accordingly. I feel that I shall be of much more use at home than I can possibly be elsewhere.

Our friend Carleton[3] has very foolishly resigned his office of Chief Justice; the act has been altogether his own, under a foolish impression that his health suffers by the labours of his Court. I feel annoyed at losing him as a Judge and much more annoyed at the apprehension that he will be succeeded by Toler, but I have reason to think that the late political struggle has made this visitation upon the people of Ireland almost inevitable. I well remember your having expressed more than once your astonishment at the consideration into which this gentleman has forced himself, and if you had the same opportunities of knowing him that I have had, you would be still more astonished. We never hear of [the] Union now and you may be quite assured that there is no possible chance of ferment or discontent at the measure.

I am much obliged to you for ensuring me a good copy of the Anti-Jacobin poems;[4] if you see Wright[5] desire him to let me know when they are published that I may desire a messenger to call upon him for my copy. (10308–9)

---

[1] Euseby Cleaver, D.D. (1746–1819). Rector of Spofforth, Yorks., 1774–83; Prebendary of Chichester, 1787; Bishop of Cork, March 1789; of Ferns, June 1789–1809; Archbishop of Dublin,1809–19. He remained Archbishop for the last eight years of his life, though a lunatic: the Archbishop of Cashel was appointed coadjutor, Aug. 1811.

[2] Charles Agar, Baron Somerton, 1795; Viscount Somerton, 1800; Earl of Normanton, 1806; Archbishop of Cashel since 1779. He was translated to Dublin, 7 Dec. 1801, and was succeeded by the Hon. Charles Brodrick, who was translated from Kilmore. Dr Randolph, Bishop of Oxford, refused the Primacy (Buckingham, *Court and Cabinets*, III, 28).

[3] Hugh Carleton (1739–1826). Solicitor-General [I.], 1779–87; Lord Chief Justice of the Common Pleas [I.], 1787–1800. Created Baron Carleton, 1789, and Viscount Carleton, 1797. An Irish Representative Peer, 1801–26.

[4] A satirical publication, published weekly, directed against revolutionary principles. It lasted from Nov. 1797 to July 1798. Canning and his friends supplied the materials.

[5] John Wright (?1770–1844), bookseller. He published the *Anti-Jacobin*, and, with Cobbett, edited the *Parliamentary History, Parliamentary Debates, and State Trials*.

2202 CABINET MINUTE,[1] *Downing Street, 24 July 1800.*

Present: The Lord Chancellor, The Duke of Portland, The Earl of Westmorland, The Earl Spencer, Lord Grenville, Mr Pitt, Mr Dundas.

Your Majesty's confidential servants humbly submit to your Majesty their opinion that, at this season of the year, and in the present circumstances of Europe and of the war, it would not be expedient to attempt the capture of Belle Isle, but that a considerable part of the disposeable force of the country should be appropriated to the purpose of destroying as much of the naval force of the enemy as can be attempted with any reasonable prospect of success.

With this view it is humbly submitted to your Majesty that, in addition to the troops now at the Isle of Houat, amounting to about 2,500 men, such further force may be immediately embarked as may compleat the number to 12,000 effectives; that the officer entrusted with the command of this corps should consult with Lord St. Vincent on the practicability of an attempt on the Port of Ferrol, and in case it should appear to present a reasonable prospect of success, that the attack should immediately be concerted between them, and be undertaken by this corps of 12,000 men and such a detachment of the Fleet as Lord St. Vincent may assign for this service, with a view of destroying the enemy's squadron and arsenals at that port. That should this service be successfully executed, or relinquished as too hazardous, in either case the force should then proceed to Gibraltar, where Sir Ralph Abercromby should also be ordered to repair with the disposeable Mediterranean force. That as soon as the two corps shall be thus united, the whole shall proceed to an attack upon Cadiz, with a view of destroying the enemy's ships & arsenals at that port: after which, or in case of its being relinquished as impracticable, a part of the force should be employed in capturing Teneriffe and such other of the Canary Islands as in the opinion of the naval & military officers may be judged best calculated for a naval & military station, and that the remainder shall rendezvous at Gibraltar to wait such further orders as future circumstances may render adviseable.[2] (9710–2)

2203 *Letters from* HENRY DUNDAS *to the* KING, *and a reply*

[*Downing Street, 25 July 1800, 11 a.m.*] Mr Dundas humbly informs your Majesty that he was about to set out for Swinley[3] this morning at six o clock when he had the honour of receiving your Majesty's note. Mr Dundas's reason of being prepared to go to Swinley was to settle the detail with his Royal Highness the Duke of York if the plans suggested by your Majesty's confidential servants had met

---

[1] Sent by Dundas, but not in his hand. The name of the Minister sending a Cabinet Minute to the King usually appeared last on the Minute.

[2] On the 24th Lord Grenville sent the following note to the King. It referred to the projected enlargement of the seating accommodation in the House of Commons in view of the coming influx of 100 Irish Members. 'It being necessary that your Majesty's answer to this Address should be reported on Monday, Lord Grenville has, at the Lord Chamberlain's request, undertaken to transmit it to your Majesty.' (Add. Georgian 2/59.) The Address was in fact, reported on Tuesday the 29th (*H. of C.J.* XLII, 647).

[3] The King reviewed the cavalry and infantry at the Camp at King's Beeches, near Bagshot on the 24th, and the Duke of York entertained the Royal family and many other guests at Swinley Lodge. The King was there again on the 25th.

with your Majesty's approbation, but wishing to avoid any delay on his part Mr Dundas thought it his duty to come immediately to town to lay your Majesty's note before your Majesty's servants. Not finding either Mr Pitt or Lord Grenville in town, Mr Dundas must of course postpone any further steps till he has an opportunity of collecting the sentiments of your Majesty's servants. (9717–18)

[*Wimbledon, 25 July 1800, 11 p.m.*] Mr Dundas humbly states to your Majesty that having no opportunity this morning to summon a Cabinet, he transmitted to Mr Pitt the note he had received from your Majesty, and has this evening received an answer from Mr Pitt, who wishes that Mr Dundas should not have recourse to a further Cabinet consultation, but humbly represent to your Majesty the joint sentiments of Mr Pitt and Mr Dundas in consequence of the doubt which your Majesty's note has been graciously pleased to suggest.[1]

They feel that if an army, collected at so much expence, and by so unusual exertions, was to remain inactive during the whole of the remainder of the season, the spirit of the country would be let down, your Majesty's Government justly censured, and the impatience and clamour for peace *on any terms* encreased every hour.

They further feel and humbly represent to your Majesty, that on a reference to the Minute of Cabinet, your Majesty will perceive that there is no intention of running any improper risk in any of the cases directed. The whole will rest on the judgement of the respectable officers to be employed, and it is not felt that too much is left to their discretion. Sir James Pultney after discreet enquiry is impressed with an opinion that Ferrol holds out a fair object of hope to the

---

[1] Pitt took a grave view of the King's opposition to the military and naval plans of his Ministers. He wrote to Dundas on Friday the 25th at 3 p.m., from Hollwood: 'I am as much astonished and hurt as you can be at the note you have sent me. But I am persuaded the difficulty cannot be persisted in; and I cannot help thinking that, to save time, it would be much best if instead of waiting for any Cabinet, you were either to write immediately to the King or go tomorrow to Windsor to lay before him a temperate statement of the various considerations to which he cannot be insensible. These seem shortly to be, first, that if he means that all the army which it has cost so much expense and unusual exertion to form, is to be kept inactive during the remainder of the campaign, he must expect to see the spirit of the country let down, the Government justly censured, and the impatience and clamour for peace *on any terms* increasing every hour. Secondly, (what you state in your note) that the expedition to Bellisle would have taken away as large a force, and would still have left sufficient here. Thirdly, that the data for thinking of the expedition, and the importance of striking *some* blow, and the opinion of a reputable officer that *this* is likely to be practicable, which are surely grounds sufficient for doing all that is proposed —viz. to refer it for decision on consultation between your Admiral and General, when they have acquired all the information they can. These topics calmly stated must I trust have their effect. If not there is only one left, in which I must most decidedly join, that of begging his Majesty to find servants whose judgments he can trust more than ours.' (Ann Arbor MSS.)

Pitt wrote again to Dundas on the 26th, from Bromley Hill, at 10.30 p.m.: 'I wish to take till tomorrow morning to think over the contents of the papers you have sent me. My first notion is that it would be best for me to write to the King stating that you have sent me his letter, and to represent to him the necessity (since he now agrees to the object) of adopting the only measure which can prevent our being too late for it. As he has given way in the main point I am sure he will in the rest; and tho' I admit you have reason enough to be personally displeased, I am sure you are above indulging that feeling especially at such a moment. And we must allow something more than usual for the effect in all other business of the irritation on the King's mind from our pressing upon him unwelcome tho' necessary counsels on the subject of negotiation. At all events have the goodness not to send your answer till you hear from me again. I would come to you in the morning but I am here in the midst of accounts which I must go thro' tomorrow.' (*Ibid.*)

enterprise of your Majesty's naval and military force, and your Majesty's servants humbly conceive that Lord St. Vincent and Sir James Pultney ought to be furnished with the means of attempting Ferrol, if they think it expedient, and that in like manner Lord Keith and Sir Ralph Abercrombie are justly entitled to a similar confidence in so far as their operations may be implicated in the propositions of the Minute of Cabinet which has been transmitted to your Majesty by your confidential servants.

Mr Dundas in his own name and that of Mr Pitt does further presume humbly to represent to your Majesty that if after the appropriation of 12,000 men to the objects in view, which is less than was destined for Belle-Isle, and for a short time, it shall be conceived by your Majesty's subjects that the various force existing in the country with an invincible fleet is inadequate to its security, they will feel themselves less comfortable than fortunately they have done for these two years past.

Mr Dundas is unwilling to trespass further on the indulgence of your Majesty, but he reposes with much confidence in the candor and integrity of your Majesty's feelings, that if those who are entrusted by your Majesty with the conduct of your Majesty's affairs, possess the confidence of your Majesty, they will not be deprived of the benefit of it at a moment when it is so essentially necessary in every particular, and in none more than the conduct of the war. (9713–16)

[*The King's reply, Windsor, 25 July 1800, 10.15 p.m.*] On returning from Swinley I have found Mr. Secretary Dundas's note forwarding a Minute of Cabinet. Not having before heard of an expedition against Ferrol and on what grounds of supposed success it is to be undertaken, nor what force will remain in this country after the sending so large force out of it, I cannot give any answer till I have received the data on which to form an opinion. (Add. MSS. 40100, f. 257.)

2204   *Letters from* WILLIAM PITT *to the* KING

[*Hollwood, Saturday, 26 July 1800.*] Mr Pitt humbly begs leave to submit to your Majesty's gracious consideration the draft of the Speech for the conclusion of the Session. He trusts that the general tone and language of it is such as your Majesty will not disapprove, as, altho he has the misfortune in common with the rest of your Majesty's servants to entertain an opinion respecting the necessity of concurring with Austria, in negotiation which is unfortunately adverse to your Majesty's personal sentiments, he nevertheless feels it of the utmost importance that every public declaration should be calculated to maintain as high as is possible the spirit of the country during the interval of negotiation. Mr Pitt will not presume to trouble your Majesty farther on this subject or on any other at present, trusting that he may have the opportunity of paying his personal duty to your Majesty at St. James's at the time fixed for reading the Speech; which he unfortunately missed doing on Wednesday from being misinformed as to the length of the Recorder's Report. (9719–20)

[*Bromley Hill, Sunday, 27 July 1800.*] Since writing the note which Mr Pitt had the honor of addressing to your Majesty yesterday from Hollwood, (and which he directed to be dispatched from town as soon as the draft of the Speech could be copied) he has received from Mr Dundas your Majesty's farther answer on the subject of the late Minute of Cabinet, and is highly sensible of your Majesty's condescension and goodness in graciously attending to the considerations which Mr Dundas and himself felt it their duty to lay before your Majesty. From the same motive Mr Pitt ventures to rely again on your Majesty's indulgence in humbly representing that if the attack on Ferrol should be found practicable, it is of the utmost importance from the advanced season of the year that it should be executed without loss of time; and also, with a view to secrecy, that the troops destined for it should be sent out as reinforcements to those now in the Bay, instead of the whole being collected here, as by these means the expedition will still be supposed to be directed against Bellisle. On these grounds Mr Pitt humbly hopes it will not be found necessary that troops so recently sent for foreign service should be brought home again previous to the expedition, but if there are any additional articles of which they are supposed to be in need, these should be sent out to them as expeditiously as possible, together with the reinforcement. [With the same object of saving time,][1] he also begs again to submit that it is very desireable to avoid the necessity of any reference home, and as the object is a very simple one, it seems safe to entrust the decision, under proper conditional instructions, to the discretion of Lord St Vincent and Sir James Pulteney on the spot.[2] (9721–2)

2205   *Letters from the* KING *to* HENRY DUNDAS *or* PITT, *and a reply*

[*Windsor, 27 July 1800, 9.02 p.m.*] The draft of the Speech seems as proper as the untoward situation of Europe will permit. If the regiment now on the coast of France can have their necessaries sent them and a sufficiency of tonnage afforded me, I shall not press their being brought to a British port for preparation, but dear

---

[1] The words within brackets are not in the copy (in Pitt's hand) in the Ann Arbor MSS.

[2] Pitt wrote to Dundas at 1 p.m. that day (the letter is inadequately dated 'Sunday, 27 July': 'I have thought it best upon consideration to write a note to the King of which the enclosed is a copy, and which is founded on much the same ideas which struck me on first receiving your paper. I trust this will have its effect, and as he has already given way in the essential point, I really cannot feel that his last note requires your returning to it such an answer as that which you have sent me is in its conclusion. All the rest seems perfectly proper, but that sentence implies a determination much too serious to be formed but on the strongest grounds, and I really do not see them in the present instance. It is surely much more dignified for yourself as well as right for the public not to suffer any sensation of personal pique to mix itself with all the higher considerations of the present moment. At any rate I trust we shall meet in town tomorrow, and I hope you will not think it necessary to take any step of this sort in the interval. I must be in town between twelve and one.

[P.S.] I was actually sending off my servant with this box when your messenger arrived. I have stated to you exactly what I think and my opinion applies equally to the one concluding sentence of your note as now proposed. What you have added respecting the approbation of force resting on the advice and responsibility of his Majesty's servants, I think perfectly just and reasonable. But after saying that, you leave the subject on manly ground and cannot be called upon to say more.

You will see by my note that I had anticipated the substance of your memorandum respecting the state of the troops. But to shew the ground you have acted upon, might it not be as well to enclose it to the King?' (Ann Arbor MSS.)

bought experience ought to teach us that if soldiers have not the conveniences that are necessary that it is impossible they can support the fatigues of service, and I cannot forget the old saying of loving more haste than good speed. (Add. MSS. 40100, f. 267.)

[*From Dundas, Wimbledon, 27 July, 10 p.m.*] Mr Dundas humbly states to your Majesty that on the receipt of your Majesty's commands on the subject of Ferroll, he immediately transmitted them to Mr Pitt, who will receive your Majesty's pleasure upon them. It only remains for Mr Dundas to remark that the delay which would arise from the preliminary steps your Majesty has pointed out as proper to be adopted previous to the measures suggested by your servants, do not correspond with the secrecy and promptitude which your Majesty's confidential servants supposed to be necessary on the present occasion.

Mr Dundas perceives with great concern that his mode of bringing this business before your Majesty has met with your Majesty's disapprobation. His only apology must be that he pursued on this occasion the same line of conduct he has uniformly done since he had the honour of a share in your Majesty's confidential Councils. In matters of smaller detail he has presumed to act on his own judgement, but in matters of such magnitude as that now in question, he has always conceived himself to be acting in the manner most respectfull to your Majesty and most beneficial to the publick service when he laid his propositions before your Majesty matured by the united wisdom of those to whom your Majesty has entrusted the conduct of your confidential affairs.

Having stated this much in apology for his own conduct, Mr. Dundas begs leave with the utmost humility and the most profound respect to state to your Majesty that in his poor judgement the appropriation of the national force must in time of war, like every other resource of the Empire, be subject to the advice and responsibility of your Majesty's confidential servants. (9723–5)

[*The King's reply, Windsor, 28 July, 7.10 a.m.*] Had Mr. Secretary Dundas stated what he has done in the note received this morning previous to calling a Cabinet and sending an opinion to me on a subject that had by no one been previously communicated to me, he would would [*sic*] have had a more explicit answer; but considering the great waste of men in the various expeditions we have attempted this war and particularly in that to Holland the last autumn, it is no wonder I wished for more explanation before I gave my consent to this proposition. My note wrote in an hurry could mean nothing also, and Mr. Pitt shewed his usual penetration in thinking it not intended for to be laid before a Cabinet meeting. As Sir James Pulteney thinks the attack on Ferrol feesible I do not object to his consulting with the Earl of St. Vincent as to the means of effecting it, but these should be laid before a Cabinet previous to putting in execution the measure. In the meantime the troops which must be collected from different places must be got together; those on the coast of France which must make a part of it must be brought to some port, that they may have all the requisites delivered to them for going on foreign service. The health of men as well as the securing success requires these precautions. Anything that will keep off making peace with France till it has an established Government on which some confidence can be placed is certainly desirable; that weighs the most with me in the present consideration if it can be effected with a reasonable hope of success and not a wanton loss of lives. (Add. MSS. 40100, f. 272.)

[*From the King, Windsor, 28 July, 7.23 a.m.*] Mr. Secy. Dundas will find from the note[1] I wrote last night to Mr. Pitt that I do not mean to press the bringing the troops from the coast of France for to prepare them for foreign service, provided they can as expeditiously have every requisite sent to them. I doubt whether by this latter mode more time will not be lost than in the other mode. The success of any enterprize must in the end depend on the arrangements being duly prepared, the want of which certainly must most frequently prevent the best intended scheme from answering. The entering into a paper war is not in the least my intention; it can answer no good purpose and certainly no agreable occupation, but after the sanguine expectations of some with regard to Belle Isle after five months its being found impracticable, gives reason for pausing on a new project till it is more fully explained. I am certain I have in no part of this business done more.[2] (Add. MSS. 40100, f. 274.)

[*From Dundas, Wimbledon, 28 July, 12 o'clock.*] Mr Dundas humbly transmits for your Majesty's signature if approved, a Commission for the Governor-General of India. Upon a reference to the Commission and the accompanying draft of the letter proposed to be wrote to Marquis Wellesley, your Majesty will be apprised of the circumstance which renders such a Commission necessary. (9726)

2206   THE DUCHESS OF WURTEMBERG *to the* KING

[*Erlangen, 28 July 1800.*] Knowing your Majesty's paternal affection for me it costs me a great deal to be always wounding your heart with wretched accounts of our situation, which grows worse and worse. Last night the Duke received a messenger to acquaint him the French have imposed six millions on the Dutchy, to be paid within a month, or all the Duke's houses to be burnt and his possessions laid waste, besides a large body of troops being sent into the Dutchy. (At present this sum amounts to six hundred thousand pounds English.) As, after all the misery and oppression the poor Würtembergers have undergone, their is no specie in the country, the Duke knowing their inability to do anything towards this contribution, has striped himself of all the money he had laid by for us to live on and sent it to pay off the first instalment, which is on the 5th, but what steps can be taken for the next, God alone knows. The French refuse to take anything but money or plate, which makes our situation infinitely worse than in the year ninety six, as then the contribution amounted to four millions, of which

[1] See the first letter in No. 2205, though it is in the Melville MSS.

[2] The King, then, had to submit to the judgement of his Ministers. The expedition to Ferrol came to nothing; a landing was effected but the capture of the port was deemed impracticable. The other objectives—Cadiz, Teneriffe and the Canary Islands were not attempted.

only one third in specie, the rest in horses, corn &c. This is a most iniquitous business as the proportion on all occasions is that the Duke pays the fifth part of all the expences of the Circle of Suabia and now they force him to pay the half, all the rest of Suabia being taxed at six millions.

This fresh blow has affected both the Duke and myself very much and I should feel still more wretched did I not place a firm confidence in your Majesty's justice and protection, who will not allow us to become the victims of the intrigues and passions of others, after the manner in which the Duke has exerted himself for the common cause.

The Austrians having abandoned our country without acquainting the Duke is shocking, not only as it is against the Treaty but doubly so when your Majesty considers that since the year ninety six the Emperor has received above fourteen millions of florins, which is double the Duke's revenues from the Dutchy. Ought we not at least to be protected after such sacrifices, instead of being yielded up to the enemy who during the Armistice make these demands to destroy the country? Trusting to your Majesty's known justice and goodness I humbly entreat you to have compassion on us and interest yourself for us at Vienna that some steps may be taken to secure the Dutchy from utter destruction.

I also beg your Majesty will be so gracious as to encourage the Loan the Duke has some thoughts of seeking to obtain in England as the only means to save his poor subjects. The moment the Duke acquainted me with this fresh calamity I wanted to give my jewels to assist the country, but he would not allow of it, as in Germany I should not receive one tenth part of their value. However, my heart is so set on being of use that can I find an advantageous opportunity in England I shall seize it with pleasure and feel more satisfaction in knowing the money has saved many families than I ever did in wearing them. It is very painful to me always to plague your Majesty with our misfortunes, but looking on you as my protector I hope you will forgive my importunity to assist us. (51607–9)

2207   HENRY DUNDAS *to the* KING

[*Downing Street, 29 July 1800, 4 p.m.*] Mr Dundas humbly transmits for your Majesty's consideration a Minute[1] containing the result of a deliberation held this day by your Majesty's confidential servants. (9727)

2208   EARL SPENCER *to the* KING, *and the reply*

[*Admiralty, 29 July 1800.*] Earl Spencer has the honor to lay before your Majesty a list of the frigates and cutters under orders to attend upon your Majesty at Weymouth; which he would have done himself the honor to present to your Majesty this day at St. James's, if there had not been so great a pressure of business. (9728)

[1] Missing.

[*The King's reply, Windsor, 30 July, 6.40 a.m.*] I am equally sensible of Earl Spencer's attention in sending the list of the frigates and ordered to Weymouth, as of his taking this method of delivering them rather than causing any delay in my going yesterday to prorogue the Parliament [*sic*].[1] (Althorp MSS.)

2209 LORD GRENVILLE *to the* KING, *and the reply*

[*Cleveland Row, 31 July 1800.*] Lord Grenville has the honour to lay before your Majesty the Minute of yesterday's Cabinet upon the Danish business, together with the drafts and other papers relating to it. Lord Whitworth is ready, if your Majesty shall approve of it, to proceed immediately on his mission. The measures for sending the squadron may, as Lord Spencer thinks, be so concerted as to prevent any suspicion of it either here or at Copenhagen till their actual arrival in the Sound. (9730)

[*Enclosure*]
[*Cabinet Minute, Downing Street, 30 July 1800.*]

Present: The Lord Privy Seal, Duke of Portland, Earl Spencer, Earl Camden, Mr Chancellor of the Exchequer, Mr Secretary Dundas, Mr Windham, Lord Grenville.

It was agreed humbly to represent to his Majesty that it may be proper, in consequence of what has passed respecting the Danish convoy, that an answer should be returned to Count Wedel's[2] note conformably to the draft which has now been read.

That a squadron of ships of the line should immediately be dispatched to the Sound, with orders to remain there till further orders, but not to commit hostilities except in the case of the detention or capture of any of the British ships in the Baltic, or of the sending away his Majesty's Minister[3] from Denmark; or lastly of any hostile conduct on the part of that Power against the squadron itself.

That Lord Whitworth should forthwith proceed on a special mission to the Court of Copenhagen.

That he should be instructed to make a demand of satisfaction, and of sufficient security for the future. And that he should be empowered ultimately to accept, as such satisfaction and security, a declaration or Convention by which the Court of Denmark shall agree not to give any further effect to the instructions on which their officer has now acted, nor to renew those orders: and that in return for this concession he should be authorized to engage for the restitution of the frigate and convoy: the same being to be detained in the meantime as a pledge for this reparation.

---

[1] The Speech from the Throne on the 29th, when Parliament was prorogued to 7 Oct., is in *Parl. Register*, LVII, 604.

[2] The Swedish Minister in London.

[3] Anthony Merry was Chargé d'Affaires at Copenhagen from 25 July 1799 until 3 Sept. 1800, when he had audience of leave of the Prince Royal. Lord Whitworth arrived at Copenhagen on his Special Mission (with full power to treat with Denmark) on 11 Aug. He left Copenhagen shortly after 26 Sept.

In the event of any such hostile conduct as is before stated, the officer commanding the squadron is to do his utmost to destroy the ships and arsenal of Copenhagen. (9731–2)

[*The King's reply, Weymouth, 1 Aug.*] The Minute of Cabinet of the 30th of July which I have received this morning from Lord Grenville on the Danish business and the drafts and other papers relating to it, as also the appointment of Lord Whitworth to proceed immediately to Copenhagen meet with [my] fullest approbation. I am pleased with Earl Spencer's opinion that the squadron may even arrive in the Sound without any suspicion either here or at Copenhagen.

P.S. Such an immense number of papers have been sent from the different Offices this day that I certainly have run them over in a more cursory manner than is desirable, and yet have kept back some boxes for tomorrow, though I have not kept back those from the Foreign Department. (Fortescue MSS.)

2210 EARL SPENCER *to the* KING, *and the reply*

[*Admiralty, 2 Aug. 1800.*] Earl Spencer has the honour to lay before your Majesty the proceedings of a court martial held at Portsmouth whereby two more of the mutineers of the Hermione have been convicted and sentenced to capital punishment, and as it appears by the evidence that they were both actually concerned in that atrocious mutiny & murder, Earl Spencer humbly submits to your Majesty that the sentence should be ordered to be carried into execution without delay. (9733)

[*The King's reply, Weymouth, 3 Aug.*] I have this morning received Earl Spencer's note accompanied by the minutes of the court martial held at Portsmouth whereby two of the mutineers of the Hermione have been convicted and are sentenced to receive capital punishment. I fully feel the necessity of allowing the above sentence to be put in force without delay. (Althorp MSS.)

2211 THE DUKE OF PORTLAND *to the* KING

[*Bulstrode, Tuesday, 5 Aug. 1800, 10.50 a.m.*] In laying before your Majesty the dispatches which arrived last night from the Lord Lieutenant, which contain a list of the Acts & a copy of the Speech which the Duke of Portland presumes to express his satisfaction in considering as the last that will ever have to receive the Royal Assent or to be delivered from the Throne but by your Majesty or your royal descendants in person, he begs leave with all humility to submit to your Majesty for your royal signature the reversionary grant, of the office of Clerk of the Pipe to the Earl of Carhampton's relation, in consequence of which, as has been represented to your Majesty, & the signification of your Majesty's consent, the Earl of Carhampton is forthwith to resign the office of Master-General of the Ordnance.[1] The Duke of Portland also begs leave to submit to your Majesty

---

[1] Castlereagh reported on 6 July 1799 that Lord Carhampton, having disposed of his estate at Luttrelstown, had parted with much of his indisposition to the Union along with it, and had announced his intention to vote for the Bill. (*Castlereagh Corresp.* II, 346.)

that it is the intention of your Majesty's servants to desire the attendance of Lord Castlereagh about the 20th of this month (the time which he states to be the most convenient to himself) in order to consider & prepare the arrangements which the new order of things arising out of the happy event of the Union will require to be submitted to your Majesty & to receive your Majesty's royal sanction in order to their being carried into effect. (9734–5)

2212 LORD SOMERVILLE[1] *to* WILLIAM PITT. (*Copy.*)

[*Hill Street, 5 Aug. 1800.*] I was unwilling to trouble you on a subject indifferent perhaps to yourself, but of no common interest to me, nor would I until the recess allowed you time to give it a moment's consideration, and the necessity for doing so is become too apparent.

The manner of my removal from the Presidency of the Board of Agriculture and the conclusions which have generally been drawn from it wound me beyond all expression, nor at the end of ten weeks since my return to England has any explanation been offered me by any of those who took part in it. I know how you, Sir, appretiate him who preceded me in that situation.[2] I must have seen into his proceedings and would not willingly suppose that I was placed there to wipe up his slops. I would not trouble you occasionally where the office I held might have justified me in doing so because your time was not to be tresspassed on, yet I did not the less regret that no notice was taken in various cases of its own institution, where with great propriety it might have been, by Parliament—well knowing that without such encouragement no individual could give such a situation its full effect whatever might be his diligence and skill. I have long exerted myself to the utmost of my little ability to forward your measures, and have made it not only my duty but my pride to serve you. This must be my excuse indeed for waiting on you when I was first appointed to that office for the purpose of receiving any hints you might think fit to give, and of course to act on them. I can therefore hardly bring myself to suppose that you, Sir, would intentionally strike at the root of my reputation and peace of mind.

I have only to add that had I known your wishes I would most chearfully have put them in execution both in the conduct or resignation of such an office, and I do most earnestly request that some means may be taken to wipe off that stain which the public thinks fit to attach to my removal—it sits too heavily on my mind to be endured any longer in silence. (9736–7)

2213 EARL SPENCER *to the* KING, *and the reply*

[*Admiralty, 8 Aug. 1800.*] Earl Spencer has the honour to lay before your Majesty the proceedings of a court martial on Lieutenant Franklin of the Marines, together with the opinion of the Honble. Mr Perceval on the sentence passed by that Court, by which it appears that their having sentenced that officer to be reduced

---

[1] John, 14th Lord Somerville (1765–1819). Scottish Representative Peer, 1796–1807; President of the Board of Agriculture, 1798–1800; a Lord of the Bedchamber, 1799–1819.
[2] Sir John Sinclair.

from his rank of First Lieutenant to that of Second Lieutenant is not warranted by law, though the offence for which the Lieutenant was tried would very well deserve such a reduction. Earl Spencer therefore humbly presumes to submit to your Majesty the propriety of your Majesty's signifying your royal pleasure that Lieutenant Franklin's name should be struck off the list of Marine Lieutenants, and that on some future occasion, in case he should express a proper sense of his misconduct, your Majesty will be graciously pleased to allow of his being appointed a Second Lieutenant of the Marines, by which means the object of the sentence will be carried into effect without being subject to the legal objections stated by Mr Perceval. (9738)

[*The King's reply, Weymouth, 9 Aug.*] I fully see the force of the opinion given by Earl Spencer as to the proper means of disposing of the sentence of the court martial on Lieutenant Franklin of the Marines, and authorize this officer's being dismissed from the service, but if he shall express a proper sense of his misconduct, permitting on some future occasion his being appointed a Second Lieutenant of Marines. (Althorp MSS.)

2214 THE DUCHESS OF WURTEMBERG *to the* KING

[*Erlangen, 9 Aug. 1800.*] The Duke has desired me to acquaint your Majesty with his humble duty, that he finds himself to his great regret obliged to go to Vienna where he will endeavour to make a very short stay, as he leaves me here.

Peace being much talked of, it is his duty to try by every exertion in his power to prevent his becoming a sacrifice to it, as he was made to the shameful Armistice of which he was only acquainted by the newspapers. The heavy contributions which have been imposed on the Dutchy seem to militate against some of the Articles of the Armistice, which made the Duke apply to the Imperial Court that it would endeavour to obtain some favourable alterations, but even this was in vain, as Monsieur de Thugut told Monsieur de Bühler the Emperor could not interfere. Moreau, to whom the Duke sent to ask that at least part of this heavy contribution might be remited, refused to diminish any part of his demands and has added requisitions in corn, cattle &c. for above two millions, which it will be impossible to furnish as there are above eight thousand men quartered in the Dutchy who eat everything up. Two hundred and fifty who are at Louisbourg cost the town eight hundred florins a day. Six Generals have lodged themselves in the Duke's houses; as yet with great difficulty they have been prevented taking possession of the Castles at Stutgard and Louisbourg. But General Richepanse, who is at Stutgard, dissatisfied with a very good house which was given him, took possession by force of the Palace we formerly inhabited and has ordered such a quantity of game to be shot that if he goes on at the same rate in three weeks there will be no more in the Dutchy. The table of each General costs sixteen guineas a day. How our poor country will ever be able to stand this God alone knows. I must again entreat your Majesty not to abandon us as without your graciously standing up for us we must be ruined, as there is so little dependance to be placed on those who can give us up a prey to the French after all our sacrifices.

I intend to remain quietly here during the Duke's absence as we can live here at present cheaper than anywhere else, though I do not like the place and long very much for the Duke's return that we may find some country house till it pleases Providence to allow us to go to Stutgard.[1] (51612–13)

2215   EARL SPENCER *to the* KING, *and the reply*

[*Admiralty, 9 Aug. 1800.*] Earl Spencer has very great satisfaction in being enabled to lay before your Majesty another instance of the distinguished intrepidity and skill of British seamen, with which he has no doubt but that your Majesty will be much pleased; and as it happens that Mr Coghlan,[2] the acting Lieutenant who commanded the party on this occasion has not served a sufficient time in your Majesty's Navy to entitle him to receive a Lieutenant's Commission according to the established rules, Earl Spencer humbly submits to your Majesty that it may be proper to distinguish this very gallant service by signifying your Majesty's pleasure that Mr Coghlan may be appointed a Lieutenant notwithstanding his want of time, for which proceeding there appears to be a precedent, a minute of which he has the honor to inclose herewith. (9739)

[*The King's reply, Weymouth, 10 Aug. 1800.*] I am much pleased with the account transmitted to me by Earl Spencer of the intrepidity with which Mr. Coglan has executed his well-planned attack on a French brig, which most properly ought to gain him the rank of Lieutenant to which the time of his service in the Navy would not otherwise entitle him. This make[s] me see with pleasure that there is a precedent for such an extraordinary promotion, which certainly must be followed on the present occasion.[3] (Althorp MSS.)

2216   THE DUKE OF YORK *to the* KING

[*Oatlands, 10 Aug. 1800.*] I have the honor to acknowledge the receipt of your Majesty's most gracious letter and am desired by Colonel Calvert to lay him at

---

[1] Lord Minto, then British Minister at Vienna, wrote of the 'lamentations and alarms of a Prince whose ruin seems so much a consequence of his relation and engagements to us...I admit...that he is no apostle of our cause, and I can easily believe all you say of the mischief done by his indiscreet and perhaps ill-affected language...He is at present struggling in the very convulsions of political death' (*Life and Letters of Lord Minto*, III, 178). Lady Minto wrote to Lady Malmesbury: 'Moreau is now living in the Duke of Wurtemberg's house at Stuttgardt. The Duke, his brother and son are here. The Duke's son has proposed to one of the Queen of Naples' daughters, and so has the Duke de Berri. She has not yet decided which she will favour. The Duke of Wurtemberg is handsome, and they are equally poor' (*ibid.* III, 177 n.).

[2] Jeremiah Coghlan (?1775–1844). Lieutenant, 22 Sept. 1800; Commander, 1804; Captain, 1810.

[3] The *London Gazette*, 9 Aug., gave Lord St Vincent's account, in a letter to Nepean, of one of the most daring exploits of the war. On the night of 29 July Coghlan, commanding the *Viper* cutter with a crew of nineteen, boarded and captured in Port Louis, under the guns of the port, a French gun-brig mounting three 24-pounders and four 6-pounders, and carrying 87 men, including sixteen soldiers. Not far away were a 74-gun ship and two frigates.

your Majesty's feet and to return your Majesty his most humble thanks for your goodness in promoting him to the command of the 5th West Indian Regiment.

I have likewise the honor to lay before your Majesty for your approbation the proceedings and sentence of a detachment court martial which has been held upon Quarter-Master Braybroke of the Royal Dragoons on account of the petition which was sent to me signed by almost every Quarter-Master belonging to the Regiments of Cavalry at Swinley Camp without the knowledge of their respective Commanding Officers. Your Majesty will find a letter from the President of the court martial in the name of the Court recommending so far Quarter-Master Braybroke to your Majesty's mercy as to commute his sentence from being reduced to being suspended during such time as your Majesty may think fit.

It is my duty however to state to your Majesty that since the brigade court martial was over, a Court of Enquiry has sat upon Quarter-Master Hughes of the 17 Light Dragoons, and after every investigation which could be made into this business it appears clearly that the whole originated in the Royals which indeed is to be seen from the petition itself, as mong other hardships complained of is that of Quarter Masters being obliged to purchase their own horses which has been ever the invariable practice of the service, except in the Royals. I must therefore in the names of Lieutenant Generals Dundas and Gwyn as well as in my own, humbly entreat your Majesty to approve of the whole sentence being put in full force and that a letter may be written to the Commanding Officers of the different Regiments ordering them to communicate the sentence to their respective Quarter-Masters, and expressing your Majesty's high displeasure at the conduct of those who signed the petition.

As Quarter-Master Braybroke has a large family and purchased his warrant for four hundred pounds, your Majesty will perhaps be graciously pleased to allow the money which he paid for his warrant to be returned to his wife.

There are some other circumstances which have come out in this investigation, which I shall think it my duty to lay before your Majesty when I have the honor to pay my duty at Weymouth, but which it is not necessary to trouble your Majesty with by letter. (9740–1)

2217   MRS CAROLINE HOWE *to the* KING

[*11 Aug. 1800.*] Mrs. Howe has so frequently been honored by your Majesty's gracious notice, and experienced so often your Royal condescension, that her gratitude cannot be encreased nor can she ever in words express the feelings of her heart, though indeed the unbounded goodness of her most dearly beloved Sovereign has more than on one occasion forced bursts of tears from her eyes.

The Countess of Altamont[1] and the Baroness Howe desire that every expression of duty & gratitude may be presented to your Majesty; they are very sensible to the truth of your Majesty's observations that they have at present more real

___

[1] John Denis, Earl of Altamont (1756–1809), who, on 29 Dec. 1800 was created Marquess of Sligo [I.] for his strenuous support of the Union, and Baron Monteagle [U.K.] on 20 Feb. 1806, married (1787) Louisa Catherine (1767–1817), daughter of Richard, 1st Earl Howe. Lady Altamont, therefore, was Mrs Howe's niece.

cause to rejoice than to lament, and Mrs. Howe with truth has the satisfaction to add that they have already acquired a composure & calmness such as she is content with. They all three pray that every happiness & prosperity during a long life may be the lot of their most admirable Sovereign, that he may be preserved a blessing to her beloved family and to his United Kingdoms.[1] (9747)

2218 LORD GRENVILLE *to the* KING, *and the reply*

[*Dropmore, 11 Aug. 1800.*] Lord Grenville has the honour to transmit to your Majesty some letters which were this day delivered to him by Baron Mylius;[2] together with the copy of his letters of recall which he has, as he says, very unexpectedly received. He is apprized by a dispatch from the Duke that the intention is to send him to Berlin, under the idea that a Congress is immediately to be opened for negotiating a general Peace, under the mediation of Russia, and Prussia.

Baron Mylius is himself very sensible of the ill impressions which this step may produce, and seems much to wish that your Majesty would authorize some intimation to be given either to him, or directly to the Duke of a wish on your Majesty's part that he should remain here: in which case he would take upon himself to wait for further orders.

Lord Grenville also humbly transmits a letter which he received a few days since from Baron Mylius on the subject of pecuniary assistance to the Duke in his present situation. As far as Lord Grenville can presume to offer an opinion he should not think that the circumstances were such as to call for such a step, unless there were any particulars unknown to Lord Grenville which might induce your Majesty to judge differently.

The Prince of Wirtemberg,[3] who is now here, came to Lord Grenville last week to ask, as he said, his advice respecting a letter which he proposed writing to your Majesty to solicit some pecuniary aid. Lord Grenville gave not the least encouragement to this idea, and proposes with your Majesty's permission to write to the Prince to dissuade him from putting your Majesty under the necessity of giving a negative to such a request.

The Turkish Ambassador having received orders from his Court to return immediately, was under much difficulty about his Audience of Leave. Lord Grenville took upon him to assure him that his taking leave under these circumstances by a letter addressed to Lord Grenville would be regarded by your Majesty as equally respectful. He has accordingly written such a letter to which Lord Grenville will with your Majesty's leave answer in such terms as may satisfy the Ambassador and his Court. (9744–6)

[1] Lord Spencer's letter of 11 August to the King, and the King's reply on the 12th, are in folio 9742 and *Spencer Papers*, III, 320, respectively. The King's letter of the 10th to Mrs Howe is in Barrow's *Life of Howe*, p. 395, and in Jesse, III, 229.

[2] The Wurtemberg Envoy in London.

[3] Prince Henry of Wurtemberg (1772–1833), the Duke's youngest brother. He married an *actrice*, who had been his mistress, and Queen Charlotte naturally wanted to have nothing to do with her. The Prince and his wife landed at Gravesend on 2 June, and returned to the Continent from Yarmouth on 9 Oct. See No. 2127.

[*The King's reply, Weymouth, 13 Aug. 1800.*] The letters transmitted to me by Lord Grenville contained the same information he sent me, namely, the recall of Genl. Melius that he might be employed at Berlin to effect indemnifications for the Dutchy of Wurtemberg.

I am perfectly of opinion with Lord Grenville as to the bad impression his being recalled would give, and it is a joke to say the Duke cannot name any other fit person to go to Berlin; I certainly will both to the Duke and to my daughter express the having desired the General to wait for further orders and send those letters tomorrow that they may be forwarded by Friday's post.

Lord Grenville will do most properly in warding off any application of pecuniary assistance for the D. of Wurtemberg, as also in the case of his brother the Prince of Wurtemberg.

The Turkish Ambassador's writing to Lord Grenville on his quitting this country is all that is necessary, to which Lord Grenville will return a proper answer in writing. (Fortescue MSS.)

2219   LORD CHARLES HENRY SOMERSET *to the* KING

[*Swinley Camp, 14 Aug. 1800.*] In obedience to your Majesty's commands, I had yesterday the honor to present to the Duke of Portland the letter your Majesty so kindly condescended to write.

The Duke will have the honor to communicate to your Majesty the result, which I fear will not be favorable to my wishes and the interest of my family. Whatever, however, may be their fate or mine in life, your Majesty I trust will believe that I shall ever retain the most lively sense of gratitude for your unbounded goodness to them and myself. For your health, prosperity and happiness shall we, gracious Sire, most fervently for ever pray. To bless you shall be the first words my children shall learn to utter. To bless you shall be the effort of our latest breath.

With every sentiment of gratitude and respect permit me to subscribe myself [etc.]. (9753)

2220   THE DUKE OF PORTLAND *to the* KING

[*Bulstrode, Thursday night, 14 Aug. 1800.*] Your Majesty's letter of the 11th instant was delivered last night by Lord Charles Somerset to the Duke of Portland.

Upon the most serious & deliberate consideration which it has been in the Duke of Portland's power to give to your Majesty's commands to lay before your Majesty his opinion of the fitness of Lord Charles Somerset to succeed to the Government of Jamaica, the Duke of Portland submits with all humility to your Majesty's superior wisdom that from various events which have taken place in that part of the world as well as in Europe, from others which are actually depending, the administration of that Government is become much more complicated & difficult than at any period since it has made a part of your Majesty's dominions. The unprecedented & peculiar circumstances in which the Island of St Domingo happens to be placed not only with regard to itself but relatively to that of Jamaica,

& the crisis which is impending over the Government of the United States, together with the introduction of negro corps into Jamaica which, however necessary, is a step now taken for the first time & has been an object of unremitting jealousy & apprehension, & in addition to that, the violent & untractable disposition which has been manifested by the Legislature & particularly by the Assembly of that Island, are some of the many reasons which oblige the Duke of Portland to represent with all deference to your Majesty that his duty suggested to him the necessity of offering to your Majesty for this very important station a person of more experience & better known in the conduct of political & military business than Lord Charles Somerset, who, from the conversation which the Duke of Portland had with him on communicating to him the purport of your Majesty's most gracious letter, seemed little aware of the nature & extent of the employment he was sollicitous to undertake, which in the variety & importance of its duties will certainly not admit of any comparison with any other of your Majesty's West Indian Governments. The Duke of Portland humbly begs leave to add that, not discouraged by the difficulties which he has hitherto met with in selecting a proper person to propose to your Majesty for the Government of Jamaica, he has in contemplation a temporary arrangement which he hopes to be able in a very few days to submit to your Majesty by which he is willing to hope your Majesty's interests in that part of the world may be as effectually secured from injury as the circumstances of the times will admit.[1] (9750-2)

2221 LORD GRENVILLE to the KING, and the reply

[*Dropmore, 15 Aug. 1800.*] In humble obedience to your Majesty's commands Lord Grenville has sent to Baron Mylius the two letters from your Majesty to the Duke and Duchess of Wurtemberg, together with a letter from himself to Baron Mylius and another to Count Zeppelin, the drafts of which your Majesty will receive with this note. (9754)

[*The King's reply, Weymouth, 17 Aug.*] The drafts of the letters communicated to me this morning which Lord Grenville has written to the Turkish Ambassador and on the proposed recall of General Melius are expressed with that clearness and elegance that constantly appear in those composed by Lord Grenville. (Fortescue MSS.)

2222 THE DUKE OF PORTLAND to the KING

[*Bulstrode, Monday, 18 Aug. 1800, 9 a.m.*] The Duke of Portland has most humbly to implore your Majesty's forgiveness for a very gross act of inadvertence & presumption which he finds, to his great shame & confusion, to have been committed at his Office by a Commission having been laid before your Majesty

---

[1] Major-General the Hon. John Knox was appointed to succeed Lord Balcarres (1752–1825), as Lieutenant-Governor of Jamaica, but he was lost on the passage out (1800). See No. 2222. Lord Balcarres had been Lieutenant-Governor since 1794, and had suppressed a dangerous revolt of the Maroon negroes.

for the appointment of Major-General Knox[1] to be Lieutenant-Governor of Jamaica without any orders having been received from your Majesty for that purpose, or your Majesty's pleasure having been taken respecting it. The Duke of Portland anxiously entreats your Majesty's condescension to suffer him to state to your Majesty the cause of this inadvertence as the only ground on which he can rest his hope for your Majesty's pardon. Mr King having been privy to several conversations which have passed between Mr Secretary Dundas & the Duke of Portland on the subject of Jamaica, & knowing that in the course of last week Major-General Knox had attended them & expressed his readiness to go to Jamaica in case your Majesty should approve of his being sent there, concluded that Mr. Secretary Dundas or the Duke of Portland could not have deferred to submit the measure to your Majesty, & knowing the importance of that station's being properly filled, he directed the Commission to be prepared forthwith, & for want of farther explanation on the part of Mr King, it found its way into the box which contained other instruments of the same form for your Majesty's signature. Since the conversations above alluded to it has been the Duke of Portland's intention, in case your Majesty should think fit to entrust the command of your forces in Jamaica to Major-General Knox, to offer him to your Majesty's consideration as the most proper person that occurred, to act in the room of the Earl of Balcarres, as Lieutenant-Governor, & until your Majesty should fix upon a Governor-in-chief, and the sanction which that idea has received by the opinion your Majesty has condescended to express of Major-General Knox encourages the Duke of Portland to acknowledge that the temporary arrangement which he had in contemplation to submit to your Majesty for Jamaica, was the appointment of a Lieutenant-Governor in the person of that General Officer, but as the Commission appointing Major-General Knox to the Lieutenant-Government of Jamaica is not distinguishable in its form from that of any Field Officer, & has consequently possibly escaped your Majesty's observation—the Duke of Portland cannot presume to countersign it until it has been again submitted to your Majesty, & that he receives your Majesty's commands to carry it into effect.

The Duke of Portland humbly begs leave to lay before your Majesty a letter he received last night from the Lord Lieutenant & to apprize your Majesty that the Peers who are junior to Lord Somerton, Archbishop of Cashel,[2] are Lord Yelverton, Chief Baron of your Majesty's Court of Exchequer, & Lord Kilwarden, Chief Justice of the Court of King's Bench. (9755–7)

2223 HENRY DUNDAS *to the* KING

[*Wimbledon, 18 Aug. 1800, 1 p.m.*] Mr. Dundas humbly begs leave to submit to your Majesty's perusal a Minute[3] with its accompanying documents upon which he proposes on Wednesday next to take [the] opinion of your Majesty's confidential servants. (9758)

---

[1] He was the son of Thomas, 1st Viscount Northland. Colonel, 1795; Major-General, 1798; Lieutenant-Governor of Jamaica, 1800. M.P. Dungannon [I.], 1790–4, and from July 1800 to December. There was no ballot on 1 Dec. 1800 as to who should represent Dungannon in the Imperial Parliament, consequently Knox became the member, but he may well have been dead at that moment. The new writ was not moved, however, until 4 Nov. 1801 (*H. of C.J.* LVII, 12).   [2] See vol. II, p. 293 n.   [3] Missing.

[*Horse Guards, 20 Aug. 1800.*] I have little to trouble your Majesty with this week except to transmit the usual weekly states, and to lay before your Majesty the recommendations for the vacant Commissions for your approbation.

I am desired likewise by Sir William Faucett as President of the Committee for managing the Fund for the relief of the widows, wives and children of the soldiers and sailors who fell in Holland, to lay at your Majesty's feet a copy of their proceedings by which your Majesty will observe that after the most liberal donations to the different objects for whom the subscription was set on foot, they have still above ten thousand pounds in hand.

In obedience to your Majesty's commands I sent an order to the 43d Regiment to form a Light Company of eighty men and to march them to Weymouth to join the other companies under Colonel Leveson, but the Commanding Officer has reported that out of the 153 men of which the whole Regiment consists he has not above forty fit for active service at present, and the rest being composed either of invalids or of raw recruits who have never had a firelock in their hands, and that besides he has neither sufficient arms or cloathing for them, under these circumstances I suppose your Majesty will approve of the detachment not being sent.

I mean with your Majesty's permission to have the honor of paying my duty to you at Weymouth next Sunday for a few days. (9759)

[*Arlington Street, 20 Aug. 1800.*] Having been inform'd by Sir Stephen Cottrell[1] that the Turkish Ambassador had received his letters of recall, and had obtained your Majesty's permission to return without his Audience of Leave, I have the honor to wait your Majesty's directions for the usual present of one thousand pounds sterling to his Excellency and one hundred and ten pounds to the Secretary of the Embassy.

I think it my duty to state to your Majesty that the Trustees of the Opera House, having declared the impossibility of performing their trust while Mr Taylor was manager, had, agreeable to a clause in the original deed bearing date in 1792, calld upon his Royal Highness the Prince of Wales, the Duke of Bedford and myself to nominate five noblemen or gentlemen to chuse a manager. In consequence of this, a meeting was held yesterday at Lord Kinnaird['s], but his Grace having taken the opinion of Mr Fontblane [*sic*], that gentleman seem'd to think that as the present deed was worded, we were not authoris'd to take such a step. Knowing Mr Taylor would lose no time in applying to me to give him a licence, I thought it proper to inform his Grace and the Trustees that I should certainly be guided by the Attorney-General, and do no act without his advice. It was agreed that a case should be laid before Mr Fontblane, that we might know what arrangement could be made for us to act under this deed, which I shall make it my duty to forward to your Majesty. (9760-1)

[1] Cottrell, the Clerk of the Privy Council, had been knighted on 21 Dec. 1796. He was also Master of the Ceremonies in the King's Household, salary, £300 a year.

[*Whitehall, Wednesday, 20 Aug. 1800.*] The Duke of Portland is warranted to think from the opinion your Majesty has condescended to express of the Earl of Shannon that it cannot be necessary for him to trouble your Majesty with a detail of the services which Lord Castlereagh has reported that your Majesty's Government in Ireland has received from Lord Shannon during the course of the rebellion & in bringing about the measure of Union, & that the favor which the Lord Lieutenant requests of your Majesty for Lord Shannon's family was totally unsollicited by him.[1] But the Duke of Portland cannot refuse Lord Castlereagh's request in acquainting your Majesty that it is the Lord Lieutenant's opinion that the measure of Union could not have been *proposed* but for the countenance it received from the Earl of Shannon, & that it would have been impossible to have effected it but for his intrepidity, exertions & firmness. (9762)

2227   *Letters from* EARL SPENCER *to the* KING, *and a reply*

[*Admiralty, 22 Aug. 1800.*] Earl Spencer having consulted with Mr Pitt on the subject of the vacancy occasioned by the death of Admiral Barrington, has the honour humbly to propose to your Majesty that Lord Bridport should be promoted to be General of Marines, and that the Lieutenant-Generalship of that corps should be conferred on the Earl of St Vincent, whose situation at present in the command of the Channel Fleet seems to make it impossible to pass him by in the disposition of the naval distinction. (9763)

[*The King's reply, Weymouth, 23 Aug.*] In consequence of Earl Spencer and Mr. Pitt's opinions, I consent to conferr the vacant General of Marines on Lord Bridport and the Lieutenant-General on the Earl of St. Vincent, though I cannot deny but my own inclination would have been more gratified in advancing the Generals of Marines and conferring the Major-General on Lord Hugh Seymour.

In my hurry the other day I believe I omitted agreeing to Admiral Kingsmill's being created a baronet, I therefore now mention it. (Althorp MSS.)

[*From Earl Spencer, Admiralty, 23 Aug. 1800.*] Earl Spencer has the honour to acquaint your Majesty that Sir Henry Harvey[2] has with great readiness accepted the offer made to him of hoisting his flag in the Channel Fleet, and will be immediately ordered to do so on board the Royal Sovereign; or with Sir Andrew Mitchell on board either of the Windsor Castle or any other ship which the Commander-in-Chief may prefer. Sir Robert Calder[3] has also been added to the Rear-Admirals under the command of the Earl of St Vincent, the present course of the service

---

[1] There seems to be no reference either in the *Cornwallis Correspondence* or in the *Castlereagh Correspondence* to this suggested mark of favour. The compensation money for Lord Shannon's Irish boroughs [Castlemartyr, Charleville (half), and Cloghnakilty (half)], amounting to £30,000, was a different matter.

[2] Admiral Sir Henry Harvey (1737–1810). Lieutenant, 1757; Captain, 1777; Rear-Admiral, 1794; Vice-Admiral, 1799; Admiral, 1804. K.B., 8 Jan. 1800.

[3] Admiral Sir Robert Calder (1745–1818). Lieutenant, 1762; Captain, 1780; Rear-Admiral, 1799; Vice-Admiral, 1804; Admiral, 1810; created Baronet, 22 Aug. 1798. K.C.B., 1815.

appearing to require a larger number of Flag Officers than had hitherto been employed: the latter officer will have his Flag in the Prince of Wales when that ship is ready for sea.[1] (9764)

2228 LORD GRENVILLE *to the* KING, *and the reply*

[*Downing Street, 25 Aug. 1800, 3 p.m.*] Lord Grenville has the honour to transmit to your Majesty by this messenger the dispatches received this morning from Lord Whitworth, and also two papers which were sent to the Office yesterday by M. Otto,[2] the French Agent for prisoners.

Lord Grenville found it impossible to collect your Majesty's servants today to deliberate on these two subjects; he has therefore sent notes to such of them as are in or near London for a Cabinet tomorrow, when he will have the honour to submit to your Majesty the result of their deliberations.

In the meantime the orders are given today for reinforcing Admiral Dixon[3] with four more ships now stationed off Goree. (9766)

[*The King's reply, Weymouth, 26 Aug.*] It seems to me impossible that Lord Whitworth could have conducted himself with greater propriety in the difficult task that has been imposed upon him either as to the mode of conducting the business or his reasoning upon it. I believe force not reason must decide the question; the only happiness is that W. cannot give way, for our existence as a great Naval Power depends on not yielding.

As to the paper from Mr. Otto transmitted at the same time by Lord Grenville, it cannot require much answer; for an amnistrie [sic] is absolutely impossible to be acquiesced in, and Austria not having opened herself as to her views, we cannot communicate them to France till we are apprized of them. (Fortescue MSS.)

2229 HENRY DUNDAS *to the* KING

[*Wimbledon, 26 Aug. 1800, 10 a.m.*] Mr Dundas humbly begs leave to inform your Majesty that with your Majesty's permission he goes this day for a fourth-night [sic] to Cheltenham. He would much rather have gone immediately to Scotland, but he is so earnestly urged by Sir Walter Farquhar and his family to make a trial of the waters of Cheltenham, he does not think himself at liberty longer to resist it.

Mr Dundas has not yet had it in his power to write anything more pointed to your Majesty on the subject of the paper[4] he took the liberty of transmitting lately to your Majesty. Mr Dundas is more confirmed in his own opinion by every

[1] The King's reply on the 24th, approving these suggestions, is in *Spencer Papers*, III, 321. Lord Spencer's letter is incorrectly dated the 29th in the Ann Arbor typescript, and there are inaccuracies, too, in the copying.

[2] For an account of this diplomatist see Pellew, I, 447 n.

[3] Archibald Dickson. Lieutenant, 1759; Captain, 1774; Rear-Admiral, 1794; Vice-Admiral, 1795; Admiral, Jan. 1801. (*d.* 1803.)

[4] Missing. See No. 2223. Dundas's plan was to send an expedition against Cuba under Sir Ralph Abercromby, recapturing Guadaloupe on the way. Pitt apparently vetoed it.

consideration he can give to it, and shall not desist from making in the meantime every proevious preparation that does not lead to any very material expence. Some of your Majesty's confidential servants seem to be actuated by two doubts, one, whether even the large force proposed would be adequate to the object. The other, whether after sending so large a force to such a distance, a sufficient security remained for your Majesty's dominions of Great Britain and Ireland. Upon the first of those doubts Mr Dundas has only to observe that the force is nearly double of that which on the former occasion captured the fort and harbour of the Havanna, and a further confirmation arises from a letter which Sir Ralph Abercrombie wrote to Mr Dundas from Martinico in 1797, wherein he states a force of fifteen or sixteen thousand men to be the force requisite for an offensive operation against the Havanna. As to the other doubt Mr Dundas trusts with some confidence that the statements which accompany this and which Mr Dundas proposes to commit to the perusal of your Majesty's servants will put an end to every apprehension that can be entertained with regard to the security of your Majesty's dominions at home. (9767–9)

2230 *Letters from* LORD GRENVILLE *to the* KING, *and a reply*
[*Downing Street, 26 Aug. 1800, 3 p.m.*] Lord Grenville has the honour to submit to your Majesty the Minute of Cabinet respecting the Danish business, and he will in the course of this afternoon trouble your Majesty with another messenger respecting the other business, which there has not yet been sufficient time to complete. (9771)

[*Enclosure*]
[*Cabinet Minute, Downing Street, 26 Aug.*]
Present: The Lord President, Duke of Portland, Earl Spencer, Earl of Liverpool, Mr Chancellor of the Exchequer, Mr Secretary Dundas, Lord Grenville.
Upon consideration of the dispatches from Lord Whitworth and Vice-Admiral Dickson, it was agreed humbly (to) submit to His Majesty,
    That Vice-Admiral Dickson should forthwith be instructed that in the event of Lord Whitworth's having actually left Copenhagen the Vice-Admiral should on the receipt of these instructions send to Copenhagen a flag of truce with a letter notifying that unless he shall within a number of hours to be limited by him in that letter receive from the Danish Government a written declaration of its accepting the ultimatum delivered by Lord Whitworth he is to commence hostilities, and that in case of his not obtaining such answer within the time so to be limited he should accordingly proceed according to the best of his judgment to take such measures as may be most effectual to annoy the arsenals, ships of war, and commerce of Denmark.
    That if Lord Whitworth should be still on the spot the Vice-Admiral is to communicate these instructions to him, and is to be wholly govern'd by his advice respecting the actual commencement of offensive operations, or the making, to the Danish Government, any such notification as is above-mentioned.

That if Mr Merry[1] should be on the spot, the Vice-Admiral is in the absence of Lord Whitworth to communicate in like manner with him, and to be governed by his advice on the two points abovementioned.

That the Vice-Admiral should carry these instructions into effect as far as his force will allow, notwithstanding any opposition on the part either of the Ministers or of the forces of Russia or Sweden.

That instructions should be sent to Lord Whitworth, highly approving his conduct in the execution of his commission, and directing him to continue to act on the same principles if these dispatches should still find him at Copenhagen. That if he should be still there, and his ultimatum not have been finally acceded to, the King entrusts to him the discretion of directing the actual commencement of hostilities, supposing that he should find it impracticable in any other way to overcome the obstinacy of the Danish Government.

That if the satisfaction shall actually have been granted, or if as a facility towards obtaining it, he should find that any advantage can be derived from the communication of the projet to be sent to him with these instructions, he is at liberty so to do, provided always that he takes sufficient care that the Danish Government shall not avail themselves of it as a means of gaining time, he being to consider it as a principal object of attention to bring the matter to a decisive issue before the Court of Petersburgh can declare a resolution of making common cause with Denmark.

That as it appears possible that Lord Whitworth may have left Mr Merry behind him at Copenhagen, a duplicate of these orders should be sent to him, with directions to act upon them in Lord Whitworth's absence. (9772–5)

[*From Lord Grenville, Cleveland Row, 26 Aug., 7.30 p.m.*] Lord Grenville has the honour humbly to acquaint your Majesty that at the meeting of your Majesty's servants this day it was agreed to send Captain George to Mr Otto to learn from him whether he was empowered to communicate the paper to which his communication relates—meaning thereby the note delivered by Lord Minto to M. de Thugut.

Mr. Otto mistaking the meaning of this message sent the original of his full-powers for concluding an Armistice, and which as it appears, relate only to an Armistice between this country and France, without any mention of Allies on either side.

In the meantime another mail arrived, and brought dispatches from Lord Minto with the copy of that note, which Lord Grenville has the honour to transmit herewith.

On considering this paper, and also the letter from M. de Thugut which accompanied it, your Majesty's servants agreed humbly to advise your Majesty that it would be right to authorize a proper person to converse with Mr Otto, in conformity to the instructions contained in the Minute which accompanies this letter.

If your Majesty should approve of this Lord Grenville thinks that the employing

---

[1] Anthony Merry. *Chargé d'Affaires* at Madrid, 1789–90, and at Copenhagen, July 1799–Sept. 1800; Secretary to the Embassy to the Congress of Amiens, 1801–2, and Minister Plenipotentiary *ad int.*, 1802; Minister to the U.S.A., 1803–6; to Denmark, 1807, and to Sweden, 1808–9.

Captain George upon this commission might perhaps be expedient as less likely to attract attention than if any other person were fixed upon. But if on discussion of this point with Mr Pitt any fitter person should occur they humbly hope that your Majesty would not disapprove of their making a different choice.

Lord Grenville does not trouble your Majesty with the remainder of this mail till the usual time. It has brought nothing else of any importance. (9776–8)

[*Enclosure*]

INSTRUCTIONS *to* CAPTAIN GEORGE

1. To declare that the Note presented at Vienna by Lord Minto contains the expression of his Majesty's sentiments, and that the King is ready to act in conformity to it.

2. To enquire whether any answer has been returned by the French Government to the proposal contained in M. de Thugut's letter to M. Talleyrand respecting a place for the meeting of plenipotentiaries to carry on joint negotiation: or whether M. Otto is authorized to agree with this Government on that point agreably to the suggestion contained in M. Thugut's letter.

3. To express in that case that either of the places named by M. de Thugut would be agreed to by his Majesty, and plenipotentiaries sent thither on his Majesty's part to meet those of Austria & France, provided that the French Government is willing to enter into sufficient engagements for the freedom of direct communication by couriers between this country and such place of negotiation.

4. That with respect to the proposal of an Armistice, the King would see with great satisfaction the moment when he could with propriety adopt any measure the immediate effect of which would put a stop, at least for a time, to the calamities of war: but that as an Armistice applying to naval operations has at no period ever been agreed on between Great Britain & France during the course of their negotiations for peace, or until the preliminaries have been actually signed, that it cannot therefore be considered as a step necessary to negotiation, and, that from the disputes to which its execution must unavoidably be expected to give rise, it might more probably tend to obstruct than to facilitate the success of those endeavours which the two parties might employ for the restoration of peace. That the circumstances of a naval war are obviously not such as to admit of such equal arrangements as are easily established with regard to military operations when suspended by such an agreement. That it appears therefore at all events premature to enter even into the discussion of this question untill, from the course of the negotiations, it shall more clearly appear how far they are likely to lead to a satisfactory issue. And that no decision could in any case be taken here on such a subject unless the French Government had previously explained in what manner it is conceived that the principles of the regulation adopted in the German Armistice with respect to blockaded towns can be applied to the naval ports & arsenals of France so as to carry bona fide into execution the respective objects as to maritime forces, those stipulations have in view with respect to the military positions occupied by the two armies. (9779–81)

[*The King's reply, Weymouth, 27 Aug. 1800.*] This morning I received Lord Grenville's note forwarding the Minute of Cabinet of the Danish business, which by the note he must have received this day from me, he must feel is perfectly agreable to my sentiments.

About forty minutes past three Shaw[1] arrived with Lord Grenville's note and the Minute on the application of Mr. Otto; I think the idea of employing Captain George in the present stage much the most proper person that could be employed; the whole conduct of Talleyrand with the *mean* Court of Vienna ought to serve as a lesson not to be too forward on our part; the demands of France will I am certain be inadmissible, consequently we must act with caution that when the negociation fails there may be no appearance of improper submission, and that we have looked for honorable terms, but that they could not be obtained. (Fortescue MSS.)

2231 THE DUKE OF PORTLAND *to the* KING

[*Whitehall, Wednesday, 27 Aug. 1800.*] The Duke of Portland most humbly submits to your Majesty the draft of the dispatch which he wrote to the Lord Lieutenant of Ireland in obedience to the commands your Majesty was pleased to signify to the Duke of Portland on the 25th inst. (9782)

2232 LORD GRENVILLE *to the* KING, *and the reply*

[*Downing Street, 29 Aug. 1800, 3 p.m.*] Lord Grenville has the honour to transmit to your Majesty Captain George's report of his conversation with Mr. Otto, in consequence of which your Majesty's servants this day agreed that a written answer should be sent to Mr Otto agreably to the tenor of the Minute which was before delivered to Captain George for the regulation of his language.

As it is probable that the answer from the French Government to Mr Otto will make it necessary that a Minister should be sent on your Majesty's part to Luneville, Lord Grenville has in obedience to the commands your Majesty was pleased to lay upon him, spoken to Mr Grenville on the subject, who has expressed his readiness to undertake any duty in which your Majesty judges that his service may be useful. (9783–4)

[*The King's reply, Weymouth, 30 Aug. 1800.*] Though perfectly convinced of the humiliating situation in which this country is placed by the unfortunate opinion lately adopted of the necessity of opening a negociation with France, after what has passed it is most probable that the leaders in that country will be too wise to neglect calling upon us to send a negociator to Luneville, as it is an additional instance to that of Lisle of our deserting the true grounds on which the war was undertaken. I certainly think Mr. Grenville the most proper person for this unpleasant business, as his honour, good sense and good principles must convince

[1] Probably John Schaw, a Foreign Office messenger.

that no good issue is to be expected from this fresh attempt for peace. He will consequently so conduct himself as to leave this country on the best ground he can when the rupture shall happen.[1] (Fortescue MSS.)

2233   THE DUCHESS OF WURTEMBERG *to the* KING

[*Erlangen, 4 Sept. 1800.*] I had yesterday the honour and happiness to receive your Majesty's most gracious letter of August 14th. It would be very difficult for me to express how delighted I was to hear from you or how deeply I am impressed with your Majesty's goodness to me. This morning I have sent off a messenger to the Duke and wrote him a long letter in which I have brought forwards every argument in my power to induce him to comply with your Majesty's gracious advice, and expressed to him how grateful we must feel for this fresh proof of goodness and for the interest you express about our affairs. I fear it will be above a fortnight before I shall receive an answer, but the moment I do shall not fail to acquaint your Majesty with its contents.

The kindness your Majesty ever shewed me convinced me you would feel for my misfortunes, particularly as your wisdom had lead to foresee what might be the case. Certainly, Sir, there is no situation of life in which there are not draw-backs, and these times double those as they not only attack all ranks but chiefly destroy the happiness of the great. However in this situation I can give your Majesty one comfort, that were it not for being parted from my parents, I can never regret the being married, as I am truly attached to my husband and ready to share any fate it may please God to send him. One advantage I have certainly gained from our misfortunes, that of being grown more serious and of feeling how much I owe my parents for having instilled into my heart good principles, which enable me to put my whole trust in God and hope that at his own time he will come to

[1] Lord Grenville naturally had unbounded faith in the ability of his brother Thomas whom he had sent on a special mission to Berlin in 1798. But the choice meant that Lord Malmesbury, who had been engaged in fruitless negotiations at Paris and Lille in 1796 and 1797, was no longer to be employed. He was consoled with an Earldom in December—presumably the result of his application to Pitt for some mark of favour from the Crown, on 7 Sept.:

'I am just informed that under the probable event of a negotiation for peace being renewed, it is the opinion of his Majesty's Ministers, that my being again employed to conduct it, might be attended with inconvenience to his Majesty's service. This consideration ought certainly to be paramount in their minds to every other; I trust, you will do me the justice to believe it is likewise so in mine, and that whatever my expectations were, or on whatever ground they rested, I forego them willingly, and chear-fully, the moment they are not to be reconciled with the publick good.

But when I thus abandon what, I must confess, was my favourite object, and that to which I looked forward as to the most flattering termination of my long publick services, I trust it will not be thought unreasonable that I should express a desire that some step may be taken to prevent an unfavourable impression with respect to myself being left on the publick mind, or a belief that motives very different from the real one, have occasioned the management of this very important and honourable mission to be now transferred into other hands.

I rely with full confidence on your goodness to rescue my character from the possibility of such an imputation. I am not at this moment prepared to point out specifically the manner in which this might the best be done; but if I am not mistaken in supposing that you will sufficiently enter into my feelings to be desirous that it should be done in some way or other, perhaps you will allow me to have five minutes conversation with you on the subject.

I shall remain in town, where I am just arrived, till I am favoured with your answer.' (W. Dacres Adams MSS.)

our assistance. I also do everything in my power to make Catherine and Paul, who are my constant companions, partake of the same comfort.

I trust that your Majesty will receive great benefit from Weymouth and that the tepid baths may do the Queen good, which will be a great joy to me. I have of late been obliged to have recourse to them having much suffered from cramps in my stomach. I rejoice very much at dear Sophia's health mending and am very happy with the thoughts of your Majesty's seeing both her and dear Amelia in good health and spirits at breakfast on the 8th. I take the liberty of offering your Majesty my congratulations on a day so dear to us all.[1] I will now take up no more of your Majesty's time. (51614–16)

2234   Letters from EARL SPENCER to the KING

[*Admiralty, 4 Sept. 1800.*] Earl Spencer has the honour to lay before your Majesty the sentence of a court martial held on one of the mutineers of the Danae and humbly to submit to your Majesty the propriety of ordering it to be carried into immediate execution, as the case is one in which there can be no circumstances of mitigation, the man having been taken on board a French privateer, and his share in the mutiny appearing to have been fully proved. (9785)

[*Admiralty, 5 Sept.*] Earl Spencer has the honour of laying before your Majesty the dispatches received yesterday evening from Vice-Admiral Dickson, and humbly begs leave to offer his sincere congratulations to your Majesty on the favourable termination of the dispute with the Court of Denmark on a question of great importance to the interests of your Majesty's Navy, which is the more satisfactory as it has been terminated without any effusion of blood.

Earl Spencer has also the honour to transmit the dispatches received this day from Sir Hyde Parker and Lord Hugh Seymour.[2] (9786)

2235   Letters from LORD GRENVILLE to the KING, *and the replies*

[*Downing Street, 5 Sept. 1800, 3 p.m.*] Lord Grenville has the honour to transmit to your Majesty Lord Whitworth's dispatches, with the copy of the Convention signed at Copenhagen, which he trusts your Majesty will find perfectly satisfactory.

The note from M. Otto which Lord Grenville has also the honour to transmit, was received yesterday after the mail coach was dispatched to Weymouth. Your Majesty's servants considering the extreme pressure of the circumstances, and the great danger to which all Europe might be exposed if hostilities were suddenly renewed with Austria at the moment when the Austrian army in Germany appears by the latest advices to be totally unequal to such a contest, were unanimously of opinion that it was necessary to lose no time in obtaining such further explanations from M. Otto as might enable your Majesty to decide finally on the question of an Armistice. Mr Nepean was accordingly sent to him, and received from him late last

[1] The King's wedding day.
[2] The King's brief reply on the 6th, expressing his satisfaction with the outcome, is in *Spencer Papers*, IV, 273.

night a projet which has this day been considered by your Majesty's servants, and found to be in almost every point highly objectionable.

Lord Grenville has taken minutes for preparing a counter-projet, on such ideas as your Majesty's servants are inclined to think might be acceded to by your Majesty, rather than to abandon Austria to the danger of renewed hostilities in this moment.

M. Otto has been informed that he may expect an answer by Sunday, & desired to require his Government to prolong the Continental Armistice till the answer to their proposal here can be received.

No further step will be taken till the whole be submitted to your Majesty, which Lord Grenville hopes to be enabled to do in the course of this evening, by a special messenger whom he will take the liberty to send as the matter presses so much in point of time. (9787–9)

[*From Lord Grenville, Downing Street, 5 Sept., 11 p.m.*] Lord Grenville has the honour to submit to your Majesty the different papers relating to the communication with Mr. Otto mentioned in his note to your Majesty this day, together with a paper of remarks prepared by him for the consideration of your Majesty's servants when Mr. Otto's projet was laid before them.

It was very much the wish of your Majesty's servants to have felt themselves enabled humbly to recommend to your Majesty to decline all further discussion of the proposal of a naval armistice previous to the negotiation: and if the state of this country only had been in question they would have had no difficulty in that respect.

But the danger to Austria, and consequently to every part of the Continent of Europe from the sudden renewal of hostilities appeared to be so great that they thought on the fullest consideration that they should not be justified in not advising your Majesty to ascertain how far the establishment of a naval armistice can be so regulated as to afford the means of giving a fair trial of the effect of joint negotiation according to the system adopted between your Majesty and the Court of Vienna. If this were not done they conceive there would be great probability of the immediate conclusion of a separate Peace on the part of Austria, a measure which it seems to them very desirable to avert, if that can be done without the sacrifice of any of the permanent interests of this country.

It is on this ground that your Majesty's servants humbly advise your Majesty to authorize the transmitting the inclosed counter-projet to Mr. Otto, with a note in which he should be informed that on those terms your Majesty would accede to the proposal of an armistice. It should seem that it would also be necessary in that note to remark in proper terms on the gross misrepresentations contained in Mr. Otto's note.

Lord Grenville thinks it his duty in a matter of so much importance to mention to your Majesty that the members of the Cabinet who have been present at the discussions of this subject yesterday and today, are the Lord President, the Duke of Portland, Earl Spencer, Earl Camden, Mr Pitt, & himself;[1] and that there has

---

[1] Windham and the Lord Chancellor were at Weymouth, in attendance on the King.

not been any difference of opinion as to the measure, though the circumstances which seem to them to make it necessary are deeply regretted by all of them. (9790–2)

[*The King's reply, Weymouth, 6 Sept.*] I entirely coincide with Lord Grenville's opinion on the judicious conduct of Lord Whitworth in the difficult business which [he] has brought to so good a conclusion. I deferr giving any opinion on what has passed with M. Otto till the arrival of the messenger expected this afternoon, who I shall find when I return in the evening from Portland. I have kept the two letters on that subject as well as the Southern letters to be sent back by that messenger. (Fortescue MSS.)

[*The King's second reply, Weymouth, 6 Sept., 6.50 p.m.*] On returning from Portland Island I have received Lord Grenville's box containing the project for an armistice from M. Otto, the remarks on it and the counter-project with an explanatory note from Lord Grenville of the members of the Cabinet who approved of the proposed measure. My sentiments are so fully known to Lord Grenville that he cannot be surprised I most unwillingly acquiesce in a naval cessation of hostilities, but I trust I am founded in the opinion that the counter-project is the ultimatum intended by the Ministers who approved of it. I think this should be entirely ascertained and that Lord Grenville should in my name ask whether they do not mean to abide by this paper as to its matter, and if not accepted in France let the war be continued.[1] (Fortescue MSS.)

[*From Lord Grenville, Cleveland Row, 6 Sept., 3 p.m.*] Lord Grenville has the honour to transmit to your Majesty for your Majesty's royal signature the ratification of the Convention with Denmark, and also the warrant for affixing the Great Seal to it. He takes the liberty humbly to request that your Majesty would have the

---

[1] Loughborough communicated his views to Pitt in a letter from Weymouth, dated Saturday evening, 6 Sept.: 'Mr. Windham and I had returned with the King from Portland Island about six o'clock, and were present at opening the packet, the contents of which you may well imagine were not very agreable. The discussion however which took place upon the subject was soon closed, and terminated in the hope that the contre projet would be adhered to on our part as the ultimate extent of concession on the question of armistice.

I did not receive your letter till after I had left the Lodge and the messenger was ready to set off again —whom I did not think it fit to delay, as the answer to Lord Grenville required no comment. I am happy to find that the latter part of that answer is conformable to your own view of the subject, and that you think the modifications proposed essentially necessary to prevent the mischiefs to be apprehended from a naval armistice. I should certainly have concurred in your opinion that no better measure could be adopted in the present conjuncture, having regard to our situation both at home and abroad, though I think the most favourable issue of the measure will be a rejection of the terms by the French Government. Windham flatters himself that a rejection on our part of this proposal would have had no bad effect at home and would even have been popular not only in the Navy but amongst a great part of the commercial men who have much to gain by the extent of trade which our naval superiority ensures to them. I hope there is some force in this observation, but there are other descriptions of men who would have felt very differently, and whom it is most essential to reconcile to the political necessity of a war in which as individuals they have no interest, and I am perfectly convinced that your judgment of the temper of the publick is as just as it has proved to be upon similar occasions. In respect to the Continent we must have brought ourselves to give up all concern for its fate had we persisted in a refusal to make this first sacrifice to the safety of Austria, which, whatever demerit it has incurred, is still the Power we must endeavor to support...' (W. Dacres Adams MSS.)

goodness to order them to be sent to the Lord Chancellor after your Majesty shall have signed them. (9793)

2236 PRINCE ADOLPHUS *to the* KING

[*Hannover, 6 Sept. 1800.*] Your Majesty will allow me to trouble you with a few lines in favor of a petition of my Aide de Camp Captain Hedemann which Baron Lenthe will present to you. It regards the survivorship of a place in the Chapter at Mariensee which is in the gift of your Majesty, and which will soon be vacant by the marriage of Miss Bussche who at present has it. Your Majesty would render Captain Hedemann infinitely happy in granting this survivorship to one of his daughters, and I can safely say that he would not be unworthy of this favor, as he has rendered me essential services ever since he has been with me, and particularly since I have had my own Establishment, all the accounts of which he has under his particular care. I must also add that he has a considerable family, and for this reason would this mark of your graciousness be doubly acceptable to him.

It is with great joy I have heard that your Majesty is in very good health, and I offer up the most fervent prayers to the Almighty that you may continue so for many years, and that you may always be able to go through with equal facility the fatigues you have had this summer. How happy should I have been to have been reviewed with my Division by your Majesty. I will answer that there is not a man in it would not have wished it, and I believe you would have been pleased with the different Batallions. I cannot enough praise the goodwill I found among all the officers and men, and I should have desired nothing more than to have been ordered with my Division on active service.

Tomorrow the twelve days notice for the cessation of the truce expire, and therefore next weeck we may expect some accounts from the Empire. Those we have of the Austrian troops are not the best, but I hope they will prove false, and that the ennemy will be repulsed. In this case very few will get back to the Rhine, for the manner in which they have treated that part of Germany which they have occupied since the truce is schocking, and has encreased very much the hatred of the inhabitants. I dare now not trespass any longer on your patience. (48554–5)

2237 LORD GRENVILLE *to the* KING

[*Cleveland Row, 8 Sept. 1800, 3 p.m.*] Lord Grenville had the honour to receive your Majesty's note yesterday, and as the rest of your Majesty's servants were out of town he could no otherwise execute your Majesty's commands than by communicating them to Mr Pitt.

In considering the note and projet to be transmitted to Mr Otto, some alterations were made in the latter, particularly in the Article respecting the blockade of the French ports, which they are confident your Majesty will approve. Till it is known what the points are to which the French Government may accede, it is not easy to speak with certainty as to the further answer which your Majesty's servants might humbly recommend to be returned to any objections urged against this projet. But it does not appear to Mr Pitt or Lord Grenville that any circumstance is likely to arise which could make a necessity for materially weakening the securities now demanded.

It appears indeed most probable from the present conduct of the French Government that they are only seeking a pretext for renewing hostilities against Austria, and thereby forcing that country to a separate peace.

Lord Grenville would see this state of things, which appears to him to be the true one, with much less uneasiness if all the reports were not so unfavourable as to the state of the German army. (9794–5)

2238 EARL SPENCER *to the* KING

[*Althorp, 9 Sept. 1800.*] Earl Spencer has the honour to lay before your Majesty the Minutes & sentence of a court martial held at Portsmouth on the surgeon of your Majesty's sloop the Beaver for striking a Lieutenant, by which, as the fact was proved, the Court have thought it necessary to pass sentence of death on the surgeon according to the Articles of War, but as the prisoner appears to have acted in some degree from ignorance, and to have very earnestly endeavoured to make every possible apology for the offence almost immediately after its commission, & appears also to have borne a good character, Earl Spencer feels it his duty humbly to recommend him to your Majesty for mercy in compliance with the wishes of the members of the court martial. (9797)

2239 THE KING *to* LORD GRENVILLE

[*Weymouth, 10 Sept. 1800.*] The accompanying paper is so curious that I think worthy of being communicated to Lord Grenville. It has been drawn up by the Bishop of Salisbury for Sir William Pulteney on the Lord Chancellor's doubting the information when given only by the Revd. Mr. Cox[1] who certainly frequently puts more faith on slight grounds than more cautious men can admit; it will be easy to collect from the actual papers either in the Secretary of State's Office or the Paper Office the foundation of the fact now stated, and it may be of use hereafter when the final determination on the Austrian Netherlands comes to be debated.[2] (Fortescue MSS.)

2240 THE DUKE OF YORK *to the* KING

[*Horse Guards, 10 Sept. 1800.*] I have the honor to lay before your Majesty the weekly and monthly states together with one of the troops under the command of Sir Ralph Abercrombie, as also the recommendations for vacant commissions which have been received this week for your Majesty's approbation.

I have at the same time to report to your Majesty that in consequence of a message which I received last Friday from the Admiralty informing me of the enemy having assembled a considerable number of flat-bottomed boats at

---

[1] The Rev. William Coxe (1747–1828), the historian, who published *inter alia* Memoirs of the House of Austria, of Walpole, of Marlborough, and of Henry Pelham.

[2] See Nos. 2241, 2253.

St Maloes, it has become necessary to reinforce immediately the guarrisons of Jersey and Guernsey which have certainly been very weak since the departure of the Russians, as also the western district, and I have the honor to inclose to your Majesty the arrangement which I have made for that purpose, which I trust will meet with your Majesty's approbation.

I wait your Majesty's orders for the disposal of the 26th Regiment of Light Dragoons vacant by the death of General Manners.[1] (9798)

2241 LORD GRENVILLE to the KING

(Copy)

[*Dropmore, 12 Sept. 1800.*] Lord Grenville begs leave to return his dutiful acknowledgements to your Majesty for the communication of the statement drawn up by the Bishop of Salisbury. He has directed a careful examination to be made of everything which can be found in the State Paper Office relating to this business: and he will have the honour to submit the result to your Majesty. (9799)

2242 HENRY DUNDAS to the KING, and the reply

[*Wimbledon, 14 Sept. 1800.*] Mr. Dundas humbly takes the liberty to mention to your Majesty that a few days before he left Cheltenham he received a copy of the projet of a Naval Armistice advised by your Majesty's confidential servants and acquiesced in by your Majesty. Under these circumstances Mr. Dundas was aware of the impropriety of obtruding any advice upon a point already decided, and nothing can be further from his inclination than to disturb the harmony of your Majesty's councils, but having never varied one iota of his opinion upon this measure from the first moment of its being mentioned, and having no opportunity of entering his dissent before the measure was resolved on, he hopes to experience your Majesty's indulgence for having taken the only method that occurred of relieving his mind from the responsibility of having concurred in such a measure. Upon that principle he found himself impelled by a feeling of duty to lodge with Lord Grenville the accompanying disapprobation in a letter[2] from Cheltenham. (9805, and Add. MSS. 40100, f. 270.)

[*The King's reply, Weymouth, 16 Sept.*] I am much pleased with Mr. Secretary Dundas's having so clearly and at the same time temperately expressed his dissent to the entering in the smallest degree into negociation on so novel and dangerous a measure as a naval suspencion of arms. The impudent manner in which Bonaparte has broken that with Austria at the moment he was giving that as a precedent

---

[1] Russell Manners. Major-General, 1777; Lieutenant-General, 1782; General, 1796. John Floyd succeeded him.

[2] Dundas wrote to Grenville from Cheltenham on the 9th: 'I perused last night the proffered projet of the Armistice which is now in discussion between this country and France. I must suppress my feelings on the occasion because I cannot express them without appearing to deviate from that respect which I ought to bear to those who are parties to the transaction. I must however, in justice to myself, request your Lordship to allow this short Minute of my disapprobation to remain with the other papers in the Office, that I may not be supposed, either now, or at any future period, to have concurred in so new, and in my judgement, so fatal a proposition.' (9796)

for what he was proposing here is now notorious, and I hardly expect he will refuse that which I own I think ought never to have been encouraged from hence and may serve as an unfortunate precedent in futurity. Mr. Wyndham clearly concurs with Mr. Dundas; I think the Lord Chancellor does also, though he is not explicit on this subject.

I desire the articles sent by the Marquis Welsley may remain at Mr. Secretary Dundas's office till I return. (Add. MSS. 40100, f. 276.)

2243   THE DUKE OF YORK *to the* KING

[*Horse Guards, 17 Sept. 1800.*] I have the honour to transmit to your Majesty the usual weekly states, as likewise to lay before your Majesty for your approbation the recommendations for vacant commissions which have been received this week.

Among them your Majesty will find the Lieutenant-Colonelcy of the 19th Light Dragoons left blank, in obedience to the remark which your Majesty was pleased to make. I trust, however, that your Majesty will allow me to state that the eldest Major is Brevet Lieutenant-Colonel Maxwell who has been nineteen years in your Majesty's service, the last four years of which he has been Major to the Regiment and commanded it since Major-General Floyd has been upon the Staff, and is very particularly recommended by Major-General Floyd as a most excellent officer.

Should your Majesty in consideration of this statement approve of Brevet Lieutenant-Colonel Maxwell being promoted to the Lieutenant-Colonelcy of the 19th Light Dragoons I beg leave to recommend the eldest Captain of the Regiment, Baily, to succeed to the Majority. He has served twenty two years, and is highly spoken of by General Floyd.

I have the honor also to report to your Majesty that in consequence of the appearance of disturbances and riots at Nottingham, Birmingham, and other towns in the interior of the country, on account of the high price of bread, I have been under the necessity of reinforcing that part of the country by ordering the 11th Regiment of Light Dragoons to march to Loughborough, not deeming it right at this moment when there are appearances of riot in London likewise to diminish the cavalry round the Metropolis, which I trust will meet with your Majesty's approbation.

I had hoped to have been able to have acquainted your Majesty this day with the arrangements proposed to be made with the forces under the command of Sir Ralph Abercrombie and Sir James Pulteney in pursuance of the orders I received from your Majesty last Sunday, but I have not as yet been able to see Mr Dundas. He has, however, appointed tomorrow morning. (9801–2)

2244   *Letters from* LORD GRENVILLE *to the* KING, *and the replies*

[*Cleveland Row, 17 Sept. 1800, 3 p.m.*] Lord Grenville has the honour to transmit to your Majesty the answer received yesterday afternoon from M. Otto. Your Majesty's servants on consideration of this paper this morning were of opinion that it would be proper to return a reply adhering to the terms of Lord Grenville's former note, & he will tomorrow have the honour to submit to your Majesty the draft which he has undertaken to prepare to that effect. (9800)

[*The King's reply, Weymouth, 18 Sept.*] Lord Grenville is so well apprised of how very unwillingly I acquiesced in the unanimous opinion of the Ministers that attended in town at the Cabinet on the proposition for a maritime cessation of arms that he cannot wonder at my concurring with them in seeing how inadmissible the alterations made in our unfortunate project are, and that we must adhere to the terms of the former note. (Fortescue MSS.)

[*From Lord Grenville, Downing Street, 18 Sept., 3 p.m.*] Lord Grenville has the honour to submit to your Majesty the draft of the answer to M. Otto's note as it has been settled this morning at the Cabinet. If, as he trusts, your Majesty should not disapprove of it in this shape, Lord Grenville will send it as soon as it is returned from your Majesty, and should M. Otto's answer, contrary to Lord Grenville's expectation, lead to any verbal communication, he requests your Majesty's permission to authorize Mr. Hammond to see him for that purpose. (9803)

[*The King's reply, Weymouth, 19 Sept.*] I trust the answer to M. Otto's [note] will put an end to a most unfortunate measure the giving in the smallest degree way to the idea of a maritime cessation of arms; should it not, I think Mr. Hammond's discretion points him out as the most proper person to communicate personally with M. Otto. (Fortescue MSS.)

2245   *Letters from the* DUKE OF PORTLAND *to the* KING

[*Weymouth, Friday, 19 Sept. 1800, 9.30 a.m.*] The Duke of Portland, in laying the letters from the Lord Mayor & Mr. King before your Majesty, most humbly submits to your Majesty his intention of immediately returning to London. (9804)

[*Whitehall, Saturday, 20 Sept.*] The Duke of Portland humbly begs leave to acquaint your Majesty that from the accounts he has received of the state of the City & of the promptitude & steadiness of the Magistrates & of the Volunteer Corps of all descriptions, he trusts he does not presume too far in representing to your Majesty that there appears reason to beleive that the spirit of impatience & disorder is so far checked that by a little longer perseverance in the means that have been used for that purpose it will be effectually suppressed, & that such measures of precaution have been taken in Westminster as encourage the Duke of Portland to hope that the tranquillity & good order of that part of the Metropolis will not suffer any material interruption. The letters from the country bring no accounts of fresh disturbances, & by the military assistance with which the Magistrates will be now furnished in those parts where riots have actually taken place or very serious disposition to outrage has manifested itself, it is to be presumed that the ill-intentioned will be awed into a sense of their duty. The judicious & spirited conduct of Lt. Genl. Rooke[1] at Bristol has had the best possible effect, & supported as the Duke of Portland is persuaded he will be by the Magistrates of

---

[1] James Rooke (c. 1740–1805), Colonel of the 38th Foot. Lieutenant-Colonel, 1779; Colonel, 1780; Major-General, 1787; Lieutenant-General, 1797; General, 1802. M.P. for Monmouthshire, 1785–1805, as a firm supporter of Administration.

that city, he trusts that it will be attended with very salutary consequences not only in that large & populous place but throughout the district which your Majesty has been pleased to entrust to Lt. General Rooke's command. (9807–8)

[*Bulstrode, Sunday, 21 Sept., 3.50 p.m.*] The Duke of Portland humbly conceiving that your Majesty will expect to receive a report of the proceedings of last night & of the result of the measures which had been taken to prevent & suppress any riots or outrages which might be attempted, begs leave with all humility to lay before your Majesty the letter he received this morning from the Lord Mayor, & to acquaint your Majesty that in the early part of the evening there appeared a strong disposition in the mob to prevent the markets in the city of Westminster from continuing open, & that it shewed itself more particularly in Clare Market, where, on the butchers receiving assurances of protection from the police magistrates, the market continued open until the usual hour of its closing; a *slight* attempt was made to molest a corn dealer in the neighbourhood of Soho, but it was almost immediately prevented by the intervention of the Westminster Volunteer Cavalry, whose conduct upon all similar occasions the Duke of Portland begs leave to represent to your Majesty as having been uniformly meritorious; & he is happy to be able to conclude this statement by observing to your Majesty that in the opinion of all the Magistrates the mob was of the meanest description, & so easily intimidated that Mr Ford, with the assistance of one constable *only*, took three out of the midst of them into custody without any molestation whatever or the smallest risk.

It is the opinion of the Magistrates that last night will see the end of the disturbances, but precautions will notwithstanding be taken this evening, in order to check any tendency that may shew itself of a dissatisfied or ill-intentioned nature. (9809–10)

[*Whitehall, Tuesday, 23 Sept.*] The Duke of Portland most humbly acquaints your Majesty that the tranquillity of this Metropolis & the freedom of the markets have not suffer'd any interruption for these last two days, & that there is no appearance of the revival of the late disturbances—that precautions, however, will still continue to be taken & every means used to trace to the source the methods that have been employed by the rioters to conduct themselves systematically, & to discover the authors & abetters of the late outrages. The Duke of Portland also submits to your Majesty the humble opinion of your Majesty's confidential servants that another circular letter should be written to your Majesty's Lieutenants of Counties to exert themselves & to call upon the Magistrates for their co-operation in impressing upon the people in general a fresh sense of the respect due to the laws & the necessity of coming forward for the protection & security of private property in order not only to prevent the calamity which they affect to apprehend but to stem that torrent which, if not effectually stopped, will lead more directly than any other circumstance to reduce this country to the same state to which France has been brought.

The Duke of Portland requests your Majesty's permission to lay before your Majesty the Lord Lieutenant of Ireland's humble recommendation of Mr. Justice

Crookshank's prayer to your Majesty that your Majesty will be graciously pleased to give him leave to resign his seat as one of the Justices of your Majesty's Court of Common Pleas,[1] & in that case the Lord Lieutenant is desirous of offering to your Majesty's consideration Mr Luke Fox,[2] one of your Majesty's Council & a person of the first eminence in his profession, as a fit successor to Mr Justice Crookshank, & the Lord Lieutenant also humbly begs leave to submit to your Majesty the name of Mr Marcus Beresford[3] as a fit person to succeed to the office of Lieutenant-General of the Ordnance in the room of Mr Pakenham whom your Majesty has been lately pleased to appoint Master-General. (9811–13)

2246   *Letters from* LORD GRENVILLE *to the* KING, *and a reply*

[*Downing Street, 23 Sept. 1800, 3 p.m.*] Lord Grenville has the honour humbly to acquaint your Majesty that Mr Otto's note and counter-project have been taken into consideration this day by your Majesty's confidential servants, and that it has been agreed that Lord Grenville should prepare a paper stating the reasons which make it impossible for your Majesty to admit the alterations proposed by France to be made in the counter-projet transmitted to Mr Otto by Lord Grenville, and that Mr Hammond should be instructed to make this communication to Mr. Otto.

Lord Grenville expects to be enabled to transmit this paper to your Majesty by tomorrow's mail.[4] (9814–15)

[*The King's reply, Weymouth, 24 Sept.*] The information given me by Lord Grenville has my fullest approbation, that the Cabinet, on considering the note of M. Otto and the counter projet which accompanied it, is of opinion that the alterations proposed by France cannot be admitted, and that a paper to that intent shall be prepared, and Mr. Hammond directed to make this communication to M. Otto.

P.S. The dispatches from Lisbon clearly point out the propriety of sending the troops under Sir Jas. Pulteney to Portugal; indeed it is impossible to send more out of this island in the present posture of affairs, and I think that preferable to sending them to the West Indies which has ever proved the obstruction of every corps sent there.[5] (Fortescue MSS.)

[1] He had been one of the Justices since Jan. 1784.
[2] Luke Fox (1755–1819), Justice of the Common Pleas [I.], Dec. 1800–July 1816. (Haydn's *Book of Dignities* dates the appointment of Fox, 27 Feb.) M.P. for Clonmines [I.], 1797–9; for Mullingar [I.], 1799–1800. On 31 May 1804 Lord Abercorn brought charges against him of libelling the Lord Lieutenant of Ireland, Lord Hardwicke, with the view of removing him from the Bench, but he was ultimately defeated in his object. (*Parl. Deb.* II, 476.)
[3] A son of John Beresford, the Irish politician. M.P. for Coleraine in the last Irish Parliament.
[4] The King endorsed the letter: 'My answer contained the fullest approbation of the conduct proposed, and a postscript proposing the troops under the command of Sir Jas. Pulteney being sent to the defence of Portugal.'
[5] Lord Loughborough sent the following note to the King from Weymouth on the 24th: 'The Chancellor begs leave most humbly to express his entire concurrence in that determination of the Cabinet which has been honoured by your Majesty's most gracious approbation' (9816). He had attended a Privy Council meeting at Gloucester Lodge on the 17th, and had not returned to London.

[*From Lord Grenville, Downing Street, 24 Sept., 3 p.m.*] Lord Grenville has the honour humbly to acquaint your Majesty that the paper of instructions has this day been settled at the meeting of your Majesty's servants. It is too voluminous to be transcribed in time to be sent to your Majesty today, but it contains directions to insist upon all the points in which the French project differs from the counter-project transmitted to Mr Otto.

The accounts received this day from Vienna seem to place in a strong light the danger to which all Europe might be exposed by the sudden renewal of hostilities on the Continent. (9817)

2247 THE KING *to* HENRY DUNDAS

[*Weymouth, 25 Sept. 1800.*] Mr. Secretary Dundas having communicated to me the copy of the note he sent to Lord Grenville from Cheltenham, I chuse to send him the draft of the note I have wrote this day to Lord Grenville on the melancholy account of the want of energy at Vienna, and my fear that if Ministers do not stop in time the dear bought conquests in the East and West Indies may [be] given up for the ideal support of continental connections and contrary to the watchword in the Seven Years War that America was conquered in Germany, that our conquests will be lost by our allies in Germany.
P.S. By some mistake I have kept back the accompanying draft. (Add. MSS. 40100, f. 282.)

2248 LORD GRENVILLE *to the* KING, *and the reply*

[*Downing Street, 25 Sept. 1800, 3 p.m.*] Lord Grenville has the honour to transmit to your Majesty the instruction to Mr Hammond. He saw M. Otto this morning, who is to send his answer in writing tomorrow, but from his conversation it does not appear likely that France will give way on the most important of the points in question. (9818)

[*The King's reply, Weymouth, 26 Sept.*] I return Lord Grenville the draft of his instructions for Mr. Hammond, and I am happy to find he is of opinion that France will not give way on the most important of the points in question, as that of course will break off the negociation. (Fortescue MSS.)

2249 EARL SPENCER *to the* KING

[*Admiralty, 27 Sept. 1800.*] Earl Spencer has the honour to lay before your Majesty the proceedings of a court martial held at Halifax on a marine belonging to your Majesty's sloop the Swan, whereby he is sentenced to death, but from the circumstances of the case, the court martial having judged it right humbly to recommend him to your Majesty's mercy, Earl Spencer submits to your Majesty the propriety of extending your royal mercy to him. (9822)

[*Whitehall, Saturday, 27 Sept. 1800.*] The suggestion that it would be adviseable that an additional circular letter should be written by the Duke of Portland to your Majesty's Lieutenants of Counties in order to render their exertions more active in the suppression of the riots which had broken out in different parts of the kingdom, having received the sanction of your Majesty's approbation, the Duke of Portland feels it to be his indispensable duty most humbly to submit to your Majesty the reasons which have influenced your Majesty's servants to be of opinion that that measure is no longer necessary. The outrages which have been committed have been confined comparatively to so small a proportion of the kingdom that it appears unnecessary to make an extraordinary call upon the vigilance of the Magistrates in those counties where good order has sufferd no interruption; & in those where disturbances have taken place the accounts which are daily received prove that the people are universally returning to a sense of their duty & of their interests, with the exception only of a part of South Wales, which, by the active & judicious conduct of Lt General Rooke, there can be little doubt, will very shortly & effectually be reduced to reason. In the correspondence which has passed between your Majesty's Lieutenants & the Duke of Portland, & which has been laid before your Majesty, your Majesty will have observed the points which have been endeavoured to have been pressed upon them, & if your Majesty is graciously disposed to attribute in any respect the restoration of good order to the line which has been pursued in that correspondence, it may be possible that your Majesty may condescend to judge it not necessary to resort to a different mode of proceeding, & that it may be most prudent in the present state of things to avoid any step which may tend to create alarm.

The Duke of Portland humbly submits to your Majesty a draft of a letter to the Lord Lieutenant of Ireland upon the subject of the reduction of the Corps of Irish Artillery, prepared in obedience to the commands your Majesty was pleased to signify to the Duke of Portland, & he requests your Majesty's permission, in consequence of a private letter from the Lord Lieutenant of Ireland, to lay the Lord Lieutenant's request at your Majesty's feet, that your Majesty will be graciously pleased to grant the reversion of the office of Remembrancer of the Exchequer, now held for life by the Marquess Wellesley, to Mr. Richard Wellesley,[1] a near relation of the Marquess's. (9451–2 and 9821)

[1] Richard Wellesley (1787–1831), Lord Wellesley's first natural son by Hyacinthe Gabrielle Roland. M.P. for Queenborough, 1810–11; for East Grinstead, 1812; for Yarmouth, Isle of Wight, 1812–17; for Ennis, 1820–6. A Lord of the Treasury, 1811–12; Commissioner of the Stamp Duties, 1826.

Cornwallis had written to Pitt on 31 March: 'I yesterday received by the express, your letter dated the 27th instant, and have great pleasure in assuring you that I have no engagement which will interfere with my giving the reversion of the Remembrancer's office to Lord Wellesley's son, and that it will afford me the most sincere satisfaction to comply with your wishes, and to gratify my friend Lord Wellesley, for whom I have great personal regard, and whose services have such strong claims upon the gratitude of his country...' (W. Dacres Adams MSS.)

Lord Bathurst wrote to Lord Wellesley on 28 May 1800: 'I am afraid there will be great difficulties in getting a title for your son [who was only thirteen and at Eton]. If it could be done at all, the way would be by a direct creation and not by descent, and that would be better managed after your return (when he and his mother would be older) than just now. His talents and his manners, which are without exception the best I ever saw any boy possessed of, together with the fortune which you will be enabled

2251 THE DUCHESS OF WURTEMBERG *to the* KING

[*Erlangen, 28 Sept. 1800.*] This moment the messenger who brings your Majesty the joyous news of Malta's being taken is arrived here and I cannot deny myself the honour & pleasure of congratulating you on this occasion.[1] I wish it were in my power to give your Majesty as favourable accounts of affairs in Germany, but alas they grow more intricate every day. The Emperor, after having joined the Army and appearing to intend to defend heartily the Empire, has concluded an Armistice by which I fear the Dutchy will remain in the hands of the enemy, but not having heard from the Duke since this was known at Vienna I cannot speak with certainty on the subject. The only hopes I have that things may turn out a little better for us, is that perhaps the Duke's being on the spot may induce the Emperor to do more in his favour than he would otherwise. I also, Sir, again seize on this opportunity to entreat your Majesty to direct your Minister to express that you wish us not [to] be abandoned to the mercy of the French. (51617–8)

2252 HENRY DUNDAS *to the* KING, *and the reply*

[*Downing Street, 28 Sept. 1800.*] Mr Dundas begs leave humbly to state to your Majesty that the state and appropriation of your Majesty's forces under the command of Sir Ralph Abercrombie and Sir James Pultney has been repeatedly under the consideration of your Majesty's confidential servants. It is universally felt among them that when negotiations for peace shall take place, your Majesty must negotiate under infinite disadvantages so long as France is permitted to remain in the undisturbed possession of Egypt; and from the most recent communications which have taken place, there seems to be no doubt of two propositions, *first*, that the French put more value upon retaining the possession of Egypt than they do upon recovering any of the possessions taken from them by your Majesty's arms in the course of the war. Mr Dundas personally never entertained a doubt that the French would make a good bargain if they allowed Great Britain to retain all its conquests, provided they were allowed to consolidate their power in Egypt, and he has reason to think that the same opinion is now generally held by all your Majesty's servants who have had occasion to consider the subject with attention. The *second* proposition is that there is little or endeed no hope of the French being expelled from Egypt by the exertions of the Turks unsupported by an European force. The Turks might probably be enabled to do their own business if the French were driven from the ports of Alexandria, Damietta and Rosetta on the one side, and from all intercourse with the Red Sea by the possession of Suez and Coshire [*sic*] on that side. The first of these objects can only be attained by a force sent from the Mediterranean, the second by a detachment to be sent from India. Your Majesty's servants had almost come to the resolution some days ago of submitting

to settle upon him if you continue in India your five years and should have no more children, which Lady Wellesley's age, you will recollect, does not make it by any means impossible on your return: all these circumstances...will make his situation in life so advantageous that his prospects must be satisfactory to you, even if you were not to succeed in this object' (*Wellesley Papers*, I, 128).

[1] Malta had surrendered to Bonaparte in 1798 on his way to Egypt. It capitulated on 5 Sept. to a British force under Major-General Pigot.

measures for your Majesty's consideration tending to effectuate these important objects, but they have been induced to hesitate whether the first of them at least should not be delayed sometime longer, and that upon two grounds, *first*, that the season would answer for the expedition better in the months of March and April than in the months of December and January. *Secondly*, that the urgent calls from Portugal rendered it necessary to give a great part of your Majesty's force to that service. The recent advices from Lisbon seem to add much force to the sentiments of those who have throughout doubted if there was any just cause for alarm in Portugal, and from information which they conceive to be accurate, Mr Pitt and Mr Dundas have received a strong conviction that the grounds are erroneous on which your Majesty's servants had been led to suppose that the later season was preferable to the earlier one for taking possession of the ports on the coasts of Egypt. In every other point of view the delay is certainly very pernicious. Under these impressions Mr Dundas thinks it his duty to give this preliminary explanation to your Majesty, meaning immediately to have the whole subject reconsidered by your Majesty's servants, as it is of much importance that no more time be lost in conveying your Majesty's orders for the direction of Sir Ralph Abercrombie's proceedings. (9823–7)

[*The King's reply, Weymouth, 29 Sept. 1800.*] The situation of Portugal certainly deserves the first attention. There is no possibility of furnishing it assistance but from the Army in the Mediterranean: that once done, after garrisoning Gibraltar and Minorca, there will remain a disposable force of 5,000 men at Minorca which may be employed in Egypt, and it may be worthy of consideration whether from the East Indies it may not be feasible to order a force to reinforce that Corps though it will not come in the early part of the expedition. Indeed the 5,000 from the Mediterranean properly lead will I should trust oblige the remains of the debilitated French Army soon free Egypt from that pest of society [*sic*]. (Add. MSS. 40100, f. 289.)

2253   LORD GRENVILLE *to the* KING, *and the reply*

[*Cleveland Row, 2 Oct. 1800, 3 p.m.*] Lord Grenville has the honour to transmit to your Majesty a précis drawn up by Mr. Goddard (transmitter of State Papers in the Foreign Office) of the negotiations with the King of Prussia, to which the paper of the Bishop of Salisbury refers, which your Majesty did Lord Grenville the honour to send him.

As this statement illustrates an interesting period of the history of this century, Lord Grenville humbly asks your Majesty's permission that it may be privately printed at the Office Press, and the copies reserved to be given to such persons only as your Majesty may be graciously pleased to allow. (Fortescue MSS.)

[*The King's reply, Weymouth, 3 Oct.*] I am pleased at the expedition with which Mr. Goddard has formed a précis of the negociation with the great King of Prussia in 1741. I willingly consent to its being printed at the Office Press as it illustrates an interesting period in the history of this century, agreable to the suggestion of Lord Grenville. (*Ibid.*)

2254. *Letters from the* DUKE OF PORTLAND *to the* KING

[*Whitehall, Friday, 3 Oct. 1800, 3.35 p.m.*] The Duke of Portland most humbly begs leave to lay at your Majesty's feet his most dutifull congratulations on the joyfull event of Princess Sophia's entire recovery which your Majesty has condescended to notify to him, & which he devoutly hopes will not suffer any interruption which can affect the satisfaction which your Majesty so feelingly expresses upon it.

Your Majesty's orders respecting Dr. Millman[1] & Admiral Kingsmill[2] would have been fulfilled today had not the meeting of your Majesty's servants continued beyond the time which the Duke of Portland expected & render'd it impossible to make out the warrants for your Majesty's signature without delaying the mail coach. (9828–9)

[*Burlington House, Friday, 3 Oct., 11.40 p.m.*] The Duke of Portland humbly conceives it to be his duty to give your Majesty the earliest notice that the Lord Mayor & Livery of London assembled in Common Hall have this day voted an Address & Petition to your Majesty praying your Majesty to call your Parliament in order to their considering the present high price of provisions & adopting measures for reducing the same. They have moreover resolved that this Address shall be presented to your Majesty *upon the Throne* by the Lord Mayor & Sheriffs, the latter of whom are desired to attend your Majesty to take your commands respecting the time at which your Majesty will please to receive them. The Sheriffs, who are but just come into office, although they are both men of good character & good intentions, had not the courage to refuse to comply with the request of the Common Hall, & notwithstanding their having been since apprized of the irregularity of the request, they still persist in considering themselves bound to fulfill it, & it is their intention accordingly to set out for Weymouth tomorrow morning at five o'clock. Your Majesty will see at one glance from the terms in which the Petition is expressed its real object, & how little the language of it is suited to promote the purpose it professes; but was it unexceptionable in that & in all othet respects, the Duke of Portland would feel it incumbent upon him to represent with all deference to your Majesty that it is not the Petition of the Corporation of London, or of a body that has any title or precedent to urge of having had the honor of having been received on the throne by your Majesty or any of your royal predecessors. The Duke of Portland received from the City Remembrancer, who very soon followed the note which he sent to the Duke of Portland containing the resolutions of the Common Hall, together with a copy of the Address & Petition to your Majesty an extract from the City Records of the answer your Majesty was pleased to return to a similar application from a Common Hall in the

---

[1] Sir Frencis Milman (1746–1821), the physician, was created a Baronet in November—a reward for his success in attending on Princess Sophia at Weymouth. The rejoicings, however, were premature. At this time he was one of the physicians to the Royal Household.

[2] Admiral Kingsmill was created a Baronet in November.

Mayoralty of the late Mr. Wilkes,[1] & had the Duke of Portland been able to procure from his own Office a copy of the minute he directed to be made upon a similar occasion in the year 1797 he would have herewith laid it before your Majesty, but as Mr. Pollock, the Chief Clerk's health makes it necessary for him to sleep out of town, & as all the Office books are in his custody, & consequently not to be got at till an hour to which the Duke of Portland is unwilling to detain the messenger, he will venture to state upon recollection to your Majesty that when the Sheriffs attended in pursuance of the direction of the Common Hall, your Majesty commanded the Duke of Portland to acquaint them that they might present their Address at the first Levée, that on the Sheriffs reporting to a Common Hall called for the purpose the answer they had received from the Duke of Portland, they were instructed to return to St. James's humbly to request an answer from your Majesty, & that your Majesty condescended to admit them into the Closet & to tell them that the answer which they had received from the Duke of Portland was given them by your Majesty's direction, & that they might bring the Address at the next Levée, the consequence of which was the same as in the former case, that they did not avail themselves of the permission your Majesty was pleased to give them. The Duke of Portland, therefore, without entering into the causes or motives which may have suggested the calling a Common Hall to petition your Majesty to assemble your Parliament, submits with all humility to your Majesty's superior wisdom the propriety of adhering to the rule which your Majesty has hitherto thought fit to observe upon similar occasions & for that purpose of directing that the Sheriffs should be acquainted, or if your Majesty should graciously please to condescend in consideration of the personal characters of the persons who hold those offices to admit them to your royal presence & let them know that they may present the Address which was voted in Common Hall at your Majesty's first Levée after your return from Weymouth. (9449–50, and 9830–1)

2255 THE DUCHESS OF WURTEMBERG *to the* KING

[*Erlangen, 4 Oct. 1800.*] Though your Majesty will long before this have received the Duke's letter it is my duty to acquaint you that I heard from him this morning by Estafette, which by some sad mistake had been ten days on the road. He mentions his having ordered General Melius to remain in England and rejoices to have this opportunity to shew your Majesty his respect and attachment. The wonderful events which continue to take place at Vienna I shall not trouble you with a repetition of, as you of course have them much better related. But if possible this fresh Armistice places us in a more miserable situation than we were, and I am sure your Majesty will have been hurt to hear that no step has been taken in our favour though everything has been done to assist the Elector of Bavaria. The greatest part of the French troops have quitted Bavaria and are quartered threefold in poor Suabia which is quite eat up and ruined by this dreadful conduct. The enemy finding they cannot feed their whole Army in our wretched country have now ordered fifteen thousand men to march into Bamberg and Würtzbourg.

[1] John Wilkes was Lord Mayor of London in 1775.

Now it is not safe to pass the Regnitz as the French behave very ill to all ranks and raise contributions without end. Even the Margravine,[1] though a Princess of Prussia, will not venture on any road but that to Nuremberg where there are Austrians. (51619–20)

2256 HENRY DUNDAS to the KING, and the reply

[*Downing Street, 4 Oct. 1800.*] Mr Dundas begs leave humbly to transmit to your Majesty a Minute of your Majesty's servants, containing their opinions and submitting their humble advice on the points therein mentioned.

Mr Dundas would have been happy if he could have stated to your Majesty that there had been no difference of opinion, but that was scarcely to be expected in matters of such difficult discussion; but the generality of your Majesty's confidential servants were of opinion that consistent with the best interests of your Majesty's Empire, at stake by the French retaining the possession of Egypt, it was impossible for them not to advise your Majesty to take the most effectual means practicable for its relief before it may become too late, and they were further of opinion that in the succours suggested for Portugal, they had gone every possible length consistently with a due attention to the various other interests of your Majesty's dominions.

Along with this Mr Dundas has thought it his duty to transmit for your Majesty's perusal the Minute he had prepared for the consideration of your Majesty's servants, and which he read to them previous to their finally deciding upon the business, and there are also sent the proposed instructions to Sir Ralph Abercrombie, and to Sir James Pultney.[2] (9832–4)

Cabinet Minute [*Downing Street, 3 Oct. 1800.*][3] (Draft)

Present: The Lord Chancellor, The Duke of Portland, The Earl Spencer, The Earl of Chatham, The Earl Camden, The Earl of Liverpool, The Lord Grenville, Mr. Pitt, Mr. Windham, Mr. Dundas.

That it is of the utmost importance that the French should not be allowed to

[1] Prince Ferdinand of Prussia (1730–1813), Frederick the Great's youngest brother, married (1755) Louise, daughter of the Margrave Frederick William of Brandenburg-Schwedt (1738–1820).

[2] Dundas communicated his views to Pitt in a letter of 1 Oct.: 'I cannot be the instrument of executing our resolution of yesterday, more than I can do that of sending the whole proposed by Lord Grenville to Portugal. To send so large a force to Minorca under a doubt of its being immediately recalled in the event of a separate Peace between Austria and France would be too ridiculous a measure, with the almost certainty of that event having happened before the troops could reach Minorca. I have read over last night the despatches from General [illegible], and Lord Elgin, and they certainly in my view lead to a very opposite conclusion than that which Lord Grenville draws from them, at least if I am to judge from his reasoning yesterday. I have wrote to him requesting these despatches to be sent in circulation and a final resolution to be taken upon them immediately after. In the meantime I feel it absolutely necessary to relieve myself from the *exclusive* responsibility which attaches itself to me of keeping the armament at Gibraltar. I have therefore sent of[f] to Sir Ralph Abercrombie a despatch of which the following is the copy.

I don't intend to be at the Cabinet today. I am by no means prepared to go the length of the measure which seems to be in contemplation. My reasons are many and various.' (W. Dacres Adams MSS.)

[3] Missing from the Archives.

avail themselves of the possession of Egypt in any negotiation that may take place between this country & France, & that effectual measures should therefore be taken for compelling them to evacuate that Province without delay.

That in order to diminish the risk of failure & loss in this expedition, & to ensure, as far as possible, its speedy termination, the land forces to be employed should not be less than 15,000 men, to be selected by General Sir Ralph Abercromby from the disposeable army in the Mediterranean, & to proceed under his command.

That by a temporary reduction in the established garrisons of Gibraltar & Minorca,[1] in the proportion of 500 men each, and by withdrawing the same number from the blockade of Malta, it appears that the disposeable force in the Mediterranean amounts to 23,000 men, leaving consequently a Corps of 8000 (after providing for the expedition to Egypt) which may, without material risk in any of the quarters above-mentioned, be appropriated to other pressing services.

It is proposed to send the whole of this Corps, in the first instance, and as soon as possible, to Portugal.

That the whole of the Dutch Corps now in the Isle of Wight, amounting to 5,000 men, should as soon as possible be embarked and sent to Lisbon, and that on their arrival such a proportion of the British forces above-mentioned as can be spared from Portugal, consistently with the promise made to that Court of completing the auxiliary Army to 15,000 men, should be brought away & conveyed to Ireland.

That the two additional Regiments of Light Cavalry intended to form a part of that Army, should be sent as soon as the means for their conveyance can be provided.

Lord Grenville wishes that his dissent may be expressed from this resolution.[2] Mr. Windham entertains the same wish with respect to himself.[2] (Add. MSS. 40102, ff. 85–8, and a copy in the Melville MSS.)

[*The King's reply, Weymouth, 5 Oct. 1800.*] I confess it is with the greatest reluctance I consent to the proposed disposal of the troops in the Mediterranean by sending 15,000 of them under the command of Sir Ralph Abercrombie to Egypt, as that service must probably prove a burial ground for them to as great an extent as St. Domingo, for unless the Army be supplied from hence as amply and as regularly as that in America was by the Treasury in the time of Lord North, nothing but famine can attend it; as to any part of it being afterwards fit for other service, that cannot be expected. I am therefore not surprised that Lord Grenville and Mr. Wyndham have dissented from the measure.

I hope everyone's eyes are now opened to the shameful pusillanimity of the Emperor and that we must avoid giving up our successes to preserve a broken reed. No good can be expected from Vienna[3]. (Add. MSS. 40100, f. 293)

[1] 'In this estimate the established Garrison of Minorca is reckoned at 5,000 men exclusive of artillery &c. & that of Gibraltar at 4,500, also exclusive of artillery, artificers &c.'
[2] In his own hand.
[3] See, too, *Glenbervie Journals*, I, 233. The King later handsomely acknowledged his error in having opposed the expedition to Egypt.

2257 THE DUKE OF PORTLAND *to the* KING

[*Whitehall, Monday, 6 Oct. 1800.*] The Duke of Portland most humbly begs leave to acknowledge your Majesty's great condescension in communicating to him the particulars of what passed when the Sheriffs of London attended your Majesty at Weymouth in pursuance of the directions of the Common Hall. The Duke of Portland is convinced that the matter will terminate exactly in the manner predicted by your Majesty.[1] (9835)

2258 LORD GRENVILLE *to the* KING

[*Dropmore, 6 Oct. 1800.*] Lord Grenville takes the liberty humbly to request your Majesty to return him the précis of the negotiations in 1741, when your Majesty has done with it, as Mr Goddard informs him that he has kept no copy of it. (9836)

2259 HENRY DUNDAS *to the* KING

[*Wimbledon, 9 Oct. 1800.*] Mr Dundas humbly begs leave to request your Majesty's permission to postpone paying his duty to your Majesty at the first Levée after your Majesty's return to town, being earnestly urged to make another and longer trial of Cheltenham, and the season for it is already far advanced.

Mr Dundas hopes to meet with your Majesty's indulgence if he takes this opportunity of humbly stating to your Majesty that he feels very severe regret in being the instrument of carrying into execution the measure of an extensive expedition for the relief of Egypt to which your Majesty's anxiety for the welfare of your army had led your Majesty to give only a reluctant consent. Mr Dundas rests confident in your Majesty's candor and justice, that your Majesty will give him the credit when he assures your Majesty that under such circumstances, nothing but a deep-rooted sense of duty could have induced him to persevere in that measure. Every day tends more to convince him that upon the success of that measure must depend the permanancy of the best interests of your Majesty's dominions. At the same time it is with much satisfaction Mr Dundas feels himself warranted to state to your Majesty that upon the best enquiry he is satisfied your Majesty may relieve your mind from any anxiety on the ground stated in your Majesty's note. With the command of the seas to preserve a communication with the shore, and in the neighbourhood of the fertile countries of Syria, Candia, Cyprus, Rhodes and every other island in the archipelago, it does not occur that any army runs the risk of a scarcity of provisions, and what further may be necessary for their welfare and comfort, Mr Dundas relies with just confidence on the continuance of the same exertions which have so successfully contributed

---

[1] *The Times* commented: 'On the return of the Royal family [from church on Sunday the 5th] to Gloucester Lodge, the King was waited on by the Sheriff and Remembrancer of London, to know when his Majesty would be pleased to receive the Petition of the Livery of London voted at the Common Hall on Friday, praying his Majesty to summon Parliament immediately to take into consideration the alarming high price of provisions. We have not heard what day his Majesty has fixed on for that purpose.' The royal family returned to Windsor on the 7th.

to the supply of your Majesty's troops in all the various and complicated services of the present war.

It is not Mr Dundas's province to enter upon the reasons which weighed with any of your Majesty's servants to dissent from the measure in question, but he perfectly knows that the extent of the force sent on the expedition, nor the want of provisions for the army, were none of the grounds of their dissent.

Mr Dundas cannot quit this subject without most humbly and at the same time most sincerely congratulating your Majesty on the surrender of Malta to your Majesty's arms, a circumstance which certainly adds much facility to this and every other operation in that part of the world.

Upon the subject of Austria, it is a considerable time since Mr Dundas was strongly impressed with serious doubts how far it was expedient to connect ourselves so closely in the negotiations of that Court. It is a wise policy at all times when we are at war with France to apply a part of the pecuniary resources of this country to create a powerful diversion on the Continent, but it is a consideration of a very different nature how far we ought in the hour of negotiation to incorporate ours with the interests of those continental Powers, especially when they have manifested either a feebleness in their councils, or an inadequacy in their exertions. Mr Dundas has reason to believe that those sentiments which your Majesty has condescended to impart to Mr Dundas are becoming daily more prevalent in the opinions of your Majesty's servants. (9837–41)

2260 PRINCE ADOLPHUS *to the* KING

[*Hamburgh, 9 Oct. 1800.*] I cannot let the quarterly messenger arrive in England without sending him a letter for your Majesty, and it is for this reason that I write from hence.

I had done myself the honor of mentioning to the Queen that I was going to make an excursion into the country of Bremen, and I begged her to mention it to you. I should certainly not have failed to do it myself had I not been afraid of troubling your Majesty too often with my letters. I left Hannover about a fortnight ago, and after passing through the Dutchy of Bremen I went to Hamburgh where I remained some days. Being only twelve miles from Eutin I could not refuse myself the pleasure of calling on my friend the Bishop who was very glad to see [me]: he kept me several days with him, and after passing through a part of Holstein on my road back I arrived here last night. I shall set off the day after tomorrow, and I shall be at Hannover on Sonday. On my return I suppose the Board which has been commissioned to examine several matters relative to the Artillery will be able to sit again: various experiments that have been necessary to be made, the result of which the Bord [*sic*] must be informed of before it go on, have stopped the Sessions for some time, and it was of this moment I profited for to make a little excursion which I trust your Majesty will not disapprove of. When this Board has finished, another will probably be commissioned for the regulating of the exercise of the infantry, and I hope you will approve of the alterations proposed, as I am convinced they are perfectly calculated and are suitable to the modern tacticks without which the ennemy never could have got the better of almost all the regular infantry in Europe. Before I conclude I must congratulate you on the surrender of Malta, and that your arms may always be attended with the most decided success both by land and by sea is the most sincere wish and fervent prayer of etc. (48556–7)

2261   THE KING *to* LORD GRENVILLE

[*Windsor, 9 Oct. 1800, 7.30 a.m.*] I did not suppose that any circumstances could have added to the disgrace of the conduct held by the Court of Vienna in the continuation of the cessation of arms she has so meanly sued for and accepted; but I should not do justice either to my feelings or to truth if I did not express to Lord Grenville that after the Emperor has placed himself in so shameful and indeed despicable a situation his alliance can only be compared to a stone tyed to a sinking man; the casting it off is the only salvation.

Mr. Otto's note gets rid of a most embarrassing question on naval cessation of arms, and I trust there is that energy in my Cabinet as well as in the country that will not allow any idea of embracing a similarity of conduct with that of Vienna.

I return the précis Lord Grenville wishes to have back. (Fortescue MSS.)

2262   THE DUKE OF PORTLAND *to the* KING

[*Bulstrode, Friday, 10 Oct. 1800, 8.08 a.m.*] The Duke of Portland humbly begs leave to lay before your Majesty a letter he has just received from the City Remembrancer informing him of the intentions of the Sheriffs to attend this day at Windsor in order to learn your Majesty's pleasure respecting the time at which your Majesty may please to receive the Resolutions of *another Common Hall*. The purport of these Resolutions the Duke of Portland is unfortunately not able to state to your Majesty, but cannot but presume that they relate to the answer your Majesty returned to the Sheriffs when they attended your Majesty at Weymouth, & that they assert a right which has never been sanctioned by your Majesty or any of your royal predecessors, & by what the Duke of Portland has been able to collect is countenanced at most by one *solitary* instance, which there is reason to believe was owing to a mistake. (9842–3)

2263   WILLIAM PITT *to the* KING

[*Downing Street, Friday, 10 Oct. 1800.*] Mr Pitt humbly begs leave to acquaint your Majesty that on a full consideration of the present circumstances your Majesty's servants have agreed to submit their opinion to your Majesty that nothing would be so likely to prevent the disaffected from availing themselves for mischievous purposes of the dissatisfaction naturally occasioned by the present high price of provisions, as an early meeting of Parliament. The discussion which would take place would tend to remove many erroneous opinions and mischievous prejudices now entertained on the subject, which have the effect both of aggravating the evil itself, and leading to riotous practices. Much real good may also be expected by renewing without delay the provisional bounty on importation granted last year for a term which has now expired, and under which greater quantities have been received from abroad than at any former period. Some other salutary regulations may perhaps also be provided. At all events the public will derive great satisfaction from the attention of Parliament being early directed to the subject, and it seems particularly desireable that the decision should take place without waiting till petitions are procured (as would almost certainly be the case) from various parts of the kingdom. On these grounds Mr Pitt trusts your Majesty will not disapprove of a Proclamation being prepared, giving notice of the meeting for the dispatch of business on the 11th Novr., and which may, if your Majesty thinks proper, be signed at the Council on Wednesday.[1] (9844–5)

2264 HENRY DUNDAS *to the* KING

[*Wimbledon, 12 Oct. 1800.*] Mr Dundas feels great regret in being obliged humbly to submit to your Majesty the propriety of recalling Sir George Yonge from the Government of the Cape of Good Hope, but his conduct during the short time he has been there has in such a variety of particulars been so wild and extravagant as to render it impossible to continue him in that Government without exposing this country to the imputation of being indifferent to the concerns of that most important settlement. Mr Dundas feels the more unpleasant in being obliged to recommend this measure, because your Majesty will have observed that there have been some differences in opinion between Sir George and General Dundas on the subject of command, and Mr Dundas from an idea of impartiality had once formed the notion of recommending to your Majesty the recall of both. But upon enquiry at the Commander-in-Chief's Office, and carefully examining the records of his own Office, Mr Dundas conceives the conduct of General Dundas has, in every situation he has held at the Cape, been so unexceptionable, and characterized by such uncommon forbearance, it would be doing real injustice to recall him. Mr Dundas believes Mr Sylvester Douglas is eminently qualified to succeed to that situation of Governor, and Mr Dundas has requested Mr Pitt in his absence to mention him to your Majesty with that view.[2]

There are some particulars relative to Ceylon which Mr Dundas wishes to take an opportunity of submitting to your Majesty, but they are not equally pressing.

Mr Dundas is sorry to mention to your Majesty *in confidence* that Mr Pitt's

[1] The King's brief reply on the 11th, in a remarkably shaky hand, approving Pitt's suggestion of an early meeting of Parliament, is in Chatham Papers, and Stanhope, III, Appendix, p. xxi. The handwriting was much more normal on the 17th.

[2] Sylvester Douglas had been thought of as Governor of the Cape in 1796, and again in Dec. 1798 (*Glenbervie Diaries*, I, 143). He was actually sworn in as Governor on 28 Jan. 1801, but the change of Government brought about a change of plan, and at Addington's request he accepted the office of Joint Paymaster of the Forces (*Ibid.* I, 165). Pitt wrote to Addington, 29 September: 'It is found necessary that Sir George Yonge should quit the Government of the Cape, and it is settled that Douglas is to succeed to it, by which means a vacancy will be made for your brother at the Treasury. The arrangement is not yet known and cannot take place till the King comes from Weymouth. It is therefore wished that nothing should be said about it just now...I should imagine no long interval need occur before the appointment takes place.' (Sidmouth MSS.)

health is by no means what could be wished, and it will require very great attention to enable him to go through the winter with any degree of energy. Sir Walter Farquhar has earnestly recommended to him to take immediate steps for that purpose.[1] Mr Pitt will probably be obliged to mention the subject to your Majesty, and Mr Dundas trusts he will receive your Majesty's approbation in conveying this information to your Majesty that he may not be allowed to procrastinate so essential a duty. (9846–9)

2265   THE DUKE OF PORTLAND *to the* KING

[*Burlington House, Tuesday, 14 Oct. 1800, 10 p.m.*] The Duke of Portland most humbly begs leave to acquaint your Majesty that the Corporation of London have voted an Address & Petition to your Majesty to convene your Parliament in order that they may adopt such measures as may lead most effectually to reduce the present high price of provisions, & that it is the intention of the Sheriffs to attend tomorrow at St. James's humbly to know your Majesty's pleasure as to the time of its being presented to your Majesty. The Duke of Portland begs leave with all humility to lay at your Majesty's feet the note which he has received upon the occasion from the City Remembrancer.[2] (9850)

2266   THE DUKE OF PORTLAND *to the* KING

[*Whitehall, Wednesday, 15 Oct. 1800, 1 p.m.*] The Duke of Portland has received the communication your Majesty has condescended to make to him of the time at which your Majesty would incline to appoint to be attended with the Address & Petition of the Corporation of London, together with your Majesty's observations upon the proceedings of that body, the wisdom & justice of which he most sensibly feels. But as it is your Majesty's intention ultimately to receive the Address in question, the Duke of Portland feels it to be his duty to submit with all humility to your Majesty's superior judgement, whether the distance of the time to which your Majesty inclines to defer the reception of it may not at such a moment as the present be subject to misconstruction, & be represented by those who are seditiously disposed as affording matter of exultation instead of conveying that reproof with which the considerate part of the community must wish to see such indecent proceedings stigmatized. (9851)

2267   THE BISHOP OF ST DAVID'S *to the* KING[3]

[*Ham, 16 Oct. 1800.*] I ever shall deem it my duty to obey your Majesties commands, and therefore, though the situation of Primate is materially changed since your Majesty was graciously pleased to communicate your wishes, the difficulties

---

[1] Pitt wrote to Addington, 8 Oct.: 'Sir Walter Farquhar even begins to threaten me with the necessity of a visit to Cheltenham or Bath, in order to be at all equal to the Session' (Pellew, I, 263). Pitt went to stay with Addington at Woodley.   [2] Timothy Tyrrell.

[3] The King's letter to the Bishop of St David's, 16 Oct., is in Jesse, III, 233; also the King's letter of the 16th to the Duke of Portland on the subject of this appointment.

of that situation increased, and its dignity and consequence considerably lessened, I do not for a moment hesitate to assure your Majesty that I will cheerfully accept the Archbishoprick of Armagh.

I trust I trust [*sic*] I never shall forget the many favours which I have received from your Majesty, but be forward to manifest, on all occasions, the inviolable attachment & gratitude with which I am Sir,[1] [etc.] (9852)

2268 THE DUKE OF PORTLAND *to the* KING

[*Bulstrode, Friday, 17 Oct. 1800, 11 p.m.*] The Duke of Portland has humbly to implore your Majesty's pardon for having neglected to lay before your Majesty the Lord Lieutenant's letter of the 3d instant which he must, to his great shame, acknowledge was only brought back to his recollection by that from the Lord Lieutenant dated 12th October which he has also to entreat your Majesty's forgiveness for having detained in order that it might be accompanied by the dispatch of the 3d (private & secret) which happened to have been left inadvertently at this place. (9853)

2269 THE KING *to* WILLIAM PITT, *and the reply*

[*Kew, 17 Oct. 1800.*] Mr. Pitt will certainly concurr with me in opinion that it will be right that some mode should be addopted of informing the House of Commons that their House cannot be ready for their reception on the 11th of Novr., for which reason I have directed the Painted Chamber to be prepared for their accommodation untill their usual place of assembling be ready for them. It has occurred to me that an Order-in-Council stating this to the Speaker, probably by a letter, would enable him to have proper notice given to the Members, and then that in the Speech mention of this should also be made. I make this suggestion thus early that Mr. Pitt may conferr with the Speaker and that some proper mode may be addopted of putting this, which may seem but a matter of form, into a shape to prevent any improper animadversion.[2] (Chatham Papers.)

[*Pitt's reply, Woodley,[3] Saturday, 18 Oct.*] Mr Pitt was honored yesterday with your Majesty's gracious commands respecting the mode of communicating to the House of Commons the steps taken for their accomodation in the Painted Chamber. He had before conversed with the Speaker on the subject, and they have since discussed it again; and Mr Pitt would humbly beg leave to submit to your Majesty

[1] Cornwallis reported on 13 Jan. that both the Archbishop of Cashel and the Archbishop of Tuam would like to succeed to the Primacy, and that the former would be a suitable person, but he thought that the King, 'according to the practice which has obtained for many years' would prefer to select one of the English Bishops (*Cornwallis Corresp.*, III, 160). On 24 March the Lord Lieutenant again suggested the appointment of the Archbishop of Cashel, adding, 'I must confess, after the kingdoms become united, I cannot see any objection to an Irish Prelate' (*Ibid.* III, 218).

[2] On 9 Oct. Pitt wrote to the Speaker: 'There is no chance of our present House being fit to receive us. The only places that have occurred are the Painted Chamber or Whitehall Chapel. I should think the former preferable. We shall probably decide this question by a Cabinet tomorrow' (Pellew, I, 265).

[3] Pitt was visiting the Speaker at his country seat near Reading. He returned to London about 5 Nov.

as the result of their consideration, that every purpose would in their opinion be answered if your Majesty should think fit to direct the Lord Chamberlain[1] (whom they conceive to be the regular channel for conveying your Majesty's commands relative to works in any of the Palaces) to write a letter previous to the day of meeting to the Speaker, stating that as the usual place of the House assembling could not be ready for their reception, your Majesty had given directions for preparing the Painted Chamber for their temporary accomodation. The Speaker would then be enabled to direct the officers of the House to give notice in the avenues to Members of the change in the place of meeting, and would on taking the Chair read the Lord Chamberlain's letter, which would naturally be followed by a vote of thanks, and might, it is conceived, preclude the necessity of anything being said on the subject in your Majesty's Speech, or of any other proceeding upon it.[2] (9854–5)

2270 THE EARL OF INCHIQUIN[3] *to the* KING

[*18 Oct. 1800.*] I throw myself at your Majesty's feet and humbly beg permission to state my present situation, which is a most mortifying one, relying on your Majesty's great goodness and feeling to pardon the liberty I take, and that your Majesty will be graciously pleased to consider the severe mortification and disappointment I have suffered in being deprived of what has always been the object of my ambition, a seat in the British House of Peers, and which I had every reason to flatter myself I should have obtained, from the promises the Duke of Portland gave me, of being returned one of the representative peers for Ireland. Trusting to his Grace's influence, I forbore exerting my own interest with my brother peers in Ireland, and knew nothing of the failure of my expectations till a few days before

[1] Pitt should have said the Lord Steward.

[2] The Irish Union increased the number of Members of the House of Commons from 558 to 658, and created new problems of accommodation. The entire side walls of the Chamber, three feet in thickness (except the buttresses supporting the ancient roof) were pulled down and rebuilt to the thickness of one foot only, two feet further back, thus making room for an additional row of seats on either side. For a short period, from 11 Nov., whilst these alterations were in progress, the House occupied another ancient part of the Palace of Westminster, the Painted Chamber, a longer but rather narrower Chamber which, after the Great Fire of 1834, was fitted up as a temporary House of Lords. It was remarked as a somewhat singular circumstance that the Parliament of Great Britain ended its career in the building formerly used as the Court of Star Chamber (the *Morning Chronicle*, 16 Oct. 1800).

When the House met on 11 Nov. in the Painted Chamber the Speaker declared that he had received 'from the Earl of Leicester, Lord Chamberlain of his Majesty's Household, a letter...:

Board of Green Cloth,
St. James's Palace, 29 Oct. 1800.

Sir—I am commanded by his Majesty to acquaint you, for the information of the Members of the House of Commons, that the Chamber in the Palace of Westminster, which has usually been appropriated to the meeting of the House of Commons, not being now in a state to receive the House, on account of the repairs and alterations which his Majesty has directed to be made there, in consequence of the Union with Ireland, his Majesty has ordered the Painted Chamber in the same Palace to be fitted up and prepared for the temporary accommodation of the House at the ensuing meeting of Parliament.' (*H. of C.J.* LV, 795.) There is, of course, an extraordinary error in the *Journals*. Lord Salisbury was Lord Chamberlain; the Earl of Leicester, who wrote the letter, was Lord Steward. *The Times*, in its report, did not fall into that error, nor did the *Parl. Register* (LVIII, 27), which, however, never mentioned the letter.

[3] See No. 1498 n. (II, 538).

the election. His Grace was disappointed, as well as myself, at finding his power inadequate to procuring me an honour, I may be bold to say, I might with justice and propriety have expected, not only from my being the head of one of the most loyal and antient familys in Ireland, but having uniformly exerted myself both in England and Ireland in favour of the Union, and tho' I had no boroughs to present to Government, I was not idle where I had influence. I procured an Address from the county of Clare, and seconded one from the county of Cork. The honour your Majesty has been graciously pleased to confer on me and my family, I receive and feel with sentiments of the most profound respect, duty and gratitude, as being a mark of your Majesty's royal favour; but with all possible submission I entreat your Majesty's gracious consideration and pardon for presuming to trouble your Majesty on the subject of my personal disappointment and embarassment, by losing the honour I fully expected of being elected one of the Representative Peers. I stand in such a predicament that I trust your Majesty will not be surprised at my saying I feel truly distressed.

All my friends and acquaintance knew of my expectations and thought them well founded, and congratulated me on the approach of the election. I was on the point of setting out for Ireland when I received from the Duke of Portland the mortifying and unexpected intelligence that his request in my favour had been disregarded, by which I have the mortification of finding placed above me, many of those peers who have not half my pretentions, either personally or otherwise.

I cannot, therefore, consistent with my feelings, continue a member of the House of Commons, especially honoured as I have so recently been by your Majesty.

Your Majesty knows that by the Union regulations, that by being a member of the House of Commons, an Irish peer loses many priviledges, and is only considered as a commoner, and his rank and titles, how high soever, places him only in the same class as those holding their titles by courtesy.

May I hope your Majesty will spare me the mortification of having it considered by the world that your Majesty's gracious favour was conferred in lieu of my being one of the Representative Peers for Ireland.

The noted loyalty of all my ancestors, as well as my loyall and steady attachment to your Majesty and your Royal House, emboldens me to entreat your Majesty will be so gracious to confer on me, only for my life (which cannot be long) the honour of a British Peerage, which my family once had. I ask this favour of your Majesty with more confidence, as I am sure your Majesty's goodness will incline you to consider the peculiar situation in which I stand, and the mortification and disappointment I have experienced; that I am not asking for more than your Majesty would be inclined to grant, first from the consideration of my family and particularly of my late uncle,[1] who was promised a British Peerage by your Majesty's royal father, and my being the head of a family who were always distinguished by rank, honours and nobleness of character.

---

[1] William O'Brien, 4th Earl of Inchiquin (*d.* 1777), M.P. for Windsor, 1722–7; for Tamworth, 1727–34; for Camelford, 1741–7; for Aylesbury, 1747–54. Gentleman of the Bedchamber to Frederick, Prince of Wales, 1744–51.

On these presumptions I humbly hope your Majesty will be graciously pleased to grant my prayer, which shall ever be acknowledged by a most gratefull and truly loyal heart, being Sir [etc.]¹ (9856–7)

2271 THE DUKE OF PORTLAND *to the* KING

[*Bulstrode, Sunday, 19 Oct. 1800, 11.45 p.m.*] The Duke of Portland most humbly begs leave to lay before your Majesty a copy of the letter which he wrote to the Bishop of St. David's in pursuance of your Majesty's commands, & the Bishop's answer which the Duke of Portland has received this evening. The Duke of Portland will give immediate directions for a search to be made for the instrument of Bishop Boulter's resignation of the See of Bristol on his being promoted to the Primacy, which the Duke of Portland believes to be the only case in point since the Reformation, but humbly submits to your Majesty that the orders to the Lord Lieutenant for the Bishop of St. David's appointment to the Primacy & the Prelacy of the Order of St Patrick need not be deferred upon that account, & requests that your Majesty will graciously condescend to signify your pleasure as to the time at which the Bishop of St David's may be permitted to kiss your Majesty's hands. (9858)

2272 WILLIAM PITT *to the* KING, *and the reply*

[*Woodley, Tuesday, 21 Oct. 1800.*] Mr. Pitt is ashamed of having appeared to defer acknowledging the honor of your Majesty's commands. What he now submits to your Majesty was written on Saturday but he deferred sending it to Windsor in the expectation of a messenger coming from town, who, from an accidental mistake, was not sent as he had desired. (9859)

¹ Lord Inchiquin renewed his application for a British peerage through Pitt, to whom he wrote on 3 Nov. from Taplow Court, his seat near Maidenhead: 'I am first to thank you, which I do with the strongest feeling of obligation, for your kind goodness in recommending me to Lord Eliot for my present seat in the House of Commons, which I mean to resign before the meeting of the United Parliaments, or sooner if you wish it. I have acquainted Lord Eliot with my intention of so doing, as I do not think it consistent for a Peer of Ireland to sit as a Commoner in the United Parliament. Permit me, Sir, to tell you how mortified & disappointed I feel at not being one of the Representative Peers for Ireland, which I was promised, & made to believe by the Duke of Portland that I was to have been, nor did I know to the contrary 'till a short time before the election, when Lord Cornwallis sent his list over here. Many of those returned have not half my pretentions, indeed some, not any, from my rank, my family, its constant loyalty, attachment & services to Government from the earliest time, makes my mortification the greater, & I have some reason to know that his Majesty thinks I have been hardly treated. I therefore once more make it my earnest request that you will be so good to recommend me to his Majesty for a seat in the British House of Peers (which my family once had) for my life only, which cannot be long, & will be no increase to the Peerage. I have been a strenuous friend to the Union, for which I procured an Address from the County of Clare, & seconded one from the County of Cork. Your granting me this favour will be a lasting obligation to, dear Sir [&].' (Hoare MSS.)

On 29 Dec. 1800 Lord Inchiquin was created Marquess of Thomond [I.], and Baron Thomond [U.K.] on 2 Oct. 1801. At his death it was said of him that he was 'celebrated rather as a *bon vivant* than a fashionable, and for many years had the reputation of being a six bottle man'. Sir Gilbert Elliot described him as 'an old fool and savage...yet he is a good-natured man and seems attached to and governed entirely by' his second wife (Minto MSS.). Sylvester Douglas, Lord Glenbervie, too, disliked him. He thought him 'very nearly quite vulgar...and not agreeable' (*Glenbervie Diaries*, I, 329).

² See No. 2114.

[*From the King, Windsor, 22 Oct.*] I have this morning received Mr. Pitt's note concerning the mode of notifying to the Speaker the Painted Chamber being prepared for the accomodation of the House of Commons till their usual place of assembling is ready for their reception, which seems fully to answer the purpose. I trust the good weather and the repose of Woodley will be of great benefit to Mr. Pitt's health.

The Bishop of St. David's has accepted the Primacy of Ireland and will kiss hands this day. I desire therefore Mr. Pitt will take the proper steps for forwarding the appointment of Lord George Murray[1] to the See of St. David's, and Dr. Heath[2] to the Canonry of Windsor. (Chatham Papers.)

2273   *Letters from* LORD GRENVILLE *to the* KING, *and the replies*

[*Dropmore, 24 Oct. 1800.*] Lord Grenville has the honour, in humble obedience to your Majesty's commands, to send your Majesty the draft of a letter from the Lord Steward to the Speaker, which Mr. Pitt and the Speaker both think right in point of form. (9860)

[*The King's reply, 25 Oct., 7.15 a.m.*] Nothing can be more proper than the draft of the proposed letter from the Lord Steward to the Speaker of the House of Commons, and he is certainly the proper officer of the Crown to make the communication. I have therefore kept it to put it this next week in the hands of the Lord Steward, who may immediately have the proper copy prepared to the Speaker.

P.S. I have no objection to the book to be published by Mr. Willick[3] being dedicated to me. (Fortescue MSS.)

[*From Lord Grenville, Cleveland Row, 29 Oct., 12 M.*] Lord Grenville has the honour to acquaint your Majesty that two messengers are arrived from Lord Minto with dispatches up to the 16th inst.

As these and the other letters received are very voluminous, Lord Grenville does not trouble your Majesty with them till the usual hour tomorrow, but he thinks it his duty not to delay acquainting your Majesty that the account of M. de Cobenzel's[4] nomination is confirmed: that M. de Thugut appears to retain the chief direction of affairs, and continues to see Lord Minto on public business as before; and that both he, and M. de Cobenzel, who is set out for Headquarters to

---

[1] Lord George Murray (1761–1803), son of the 3rd Duke of Atholl. Bishop of St David's, 1801–3. He was consecrated on 11 Feb. 1801.

[2] Dr George Heath (*c.* 1748–1822), Assistant Master at Eton, 1775–91; Head Master, 1792–1801; Canon of Windsor until his death, and a Fellow of Eton. Rector of Monks Risborough, Bucks., 1789–1800; Rector of Brasted, Kent, 1800–5; Rector of Piddlehinton, Dorset, 1805; Vicar of Sturminster-Marshall, 1805. His mother applied unsuccessfully to Pitt on 7 Feb. 1800 for the Bishopric of Bangor for him. 'He has at present a wife and nine children on the very small Living of Hunton in Kent...He is a most worthy clergyman and most strenuously well affected to our good King and glorious Constitution.' She concluded: 'I hope I shall not plead in vain for one who, by his merit and his rank, has had long reason to expect promotion' (W. Dacres Adams MSS.) Charles Grey described him as 'one of the best and most amiable men that ever lived.' (Gore, *Creevey's Life and Times*, p. 8).

[3] Presumably Anthony Florian Madinger Willich, who published various books on diet and philosophy between 1798 and 1802.   [4] Variously spelt. See No. 1850.

negotiate the prolongation of the Armistice, have given to Lord Minto the strongest assurances that the Emperor is determined to enter into no negotiation for peace except in conjunction with your Majesty.[1] (9861–2)

[*The King's reply, St James's, 30 Oct., 12.46 p.m.*] I have just received Lord Grenville's very attentive note, as it has informed me with the situation of affairs at Vienna, and approve of his not sending the dispatches till tomorrow morning at the usual hour. (Fortescue MSS.)

[*From Lord Grenville, Cleveland Row, 31 Oct., 3.55 p.m.*] Lord Grenville has the honour to transmit to your Majesty a letter from Count Cobenzel, brought by courier from Paris. He is preparing the draft of the answer, which will be in substance that the arrival of a Minister from your Majesty in France does not depend on your Majesty, but on the French Government, which has refused to admit him except on the inadmissible condition of treating separately.

If your Majesty approves of this general idea, the draft may be laid tomorrow before such of your Majesty's servants as are in town, and the letter may be dispatched tomorrow. (9863)

[*The King's reply, Windsor, 31 Oct., 7.30 p.m.*] I have this instant received Lord Grenville's note and most cordially coincide in opinion with him as to the answer he must write to Count Cobenzel. Indeed, any other would be most improper, and therefore hope that after he has communicated it to the Ministers that may be tomorrow in town, that he will instantly send it to Paris. (Fortescue MSS.)

2274   THE DUKE OF PORTLAND *to the* KING

[*Whitehall, Friday, 31 Oct. 1800.*] Considering the magnitude of the subjects upon which your Majesty has determined to declare your royal pleasure in Council on next Wednesday the 5th of November, the Duke of Portland submits with the utmost deference to your Majesty's superior judgement the expediency of appointing the Council to be held in the Great Council Chamber, & most humbly requests the signification of your Majesty's commands respecting it.[2] (9864)

[1] Thugut resigned on 26 Sept. at a Council at Schönbrunn, disapproving of the armistice authorised by the Emperor, which led to the Treaty of Lunéville in Feb. 1801.

[2] Amongst the Councillors present were the Archbishops of Canterbury and York. Amongst the subjects discussed, it was said, was a proposition to be submitted to Parliament on the subject of the King's being crowned 'Emperor of the British Isles' (*The Times*, 6 Nov.). 'His late Majesty…was advised, at the time of the Union with Ireland, in compensation for H.M.'s abandonment, then voluntarily made, of the title of King of France, which had been so long annexed to the Crown of England, to assume the title of Emperor of the British and Hanoverian Dominions; but his late Majesty felt that his true dignity consisted in his being known to Europe and the world by the appropriated and undisputed style belonging to the British Crown.' (A. G. Stapleton, *Pol. Life of George Canning* (1831), II, 361–2. Stapleton, who was Canning's private secretary, doubtless derived his information from Canning himself.)

Cornwallis's letter to Portland, 1 Nov. 1800 on the subject of fortifications in Ireland (9865–6) is in Ross, III, 296–7. His secret and confidential letter to Portland, of the same date (f. 9869), is in *ibid.* III, 299–300.

[*Hartlebury, 8 Nov. 1800.*] I have but this day received the honour of your Majesty's most gracious letter from Windsor of Octr 31st, inclosed in a packet containing the Gottingen exercises for the present year: for both wch. fresh marks of your Majesty's favour I humbly beg leave to return my warmest thanks. I have to lament that living at this distance from Worcester I have so late received the packet, wch. I should have sent a messenger for if I could have flattered myself that so welcome a present had lain at my house there.

Permit me, Sir, in the first place, to present my sincere congratulations on your safe return to Windsor, & the benefit as well as relaxation wch. your Majesty, the Queen, and the Royal party have, I trust, found in the sea air & exercises of Weymouth.

From all I have heard of the new Archbishop of Armagh (for I have not the honour of a personal acquaintance with him) I have no doubt of his possessing those qualities wch. will enable him to discharge that important trust. And when your Majesty condescends to say that you have *persuaded* him to undertake this charge, I the more confidently believe that he is fully equal to it. If it should be so, what thanks will the Church of Ireland have to return to your Majesty for such a benefit, tho' indeed it be but small when compared with that immense service done to your whole kingdom of Ireland by the Union, wch your Majesty's persevering & wise counsels have effected.[1]

Your Majesty is pleased to mention a new, & what is more, a *good* book, received from Paris, & to intimate to me your Majesty's gracious design of ordering a copy of it to be sent to Worcester. I need not say how thankful I should be for this notice of me, & with what curiosity I should read such a book, at least so much of it as my bad head and inability to attend to anything, would permit me to do.

I am singularly affected, Sir, by your Majesty's inquiry after my health. I thank God it has been as well this summer as I can expect it to be, but at the close of eighty one, it must only be *labour & sorrow*, as the Psalmist assures us. My chief satisfaction is in hoping & trusting that it will please God to prolong your Majesty's health & enjoyment of it, to as long a term as humanity admits.

We are busy here in sending up such returns of the state & price of provisions to the Secretary's Office as may be useful on the meeting of Parliament. The account is not pleasant; but your Majesty & your Parliament will do all that can be done to relieve the distresses wch. the poor, and indeed all sorts of people feel. (9877–8)

2276 WILLIAM PITT *to the* KING, *and the reply*

[*Downing Street, Tuesday, 11 Nov. 1800, 10 p.m.*] Mr Pitt humbly begs leave to acquaint your Majesty that the Address this day was moved by Sir John Wrottes-

---

[1] Cornwallis wrote to his brother, the Bishop of Lichfield and Coventry, on 22 Dec.: 'Our Primate is rather reserved, but he seems to like his situation better than he did at first, and appears to be disposed to be as civil and accommodating to Government as could reasonably be expected after the manner of his appointment. I have lost my poor Bishop Young [see No. 2301], of whom I was so proud, and the effects of our late political contest will prevent my getting as much credit by his successor.' (Kent R.O. MSS.)

ley[1] and seconded by Mr Wm. Dickenson. It was opposed by Sir Francis Burdett, Mr Jones, Mr Robson[2] and Mr Nicholl on the ground chiefly of the war being the cause of the scarcity, and an Amendment was moved by Mr Grey to omit the expressions of reliance on the disposition of Government to peace. The Address was supported by Mr Pitt, Mr Dundas, Dr Lawrence and Mr Wilberforce, and Mr Grey's Amendment was objected to by Mr Sheridan, who wished to confine the discussion to the subject of provisions, and to avoid anything which could prevent unanimity. The Address was agreed to without a division.[3] (9887)

[*The King's reply, Queen's House, 12 Nov., 7.46 a.m.*] The last night I received Mr. Pitt's notice of the Address having been agreed to without a division, though not without some remarks from the Opposition and Amendment from Mr. Grey, which after animadversion was withdrawn.

I suppose a Committee on the high price of provisions will be immediately assembled, and that it will as much as possible be kept to effectuating a regular line of conduct in the corn trade rather than a trying of experiments which on so delicate a subject are always hazardous, but [will] encourage the importation of corn on the lowest bounty that can answer the purpose, diminish the consumption of bread unless the wheat be mixed with barley, rye, or oats, and propose the use of rice and potatoes in lieu of it for some days in the week; this latter proposition I own I should prefer to the stale bred introduced the last year. (Chatham Papers.)

[1] Sir John Wrottesley, 1st Baron Wrottesley (1771–1841), succeeded his father as 9th Baronet, 1787; a Coronation peerage, 1838. Retired from the Army, 1795. M.P. for Lichfield, 1799–1806; for Staffordshire, 1823–32; for South Staffordshire, 1832–7.

[2] Richard Bateman Robson (*d.* 1827), M.P. for Okehampton, 1796–1802, 1806–7; for Honiton, 1806; for Shaftesbury, 1812–13.

[3] *Parl. Register*, LVIII, 27–74. This curious divergence of opinion between these two prominent members of Opposition is referred to in Fox's letter to his friend O'Bryen on the 20th: 'There is some ill blood between them upon private accounts relative to money transactions, and...S[heridan] very foolishly let it out upon this occasion, for I understand he was quite hostile to G[rey] in his second speech. These things cannot be helped, but they are additional reasons to make me satisfied with secession as far as relates to myself. I have said all I could to soften Grey in regard to Sheridan, and know him enough to think that, if occasions call for their acting together, it will not be his fault if they do not...S. will never do anything quite wrong in politics, but whether he will ever go on very steadily and straightforward I doubt.' (Howick MSS.) Sheridan sent Grey a long letter of explanation, dated Sunday evening. (*Ibid.*) Grey himself wrote: 'We had a most miserable debate, in which I made a long speech, which had no other effect than that of creating a difference between me and Sheridan. I think, and I believe everybody thinks he was quite in the wrong, but this does not make it less provoking.' (Howick MSS.)

Canning thus commented on the contents of the Speech: 'The King's Speech *promises* the papers to be laid before Parliament. This is a little but very little better than publishing them in the way originally intended. The change (such as it is) they are good enough to attribute to my remonstrance. But this is very grievous & very impolitick. My only hope is that people may be so much occupied with the question of scarcity, as to pay little attention to that of Peace: it will of course be our endeavour to keep Parliament as much as possible to the former subject—and accordingly no other business of importance will be brought forward by Govt. & no *private* business allowed, if it can be prevented. It will be impossible to avoid at least one Motion from Opposition...' (Harewood MSS. [11 Nov.].)

In another letter (6 Dec.) Canning described Tyrwhitt Jones, Robson and Nicholls as 'the three Horatii' who had 'concluded the Opposition campaign...in a manner that really throws a ridicule on the whole of their joint efforts. It was very shabby in the leaders not to support their forlorn hope [in a debate on 4 Dec.] and still more so to laugh as heartily as we did at them'. (Add. MSS. 38833, f. 11.)

2277 PRINCE ADOLPHUS *to the* KING

[*Hannover, 12 Nov. 1800.*] I must do myself the honour of troubling your Majesty with a few lines to inform you that I have lately been at Brunswick, and that I found the Duchess in very good health and spirits. She was exceeding kind to me during the three days that I passed there, and she seemed very glad to see me. I should certainly not have failed to have written your Majesty word of this little excursion, but as I had lately written, and trusting you would have no objection to it, I postponed my letter till my return to Hañover. This trip to Brunswick was occasioned by a visit I paid to Count Schwicheldt, one of your Chamberlains, whose estate is but ten English miles from that town. I therefore could not refuse myself the pleasure of calling on the Duchess whom I had not seen for three years, and I hope your Majesty will approve of what I have done, the more so as the Duchess reproached me for not having been at Brunswick for so long a time. I cannot express what I felt on seeing my aunt on account of her likeness to your Majesty; and she rendered me very happy in talking of you in a manner as did my heart good to hear. I hope that soon the time will come when you will allow me to go over to England for a short time, and I do assure your Majesty that nothing can render me happyer than to have the opportunity of waiting on you. (48558)

2278 LORD GRENVILLE *to the* KING, *and the reply*

[*Cleveland Row, 12 Nov. 1800, 11 p.m.*] As Lord Grenville is not quite sure that what he had the honour to mention to your Majesty today respecting the rice was correct, he has taken the liberty to send your Majesty a small pamphlet containing the printed receipt, which Lady Grenville[1] informs him she has exactly followed, except that she thinks it better to put the rice into cold water instead of hot, as is there mentioned.[2] (9888)

[*The King's reply, Queen's House, 13 Nov. 1800, 7.50 a.m.*] I am sensible of Lord Grenville's attention in sending a pamphlet containing the printed receipt of the mode of dressing rice for the poor; I have no doubt that Lady Grenville is perfectly right in preferring the putting rice into cold water to boiling water. (Fortescue MSS.)

[1] Lord Grenville married (1792) Anne (1772–1864), daughter of Thomas Pitt, 1st Baron Camelford.
[2] Letters were pouring into the Home Office at this time on the subject of the food shortages and the resulting disturbances, with requests that the Government should adopt such remedial measures as were practicable. Lord Auckland wrote to Lord Sheffield on 24 Dec. from Palace Yard, Westminster: '... You will be surprised at the economy of the tables here. Mr. Fagel, who has just been with me, tells me that he dined two or three days ago with Lord Grenville, and there was no bread whatever. I dined yesterday with Mr. Pitt. We each of us had a small bit of old (and bad) bread weighing about an oz.½, and there was no more in the bread basket—nor (of which I complained) any rice on the table—and I understand that the same plan is following at all the tables at this end of the town, but (as yet) operates slowly among the sleek and greasy citizens.'

2279   WILLIAM PITT *to the* KING, *and the reply*

[*Downing Street, Thursday, 13 Nov. 1800.*] Mr Pitt humbly begs leave to submit to your Majesty what he has taken the liberty of preparing as an answer to the Address of the House of Commons[1] to be presented this day. (9889)

[*The King's reply, Queen's House, 13 Nov.*] The proposed answer to the Address the House of Commons will present this day as transmitted by Mr. Pitt, meets with my fullest approbation. (Chatham Papers.)

2280   EARL SPENCER *to the* KING

[*Admiralty, 15 Nov. 1800.*] Earl Spencer has the honour of laying before your Majesty the proceedings of a court martial on a deserter who afterwards entered into the enemy's service & was taken in a prize recaptured from a French privateer. The case appears to have much aggravation in it, and the man's character to have been very bad. Earl Spencer therefore humbly submits to your Majesty that it will be adviseable to order the sentence to be carried into immediate execution. (9890)

2281   LORD GRENVILLE *to the* KING, *and the reply*

[*Cleveland Row, 16 Nov. 1800, 11 p.m.*] Lord Grenville has the honour humbly to submit to your Majesty the draft, which was this day settled at the meeting of your Majesty's servants, for the answer to M. de Cobentzl's letter. (9891)

[*The King's reply, Windsor, 17 Nov., 7.35 a.m.*] The answer prepared by Lord Grenville seems perfectly proper according to diplomatic etiquet, but I confess my nature would have inclined to a little more national dignity, the explicitly declaring that as the enemy have so long abstained from granting passports for a British negociator that it would now be unbecoming to receive them if sent. (Fortescue MSS.)

2282   EVAN NEPEAN *to the* KING

[*Admiralty, Tuesday night, 18 Nov. 1800.*] Mr. Nepean communicated to Mr. Pitt yesterday all the circumstances that had recently taken place in respect to Ernst[2] and after a full consideration of the subject Mr Pitt was of opinion that the best thing to be done would be to prevent (if possible) his Majesty's being farther troubled by this man, and with that view has directed a warrant to be prepared appointing him to be Comptroller of the Customs at Surinam, worth about £800 per annum.

Mr. Nepean explained very fully to Mr. Pitt the opinions entertained by his Majesty of the inconvenience which may hereafter be felt by the allowing a man

---

[1] The Address in reply to the King's Speech delivered at the opening of the Session.

[2] G. Ernst was a Page of the Backstairs (salary, £80 a year). His name disappears from the Royal Kalendar.

who has behaved so improperly to carry his point; and, that though his Majesty did not think proper to oppose his being provided for in the manner proposed, his Majesty wished it to be distinctly understood that this appointment was not given to him in consequence of any interposition of his Majesty in his favour. Mr Pitt's opinions so exactly coincided with those of his Majesty on the subject, that nothing but the consideration of getting Ernst out of the way would have induced him (unless his Majesty had been pleased to signify his commands to him to do so) to have bestowed the office upon him.

Mr. Nepean apprized Mr Pitt at the same time of his Majesty's intention of appointing a successor to Ernst in the office he now holds, and on Mr Nepean's explaining to Mr Pitt the effect that this arrangement would have on the mother, (Mrs Ernst) he at once removed all difficulties on that head, by expressing his intention of giving her an ample compensation for the loss she would sustain by being deprived of the advantage of her son's apartments at St. James's.

Mr Pitt advised Mr Nepean to make this communication directly to his Majesty rather than convey it to his Majesty thro' any other channel. This explanation he trusts will be accepted as an apology for his presuming to write to his Majesty on the subject. (9892–3)

2283 WILLIAM PITT *to the* KING

[*Downing Street, Wednesday noon, 19 Nov. 1800.*] Mr Pitt being prevented from paying his duty to your Majesty at St James's this day (which he trusts your Majesty will have the goodness to excuse on account of his necessary attendance at the Committee) takes this mode of humbly acquainting your Majesty that he received some time since a letter from Lord Pembroke, expressing in the warmest terms his grateful sense of your Majesty's condescension and goodness in graciously thinking of him in the creation of Marquisses, but begging upon the whole to be permitted to remain in his present rank. Mr Pitt's motive for troubling your Majesty at this time is that he believes Lord Pembroke may be desirous of soliciting an audience to repeat his thanks to your Majesty.[1] (9894)

[1] Lord Pembroke's letter to Pitt is dated 21 Oct.: 'I trust the short period which will have elapsed between your receipt of my last letter and of this, will not be deemed an unreasonable use of the indulgence which I conceive was granted me, that I might be enabled thereby to consult my friends and the better to make up my own mind on a subject which so materially concerns my family. I have made the best use in my power of this time by giving the subject the most attentive consideration I could bestow on it, and the result is, that I beg leave with all humility and respect to decline the promotion which his Majesty has been graciously pleased to place within my reach. In doing this I trust I shall not appear in any degree less sensible than I ought to this fresh instance of his Majesty's goodness towards me, or to that kind protection with which his Majesty has uninterruptedly honored me even from my childhood. I am well aware of the King's extreme condescension in having been thus pleased to express his willingness to gratify me with so honorable an encrease of my rank in the Peerage, but there are reasons, unnecessary for me to detail, which yet appear to my mind a sufficient inducement for my declining to avail myself of it on the present occasion. At the same time I must allways recollect with the most heartfelt gratitude this proof added to so many which I have before experienced of his Majesty's favorable opinion of me, and if it were possible I should find in it a new motive for my unalterable attachment to his person and for the zeal with which I am devoted to his service ' (W. Dacres Adams MSS.)

The Times suggested that he refused the higher rank on account of his younger children whose courtesy titles might incapacitate them from, or disincline them to follow, other active professions.

2284 EARL SPENCER *to the* KING

[*Admiralty, 20 Nov. 1800.*] Earl Spencer has the honour of laying before your Majesty the proceedings of a court martial on a corporal of marines on board the Isis for striking a serjeant. The Court have adjudged the offender to suffer death, but as there appear to be strong circumstances of mitigation and the corporal has borne an excellent character, they have humbly recommended him to your Majesty's mercy, and Earl Spencer on the above considerations humbly submits to your Majesty that it may be proper to grant him your Majesty's pardon. (9895)

2285 THE DUKE OF PORTLAND *to the* KING

[*Burlington House, Saturday, 22 Nov. 1800.*] The observations which your Majesty had condescended to make on the Lord Lieutenant's letter on the subject of the Privy Council, & your Majesty's orders to the Duke of Portland to consult the Lord President & Mr Pitt were received by him this morning, & his endeavours were immediately used to obey them, but without success; he had however the good fortune to meet the Lord Chancellor & Lord Grenville who unite with him in most humbly submitting to your Majesty that however inaccurately or indistinctly the Lord Lieutenant may have expressed the motion he wished the Duke of Portland to offer to your Majesty's consideration for calling the Lord Primate & the other persons mentioned in that letter to the Council Board, the Lord Lieutenant's object was solely to obtain places for them at the Council Board in Ireland, the continuance of which is expressly provided for by the third & last clause of the Act of Union, which enacts, besides the future use of the Great Seal of Ireland, that, 'Your Majesty may, so long as you shall think fit, continue the Privy Council of Ireland, to be your Majesty's Privy Council for that part of the United Kingdom called Ireland', it would therefore seem to the Duke of Portland, & in that conclusion the Lord Chancellor & Lord Grenville concur, that if your Majesty shall be graciously pleased to consent to the Lord Lieutenant's request in favor of the Lord Primate & the other persons named in his letter of the 15th instant, that they will be exclusively members of the Privy Council in Ireland, and be no more intitled to sit at your Majesty's Council Board in this kingdom than they would have been if the Union had not taken place.

In laying at your Majesty's feet the dispatches which have been this day received from the Lord Lieutenant, the Duke of Portland feels it to be his duty to represent to your Majesty that the appointment of an efficient Master of the Rolls is a measure which the Lord Chancellor of Ireland, when he was last here, frequently & fully discussed with several of your Majesty's servants & particularly with the Lord Chancellor, who is fully persuaded of the propriety & necessity of it, & who is therefore the forwardest of your Majesty's servants in most humbly recommending the appointment as well deserving the sanction of your Majesty.[1] (9896–8)

---

[1] The 2nd Earl of Glandore (1752–1815) and the 1st Earl of Carysfort (1751–1828) were the Joint Masters of the Rolls [I.], 1789–1801. Sir Michael Smith (1740–1808), who was created an Irish Baronet in 1799, was appointed Master of the Rolls [I.], in June 1801. He resigned in June 1806.

The Marquess of Buckingham wrote to Pitt on 4 Sept.: 'The Mastership of the I[rish] Rolls is most uncertain in its profits, depending on the sale of the inferior offices. This and the expediency of assimilat-

[*26 Nov. 1800.*] Your Majesty's goodness to me has been unbounded: it is impressed on my mind beyond all power of utterance, but it leads me most humbly to represent that a slight has most undeservedly been put on me by the manner in which I was removed from that office to which it was your Majesty's pleasure that I should be called,[1] and it leads me to cherish some hope that the means of doing it may not incur your Majesty's disapprobation, or so long as I live it should remain unsollicited.

It is my misfortune to feel acutely the wrong done me; to this moment it has remained unexplained, and I regret that I should accidentally have stood in the way of any design Mr. Pitt might have formed, but of all men I least deserved it at his hands, for I laboured to serve your Majesty's cause thro' him and never asked the slightest favor at his hands.

Born in England and representing a family which some centuries ago was honoured with an English Peerage, it will not be wondered at that with all humility I express a hope that this honor might now be accorded to me, not as a reward, for I merit none, but as the means of publickly doing away that stain which my conscience says I have not merited.

To your Majesty's judgement and benevolence I most humbly submit this request. (9899)

2287 *Letters from* LORD GRENVILLE *to the* KING, *and a reply*

[*Cleveland Row, 27 Nov. 1800, 11 p.m.*] Lord Grenville has the honour humbly to submit to your Majesty a letter received this day from one of the Russia merchants; and as the measure there proposed appears both to Mr Pitt & to Lord Grenville to be indispensably necessary, and to be very pressing in point of time, Lord Grenville trusts your Majesty will excuse the liberty he takes in humbly requesting to be honoured with your Majesty's commands, respecting the holding of a Council tomorrow at such hour as your Majesty may be pleased to appoint.

Lord Grenville has but just received from the House of Commons Mr Pitt's answer; which has prevented his writing to your Majesty earlier.[2] (9900–1)

[*The King's reply, Queen's House, 27 Nov. 1800, 11.35 p.m.*] When any public business calls pressingly for my attendance I never make the smallest difficulty. I desire therefore Lord Grenville will give notice that I shall hold a Council here as early as may be convenient for the members of the Privy Council. I highly approve of the measure proposed and I am certain with such a *strange* character as that of the Russian Emperor nothing can be gained but by shewing him he is

ing Irish to English courts would be a sufficient reason for the new modelling the office. I gave (in 1789) the office jointly to Lords Glandore and Carysfort, who have both expressed and even lately to me their earnest wish to get the value of it in some other way. It is tenable with a seat in our House of Commons, for Rigby held it for 26 years.' (W. Dacres Adams MSS.)

¹ See No. 2212.

² News had just reached England from Hamburg that the Tsar had again ordered an embargo on all British ships in Russian ports, of which there were about 70 in Riga and 120 at Petersburg.

not feared. I desire I may know what hour Lord Grenville proposes for assembling the Privy Council as I totally leave it [to] his decision. (Fortescue MSS.)

[*From Lord Grenville, Cleveland Row, 27 Nov., 11.45 p.m.*] Lord Grenville is this moment honoured with your Majesty's commands. He has written to Mr. Fawkener to desire him to take the necessary measures for a Privy Council at twelve tomorrow; as he imagines that to be as early an hour as it will be possible to collect, (with such short notice) the necessary number of Privy Counsellors.[1] (9902)

2288 *Letters from* WILLIAM PITT *to the* KING, *and a reply*

[*Downing Street, Friday, 28 Nov. 1800, 1.30 a.m.*] Mr Pitt humbly begs leave to acquaint your Majesty that a Motion was made by Mr Tierney grounded on the conduct of the war, the state of alliances, and the finance and internal state of the country for a Committee on the State of the Nation. The Motion was opposed by Mr Pitt, Mr Canning, Mr S. Thornton and Mr Secretary Dundas, and was supported by Mr. Grey, Mr W. Smith, Mr Bouverie, and Mr Tyrwhitt Jones. The Motion was negatived on a division by 154 to 37.[2] (9903)

[*From Pitt, Downing Street, Monday, 1 Dec. 1800, 11 p.m.*] Mr Pitt humbly begs leave to acquaint your Majesty that an Address was this day moved by Mr Sheridan, requesting your Majesty to enter into no new engagements with Austria which could prevent a separate peace with France. The Motion was supported by Mr Grey and opposed by Mr Windham and by Mr Secretary Dundas whose speech produced the greatest effect on the House, and (with the exception of a short and feeble reply from Mr Sheridan) terminated the debate, when the Motion was rejected by 156 to 35.[3]

[1] At this meeting of the Privy Council it was decided to lay a counter-embargo on all Russian ships in British ports. (Stanhope, III, Appendix, p. xxii.)

[2] *Parl. Register*, LVIII, 267–317. Canning, whose speech was reported in *Th e Times* and at greater length in the *Parl. Register*, referred to it in a letter to his uncle, the Rev. W. Leigh, on the 28th: 'Well— are you satisfied? I suppose you will say No, for you see no account of my speech in the papers; but that you know cannot be helped on a day when Pitt speaks for three or four hours, & goes through the whole of a subject. But I did speak, & in answer to Grey, as you desired—& by answer I do not mean only next after him, but speech against speech & topick against topick—I have no notion of his setting up for an ex-Minister, pretending to CLOSE the debate forsooth with a pompous no-meaning speech, expressive of his approbation or disapprobation of what Pitt has said, & in a tone as if he were not to be answered. I shall not suffer that—I can tell him—& so I believe I shewed him yesterday to the great indignation, I believe, of himself & of his friends who had just elected him Leader of the Party; & to the great amusement (as I could plainly see) of Sheridan, who was not easily persuaded to concur in such an election...' (Harewood MSS.)

The King's reply at 7.48 a.m. that day is in Stanhope, III, Appendix, p. xxii.

[3] *Parl. Register*, LVIII, 327–70. Canning thus referred to the debate in a letter to Frere, 2 Dec.: 'The debate last night went off very well (publicly) but not so well (privately), as it afforded me no opportunity of speaking. As Windham had given way to me the night before, I did not contest with him the following Sheridan (and indeed I am not fond of following Sheridan, speech for speech, on a Motion of his own, though I do not mind jostling with him in debate)—and after Grey (who spoke with great ability and some effect, but very *answerably*) Dundas started, and of course was called to by the Speaker. I saw it would not do, and therefore did not rise, especially as Jinksbury [i.e. Hawkesbury] was extremely anxious to make a demonstration. The worst is that Grey, I am afraid, has exhausted himself and has

Mr Pitt humbly takes the liberty of submitting a warrant giving an authority to Mr Wickham, which seems requisite, to give him a regular superintendance of the pecuniary points under his directions.[1] (9904–5)

[*The King's reply, Windsor, 2 Dec. 1800.*] It gives me much satisfaction to be apprized by Mr. Pitt's note of Mr. Sheridan's Motion being rejected by so considerable a majority the last night, and that Mr. Secretary Dundas's speech in opposition to the proposal had so much [effect] on the House; indeed, the idea of Mr. Sheridan on the first view seems so improper that it might easily be answered by one of less Parliamentary abilities.

The appointment for Mr. Wickham seems highly necessary, as it frees him from any other controul but the Treasury which his present situation requires. (Chatham Papers.)

2289 THE EARL OF ASHBURNHAM[2] *to the* KING

[*2 Dec. 1800.*] I most humbly beseech your Majesty to pardon an old servant of the Crown (perhaps the oldest, I having had the honor to be appointed in 1748 a Lord of the Bedchamber to your Majesty's grandfather), in presuming with great humility to request your Majesty that whenever you shall be pleas'd to add to the list of Marquis's, that your Majesty would be graciously pleas'd to include me amongst those on whom you intend to confer that honor. My age & infirmity have occasion'd me to lead to a degree a retir'd life, but I have the pleasing consolation to be certain that in the person of my son[3] that your Majesty will find a subject zealously & actively attach'd to your person and Government. (9906)

2290 *Letters from the* DUKE OF PORTLAND *to the* KING

[*Burlington House, Tuesday even., 2 Dec. 1800.*] The Duke of Portland most humbly begs leave to lay himself at your Majesty's feet & to implore your Majesty's forgiveness for having presumed, without having previously received your Majesty's commands, to signify to the House of Lords that your Majesty would please to be attended with the joint Address of the two Houses touching the high price of provisions tomorrow at two o clock at your Majesty's Palace of St James.

Some inadvertence or misunderstanding on the part of the Lords with White Staves, who were ordered by the House on Friday last to request your Majesty's

nothing left for a Motion of his own. Indeed he said something like this last night. If so, I am, very much against my will, a speech in *pocket*, which, what to do with, I cannot tell.' (Add. MSS. 38833, f. 9.)

In another letter of the same date Canning remarked: 'Dundas's [speech] one of the greatest *effect* that I ever heard in the House of Commons. Sheridan's opening speech very much below himself, & his reply stupid & feeble. Windham's not very good upon the whole, nor very useful, though (as is always the case) with much good matter in it.' (Harewood MSS.)

[1] In the Ann Arbor typescript the date of this letter is wrongly given as 1 Oct.

[2] John, 2nd Earl of Ashburnham (1724–1812); succeeded his father, 1737. A Lord of the Bedchamber, 1748–62; Master of the Great Wardrobe, 1765–75; First Lord of the Bedchamber and Groom of the Stole, 1775–82.

[3] George, 3rd Earl of Ashburnham (1760–1830), his father's second but first surviving son. A Lord of the Bedchamber to the Prince of Wales, 1784–95. Summoned by writ, March 1803 in his father's Barony, as Lord Ashburnham. He had been styled Viscount St Asaph until that date. See No. 365 n.

pleasure upon this subject, having kept the House in ignorance respecting it, & the House of Commons finding itself consequently in the same state, Mr Ryder was desired by the Speaker & some of the most respectable members to represent to the Duke of Portland the dilemma in which the House of Commons would be placed, should your Majesty have appointed tomorrow to be attended with the joint Address, which it was presumed had been your Majesty's determination upon account of the importance of your Majesty's sanction being given to the measure with the least possible delay, & that the House of Commons should rise today without being informed of it. The Duke of Portland therefore immediately consulted with such of your Majesty's confidential servants as happened to be in the House of Lords, & accordingly took upon himself to make use of your Majesty's royal name in the manner he has stated, & a Message[1] was sent to the House of Commons to acquaint them that your Majesty would be attended with the joint Address at the place & time above-mentioned. For these reasons, which are with all humility submitted to your Majesty, the Duke of Portland ventures to hope that your Majesty will graciously condescend to pardon his presumption. (9907–8)

[*Burlington House, Friday even., 5 Dec.*] The laying before your Majesty the Lord Lieutenant's dispatch (Military) of the 13th of last month, the Duke of Portland feels it to be his duty to represent most humbly to your Majesty that the Duke of York, to whom, by his Royal Highness's permission the Duke of Portland is in the habit of submitting the Lord Lieutenant's correspondence upon military arrangements prior to its being offer'd to your Majesty's consideration, has been pleased to observe that, in regard to a successor being appointed to Captain Longfield[2] of the 6th Dragoon Guards by purchase, as Captain Longfield does not appear to have purchased any of his Commissions and as he has not served twenty years, his Royal Highness does not consider him entitled to receive the value of a troop on retiring from the service unless there are particular circumstances in his case known to the Lord Lieutenant which may afford a plea for this mark of your Majesty's favor being extended to Captain Longfield. His Royal Highness has also further observed on the proposed exchange between Captain Ridge of the 46th Regiment and Captain Shawe on the half pay of the 60th, that unless Captain Shawe did not receive a pecuniary difference when placed on half pay, and admitting that he did not, unless he declared upon his honour that on being restored to full pay, it is his intention to serve, the exchange ought not to be allowed. The Duke of Portland most anxiously hopes that your Majesty will graciously condescend to receive the remarks herewith submitted to your Majesty as a mark of his dutifull attention to your Majesty's service, & that your Majesty will not refuse your sanction to the means he has taken to obtain them. (9909–10)

[1] Mr Ord and Mr Walker brought the following Message from the House of Lords: 'The Lords have commanded us to acquaint the House that his Majesty has appointed tomorrow at two of the clock, to be attended with the Address of both Houses of Parliament at his Palace of Saint James; and that their Lordships have ordered the Lord Steward and the Lord Chamberlain of his Majesty's Household to attend his Majesty therewith on the part of the Lords, and do desire this House to appoint a proportionable number of their Members to go with them.' (*H. of C.J.* LV, 890.) Ryder, William Dundas, Canning and Viscount Belgrave were appointed to go with the Lords to attend his Majesty with the Address.

[2] Lord Longueville's nephew. See No. 2301.

2291 HENRY DUNDAS *to the* KING, *and the reply*

[*Downing Street, 9 Dec. 1800, 4 p.m.*] Mr Dundas humbly transmits the accompanying papers for your Majesty's perusal. Mr Dundas has conceived it most expedient not to allow them to be the subject of circulation even amongst your Majesty's confidential servants, as the discussions they might create could only tend to encrease jealousy and disunion in the two branches of your Majesty's military service, than which nothing can be more fatal to the credit and utility of both. But as the accompanying letter and its enclosure contain, in Mr Dundas's judgement, the most correct detailed account of what passed at Ferroll and Cadiz in the course of last autumn, he did not think himself at liberty to keep them back from your Majesty's confidential perusal. (9911–12)

[*The King's reply. Windsor, 10 Dec., 8.13 a.m.*] The papers Mr. Secretary Dundas has communicated to me are curious, but it must be remembered they are drawn up by a warm man, and one perhaps not pleased at not having more the ear of both Generals, and as such a little inclined to view their conduct with a jaundiced eye. I am clear of opinion that these papers ought not to be shewn to any of the Ministers; it could not do any good and might encourage ill humour between the two services if the contents transpired; in general to them no communication ought to be made but when it is with a view to give them lights to form an opinion on a subject on which they are to be consulted, but where it is to explain the causes of the failure of any measure it is better avoided, as it must ever tend to make them talk too freely of the persons employed, which can never be desirable. (Add. MSS. 38736, f. 269.)

2292 THE DUCHESS OF WURTEMBERG *to the* KING

[*Erlangen, 10 Dec. 1800.*] I had just begun to write to your Majesty on Sunday when we received the sad news of the defeat of the Austrians on the third.[1] Your Majesty will imagine how cruel a blow this must be to us who have our all at stake and from the advantages on the 1st had flattered ourselves that things would take a better turn; though much could not be expected from a boy who had never been out of his nursery till he was sent to command the Army. It is very vexatious to those who wish well to the good cause to see our brave Archduke Charles left at Prague, and this child sent instead of him who has twice saved Germany, to command an Army on which the fate of the Continent depends.

We are now in a very unpleasant situation here, General Simschen having quitted Nuremberg and taking his whole Corps to Lauff, the French have taken possession of Nuremberg and their troops are constantly marching through this town and are quartered in all the villages round about, which makes me an absolute prisoner, as yesterday I attempted to walk round the town and at a very small distance we saw a patrol, which prevents our going out at all as in Erlangen there is no end of the French soldiers who are to be met with constantly in the streets.

[1] Moreau defeated the Austrians commanded by the Archduke John (1782–1859), one of the Emperor Francis II's younger brothers, at Hohenlinden on 2 Dec.

I imagine your Majesty will have found the new Lodge at Kew much advanced, though I fear a stop will be put to the building by the weather which begins here to be very severe and we suffer much from the cold in this paper house. If ever it pleases Providence to allow us to return home we shall enjoy every thing doubly from the uncomfortable way we have lived in now above six months. (51621–2)

2293 THOMAS COUTTS *to the* KING

[*11 Dec. 1800.*] Mr Coutts has been forced by a continual progressive increase of business to enlarge his offices and repositories—and for that purpose to apply to Parliament for an Act to throw a bridge of communication cross a street immediately behind his house in the Strand. The whole has been nearly compleated and is thought to be executed in a masterly manner and to be the first thing of its kind. He has had the honour of showing it to his Royal Highness the Duke of York, and would be too happy were it ever to be thought worthy of superior inspection. His aim through life has been that himself and his house should deserve the good opinion of his friends. He has always valued it more than any acquisition of fortune. He has happily succeeded, and in no instance has it ever been withdrawn from him —which indeed would have been a wound he could never have recovered—tho' with pride he flatters himself it never could have been deserved.

The greatest object of his honest ambition is the confidence of his Sovereign, the possession of which he would prefer to every distinction of rank or fortune. (9913)

2294 THE BISHOP OF WORCESTER (RICHARD HURD) *to the* KING

[*Hartlebury, 11 Dec. 1800.*] I had the honour of your Majesty's gracious letter from Windsor of Novr 14th, & on Monday last the 8th inst. I received M. Laharpe's[1] *Cours de literature ancienne & moderne*, wch. your Majesty was pleased to send me.

Mr Giffardiere[2] is so conversant in the French language & literature, that he cannot be mistaken about the general merit of the composition.

As to the *work* itself, it is so long, branching out into ten volumes, that I despair of ever reading it through in any reasonable time & with any degree of attention. But in running over the contents, & casting an eye on some chapters, I find some things well & properly said, others with less care & judgement. His criticism seems slight, but expressed in the French manner, that is, in many words, & those rather too fine & florid. I suppose *M. Laharpe* to be a poet by profession, for he enlarges most on the subject of poetry. Yet he says little of the English poets; & I do not wonder at it, for they are very different from the French. I have not observed any traces of licentiousness in this miscellany: but there was little room for it in a treatise on polite letters. What of this sort may insinuate itself into the remaining volumes, wch. are to treat of *the Philosophy of the 18th century*, I cannot say.

[1] Jean François de La Harpe (1739–1803). He published his lectures, *Lycée, ou Cours de Littérature* between 1799 and 1805.
[2] The Rev. Mr Guiffardière had been the Prince of Wales's and Prince Frederick's French Master, at a salary of £200 a year.

On the whole, if we are to form an idea of antient literature from any modern compilation, I should prefer the sage *Rollin*[1] to this brilliant Master of the *Lyceum*; an affected word, which the modern French have adopted instead of University.

But I must not trouble your Majesty with more words, at so busy a time, & on such a subject. I only beg leave to return my humble thanks for this literary present. (9914)

2295   LORD GRENVILLE *to the* KING, *and the reply*

[*Cleveland Row, 12 Dec. 1800, 11 p.m.*] Lord Grenville is very sorry to acquaint your Majesty that French papers received today contain the account of a victory obtained by General Moreau over the Austrians, on the 3d of this month.

Lord Grenville incloses a copy of the letter published at Paris. (9916)

[*The King's reply, Windsor, 13 Dec., 9.02 a.m.*] I am infinitely sorry, though the account as yet is only from France, that Genl. Moreau has obtained a victory over the Austrians on the 3rd. I must hope the disproportion of loss cannot have been so great as it is stated, but any disaster at the beginning of the fresh contest I should fear will have a bad effect on the too timid counsels of Vienna. (Fortescue MSS.)

2296   PRINCE EDWARD *to the* KING

[*Kensington, 13 Dec. 1800.*] Relying on your Majesty's justice and goodness, which I have so often experienced, I have at last brought myself to intrude for a moment upon your time, humbly to represent that the apartments in Kensington Palace which you were graciously pleased to allot for my town residence are at present so comfortless as to be almost uninhabitable, unless they undergo some indispensable repairs and a few alterations which, though in themselves trifling, are such that without them my accommodations must ever remain extremely incomplete. I am sensible that the application should have been made through the Lord Chamberlain, but he declines all interference, saying that he had your Majesty's positive orders that the appartments should only be made wind and water tight. Thus circumstanced, as the regular channel of application is closed, I felt confident that you would excuse my presumption in communicating my situation directly to yourself. In order not to be under the necessity of taking up any part of your Majesty's time with a detail of the inconveniences from which I am at present suffering at Kensington I have ventured to request Mr. Wyatt to call in here, on his way to Windsor, to whom I have shewn every part of my Appartments, and fully explained their defects. If therefore you condescend to give my humble representation a moment's thought, permit me to sollicit that you would allow him to state what he has seen. I shall then hope that your Majesty, being convinced of the urgency of something being done for me, may be induced to give him such orders as will insure some plan being adopted to add those comforts to my residence with which I am sure it was your gracious intention that I should be indulged. (45993)

---

[1] Charles Rollin (1661–1741), who published his *Histoire Ancienne* between 1730 and 1738.

[*Cleveland Row, 13 Dec. 1800, 11 p.m.*] Lord Grenville has the honour to acquaint your Majesty that he has this day seen M. Ehrensward,[1] who, contrary to what had been stated, appears to be charged with credentials to your Majesty, the copy of which Lord Grenville has the honour to inclose.

Your Majesty's servants were of opinion (Lord Grenville having this day stated the question to them) that the difficulties which have arisen respecting the reception of Mr Talbot & Mr. Netzel ought not to prevent M. d' Ehrensward's being received and admitted to present his credentials to your Majesty in the character with which he is invested for this special Mission.

If your Majesty should be graciously pleased to approve of this opinion, Lord Grenville will, with your Majesty's permission, appoint M. d' Ehrensward for Wednesday next. (9917–18)

[*The King's reply, Windsor, 14 Dec., 8.58 ?p.m.*] As M. Ehrensward has credentials the difficulties concerning Mr. Talbot cannot be admitted as sufficient reason to decline giving him an audience. Lord Grenville may therefore appoint him for Wednesday.

My son Augustus has been so unfixed about his wintering in Portugal that I have never mentioned his intention to Lord Grenville. He came yesterday and expressed a wish to embark on Wednesday at Portsmouth. I desire therefore that Lord Grenville will by the Endymion, which is the frigate that carries him, write to Mr. Frere[2], that he may notify his arrival to M. de Pinto,[3] and express that it is for the benefit of the climate; that he is to be there incognito under the name of one of my Hannoverian courtiers.[4] (Fortescue MSS.)

[*From Lord Grenville, Cleveland Row, 14 Dec. 1800, 11 p.m.*] Lord Grenville has been honoured with your Majesty's commands respecting his Royal Highness Prince Augustus, and he will immediately write to Mr Frere in the manner your Majesty has been pleased to direct.

Count Starhemberg received yesterday a dispatch from Count Cobenzl, of which he has this day delivered to Lord Grenville the inclosed copy. His messenger, who had conversed with the officer who brought to Lunéville the account of General Moreau's late success, reports it to have been much less considerable than it was represented by the French. But Lord Grenville does not think much stress can be laid on this sort of information. It is however satisfactory to observe that this event has not altered M. de Cobenzl's intention as to his quitting Lunéville. (9919–20)

[1] Baron Ehrensvärd, Envoy from the King of Sweden. Grenville wrote on the 16th: 'I see no appearance in Ehrenswerd's conversation of a better disposition on the part of Sweden. We have as yet had only one unofficial conversation, but he is presented tomorrow, and in our first ministerial conference I am to make the same categorical demand as we now make to Denmark for an explanation of their negotiations or engagements on the subject of armed neutrality, and to tell him plainly that till we are satisfied on that head we will discuss nothing else.' (*Dropmore Papers*, VI, 408.)

[2] Frere, the British Minister to Portugal, arrived at Lisbon at the end of December.

[3] The chief Minister at Lisbon.

[4] Prince Augustus sailed from Portsmouth on Sunday the 28th.

[*The King's reply, Windsor, 15 Dec., 7.57 a.m.*] Considering the magnitude of the object entrusted to Count Cobenzl, it seems rather extraordinary that he should so long have deferred acknowledging the receipt of Count Starhemberg's [despatch], and I think in it he has let out more than he meant, I mean an appearance that, could he have secured the evacuation of Tuscany, he might not have been found so firm on the joint negociation, but on which he now holds a firm language, the other object having failed.

The account given by the messenger of the language of the French officer who brought the account of Moreau's success seems probable, and I trust the check, though it may have cost some lives, will prove no more than a failure of an attack on the enemy which, if it had succeeded, might have given good spirits to the Austrian troops. But the account in the French papers is coloured so highly that it gives that degree of comfort, the shewing that at the present moment a supposed great success is necessary to feed the hopes of the Parisians, and consequently that a reverse of fortune would soon prove fatal to Bonaparte. (Fortescue MSS.)

[*From Lord Grenville, Cleveland Row, 15 Dec., 11 p.m.*] Lord Grenville has the honour humbly to acquaint your Majesty that Mr. Moberley,[1] one of the members of the Russian factory, arrived this day from Petersburgh, having received a passport from that Government, in order that he might communicate to your Majesty's servants some general insinuations for the restoration of good understanding between the two Courts, by your Majesty's agreeing that the Maltese flag should be hoisted at Malta.

Lord Grenville also transmits to your Majesty a letter he has received from Mr. Elliot[2] on the same subject.

This business, together with the situation of affairs with respect to the Courts of Copenhagen & Stockholm, having been laid by Lord Grenville before your Majesty's servants, they this day came to an unanimous resolution on the subject, the result of which Lord Grenville has the honour humbly to submit for your Majesty's consideration.

If your Majesty should be pleased to approve of the ideas there stated, they will be executed by tomorrow's mail. (9921–2)

(*Enclosure*)
[*Cabinet Minute, Downing Street, 15 Dec.*]

Present:[3] The Lord Chancellor, Duke of Portland, Earl Spencer, Mr Chancellor of the Exchequer, Mr Secretary Dundas, Lord Grenville.

[1] He belonged to the English Factory at Petersburg, and, returning home *via* Berlin and Hamburg, he brought to the Foreign Office information about the state of Russian opinion, which was said to be inflamed against the Tsar for his recent acts of violence against British ships and seamen.

[2] Hugh Elliot, the British Minister at Dresden. His letter of the 11th from Dresden referring to Kalitschev's appointment as Russian Vice-Chancellor in succession to Count Panin, is in *Dropmore Papers*, VI, 405.

[3] It will be noticed that Lord Liverpool's name is often missing from Cabinet Minutes. His health was deteriorating. He wrote to the Duke of Portland from his seat, Addiscombe Place, on 9 Oct.: 'I

It was agreed humbly to recommend to his Majesty,

That with respect to the insinuations received from Russia thro' Mr Maberley, and M. de Kalitcheff,[1] the answer to be returned should be by transmitting to the latter, thro' Mr Elliot, the copy of Lord Grenville's letter to Count Rostopchin; adding that his Majesty will not enter into any negotiation untill the embargo is removed, and the Ministerial communications renewed between the two Courts by persons properly accredited.

That if this is now done, the King will be ready to enter into confidential explanations with the Emperor, respecting the grounds of every part of his Majesty's conduct with respect to Russia since the beginning of the misunderstanding between the two Courts.

That orders should be sent to Mr Drummond[2] to demand a categorical explanation as to the existence, nature and extent of the engagements reported to be entered into by Denmark with other Powers respecting the privileges of neutral navigation.

That M. d'Ehrensward should, in the first conference he may desire with Lord Grenville after the delivery of his letters of credence, be apprized that the King requires a similar explanation from the Court of Stockholm, before any Ministerial discussion of any other point can be entered into. (9923–4)

[*The King's reply, Windsor, 16 Dec., 9.02 a.m.*] It is impossible that a Minute of Cabinet could be drawn more congenial to my sentiments than that transmitted this morning by Lord Grenville. It contains the dignity and good temper which becomes the occasion. It may be of great use in hindering the Northern Powers from entering into measures that must be withstood from hence with open force, and to Russia shews a willingness of treating, provided the abominable act of aggression is conceded. I desire no time may be lost in putting the whole into effect. (Fortescue MSS.)

2298   EARL SPENCER *to the* KING, *and the reply*

[*Admiralty, 16 Dec. 1800.*] Earl Spencer is concerned to be under the necessity of laying before your Majesty the proceedings of a court martial on two men of the St George by which they have been sentenced to suffer death for the commission of a most detestable and unnatural crime; and the proofs being very clear, Earl Spencer humbly submits to your Majesty that the sentence should be carried into immediate execution. (9925)

am so very ill with the rheumatism, a disorder I never had before, that I cannot walk at all except on plain ground, and from the great pain it gives me I have had no rest for some nights, so that my general health begins to be affected by it, I went to town yesterday to attend the Cabinet.' (Add. MSS. 38311, ff. 79–83.) By 24 Oct. he was incapable of writing, and his private secretary, Thomas Lack, attended to his correspondence. In Oct. 1803 he was still, in a great degree, deprived of the use of his arms and legs. (Add. MSS. 38191, ff. 94, 162.)

[1] His name was variously spelt. He had been Russian Minister in Vienna for about a year, and he took up his new appointment at home in Dec. 1800.

[2] See No. 1637.

[*The King's reply, Windsor, 17 Dec., 7.40 a.m.*] There cannot be a doubt of the propriety of the sentence of the court martial on the two seamen of the St. George for the commission of a most detestable and unnatural crime. Earl Spencer is therefore to give the proper order for its being enforced. (Althorp MSS.)

2299   WILLIAM PITT *to the* KING

[*Downing Street, 17 Dec. 1800.*] Mr. Pitt having been prevented, by the necessity of attending the Corn Committee on some points which did not admit of delay, from paying his duty to your Majesty at St James's, feels himself obliged to trouble your Majesty by submitting an application which he has received from Lord Buckingham, and of which the circumstances may, he trusts, appear not undeserving of your Majesty's favorable consideration. Lord Buckingham's property and connections in Ireland have rendered him desirous of preserving the Nugent title in his family, and with that view he is anxious to obtain from your Majesty's gracious favor the grant of an Irish Barony of Nugent to Lady Buckingham,[1] with a remainder to his second son on whom he means to settle his Irish estate. Mr Pitt ventures to submit this request to your Majesty in the hope that the motive to it will appear to be not unreasonable, and the compliance with it (if your Majesty should be graciously pleased to approve of it) not likely to be attended with any inconvenience.[2] (9926–7)

2300   THE DUCHESS OF WURTEMBERG *to the* KING

[*Erlangen, 20 Dec. 1800.*] By the last letter that I had the honour to write to your Majesty you will have seen that the French had taken possession of Nuremberg, which I understand they have left this morning at four o'clock after having kept the town quite shut these last two days. The day before yesterday there was an action between Klenau's[3] and Augerau's[4] Corps; one could hear every shot as distinctly as if we were at a Review. I own that the idea that every shot took away some lives had great effect on me, but the trusting Providence would at last have mercy on us and let the good cause have success gave me great courage. However the affair that day, though sharp, had no decided advantage. Yesterday the Austrians took four canons and would have taken the military chest but the carriage broke down and the peasants harnassing the horses to the chest itself drew it into a Prussian village, which being unfortunately neutral the Austrians did not dare

---

[1] The Marquess of Buckingham (1753–1813) married (1775) Mary Elizabeth (*d.* 1812) daughter of Earl Nugent [I.] (*c.* 1702–88). On 26 Dec. she was created Baroness Nugent [I.], with a special remainder to Lord George Nugent-Grenville, her second son (1789–1850). Lord Nugent was M.P. for Buckingham, 1810–12; for Aylesbury, 1812–32 and 1847–50; a Lord of the Treasury, 1830–2, and Lord High Commissioner to the Ionian Islands, 1832–5.

The Marquess had sounded his brother Lord Grenville about a Nugent Barony as early as 21 July (*Dropmore Papers*, VI, 273).

[2] The King's favourable reply on the 18th is in Stanhope, III, Appendix, p. xxii.

[3] The Austrian General.

[4] Pierre François Charles Augereau (1757–1816), Duke of Castiglione, Marshal of France. He fought at Lodi, Castiglione, Roveredo, Jena, Eylau and Leipzig.

carry it off. Afterwards General Keim sent an Officer to the French to assure them if they did not leave Nuremberg he would attack them this morning, which induced them to leave it a[t] four o'clock and to go towards Furth; this whole day there is nothing but firing to be heard. God grant the Austrians success. It is dreadful to hear every shot without being able to know if the enemy is likely to be beat. I assure your Majesty that I cannot be sufficiently thankful to God for allowing me to feel quiet and composed though in the midst of the armies. It is now above ten days that I have been obliged to stay quite at home as the marching of the French through the town would make it very imprudent for me to venture out. As I fear I shall hear nothing certain of this affair till after the post is gone out I shall not fail on Monday to acquaint your Majesty with the event. (51623–4)

2301 *Letters from the* DUKE OF PORTLAND *to the* KING

[*Burlington House, Saturday even., 20 Dec. 1800.*] The Duke of Portland most humbly begs leave to lay at your Majesty's feet a letter which he has received today from the Lord Advocate of Scotland containing accounts which will probably be the last he will think it necessary to send of the proceedings under the new Militia Act, a measure which has been brought to so successfull a conclusion by the exertions, the energy, the firmness & the temper of those in general whose duty it has been to carry it into effect that it is a great mortification to the Duke of Portland to have to submit to your Majesty the apprehensions expressed by the Lord Advocate that the seditious & malignant spirit to which the late disturbances are to be attributed still remains in a sufficient state of force & activity to give uneasiness & demand the vigilant attention of all your Majesty's servants in that part of the kingdom. As those circumstances are unhappily supposed to exist, your Majesty will permit the Duke of Portland to consider it as a great consolation that the conduct of the measures which are to be taken for the discovery of the parties concerned in resisting the law & for the prevention of any violence or outrage is in the hands of a person so capable to perform that task as the present Lord Advocate.

As there does not appear to be any circumstance in the cases of the four gentlemen whose names are inclosed in a separate paper, whom your Majesty has determined to raise to the dignity of the Peerage, which enables the Duke of Portland to form a decided opinion of the precedence to which they may be intitled among themselves, & that he cannot learn that any rule has been positively laid down by your Majesty in such cases, although he has been informed that in one or two of the later instances your Majesty was graciously pleased to order that those who had no determinate rank should be placed in the Peerage according to their seniority in the House of Commons, he requests with all humility to have your Majesty's commands signified to him in that respect, & also the dispatches from the Lord Lieutenant of Ireland, which the Duke of Portland herewith submits to your Majesty, are so voluminous that he humbly conceives it may not be disagreable to your Majesty to have a summary of their contents laid before your Majesty, & he therefore ventures to inform your Majesty that the dispatches of the 13th contain the Lord Lieutenant's most humble recommendation to your Majesty of the Reverend George Beresford,[1] son of Mr Beresford, the First Commissioner of your Majesty's Revenues, & Dean of Elphin, to succeed to the Bishoprick of Clonfert vacant by the death of Dr Young[2] on whom your Majesty was pleased in the year 1798 to confer that See for the eminence of his learning & character— & a letter from the Viscount Oxmantown[3] to the Duke of Portland desiring that his most humble request may be laid before your Majesty that your Majesty may graciously condescend to confer the dignity of the Peerage on Colonel Robert King,[4] a grandson of the late Earl of Kingston's,[5] who married Lord Oxmantown's only daughter, in consequence of which Lord Oxmantown states that Col. King, who is in possession of landed property to the amount of upwards of twelve thousand pounds a year, will be intitled in reversion to ten thousand a year more, besides personal property amounting to between ninety & one hundred thousand pounds in money. The Duke of Portland begs leave to observe to your Majesty that he has not the least acquaintance with Lord Oxmantown, & that this letter is addressed to him in consequence of the Lord Lieutenant's assurance to your Majesty that his recommendation of Mr Trench[6] of Woodlawn should be the last he would offer to your Majesty. He therefore only vouches for his belief in the correctness of Lord Oxmantown's assertions respecting Colonel King's fortune in possession & reversion, & that the Colonel is universally esteemed & respected.

One of the dispatches of the 15th instt. is an humble representation to your Majesty by the Ld. Lieutenant that he was induced, by the services of Lord Longue-ville[7] in the severe political contest for the Union, & the anxiety he expressed for some provision for his nephew Capt. Longfield of the 6th Dragoon Guards, to request your Majesty's leave that the Capt. might dispose of his troop, & that,

[1] The Rev. George de la Poer Beresford was nominated Bishop of Clonfert on 23 Dec., and was consecrated 1 Feb. 1801; Bishop of Kilmore, 1802–41. (1765–1841.) He was the second son of the Right Hon. John Beresford (1738–1805).

[2] The Rev. Matthew Young (1750–1800), Bishop of Clonfert, 1799–1800 (nominated, 15 Jan. 1799).

[3] Lawrence Harman Parsons (1749–1807), 3rd son of Sir Lawrence Parsons. M.P. for Co. Longford, 1776–92; created Baron Oxmantown [I.], 1792; Viscount Oxmantown [I.], 1795; an Irish Representative Peer, 1801–7; created Earl of Rosse [I.], 3 Feb. 1806.

[4] Robert Edward King (1773–1854), second son of Robert, 2nd Earl of Kingston [I.]. (1754–99.) Colonel, 1801; Major-General, 1808; Lieutenant-General, 1813; General, 1830. M.P. for Jamestown, 1796–7; for Boyle, 1798–1800. Created Baron Erris, 29 Dec. 1800, and Viscount Lorton [I.], May 1806. Irish Representative Peer, 1823–54. He married (Dec. 1799) his cousin Frances (1775–1841), daughter of the Earl of Rosse by Jane, daughter of the 1st Earl of Kingston. In April 1798 he was acquitted at Cork Assizes on a charge of having, together with his father, murdered Henry Gerald Fitzgerald, an illegitimate son of his mother's brother. Fitzgerald, a married man, had eloped with and seduced King's sister.

[5] Edward, 1st Earl of Kingston (1726–97), 2nd son of Sir Henry King, 3rd Baronet [I.], created Baron Kingston [I.], 1764; Viscount Kingston [I.], 1766; Earl of Kingston [I.], 1768.

[6] Frederick Trench (1755–1840), of Woodlawn (earlier called Moate) in Kilconnel, Co. Galway. M.P. for Maryborough, 1785–90; for Portarlington, 1798–1800, and 1800 [U.K.]. Created Baron Ashtown [I.], 27 Dec. 1800 as a reward for changing sides on the Union. His creation as an Irish Peer prevented him from taking his seat in the United Parliament, though he would have been eligible for an English or Scottish constituency.

[7] Richard Longfield (1734–1811), M.P. for Charleville, 1761–8; for Cloghanikilty, 1768–76; for Cork, 1776–83 and 1790–5; for Baltimore, 1783–90. Created Baron Longueville [I.], 1795, and Viscount Longueville [I.], 29 Dec. 1800. An Irish Representative Peer, 1801–11. In one of his querulous letters, remarked Ross, Lord Longueville claimed Cork and Mallow, and six other seats, as his own. (*Cornwallis Corresp.*, III, 324.)

on these considerations together with that of Captain Longfield's having served
16 years & been with his regiment on the Continent he presumes to hope that your
Majesty may still graciously please to grant that indulgence to Capt. Longfield.

The other dispatch of the same date contains the monthly reports by the General
Officers of the state of the respective Districts in which they command, from whence
it appears that the publick tranquillity has sufferd very little & no material interruption, that the scarcity & high price of provisions have created little sensation
excepting in the neighbourhood of Limerick & some parts of the counties of
Tipperary & Kilkenny, & that no apprehension of disturbance is entertained except
in the case, which seems not very likely to happen, of actual invasion. The dispatches of the 16th contain the Lord Lieutenant's most dutifull acknowledgments
of your Majesty's great goodness in condescending to raise Genl. Massey[1] & Mr
Trench of Woodlawn to the Peerage & to continue the title of Clanricarde by the
grant of a new earldom to the daughters & their issue male of the present Earl[2]
in default of issue male of himself; whose estate, which amounts to upwards of
ten thousand pounds a year in Ireland, the Earl has assured the Lord Lieutenant
is settled in that manner upon his daughters by the late Marquess his brother,[3]
who had the absolute power of disposing of it, & that it was that circumstance
which suggested to him the wish in which your Majesty has condescended to
gratify him.

[1] Eyre Massey (1719–1804), who served at Culloden, with Wolfe in Canada, and at the taking of
Havannah. Major-General, 1777; Lieutenant-General, 1782; General, 1796. M.P. for Swords, 1790–7;
Governor of Limerick, 1797–1804. Created Baron Clarina, 28 Dec. 1800. He had seen active service for
more than sixty years.

[2] John Thomas de Burgh, 13th Earl of Clanricarde [I.] (1744–1808) succeeded his brother in the
Earldom, 1797. Major-General, 1793; Lieutenant-General, 1798; General, 1803. On 29 Dec. he was
created Earl of Clanricarde [I.], with remainder (he then had no son) to his daughters in succession, and
their issue male. He was an Irish Representative Peer, 1801–8. His only son Ulick John (1802–74)
succeeded him. Lord Clanricarde had asked Pitt for promotion in the peerage, on 12 Sept. 1798: '...A
sollicitation for favors ought to be backed perhaps with better claims than I can adduce in support of
mine, for I can scarcely consider a mere acquittal of professional duties, as a foundation to build a claim
upon. Nevertheless it may be allowable to me to say, that in a military service of many years standing,
I have in no instance declined any duty which came in my way, and I trust I have been so fortunate,
as always to have received an approbation of my conduct. I have never sollicited nor received a favor or
gratification of any kind but what reached me in the ordinary course of promotion, beyond what has
arose from a consciousness of a correct performance of my duty.

An unfortunate family event not long since happened has placed me in a situation, which probably,
I do not presume too much in supposing you may be acquainted with. My late brother was honored
with a creation of a *Marquisate*, and he was not the first of the family who had borne it. The Patent did
not extend to me because it was declared to be unusual to extend *that rank* to any but the imediate issue.
The title of Clanricarde, which from the first existence of peerages in this kingdom, to the present day,
has always been at the head of the Irish Peerage, from the above circumstances, in my instance now loses
its ancient station. I am by no means, Sir, of a disposition to court distinctions of this description, and I
should not have become a sollicitor for an advancement in the peerage, but that I feel circumstanced as
I am, a most sensible mortification that in my person the family should lose a pre-eminence in rank which
has so long distinguished them. Allow me Sir, to observe that could a Marquisate be obtained, it would
be no object to me, as (if I may be permitted the expression) it would but give me precedence over
myself.

Should there be a disposition to favor my views and wishes, the only gratification to them, would
be a Dukedom in the Irish Peerage, or a seat in the English House of Lords, an honor which has already
more than once been enjoyed by my ancestry, who like myself have never been wanting in their endeavors
to support the measures of Government in either country...' (Chatham Papers, 123.)

[3] Henry de Burgh, 12th Earl of Clanricarde (1743–97), *d.s.p.* Created Marquess of Clanricarde [I.] 1789.

The other dispatch of the same date only serves as a cover to the return by the Clerk of the Hanaper of the members who are to serve in the Parliament of the United Kingdom on the part of Ireland with the addition of the names of Ld Sudley[1] & Mr Sneyd,[2] the first of whom has been chosen for the county of Donegall, & the latter for the county of Cavan since the return was made.

By Ld. Castlereagh's letter it appears that he may be expected the beginning of next week, that he will collect what information he can to satisfy the inquiries made by the Duke of Portland respecting the means of growing hemp in Ireland & of assisting Scotland with flax, which by the arrival of some cargoes from Russia is now no longer in want of that article; that Sir George Hill,[3] Mr Beresford's son-in-law, is likely to succeed for the county of Londonderry, & that the number of candidates will probably ensure Mr George Ponsonby's being chosen for the county of Wicklow;[4] & from the favorable sentiments your Majesty condescended to express of the Earl of Inchiquin the Duke of Portland has great satisfaction in adding that there seems to be no obstacle on the part of the Lord Lieutenant to Lord Inchiquin's becoming one of the representatives of the Peerage of that part of the United Kingdom on the first vacancy.

Mr Cooke's letter to Mr King contains nothing more than the copy of a letter which he was directed by the Lord Lieutenant to write to the Mayor of Limerick in consequence of information having been received of the appearance of a disposition to obstruct the exportation of grain from that port. (9928–31, and 9124–5)

[*Burlington House, Sunday even., 21 Dec.*] The Duke of Portland conceives it to be his duty, in laying before your Majesty the letters to the Lord Lieutenant for your Majesty's royal signature, which have been prepared in obedience to the commands which the Duke of Portland received this morning from your Majesty, most humbly to represent to your Majesty that blanks are left for the titles which the Earl of Clanricarde & Mr King may wish to assume, for the following reasons, which are submitted with the utmost deference to your Majesty—namely, that on the part of the Earl of Clanricarde none has been offer'd to your Majesty's consideration, & on that of Mr King, the one he has proposed being that of Rockingham, could not be taken without giving considerable uneasiness to the heirs & other near connections of the person who last bore that title,[5] & is consequently

---

[1] Arthur Saunders Gore (1761–1837), who succeeded his father as 3rd Earl of Arran, 8 Oct. 1809. Styled Viscount Sudley, 1773–1809. M.P. for Baltimore, 1783–90; for Co. Donegal, 1800–6.

[2] Nathaniel Sneyd (1767?–1833), M.P. for Cavan, 1801–26. He was a Dublin wine merchant. The fantastically wealthy Lady Andover (1717–1803), gave him £10,000 about this time. He was one of Canning's friends. Later (1819) he was Governor of the Bank of Ireland. He was murdered by a lunatic.

[3] Sir George Fitzgerald Hill (1763–1839), succeeded his father as 2nd Bart., 1795. M.P. for Coleraine, 1790–5; for Londonderry, 1795–8; for Londonderry Co., 1801–2; for Londonderry City, 1802–30. A Lord of the Treasury [I.], 1806; Vice-Treasurer of Ireland, 1817–30. In Jan. 1798 he was appointed Clerk of the House of Commons [I.], for which office he received compensation at the Union amounting to £2265 a year. He married (1788) Jane (1769–1836), daughter of the Right Hon. John Beresford.

[4] Only two candidates went to the poll in Co. Wicklow in Jan. 1801, the by-election being occasioned by the death of Nicholas Westby on 29 Nov. George Pondonby, with 695 votes, defeated Lord Proby by a majority of 73 (*The Times*, 5 Feb. 1801). 'It has occurred to me', wrote Fox to his friend O'Bryen on 11 Dec. 1800, 'that Fitzwilliam determined against bringing [in] Ponsonby, Mrs. Grey's brother, chiefly on account of his (P.'s) opinion on parliamentary reform.' (Add. MSS. 47565, f. 56.)

[5] The Marquess of Rockingham, the Prime Minister (1730–82). Lord Fitzwilliam, his nephew, was his heir.

inconsistent with the injunctions which your Majesty has been graciously pleased to lay upon the Duke of Portland in this respect. The Duke of Portland feels himself also called upon by his duty to observe to your Majesty that he has dared to depart from the letter of your Majesty's orders respecting the Peerage for Colonel Robert King which, according to the terms in which your Majesty's commands are expressed, should have been reversionary on the death of Lord Oxmantown & not an immediate grant. But as Lord Oxmantown's petition to your Majesty was for an immediate Peerage for Colonel King, & that the Colonel is actually in possession of upwards of twelve thousand pounds pr. annum besides personal property to a considerable amount & reversions of some thousands a year more, independent of Lord Oxmantown's contingency, the Duke of Portland has ventured to suppose that your Majesty might condescend to think these circumstances sufficient to dispose your Majesty to grant the whole of Lord Oxmantown's request, & to forgive the Duke of Portland's presumption in offering for your Majesty's signature a letter which so far deviates from the words in which your Majesty's order is expressed. (9932–3)

2302 LORD GRENVILLE *to the* KING, *and the reply*

[*Cleveland Row, 22 Dec. 1800, 11 p.m.*] Lord Grenville has the honour to transmit to your Majesty the copy of a letter which M. de Pombeiro[1] is charged to deliver from the Prince of Brazil[2] to your Majesty—and he humbly requests to know whether your Majesty would approve of his appointing M. de Pombeiro for New Year's day to have his Audience of your Majesty. (9934)

[*The King's reply, Windsor, 23 Dec.*] As I shall be at St. James's on New Year's Day to do the business in the Privy Council which is necessary as the Union of the Kingdoms that day takes effect, I do not object of [*sic*] receiving Mr. de Pombeiro, though I shall not have a Levée; but if Lord Grenville wishes to introduce him the first time I shall be in town, that might easily be the day when I go to end the present session of Parliament; the Chancellor had promised to send me timely notice, and I am rather surprised not yet to have heard when the Bills will be finished in Parliament that I may attend for that purpose. (Fortescue MSS.)

2303 THE DUCHESS OF WURTEMBERG *to the* KING

[*Erlangen, 23 Dec. 1800.*] I defered writing to your Majesty till the last moment, flattering myself before the departure of the post to have something good to say, but alas everything has taken a worse aspect since I wrote to the Queen this morning. The French have received a reinforcement of nine thousand men and

---

[1] Sometimes spelt Pombeira (e.g., *Dropmore Papers*, VI, 422).

[2] John Maria Joseph Lewis, Prince of Brazil (1767–1826), the only surviving son of Peter III (1717–86) who married (1760) his niece, Maria, Queen of Portugal (1734–1816), she succeeding her father Joseph, King of Portugal, in 1777. The Prince of Brazil was declared Regent of Portugal in 1792 on account of his mother's incapacity, and he succeeded her in 1816 as John VI. He married (1790) Charlotte (1775–1830), daughter of Charles IV of Spain.

are again I believe at Nuremberg; the cannonading is since ten o'clock without end and we must now tremble for the Austrians as the French have many more troops. What is particularly unfortunate is that if even the Austrians were to be successful it would be to no purpose as the French have passed the Inn and are according to some accounts at Lintz. It would be impossible for me to describe to your Majesty the effect this melancholy news has on me, as I see nothing but the most wretched events likely to happen. Since these misfortunes I hear the Archduke Charles has joined the Army. Had he been there three weeks ago everything would have had another aspect and we might have had a chance of recovering part of the ground that had been lost by General Kray.

As the post is going off I can only add the Duke's humble duty and shall not fail to acquaint your Majesty with any fresh event that takes place. (51625–6)

2304   LORD GRENVILLE *to the* KING, *and the reply*

[*Cleveland Row, 23 Dec. 1800, 11 p.m.*] Lord Grenville was this morning honoured with your Majesty's commands and in consequence of them enquired of the Lord Chancellor respecting the day of the prorogation of the Parliament: which the Lord Chancellor desired him to acquaint your Majesty cannot take place till Monday as several bills were brought up from the House of Commons today. The Lord Chancellor would have written to your Majesty on this subject, but he did not know the day till yesterday, and he then desired the Archbishop of Canterbury, (who he understood was to have the honour of seeing your Majesty today) to mention it to your Majesty.

Lord Grenville took the liberty to mention New Year's day to your Majesty for M. de Pombeiro's audience, because he wished to ask your Majesty's permission to remain till that day at Dropmore, where he goes tomorrow, unless any fresh business should arise, or your Majesty should have any other commands for him.

If it should be your Majesty's pleasure to receive M. de Pombeiro on Monday next, the Duke of Portland will, with your Majesty's permission, have the honour of introducing him. (9935–6)

[*The King's reply, Windsor, 24 Dec.*] I shall certainly be at St. James's on Monday to hold the Council for the Speech on concluding the session of Parliament that day in consequence of Lord Grenville's information, which the adjournment of the House of Commons to that day made me suppose was the time that would suit Parliament. As Lord Grenville comes this day to Dropmore, I certainly shall not wish to call him earlier to town than on Thursday, and therefore fix on that day for receiving M. de Pombeiro. (Fortescue MSS.)

2305   THE ARCHBISHOP OF CANTERBURY (DR MOORE) *to the* KING

[*Friday, 26 Dec. 1800.*] The Archbishop of Canterbury having received a report from the Lord Chancellor on the subject of the King's stile & title, which it is his duty to communicate to his Majesty, will hold himself in readiness to obey his Majesty's commands when honoured with them. (9940)

2306 THE DUKE OF PORTLAND *to the* KING

[*Burlington House, Friday even., 26 Dec. 1800.*] The Duke of Portland most humbly begs leave together with two dispatches from the Lord Lieutenant of Ireland, to submit to your Majesty a letter to the Lord Lieutenant for continuing the Privy Council of Ireland to be your Majesty's Privy Council for that part of the United Kingdom, & a warrant empowering him to direct the present Great Seal of Ireland to be used after the Union within that part of the United Kingdom in the same manner as before the Union, except where otherwise provided by the Act of Union. The Duke of Portland must acknowledge to your Majesty that it had not occurred to him or to any of your Majesty's servants that it would be necessary that either of these orders should be laid before your Majesty for your royal signature before the day on which the Union of the Kingdoms is to take place; but on opening the Lord Lieutenant's Dispatches the necessity of the measure struck the Duke of Portland so forcibly & has made so exactly the same impression upon such of your Majesty's servants as he has had an opportunity of communicating with, that there does not remain a doubt in the mind of any of them that the Privy Council of Ireland would cease to exist & the Great Seal of Ireland have no longer any force on the first of January, unless they are preserved by the interposition of your Majesty's authority. The Duke of Portland therefore feels it to be his duty to sollicit your Majesty's sanction of the orders he herewith humbly submits to your Majesty for the purpose of obviating the inconveniences which might ensue from the want of them. (9941–2)

2307 PRINCE AUGUSTUS *to the* KING

[*Portsmouth, 26 Dec. 1800.*] I have constantly delayed writing in hopes of being able to inform your Majesty of my sailing. There are hopes now of the wind coming fair, in which case not a moment will be lost. The weather has been extremely mild ever since my arrival here, so much so that there has not been even a fog. This change in climate has worked an equal one on my constitution, for ever since my coming here I have been able to sleep in bed like any other person. This of course has improved my health in no small degree, therefore I have no reason to complain. I have employed part of my time in viewing the different works that are going on here, which do as much credit to the projector as well as to the builder. The new dock will be finished in a very few months, and from its solidity bids fair to be as lasting a monument of our naval grandour as any Roman edifice I recollect to have seen in my travels abroad. Yesterday I went on board the Malta (formerly the Guillaume Tell); she is one of the largest ships of her size existing and I understand from naval officers almost similar to the *Ca Ira*. Though repaird at Minorca for to be sent home one can still see the marks of her brave defense as well as of the scientific manner in which she was attacked, almost all the fire having been directed either at her stem, or her forecastle. She carries the largest masts of any ship in our service the diameter of her mainmast being three feet three inches. Not far from her lies at this moment in ordinary the Flagship of the hero of the Nile, the Vanguard; it was not without some grief I look'd at her forlorn situation and mourn'd for the blinding of her chief whose superlative bravery should [not] for a moment be forgotten on account of his present imprudent conduct. We are all men, Sir; to err is human, and to bear good fortune with calmness in its rapidity is almost supernatural; besides the great attention he must have given to his profession in order to make himself so useful a conductor, must have naturally prevented him from learning perfectly those doctrines of society which would have prevented weaknesses on his part that merit in him I truly believe more compassion than censure. I trust and believe that when again on board the *San Joseph*, should an opportunity offer, he will give your Majesty reason to be satisfied with his conduct. With every wish for your Majesty's welfare and happiness, with every sentiment of gratitude and filial attachment, I have the honor [etc.]¹ (48204–5)

¹ There is no copy of the Queen's letter to Dundas dated Queen's Lodge, Windsor, 26 Dec. 1800, in the Royal Archives, but it shows her in an unusual light. Lady Louisa Paget, sister of Sir Arthur and of the 1st Marquess of Anglesey, married Colonel, afterwards Major-General Sir James Erskine, in 1801.

'I am pretty sure that you are not ignorant of the attachment which has, and does now at this hour, subsist between Colonel Erskine & Lady Louisa Paget, how it was opposed by Lord Uxbridge & at last given up on the lady's side, which determined the Colonel to go upon service abroad and almost completely broke Ldy. Louisa's heart and consequently rendered a family who had every reason to be happy completely the contrary. In this situation have I seen them every day for three months without the least amendment, and as the young lady's health is visibly declining I took an opportunity the other day to talk it over with both Lrd. and Ldy. Uxbridge, & to assure them that tho' the match could never be looked upon as prudent in point of circumstances, & that their opposing it at the time they did was justifyable to the world, I was of opinion that if they would, for the sake of preserving their child, only promise that whenever Colonel Erskine's income did increase they would agree to the match, it might be the means of making all parties easy and restore health and tranquility again into the family. The tryal was a severe one. For the love of the father was always for yielding on one side & on the other honour always opposed it. At last, after two hours conversation, I stated that out of two evils they must choose one, namely, poverty & happiness on one side, & the death of a beloved child on the other, & that they would feel happy, let the event be at the end what it might, that they would have nothing to reproach themselves with. After two days consideration I received a message through Ldy. Uxbridge that My Lord would *acquiesce* whenever Colonel Erskine could obtain a permanent place in addition to his present income, & that he wished somebody would apply to you. This I undertook to do, as likewise to break his *acquiescence not consent* to his daughter. I did mention this to the Kg., by which I do not mean to imply that his Majesty said you should do it but only to shew that I act openly.

I know Sir William Erskine was a friend of yours, & likewise that you wish well to the son, I should do injustice to yr. character if I was to doubt your readiness to assist those that are in distress. I shall therefore only ask whenever it is possible to provide for the son of a friend, not for my sake, but for the sake of him whom you honoured with your friendship, & for the sake of two young people who by your means may become happy & contented.

I beg my compliments to Lady Jane & hope to hear she is better than she was when I left town.' (Melville MSS., Scottish Record Office.)

Dundas replied to the Queen's letter on the 27th: 'I have this morning received the letter with which your Majesty has been pleased to honour me on the subject of Col. Erskine, & the comfortable relief to his mind which your Majesty's gracious interposition has accomplished. Every person with a heart capable of just & honourable feelings must venerate the condescending benevolence with which your Majesty has entered into the interesting concerns of a very amiable young couple, who I trust, will live long in comfort together to acknowledge with gratitude the happiness which your Majesty's goodness has procured for them. In any case it would be my duty to forward by every means in my power, a cause which your Majesty has been graciously pleased to espouse, and in the present instance your Majesty's wishes are connected with so many circumstances of a tender & interesting nature as to command my earliest & best attention. I shall without delay revolve the subject in my mind, and after taking the first opportunity which offers of speaking to Mr. Pitt upon it, I will humbly submit to his Majesty the result of my consideration.' (*Ibid.*)

[*27 Dec. 1800.*] The Chancellor had the honour to receive your Majesty's commands from the Archbishop of Canterbury this morning. It is uncertain when the Lord President of the Council, to whom he was directed to communicate them may be in town, but the Chancellor has presumed to desire Sir Stephen Cottrell to prepare the Minute of the Order of Council for your Majesty's approbation, and has also communicated it to Mr Pitt, who will have the honour to inform your Majesty that the business remaining in the House of Commons is likely to prevent the Prorogation on Monday.

All the Bills are passed in the House of Lords this day, but it seems there are reports to be made, and discussions which may possibly arise upon them, which would interrupt the time of Prorogation on Monday as originally intended.

The variance from the precedent in the reign of Queen Anne upon the Union with Scotland does not appear to be of any moment; the only difference will be that on the final close of the Parlt. on Wednesday, which of necessity must cease to exist at the close of that day, your Majesty will make that formal declaration of your pleasure to your Parliament to be there deposited, which in effect you have already been pleased to express, and which, by the interval of a Prorogation Queen [Anne] was pleased to do by *a Commission,* and there can be no possible doubt that whatever your Majesty is pleased to direct by Commission to be done, must be done with more force by your own commands delivered in full Parliament.[1] (9945–6)

[*The King's reply, Windsor, 28 Dec. 1800.*] This morning I have received the Lord Chancellor's information of the steps he has taken that Sir Stephen Cottrell may have the proper minute of the Order of Council prepared for the title to be used on the Union of the Kingdoms. I cannot but feel surprised that the absurdity of looking back to antient times should have arisen when the modern one so fully answered the purpose; but some men love to shew their erudition and positiveness as much as what is more useful at least their discression [*sic*].

I have been also this morning apprized by Mr Pitt of the necessity of postponing the Prorogation. I have strongly expressed my opinion in favour of Wednesday in preferrence to Tuesday which Mr Pitt seemed to think the Speaker would incline to; but the Lord Chancellor's note compleatly decides me for Wednesday. I have therefore just sent counter-orders for tomorrow and named Wednesday as the day of my going to Parliament. (9950)

2309 *Letters from* WILLIAM PITT *to the* KING, *and the replies*

[*Downing Street, Saturday, 27 Dec. 1800.*] Mr Pitt humbly begs leave to acquaint your Majesty that on conversing fully with the Chancellor and consulting Mr Lee,[2]

---

[1] The Archbishop of Canterbury sent this note to the King, undated, but written at 7.30 a.m., and endorsed 'Saturday, 27 Dec. 1800': 'The Archbishop having this moment received the enclosed letter from the Lord Chancellor, thinks it his duty to transmit it to his Majesty' (9944).

[2] John Ley, Deputy Clerk of the House of Commons. John Hatsell was the Clerk.

he finds there would be a risk of some inconvenience, if the Prorogation of Parliament were to take place on Monday; and that considerable doubts are entertained whether instead of deferring the Prorogation to Tuesday, and then proroguing for a single day, it would not be a more simple and correct mode of proceeding that the Prorogation should be wholly omitted; and that instead, if your Majesty is graciously pleased to approve it, the Speech to terminate the Session should be delivered on Wednesday, and the Proclamation for the sitting of the United Parliament be then read, as was practised in 1706 [*sic*], on the day immediately preceding that on which the Union was to take place. The only difference will be that Parliament in that case met on that day, after a Prorogation of four days, and that in the present case they will have continued sitting without Prorogation, but this circumstance does not appear to render the proceeding less applicable.

Mr Pitt has thought it best under these circumstances to send a messenger to the Speaker, who is at Woodley, in order to learn his opinion on the two alternatives; and he ventures to hope that if the choice of the day makes no material difference in point of convenience, your Majesty will have the goodness to permit either Tuesday or Wednesday to be fixed, as it shall be found adviseable on the whole to adopt the mode of prorogation or to omit it. He also takes the liberty of submitting for your Majesty's consideration a rough draft of the Speech. (9947–8)

[*The King's reply, Windsor, 28 Dec.*] The moment Mr. Pitt's [*sic*] expresses that it is of consequence that the Parliament should not be prorogued till Wednesday, I cannot make a difficulty of postponing it to that day, which seems a more natural mode of ending the Parliament than on the Tuesday. I shall therefore give orders for Wednesday, but come on Tuesday if on farther consideration Mr. Pitt shall by tomorrow morning's messenger propose that as the more convenient time.

The speech seems very proper. The Council should be summoned for that to be held at St. James's just before I go to the House. (Chatham Papers.)

[*From Pitt, Downing Street, Sunday, 28 Dec. 1800.*] Mr Pitt humbly begs leave to acquaint your Majesty that he has received an answer from the Speaker, who entirely concurs in thinking it most desireable that the Session should end on Wednesday in the mode proposed, without any Prorogation. (9949)

[*The King's reply, Windsor, 29 Dec.*] The note just come from Mr. Pitt that the Speaker of the House of Commons concurrs in the propriety of not ending the session till Wednesday and that consequently without a prorogation is most satisfactory to me, as after writing yesterday to Mr. Pitt, I found in the green box a letter from the Lord Chancellor proposing also Wednesday and giving very conclusive reasons that seem to end the Parliament and prepare for that of the Union in a more neat manner than the mode adopted on the Union with Scotland. I suppose this will require a few words being added at the conclusion of the Speech or perhaps the intimation may be given by the Lord Chancellor in my name in the same manner as he declares the prorogation and the conclusion of common sessions of Parliament.

I have just received from the Lord Lieutenant of Ireland an application without any private explanation, which has always been the case on new reversions, that I will revoke the Patent during pleasure of a place in the Chancery of Ireland[1] now held by the Marquess of Downshire and two of his sons, and grant a Patent of the same office for the two lives of a Mr. Yelverton[2] and his son, which I shall certainly postpone till I am fully acquainted with the case, as I am by no means inclined to add to the offices for life in Ireland. (Chatham Papers.)

2310   EARL SPENCER *to the* KING, *and the reply*

[*Admiralty, 31 Dec. 1800.*] Earl Spencer has the honour of laying before your Majesty the list of officers he humbly proposes to your Majesty to promote to the several ranks therein expressed, as also an abstract of the numbers of the respective ranks as they will stand after the promotion has taken place. Your Majesty will be pleased to observe that the names of the Captains proposed to be left out are written in red ink; four of them, Captains Carlyon,[3] Boston,[4] Charrington,[5] and Richard Graves[6] have not been employed either on shore or afloat during the present war; Captain Alexander Christian[7] was employed in the Grampus, but having thought fit to give up the command of that ship on her being ordered to the West Indies in the year 1795, Earl Spencer humbly submits to your Majesty that he should not succeed to a Flag; and Captain George[8] being a Commissioner of Transports and wishing to remain so, is likewise proposed to be omitted. The rest having all been employed in the course of the war either afloat or ashore are humbly recommended to your Majesty for Flags. The three Colonels of Marines being promoted by this arrangement, Sir Edward Pellew, Captain Domett[9] and Sir Thomas Troubridge are submitted to your Majesty's approbation to succeed them.

Earl Spencer has also the honour to lay before your Majesty the proceedings of a court martial on a private marine on board the Royal George, for having struck or rather pushed his superior officer; the Court has adjudged him to be hanged, but a letter from the President, Sir Henry Harvey, accompanies the sentence signifying their unanimous recommendation of the prisoner to your

[1] That of Joint Registrar of the Court of Chancery. Lord Downshire's eldest son, who succeeded him on 7 Sept. 1801, was at this time a boy of twelve. The other sons were born in 1792, 1798 and 1800.

[2] William Charles Yelverton (1762–1814), Principal Registrar of the Court of Chancery [I.]. He succeeded his father, Barry Yelverton (1736–1805) [see No. 1210], who was created Lord Yelverton, Baron Avonmore in 1795, and Viscount Avonmore on 29 Dec. 1800.

[3] William Carlyon. Lieutenant, 1773; Commander, 1777; Captain, 1781; superannuated as Rear-Admiral, 1800.

[4] Thomas Boston. Lieutenant, 1762; Commander, 1779; Captain, 1781; superannuated as Rear-Admiral, 1801.

[5] Nicholas Charrington. Lieutenant, 1773; Captain, 1781; Superannuated as Rear-Admiral, 1801.

[6] Richard Graves. Lieutenant, 1775; Captain, 1781; superannuated as Rear-Admiral, 1804.

[7] Alexander Christie. Lieutenant, 1775; Commander, 1781; Captain, 1781; superannuated as Rear-Admiral, 1801.

[8] Sir Rupert George. Lieutenant, 1770; Captain, 1781. He was superannuated. Created Baronet, 1809.

[9] Sir William Domett (1754–1828). Lieutenant, 1777; Captain, 1782; Rear-Admiral, 1804; Vice-Admiral, 1809; Admiral, 1819; K.C.B., 1815; G.C.B., 1820.

Majesty's mercy. Earl Spencer therefore thinks it his duty humbly to solicit your Majesty to grant him your royal pardon accordingly. (9952–3)

[*The King's reply, Queen's House, 31 Dec.*] The list of the promotion of Admirals, Vice-Admirals and Rear-Admirals which I have just received from Earl Spencer, seems formed with great attention; those omitted are properly accounted for. I desire therefore it may be tomorrow ratified, as also the advancement of Sir Edward Pellew, Capt. Domett and Sir Thomas Troubridge to the Colonelcies of Marines.

I consent to the pardon of the marine on board the Royal George agreable to the application of Sir Henry Harvey, the President of the court martial. (Althorp MSS.)

2311   THE DUCHESS OF WURTEMBERG *to the* KING

[*Erlangen, 31 Dec. 1800.*] It gives me great pleasure to have it in my power to write openly to your Majesty as the post is too dangerous a conveyance for me to feel at ease when I wish to acquaint your Majesty with any particulars of our situation, which since yesterday morning is very wretched, as the Duke then received the cruel news of the retreat of the Austrians and the total disorganisation of their Army. It is dreadful to hear that those troops formerly so brave now throw down their arms at the approach of the enemy. Thank God the Württemberg troops continue doing their duty and behave nobly on all occasions notwithstanding the hardships they have undergone; but it is always to be feared that at last they may be induced to follow the wretched example the Austrians set them. If we can credit what the French report we have also reason to fear that the Emperor has been obliged to sign the Preliminaries of Peace. Should this prove true I have recourse to your Majesty's justice and goodness for to entreat you not to abandon the Duke and allow us to suffer for having adhered to the good cause, notwithstanding our country was the first yielded to the enemy by the Armistice; that the French have quite ruined it by draining it of money and of corn, and even threaten to treat us with greater severity. I am sure these considerations will have some weight with your Majesty and that your generosity will induce you to protect us.

I shall also take the liberty to mention another subject which I have much at heart. Your Majesty certainly remembers my having entered into a particular account concerning the bad behaviour of the States of the Dutchy and that the Emperor by a decree had enabled the Duke to dissolve the Committees as well as the Assembly. On the 29th of April the new Assembly of the States was opened and I believe, had these misfortunes not befallen the country, would have avoided following the bad example of their predecessors, but the distresses which drove the Duke from Württemberg encouraged them again to forget their duty and fearing that hereafter they may be called to account for this, they seek support every where. The Duke has heard that they have applied at Hanover to have somebody named in Monsieur de Kneble's place and that there is an idea of proposing to your Majesty a person who is not a gentleman to succeed him. I am convinced that your Majesty is too good and just to give any encouragement to those who only distress their Sovereign and in the end hurt the people. I hope your Majesty will not be offended at my entreating you not to name anybody who is not a gentleman as it would distress us both very much to have any person at Stutgard in your service to whom the Duke and myself could not shew every attention which can denote our respect and attachment to you. According to the etiquette established at all the German Courts it is only a Minister Plenipotentiary that has the right to be invited to dinner, and even with Kneble, as he was only Minister Resident, it would have made great difficulties had his birth not entitled him to those attentions which otherwise he could not have obtained. I think it my duty to mention this to your Majesty and hope you will forgive my troubling you on this subject as I am sure you will feel that I am ever guided by the desire to shew my attachment to you. (51627-30)

2312   PRINCE ADOLPHUS *to the* KING

[*Hanover, 31 Dec. 1800.*] I cannot refuse myself the honour and pleasure of presenting your Majesty my most humble congratulations on the beginning of the New Year and century. That you may pass many and many very happy years in it, and enjoy at the same time the most perfect health is the sincerest wish, and I join with many thousand of your subjects in offering up the most ardent prayers to the Almighty for your preservation. Your Majesty will also allow me to renew here the humble assurance of my ever striving to act in such a manner as may meet with your approbation; and that I wish nothing more than to be successful in this point. I rejoice in being able to inform you of the arrival of the Archduke Charles on the 16th inst. There was yesterday a report that he had attacked and beat the French on the 19th or 20th; but, as the post from Franfortt is not yet arrived, I am unable to answer for its authenticity. The affair of the 18th near Nurenberg between the Corps commanded by General Augerau, and that com̄-anded by General Klenau has been confirmed: the French have retreated to Bomberg and the siege of Wurzbourg has been changed into a blockade in consequence of this affair. Happy should I be to be able to write your Majesty some good news by today's post. It would be a fine end of the century: the arrival of the Archduke Charles to the Army has caused an universal joy among the troops, and I am convinced that they will act very well under him.

I dare now not trespass any longer on your patience. (48559)

2313   HENRY DUNDAS *to the* KING, *and the reply*   (Copy)

[*Downing Street, 31 Dec. 1800, 12.30 p.m.*] Mr. Dundas is humbly confident he will meet with your Majesty's indulgence in transmitting for your Majesty's perusal the last letter he can ever receive from a much respected and venerable friend. It contains a small and moderate request which Mr. Dundas feels will meet with a gracious reception in your Majesty's breast. (Melville MSS., Scottish Record Office.)

[*The King's reply, Queen's House, 31 Dec.*] Dundas's note enclosing the one he had from the Solicitor-General for Scotland forwarding that of the late Doctor Blair[1] whose sermons and other publications do so much credit to the erudition and good principles of that part of my dominions. I desire therefore that his dying request may be granted in the manner he has proposed, and that Mr. Secy. Dundas will have this immediately communicated to Miss Elizabeth Hunter, the great-niece of the worthy man now deceased. (Melville MSS., Scottish Record Office.)

2314 [SIR] WILLIAM COCKBURN[2] *to* [   ]

[*Thursday (?1800).*] My dear Sir, On account of leaving my family, and all that is dear to me in this country, I am sorry to inform you that I am again on the eve of departure for India, but his Royal Highness, the Duke of York, having thought my services in that country necessary, I with pleasure sacrifice my private happiness to the service of our most gracious Sovereign. As I am told his Majesty frequently writes to the Nabob of Arcot, I shall esteem it a most particular favor if you will endeavour to procure me the honor of bearing his Majesty's letter, the more so as I am particularly acquainted with the Nabob, and had the honor of bringing his Highness's dispatches to his Majesty when I left India. With best respects to Lady Catherine. (9955)

2315 PROPOSED REPRESENTATIVE PEERS TO WHOM PROMISES HAVE BEEN MADE[3]

Earls: Clanricarde, Westmeath,[4] Bective,[5] Roden,[6] Altamont,[7] Glandore,[8] Longford,[9] Erne,[10] Desart,[11] Leitrim,[12] Lucan,[13] Conyngham,[14] Landaff.

[1] The Rev. Hugh Blair (1718–1800). Five volumes of his Sermons were published between 1777 and 1801.

[2] Sir William Cockburn (1768–1835), succeeded his father as Baronet, 1801. Ensign, 1778; Captain, 1783; Lieutenant-Colonel, 1798; Colonel, 1801; Major-General, 1811; Lieutenant-General, 1821; served in India for many years.

[3] The italicised names are those of the 28 Peers actually elected as Representative Peers (for life). The influence of Government, then, was decisive. It was the list originally proposed by Cornwallis, to which the Duke of Portland strongly objected—with one exception; Lord Londonderry's name was substituted for that of Sir John Blaquiere.

Londonderry was not anxious for a U.K. peerage at this time, and contented himself with an assurance from the British Government that either he or his descendants could have one whenever they cared to apply for it. The other four were given U.K. peerages in Jan. 1801: Drogheda took the title of Baron Moore; Ormonde that of Baron Butler; Carysfort that of Baron Carysfort; Ely that of Baron Loftus.

[4] George, 7th Earl of Westmeath (1760–1814). Styled Lord Delvin until 1792; succeeded his father, 1792. M.P. for Fore, 1780–92; Auditor of Foreign Accounts and Imprests [I.], 1784–98; Clerk of the Crown and Hanaper, 1807–14.

[5] Thomas, 2nd Earl of Bective (1757–1829). Succeeded his father, 1795, having been styled Viscount Headfort, 1766–95. Created, 30 Dec. 1800, Marquess of Headfort [I.]; a Lord of the Bedchamber, 1812–29.

[6] Robert, 2nd Earl of Roden (1756–1820); styled Viscount Jocelyn, 1771–97. Auditor-General of the Exchequer [I.], 1797–1820. K.P., 1806.

[7] John, 3rd Earl of Altamont (1756–1809); succeeded his father, 1780; created Marquess of Sligo, Dec. 1800, and (Feb. 1806), Baron Monteagle [U.K.].

[8] John, 2nd Earl of Glandore (1752–1815). Succeeded his father, 1781. Joint Master of the Rolls [I.], 1789–1801.

(*continued opposite*)

Viscounts: Wicklow,[1] *Northland,*[2] *Oxmantown, O'Neil,*[3] *Bandon,*[4] *Donoughmore*[5]*, Carleton.*

Barons: Caher,[6] *Glentworth,*[7] *Callan,*[8] *Somerton, Longueville, Rossmore, Tyrawley,*[9] [also] *Sir John Blaquiere.*[10]

N.B. The following it is supposed will be created British Peers, vizt., The Marquis of Drogheda,[11] The Earl of Ormonde & Ossory, Carysfort, Ely,[12] Londonderry.[13] (10018)

[9] Thomas, 4th Earl of Longford (1774–1835). Succeeded his father, 1792, as Baron Longford, and his grandmother as Earl, 1794. Created Baron Silchester [U.K.], 1821.

[10] John, 1st Earl Erne (1738?–1828). Succeeded his father as Baron Erne, 1772; created Viscount Erne, 1781, and Earl, 1789.

[11] Otway, 1st Earl of Desart (1737–1804). Created Viscount Desart, 1781; Earl of Desart, 1793.

[12] Robert Clements, 1st Earl of Leitrim (1732–1804). Created Baron Leitrim, 1783; Viscount, 1793, and Earl, 1795.

[13] Richard, 2nd Earl of Lucan [I.] (1764–1839). Succeeded his father, 29 March 1799. M.P. for St Albans, 1790–1800; styled Lord Bingham, 1795–9. His sister Lavinia (1762–1831) married Lord Spencer, Pitt's colleague, who had arranged that he should be elected a Representative Peer, and, to avoid trouble at St Albans, that he should vacate his seat before the election. The new writ was issued on 17 June and William Stephen Poyntz was elected on the 23rd.

[14] Henry, Earl Conyngham (1766–1832). Succeeded his father as 3rd Baron Conyngham, 1787; created Viscount, 1789, Earl, 1797, and Marquess, 1816; U.K. peerage, 1821, title Baron Minster. His wife Elizabeth, daughter of Joseph Denison (married 1794) succeeded Lady Hertford as the Prince of Wales's reputed mistress in 1819.

[1] Robert, 2nd Viscount Wicklow (1757–1815), succeeded his father as Viscount, 1789, and his mother as 2nd Earl of Wicklow in 1807.

[2] Thomas Knox, 1st Viscount Northland (1729–1818); created Baron Welles, 1781, and Viscount Northland, 1791.

[3] Charles, 2nd Viscount O'Neill (1779–1841), succeeded his father, 1798; created Earl O'Neill, Aug. 1800; Joint Postmaster-General [I.], 1807–31.

[4] Francis Bernard, 1st Earl of Bandon (1755–1830); created Baron Bandon, 1793; Viscount, 1795; Earl, Aug. 1800.

[5] Richard, 1st Viscount Donoughmore (1756–1825); succeeded his mother as 2nd Baron Donoughmore, 1788; Commissioner of Revenue [I.], 1785–93, and of Excise, 1793–1806; Major-General, 1805; Lieutenant-General, 1812; General, 1825. Created Viscount, 1797, and Earl of Donoughmore, Dec. 1800.

[6] Richard Butler, 1st Earl of Glengall (1775–1819); succeeded his father in 1788 as 10th Baron Caher; created Earl of Glengall [I.], 1816.

[7] Edmond Henry Pery, Baron Glentworth (1758–1844). Succeeded his father, the Bishop of Limerick (who in 1790 had been created Baron Glentworth), in 1794. Keeper of the Signet and Privy Seal [I.], 1795–7; Clerk of the Crown and Hanaper [I.], 1797–1806; created Viscount Limerick, Dec. 1800, and Earl of Limerick [I.], 1803; U.K. peerage, 1815, as Baron Foxford.

[8] George Agar, Baron Callan (1752?–1815), M.P. for Callan, 1777–90; peerage, 1790.

[9] James Cuffe, Lord Tyrawley (1748–1821); M.P. for Co. Mayo, 1768–97; peerage, 1797; Commissioner of Barracks [I.], 1798–1803. Castlereagh reported (7 Jan. 1799) that he had 'enlisted heartily' in support of the Union. 'The necessary personal attention being paid him will gain many very respectable county members from Mayo, together with his other friends.' (*Castlereagh Corresp.* ii, 85.)

[10] Sir John Blaquiere, Baron De Blaquiere (1732–1812), the son of a Huguenot refugee; Secretary of Legation in France, 1771–2; Irish Secretary, 1772–7; M.P. for various Irish constituencies, 1773–1800; K.B., 1774; created a Baronet, 1784; peerage, for supporting the Union, July 1800; M.P. for Rye, 1801–2; for Downton, 1803–6.

[11] Charles Moore, Marquess of Drogheda (1730–1822); succeeded his father as 6th Earl of Drogheda, 1758; created Marquess, 1791, and (U.K. peerage) Baron Moore, Jan. 1801. Master-General of the Ordnance [I.], 1770–97; Major-General, 1770; Lieutenant-General, 1777; General, 1793; Muster Master General [I.], May–Nov. 1807; Field Marshal, 1821. Joint Postmaster-General [I.], 1797–1806.

[12] The Duke of Portland had reported in Nov. 1798 that Lord Ely, relying on the favour of the Crown in an object personal to himself, was prepared to give the Union his utmost support. (*Castlereagh Corresp.* ii, 25.)

[13] Robert Stewart, 1st Marquess of Londonderry (1739–1821), Castlereagh's father. M.P. for Co.

[*Erlangen, 1 Jan. 1801.*] As I cannot in person have the honour to offer your Majesty my humble congratulations on your having effected the union of your Kingdoms, allow me to express my wishes that this event may contribute to the prosperity of Britain and that every English heart may date from the begining of this century their quiet and happiness and ever look up to your Majesty as the cause of the comfort they enjoy.

I hope also that your Majesty may in this new century as in the last continue to be particularly under the protection of the Almighty who preserved you so wonderfully last year for the good of Europe and the happiness of a family which feels the blessing of belonging to you.

The Duke desires me to present his humble duty to your Majesty with his congratulations on the Union and on the New Year, which begins most wretchedly for us, as we have just received the news of the dreadful Armistice[1] which destroys every hopes of ever seeing Germany restored to its ancient glory. As I am sure your Majesty will have the shameful particulars long before you can receive this letter I shall not trouble you by repeating them. (51631–2)

2317 EARL SPENCER *to the* KING

[*Admiralty, 2 Jan. 1801.*] Earl Spencer has the honour to lay before your Majesty the three Commissions for Colonels of Marines for your Majesty's signing, as also a scheme for a small augmentation in the Marine Corps which is become necessary from the present extended state of the Service and the numbers of supernumerary recruits which have lately been obtained. The augmentation is calculated upon a plan to make as small an increase of expence as can well attend such a measure, and Earl Spencer hopes that it will meet with your Majesty's approbation. (9974)

2318 THE DUKE OF PORTLAND *to the* KING

[*Bulstrode, Saturday, 3 Jan. 1801.*] The Duke of Portland begs leave with all humility to lay at your Majesty's feet two dispatches of the 23d & 27th of last month from the Lord Lieutenant of Ireland which were received in the course of yesterday & of this day. The first of them relates to a military transaction in which the conduct of the inferior officer appears to have been so highly reprehensible & subversive of discipline that it is suggested to the Duke of Portland (by the same high authority by whom it was heretofore suggested to him to submit an opinion to your Majesty respecting the sale of Captn. Longfield's commission which received the sanction of your Majesty's approbation) most humbly to represent to your Majesty that the conduct of Lieutenant Wilson of the 15th Regiment of Foot calls for the heaviest mark of your Majesty's displeasure, & to submit with all deference to your Majesty that your Majesty's dismissal of him

Down, 1771–83; created Baron Londonderry, 1789; Viscount Castlereagh, 1795; Earl of Londonderry, 1796; Marquess, 1816. Lord Camden wrote to Pitt on 10 July 1800: 'I enclose you a letter I received from Lord Castlereagh a few days ago by which you observe that he relinquishes for the present the English peerage.' (W. Dacres Adams MSS.) [1] Signed at Steyer, 25 Dec.

from the service, should be publickly declared at the head of the 15th Regiment & also promulgated to the army serving in Ireland. The other letter from the Lord Lieutenant only contains the alteration which in consequence of your Majesty's orders has been made in the title to be assumed by Col. Robert King, & the Lord Lieutenant's most dutifull & gratefull acknowledgements of your Majesty's most gracious condescension in granting all the favors which the success of the great measure of the Union made it necessary for him to sollicit of your Majesty. The Duke of Portland requests your Majesty's permission to lay before you the expression of similar sentiments on the part of the Earl of Clanricarde for the great favor your Majesty has been pleased to confer on his family by the grant of an Earldom to his daughters in succession. The Duke of Portland also presumes to offer to your Majesty two reports of Mr Graham[1] the Magistrate whom your Majesty was pleased to approve being sent into the Midland & manufacturing part of the kingdom which the Duke of Portland trusts will not be unsatisfactory to your Majesty, & he has ventured to add a letter which was only put into his hands this afternoon from a Mr Dyneley, a nephew of your Majesty's Advocate, containing, as the Duke of Portland is inclined to believe, some facts relative to France & the United Provinces which has not been observed before, & of which he has reason to beleive that the authenticity may be fully relied upon. (9975–6)

2319 LORD GRENVILLE *to the* KING, *and the reply*

[*Dropmore, 6 Jan. 1801.*] Lord Grenville has the honour to transmit to your Majesty a Paris paper containing the account that another Armistice has been signed in Germany, on such terms as must ensure the signature of a separate peace, such as the enemy may chuse to dictate. Lord Grenville thinks it very doubtful whether, considering the last accounts received of the state of the Austrian army, this event is on the whole unfavourable to the interests of your Majesty's dominions. (9977)

[*The King's reply, Windsor, 7 Jan.*] The French paper communicated this morning by Lord Grenville shews that the Emperor yields entirely to the orders of the enemy. I cannot in the present state of the Austrian troops look on this as by any means disadvantageous to my dominions; on the contrary it removes the necessity of sending money to assist a dispirited Court, and will consequently concentrate our means to defend ourselves, and I trust with both vigour and effect. (Fortescue MSS.)

2320 THE EARL OF CHESTERFIELD *to the* KING

[*London, 10 Jan. 1801.*] In obedience to your Majesty's commands I wrote on Wednesday last to Coll. FitzRoy[2] to acquaint him with your gracious intentions to appoint him one of your Majesty's Equerries Extraordinary. I have the honour

---

[1] Aaron Graham, the Hatton Garden Magistrate (salary, £400 a year). Before the end of the month he was moved to Bow Street.

[2] Charles Fitzroy (1762–1831), second son of Charles, 1st Lord Southampton (1737–97), for whom see No. 34. Lieutenant-Colonel, 1794; Colonel, 1797; Major-General, 1803; Lieutenant-General, 1810; General, 1821. In 1816, six years after the death of Princess Amelia, he married Eliza (*née* Barlow) widow of Clavering Savage.

to lay before your Majesty Colonel FitzRoy's answer to my letter. I find that the Clerk Martial[1] is sworn in before the Board of Green Cloth. (9978)

2321 LORD GRENVILLE *to the* KING, *and the reply*

[*Cleveland Row, 12 Jan. 1801.*] Your Majesty will receive in these boxes a letter from the Emperor of Germany transmitted by Lord Minto. As the returning an early answer may much add to the impression of those friendly sentiments which Lord Grenville imagines your Majesty would think it proper to express on this occasion, he has taken the liberty to submit to your Majesty the draft of an answer, which, if your Majesty should be graciously pleased to approve it, may be sent tomorrow night. (9979)

[*The King's reply, Windsor, 13 Jan.*] Lord Grenville having by his note expressed a wish that the answer to the letter of the Roman Emperor should be dispatched this night, I have sent it in *manu propria* for that purpose. (Fortescue MSS.)

2322 THE DUCHESS OF WURTEMBERG *to the* KING

[*Erlangen, 13 Jan. 1801.*] As it ever gives me great pleasure to write openly to your Majesty I seize on the opportunity of a messenger going to General Melius to send you a letter.

The Duke has ordered the General to acquaint Lord Grenville that after the unexpected misfortunes of this campaign, and the steps the Court of Vienna has taken in consequence of them, he has found himself obliged to send a person to Paris who has orders to keep in the background and not to come forwards unless he finds there is no thoughts of continuing the war, and then not till he see[s] that the other Courts seek to conclude separate Treaties. As the Duke is determined strictly to keep his Treaty as long as it lays in his power, and has already maintained it notwithstanding his severe losses and the offers made him to break it your Majesty will I am sure do the Duke the justice to believe that whatever he may find himself obliged to do, it will be against his inclination, but you must yourself feel it quite impossible for him with his seven thousand men to continue alone the war, should Austria give up the contest and make Peace.

Your Majesty is I trust too well acquainted with my character not to be convinced that I detest interfering or speaking of things out of my sphere. However I cannot conceal the regret I feel at seeing by the papers that in addition to the many painful hours you have spent owing to this unfortunate campaign the breach between the Northern Powers will be a fresh source of uneasiness to your Majesty and of great distress to the rest of Europe. Far be it from me to pretend to judge of the merits of the cause; my attachment to your Majesty and Great Britain must ever make me too partial to attempt investigating the subject; which ever important is doubly so at this awful crisis. This alone induces me to break my deter-

---

[1] Major-General Robert Manners kissed hands on the 14th on being appointed as Clerk Martial and First Equerry to the King, *vice* General Goldsworthy, *dec.* (salary as Clerk Martial, £60 a year, as First Equerry, £500).

mination of never speaking to your Majesty on political subjects, and my dutiful affection for you makes me overlook every other consideration and on this occasion alter my conduct and speak to your Majesty with the sincerity due to the best of parents. This I hope is a sufficient apology for my offering some hints concerning Russia as I happen by my connexions to be pretty well acquainted with that Court, and from what I have heard the Duke say of those he lived with in Russia have been able to form some judgement of the Emperor's character. On the subject of the present misunderstanding the Duke has had the delicacy never to speak to me, feeling that it must be a painful one to me, and his being related and attached to both Courts makes him think it prudent to be silent.

From the various things that I have collected I fear that the making use of Ministerial discussions to set things to rights will only lose much time and perhaps not be crowned with success, as at that Court it is difficult to have them brought to the Sovereign's knowledge: and it appears to me that many difficulties might be removed if your Majesty wishes things to be brought round and a spunge passed on all sides over the unpleasant transactions which have taken place, if you would try to employ a person who being fortunately equally attached and related to both Courts might more easily succeed in softening things without exposing the dignity of either Monarch. I mean the Duke who, being your son-in-law and the Emperor's brother,[1] (to whom the Emperor has to my knowledge constantly shewn great friendship and confidence) could have no other object but the uniting two great Powers on whom the good of Europe depends. Though I know the Duke dislikes the interfering in any business which does not directly regard him, still I am sure he is too much attached to both Sovereigns and has too much at heart the good of Europe not to undertake to do everything in his power if your Majesty would write to him and express your wishes on the subject.

Your Majesty's constant goodness to me has encouraged me to venture to speak thus freely to you and to repose my whole confidence in your breast, only intreating you never to mention to anybody my having taken this liberty, as I should be wretched whatever your decision may be on this subject, that the Duke should ever hear of this from anybody but yourself, as it is the only time in my life that I have kept anything from him and I should be miserable could he think me wanting in confidence towards him. If your Majesty should dislike the liberty I have taken I hope my goodwill will obtain my pardon. (51633–7)

2323   LORD AVONMORE *to the* MARQUESS OF DOWNSHIRE

[*13 Jan. 1801.*] Tho' you must have learned that the Office of Register in Chancery has been granted to my son, yet when I assure your Lordship, which I can with truth, that this arrangement has been the voluntary act of Administration and neither solicited nor forseen by me, I hope you will permit me to express a wish which is near my heart, which is, that it may not excite in your mind any jealousy of me or cause any interruption of that intercourse which has hitherto subsisted between us, and which, if not forbidden by your Lordship, it shall be

---

[1] The Duke's sister Sophia Dorothea Augusta (1759–1828) had married the Tsar Paul I in 1776.

my ambition to cultivate. If the office had not been granted to one of my family it would probably have fallen into the hands of some person who might not entertain for your Lordship the same respect and esteem with which I have the honor to be [etc.]. (9980)

2324 THE DUKE OF PORTLAND *to the* KING

[*Burlington House, Tuesday eve., 13 Jan. 1801.*] Your Majesty's gracious condescension in approving the Duke of Portland's having submitted to your Majesty a summary of the contents of the inclosures which accompanied a former dispatch of the Lord Lieutenant's, encourages the Duke of Portland on the present occasion most humbly to acquaint your Majesty that it appears by the reports of the General Officers commanding in the different districts that in the provinces of the south & north general quiet prevails & that in the counties of Tipperary & Kilkenny & generally throughout the province of Ulster the people are as industrious as they were ever known to be, that the same spirit & temper prevail in general through the province of Leinster, & that there is no appearance of the contrary in Connaught but a sort of whisper that something is in agitation, & the Duke of Portland cannot but fear that the late unfortunate events in Germany will tend to revive & invigorate that restless spirit & disposition to outrage to which the generality of the Irish are but too much addicted. (9982–3)

2325 HENRY DUNDAS *to the* KING

[*Downing Street, 14 Jan. 1801, 3 p.m.*] Mr Dundas humbly submits to your Majesty's consideration the accompanying drafts[1] which he has prepared in concurrence with the opinions of your Majesty's confidential servants, and which, if they meet with your Majesty's approbation, Mr Dundas proposes to dispatch without delay.[2] (9984)

2326 LORD GRENVILLE *to the* KING, *and the reply*

[*Cleveland Row, 14 Jan. 1801, 11 p.m.*] Lord Grenville omitted to mention to your Majesty today that Monsieur d'Ehrensward was to have had an audience of the Queen tomorrow. But as he will receive tomorrow morning a note apprising him of the measures taken this day, Lord Grenville proposes with your Majesty's permission to send Sir Stephen Cottrel to him, to say to him that under the present circumstances it is concluded that it will be more agreeable to him that this ceremony should not take place tomorrow. (Fortescue MSS.)

[1] To the Admiralty, to the Commander-in-Chief in the Leeward Islands, and to the Governor-General of Bengal (on resisting the claims of the Armed Neutrality that free bottoms make free goods).
[2] The King's reply on the 15th is in Pellew's *Life and Correspondence of Viscount Sidmouth*, I, 365 (subsequently cited as Pellew). In line 3, for 'proposed' read 'prepared'. See also, Add. MSS. 38736, f. 275, and 40100, f. 297.

[*The King's reply, Queen's House, 15 Jan.*] On returning the boxes received this day from the Foreign Office I cannot help just writing a line to Lord Grenville approving of his having intimated to Sir Stephen Cottrell that it will probably be more agreable to Monr. Ehrenswerdt not to have his audience this day of the Queen under the present circumstances. (*Ibid.*)

2327   *Letters from* WILLIAM PITT *to the* KING

[*Downing Street, 22 Jan. 1801.*] Mr Pitt humbly begs leave to submit to your Majesty a draft for the Speech,[1] the sentiments of which are he trusts likely to receive your Majesty's approbation.[2] (9985)

[*Downing Street, Saturday, 24 Jan.*] Mr Pitt humbly begs leave to submit to your Majesty that from the small number of Members sworn yesterday and today, it may be adviseable that the delivery of your Majesty's Speech should be deferred till Wednesday or Thursday.[3] He has consulted on this point with the Speaker, and therefore takes the liberty of requesting your Majesty's commands which of those days will be least troublesome to your Majesty. The latter of the two days, if equally convenient to your Majesty's arrangements, will probably be the most so to the House. (9986)

2328   THE DUKE OF PORTLAND *to the* KING, *and the reply*

[*Burlington House, Sunday, 25 Jan. 1801.*] The commands your Majesty was pleased to lay upon the Duke of Portland have been obeyed & the necessary orders have been given accordingly for deferring the Council[4] from tomorrow to Wednesday next at St. James's.

As the person who has of late been employed to transcribe your Majesty's

[1] The Speech from the Throne delivered at the opening of the first Session of the United Parliament on 2 Feb.

[2] The King replied from the Queen's House on the 23rd (the letter is inaccurately given in Stanhope, III, Appendix, p. xxiii): 'The general tone as well as matter of my proposed Speech for Tuesday meets with my fullest approbation, and no want of exertion shall be wanting in me to deliver it with the force it deserves. I trust, therefore, that Mr. Pitt will not make any material alterations in it, and that I shall find it as perfect when, on Monday, it will be communicated here to the Cabinet as it has come this morning from him' (Chatham Papers).

[3] As the Parliament of Great Britain had now become the Parliament of the United Kingdom of Great Britain and Ireland, not merely the new comers but all the Members of the House of Commons were required to take the usual oaths, as if there had been a General Election. This applied too to the Peers. Addington was re-elected Speaker on the 22nd. Notice, however, that Ley, the Deputy Clerk of the House of Commons, had written to the Speaker on the 16th: 'Mr. Pitt has desired me to let you know the result of the conference today at his house. There were present, Lord Grenville, Lord Castlereagh, Master of the Rolls and Attorney and Solicitor-General. He entered largely upon the whole subject. The result is as far as matters can be settled, that the present Members, British and Irish, are *not* [to] take the qualifyg. oath; that future British are to take it; that future Irish ought to have a qualifn. and that an Act is to be passed immediately declaring where that qualifn. is to lie...The questions respecting the cases of writs issuing before 31 Decr. and the electn. afterwards must be determined by the House. Perhaps the best way of deciding this qn. will be to let things go on as they would have done in their respective Houses.' (Sidmouth MSS.)

[4] The Council for the Speech. The Grand Cabinet, that is.

Speech is incapable at this time through illness of doing so, the Duke of Portland has had a fair copy made of it by another of the clerks in his Office, & herewith submits it with all humility to your Majesty in order that he may receive your Majesty's pleasure with respect to the form & size of the character in which it is written.[1] (9987)

[*The King's reply, Windsor, 26 Jan., 8.44 a.m.*] The draft of the Speech is written in so very legible a manner that I desire the Duke of Portland will direct the copy for my reading in the House of Lords on Thursday to be prepared in the same hand; I think it more easy to read than when the characters are larger.

As I am not wanted this day in town, I shall deferr returning till tomorrow. (Ann Arbor MSS.)

2329   THE KING *to the* LORD CHANCELLOR (LORD LOUGHBOROUGH), *and the reply*

[*Queen's House, 28 Jan. 1801.*] In consequence of the information given me this day by the Lord Chancellor that it is supposed the Lord Primate of Ireland is to consent that Mr Duigenan,[2] member for the Borough of Armagh, shall vacate his seat in favour of Mr Corry,[3] the Irish Chancellor of the Exchequer, I am certainly very willing to apprize the Lord Primate of the ill effect it would produce should he assist any person to a seat in Parliament who is supposed to be favorable to the Roman Catholic question, and that at the expence of one supposed a strong friend to the present Church Establishment; but before I take any step to that effect, I have put a few lines on paper for the Lord Chancellor's opinion as to the propriety of my writing on the subject, and whether I have said more than he thinks I ought on this occasion; when perused I desire it may be returned.[4] (9988 and [draft] 9989)

[1] The King's eyesight was failing, and he already had had trouble with one Speech owing to the negligence of the Home Office. *The Times* had had this paragraph on 4 Nov. 1797: 'When his Majesty went to the House of Lords on Thursday to read the Speech from the Throne, a very extraordinary embarrassment arose from a blunder in the Office of the Home Department which has the charge of delivering to his Majesty a fair copy of the Speech. After his Majesty was robed, it was found that the box that had been sent him contained only a rough draft of the Speech, written on half sides of paper and in so small and illegible a hand that when the King mounted the Throne he could hardly proceed to read it. The King put on his spectacles, but even that could not assist him. The confusion was very great; messengers were dispatched in all directions for a fair copy and it was not until his Majesty came to that part which relates to Lord Duncan's victory that he was relieved from his embarrassment by having a fair copy procured for him.'

[2] Patrick Duigenan (c. 1735–1816), a fanatical anti-Catholic. M.P. for Old Leighlin, 1791–7; for Armagh City, 1797–1816. He did not vacate his seat. See No. 2333.

[3] Isaac Corry (1755?–1813). M.P. for Newry, 1776–1800; for Dundalk, 1801–2; for Newry, 1802–6; for Newport, Isle of Wight, 1806–7. Surveyor-General of the Ordnance [I.], 1788; Commissioner of Revenue [I.], 1789–98; Chancellor of the Exchequer [I.], 1799–1804; Surveyor-General of Crown Lands, 1799–1813. A new writ for Dundalk was ordered on 2 Feb. 1801, both the late Members having resigned their seats, and Corry was elected on 28 Feb. He had lost his seat for Newry by the luck of the draw.

[4] The Duchess of Devonshire wrote on 25 February: 'I saw my brother [Lord Spencer] and I find that the poor King certainly showed proofs of derangement on the 28th January, the day he accused Dundas at the Levée of Jacobinical principles for opposing him' (Chatsworth MSS.).

[*Lord Loughborough's reply, 28 Jan., 8 p.m.*] Your Majesty will probably receive very soon a distinct & ample communication of all the considerations which have engaged the most serious deliberations of those servants in whom you have graciously been pleased to place your confidence. Any step taken (however slight it might appear to be) to anticipate the decision your Majesty may form on that re-presentation of the subject, would in my apprehension be premature. I am humbly to request your forgiveness for my indiscretion in mentioning a circumstance which may bear an application to that subject, & which at the time I referred to it, I had reason to think your Majesty might have heard from the Archbishop of Canterbury.

With every feeling of distress for having given your Majesty the trouble of discussion upon a point which, upon my best reconsideration, I think requires no immediate measure, I humbly advise that no *formal* communication should be made by your Majesty to the Primate of Ireland on this subject.

No reason has yet been offerred to my understanding which varys the opinion I have declared on the great question, & by which I shall abide.[1] (9990–1)

2330 WILLIAM PITT *to the* KING, *and the reply*

[*Downing Street, Wednesday, 28 Jan. 1801, 6 p.m.*] Mr Pitt humbly begs leave to submit to your Majesty that as progress made in swearing Members today has not been considerable,[2] it would be very desireable, if it can be done without inconvenience to your Majesty, that the delivery of the Speech should be post-poned from tomorrow till Monday; and as the House could not sit on Friday[3]

[1] Portland had communicated his views to Pitt on Saturday the 24th: 'I so entirely agree with you in the necessity of determining on the language to be held in case the Catholick question should, as is most likely, be forced into Tuesday's debate, that I am quite ashamed of having forgot a principal object of my intention in calling upon you yesterday, which was to express my own apprehensions of the consequences of countenancing that measure, & the necessity of coming to a decision upon it. I wish I could, with any convenience, accept your proposal in the course of this morning, but I have been induced to submit to an operation which makes it necessary for me to stay at home & is not unaccom-panied with unpleasant sensations which rather make me wish to defer calling upon you till tomorrow, when I am assured that I may go out without any inconvenience & when I will call upon you about twelve o'clock in my way to the Cabinet...' (Chatham Papers, 168.)

The Lord Chancellor communicated his views to the King after the Cabinet meeting that day. Wind-ham wrote in his diary: '*28 Jan.* Cabinet, in which last discussion of the Catholic business, when Pitt declared that he must go out if it was not carried' (Add. MSS. 37924, f. 86).

George Rose wrote in his diary: 'On Wednesday the 28th of January, Mr. Pitt first had distinct and clear proof of the Speaker taking an eager and anxious part in influencing persons against the measure of Catholic emancipation.' Rose was astonished to hear a few days later that Addington had been rash enough to accept the Premiership. 'I was not in the remotest *possible degree* prepared for it, not having had the most distant intimation of anything tending to a misunderstanding between them [the King and Pitt.]...The Speaker, to my utter astonishment, to be Mr. Pitt's successor. To what length will vanity not carry a man? Amiable and good in private life, and I am persuaded honestly attached to Mr. Pitt, he is no more equal to what he has undertaken than a child.' (Pretyman MSS.)

Rose has an interesting reference to the Court influence against Pitt and the advocates of Catholic emancipation, in a letter dated 18 Nov. 1801 to the Bishop of Lincoln: 'Mr. Pitt...is much more sore about the King's interference with the Lords of the Bedchamber, etc., on the Catholic question than he was in the summer.' (Pretyman MSS.)

[2] According to *The Times* about 350 members had been sworn in by Wednesday.

[3] That being the anniversary of the execution of King Charles the Martyr. It was, customarily, a holiday at all the Public Offices, and the Theatres were closed. On 30 Jan. 1800 many people attended the usual service in Westminster Abbey in the expectation of hearing a sermon from one of the Bishops,

there would in fact be no material time lost in the course of business.[1] It is also some additional reason for this measure, that in the interval some further explanation may naturally be expected of accounts which have been brought by this day's mail from Hamburgh in private letters to several respectable merchants in the city, of the Danish Minister having been suddenly sent away from Petersburg; an event which, if it proves true (as there seems little reason to doubt) may probably lead to very interesting consequences. (9992–3)

[*The King's reply, Queen's House, 29 Jan. 7.05 p.m.*] I have this instant received Mr. Pitt's proposing the suspension of my delivering the Speech from tomorrow to Monday. The moment it is thought more advantageous to the conducting the public business I cannot have the smallest objection to it. (Chatham Papers.)

2331   THE KING *to* HENRY ADDINGTON,[2] *and the reply*

[*Queen's House, 29 Jan. 1801.*] The Speaker of the House of Commons, I trust, is so sensible of the high regard I have for his upright private character, as well as of his ability and temper in the fullfilling his public employment that he will not be surprised at my desire of communicating to him the very strong apprehensions I conceive that the most mischievous measure is in contemplation to be brought forward in this first Session of the Parliament of the United Kingdom, and this by one styling himself a friend to Administration, I mean Lord Castlereagh. This is no less than the placing the Roman Catholics of the kingdom in an equal state of rights to sit in both Houses of Parliament and hold offices of trust and emolument with those of the Established Church. It is now suggested by those best informed that Mr Pitt favours this opinion; that Lord Grenville and Mr Dundas do I have the fullest proof as they have intimated as much to me, who have certainly not disguised to them my abhorrence of the very idea, and my feeling it as a duty, should it ever come forward, publicly to express my disapprobation of it, and that no consideration could ever make me give my consent to what I look upon as the destruction of the Established Church which by the wisdom of the Parliament of England I as well as several of my predecessors have been obliged to swear the support of at our Coronations, besides its being contrary to the wisdom of every other European Government who have seen the necessity of having an Established Church and consequently admit no one into civil employment not members of

but they were disappointed, as the service was omitted, for the first time, it was said, since the custom was started.

[1] This Speech from the Throne, which opened the first Session of the first Parliament of the United Kingdom of Great Britain and Ireland, was the first which was not read in the customary way at the Cockpit on the eve of the Session. The change was made, as *The Times* later remarked, because 'Ministers have judged (and we believe the public opinion has sanctioned theirs) that there is a great indecorum in anticipating (if one were able) the contents of the Royal communication to Parliament.' Addington wrote to Lord Pelham on 17 Oct. 1801: 'As the practice of reading the King's Speech at the Cockpit was dropped last year, I have no thoughts of resuming it, but as I shall have a dinner party on Wednesday, consisting chiefly of Privy Councillors, I propose to read the Speech to them before dinner, as was done by Mr. Pitt in November and in January last.' (Add. MSS. 33108, f. 175.) See, also, A. Aspinall, *The Grand Cabinet, 1800–1837*, in *Politica*, Dec. 1938, p. 332.

[2] There is a very different version of this letter in Pellew, I, 285–6, which is accurately printed except that in line 16 of the first paragraph, 'they' should be 'their'.

it. I should be taking up the Speaker's time very uselessly if I expatiated farther on this subject as I know we both view it in a similar point of view. I wish he would open Mr Pitt's eyes as to the danger arising from the mere agitating so improper a question, that whatever evils have been cured by his manly recantation of his former opinions for Parliamentary reform, his shewing any countenance to a measure striking our Church Establishment at the heart, besides unhinging every political tye our forefathers have thought sacred, must affect every man attached to the principles on which our happy Constitution is founded; indeed it is exactly following the steps of the French Revolution where every consideration of religion has been destroyed.

My eagerness has again forced my pen to detain the Speaker longer than I intended. I will therefore conclude with remarking that my conveying my thoughts in this private manner I have adopted least if I had desired to see him, which I should have preferred, it might have put him under difficulties if questioned how he came to have been desired to come here.

If unfortunately this measure shall be brought forward it will then be impossible for me not from the urgency of the case to set all etiquettes aside and desire the Speaker to come to me, as I must then know the true sentiments of all those who view this dangerous business in the same light I have uniformly done from the time I could speculate on either religious or political subjects. (9994–5)

[*Addington's reply, Palace Yard, 29 Jan.*] The Speaker is deeply sensible of that condescension and goodness with which your Majesty has upon all occasions been pleased to honor him, and of the peculiar mark of your Majesty's confidence, conveyed to him on the highly interesting and anxious subject to which your Majesty's note relates. He has lost no time in obeying your Majesty's commands by endeavouring to ascertain whether he can be instrumental in preventing the embarrassments which would arise from any dissatisfaction in your Majesty's mind in consequence of the line of conduct which your Majesty's Ministers may think of recommending on a subject of great public importance. He has had an opportunity of communicating with Mr. Pitt of which he has availed himself in the manner that he thought best suited to the occasion. The result of what passed he is not without hopes it might be useful to submit to your Majesty's consideration, but he feels that it would be hardly possible to do so as fully and particularly as your Majesty would naturally expect under such circumstances, within the compass of a letter, and he therefore ventures to avail himself of your Majesty's indulgence so far as to say that he is not aware of any inconvenient observations which would be attracted if your Majesty should think proper to lay your commands upon him to attend you at the Queen's House either tomorrow or Saturday evening. (9999–10,000)

2332 THE ARCHBISHOP OF CANTERBURY (DR MOORE) *to the* KING

[*Lambeth House, 29 Jan. 1801.*] Since I had the honor of mentioning to your Majesty yesterday the circumstance of the Primate of Ireland's promise to favor the election of Mr Corry, Chancellor of the Exchequer, to represent a borough in the present Parliament of the United Kingdom, I have been informed by Lord Hobart of his having spoken to the Primate upon that subject, stating to him the design of bringing in a Bill for the emancipation of Irish Roman Catholicks from the Test Oaths &c &c, & Mr Corry's known determination to support that Bill. His Grace called upon me this morning in order to express his concern at not having sooner been informed that such a Bill was in contemplation, nor that it would have Mr Corry's support. He added that, under such circumstances, he should not hesitate to inform Lord Castlereagh immediately of his determination to withdraw the support of his recommendation of Mr Corry, feeling it to be his duty to oppose to the utmost of his power a Bill so hostile to the United Church of England & Ireland & to the Constitution in Church & State. Under this state of the case, I presume your Majesty will not think it necessary to write to the Primate upon the subject.

It will not be unacceptable to your to your Majesty [*sic*] to know that I have mentioned to my friend Ld Ch. Justice Eldon the intended Bill before-mentioned, which I found he had not before heard of. And I am happy to assure your Majesty that his sentiments upon it are such as I expected, & as your Majesty would wish them to be, firm & decisive against it. What I have farther heard upon the subject is favorable—so that I am willing to hope there is good foundation to believe that when Mr Pitt sees what the general sentiments of so respectable persons are upon the subject, which he must soon see & be sensible of, he will cease to persevere in what he has too hastily taken up (if it be certain that he *has* taken it up) & determine no longer to give support to it.

I have presumed to trouble your Majesty with the above statements under a persuasion that they will not be unacceptable to your Majesty. (9996–7)

2333   THE KING *to the* LORD PRIMATE OF IRELAND[1]

[*Queen's House, 29 Jan. 1801.*] The King does not think he should act right towards the Lord Primate of Ireland if he did not acquaint him that the Lord Chancellor informed him that it is supposed his Grace has engaged to give his interest in the Borough of Armagh in favour of Mr Corry, the Irish Chancellor of the Exchequer, on Mr Duigenan's resigning his seat in Parliament; but that the Lord Primate is probably not informed that Mr. Duigenan is a strong friend to the Established Church, and the other gentleman supposed engaged in favour of the highly dangerous proposition the total emancipation of the Roman Catholics, and consequently the destruction of the National Church as a Test necessary for sitting in Parliament or holding public employments. In this view I should trust the Lord Primate must think his giving his support to anyone who does not declare his adherence to the Established Church, and resolution to oppose any enovation in favour of Popery would be highly improper. I therefore give him this notice privately, as I know his warm attachment to our Church Establishment, and that on this hint he will thoroughly consider the proper conduct he ought to follow.[2] (9998)

[1] Endorsed by the King, 'Not sent'.
[2] The King later spoke of this episode to Lord Glenbervie who thus reported the King's statement: 'Upon the new Parliament after the Union it had been settled that Dr. Duigenan was to retire from

2334 HENRY ADDINGTON *to the* KING

[*Palace Yard, 30 Jan. 1801.*] The Speaker is truly grateful for your Majesty's gracious indulgence, and will not fail to pay his humble duty to your Majesty at the Queen's House, at eight o'clock this evening.[1] (10001)

2335 *Letters from the* EARL OF CHESTERFIELD *to the* KING

[*Chesterfield House, 30 Jan. 1801.*] Your Majesty will, I hope, forgive the liberty I take in acquainting you that I have just received an account of the death of Edward Beard, Mewskeeper at Windsor. The emoluments of the situation consist of a weekly allowance of half a guinea and an allowance of twenty pounds per annum for a house, making in the whole forty seven pounds sterling & six shillings per annum. When I have the honor to pay my duty this evening at the Queen's House I shall beg to be honoured by your Majesty's commands as to the disposal of the place. (10002)

[*Friday, 30 Jan.*] Your Majesty will, I hope, pardon the liberty I take in submitting to you that as the situation of the Keeper of the Mews at Windsor is almost a sinecure it might be a comfortable addition to the situation of any of your Majesty's Pages who have a large family. The Mews Keeper at Windsor never wears the livery, nor is he allowed one. In every case I beg to submitt the disposal of the place to your Majesty. I heard today that the Mews Keeper at Kensington[2] is much worse & not likely to live long, and in obedience to your Majesty's commands I had reserved that place (which cannot be done by Deputy) for Sturkey. (10003)

2336 THE KING *to the* ARCHBISHOP OF CANTERBURY, *and a reply*

[*Queen's House, 31 Jan. 1801.*] The King is much pleased with the attention of the Lord Archbishop of Canterbury in having last evening[3] communicated to him what has passed with the Primate of Ireland, whose conduct seems highly becoming his station. The language of Lord Eldon is just what, from his char-

representing the borough of Armagh or rather to vacate...to make room for Corry, but that one day as he was going from the Levée to hold a Council, a person...whispered to him that he ought to write a letter to the Primate...to warn him of this and to desire that he would not suffer so good a friend of the Church to vacate in order to make room for one so great an enemy to it. That the King observed that he thought this would be a strong measure... The King on going home to dinner drew up a letter to the Primate in which he made the application, mentioning that it was by Lord Rosslyn's advice, which he sent over to Lord Rosslyn, desiring his opinion whether it would be right for him to send it, and that Lord Rosslyn then wrote him back that upon consideration he thought it more prudent not to do it... That his letter of course was never sent, but that somebody else...had persuaded Stewart not to permit Duigenan to vacate.' (*Journals*, I, 394.)

[1] The King's letter to Addington, 31 Jan., is in Pellew, I, 287. Rose believed that on the 30th Addington was at the Queen's House for four hours (*Diaries and Correspondence*, I, 286, 292, 309). Pitt wrote to his brother on 5 Feb.: 'I have long been persuaded that, whenever he [the King] might have occasion to do so, the Speaker would be the person to whom he would resort' (Ashbourne's *Pitt*, p. 311).

[2] James Pye. He died in his apartments in Kensington Palace on 21 Feb., and was succeeded by William Sturkey. Beard was succeeded by James Cocum.

[3] This letter is the reply to the Archbishop's letter of the 29th (No. 2332), so there may be an inaccuracy in the dating of one of them.

acter and tallents must have been expected, and the inference drawn by the Lord Archbishop of the supposed effect on Mr Pitt's mind of the general sentiments of wise and dispassoniate men, it is justly to be hoped will prove founded.[1] (10005)

[*From the Archbishop of Canterbury, Lambeth House, 31 Jan. 1801.*] The Archbishop of Canterbury has received the honor of his Majesty's commands, & will pay his duty to his Majesty at the time appointed, three o'clock, this afternoon.[2] (10004)

[1] The letter is endorsed, in no recognizable hand: 'From the King to the late Archbishop Moore'—so the Papers were arranged after the Archbishop's death in 1805.
[2] Pitt's letter to the King, 31 Jan., on the Catholic question (10006–13), and the King's reply on 1 Feb. (10021–2) are in Stanhope, III, Appendix, pp. xxiii–xxx.

Windham wrote in his diary on the 30th: 'Saw Mr. Pitt and found that all was changed from the time of the Cabinet on Wednesday, and that he conceived he must give way.' (Add. MSS. 37924, f. 86.)

As Joint Postmaster-General, Auckland was not in the Cabinet, but his views were of some importance, and they were communicated to Pitt on the 31st:

Most private and confidential

'I write this letter after the first night, in the course of 56 years, that I recollect to have passed without any disposition to sleep.—I write it rather to avoid the self-reproach of inactivity and reserve in a conjuncture the most unhappy that I have known, than from any vanity of spirit, or from any hope that my openness will meet with a return, or that what I shall say will make any impression. I write, because it is not in my nature to preserve a sullen silence under the knowledge which I have of what is going forwards. And yet it nearly throws my reason off its hinges, when I am to advert to particulars impossible to have been expected by me, after all that had passed on your part in 1790, in 1795, and through the whole course of our preparing the fatal measure of the Union in 1799 and 1800. Still, however, if considerations hitherto unforeseen by either of us, and at this hour utterly beyond the reach of my imagination, have decided you to an experiment, momentous beyond example, contrary to your supposed opinions, and adverse to the known and fixed opinion of one who has long merited your confidence, and who has shewn himself warmly and affectionately attached to you, surely it is neither petulant nor unreasonable to say that a wound from a friend's hand may be aggravated beyond mortal sufferance by the neglectful and indifferent manner in which it is inflicted.

I well know and I make allowances for the unwillingness of a great mind to hold conference and controversy with those whose opinions on essential subjects cannot have either complaisance or pliancy. But I know also that the same great mind is candid and generous when the first moments of impatience have subsided; and that it is capable of self-examination, self-conviction, and self-correction. It is under this impression that I shall now submit a few questions in the order in which they occurred to me, when I first heard that it is seriously in contemplation to strike down all the barriers which the wisdom of our forefathers thought necessary for the security of our civil and religious establishment.

Is such an enterprize necessary? Is it expedient? Cui bono? With what view? To what end? Will it convert disaffection to loyalty? Will it change antipathies and intolerance into mutual love and indulgence? Will it reconcile sects which a long and bloody experience has shewn to be irreconcileable? Will it stand clear of the imputation (however unjust) of unconcern and apathy respecting truths the most essential both to present and future life? Will it not be considered as tending to revolution, either through the influence of irreligion by the equipoise, or rather by the confusion, of all creeds and worships as so many State-juggles; or through the effect of a religious alarm, distrust and animosity which may possibly burst forth in every part of the Empire.

But admitting for a moment that the measure is sound in its principles—is it consistent with good faith to push forwards, as a postscript to the Union, a proposition which is repugnant to the feelings, because it is deemed ruinous to the safety and interests, of those who principally supported the Union; and who supported it under a very different expectation known to prevail in their minds, and warranted (as they thought) by what had passed in 1795?

There is however a larger point of view. Is the measure applicable to the actual circumstances of the British Empire? Is it eligible and wise? Is it moral and justifiable before God and man to force a dis-union among your friends and to expose the whole Government of the country to the mockery and mischief of our enemies, and to eventual subversion; and all this in a crisis and conjuncture of the most complicated and accumulated difficulties?

Permit me to advance one step further! I will again admit for a moment that the measure is so right

2337 HENRY ADDINGTON *to the* KING

[*Palace Yard, 1 Feb. 1801.*] The Speaker of the House of Commons cannot fail, from various considerations, to be deeply affected by your Majesty's note.[1] He proposes to pay his duty at the Queen's House at ¼ past one o'clock today, and to attend your Majesty in the manner which you have condescended to direct. (10020)

2338 THE ARCHBISHOP OF CANTERBURY (DR MOORE) *to the* KING

[*Lambeth House, 2 Feb. 1801.*] I have the honour to return to your Majesty, with my humble thanks for your Majesty's confidential communication of thanks, the enclosed papers relative to Ireland.

It is my duty to inform your Majesty that it appears impracticable to propose to the Primate of Ireland, in the present state of the case, to revoke the purport of his letter to Lord Castlerea[g]h, because I find it is a fact that, on the same day he wrote to Dr. Duigenan and committed himself so entirely that he must unavoidably wait for the answer. The decision with which he took the measure, certainly arose from an honourable anxiety for the essential Interests of the Church and the safety of the Throne and the Constitution, strongly impressed by the necessity and sacred duty of not suffering himself to be in any degree an indirect instrument of contributing to the success of what appeared to him so dangerous. (10023)

2339 *Letters from* WILLIAM PITT *to the* KING, *and a reply*

[*Downing Street, Monday, 2 Feb. 1801, 11.30 p.m.*] Mr Pitt humbly begs leave to acquaint your Majesty that the Address was moved this day by Sir Watkin Williams[2] in a speech of great manliness and good sense, and seconded with great ability by

in its principles, and so beneficial in its tendency, as to justify you in sacrificing many friends to it, and in exposing the Kingdom to great embarrassments in the pursuit of it. Still, is it *so clear*, is it *quite so clear* that it will have the concurrence of any one branch of the Legislature? If it be likely to fail in any of those branches (and God avert the effects which it may possibly have on one of them); if it be certain to meet with a great and serious obstruction in each of those branches; will the inevitable agitation and impression of such a struggle, even if the point could be carried, be compensated by any good to be derived from the modern theory of "adapting old establishments to new circumstances," of weighing religious tenets in the scale of population, and of being guided by what is called the will of the people and the freedom of religious opinion?

Is it, in plain words, advisable or right to try such a measure without previously ascertaining that it will have the concurrence or at least the acquiescence of the Crown, of the Church, of the Law, and also of the leading individuals and great interests of the Country, by which your Government has been so steadily and so honorably supported?

Lastly if these suggestions be solid only in part, are they not at least sufficient to require a pause: and will it not be consonant to the manly wisdom of your mind to bear down in the interval all attempts to move a business replete with mischief and with the danger of mischief beyond all calculation?

I shall close with a last request. I wish this letter to be shewn to the Speaker; I am sure that it is not fit for any other eye: I do not know that it is fit for his. I have not had the means of seeking or learning his opinions on the subject. And I look with diffidence to my own sense respecting others in a period when the hand of Providence for some dreadful purpose seems to be influencing men's minds to involve in calamity and destruction every establishment, every principle and every public and individual interest that is near and dear to my mind and heart.' (W. Dacres Adams MSS.)

[1] The King's letter of the 1st, to which Addington is replying, is in Pellew, I, 288, where, in line 8 'as' should read 'after'.　　　　　　　　　　　　　　[2] Sir Watkin Williams Wynn.

Mr Cornwallis.[1] An Amendment was moved by Mr Grey[2] which was supported by Dr Laurence, Mr Tierney, and Mr Sheridan, of which the principal object was to avoid any pledge on the question in dispute with the Northern Powers. The Amendment was opposed and the decisive language of the original Address was supported by Mr Pitt, the Solicitor General (who spoke with peculiar force and effect) and Mr Secy. Dundas. On a division the Amendment was negatived by 245 to 63, and the original Address was then agreed to.[3] (10024)

[*The King's reply, Queen's House, 3 Feb.*] I am learn [*sic*] from Mr. Pitt that the mover and seconder of the Address have acquitted themselves with propriety, as also that the Amendment to it moved by Mr. Grey and supported by Dr. Lawrence, Mr. Tierney and Mr. Sheridan was rejected by 245 to 63, after having been objected to, and the original Address supported by Mr. Pitt, the Solicitor General and Mr. Secy. Dundas. The Amendment was I suppose the same I have received this morning as moved by Earl Fitzwilliam and rejected by 73 to 17.[4] I should hope no farther trouble will be given on the Report today in the House of Commons and that I may receive that Address tomorrow at three.[5] (Chatham Papers.)

[1] James Cornwallis (1778–1852), M.P. for Eye (the family borough), 1799–1806, and Jan.–April 1807. In 1814, on the death of his maternal uncle, Sir Horace Mann, Bart., he took the name of Mann. In 1824 he succeeded his father, the Bishop of Lichfield and Coventry (1743–1824), who was the Marquess's younger brother, as 5th Earl Cornwallis. The Marquess wrote to his brother, the Bishop, 22 Dec. 1800: 'I most perfectly approve of James's moving the Address [*sic*]. The first meeting of the United Parliament affords a most propitious occasion, and I most sincerely hope that he will acquit himself to his own satisfaction so as to induce him to persevere in taking some share in the business of Parliament.' (Kent R.O., MSS.) Very curiously, the invitation to second (not move, as the Marquess wrote) went to the wrong person in the first instance—to Admiral Cornwallis, M.P. for Eye and the Marquess's brother. He must have been very surprised to receive the invitation. (Kent R.O., MSS., 7 Feb. 1801.)

[2] The Duchess of Devonshire wrote on the 8th, the reference being to this debate: 'Mr. Grey told us that on Monday the Speaker made excuses to him and said he had not slept half an hour the preceding night—of which Mr. Grey said he felt glad, as he perceived the Speaker sleeping during this speech' (Chatsworth MSS.).

[3] *Parl. Register*, LIX, 31–72. Canning wrote, earlier in the day: 'You need not be frightened. Pitt is not out, nor likely to be so. The lies that have been in circulation for these last three days are inconceivable. They will be all dissipated & destroyed today, however, after a debate which for length & violence is expected to be such as we have not for some years been accustomed to. The meeting of Parliament is always a good thing, but it never was more wanted than at present.' (Harewood MSS.)

[4] See *Parl. Register*, LIX, 19 (a similar Amendment).

[5] Pitt's letter of the 3rd to the King (a draft which differs from the one the King received) is in Rose, p. 244. He wrote: 'In addition to the letter with which Mr Pitt has felt it his duty to trouble your Majesty in consequence of that with which your Majesty honored him on Sunday, he ventures, in full reliance on the gracious indulgence and goodness which your Majesty has condescended to express, humbly to solicit your Majesty's attention to an object which he confesses he has peculiarly at heart. He would have taken the liberty of doing so some days sooner, if, very soon after forming that intention, the circumstances had not intervened on which he has been recently under the painful necessity of submitting his sentiments to your Majesty, but which were not at that time in his contemplation. The object itself relates to the situation of Mr Long, who has been now for ten years in the laborious situation of one of the Secretaries of the Treasury, and has discharged its duties not only to Mr Pitt's entire satisfaction, but he believes, he may truly add, to that of every description of persons with whom he has had intercourse, and with great advantage to the public service.

Neither Mr Long's private fortune nor any which he has reason to expect is such as would leave him, in the event of his at any time retiring from office, with a provision at all adequate to the situation he has so long filled. Under these circumstances Mr Pitt had flattered himself that your Majesty would not

[*From Pitt, Downing Street, Wednesday, 4 Feb.*] Mr Pitt humbly presumes to submit for your Majesty's consideration the answer which he takes the liberty of proposing to the Address from the House of Commons.[1] (10032)

2340 JOSIAH BOYDELL *to the* KING

[*4 Feb. 1801.*] May it please your Majesty. By the death of Mr. Markham, a certificate Commission in the Lottery is now vacant. I have been a single Commissioner for these last one & twenty years, the last twenty of which I have put an entire stop to the forging of lottery tickets, which before that period were very frequent & which caus'd several Lottery Boards to meet upon the subject to devise means to put a stop to a practice so detrimental to its credit. I have the further satisfaction to hope by this prevention many valuable lives have been saved to their country. It has been a further gratification for me to know that the clauses I recommended have been inserted in the Lottery Acts which have very materially check'd illegal insurance, whereby one of the greatest evils attendant upon Lotteries has been lessen'd.

disapprove of his requesting the grant of a contingent pension (with the remainder of one-half of it to Mrs. Long) to the amount of £1500 pr annum, which is not more than was granted to a former Secretary of the Treasury above thirty years ago, and is very inferior to the value of patent offices by which others of his predecessors have frequently been provided for, but which are no longer remaining disposeable. Mr Pitt only entreats your Majesty's permission to add that altho he had meant to submit this request under different circumstances, it is certainly since become doubly interesting to him, and that he should most sensibly feel your Majesty's gracious compliance as a strong addition to the many marks he has received of your Majesty's kindness and goodness to himself.' (10030–1)

Long explained to Pitt (10 Jan.) that, although he had been in office for ten years he had saved nothing, and that, as his and his wife's private income amounted in all only to about £1,700 a year, he would have to alter drastically his style of living. His own suggestion was a contingent pension of £1,200, not £1,500 a year. (W. Dacres Adams MSS.)

Though, later, Long voted against Catholic relief, he now refused to remain in office—writing to Pitt on 4 Feb.: 'Nothing but the suggestion coming from you would induce me to admit the idea of remaining in any situation under Government one moment after your resignation. I trust you will not see the necessity of pressing it. If I am capable of being in any degree useful I am only capable of being so where my zeal is as much engaged as I may truly say it will ever be towards you. I certainly can have no objection to talk the subject over with you, but if you press me to remain you will force me to the most painfull sacrifice I ever made in my life. You know I say this without affectation. I have really no wish beyond that of following your fortunes whatever they may be.' (W. Dacres Adams MSS.) See also, Long's letter to Addington, 8 Feb., though inaccurately copied, in Pellew, I, 318.

George Rose wrote on the 12th, 'Mr. Long (who told me that he thought he should quit) is to remain in for some time at least' (*Diaries and Correspondence*, I, 298). He quitted in March.

[1] The King's formal answer to the Address is in *H. of C.J.* LVI, 19. The King's letter to Pitt on the 5th is in Stanhope (inaccurately copied); the King's copy, in the Archives, is not identical with the one in the Chatham Papers. He wrote: 'The box from Mr. Pitt contained two letters and a warrant in favour of Mr. Long. I cannot have the smallest difficulty in signing the proposed warrant as I think him a very valuable man and know how much Mr. Pitt esteems him.

I had flattered myself that on the strong assurances I gave Mr. Pitt of keeping perfectly silent on the subject whereon we entirely differ, provided on his part he kept off any disquisition on it for the present, which was the main object of the letter I wrote to him on Sunday, we both understood our present line of conduct, but as I unfortunately find Mr. Pitt does not draw the same conclusion, I must come to the unpleasant decision, as it will deprive me of his political service, of acquainting him that rather than forego what I look on as my duty, I will without unnecessary delay attempt to make the most creditable arrangement, and such as Mr. Pitt will think most to the advantage of my service as well as to the security of the public, but he must not be surprised if I cannot fix how soon that can possibly be done, though he may rest assured that it shall be done with as much expedition as so difficult a subject will admit.' (10039)

If your Majesty should condescend to think my long & faithfull services deserving of your Royal consideration, might I humbly hope your Majesty would condescend to recommend me to Mr. Pitt to succeed the late Mr. Markham in the certificate Commission now vacant by his death? This condescention of your Majesty would add to the many gracious favours already granted by your Majesty to [etc.]. (10036–7)

2341 *Letters from* HENRY ADDINGTON *to the* KING[1]

[*4 Feb. 1801.*] As it unfortunately appears that the earnest wishes of your Majesty, in which every public and private feeling have led the Speaker of the House of Commons to concur, have been frustrated, he conceives it to be his duty to express his humble acquiescence in that part of your Majesty's determination which relates immediately to himself. He trusts your Majesty is persuaded that he must be impressed with all the gratitude, so justly due for those gracious assurances of confidence and support with which your Majesty has condescended to honor and encourage him.

Nothing, he is sure, could be more grateful to the feelings of Mr. Pitt, as nothing could be more kind and explicit than the manner in which your Majesty proposes to express your sentiments to him on the general result of what has passed. But the Speaker ventures to assure your Majesty from his own personal knowledge, that Mr. Pitt has not an idea of bringing forward the measure in question or of promoting the agitation of it from any other quarter. The wish, stated in Mr. Pitt's letter, is founded solely on the considerations which he has there explained and which were dictated by what he conceived would be most conducive to your Majesty's service. The Speaker therefore presumes to express a hope that in signifying to Mr. Pitt your Majesty's gracious compliance with his wishes respecting Mr. Long, your Majesty may think it proper to omit the reference to Mr. Pitt's supposed motive for sending the warrant at this time,[2] which the Speaker is empowered to assure your Majesty did not operate in any degree upon Mr. Pitt's mind, as he was on the point of making this request when the circumstances took place which led to the late discussion. The Speaker is at the same time authorised, and indeed impelled, to state in terms suggested by Mr. Pitt himself, 'That it is his genuine and decided opinion that the strength and efficiency of your Majesty's Government require that there should be no delay in carrying into effect those measures which he conceives are become necessary in consequence of the unalterable opinions of your Majesty and himself'.

The Speaker will not defer communicating with Mr. Pitt respecting the time and mode of taking those measures. It cannot but be highly desireable that the first intimation to the persons, particularly named in your Majesty's note, of the wish that they should retain their respective situations should proceed from your

---

[1] This letter, with many variations, appears as a draft in Pellew, 1, 292, and is there dated the 5th. The King's reply on the night of the 5th is in Pellew, 1, 294.

[2] Writing to Addington on the 6th the King said he had omitted this, in writing to Pitt the previous evening. The King said that he ought to have made some communication to the Lord Chancellor, and would, if possible, write to him that day (Pellew, 1, 295. In line 6, for 'to whom', read 'to who').

Majesty in the first instance. But he presumes to intreat that the intimation may be suspended till he has been enabled to communicate to your Majesty the result of further conversation on those points with Mr. Pitt. He is not aware of any circumstance which need interfere with your Majesty's intentions of going to Windsor on Friday, to which place he will not fail to transmit whatever it may be material for your Majesty to be made acquainted with previous to your return to town. (10033–5)

[*Palace Yard, 5 Feb., 8.30 a.m.*] The Speaker of the House of Commons humbly submits to your Majesty his opinion, that the suggestion contained in your Majesty's note of yesterday should be this day carried into effect, though he is concerned to think that the hopes entertained respecting Earl Spencer in particular may not be accomplished. The Speaker ventures also to express a wish that it may not be thought by your Majesty to be undesirable to extend the communication to the Lord Chancellor, so far as to apprize him in general terms of what has passed, of the wish to create as little change in the present distribution of offices and in subsisting arrangements as circumstances will admit of, and as may be deemed to be consistent with the strength and efficiency of your Majesty's Government.[1] The Speaker proposes to write to the Earl of Chatham this day.

On the part of Mr Pitt there is the utmost disposition to afford all possible accommodation in point of time and every facility towards the forming of new arrangements, but, till the business is more matured, it cannot but be highly desireable that no communications should be made but such as are calculated to surmount difficulties and to promote the attainment in the best manner possible of the important object now in view. In these sentiments the Speaker is persuaded that your Majesty will be pleased to concur, and he has been chiefly induced to mention these as the guide by which his own conduct will for a time be regulated. (10038)

2342 LORD LOUGHBOROUGH *to the* KING

[*Thursday, 5 Feb., 7 p.m.*] The Chancellor would not delay returning to your Majesty the box, knowing your intention to transmit [it] to the Duke of Portland. Deeply as he is affected by the contents of it, he begs leave to convey his sentiments on the occasion as soon as he is able to collect & state them with less agitation than he *now* feels, when all that occurs to him is only a repetition of what he had the honour to utter with no less sincerity than pain, his entire resignation of every personal consideration, to any disposition H.M. may think fit to make of him in this important & alarming crisis.[2] (10040)

[1] According to Pellew (I, 315) Addington at first intended to offer Loughborough the office of Lord President, but Chatham was appointed.
[2] See Campbell, *Lives of the Chancellors*, VIII, 183, 189 [1868 edn.] for undated letters from him to the King.

[*Burlington House, Thursday, 5 Feb. 1801, 11.45 p.m.*] The Duke of Portland in pursuance of your Majesty's commands returns the box containing the papers your Majesty condescended to put into his hands this evening. He cannot but feel the present crisis as the most awfull in which he has ever known this country to be placed, & most humbly begs leave to assure your Majesty that his duty & attachment to your Majesty & the Constitution make him feel himself bound to contribute every assistance which he has the means of affording to the stability & security of your Majesty's Government. (10041)

2344 LORD GRENVILLE *to the* KING, *and the reply*

[*Cleveland Row, 5 Feb. 1801.*] Mr. Pitt having communicated to Lord Grenville the notes which he has had the honour to receive from your Majesty on the subject of the unfortunate difference of opinion which has arisen, and of the events to which it is about to lead, Lord Grenville would be fearful of appearing to your Majesty deficient in those sentiments which, in the moment of quitting your Majesty's service, are the most strongly impressed on his mind, if he delayed any longer humbly to offer to your Majesty the warm and dutiful acknowledgements of a grateful heart for all your Majesty's uniform goodness and indulgence towards him.

He begs leave to assure your Majesty that his veneration, gratitude, and, he hopes your Majesty will allow him to add, his affectionate attachment to your Majesty will be the rule of his conduct in all situations and circumstances of his future life: and he trusts your Majesty will not think it presumption in him to add that nothing will afford him so much gratification as the being enabled on any occasion to contribute by any feeble aid of his to the ease and honour of your Majesty's Government.

That the same Providence which has so often and so signally protected your Majesty may preserve and defend your Majesty in all difficulties and dangers, and may crown with success your Majesty's endeavours for the safety and happiness of your people, will ever be his warmest wish and most fervent prayer. (Chatham Papers, 140; and Fortescue MSS.)

[*The King's reply, Queen's House, 6 Feb.*] However my mind is hurt at the finding that without abandoning what ought to be the object of every well-grounded mind, the acting up to what appears to be a religious and political duty, I must submit to a change in Ministry that I had ever hoped could never have happened; I cannot receive so kind a letter from Lord Grenville without expressing that the esteem I have always had for him adds to my uneasiness, and the conduct he seems inclined to take will certainly not remove those sentiments in his favour. I cannot but add, if more confidence had been placed in me whilst the subject of contention was in contemplation, perhaps persons would not have pledged themselves when they had known the real dictates of my mind; theirs can only be the opinion of expediency, mine are grounded on a solemn oath taken and the uniform conduct of this kingdom and I think most wisely since the exclusion of the House of Stuart.[1] (*Ibid.*)

2345 EARL CAMDEN *to the* KING

[*London, 6 Feb. 1801.*] Lord Camden entreats your Majesty's permission with all humility to submit to your Majesty that he has been informed by Mr. Pitt that your Majesty considers it inconsistent with the duty your Majesty owes to yourself & to the public to entertain a question which the majority of those whom your Majesty has called to your Councils had proposed to submit to your Majesty's consideration; and as Lord Camden concurred in an opinion in which he has the misfortune to learn your Majesty cannot agree, he feels it incumbent upon him humbly to entreat your Majesty's permission to relinquish that flattering distinction & proof of confidence with which he was honored by your Majesty's especial grace, when he returned from Ireland.

Impressed as he is with the most lively gratitude for the marks of confidence & favor which he has received from your Majesty, it is with the most unfeigned regret that Lord Camden is compelled humbly to submit this sentiment to your Majesty; intreating at the same time your Majesty's permission to assure your Majesty that no one of your subjects feels a more devout attachment to your Majesty's person, or possesses a more determined resolution by every means within his limited power to support your Majesty's Government.

Lord Camden ventures to express an anxious hope that he may be permitted at some convenient period to lay with all humility before your Majesty those reasons which have induced him to entertain the opinion that, under all the circumstances of the present times and with all the limitations which a scrupulous attention to the interests of the Church had suggested, it became him to concur in the advice that such a proposition should be submitted to your Majesty as the one which your Majesty's confidential servants had intended with all humility to have laid before you for your Majesty's royal consideration. (Camden MSS.)

2346 THE KING *to* HENRY DUNDAS

[*Windsor, 7 Feb. 1801.*] I cannot but regret that on the late unhappy occasion I had not been treated with more confidence previous to forming an opinion which

[1] Charles Abbot wrote, on the 26th: 'The Bishop of Durham told me Lord Grenville, in taking leave of the King, has asked a pension of £1500 a year for Lady Grenville. Lord G. has let his house in Cleveland Row for £1,000 a year to Lord Temple.' (*Colchester Diary*, 1, 247, and MS.)

Thomas Coutts, believing that Pitt too would be in rather straitened circumstances out of office, wrote to him on the 22nd, suggesting, truly enough, that as Prime Minister, he might not have been able to pay sufficient attention to his private affairs, and that the consequences might prove unpleasant and inconvenient. Pitt, therefore, should resume his legal practice; and in a few years he could become Lord Chancellor: 'A silk gown you may wear immediately and the Northern Circuit by Mr. Law's elevation presents you at once with at least £3000 a year—Every line is open for you and there cannot be a doubt of your rising *instantaneously* to the very summit of the profession, and there is not a moment to lose. Who is there with a brief, that would not fly to put it into such hands? So far from *lessening*—such a determination would *elevate* your character, beyond every point you have yet attained, and make you *sought* for to be *again* the Minister, with more eclat than ever, in case you should wish it on any future occasion.' (W. Dacres Adams MSS.)

to my greatest surprize I learnt on Thursday from Earl Spencer has been in agitation ever since Lord Castlereagh came over in August, yet of which I never had the smallest suspicion till within very few weeks; but so desirous was I to avoid the present conclusion that except what passed with Earl Spencer and Lord Grenville about three weeks past and an hint I gave to Mr. Secy. Dundas on Wednesday sennight, I have been silent on the subject, and indeed hoping that Mr. Pitt had not pledged himself on what I cannot with my sentiments of religious and political duty think myself at liberty to concurr. Mr. Secy. Dundas has known my opinions when he corresponded with the Earl of Westmoreland, when Lord Lieut. of Ireland, and at least will do me the justice to establish that both then and when afterwards brought forward by the Earl Fitzwilliam, my language perfectly coincided with my present conduct.[1] (Add. MSS 40100, f. 300.)

2347 PRINCE ADOLPHUS *to the* KING

[*Hanover, 7 Feb. 1801.*] I cannot find words to express my feelings on receiving from Baron Lenthe the account of the new rank your Majesty has been pleased to confer on me.[2] It certainly is much more than I could expect and it has made me infinitely happy. Your Majesty will allow me to add to my most humble thanks the assurance of my constant endeavours to act and to behave in such a manner as to meet with your approbation. This has been my constant aim ever since I

[1] This letter caused Dundas to write to Pitt the same day, from Wimbledon: 'I know not to what stage the Speaker's endeavours to form an arrangement have proceeded, but it is impossible for me not to whisper into your ear my conviction that no arrangement can be formed under him as its head that will not crumble to pieces almost as soon as formed. Our friends who as an act of friendship and attachment to you agree to remain in office, do it with the utmost chagrin and unwillingness, and among the other considerations which operate upon them, the feeling that they are embarking in an Administration under a head totally incapable to carry it on, and which must of course soon be an object of ridicule, is almost uppermost in all their minds. Add to this that altho' they will not certainly enter into faction and oppose him, all the aristocracy of the country at present cordially connected with Government and part of it under you, feel a degradation in the First Minister of the country being selected from a person of the description of Mr. Addington without the smallest pretensions to justify it and destitute of abilities to carry it on. Depend upon it I am not exaggerating the state of the case, and a very short experience will prove that I am right, and the Speaker will ere long feel that he has fallen from a most exalted situation and character into one of a very opposite description. Save him from it if not too late. Yourself excluded from it I am afraid nothing permanent can be formed, but if the Speaker was to advise the King to call upon the Duke of Portland to form an Administration, I am persuaded his Grace at the head of it with either Steele, Ryder, Lord Malmesbury or even Mr. Abbott as the Chancellor of the Exchequer would fill the publick eye infinitely more than anything that can be formed upon the plan now in agitation. By the answer I have received from the King to my resignation I must entreat you without delay to send for my correspondence with Lord Westmorland in order that I may be sure of what my recollection suggests, that I refused to give the promise of the Government at home, that what was then proposed, was the ultimatum of concession.' (Chatham Papers, 157.)
'Lord Westmorland says he had a regard for Pitt and thought him a man of talents, but the King was the only thing of real consequence' (The Duchess of Devonshire's Diary, 9 Feb. 1801). She added: 'I believe, if the truth was known, though the King is sincere in saying that he feels scruples about the emancipation, yet that he has been for months listening to underhand courtiers, and that Pitt, though he never thought the King would give him up, yet did not like to bring the thing till necessary to an absolute decision, and that in this the King humoured them by not coming to an explanation till, when forced to do, he absolutely refused'. (*Ibid.*)
[2] Probably promotion in the Hanoverian Army. It was not until 27 Nov. of this year that he was created Duke of Cambridge (subordinate titles, Baron of Culloden and Earl of Tipperary); but the letter is accurately dated: it could not have been written in 1802, for he was in England on 7 Feb. of that year.

have begun to act in the world and I hope I may always succeed in it. At least I will do my best and I have a double reason for it as this is the only way I have to prove to you my gratitude for the many gracious proofs of your kindness to me, which certainly make the happyness of my life.

I dare not trespass any longer on your patience than to add [etc.].[1] (48560)

2348 WILLIAM WINDHAM *to the* KING

[*Park Str. Wesr., 7 Feb. 1801.*] Mr Windham was apprized only this morning that the moment was arrived when it would be proper for him to execute the painful task of requesting your Majesty's permission to relinquish the situation which he has hitherto had the honour of holding in your Majesty's Government.

In the midst of the many afflicting sensations which this event produces in his mind, his hope is that your Majesty will do justice to the purity of his motives & not conceive for a moment that he is either less sincerely or zealously attached than he has been at every preceding period to your Majesty's person & Government, or has relinquished any of those principles or sentiments which have on different occasions appeared to recommend him to your Majesty's gracious favour.

Mr Windham will not presume to obtrude on your Majesty any reasoning on a subject on which your Majesty's mind appears to be finally made up. He is anxious only to explain to your Majesty that it is not from want of reverence for a maxim on which he has so often had the happiness of concurring with your Majesty— that principle & not expediency ought to guide in political conduct; but from thinking that what principle prescribed in the present instance is only that the Church be preserved, and that it is for discretion & prudence afterwards to chuse such means as in the varying state of human affairs shall appear best calculated for that end. It has been Mr Windham's firm & conscientious persuasion that in the present state of the world such means were only to be found in the measures lately proposed; and feeling that persuasion, & having in concert with others acted upon it, your Majesty would, he is sure, be the first to pronounce that no option remained to him but to take the course which, with your Majesty's concurrence, he has above expressed his wish to pursue. To relinquish his present situation is not in itself a sacrifice that would cost him much. He has in various respects long found it to be such as to place him more than once on the point of soliciting your Majesty's permission for that purpose. But he should indeed consider his departure from office as a circumstance of heavy affliction, if the effect were to be to forfeit any part of that good opinion with which your Majesty has hitherto appeared to honour him; or to call in question those sentiments of duty, of gratitude & of affection which your Majesty's goodness has so deeply engraven upon his mind, & which in every situation, whether in or out of office, will never cease to be the guide of his conduct.[2] (10044–5)

[1] Addington's letter to the King on the 7th is in Pellew, I, 296, and the King's reply at midday the same day, on p. 297. In paragraph 2, line 3, for 'intention to retire', read 'intended retiring'; for 'Lord Fitzwilliam' read 'Earl Fitzwilliam', and the four lines further down should not be italicised.

[2] The King's reply on the 9th is in the *Windham Papers*, II, 169.

[*Admiralty, 8 Feb. 1801.*] Deeply penetrated by the very flattering and undeserved condescension with which your Majesty was graciously pleased to receive what Earl Spencer most reluctantly thought it his duty to represent on Thursday last, he now presumes once more to approach your Majesty on the same subject, and painful and distressing to him as the task must necessarily be, most humbly to submit to your Majesty that, finding from a communication he had yesterday with the Speaker of the House of Commons that the faint hopes he had even till then cherished in his mind of the possibility of averting the dissolution of your Majesty's present Administration had no longer any foundation, he now finds himself reduced to the indispensible necessity of intreating your Majesty to accept his resignation of the office of First Commissioner of the Admiralty, and of beseeching your Majesty that as little delay as possible may intervene in the appointment of his successor.

Earl Spencer feels on this occasion so unable to do justice to the profound sentiments of duty, veneration and gratitude with which he must ever be impressed towards your Majesty, that it only remains for him to implore your Majesty to believe that they are such as will never terminate but with his life.[1] (10046–7)

[*From Lord Spencer, Admiralty, 9 Feb.*] Earl Spencer has the honour of laying before your Majesty the proceedings of a court martial on a man belonging to the Warrior for striking a boatswain's mate, together with a letter from the President of the Court recommending the prisoner to your Majesty's mercy for certain reasons therein contained; and in consequence Earl Spencer humbly submits to your Majesty that it may be proper to grant him your Majesty's most gracious pardon. (10049)

[*The King's reply, Queen's House, 9 Feb.*] The sentence of the court martial seems very properly to have sentenced John Robbins of the Warrior for striking his superior officer; and the letter of the President gives just room for my granting a pardon, which I desire Earl Spencer will have notified in the proper manner. (Althorp MSS.)

[1] The King's reply on the 9th, reluctantly consenting to Spencer's resignation, is in *Spencer Papers,* IV, 303. The Duchess of Devonshire received what she described as 'a most curious detail' from her brother on the 7th: 'He says he gives up his place because his strongest principles went to emancipation and not yielding in the Cabinet. He says the King is sincere and really thinks it his duty. That this has been suggested by the Chancellor (who is now frightened) and others. That the Bishops, all except Watson, are against them. That the Irish Primate Stewart, Lord Bute's brother, is violently so; and Meath, he supposed, as he was once a Catholic, and proselytes are most violent. He says the King is fixed; that perhaps Pitt delayed too long laying it officially before him, but he has no hopes, he says, that he will not join Opposition, and with Pitt wishes success to these new men...He says that those who are against emancipation are right to stay in, but he is astonished at the Duke of Portland, whom he thought as much decided as himself.' (Chatsworth MSS.) 'My brother...only said that Pitt had not dared to affront him by supposing he would stay in.' (*Ibid.* 8 February.)

[From the King, Windsor, 9 Feb.][1] I have read over with attention the proposed plan for arranging the dockyards. One part in particular appears to me highly commendable, namely, the Admiralty's having advanced the salaries of the officers of the Yards which, according to the establishment laid down by the Commissioners for examining the Public Offices, certainly were not adequate to their responsibility. I therefore shall most willingly sanction the Report when brought for that purpose to the Privy Council. (Althorp MSS.)

2350   *Letters from* HENRY ADDINGTON *to the* KING

[Palace Yard, 9 Feb. 1801, 8 a.m.][2] In returning the inclosed papers, the Speaker of the House of Commons has the satisfaction of informing your Majesty that the progress towards such an arrangement as, he humbly trusts, will meet with your Majesty's approbation, has during the last two days nearly equalled his wishes; indeed it has done so with one exception only, occasioned by Mr. Pelham's having declined taking any official situation, tho' he has given the strongest assurances of concurrence and support.

The proposed law arrangements are those which the Speaker ventures to believe will be most acceptable to your Majesty, but he feels it to be due to the Lord Chancellor, whose conduct has been handsome and becoming in the highest degree, to leave it to his Lordship to make a particular communication to your Majesty of the steps which have been taken towards the accomplishment of this very important object.

The difficulty of supplying in an adequate manner the vacancy which unfortunately will take place at the Admiralty cannot but have impressed itself forcibly on your Majesty's mind. After the best consideration which the Speaker has been enabled to give to this subject he has formed the opinion that it is by Earl St. Vincent that the duties of the situation, now filled so ably and honourably by Earl Spencer, would, upon the retirement of the latter, be executed most beneficially to the country at the present crisis. The talents, experience and name of Earl St. Vincent would, the Speaker is convinced, have the best effect in the management and discipline of the Navy, and in combining the duties and the feelings of subordination and enthusiasm. The Speaker is, however, fully aware that the proposition which he now ventures to submit to your Majesty's consideration is liable to weighty and serious objections, which were not surmounted, or rather counterbalanced in his own mind, except after much reflection and communication with a few persons whose opinions were best calculated to be useful to him in forming his own. The union of a professional and official character, each being of such a description, in the same person, and the mere consideration that Earl St. Vincent is a professional man, suggest observations which can only be rendered unavailing, according to the Speaker's conceptions, by a conviction that the war henceforth to be carried on will be of a nature to require all the promptitude, energy and

[1] This is the reply to Lord Spencer's brief note dated the 6th: 'Earl Spencer has the honour to lay before your Majesty a copy of the Report on the Dockyards for your Majesty's perusal before it comes under the consideration of the Council' (10042).   [2] A portion of this letter is in Pellew, I, 299.

ability which eminently distinguish the person in question. The Speaker thinks it incumbent upon him to add that he has the best reason for believing that Earl St. Vincent has no political convictions whatever,[1] and that he would not hesitate to give a fair and firm support to the measures of your Majesty's Government.

It is a great satisfaction to the Speaker to be enabled still further to state that he finds, from the opinions of intelligent men and from former instances, that the situations of First Lord of the Admiralty and of Commander-in-Chief of the Channel Fleet are by no means incompatible with each other, with a view to the conduct of official business, and the active duties of Naval service. Upon this point, and upon others connected with it, the Speaker hopes to be allowed to explain himself more fully when he next pays his duty to your Majesty. On the main point it appears to be of the highest and more urgent importance that there should be as little delay as possible.

It is with great reluctance and concern that the Speaker has trespassed so long on your Majesty's time. He has only further to request your Majesty's permission to notify to the House of Commons tomorrow his resignation of the office he now holds. This step, he is well convinced, will appear to your Majesty to be equally due to decorum and convenience.

[P.S.] The Speaker has opened his note for the purpose of affording to your Majesty the satisfaction of knowing that he has just received a most gratifying letter from the Earl of Chatham, who will be in town in the course of two or three days.[2]

The Speaker hopes to be pardoned for having omitted to state in his note that Sir John Mitford is the person intended to be proposed as the Speaker's successor

---

[1] See, however, No. 2357.

[2] Chatham had taken no part in the Cabinet discussions which resulted in the break-up of the Government: he had been in the country. He wrote to his brother from Winchester on the 6th in reply to Pitt's letter of the 5th: 'If it were not for the wish you expressed of having the enclosures you sent me, returned today, I shou'd have been glad to have given more consideration to the subject, before I wrote, than I have yet been able to do. I shall confine myself therefore principally, to expressing the deep sorrow your letter has given me. I so far agree with you that we have had experience of unexpected difficulties, and therefore, are not unprepared to meet them, but, alas, here, with the resolution you have taken, I fear, the means of encountering them in future, in a great degree cease. Upon the measure itself of granting further indulgence to the Catholics, I have neither time, nor indeed wou'd it be of any use to say anything at present. I will only observe that, if by being on the spot, I cou'd in any degree have contributed even to put off the extremity to which the agitation of it has led, I shou'd think I had done much, and I shou'd be most unhappy in having been absent, otherwise I consider myself as fortunate, in having avoided a discussion which cou'd only have been painful to me, in many respects. As things stand, I shall certainly think it my duty to come to town in a few days, and I will defer, till we meet, any further remarks. I will only add that if your part is irrevocably taken, the King cou'd not have acted more wisely than in having recourse to the Speaker, on every account, and on none more, than that, I am sure, no one man, will feel a more sincere concern than himself, for the occasion which has called him forth. While I remain here, I shall not abandon the hope that the same good fortune which in so many instances has watched over the affairs of this country, may yet ward off a blow which I assure you (independent of all private feeling on which I say nothing) I consider as a most serious one indeed. At ye same time, I will not disguise, that I see all the difficulty and delicacy of your situation.' (Chatham Papers, 122. And see Ashbourne's *Pitt*, p. 309.)

'Lord Grenville said to the Bishop of Lincoln he thought Lord Chatham should not remain in office' (Rose, *Diaries and Corresp.* I, 295). On 6 March George Rose wrote in his Diary, 'Lord Chatham told the Bishop of Lincoln he had not made up his mind decidedly on the Catholic question, but that the inclination of his opinion was against the question and of course favourable to his Majesty's view of the subject' (Rose, *Diaries and Corresp.* I, 328).

in the Chair of the House of Commons, the duties of which no man appears to be better qualified to discharge to the satisfaction of the House and of the public. On this ground the Speaker presumes to hope that the nomination of Sir John Mitford will be honoured with your Majesty's approval.[1] 2.30 p.m. (10050–4)

[*Palace Yard, 9 Feb., 6.30 p.m.*] It is not possible for the Speaker of the House of Commons to express the satisfaction he derives from the manner in which your Majesty has condescended to receive his note of this day. An immediate communication of your Majesty's pleasure shall be made to Earl St. Vincent, who, the Speaker has reason to believe, may come to town for a few days without any inconvenience to the public service.

With your Majesty's permission, the Speaker will be most happy to pay his duty to your Majesty at the Queen's House at any time to-morrow evening that you may be pleased to command. (10055)

[*The King's reply, Queen's House, 9 Feb. 1801.*] It gives me infinite satisfaction to learn from the Speaker that he has made so much progress in preparing the necessary arrangements, and he will find me as I have before mentioned open to whatever he may have to suggest on that head. I am sorry Mr. Pelham declines office, though his assurances of support are not doubted; but that is over-ballanced by the hopes of the Law arrangements proving satisfactory, though not as yet stated.

---

[1] Addington resigned the Speakership on the 10th, and on the 11th Mitford was elected as his successor. Addington first suggested Charles Bragge as Speaker, but the King objected to it (Rose, *Diaries and Corresp.* I, 307). Charles Abbot, who became Speaker on 10 Feb. 1802, wrote in his diary on 9 Feb. 1801: 'Several persons said to me that I was the fittest person to be Speaker, and *all* shrugged up their shoulders when they were told Mitford was to be proposed.' (Omitted from Colchester, I, 231.)

Mitford's own analysis of the situation is given in his letter to Pitt on the 6th:

Private

'I hope you will pardon my again troubling you on the subject of our conversation this morning. I have again seen the Speaker, and I have also conversed with Lord Eldon. I will freely lay before you all my thoughts on the subject, and intreat your unreserved opinion, begging you will consider *yourself*, and *your* future views, as well as *me*, and *my* views. I feel, upon reflection, a thorough conviction that the Administration now forming cannot last. I also feel that if the country remains in its present state, imperious necessity will compel you again to take the lead. I therefore consider you as materially interested; and on this account request you to state to me freely, whether, if by any accident the Chair had become vacant whilst you remained in office, you should have thought of proposing me as the person whom you would wish to take it. If I thought you would not, that would decide me. I must also request your advice, as a friend, with respect to my actual situation. Putting my office of Attorney-General out of the question, I have an income from my profession beyond my expenditure, and if I ceased to be Attorney-General my professional income might, I think, be considerably increased. My private fortune *ought* to have been considerable, but it is not so, from a variety of circumstances with which I need not trouble you, notwithstanding I have had from my family about thirty thousand pounds. The income of my private fortune, therefore, would not maintain me as I now live; and if I should be reduced to that income I must curtail my expences. The income of the office of Speaker I think not more than the necessary expenditure which the office requires; so that, at even a distant time, I should hardly be enabled by it to put myself on my *present* establishment on quitting the office. You suggested the improbability that the House itself would suffer a person retiring from that office, to sink much below the situation he had filled. I must confess I cannot bear that idea. I have nourished notions of independence which perhaps are foolish, but which at present I am not disposed to give up. Under these circumstances I am called upon to give up my profession for high dignity and a splendor of living which I am growing too old for. You now know my feelings. Have the goodness to decide for me, as I must decide.' (W. Dacres Adams MSS.)

I am clear that the Earl of St. Vincent is the best choice that could be made on the present occasion for head of the Admiralty, and I should hope his official fitness will counter-ballance any warmth of temper which might otherwise be alledged against him.

Mr. Speaker is highly right, as he is prepared for it, to notify to the House of Commons his resignation of the Chair, which I must think he has filled to the honour of that House, the advantage of the public, and to his own personal credit. The King will be happy if Sir John Mitford is able to say as much after so long a service.

I am happy indeed that the Earl of Chatham has answered to the Speaker's satisfaction.

I do not press Mr. Speaker to come here but shall be glad to know when that will be convenient to him.[1] (Sidmouth MSS.)

2351   THE DUKE OF PORTLAND *to the* KING

[*Burlington House, Monday, 9 Feb. 1801.*] The Duke of Portland humbly begs leave to lay before your Majesty a letter from the Lord Lieutenant which contains the long expected plan for the incorporation of the civil & military branches of the Ordnance Departments of this part of the United Kingdom & Ireland, for the delay of which the Duke of Portland humbly conceives your Majesty will admit the satisfactoriness of the reasons assigned by the Lord Lieutenant.[2]

The Duke of Portland also humbly submits to your Majesty the request of the Bishop of St. David's (whose consecration took place yesterday[3]) to be informed of the time at which your Majesty will please to permit him to do his homage.[4] (10048)

2352   THE EARL OF WESTMORLAND *to the* KING, *and the reply*

[*London, 9 Feb. 1801.*] Lord Westmorland takes the liberty of intruding upon your Majesty with his most respectful excuses for not having had the honor of attending your Majesty at the Levée or Drawing Room, being prevented by indisposition & ignorant of the unfortunate state of affairs—humbly hopes your Majesty will permit him in this manner (till he can do it in person) to humbly make to your your [*sic*] Majesty his most grateful expressions of duty & attachment. (10056)

[1] Part of this letter (and parts of other letters from the King to Addington) are given, usually inaccurately, in Pellew. The King's letter of the 11th to Addington, is in I, 303. In line 18, for 'who, from his' *read* 'whose'.

[2] Glenbervie wrote on 30 March: 'Pelham says he foresaw and stated that Lord Cornwallis might wish to keep the Ordnance, and accordingly it seems he has said he wishes to continue in that and his other offices till the incorporation of the Irish and English Ordnance and artillery establishments shall be completed, as with his joint powers he can better execute that service than any other person. But Pelham also thinks Ld. C. may wish to retain his great military situation, as he has always professed that an officer has nothing as such to do with politics. . . The Seals remain still untransferred. I thought I saw that Pelham still longs for the War Department.' (MS. Diary.)

[3] In the Royal Historical Society's *Handbook of British Chronology*, p. 280 [1961], the date given is the 11th.   [4] The Bishop did homage to the King after the Levée on the 11th.

[*The King's reply, Queen's House, 11 Feb.*] The King is too much impressed with the solidity of the Earl of Westmorland's opinion on the unhappy question which has caused many of the Ministers to retire, and particularly the one on whom his Majesty not only from esteem for his talents but real affection placed his chief confidence, to have the least doubted of the Lord Privy Seal's zeal on the present occasion. As the King did not see the Earl of Westmorland last week he desires he will call here in his morning dress at three this day.[1] (Lonsdale MSS. [copy].)

2353   EARL SPENCER *to the* KING, *and the reply*

[*Admiralty, 11 Feb. 1801.*] It being necessary that your Majesty should make the declaration of sea provisions for the remaining ten lunar months of the present year in the Council today previous [?] to the Estimates being regularly laid before the House of Commons, Earl Spencer begs permission humbly to submit to your Majesty that the number of men declared should be one hundred and thirty five thousand, including thirty thousand marines. (10060)

[*The King's reply, Queen's House, 11 Feb.*] I have received Earl Spencer's notification that for the remaining ten lunar months the number of men required for the Navy are 135,000, including 30,000 marines, of which I shall certainly make the declaration in the Privy Council this day.[2] (Althorp MSS.)

2354   HENRY ADDINGTON *to the* KING, *and the reply*

[*Palace Yard, 11 Feb. 1801, 11.30 p.m.*] Mr. Addington thinks it incumbent upon him to acquaint your Majesty that Sir John Mitford was this day chosen Speaker of the House of Commons without a division. It is extremely material that your Majesty's pleasure upon the election should be notified tomorrow; if your Majesty thinks proper that it should be declared by Lords Commissioners, Mr. Addington, upon receiving your Majesty's commands, will immediately make them known to the Lord Chancellor, who will cause a Commission to be prepared for your Majesty's signature in the course of the morning.

Mr. Addington has great satisfaction in adding that he has seen the Earl of Chatham this evening, who is only anxious to give your Majesty every possible proof of his devotion to your service. (10059)

[*The King's reply, Queen's House, 12 Feb. 1801.*] There could not be a more strong pressage of our joint endeavours to save this dear country than the event of the choise of Sir John Mitford as Speaker of the House of Commons just notified

---

[1] The Earl attended the Levée on the 11th. There is a slightly different rendering of this letter in Jesse, III, 247.

[2] The Council was held primarily for the purpose of pricking the Sheriffs for the ensuing year. Glenbervie wrote on the 15th: 'Lord Liverpool told me yesterday that Pitt cried profusely at the audience he had, to signify his resignation to the King, after the Levée last Wednesday, and that he appeared much agitated when he came out of the Closet.' (*Glenbervie Journals*, I, 169.) Bishop Tomline's account of the Levée on Wednesday the 11th is in Ashbourne's *Pitt*, p. 315.

to me by Mr. Addington; the being without a division arises not from the sense of Opposition but the extreme folly of having proposed [a] person not eligible.[1] I desire the Commission may be instantly prepared for approving the choice the House of Commons have made, and that Mr. Addington will desire the Lord Chancellor to have sent as soon as ready for my signature.

Mr. Addington's account of the Earl of Chatham sets my heart quite at ease, for I not only see the utility of his remaining but I truly bear the warmest affection for him.

I trust Mr. Addington will be at the Queen's Drawing Room this day and bring his brother and Mr. Bragge[2] with him; if they come early they may soon get back to their various occupations to forward the proposed arrangements.[3] (Sidmouth MSS.)

2355   THE EARL OF CHESTERFIELD *to the* KING

[*Chesterfield House, 12 Feb. 1801.*] Your Majesty will I hope pardon me if at a moment like the present, when so many persons have thought it became them to resign the situations they held in your Majesty's Government, I take the liberty to state my sentiments on the great question which now agitates the public mind.

So long since as the period of the recall of the Earl Fitzwilliam from the Government of Ireland, I have decidedly formed my opinion on the subject of the repeal of the Test Act & of Catholic Emancipation, and had the question been at that time brought before the consideration of the British Parliament, I should have felt it to be my duty to have opposed it. Nothing has occurred since that period to weaken, many things to strengthen that opinion.

The affectionate attachment I feel for your Majesty belongs to my heart, to my gratitude & to my existence, and is perfectly independent of the high situation in which your Majesty's goodness has placed me.

If therefore in any arrangement to be made, the putting the office of Master of your Horse into any other hands may strengthen the new Administration, I humbly beg your Majesty not to hesitate to do so, upon the full conviction that I shall most cordially & chearfully acquiesce in any sacrifice which may even eventually contribute to your Majesty's comfort and happiness. (10061–2)

2356   THE DUKE OF YORK *to the* KING

[*York House, 13 Feb. 1801.*] I have the honor to return your Majesty the papers which you was graciously pleased to allow me to peruse.

If my sentiments upon the question of Catholick Emancipation and of the repeal of the Test Act had not been already immutably fixed, the arguments adduced in

---

[1] Sheridan would have liked to propose the Whig Charles Dundas, but his eligibility was disputed on the ground that he had not, it was alleged, taken the required oaths (Sheridan, however, stated that he had). Sheridan did not persist and Charles Dundas was not nominated.

[2] See Nos. 1480, 1793. On 6 Feb. George Rose had written: 'I conjecture Bragge will be Speaker.' (Pretyman MSS.) At this time he was Chairman of Ways and Means.

[3] There is a garbled version of part of this letter in Pellew, II, 304.

favor of the measure would alone have been sufficient to have convinced me of the danger, if not of the absolute certainty, of the dreadfull consequences of its being carried into execution.[1] (10063)

2357 *Letters from* HENRY ADDINGTON *to the* KING, *and the replies*

[*Palace Yard, 13 Feb. 1801, 8 a.m.*] Mr. Addington humbly submits to your Majesty's consideration the importance of taking measures without delay to complete the law arrangements: the following are the appointments which he presumes to recommend to your Majesty on the only grounds which your Majesty could approve:

Lord Eldon	Lord Chancellor
Sir Richard Pepper Arden	Chief Justice of the Court of Common Pleas
Sir William Grant	Master of the Rolls
Mr Law[2]	Attorney General
Mr Perceval	Sollicitor General

As soon as your Majesty's pleasure is known, he will cause the necessary steps to be taken.[3] (10064)

---

[1] The King's letter of the 13th to Lord Kenyon, the Lord Chief Justice, is in H.M.C., Kenyon MSS., p. 555. Lord Kenyon replied, the same day: 'As your Majesty is pleased to name tomorrow or Sunday, and as I should be at Westminster Hall tomorrow, I will attend your Majesty at the Queen's House at one on Sunday.' (10067)

The King's letter to the Bishop of Worcester, 13 Feb., on the subject of the change of Prime Minister, is in Jesse, III, 248.

[2] Edward Law (1750–1818), M.P. for Newtown (Isle of Wight), 1801–2; Attorney-General (without having been Solicitor-General), 1801–2; knighted, 22 Feb. 1801; Lord Chief Justice of the King's Bench, 1802–18. Created Baron Ellenborough, 19 April 1802; in the Cabinet in the 'Talents' Ministry, Jan. 1806–March 1807, as a member of Lord Sidmouth's party.

[3] Pitt knew of all these proposed appointments as early as the 10th (Rose, *Diaries and Corresp.* I, 296). Loughborough had a conversation with the King after the Levée on the 11th, and declared that the suggestion that he should resign the Seals came from Addington on Sunday the 8th. This is confirmed by Charles Abbot: Addington told him before the 8th that 'he should endeavour to persuade the Chancellor to take the Pres[identshi]p of the Council' (Colchester, *Diary and Corresp.* I, 223, 228). Addington told Loughborough that his retirement would greatly strengthen the new Government by securing the assistance of that great lawyer, Sir William Grant, who, by being appointed Master of the Rolls (the great prize of the legal profession, on account of its being tenable for life, its magnificent salary, and its being tenable with a seat in the House of Commons) would sensibly add to the speaking strength of the Government front bench. The King readily accepted this suggestion and offered Loughborough some compensating mark of favour. On 21 April Loughborough became Earl of Rosslyn, though in February he had told George Rose that he would not accept an Earldom (*Diaries and Corresp.* I, 307). Eldon later declared that he was the King's Lord Chancellor, not the Minister's (Twiss, *Life of Eldon*, I, 367 [1844 edn.]). On the 22nd Eldon told George Rose that 'the first proposal [was made] to him on Sunday the 8th...[He spoke of] his determination not to accept it but on Mr. Pitt's earnest entreaty and engagement that he would be Chancellor if he (Mr. Pitt) should ever come into office again; pension to him (£4,000 a year) to be secured immediately' (Rose, *Diaries and Corresp.* I, 310). This seems to conflict with Eldon's statement later that in 1799 he had promised the King to take the Great Seal if called upon to do so. Glenbervie, too, says that Eldon at first (that is, on the 8th) refused: 'When Addington offered him the Seals he declined. Addington had been told by the King that he (Lord Eldon) had promised to be his Chancellor when he should ask him. On a second interview with Lord Eldon, after pressing him again in his own name without success, he produced a letter he had procured from the King to Lord Eldon to the same effect, which Lord Eldon yielded [*sic*].' (MS. Diary, 29 February.) Reminiscing in 1804 Eldon wrote to Lord Redesdale: 'If I could have foreseen the lacerations of private

[*The King's reply, Queen's House, 13 Feb., 9.05 a.m.*] The King has this instant received Mr. Addington's information of the importance of compleating the law arrangements without delay. His Majesty therefore authorises Mr. Addington to take such necessary steps as may be required for putting that part of the new Administration into effect, and his Majesty is very desirous, if not highly inconvenient to Mr. Addington, that he would call here in his morning dress either before or after Church.[1] The King must go to St. James by eleven, and will return about half hour past two.[2] (Sidmouth MSS.)

[*From Addington, Palace Yard, 13 Feb., 9 a.m.*] Mr. Addington thinks it incumbent upon him to transmit to your Majesty without delay the inclosed letter which he has just received from the Earl of St. Vincent.[3]

Mr. Addington has opened his note for the purpose of inclosing one this moment arrived from Mr Nepean.[4] (10065)

[*The King's reply, Queen's House, 13 Feb., 10 a.m.*] The King is highly pleased with the very handsome letter Mr. Addington has communicated from the Earl of St. Vincent, which H.My. returns. (Sidmouth MSS.)

[*From the King, Queen's House, 13 Feb.*[5]] As it is my inclination not to have a thought that can tend to the assistance of the Administration now forming and delay communicating it to Mr. Addington, as I mean to have his affection as well as zeal, it has occurred to me this morning that Mr. Abbott[6] could stand much more

friendship, in themselves heart-breaking, in their consequences tremendously injurious to the public interest, which have taken place...I believe I never should have been able to have worked myself up to the resolution of taking the Seal into my hands. It came into them, as you know, at Mr. Addington's request, with the fullest approbation, to say no more, of Mr. Pitt, and with more than approbation on the part of his Majesty.' (Redesdale MSS.)

[1] The Royal family attended divine worship at the Chapel Royal that day because it had been appointed for the observance of a General Fast and Humiliation. Pellew thought that the letter should have been dated Sunday the 15th, but a dignitary of the Church (he was Dean of Norwich) should have known that the King did not go to church merely on Sundays. There were always special services on Fast Days, and, as on 30 January, Parliament did not meet.

[2] Pelham had contributed to Addington's difficulties by refusing the office of President of the Board of Control with a seat in the Cabinet and a peerage. (Rose, *Diaries and Corresp.* I, 309; Malmesbury, *Diaries and Corresp.* IV, 11; *Glenbervie Diaries*, I, 172.)

[3] Lord St Vincent wrote to Addington from Tor Abbey on the 11th: 'I am honor'd with your letter of the 9th and will set out for London the moment I have made a few necessary arrangements for carrying on the public service in my absence. All the knowledge and sense I possess on naval subjects shall be (as they always have been) devoted to the service and support of Government: and lamenting as I do most sincerely that any reverse in this arduous contest should make it necessary for Mr Pitt to retire from his situation, I deem it a most fortunate event for the country that his Majesty's choice has fallen upon you.' (10066) There was also the question of St Vincent's attitude to the repeal of the Test and Corporation Acts, in support of which questions, so far as it concerned Dissenters, he had committed himself. Pitt, however, told him that 'he was not bound by his acceptance of the office to any particular line in Parliament' (Rose, *Diaries and Corresp.* I, 299).

[4] Nepean wrote to Addington from the Admiralty, Friday morning, 13 Feb.: 'Lord St Vincent reached town last night, and will wait on you as soon as he can' (10066).

[5] The date is not clear, but the 13th is confirmed by Abbot's *Diary*, I, 236, and Pellew's inaccurate and incomplete version has that date (I, 305).

[6] Charles Abbot, 1st Baron Colchester (1757–1829), M.P. for Helston, 1790 and 1795–1802; for Woodstock, 1802–6; for Oxford University, 1806–17. Clerk of the Rules in the Court of King's Bench (worth £2,000 a year), 1794–1801; Irish Secretary, 1801–2; Speaker of the House of Commons, 11 Feb.

creditably as Secretary of State for Ireland if he relinquished his employment in the Court of King's Bench. If Mr. Addington sees it in the same light, I should think a message from him to Lord Kenion would easily gain that Lord's consent to some creditable man being allowed to arrange with Mr. Abbott for that employment. If I am not right on this occasion, I desire the matter may rest here.

I think it right to acquaint Mr. Addington, for himself alone, that I have obtained information as to the cause of Mr. Pelham's reluctance at first to come into office. It was Lord Camden that expressly advised him to decline; and my informer, on learning it, decided his change of conduct.[1] Now when I couple that with Dundas's assurance that he did not know of Mr. Pitt's first letter[2] till after I had received it, and that he protests he did not look on the last conversation on the enabling Catholics to sit in both Houses of Parliament as a final decision, but explains it as those of the Ministry that remain, I think I am right (though it appears most extraordinary), that Lords Camden and Castlereagh and Mr. Canning are the persons that led Mr. Pitt to the rash step he has taken, and that his own good heart now makes him, by exertion in favour of my service, take the line most to his own inclination as well as honour. I should add that Mr. Dundas assured [me] that, during the latter conflict, he has neither seen nor heard of Mr. Canning.[3] (Sidmouth MSS.)

1802–17; peerage, 3 June 1817. Addington's original idea had been to make Abbot a Lord of the Treasury, but Abbot declined it on 6 Feb. as 'a situation quite inconsistent with my office in Westminster Hall' (*Colchester Diary*, 1, 225). Lord Minto wrote (8 Feb. 1802): 'Sir John Mitford to be Chancellor of Ireland, an appointment which is generally approved of. Mr. Abbot is to be Speaker, but this nomination does not give the same satisfaction. He is a clever man, but besides being a dwarf, his manner is rather pert than dignified, and he has the *tournure* of a clerk, which he was, rather than of a Speaker. However, he is fixed. The day before yesterday I found Lord Glenbervie had a violent desire for that office, and that he wished this to be known before the choice was finally settled. He is better qualified than any other person for the Chair, and so he is generally thought to be. He had, indeed, been mentioned amongst other names, tho' never by Government. He hoped that the Pay Office might have been an inducement as it is a good thing to give away, and is wanted for Tierney. As there was no time to lose I volunteered on the occasion and ran up to Pelham with this information, who approved of the thing so much that he wrote immediately to Mr. Addington on the subject, but Addington himself told Douglas that Abbot had asked for it a year ago, and as nobody else had appeared to desire it, it was already proposed to him.' (Minto MSS.)

[1] Portland wrote to Pelham on the 14th: 'I am extremely sorry to find from Addington that it is *impossible* at *present* to place you where *you particularly* ought to be, & that it is almost impossible for you not to go to the Board of Control. I am happy, however, to feel that I shall have your assistance in the House of Lords immediately.' (Add. MSS. 33107, f. 23.) Lord Glenbervie heard that Lord Hobart and Pelham were to change places; that Hobart was to be Home Secretary and Pelham Secretary for War and the Colonies; and he commented (17 March): 'I am persuaded the D. of Y[ork] is working very hard for Pelham, hoping, with him, to be in fact, the War Minister' (MS. Diary).

[2] 31 Jan. Dundas wrote to Pitt, evidently that day (the letter is dated merely 'Saturday morning'): 'In consequence of a note from Lord Grenville I called on him this morning, and at his suggestion I have called to talk with you on the subject of the last Cabinet. He has explained to me your idea in which I entirely concur, with this difference, that after the publicity which must of necessity attend this unfortunate difference of opinion between the King and his Ministers, it is impossible to postpone the point being brought to its issue beyond either. Till that time the King ought to be allowed to arrange his Government, it being distinctly explained to him, that although it is impossible for us in conscience to remain in the possession of a Government, which we are deprived of the means of carrying on, nothing can be further from our ideas than the exercise of any one factious line of conduct, and that except in this point it is equally our intention as ever to bear up the strength and efficiency of his Government...' (W. Dacres Adams MSS.)

[3] 'Lord B[oringdon] told me Pitt had prevented the Speaker going with his message to Canning, because he was afraid of Canning's violence, who certainly would have answered him. Canning said he

[*From the King, Queen's House, 14 Feb., 7 p.m.*] It seems to the King rather necessary that Mr. Addington should be acquainted with [the] general language of the Earl of St. Vincent. It was explicit, and shewed, on being rather closely pressed, that since he went to the Mediterranean he has not had the smallest intercourse with the Marquess of Landsdown, that his former connection arose entirely from the intimacy with Mr. Barré, and when that gentleman could no longer bear the insolence of the Marquess he also quitted the acquaintance.[1] He speaks well of all the Officers who have served under him but wishes to relinquish the command in favour of Admiral [   ] with whom he is not much acquainted, but values his military services. Captains Trowbridge and Markam[2] are the two Naval Officers he wishes to bring to the Board of Admiralty. His choise seems to be excellent on this occasion.

I have heard a rumour that great address is using to persuade Mr. Pitt to support the emancipation of the Papists, but I do not credit it, yet think it is right Mr. Addington should be informed of it.[3] (Sidmouth MSS.)

2358   THE DUKE OF KENT *to the* KING

[*Kensington, 14 Feb. 1801.*] Sensible as I am that every moment of your Majesty's time must at this period be taken up with concerns of the utmost importance, I should not presume to trespass even for an instant upon your indulgence if I did not hope that the shortness of this letter, and the subject of it, which is to lay the humble offer of my services at your Majesty's feet, would be deemed a sufficient excuse.

Amongst the various changes that are about to take place it has occurred to me as a thing possible that the Master-Generalship of the Ordnance might become vacant: should your Majesty in that event condescend to think me capable of discharging the duties of that important office, it would be the height of my ambition, by the most zealous attention to every part of them, to prove myself not unworthy of your confidence. I shall now only add, that not having mentioned to any person living my intention of addressing your Majesty on this subject, it will rest with you to forget that I have ever even named it, should you not conceive this letter to merit consideration. (45996)

was sorry he had not an opportunity of advising the Speaker to fall at the King's feet and implore forgiveness for his presumption.' (The Duchess of Devonshire's Diary, 9 Feb. 1801.)

¹ Cf. *The Times*, 19 Feb.: 'Previous to his Lordship's final acceptance of his new office he consulted his old friend the Marquis of Lansdowne, to whose party the noble Admiral has always been attached. The Marquis advised him by all means to accept of so distinguished an honour... but he recommended to his Lordship to interfere as little as possible with anything that did not immediately regard his own Department, and only to attend the Cabinet when naval affairs were under discussion. It is generally believed that Earl St. Vincent has accepted the office he holds under this express avowal of his intentions.'

² John Markham (1761–1827). Captain, 1783; Rear-Admiral, 1804; Vice-Admiral, 1809; Admiral, 1819. M.P. for Portsmouth, 1801–18, 1820–6. A Lord of the Admiralty, Feb. 1801–May 1804, and Feb. 1806–March 1807.

³ The King's earlier letter to Addington that day is in Pellew, 1, 306. There should be no exclamation marks after the date, and in paragraph 2, line 3, after 'consequently' add 'this morning'.

[*Downing Street, Sunday, 15 Feb. 1801.*] Mr Pitt humbly begs leave to submit to your Majesty a Message which, if it should receive your Majesty's approbation and signature, he should feel great satisfaction in being enabled to deliver to the House of Commons, because he considers the acknowledgment of Sir Sidney Smith's services as a debt of justice on the part of those who have had the best means of observing them.[1] (10070)

[*Downing Street, Monday, 16 Feb., 11 p.m.*] Mr Pitt humbly begs leave to acquaint your Majesty that the Motion for the Committee of Supply this day was opposed by Mr Harrison,[2] but after some debate in which Mr Pitt, Mr Sheridan, Mr Hiley Addington, Mr Whitbread, and Mr Dundas took part, was agreed to without a division. The Estimates for the Army and Navy were then voted.

Mr Pitt takes the liberty of troubling your Majesty with a duplicate for the House of Lords of the Message respecting Sir Sidney Smith, which he inadvertently omitted to send with that to the House of Commons. (10071)

2360   THE BISHOP OF WORCESTER (RICHARD HURD) *to the* KING

[*Hartlebury, 16 Feb. 1801.*] I know not in what words to express my sense of the honour done me in your Majesty's kind remembrance of me at such a moment. I had heared [*sic*] & lamented the change that had happened or was likely to happen. I felt with great concern for the trouble it was likely to occasion to your Majesty. But I knew your Majesty would be well advised, & I also knew that your Majesty was able to advise yourself. I now rejoyce to find that appearances are so favourable, and that there is so general a concurrence in support of the new arrangement.

As to your Majesty's part in this matter, you have done, & will always do, what conscience dictates, than wch. there is no safer or better rule for all to follow.

It is of no moment what so inconsiderable a person as I am thinks on the subject in question. And indeed I am little able to enlarge upon it. But the result of all I have thought & read upon it is this, that toleration should be allowed to those who dissent from an Establishment, & that such Establishment should be guarded by a Test Law. Both these things are provided for in our happy Constitution, & it is not easy to see what should incline wise & good men to think otherwise.

My dayly & fervent prayer is that it will please God to preserve your Majesty's life & health, & to give a blessing to all your endeavours for his honour and service. (10072)

---

[1] The King's brief letter of approval on the 16th is in Stanhope, III, Appendix, p. xxxii.

The Message is in *H. of C.J.* LVI, 38 (16 Feb.): 'His Majesty, being desirous of conferring a signal mark of his favour and approbation on Captain Sir Sidney Smith, in consequence of the eminent services which he has rendered, and the valour and ability which he has displayed during the whole period of the important operations, with the conduct of which he has been entrusted on the coast of Egypt, and particularly in the gallant and heroic defence of the fortress of Acra [*sic*], recommends it to the House of Commons to enable his Majesty to make provision for securing to the said Sir Sidney Smith a pension of one thousand pounds per annum for the term of his natural life.'

[2] John Harrison (1738–1811), M.P. for Great Grimsby, 1780–96; for Thetford, 1796–1806. A Foxite Whig.

2361   THE KING *to* HENRY ADDINGTON

[*Queen's House, 16 Feb.*[1]] In consequence of my promise to Mr. Addington to give him my thoughts as they occurr, I think he might do a very agreable thing both to the Duke of Portland and to the Bath familly if he could offer a seat at the Admiralty to the D. of Portland for Lord George[2] or Lord John Thynne.[3] If it in the least clashes with other arrangements I desire it may not be attend[ed] to; excuse my writing so ill, for I am in bed from a severe cold. (Sidmouth MSS.)

2362   THE DUKE OF PORTLAND *to the* KING

[*Burlington House, Tuesday, 17 Feb. 1801, 11.35 p.m.*[4]] The commands which your Majesty is pleased to signify to the Duke of Portland will be immediately obeyed; the Lord President will be informed of your Majesty's pleasure, & the Earl Camden will be acquainted with the permission your Majesty has condescended to grant him. The Duke of Portland will be in waiting to pay his humble duty to your Majesty. The Duke of Portland most humbly requests your Majesty's permission to offer his most anxious wishes for the speedy & perfect re-establishment of your Majesty's health. (10075)

2363   LORD LOUGHBOROUGH *to* HENRY DUNDAS

[*Tuesday evening,* [*17 Feb. 1801*][5].] I had neglected to inquire about Mr. Lushington till I received your letter this morning. I wrote to Mr. Law upon it & have received from him the most ample & satisfactory account of the qualifications of Mr. Edmund Henry Lushington[6] which are such as to recommend him to any judicial situation, however eminent, & I have so much confidence in the recommendation that I am persuaded that this nomination will be an additional proof of your unremitting care to make the best choice of the persons for judicial offices on whose abilitys & integrity the honour of Governt. so essentially depends.
[P.S.] I enclose Law's letter to you & I must add that tho' he addresses his thanks to me, my note to him distinctly stated that you had decided in favour of Mr. Lushington & only suspended the actual nomination till you were more fully

---

¹ Another letter of this day's date is in Pellew, I, 308. In line 2, for 'with' read 'and'. The King had not been downstairs that day; James's powder was removing his cold, which was mentioned in the newspapers on the 17th. On the 18th they said he was much better and would have a Levée that day at St James's. He was, however, unable to be present, his cold persisting.

² Lord George Thynne (1770–1838), second son of Thomas, 1st Marquess of Bath (1734–96) by Elizabeth (1735–1825), daughter of the 2nd Duke of Portland. M.P. for Weobley, 1790–1812; a Lord of the Treasury, 1801–4; Comptroller of the Household, 1804–12. Succeeded his uncle, 1826, as 2nd Baron Carteret.

³ Lord John Thynne (1772–1849), Lord George's brother. M.P. for Weobley, May–Dec. 1796; for Bath, 1796–1832; Vice-Chamberlain of the Household, 1804–12. Succeeded his brother as 3rd Baron Carteret.

⁴ Written after Addington's first Cabinet dinner (Pellew, I, 347).

⁵ The letter is endorsed, received, 18 Feb. 1801.

⁶ He was appointed a Puisne Judge in Ceylon, and was later Chairman of the Colonial Office Audit Board, and Master of the Crown Office (1766–1839).

informed of his qualifications, which I undertook to examine. The favour therefore (if any there is any [*sic*]) belongs to you & not to me.[1] (10076–7)

2364   WILLIAM PITT *to the* KING

[*Downing Street, Wednesday, 18 Feb. 1801, 7.30 p.m.*] Mr Pitt has great satisfaction in being enabled humbly to acquaint your Majesty that the proposal for
raising the Ways & Means for the present year by a loan of £25,500,000 on the
part of Great Britain and of £2,500,000 on the part of Ireland, and for providing
the necessary taxes, was this day agreed to in the Committee of Ways & Means
without any debate, and apparently to the satisfaction of the House.[2] (10081)

2365   *Letters from the* KING *to the* EARL OF CHATHAM, *and the replies*

[*Queen's House, 18 Feb. 1801.*] The King is so much convinced of the attachment and he flatters himself affection of the Earl of Chatham that he prefers writing
to the Lord President than in conversation calling upon him (when the Marquiss
Cornwallis's resignation of the Lieutenancy of Ireland shall arrive) to accept that
office. The manners, integrity and correct line of conduct of the Earl of Chatham
certainly point him out as the person most proper for the station; besides his
having returned to his military profession, he as Lord Lieutenant must of course
take the supreme command of the troops stationed in Ireland, and the Commander-in-Chief only act under his orders; the military business must conse-

---

[1] Addington was prepared to allow Dundas considerable influence so far as Indian affairs were concerned, and seemed also disposed to leave the management of Scotland in his hands. Glenbervie wrote
(5 April): 'Addington...settled that William Dundas was, under Lord Lewisham, to bring forward
India business in the House of Commons, but that there is to be no Vice-President because of the jealousy
of Lord Belgrave; that William Dundas would be the best channel of communication between Lord
Lewisham and Henry Dundas, whom, of course, he would wish to consult very much. I said I could
have no objection, that for many reasons I should think Lord Lewisham would like to communicate
with me, but that I thought it would look ill in the world if I were to be left out of the Commission or
not to have the communication of papers...Dundas, I find, is also to continue Minister for Scotland.
But God help them. Are they so inconsiderate as not to see that he cannot govern India and Scotland
without remaining in the Cabinet, or by acting so much as a puppet master that neither the puppets nor
the public will bear it?' (MS. Diary). Glenbervie added, shortly afterwards, 'Coutts Trotter told Arbuthnot today that William Dundas is fixed on as Minister for Scotland (with the aid of his brother the
Advocate). William Dundas Minister for Scotland and India! Will Dundas push for the Cabinet for
him, or add to his present £1,500 the Paymastership of the Navy? I do not think the public of England
or Scotland will bear to see William Dundas in those stations and governing either at second or first
hand. His temper at least and manner, and I think his talents, are against him. As to me I feel no illwill
to him, but he plays the Minister already too much, and I shall therefore act in suspense and reserve.'
(*Ibid.*)

[2] *Parl. Register*, LIX, 184–201; Pellew, I, 347. The King's brief reply, beginning, remarkably enough,
'My dear Pitt', is in Stanhope, III, Appendix, p. xxxii. 'As you are closing, much to my sorrow, your
political carreer [*sic*], I cannot help expressing the joy I feel that the Ways and Means for the present year
have been this day agreed to in the Committee without any debate, and apparently to the satisfaction
of the House.' (Chatham Papers.)

According to a Memorandum in the Sidmouth MSS. 'Lord Eldon had on Friday, the 18th [*sic*], two hours
conversation with the King from 12 to 2, and never saw him in a state to talk more rationally, nor heard
truer wisdom upon any subject than from the King in that audience. It had been then proposed that Lord
Eldon should have surrendered his Office immediately to accelerate the other arrangements, but the
King said, "Stay till you have the Seals before you part with your Chief Justiceship", and tomorrow
(Wednesday) he was to have taken them.' Cf. *Colchester Diary*, I, 244.

quently be transmitted by the Lord Lieutenant to the Duke of York as Commander-in-Chief of my Army, who, when he has received my approbation to the successions proposed, will transmit them to the successor of Mr Wyndham and the Commissions be prepared by the Secretary of State as those of the rest of the Army.[1] (10078)

[*Lord Chatham's reply, Dover Street, 18 Feb.*] Lord Chatham has received with the deepest sense of your Majesty's goodness the very gracious communication with which your Majesty has been pleased to honor him. Lord Chatham has been long persuaded that the office of Lord Lieutenant of Ireland was one which he cou'd neither hold with any comfort to himself or with any prospect of advantage to your Majesty's service. At the same time, if personal difficulties (however strong) alone stood in the way of the possibility of his undertaking that situation, Lord Chatham would have readily sacrificed them at such a moment as this, to a sense of dutiful obedience to your Majesty's commands. But being firmly convinced, on considering all the circumstances of the present times, as well as on a review of the pas't, that he shou'd be, of all others, the most unfit to advance (what must be always nearest his heart) your Majesty's service, he presumes to hope that he cannot more strongly evince the sincerity of his attachment or the warmth of those sentiments which he must ever gratefully entertain towards your Majesty, than by supplicating your Majesty to permit him to decline a station to which your Majesty's partiality has induced you to call him. (10079–80)

[*From the King, Queen's Palace, 19 Feb.*] The King should not do justice to his affection for the Earl of Chatham if he pressed him farther on a station in his service which his Majesty is convinced the Earl of Chatham is more capable to fill with efficiency than any person. The King thinks the Marquess of Cornwallis will certainly resign the office of Master-General of the Ordnance. The Irish Ordnance ceasing, the King will think it but right on the encrease of business to raise the salary of that office to an equality with [the] President of the Council. In that case he should hope the Earl of Chatham would take that employment; his integrity would be highly useful in controuling that great branch of military service. (10085, and, with trifling variations, Chatham Papers, 364.)

[*From Lord Chatham, Dover Street, 19 Feb., 6.15 p.m.*] Lord Chatham will not trespass further upon your Majesty at present than humbly to assure your Majesty that he shall be earnestly desirous on all occasions to regulate his conduct by whatever may be the most for the good of your Majesty's service. There are some circumstances which Lord Chatham feels to be so nearly connected with it, and which arise out of the very gracious communication your Majesty was pleased to make to Lord Chatham this morning, that he is extremely anxious to be permitted

[1] The King had suggested Chatham's appointment as Lord Lieutenant in his letter of the 11th to Addington (Pellew, I, 303). 'It is necessary to fill up that office with a person that shall clearly understand that the Union has closed the reign of Irish jobs; that he is to be a kind of President of the Council there, and that the civil patronage may be open to his recommendation, but must entirely be decided in England.' See also, Colchester, I, 224.

to offer some explanation upon to your Majesty when he has the honor of attending your Majesty's commands. (10086–7)

[*The King's reply, Queen's House, 19 Feb., 7 p.m.*] The King has this instant received the answer from the Earl of Chatham to the note his Majesty wrote early this morning. He cannot but attain [*sic*] with kindness any ideas the Earl of Chatham may have to state; and when the Lord President will attend at the Queen's House tomorrow, that the Clerk in Waiting of the Privy Council may administer the oaths of office to the new Chancellor of the Exchequer, the two new Secretaries of State,[1] the Master of the Mint[2] and the Joint-Postmaster.[3] His Majesty will in his closet with attention accept the ideas of the Earl of Chatham in case the Master-General of the Ordnance shall resign. (10084, and, with slight variations, Chatham Papers, 364.)

2366   EARL SPENCER *to the* KING, *and the reply*

[*Admiralty, 19 Feb. 1801.*] Earl Spencer would not again have presumed to intrude upon your Majesty's gracious indulgence on any plea less urgent than the one which he now humbly ventures to lay before your Majesty appears to him to be.

[1] Lord Hawkesbury (Foreign) and Lord Hobart (War). Lord Malmesbury wrote on the 12th: 'Pelham told me the King had mentioned me for the Foreign Department, and regretted my being too unwell to accept it' (*Diaries and Corresp.* IV, 7). Hawkesbury proved to be a rather inefficient Foreign Secretary, and in May 1804 Pitt, returning to office, did not reappoint him. According to Glenbervie, Addington wished him to go to the Admiralty but he had declined (Glenbervie MS. Diary). Lord Grenville resigned the Foreign Secretaryship on the 20th (Buckingham, *Court and Cabinets*, III, 138). The King agreed that Lady Grenville should be given a pension, to date from her husband's death. (*Ibid.*)

Lord Wellesley, the Governor-General of Bengal, believed that it was still Lord Hobart's ambition to succeed him. 'I must enter my protest against his appointment,' Wellesley wrote on 4 Oct. 1800. 'Lord Hobart's temper, prejudices and reputation in Bengal disqualify him for this Government... He never will be respected here...He will...overthrow all my institutions and frustrate all my plans. He will be the more inclined to this violence from his natural temper as displayed at Madras, and from his personal resentment against me, and his jealousy of my reputation...On private grounds...I think I may claim from the justice and merited gratitude of my country, that my most bitter and implacable enemy, whose hatred is derived from the consciousness of his own base ingratitude and flagrant injustice towards me, should not be my immediate successor.' (W. Dacres Adams MSS.)

On 10 Feb. Addington, with Pitt's approval, offered Hobart the War Secretaryship. Hobart pointed out that as the Secretaryship was now to be separated from the Board of Control, his office would cease to exist at the peace. Addington replied that in some way or other the Secretaryship should be made permanent; he had no doubt that the country's business would require a Third Secretaryship. After seeing Pitt, Hobart accepted the office. At the end of July the colonial business was transferred from the Home Department to the War. See No. 2498 n. As early as 18 Feb. Glenbervie reported that Hobart was 'in full possession of the office in Downing Street. Arbuthnot saw him there yesterday coming downstairs, calling for clerks, boxes, etc. Yet Dundas is still in possession of the Seals and Hobart is not to kiss hands I believe till Friday.' (MS. Diary.)

The Duke of Portland would have liked the Duke of Montrose to be seriously considered for the Foreign Secretaryship. He wrote to Addington on the 11th: 'If it were possible to bring him forward in such a situation I cannot but think he would be more useful in the House of Lords than any other *layman* to be met with there.' (Sidmouth MSS.)   [2] Lord Arden. See No. 1632.

[3] Lord Charles Spencer. See No. 22. The other Joint Postmaster, Lord Auckland, did not have to be re-sworn, as he had held the office since March 1798. An earlier idea had been to appoint Lord Charles Spencer Joint Paymaster-General. 'It would be so agreeable to *all his family* as well as to himself...It would open the county for the Duke of M[arlborough]'s youngest son who wishes much to be in Parliament, and would render other situations for that purpose unnecessary which would give the Duke of M. a certain degree of trouble which it is the study and *trouble* of his life to avoid', Portland told Addington on the 11th (Sidmouth MSS.).

Sir James Saumarez,[1] of whose merits and services your Majesty has already been on various occasions informed, has more than once very earnestly solicited Earl Spencer to recommend him to your Majesty for the distinction of a Baronetage; and in consideration of the many instances in which it has been this Officer's good fortune to distinguish himself in your Majesty's service,[2] Earl Spencer had encouraged him to hope that at some future period he would lay his humble solicitations at your Majesty's feet. Having held out, though distantly, this expectation, he does not feel that he should act fairly by a most gallant and meritorious Officer, were he to retire from the Admiralty without acquainting your Majesty with this circumstance, and adding that, should your Majesty be graciously pleased to include Sir James Saumarez in the next promotion of Baronets which may be made, Earl Spencer will esteem it as another mark of your Majesty's unmerited grace and condescension to himself, in addition to the many former ones with which your Majesty has already honoured him.[3] (10082–3)

[*The King's reply, 19 Feb.*] The Earl Spencer's recommendation of Sir Jas. Saumarez for a patent of Baronet I highly approve, and think no time so proper as the present hour for the distinction. (Althorp MSS.)

2367   WILLIAM PITT *to the* KING

[*Downing Street, Thursday, 19 Feb. 1801, 11.30 p.m.*] Mr Pitt humbly begs leave to acquaint your Majesty that a Motion was this day made by Mr Sturt for a Committee to enquire into the failure of the expedition to Ferrol, which produced from Sir James Pulteney a very able and satisfactory explanation of his conduct. The Motion was afterwards supported, on a variety of opposite grounds, by Mr Jekyll, Mr Dent, Col. Gascoyne, Mr Ellison, Lord Temple and Mr Grey, and was opposed by Mr Dundas, Mr Pitt, Lord Belgrave, and Genl. Loftus and General Norton. In the course of the debate, Mr Horne Tooke made a speech which seemed to aim only at quaintness and singularity in its turn, and deserves very little remark.[4] The question was negatived by 149 to 75.[5]

[1] Lieutenant, 1778; Captain, 1782; Rear-Admiral, Jan. 1801; Vice-Admiral, 1810; Admiral, 1814. Knighted, Nov. 1793; Baronetcy, June 1801; K.B., 5 Sept. 1801; G.C.B., 1815; created Baron De Saumarez, 1831 (a Coronation peerage). [1757–1836.]

[2] He was, for example, second in command at the Battle of the Nile, 1 Aug. 1798.

[3] Lord Spencer resigned office on the 20th. 'Under his Administration the British Navy reached the pinnacle of renown, and redeemed and balanced the disappointments we have experienced in other departments of the war. To him the new Ministers owe that they have a Government to inherit and an Empire to defend.' (*The Times*, 21 Feb.)

[4] The story went that Lord Camelford, who brought in Horne Tooke for Old Sarum, and who was himself an eccentric (Malmesbury said that he deserved to be confined 'for this act of madness and wickedness', and that his choice of Member was the effect of malice and insanity mixed in nearly equal proportions in his mind), declared that if his Member was turned out of the House as a person in holy orders, he would bring in his black servant. 'Dudley North said, on Lord Camelford's having expressed his wish to find a naturalised negro for Old Sarum, that Horne Tooke might serve him in that light if he turned him inside out' (The Duchess of Devonshire's Diary, 21 Feb. 1801). Glenbervie thought that Horne Tooke was now looking very old and was very lame, and Malmesbury said that no notice at all had been taken of him in this debate (*Glenbervie Diaries*, I, 171; Malmesbury, *Diaries and Corresp.* IV, 9, 13).   [5] *Parl. Register*, LIX, 216–46.

Mr Pitt cannot omit the opportunity of entreating your Majesty's permission to express, tho very insufficiently, how deeply he feels the affecting and condescending mark of your Majesty's goodness and personal kindness conveyed in the expressions of the note[1] with which your Majesty honored him yesterday evening, and which he must ever recollect with the warmest gratitude.[2] (10088–9)

2368 LORD HAWKESBURY to the KING

[*20 Feb. 1801.*] Lord Hawkesbury has the honour to return to your Majesty the letters you were graciously pleased to entrust to him this morning. The account your Majesty gives of what passed on the day when the messengers of the Lords & Commons waited upon you with the Articles of the Union was perfectly fresh in the recollection of Lord Hawkesbury, and is stated in your Majesty's letter to Mr Pitt correctly according to his recollection.

Lord Hawkesbury is sensible to the greatest degree of the confidence your Majesty has been pleased to repose in him, by communicating to him this correspondence, and begs to assure you that nothing can ever obliterate from his mind the highly flattering manner in which your Majesty was pleased to deliver to him the Seals.[3] (10090)

[1] No. 2364 n.

[2] The King's reply on the 20th is in Stanhope, III, Appendix, p. xxxiii.

[3] George Rose has some interesting remarks about the onset of the King's illness and the ministeria changes, in a letter of the 25th, a Wednesday: 'I had a full hour's conversation with Mr. Pitt last night, and I think I scarcely ever saw him in higher spirits. He began by giving me the history of the King's illness which first shewed itself at his evening party last Thursday, but now some of the Princes and Princesses say that they have seen it approaching for some time. A gentleman who was at this party represented the King's conversation and conduct as very extravagant, but Lady Chatham, Lady Jane Dundas, and Lady Grenville, who were all there, said that the marks of derangement were not so strong; still, however, it was evident to them that his Majesty's mind was not in a proper state. On Friday he discharged a great quantity of bile, and was better. He had a Council at the Queen's House, and talked to the Ministers nearly in his usual manner; particularly with the greatest kindness to Mr. Dundas about himself and Mr. Pitt. On Saturday Mr. Pitt heard nothing and concluded that all was well. On Sunday the King, after a very bad night, was evidently deranged, and the Duke of York gave notice of it to Mr. Addington and Lord Chatham. The Willises were immediately sent for. The Queen and Princesses went to St. James's Chapel. Since that time the King has had fever and not been in general as he should be— but at intervals he has been quite well. He saw the Queen and Duke of Cumberland yesterday. He saw Mr. Addington on Sunday. Mr. Pitt has not seen him—he had two notes from him (one on Friday) not written quite in his usual style—they were more familiar, and he did not use the first person. Dr. Willis is not himself in town, but his three sons attend the King; they say they can by no means answer for the time of the King's recovery. Mr. Pitt seems to think that he may be well in six or seven days, and in any such interval the public business may go on without any material mischief or inconvenience.

I then talked to Mr. Pitt about the new Administration, and spoke very strongly my own opinion and that of everyone with whom I conversed that it could not continue—that even those who were in office had no confidence in their leader; that I could not consider his abilities as in any degree equal to his situation and that the consequence of Mr. Addington being obliged to retire would be either that a *Jacobin* Government must take place or that Mr. Pitt must return to office. I said that the country at large, or at least, great number of people, believed that Mr. Addington had made use of improper means to get into office, and considered him as very incompetent to govern the nation at the present critical moment. Mr. Pitt answered that the latter was matter of opinion, but that there was not the slightest ground for the former suspicion. I told him that people would not believe that there was not some cause not yet declared for his quitting office, and that credit was given to him for not deserting the country in its present state without some adequate cause. He intimated that he would declare in Parliament that there was no other reason but the one *avowed*, but I told him that even that would not remove the

[*Palace Yard, 22 Feb. 1801, 8 a.m.*] Mr. Addington humbly acquaints your Majesty, that the Earl of Hardwicke has accepted the situation of Lord Lieutenant of Ireland;[1] as has Lord Lewisham that of President of the Board of Controul.[2] Both expressed in the strongest terms their deep sense of your Majesty's con-

suspicion. When once an idea prevailed of intrigue or of undue means being used to supplant, it was next to impossible to do away such impressions—and that even his support, however active and zealous, would not affect it. I instanced Lord Shelburne. He said that the cases were not similar. I admitted that there was some difference, but contended that they both depended upon the same principle of the human mind, namely, the difficulty of removing any impression of duplicity, insincerity, etc. Mr. Pitt in talking of Mr. Addington's abilities said that he would certainly *assert himself* in a manly way, and that he would have some stout supporters who would stand forward in his defence. I said that would not do— after the House of Commons had been for 17 years accustomed to see the First Minister fight his own battles, they would not be contented with seeing another person in that situation acting a second part in debate. I said that very much depended upon the manner in which Mr. Addington conducted himself in the House of Commons, and that really he had so little experience in debate that no one could speak very confidently about his talents in that way. To both these positions, particularly the former, Mr. Pitt assented warmly. He never once spoke of Mr. Addington as likely to distinguish himself as a debater. We afterwards came to the important point of the Catholic question, about which we talked a long time. He said that he had intended to pledge himself never to come into office without full permission to propose that measure, upon the ground of thinking that by so doing he should keep the Catholics of Ireland more quiet from the hope that they might succeed in their wishes at some future time. I argued warmly and strongly upon this point, and Mr. Pitt owned that even what had now happened to the King in some sort shook his determination. I endeavoured to persuade him on public grounds that he ought to leave himself at liberty, and indeed in the very beginning of our conversation we both declared that no *personal* or *private* considerations ought to weigh in such a situation as the present of the country. I told him that Opposition would endeavour to draw such a pledge for him—that in thinking of the Catholic interest he was not to forget the Protestants of England—that there was still, and ought to be, a great prejudice in this country against Popery—and that the state of things might become such as to leave only the alternative of his taking office without proposing that measure or of abandoning the country to be ruined by a Jacobin Government. In such a case, surely the higher duty of saving his country was to prevail over his wish to grant this indulgence, or, if he pleased, this right, to the Catholics and Dissenters. He would not absolutely promise not to pledge himself, but I am satisfied that he will not.' (Pretyman MSS.)

[1] The Duke of Montrose, Lord Winchilsea and Lord Chatham had refused the offer of that office (Malmesbury, *Diaries and Corresp.* IV, 13; *Colchester Diary,* I, 240, 242). The Duke of Montrose's letter declining the appointment is in Pellew, I, 346. Winchilsea said he 'felt himself so entirely unfit that he should ever reproach himself if he undertook it, and should not have any peace of mind upon it.' Hardwicke supported the Catholic question and the repeal of the Test Act, but he was 'not for trying it now, against the positive refusal of the Executive Government' (*Colchester Diary,* I, 239).

[2] Viscount Lewisham (1755–1810) had been Lord Warden of the Stannaries, 1783–98. He was President of the Board of Control, 1801–2; Lord Steward of the Household, 1802–4, and Lord Chamberlain, 1804–10. See No. 64. He was summoned to Parliament by writ, 15 June 1801 in his father's Barony of Dartmouth, but did not take his seat, as he succeeded to his father's Earldom of Dartmouth on 15 July following. 'Ministers,' wrote Glenbervie (18 Feb.) 'had never offered him any situation. Knowing his worth and parts, and believing him to be an enemy to innovation and democracy, knowing also the religious turn of his father and mother and that they have been great courtiers, and aware that he has a large family and very narrow income I...ventured to suggest to Bragge that it might be worth his brother-in-law's while to consider whether by the offer of some respectable office to him would not tend to give credit and strength to his Administration...He...seemed a good deal impressed with the reasons for wishing to have Lord Lewisham. He said it was a pity that he had not occurred before.' (MS. Diary.)

Hardwicke was gazetted on 17 March but was sworn in only on 25 May, the delay being due to the illness of the Commander-in-Chief elect in Ireland, Sir Charles Stuart. Cornwallis could not very well abandon the command of the Army there until the arrival of a military successor. Stuart died before he could take up his appointment (25 March) and Sir William Medows was subsequently appointed

descension and goodness in deeming them worthy of those proofs of confidence, with which your Majesty is disposed to honor them.[1] (10091)

2370 PRINCE AUGUSTUS *to the* KING

[[*Lisbon*], *28 Feb. 1801.*] It is not without the sincerest anxiety as well as warmest interest that I learnt by the last post the late political changes that have taken place in your Majesty's Cabinet, knowing how much this must have agitated you, and feeling by nature, as well as by duty, the most real concern in everything that regards your personal welfare and happiness. I trust by this time that everything will be settled to your Majesty's satisfaction, and may contribute towards your tranquillity. I cannot say, Sir, how truly unhappy I feel at being out of England at this moment, as every incident gives rise to various reports which gradually encrease according to the distance they have to travel, and of course afford a more inexhaustible source of uneasiness, to which the human mind is but too prone to give way.

There is little or nothing new in this disagreable place, except the report still prevails of hostilities being upon the eve of breaking out betwixt this Court & that of Spain. The Spanish Ambassador has removed from this place already ten days, but the little Spanish Infant, the Regent's[2] nephew, still continues here, which makes the politicians believe, that this rumor of a war is still a farce, and that underhand this Court is patching up a peace, for at best I believe it will be a bad one. Thus far is certain that the military preparations that they have made till now, are very insignificant, except that today I have heard it was the intention of this Government to encrease the private soldier's pay for which additional taxes are to be levied, upon servants, carriages, horses, and various other articles of luxury. As for magazines they are incapable of forming any in their present situation, as I am told from authority, that they have not sufficient provisions to feed their own subjects for upwards of two months. The Spaniards have neither magazines of corn, except at *Salamanca*, but I have heard they can easily form them, as at the end of the last harvest, the Spanish Government caus'd a return to be made them of all the corn that had been reaped in the Provinces that border on this Kingdom, and had only allowed the peasants to sell such a quantity of it, as was thought absolutely necessary for their own immediate consumption. If in consequence of these events it should be thought necessary to send here again English troops for the defense of this country I can assure your Majesty that it will be absolutely necessary to insist upon the following points.

1st. That the English General should have the supreme command not only of our troops but also of those of this Government, for the foolish Court intrigues are so numerous and the pride of the nobility such, that every plan will not only be opposed but positively thwarted in every manner for the Duke de la Fuenza

---

[1] There was no reply to this letter. The King's illness now took a decided turn for the worse, and it was said that he was as bad as he had been at his worst period in 1788 (Malmesbury, *Diaries and Corresp.* IV, 14).

[2] The Regent, John, afterwards John VI, King of Portugal (1767–1826) married (1790) Charlotte (1775–1830), daughter of Charles IV of Spain (1748–1819).

will not allow any one to meddle in anything that he blindly directs himself, and has such an opinion of the Portuguese knowledge in military tactics that whoever from his situation wishes to put him right upon this point, which is absolutely necessary before any change can be thought of, is treated by him not only as a liar but also as guilty of a libel against the Government, and yet, Sir, I can assure your Majesty that they have not in their forts a single cannon properly fit for service, the frames or carriages being rotten, and the balls not of the same calibre as the cannons.

2ly. It is absolutely necessary to maintain our own discipline independant of this Government. It stands to reason that if we come here as Allies [the rest is missing][1]. (48208–9)

2371 THE KING to HENRY ADDINGTON

[*Friday, 13* [?] *March 1801, 10 a.m.*[2]] His Majesty cordially approves of the Minute of Cabinet transmitted by his Majesty's Chancellor of Exchequer in the box, accompanied by Mr. Addington's letter dated yesterday at $\frac{m}{40}$ p.m. The King authorizes his Minister to acquaint his Majesty's newly appointed Cabinet of his approbation of their Minute. (Sidmouth MSS.)

[1] General Simon Fraser commanded the British forces in Portugal, and Prince Augustus reviewed the *émigré* regiments which were preparing to face a Franco-Spanish invasion. In the summer, however, the Portuguese Government made overtures for peace, and the Foreign Minister, the Chevalier de Pinto, signed the Treaty.

[2] Printed (inaccurately) in Pellew, I, 350, and there dated the 10th. The MS. is endorsed by Pellew 'in reality, Tuesday'. The date is not clear in the MS. (the King's handwriting was, not unnaturally, worse than usual), but if he knew on which day of the week he was writing (he was, in fact, recovering fast), the date is obviously the 13th, unless, indeed, he was so far out of his reckoning that he meant the 20th, in which case he could be replying to Addington's letter of the 19th, enclosing the Cabinet Minute. The phrase 'newly-appointed Cabinet' almost suggests the 20th, but Addington's letter of the 19th was written at 4.45 p.m.

The King's letter of the 15th to Addington is (inaccurate as usual) in Pellew, I, 353. Damp has now destroyed the first part of the MS., but it should probably read: 'His Majesty has received the box containing the new appointment of Postmaster, as also that of the Joint Paymaster. The King cannot find words sufficiently expressive of his Majesty's cordial approbation of the whole arrangements which *his own Chancellor of the Exchequer* has wisely, and, his Majesty chuses to add, most correctly recommended.' (Sidmouth MSS.)

The following drafts of Cabinet Minutes, in the Liverpool Papers, all in Hawkesbury's hand, were obviously written between the last week in February and Pitt's resignation on 14 March. The King may never have received them. See A. Aspinall, *The Cabinet Council, 1783–1835* (*Proc. of British Academy*, XXXVIII, 149, for a comment on the extraordinary character of these Cabinet meetings).

Cabinet Minute [? shortly before 12 March 1801]

Present: The Lord Chancellor, The Lord President, The Lord Privy Seal, The Duke of Portland, Earl St Vincent, Lord Hobart, Lord Eldon, Mr. Addington, Lord Hawkesbury.

After a full consideration of the subject, your Majesty's servants are strongly impress'd with the importance of bringing the differences subsisting between this country and Denmark to an issue, before the Fleet of Denmark can be joined by those of Sweden and Russia. They therefore humbly submit to your Majesty the expediency of ordering the Fleet destined for the Baltic to sail without delay.* That on its arrival in the Categat, the Admiral should communicate with Mr. Drummond, your Majesty's Minister at Copenhagen, who should be authorised to require from the Danish Government an explicit answer in the course of 48 hours to the propositions which will have been made to them, in consequence of the

* It sailed from Yarmouth on 12 March under the command of Sir Hyde Parker, with Nelson under him, and entered the Sound on the 30th.

[*Downing Street, Monday night, 16 March 1801.*] Mr Pitt humbly begs leave to submit for your Majesty's signature the accompanying warrants, which, if they should receive your Majesty's approbation, he naturally wishes to see compleated, and therefore presumes to trouble your Majesty with them in the interval before the new patent for the Treasury passes.[1] (10099)

instructions of Lord Grenville to Mr. Vansittart. That in the event of their refusing to acquiesce in either of the alternatives therein proposed, he should be directed to leave Copenhagen together with all the persons attached to the Mission, and that the Admiral should in that case proceed to the most vigorous hostilities.

That if upon the arrival of the Fleet in the Categat the Admiral should find that Mr. Drummond had been under the necessity of leaving Copenhagen, or if the Danish Government should attempt to prevent any communication between the Fleet and the shore, the Admiral should be directed to commence hostilities without waiting for further orders.

Mr. Pitt & Mr. Dundas attended the meeting for the purpose of giving any information in their power, and perfectly approved of the decision. (Add. MSS. 38357, f. 146.)

Cabinet Minute

Present: The Lord Chancellor, The Lord President, The Lord Privy Seal, The Duke of Portland, Earl St. Vincent, Lord Hobart, Lord Eldon, Mr. Pitt, Mr. Dundas, Mr. Addington, Lord Hawkesbury.

A Memorial of Count Wedel Jarlsberg dated the 23 of this month having been communicated to your Majesty's servants, they humbly agree to submit to your Majesty their unanimous opinion that the following answer should be returned to it: that your Majesty had taken the most convenient mode of sending your ultimatum to the Danish Government; that to that ultimatum you continue to adhere; that if consistent with the principles therein contained, an amicable arrangement could still be formed, it would give your Majesty the greatest satisfaction, but that if the Danish Government should continue to persist in the principles laid down in Count Wedel Jarlsberg's Note & in the Treaty to which it refers, there is no other alternative left to your Majesty, but that of having recourse to immediate & vigorous hostilities. (Add. MSS. 38357, f. 148.)

Cabinet Minute [1801] [In Hawkesbury's hand]

Present: The Lord Chancellor, The Lord President, The Lord Privy Seal, The Duke of Portland, Earl St. Vincent, Lord Hobart, Mr. Pitt, Mr. Dundas, Mr. Addington, Lord Hawkesbury.

After fully considering the Intelligence received from Lisbon, your Majesty's servants have agreed to submit to you as their opinion that the Government of Portugal should be informed that in the present state of the war in Europe it is not in the power of your Majesty, consistent with a due regard to the safety of your Kingdom, to afford any assistance to Portugal by sending any British forces into that country. That under these circumstances, it should be recommended to the Prince Royal of Portugal to endeavour to make peace on such terms as he may be enabled to procure, without any reference to his engagements with Great Britain.* That if the Government of Portugal are however determined to have recourse to arms rather than submit to the conditions which have been proposed through the Spanish Government, your Majesty's servants would propose to Parliament to furnish £300,000 as a subsidy, & would endeavour to negociate a loan of £500,000 on the security the Portuguese Government have proposed, they undertaking to provide the interest that may be judged sufficient. But on this latter point your Majesty's servants cannot give a positive answer without further consideration & enquiry. That in the event of any negociation for peace being open'd between your Majesty and France (before Portugal should conclude a seperate Peace) the Government of this country will press for including Portugal in any pacification that may take place. (Add. MSS. 38357, f. 149.) It was not until 18 May that Lord Hawkesbury asked the House of Commons to grant a subsidy of £300,000 to the Queen of Portugal.

[1] On Saturday the 14th at 3 p.m. Pitt had an audience of the King and resigned his office. The seals were at once delivered to Addington. Pitt gave George Rose an account of what happened (Rose, *Diaries and Corresp.* I, 337). Rose explained what the two warrants were about: 'In the evening [of the 14th]

---

* Napoleon, determined to compel Portugal to abandon its alliance with Great Britain, made an alliance with Spain on 1 Oct. 1800 providing for the partition of Portugal, and on 8 March 1801 Spain declared war on Portugal. The British Government felt unable to send any effectual military aid, the chief disposable force being engaged in Egypt, and in June the Portuguese Government signed with Spain preliminaries of peace.

[*Downing Street, 19 March.*] Mr Pitt humbly begs leave to submit for your Majesty's signature several warrants for small pensions on the Scotch Fund, which are in consequence of engagements of some standing, and were only deferred from a deficiency for a time in the produce of the Fund which is since become ample. (10100)

2373   *Letters from* HENRY ADDINGTON *to the* KING, *with a Cabinet Minute*
[*Palace Yard, 19 March 1801, 4.45 p.m.*] Mr. Addington humbly communicates to your Majesty a Minute of Cabinet expressive of an opinion and recommendation in which, Mr. Addington thinks it his duty to state that your Majesty's confidential servants unanimously concurred. (10101)

[*Enclosure*]
Cabinet Minute [*Palace Yard, 19 March 1801, 4.30 p.m.*]

Present: The Lord Chancellor [Lord Loughborough], The Lord President, The Lord Privy Seal, The Duke of Portland, The Earl of St. Vincent, Lord Hobart, Lord Eldon, Lord Hawkesbury, Mr Addington.

Lord Liverpool was prevented by indisposition from being present; but Lord Hawkesbury declared himself authorized to express his Lordship's concurrence in the sentiments contained in the Minute of Cabinet.

It is humbly recommended to your Majesty that steps should be taken without delay to make known to the French Government your Majesty's disposition to enter into an immediate negotiation for the restoration of peace.[1] (10102)

[*From Addington, Palace Yard, 26 March 1801, 5 a.m.*] Mr. Addington humbly acquaints your Majesty that the numbers in the House of Commons, upon Mr. Grey's Motion for an enquiry into the State of the Nation were, for the Motion 105, against it 295.[2] (10108)

...Dr. Thomas Willis came to me by his Majesty's command, to desire I would give what furtherance I could to two pension warrants for £600 a year to Lady Louisa Paget, about to be married to Colonel Erskine, which message he had received from the King while playing at cards with the Queen and Princesses.' (*Ibid.* 1, 336.)

On the 28th Rose remarked, 'The state of the King's health cannot be perfectly good. There are at least eight hundred warrants unsigned, and none are returned that were lately sent' (*Ibid.* 1, 339).

The Duke of Cumberland's undated letter (? to Pitt's private secretary) was probably written at this period: 'The news is still better, his Majesty has eat three platesfull of bread and butter, has spoken as collectedly as ever he did in his life to *all* his Phisicians, and has gone to bed remarkably well. The brothers Willis own they are astonished at the amendment, and we are overjoyed, God grant now he may go on as he is now & we shall be the happiest family on the globe. I hope this good news will act as a charm upon you my dear friend, pray if you think this worthy of Mr. Pitt's notice pray read it him, he will excuse the style of this note from the overjoy I feel.

P.S. I make Dr. J. Willis add a few lines to empasis the above. "A day of sunshiny showers ending with a steady gleam and hatching every good we all so firmly wish for. J.W."' (W. Dacres Adams MSS.)

[1] Endorsed by the King: 'I fully approve of the above Minute.—George R. 20th M. 1801.' On the 20th he was reported to be 'extremely nervous and low spirited', and there is another gap in the correspondence. Malmesbury said on the 22nd he was 'unequal to business'.

[2] *Parl. Register*, LIX, 559–659 (25 March). The correct numbers are 291 v 105. Addington himself, showing every sign of exhaustion, did not rise to speak until 4 a.m., and the House rose at 4.45 a.m. This

[*Burlington House, Friday, 27 March 1801, 11.10 p.m.*] The Duke of Portland most humbly begs leave, in the absence of Lord Hobart, to lay at your Majesty's feet the list of the Lords who were present, & the order of the speakers in the debate on the clause proposed to be added to Taylor's Divorce Bill for the purpose of preventing the adulteress from marrying the person who was the party to her crime.[1] (10111)

2375 THE DUKE OF CUMBERLAND *to the* KING

[*St. James's, 29 March 1801.*] I return your Majesty my most humble thanks for the favour you have graciously conferred on me in giving me the command of the 27th Regt. of Light Dragoons, as well as for your gracious promise that whenever an exchange can be made, I may flatter myself I shall receive the 15th Regt., your Majesty's Own Regt. of Light Dragoons, which has always distinguished itself; whenever that happy moment shall arrive I shall endeavour to prove myself worthy of the command entrusted to my care.[2] As to your gracious approbation of my conduct I beg leave to observe, had I behaved otherwise I should be unworthy of the blessing Providence has conferred on me in giving me the best of fathers and mothers. God grant I may always behave so as to merit their approbation, & affection. (47188)

2376 THE KING *to the* DUKE OF YORK, *and a reply*

[*Sunday, 29 March 1801.*] I approve in general of your proposed [*sic*], but think my partiality to the Earl of Aylesford not too strongly marked, considering the unfortunate wound of Col. Edward Finch[3] of the Coldstream Regt. of Guards, as well as his willingness to take the command of the 2d Bat. now in Egypt, in naming his brother to the command of the 59th Regt. of Foot. As I shall wish to

helps to account for the brevity of his report. Glenbervie has an interesting account of this debate (*Journals*, I, 204). Dundas, Pitt, Castlereagh and Canning sat together in the third row behind the Treasury bench. See also Malmesbury, *Diaries and Corresp.* IV, 51, where the majority is given as 293, and *Colchester Diary*, I, 261.

Grey himself wrote, on the 24th: 'I am very nervous about the debate tomorrow, and as usual deprived of sleep by it, so that instead of being in full strength as I ought to be, I shall be all to pieces, and I am afraid my speech will be something like the Archbishop of Granada's sermon.' (Howick MSS.) He must have been disappointed with the division: he had written: 'If we have a strong division tomorrow, of which I am not quite so confident as I was, the new Administration will be shaken to its centre.'

[1] George Taylor, of Totnes, married Catherine Birchall Elken on 28 May 1792, and in 1800 the Court of King's Bench awarded him £500 damages, with costs, against the Rev. William Ilbert Birdwood, who was proved to have committed adultery with the plaintiff's wife. The Bishop of Exeter, who had the misfortune to be related to the co-respondent, said that the affair had 'planted daggers in the breasts of his afflicted relations'. Mrs Taylor had entangled the young man in her snares even before he was ordained. (*Parl. Register*, LIX, 665.) Birdwood was eighteen in April 1793 when he matriculated at Balliol, and he graduated in 1797.

[2] See No. 2380.

[3] See Nos. 905 and 1329. He was a younger brother of Lord Aylesford. Captain, 1783; Lieutenant-Colonel, 1792; Colonel, 1796; Major-General, 1801; Lieutenant-General, 1808; General, 1819. M.P. for Cambridge, 1789–1819. (1756–1843.)

get by the middle of June to Weymouth to Weymouth [*sic*], I should think the coming sometimes to Farrington Field near Dorchester Barracks might be conducive to my spirits and make my quiet riding most pleasant. I desire therefore that you and the Dutchess of York will come about that time to Mrs. Stuart's at Weymouth and that you will look on yourselves as lodged there by me; my table, house and box at the Play will be heartily at the dear Dutchesses service.[1] I would propose, that Lieut. Genl. Harrington should under you command the cavalry, having Lt. Genl. D. of Cumberland as second in command with [*sic*]. (10112)

[*From the Duke of York, Horse Guards, 30 March 1801.*] I have the honor to acknowledge the receipt of your Majesty's letter of this day returning the memoranda papers for the last two weeks of which your Majesty is graciously pleased to approve.

Had I had the honor of paying my duty to your Majesty in person yesterday, and laying the papers before you myself, it had been my intention to explain to your Majesty the reasons for my venturing to propose Major-General Ross for the command of the 59th Regiment in succession to Lieutenant-General Gordon[2] removed to the 26th Regiment by the death of Sir Charles Stuart,[3] as likewise of Lieutenant-General Ogilvie to the 89th and Major General Vilettes to the 3d Batallion of the King's Own. I therefore beg leave to lay them now before your Majesty and to wait your pleasure before the succession is published.

In consequence of the Marquess Cornwallis's intended resignation of the Ordnance[4] I understand that it is wished that Major-General Ross should likewise resign the Surveyor Generalship, and this measure will, it is thought, more easily and expeditiously be accomplished by his being removed to an old Regiment.[5]

With regard to Lieutenant-General Ogilvie I took the liberty of laying his name before your Majesty as a very old and respectable officer, who has had the honor to serve your Majesty near fifty years, and to whom such a remove would be a promotion, and in venturing to propose Major-General Vilettes for the 3d Batallion of the King's Own, I was actuated by the peculiarity of his situation, who, having been removed from the Lieutenant-Colonelcy of the King's Dragoon Guards upon the idea of raising one of the Albanian Regiments, now finds himself after the failure of that project, after two years and without receiving any advantage from it upon the eve of being reduced to half pay. (10113–4)

[1] The Duchess, whose health was always delicate, had been at Bath for some time.

[2] Andrew Gordon (*d.* 1806), referred to in No. 303. Colonel, 1790; Major-General, 1794; Lieutenant-General, 1801. At the time of his death he was commanding the forces in Jersey.

[3] On 25 March.

[4] Cornwallis wrote to his brother, the Bishop, on 12 March: 'When I come to London I shall resign the Ordnance, and it is then my determination to retire absolutely from all public and political life, and to pass the remainder of my days in Suffolk. I have taken such measures as will, I trust, for some time insure the tranquillity of Ireland, unless my successor should be weak enough to suffer some of it's old and violent rulers to resume the power which they have hitherto so much abused, and which they would again employ to plunge this wretched country into all the miseries and horrors from which it has with so much difficulty been rescued.' (Kent R.O.)

[5] He retained his office until 1804.

2377 THE DUCHESS OF WURTEMBERG *to the* KING

[*Erlangen, 31 March 1801.*] Having just heard from my brother that he is going to leave Germany I cannot deny myself the pleasure of writing to your Majesty and congratulating you on your recovery. The gracious message you honoured me with through Elizabeth made me very happy, as it is a fresh proof of your constant goodness to me which is most deeply felt by me, who am very dutifully attached to your Majesty and have been very wretched to hear that you were ill. I trust the country air will strengthen your Majesty and that the Almighty will long preserve you a blessing to us all.

The Duke had intended to have written to your Majesty but as I feared it might be troublesome I undertook to present his humble duty to you and take on myself this apparent neglect which I thought would avoid your Majesty trouble. I cannot sufficiently express how much affection and kindness the Duke shewed me during the uneasiness I underwent on account of your Majesty, but thank God you are now quite well and I trust will be able to enjoy the Easter week in the country. (51638-9)

2378 THE DUKE OF PORTLAND *to the* KING

[*Burlington House, Tuesday, 31 March 1801, 10.15 p.m.*] In obedience to your Majesty's commands the Duke of Portland most humbly lays before your Majesty the list of the Lords who were present in the House today & of those who took a part in the debate which lasted till near ten o'clock, which was opened with great force by the Earl of Clare & supported with great powers of argument & eloquence by Lord Eldon in particular & several other Lords & as feebly combated by the Lords who spoke on the other side.[1] (10115)

2379 *Letters from* HENRY ADDINGTON *to the* KING

[*Downing Street, 9 April 1801, 3.30 p.m.*] I am really unable to describe the relief and consolation afforded to my mind by the note with which your Majesty has been pleased to honor me. That which I received on Tuesday last, accompanied by a most affecting communication to your Majesty from the Queen, gave me, I venture to acknowledge, great uneasiness, and confirmed what I could not but feel when I paid my duty to your Majesty at the Queen's House. It was certainly on Tuesday ye 31st of March, as stated in your Majesty's note of this morning, and not on Saturday ye 28th, as mentioned in that of Monday last, that I waited on your Majesty. My anxiety on account of your Majesty's indisposition has now given way to the conviction, that, in a few days, all traces of it will be removed,

---

[1] *Parl. Register*, LX, 21. The debate, on the martial law in Ireland Bill, was unreported, strangers being excluded.

Addington told Glenbervie on 5 April that 'efforts had been made to place Lord Clare in this Cabinet, and I said I had clearly seen that to be his aim. He said it would be declaring too strongly to the Irish Catholics that the power which had been employed against them there was only transferred to London. I mentioned Lord Clare's influence over Lord Hobart. He said that was an additional reason against admitting him into the Cabinet.' (MS. Diary.)

without the danger of a relapse, which is so much to be guarded against; and that your Majesty will be thus restored to every domestic comfort and to the full exercise of every function which the public interests may require. To that period I need not assure your Majesty that I look forward with a degree of impatience which is only restrained by an extreme sollicitude that it may not be so accelerated as to interfere with the completion of your Majesty's recovery, or endanger the continuance of that state of health which is so important to your Majesty's family, to your subjects, and to Europe. (10123–4)

[*Downing Street, 11 April, 12.45 p.m.*] Mr. Addington humbly acknowledges the return of the two Treasury warrants with your Majesty's signature to each of them.

Mr. Addington hopes to be allowed to pay his duty to your Majesty tomorrow. He is now going to the Committee of Secrecy at the House of Commons where he expects to be unavoidably detained till late in the day.[1] (10127)

2380 THE DUKE OF CUMBERLAND *to the* KING

[*St James's, 11 April 1801.*] I am this moment honoured with your Majesty's gracious letter and cannot find words sufficiently strong to express to your Majesty my gratitude for your gracious approbation of this exchange with Lord Dorchester. Having now the honour of commanding your own Regiment of Light Dragoons I shall endeavour to prove to your Majesty by a faithful and zealous discharge of my duty that my utmost ambition will ever be to prove myself not unworthy of the honour so graciously conferred on me. (47189)

2381 THE KING'S *Memorandum*

[*12 April 1801.*] No. 1. Paper[2] drawn up on the Earl Fitzwilliam's pressing a farther emancipation of the Irish Papists, and transmitted to Mr. Pitt, who, having approved it then, ought not on the 31st of January to have made a similar proposal and seemed surprized I would not follow him in changing my opinion; his ground of *expediency* certainly was futile, and the more [so] as every Irish Protestant felt the ruin of the measure if adopted. And I certainly feeling the duty I owe to my Coronation Oath, could not have given my assent to any Bill that had but [?] the shaddow of putting Papists and Presbiterians on a state of equality with the Church of England.[3] (Sidmouth MSS.)

[1] The Secret Committee, which was appointed to inquire into the disturbed state of Ireland, was ballotted for on the 2nd, and the names of the 21 members are in *H. of C.J.* LVI, 269, and *Parl. Register* XL, 50.
[2] In Stanhope, II, Appendix, p. xxiii (6 Feb. 1795).
[3] The Catholic question was still preying on the King's tortured mind. When Loughborough attended the King to deliver up the Great Seal, 'the King', wrote George Rose, 'put into his hand a paper which he wrote in 1795, testifying his approbation of the recall of Lord Fitzwilliam, and the reasons for that, which paper his Majesty said, would be a decisive proof that *he* had not changed his mind on the subject of the Irish Catholics; and he added that he had a duplicate of it which he should soon put into the hands of another person' (Rose, *Diaries and Corresp.* I, 349).

2382 THE EARL OF ST VINCENT *to the* KING

[*Admiralty, 15 April 1801, 1.15 p.m.*] Lord St Vincent humbly presumes to transmit to his Majesty the substance[1] of a dispatch he has just received by Capt. Otway[2] of the London from Admiral Sir Hyde Parker, containing an account of his operations against Copenhagen, and begs leave to offer to his Majesty his congratulations on the success which has hitherto attended his Majesty's Fleet. (10128)

2383 LORD ELDON *to the* KING[3]

[*18 April 1801.*] The Lord Chancellor, submitting his most humble duty to your Majesty, has presumed to transmit to your Majesty the titles, containing in effect the substance, of some Bills which have passed both Houses of your Majesty's Parliament, and to which your Majesty's Royal Assent is humbly prayed. One of them is a Bill for reviving certain Acts, passed for suspending the Habeas Corpus Act, in part, in cases of treason or treasonable practices, and which has been thought so necessary to the public safety that each House of your Majesty's Parliament has read the Bill three times in as short a space of time as their modes of proceeding would admit. If your Majesty should be graciously pleased to give your Royal Assent to this Bill, it is thought that the public interest requires, if your Majesty should so think fit, that such Assent should be given today by commission: and the Lord Chancellor humbly proposes with your Majesty's gracious leave to wait upon your Majesty today, somewhat before three o'clock, to learn your Majesty's pleasure upon the subject. The nature of the other Bills does not seem to call for particular observation.[4] (10139–40)

2384 THE EARL OF ST VINCENT *to the* KING

[*Admiralty, 21 April 1801, 10 p.m.*] Lord St. Vincent thinks it his duty to acquaint your Majesty that on a consideration of all the circumstances that have occurr'd since Sir Hyde Parker was first entrusted with the command of the Baltic Fleet, and the difficulties which he has rais'd on every occasion, wherein a prompt and vigorous execution of his duty has been requir'd, he is under great apprehensions that your Majesty's service will derive no advantage from Sir Hyde's continuance in that command. Lord St. Vincent therefore most humbly presumes to submit to your Majesty's consideration whether it may not be adviseable that Sir Hyde should be recall'd, and that a commission should be sent to Lord Nelson, vesting

[1] Folio 10129.
[2] Sir Robert Waller Otway (1770–1846). Lieutenant, 1793; Captain, 1795; Rear-Admiral, 1814; Admiral, 1830; created Baronet, 1831; K.C.B., 1826; G.C.B., 1845. He was now in command of Sir Hyde Parker's flagship, *London*.
[3] Lord Eldon had taken his seat in the Court of Chancery on the 15th. Throughout the Easter Term he continued to discharge the duties both of Lord Chancellor and of Lord Chief Justice of the Common Pleas—resigning the Chief Justiceship only on 21 May (Twiss, I, 371).
[4] The King sent the following note to Lord Hobart, Secretary of State for War, on the 19th at 1.20 p.m.: 'The King is highly gratified by the account transmitted to him by Lord Hobart of the intelligence received from Egypt by the French as stated in the Moniteur' (Bucks. R.O.).

him with the chief command of the Baltic Fleet. When Lord St. Vincent has next the honor of paying his duty to your Majesty, he will take the liberty of explaining fully to your Majesty the various circumstances which have occurred to induce him to offer this opinion.

Lord St. Vincent stated fully to your Majesty's confidential servants today all that has passed on this unpleasant subject, and he had the satisfaction of finding an unanimous opinion of the propriety of the measure now propos'd.[1] (10141)

2385 THE DUKE OF PORTLAND *to the* KING

[*Burlington House, Thursday, 23 April 1801, 11.10 p.m.*] In laying before your Majesty the inclosed dispatches from the Lord Lieutenant of Ireland the Duke of Portland conceives it to be his duty to represent with all humility to your Majesty that the recommendations which they contain, & which had provisionally received your Majesty's sanction, have been necessarily withheld until the Act to empower your Majesty to make the office of Master of the Rolls in Ireland an efficient office had received your Majesty's Royal Assent, for which it was not ready until last Saturday. The Duke of Portland also humbly submits herewith a warrant for your Majesty's royal signature for the appointment of the Earl of Hardwicke to the Lieutenancy of Ireland.

The Duke of Portland farther hopes that your Majesty's great goodness & condescension will not dispose your Majesty to blame him for giving way so far to the sollicitations of the parties interested as most humbly to represent to your Majesty that a large box containing military letters & lists of successions from the Lord Lieutenant of Ireland, & two boxes containing commissions for the Royal Regiment of Artillery, were some days since submitted to your Majesty's consideration. (10144–5)

2386 *Letters from* LORD HAWKESBURY *to the* KING, *and a reply*

[*London, 23 April 1801.*] Lord Hawkesbury has the honour to send to your Majesty the credentials & full powers intended for Lord St Helens as Ambassador to the Court of St Petersburgh which he requests your Majesty will sign if they meet with your approbation.

Lord Hawkesbury has conversed with Count Woronzow & Lord Whitworth respecting the person who would be most likely to be acceptable to the Russian Government at the present moment, and they both recommend Lord St Helens as well acquainted with that Court and peculiarly qualified to accomodate the differences which have unfortunately subsisted between the two countries. Lord Hawkesbury is highly gratified that the appointment of Mr Garlike[2] meets with your Majesty's approbation. (10146)

[1] On 5 May Parker, to his 'astonishment and surprise', received the dispatches which relieved him of the Command, and, on his arrival at Yarmouth on the 13th addressed a letter of protest to the Admiralty.

[2] As Secretary of Embassy and *Chargé d'Affaires* at Petersburg (until the arrival of St Helens on 28 May). See Appendix.

[*The King's reply, Kew,*[1] *24 April 1801.*] I am infinitely pleased at the proposal of Lord Hawkesbury that Ld. St. Helens shall be appointed Ambassador to the Emperor Alexander;[2] I had suggested his name to Mr. Addington, who most erroneously thought he wd. not please in Russia. I think it so handsome of Lord St. Helens that I authorize Lord Hawkesbury to acquaint him in my name that he must on this occasion be an English Peer, and that I recommend his keeping the title of St. Helens only adding of the Isle of Wight [*sic*].[3] I first thought of writing to him but I desire you will shew him this note.

I wish to know how *my friend* the Earl of Liverpool continues, and wish he may be acquainted how perfectly I am satisfied with his eldest son's tallents, assiduity and good temper.

P.S. Lord Hawkesbury is desired to send the enclosed to my son P. Adolphus[4] at Kew by a messenger, as difficulties are made of letting me send it to him though but two rooms off. (Add. MSS. 38190, f. 1.)

[*From Lord Hawkesbury, 24 April 1801.*] Lord Hawkesbury humbly submits it to your Majesty whether it would not be better to defer conferring an English Peerage on Lord St Helens till his return from Petersburgh. Lord Hawkesbury is led to make this suggestion to your Majesty, not from any insensibility to the merits of Lord St Helens, but from the high value he has always placed on the honours of the Crown, and from an opinion that the precedent of conferring them on individuals at the time they accept publick situations, and before they can have render'd any services in those situations, may be attended with considerable inconvenience.

The Earl of Liverpool is considerably better; he is settled in the country.

Lord Hawkesbury knows not how sufficiently to express his thanks to your Majesty for the approbation you are graciously pleased to express of his official conduct.

Lord Hawkesbury has sent the letter to Prince Adolphus in obedience to your Majesty's orders. (10147)

---

[1] The King was sufficiently recovered to move with his Family to Kew on Monday the 20th. He rode there with the Prince of Wales.

[2] The Tsar Paul I had been assassinated during the night of 23–24 March, and his eldest son by his second wife succeeded him as Alexander I (1777–1825).

[3] Lord St Helens had been only an Irish Peer (since 26 Jan. 1791); on 31 July he was given a U.K. peerage, with the title Baron St Helens of St Helens, Co. Southampton. The King wrote to Addington, 12 May: 'The King most cordially thanks his Chancellor of the Exchequer for the communication of the very affectionate letter of Lord St. Helens, for it has given most sincere satisfaction. His Majesty desires this may be made known to him, & that the King feels most sensibly having made a great sacrifice to public duty in having consented that Lord St. Helens should absent himself from him by his mission to Russia; but the King is thoroughly convinced that the temper and manners of Lord St. Helens particularly suit the relative situation of the two countries; and as the King relies on everything being settled to the mutual advantage of both countries, he shall feel much personally gratified in rewarding Lord St. Helens on the completion of the business by placing him in the British House of Peers.' (Sidmouth MSS., merely signed by the King.)

[4] Prussian troops having occupied the Electorate, Prince Adolphus left the country, and on 16 April landed at Yarmouth from the *Shark* sloop.

[*Kew House, 24 April 1801.*] I hasten to return your Majesty my most humble and sincere thanks for your very gracious letter which I have just received through Lord Hawkesbury.

Your Majesty will allow me to recall to your memory the promise you made me that I should never marry any woman unless I approved of her myself, and for this reason I take the liberty of humbly representing to your Majesty whether it would not be better to postpone writing to my sister on the subject of her daughter-in-law[1] till I had seen the young Princess myself, as it might otherwise put your own daughter in a very awkward situation till she should be assured of our mutual attachment.

I have not failed in conformity to your Majesty's orders to communicate this answer to my mother the Queen, which she has totally approved of.

I now dare not trouble your Majesty any further than just to add the most humble assurance of my ever remaining [etc.].

As your Majesty has left the subject to me, I have kept the draft as a most precious mark of your affection for me. (48562)

2388   THE DUKE OF YORK *to the* KING

[*Horse Guards, 26 April 1801.*] I have the honor to transmit to your Majesty the weekly states and monthly returns, as well as to lay before your Majesty for your approbation the recommendations for the vacant commissions for the last week.

I had the honor to mention to your Majesty some time before the resignation of Mr. Dundas that a proposal had been made to raise two Corps of the inhabitants of the island of Ceylon upon the footing of the Seapoy Batallions in the East India Company's service. This plan, however, could not from circumstances be brought to maturity till now, and I therefore beg leave to lay it before your Majesty, and if it meets with your Majesty's gracious approbation I beg leave to recommend Colonels Champage and Ramsay, two very old and meritorious Officers and who are actually upon the spot (being both in the 80th Regiment) for the command of them.

The Secretary at War has desired me to lay before your Majesty for your signature a warrant fixing the period for the commencement of the cloathing of the Army in each year.[2] (10148)

---

[1] The Duke of Wurtemberg's sole surviving daughter, Catherine (1783–1835), by his first wife Augusta, daughter of Charles William Ferdinand, Duke of Brunswick. On 22 Aug. 1807 she married Napoleon's brother Jerome, King of Westphalia (1784–1860).

[2] Princess Mary wrote to the King from Kew House on 26 April (in reply to a birthday letter): 'My heart overflows with gratitude for your gracious and most affectionate letter. I feel unequal to answer it in terms that will do justice to the dictates of my heart, but I trust my conduct through life will prove me deserving of the best of fathers as my pride has ever been to meet with the joint approbation of you and dear mama, and not a little delighted at your saying I am the declared favourite of my dear Dolly.

With the most ardent prayers for your speedy & perfect recovery give me leave to subscribe myself your dutiful and affectionate daughter.' (Add. Georgian 12/22.)

[*Burlington House, Monday, 27 April 1801, 11.15 p.m.*] The Duke of Portland most humbly begs leave to represent to your Majesty that six months have now elapsed since the date of the last account of Major-General Knox, & that his family & friends have renounced all hope of his existence. The Duke of Portland therefore feels himself called upon by a sense of his duty not to delay any longer to inform your Majesty of these melancholy circumstances, & to submit with all humility to your Majesty's superior wisdom the continuance of the necessity of giving effect to the determination your Majesty had taken to remove the Earl of Balcarres from the Lieutenant-Government of Jamaica, in consequence of which, & after much deliberation with the rest of your Majesty's servants, the D. of Portland ventures to offer M. Genl. George Nugent to your Majesty's consideration as the fittest person who has occurred to them to be appointed to succeed to M. Genl. Knox in the very important Government & Military Command of your Majesty's island of Jamaica at this momentous crisis, & an instrument for your Majesty's signature is herewith submitted in case the proposal should be so fortunate as to meet with the sanction of your Majesty's royal approbation. (10149–50)

2390 THE DUKE OF YORK *to the* KING

[*York House, 28 April 1801.*] I beg leave to return your Majesty my humble thanks for your most gracious letter and to express to your Majesty the happiness I feel in learning that your Majesty is so nearly recovered, and I trust in God that by persevering a short time longer, your Majesty's health, which is of such essential consequence both to us and to your dominions, will be compleatly restored.

I shall not fail to obey your Majesty's orders concerning Colonel Dyott.[1]

Having made enquiry of General Frederick's Agents, they have acquainted me that no certain information has been yet received of his death. Perhaps however, as accounts may be hourly expected from Sir Ralph Abercrombie, your Majesty would approve of not disposing of the 54th Regiment if it should become vacant or of the Batallion of the 9th which was poor General Knox's, until your Majesty learns if any of the General Officers upon that expedition have particularly distinguished themselves, as Major-General Finch, though a most excellent and meritorious officer, is the junior Major-General upon that service and there are even two in the Guards senior to him in Egypt.[2]

I shall as expeditiously as possible endeavour to assemble the Regiments which your Majesty has been pleased to specify should be encamped at Weymouth during your Majesty's residence there this summer, but I am afraid that it will require some time, as from the very disturbed state the country in general has been in for some weeks on account of the high price of provisions, and particularly the West of England, the Regiments of Cavalry as well as infantry have been

[1] William Dyott (1761–1847). Colonel, 1800; Major-General, 1808; Lieutenant-General, 1813; General, 1830. A.D.C. to the King, 1801.
[2] Colonel Finch had been made a Major-General as recently as 1 Jan.

necessarily so much dispersed and the Magistrates so clamorous at the least idea of their being removed that it will require great care and precaution to assemble any Corps without endangering the general tranquility of the country. (10151–2)

2391 LORD HAWKESBURY *to the* KING

[*London, 28 April 1801.*] I have the honour to send to your Majesty the dispatch received this day from Lord Elgin which gives an account of the landing and of the first operations of the British army in Egypt. As French papers have been received of as late a date as the 25th inst. and as they make no mention of any events in Egypt of a date ulterior to the 14th of March, there is strong reason to presume that they either know more than they are disposed to tell, or that the success of your Majesty's arms has prevented their receiving any further accounts. Lord Minto has been for some time desirous of resigning his situation as your Majesty's Minister at Vienna. I humbly suggest to your Majesty the propriety of appointing Mr Paget to succeed him. I know no person in the Diplomatic line more equal to the business & more likely to give satisfaction to your Majesty, than he is.[1]

I saw my father the Earl of Liverpool on Sunday. He is considerably recover'd from his complaint, and felt gratified to the greatest degree and highly honour'd by the inquiries your Majesty had the goodness to make respecting him.[2] He requests your Majesty would sign two Duchy Warrants. (10153)

2392 *Letters from* LORD ELDON *to the* KING

[*29 April 1801, 10.30 a.m.*] The Lord Chancellor, submitting his most humble duty to your Majesty, begs permission to request that your Majesty would be graciously pleased to signify whether, consistently with your Majesty's pleasure, he may transmit tomorrow for your Majesty's royal signature the proper warrant for giving your Majesty's Royal Assent to the Bills which shall previously have passed in both your Majesty's Houses of Parliament. The Lord Chancellor is chiefly induced to request, most dutifully, your Majesty's indulgence in this respect on account of its being necessary that he should, for the convenience of the suitors, if possible, attend in the Court of Chancery.

One of the Bills, that for reviving the Act against Seditious Meetings, is undoubtedly an important Bill. The former Act your Majesty was pleased to give your Royal Assent to: and meetings of a dangerous tendency having taken place since the Act expired, your Majesty's Houses of Parliament have thought it proper and necessary to renew the Act.

The Lord Chancellor is not aware that the other Bills proposed to your Majesty for your Royal Assent, call for particular observation.[3] (10154–5)

[1] Arthur Paget was appointed to succeed Lord Minto, and he arrived at Vienna on 12 Sept.

[2] Visiting Addiscombe Place on 23 July Lord Glenbervie found Lord Liverpool 'in tolerable spirits, but so weak in his limbs as to be unable to rise from his sofa without help. When got up he walked about a good deal, but after two hours conversation...he appeared so much exhausted that Lady Liverpool...seemed uneasy about him.' (*Glenbervie Diaries*, 1, 240.)

[3] The King's reply, written sometime after 1 p.m., is in Twiss, 1, 372. There is no draft in the Archives.

[*Wednesday, 29 April, 9 p.m.*] The Lord Chancellor, offering your Majesty his most humble duty and his most grateful thanks for the very gracious communication which he has received of your Majesty's pleasure upon the subject, takes leave to transmit the commission for passing the Bills, which are humbly offered for your Majesty's Royal Assent, together with their several titles.[1] (10156)

2393 LORD HAWKESBURY *to the* KING

[*Downing Street, 30 April 1801, 1 p.m.*] I have the honour to inform your Majesty, that Mr Charles Locke,[2] Consul at Naples, arrived in town this morning; he left Paris on Friday. On the Thursday night he saw the Marquis de Lucchisini,[3] who informed him that intelligence had been that day received from Egypt of the defeat of the French army & that Menou was taken prisoner.[4] The fate of Egypt was considered by these accounts as decided. As this intelligence is not official it is thought more prudent not to represent it as certain. At the same time I cannot entertain any doubt of its being substantially true. I most sincerely congratulate your Majesty on this important event, which will reflect the highest honour on your Majesty's arms & must lead to consequences which cannot be too greatly appreciated.[5] (10158)

2394 LORD HOBART *to the* KING, *and the reply*

[*Downing Street, 1 May 1801, 1.30 p.m.*] Lord Hobart begs leave most humbly to transmit the accompanying intelligence this instant received from the East India House.[6]

The important consequences to the interests of the British Empire & the additional lustre reflected upon your Majesty's arms by this brilliant victory

[1] The following undated note from Eldon to the King, is endorsed April 1801: 'Lord Eldon most humbly tenders to your Majesty his duty and his determination earnestly to express his gratitude by the fidelity and integrity of his conduct. In obedience to your Majesty's commands he returns without delay the inclosed papers, for the communication of which he offers to your Majesty's acceptance his most humble and most dutiful thanks.' (10159)

[2] Sometimes spelt Lock. (Buckingham, *Court and Cabinets*, III, 157.)

[3] Lucchesini, the Prussian Minister in Paris. Thomas Grenville said he was always better informed than any other Foreign Minister. (*Ibid.*) He was a Florentine. Sir Herbert Taylor described him as 'a very sharp, clever man, very civil, and had the character of being a consummate political intriguant. He retired after the Prussian catastrophe at Jena, and went to Florence, where he died' (*Taylor Papers*, p. 19 n.).

[4] General Kléber, commanding the French army in Egypt after Bonaparte's return to France, had been assassinated by a Muslim fanatic on 14 June 1800, and General Menou succeeded him. In March 1801 a British force under General Sir Ralph Abercromby, landed at Aboukir to expel the French, and soon after the battle outside Alexandria, in which Abercromby was killed (21 March) the French garrison under General Belliard surrendered Cairo, and on 30 Aug. Menou capitulated at Alexandria with over 10,000 men.

[5] For the reply see Appendix.

[6] 'By a dispatch received this day by the East India Company from Mr Tooke, their Agent at Constantinople, dated the 4th of April last, it appears that General Menou on his march from Rahmanie, was, on the 21 of March attacked by General Abercromby, & after a very obstinate battle, defeated with the loss of 2000 killed & 500 taken prisoners. The English had 300 killed & 1200 wounded, amongst the latter are Genls. Abercromby, Moore & Parker, & Sir S. Smith. The French were pursued in every direction. The French cavalry in the stile of the Mamalukes attacked the English infantry with all the impetuosity peculiar to the Arab cavalry; but were defeated in every attack. *Aboukir* had surrendered— & Alexandria was suposed by Lord Keith, if not taken, on the point of surrendering.' (10163)

have made an impression upon Lord Hobart's mind which he shou'd certainly not be able to convey to your Majesty by any attempt to describe it.

He trusts your Majesty will permit him to offer his congratulations upon the occasion.

It may be proper for Lord Hobart to observe to your Majesty that there is no officer of the rank of General of the name of Parker serving under Sir Ralph Abercrombie. (10160)

[*The King's reply, Kew, 1 May, 3.19 p.m.*] No event could have been more providential than the defeat of the French in Egypt, and I trust it will effect that kind of consternation in France which may occasion some great event. To a thinking mind it gives a certain composure, as it has the appearance of the interposition of the Divinity in favour of a just cause against the open enemies of religion, morality and civil society. (Bucks. R.O.)

2395   PRINCE ADOLPHUS *to the* KING

[*Kew House, 1 May 1801.*] I take the liberty of sending your Majesty the enclosed[1] which I have just received from Baron Lente; you will find in it the confirmation of the report I had written from Berlin relative to the King of Prussia's intentions concerning the Electorate, and I am now confident that in a very short time everything will be arranged and that the Prussian troops will leave your dominions as soon as they are sure of the good intentions of the new Emperor of Russia & of those of the French. For, supposing the latter were to venture to attack the Electorate, it is certainly better that an army should be in the country ready to act in conjunction with your own troops than that the ennemy should march into it and pillage any part of it before they met with proper resistance. It is under this point of view that I beg your Majesty to look upon the present stay of the Prussians in your dominions, and I trust you will not find my opinion erroneous.

Before I conclude I must congratulate your Majesty on the important news arrived from Egypt which undoubtedly must make every British subject happy. We cannot enough thank the Almighty for having blessed your arms with this success, and we and all your children join in prayers for the preservation of your health, which is of the utmost consequence for us and for all Europe. We all rejoice that the present quiet which you enjoy has been so beneficial to you, and we trust in a very short time to see you perfectly recovered, at which no one can be happyer than he who ever will remain [etc.]. (48563)

2396   *Letters from* LORD HAWKESBURY *to the* KING

[*London, 1 May 1801.*] Lord Hawkesbury has the honour to send to your Majesty a dispatch from Lord Carrysfort[2] which came by a boat without any mail to

---

[1] A long letter in French, dated Arlington Street, 30 April 1801 (48564–5).

[2] The British Minister at Berlin from Aug. 1800 to Oct. 1801. The King's reply on the 1st, at 12.50 p.m. is in Yonge's *Liverpool*, I, 55 n.

Harwich. It confirms the account received yesterday from Paris, at least as far as respects a compleat victory obtained by Sir Ralph Abercrombie over the French army on the twenty first of March. (10161)

[*London, 1 May, 11.45 a.m.*] Lord Hawkesbury has the honour to send your Majesty a dispatch he has received from Lord Elgin, and likewise a private letter from Lord Elgin to his Royal Highness the Duke of York, and a letter from Col. Anstruther to Col. Brownrigg. The last contains a very satisfactory account of the first operations of the British army on landing in Egypt. The two former contain very imperfect details of the action of 21st of March, but leave no doubt that the result has been as favourable to your Majesty's arms as we had reason to expect. (10162)

[*London, 2 May 1801.*] Lord Hawkesbury has the honour to send your Majesty the instructions intended for Lord St Helens,[1] which he requests your Majesty will have the goodness to sign if they meet with your approbation. (10164)

2397 *Letters from the* KING *to* CHARLES PHILIP YORKE, *and a reply*

[*Kew, 1 May 1801, 11.31 a.m.*] The King cannot help remarking that since the very judicious appointment of Mr. Yorke to be Secretary at War there is an appearance of regularity in the War Office which was much wanted.[2] (Adeane MSS.)

[*Charles Yorke's reply, War Office, 2 May.*] Mr Yorke humbly desires permission to offer his most grateful thanks for the very high & unexpected honor conferred upon him yesterday by your Majesty's most graciously condescending to notice his humble endeavours regularly to discharge the duties of the important office to which your Majesty's favor & goodness has been pleased to appoint him; and to assure your Majesty that his zeal & devotion to your Majesty's service can never cease but with his existence. (10165)

[*From the King, Kew, 2 May.*] The King is so pleased with the note he has received from Mr. Yorke, accompanying the warrants for holding court martials, and the

---

[1] His instructions dated 30 April, on his appointment as Ambassador to Russia.

[2] 'The consenting to fill up the breaches occasioned by this convulsion, is considered by us all as a matter of *necessity* & *duty*, not of *choice*, as a means of preventing the country from falling into the very worst hands, & the K. from being delivered up to some of his worst enemies. For my own part, I reflect upon it as a most arduous responsible & difficult task which I have undertaken; that my situation is equally unlooked for & *precarious*; & that one ought not to calculate upon remaining in it for six *months*, perhaps not for six *weeks*. But I think as a great & terrible conflict may be expected that it is more glorious to combat in the *first* ranks than in the *rear*; & that in what relates to myself personally; that the *call* upon me *is honorable*; *may* be advantageous, *cannot* probably be attended with *much* inconvenience to private affairs, is compatible with my former views & conduct, & therefore was not to be declined... That some parts of the new Administration are greatly inferior in talents & abilities to those of the former no man living can doubt; that is to be deplored & regretted, but it *must* be formed as it is, or Messrs. Sheridan, Grey & Tierney sent for. Honesty, right intentions, & true patriotism will be found, & for the rest we must put ourselves on God & our country...' (Bodleian MSS., Yorke to his mother, 11 Feb.).

others, that he cannot help expressing his feelings on the occasion; he has ever had a most sincere regard for the family of Yorke, and the uniform conduct of his Secretary at War has made him long wish to see him in office. Colonel Manningham has long been apprised of this, for at Christmas last his Majesty thought Mr. Yorke the only person fit to succeed Mr. Addington as Speaker, should the latter have been called from that situation; but the King is much pleased things have turned out otherwise. He thinks Sir John Mitford will with practise make a good Speaker of the House of Commons, and he is certain Mr. Yorke's tallents are such as will be of advantage to the service in any post of business, for with most considerable abilities and a very honourable mind, he has the advantage of having had a grandfather and father[1] whose memory must be ever revered by those who value the laws and Constitution of this enviable country. (Adeane MSS.)

2398 THE DUKE OF YORK *to the* KING

[*Horse Guards, 3 May 1801.*] I have the honor to acknowledge the receipt of your Majesty's most gracious letter, and will not fail to obey your Majesty's commands in relieving the Staffordshire Militia at Windsor and Kew by a detachment from the Brigade of Guards, which duty the Brigade is perfectly equal to, as soon as the invalids can occupy the Tower.

I most sincerely congratulate your Majesty upon the signal success which your Majesty's arms through Divine Providence have had in Egypt. I trust that your Majesty will soon receive detailed accounts of this great event, and that you will find that Sir Ralph Abercrombie and General Moore are not dangerously wounded. The third General Officer said to be wounded is supposed to be Brigadeer-General Oaks,[2] as there is no General Officer of the name of Parker in Egypt and General Oaks was attached to the reserve of the army under General Moore.

As there have been some courts martial during your Majesty's illness, upon which the Judge Advocate General is anxious to receive your Majesty's commands I thought it would be more agreable to your Majesty to receive his opinion upon them in writing, and I have now the honor to transmit them to your Majesty for your Majesty's approbation. (10166)

2399 *Letters from* CHARLES YORKE *to the* KING, *and a reply*

[*War Office, 4 May 1801.*] Your Majesty's faithful & devoted Secretary at War is utterly unable to find expressions adequate to the feelings of veneration & gratitude excited in his breast by the contents of the note he had the distinguished honor of receiving on Saturday night. The impression made by a communication so condescending, but too flattering, can never be effaced. To know that he has

[1] Charles Yorke was the son of Charles Yorke (1722–70), the Lord Chancellor, who was the son of Philip Yorke, 1st Earl of Hardwicke (1690–1764), Lord Chancellor, 1737–56. On 1 July 1790 he married Harriott, daughter of Charles Manningham of Thorpe, Surrey.

[2] Sir Hildebrand Oakes (1754–1822). Entered the army, 1767; Major, 1791; Lieutenant-Colonel, 1795; Colonel, 1798; Major-General, 1805; Lieutenant-General, 1811; Baronetcy, 1813; G.C.B., 1820. Lieutenant-General of the Ordnance, 1814–22.

the happiness of possessing your Majesty's favorable opinion, (much too favorable!) must be his highest pride; the hopes of meriting in some degree the continuance of it cannot fail to stimulate his best exertions. Above all, your Majesty's most benign recollection of services performed by faithful servants who are gone before, expressed in a manner so infinitely kind & gracious, is at once the strongest incentive, & the best reward that can be proposed to their descendant, who, conscious, as he must be, of his extreme inferiority to them in all respects, hopes at least that he inherits some portion of their zeal for the happiest Constitution of civil society existing upon earth, and of their love & attachment to a Sovereign who has proved himself on all occasions the father & the friend of his people. (10167–8)

[*From the King, Kew, 5 May.*] The King is so much pleased at the sensibility of heart of his Secretary at War, and with finding that inheriting the tallents of his ancestors he also possesses their sentiments of attachment to his Majesty and to our excellent and unparalleled Constitution, that he could not refrain on returning the box with the warrant to express his feelings on this occasion. (Adeane MSS.)

[*From Charles Yorke, War Office, 6 May 1801.*] Mr. Yorke most humbly submits the accompanying warrants for your Majesty's Royal signature and once more entreats permission to express his most dutiful and grateful acknowledgments of the repeated marks of your Majesty's most gracious favor and condescension towards him. (10174)

2400 THE DUKE OF CUMBERLAND *to the* KING

[*Kew House, 5 May 1801.*] I return your Majesty my most humble thanks for the valuable present you was so good to send me of the new Common Prayer Book which from henceforth I shall always make use of.[1] It is with infinite satisfaction I hear your Majesty's health improves so much, & I hope that now in a very short time you may be restored to us all & that we may pass many many happy years in the company of the best of fathers.[2] (47190)

2401 THE MARQUESS OF SALISBURY *to the* KING, *and the reply*

[*Arlington Street, 5 May 1801.*] When I last had the honor to lay before your Majesty a plan for alterations to be made in Kensington Palace for the accommodation of his Royal Highness the Duke of Kent, I receiv'd your Majesty's commands to do nothing but what was essentially necessary; and I should not think myself justified in troubling your Majesty at present if it had not been for the letter receiv'd from his Royal Highness last night, which I have the honor to submit

---

[1] Cp. Lady Salisbury's Diary, 13 July 1833, quoting the Duke's remarks to the Archbishop of Canterbury: 'By God, my Lord, I am a d——d infernal sinner, and I know it, but I think it right to go to church for the sake of example.' She added, 'It is curious that circumstances should have made this man the champion of the Protestant Church at the most critical moment of its existence.' (Hatfield MSS.)

[2] Lord Eldon's letter of 5 May to the King (10169) is in Twiss, *Life of Eldon*, I, 373.

to your Majesty. I shall wait your Majesty's commands for my further guidance. (10170)

[*The King's reply, Kew, 5 May.*] The King has just received the Marquess of Salisbury's letter accompanying the one received from the Duke of Kent. His Majesty certainly on a former occasion directed his Lord Chamberlain to authorise no other repairs in the Duke of Kent's appartment at Kensington but such as were necessary for keeping the Palace in a proper state as to durability and cleanliness; but, prior to the severe illness his Majesty has laboured under, Mr. Wyatt by the direction of Mr. Pitt brought a plan of the alterations the Duke of Kent seemed to think necessary for his comfort, with an assurance that the Treasury would consent to them provided the expence did not exceed a specific sum every quarter. I therefore now approve to the Marquess of Salisbury's consenting to these alterations, agreable to the plan settled by Mr. Wyatt with the late Chancellor of the Exchequer. (Hatfield MSS.)

2402   PRINCE ADOLPHUS *to the* KING

[*Kew House, 5 May 1801.*] I cannot refuse myself the pleasure of troubling your Majesty with a few lines to return you my most humble thanks for the gracious present of the Prayer Book I received this morning. Nothing could be more precious to me than this mark of your goodness, and this book will ever be read by me with double interest as it comes from your hands.

I rejoice most sincerely at the excellent accounts of your Majesty's health, and no one can rejoice more at the prospect of seeing you soon again than he who has the honour to be with the most respectful attachment [etc.]. (48566)

2403   THE DUKE OF PORTLAND *to the* KING

[*Whitehall, Tuesday, 5 May 1801, 3.35 p.m.*] The Duke of Portland most humbly begs leave to acquaint your Majesty that he has received the request of the Lord Chief Baron of your Majesty's Court of Exchequer in Scotland[1] most humbly to lay him at your Majesty's feet & to sollicit your Majesty to permit him to resign that office which he has now filled for twenty-six years very much, as the Duke of Portland has reason to beleive, to his own credit & to the intire satisfaction of your Majesty's subjects. The Duke of Portland has upon these accounts farther to submit to your Majesty that the Lord Chief Baron most humbly hopes that your Majesty will be graciously pleased to confer upon him the usual mark of favor which your Majesty has condescended to bestow upon your servants on similar occasions by the grant of a pension equivalent to two-thirds of his present appointment, which will amount to the annual sum of £2000. Should it be your Majesty's pleasure to grant the Lord Chief Baron's request, the Duke of Portland would

---

[1] Sir James William Montgomery (1721–1803), M.P. for Dumfries Burghs, 1766–8; for Peeblesshire, 1768–75; Joint Solicitor-General [S.], 1760; sole Solicitor-General, 1764–6; Lord Advocate of Scotland, 1766–75; Lord Chief Baron of the Exchequer [S.], 1775–1801; created Baronet, 16 July 1801.

take the liberty of offering the present Lord Advocate[1] to your Majesty's consideration as a proper person to succeed to the office of Lord Chief Baron. The Lord Advocate has now been eighteen years in your Majesty's service during which time he has, as the Duke of Portland has always understood, discharged the duties of his very laborious & important office with equal fidelity & ability; & for the last seven years of that period, with which the situation in which your Majesty in your great goodness has been pleased to place the Duke of Portland, has given him the opportunity of being immediately & intimately acquainted, he must beg your Majesty's leave to offer his most unqualified testimony of the meritorious & exemplary conduct of the Lord Advocate & of his unremitting attention to your Majesty's service & interests. In the humble hope that your Majesty may condescend to think the Lord Advocate worthy of the appointment of Chief Baron, your Majesty's Sollicitor-General in Scotland, Mr Blair, would naturally have been the successor whom the Duke of Portland would have submitted to your Majesty for the Lord Advocate's office, but Mr Blair's diffidence & infirmity made him decline the seat which your Majesty directed the Duke of Portland to offer him on the Scotch Bench, & would not suffer him to accept the situation of your Majesty's Advocate which necessarily requires so much more activity & exertion. The gentleman, therefore, whom the Duke of Portland's duty requires him to propose to your Majesty is Mr Charles Hope,[2] an advocate of such acknowledged eminence & of such established moral & political character that the Duke of Portland beleives himself warranted in assuring your Majesty that, with the exception of Mr Blair who for personal reasons declares it to be inconsistent with his sense of duty to undertake the office, the Bench, the Bar & that part of the Kingdom at large would concur in their humble representations to your Majesty of Mr Hope's superior fitness to execute the office of your Majesty's Advocate for Scotland.

The Duke of Portland is desired by the Lord Chancellor to transmit to your Majesty the letter which accompanies this.[3] (10171–3)

2404 THE EARL OF HARDWICKE *to the* KING, *and the reply*

[*St James's Square, 7 May 1801.*] Lord Hardwicke flatters himself he may be excused the liberty he takes in expressing, with his humble duty to your Majesty, his heartfelt acknowledgements for the very gracious manner in which your Majesty has condescended to allude to his late illness in a note to the Secretary at War. He finds his health so far re-established as to enable him to fix his departure for Ireland in the course of a few days, to undertake the duties of the important situation to which your Majesty has been graciously pleased to appoint him: a situation to which he is conscious he can only claim the merit of carrying an heart

[1] Robert Dundas.
[2] Charles Hope, Lord Granton (1763–1851), M.P. for the Dumfries Burghs, 1802; for Edinburgh, 1803–4. Lord Advocate of Scotland, 1801–4; Lord Justice Clerk, 1804–11; Lord President of the Court of Session, 1811–41.
[3] Lord Eldon's letter to the King, 5 May, thanking him for having appointed him, Lord Kenyon and Sir John Mitford as trustees of part of the King's property, is in H.M.C. Report, Kenyon MSS. p. 557, also Twiss, I, 373, and folio 10169.

filled with the most lively gratitude, duty and zeal for your Majesty's service. (10177, and Add. MSS. 45031, f. 1.)

[*The King's reply, Kew, 8 May.*] The King is much gratified in receiving from the Earl of Hardwicke the assurance that he finds his health so much re-established that he hopes in a few days to be in a situation with safety to undertake his journey to Ireland.

In the formation of the new Administration no part has given his Majesty more confidence than the having brought the Earl of Hardwicke and Mr. Yorke into active employment; the opinion the late Lord Dover[1] had ever given of his two valuable nephews has certainly given the best impression in their favour, and their uniform conduct in very trying times has with justice rivetted that opinion.

The Earl of Hardwicke's good sense and prudence will certainly point out to him that whilst on the one hand he shall treat the Irish with civility he must not get too familiar with them and must shew them that the season of jobs is at an end. The King recommends the Lords Primate and Chancellor as men that will not deceive the Lord Lieutenant, but he should not deal with the openness necessary if he did not hint that the latter may be an useful instrument in the Earl of Hardwicke's hands, but if not attended to may attempt to guide, which can neither be expedient nor creditable. Lord Shannon and Mr. Beresford are also fair and useful men. (B.M. Add. MSS. 35349, f. 73, and 45031, f. 2 [copy].)

2405   HENRY ADDINGTON *to the* KING, *and the reply*

[*Downing Street, 7 May 1801, 11.30 p.m.*] Lord Castlereagh having requested permission to resign the office of Keeper of the Signet or Privy Seal of Ireland, Mr Addington humbly begs to bring to your Majesty's recollection your gracious intention of appointing Mr Abbot to succeed him.[2] Mr Abbot has divested himself of an ample independence for a very inadequate compensation, with the sole view of being better enabled to devote his time and talents to the immediate service of your Majesty; but your Majesty's goodness and justice preclude any apprehension on his part, or on that of his connections, that the smallest injury can arise to himself or his family, from the readiness with which he obeyed a call of public duty at a most critical and important conjuncture. Mr Addington trusts that, under these circumstances, it will be thought right to confirm by patent the appointment to the office, for the life of Mr Abbot. (10178–9)

[1] Lord Dover (see No. 376) was the third son of Philip, 1st Earl of Hardwicke.

[2] Addington had suggested that Castlereagh should retain the office of Privy Seal of Ireland and hold it for life. When Castlereagh decided against this, Addington offered Abbot the office, also for life, as compensation for the loss of his office in the Court of King's Bench. 'Value £1500 a year, with a floating pension of £1000 a year, to go in part of the £5000 a year during my holding the Chief Secretaryship, and to be afterwards in lieu or in part of the emoluments of any situation of equal or greater emolument which I might hold under the Crown, such as the Pells or the like.' (*Colchester Diary*, I, 262.) 'Barré dying', Abbot wrote on 9 June. 'I immediately to have the Pells. Pelham to be Privy Seal of Ireland.' But Abbot's information proved to be inaccurate (*Colchester MS. Diary*).

[The King's reply, Kew, 8 May, 2.07 p.m.] The King perfectly remembers what passed on the subject of Mr. Abbot, and very gladly authorizes Mr. Addington to accept Lord Castlereagh's resignation of the office of Keeper of the Signet and of its being conferred on Mr. Abbot, who will certainly prove a very useful servant of the Crown. (Sidmouth MSS.)

2406 LORD HAWKESBURY *to the* KING

[London, 8 May 1801.] Lord Hawkesbury has the honour to send your Majesty a dispatch received this day from Sir James Craufurd, enclosing a letter from Count Bernstorff by which it appears that the King of Denmark has appointed him to come to this country for the purpose of adjusting all differencies between your Majesty and the Court of Copenhagen. Lord Hawkesbury humbly submits it to your Majesty that this intelligence is of the greatest importance, as it proves that the Northern Confederacy is dissolved, that one of the most active members of it is disposed to make a seperate Peace, and that there can be little doubt that this most essential question will be decided in a manner the most satisfactory to your Majesty.[1] (10180)

2407 *Letters from* DR THOMAS GISBORNE *to the* KING

[Kew, 8 May 1801.] The infinite satisfaction which your Majesty's goodness has bestow'd on all around you in the establishment of your health by quiet and retirement is what neither I nor anyone can express, and it is become the wish of all that you shou'd now soon be restor'd to the comfort and company of your family, and so on, in the usual way, to the benefit of your subjects and the world in general, of which, alas !, in these times there is so much need.

It is my hope not to be thought presumptuous in this address to your Majesty when I am permitted to assure you that, in the situation in which I have the honour to be plac'd by your Majesty, my conscience will not suffer me to omit hinting at anything which might be beneficial to your health; and therefore 'tis fit I shou'd mention that the heat and hurry of the Birthday is what it is adviseable your Majesty should in your own person decline. When that is over, the consideration of going steadily and quietly to Weymouth, and of staying there a considerable time, will naturally take place, where, if the heat of the ensuing summer shou'd at all resemble the last, it may be prudent to avoid too much exposure to the sun.

If the observance of these circumstances shall prove useful to your Majesty (as I trust they may), the remembrance of having deliver'd them, believe me, Sire, will ever give me more pleasure than anything besides which the whole world can give me, being sure to remain, for the short time I have to live, unalterably, [etc.].[2] (10181)

---

[1] The King's reply at 7 a.m. on the 9th is in Yonge's *Liverpool*, I, 55 n.
[2] Next day the Duke of York spent three hours with the King, who saw Addington during that time 'He is described to be still thin, but better in flesh than he was before he went to Kew', wrote Thomas Grenville, on the Duke's authority (Buckingham, *Court and Cabinets*, III, 160).

May it please your Majesty to permit me humbly to lay before you what appears to me the best and likeliest means of establishing your health after so severe an illness, & of preventing any similar return for the time to come; & in doing this, I cannot but flatter myself your Majesty will have the goodness to beleive me when I assure you that I am actuated by no whimsical conceits of a medical or any other kind, but by the sole motive of discharging my duty as your physician, for an omission of which I am sure my conscience wou'd never forgive me, & without which I cou'd never be happy as long as I live.

It seems to me particularly necessary that you shou'd determine at present to set apart an hour or more every day when you wou'd be free from the company or conversation of everyone; after this has been the case for a week or two I shou'd hope your Majesty will have acquir'd that sedate composure over your spirits as to prevent them from hurrying you into the smallest prejudicial agitation. Of your Majesty's having the power of doing this, beleive me, Sire, you have of late given so many happy proofs as have been exceedingly gratifying to myself, as well as to all your other medical attendants & servants.

Besides all this, if your Majesty wou'd be pleas'd for a short time at present to refrain from going much into public, it wou'd probably be of use, & enable you hereafter to resume your usual way of life with the utmost comfort.

Your Majesty has apparently receiv'd so much benefit by bathing in the sea, that it is sincerely my wish that you wou'd immediately take into your consideration the idea of going to Weymouth much earlier, & of staying there much longer than usual; & whilst you are at Kew, your Majesty may direct for a short time that any of your medical attendants or myself shall occasionally call upon you, if wanted.

Your Majesty's wonted goodness to me will I trust not suffer you to be offended with my thus saying before what my duty suggests to me I ought to do, in order to prevent the possibility of a relapse into your former illness, which an attention to these hints will I trust for ever prevent.

With my incessant prayer to Almighty God for your Majesty's health so essentially necessary to the happiness of your family, your subjects, & the world in general, permit me to subscribe myself[1] [etc.]. (10767–8)

2408 THE EARL OF HARDWICKE *to the* KING, *and the reply*

[*St James's Square, 9 May 1801.*] Lord Hardwicke feels so sensibly the high honour conferred upon him by your Majesty's gracious letter that he ventures to intrude himself once more upon your Majesty to express his gratitude for so distinguished a mark of your condescension and goodness. At the same time that he acknowledges the value of your Majesty's confidential hints in regard to individuals in Ireland, he is fully impressed with the wisdom and justice of your Majesty's observations, which he considers as at once a proof of your Majesty's judgment and knowledge of that country, and of your favour towards those who have the happiness of being employed in your Majesty's service. (10182, and Add. MSS. 45031, f. 2.)

[1] The Ann Arbor typescript of this undated letter suggests the date May 1801, which may be more correct than the endorsement of the MS. '1802'.

[*The King's reply, Kew, 10 May.*] The Earl of Hardwicke's soon departure for Ireland inclines the King to write again as he finds his confidential hints have been taken as meant. The situation of the Lord Lieutenants of Ireland has been rendered more difficult from their not acting on one steady plan, but by degrees becoming the tools of some one of the parties which unfortunately by that conduct have been constantly fostered in that uncivilised island. The King is certain that the good private character of the Earl of Hardwicke, and his having seen the rocks on which his predecessors have split, will be the best guide for his taking the right path. Ireland must be with temper taught to feel that, till a better mode of education is established and that obedience to law which alone can render men advantageously industrious or their property secure, the solid good to be obtained from the Union with this country cannot be effected. Another most necessary measure is the encouraging the residence of the clergy of the Established Church and the attending to calling on the Bishops by their examples, as well as precepts enforcing it, the obliging them to keep their Cathedrals in good repair and having the choir service performed with great punctuality and decorum, that will certainly by degrees draw some of the Roman Catholics to our Church. His Majesty will not add more than his sincere wishes that the Earl of Hardwicke and all his family may enjoy good health and find Ireland a pleasant abode. (B.M. Add. MSS. 35349, f. 75, and 45031, f. 3.)

2409   *Letters from the* EARL OF ST VINCENT *to the* KING

[*Admiralty, 10 May 1801, 10 p.m.*] Lord St Vincent has the honor of sending to your Majesty the dispatches[1] this moment received from Rear-Admiral Duckworth brought by Capt Ekins, late of the Amphitrite, containing an account of the capitulation of the following islands in the West Indies

St. Bartholemew — Swedish
St. Martins   — French & Dutch
St. Thomas's ⎫
St. John's   ⎬ — Danish
St. Croix   ⎭   (10203)

[*Admiralty, 11 May, 5 p.m.*] Lord St Vincent has had the honor of receiving your Majesty's commands for preparing the Royal Charlotte and Princess Augusta yachts for the purpose of attending your Majesty during your intended residence at Weymouth, and will give the necessary directions in consequence immediately.

As Capt. Browell,[2] who now commands the Princess Augusta, is not in a condition for active service, Lord St Vincent begs to be honor'd with your Majesty's commands to whom the temporary command of her should be given. The officer that occurr'd to Lord St Vincent as the fittest among those out of employment,

[1] See *London Gazette*, 12 May 1801.
[2] William Browell (1759–1831), Lieutenant, 1778; Captain, 1794. Lieutenant-Governor of Greenwich Hospital, 1809–31.

is Lord Mark Ker,[1] whose conduct while in the Mediterranean, under Lord St Vincent's orders, merited much approbation. He however understands, that his Lordship is engag'd in a law suit in Ireland which may possibly render his employment a matter of great inconvenience, and if that should be the case, perhaps your Majesty would be pleased to allow him to decline it. The only other person that immediately occurs to Lord St Vincent is Capt Grey,[2] late Captain of the Ville de Paris, the son of Sir Charles, who is now on half pay: but whatever arrangement may be most agreeable to your Majesty Lord St Vincent will feel the highest satisfaction in carrying it into execution. He only mentions these officers as persons likely to conduct themselves properly in the command of a yacht, for which every officer is not exactly fitted.

Lord St Vincent wishes also to receive your Majesty's commands in respect to the appointment of a Lieutenant to the Royal Charlotte, under the impression that your Majesty might be desirous of bringing some officer forward, who might, on your Majesty leaving Weymouth, if your Majesty thought fit, be promoted. This, and some other inferior arrangements, are not necessary to be decided on immediately. Lord St Vincent only mentions them for your Majesty's consideration at your leisure.

Lord St Vincent takes the liberty of mentioning to your Majesty that he understands from the friends of Admiral Duckworth that a Baronetcy would be much more acceptable to the Rear-Admiral than a Red Ribbond, and if your Majesty should be graciously pleas'd to consent to confer that honor on the Rear-Admiral, he is persuaded that he will feel that mark of Royal approbation of his conduct in the way he ought to do. Lord St Vincent has already mention'd the subject to Mr Addington, who concurs with him in opinion that the Baronetcy would be preferable to the Red Ribbond.[3] (10183–4)

2410 LORD HAWKESBURY *to the* KING

[*London, 11 May 1801.*] Lord Hawkesbury has the honour to send your Majesty the Message[4] which it is humbly proposed to deliver from your Majesty to the House of Commons. If it should meet with your Majesty's approbation, Lord

[1] A younger son of the Marquess of Lothian (1776–1840). Lieutenant, 1794; Captain, 1797; Rear-Admiral, 1821.

[2] Sir George Grey (1767–1828), fourth son of Sir Charles Grey, 1st Earl Grey. Lieutenant, 1781; Captain, 1793; Captain of the *Royal Charlotte* yacht; Resident Commissioner at Portsmouth Dockyard. Baronetcy, 1814.

[3] He was not made a Baronet until 1813, but became a K.B. on 6 June 1801. Lord St Vincent wrote to him on 21 Sept.: 'You cannot be unapprised that a Baronet is higher in rank than a Knight of the Bath, and I had every reason to believe that you ambitioned the former, and I really made the choice for you in the belief thereof, and until Mr. Baker gave me reason for judging otherwise, I was in complete error.' (*Letters of Lord St. Vincent*, I, 273.)

[4] 'His Majesty, taking into his most serious consideration the imminent danger with which the Kingdom of Portugal, the ancient and natural ally of his Crown, is threatened by the Powers now at war with his Majesty, as well as the importance of the commercial relations subsisting between the two Kingdoms, and relying on the known zeal and affection of his faithful Commons, recommends it to them to consider of empowering his Majesty to afford, by way of subsidy, to the Queen of Portugal, such assistance as may enable her most Faithful Majesty to take such measures for the defence of her dominions against her enemies, as the exigencies of affairs may appear to require.' (*H. of C.J.* LVI, 409 [14 May].)

Hawkesbury intends presenting it tomorrow. The assistance proposed to be given is not very considerable, but will at least prove to the Government of Portugal the disposition of your Majesty to do everything in your power to protect them, a protection which their conduct during all the circumstances of the present war appears most fully to have deserved.[1] (10185)

2411 HENRY ADDINGTON *to the* KING, *and the reply*

[*Downing Street, 11 May 1801, 12.15 p.m.*] Mr Addington has been frequently pressed to apply to your Majesty on a business of some importance, which is now so circumstanced as not to admit of further delay. It has been represented to Mr Addington that a surplus, which had gradually arisen in the Civil List of Ireland, and which is at your Majesty's disposal, was, in consequence of a warrant from your Majesty, paid over, towards the end of last year, to Lord Cardigan[2] for your Majesty's Privy Purse, with the view of being afterwards paid over, by your Majesty's directions, to Mr King, for the purpose of being remitted by him to Ireland for secret service, to discharge engagements the nature of which, Mr Addington understands, has been submitted to your Majesty. This being the case Mr Addington humbly suggests to your Majesty the expediency of giving such directions to Lord Cardigan as may be requisite to carry this measure into effect. (10187–8)

[*The King's reply, Kew, 11 May, 2.13 p.m.*] The King has just received Mr. Addington's note, which has rather surprised him, as on Mr. Pitt's resignation and assuring his Majesty he had no call for any money, the King had directed Lord Cardigan to pay the money to Mr. Drummond who was to place it to his private account with the King, and was to pay off some large demands which must now be satisfied. When the King next sees Mr. Addington he shall hope to have some explanation as to this business; as he certainly does not mean to screen those concerned in corrupt measures in Ireland by being supposed to have taken the money to his Privy Purse.[3] (Sidmouth MSS.)

2412 *Letters from* LORD HOBART *to the* KING, *and the replies*

[*Downing Street, 12 May 1801, 6 p.m.*] Lord Hobart begs leave humbly to submit to your Majesty the copy of a letter he has receiv'd from Mr. Huskisson, the Under-Secretary of State in the War Department, with Lord Hobart's answer. (10189)

[*From the King, Kew, 13 May, 6.55 a.m.*] The King has no doubt but Mr. John Sullivan[4] will prove himself well qualified for the employment in which he is

---

[1] For the reply see Appendix.   [2] Keeper of the Privy Purse. See No. 51.
[3] There is in Pellew, 1, 386, the copy of a letter from the King to Addington dated the 12th, on the subject of Lord St Helens' diplomatic Mission to Russia, and the promise of a U.K. peerage on his return.
[4] Sullivan (1749–1839), who was now appointed Under-Secretary of State in the War Department, was M.P. for Old Sarum, 1790–6; for Aldborough, 1802–6; for Ashburton, 1811–18; a member of the Board of Control, Feb. 1806–March 1807, and April 1812–1839. He had married one of Lord Hobart's sisters in 1789. His 'long residence in India, and habits of business, well qualify him for any public situation' (*The Times*, 21 May).

placed by Lord Hobart; and I cannot but rejoice at Mr. Huskisson's retiring, as his style and manner rather gave disgust to those obliged to conferr with him. (Bucks. R.O.)[1]

[*From Lord Hobart, Downing Street, 12 May, 6 p.m.*] Lord Hobart humbly begs leave to present his duty to your Majesty and sends the draft of instructions which has been prepar'd for Mr. Cameron whose name he humbly takes the liberty of submitting to your Majesty as a fit person to fill the office of Civil Commissioner upon the island of Malta.

Lord Hobart is fully aware of the consideration that is due to the opinions of Capt. Ball[2] on account of the essential advantage deriv'd to the publick interests from his services upon the island of Malta, but he trusts that all the purposes which wou'd appear to have been in his contemplation may be answer'd by the nomination of a Civil Commissioner without hazarding the inconveniences and embarrassment that might arise under existing circumstances from the appointment of a Civil Governor. (10190)

[*From the King, Kew, 13 May, 6.55 a.m.* [*sic*]] The King perfectly coincides in opinion with Lord Hobart as to the impossibility in the present state of affairs of appointing a Civil Governor at Malta, and the propriety of naming a Civil Commissioner, and he doubts not but Lord Hobart has fully examined into the ability of Mr. Cameron to fill that employment. (*Ibid.*)

2413   *Letters from the* EARL OF ST VINCENT *to the* KING

[*Admiralty, 13 May 1801.*] Lord St. Vincent has had the honor of receiving your Majesty's commands on the subject of the Princess Augusta yacht and has, in consequence, directed that an order may immediately be sent to Capt. Grey to command her.

[1] Though Huskisson's resignation was delayed until May, the decision had been taken in February. He wrote, 12 Feb.: 'The more I think of our unprecedented situation, and the more I learn in several quarters, (but from Mr. P. in particular) the more I am satisfied that having no option but between two prospects, both of great distress and difficulty, he has taken that course which, whilst it best consisted with his honor and personal feelings, is likely in this choice of misfortunes, to be attended with the fewest to the country. You may implicitly rely upon what I mentioned to you yesterday respecting the light in which the K. views the question—Had his objection rested solely on his sense of the inexpediency of the measure, it would (as on many other occasions) have been overcome; but on the other ground he is prepared for any extremity, rather than yield up the point—and I leave to your Lordship and every well meaning friend to the Catholic claim, and indeed to every honest Catholic himself, to decide whether in the present state of the country, and with this impression on the King's mind the question ought to be pressed to a decision in Parlt. with a certainty of its being defeated in the last stage, if not by the King of England residing in England, by the K. of England, exercising his constitutional right from his Palace in Hanover—This (tho' too delicate to meet the public ear) I have very good reason to believe was the final determination.' (Carlisle MSS.)

[2] [Sir] Alexander John Ball (1757–1809), who, said Nelson (21 Sept. 1799) 'is named by his Sicilian Majesty...at my request, and by the unanimous desire of the Maltese people, Chief of the Island of Malta' (Nelson's *Despatches and Letters*, IV, 25). Lieutenant, 1778; Captain, 1783; Rear-Admiral, 1805. Baronetcy, 24 June 1801.

Lord St. Vincent finds it will hardly be possible to bring Lieut. Braun[1] to England in time to be appointed to the Royal Charlotte yacht as, by the last accounts from Gibraltar that he had proceeded up the Mediterranean to join his ship, probably at this moment on the coast of Egypt, but as the great object to Lieut. Braun is that of early promotion, Lord St. Vincent hopes that he shall have anticipated your Majesty's wishes touching that Officer and make some amends to him for the disadvantage he must sustain by being out of the way, by promoting him to the command of the Strombolo Bomb, now in the Mediterranean.

Mr. Nepean has fully inform'd Lord St. Vincent of the interest your Majesty has been pleas'd to take in favor of this young Officer, and as it may possibly be agreeable to your Majesty to mark your gracious attention towards the worthy father[2] in a way that cannot fail of being highly gratifying to his feelings, Lord St. Vincent has presum'd to send the Commission in the box, that your Majesty may dispose of it in any manner your Majesty may judge fit. (10191–2)

[*Admiralty, 13 May 1801.*] Lord St Vincent has the honor to transmit to your Majesty the sentence and minutes of a court martial, held some time since, at Yarmouth, on William Lander, John Johnson, and John Gray, three men belonging to the Squirrel, for mutiny. The case appears to Lord St Vincent to be of so atrocious a nature as to induce him most humbly to submit to your Majesty's consideration, whether it may not be proper to order the sentence of death to be carried into execution on the return of Admiral Dickson with his squadron from the coast of Holland, to Yarmouth, where he may be expected to arrive in a few days. (10193)

2414 LORD HAWKESBURY *to the* KING

[*London, 13 May 1801.*] Lord Hawkesbury has the honour to send your Majesty a Message[3] respecting Portugal, in substance the same as that which your Majesty was graciously pleased to sign a few days ago. Upon referring to precedents, it was found that the specification of the sum of money in the former Message was not usual, and the better opinion appeared to be that the terms of that part of the Message should be general. Lord Hawkesbury therefore humbly requests that your Majesty would sign the Message, as it is alter'd, if it should meet with your royal approbation. (10194)

2415 THE DUKE OF YORK *to the* KING

[*Kew, 15 May 1801.*] In consequence of your Majesty's very gracious letter of yesterday, I had determined to pay my duty to you this day, and should have been here before your Majesty had done your dinner if I had not been detained by a message from your Majesty's Ministers who were anxious to see me immediately

---

[1] Ernest Braun. Lieutenant, 1799; Commander, 13 May 1801; Captain, 29 April 1802. The name was sometimes spelt *Brawn*.

[2] Probably Robert Braun, the King's barber. See No. 1754.

[3] No. 2410 n.

upon some arrangements which they wished should be proposed to your Majesty in consequence of the intelligence received this morning from Egypt. As soon therefore as I had finished with them I set out, and unfortunately arrived soon after your Majesty had begun your walk. I must therefore humbly beg your Majesty's pardon, and sincerely regret having missed the happiness of paying my duty to you.

I beg leave to congratulate your Majesty upon the glorious success of your Majesty's arms on the 21 of March. The courage and intrepidity displayed by your Majesty's army in Egypt upon this and every former occasion does the officers and men the highest honor, but the cruel loss which your Majesty's service has sustained in my worthy friend Sir Ralph Abercrombie is most serious, and I am affraid at this moment not to be fully repaired.

After full consideration your Majesty's Ministers wish me to express to your Majesty their opinion in which I fully coincide that though Major-General Hutchinson[1] may not fully supply the place of Sir Ralph Abercrombie, yet as he is a very sensible, well-informed man, now thoroughly acquainted with that army of which he will have been for some months in the chief command before it would be possible for Lieutenant-General Fox to arrive in Egypt, it would be most advisable to appoint him to it.

Should your Majesty approve of this suggestion I beg leave to recommend that Major-General Hutchinson may have the brevet of Lieutenant-General in Egypt.

Your Majesty's Ministers have likewise desired me to mention to your Majesty the necessity of sending as strong a reinforcement to Egypt as can possibly be spared both from the guarrisons in the Mediterranean as from this country, and that it should be dispatched as expeditiously as possible.

From this country it is totally impossible for us to spare more than two batallions without diminishing too much our force here, and should your Majesty approve of it, the only two batallions which could be sent immediately are the 25 and 26 Regiments who lie the one in Horsham, and the other in Portsmouth as the only other batallions in England who can serve out of Europe are the 24 and 26 which are dispersed all over Devonshire and Cornwall on account of the riots, and the two batallions of the 85th who are, I am sorry to say, in consequence of the disputes among their officers of whom your Majesty has dismissed lately nine, perfectly unfit at present for service. (10195–6)

2416   LORD HOBART *to the* KING, *and the reply*

[*Downing Street, 15 May, 1801, 1 p.m.*] Lord Hobart presents his humble duty to your Majesty and transmits despatches received this morning from Major-General Hutchinson.

The loss which your Majesty's service has sustain'd by the death of that excellent

[1] John Hely-Hutchinson (1757–1832). Entered the Army, 1774; Lieutenant-Colonel, 1783; Colonel, 1794; Major-General, 1796; Lieutenant-General, 1803; General, 1813. He succeeded Abercromby as Commander-in-Chief in Egypt, and to him the French soon capitulated. Created Baron Hutchinson, 16 Dec. 1801; K.B., 28 May 1801; G.C.B., 1815; succeeded his brother as 2nd Earl of Donoughmore, 22 Aug. 1825.

and gallant Officer General Abercrombie cannot but be most severely felt both by his country and his friends. They will however derive no small consolation from the reflection that, directed by his military experience and talents, and animated by the example of that intrepidity and coolness for which he has at all times been so conspicuous, the gallantry and conduct of the British troops has never been more distinguish'd than in the several actions which have taken place under his command in Egypt.

Lord Hobart humbly takes the liberty of sending to your Majesty a sketch of the ground upon which the actions of the 8th and 13th were fought, conceiving that it may be of use to your Majesty in considering Major-General Hutchinson's despatches.

For your Majesty's further information Lord Hobart also forwards a private letter from Major-General Hutchinson to Mr. Dundas. (10197–8)

[*The King's reply, Kew, 15 May, 5.20 p.m.*] The King is sorry for the loss of Sir Ralph Abercrombie, he always urged the necessity of sending a Lieutenant General with him though it has not been attended to; when Lt. Gen. Fox arrives he trusts the Service will [not] suffer by the change. (Bucks. R.O.)

2417   THE EARL OF ST VINCENT *to the* KING

[*Admiralty, 16 May 1801.*] Lord St. Vincent has the honor of transmitting to your Majesty a plan of the proposed alterations in the Royal Charlotte yacht which has been submitted by the Navy Board. If they meet your Majesty's Royal approbation Lord St. Vincent will give orders for their being immediately made.

Lord St. Vincent has, in obedience to your Majesty's commands, given the rank of Post Captain to Capt. Farnall,[1] and an order will be given to him for commanding the Royal Charlotte yacht whenever your Majesty shall be graciously pleas'd to require the attendance of Sir Harry Neale in any of the ships which may attend your Majesty at Weymouth. (10199)

2418   THE DUKE OF PORTLAND *to the* KING

[*Bulstrode, Saturday night, 16 May 1801.*] The Duke of Portland most humbly begs leave to lay at your Majesty's feet the humble request of the Bishop of Rochester[2] that your Majesty will graciously please to permit him to dedicate to your Majesty a translation of the Prophet Hosea with critical & explanatory notes which he has prepared & which are now ready for the press.

The Duke of Portland has been also desired by the late Lord Advocate on whom your Majesty has been pleased to confer the appointment of Chief Baron of the Court of Exchequer in Scotland, to lay his most gratefull acknowledgements for this high mark of your Majesty's favor at your Majesty's feet; & to entreat

---

[1] Harry Farnall. Lieutenant, 1793; Captain, 14 May 1801.
[2] Samuel Horsley (1733–1806). Bishop of St David's, 1788; of Rochester, 1793; of St Asaph, 1802–6. The translation was published during the year.

your Majesty to beleive that no endeavour will be omitted on his part to fulfill with his utmost zeal & fidelity the important trust your Mastery has condescended to place in his hands—& the Duke of Portland has also been desired by Mr Hope, to whom your Majesty has thought fit to give the appointment of your Majesty's Advocate for Scotland, to lay him most dutifully at your Majesty's feet & to assure your Majesty that the sense he has of your Majesty's paternal regard for your people must make him consider an active & zealous discharge of his publick duty the most acceptable return which he can make to your Majesty for the gracious mark of favor which your Majesty has been pleased to confer upon him. (10200–1)

2419   THE DUCHESS OF WURTEMBERG *to the* KING

[*Louisbourg, 17 May 1801.*] The constant goodness with which your Majesty has honoured me encourages me to seize on the earliest opportunity to acquaint you that I arrived here yesterday. I am happy to be able to say that all ranks appear equally delighted with the Duke's return and though we had both declined any public reception the people insisted on shewing him every mark of respect and affection. I shall never forget the way in which they received me; the whole road from Lorch to Louisbourg was crouded with people. The Duke and his sons came three miles to meet me. Words can but feebly express the gratitude we feel to the Almighty for having restored us to our home. Louisbourg is in great beauty and appears even more so after having been a whole year condemned to live in Franconia, as round Erlangen there is nothing but sand and firs; near Anspach the country mends, but even there it is very inferior to Suabia.

I rejoice very much to hear that your Majesty begins already to reap the benefit of the country air and hope that very soon you will feel quite strong. (51640–1)

2420   THE DUKE OF YORK *to the* KING

[*Horse Guards, 17 May 1801.*] Having met your Majesty's Ministers by appointment this day, I am desired by them to submit to your Majesty their decided opinion of the necessity of reinforcing the army now in Egypt with a larger force than was first proposed, and therefore humbly entreat your Majesty's approbation to the following arrangement, that in addition to the 25 and 26th Regiments the 24th should be ordered to embark for Egypt, as likewise the York Hussars with their horses, and a Regiment of Light Dragoons dismounted from Ireland, and also a draft of one hunderd and fifty men should be sent to each of the batallions of Guards in order to fill up the vacancies which have happened.

Should your Majesty be graciously pleased to approve of this proposal, Lord St. Vincent has undertaken to find troop ships sufficient to convey the detachment of Guards and the Horse Regiments of Infantry in the course of this week. (10202)

2421 HENRY ADDINGTON *to the* KING

[*Downing Street, 19 May 1801, 4.15 p.m.*] It is with extreme reluctance and regret that Mr Addington presumes to intrude upon your Majesty a second time[1] in the course of the day, but as a cutter is to be dispatched to Egypt without loss of time, he cannot forbear submitting to your Majesty's consideration the propriety, and the probable advantage of conferring the Red Ribband of the late Sir Ralp[h] Abercrombie on Major-General Hutchinson, as a reward and an encouragement to that zealous and deserving officer, and as an incitement to the army under his command to persevere in that conduct by which they have already done themselves so much honor, and to manifest the same obedience to his orders which was invariably paid to those of his highly distinguished predecessor. (10204)

2422 LORD ELDON *to the* KING

[*21 May 1801, 10 a.m.*] The Lord Chancellor, offering his most humble duty to your Majesty, begs leave to transmit the titles of several Bills which have passed both Houses of Parliament, and humbly mentions to your Majesty his intention of taking your Majesty's pleasure at the Council this morning whether your Majesty may think proper to give the Royal Assent to them by Commission today. The first eight of these Bills are of a public nature, and the effect of them is fully expressed in their respective titles: the others, fifty in number, are all of a private nature. (10205)

2423 THE DUKE OF YORK *to the* KING

[*Horse Guards, 23 May 1801.*] Your Majesty having been pleased yesterday to express your regret at the York Hussars being ordered to Egypt, I beg leave to propose to your Majesty that they may remain in this country and that the remainder of the regiment of Hompesch[2] of which there is already a detachment with Major-General Hutchinson may be ordered to embark from Ireland in their stead.

The only reason for sending the York Hussars was the desire of sending a mounted Regiment to Egypt and the difficulty of embarking horses at Cork, but this being now found impossible as the Transport Board cannot find sufficient Horse Transports it will be infinitely more advantageous to your Majesty's

---

[1] Addington's earlier letter seems to be missing from the Archives. The King's replies on the 19th are in Pellew, I, 394–5, the second being written at 5.53 p.m. (for 'General Hutchinson' read 'M. Genl'.). He approved of the proposal of a Barony for Lady Abercromby, together with a pension of £2,000 a year, and the Red Ribband for Hutchinson.

[2] The reference, apparently is to Ferdinand, Baron Hompesch, rather than to his brother Charles, Baron Hompesch (Colonel, Sept. 1796; Major-General, 1802; Lieutenant-General, 1803), who died in June 1812. They came of a Rhineland family, and both had been in the Austrian service before entering that of Britain. Sir Herbert Taylor wrote: His [Charles's] brother Ferdinand had…raised a corps of *chasseurs à cheval* which did good service under his orders in Ireland, proceeded without him to Egypt, and was reduced after the Peace of Amiens…Ferdinand also rose to the rank of Lieutenant-General, and, having survived his brother, inherited large property on the Rhine and in Bavaria from an uncle.' (*Taylor Papers*, p. 66.)

service that the remainder of the Regiment of Hompesch should be dismounted and sent to join their detachment than to detach a fresh corps which is now improving rapidly.

Should your Majesty be graciously pleased to approve of this change, the York Hussars may attend your Majesty at Weymouth and be encamped upon the same ground they were last year. (10206)

2424   *Letters from the* EARL OF CHESTERFIELD *to the* KING

[*Bretby Hall,*[1] *23 May 1801.*] That no time may be lost in carrying into effect those arrangements which your Majesty, by your very gracious letter which I have just received, has been pleased to command, I have by tonight's post sent a copy of them to Mr. Parker.[2]

As I propose having the honor to pay my duty to the Queen on your Majesty's birthday, I shall while in London see Mr. Parker in order to be enabled to lay before your Majesty the state and amount of such compensations and pensions as you are graciously pleased to direct to be allowed. I will also ascertain whether the last appointed Hobby Groom chooses to change his situation for the one your Majesty has pointed out.

Lady Chesterfield[3] and I shall be highly gratified in availing ourselves of your Majesty's gracious permission to pay our duty at Weymouth. (10207)

[*Bretby Hall, 24 May.*] In obedience to your Majesty's commands, I have by this night's post written to Mr. Parker directing him to prepare for your Majesty's signature a warrant appointing Coll. Brent Spencer[4] Equerry in Extraordinary to your Majesty. I am confident I cannot announce to Coll. Spencer this instance of your Majesty's goodness to him in any manner so flattering or gratifying to him as by enclosing him a copy of your Majesty's letter commanding that appointment. (10209)

2425   THE EARL OF ST VINCENT *to the* KING

[*Admiralty, 24 May 1801.*] As some discussion took place on Wednesday last, in the House of Commons, on the subject of Sir Hyde Parker's being superseded in his command of the Baltic Fleet, and will, probably, from what Lord St. Vincent saw of the Admiral's disposition, in an interview with him, since his return, be brought again into discussion in some shape or other, Lord St. Vincent thinks it his duty to transmit to your Majesty copies of all the private letters which passed between him and Sir Hyde from the time of his leaving Yarmouth to the time of his return.[5]

---

[1] Near Burton-on-Trent.

[2] Probably David Parker, Clerk of the Stables, Lord Chesterfield being Master of the Horse.

[3] Lord Chesterfield married, as his second wife (1799) Henrietta (1762–1813), daughter of the 1st Marquess of Bath. She was a Lady of the Bedchamber to the Queen, 1809–13.

[4] Sir Brent Spencer (1760–1828). He had served in the Helder expedition and in Egypt. Lieutenant-Colonel, 1794; Colonel, 1798; Major-General, 1805; Lieutenant-General, 1811; General, 1825. K.B., 1809; G.C.B., 1815.

[5] The honours for the Copenhagen action were announced in the *London Gazette* on the 19th, Nelson

Lord St. Vincent understands that, previously to Sir Hyde's recieving the directions of the Admiralty Board to return home, Lord Nelson had applied for and obtained his permission to quit his station in the Baltic Fleet, and was to have shifted his Flag to the Blanche frigate for that purpose on the day Sir Hyde left it. Lord Nelson, who is in the habit of complaining of ill health and stated it to be the cause of his taking that step, has, it appears, recieved considerable benefit from the additional responsibility which has recently been thrown on him, and will, Lord St. Vincent has no doubt, be able to continue in the command.

Lord St. Vincent finds, by the last letter received from Lord Nelson, (a copy of which is sent in the Box) that he had left Kioge Bay on the 6th, and was, on the following day, proceeding off Revel, not having at that time been joined by Rear-Admiral Totty,[1] but by letters which have been recieved from other persons it appears that the Rear-Admiral had reached Elsineur on the 9th instant, and would of course avail himself of the first opportunity of proceeding from thence into the Baltic for that purpose. (10210–11)

[*Enclosure*]

[*Lord Nelson to Evan Nepean, St George, at anchor off Falsterborn, 7 May.*] (*copy*)

I beg leave to inform you that I directed the fleet to be got under sail yesterday morning, but the wind coming strong to the eastward I was obliged to anchor here. It is my intention to leave Capt. Murray till relieved by Rear-Admiral Totty off Bornholm with 7 sail of the line and a proper number of attendant frigates and small craft, under the present circumstances. I have thought it right to address a letter to the Swedish Admiral in respectful terms, signifying my wish that the Swedish fleet would not come to sea as I should be sorry, out of respect to the Emperor of Russia, to see hostilities committed, which must be the case if they put to sea. I have directed all the bombs, fireships and gun brigs to be placed under the direction of Capt. Inman of the Desirée and to keep them as much as possible at anchor under Bornholm, for in bad weather they are bad cruizers.

With 11 sail of the line, a frigate and two sloops, it is my intention to shew myself in the Gulph of Finland, but in such a manner as I trust will be taken as a compliment by the Emperor of Russia, and at the same time with the precautions that if the whole Empire of Russia was hostile to us, that their Lordships may be perfectly at ease for the safety of the squadron in spite of all the power of Russia.

I cannot omit this opportunity of testifying that I never saw more zeal or a desire to distinguish themselves than in this Fleet, and it must be with real sorrow when I am forced to state that the probability is that very soon that I must be separated from them; either my decline must finish my earthly career, or a change of climate is the only prospect of the restoration of my health. I send this by way of Hamburgh through Sir James Crauford. (10175–6)

was given a Viscountcy, Graves a K.C.B., and Parker was passed over. Tierney raised the matter in the Commons on the 20th, but strangers were excluded and the debate went unreported. Parker was refused a court martial as well as a peerage.

[1] Thomas Totty. Lieutenant, 1775; Captain, 1782; Rear-Admiral, 1 Jan. 1801. (*d.* 1802.)

2426 LORD HAWKESBURY *to the* KING

[*London, 25 May 1801.*] Lord Hawkesbury has the honour to send your Majesty the Chevalier D'Almeida's[1] letter of recall. Monsr De Lima, the successor of Monsr. D'Almeida, is arrived. Lord Hawkesbury begs to receive your Majesty's commands whether the letters of credence of Monsr. De Lima should be deliver'd through him or if not in what other way they should be transmitted to your Majesty.

Lord Hawkesbury humbly submits to your Majesty the following arrangements, and if they should meet with your gracious approbation Lord Hawkesbury will order the warrants to be made out for your royal signature.

Lord Hawkesbury proposes that Mr Drummond should succeed Mr Paget as Minister to the King of Naples, that Mr Stratton[2] should be appointed Secretary to the Embassy at Constantinople. He has been nineteen years at Vienna,[3] and appears to be fairly entitled to a promotion; and that Mr Charles Stuart,[4] the eldest son of Sir Charles Stuart, should succeed, as Secretary of Legation at Vienna. Lord Hawkesbury is induced to submit this last recommendation to your Majesty in part from the respect he entertains for the memory of Sir Charles Stuart, and from a conviction that Mr Stuart's talents and education render him particularly qualified for the line in which he wishes to be placed.[5] (10212)

2427 HENRY ADDINGTON *to the* KING

[*Downing Street, 26 May 1801.*] With your Majesty's gracious permission, the Lord Chancellor and Mr. Addington will pay their duty to your Majesty at Kew tomorrow, a little before twelve o'clock.[6] (10213)

2428 THE BISHOP OF NORWICH (DR MANNERS-SUTTON) *to* GENERAL [? BUDÉ]

[*Clifford Street, May ye 28th 1801.*] In obedience to his Majesty's commands, I have ye honor of transmitting for his Majesty's signature ye dispensing warrants for their Royal Highnesses ye Duke of Clarence, ye Duke of Kent, ye Duke of Cumberland, Prince Augustus, & Prince Adolphus. When his Majesty shall have signed them you will have ye goodness to return them to me. I shall trouble you at ye same time to take his Majesty's pleasure whether ye warrants when completed shall be again returned to his Majesty, or whether they shall be conveyed

---

[1] The Portuguese Minister in London, who had been appointed Foreign Minister of Portugal. The Marquis Lorenzo de Lima delivered his credentials to the King at the Queen's House on the 29th.

[2] Straton. See No. 505. Later, he was appointed Minister *ad interim* to Turkey (1803), and Minister to Sweden (1807).

[3] He had been appointed Secretary of Legation at Vienna in July 1789.

[4] Charles Stuart (1779–1845), son of Lieutenant-General Sir Charles Stuart (*d.* 1801, he being the fourth son of the 3rd Earl of Bute). Secretary of Legation at Vienna, 1801–4, and Chargé d'Affaires, 1803–4 and 1805–6; Secretary of Embassy at Petersburg, 1804–8, and Minister *ad interim*, 1806–7; Special Mission to Spain, 1808–9, and to Vienna, 1809; Minister to Portugal, 1810–14; Minister *ad interim* to France, 1814; Ambassador to the Netherlands, 1815; Ambassador to France, 1815–24; Special Mission to Portugal, 1825, and to Brazil, 1825–6; Ambassador to France, 1828–31, and to Russia, 1841–4. K.B., 1812; G.C.B., 1815. Created Lord Stuart de Rothesay, 22 Jan. 1828.

[5] See Appendix.

[6] The King's brief reply from Kew on the 27th, 7.50 a.m., is in Pellew, I, 406.

by me in person to their Royal Highnesses respectively. The remaining warrants will be ready tomorrow.[1]

I am at a loss in what manner ye most respectful to signify to his Majesty ye receipt of four hundred pounds which his Majesty has been pleased to subscribe for their Royal Highnesses ye Dukes of Kent & Cumberland & ye Princes Augustus & Adolphus, to ye Fund for maintaining & keeping in order ye painted windows in St George's free Chapel in Windsor Castle. I am fearful of doing anything that may appear obtrusive or presumptuous in so humble a subject as myself, & most anxious to express to his Majesty what I feel from ye bottom of my heart, every sentiment of duty & veneration. You will perhaps have ye goodness to state to his Majesty ye difficulties I labour under, & to rescue me from ye consequences of them.

I shall order my servant to receive your instructions, whether he shall wait for ye warrants or return without them. (10214)

2429   THE EARL OF ST VINCENT *to the* KING

[*Admiralty, 30 May 1801.*] Lord St Vincent has the honor of informing your Majesty that he has received from Lieut.-Colonel Hutchinson of the 49th Regt., who has been serving in the Baltic Fleet, and arrived in town a few hours ago, from Yarmouth, (having taken his passage in the sloop which brought Vice-Admiral Lord Nelson's dispatches of the 17th, sent to your Majesty this morning) a lamentable account of the state of Lord Nelson's health and spirits, insomuch that Lord St. Vincent is very apprehensive, unless his Lordship is immediately reliev'd, his life will be in danger.

On a careful examination of the list of Flag Officers, Lord St. Vincent finds extreme difficulty in pointing out to your Majesty an officer in all respects fitted for such an important command, considering the present critical situation of affairs with the Northern Powers, and after weighing the objections which occur to different people, the officer who appears to him as most likely to be employed therein with advantage to your Majesty's service is Admiral George Montagu.[2]

Lord St. Vincent is aware that from his having remained so long unemployed, objections may be stated to his being at once placed in such a responsible situation, but, notwithstanding the extent of the list of Flag Officers, there is not one to whom greater objections do not arise than to the officer he has presumed to name to your Majesty.

If your Majesty should approve of the arrangement Lord St. Vincent has taken

---

[1] The Bishop was Registrar of the Order of the Garter. The King's letter to Addington, Kew, 1 June (inaccurately, as usual, given in Pellew, 1, 406), explains the Bishop's letter: 'The King thinks it proper to acquaint Mr. Addington that, in consequence of a very judicious intimation yesterday by letter from the Lord Chancellor, he has postponed his journey to Hampshire and Weymouth till it shall be ascertained that no message can be necessary to the Houses of Parliament consequently to the day or day before the rising of Parliament. His Majesty trusts *his* Chancellor of the Exchequer will be at the Queen's Palace on Wednesday at one o'clock; and transmits the account of the fees for his five sons and the two foreign Knights of the Garter, which should be paid by a Treasury warrant, and that immediately prepared.' (Sidmouth MSS.)

[2] Sir George Montagu (1750–1829). Lieutenant, 1771; Captain, 1774; Rear-Admiral, 1794; Vice-Admiral, 1795; Admiral, 1 Jan. 1801. Commander-in-Chief at Portsmouth, 1803; G.C.B., 1815.

the liberty to suggest, it is his intention to desire Admiral Montagu (who is now in Sussex) to come to town, and, should no unforeseen objection arise, to offer the command to him, leaving Rear-Admirals Graves[1] and Totty in their present stations.[2] (10215–16)

2430   THE EARL OF ELGIN *to the* KING

[*Constantinople, 30 May 1801.*] I am at a loss to apologize for the liberty I venture to take in addressing myself directly to your Majesty. But knowing no person now in your Majesty's Councils acquainted with the circumstances of my publick life, I feel embolden'd by the recollection of the good will with which your Majesty has ever honored my family, to lay myself in this way at your Majesty's feet.

From the year 1786 that your Majesty was graciously pleased to give me a Commission in the 3d Regt. of Guards, I have ever been in your service. My diplomatick career began at the earliest commencement of the French Revolution, since which time I have had the honor of being constantly employed, passing thro' the various gradations of this line, always in very active & busy situations, sometimes in very painful ones, till I have now attained the summit of my profession, and have the pride of representing your Majesty in a post infinitely more important & more brilliant than any other that has offer'd during the course of this eventful period.[3]

Sire, my career has involved me in great pecuniary embarassements: it has necessarily withdrawn me from every opportunity of forming political connexions in England: and I have never once, in the course of it, received any publick testimony of your Majesty's favor, while all my colleagues of my standing, have obtained peerages and the order of knighthood.

I have not the presumption to draw comparisons with any man's abilities, but I trust your Majesty is persuaded that no act or effort by which I could hope to contribute to my country's good or to your Majesty's glory, ever cost me a thought.

Sire, in solliciting from your Majesty a proof of your royal approbation, similar to what has been bestowed on my colleagues, I sollicit a proof that I have served your Majesty faithfully and zealously under the most arduous circumstances that our country & Europe ever saw. I sollicit it, earnestly, from the prospect which I now, thank God, have, of a child to inherit the benefits that may accrue from my services. And I must be allowed to declare that I sollicit it as a personal mark of the favor of your Majesty, the extensive & beneficial influence of whose virtues & character I have had more opportunity of observing & admiring than perhaps any individual among your Majesty's subjects. (10217–8)

[1] Sir Thomas Graves (1747?–1814). Lieutenant, 1782; Captain, 1794; Rear-Admiral, 1 Jan. 1801; Vice-Admiral, 1805; Admiral, 1812. K.B., 1801.

[2] The King's reply on the 30th is in *Letters of Lord St. Vincent* (Navy Records Society, I, 98). The King's letter of 31 May to the Bishop of Worcester is in Jesse, III, 278.

[3] Sent on a Special Mission to Austria, 1790–1; Envoy to the Austrian Netherlands, 1792–4; Minister to Prussia, 1795–9. He received no mark of the King's favour. He married (1799), as his first wife, Mary, daughter of William Hamilton Nisbet, and his first son, George, Lord Bruce (*d.* 1840), who predeceased him, was born on 5 April 1800.

[*Downing Street, 31 May 1801, 11 p.m.*] As there are two or three points upon which it is material that Mr. Addington should know your Majesty's pleasure, he humbly hopes that he may be permitted to pay his duty at Kew tomorrow. If your Majesty should grant him this indulgence he proposes to be at Kew by twelve o'clock, unless he should be directed to attend your Majesty at any other hour. (10219)

2432   LORD ELDON *to the* KING[1]

[*Sunday morning, 11 a.m.* [*31 May 1801*].] The Lord Chancellor, offering his most humble duty to your Majesty, presumes to submit to your Majesty's gracious consideration that it appears to him that great difficulties may arise in matters of public concern if your Majesty should be pleased, during the time of its sitting, to remove to any considerable distance from your Majesty's Parliament. It cannot but happen that, before Parliament can be closed, some intelligence should be received from abroad upon which it may be absolutely necessary to learn promptly & perhaps instantly your Majesty's pleasure, and to learn it by communications more ample than your Majesty, however gracious to your servants, could probably allow to them if they were not personally attending, in the discharge of their duty, upon your Majesty. Communications from your Majesty in the form of Messages to your Parliament, not admitting of delay, may also become necessary. Impressed at this moment with a deep sense that it is extremely important, on all accounts, to your Majesty's welfare that your Majesty should be graciously pleased to secure to your servants the power of personally communicating with your Majesty, at least during the short interval which must elapse before Parliament seperates, at the close of which they may, in obedience to any commands which your Majesty may think proper to give, attend your Majesty anywhere, the Lord Chancellor ventures to hope that your Majesty will not think it inconsistent with his duty that he should have thus most humbly but most earnestly submitted to your Majesty the expression of his conscientious conviction that such a measure is of the highest expediency.

The Lord Chancellor also requests your Majesty's gracious permission to introduce to your Majesty the Master of the Rolls and the Solicitor-General previous to your Majesty's birthday. As Tuesday is the Seal-day in the Court of Chancery, your Majesty may probably have the goodness to give that permission for Wednesday.

The Lord Chancellor throws himself at your Majesty's feet, requesting pardon for giving your Majesty this trouble.[2] (10220–1)

---

[1] Eldon's draft, differing in many respects from the letter sent, is in Twiss, I, 377, without a date.

[2] The King's reply on the 31st is in Twiss, I, 378. He agreed to postpone his journey to Weymouth until after the close of the Session (2 July). See also the King's letter to Addington from Kew, 1 June (Pellew, I, 406).

2433   THOMAS COUTTS *to the* **KING**

[*Strand, 2 June 1801.*] The happiness I have felt upon being assured of your Majesty's recovery is more than I am able to express, and it could only be exceeded by my being permitted to approach your person remembring, as I shall ever do, the kind words and manner in which your Majesty spoke to me the last time I had that honour.

The inclosed paper contains truths that have plung'd me in affliction. I hope my inclosing it may not be thought improper. I could not resist the impulse I felt to lay it before your Majesty, as indeed the matter has touch'd me in the tenderest part. (10222)

[*Enclosure*]

[*2 June 1801.*] On the 29th of April the account kep'd at my house in Lord Cardigan's name was finally shut by the ballance being drawn out—& no transactions having since follow'd.

If the alteration has been made by the King's command—I must submit—and I will do so in respectful silence, 'tho' my suffering in consequence of so severe a blow can never end but with my life.

If besides it were possible for me to suppose myself accused or suspected of any impropriety of conduct (and who can always escape from the baneful blasts of malice and envy?) I should feel a terrible addition of unhappiness. Yet conscious of rectitude, and nothing in my heart but duty and attachment, I would trust in Heaven and the King's goodness and justice that the day of my honourable acquittal from such foul slander would not be far distant. (10223)

2434   THE DUKE OF PORTLAND *to the* **KING**

[*Burlington House, Tuesday, 2 June 1801, 9.45 p.m.*] The Duke of Portland humbly begs leave to acquaint your Majesty that Mr. Stuart, the son of the late Sir Charles Stuart, has requested the Duke of Portland to receive your Majesty's pleasure with respect to the manner in which Mr. Stuart is to deliver up the badge of the Order of the Bath which your Majesty was pleased to confer on his late father.[1] The Duke of Portland farther begs leave to inform your Majesty of the Marquess Cornwallis's return; he arrived in town this afternoon. (10224)

2435   HENRY ADDINGTON *to the* **KING**, *and the reply*

[*Downing Street, 3 June 1801, 10 p.m.*] Mr. Addington humbly acquaints your Majesty that, as the embargo on British ships in the ports of Russia has been taken off, and as the Court of Denmark has manifested a disposition the most conciliatory, and pacific, it has been judged adviseable by your Majesty's confidential servants that the ships belonging to those countries and now detained in our ports, should be forthwith released. These measures cannot however be

---

[1] On 8 Jan. 1799. He was actually invested on 8 Jan. 1800, but not installed.

properly carried into effect except by the authority of an order of your Majesty in Council, and it is obvious that if right in themselves, they should be executed without delay. Mr. Addington hopes it may not be very inconvenient to your Majesty to hold a Council tomorrow: if not, he will, upon receiving your Majesty's commands, cause summonses to be issued for a due attendance at any hour that your Majesty may please to appoint. (10225–6)

[*The King's reply, Queen's Palace, 4 June, 7.05 a.m.*] The King desires Mr. Addington will send to the Earl of Chatham this morning, that [a] Privy Council may be held here at three o'clock for taking off the embargo on the Russian and Danish ships; which, I should hope, will not be inconvenient to my Ministers, as they may make their bow to the Queen in the Entrée room, and by ordering their coaches to the Friary in St. James's Park, shall be shewn down my private stairs, and come here without inconvenience. (Sidmouth MSS.)[1]

2436   THE BISHOP OF WORCESTER (RICHARD HURD) *to the* KING

[*Hartlebury, 4 June 1801.*] The receipt of the gracious letter wch. your Majesty had the goodness to write to me from Kew on the 31st past, gives me a pleasure wch. I cannot easily express. I had heard indeed from all quarters that your Majesty's health was recovering, but having the assurance of it under your own hand & on *this* auspicious day, completes my satisfaction. I hope, Sir, the change of the scene, together with the moderate exercise wch. your Majesty will take at Weymouth, & above all a relaxation of that attention wch. your Majesty gives to public business, will perfectly restore your former strength & spirits.

It was agreable, Sir, to your Majesty's piety to make your devout acknowledgments at the Altar for this instance of the Divine goodness to yourself & to all your subjects, & to carry with you to that sacred place so many ornaments of the Royal family, trained up in the principles of that religion wch. your Majesty exemplifies as well as professes. It is a sensible concern to me that I could not be a witness, at least, of this hallowed scene, and that the unworthy Clerk of your Majesty's Closet is wholly disabled from bearing a part in it: but the goodness to me & Cambridge[2] in the choice made of the officiating Bishop on this occasion is in the usual strain of your Majesty's condescending politeness.

I conclude with every wish for your Majesty's perfect health & long life & prosperity in all your great affairs & am [etc.]. (10227–8)

2437   THE DUCHESS OF WURTEMBERG *to the* KING

[*Louisbourg, 4 June 1801.*] I hope your Majesty will allow me with the Duke's humble duty to present our joint congratulations on this day. I hope the Almighty will long watch over your Majesty and grant you his choicest blessings. Every day I feel more rejoiced at being at home and having it in my power to walk out in this

---

[1] There is a much-edited version of this letter in Pellew, 1, 407.
[2] The Bishop was a Fellow of Emmanuel College, Cambridge.

fine country which is as beautiful as Erlangen and all Franconia is frightful. Few countries are so totally deprived of everything that is pleasant, hardly any trees and those only firs; no verdure and nothing but deep burning sand. Here we have the advantage of having all the finest forest trees and many exotics. Since the Duke was in England he has had some plants left out in the winter which used formerly to be housed, and they have succeeded very well, which will now encourage us to make more trials. The kongaroos are in very good health and two young ones are born which are great beauties. Everybody comes to see them and they are much admired. (51642–3)

2438 LORD BRAYBROOKE[1] to GENERAL BUDÉ

[*Grosvenor Street, 5 June 1801*.] When you did me the honor to signify to me this morning his Majesty's commands respecting a painting of King George the Second, I was not without hopes of having it in my power to offer to his Majesty, with my humble duty, a very valuable whole-length portrait of the late King, painted by Pine[2] in 1759: upon further reflexion, however, it is quite clear that this picture is amongst the heirlooms at Audley End.

I have not in my possession any other painting of that great personage, but I have a proof print from Pine's picture, (& indeed the only remaining one) which is at his Majesty's service, if he should condescend to accept it.

If his Majesty should also be pleased to express a wish of having a copy of Pine's *portrait*, I will either give directions that the artist who may be employed to copy it, shall have access to it at Audley-End, or I will order the picture to be carefully packed up, & sent to any place which may be named, in order that the copy may be taken.

As the picture is really curious, perhaps it may not be unacceptable to you, tho' it may be rather tedious, if I mention a few particulars upon the subject which Lord Howard[3] related to me, & which make me quite anxious that a faithful copy may at least find its way into the King's Collection, and particularly as there are difficulties in introducing the original.

Upon Ld. Howard's expressing a wish to some friend to have the portrait of King George ye 2d, and his fears that there were no original portraits of him except those which were painted early in his life, it was suggested that this picture by Pine existed, but that it was at that time sent to America. Lord Howard applied to the painter who informed him that he had taken the likeness, unseen by the King, as he was speaking to one of his attendants at the top of the great staircase at Kensington Palace. Lord H. pressed Mr. Pine to try to recover the portrait, which was after a long time effected, at a large price, together with the plate itself from which the engravings had been taken, and which is in my possession, uninjured.

[1] Richard Aldworth Neville (1750–1825), M.P. for Grampound, 1774–80; for Buckingham, 1780–2, and for Reading, 1782–97, succeeded his cousin John Griffin, 1st Lord Braybrooke, as 2nd Baron in 1797, and also to the Griffin family estates at Audley End in Essex.

[2] Robert Edge Pine (1730–88), the portrait painter.

[3] Lord Braybrooke's cousin, the 1st Lord Braybrooke, bore the title of Lord Howard de Walden (from Aug. 1784), being the heir to his great-grandmother, one of the two co-heirs to that dignity.

I have as yet taken no new impressions from this plate, but if his Majesty should be desirous of more copies than the remaining one which I have already taken the liberty to offer, I will order as many to be struck off as his Majesty may be graciously pleased to accept.

P.S. The picture of the late King, at Audley End, is 8 feet 6 inches in height, (with the frame) and 5 feet 7 or 8 inches wide.[1] (10229–30)

2439 HENRY ADDINGTON *to the* KING

[*Downing Street, 5 June 1801.*] In transmitting the warrants herewith inclosed Mr. Addington thinks it incumbent upon him most humbly to acquaint your Majesty that they have been seen by Mr. Pitt who has stated in a note to Mr. Addington that they are quite conformable to his recollection of what he had agreed to propose.

Mr. Addington ventures also to lay before your Majesty the form of a Message for a Vote of Credit to the two Houses of Parliament and intreats your Majesty's signature to each of the copies. (10231)

2440 LORD HAWKESBURY *to the* KING

[*London, 8 June 1801.*] Lord Hawkesbury has the honour to send your Majesty the answer to the Duke of Modena[2] and drafts of answers from your Majesty and the Queen to the Archduke and Archduchess Ferdinand[3] for your Royal approbation. (10232)

2441 THOMAS COUTTS *to the* KING, *with a Memorandum*

[*Strand, 9 June 1801.*] I hope I shall not be thought too presumptuous or departing in any shape from propriety or the modest humility becoming my character and situation—far less from the respect and duty with which my heart will ever be fill'd, in laying the inclosed before your Majesty.

A person who has receiv'd the marks of condescending goodness from your Majesty that I have been honour'd with, ought to feel something due *on that account* to himself on all occasions added to the general desire of supporting the character of a gentleman.[4] (10233)

---

[1] Sir Owen Morshead added the following note to the foot of the MS.: 'I sent a copy of this letter to Lord Braybrooke 29th June, 1946. The picture is still at Audley End—the only likeness of George II taken *ad vivum*. The circumstances of its execution are well known—and narrated in the printed history of Audley End by a former Lord Braybrooke.'

[2] Ercole III, Duke of Modena, of the ancient House of Este (1727–1803); succeeded his father, 1780.

[3] The Emperor's brother, the Archduke Ferdinand (1769–1824), Grand Duke of Tuscany, married (1790), Louisa (1773–1802), daughter of Ferdinand I, King of Sicily. She died on 19 Sept. 1802.

[4] Glenbervie wrote, 23 Aug. 1802: 'I asked Rose the reason why the King's money had been taken from Coutts. He said he heard it in a way which precluded him from mentioning; that the reason had nothing to do with politics. That it had been some answer or transaction which had been felt to be unaccommodating. That the Drummonds had become more agreeable to the King.' (*Glenbervie Diaries*, I, 330.)

[*9 June 1801.*] I had the impression of integrity and honesty made on my mind at a very early period by the best of fathers, and I learnt by his powerful example as well as by his precept that honour and character were the first acquirements to be desired in the world—and that fortune should be considered as the last, or rather as a thing which would follow to the full extent of all that is useful or desireable in the train of common prudence and good conduct. On this plan I have ever uniformly acted, and on conviction if I had fifty sons I would impress the same upon them by every means in my power. My family both by my father and my mother have been remarkable for an uncommon degree of sensibility of heart—overflowing with gratitude and feeling for kindness receiv'd—It cannot be matter of surprise that such a person, in particular, shoud have been proud of any degree of notice from the Sovereign of his country, & of a Sovereign who has long reign'd in the hearts of his own subjects and is justly honour'd and rever'd by those of other nations—and look'd up to by all good men.

Lord Cardigan having said abroad that your Majesty had withdrawn your money from my House (and many who had often flatter'd me with the appellation of your Majesty's Banker having express'd both surprise and regret in showing me drafts in the royal signature on another House) cannot fail to operate strongly against my character and interest—but the mortification to which it has subjected me is inexpressible—and tho' certainly I can make no claim—and tho' in the face of Heaven my mind is clear of every inward reproach—yet it has been almost more than I have been able to bear. The blow comes heavily from such an eleva-tion—and my family and friends have express'd with much concern the appearance of wasting and decay visible in my countenance—the true cause of which remains a secret in my own breast, having never mention'd it even to those nearest to my heart; and there it will remain for the little time remaining of my life—without murmur or complaint. My only wish is that I may *appear as I am* in your Majesty's eyes—and if I have been accused, that I may not be condemn'd unheard, as face to face I am convinced there is no man would dare to injure me so falsely. (10234)

2442   THE DUCHESS OF WURTEMBERG *to the* KING

[*Louisbourg, 9 June 1801.*] I am too much overcome by your Majesty's gracious remembrance not to hasten to make my humble acknowledgements for the message you were pleased to send me through Elizabeth. My heart is too full of gratitude for my pen to do justice to my feelings. The two beautiful numbers of the Kew plants are invaluable to me as they are your Majesty's gift and a proof of the continuance of your goodness to me which it will ever be my object through life to try to deserve.

Sir Joseph Banks has sent us some fine plants and seeds which are a great addition to our collection and from which I hope to receive great amusement. At present much of my time is taken up in my flower garden and examining the various sorts of roses which form the fence. After having been so many months deprived of flowers I feel double pleasure in attending to them and to a very pretty aviary the Duke has been so good as to build for me and to fill with common birds, as I object much to fine foreign ones which would not give me more pleasure and would cost much more trouble. (51644-5)

2443 LORD HAWKESBURY *to the* KING, *and the reply*

[*London, 12 June 1801.*] Lord Hawkesbury has the honour to send your Majesty the answer to the Chevalier D'Almeida's Letter of Recall for your royal signature. Lord Hawkesbury wishes to receive your Majesty's commands whether a letter should be prepared for the Princess of Brazil.[1] The Court of Lisbon appear'd rather disappointed that Mr Frere had no letter from your Majesty to the Princess at the time he presented his Letter of Credence to the Prince Regent. Lord Hawkesbury has not been able to find any precedent analagous to the present in the books of the Office. (10235)

[*The King's reply, Kew, 13 June 1801.*] The unhappy state of the Queen of Portugal's mind having rendered a Regency necessary, there cannot be any precedent in the Office for this case; but as the Court of Portugal wish a letter should be written to the Princess of Brazil the King cannot see any reason to decline gratifying this wish, and consequently authorizes Lord Hawkesbury to have a letter on the recall of the Chevalier d'Almeida prepared for her. (Add. MSS. 38564, f. 44)

2444 THE DUKE OF PORTLAND *to the* KING

[*Burlington House, Friday night, 12 June 1801.*] The Duke of Portland most humbly begs leave to represent to your Majesty, at the instance of the Viscount Howe, the apprehensions of that Lord & the other Officers of the Board of Ordnance that in consequence of your Majesty's having only expressed your approbation of the augmentation, & having not taken any notice of the Regulations proposed in the Civil Branch of that Department, that they will not be authorized to carry the latter into effect, an opinion in which, although the Duke of Portland does not concur, he trusts your Majesty will pardon him for submitting to your Majesty the docket which your Majesty was pleased to make on the cap which contained the letter & the propositions of the Lieutenant-General of the Ordnance, in order that if your Majesty shall think fit, the words '*& Regulations*' may be added by your Majesty & the letter with such alterations as are marked in red ink may, in consequence of it, be written to the Lieutenant-General by the Duke of Portland. The Duke of Portland farther humbly begs leave to lay before your Majesty for your Royal signature a letter to the Lord Lieutenant of Ireland for

[1] The Prince of Brazil, afterwards John VI, King of Portugal, married (1790) Charlotte (1775–1830), daughter of Charles IV, King of Spain. John Hookham Frere, who had received his credentials on 14 October 1800, arrived at Lisbon towards the end of December 1800 and presented his credentials on 1 January 1801.

revoking the patents of the Officers of the Board of Ordnance in that part of the United Kingdom.

Lord Craven,[1] who requests to be laid at your Majesty's feet & to offer to your Majesty his most gratefull acknowledgements for the honor your Majesty has been most graciously pleased to confer upon him, proposes to take for his second title the name of Uffington, which has been formerly a title in his family & is a place in which a very considerable part of his property lays. (10237–8)

2445 *Letters from* HENRY ADDINGTON *to the* KING

[*Downing Street, 12 June 1801, 11 a.m.*] Mr. Addington has too long delayed to communicate to your Majesty the grateful submission of Sir Charles Grey to your Majesty's pleasure; and he now humbly requests permission to lay before your Majesty the sentiments of Sir Charles Grey as he has expressed them to the Earl of St. Vincent and himself.

Mr. Addington has only to trespass further on your Majesty's time by stating the humble hope of Lord Pelham[2] that he may be allowed to avail himself of your Majesty's gracious intentions towards him by taking the title of Earl of Chichester. (10236)

[*The King's reply, Kew, 12 June, 1.51 a.m.* [*sic*].] The King is much gratified at the manner Sir Charles Grey expresses himself to the Earl of St. Vincent and Mr. Addington on his advancement to a peerage; and approves of the Patent being prepared as Baron Grey of Howick,[3] as also that Lord Craven be Earl of Craven, Ld. Onslow Earl of Onslow, Lord Romney Earl of Romney and taking Marsham as his second title, Lord Pelham as Earl of Chichester, and Lord Grey de Wilton as Earl of Wilton, and directs that the warrants for that purpose shall be immediately prepared.[4] (Sidmouth MSS.)

[1] William, 7th Baron Craven (1770–1825), a Colonel in the Army, Major-General, 1805; Lieutenant-General, 1811; and General, 1825; was an A.D.C. to the King, 1798–1805. On 18 June 1801 he was created Viscount Uffington, Co. Berks., and Earl of Craven, Co. York.

[2] Thomas Pelham (1728–1805), Baron Pelham since 1762, when he succeeded his cousin the Duke of Newcastle, was created Earl of Chichester on 23 June 1801. It had taken him a long time to decide about his title. His son Thomas wrote to him on 20 March: 'I am going to Chichester, but before I go, I must inform you that I spoke to the Duke of Portland about the title of Hastings, to which he thought there might be some objection, and suggested that you might be Earl Pelham of Laughton and I might be called up by the title of Lord Pelham of Stanmer; the only objection is the possible confusion arising from the same name in common conversation, but I do not think it very material; will you consider it and let me know your sentiments by a letter on Sunday which I shall receive in London on Monday night or Tuesday morning?... Lord Sheffield is just come in—says that Earl of Pevensey would be a good title, and certainly there is this reason for it that most of your property is in the Rape—but Lord Sheffield adheres to his opinion that Hastings would be best.' (Add. MSS. 33130, f. 228.)

[3] Charles Grey derived no pleasure from his father's promotion to the peerage.

[4] The King wrote again to Addington on the 13th, ordering him to bring his family in his sociable to the Lodge in Richmond Park that evening, and expressing the hope that 'the lively and engaging youngest daughter will not be omitted' (Pellew, 1, 410). The King now assigned to Addington the occupation of the Royal Lodge in Richmond Park, and had it extensively repaired and adapted as a family residence at his own expense. For an account of this mark of the King's favour, see Pellew, 1, 408–10.

[*From Addington, Downing Street, 13 June, 11 p.m.*[1]] Mr. Addington most humbly and earnestly hopes, that he shall be forgiven by your Majesty, if, before he goes to rest, he ventures to indulge the feelings, with which he is deeply affected, in consequence of the condescension and goodness which have been recently manifested towards himself and those most dear to him.

It will be his constant aim and anxious endeavour to prove himself not altogether unworthy of the confidence and kindness with which your Majesty has been invariably pleased to honor him, and which are perpetually animating the obligations of duty by the strongest sentiments of reverential attachment and gratitude.[2] (10239)

[*From Addington, Downing Street, 16 June, 1.30 p.m.*] With your Majesty's permission, Lord Alvanley[3] and Mr. Abbot[4] will be most happy to pay their duty to your Majesty at the Queen's House at two o'clock today; the former on account of his elevation to the Peerage; the latter in consequence of his appointment to the office of Keeper of the Privy Seal in Ireland. (10240)

2446   THE EARL OF MALMESBURY *to the* KING

[*Park Place, Tuesday, 16 June 1801.*] Your Majesty will, I hope, not deem me guilty of an unwarrantable liberty in thus presuming to address myself to you, humbly to solicit your royal permission to dedicate to your Majesty a new edition of my father's works, now preparing for publication.

The very gratious and condescending manner in which your Majesty has often been pleased to recollect my father and to mention his name, joined to the strong desire which prevails in me to manifest my filial affection for him by being allowed to do what now is the most honorable and most grateful to his memory, as it would have been was he still living, the most consonant and the most soothing to his feelings, emboldens me to lay this my most humble request at your Majesty's feet.[5] (10241–2)

[1] The reply to the King's invitation, and for the assignment to him of the Royal Lodge.

[2] There is an inaccurate version of the King's reply on the 14th (7.02 a.m.) in Pellew, I, 407. 'The King is highly gratified at the repeated marks of the sensibility of Mr. Addington's heart, which must greatly add to the comfort of having placed him with so much propriety at the head of the Treasury. He trusts their mutual affection can only cease with their lives. As Mr. Addington could not fix last night when the Parliament will actually close, his Majesty thinks he may trust that, with dilligence, that may be either on Saturday the 27th, or, at farthest, Tuesday the 30th, in which case he may leave Kew on the 29th—the day before, which cannot require any latter [*sic*] Message to Parliament.' (Sidmouth MSS.)

[3] Sir Richard Pepper Arden, who had succeeded Lord Eldon as Lord Chief Justice of the Common Pleas in May, was created Baron Alvanley on 22 May.

[4] Charles Abbot had been appointed Irish Secretary on 25 May. See his *Diary*, I, 272. He proved to be such a thorough-going reformer of abuses that he made himself obnoxious to Lord Clare, the Lord Chancellor. Commenting on the circular letter sent to every office in the Civil and Military Departments of the country, Lord Clare denounced it as an insolent proceeding, marked by unexampled arrogance. 'Is there wisdom, justice or policy in suffering this upstart prig to disgust and offend the gentlemen to whose support we are indebted for carrying the Union?...I understand that Mr. Abbot, who commenced his official career by securing to himself a sinecure office in Ireland for life, has openly declared that he has come here for the sole purpose of effecting reformation in every Department' (Ashbourne's *Pitt*, p. 272).

This letter suggests the inaccuracy of the dating of Willis's letter to Eldon, in Twiss, I, 381.

[5] Lord Malmesbury's father was James Harris (1709–80), M.P. for Christchurch, 1761–80; a Lord of the Admiralty, Dec. 1762–April 1763; a Lord of the Treasury, 1763–5; Secretary and Comptroller

2447 THE DUKE OF PORTLAND *to the* KING

[*Burlington House, Wednesday, 17 June 1801, 11.20 p.m.*] The Duke of Portland humbly begs leave to offer to your Majesty a list of the Lords who were present today in the House, together with one of those who took a part in the debate upon the Martial Law Bill,[1] & also to acquaint your Majesty that the House having continued to sit 'till about nine o'clock it seemed to be the wish of everyone that the second Reading of the Indemnity Bill should not be proceeded to, & it was adjourned accordingly to Friday next.[2] (10243)

2448 LORD ELDON *to the* KING

[*Friday, 19 June, 8 p.m. [1801].*] The Lord Chancellor, offering his most humble duty to your Majesty, transmits herewith the titles of the several Bills, to which it is humbly wished that your Majesty should be graciously pleased to give your Royal Assent. The titles express, in general, the substance of these Bills with reasonable sufficiency, and the Lord Chancellor is therefore unwilling unnecessarily to give your Majesty the trouble, which saying more respecting them would occasion. The Lord Chancellor has also taken the liberty of sending to your Majesty the Commission for your Majesty's Royal Sign Manual, if your Majesty shall be graciously pleased to give your Majesty's Royal Assent. (10245–6)

2449 LORD PETRE[3] *to the* KING

[*Park Lane, 20 June 1801.*] It is with the most sincere attachment to your Majesty I presume, in my present decline of health, which has long prevented my dutiful

to the Queen, 1774–80; and author of *Hermes, or a Philosophical Inquiry concerning Universal Grammar* (1751). His collected works were published in 1801, with 'Some account of the Author' by his son. Malmesbury wrote, later in the year: 'Part of the 26th, the 27th and 28th of November I was at Windsor. I went there to present to the King and Queen copies of the new edition of my father's Works' (*Diaries and Corresp.* IV, 62).

As for Malmesbury himself, the King had thought of him in Feb. for the Foreign Secretaryship, 'and regretted my being too unwell to accept it' (*Ibid.* IV, 6–7).

[1] A Bill to continue the operation of the Irish Martial Law Act for the duration of the War and for one month after the signing of a definitive treaty of peace. There had been what Lord Hardwicke described as a 'very singular and awkward' debate on the Bill in the Commons on the 10th. Hardwicke wrote to his brother, Charles Yorke, on the 15th, from Dublin Castle: 'Abbot...seems to have been rather ill treated, I think, and the whole seems to have been wonderfully ill managed. For it was indifferent whether the Martial Law Bill was extended to the end of the War or to Lady Day next; though when it was once moved, it might as well have been permitted to go on. At any rate it ought to have been a Cabinet measure, and as you observed, was a pretty good lesson to Ministers to act more in concert in future. Such things always give the enemy advantage, and disgust friends. Surely it would have been better to have consulted with such a man as Dawson and other Irish Members, because no bad effect would have resulted from moving the continuance of the Bill to the 25th of March next, though perhaps, with a view to the disaffected only, the duration of the War would have been the best period to have taken.' (Add. MSS. 35771, f. 15.)

[2] *Parl. Register*, LX, 638–54. It was customary for an Act for the Suspension of the Habeas Corpus Act to be followed by an Indemnity Act, indemnifying persons concerned in securing and imprisoning persons under the Suspension Act, from the consequences of any illegal acts which they might have committed.

[3] Robert Edward, 9th Lord Petre (1742–1801), a leading Catholic Peer, who worked hard to liberate his co-religionists from the penalties and restrictions imposed on them by the penal laws. The peerage dated from July 1603. He died on 2 July 1801. His successors never attained higher rank in the peerage.

attendance in person on your Majesty, to address your Majesty with the strongest assurances of affection, which during your Majesty's reign I have zealously endeavoured to evince by the most loyal exertions in your Majesty's service my limited situation would permit, and having at an humble distance partook of the general blessings of your Majesty's reign I hope my earnest desire of receiving from your Majesty's own handsome mark of your royal countenance will be considered as a further proof of my affection, and of the high value & the esteem I place on any favour flowing spontaneously from your royal benevolence.

Permit me, royal Sir, to mention that it is now near two hundered [*sic*] years since my family have held the same rank in the peerage. Should your Majesty condescend to take it into your royal consideration & advance my family to the honors of a higher rank it would for ever be remembered & esteemed as a most lasting and valuable mark that during my lifetime I enjoyed the favour & countenance of my beloved Sovereign.

It is with the most unfeigned loyalty and affection I have the high honor [etc.]. (10247)

2450   THE DUKE OF YORK *to the* KING

[*Oatlands, 20 June 1801.*] I have the honor to acknowledge the receipt of your Majesty's most gracious letter, and beg leave to assure your Majesty that I see no danger of your Majesty's favourable intentions towards Major Irby in permitting him to sell the Majority of the 13th Light Dragoons, which he did not purchase, becoming a precedent if your Majesty will be pleased to allow it to be done at your express command. (10248)

2451   LORD ELDON *to the* KING

[*21 June* [*1801*], *11 a.m.*] The Lord Chancellor offers to your Majesty his most humble duty, and his grateful thanks for the honour done him by your Majesty's gracious letter of yesterday. He is afraid that the necessity for passing the Martial Law Bill for Ireland, and the Indemnity Bill afterwards, will oblige him to trouble your Majesty by offering a Commission for the Royal Sign Manual on Tuesday morning, and another on Wednesday or Thursday.

The Lord Chancellor, under the influence, as he can most sincerely assert, of an anxious concern for your Majesty's health, has hitherto abstained from expressing, as he wished to express, his gratitude to your Majesty for the unmerited favours which he has received. He meant so to do soon after your Majesty was pleased to place the Great Seal in his hands, & to tender in terms which, in consequence of your Majesty's indisposition, he had not an immediate opportunity of representing his gratitude for the goodness which he had experienced for many years, & especially for that goodness which had induced your Majesty to place him in the Common Pleas, & to permit him to enjoy in that Court the professional situation which throughout his life he had ever considered as the most to be wished for, more especially as the duties of it were such, as, with attention, he might hope to discharge with reasonable sufficiency. He has since abstained from expressing these sentiments because he felt the importance to your Majesty's health of abstaining from giving your Majesty the trouble which he now occasions. He resigned the Common Pleas with a degree of pain to which nothing could have reconciled him but the consideration which most effectually reconciled him to it— the consideration that duty & gratitude called for the most prompt obedience to your Majesty's pleasure. It was therefore that, when your Majesty was pleased to call him to a higher station, he represented, what he now repeats, that, as your goodness had enabled him in the retirement which he enjoyed in his former office to regain his health, he was most ready, as he ever will be, to sacrifice it again in your Majesty's service. It would be arrogant presumption, unpardonable in any subject, & especially in one who ought to deem humbly of himself, not to consider his having been placed but for a day in the office of Chancellor, as an honour of the highest nature: for him it is honour more than abundant: & his happiness is as compleat as in this world it can be, if it shall only happen that, whenever your Majesty, sooner or later, dismisses him to a private situation, he can carry into it the approbation of his own heart, & the assurance that in it he may hope to possess your Majesty's regard. It is on account of his most anxious wish so to do that he now proceeds to recall to your Majesty's recollection that, soon after he had the Great Seal, it became his painful duty in some of the conversations, with which your Majesty honoured him, to state that he trusted in Providence that the time would soon come, & he offers his humble thanks to that Providence that it has arrived, when he should throw himself at your Majesty's feet to implore your pardon with respect to circumstances which he need not present to your Majesty's recollection; and he now relieves his mind from what has deeply oppressed it, by most humbly asking your Majesty's forgiveness for himself & for all others, who, with him, have been actuated in what has past of that, to which he alludes, as he can most solemnly assure your Majesty, by a loyal, dutiful & heartfelt concern for your Majesty's health and welfare. He looks back with a consciousness that there is too much in what has past, that requires your Majesty's gracious consideration as to the good intentions of all that have been concerned in the restoration of your Majesty's health, to have presumed to take any further step which, by any construction or possibility, could appear to your Majesty to be improper. He had however your Majesty's permission, repeatedly given, to mention his humble opinion to your Majesty, respecting the degree of attendance of your Majesty's physicians & others employed by them, as anxiety regarding your Majesty's health and honour might require. He considers that health as, under the blessing of Providence, compleatly restored, but gratitude to Providence calls even for the over-cautious exertion of all human means that are proper to secure, what he trusts is secure, the continuance of that great blessing. This consideration induces him humbly to state, and, he hopes, makes it in some degree excuseable to state, before your Majesty goes to Weymouth, his anxious hope & wish that your Majesty would be graciously pleased for your own sake & your family's, if you can so think fit, to command the attendance, at least for the present, of Dr Robert

Willis,[1] who, *as being of the College*, attends your Majesty as a regular physician. This caution cannot be extreme, even if it be unnecessary, in a matter of such high importance. It will be altogether for your Majesty's own gracious consideration to decide whether you will command, & in what degree, occasional visits from both or either of the other gentlemen of that name.[2] As to inferior persons who were employed in this service, when yr Majesty was indisposed, God grant, and I have an humble confidence in His Providence that he will grant it to me, ever to say, what I now humbly, dutifully and anxiously state to your Majesty, that I should betray my duty to you if I did not, under the permission you gave me, express my conviction that the most mischievous thing possible would be that, for any reason whatever, any of them should be about your Majesty's sacred person. They are all necessarily taken from situations & occupations in life which render it wholly unfit that they should be in stations of such high & delicate trust & honour. But, if they were of the highest character, your Majesty will feel that the attendance of any one or more of them must occasion suspicions about your Majesty's health which, God be thanked, there is no ground to entertain, and un-easiness in the minds of your people, when, God be thanked, they have occasion in your Majesty's health for joy & exultation. Under such suspicions & such un-easiness, both unnecessary, it is too obvious that your Majesty's Government would be weakened. It is, therefore, under a sense of imperious duty that I have presumed to trouble your Majesty as to this point. Your Majesty's gracious nature cannot admit that you should be without intentions of kindness to these people, & other means may be found of most liberally indulging that kindness. It has occurred to the Chancellor to mention this topic to your Majesty from having heard that there are those who judge of what most concerns your Majesty's interest and honour by the inferences which they draw from facts of this kind.

The Lord Chancellor now throws himself most humbly at your Majesty's feet, praying that, when he shall have the honour of seeing your Majesty on Wednesday, you will graciously condescend to intimate that you can, & do, pardon what has past, and the additional presumption, of which he is now guilty: he has unburthened his mind, and, acting from a conviction of duty, he can submit chearfully to any consequences but your Majesty's displeasure. May God Almighty preserve your Majesty in that health which He has restored. May He continue to your illustrious & beloved family the blessing they enjoy in the restoration of it— and may He prolong to the great family of your people, dutifully, loyally & cordially attached as He knows them to be to your Majesty, a security in the enjoyment of that health by yr. Majesty for the continuance of those blessings which they have derived from your parental attention, and from that example which has diffused amongst them those principles of morality & religion, without which a people cannot be great or happy![3] (10249–52)

[1] Robert Darling Willis (1760–1821), one of Francis Willis's five sons by his first wife.
[2] Dr Francis Willis (1718–1807) and his son Dr John Willis (1751–1835), who now attended the King, as in 1788–9. (Twiss, *Eldon*, I, 376.)
[3] The King's reply on the 21st is in Twiss, I, 382. He refused to have Dr Robert Willis about him. 'The line of practice followed with great credit by that gentleman renders it incompatible with the King's feelings that he should, now by the goodness of Divine Providence restored to reason,

[*Ham Common, 21 June 1801, 4.30 p.m.*] Lord Hobart presents his humble duty to your Majesty and begs leave to acquaint you that at a meeting of your Majesty's confidential servants it has been determined to recommend to your Majesty that a detachment of one thousand Infantry and about fifty Artillery should be immediately sent to the Island of Madeira.

The situation of Portugal with regard to France has excited a strong apprehension that either by force or artifice the enemy may endeavour to obtain possession of that valuable island, and as in that case property to a very large amount belonging to your Majesty's subjects wou'd in all probability be confiscated, it is judg'd advisable without loss of time to embark the propos'd force for that place with a view to prevent so serious a mischief—as well as to deprive the enemy of those means of annoying the trade of your Majesty's dominions which wou'd be the inevitable consequence of Madeira's falling into their hands.

It is not intended that force shou'd be resorted to for the purpose of introducing your Majesty's troops into the island—and therefore much difficulty may occur in effecting the object—but it is imagin'd that by selecting an officer for this service upon whose firmness and address a well-founded confidence can be plac'd, the most sanguine expectation of success may be entertained.

Under this impression, from a thorough knowledge of the character and talents of Colonel Fullarton, Lord Hobart humbly takes the liberty of submitting his name to your Majesty. (10253–4)

[*The King's reply, Kew, 21 June.*] The King has just received Lord Hobart's letter informing him of the proposal that one thousand infantry and fifty artillery be sent to the island of Madeira. His Majesty authorises Lord Hobart to consult the Duke of York as to the best mode of collecting this force and as to the person that on mature consideration may be thought most eligible for the command, he should doubt whether some difficulties might not arise in giving the command to a temporary officer. (Bucks. R.O.)

[*From Lord Hobart, Ham Common, 21 June, 10 p.m.*] Lord Hobart presents his humble duty to your Majesty and begs leave to acquaint your Majesty that he this morning paid his respects to the Duke of York at Oatlands for the purpose of communicating with his Royal Highness upon the subject of the propos'd detachment for Madeira.

That Lord Hobart intimated to his Royal Highness his intention of submitting to your Majesty the name of Colonel Fullarton as an officer peculiarly qualified for the command of that detachment—and that his Royal Highness having suggested an objection to Colonel Fullarton upon the ground of there being a

consult a person of that description. His Majesty...cannot bear the idea of consulting any of the Willis family.'

Eldon, who was wondering whether he should be able to attend a Council meeting at Weymouth 'respecting the change of Secretary of State', had not found time to attend a Cabinet meeting on the 16th.

difficulty in recommending to your Majesty that he shou'd have a special commission for the purpose of that command, on account of the particular circumstances under which he holds the rank of Colonel in your Majesty's service, it was conceiv'd that the difficulty might be remov'd by a small detachment from Colonel Fullarton's Regiment being order'd upon the service in question—and the Duke of York being pleas'd to agree with Lord Hobart that such an arrangement might be calculated to obviate the objection, intimated his intention of issuing orders accordingly.

Lord Hobart has with great deference to submit to your Majesty that the object in view wou'd seem to require that some step shou'd immediately be taken, and that he humbly waits your Majesty's commands.

Lord Hobart has been honour'd with your Majesty's commands of this day's date. (10255–6)

[*The King's reply, Kew, 22 June.*] The King does not mean to negative the nomination of Colonel Fullarton to the command at the Madeira, but should not have thought he shewed a proper attention to his military service had he not suggested that perhaps a regular officer might have been more desirable, as certainly more congenial to the feelings of the whole profession; but as the Duke of York seems to think the addition of a few of Colonel Fullarton's men may in some degree alleviate difficulties the King will not object to the appointment of Colonel Fullarton for the expedition to Madeira, but hopes in future Lord Hobart will avoid what cannot be agreeable to the profession he formerly belonged [*sic*]. (Bucks. R.O.)

2453   LADY ANNE HORATIA SEYMOUR[1] *to the* KING

[*Clifton, 22 June 1801.*] When I think of my presumption in adressing your Majesty I can scarcely hold my pen—but let me humbly request my situation will plead my excuse, with that excellent heart which your Majesty possesses, as it is written by a person to whom Providence has preserv'd for three years in a wonderful way—but I have relaps'd, and I do not feel I can now last. When I left Jamaica Lord Hugh Seymour said, 'that Providence which has preserv'd you hitherto will I am confident make the voyage recover you—and then being restor'd to six of your children. If not, go to Bristol, and that you like the idea of. If you recover I have no wish to form but for the happiness of my children—and here my ambition steps in, and I own if I could but *distinguish* myself in my *profession*—and that the King would make me an English peer I should be truly gratified.' Unless Gantheaume[2] should be coming here there is no chance of that. At the same time he feels most sensibly your Majesty's *goodness* in giving him,

---

[1] Lady Anne Horatia Waldegrave (1762–1801) daughter of the 2nd Earl Waldegrave, married (1786) Hugh Seymour-Conway (who dropped his father's additional surname of Conway after his father's death in 1794.) He died at sea, on board the *Tisiphone*, whither he had been ordered by his physicians for the benefit of his health, on 12 Sept. 1801, whilst commanding the Fleet on the Jamaica station. She died, at Bristol, on 11 or 12 Sept. 1801, leaving six children, of whom the youngest, Mary Seymour, was born in 1798. A seventh child, a son, had recently predeceased his parents.

[2] The French Vice-Admiral.

(so young an Admiral) such an appointment. Altho' he has not been fortunate may I petition her Majesty to join me in begging forgiveness of your Majesty, but I do think if your Majesties could see the object I am [*sic*], your Majesties would forgive me for thinking of Ld. Hugh's last speech to me almost. May God ever preserve your Majesty is the constant prayer of [etc.]. I have been held up to write. (10261–2)

2454   LORD HOBART *to the* KING, *and the reply*

[*Grosvenor Place, 22 June 1801, 10 p.m.*] Lord Hobart presents his humble duty to your Majesty and begs leave to offer his gratefull acknowledgments to your Majesty for your having been pleas'd to acquiesce in his recommendation of Colonel Fullarton, and at the same requests permission to be allow'd to submit to your Majesty the reasons which induc'd him to believe that such a nomination wou'd not have been objectionable in a military point of view. Lord Hobart had understood that Colonel Fullarton had commanded an army in India during the years 1783 and 1784, and that he had receiv'd the most honorable testimonies of approbation from Lord Macartney under whose Government he then serv'd.

Lord Hobart had also been inform'd that Colonel Fullarton had been selected in the year 1796 for the chief command of the land forces upon an expedition which it was at that time in contemplation to send to Spanish America under Lord Hugh Seymour.

These circumstances connected with the knowledge Lord Hobart had of the address and conciliatory manners of Colonel Fullarton, had led him to think that he was well calculated to succeed in the very critical and important service upon which it was propos'd to employ him.

Lord Hobart, having thus ventur'd to explain to your Majesty the motives which actuated his conduct, wou'd not discharge his official duty in the manner which he feels it incumbent upon him to perform it, if, now he is appriz'd of your Majesty's sentiments upon the subject, he did not humbly solicit your Majesty to be permitted to withdraw the name of Colonel Fullarton and to be authoriz'd by your Majesty to mention Colonel Clinton to his Royal Highness the Duke of York for the command of the detachment under orders for Madeira. (10259–60)

[*The King's reply, Kew, 23 June.*] The King fully enters into the grounds on which Lord Hobart in the first instance turned his thoughts towards Colonel Fullarton, and is pleased with the candid manner with which Lord Hobart has now stated them; his Majesty most cordially consents to Colonel Clinton being now proposed as the commander of the expedition to Madeira, both the brothers are men of uncommon abilities and are well respected in their profession. (Bucks. R.O.)

2455   J. MARTYN *to* [?   ]

[*Greenwich, 23 June 1801.*] In answer to your favour of the 17th inst. (which I beg to apologize for not having sooner noticed) I have to inform you that the house at this place occupied by the Princess *of Wales* (not the Princess Royal) is not the property of Dr. Robertson, but that of his Grace the Duke of Buccleugh. The house now occupied by Lord Lewisham at Blackheath was about three years ago used as a residence for the Princess *Charlotte* of Wales. The late Dr. Robertson formerly held a lease of this house under the Earl of Dartmouth,[1] but about a year before his death he disposed of his interest in it, to Lord Lewisham. We never were concerned for Dr. Robertson in his lifetime, nor are we now for his representatives. (10263)

2456 THE KING *to* HENRY ADDINGTON, *and two replies*

[*Kew, 23 June 1801.*] The King thinks it right to inform Mr. Addington that he shall be at the Queen's Palace tomorrow to knight two Judges going to the East Indies.[2] He shall therefore hope to see Mr. Addington there at one, and then if possible to learn the Duke of Portland's decision of accepting the high office of President of the Council, which may very properly take effect in Council that day, and Lord Pelham[3] receive the Seals of the Home Department. (Sidmouth MSS.)

[1] The 2nd Earl of Dartmouth, Lord Lewisham's father, died on 15 July at Blackheath.

[2] Only Codrington Edmund Carrington, Chief Justice of the Supreme Court of Judicature of Ceylon was knighted on the 24th. So, however, were John Royds and Henry Gwillim on the 30th, before going to Calcutta as Judges of the Supreme Court; and Benjamin Sullivan, a Judge of the Supreme Court at Madras.

[3] Thomas Pelham, who in February had twice been urged to take a Cabinet office, had just been summoned to the House of Lords, on his father's elevation to the Earldom of Chichester, in his father's Barony, as Lord Pelham. He had evidently refused an offer of a temporary diplomatic appointment; Lord Hawkesbury had written to him on 17 April: 'Addington informs me that he mentioned to you before you left town how desirous we both of us were that you should go to Petersburgh at the present moment, for the purpose of congratulating the new Emperor and of endeavouring to renew the connection between the two countries. The subject has been mentioned to his Majesty this morning; his only objection to you was, that your rank was not sufficient, but he immediately said that he would remove that objection, by creating you a Peer for the purpose. It is of essential consequence that the person who is appointed to this important mission should go without delay. If you feel therefore inclined to accept it, I am convinced you will think it right to come to town immediately & to make your preparations for departure. Instructions have been sent this morning to Sir Hyde Parker to suspend all hostilities against Russia, & I have written to Count Pahlen in answer to the letter I received from him, to say that a proper person would be sent immediately to congratulate the Emperor on his accession.' (B.M., Add. MSS. 33107, f. 31.)

His friend William Elliot advised him (18 April) to insist on his being appointed Secretary of State before going to Russia: 'When Lord Spencer went to Vienna, he retained his seat in the Cabinet, and your mission would be very much of the same nature. Should it be urged that the presence of one of the Secretaries of State cannot at this juncture be dispensed with, that would of itself be a conclusive objection to your undertaking the mission. Many other persons are to be found, who are well qualified for it, and you must feel that you can render your country more essential service by remaining at home in considerable power, than by going abroad without power. In truth it is to you alone that one can look for the infusion of any thing good into the present Councils. Depend on it there is a very ardent wish to have you in the Cabinet, and if you suffer yourself to be banished without the actual possession of a place in it, many plausible reasons will be assigned for protracting your exile, and in the interval the Government may acquire such a degree of stability and strength as may enable it to oppose obstacles to your even ultimately obtaining that situation which was the express condition of your connexion with it. I trust therefore you will come to town armed with a firmness on this topick *not to be shaken*. I well know how reluctant you are to press *personal* points, but remember that in this case you will, by insisting to be put into the situation in which the country expects to see you placed, be acting not so much on a principle of justice to yourself as of indispensable duty to the publick...' (Add. MSS. 33107, f. 39.)

When Lord Hobart heard that Pelham was to be called up to the House of Lords he began wondering

[From Addington, Downing Street, 23 June, 10 p.m.] With your Majesty's gracious permission, Lord Arden will pay his duty tomorrow at the Queen's House, and humbly submit to your Majesty a design for the new gold coin, adapted to the Union between Great Britain and Ireland.

Mr. Addington will not fail to obey your Majesty's commands a little before one o'clock tomorrow, when he hopes to lay before your Majesty some information which he trusts will prove satisfactory respecting the proposed arrangements in your Majesty's Government.[1] (10264)

[From Addington, Downing Street, 25 June, 11.15 p.m.] Mr. Addington humbly desires to receive your Majesty's commands respecting the time of holding a Council previous to your Majesty's removal to Weymouth. If it should be your Majesty's pleasure that it should take place tomorrow, Mr. Addington will cause directions to be given for convening it at the hour which your Majesty may appoint, but he ventures to add that a delay till Saturday would be attended with the probability of such steps being taken as would remove the impediments which have deferred the completion of the remaining arrangements in your Majesty's Government. (10265)

[From the King, Kew, 26 July [June].] The King finds by Mr. Addington's note that it will be convenient he shall hold a Council previous to going to Weymouth, and that it will be advantageous it be not held till Saturday. His Majesty will therefore be at the Queen's Palace at half hour past one that day to receive Mr. Addington, and desires the Council may be assembled by two o'clock, when he hopes Mr. Addington will have arranged what he alludes to, though the Duke of Portland with every expression of good humour as well as attachment seemed to think till late in the autumn it would be impossible to conclude the business.[2]
P.S. Since writing the above an application is come from the Recorder for his making another Report. The King desires Mr. Addington will acquaint the Lord Chancellor that it will be made immediately tomorrow after the Privy Council. (Sidmouth MSS.)

how his own position would be affected. 'The management of the House of Lords is the question. Should I leave it to Pelham or should I assume that I am to have it, which you know would be a tolerably laborious task?...The danger from this other Secretary of State is a possible clashing between us on some future arrangement. Should that be out of the question I should most heartily rejoice in it.' (Add. MSS. 34455, f. 419.)

[1] The King's brief reply on the 24th, expressing satisfaction with the contents of Addington's letter, is in Pellew, I, 410. A note from the King to Eldon on the 23rd is in Twiss, I, 383.

[2] On 11 June the Duke of Portland wrote a remarkable letter to Pelham, which helps to account for the delay in effecting this change: 'It is so painful to me to write upon what must make the subject of this letter that I have abstained from it as long as I could entertain an hope of your calling here, & I should have acquiesced probably in your wishes, & have abstained from writing altogether, could I reconcile it to the motives which have ever influenced my conduct towards you, & which I am convinced operate as strongly in prompting me to urge you to reconsider the opinion which you communicated to me yesterday & to accede to the proposal I submitted to you the other day as they did in the preference which I consider your services to the publick entitled to over those I can render it, & as they did at the time of the offer I made of relinquishing the employment I hold in your favor—It cannot be a question but that it must be the first wish of a Minister, & little less than his duty, to be as well as he can make himself with the Prince he serves, & equally not to force himself into a situation against the inclination

[*Park Place, Friday, 26 June 1801.*] (Private.) As I understand any farther delay in Mr Cooke's return to Ireland[1] would be attended with inconvenience, and as he cannot well venture to go back till he is enabled to settle the secret account on which we have had occasion to converse, I have thought it best to send you a written statement of the circumstances relative to it. It appears in the course of last autumn that there had occurred a saving on different articles in the Irish Civil List, which left a sum disposeable by the Lord Lieutenant with his Majesty's approbation to the amount of £18,000. This sum it was proposed to apply to a very important and pressing purpose which was then explained to his Majesty and which he was pleased to approve; and as the best mode of doing so, the sum was directed to be paid over to his Majesty's Privy Purse, it being understood to be his Majesty's gracious intention that it should afterwards be paid into the hands of Mr King, the Under-Secretary of State, or of Lord Castlereagh or Mr Cooke.

The money has under these circumstances been expended by the Irish Govern-

of his Sovereign. It therefore is necessary that you should know that on my first opening to the King the change of my situation, he interrupted me by saying that the most agreeable thing I could do to him would be to retain the employment I hold; that he had taken every opportunity & means of manifesting that sentiment to me since the idea of a change had first been mentioned to him. On my stating to him the objections which had occurred to you, he observed that the buying a man off by giving him less than he expected to have was a mode of purchase quite new, & what you certainly had not learnt in Ireland, but could not certainly be to any one's discredit who so disposed of himself, & that as for first & last there was no difference in the Cabinet, that all those who sat there were upon an equality & consequently that no change of office could in that respect affect the importance or character of those who composed it, which he illustrated by asking whether any man would think less highly of Ld. Chatham when he was Master-General of the Ordnance than now that he is President. Upon my telling him that if such was his opinion upon the point of honor or delicacy I would venture to submit to him the arrangement I had thought of. He expressed the highest approbation of it, said it was what Lord Liverpool must *jump* at & such an one as would place you in as respectable a situation as you could fill, & give you as much business as you liked, but upon that I do not know that he added anything that I have not before stated to you respecting it. But since I returned from Kew a circumstance has been represented to me by King at the instance of old Pollock & which I did not fully comprehend until yesterday afternoon, which makes me more particularly anxious for the consideration which I have pressed upon you, & for your revoking the determination you are inclined to come to, because with every disposition your friend thinks you entitled to experience on my part in putting you in possession of the Seals, the time of my doing it cannot but be indefinite, & would be impracticable at present unless I could advance between £20,000 & £30,000 at least out of my own pocket & wait for events & circumstances to reimburse me, which may be nine, twelve or eighteen months in taking place, & for which, although as you may believe not a sixpence has remained with me, I am answerable for & is a risk I must have been exposed to had any change of Administration taken place which had removed me from my present office. But this...if you see King will be explained to you in such a manner as will not admit of a doubt & will not I hope at such a crisis as this & under the circumstances which impelled you to offer to take a part in the present Government suffer you to withhold your services until a specifick employment can be opened for you, by waiting for which you must allow me to say that I am clearly of opinion that you would expose your-self much more obviously to animadversion than you would be subjected to by the acceptance of any situation whatever that gives you a seat in the Cabinet...' (Add. MSS. 33107, f. 75.)

Charles Yorke, the Secretary at War, wrote, 29 June: '*The Duke of P.* did *not* resign the Seals at the Council on Saturday, tho' Pelham went on purpose to take them. It is adjourned for ten days to be performed at Weymouth' (Add. MSS. 37511, f. 61). Few people had any idea of the cause of the extra-ordinary delay. 'Surely his Grace must have a great arrear of bottoms to wind up', suggested Cresset Pelham. (Add. MSS. 33107, f. 125.)

[1] 'Cooke', wrote Abbot, 'dissatisfied with his situation under a Lord Lieutenant and Secretary, whose confidence he forfeited by his insolent language and froward manner, withdrew himself in October by desiring to resign upon a sinecure office and pension' (*Colchester Diary*, I, 279).

ment, who borrowed it from a Fund to which they are indispensably bound to replace it but which they have no means of doing but by his Majesty's being graciously pleased to give effect to what I conceived to be his Majesty's intentions. I hope when these circumstances are submitted to his Majesty they will sufficiently explain the nature of the transaction. (10266–7)

2458 LORD HAWKESBURY *to the* KING

[*London, 29 June 1801.*] Lord Hawkesbury would not have intruded upon your Majesty's time at present, but he could not resist the satisfaction of informing your Majesty that the attack upon Rhamanie had been attended with compleat success, and that the loss on the part of your Majesty's forces had been very inconsiderable.

The two mails which were received in the course of the night bring no other intelligence of any importance. (10268)

2459 THE DUKE OF PORTLAND *to the* KING

[*Burlington House, Tuesday, 30 June 1801, 9.20 p.m.*] The Duke of Portland most humbly begs leave to acquaint your Majesty that in consequence of the necessity which has been represented to your Majesty of obtaining your Majesty's Order-in-Council for the prorogation of the Parliament, the Duke of Portland, Lord Glenbervie,[1] Mr. Vice-Chamberlain[2] & Mr. Corry will attend your Majesty's orders tomorrow at Cufnells at so early an hour in the afternoon as to constitute a Council, if it shall be your Majesty's pleasure, in the course of it, so as that the Commission may be returned in time sufficient the next day for proroguing the Parliament. Every means will be taken to procure the attendance of two other Privy Councillors, but the Duke of Portland entreats & ventures to flatter himself that your Majesty's goodness will dispose your Majesty to forgive his presumption in observing to your Majesty that it has been suggested to him that his Royal Highness the Duke of Cumberland is at Southampton.[3] (10269–70)

[1] He had succeeded Canning as Joint Paymaster-General. He wrote, 2 April: 'I spent two hours yesterday at the Pay Office. It is a very complicated machine and I shall find it difficult, with all the assistance Steele and the other officers may give me, to understand it. In the hands of Steele it has been almost the second Finance Office in the State, and I fancy between Pitt and the Treasury, and the Pay Office, much accommodation has taken place during the war, which, though very honest, has not been strictly regular nor very justifiable. Query, if the execution of the law as to strict appropriations is either practicable or advisable' (MS. Diary). Cp. Portland's awkward situation with regard to public balances in his private possession (No. 2456) and Canning's equally embarrassing situation on the eve of his duel with Castlereagh in 1809.

Lord Minto wrote (11 Dec. 1801): 'Lord Glenbervie has told me that he was offered the President-ship of the Board of Control, and he seems to have declined it because it was not to be a Cabinet office as before. He says, indeed, besides, that his present place is better in point of income and house, and he thinks it may outlive a change better.' (Minto MSS.)   [2] Charles Francis Greville (1749–1809).

[3] On Monday, 29 June, the royal family set off from Kew at 6 a.m. for Weymouth, breaking their journey at Cuffnells, George Rose's seat near Lyndhurst, where they arrived about nine hours later. Rose found the royal visit a nerve-racking experience (Twiss, 1, 386). On Friday, 3 July, they embarked on the royal yacht which was anchored in the bay opposite Rose's cottage near Christchurch, some distance from Cuffnells, being received there by the Christchurch Volunteers. They arrived at Weymouth after midnight, being delayed in their voyage by a fresh breeze from the west. Then they proceeded to Gloucester Lodge.

[*Tuesday evening, 30 June 1801, 11 p.m.*] The Lord Chancellor, offering his most humble duty to your Majesty, has the honour to transmit a Commission for pro- roguing the Parliament to be signed in the usual manner with your Majesty's Royal Sign Manual, if your Majesty shall graciously so think fit, after your Majesty shall have been pleased to make an Order-in-Council that the Parliament shall be prorogued. The Lord Chancellor has also the honour of sending to your Majesty a Commission for passing Bills, which are ready to receive your Majesty's Royal Assent, if your Majesty is pleased to approve them. He transmits also the titles of the Bills, which, in general, express their contents or the substance of their contents, and he is not aware that his duty to your Majesty requires that he should give your Majesty the trouble of more particularly stating the effect of any of them.

He cannot conclude this without expressing the heartfelt satisfaction which he enjoyed when he had last the honour of being admitted to your Majesty's presence, from perceiving in your Majesty's compleatly restored health the blessings which have resulted from your Majesty's condescending to be your own physician: a satisfaction so great that he could not have resisted his wishes to offer in person the papers which he transmits for your Majesty's Royal Sign Manual if he did not know that your Majesty would more approve his attending his duty in administer- ing your Majesty's justice in Court to your subjects.[1] (10271–2)

2461   HENRY ADDINGTON *to the* KING, *and the reply*

[*Wimbledon, 30 June 1801, 10 p.m.*] Mr. Addington most humbly informs your Majesty that in consequence of an accidental omission at the Queen's House on Friday last, it is very material that a Council should be held without delay for the purpose of receiving your Majesty's commands respecting the prorogation of Parliament. The Duke of Portland, and some other members of the Privy Council, accordingly intend to proceed to Cuffnalls to-morrow to learn your Majesty's pleasure on this subject. Mr. Addington herewith transmits to your Majesty a paper of the contents of which he earnestly hopes that your Majesty will not disapprove; and he has only further to express his regret that any circumstance should have arisen to break in upon your Majesty's convenience during your residence in Cuffnalls. (10273)

[*The King's reply, Cuffnals, 1 July 1801, 9.50 a.m.*][2] The King has received Mr. Addington's box as he was going out on horseback for Southampton. He had this morning from the D. of Portland an account of the omission on Saturday which

---

[1] The King's brief reply, from Cuffnells next day, is in Jesse, *Memoirs of the Life and Reign of George III*, III, 288. He said he was daily improving in strength, sleeping better, and doing without Dr Gis- borne's medicine.

[2] A garbled version of the King's letter to Addington, dated Cuffnals, 3 July, is in Pellew, I, 427. 'The King cannot leave this place without entrusting the senior messenger with a line, to be left in Downing Street, for his Chancellor of the Exchequer, to acquaint him that the gentle exercise, new objects of admiration which this country affords, and the real comfort and hospitality of this place, has been

occasioned the necessity of holding a Privy Council here this afternoon.[1] His Majesty will certainly return in time for that purpose. The King highly approves of the sentiments and language of the Speech on the close tomorrow of the Session, as he thinks it equally calculated to support the national character abroad as well as at home. All are doing well here, Sophia had yesterday one of her cramps in the stomach but is now greatly releaved and will be able to proceed on Friday for Weymouth. (Sidmouth MSS.)

2462   THE SUPREME BOARD OF COMMISSIONERS FOR THE AFFAIRS OF THE ROYAL MILITARY COLLEGE *to the* KING

[*Horse Guards, 1 July 1801.*] Present: His Royal Highness the Duke of York, Commander in Chief; Right Honorable Charles Yorke, Secretary at War; Honorable General Harcourt; Lieutenant-General David Dundas, Quarter Master-General; Lieutenant-General Lord Cathcart; and Colonel Calvert, Adjutant-General.

Your Majesty's warrant, bearing date the 24th June 1801, was read, constituting and appointing Commissioners for the affairs of the Royal Military College.

In pursuance of your Majesty's said warrant, the Commissioners present having formed a Supreme Board, proceeded to examine the several papers and documents produced to them by Lieutenant-Colonel Le Marchant,[2] Superintendant of the Military Institution at High Wycombe, and having considered the matters before them with the attention due to the importance of the objects confided to their direction, the Supreme Board do now most humbly propose, for your Majesty's Royal approbation, that Lieutenant-Colonel Le Marchant be appointed Lieutenant-Governor and Superintendant General of the Royal Military College.

That that part of the Royal Military College intended to be called the First or Senior Department, be forthwith established and called into operation, and that General Jarry be appointed the Commandant thereof.

That the Officers, Professors and Masters now employed at High Wycombe be considered as transferred for the present to the establishment of the Royal Military College and be accordingly authorized to act in their several capacities with the pay and salaries affixed to their respective names in the schedule hereunto annexed.

beneficial to the healths of all the party. Princess Sophia's spasm has proved shorter than on former occasion[s], and she is able to proceed to Christchurch where the yachts are waiting to convey the whole family to Weymouth. If the wind remains as at present, it will be reached in four or five hours.' (Sidmouth MSS.)

[1] 'The Council', wrote Glenbervie (3 July), 'having been suffered to pass last week without the King having signed a commission to prorogue it [Parliament, that is], it was necessary that a Council should be held at Cuffnells on Wednesday for that purpose, and Addington having sent Lord Hobart to desire that I would make one to go there, I went with Mr. Corry, and we, together with the Duke of Portland (who is still Secretary of State), the Duke of Cumberland, Lord Harrington and Mr. Charles Greville constituted the Council.'

The King had originally intended to break his journey for a day or two at Dogmersfield Park, Winchfield, Hants. (Sir Henry Mildmay's seat), but, declared Glenbervie, 'Rose had said he should be much mortified if, having himself a house much more conveniently situated, his Majesty should not honour him by using it' (*Glenbervie Journals*, I, 234–5).

[2] John Gaspard Le Marchant (1766–1812). Ensign, 1781; Major, 1795; Lieutenant-Colonel, 1797; Colonel, 1805; Major-General, 1810; mortally wounded at Salamanca.

The Supreme Board do further submit to your Majesty the expediency of immediately appointing a Treasurer and a Secretary for the affairs of the Royal Military College, and in case your Majesty shall be pleased to approve thereof, they do most humbly recommend Charles Greenwood,[1] Esqre., to be the Treasurer, and Lieutenant-Colonel McKenzie,[2] Assistant Barrack Master-General, to be the Secretary.

Your Majesty's Commissioners, in obedience to your Majesty's commands expressed in the said warrant, will next proceed with all possible diligence to prepare and submit for your Majesty's approbation and authority such rules and orders as may be necessary for the conduct and good government of the said First Department of the Royal Military College. [*Signed*] Frederick, C. in C., Wm. Harcourt, General, C.Yorke, D. Dundas, Harry Calvert, A.G., Cathcart, Lt.-Gen.[3] (10275–6)

2463 THE DUKE OF YORK *to the* KING

[*Oatlands, 4 July 1801.*] I have the honor to transmit to your Majesty the usual weekly states, together with the monthly return of quarters, from the Quarter

[1] The well-known army agent and friend of the Duke of York and the Prince of Wales. (*c.* 1747–1832.) He died at the Pavilion, Brighton, in the arms of Sir Herbert Taylor, after having dined and played cards with the King. 'To the undeviating confidence of the Duke of York he was indebted for a great part of his very extensive business. He was always the judicious counsellor and able advocate of officers whose want of family influence seemed to be at a loss for an easy and unembarrassed medium of communication with the Commander-in-Chief...He was also a great favourite with George IV, and much noticed by his present Majesty [William IV], but the estimation of royalty never inflated his mind; few men have been more unassuming, and few have so completely applied themselves to acts of disinterested kindness and practical philanthropy' (*Gent. Mag.*, 1832, I, 650). Greenwood's great-aunt Mary had married the son of Richard Cox, who founded (1758) the first English Army Agency under the name of Cox and Co., of which firm Greenwood, his cousin, became a partner in 1770 on leaving Cambridge, and remained the chief manager for sixty-one years. It is said that when the Duke of York introduced him to the King as 'the gentleman who keeps my money', Greenwood remarked, 'I think it is rather his Royal Highness who keeps my money'. This remark, which delighted the King, was actually true, for the large advances made to the Duke of York were not repaid until long after the Duke's death in 1827. Greenwood's appointment was gazetted on 29 Aug.

[2] Lieutenant-Colonel Frederick Mackenzie. Lieutenant-Colonel, 1799.

[3] The following Schedule is annexed to the Report:

Lieutenant-Colonel J. G. Le Marchant as Lieutenant-Governor and Superintendant-General,	at 40s. p. diem for 365 days	£730 : –
Ditto, with a Clerk	1s. p. diem	18 : 5
		748 : 5 : –
Charles Greenwood, Esqr. as Treasurer and Agent		300 : – : –
Lieutenant-Colonel McKenzie as Secretary to the Supreme Board for the affairs of the College p. annum		200 : – : –
General Jarry, as Commandant of the Senior Department		790 : 9 : 7
Mr. Dalby, as Professor of Mathematicks		250 : – : –
Mr. Dowson, Senior Draftsman		200 : – : –
Chevalier St. Dennis, Master of Fortification		200 : – : –
Mr. Stephens, Assistant Draftsman		100 : – : –
Baron D'Agrain, French Instructor		100 : – : –
Revd. Mr. Ghebart, German Instructor		100 : – : –
Mr. William Bennett, as Acting Adjutant		80 : – : –

(10274) [*sic*] £2,768 :14 : 7

Master-General, as likewise the recommendations for vacant commissions which have been received this week for your Majesty's approbation.

I have little to report to your Majesty this week except the arrival of the 45th Regiment, and of a detachment of the 70th from the West Indies. Both these corps are perfect skeletons having, as usual, allowed such men as chose to turn out volunteers to inlist into the Regiments remaining in the West Indies. As there is a very strong detachment of the 70th in Jersey, I beg leave to recommend that the part of that corps returned from the West Indies be ordered there to join it, and that the 45th Regiment which is ordered to recruit boys be stationed at Chatham.

I was rejoiced to hear that your Majesty had had so pleasant a journey to Cuffnalls and that you have been pleased with your stay there, and I trust that we shall have as good accounts of your Majesty's passage and safe arrival at Weymouth. (10277)

2464   SIR HENRY STRACHEY[1] *to the* KING

[*Hill Street, 5 July 1801.*] Altho' it appears that a considerable saving will arise from the new arrangement which your Majesty hath been pleased to command for the Royal Gardens at Windsor, and for the Queen's Garden in town, Sir Henry Strachey is apprehensive that the amount of saving will not completely defray the expence of your Majesty's Botanic Garden, on account of the constant employment of laborers there, and the necessary consumption of coals and tan, which are always at high prices. He finds that the Botanic Garden, upon a fair average of the last four years, has cost your Majesty £1,070 pr. annum.

Your Majesty will be pleased to determine, whether, in order to reduce the expence to a certainty, Mr. Aiton shall have a contract for that sum, to be paid nett, in the ordinary course of the Household Establishment, or whether he shall be paid his bill of expences, quarterly, by disbursements, at the Board of Green Cloth; the bills being previously examined and passed by the Master of Your Majesty's Household.

Sir Henry Strachey, most humbly presumes also, to submit to your Majesty's consideration, the short matter of the enclosed paper, as he is anxious to forward the preparation of the contracts, according to your Majesty's instructions of the 30th May last; and that the whole arrangement may take place at Michaelmas next, conformably to your Majesty's most gracious note of the 27th of June. (10278)

2465   THE DUKE OF PORTLAND *to the* KING

[*Whitehall, Sunday, 5 July 1801, 1.50 p.m.*] The Duke of Portland humbly conceives it to be his duty, in laying before your Majesty the warrants herewith submitted to your Majesty for your royal signature, to represent to your Majesty that they comprise the grants of those Baronetages *only* which your Majesty had

[1] M.P. for Pontefract, 1768–74; for Bishop's Castle, 1774–8, 1780–2; for Saltash, 1778–80; for East Grinstead, 1802–7. (1737–1810.) Under-Secretary of State, Home Department, July 1782–April 1783; Clerk of Deliveries, Ordnance Department, April–Dec. 1783; Master of the King's Household, 1794–1810; Baronetcy, 15 June 1801.

graciously condescended to create at the instance of the Marquess Cornwallis antecedent to the Union, & were intended to have taken place prior to that event. By some accident however, with the particulars of which the Duke of Portland is not sufficiently acquainted to state them in detail to your Majesty, the official recommendations were not received from the Lord Lieutenant until the 20th of last January, when it was the opinion of your Majesty's late servants, considering the approaching *opening* of the Session, that it would be more adviseable to defer carrying your Majesty's gracious intentions into effect to a later period, & the concurrence of your Majesty's present servants in the same opinion, & that it might be desireable to wait for the conclusion of the Session, have occasioned the Duke of Portland to abstain hitherto from bringing this subject under your Majesty's consideration. But as the prorogation has now taken place, as the late Lord Lieutenant of Ireland has renewed his instances with the D. of Portland for the accomplishment of those wishes which the Duke of Portland has authorized him to encourage in this respect, & as the importunities of the gentlemen interested become daily more urgent, the Duke of Portland ventures with the utmost deference & humility to offer to your Majesty the warrants in question in the dutifull but anxious hope that they will receive the sanction of your Majesty's signature. The Duke of Portland humbly hopes your Majesty will forgive his presumption for expressing the joy with which he learnt your Majesty's safe arrival at Weymouth after being detained so much longer on board the yacht than he was led to expect. (10279–80)

2466   PRINCE ADOLPHUS *to the* KING

[*Weymouth, 5 July 1801.*] At the present moment where this country is threatened by an invasion from the ennemy I think it the duty of everyone who is attached to the good cause to come forward and offer his services to his Sovereign. It is for this reason that I venture to trouble your Majesty with these lines to assure you that I shall be proud of serving you in any way you should think fit. I must at the same time add that it is not at all my wish to remain in the British Service, but that being at the present moment in England and unemployed I thought it a duty to make you this proposal. I therefore dare hope that your Majesty will not take these lines amiss, and that you will look upon them as dictated by a heart overflowing with gratitude for all your goodness to me.[1] (48568)

2467   HENRY ADDINGTON *to the* KING, *and the reply*

[*Wimbledon, 6 July 1801, 10.30 p.m.*] Mr Addington could not be satisfied in forwarding the inclosed warrant, to which he humbly intreats your Majesty's signature, without offering his grateful acknowledgments for the satisfaction he received from the note with which your Majesty was pleased to honor him almost immediately previous to your departure from Cuffnall's. The safe arrival of your

---

[1] W. H. Fremantle, who saw Prince Adolphus at Weymouth, described him as 'a remarkable gentlemanlike amiable young man, uncommonly attentive and affectionate in his behaviour to the King' (Buckingham, *Court and Cabinets*, III, 173).

Majesty and the Royal family at Weymouth, and the favourable accounts since brought from thence, are also subjects of the utmost satisfaction to him.

Mr. Addington cannot forbear adding that he was indeed highly gratified by the approbation which your Majesty condescended to express, of the draft of the Speech delivered by the Lords Commissioners on Thursday last in the House of Lords. (10281)

[*The King's reply, Weymouth, 8 July.*] The King received Mr. Addington's box this morning; but the key having broke in opening that of the War Office yesterday, he has sent for a new one to Davis at Windsor, which cannot, at soonest, arrive before tomorrow, when his Majesty will answer its contents.

He is certain Mr. Addington will be pleased at hearing all the family here are now well. The King finds his sleep now perfect, but that it is necessary to avoid any hurry: even the event of the breaking the key gave more uneasiness than it ought, but the nerves certainly are regaining their proper tone, though not so quickly as wished, but probably as much so as can reasonably be expected. (Sidmouth MSS.)

2468 THE KING *to* LORD HOBART

[*Weymouth, 8 July 1801.*] The failure of the key yesterday is the cause of the box not being returned this day; the new one will probably arrive tomorrow, in which case the business will return to its former order. (Bucks. R.O.)

2469 THE KING *to* HENRY ADDINGTON

[*Weymouth, 9 July 1801, 4 p.m.*] The King has received the key from Davis and has instantly signed the warrant to be returned to Mr. Addington. He at the same time acquaints him with having for the second time bathed in the sea and found the usual mark of its agreeing, the glowing on coming out of the water. His Majesty has made one change this year, the getting on horseback the bathing days, instead of walking before breakfast, this seems also to agree.

The King trusts the messenger that returned from Cuffnalls agreable to order called at Winchester that Mr. Addington might hear of his son.[1] (Sidmouth MSS.)

2470 THE DUKE OF YORK *to the* KING

[*Horse Guards, 9 July 1801.*] I have the honor to send your Majesty the usual weekly and monthly returns of the army both in Great Britain and Ireland, together with the monthly report of the Irish Medical Board, and likewise to lay before your Majesty for your approbation the recommendations for vacant commissions which have been received this week.

---

[1] Henry Addington (1786–1823), his father's eldest son, who became a lunatic and tried to commit suicide in Oct. 1805. In July 1802 his father appointed him to the lucrative sinecure office of Clerk of the Pells in succession to Col. Barré, after it had been declined both by Pitt's friend, Thomas Steele, and by Pitt himself. (Stanhope, III, 385.) Pitt wrote to Addington, 29 July: 'I rejoice most sincerely that you have found it practicable to dispose of the Pells as you have done. Under all the circumstances it is infinitely preferable to any other use you could make of it.' (Pellew, I, 499 n.)

I have also the honor to report to your Majesty that in consequence of an account received from the Admiralty that a considerable number of gun and flat bottom'd boats had escaped out of Havre and were arrived at Boulogne I have thought it necessary to reinforce the Southern District and have therefore ordered the Brigade of Guards to march from Colchester, and to move ultimately to Chatham, from which point they will be ready to support either the coast of Kent or that of Essex. At present the barracks at Chatham requiring some repairs I am affraid that it will be impossible to procure more ground than will be necessary to encamp one batallion. If so I propose to encamp the Light Infantry batallion and to station the other two batallions of Guards at Chelmsford till Chatham Barracks are ready for their reception, which arrangement I trust will meet with your Majesty's approbation.

I must also add the arrival of the 55th Regiment from Guernsey, being relieved by the Dutch troops, this batallion is ordered to march to Lewes.

I am most sincerely rejoiced to learn from your Majesty's most gracious letter that your Majesty did not suffer from the unpleasant passage which you had from Christchurch to Weymouth, and I trust in God that your Majesty will feel the most beneficial effects from the sea bathing.[1] (10282-3)

2471 CHARLES YORKE to the KING

[*War Office, 9 July 1801.*] The Secretary at War had the honor of receiving your Majesty's note accompanying the warrants which had received the Royal signature. Presuming that the key which had been broken may have been replaced, the Secretary at War has ventured to make up another box of warrants for your Majesty's signature, which will complete the number of those which were in arrear. For the future, it will not be necessary to trouble your Majesty with so many; as the current business will be easily kept under.

Your Majesty will find the First Report of the Commissioners for the Royal Military College,[2] humbly submitting the establishment of the *Senior* Department; and the names of the Officers and Professors proposed to fill the situations in it. Upon your Majesty's gracious approbation being signified, the necessary steps will be taken accordingly. (10284)

2472 THE EARL OF ST VINCENT to the KING

[*Admiralty, 10 July 1801.*] Lord St. Vincent has the honor of sending to your Majesty the sentence and minutes of a court martial held a few days since at Portsmouth on two of the mutineers of the Hermione, and a correspondence which has taken place, in consequence, between the Secretary of the Admiralty[3] and the members of the Court.

Lord St. Vincent felt himself so much embarrass'd by the extraordinary conduct of the Court that he thought it right to consult the Lord Chancellor, as your Majesty will perceive by Lord St. Vincent's letter to his Lordship and his answer

---

[1] The King replied next day: 'The removal of the Brigade of Foot Guards from Chelmsford to Chatham is very proper, as Kent or Sussex are certainly more likely to be attacked this summer than Essex...' The letter was sold at Sotheby's on 28 July 1913.　　　[2] No. 2462.　　　[3] Nepean.

thereto, and on a due consideration of what his Lordship has stated, Lord St. Vincent begs leave humbly to submit to your Majesty whether it may not be adviseable to order the immediate execution of Powelson and to pardon Johnson, on condition of being transported for life. (10285)

2473 LORD HAWKESBURY to the KING

[*Downing Street, 11 July 1801.*] Lord Hawkesbury has the honour to send your Majesty the dispatches of Lord St Helens together with the copy of the Convention signed at St Petersburgh on the 17th of June.[1] Lord Hawkesbury humbly begs leave to offer to your Majesty his sincere congratulations on the successfull and creditable termination of this important business. The talents and experience of Lord St Helens have been eminently conspicuous in the progress of it, and Lord Hawkesbury ventures therefore to suggest to your Majesty the expediency of conferring the dignity of a peer of the United Kingdom on Lord St Helens for his essential services on this occasion.[2] (10286)

2474 *Letters from* HENRY ADDINGTON to the KING

[*Wimbledon, 11 July 1801.*] Mr. Addington is particularly thankful for the two notes with which your Majesty has been pleased to honor him, and is happy in indulging the hope that a speedy and complete renovation of strength will be the effect of the plan which your Majesty is now pursuing at Weymouth. He also humbly acknowledges your Majesty's great goodness in the communication made to his son, who has also mentioned it in terms of sensibility, and gratitude.

It is with extreme satisfaction that Mr. Addington informs your Majesty of the termination of the difficulties which have arisen respecting the offices of Secretary of State for Great Britain and Ireland, and that of President of the Council. The Duke of Portland has manifested upon this occasion, as upon every other, the utmost readiness to bend his feelings and wishes to the convenience of the public service, and to the important object of facilitating the arrangements of your Majesty's Government.[3] It seems to be material and requisite that the proposed distribution of the business of their respective offices should be notified to Lord Hobart and Lord Pelham as soon as the appointment of the latter has taken place;

---

[1] The signing of this Convention completed the reconciliation of Britain and Russia, and it formally defined the maritime rights of the neutral Powers.

[2] On 31 July Lord St Helens was created Baron St Helens of St Helens, Co. Southampton (a U.K. peerage). For the King's reply see Appendix.

[3] On 29 June Pelham told his friend Malmesbury of the 'extraordinary proceedings' on the previous Friday and Saturday (the 26th and 27th): '...I went to Addington on Friday morning with Lord Abergavenny upon some business of his, and Mr. Addington shewed me three letters from the King, written on Wednesday and Thursday, in which I was very glad to see that his Majesty expressed some impatience at the delay of my business, and it appeared that after surmounting all the Duke of Portland's difficulties it was at last determined that the Duke was to resign the Seals on the Saturday and that I was to receive them on the same day. On Friday night I received a note from Addington desiring to see me on Saturday before 12 o'clock. I confess I suspected some fresh difficulty, but on the contrary I found that all my share of the transaction was settled. I was desired to be at the Queen's House at ½ past one o'clock but it appeared that the Duke had some difficulty about taking the Presidentcy of the Council. Accordingly I went to the Queen's House and Mr. Addington told me that the Duke had completely made up his mind

and Mr. Addington ventures to submit to your Majesty the advantage that might arise, if the communication of your Majesty's pleasure was made in such a manner as to render it a matter of reference and record. This would prevent discussion at present, and all ambiguity and collision in future.[1] (10287–8)

[*Wimbledon, 12 July*] Mr. Addington humbly requests permission to offer to your Majesty his warmest congratulations on the satisfactory intelligence from Petersburgh. As your Majesty has been graciously pleased to declare your intention of conferring upon Lord St. Helens the dignity of a Peer of the United Kingdom on the successful termination of his mission Mr. Addington ventures to transmit a warrant to your Majesty for that purpose, being fully persuaded that it will not be less satisfactory to your Majesty to bestow an early mark of distinction on a service so meritorious and important as that performed by Lord St. Helens, than to his Lordship to receive such a proof of your Majesty's approbation and favor. (10289)

2475 LORD HAWKESBURY *to the* KING

[*Roehampton, 16 July 1801.*] Lord Hawkesbury has the honour to send your Majesty a Minute of Cabinet together with the Convention drawn up in the usual form for ratification.

Lord Hawkesbury has the honour to send your Majesty at the same time according to your command an answer to the letter of Monsieur announcing the arrival in London of the Prince of Condé for your Majesty's royal signature, if it shall meet with your approbation.[2] (10293)

[*Enclosure*]

Cabinet Minute [*Downing Street, 15 July 1801.*]

Present: The Lord Chancellor, The Lord Privy Seal, The Duke of Portland, The Earl of Chatham, The Earl of St Vincent, Lord Hobart, Mr Addington, Lord Hawkesbury.

to resign the Seals, but that he intended asking the King on what day it would be convenient for him to do so at Weymouth. I confess that I was a little vexed at this and said that I must insist upon seeing the King and explaining my conduct to him. Addington admitted the propriety of my demand and the King gave me a very long audience in which I stated the whole transaction from the beginning, and stated strongly to him, that I had made a great sacrifice of my private feelings to his wishes, in taking any share in an Administration which Lord Spencer, Lord Camden and Windham had left, and that nothing but an understanding that it was his Majesty's express desire that I should be in his councils would have induced me to take office; that I wished to be acquitted of any presumption in insisting upon the Seals or of any backwardness in serving his Majesty which the delay might give the appearance of; that I was very sorry to appear to be in competition with the Duke of Portland, but I was so circumstanced at present that I could not take any situation but that of Secretary of State, without a loss of credit, which would make my services less useful to his Majesty. He said that it was impossible for me to be in any other situation at present, that the Presidentcy of the Council was the best situation for the Duke of Portland, and he wondered at his hesitating about it. He then entered into some details about my office and talked a good deal about Ireland and Irish politics, touched a little upon the Catholic question with great goodwill towards Pitt, but more hostility towards Lord Grenville.'

[1] The King's reply, at 4 p.m. on the 12th, is in Pellew, I, 411–12. On page 412, line 10, 'trade; and' should read 'trade. He.' Line 11, 'merchants. Through' should read 'merchants, and as'. Line 15, 'the Duke's' should read 'the decision as to the Duke's'. Line 17 should read 'Lord[s]'. Line 21 should read 'Department'. Line 28, 'draw' should read 'naturally drawn [*sic*]'.   [2] See Appendix.

Your Majesty's confidential servants humbly submit their opinion to your Majesty that the Convention signed at St Petersburgh on the 17th of June by Lord St Helens & Count Panin on the part of your Majesty and the Emperor of Russia should be ratified. (10291, and Add. MSS. 38237, f. 107.)

2476 THE DUKE OF YORK *to the* KING

[*Horse Guards, 16 July 1801.*] In transmitting to your Majesty the usual weekly states, and recommendations for vacant commissions which have been received this week for your Majesty's approbation, I have little to trouble your Majesty with except to report the arrival of the three batallions of the Ninth Regiment from Jersey at Portsmouth, where by the desire of the Admiralty, who are anxious to have the ships cleared as expeditiously as possible, orders have been sent to them to disembark and to march to Silver Hill and Riding Street barracks in the Southern District.

As by Lord Elgin's letters received yesterday it appears that Colonel Wellesley[1] is arrived in Egypt with the corps under the command of Major-General Baird[2] from the East Indies, I beg leave to recommend to your Majesty to appoint him to the local rank of Brigadier-General in Egypt as he will be the senior Colonel but two in that army.

Your Majesty will remark that the weekly state of the depot and the recruiting return are wanting this week, which is in consequence of the removal of the depot to the Isle of Wight, where they could not arrive time enough to be made out, but they shall be sent with those of next week. (10294)

2477 E. J.[3] STEWARD *to the* EQUERRY IN WAITING

[*Weymouth, 16 July 1801.*] I take the liberty of enclosing, at the request of several of the respectable inhabitants of this town, a petition to his Majesty for leave to lay before him a plan for the establishment of a Charity School, and at the same time I beg leave to enclose the plan, and to request the favor of you to make it known to his Majesty at some convenient period.[4]

[1] Afterwards Duke of Wellington. (1769–1852.) He had been a Colonel since May 1796, and had been serving in India since 1797, taking a leading part in the campaign against Tipu of Mysore.

[2] General Sir David Baird (1757–1829). Entered the Army, 1772; Major, 1787; Colonel, 1795; Major-General, 1798; Lieutenant-General, 1805; General, 1814. Knighted, 1804; K.B., 1809; G.C.B., 1815; created Baronet, 1809.

[3] The initials are not absolutely clear. He was Mayor of Weymouth at this time.

[4] '*Weymouth, July 1801.* It is intended to promote a scheme for the education of poor children by printing and publishing the following

HINTS FOR THE ESTABLISHING A FUND FOR A PERMANENT CHARITY SCHOOL.

The number of excellent Charity Schools established in the Metropolis and its vicinity, and indeed in almost every principal Town in the Kingdom, cannot but strike every rational observer with admiration. No one can moralize on the consequences resulting from such Institutions, but must wish them to be established more extensively. No great town should be without a seminary, where the orphan and friendless poor of both sexes might find a shelter from distress: they want a protecting hand that will lead them into the paths of religion, virtue and industry by affording them the salutary aid of that system of education which bids fair to produce all the benefits, naturally to be expected from the proper cultivation of the mind. Under such a guidance, and by a careful attention to their behaviour and conduct, the

I beg at the same time to send you for his Majesty's information, a short statement[1] of the Corporate Funds—as I think his Majesty expressed a desire to know what resourses they had. (10295)

baneful effects of vice and immorality, sloth and idleness will be impress'd, and the acquirement of a suitable education will render them capable of such attainments in life, as will make them at least useful members of society, if not capable of filling higher situations, to the honor of their country and themselves, and perhaps ultimately to the benefit of the Institution, by a grateful retrospect to the origin of their good fortune.

To arrest the hand of poverty in the infant offspring of our fellow creatures, ere it has consigned them to irredeemable misery; to lead them with a fostering care by affording if possible a home, suitable clothing and a proper education, by which the comforts of life are obtained, and the seeds of knowledge implanted, and above all to inculcate the true principles of religion, from which they will learn to do their duty in this life, and secure to themselves eternal rewards in a future state. This will not only be a prop to youth, but a comfort to the aged. The dying sailor or soldier bleeding in his country's cause, may receive consolation in his last moments, in knowing there is an asylum for the fatherless child of sorrow: and the unfortunate of every class may anticipate for their children and descendants that seasonable bounty of a generous public which has never been extended to themselves. Under such impressions and from such motives, it is to be hoped there will not be wanting a numerous support to countenance a Plan that has for its object so much good.

In the commencement of such an undertaking many difficulties will arise, yet time and perseverance may subdue them all. Therefore it is necessary to draw, as into one focus, the different means of support that now present themselves, and with that aid to make a beginning, not doubting but the end will be crowned with success; and relying on that protecting Power who stimulates the good to generous deeds, and who blesses tenfold those acts which spring from a charitable heart.

Benefactions for establishing a fund or communications of intended benefactions will be received at the Bank and Libraries, and in maturity of time a Committee will be formed and plans entered into, agreeable to the means furnished, which may be enlarged as the fund shall increase.

The intention is, 'tho it may begin, with merely the educating a few children, yet, when the means will admit, that a house shall be purchased and proper persons appointed for educating the children and conducting the establishment, with suitable salaries; and that from the list of subscribers, Governors will be chosen, and Trustees appointed, and that general and other meetings be established.

The smallest donations to be received.

Some regulations, on the following or similar plan are suggested, that the liberally disposed may have an interest in the Establishment.

A SUBSCRIPTION

of £1   1.   0. pr annum, to constitute the subscriber, whether lady or gentleman, a Governor.

And a donation

of £20   0.   0.   a Governor for Life, who shall be intitled to have one child in the school at one time.
of £50   0.   0.   two children
of £100   0.   0.   and upwards,   three children

Each Governor to have a vote at all elections for appointments to the Charity.

It is intended to follow up the present opening of the plan with a more digested and particular scheme, as soon as a sufficient number of patrons have appeared to support it, who may meet for that purpose. (10322–3)

[1] '[15 July 1801] The Corporation of Waymouth have at this moment in hand on account of the harbour and general fund, about   £546 : – : –
To this may be added about £63 receivable from different people for their frontages   63 : – : –

                                                                                                                        £609 : – : –

Out of this is to be paid for debts to the contractors for the wall and other persons, upwards of   360 : – : –

                                                                        And this remaining balance of   £249 : – : –
is all that will be left to the harbour fund which at this moment requires an expenditure of upwards of £1,000, and nothing remains applicable to defray the current annual expences of the Corporation till next midsummer, which expences in the last year exceeded £370 and will be probably increased.' (10292)

[*Teinach*, *16 July 1801*.] I am so much overcome by your Majesty's most gracious letter of June 28th that I fear I shall have great difficulty in doing justice to my heart which is full of gratitude and joy. Little did I expect when I awoke this morning the having such a blessing; it diffused on my whole countenance such a look of happiness that the first question my children asked me was what had given me so much pleasure, that they might share in it, and I must acknowledge that when I had told them my happiness they were very much rejoiced. I hope your Majesty will receive great benefit from sea bathing; its having been every year of great service to you makes me trust that it will quite restore your strength and enable you to go through the winter without any complaint. I am now on a party for a few days to see the Black Forest, which is quite a different sort of country to that we inhabit. Nature is most beautiful in this part of the Dutchy and I should like very much to spend some time in visiting the many pretty spots which surround Teinach. Culw is a very considerable town from its extensive trade and has many good manufactures. Its houses are better built than those at Stutgard, being chiefly stone and I hear that the furniture in most of the merchants houses is made of mahogany, which is an expense few people are able to make in Suabia. I am today going to Liebenzel and tomorrow to Wildbad, from which I shall soon return to Louisbourg. (51646–7)

2479 HENRY ADDINGTON *to the* KING

[*Wimbledon*, *16 July 1801*.] Intelligence having been received of the death of Dr. Vivian,[1] late Regius Professor of Physick in the University of Oxford, Mr. Addington humbly recommends Sir Christopher Pegge to your Majesty, to succeed him. Sir Christopher Pegge has the good wishes of the Duke of Portland, and is universally esteemed as an able physician, and a respectable man.[2] (10296)

2480 LORD HAWKESBURY *to the* KING

[*Downing Street*, *18 July*[3] *1801*.] Lord Hawkesbury has the honour to send your Majesty a letter he received yesterday from Lord St. Helens by which it appears that the state of his health will not permit him to remain in Russia. Lord Hawkesbury has with very great regret been under the necessity of directing that the usual Letter of Recall should be made out, which he requests your Majesty would be graciously pleased to sign as well as the Letter of Credence for Mr. Garlike.

[1] William Vivian, M.D., Regius Professor since 1772, died on 14 July. He had been a Fellow of Corpus Christi College. (?1727–1801.)

[2] The King's reply on the 18th is of particular interest. 'The King is highly pleased that the first vacancy of a Regius Professor should have enabled Mr. Addington to recommend a man so universally esteemed as Sir Christopher Pegge, the more so as the King knows how very deservedly Mr. Addington considers the importance to Science that these University situations should be bestowed on merit, not solicitation.' (Sidmouth MSS., and Pellew, I, 429.)

[3] The letter was wrongly endorsed by the King, the 11th.

Lord Hawkesbury humbly recommends to your Majesty to appoint Mr A'Court[1] Secretary of Legation at Naples. The warrant will be forwarded for your royal signature.

Lord Hawkesbury has the honour to send your Majesty a letter from Baron Hompesch on which he wishes to receive your Majesty's commands.

Lord Hawkesbury has been desired by Mr Drummond and Mr Garlike to request your Majesty's permission to wear your uniform which they will both consider as a high honour confer'd upon them, and as a mark of your Majesty's approbation of their conduct. (10298)

2481   THE DUKE OF YORK *to the* KING

[*Horse Guards, 21 July*[2] *1801.*] I have the honor to acquaint your Majesty that in consequence of a conversation which I have had this morning with Mr Addington in which he informed me of the great probability of some immediate attempt being intended to be made by the French upon the coasts of this kingdom, and particularly upon those of Essex and Kent, I have thought it necessary to take every precaution to concentrate as much as possible the force in the Southern and Eastern Districts, and have therefore ordered the troop of Horse Artillery which has been detached to Stafford to return immediately to Colchester, as well as the 15th Light Dragoons to approach London, and shall hold in readiness two batallions of Guards to march from London. Mr. Addington has likewise agreed with me in the expediency of moving the French prisoners from Portsmouth and Plymouth into the interior of the country, and as there are no unoccupied buildings to be found in situations proper to place them in, General Delan[c]ey has proposed to prepare a piece of ground upon Salisbury Plain, strongly stockaded within which they can be encamped, as a temporary place of confinement, while a more permanent situation is provided for them for the winter.

Lord Cornwallis having mentioned to your Majesty when he resigned the Ordnance his anxious wish to be employed whenever and wherever your Majesty might think his services usefull, both Mr. Addin[g]ton and myself beg leave to propose to your Majesty his being placed in the command of the Eastern District.

All these arrangements I trust will meet with your Majesty's approbation.

I take this oportunity of reporting to your Majesty the death of General Mocher,[3] who died on Saturday last, by which event the 9th Light Dragoons are become vacant, and beg leave to mention to your Majesty that Sir James St. Clair[4] is the senior Major-General of Cavalry without a Regiment.

[1] Sir William A'Court (1779–1860), son of Sir William Pierce Ashe A'Court, 1st Baronet. Secretary of Legation at Naples, 1801–7, and Chargé d'Affaires, 1801–2 and 1803; Secretary to Special Mission to Vienna, 1807; Special Mission to Algiers, to Morocco, to Tripoli, and to Tunis, 1813; Minister to Sicily, 1814–22, and to Spain, 1822–4; Ambassador to Portugal, 1824–8, and to Russia, 1828–32. Succeeded to Baronetcy, 1817; G.C.B., 1819; created Baron Heytesbury, Jan. 1828; Lord Lieutenant of Ireland, 1844–6. K.P., 1844.   [2] Wrongly endorsed by the King, the 24th.

[3] Flower Mocher. Entered the Army, 1744, and fought at Fontenoy and Minden. Major-General, 1777; Lieutenant-General, 1782; General, 1796. (*c.* 1729–1801.)

[4] Son of Lieutenant-General Sir Henry Erskine, 5th Bart. [S.]; succeeded to Baronetcy, 1765. Lieutenant, 1778; A.D.C. to Lord Lieutenant of Ireland, 1782; Lieutenant-Colonel, 1792; A.D.C. to the King,

I had intended to have paid my duty to your Majesty in the course of next week at Weymouth, but in consequence of the intelligence received of the enemy's intentions I am affraid I shall be under the necessity of postponing that happiness, till we can judge more clearly what is likely to happen. (10299–300)

2482 HENRY ADDINGTON *to the* KING

[*Downing Street, 21 July 1801, 1.30 p.m.*] In the absence of Lord Hobart from London, Mr. Addington presumes to submit to your Majesty the expediency, under the present circumstances, of sending a letter to the Lord Lieutenant of every county in Great Britain, pursuant to a form, which will be inclosed herewith, and which he humbly hopes will meet with your Majesty's approbation. (10301)

2483 *Letters from the* KING *to* LORD HOBART, *and the replies*

[*Weymouth, 22 July 1801.*] The King has read and approves of the proposed circular letter to the Lord Lieutenants of Counties, for the not having had any attempt of invasion has certainly in a great measure cooled the ardour and dilligence of the Volunteer Corps and perhaps of the embodied militia. It is highly expedient this letter should be sent without loss of time which Mr. Addington will certainly direct. (Bucks. R.O.)

[*From Lord Hobart, Downing Street, 22 July[1].*] Lord Hobart presents his humble duty to your Majesty and submits to your Majesty several drafts of instructions which have been prepar'd for Lieutenant-General Fox, Lieutenant-General Sir John Hutchinson and Major-General Pigot.[2]

Lieutenant General Fox is now the senior officer upon the Staff serving in the Mediterranean, and from the extent and importance of the duties propos'd to be confided to him, Lord Hobart wou'd humbly submit to your Majesty that Lieutenant-General Fox should have the commission of Commander-in-Chief in the Mediterranean—and in the event of your Majesty's approving of Lord Hobart's suggestion to that effect, a commission is sent for your Majesty's signature, which it is propos'd to transmit with the accompanying instructions by a sloop of war now under orders for the Mediterranean.

The consequences that wou'd inevitably result from the French obtaining possession of the Island of Sicily wou'd appear too obvious for Lord Hobart to take up your Majesty's time with many observations respecting the provisional instructions upon that subject.

May 1792; Colonel, 1795; Major-General, 1798; Colonel 9th Light Dragoons, 1 Aug. 1801; Lieutenant-General, 1805; General, 1814. M.P. for Castle Rising, 1782–4; for Morpeth, 1784–96; for Kirkcaldy Burghs, 1796–1805; took name of St Clair before that of Erskine on succeeding to the St Clair estates, 1789; succeeded to the peerage as 2nd Earl of Rosslyn, 2 Jan. 1805, on death of his maternal uncle, Lord Loughborough, who had been created Earl of Rosslyn, 21 April 1801, with a special remainder in favour of male issue of his sister, Dame Janet Erskine. Lord Privy Seal, 1829–30; a Lord of the Treasury, Nov.–Dec. 1934; Lord President of the Council, Dec. 1834–April 1835.

[1] Wrongly endorsed by the King, 22 June.

[2] General Sir Henry Pigot (1750–1840). Entered the Army, 1769; Lieutenant-Colonel, 1783; Colonel 1793; Major-General, 1795; Lieutenant-General, 1802; General, 1812. G.C.M.G., 1837.

To secure a retreat for the King of the Two Sicilies,[1] to strengthen the situation of your Majesty's troops upon the Island of Malta, and eventually to facilitate military operations in the south of Italy are the principal grounds upon which your Majesty's confidential servants have considered it their duty to recommend that the propos'd instruction relative to Sicily shou'd be submitted to your Majesty.

Lord Hobart has also to present his humble duty to your Majesty, and to transmit a private letter from Lieutenant-General Sir John Hutchinson. (10304–5)

[*The King's reply, Weymouth, 23 July.*] The King very much approves of the instructions which Lord Hobart has prepared for Lieutenant-General Fox, Lieut.-Genl. Sir John Hutchinson and Major-Genl. Pigot, and has signed the commission of Commander-in-Chief in the Mediterranean for Lieutenant-General Fox. (Bucks. R.O.)

Copy.

[*From Lord Hobart, Downing Street, 23 July.*] Lord Hobart presents his humble duty to your Majesty and takes the liberty of submitting the name of Lord George Seymour[2] to your Majesty for the appointment of Governor of the Cape of Good Hope.

His high rank, conciliating manner, with a very large share of talents, and a strong desire on his part to succeed to the situation afford the best founded expectations of his discharging the duties of it with advantage to your Majesty's service—and Lord Hobart therefore venture[s] to recommend him to your Majesty for the appointment. (Bucks. R.O.)

[1] Ferdinand I.

[2] A brother of Lord Hugh Seymour (Seymour-Conway until 1794). (1763–1848.) M.P. for Orford, 1784–90; for Totnes, 1796–1801. Appointed a Commissioner of Excise, 1801; Chairman of the Board, 1822–33. Father of Sir George Hamilton Seymour, the diplomatist. He and his brothers were descendants of Charles II: their maternal grandfather was the King's grandson.

Referring to his appointment as a Commissioner of Excise, Glenbervie remarked that it was 'an office hitherto considered as beneath the rank of persons of his description, and would thereby have vacated his seat for Totnes, but it being thought by Mr. Addington and others that this would read ill on the Journals, he did vacate by the Chiltern Hundreds—much against his own inclination, as Coleman told me, as the fees for the Chiltern Hundreds amount to £20 and he is miserably poor, and, as Conway, probably very fond of money' (MS. Journal, 28 June 1801).

Earlier, Lord George had written to Pitt (the letter is undated): 'Will you allow me to say three words in reference to a conversation which I had ye honor of holding with you a few days since—when you did me ye honor of entering into my situation so far as to say you had not thought of me as a successor to Mr. Bates in ye Commissioners' Office, imagining I should not wish to hold any thing incompatible with a seat in Parliament? I partly acquiesced, feeling that in point of delicacy I had no right to call upon you to put me at once into an independent situation, & in which, except in private life, I should not have it in my power to make you any acknowledgement. Under any other view of ye subject it must be an appointment highly desirable in my situation, ye part I act in Parliament being (unfortunately) purely mechanical, & my seat being equally well to be held by any other part of my family. At ye same time I take ye liberty of stating this preference, I can not help adding my hopes that it may not form a bar to my holding any other situation, differently circumstanced, which may fall vacant, & which you may udge me worthy of.' (Chatham Papers, 177.)

[*London, 24 July 1801.*] Lord Hawkesbury has the honour to inform your Majesty that Count Woronzow has received his Letter of Credence as Ambassador and is desirous of presenting it to your Majesty at any time which you may be graciously pleased to appoint. Lord Hawkesbury can perceive from Count Woronzow's manner that he is desirous of going down to Weymouth for that purpose. As he has been so very instrumental in settling the differences which had unfortunately arisen between your Majesty and the Russian Government, and as he is so warm a friend to this country, your Majesty will perhaps be pleased to indulge him.

Lord Hawkesbury expects to receive the answer of the French Government to the last note of your Majesty's Government the beginning of next week; he hopes that he should then be able without inconvenience to your Majesty's service to attend Count Woronzow to Weymouth for a few days, by which means he should have the satisfaction of paying his duty to your Majesty. (10302–3)

2485 THE EARL OF ST VINCENT *to the* KING

[*Admiralty, 24 July 1801, 6.30 p.m.*] Lord St Vincent has the honor of acquainting your Majesty that on a consideration of the measures necessary to be taken for the defence of the coast, and guarding against any attempts, which may be meditated by the enemy for forcing the passage of the Thames, or effecting any landing on the coast of Sussex, Kent and Essex, it has occurr'd to him that it will be of advantage to your Majesty's service, to employ Vice-Admiral Lord Viscount Nelson in the command of all the ships of war, gun vessels and craft intended to be employ'd on that particular service, limiting the extent of his command from Beachy Head to Orford Ness. Lord St Vincent has no idea of interfering with the command in the Downs and at the Nore now held by Admiral Lutwidge,[1] and Vice-Admiral Graeme,[2] but to leave them in the exercise of what is generally considered the Port duty.

As the Mary yacht is in all respects ready to receive men, and may be of use in the river during the absence of the Princess Augusta, Lord St. Vincent humbly recommends that she may be put into commission, and if your Majesty should not have any particular wishes in respect to the choice of an officer to command her, he begs permission to submit to your Majesty whether it may not be proper to appoint Sir Thomas Boulden Thompson, late Captain of the Bellona, who lost his leg off Copenhagen, to the yacht. If your Majesty shall be pleas'd to approve of the measures Lord St Vincent has taken the liberty to propose, he will, immediately on receiving your Majesty's commands, carry them into execution and direct the draft of the instructions to Viscount Nelson to be sent to your Majesty when it shall be completed.

Lord St. Vincent takes this occasion to mention to your Majesty that no account

---

[1] Skeffington Lutwidge. Lieutenant, 1759; Captain, 1773; Rear-Admiral, 1794; Vice-Admiral, 1799; Admiral, 1801. (?1737–1814.)

[2] Alexander Graeme. Captain, 1778; Rear-Admiral, 1795; Vice-Admiral, 1799; Admiral, 1804. (*d.* 1818.)

either public or private has reach'd him of the capture of the Hannibal, excepting through the medium of the French papers. Lord St. Vincent is unable to form any opinion of the extent of the injury the squadron may have received from that hazardous undertaking, but in order to give every consistent support to Sir James Saumarez, and to enable him, if possible, to preserve his station before Cadiz, has directed him to be reinforc'd with four ships of the line. The ships intended to form that detachment are to be selected out of the six seventy four gun ships which lately left the Baltic and proceeded round the north of Ireland to Cork, from whence, or off Cape Clear, if they should be met with there, they will be dispatch'd.

Lord St. Vincent is very happy to learn that the Royal Charlotte and Princess Augusta yachts answer your Majesty's expectations—a great deal depends on the good management of their Commanders. (10306–7)

2486   THE DUKE OF YORK *to the* KING

[*Horse Guards, 24 July 1801.*] In transmitting to your Majesty the usual weekly returns, and successions for vacant commissions for your Majesty's approbation I have the honor to acknowledge the receipt of your Majesty's very gracious letter of the 22d instant, expressing your approbation of the different steps which have been taken in consequence of the threatening appearance of the enemy.

As your Majesty is pleased to consider Sir James St. Clair as too young an Officer to succeed immediately to the command of the 9th Regiment of Light Dragoons, and has directed that a senior General should be appointed to it, to whose Regiment Sir James St Clair may succeed, I beg leave to lay befor[e] your Majesty Lieutenant-General Tarleton's[1] name as being the senior General Officer commanding a young Regiment, for the 9th and Sir James St Clair to be appointed to the 22d.

As Lord Chatham has reported to me a great want of artillery men for the different parks, and the necessity of some immediate assistance being given to the Artillery, I have directed three of the small Welsh corps to be attached to the Artillery and instructed in the use of the great guns which I trust will meet with your Majesty's approbation. (10310)

2487   THE DUKE OF PORTLAND *to the* KING

[*Burlington House, Saturday, 25 July 1801, 8 a.m.*] The Duke of Portland most humbly begs leave to represent to your Majesty that Thursday the 6th of August being the day to which the Parliament is prorogued, it would be desireable that it should suit your Majesty to hold a Council in the course of next week for the purpose of ordering another Prorogation & for other business which the Duke of Portland is informed is ready to be laid before your Majesty in Council; and also to permit the Duke of Portland to resign the seals of the office, which he fears he has too long unworthily held, into your Majesty's hands. The Duke of Portland

---

[1] Sir Banastre Tarleton (1754–1833). Entered the Army, 1775, and served in the American War of Independence. Colonel, 1790; Major-General, 1794; Lieutenant-General, 1801; General, 1812. M.P. for Liverpool, 1790–1806 and 1807–12.

would submit with all humility to your Majesty that next Thursday the 30th inst. might be the day on which Lord Pelham as well as the Duke of Portland might be permitted to attend your Majesty & will humbly hope to receive your Majesty's commands respecting it.[1]

Your Majesty's University of Oxford having put into the hands of the Duke of Portland the new edition of what is called the *Grenville* Homer to be laid at your Majesty's feet, the Duke of Portland humbly requests to know whether it is your Majesty's pleasure that he should bring it with him to Weymouth or send it to your Majesty's Librarian[2] at the Queen's Palace. (10311–12)

2488 THE DUCHESS OF WURTEMBERG *to the* KING

[*Louisbourg, 26 July 1801.*] I hope your Majesty will now allow me to write to you constantly once a fortnight; nothing but the fear of being troublesome could have kept me so long silent.

I have been delighted with the beauties of the Black Forest, particularly with a fine ruin at Hirschau which I am sure could your Majesty see it would lead you to build a tower in the Great Park on the same plan. It is quite Gothic, having been part of a monastery; the outward walls remain perfect and in the midst has grown a fine elm which spreads its branches some feet above the tower. The whole road from Hirschau to Liebenzel is like the drive we once took in Lord Dorchester's[3] Park, only the trees are full grown and the mountains on either side of the road much higher. I prefer Wildbad to Teinach as nature is on a much grander style. The river Ens [*sic* ? Ems] which runs through the public walk has a fine effect; its bed is very rocky and forms many pretty cascades as it falls over the stones. Down this river is floated all the rafts which go to Holland: I saw two floated down, it is a very curious sight, there were ten or twelve men on each of them. Since my return home I have been much taken up with a garden I have bought and which I hope next year will afford me much amusement; it now consists of seven acres but will be considerably enlarged by a peice of ground the Duke has given me. The house, though in good repair, is like old Frogmore and I have made it very comfortable by papering some of the rooms. (51648–9)

[1] Lord Liverpool told Glenbervie that Portland 'had made various attempts to persuade Pelham to accept some other situation and had declared a decided wish to continue [Home] Secretary himself. He did not add that, among other offices, his own place of Chancellor of the Duchy had been proposed to him. He says the Duke of Portland's distressed circumstances is the chief motive of his tenacity' (*Glenbervie Journals*, I, 241).

Pelham was made Leader of the House of Lords, although, as Hobart remarked, 'in point of strict official propriety and practice (except in the instance of the Duke of Portland and perhaps other exceptions that I know nothing of) it would seem to belong to the Home Department' (*Auckland Corresp.* IV, 139).

[2] Frederick Barnard.

[3] Not Baron Dorchester (formerly Sir Guy Carleton) but Joseph Damer, 1st Earl of Dorchester (1718–98), created Baron Milton, 1762, and Earl of Dorchester, 1792—or else his son, the 2nd Earl (1746–1808). Milton Abbey, Dorset, was the family seat, which the Royal Family visited more than once whilst holidaying at Weymouth.

[*Downing Street, 27 July 1801, 2.30 p.m.*] Mr. Addington humbly trusts that, in consideration of the eminent and unexampled services of Viscount Nelson, the preservation of his Lordship's Barony in his father's[1] family, conformably to the suggestion contained in the inclosed paper, will not be disapproved of by your Majesty. Mr. Addington also ventures to submit to your Majesty a petition from his Grace the Duke of Beaufort, who, having succeeded to the estates of his uncle,[2] humbly prays that your Majesty will be pleased to bestow upon him the Barony of Botetourt.[3]

The arrangement of the business in the offices of Home Secretary, and of Lord Hobart, which Mr Addington conceives to have been approved of by your Majesty, is that the concerns of the Colonies should be transferred to Lord Hobart, and that those of Great Britain and Ireland should belong to the Secretary for the Home Department. (10313)

[*The King's reply, Weymouth, 28 July.*] The King is so perfectly satisfied with the services and ardour of Viscount Nelson that he cannot make the smallest objection to the preservation of his Barony in his father's family agreable to the paper Mr. Addington has transmitted and is now returned, as also to securing in the Duke of Beaufort the old Barony of Botetourt.

Mr. Addington has most exactly arranged between the two Departments of Secretaries of State of the Home and War Departments [*sic*] which must prevent any future misunderstanding; the Duke of Portland and Lord Pelham arrive on Thursday morning for the resignation and acceptance of the Seals of the former Department. (Sidmouth MSS.)

2490   The Earl of St Vincent *to the* King

[*Admiralty, 28 July 1801, 3 p.m.*] Lord St. Vincent has the satisfaction of transmitting to your Majesty a letter he has received from Admiral Cornwallis giving an account of a very distinguish'd service perform'd by the boats of some of the ships employed off Brest, in which he thinks as much valour has been shown as has appear'd in any instance that has occurred during the present war. Lord St Vincent is not exactly informed of all the circumstances which took place in the performance of this service, but will take care to concert with Admiral Cornwallis

---

[1] Nelson was the fifth son of the Rev. Edmund Nelson (*c.* 1722–1802), Rector of Hilborough and Burnham Thorpe, Norfolk. Nelson was created Baron (1798) and Viscount (22 May 1801) Nelson of the Nile and of Burnham Thorpe; and (18 Aug. 1801) Baron Nelson of the Nile and of Hilborough, Norfolk, with a special remainder to his father and his male heirs, or in default, to the male heirs of his two sisters in succession. His elder and only surviving brother succeeded him in 1805.

[2] The Barony of Botetourt had been in abeyance since 1406. Norborne Berkeley (*c.* 1717–70) having proved himself coheir (heir to one-third) of this Barony, the abeyance was terminated in his favour in 1764. He was M.P. for Gloucestershire, 1741–63; Groom of the Bedchamber, 1760–4, and Governor of Virginia, 1768–70. On his death the Barony again fell into abeyance.

[3] The Duke of Beaufort's mother Elizabeth (*c.* 1719–99), sister of Lord Botetourt, was co-heiress (heiress to one-third) of the Barony; the Duke obtained a confirmation of this by patent dated 4 June 1803 (G.E.C.), and the abeyance of the Barony was terminated in his favour. See No. 2502 n.

the means of noticing in a proper manner the gallant conduct of the persons who best deserve it.

Lord St. Vincent takes this occasion of acquainting your Majesty that learning by the French newspapers and other channels of the capture of the Swiftsure, and of the preparations making at Cadiz, he thought it his duty to propose to some of your Majesty's confidential servants the sending a considerable force off Cadiz instead of the detachment of four ships of the line directed to proceed from the coast of Ireland, in which they most readily concurred. If your Majesty should be pleased to approve of his so doing he humbly begs leave to propose to your Majesty that Vice-Admiral Pole[1] should on his return from the Baltic (which may be hourly expected) be sent with 12 ships of the line, viz. two three-decked ships and ten of 74 guns, as soon as possible; that force Lord St Vincent thinks may be spar'd, and still leave sufficient fleets for the Channel and the North Sea, which will stand nearly in the manner stated in the inclos'd paper. (10317–18)

2491   THE EARL OF CHATHAM *to the* KING

[*Dover Street, 28 July 1801.*] Lord Chatham is still so unwell as to be under the necessity of entreating your Majesty's indulgence to excuse his not being present at the Council to be held at Weymouth on Thursday next, and at which he under-stands that it is your Majesty's intention to declare the Duke of Portland to be Lord President. Lord Chatham cannot suffer this event to take place without feeling an anxiety to be allowed to offer his humble acknowledgements for all your Majesty's goodness to him, as well as to renew the assurances of his dutiful and affectionate attachment to your Majesty. Lord Chatham has too deeply imprinted on his mind the recollection of those expressions of approbation and kindness, with which your Majesty was pleased to honor him, when you bestowed on him the Presidency of the Council, not to indulge the earnest hope that he may be permitted to consider the important trust to which your Majesty has been recently pleased to call him, as a mark of the continuance of the same gracious sentiments, and which it will be ever Lord Chatham's first ambition to retain.

Lord Chatham will only beg to trespass further on your Majesty to express the sincere happiness with which he has learn't how much your Majesty's health has benefitted by the sea air. It is a most real mortification to him to have been pre-vented from paying his duty at Weymouth before this time, and availing himself of your Majesty's condescension and goodness, but he has neither been well enough nor wou'd the state of publick business and preparation have as yet per-mitted him to leave town. (10315–16)

2492   THE EARL OF ST VINCENT *to the* KING

[*Admiralty, 30 July 1801, 3 p.m.*] The Earl of St. Vincent has the honour of acquainting your Majesty that he has received information from different quarters,

---

[1] Sir Charles Morice Pole (1757–1830). Lieutenant, 1777; Captain, 1779; Rear-Admiral, 1795; Vice-Admiral, Jan. 1801; Admiral, 1805. M.P. for Newark, 1802–6; for Plymouth, 1806–18. Baronetcy, 12 Sept. 1801; K.C.B., 1815; G.C.B., 1818.

that there are a great many deserters from your Majesty's ships and from the Marine now in concealment who are deterr'd from returning to their duty by the fear of punishment, and begs leave humbly to submit to your Majesty whether, considering the great want of men, it may not be adviseable that a Proclamation should issue under the usual form for pardoning deserters from the Navy and Marine. (10319)

2493   THE DUKE OF YORK *to the* KING

[*Horse Guards, 31 July 1801.*] In transmitting to your Majesty the usual weekly states and returns, together with the recommendations which have been received this week for vacant commissions for your Majesty's approbation, I have little to trouble your Majesty with.

Lord Hobart will report to your Majesty the substance of a conference which was held yesterday at Mr Addington's, at which it was determined to propose to your Majesty to call out immediately the Supplementary Militia, as likewise to order all half-pay officers to send in their names to the Generals in whose districts they reside, in order that they may be employed in case of invasion, under pain of having their half pay suspended if they do not obey the order within one month, and also to publish an exhortation to all those who have retired from your Majesty's service, and who have served in the Fencibles or Militia, or in the India Company's Service, to come forward at this moment and offer their services.

It was likewise determined that immediate steps should be taken to remove the French prisoners to the Isle of Lundy in the Bristol Channel, which by a report which I have received from Lieutenant-General Delancy will easily be made fit to contain almost any number of prisoners, and by being three leagues in the sea, with a very small water force to prevent boats landing in two small creeks, and a work properly fortified to command the principal landing place, in which all the provisions must be kept with a guarison of between two and three hunderd men, the prisoners will be perfectly secure. (10320)

2494   THE KING *to the* EARL OF CHATHAM

[*Weymouth, 31 July 1801.*] Yesterday the Duke of Portland delivered to the King the letter from the Earl of Chatham. It is with much concern his Majesty finds the Earl of Chatham continues indisposed, but trusts when country air and horse exercise can be obtained that more advantage will be gained than from medicine, and a few days will probably so far compleat the military arrangements of the Ordnance as to enable the Earl of Chatham finally to decide whether he must visit Cheltenham previous to joining his Brigade.

The King certainly finds the best effects from the sea bathing, but after so severe an attack it is not to be wondered that the nerves have not yet gained their usual tone, but idleness and quiet will probably produce it. (Chatham Papers, 364)

[*Downing Street, 1 Aug. 1801.*] Lord Hobart presents his humble duty to your Majesty and takes the liberty to inform you that in communication with his Royal Highness the Duke of York it has been judg'd advisable to recommend to your Majesty to call out the disembodied Militia without delay. Warrants are therefore transmitted for your Majesty's signature. (10325)

2496   THE EARL OF ST VINCENT *to the* KING

[*Admiralty, 3 Aug. 1801, 12 a.m.*] Lord St. Vincent has the satisfaction of sending to your Majesty some dispatches brought by Lieutenant Dumaresq, late last night, from Rear-Admiral Sir James Saumarez, containing an account of an attack made by the squadron under his orders on the combin'd force of the enemy on its passage from Algeziras to Cadiz in which it appears that he has had the good fortune to capture one of the Spanish line of battle ships under French colours, and that the two Spanish first-rates, the Real Carlos and Herminegeldo, had, after the commencement of the action, taken fire and blown up.

Lord St. Vincent cannot too much admire the intrepidity and zeal, which has been manifested by Sir James Saumarez and all the officers and men of the squadron who were able to get into action, and begs permission, most heartily to congratulate your Majesty on the occasion.[1] (10327)

2497   LORD HOBART *to the* KING, *and the reply*

[*Downing Street, 4 Aug. 1801.*] Lord Hobart presents his humble duty to your Majesty and takes the liberty of submitting Capitulations for the purpose of extending the services of the foreign corps now employ'd in Portugal.

---

[1] At 4 p.m. on the 5th Lord St Vincent wrote the following note to the King: 'Lord St. Vincent has the honor of sending to his Majesty a copy of a private dispatch just received from Lord Nelson' (10331). It was dated 'Medusa, off Boulogne, 3 Aug. 1801': 'I was in hopes that the wind would have sprung up from the westward and have enabled me to have let the bombs have a good knock at the Mole and vessels outside of it, but the wind falling nearly to a calm, and what was worse, coming to the northward, I called the bombs off after they had fired 10 or 12 shells, some of which went as far as the town but without any effect that we could see, but we have ascertained that we can bombard the vessels at proper times of tide and with the wind to the southward of west with great facility. The fishing boats do not come out, which is very odd; perhaps an embargo is laid on. I hope the wind will come westerly when we can fully try the effect of shells; if it does not before Captn. Ferrier or Trotter, on Captn. Nichols arrival, I shall leave this business to be done by him, and looking at Dunkirk and Flushing get over to our own coast and arrange our plans of defence, or rather be ready to assault the scoundrels should they dare to come over. In these parts we are so well guarded that I cannot think they will come from their coasts. Augt. 4th: the wind being at NE the bombs anchored at ½ past 5 abreast of the town; what damage has been done cannot be ascertained. On the inside the pier, on the outside two large floating batteries are sunk, and one large gun brig cut her cables & run on shore, where she lays abandoned. The bombs are very well placed by their Captains, and the Artillery officers and men have the greatest desire to do their business. Boulogne is certainly not a very pleasant place this morning, but it is not my wish to injure the poor inhabitants, and the town is spared as much as the nature of the service will admit. Very little damage has been done to our bombs: Captn. Fyers of the Artillery is slightly wounded in the thigh, but remains at his post. I have paid them all a visit, and the Medusa is at anchor one cable's length from them. [P.S.] One or two more gun vessels are destroyed since I finished my letter.' (10332-3)

The probability of their being immediately withdrawn from that country, and the convenience that wou'd arise from your Majesty's being enabled to order them out of the limits of their present engagements has suggested the propriety of humbly requesting your Majesty's authority for entering into the propos'd Capitulations. (10328)

[*The King's reply, Weymouth, 5 Aug.*] The King perfectly coincides with Lord Hobart in opinion as to the propriety of extending the services of the Foreign Corps employed in Portugal. (Bucks. R.O.)

2498 HENRY ADDINGTON *to the* KING, *and the reply*

[*Wimbledon, 4 Aug. 1801.*] In obedience to your Majesty's commands Mr Addington communicated with Lord Hobart and Lord Pelham on the subject of the arrangement of business, which had been long since submitted to, and approved of by your Majesty, in the office of Secretary of State. Of the plan in contemplation their Lordships were apprized very early in the spring.

Upon being informed that Lord Pelham had received from your Majesty the Seals lately in the possession of his Grace the Duke of Portland, Mr Addington sent a letter to Lord Hobart, of which he presumes to lay a copy[1] before your Majesty; and on the same day he made a communication to the same effect to Lord Pelham. These steps, Mr Addington humbly hopes, will be honor'd with your Majesty's approbation.

Mr Addington is impatient to pay his duty to your Majesty at Weymouth, and would be particularly happy at the present moment to offer his congratulations in person on the late intelligence from Sir James Saumarez, who has derived success from failure, and given new lustre to your Majesty's arms and to the naval glory of his country. (10329–30)

[*The King's reply, Weymouth, 5 Aug., 6.40 p.m.*] The King on coming on shore has found Mr. Addington's box. He highly approves of the communication made to Lord Hobart which was to be accompanied with a similar one to Lord Pelham, which must prevent any future misunderstanding between the two Departments.[2]

---

[1] Addington's letter to Hobart is dated Wimbledon, 2 Aug.: 'I have it in command from his Majesty to acquaint your Lordship that for the convenience of the public service & in consequence of an arrangement long since recommended to, and approved of by, the King, the business of the Colonies is henceforth to be transacted in the Office over which your Lordship presides as one of his Majesty's principal Secretaries of State. A communication to this effect will be made forthwith to Lord Pelham, to whom his Majesty has been pleased to deliver the Seals of Secretary of State for the Home Department.' (10326)

[2] Lord FitzHarris, Lord Malmesbury's son, who was appointed précis writer in the Home Department later in the month, had no great respect for his superiors in office. He wrote on the 29th: 'Pitt very hard at work at the Peace, a strenuous advocate for it. Addington a mere doll of his, a fair weather Minister thinks of nothing but the good, lets the bad take its course. Lord Hawkesbury I should fear not by any means equal to the task imposed on him but much more so than Lord Hobart of whom I've the most despicable opinion as a statesman. He has been in hot water ever since he has been in power yet he has always been endeavouring to increase the business already on his hands or rather to increase his income and secure himself a permanent place after the Peace. He is and must be a strong advocate for the strongest but worst reason possible—selfishness. He knows he is not equal to the place he now holds, yet he is fond of power—and he wants to have *otium cum dignitate* at any price. They none of them

The second enterprize of Sir James Saumarez adds fresh lustre to the brilliant exploits of the Navy, and may perhaps yet be followed by some further loss to our enemies.

The King trusts Mr. Addington will come here when he thinks he can be best spared from the neighbourhood of London. (Sidmouth MSS.)

2499   THE DUKE OF YORK *to the* KING

[*Horse Guards, 6 Aug. 1801.*] I have the honor to send your Majesty the usual weekly states together with the monthly returns and the quarters of the troops, as also to lay before your Majesty for your approbation the recommendations received this week for vacant commissions.

In obedience to your Majesty's commands contained in your letters of the 1st instant, for a Proclamation to be issued for the pardon of deserters, I took the earliest oportunity to see the Secretary at War, and the Proclamation will be published in the Gazette of next Saturday night.

The alterations which we have made in this from former Proclamations, and which I trust will meet with your Majesty's approbation, are, first, to limit the term of its being in force to the tenth of next month, secondly, to oblige deserters to surrender for general service only, giving the Regiments from whom they deserted the option of taking them back.

I have no new circumstance to report to your Majesty this week except the arrival of the whole of the 49th Regiment and the detachment of the Rifle Corps from the Baltic Fleet. The whole of the 49th are ordered to Colchester, and the detachment of the Rifle Corps to join the rest at Weymouth. (10324)

2500   *Letters from* LORD PELHAM *to the* KING, *and a reply*

[*White Hall, 6 Aug. 1801.*] Lord Pelham begs leave with all humility to represent to your Majesty that Mr Addington has communicated to him your Majesty's pleasure that the business which relates to the Colonies should henceforth be conducted by the Secretary of State who has the charge of what is termed the War Department, & that the concerns of Great Britain & Ireland will constitute the trust committed to the Secretary of State for the Home Department.[1]

Lord Pelham will not fail to carry into effect with every possible dispatch these your Majesty's intentions as soon as he shall receive your Majesty's commands, & relies upon your Majesty's indulgent interpretation of the motives of his request to have your Majesty's orders upon this subject. He conceives that, respectable as was the channel by which he received the communication, your Majesty's orders alone can justify him in the execution of the duties of his office, & therefore without presuming to offer any doubts upon the expediency of the arrangement

act with that cordiality to Lord Pelham that they ought to—which makes me sure that they all act on selfish or pusillanimous motives, and they find he is the only one amongst them who does not.' (Malmesbury MSS.)

[1] Addington's letter of 2 Aug. is in Add. MSS. 33107, f. 212.

he requests only your Majesty's commands for carrying it into execution.[1] (10335–6)

[*The King's reply, Weymouth, 7 Aug.*] The communication made [by] Mr. Addington to Lord Pelham in the King's name was to have been done previous to Lord Pelham's receiving the Seals of the Home Department, or his Majesty would have on that occasion mentioned the transferring the Colonies to the War Department. The additional business which ought hourly to increase in the Home Department from the Union with Ireland, added to that of this island, is full employment for any man, and the King is thoroughly convinced that the zeal, talents and assiduity of Lord Pelham will enable him with advantage to the public and credit to himself to superintend the Department he has accepted. (Add. MSS. 33107, f. 238.)

[*From Lord Pelham, Whitehall, 7 Aug.*] Lord Pelham humbly begs leave to represent to your Majesty, that some difficulties have arisen in carrying into execution your Majesty's royal pleasure for consolidating the Boards of Ordnance, owing principally to the powers of the Lord Lieutenant & Master-General of ye Ordnance not being sufficiently defined. With a view therefore of removing all clashing of authorities Lord Pelham humbly submits to your Majesty whether it might not be expedient to revoke the 13th Article of your Majesty's instructions to the Lord Lieutenant, which gives him the command of the forts, guarrisons & trains of artillery in Ireland.

Lord Pelham takes the liberty of inclosing a copy of the Article for your Majesty's information & the proposed revocation of it. Lord Pelham has communicated with Lord Chatham upon the subject, who is of opinion with Lord Pelham that if this suggestion should receive your Majesty's approbation, all the essential parts of the service may be immediately carried into execution. (10337–8)

2501   THE DUCHESS OF WURTEMBERG *to the* KING

[*Louisbourg, 8 Aug. 1801.*] I hasten to express my gratitude to your Majesty for your most gracious letter of July 12th which I have just received. It would be most

---

[1] Lord Pelham wrote to Addington, rather tartly, on 3 Aug.: 'Between three & four o'clock this morning, the messenger arrived here with your letter of the 2d, inclosing the copy of one to Lord Hobart of the same date. I confess that I did not expect that you would have attempted to preclude all discussion upon the expediency & practicability of separating the Colonies from the office of Secretary of State for the Home Department, by writing a letter to me & to Lord Hobart in the King's name & using his authority for making that division in the duties of our offices; I say that I did not expect that you would have taken such a step after the conversation I had with you at Putney:—when you must have observed the greatest readiness on my part to accede to any arrangement for the benefit & convenience of the public service, & a strong disinclination to allow any private considerations of advantage to influence such arrangements. At present I shall confine myself to a mere representation against any steps being taken towards the accomplishment of this arrangement untill I come to London & untill I can have an opportunity of laying the case before the King either in person or in an humble Memorial: for as I received the Seals from the King which His Majesty had a few minutes before taken from the Duke of Portland & that His Majesty did not express any intention of making any difference in the duties annexed to the possession of those Seals, I can not consent to any alteration without His Majesty's express commands: & allow me to say that I can not receive any commands or directions respecting my office but from His Majesty's mouth or hand: excepting that of attending His Majesty to return the Seals which it is thought my hands are not equal to the management of...' (Add. MSS. 33107, f. 219.)

difficult for me to express how deeply I feel your goodness in writing to me. I am quite overcome by it and wish it were in my power to shew your Majesty my respect and attachment.

I rejoice at your Majesty's having taken to Botany as I am convinced that you will find it a constant source of amusement. Since I have bought a garden I try to acquire some fresh knowledge every day, and have been fortunate in finding a very good gardener, who understands both the kitchen garden and the flower garden. In two months I shall have a large addition, as the Duke has given me a peice of ground which contains three acres and joins my wall. I have a thousand different plans how to lay it out to the best advantage. In my original purchase I have a good hot-house and green-house which will furnish me with flowers the whole winter. In a few days I shall have two cows which the Duke has promised me; they are of the Swiss breed, very beautiful and large. In general the cattle is fine in this part of Germany and I am convinced would be healthier if it was not so much confined. Of late years the distemper has destroyed a great deal of it, which is a sad misfortune, the chief riches of our peasants consisting in oxen, cows and horses. Their obstinately refusing to kill those which are first attacked with this illness certainly is one of the causes of its spreading so much. (51650-1)

2502   *Letters from* HENRY ADDINGTON *to the* KING, *and a reply*

[*Downing Street, 11 Aug. 1801, 4.30 p.m.*] Mr Addington humbly hopes that in consideration of the long and meritorious services of Vice-Admiral Pole, your Majesty may be graciously pleased to confer upon him the dignity of a Baronet. Mr Addington has the satisfaction of adding, that in this hope the Earl of St. Vincent entirely concurs. (10339)

[*The King's reply, Weymouth, 13 Aug.*] The King most willingly consents to Mr. Addington's application for advancing Vice-Admiral Pole to the dignity of a Baronet, and at the same time expresses his satisfaction at the news imparted by a private letter from Lord Minto just forwarded by Lord Hawkesbury of the surrender of Cairo and the whole French force in that quarter.[1] (Sidmouth MSS.)

[*From Addington, Wimbledon, 13 Aug. 1801.*] At the request of his Grace the Duke of Beaufort, Mr. Addington has the honor of laying before your Majesty

---

[1] Hawkesbury wrote to the King on the 12th from Roehampton: 'Lord Hawkesbury has the honour to send your Majesty a private letter which he has just received from Lord Minto containing an account of the surrender of Cairo and the whole French force in that quarter. Lord Hawkesbury humbly begs leave to offer to your Majesty his most sincere congratulation on this fortunate event.' (10341)

And he wrote to his father, Lord Liverpool, from Weymouth on the 9th: 'I found the King looking remarkably well and wonderfully recover'd in all respects since he left town. I sailed with him yesterday from six o'clock in the morning till six. I understand he passes several days of the week in this manner, and it does him more good than anything, as it gives him air and amusement without fatigue...Though the King does not like Wyndham [*sic*] as a man of business, I can perceive he is in great personal favour. Indeed I cannot wonder at it, as his conversation is very agreeable and his manners to the royal family particularly respectful.' (Add. MSS. 38235, f. 172.)

a letter transmitted to him by his Grace from Badminton by yesterday's post.[1] (10342)

2503 THE DUKE OF YORK *to the* KING

[*Horse Guards, 13 Aug. 1801.*] I have the honor to lay befor[e] your Majesty the usual weekly states together with the recommendations for vacant commissions for your Majesty's approbation, as also a small treatise upon the duties of officers of Light Infantry drawn up by General Jarré[2] which appears to me to contain such very useful instruction that I have had it printed and trust that it will be found of advantage to your Majesty's service.

I have little to report to your Majesty this week except the death of Lord Rossmore by which the Government of Kinsale is become vacant, and have at the same time to add that a strong application has been made by the Lord Lieutenant of Ireland for a Lieutenant-Government for Lieutenant-Colonel Creighton,[3] son of Lord Erne,[4] upon the plea of being a promise made by Marquess Cornwallis on account of the Union. Under these circumstances perhaps your Majesty will be graciously pleased to take this oportunity of complying with the Lord Lieutenant's wishes, by promoting Lieutenant-General Gardiner from the Government of Hurst Castle to that of Kinsale, and appointing Lieutenant-Colonel Creighton to succeed Lieutenant-General Gardiner in Hurst Castle.[5] (10343)

2504 THE EARL OF ST VINCENT *to the* KING

[*Admiralty, 14 Aug. 1801, 11 a.m.*] Lord St Vincent has the honor of transmitting to your Majesty the draft of the instructions intended to be given to Vice-Admiral Pole for proceeding, with six ships of the line, off of Cadiz, to take the command of your Majesty's ships and vessels employed on the coasts of Portugal and Spain, bordering on the Atlantic.

The directions which had been sent to Lord Gardner for countermanding the orders to the four ships of the line, which had been appointed to reinforce Sir James Saumarez from Cork, did not arrive in time; and, considering all circumstances, Lord St Vincent thinks it fortunate that it has so happened, as Sir James will thereby be put in considerable force, long before the arrival of Vice-Admiral Pole. Lord St Vincent calculates that the four ships from Cork must have arriv'd off Cadiz about the 5th or 6th of this month, and united with the ships which

[1] The Duke of Beaufort wrote to the King on the 11th: 'Not being able from the present state of my health at this time personally to wait on your Majesty, I presume in this manner to return your Majesty my most sincere thanks for the honor your Majesty has been graciously pleas'd to confer on me by calling out in my person the Barony of Botetourt. I beg leave to assure your Majesty that this and the repeated marks of your Royal favor which I have experienc'd will ever be most gratefully remember'd by me and that it always will be my greatest pride to prove myself [etc.]' (10340)

[2] General Jarry died in March 1807, aged 74. He had been Inspector-General of Instruction at the Royal Military College at Marlow.

[3] John Creighton (1770?–1833), Lieutenant-Colonel and Governor of Hurst Castle.

[4] John Creighton (1738?–1828) succeeded his father as 2nd Baron Erne in 1772. Created Viscount Erne [I.], 1781; Earl Erne [I.], 1789; Irish Representative Peer, 1801–28.

[5] These appointments were gazetted on 22 Aug.

were before under Sir James, will form a squadron of ten sail, fit for any service that may present.

Lord St Vincent takes this occasion of expressing his regret at the probability which appears of his being prevented of the opportunity of paying his duty to your Majesty at Weymouth. It was his intention to have done so in the course of the next week, but so many important questions are now under consideration on which it is thought desireable that the opinion of all your Majesty's confidential servants should be taken, he has been induc'd to give way to the wishes, expressed by Mr. Addington, for his continuance in town, and humbly to beg he shall stand excused to your Majesty for failing to wait on your Majesty, which, from a strong sense of duty, as well as from inclination, he hoped to have been able to do. (10344–5)

2505   LORD HOBART *to the* KING, *and the reply*

[*Downing Street, 14 Aug. 1801.*] Lord Hobart presents his humble duty to your Majesty and has very great satisfaction in transmitting the enclos'd extract receiv'd this morning from the India House, and trusts that in the course of a very few days he shall have the happiness in the execution of his official duty of sending to your Majesty a more detail'd account of proceedings so honorable to your Majesty's arms, and of such incalculable importance in the present situation of affairs.

Lord Hobart humbly informs your Majesty of the arrival of Sir Alured Clarke from the East Indies. (10346)

[*The King's reply, Weymouth, 15 Aug.*] The King is happy to find confirmed by the extract of the letter from Constantinople the account forwarded yesterday by Lord Hawkesbury which he had received from Lord Minto. Official accounts must soon follow. (Bucks. R.O.)

2506   *Letters from the* EARL OF ST VINCENT *to the* KING

[*Admiralty, 17 Aug. 1801, 3.30 p.m.*] Lord St Vincent has the honor of transmitting to your Majesty the copy of a letter he has received from Lord Nelson, and has to lament that the zeal and gallantry of the officers and men employed on the enterprize have not been attended with the success which could have been wished. Lord St Vincent has ordered men to be sent to the Downes to supply the place of those who have been killed & wounded.

Lord St Vincent takes the liberty of mentioning to your Majesty that the East India Company have applied to the Board of Admiralty for a frigate to carry some treasure to China, for which a freight will be paid to the Captain of above 16 or 1700£. If your Majesty should be desirous of shewing a mark of your gracious attention to Capt Foote[1] or to either of the Captains of frigates who have been attending your Majesty at Weymouth, Lord St Vincent will feel highly gratified in the opportunity of making an arrangement suitable to your Majesty's wishes. (10347)

---

[1] Edward James Foote (1767–1833). Lieutenant, 1785; Captain, 1794; Rear-Admiral, 1812. K.C.B.,1831.

[*Admiralty, 17 Aug., 3.30 p.m.*] Lord St Vincent has the honor of transmitting to your Majesty the minutes of a general court martial held at Chatham on two private marines for desertion and attempting to murder the serjeant of marines and a private soldier of the Guards who apprehended them.

The sentence passed on Tilbury who appears to have made the least resistance is, that he shall serve abroad during the remainder of his life; the sentence on Cashman, that he shall receive 1000 lashes, but in consideration of wounds he has receiv'd on the head, the Court has recommended a remission of his punishment. Lord St Vincent takes for granted that the Court saw sufficient ground for that recommendation, and most humbly submits to your Majesty, whether it may not be proper to confirm the sentences and remit the punishment ordered to be inflicted on Cashman, letting it be distinctly understood that the circumstances of his probable derangement at the moment has alone occasioned this favorable consideration of his case. (10348)

2507 THE DUKE OF YORK *to the* KING

[*Horse Guards, 20 Aug. 1801.*] In transmitting to your Majesty the recommendations for vacant commissions received this week for your approbation, together with the usual weekly states and monthly returns, I have the honor to report to your Majesty the death of Lord Adam Gordon which happened on the 13th instant, owing to his Lordship having drunk some cold water when heated.

By this event the Royals, and the Government of Edinburgh Castle are become vacant.

I trust your Majesty will pardon my hinting that I believe the Duke of Kent would feel himself highly gratified if your Majesty should be graciously pleased to promote him to the command of the Royals.[1]

Should this meet with your Majesty's approbation, probably Sir Alured Clark would be happy to be removed to the command of the Fusileers, in which Regiment he served so long. This would give an opening to Major-General England, who is at present Colonel Commandant of the 2d Batallion of the 5th, to succeed to the command of the Regiment; and as your Majesty was graciously pleased to promise the Duke of Gloucester to remove Lieutenant-General Drummond[2] out of the 1st Regiment of Guards, your Majesty would have the oportunity of appointing him Colonel Commandant of the 2d Batallion of the 5th Regiment.

With regard to the Government of Edinburgh Castle which is one of the best in your Majesty's gift, among the General Officers whose rank and services would entitle their names to be laid before your Majesty for a Government, none seem to have stronger claims than Lieutenant-General Sir Robert Abercrombie who has not received any mark of your Majesty's favor since his return from India. His greatest ambition I know would be to be appointed Governor of Stirling Castle. I therefore beg leave humbly to propose to your Majesty to remove General

---

[1] The Duke's appointment as Colonel of the 1st (or Royal) Regiment of Foot was gazetted on the 21st.

[2] Andrew John Drummond. Colonel, 1793; Major-General, 1795; Lieutenant-General, 1802 [*sic Royal Kalendar*]; General, 1812.

Grant[1] from Stirling to Edinburgh, who in all human probability will not keep it long, and to appoint Sir Robert Abercrombie to Stirling.[2]

In consequence of the remark which your Majesty was pleased to make in your last very gracious letter, upon the alteration which has been made in the Lord Lieutenant's instructions in regard to the Ordnance in Ireland, and your wish that a similar alteration might take place in regard to the army, I took the earliest oportunity of speaking confidentially upon the subject with Lord Pelham, who, though not prepared to give a decided opinion, appears willing to give it every consideration, I beg leave to say that every day proves more and more the necessity of taking compleatly out of the Lord Lieutenant's hands the controul of the army, and to add confidentially to your Majesty, that he is using every effort in his power to regain that patronage, and states openly the importance of it as a necessary means of carrying on his government. (10349–50)

2508   *Letters from* LORD HOBART *to the* KING, *and the reply*

[*Downing Street, 21 Aug. 1801.*] Lord Hobart presents his humble duty to your Majesty and has the satisfaction to transmit a despatch receiv'd yesterday evening from Colonel Clinton, by which your Majesty will see justified the opinion you was graciously pleas'd to express of that officer, when Lord Hobart took the liberty of humbly submitting his name to your Majesty for the command of the troops destin'd for the Island of Madeira. (10351)

[*The King's reply, Weymouth, 22 Aug.*] The King is highly pleased with Colonel Clinton's having executed the delicate commission entrusted to him with so much delicacy, prudence, and activity, which will encourage the employing him when occasions offer. (Bucks. R.O.)

[*From Lord Hobart, Ham Common, 22 Aug., 6 p.m.*] Lord Hobart presents his humble duty to your Majesty and with the most heartfelt satisfaction ventures to take the liberty of congratulating your Majesty upon the success of your arms against that part of the French army in Egypt employ'd in the defence of Cairo— and which Lord Hobart is persuaded must speedily be follow'd by the evacuation of the whole of that country by the French troops.

Lord Hobart humbly transmits to your Majesty the despatches received this day from the Honorable Sir John Hutchinson. (10352)

[*The King's reply, Weymouth, 24 Aug., 6.34 a.m.*] The King received the last evening Lord Hobart's note accompanied by the dispatches from Sir John Hutchinson giving an account of the surrender of Cairo; but it seems by parts of the narrative as if the subsequent dislodgement of the enemy will take further time. (Bucks. R.O.)

[1] James Grant (1720–1806). Captain, 1744; Lieutenant-Colonel, 1760; Colonel, 1772; Major-General, 1776; Lieutenant-General, 1782; General, 1796. M.P. for the Tain Burghs, 1773–80; for Sutherlandshire, 1787–1802. Governor of Stirling Castle, 1789–1806.

[2] Sir Robert Abercromby was appointed Governor of Edinburgh Castle (gazetted, 25 Aug.).

2509   THE DUKE OF KENT *to the* KING

[*Castle Hill,*[1] *23 Aug. 1801.*] Having last night been informed by the Duke of York of your Majesty's goodness in conferring upon me the command of the Royals, I hope you will excuse this intrusion, as it is for the purpose of offering my most humble and grateful thanks for this distinguished favor. Flattered as I must be at all times by every mark of your Majesty's goodness to me, I trust I may be permitted to say that I am doubly gratified on this occasion, as I humbly hope I may be allowed to consider my promotion as a proof of your having condescended to approve of my past conduct in the line of my profession. I shall beg leave to add that to merit the continuance of your good opinion will ever be my first object in life, and I flatter myself I shall never be capable of doing any thing to make me forfeit it. (46015)

2510   THE EARL OF HARDWICKE *to the* KING

[*Dublin Castle, 25 Aug. 1801.*] The peculiarly flattering and gracious manner in which your Majesty was pleased to call me to your service, and the condescension of your Majesty's personal and confidential kindness before I left England, encourage me to hope that the liberty I now take in offering myself to your Majesty's notice will be attributed to the only motive which could have operated upon my mind, viz. a just sense of duty to your Majesty and a real anxiety to promote the true interests of your Majesty's Government in this country.

With these views and feelings of duty to your Majesty I beg leave humbly to submit to you the following statement of what has passed in regard to the vacancy in the representation of the Irish Peerage. The first application which was made upon this subject was from Lord Charleville,[2] who stated to me on the 7th July a wish that his pretensions to succeed to the first vacancy in the representation of the Peerage of Ireland might be favourably entertained by your Majesty's Government. I, of course, declined giving him any positive assurances, but I lost no time in apprising Mr. Abbot of the application, and of my opinion that his claims deserved attention upon the first vacancy. That opinion was founded, first, upon the honourable manner in which he had supported the Union, without any engagement either for himself or any of his friends; secondly, upon the favourable opinion entertained of him by Lord Cornwallis, who would have proposed him for the original list if he had not been prevented by circumstances which arose at that embarrassing period; and lastly, upon the circumstance of the Government having recently accepted from him a seat in Parliament for the Borough of Carlow, for which he had unconditionally upon their recommendation brought in a

---

[1] Glenbervie said that the Duke bought a house at Ealing in 1800 which had belonged to Mrs Fitzherbert (*Diaries*, 1, 258). In March 1802 Lord St Vincent heard that the Duke was to be given an appointment at Gibraltar which would not subject him to residence, and that General Fox was to be his locum tenens. But the report was groundless (*Letters of Lord St Vincent* [Navy Records Society], 1, 213). The Duke succeeded General O'Hara as Governor.

[2] Charles William Bury (1764–1835), M.P. for Kilmallock, 1789–90 and 1791–7. Created Baron Tullamore [I.], Nov. 1797; Viscount Charlesville [I.], Dec. 1800. An Irish Representative Peer, 1801–35; created Earl of Charleville [I.], 16 Feb. 1806.

gentleman of character and useful parliamentary talents.[1] In a second letter to Mr. Abbot, who, being then in England, was the proper channel for so confidential a communication, I again stated my opinion of Lord Charleville's pretensions, and he was so much of that opinion, that he immediately forwarded my letter to Mr. Addington. On the sixth inst., the day Lord Rossmore died, I dispatched a messenger to England with a letter to Mr. Addington, and on the 13th, received a letter from him of the 10th, in which he expresses his concurrence in my recommendation of Lord Charleville to the Peers of Ireland, the substance of which was accordingly communicated to Lord Charleville himself. On the 7th inst. in a conversation with Lord Clare on the subject of the details to which it would be necessary to attend in the filling up of the vacancy, I communicated to him confidentially what had then passed in regard to Lord Charleville, and had the satisfaction of finding that he entirely approved of the recommendation which was proposed describing him as a man of strict honour and gentlemanlike feelings and highly deserving of the distinction.

After matters had been so far adjusted, I received on the 16th a letter dated the 12th from the Duke of Portland, in which his Grace informed me that your Majesty had some time since expressed a wish in favour of the Marquis of Thomond. I need not say that I should at all times consider every wish of your Majesty as a command which should receive from me the most cheerful obedience, and the embarrassment which exists at present arises solely from a want of timely communication.

In a publick view it is certainly indifferent in itself on which of the two Peers the choice should fall, and it is no otherwise material to myself personally than as it involves the essential stability of the Government here; which cannot be useful or efficient in hands from which the means of executing the promises of your Majesty's Ministers are withheld. This degree of weight and authority was at all times important but never more so than at the present moment, when the general state of the country is unsettled, and when cabals are on foot hostile to the joint interest of the Empire as cemented by the Union, the full benefits of which, so far as respects the due collection of the revenue, the necessary economy in its expenditure, and the improvement of the internal resources of the country, can never be fully obtained but by an impartial and uncorrupt Government, supported by your Majesty's unquestionable favour and protection.

I am aware that a direct address to your Majesty may be considered as unusual; but being assured that the difficulty of my present situation arises wholly from the supposition that your Majesty's wishes in favour of Lord Thomond prevent that, which on account of what has passed, so deeply concerns the lasting interest of your affairs, I beg leave humbly to lay before you this statement which I presume to hope may induce your Majesty to see the question in a different point of view;

[1] On 30 July, Charles Montague Ormsby (1767–1818) was elected for Lord Charleville's pocket borough. Charles Abbot, the Irish Secretary, wrote to Hardwicke on 30 June: 'The person whom I have recommended...is Mr. Ormsby, newly-appointed Counsel to the Commissioners of the Revenue. He was a strong Unionist in the last Parliament of Ireland, an able debater and a good lawyer...We think he will strengthen our ranks very much next winter on Irish discussions and assist us in our Revenue Bills.' (Add. MSS. 35711, f. 65.) M.P. for Carlow, 1801–6. Baronetcy, Dec. 1812.

and that Lord Thomond may be prevailed upon to postpone his expectations to a future vacancy. Unless some arrangement can be made which shall enable me to fulfil the promises which I was regularly authorised to make, I shall feel that nothing can repair diminution of weight and authority which your Majesty's Government in this country will experience, and that it will be impossible for me to continue in this situation with any farther prospect of being useful to your Majesty's service.[1] (Add. MSS. 35771, f. 48.)

2511 THE DUKE OF YORK *to the* KING

[*Horse Guards, 27 Aug. 1801.*] I have little or nothing to trouble your Majesty with this week except the usual returns and the recommendations for vacant commissions for your Majesty's approbation.

As your Majesty has not made any remark upon the proposed arrangement of the disposable force of Great Britain into brigades and the stationing of the Major-Generals, I suppose that your Majesty will approve of its being carried into execution.

[1] There is no copy of this letter in the Archives: an accident prevented the King from receiving it. Hardwicke wrote to his brother Charles Yorke on 8 Sept.: 'I cannot help being mortified at the accident by which my letter was prevented from reaching the King, and sincerely wish you had forwarded it to Weymouth even after the unlucky delay of its being sent to Tyttenhanger.' Yorke replied three days later: 'I am anxious to hear your opinion upon the step I presumed to take of stopping your letter to his Majesty, which fell accidentally into my hands, having been detained till after the *final* arrangement for the peerage had been settled with his Majesty. The circumstance is not known and never will be, should you approve of my proceeding, as I have no doubt you will.' He added: 'The King is perfectly well and has recovered his flesh, but he complains at times that his spirits are not good. In truth, he cannot be otherwise than full of anxiety and solicitude.' (Add. MSS. 35701, f. 92.)

Hardwicke had written to Yorke on 26 Aug.: 'The letter to the King I sent to Colonel Manningham under cover, requesting him to deliver it at a proper opportunity; probably the point may be determined before the King receives it; or possibly it may have no effect, and in that case, I must beg that my leaving this Government, may make no alteration in your situation at home. I shall never be induced to lend my aid to any factious opposition, but shall give the same support as if the case had never happened, tho' I shall feel that I have some reason to complain, and that is worse, that the Ministry will weaken itself, not by obliging me to return, but by retracting a promise made by the Prime Minister, and shaking all confidence in future and past engagements.' (Add. MSS. 35701, f. 76.)

Charles Yorke advised his brother against taking precipitate action (28 Aug.): 'I...deprecate for your own sake, and for the sake of the Government and the country at this *most critical* conjuncture, any violent resolution, tending to make a breach which can never be healed and which may be fatal in its effects. From Abbot's letter it should seem, as if he was only looking to the carrying this point, (which in itself is really of no *public* importance, tho' I admit it involves much embarrassment and mortification) without ever considering the situation of the King's health, the extreme danger of adding at this moment to the anxieties and disquietudes of his mind, which ought on all accounts to be kept in as serene a state as possible, and which it is obvious, must be harassed and vexed in an extraordinary degree, by so *sudden and unexpected*, so *distressing* and *embarrassing* a change, as your quitting the Government of Ireland, almost as soon as you had taken possession of it, and *for such a reason*.

As little does Abbot seem to reflect upon the immense inconvenience and mischief which would be brought upon Government, and the operation to be produced on the public opinion. And for what? Let me beseech you to consider this affair coolly and with a view to the *public* interest; you will besides be convinced, I am sure, that neither Addington or Lord Pelham, *are in the least* to blame; that it [is] to the King's *word* and *engagement* that Lord Charleville is called upon to give way; and if he does it with a good grace, (as I am sure he will if he is at all worthy of the honour intended him) what possible reason can there be for yourself and Abbot remaining at all uneasy?...' (Add. MSS. 35701, f. 78.)

Addington saw Hardwicke's letter to the King, and agreed, on being consulted by Charles Yorke, that the letter should not be sent on to Weymouth.

The first Board of the Royal Military College was held yesterday, when General Delancy[1] delivered in the plans for the interior dispositions of the buildings, which, in obedience to your Majesty's orders, were transmitted to Mr Wyatt, in order that he might form the design for the fronts of them for your Majesty's approbation. (10353)

2512   Letters from LORD PELHAM to the KING

[*White Hall, 28 Aug. 1801, 3 p.m.*] Lord Pelham humbly begs leave to lay before your Majesty the wish of Monsieur to have your Majesty's permission to occupy the apartments in Holyrood House, lately inhabited by Lord Adam Gordon; in the event of its being thought desireable that Monsieur should return to Edinburgh; the apartments which your Majesty was graciously pleased to allot to Monsieur, during his former residence, are adjoining to the late Lord Adam Gordon's & as Monsieur hopes to be permitted to have Monsieur & Madame Angoulême with him, the addition of Lord Adam Gordon's apartment would enable him to make so desireable an addition to his domestick happiness.

Lord Pelham has been desired by Lord Elcho[2] to lay him at your Majesty's feet with his most humble request that he may have the apartments in Holyrood House become vacant by the death of Lord Adam Gordon. (10354–5)

[*Whitehall, 28 Aug. 1801.*] Lord Pelham begs leave with all humility to represent to your Majesty that it would be desirable to have a Council on Monday the seventh of September for the purpose of further proroguing the Parliament; & Lord Pelham sollicits your Majesty's commands thereon. (10356)

2513   THE EARL OF ST VINCENT to the KING

[*Admiralty, 28 Aug. 1801, 3.15 p.m.*] Lord St. Vincent has the honor of transmitting to your Majesty the sentence and minutes of a court martial held a few days since at Portsmouth, on John Pearce one of the mutineers of the Hermione, and begs leave humbly to submit to your Majesty whether it will not be adviseable to order that the sentence may be carried into execution immediately. (10357)

2514   LORD HAWKESBURY to the KING

[*Downing Street, 29 Aug. 1801, 3 p.m.*] Lord Hawkesbury has the honour to inform your Majesty that there is every reason to believe, from private communications, that the negociation with the French Government is likely to take a favourable turn. Under these circumstances Lord Hawkesbury has thought it adviseable to direct that his full powers should be made out in the usual form, which he has the honour of herewith forwarding to your Majesty for your royal signature. Your Majesty may be assured that these full powers will not be made

---

[1] See No. 692. The more usual spelling is De Lancey. Lieutenant-General, 1801; General, 1812.

[2] Francis Charteris (1749–1808), formerly Wemyss, styled, from April 1787, though never officially recognised, Lord Elcho, as the eldest son of the self-styled Earl of Wemyss (this being a forfeited Jacobite peerage). M.P. for the Haddington Burghs, 1780–7. He died on 20 Jan. 1808, seven months before his father.

use of untill the Treaty has been communicated to your Majesty and has received your approbation, and that the terms of it shall be such as in the opinion of your confidential servants are consistent with the honour of your Majesty's Crown and the interests of your people.

Lord Hawkesbury humbly recommend[s] to your Majesty, to appoint Mr Bartholomew Frere[1] who has acted as Private Secretary to Lord Minto during the whole of his Mission to Vienna, to be Secretary of Legation at Lisbon. (10358–9)

2515   HENRY ADDINGTON *to the* KING, *and the reply*

[*Wimbledon, 31 Aug. 1801.*] Mr Addington hopes to be pardon'd for troubling your Majesty in consequence of a letter which he understands has been address'd to your Majesty by the Lord Lieutenant of Ireland.

Upon the death of Lord Rossmore a wish was express'd by the Lord Lieutenant to Mr Addington that the support of Goverment might be given to Lord Charleville, as a proper person to succeed his Lordship as one of the Representative Peers for Ireland. As Mr Addington was not apprized of any engagement which could interfere with this recommendation, he had no hesitation in acceding to it, but he afterwards learnt that great encouragement had been given some months before to the Marquis of Thomond, in the event of such a vacancy, & that your Majesty's wishes had been strongly expressed in his Lordship's favor. This being the case, Mr Addington was induced by a sense of duty to your Majesty to inform Lord Hardwicke, that, having learnt the wish which your Majesty had conceiv'd & previously signified upon the subject, he must regard that wish as paramount to every other consideration. With this view, Mr Addington has used his best endeavours to avoid giving your Majesty any trouble upon this occasion; but finding from Lord Hardwicke's letter, received this day, that difficulties may arise, tending to a change in the Government of Ireland, which Mr Addington is most anxious to prevent, he has been led to consider the best means of avoiding so great an inconvenience; and he would therefore humbly submit to your Majesty that if it should be thought proper to confer the dignity of a Peer of the United Kingdom on the Marquis of Thomond, all future discussion and difficulty will be precluded. He therefore humbly hopes that your Majesty will be graciously pleased to approve of this suggestion, in which case the vacancy occasion'd by the death of Lord Rossmore may be supplied by the election of Lord Charleville to succeed him.[2] (10360–1)

[*The King's reply, Weymouth, 1 Sept., 6.30 p.m.*] The King on coming on shore found Mr. Addington's letter on the subject of the vacancy occasioned in the representation of the peerage of Ireland by the death of Lord Rossmore.

[1] A younger brother of Canning's friend John Hookham Frere (1778–1851). Secretary of Legation at Lisbon, 1801–2, and Chargé d'Affaires, Oct.–Nov. 1802; Secretary of Legation in Spain, 1802–4 and Chargé d'Affaires, July–Nov. 1804; Secretary of Legation, 1808–9, of Embassy, 1809, and Minister, in Spain, *ad interim*, 1809–10; Secretary of Embassy at Constantinople, 1811–21, and Minister *ad interim*, 1815–17, and 1820–1.

[2] Lord Hardwicke wrote to his brother Charles Yorke on the 20th from Phoenix Park, regretting the lack of firmness evidently being displayed by 'our friend A[ddington]': 'Lord Charleville's application

It seemed highly unjust that the Marquess of Thomond, descended from one of the most illustrious families in Ireland and near the head of that peerage, should be omitted on the first election. The Duke of Portland therefore obtained my leave to press the Marquess Cornwallis who promised his support as Lord Lieutenant on the first vacancy. Thus it now stands, and it certainly is unfortunate that the present Lord Lieutenant is so forward in entering into promises that cannot but distress Government; but Mr. Addington has proposed an unexceptionable means of getting out of the present difficulty. A peerage of the United Kingdom extending no farther than to the male heirs lawfully begotten by the Marquess of Thomond will be only a peerage for his life, which the King will most willingly grant.[1] (Sidmouth MSS.)

for the recommendation of Government upon a vacancy of the representative Peerage was made to me on the 7th of July, and immediately communicated to Addington through Abbot who was then in England. When Lord Rossmore died, I immediately wrote to Addington stating my reasons for thinking Lord Charleville's pretensions just and proper, and received full authority by his letter of the 10th inst. to recommend him to the Peers of Ireland. After this, judge of my surprise in receiving a letter dated the 12th inst. from the Duke of Portland in which he mentions the King's engagement to Lord Thomond, and of my still greater surprise on receiving on Tuesday, Addington's letter of the 13th. I am sure you will think I cannot remain here with honour or with any chance of being useful, if the forgetfulness of an Ex-Secretary of State is to be indulged by superceding a positive engagement of the Prime Minister, signified to me in precise terms. After all, Littlehales tells me that Lord Thomond and Lord Sheffield were recommended by the Duke of Portland to be placed on the original list; but that Lord Cornwallis stated the impropriety of recommending absentee Peers who always resided in England, to be amongst the Representatives of the Irish Peerage, and that the King approved of the idea.' (Add. MSS. 35771, f. 44.)

[1] The Marquess of Thomond was created Baron Thomond [U.K.] on 2 Oct. 1801. Hardwicke explained his peculiar difficulties arising out of the vacant Representative Peerage, in a letter to Addington on 26 Aug.: '...I am sorry to find by your letter of the 21st that I have not succeeded in putting you in possession of the real question to be considered. If it were merely a question between Lord Charleville and Lord Thomond I have no doubt the former might be prevailed upon to waive the engagement which has been made to him; but though it would be very easy to explain to Lord Charleville the circumstance of the King's wish as stated to have been expressed in favour of Lord Thomond, and the accident of that wish not having been communicated either to you or to myself till after the application had been received and sanctioned, yet as it would not be possible to give an explanation to the publick, the idea that would be generally and I believe industriously propagated would be that the power of fulfilling promises and engagements was so far weakened as to render nugatory any reliance upon such as might be made here. The cabals to which I have alluded are not merely those of anti-Unionists or half-traitors; they are those of persons, some of whom perhaps are of no small consequence in this country, who, tho' they supported the Union, supported it in the expectation of a change in the system of Government by which their weight, influence and power in this country would be increased. Of those who imagined that one consequence of the Union would be, the governing of Ireland by means of some of its leading men, formerly known by the name of Undertakers, aided by the co-operation and agency of others, who by such an arrangement would be raised from a more subordinate situation to that of the real Ministers of this country. To such men (and that there are such is an undeniable fact) the continuing to govern Ireland by a Lord Lieutenant from England, has been a subject of mortification and disappointment, and without referring it to any personal dislike of myself, accounts for some things which I have unavoidably observed. Any thing therefore that would tend to lower either the real or supposed weight of the Lord Lieutenant would be to them a subject of triumph; and the real and immediate consequence would be, an inability to carry on with effect any of the proposed and necessary enquiries into the different offices and departments, and the best mode of ensuring in future, the due collection and expenditure of the publick revenue...

The circumstance of antiquity of peerage might have been urged in favour of Lord Thomond if the question had rested upon that ground instead of priority of promise; but in justice to the original recommendation of Lord Charleville it is right to observe, that Lord Rossmore and Lord Tyrawly are of very recent creations, though Representative Peers; and that Lords Somerton, Callan and Carleton are not of much earlier date. Lord Thomond too was raised lately to the Marquisate by Lord Cornwallis;

[*Louisbourg, 1 Sept. 1801*] I have this instant been honoured with a most gracious letter from your Majesty for which I return my most humble thanks. I am quite overcome by the kind things you are pleased to say, and entreat your Majesty to be convinced that the seeking to deserve your good opinion and affection will ever be a strong inducement for me to fulfil my duty. After the pains which were bestowed on me at home I must be devoid of every good principle if I did not try to follow the examples I had so long the happiness of having daily before my eyes.

I am very happy that Mr Wickham has given your Majesty a good account of our eldest son; he is a fine young man and I hope will be a great comfort to his father who doats on him. Had my little Paul been older I think he would have pleased Mr Wickham very much as he is a very comical boy and in my partial eyes his manners are like Adolphus's, but I must acknowledge that the Duke always accuses me of spoiling him and Catherine, who certainly puts me much in mind of dear Elizabeth and has a very amiable good heart.

Though the harvest is fine we have a sad distress in the Dutchy, which is the quantity of field mice that eat up everything: they make it quite dangerous to ride or walk out in the fields from the holes they make. My garden is full of them and notwithstanding traps and cats they continue to encrease. It is said that nothing but a heavy snow will destroy them. (51652-3)

2517 THE ARCHBISHOP OF CANTERBURY (DR MOORE) *to the* KING

[*Lambeth House, 2 Sept. 1801.*] The Archbishop of Canterbury humbly begs leave to submit to the King's consideration our duty as a nation to offer up with

who declined recommending him as a Representative Peer, because he was not bonâ fide a resident Peer of Ireland.

Independently of this question, it is well worth consideration whether it would not be better to confine the honour to such as are resident Peers, and whether a contrary practice may not be attended with inconvenience and be felt as a step towards excluding the resident Irish Peers from their due share of the Parliamentary priviledge allotted to them by the Union.' (Add. MSS. 35771, f. 51.)

Addington's proposal, acceptable to the King, ended the affair, though with ruffled feelings. Charles Yorke emphasised the fact that Addington had not been to blame. 'I *know* that he has suffered as much pain and anxiety as it [is] possible for a man to have done.' In this letter to his brother, the Lord Lieutenant, he declared (2 Sept.): 'I can easily enter into all the feelings of yourself and Abbot on this occasion as arising from the view you have of the intrigues and cabals in Ireland; and I can further assure you that the fullest credit is given on this side of the water for your having acted entirely on *public* grounds in the course of this transaction; and had it been a question between the Irish Government and any *individuals* or set of men, *here* or *there*, I am perfectly persuaded that the hesitation would not have been permitted for an instant. In like manner, if *subsequent* to your recommendation his Majesty had thought proper to propose and *support another* person you would have had the strongest reason to complain; and would have been cordially supported in any representation you might have thought proper to make. But the embarrassment in this case arose from a *previous* encouragement given by his Majesty which was known only to the D of P. and unluckily kept by him (unintentionally I am persuaded) from your knowledge as well as Addington's till the pledge had been unwarily given. It is obvious, that if it had been known *beforehand* no one would have thought of insisting upon Lord Charleville's nomination; and on the other hand, the point *really* in issue (abstracted from the feelings created by the jealousy of cabals and parties *in Ireland*) was merely whether Lord Charleville should or should not sacrifice his pretensions for this time, to the *previously declared* wishes, and pledge of his Majesty; especially at a juncture the *most critical* to Government and the public, and to the complete re-establishment of the King's health, which essentially depends on quiet and composure.' (Add. MSS. 35701, f. 82.)

grateful hearts a general prayer to Almighty God for the great blessing which in His mercy & goodness He hath vouchsafed us, in our favourable & abundant harvest—and he humbly requests to receive his Majesty's command for that purpose. (10362)

2518 HENRY ADDINGTON *to the* KING, *and the reply*

[*Downing Street, 2 Sept. 1801.*] Mr. Addington humbly hopes that, in consideration of the extraordinary merits and services of Rear-Admiral Sir James Saumarez,[1] your Majesty may be graciously pleased to bestow upon him the Red Ribbon become vacant by the death of Sir George Warren.[2]

Mr. Addington trusts he shall be pardon'd for adding that he cannot sufficiently express the relief and satisfaction which have been afforded to his mind by your Majesty's approval of his suggestion respecting the Marquiss of Thomond. (10363)

[*The King's reply, Weymouth, 2 Sept.*] By the death of Sir George Warren, the Senior Extra Knight of the Bath of course succeeds to his stall, that is, Lt. Genl. Trigge. The King will very willingly bestow an Extra Ribband on Sir James Saumarez, of which Mr. Addington may give due notice, as it may on the first occasion be forwarded to the Mediterranean, and Sir Charles Pole invest him.[3]

In the box the King found a letter from the Archbishop of Canterbury recommending the ordering a Thanksgiving Prayer on account of the very abundant harvest. I certainly approve of it, but hope, though by the goodness of Divine Providence it has proved so favorable, that every care will be taken to be moderate in the expenditure of it. The King wishes to suggest whether even in the Prayer some words to that effect would not be proper.[4] (Sidmouth MSS.)

2519 THE DUKE OF YORK *to the* KING, *and the reply*

[*Horse Guards, 2 Sept. 1801.*] I should not have troubled your Majesty with my report a day sooner than usual if I did not think it my duty to acquaint your Majesty as early as possible with the result of a conference which I had yesterday with Mr. Addington and others of your Majesty's Ministers in which they urged in the strongest manner the necessity of reinforcing as expeditiously as possible the coast of Sussex as well as Essex, and in general the Eastern District, stating as their reason the forwardness of the enemy's preparations upon their coast,

---

[1] K.B., 5 Sept. 1801. Invested at Gibraltar by General O'Hara, 17 Nov. 1801.

[2] Sir George Warren (1735–1801), M.P. for Lancaster, 1758–80, 1786–96; for Beaumaris, 1780–4. K.B., 1761. He died on 31 Aug.

[3] Notwithstanding marks of favour from the Crown, Sir James was dissatisfied. Lord St Vincent wrote to Addington on 6 Aug. 1802: 'Sir James Saumarez, in a conversation I had with him yesterday, amongst other grievances, stated his disappointment at not having a pension given him to support the titles conferred upon him for his services during the late war, which his circumstances required, and I understood him to say that £1,000 a year was what he hoped would not be considered too much. I replied to him by observing how very kind you had been in giving a very lucrative employment to his brother.' (*Letters of Lord St Vincent*, I, 214.)

[4] The King being at Weymouth, one of these letters may be slightly misdated.

and the failure of the attempts which have been made to destroy their flotillas, as also from the nature of the enemy's boats the impossibility of their making any attempt beyond what they can effect in one tide, and therefore that their efforts must be confined between Harwich and Portsmouth.

These being points upon which, from the intelligence which they are in possession of, they ought to be able best to judge, I could only lay before them the present distribution of the troops, pointing out those who from being placed in the interior might be brought forwards, and stating at the same time that though Sussex was a county particularly adapted for cavalry, yet that no more could be placed there unless temporary arrangements were taken, as every barrack and quarters was already occupied.

The urgency of the moment, however, appears so strong to your Majesty's Ministers, that they think that from the present prevailing good disposition of the country, there will be no risk in withdrawing the greater part of the troops from the interior. I have therefore made the inclosed disposition, which I trust will meet with your Majesty's approbation.

With regard to the cavalry intended to be sent into Sussex, an Officer of the Barrack Department is ordered down immediately to provide such temporary accommodation for them as the country affords and which General Delancy assures me will be ready for them by the end of the present month, after which it certainly would be very detrimental to cavalry to remain in camp.

In order to supply in some degree the deficiency occasioned by the moving of two Batallions of Guards to Chelmsford, I have ordered the 2d Tower Hamlet and the West London Militia to return to London, and until the Stafford Militia return to Windsor I propose that the duty shall be done there by a detachment from the 10th Light Dragoons.

Your Majesty's Ministers have also pointed out to me the expediency of my making a tour round that part of the coast which is threatened, which I shall undertake as soon as I can ascertain exactly when the troops will be able to arrive upon their stations, and the only circumstance which I have to regret is that this will necessarily oblige me to postpone paying my duty to your Majesty at Weymouth which I had intended at the beginning of this month.

I have the honor to transmit to your Majesty the usual weekly states and returns, together with the recommendations for vacant commissions for your Majesty's approbation, as also Sir Charles Morgan's opinion upon the case of Lieutenant Col. Sankey of the City of Dublin Militia, upon which I beg to receive your Majesty's commands. (10364–5)

[*The King's reply, Weymouth, 3 Sept.*] The new arrangement of the troops by moving from the interior to strengthen Essex and Sussex meets with my approbation, as also that the 10th Regiment of Light Dragoons shall do the infantry duty at Windsor and Kew till the return of the Stafford militia from hence.

The usual returns are arrived, and I approve of the recommendations of the successions in the Army. (Huntington MSS.)

2520 HENRY ADDINGTON *to the* KING

[*Wimbledon, 6 Sept. 1801, 1.30 p.m.*[1]] Mr. Addington extremely regrets that it will not be possible for him to attend the Council at Weymouth tomorrow, but he humbly hopes to be permitted to pay his duty to your Majesty on Tuesday next, on which day he trusts that he shall reach Weymouth by or before three o'clock.

The death of Mr. Yorke[2] having open'd a reversion in the Office of Clerk of the Crown Mr. Addington has reason to believe that in consequence of it the Lord Chancellor will be induced to resort to that gracious indulgence and favor which his Lordship has experienced from your Majesty upon every occasion.[3] (10367)

2521 THE DUCHESS OF WURTEMBERG *to the* KING

[*Louisbourg, 8 Sept. 1801.*] I cannot deny myself the pleasure of offering your Majesty my congratulations on this day[4] which is so dear to us all. I hope the Almighty will attend to my prayers and grant that you may see many happy returns of it. I envy all those who will have the honour of complimenting your Majesty in person. The Duke desires me to present his humble duty; had I not prevented him he would have wrote himself but I feared it would be troublesome.

I wish it were possible for your Majesty to see the See Haus where the Duke has a very large farm. The sheep are all of the Spanish breed and the wool has been sold this year for above twelve guineas a hundredweight which appears to me dearer than it used to be in England. Much pains is taken to improve the wool as there is a very good cloth manufactory here. The troops as well as all the livery are clothed in it, and some of the cloths are so good that the Duke often wears them. In general the spirit of industry which the people exert in agriculture is very pleasant to see, and I hope the encouragement the Duke gives them will do a great deal of good. Your Majesty having taken so much to farming is very much admired abroad and looked on as one of the great causes of the improvements in England. (51654–5)

2522 *Letters from* LORD HAWKESBURY *to the* KING

[*Downing Street, 9 Sept. 1801.*[5]] Lord Hawkesbury has the honour to send your Majesty the full powers to enable Lord St. Helens to receive the accession of Denmark & Sweden to the Convention of the 17th of June, for your royal signature. Lord Hawkesbury has been enduced to take this step from the earnest wish which has been express'd by his Imperial Majesty that the accession of those two Powers to the Convention should take place at St. Petersburgh, & because he is of opinion that it is much more for your Majesty's interest that the business should be finally settled in Russia, than by seperate negociations with the different Powers in this country. (10370)

---

[1] Wrongly endorsed by the King, the 5th.

[2] John Yorke (1728–1801), fourth son of the 1st Earl of Hardwicke, the Lord Chancellor. M.P. for Higham Ferrers, 1753–68; for Reigate, 1768–84. A Lord of Trade, 1761–3 and July–Dec. 1765; a Lord of the Admiralty, 1765–6.   [3] See on this point *Colchester Diary and Correspondence*, I, 144.

[4] The King was married on 8 Sept. 1761.   [5] The King wrongly endorsed the letter, the 4th.

[*London, 14 Sept.*] Lord Hawkesbury has the honour to send your Majesty the full powers which are necessary to enable him to sign a Convention with the Minister[1] from the United States of America relative to the differences which have so long subsisted in consequence of the sixth Article in the last Treaty.

The American Government have offer'd to give six hundred thousand pounds to satisfy the claims of such creditors as may be unable to recover their debts (from lapse of time) in the American courts[2] & to leave the Courts open to the others; your Majesty's confidential servants are of opinion that under all the circumstances of the case, it is wise to close with this offer.

Your Majesty may depend on Lord Hawkesbury using every endeavour to encourage the better disposition which has of late appear'd in the Court of Berlin, and of providing as far as is in the power of this country, for the security of your Majesty's Electoral dominions and of the North of Germany. Lord Hawkesbury entertains hopes, however, that the speedy and successfull termination of the contest with France will avert for the present any danger which may be apprehended in that quarter, and will give Europe time to recover itself from the effects which have so naturally follow'd the feebleness & contracted policy of most of the Continental Governments. (10371)

2523 Sir Charles Morgan's Memorandum

[*Tredegar, Monmouthshire, 15 Sept. 1801.*] The Judge Advocate General has now the honor of representing to his Majesty, that by a general court martial held at Bristol Thomas Bailey, a private Militia man of the Oxfordshire Regiment has been tried and found guilty of 'being drunk in the streets between the hours of eleven and twelve o'clock at night of the 28th of last month and of striking Lieutenant Fowler of another Regiment, then Officer of the Guard,' and has been sentenced to receive eight hundred lashes.

The charge is fully established by evidence, and the prisoner ingenuously admits having been in a state of extreme intoxication, nor does he controvert the fact of having struck the Officer, but declares most solemnly he has not recollection of that or of any other circumstance which passed at the time, and professes the utmost penitence and contrition for so flagrant a crime.

Altho' the lesser offence cannot be admitted in excuse for the greater, yet as the prisoner is not habitually addicted to an immoderate use of liquor, and as the striking of Lieutenant Fowler has not proceeded from any ill will or intentional disrespect to that officer personally, nor from any settled contempt of authority, and more especially as both his immediate Captain and Lieutenant state him to have so conducted himself, untill this unhappy instance of transgression, as to be reputed by them one of the best soldiers in the company, possibly his Majesty may be graciously disposed to remit a moiety of the punishment awarded by the court martial, and to direct that the prisoner receives no more than *four* hundred lashes.

[1] Rufus King.
[2] Dating from the War of the American Revolution.

There seems to be fair ground for hope that this prisoner will avoid any excess of liquor, which may again betray him into disorderly behaviour, but it may be indispensibly necessary that he should undergo some open disgrace and punishment for the sake of deterring others. (10372)

2524 THE DUKE OF YORK *to the* KING

[*Horse Guards, 15 Sept. 1801.*] I take the earliest oportunity to report to your Majesty that I returned yesterday evening from my tour to Portsmouth, and from thence along the coast of the Southern District to Dover.

As I think it my duty to lay before your Majesty a detailed report of the different points which appear to require immediate attention for the protection of that part of the coast I shall not tresspass upon your Majesty's leisure by entering upon that subject in this letter.

I have in general found the regiments of infantry and militia very fine in point of men, and some of them well exercised, but I am sorry to say that sufficient attention has not been paid to the exactness and equality of their movements.

I am also sorry to add that it is not in my power to make a favourable report of the cavalry in the Southern District to your Majesty; some allowance may be made on account of Major-General Wilford's[1] having been alleged to be absent on account of illness. He has however now joined again, and I trust that upon a future oportunity their movements and appearance will be more exact and more creditable to them.

I trust that your Majesty will be graciously pleased to excuse my delaying to lay before your Majesty the usual weekly states for last week till the day after tomorrow when they shall be sent with those of this week. (10373)

2525 LORD HOBART *to the* KING, *and the reply*

[*Downing Street, 16 Sept. 1801.*] Lord Hobart presents his humble duty to your Majesty and takes the liberty of submitting the draft of a letter to the Lords of the Admiralty which he conceives necessary in order to guard against the possibility of your Majesty's Government being liable to the charge of having acquiesc'd in a measure calculated to bring the good faith of the British nation into question. (10374)

[*The King's reply, Weymouth, 17 Sept.*] The King fully enters into the propriety of Lord Hobart's draft to the Admiral on the ill-tempered conduct of Lord Keith, which if not taken notice of might occasion service difficulties. (Bucks. R.O.)

2526 THE DUKE OF YORK *to the* KING

[*Horse Guards, 17 Sept. 1801.*] I have little to trouble your Majesty with this week except the weekly states for two weeks, and monthly returns, together with

---

[1] Richard Rich Wilford (c. 1754–1822). Colonel, 1795; Major-General, 1797; Lieutenant-General, 1805; General, 1814. A.D.C. to General Burgoyne at Saratoga.

the recommendations for vacant commissions which have been received during my absence, for your Majesty's approbation.

As so large a reinforcement of troops has been moved into Sussex your Majesty I suppose will think the command a great deal too considerable and important for Major-General White,[1] and will therefore approve of a Lieutenant-General being sent there to command under Lieutenant-General Hulse. I therefore beg leave to recommend that Lieutenant-General Sir James Pulteney be placed upon the Staff for that purpose. (10375)

2527 SIR CHARLES MORGAN *to the* KING

[*Tredegar, Monmouthshire, 20 Sept. 1801.*] The Judge Advocate General is concerned to have so frequent occasion to trouble his Majesty, but feels it to be his duty to make a report of the sentence of a general court martial lately held at Colchester, together with a peculiar circumstance which has attended the proceeding. The object of the trial was a charge preferred against Lieutenant Richard Johnston of the 49th Regiment of Foot of having 'Misbehaved himself before the enemy in the action off Copenhagen on the 2nd April 1801', of which crime he was found *guilty*, and was adjudged 'to be dismissed his Majesty's service with every mark of infamy and disgrace, and for the sake of example in as publick a manner as possible at such time and place as his Majesty may be pleased to direct'. The instance of misbehaviour adduced against the prisoner consists in going down to the cockpit of the ship and remaining there during the action, which fact has been established by evidence to the satisfaction of the Court, and the Judge Advocate General has nothing to object to their decision.

The circumstance before alluded to, and which seems proper to be stated for his Majesty's consideration is this: the court martial has been held, not in consequence of a special warrant, which the case required, but under an order from General Marquis Cornwallis, as commanding the forces in the Eastern District, who conceived himself to be thereunto authorized by a general warrant which was issued soon after the passing of the Mutiny Act, addressed to Lieutenant-General Balfour[2] who at that time had the command of that District 'or to the General Officer Commanding the forces there', which warrant was calculated to confer a power for appointing courts martial from time to time to try any officer or soldier belonging to the forces within that District who should be charged with committing any offence against the rules of military discipline, but no authority could be derived from that warrant for giving cognizance of an offence charged to have been committed in another District or Station, as in the present instance, in which the crime imputed to the prisoner was alledged, and is found to have been committed on board one of his Majesty's ships of war off the coast of Denmark. It may not however be advisable, unless it should become absolutely necessary, that a doubt respecting the competency of the Court's jurisdiction should be held out to public

[1] Sometimes spelt Whyte. Colonel, 1793; Major-General, 1795; Lieutenant-General, 1802; General, 1812.

[2] James Balfour. Colonel, 1790; Major-General, 1794; Lieutenant-General, 1801; General, 1809 (d. 1823).

notice. The expedient which has suggested itself to the Judge Advocate, and which he takes leave humbly to submit to his Majesty, is that in the notification of his royal pleasure touching the sentence of the court martial, it may be stated that his Majesty, having adverted to some particular circumstances in the case as well as to the character of the prisoner, which untill the point of time in question had stood unimpeached, and more especially to the testimony of an officer of the same Regiment who has represented him as having behaved with much propriety as an officer in an action in Holland on the 2d October 1799, has not thought fit that the adjudication of the court martial should be carried into execution; but has nevertheless directed that it be intimated to the prisoner, Lieutenant Johnston, that his Majesty has not any further occasion for his service. (10377–8)

2528   THE DUCHESS OF WURTEMBERG *to the* KING

[*Louisbourg, 20 Sept. 1801.*] I rejoice to hear from all those who have the honour of attending your Majesty at Weymouth that you reap great benefit from the sea bathing, which I hope will give you strength to bear the fatigues of the winter. When the season for Weymouth is over I flatter myself that your Majesty will find your buildings at Windsor and Kew much advanced and that the farms will be in great beauty. Thank God our harvest has been very fine, but the plague of the field mice increases so much that in general people will be obliged to gather the potatoes much earlier than is usual. In some parts of the country they have drove the hogs into the fields which have devoured the mice, but most people are against this as they imagine that it gives the hogs an epidemal illness which our peasants cannot well afford after the severe losses they have had this last year. The most unpleasant thing here is the not being able with the greatest care to obtain the English verdure. Clover alone always keeps green which I believe is owing to its being mowed once a month. In my small field I have this year been able to make hay three times, which just gives me sufficient fodder for my cows during the winter and for a little calf which was born this week. I must acknowledge to your Majesty that I had no idea that I should ever have found so much pleasure as I do in my garden; it is my greatest amusement and it delights the Duke to see me so much taken up with my plants. (51656–7)

2529   HENRY ADDINGTON *to the* KING

[*Downing Street, 21 Sept. 1801.*] Mr. Addington most humbly intreats your Majesty's forgiveness for venturing to lay before your Majesty a letter which he received this day from his old master and friend, the Revd. Mr. Gilpin,[1] by whom Mr. Addington's presumption in making such a communication will never be known. (10376)

[1] The Rev. William Gilpin (*c.* 1726–1804), Master of Cheam School, Vicar of Boldre, Hants., Prebendary of Salisbury. Addington was sent to his school in June 1762 at the age of five, and was then described as 'an engaging, sweet boy, obliging to everybody, and tractable in the highest degree.'

2530 LORD HAWKESBURY *to the* KING

[*Downing Street, 22 Sept. 1801.*] Lord Hawkesbury has the honour to submit to your Majesty two communications which have been made to him by his Serene Highness the Prince of Orange, on the subject of which he humbly requests to receive your Majesty's commands. (10379)

2531 THE JUDGE ADVOCATE GENERAL (SIR CHARLES MORGAN) *to the* KING

[*Tredegar, Monmouthshire, 23 Sept. 1801.*] Sir Chas Morgan, before he troubles his Majesty with the proceedings of some courts martial which have been held in Jersey and Guernsey for the trial of soldiers who have attempted to desert from the Dutch Corps stationed at present in those islands, and (as the proximity of the French coast affords reason to suspect) to the enemy, esteems it to be an indispensible duty to state a doubt which has occurred to him in respect of a sentence of death passed upon four prisoners, one of whom has been upon account of his youth recommended as a fit object of his Majesty's clemency.

The doubt, if it may be so termed, is so considerable that the Judge Advocate General cannot reconcile it to himself to propose to his Majesty an approval of the sentence, which, fully impressed with a sense of the expediency of a public example, he would otherwise have felt himself obliged to do. The measure, which under these circumstances he presumes humbly to offer to his Majesty is, that the court martial should be reassembled and directed to reconsider their sentence. A revision upon this ground, which turns upon a question of law, seems not to be of so delicate a nature as when it respects the degree of credit to be given to witnesses, or the inference to be drawn from the evidence. The circumstance which has given occasion to the revision, the Judge Advocate General purposes to state in a letter to be laid before the court martial by the Depy Judge Advocate[1] who assisted at the trial, and takes leave to inclose herewith a draft of the intended letter for his Majesty's consideration. (10380)

2532 LORD PELHAM *to the* KING

[*Whitehall, 24 Sept. 1801.*] Lord Pelham humbly begs leave to represent to your Majesty that a Poor Knight's place belonging to St. George's Chapel at Windsor Castle is vacant, & he takes the liberty of naming to your Majesty Mr. William Denman of Willingdon in ye county of Sussex as a person whom Lord Pelham has long known, & for whom he feels a particular interest as he is now reduced to very low circumstances. (10381)

2533 THE DUKE OF YORK *to the* KING

[*Horse Guards, 24 Sept. 1801.*] I have the honor to transmit to your Majesty the usual weekly states together with the recommendations for vacant commissions

[1] Augustus Oldham.

for your Majesty's approbation as also the proposed quarters for the regiments now at Weymouth, after your Majesty's return from thence.

By the death of Colonel Forster which was reported to me a few days ago, the Loyal Somerset Regiment of Fencible Infantry has become vacant, and I beg leave to lay before your Majesty the name of Brigadeer Scot[t], who is serving upon the Irish Staff where that regiment now is and who is a most excellent and deserving officer to succeed to it. He has been recommended in the strongest manner by the Marquess Cornwallis for some such mark of your Majesty's favor, as he would probably otherwise at the end of the war be obliged to retire again upon the half pay of a Lieutenant-Colonelcy of Infantry.

Mr Addington has urged me strongly to lay before your Majesty Prince William's wish to be placed upon the Staff at this moment. The only difficulty is his being so old a Lieutenant-General, which in most stations would intitle him to a command which I should not think that your Majesty would approve of being intrusted to him. He can however be placed in the command of the North West District where there is hardly any troops and where from the little likelihood of the enemy making any attempt there will be less reason to fear the responsibility for him.

I am most rejoiced to learn by your Majesty's last most gracious letter that you intend to return to Windsor on the 2d of next month, as it is a clear proof of your Majesty feeling yourself thoroughly recovered. It has given me great pain not to have been able to pay my duty to your Majesty during your residence at Weymouth, and I shall not therefore fail to be at Windsor when your Majesty arrives there on Friday. I have in consequence arranged my tour round the coasts of Essex for next Sunday and shall return again in the course of Wednesday.[1] (10382)

2534 CABINET MINUTE, *29 Sept. 1801, and the King's reply*

At a Meeting of your Majesty's Confidential Servants.

Present: The Lord Chancellor, The Lord President, The Earl of Chatham, The Earl of St. Vincent, Lord Hobart, Lord Pelham, Mr Chancellor of the Exchequer, Lord Hawkesbury.

It was agreed that Lord Hawkesbury should submit to your Majesty the annexed Minute. (10385)

[*Enclosure*]

LORD HAWKESBURY *to the* KING

[*Downing Street, 29 Sept., 9 p.m.*] Lord Hawkesbury has the honour to send your Majesty the copy of a note which has been deliver'd to Mr Otto this evening and which must bring the negociation so long depending between this country and France to an immediate issue. Lord Hawkesbury has since seen Mr Otto and has

---

[1] The King's reply on the 25th is in Wheeler and Broadley, *Napoleon and the Invasion of England*, I, xvii. 'I cannot say I very willingly would put Prince William in any Command where much talents were required, but there is little probability of any attempt on the North West District that he will there be most out of the way.' Prince William was, of course, the 'Silly Billy' of contemporary satirists.

reason to think that the French Government will withdraw the demands to which the note refers. A great point however is made that the Preliminaries should be signed with as little delay as possible. Under these circumstances your Majesty's confidential servants humbly recommend to your Majesty to conclude the Treaty on the following terms. Ceylon & Trinidad, the two most important naval stations in the two hemispheres and not less important when their value as colonies is consider'd, to be annexed to your Majesty's dominions.

The Cape of Good Hope to be made a Free Port.

Malta to be made independant by being restored to the Order under the guaranty and protection of a third Power.

The rest of your Majesty's conquests to be restored to the Powers to which they belonged previous to the commencement of the war.

The integrity of the Dominions of your Majesty's remaining allies Turkey and Portugal to be preserved. The Kingdom of Naples & the Roman territory to be evacuated by the French.

Under all the circumstances of the times and in the present state of the continent of Europe, your Majesty's confidential servants are induced to hope that a peace founded on these conditions will be considered by your Majesty as consistent with the honour of your Crown, and the permanent interests of your dominions.

Lord Hawkesbury thinks it right further to inform your Majesty that the French Government have offer'd to consent to an arrangement by which Tobago should be ceded to your Majesty in the Definitive Treaty. (10386)

[*The King's reply, Weymouth, 30 Sept., 1.55 p.m.*] The King has received the Minute of Cabinet on the proposed Peace with France. To repeat his doubts whether any confidence can be placed in any agreement to be made with that country till it has a settled Government would be in reality a stop to all negociation; he will not oppose the concluding Peace, though he cannot place any reliance[1] on its duration, but trusts such a Peace establishment will be kept up as may keep this country on a respectable footing without which our situation would be most deplorable.[2] (10388)

2535   LORD HAWKESBURY *to the* KING, *and the reply*

[*Downing Street, 1 Oct. 1801.*] Lord Hawkesbury has the honour to acknowledge the receipt of your Majesty's note of yesterday and has great satisfaction in

[1] Altered from 'shall certainly place no reliance'.

[2] A copy of the Preliminary Articles of Peace, signed in London on 1 Oct., is in the Archives (ff 10389–96). The following is a copy of the Secret Article: 'It is understood between the contracting Parties that by the 6th Article concerning Portugal no obstacle is opposed either to the arrangements which have taken place between the Courts of Madrid and of Lisbon for the purpose of settling their frontiers in Europe, or to those which may be settled between the Governments of France and of Portugal for fixing the Limits of their territories in Guyana, provided that this settlement of limits shall not exceed what was fixed by the Treaty signed at Badajoz on the 6th of June last between the Ministers of France and of Portugal and communicated by the French Plenipotentiary at London in his note of the 18th of the same month.

In witness whereof we etc.

Hawkesbury.   Otto.' (10397)

informing you that preliminaries of peace between your Majesty and the French Government were signed this evening by Lord Hawkesbury and Mr Otto.[1] (10398)

[*The King's reply, Andover, 2 Oct. 1801, 9.10 a.m.*] The King has this instant received Lord Hawkesbury's note acquainting him with the signature of the Preliminaries of Peace. He trusts therefore every attention will be given to put this country on the most respectable state of defence; for he can never think any Treaty with France can be depended upon till it has a settled and regular form of Government. (10398)

2536 HENRY ADDINGTON *to the* KING, *and the reply*

[*Wimbledon, 3 Oct. 1801, 9.30 p.m.*] It appears to your Majesty's confidential servants to be extremely important that the meeting of Parliament for the dispatch of business, should not be delayed beyond ye 29th of October, and it is material that your Majesty's authority for this purpose should be given on Monday or on Tuesday morning at latest, that timely notice may be given to those members who reside at a considerable distance. Mr. Addington therefore humbly sollicits your Majesty's commands respecting the place for holding a Council on this subject, and the day and hour which may best suit your Majesty's convenience. (10399)

[*The King's reply, Windsor, 4 Oct.*] The King has received Mr. Addington's note proposing the holding a Privy Council for assembling the Parliament on the 29th of this month. The King will certainly be at the Queen's Palace on Tuesday at one o'clock for that purpose, and desires the Counsellors may be desired to be there at that hour, as he means to make as short a stay that day in London as may be required.

The King desires Mr. Addington will send this day due notice to the Lord President for that purpose.[2] (Sidmouth MSS.)

2537 LORD HAWKESBURY *to the* KING

[*Roehampton, 5 Oct. 1801.*] Lord Hawkesbury has the honour humbly to recommend to your Majesty Marquis Cornwallis to be appointed Plenipotentiary to the

---

[1] A *Gazette Extraordinary* published the news the following morning. Glenbervie wrote that day, 'I suppose no State secret was ever so well kept. It was not suspected by any news writer, nor by the public in general. Stocks have risen today, three per cent Consols from 59 to 68' (*Diaries*, 1, 254).

Pitt was told the news at once, 'The terms', he said, 'though perhaps not in every point exactly what one should wish, are, on the whole, advantageous, and certainly very creditable to the country.' (Rose, *Diaries and Corresp.* 1, 430.) And to Dundas he wrote (2 Oct.): 'I find Windham (as might be expected) in agonies, but the rest of the world as far as one can yet judge, very much delighted with the Peace.' 'It is remarkable that an ex-Speaker and the head of the Treasury made the Peace of Utrecht at the beginning of the last, and that an ex-Speaker now at the head of the Treasury has made a Peace at the beginning of this century, which is likely to occasion as much discussion and as great difference of opinion as the former did.' (Glenbervie's MS. Diary, 2 Oct.)

[2] The King sent Addington a brief note on the 18th, from Windsor: 'The King returns the warrants which he has signed. He trusts this fine day will enable Mr. Addington to conclude his arrangements at Woodley to his satisfaction.' (Sidmouth MSS.)

Congress at Amiens. Lord Hawkesbury trusts that this choice will be agreable to your Majesty, as he is convinced that the military reputation and character of Marquis Cornwallis will give him advantages in treating with the French Government which no other person would possess in an equal degree. Your Majesty may depend on every measure being taken for placing the country in a respectable state of defence. (10400)

2538 THE DUCHESS OF WURTEMBERG *to the* KING

[*Louisbourg, 7 Oct. 1801.*] I think it my duty to offer your Majesty my most humble congratulations on the signature of the peace, which I have this moment been apprized of. I trust that this fortunate event will enable your Majesty to pass a quiet winter and will ensure to Great Britain as well as to the continent many years of happiness and plenty to make up for the last wretched years we have passed. I rejoice most sincerely at the prospect of comfort your Majesty will enjoy; now that you are freed from constant uneasiness you will take double pleasure in your farms at Windsor and your buildings at Kew which I hope will many years prove an amusement to your Majesty's leisure hours.

To my great regret I am to leave this place on Monday for five months as the inhabitants of Stutgard are very anxious that the Duke should spend some time amongst them. Everybody assures me that this [is] a necessary step to keep all parties in good humour. I intend however frequently to visit my garden and watch the planting. (51658–9)

2539 LORD HAWKESBURY *to the* KING

[*Downing Street, 10 Oct. 1801, 6 p.m.*] Lord Hawkesbury has the honour to send your Majesty another copy of the ratified Treaty for your royal signature. The reason of Lord Hawkesbury's giving your Majesty this trouble will he trusts be approved of by you.

The Treaty was signed in English and French, and Lord Hawkesbury expected that the ratification of the French Government would be in both languages, and order'd the former copy to be prepared accordingly, but as the ratified copy of the French Government is only in French, Lord Hawkesbury is of opinion that your Majesty's copy should be only in English. Lord Hawkesbury received the ratification this morning from Genl. Lauriston,[1] he has carefully examined it, and it is exactly conformable to the original Treaty in French.

Lord Hawkesbury hopes to have the honour of paying his duty to your Majesty tomorrow at Windsor.[2] (10401)

---

[1] The French General and Marshal (1768–1828). At this time he was Napoleon's Aide-de-Camp (see *Auckland Corresp.* IV, 140). He fought in the later campaigns and was taken prisoner at Leipzig. Louis XVIII made him a peer and (1821) Marshal. 'To the great disgrace, I think, of John Bull,' wrote Glenbervie, 'the populace drew him [Lauriston] in Otto's carriage, from Pero's [*sic.*? Nerot's] hotel, first to Downing Street, and afterwards across the Park…to the door of the Admiralty Garden, whence he and Otto alighted and paid a visit to Lord St. Vincent…' (*Journals*, I, 256.)

[2] See Appendix.

[*London, 18 Oct. 1801.*] Lord Pelham begs leave with all humility to lay before your Majesty the inclosed papers.

Your Majesty will naturally observe, upon seeing the dates of some of them, that they might have been sooner taken into consideration, but Lord Pelham hopes that your Majesty will receive as an excuse the unusual circumstance of Colonel Littlehales[1] coming from the Lord Lieutenant with instructions to discuss with your Majesty's confidential servants almost all the material points in the administration of the Government in Ireland.[2]

It was on this account that Lord Pelham thought it most adviseable to bring the various points for consideration, before the Cabinet, at one time, having previously sent in circulation his observations upon the Lord Lieutenant's instructions, & his opinion upon the relation in which the Lord Lieutenant was to stand in future, in respect to this country. Having done so, it would have been Lord Pelham's duty to have sollicited an Audience of your Majesty in order to give such explanations as your Majesty might require at the time that your Majesty might think fit to give your commands upon the several subjects under consideration; but Lord Pelham well knowing how much your Majesty approves of those attentions which are due to departed friends & relations, has presumed that your Majesty would consider with indulgence this temporary suspension of the duties which he owes to your Majesty, & that your Majesty will forgive Lord Pelham for not paying his duty in person to your Majesty, untill after the funeral of Lady Holdernesse.[3] (10407-8)

2541 LORD GRENVILLE *to the* KING

(Copy)

[*Dropmore, 19 Oct. 1801.*] A sincere reluctance to intrude myself on your Majesty's time by any statement relating solely to my own conduct has hitherto prevented me from venturing upon the liberty which I am now presuming to take.

Strong as the sense is which I must ever entertain of all your Majesty's goodness towards me, yet of the many proofs of it which I experienced on quitting your Majesty's service there was none for which I felt more truly grateful than for the gracious assurance that I might always rely on your Majesty's favourable interpretation of my future conduct. I valued this assurance highly in proportion to the

[1] Edward Baker Littlehales (1765–1825). Lieutenant-Colonel, 1797; Under-Secretary of State, Military Department [I.], May 1801–19. He accompanied Cornwallis to France when the Marquess went to negotiate the Treaty of Amiens. Created Baronet, Sept. 1802.

[2] On the 20th Addington wrote to Pelham, 'Many thanks for the contents of your box. The King's notes show that insight into men's characters which is the result of close observation and long experience.' (Add. MSS. 33108, f. 191.)

[3] Lady Holdernesse (?1721–1801) died on 13 Oct. and was buried on the 28th at Hornby, Yorks. Her furniture was subsequently auctioned. Lord Pelham married, 16 July 1801, Mary Henrietta Juliana (1776–1862), daughter of the 5th Duke of Leeds by his first wife, Baroness Conyers, who was Lady Holdernesse's daughter. Lord Auckland was told about 'the terrible operation to which my respectable old friend Lady Holdernesse has been obliged to submit, for a cancer in the breast. She had kept it a secret from everybody, and preserved her cheerfulness and courage in an astonishing degree' (To Lord Sheffield, 26 April [1801]).

earnest desire which I must ever feel to stand well in your Majesty's opinion, from whom I have received such uniform and affecting kindness. And I am therefore particularly desirous to solicit that indulgence which your Majesty thus allowed me to hope for, at a moment when my duty appears to me to require of me that I should express in public how much I have the misfortune to differ from your Majesty's servants, on points of the highest national importance.

As an individual who, both on public and on private grounds, was deeply interested in the subject, I have looked with increasing anxiety at all I have seen of the course of the late negotiations with Russia and France. Both appear to me to have been marked throughout by a tone of unnecessary and degrading concession. And after the fullest and most deliberate consideration I remain convinced that the result of both, instead of contributing to the credit or security of the country, has involved your Majesty's dominions in new dangers, and has created a fresh and urgent necessity for measures of increased precaution at home, and for the most extensive scale both of military and of naval establishments.

These opinions, for the freedom of which I ought perhaps to apologise to your Majesty, it is by no means the object of this letter to obtrude where it does not in any manner belong to me to offer them, but solely to submit them with all humility as the grounds of the part which I myself am compelled to take. They appear to me to be so entirely consonant with those on which I have so long been acting, and from which I am not conscious of having ever departed, even in a single instance, that I flatter myself your Majesty will at least think them sincere, even if they are mistaken, and will impute them to the effect of deep and permanent impressions, strengthened by continual reflection and confirmed by long experience.

If therefore after having hitherto endeavoured as far as was in my power to support the persons to whom your Majesty has committed the administration of your affairs, I am now compelled to express in public the deep concern and apprehension with which I have seen their last and most important measures, your Majesty will I trust do me the justice to believe that I can be influenced by no other motive than those by which your Majesty always wishes that every man should regulate his conduct. Above all I hope that your Majesty will never suspect that I can either forget my sense of personal obligation, or lose sight of those feelings of public gratitude which are indeed due to your Majesty from all your subjects, but which can be fully appreciated by those only who in times of difficulty and alarm have been honoured with your Majesty's confidence.

That all your Majesty's endeavours for the happiness of your people may be crowned with success, and that a protecting Providence may remove far from your Majesty all danger and misfortune, will ever continue to be my constant and earnest prayer. (Fortescue MSS., and Chatham Papers, 140.)

2542 THE DUC DE MORTEMART *to the* KING

[*London, 22 Oct. 1801.*] In those unhappies times [*sic*], when all sorts of misfortunes have befallen us, it is to your Majesti's goodness that I owe my existence and that of my large family. The command with wich your Majesty honored me has been almost my only ressource since he gave us an azilum in his dominions. It is my greatest consolation, and of those belonging to me, that we owe this blessing, to so great and generous a King. But, Sir, in the arrangements following the peace that your Majesty has just given to his subjects, I am in the greatest anxiety that the French regiments in his service should be disbanded. By that I schould fall again in that dreadfull situation from wich your Majesty saved me. By the very great goodness your Majesty gave me so many proofs of I dare take the liberty of beseching him to preserve stil in his service me, my brother, and the galants and ever loyals French officers now under my command [*sic*]. I trust I may assure him that in any country or situation watsoever it may please your Majesty to employ us, he cann never have more zealed, and devoted servants [*sic*]. But whatever may be the resolution, dict[at]ed by his generosity, I take the liberty to intreat your Majesty to be convinced, that nothing cann ever equal the very great gratitude, I shal preserve for him till the least breath of my existence. (10409)

2543   LORD ELDON *to the* KING

[*Friday morning, 23 Oct. 1801.*] The Lord Chancellor offering his most humble duty to your Majesty, takes leave to mention that the City of London propose to name, for your Majesty's Royal approbation, Sir John Eamer as a proper person to fill the high office of Lord Mayor in the ensuing year.[1] It will be the Lord Chancellor's duty to signify your Majesty's Royal approbation early in the next week, if your Majesty shall graciously so think fit, and he has particular satisfaction in assuring your Majesty that his own observation upon that gentleman's conduct, whilst he was Sheriff, fully justifies him in saying that he is eminently loyal & cordially attached to your Majesty's person & Government.[2] (10506)

2544   THE DUCHESS OF WURTEMBERG *to the* KING

[*Stutgard, 24 Oct. 1801.*] Though I have already had the honour of congratulating your Majesty on the Peace I cannot neglect to accompany the Duke's letter with a few lines, and entreat your Majesty with your wonted goodness to take into consideration the great losses which the Duke has suffered owing to the war, and to beg you will order your Ministers to attend to the Note which will be delivered to them on this subject. I must also beseech your Majesty to be so gracious as to give Lord Cornwallis some directions to press at Amiens the indemnifications which have so long been promised to the Duke and particularly so by the Treaty of Louisbourg which promises territorial indemnifications at the Peace.

Your Majesty is already apprised in great measure of our losses, but I hope you will allow me to make a short statement of them that you may at once be able

---

[1] On Tuesday, 29 Sept. Sir John Eamer was nominated Lord Mayor of London for the ensuing year. The Lord Chancellor appointed Wednesday 28 Oct. to receive the Lord Mayor elect at his house in Bedford Square. On that day the Recorder of London, some of the Aldermen and the Sheriffs went in procession to Bedford Square to present Sir John to the Lord Chancellor for the approbation of the King. Sir John attended the Levée on Friday the 30th.

[2] The King's reply on the 25th, approving the choice of the new Lord Mayor, is in Twiss, I, 397.

to judge of their extent. The Principality of Montbeillard, the Sovereignties in Alsatia and in Franche Comté and since the year 1799 near ten millions of florins besides the Fortress of Hohentweil, whose fortifications cost some millions and which the enemy has blown up.

I am sure your Majesty will be struck with the misfortunes this war has brought on us and consider how dreadful the weight of these calamities would be on all countries but doubly so on one of this size which, though not half so extensive as Bavaria, has been forced to pay larger contributions. Your Majesty's goodness encourages me to hope you will forgive my dwelling so long on this subject and that you will be so gracious as to assist us in obtaining the advantages which through the Peace of Luneville have been promised to the secular Princes and which our heavy losses gives us some right to expect, particularly if your Majesty will be so gracious as to take us under your protection. (51660–1)

2545   THE BISHOP OF WORCESTER (DR HURD) *to the* KING

[*Hartlebury, 26 Oct. 1801.*] Your Majesty's gracious notice of me in sending the Gottingen exercises, & especially the letter wch came with them, is almost the only, certainly the greatest, satisfaction I can receive. That your Majesty found benefit by your late residence at Weymouth is most welcome news. But it is no wonder that some remains of so severe an illness are felt; which, however, gentle exercise, & the care to avoid as much as possible the fatigue of business, will, I trust, gradually remove.

As to the Peace, tho' I am no politician, I would fain persuade myself that it will be lasting. The moderation & magnanimity of your Majesty's counsels promise this effect. And as to the rest of the world, necessity will sometimes do more than principle. But I forbear to enlarge farther on a subject I so little understand.

The close of your Majesty's letter affects me infinitely. If I could have paid my duty & gratified my own inclination by seeing Windsor, I should certainly have done it long since. But I am wholly incapable of doing myself that honour. My bodily weakness is not the worst. My memory is almost entirely gone, & my powers of attention so weak that conversation with a common friend, for a few minutes, is almost too much for me. In this enfeebled state I support myself as well as I can in this quiet scene, & employ the little recollection I am master of, in calling to mind the innumerable obligations I have to your Majesty, & in putting up my prayers to Heaven for a long continuance of health and every other blessing to your Majesty, and the Queen, & the Royal Family.[1] (10412)

2546   LORD PELHAM *to the* KING

[*Stratton Street, 26 Oct. 1801.*] Lord Pelham takes leave with all humility of laying before your Majesty a private letter from the Lord Lieutenant suggesting an arrangement of Church preferment in Ireland in consequence of the death of

---

[1] Dr Hurd, in spite of his feeble physical and mental condition, retained his See until his death in 1808, at the age of 88. This was the custom of the time.

the Archbishop of Dublin.[1] Lord Pelham sollicits your Majesty's indulgence while he ventures to add his own recommendation to that of the Lord Lieutenant, being well acquainted with the merits of the present Archbishop of Cashel in his diocese where he has enforced residence & established a discipline amongst his clergy that reflects the highest honour upon his character, & Lord Pelham feels very particular satisfaction in being able to give full scope to those feelings which a long & intimate connection with ye Bishop of Kilmore give rise to, without any risk of exceeding the limits of what is due to your Majesty & the publick service, for Lord Pelham is convinced that the Bishop of Kilmore's intimate knowledge of ye Irish, (a qualification possessed by very few Englishmen) his firm attachment to ye Protestant Establishment, the unshaken correctness of his own conduct, his candour towards others, the encouragement he has always given to the clergy within his diocese, who have recommended themselves by a diligent discharge of their parochial duties, qualify him in an eminent degree for advancement in rank & authority.[2]

With respect to the other promotions suggested by Lord Hardwicke, Lord Pelham humbly submitts to your Majesty that as the persons are certainly very respectable it would be considered as an act of grace on the part of your Majesty, to confirm the encouragement which Lord Cornwallis had held out at the Union.

Lord Pelham begs leave farther to ask your Majesty's commands, as to the time when your Majesty will be graciously pleased to receive your confidential servants for the purpose of reading the Speech. (10413–16)

2547   THE EARL OF ST VINCENT *to the* KING

[*Admiralty, 31 Oct. 1801, 8 a.m.*] It is a very painful part of my duty humbly to apprize your Majesty that a message by telegraph was sent up from Portsmouth late last evening, imparting the death of Vice-Admiral Lord H. Seymour, and that his body was arriv'd at Spithead in a sloop of war.[3] In making this communication to your Majesty, I cannot refrain from expressing the deep concern I feel for the heavy loss your Majesty, his country and family have sustained in the loss of this excellent officer.[4] (10418)

2548   THE DUKE OF YORK'S MEMORANDUM ON THE PROPOSED PEACE ESTABLISHMENT FOR 1802

(*Copy*)

[*1 Nov. 1801.*] Upon a consideration of the two plans proposed for the Peace Establishment of 1802, it is evident that they do not differ more in the number

[1] Dr Fowler, the Archbishop (1726?–1801) died on 10 Oct.

[2] Charles Agar, Lord Somerton, Archbishop of Cashel, succeeded Dr Fowler as Archbishop of Dublin. Dr Brodrick [Broderick], Bishop of Kilmore, became Archbishop of Cashel.

[3] Lord Hugh Seymour died on 12 Sept. on board the Tisiphone, a victim of yellow fever. He was buried in the family vault in Warwickshire.

[4] The King's letter to Cornwallis on the subject of his Electoral dominions (10425 [1 Nov.]), and Cornwallis's reply at 6 p.m. that day (10424), are in Ross, III, 384–5.

of men for which the calculations are made, than in the principles upon which they are formed.

The principle upon which that for 117,600 men rests is in the first instance a consideration of the gross number of troops supposed necessary for the defence and the protection of every part of his Majesty's dominions, founded upon past experience and under present circumstances; in the next instance, the formation of a plan of establishment for that gross number, which should render the force as efficient as possible, (paying due attention to the necessary proportions of cavalry and infantry) at the least expence to the public.

The other plan appears to have been formed upon principles diametrically opposite, first by fixing an ideal number of troops to be kept up, secondly by forming an establishment for that number having for its object the preserving every battalion of the line which is numbered, the reducing the second and third battalions, and then raising eight additional corps, without adverting to the relative proportions of cavalry and infantry, the first of which is in every respect from its nature the most difficult to form, and lastly by endeavouring to allot the force so formed to the different parts of his Majesty's Dominions, not with a view to local circumstances and situations, but to an unqualified division of a given number.

Experience at the commencement of the two last wars has proved how serious are the disadvantages which must ever arise from the system of keeping up many Regiments at low establishments. Besides its being more expensive, from the number of officers which it requires, it must be evident to all persons conversant with the service, that the various demands which are equally made upon every Battalion, whether strong or weak, of bat men, additional gunners &c, cause (proportionably speaking), a much greater diminution of effectives in a weak corps than in a strong one, which reasoning applies equally to the cavalry.

The nature of our Constitution furnishes an additional argument in favour of strong corps in the British service, as it precludes the possibility of secretly augmenting the army previous to the breaking out of a war. The necessity which results from such an event of instantaneously reinforcing our foreign possessions, allows no time for adding to the strength of Regiments, and obliges us to employ Battalions at their low establishments, whereby we deprive ourselves of the most effectual means of creating an efficient force.

Having stated generally the grounds of objection which appear to me to attach to the plan prepared at the War Office, I shall proceed to observe upon such distinct points in it as require particular animadversion. Of these the most prominent is the proposed reduction of one squadron in each of the Regiments of Life Guards, and of one Battalion in each Regiment of Foot Guards.

Upon the reduction of the Horse and Horse Grenadier Guards in 1787, two Regiments of Life Guards of 200 men each were raised. This number however was found so inadequate to the common duties required, that in a very few months an additional troop was added to each Regiment. This addition was still insufficient, and after the experience of some years, Government found itself under the necessity of making a further augmentation of one troop to each, the whole thus amounting to 600 men, a number exceeding in a trifling degree only that of the Horse and Grenadier Guards previous to their reduction in 1787. It is therefore evident that no reduction in their numbers can with propriety be made in these corps.

Without entering into the policy of reducing in times like the present the number of his Majesty's Foot Guards who have existed since the Restoration, and who during all subsequent periods of the strictest oeconomy and the lowest peace establishments, have been kept up even at a higher establishment than the Regiments of the Line—it must at least appear singular that the very moment when their services have been most called for and have been most distinguished, should be that chosen for their reduction. The chief support of a due military spirit in the Foot Guards has hitherto been the prospect of being upon every occasion employed upon actual service, being from their numbers and station the corps which Government has always the power of calling upon in moments of emergency. It is this expectation which keeps up the respectability of the officers, as no young man of spirit who really wished to make the Army his profession could possibly reconcile to himself the idea of entering into a corps which had not the prospect of being employed upon actual service, which could not be the case if the number of Battalions are reduced as suggested. Should such a measure be determined upon, a class of persons altogether the reverse of the present would compose the officers of the Guards, which part of the Army from that moment could only be considered in the light of a body of armed constables.

A recollection of the fatal events which have recently occurred in France, where the French Guards (officered and constituted as ours would then be) were the first to throw down their arms and to join against their Sovereign, affords room for the most serious reflection.

The only objections which have ever been made to the Guards as a part of the Army, are the advantages which they enjoy in point of rank and additional pay, and that from the manner in which the soldiers are quartered, being unavoidably dispersed in public houses throughout London, the officers are less in connection with their men than those of other corps. That the pay of the Foot Guards should be higher than that of the Line, has always been considered the necessary consequence of the higher rate of every article of living in the Metropolis.

Whatever troops therefore are stationed in London must unavoidably receive a higher pay, and upon those grounds it is clear that no saving would accrue to the public from employing in the capital any other description of troops than the Guards. This observation is equally applicable to the officers, indeed more forcibly still, for no one can suppose that their pay alone, although somewhat higher than that of the Line, suffices to the support of their situation; they must therefore necessarily be possessed of some private fortune, and it therefore naturally follows that they must in general be of a higher description of men than those of the other branches of the service. Some advantages must be held out to persons engaging in any profession which from its nature entails extraordinary expence—these advantages in the Army can only be rank or increased pay, to the latter of which one great objection presents itself, which is, that it would induce persons to enter the service for that sole object, and men who become officers with views so sordid and so limitted cannot be supposed to possess that military ardour and ambition which must cause every officer to look forward to rank as his greatest reward. The only remaining inducement therefore is superior rank, which, however it may be considered with a jealous eye by other branches of the service, when placed in its proper light must operate in a partial degree only (if in any) to the prejudice of the rest of the Army; and in a general view of the subject is attended with solid advantages both in a political and a military sense.

There can be no doubt of the great advantage of young men of high rank and fortune entering into the Army with every degree of military ardour, many of them from their own situation or from family reasons could not make it a profession, if they were under the necessity during peace of being for any length of time absent from this country. To these therefore the Guards offer an opportunity of honorably pursuing the military profession without subjecting themselves to those inconveniences which would otherwise preclude their belonging to the service. They offer also almost the only means which his Majesty has in time of peace of conferring rank on young men of fashion and fortune, as it has always been the policy to dispose of a certain proportion of vacancies in the Guards out of the Regiments, nor can the quick promotion of persons purchasing from the Line into the Guards be brought forward as an objection to the latter, as rank must be an object with them, and unless obtained in the Guards, would be gained in the Line where it would certainly be more severely felt.

The last objection on the score of rank which has been [made] to the Guards, is its clashing with that of officers of the Line upon service. To this it is only observed that no serious inconvenience has ever been known to have resulted from it, and indeed it can only operate to the inconvenience of the Guards themselves by loading the subalterns with a greater proportion of duty from the Captains having the rank of Field Officers. The service in general this war certainly does not admit of bringing forward any objection to the rank of the Guards, for to that corps we are indebted for many of the officers who have most distinguished themselves in command.

The third objection which has been made to the Guards is the want of a more immediate connexion between the officers & men. This however may be urged against any body of troops placed in the same situation, as from the immense extent of the Metropolis, & the consequent widely scattered situation of the soldiers quarters, it is impossible for the officers to see so much as could be wished of their men, although late regulations have in a great degree removed this evil. This is an additional reason for its being so strongly urged that the Guards should be kept at such an establishment as to admit of a part being constantly detached from London so as to afford the officers an opportunity in Barracks, or in streightened quarters of becoming more acquainted with their men, and of learning the detail of regimental duty, which they have less opportunity of doing in London.

In examining the proposed establishment of the cavalry, every one must be struck with the great disproportion between that and the infantry. The superior advantage of cavalry for the preservation of tranquillity in the country is evident from the experience of the last ten years and is enforced by the constant demand which there is for the infantry for our distant possessions; and the great credit which the cavalry have gained on foreign service is a signal proof of their pre-eminence in war. So powerfully indeed has this been impressed on the minds of Government, that within a very short period before the Peace a considerable augmentation had taken place in this part of the service. It has been already observed that cavalry is an arm which requires time and much trouble to be brought to a state of perfection. In former wars, cavalry was a very secondary consideration in the active operations of a campaign, but in the present war, cavalry and artillery have been the principal instruments employed in all great movements. It cannot be disputed that these arms are the most expencive, but if the enemy finds an advantage in adopting them, no choice is left, and he must be met upon equal grounds.

From the above considerations the first proposal for the peace establishment of the cavalry was formed, and although a partial diminution might be made in the number of Regiments, yet any essential alteration of that number would be attended with great prejudice to the general interests of the country.

In regard to the proposed establishment of the infantry, it is unnecessary to repeat the objections which have been adduced in the beginning of this paper to the keeping up of many Regiments at low establishments; but it is impossible to avoid noticing the proposal of reducing seventeen existing Battalions and raising five new ones, under the idea of forming the latter into Light Corps. This measure is presumed to be equally inconsistent with oeconomy and justice; and although the utility and necessity of Light troops are admitted to the fullest extent, it surely is preferable that a proportionate number of the present Regiments of the Line should be armed and trained to that particular service, rather than raise new corps; which arrangement can be made with the greatest facility, and the Battalions can be rendered fit for that service much more expeditiously in every respect than new ones could possibly be formed.

The last point to be considered is the proposed distribution of the troops. In the first part of both proposals the necessity of maintaining a large force in Great Britain and Ireland appears to be equally admitted, although that drawn up at the War Office does not seem to connect the important objects of security at home and the preservation of a force adequate to afford reliefs for our foreign possessions.

In the allotment of a force for India and of garrisons for our colonies the proposals differ widely. In a former paper the East India establishment of 1792 was detailed, and it might have been presumed that the acquisition of the Mysore country and the Island of Ceylon would have been a reason for augmenting, rather than diminishing the European force in that country.

In the most peaceable times 3,500 men have been allotted for Jamaica, but at this moment, when the whole Island of St. Domingo is in the hands of France, or (what is considered more dangerous still by the proprietors in Jamaica) in the power of the blacks, no augmentation is intended.

Both Lord Grey and the late Sir Ralph Abercromby gave it as their opinion that between 7 and 8,000 men were absolutely necessary for the garrisons of the

Leeward and Charribbee Islands in the possession of Great Britain previous to the war. To these must now be added the Island of Trinidad, which from its proximity to Spanish America must be supplied with a garrison capable of resisting any sudden attack. For the whole of these however 8,800 men only are proposed, which it is intended should comprehend 2,400 Europeans and 6000 blacks, making the proportion of the latter nearly as three to one—a proposal which surely cannot be acceptable to the proprietors or inhabitants of the West India Islands. (10426–38)

2549 LORD PELHAM *to the* KING

[*Thursday, 5 Nov. 1801.*] Lord Pelham humbly begs leave to inform your Majesty that on account of certain circumstances which make it desireable for the Algerine Embassador to prolong his stay in England, he wishes to avail himself of your Majesty's gracious consent to give him an audience on some distant day instead of tomorrow.

Lord Pelham has taken the necessary means for communicating to both Houses of Parliament your Majesty's commands about receiving their Addresses tomorrow. (10441)

2550 LORD HAWKESBURY *to the* KING

[*Roehampton, 7 Nov. 1801.*] Lord Hawkesbury has the honour to send your Majesty a dispatch and a private letter which he has just received from Lord Carrysfort. It is with the most sincere and heartfelt satisfaction that Lord Hawkesbury is enabled to inform your Majesty that the Prussian troops have actually begun to retire from your Majesty's Electoral dominions. (10444)

2551 THE DUCHESS OF WURTEMBERG *to the* KING

[*Stutgard, 8 Nov. 1801.*] I cannot deny myself the honour of writing to your Majesty by Lord Minto though I fear it will not be quite so legible as usual, having contrived to strain my arm.

It gave me great pleasure to see Lord Minto as he had had the pleasure of seeing your Majesty so much later than myself; indeed it is impossible for those who have not been parted from their family to imagine the joy one feels at meeting with anybody who can give some account of all those one loves. I am like an infant on those occasions and though perfectly satisfied with my situation and sincerely attached to the Duke, can never one moment forget the strong ties of duty and attachment which I feel for the best of parents. Lord Minto has promised to take Louisbourg on his road that he may give your Majesty some account of my favourite spot, though it is not in beauty at present. If possible I contrive to spend one day there every week and watch a little my workmen who grow very idle if they are not followed. (51664–5)

2552　LORD PELHAM *to the* KING

[*Stratton Street, 9 Nov. 1801.*] Lord Pelham having been informed by Mr Addington that your Majesty is graciously disposed to create their Royal Highnesses Prince Augustus & Prince Adolphus Dukes & Peers of the Realm, he humbly sollicits your Majesty's commands for making out the necessary Patents. (10445)

2553　THE EARL OF CHESTERFIELD *to the* KING

[*Bradby Hall, 14 Nov. 1801.*] Your Majesty will I hope forgive the liberty I take in acquainting you that I received on Thursday evening last a letter from Coll. Spencer, dated Camp before Alexandria, September 12, 1801. I can I think in no way convey to your Majesty the gratitude Coll. Spencer feels for your gracious kindness in appointing him one of your Equerries in Extraordinary so well as by having the honor to enclose his letter to your Majesty.[1] (10446)

2554　HENRY ADDINGTON *to the* KING, *and the reply*

[*Downing Street, 16 Nov. 1801, 11.30 p.m.*] As Mr. Ryder has resigned the office of Treasurer of the Navy, Mr. Bragge will not fail to attend at St. James's on Wednesday next, to acknowledge your Majesty's goodness in directing that he should succeed him;[2] and Mr. Addington ventures to hope that your Majesty may be graciously pleased to allow Mr. Bragge to be sworn a member of the Privy Council on that day.[3] (10449)

[*The King's reply, Windsor, 17 Nov., 8 a.m.*] The King very much approves Mr. Bragge's being admitted tomorrow of the Privy Council, as he would not have him

---

[1] Colonel Brent Spencer wrote to Lord Chesterfield on 12 Sept.: 'I had not the honor of receiving until yesterday your Lordship's letter of the 24th May in which a copy of the one from his Majesty was enclosed. If in the mere performance of my duty I had been honored with the smallest mark of approbation from his Majesty I should consider it greatly exceeding what I could possibly deserve. To express, therefore, the sense I entertain of his gracious kindness to me in the appointment of Equerry as well as in several other instances, is far above my abilities, and must ever excite sentiments of the sincerest gratitude and the most devoted attachment. Could anything add to the pleasure I naturally feel on this occasion it would be from the polite manner in which the intelligence has been communicated to me.' (10447–8)

[2] As early as 3 July William Wellesley-Pole had said that this arrangement was to be made. 'Dudley Ryder is dying [he died in 1847]. He has had a fever which ended in an abscess in his side that is killing him. Bragge will be his successor as Treasurer of the Navy' (*Wellesley Papers*, I, 141). Charles Yorke however, had the first refusal. He wrote to his brother, Lord Hardwicke on 28 July: 'Addington... told me that in case of poor Ryder's death... he was empowered by his Majesty to offer me the *Treasurership of the Navy* in case I chose to prefer it to my present office...Bragge is intended for the office which I do not take. The Treasurership is £4,000 per annum and a good house; my present office is £2,400 and no house; indeed, considering its rank, *much* underpaid, and I am not one jot *richer* in fact than I was before. On the other hand the business of the War Office, such as it is, suits me well. I like the people I have found there, and they appear well enough satisfied with me, and the Duke of York is on very comfortable terms. Besides this, there must be another *county election*. If the War Office was £3,000 per annum I don't think I should hesitate.' (Add. MSS. 35701, f. 55.) On 4 Nov. Yorke said he had again been offered the Treasurership of the Navy, but that he had decided to remain where he was. Addington, to whom he wrote on the 5th, had proposed to increase the salary of that office to £3,000. (Add. MSS. 35701, f. 145; Bodleian MSS.)

[3] Before 11 Feb. Addington had expressed a wish that Bragge, his brother-in-law, should be proposed as Speaker, but the King had objected to the suggestion (Rose, *Diaries and Corresp.* I, 307).

by any means stood in a less conspicuous light than any of his predecessors. Mr. Addington is therefore to give notice of this to the Lord President of the Council.[1] (Sidmouth MSS.)

2555   THE EARL OF ST VINCENT *to the* KING

[*Admiralty, 18 Nov. 1801.*] Lord St. Vincent has the honor of transmitting to your Majesty the sentence and minutes of a court martial lately held at Portsmouth for enquiring into the conduct of Vice-Admiral Sir William Parker;[2] the minute of the Board of Admiralty containing the grounds for recalling the Vice-Admiral from his station, which is annexed to the minutes, and the charge as recited in the sentence, are so full and explicit that Lord St. Vincent thinks it unnecessary for him to enter into any explanation upon the subject. He cannot however help observing that of all the sentences which have come to his knowledge, no one ever appeared so extraordinary as the present, indeed even the ordinary forms of pronouncing whether the charges were or were not proved, have not been observed.

Lord St. Vincent has been for some days indisposed, and is thereby prevented of the honor of paying his duty to your Majesty at St. James's today, which he wished very much to have done. (10450)

2556   *Letters from* LORD ELDON *to the* KING

[*20 Nov. 1801.*] The Lord Chancellor most dutifully acknowledges the honour of receiving your Majesty's letter this morning, and he takes leave to avail myself [*sic*] of your Majesty's gracious authority to consult Mr. Addington on this occasion. As soon as he can see that gentleman, and he hopes so to do this evening or early tomorrow morning, he will immediately return to your Majesty the draft, with the perusal of which your Majesty has been pleased to honour him. (10451)

[*Downing Street, 22 Nov. 1801.*] The Lord Chancellor offers his most humble duty to your Majesty, and, having, according to your Majesty's gracious permission, communicated the inclosed draft to Mr. Addington, takes leave to return it to your Majesty. Mr. Addington and the Chancellor agree in presuming to state to your Majesty their humble opinion that it is perfectly well calculated to continue to the Princess[3] that happiness, which she has derived from your Majesty's goodness and protection. (10452)

---

[1] Yorke wrote to his brother Lord Hardwicke on the 6th: 'I was in the *Closet* today for some time. The K. was more gracious than I can express; accepted of my refusal in perfectly good part, and said that tho' he was determined that the office in question should not be vacant without its being offered to me, yet he was much better pleased that I remained where I was; that he had a very high opinion of my integrity as well as of my talents, etc....I never saw his Majesty look better, clearer, or more himself. To Addington I have certainly done a great favour by refusing the Treasurership.' (Add. MSS. 35701, f. 148.)

[2] Sir William Parker (1743–1802). Lieutenant, 1766; Captain, 1777; Rear-Admiral, 1794; Vice-Admiral, 1799. Created Baronet, 24 June 1797. He was Commander on the Halifax station, 1800–1, being recalled for a technical offence.

[3] The Princess of Wales, who had informed the King on the 18th that her allowance from the Prince was three quarters in arrear, that she was in debt and her situation uncomfortable. See *Corresp. of George, Prince of Wales*, no. 1619.

2557 LORD PELHAM to the KING

[*London, 23 Nov. 1801.*] Lord Pelham most humbly begs leave to submit to your Majesty an observation respecting the title of Cambridge for which a warrant is prepared in obedience to your Majesty's commands for his Royal Highness the Prince Adolphus; the Dukedom of Cambridge being vested in your Majesty by letters patent entailing it on your Majesty's heirs male, it might happen that if in the course of events the Crown should descend to a female there would be two Dukes of Cambridge.

Lord Pelham has inclosed a note respecting the title of Cambridge which he received from the Herald's Office and also a list of extinct titles in case your Majesty should think the foregoing observation of sufficient importance to induce your Majesty to order a fresh warrant. (10453–4)

2558 THE DUKE OF CUMBERLAND to the KING

[*St James, 25 Nov. 1801.*] On my return to town I sent for Bott and had a long conversation with him, & again this morning. He saw Keling this very morning and he positively asserts that Bowman was the person who ordered your Majesty to be blindfolded, that he quarrelled with the men for not tying your Majesty tighter, that he had you placed nearer the fire, was the person who felt you & stirred himself the fire to make it hotter, using expressions too gross to be written & makes one shudder to think of.[1] (47191)

2559 DR GEORGE HEATH to the KING

[*Eton, 25 Nov. 1801.*] Although I am well aware how great a liberty I am taking in addressing these lines to your Majesty, when I state the grounds on which I presume to do it I hope I shall be forgiven.

My mind is deeply impress'd with so strong a sense of gratitude towards your Majesty, for the very gracious notice with which I am occasionally honor'd, and the zealous warmth with which your Majesty has condescended to patronize me, that I never can express in adequate terms my feelings on the occasion. I am therefore in duty bound not to take any step of such consequence as what I am about to communicate, without humbly requesting your Majesty's gracious permission.

A Fellowship is now vacant in Eton College: I have hopes that my pretensions to success, if I offer myself a candidate, are fair and flattering. I have now been engaged in teaching at Eton thirty five years; eight as a private tutor, seventeen as assistant, and ten as Master. I feel my health and spirits much on the decline. I feel my mind hardly competent to the exertion necessary in a situation of such constant anxiety and responsibility, from nervous agitation and frequent indisposition. I have for some time past found myself so alter'd that I have several times had thoughts of solliciting your Majesty's permission to withdraw myself

[1] Bowman was one of the King's Pages, and is mentioned in R. F. Greville's Diary, 7 Jan. 1789, as one of 'Dr. Willis's men', but Greville does not corroborate this story.

from so laborious a life before it shall be too late for me to enjoy any domestic comfort in retirement, even without any additional preferment to make up for the great sacrifice of emolument by resigning the School. An opportunity now offers, probably, of which I wish to avail myself, as quiet, after so long and unremitted fatigue, seems almost indispensably necessary to my health if not to my life.

I should be more scrupulous about proposing myself as a candidate for the vacant Fellowship, were I not certain of my successor, who stands out, as a man of such superior abilities, as so eminently qualified to fill such a situation. I ought not probably to omit mentioning to your Majesty that, Dr Goodall[1] having offer'd himself as a candidate for the Fellowship, may possibly, if I should withdraw my pretensions, be elected, in which case the School would be deprived of his services, which I conceive are of much more consequence to it than mine, as he has health and unimpair'd youth, I have only the dregs of a laborious life to dedicate to my Alma Mater.

I have therefore humbly to request your Majesty's gracious permission to accept the vacant Fellowship, if I should be fortunate enough to succeed in my application: the income of which, in addition to the Canonry of Windsor, which your Majesty has been pleased so graciously to confer upon me, and for which I shall ever be impress'd with the most heart-felt gratitude, will enable me, I trust, to support my family in a quiet and comfortable stile. At the same time I am bound to add, and I do it with all my heart, that, if it be your Majesty's wish that I should at all events continue longer in my present situation, I shall not hesitate a moment to obey your Majesty's commands, and will exert myself still to discharge the arduous duties of it to the best of my power.

With a heart fully sensible of all your Majesty's goodness and condescension to me, and with the most profound respect, I have the honor to subscribe myself etc. (10456–7)

2560   *Letters from* LORD PELHAM *to the* KING

[*London, 28 Nov. 1801.*] Lord Pelham begs leave with all humility to lay before your Majesty two letters from the Lord Chief Baron of Scotland, one to Lord Pelham & the other to Mr. King.

Lord Pelham conceives that your Majesty's gracious comands in consequence of his Royal Highness Monsieur's original application thro' Lord Pelham would have warranted him in giving directions to the Chief Baron to carry those commands into effect; at the same time Lord Pelham flattered himself that it would not appear inconsistant with his duty & obedience to your Majesty's commands already expressed, if he laid these papers before your Majesty & sollicited a confirmation of the orders. (10458–9)

[*Tuesday, 1 Dec. 1801.*] Lord Pelham humbly begs leave to represent to your Majesty that the Algerine Embassador sollicits an audience of leave, having

---

[1] Joseph Goodall (1760–1840). Assistant Master at Eton, 1783; Headmaster, 1802; Provost, 1809–40; Canon of Windsor, 1808–40. 'A man of high reputation as a teacher', said Lord Glenbervie (*Journals*, I, 300). Heath had 'suffered the discipline of the school to go to ruin', he added.

received intimation that the ship which your Majesty has been graciously pleased to order to convey him to Algiers is now ready. (10488)

2561 LORD HAWKESBURY *to the* KING

[*Downing Street, 1 Dec. 1801.*] Lord Hawkesbury has the honour to send your Majesty a Letter of Credence for Mr Jackson[1] to reside as Minister Plenipotentiary at Paris during the sitting of the Congress at Amiens. Lord Hawkesbury humbly submits it to your Majesty that it may be convenient and tend to forward the business in discussion to have an authorised Minister at Paris, as well as one from France in London, who may be able to enter into explanations upon such points as may require it & who may furnish your Majesty with regular information respecting the state of affairs in France. Lord Hawkesbury trusts that the form of the Letter of Credence will meet with your Majesty's approbation. It is nearly conformable to what has been usually sent to the President of the United States of America. (10489)

2562 LORD PELHAM *to the* KING

[*3 Dec. 1801.*] Lord Pelham most humbly reports to your Majesty that the Governors at the Charterhouse having omitted to choose a Governor within the time prescribed, the nomination has lapsed to your Majesty. Lord Pelham does not presume to sollicit your Majesty to name him; at the same time he cannot help availing himself of the indulgence with which your Majesty has been graciously pleased to consider his conduct & to represent to your Majesty how much he would be gratified & feel himself honoured, if yr. Majesty should think him deserving of being named by yr. Majesty. (10490–1)

2563 THE DUCHESS OF WURTEMBERG *to the* KING

[*Stutgard, 6 Dec. 1801.*] I am too happy to have it in my power to recall myself frequently to your Majesty to neglect troubling you with a few lines by the messenger.

I hope that the weather allows your Majesty to enjoy your works at Windsor and Kew and does not by constant rain prevent your taking exercice as is the case here. Though I am both planting and altering my house the damp has kept me at Stutgard near three weeks and even the Duke has not been able to shoot or hunt which is a great vexation to him. On me this weather has a worse effect as it gives me violent headachs which stop my drawing or working. At this time I am employed in drawing some dogs after Reidinger which I flatter myself your Majesty would approve of. We have here a very fine engraver, Müller, whose works are known in England and who I generally consult before I think a drawing quite finished, and he appears satisfied with those I have finished of late, which encourages me very much to apply. By chance I have met here with a good Baptiste and

---

[1] See No. 538. He was Sir George Jackson's elder brother, and is frequently mentioned in Sir George's *Diaries and Letters* (2 vols., 1872).

able, gallant man, was also immediately dismissed, unheard, from the Majority of the Regiment & from another situation of about £400 pr. annum that Lord Downshire had requested for him as a small reward for his merits. And about ten months afterwards Ld. Downshire was dismissed, & our two dear eldest sons, from the only remaining office held by my family, namely that of Register to the Court of Chancery in Ireland which had come from Sr. Wm. Cooper[1] to the first Marquis of Downshire,[2] from him to my dear Lord, & in the year 1795 had been granted by your Majesty to him & those two sons & the survivors & survivor of them;[3] all equally innocent of any real offence, much less guilty of any crime.

The loyalty and fidelity of my dear Lord to your Majesty were not to be shaken or in the least diminished by any injury, however ruinous, by any persecution, however unmerited. On the contrary his first care was to exhort those whose exertions in your Majesty's service were likely to be lost or abated on account of the treatment he had received, to a continuance of their duty. The opinion he had formed upon the subject of the Union was founded upon that knowledge & experience of Ireland & its interests which few had such an opportunity to possess. It was the honest opinion of one who had long expressed to your Majesty's Ministers his apprehension of the dangerous consequences that might arise from the measure of an Union. His nature, his allegiance, would not permit him to yield his acquiesence to a measure which his judgement, his conscience, his un-bounded affection for his Sovereign & his country told him he ought not to consent to. His speech in the House of Lords of Ireland on the 10th of February (after his suspension) of which I most humbly trouble your Majesty with a public account (No. 11.) that I have been told by persons who heard it delivered is very correct; the whole of his conduct to the last, his inmost thoughts which were always communicated to me & which as far as the expression of them related to the subjects of this statement I now possess in his letters, all justify me in asserting to your Majesty that if he erred in judgement, his was the error of a devotion to loyalty & patriotism.

The consequences following his degradation have been, & without your Majesty's benevolent protection must continue to be, afflicting & detrimental to my family & its dearest interests. The command of the Downshire Militia was in his life time given to others, & Capt. Boyd was raised to the Majority from which Major Matthews had been dismissed. The Office of Register was granted to the son[4] of Lord Avonmore, without any solicitation from him (No. 12.), & immediately after the departure of my dearest Lord, the Government of the County of Down (for the good order, civilization & prosperity of which he had unceasingly exerted himself, & to effect those objects had also made very great pecuniary

---

[1] Sir William Cooper, LL.D. (c. 1689–1761), a Master in Chancery [I.], 1740–54. Created a Baronet [I.], 1758.

[2] Wills Hill (1718–93), third son of 1st Viscount Hillsborough [I.]. Succeeded to his father's peerage, 1742; created Earl of Hillsborough [I.], 1751, and Earl of Hillsborough [G.B.], 1772; created Marquess of Downshire [I.], 1789. Joint Registrar in Chancery [I.], 1759–93; Joint Postmaster-General, 1766–8; Colonial Secretary, 1768–72.

[3] This grant is not mentioned in the Complete Peerage.

[4] William Charles Yelverton (1762–1814) succeeded his father as 2nd Viscount Avonmore in 1805. He was Principal Registrar of the High Court of Chancery [I.].

sacrifices) was presented to the Earl of Londonderry, who but very recently had become a supporter of your Majesty's Government.

In stating these facts & circumstances to your Majesty I have been careful to assert nothing, however true, that I am not prepared to prove. Had my most revered Lord been spared a little longer he would have taken a proper opportunity to justify himself. He had always felt the necessity of doing so, and the times had the appearance of becoming suitable for so important a discussion, but it pleased God to preclude us from that most wished-for investigation.

For myself & my children, who will be taught to emulate the virtues of their father & his attachment and fidelity to his King, I most earnestly implore your Majesty's pardon for the liberty I have thus taken, & the pain & trouble I fear this letter must occasion. If it should appear to your Majesty that in presenting this statement I have not outstepped my duty, I shall be happy; if on the contrary it should seem to your Majesty that I have in any aspect addressed or expressed myself improperly, I most humbly entreat your Majesty's forgiveness & that my zeal may be attributed to its true cause, a sense of the allegiance I bear & of the conviction that a heavy duty & responsibility called upon me thus to address myself to that benevolent father of all his subjects from whom I & my dear family may confidently expect such justice and protection as from the nature of our case we may appear to be intitled to. That the Almightly may grant to your Majesty the enjoyment of health & every earthly comfort till at a remote period you shall be elevated to the mansions of the just is the sincere prayer of[1] [etc.].[2] (9956–68)

The following British Museum letters reached the printer too late for insertion in the appropriate places; the numbering indicates their proper location.

2386A THE KING *to* LORD HAWKESBURY

[*Kew, 23 April 1801.*] The King is highly satisfied with the choise that has been made of Mr Garlike to go as Chargé d'Affaires to Petersburgh. His education in the line of foreign affairs has been regular. He was private secretary of Lord Auckland at The Hague,[3] went to Denmark with the late most promising Lord Henry Spencer[4] and followed him to Berlin where he has remained much to the satisfaction of that Court as well as of the various English Ministers that have been employed there.[5] (Add. MSS. 38564, f. 39.)

2393A [*The King's reply, Kew, 30 April 1801, 3.22 p.m.*]

Lord Hawkesbury may easily conceive what a balm to my heart so essential a piece of news as that he has just sent me must prove. I feel most fully the honour that

---

[1] The enclosures (9493, 9496–9509) are much too long to be printed here.
[2] She signed herself 'Mary Downshire Sandys'.
[3] William Eden was Envoy at The Hague, 1786–88.
[4] See No. 1223.
[5] Garlike was Secretary of Embassy, 1801–3, and Chargé d'Affaires at Petersburg, May 1801.

must accrue to the British arms, but give me credit for saying that I more weigh on the manifest interposition of Divine Providence in a just cause, and for the destruction of the enemies of His Holy Word and of all civil and domestic happiness. (Add. MSS. 38564, f. 41.)

2410A [*The King's reply, Kew, 12 May 1801, 7.25 a.m.*]

The Message to the House of Commons in favour of the Court of Portugal is very judicious; a similar one ought to be sent to the House of Lords. Lord Hawkesbury is desired therefore to give due notice to the D. of Portland that it may be prepared. (Add. MSS. 38564, f. 42.)

2426A THE KING *to* LORD HAWKESBURY

[*Kew, 1 June 1801.*] The King directs the Lord Hawkesbury to give notice to the Foreign [Ministers] either by a note or through the Master of the Ceremonies that he will see them at the Queen's Palace on Wednesday at two o'clock. The King, after his illness eleven [*sic*] years ago received them in the same manner at Kew. Lord Hawkesbury will of course attend on this occasion. (Add. MSS. 38564, f. 43.)

2473A [*The King's reply, Weymouth, 12 July 1801, 4.04 p.m.*]

The King is highly gratified with the information of Lord St Hellens's having so perfectly succeeded in the business entrusted to him, and with personal satisfaction authorizes Lord Hawkesbury to acquaint him that he is advanced to a seat in the House of Lords of the United Kingdom by the title of Lord St Hellens of the Isle of Wight, and that notice be given to the Home Department that the warrant for the patent be immediately prepared. (Add. MSS. 38564, f. 45.)

2475A *Letters from the* KING *to* LORD HAWKESBURY

[*Weymouth, 14 July 1801, 4 p.m.*] The King desires Lord Hawkesbury will prepare the draft of an answer to the Count d'Artois. It seems as if his bringing the P. of Condé here would be making an unnecessary parade; it ought therefore civilly to be declined. (Add. MSS. 38564, f. 46.)

[*Weymouth, 17 July 1801, 4 p.m.*] The King having signed the warrant for passing the ratification of the Russian Convention under the Great Seal and signed the ratification, returns [them] to Lord Hawkesbury for completion, as also the letter to Monsieur which he has signed. (Add. MSS. 38564, f. 47.)

2539A THE KING *to* LORD HAWKESBURY

[*Windsor, 24 Oct. 1801, 8 a.m.*] The King returns to Lord Hawkesbury a number of commercial passports which he has signed, that they may be ready when called for by the mercantile vessels. He will finish the rest so as to return them when another cargo arrives for signature. (Add. MSS. 38564, f. 48.)

INDEX

Abbot, Charles, 1st Baron Colchester (1757–
1829), 2346 n., 2357, 2357 n., 2405, 2445,
2510, 2510 n., 2515 n.

Abercorn, 9th Earl of (1756–1818), 1983

Abercromby, Lieut.-Gen. Sir Ralph (1734–
1801), 1701 n., 1709, 1709 n., 1711, 1720,
1752, 1755 n., 1825, 2005, 2011, 2013,
2016, 2022, 2027, 2037, 2048, 2136, 2171,
2175, 2175 n., 2202–3, 2229, 2240, 2243,
2252, 2256, 2256 n., 2390, 2394, 2394 n.,
2396, 2398, 2415–16, 2421, 2548
letter from, 2032
his son's marriage, 1900
question of a peerage for, 2054, 2054 n.
his wife, 2054 n.
his children, 2054 n.

Abercromby, George (d. 1800), father of Sir
Ralph Abercromby, 1900

Abercromby, George, 2nd Baron (1770–
1843), 1900

Abercromby, Montague, Lady (1772–1837),
1900

Abercromby, Sir Robert (1740–1827), 2032,
2507
why he entered Parliament, 2054 n.

Abergavenny, 2nd Earl of (1755–1843), 2474 n.

Aboukir, battle of, 2128

A'Court, Sir William, Ld. Heytesbury (1779–
1860), 2480

Adams, James (1752–1816), 1664 n.

Adams, William (c. 1752–1811), 1664 n.

Addington, Henry, 1st Viscount Sidmouth
(1754–1844), 1760, 1764 n., 1793, 1796,
1922, 1932, 1981, 2174, 2269, 2272–3,
2288 n., 2290, 2308–9, 2327, 2329 n.,
2336 n., 2339 n., 2346 n., 2349, 2357 n.,
2363 n., 2365, 2365 n., 2368 n., 2369 n.,
2386, 2397, 2409, 2456 n., 2461 n.,
2474 n., 2481, 2483, 2493, 2500, 2504,
2510, 2510 n., 2515 n., 2519, 2533,
2536 n., 2552, 2554 n., 2556, 2572
letters from, 1932 n., 2189 n., 2331, 2334,
2337, 2341, 2350, 2354, 2357, 2369, 2373,
2379, 2405, 2411, 2421, 2427, 2431, 2435,
2439, 2445, 2456, 2461, 2467, 2474, 2479,
2482, 2489, 2498, 2498 n., 2502, 2515,
2518, 2520, 2529, 2536, 2540 n., 2554,
2570, 2572

letters to, 1793 n., 2060 n., 2264 n., 2327 n.,
2331, 2354, 2357, 2357 n., 2361, 2371,
2371 n., 2386 n., 2405, 2411, 2428 n.,
2435, 2445, 2445 n., 2456–7, 2461,
2461 n., 2467, 2469, 2479 n., 2498,
2500 n., 2502, 2515, 2515 n., 2518, 2536,
2536 n., 2554, 2570, 2573

Addington, Henry, jun. (1786–1823), 2469,
2474

Addington, John Hiley (1759–1818), 2189,
2264 n., 2354, 2359
letter from, 2189 n.
letter to, 2189 n.

Adjutant-General, the, *see* Calvert, Sir Harry

Adolphus Frederick, Duke of Cambridge
(1774–1850), 1738, 1817, 1863, 1945,
1953, 2377, 2386, 2388 n., 2428, 2516
letters from, 1696, 1703, 1714, 1735, 1749,
1789, 1810, 1842 n., 1866, 1884, 1905,
1944, 1949, 1955, 1967, 1989, 2001, 2047,
2059, 2118, 2128, 2154, 2162, 2188, 2236,
2260, 2277, 2312, 2347, 2387, 2395, 2402,
2466

his near-engagement, 1905, 1955
returns to England, 2386 n.
idea of his marrying Catherine, Princess of
Wurtemberg, 2387
asks for employment (1801), 2466
his peerage, 2552, 2557

Agar, Charles, Lord Somerton, Archbishop
of Cashel (1736–1809), 2201, 2222, 2315,
2515 n., 2546

Agriculture, Board of, 2212

Ahrens, M., 1734

Aiton, William Townsend (1766–1849), the
King's gardener, 1931, 2464

Albemarle, 4th Earl of (1772–1849), 1983

Alessandria, Armistice signed by Austrians at,
2181, 2188, 2193, 2198, 2214

Alexander I, Tsar (1777–1825), 2386, 2395,
2425, 2456 n., 2475, 2522, 2566

Allen, John, 1691, 1694

Alley, *see* Allen

Altamont, Countess of, *see* Sligo

Altamont, 3rd Earl of, *see* Sligo

Alvanley, Lord, *see* Arden, Richard Pepper

Amelia, Archduchess of Austria (1780–98),
1848

Fitzgerald, Lord Robert Stephen (1765–1833), 1783

Fitzgibbon, Lord (later, Earl of Clare) (1749–1802), 1686, 1820, 1824, 1839, 2285, 2378, 2378 n., 2044, 2510
letter from, 2201

Fitzherbert, Alleyne, Lord St Helens (1753–1839), 1917, 2386, 2386A, 2396, 2473, 2475, 2480, 2522, 2566

Fitzpatrick, Gen. Richard (1748–1813), 1950
letter to, 2114 n.

Fitzroy, Col. Charles (1762–1831), 2320

Fitzwilliam, 2nd Earl (1748–1833), 1678, 1686, 1983, 2301, 2339, 2346, 2355, 2381
letter to, 1686 n.

Floud, John, police magistrate at Worship Street, Shoreditch, 1717

Floyd, Sir John (1748–1818), 2243

Fontblane [*sic*], 2225

Foote, Sir Edward James (1767–1833), 2506

Ford, Sir Richard, police magistrate (1759?–1806), 2245

Forster, Col. (d. 1801), 2533

Foster, John, Baron Oriel (1740–1828), 1889, 1896, 1913, 2169

Fowler, Lieut., 2523

Fowler, Robert, Archbishop of Dublin (1726?–1801), 2546

Fox, Charles James (1749–1806), 1664, 1664 n., 1678 n., 1680, 1680 n., 1722 n., 1729, 2108, 2108 n.
letter from, 2276 n.

Fox, General Henry Edward (1755–1811), 2415–16, 2483

Fox, Luke (1755–1819), Justice of the Common Pleas [I.], 2245

Francis II, Emperor (1768–1835), 1750, 1817, 1845, 1848, 1905, 1908, 1936, 2072, 2082, 2115, 2119, 2127, 2199, 2206, 2214, 2251, 2256, 2261, 2273, 2311, 2319, 2321

Franklin, Lieut., 2213

Fraser, Major-Gen. Simon (1738–1813), 1852, 1935

Frederica of Mecklenburg-Strelitz, Princess [later, Duchess of Cumberland] (1778–1841), 1905

Frederica, Duchess of York (1767–1820), 1716, 1858, 2139, 2376

Frederick, Prince of Wales, father of George III (1707–51), 1754, 2270

Frederick, Duke of York (1763–1827), 1678 n., 1716, 1718–19, 1748, 1858, 1916, 1919, 1979, 2001, 2011, 2025–7, 2029–30, 2032–3, 2040–3, 2051, 2053–4,

2057, 2060, 2062–3, 2066–7, 2070 n., 2073–4, 2079 n., 2081, 2087, 2087 n., 2094, 2098, 2116, 2134, 2139, 2155, 2155 n., 2184, 2203, 2290, 2293, 2314, 2375 n., 2365, 2368 n., 2396, 2452, 2454, 2462, 2495, 2509, 2554 n.
letters from, 1700, 1702, 1748 n., 1752, 1765, 1769, 1774, 1788, 1819, 1821, 1825, 1833, 1837, 1852, 1857, 1880, 1910, 1931, 1935, 2005, 2008, 2013, 2022, 2028, 2037, 2048, 2054 n., 2065, 2066 n., 2113, 2132, 2136, 2216, 2224, 2240, 2243, 2356, 2376, 2388, 2390, 2398, 2415, 2420, 2423, 2450, 2463, 2470, 2476, 2481, 2486, 2493, 2499, 2503, 2507, 2511, 2519, 2524, 2526, 2533, 2564
letters to, 2013, 2054 n., 2165 n., 2376, 2519
memo by, 2548

Frederick, General Moriscoe (c. 1723–1801), 1935, 2390

Frederick II, King of Prussia (1712–86), 2037, 2253

Frederick William III, King of Prussia (1770–1840), 1670–1, 1673, 1675, 1689, 1696, 1719, 1848, 1863, 1867, 1888, 1908, 1920, 1943–4, 1954–5, 1967, 1973, 1985, 1997, 2000, 2010, 2082, 2127, 2395

Fremantle, Sir William Henry (1766–1850), 1710

French, *see* Ffrench

Frere, 1710

Frere, Bartholomew (1778–1851), 2514

Frere, John Hookham (1769–1846), 2082 n., 2173 n., 2297, 2443
letters from, 2101, 2173

Freytag, Field Marshal William von (1711–98), 1669

Frogmore, 2488

Fuenza, Duke de la, 2370

Fullarton, Col. William (c. 1754–1808), 2452, 2454

Fyers, Capt., 2496 n.

Gallo, Marchese di, Neapolitan Minister at Vienna, 1777

Gantheaume, Rear-Admiral, (1755–1818) 2453

Gardens, the Royal, 2464

Gardiner, General William (1748–1806), 1826, 1935, 2503

Gardner, Alan, 1st Baron (1742–1809), 2024, 2504

Garlike, Benjamin, 1848, 1863, 1883, 2107, 2386A, 2386, 2480

Garter, Order of the, 1918

Grenville, Elizabeth (d. 1769), 1933

Grenville, George, the Prime Minister (1712–70), 1933, 2099

Grenville, Lord George Nugent, Lord Nugent (1789–1850), 2299

Grenville, General Richard (1744–1823), 2132

Grenville, Thomas (1755–1846), 1759, 1783, 1879, 1886, 1890, 1894, 1898, 1908, 1912, 1930, 1933, 1936, 1938, 1952, 1954, 1959, 1997, 1999, 2017, 2031, 2034, 2082, 2192–3, 2232

Grenville, William Wyndham, Lord (1759–1834), 1670, 1678 n., 1708, 1713, 1727 n., 1736 n., 1768, 1775, 1787, 1790, 1792, 1803, 1817, 1889, 1937, 1964, 1978, 2007, 2011, 2020, 2027, 2072, 2101, 2173 n., 2199, 2203, 2235 n., 2242, 2247, 2256, 2256 n., 2278 n., 2285, 2322, 2327 n. 2331, 2344 n., 2346, 2357 n, 2371 n., 2474 n.

letters from, 1671, 1673, 1675, 1682, 1689, 1693, 1698, 1704, 1719, 1721, 1725, 1731, 1734, 1762, 1777, 1782, 1791, 1795, 1798, 1814, 1827, 1841, 1843, 1845, 1850, 1854, 1879, 1883, 1886, 1890, 1894, 1898, 1908, 1908 n., 1912, 1917, 1923, 1930, 1933, 1936, 1938, 1952, 1954, 1959, 1964, 1973, 1985, 1987, 1995, 2031, 2072, 2080, 2082, 2082 n., 2095, 2097, 2100, 2103, 2107, 2120, 2123, 2142, 2176, 2181, 2193, 2201, 2202 n., 2209, 2218, 2221, 2228, 2230, 2232, 2235, 2237, 2241, 2244, 2246, 2248, 2253, 2258, 2273, 2278, 2281, 2287, 2295, 2297, 2302, 2304, 2319, 2321, 2326, 2344, 2541

letters to, 1673, 1682, 1689, 1693, 1698, 1704, 1719, 1721, 1725, 1731, 1734, 1758, 1766, 1777, 1782, 1791, 1795, 1814, 1827, 1841, 1843, 1845, 1854, 1879, 1883, 1886, 1894, 1898, 1908, 1919, 1923, 1930, 1933, 1936, 1938, 1952, 1954, 1959, 1964, 1973, 1985, 1987, 1995, 2003, 2031, 2034, 2072, 2080, 2082, 2090, 2095, 2097, 2099, 2100, 2103, 2107, 2120, 2123, 2142, 2176, 2181, 2193, 2209, 2218, 2221, 2228, 2230, 2232, 2235, 2239, 2242 n., 2244, 2246, 2248, 2253, 2261, 2273, 2278, 2281, 2287, 2295, 2297, 2302, 2304, 2319, 2321, 2326, 2344

Greville, Charles Francis, Vice-Chamberlain of the Household (1749–1809), 2459, 2461 n.

Grey, Sir Charles, 1st Earl Grey (1729–1807), 1709 n., 1736 n., 1755 n., 1990, 2011,

2013, 2020, 2022, 2077 n., 2409, 2445, 2548

Grey, Charles, 2nd Earl (1764–1845), 1667, 1678 n., 1922, 2135, 2137, 2140, 2140 n., 2276, 2276 n., 2288, 2288 n., 2339, 2339 n., 2367, 2373, 2373 n., 2397 n.

letters from, 2077 n., 2114 n.

Grey, Sir George (1767–1828), son of 1st Earl Grey, 2409, 2413

Grey de Wilton, Lord, see Egerton, Sir Thomas

Guiffardière, Rev. Mr., 2294

Gwynn, Major-Gen. Francis Edward (d. 1822), 2216

letter to, 1745

Habeas Corpus Act, Suspension of, 1722, 2383

Hadfield, James (c. 1772–1841), lunatic, 2153

Hale, John, a Gentleman Usher of the Privy Chamber, 1754, 2035

Hale, Capt., 1818

Halkett, Capt., 2032

Hall, Sir Robert, 2200

Halliburton [Haliburton], surgeon in Nova Scotia, 1818, 2200

Hamilton, Admiral Sir Edward (1772–1851), 2105

Hamilton, Sir William, diplomatist, (1730–1803), 1692, 1695, 1713, 1727, 1727 n., 1744, 1750, 1768, 1777, 1782, 1792, 1803, 1843, 1917

memo by, 2099

Hammond, George (1763–1853), Under-Secretary of State, 1675, 1894, 2244, 2246, 2248

letter from, 1783

Handfield, William (Lieut.-Col., 1783), 1852

Harcourt, Duc d', the Comte de Provence's representative in London (1726–1802), 1673, 1725

Harcourt, William, 3rd Earl (1743–1830), General, 2462

Hardwicke, 3rd Earl of (1757–1834), 1885, 2369, 2385, 2444, 2503, 2507, 2510 n., 2515, 2540, 2546

letters from, 2404, 2408, 2510, 2510 n., 2515 n.

letters to, 2404, 2408, 2510 n., 2515 n.

Hare, James (1747–1804), 2114 n.

Harrington, Lieut.-Gen. the Earl of (1753–1829), 2376, 2461 n.

Harris, James (1709–80), father of Lord Malmesbury, 2446

Keling [*sic*], 2558
Kelly, a mutineer, 1779, 1834
Kenmare (titular), 4th Viscount (1726–95),
    1666
Kenmare, 1st Earl of (1754–1812), 1666
Kennedy, Richard, mutineer, 1834
Kensington Palace, shabby state of, 2296,
    2401
Kent, Duke of, *see* Edward, Duke of Kent
Kenyon, Sir Lloyd, Lord Kenyon (1732–
    1802), 1968, 2158, 2165, 2165 n., 2167,
    2357
  letter from, 2356 n
Kenyon, Lloyd (1775–1800), 2158
Kerr, Lord Mark Robert (1776–1840), 2409
Kerry, 'one of the least civilised' counties,
    1666
Kew, the new Lodge at, 2292
Killala Bay, French landing in, 1808
Kilmore, Bishop of, *see* Broderick, Charles
Kilwarden, Lord, *see* Wolfe, Arthur
King, John (1759–1830), Under-Secretary of
    State, 1684, 1686, 1740, 1975, 2102, 2146,
    2153, 2222, 2245, 2301, 2411, 2456 n.,
    2457, 2560
King, Sir Richard (1774–1834), 1869
King, Col. Robert Edward, Viscount Lorton
    (1773–1854), 2301, 2318
  his wife Frances (1775–1841), 2301
King, Rufus (*c.* 1754–1827), the American
    Minister in London, 1868, 2522
Kingsmill, Admiral Sir Robert Brice (1730–
    1805), 2227, 2254
Kingston, Edward, 1st Earl of (1726–97), 2301
King's Theatre, Masquerade forbidden at the,
    1730
Kinnaird, 7th Baron (1754?–1805), 2225
Kinsale, Government of, 2503
Kinsey, Lieut.-Col. John, 1857
Klenau, Count Wensel von, the Austrian
    General, 2300, 2312
Klösst, Mme de, M. de Jacobi's daughter, 1953
Kneble, M. de, 2311
Knox, Major-Gen. John (*c.* 1757–1800),
    2220 n., 2222, 2389–90
Korsakoff, Alexander Rimsky-, Russian
    General (1753–1840), 1993, 2059
Kotzbue, August Friedrich Ferdinand von
    (1761–1819), 1902
Kray, General, the Austrian commander,
    1949, 2118, 2151, 2161, 2172, 2303
Kutzleben, Baron de (d. 1798), Minister to
    Landgrave of Hesse-Cassel, 1814
  his family, 1814

Lack, Thomas, 1st Lord Liverpool's private
    secretary, 2297 n.
Laffin, Thos., mutineer, 1834
La Grasini, *see* Grassini
La Harpe, Jean François de (1739–1803), 2294
Lake, Gerard, 1st Viscount (1744–1808),
    1709, 1709 n., 1711, 1755 n., 1757 n.,
    1772, 1776, 1816, 1825, 2116
Land Tax Sale Bill, 1724
Landaff, Earl of (?1738–1806), 2315
Lander, a seaman, 2413
Lansdowne, Marquess of, *see* Shelburne
Larrey, 1933
Lascelles, General Francis (1744–99), Groom
    of the King's Bedchamber, 2022
Latouche, 1684
Laurence, an Englishman at Stuttgart, 1902
Laurence, French (1757–1809), 1914, 2137,
    2140, 2276, 2339
  letters from, 1686 n.
  letters to, 1686 n.
Laurie, Lieut.-Gen. Sir Robert (*c.* 1738–
    1804), 1769, 2022
Lauriston, Jean Alexandre Law, Marquis de
    (1768–1828), Marshal of France, 2539
Law, Edmund (1703–87), Bishop of Carlisle,
    2062
Law, Edward, 1st Lord Ellenborough (1750–
    1818), 2344 n., 2357, 2363
Leary, Jeremiah, 1691, 1694
Le Blanc, Sir Simon (d. 1816), 1968
Lefevre, Charles Shaw- (*c.* 1758–1823), 1664
Leicester, Earl of, *see* Townshend, George
Leigh, Rev. William, Canning's uncle,
    letters to, 1881 n., 1932 n., 2288 n.
Leighton, Sir Baldwin (1747–1828), 1852
Leitrim, 1st Earl of (1732–1804), 2315
Le Marchant, John Gaspard (1766–1812), 2462
Lennox, Col. *see* Richmond, 4th Duke of
Lens, John, Serjeant at law (1756–1825),
    1968
Lenthe, Ernst Ludwig Julius von (1744–
    1814), 1795, 1810, 1884, 2236, 2347,
    2395
Leveson, Col., 2224
Leveson-Gower, Lord Granville, later, Earl
    Granville (1773–1846), 1881, 2067–8,
    2070, 2070 n., 2074 n., 2079, 2084, 2180,
    2192
  letters from, 2079 n., 2180 n.
  letter to, 2180 n.
Lewes, Sir Watkin (1736–1821), 2157
Lewis, of the War Office, 2028
Lewisham, Lord, *see* Dartmouth, Earl of

(659)

Manners, General Robert (?1758–1823), 1935, 2320

Manners, General Russell (d. 1800), 2240

Manners-Sutton, Charles, Archbishop of Canterbury (1755–1828), *letter from*, 2428

Manningham, Col. Coote (d. 1809), 2008, 2397, 2510 n.

Mansel, William Lort (1753–1820), Master of Trinity Coll., Camb., 1733

Mansfield, Sir James, Chief Justice of Chester (1734–1821), 2138

Mantin, 1691

Maria Theresa, wife of Emperor Francis II (1772–1807), 1848

Maria Theresa, wife of Duc d'Angoulême (1778–1851), 1848

Markham, 2340

Markham, Admiral John (1761–1827), 2357

Marlborough, Duke of (1739–1817), 2365 n.

Marriott, Sir James (c. 1720–1803), 1683, 1859, 1957

Marsden, William (1754–1836), 1820

Marsh, John, a Commissioner of the Transport Office, 1826

Marsham, Charles, 3rd Baron and 1st Earl of Romney (1744–1811), 1976, 1986, 2445

Martial Law Bill [Ireland], 1927, 1940, 2447, 2451

Martin, James (1738–1810), 2189

Martyn, J., *letter from*, 2455

Mary, Princess, later, Duchess of Gloucester (1776–1834), *letter from*, 2388 n.

Masséna, Marshal (1758–1817), 1944

Massey, General Eyre, 1st Baron Clarina (1719–1804), 2301

Matthews, George, 2575

Maxwell, 1691

Maxwell, Lieut.-Col. Patrick, 2243

Mecklenburg-Strelitz, Adolphus Frederick, Duke of (1738–94), 1687, 1708

Mecklenburg-Strelitz, Charles, Duke of (1741–1816), 1673, 1687, 1708

Mecklenburg-Strelitz, George, Hereditary Prince of (1779–1860), 1687, 1708

Medows, Edward, Commissioner of Taxes, 1685

Mehrfeld, *see* Merveldt

Melas, General, 2188

Melius, *see* Mylius

Menou, Baron de (1750–1810), French General, capitulates in Egypt, 2393, 2394 n.

Menzies, Sir John (d. 1800), 2124

Merry, Anthony, diplomat, 2230

Merveldt, General, 2015, 2161

Metternich, Countess, 1948, 1951

Metternich, Prince (1773–1859), 1948, 1951

Milbanke, Admiral Mark (?1725–1805), 2024

Milman, Sir Francis (1746–1821), 2254

Minorca, expedition against (1798), 1901

Minto, Lord, *see* Elliot, Sir Gilbert

Mitchell, 1894

Mitchell, Vice-Admiral Sir Andrew (1757–1806), 2006, 2011, 2016, 2018, 2021, 2032, 2046, 2227, 2572–3

Mitford, Sir John Freeman-, Lord Redesdale (1748–1830), 1724, 1794, 1800, 1824, 1897, 2170, 2174, 2187, 2225, 2327 n., 2357 n., 2397

letters from, 2158, 2350 n.

and the Speakership, 2350, 2350 n., 2354

Moberly, Edward, a Russia merchant, 2297

Mocher, General Flower (c. 1729–1801), 2481

Modena, Ercole III, Duke of (1727–1803), 2440

Moira, Francis Rawdon-Hastings, 2nd Earl of (1754–1826), 1688, 1896, 2149

Möllendorff, Field Marshal (1724–1816), 1673

Monsieur, *see* Artois, Comte d'

Montagu, Admiral Sir George (1750–1829), 2429

Montbéliard, Principality of (Wurtemberg Territory, 1407–1801), 2544

Montgomery, Sir James William (1721–1803), 2403

Montpensier, Antoine Philippe, Duc de (1775–1807), Louis Philippe's brother 2102

Montrose, Duke of (1755–1836), 2365 n., 2369 n.

Moore, Mrs Catherine, wife of the Archbishop, 2010

Moore, John, Archbishop of Canterbury (1730–1805), 1870, 2098, 2145, 2304, 2308, 2329, 2518

letters from, 1730, 1847, 1856, 2156, 2305, 2308 n., 2332, 2336, 2338, 2517

letters to, 1851, 2010, 2091, 2336

Moore, Lieut.-Gen. Sir John (1761–1809), 2048, 2051, 2394 n., 2398

Moreau, General (1761–1813), 1993, 2214, 2295, 2297

Morgan, Sir Charles, *see* Gould

Morley, 1710

Morning Chronicle, the, 1729

Morning Post, the, 1729

O'Neill, 2nd Viscount (1779–1841), 2315

Ongley, William, a clerk in the Navy Pay Office, 2152

Onslow, George, 1st Earl of (1731–1814), 1729, 2445

Opera House, the, 2092, 2225

Orange, Frederick, Prince of (1774–99), 1670–1, 1673, 1725, 1817, 1906, 1917, 1930, 1933

Orange, Wilhelmina, Princess of (1751–1820), 1906, 1917, 1919

Orange, William V of (1748–1806), 1719, 1883, 1906, 1908, 1917, 1919, 2011, 2123, 2530

Orange, William, Hereditary Prince of (1772–1843), 1670, 1906, 2032, 2037

Orde, Sir John, 1st Bart. (1751–1824), 2055

Orde, Thomas, 1st Baron Bolton (1740–1807), 1983

O'Reilly, Sir Hugh, 1st Bart., 1772

Orleans, Duke of, see Louis Philippe

Ormonde, 18th Earl of (1770–1820), 1684, 2315

Ormsby, Sir Charles Montague (1767–1818), 2510

Osborne, Lord Francis Golodphin, later, Lord Godolphin (1777–1850), 2110

Osborne, Lady Mary, later, Countess of Chichester (1776–1862), 2110

Otto, Louis Guillaume, Comte de Mosloy, (1754–1817), French Commissioner in London, 2228, 2230, 2232, 2235, 2237, 2244, 2246, 2248, 2261, 2534

Otway, Capt. Robert Waller (1770–1846), 2382

Oughton, Capt. James, 2018, 2032

Oxford, University of, 1870, 2153, 2479, 2487

Oxmantown, Viscount and (1806), Earl of Rosse see Parsons

Paget, Sir Arthur (1771–1830), 1827, 2082, 2099, 2391, 2426

Paget, Henry, Earl of Uxbridge (1744–1812), 1710, 2307 n.

Paget, Sir Henry William, 2nd Earl of Uxbridge and 1st Marquess of Anglesey (1768–1854), 2008, 2048

Paget, Lady Louisa, see Erskine

Painted Chamber at Westminster, the, 2269, 2272

Pakenham, Hon. Thomas, Master-Gen. of Ordnance [I.], 2245

Paley, William (1743–1805), 2062

Panin, Count (1771–1837), Russian diplomat-

ist, and later Alexander I's Vice-Chancellor, 2082, 2475

Paper Office, the, see State Paper Office

Parker, Miss Anne, 1804

Parker, David, 1710, 2424

Parker, Admiral Sir Hyde (1739–1807), 2105, 2234, 2382, 2384, 2425, 2456 n.

Parker, Admiral Sir Peter (1721–1811), 1712 n., 2024

Parker, Vice-Admiral Sir William (1743–1802), 2555

Parnell, Sir John, 2nd Bart. (1744–1801), Chancellor of the Exchequer [I.], 1686, 1707, 1824 n., 1889

Parsons, Lawrence Harman, 1st Baron Oxmantown and (1806), Earl of Rosse (1749–1807), 2301, 2315

Parsons, Sir Lawrence, 2nd Earl of Rosse (1758–1841), 2157

Parsons, Thomas Zachariah, 2574

Paul, Tsar (1754–1801), 1670, 1817, 1845, 1854, 1888, 1908, 1908 n., 1960–1, 1979, 1987, 1997, 2007, 2027, 2072, 2080, 2082, 2123, 2142, 2181, 2287, 2297, 2322, 2566

Paulet, Lady Mary, see Poulett

Payne, Col. Wm. (d. 1831), 1833

Pearce, John, seaman, 2513

Pegge, Sir Christopher (1765–1822), 1973, 2479

Pelham, Thomas, Lord, and 1st Earl of Chichester (1728–1805), 2445

Pelham, Thomas, Lord, later 2nd Earl of Chichester (1756–1826), 1666, 1707, 1709 n., 1759, 1820, 1824, 2357 n., 2456, 2456 n., 2474, 2487, 2489, 2498, 2498 n., 2507, 2510 n.

letters from, 2474 n., 2500, 2500 n., 2512, 2532, 2540, 2546, 2549, 2552, 2557, 2560, 2562, 2574

letters to, 1868 n., 2456 n., 2500

his illness, 1701, 1701 n.

reluctance to take office (1801), 2350, 2357, 2357 n.

Pellew, Sir Edward, 1st Viscount Exmouth (1757–1833), 2310

Pemberton, Christopher Robert, physician (1765–1822), 1931

Pembroke, 11th Earl of (1759–1827), 1769

letter from, 2283 n.

refuses a Marquessate, 2283

Penleys, the, of the Weymouth Theatre, 2042

Pepys, Sir Lucas (1742–1830), 1875

Perceval, Spencer (1762–1812), 1664, 1664 n., 1793, 1793 n., 2174, 2213, 2357, 2432

Portland (*cont.*)

letters to, 2297 n., 2328

Portugal, Maria, Queen of (1734–1816), 2443A

Portugal, Prince Regent of, *see* John VI

Postlethwaite, Thomas (1731–98), Master of Trinity College, Cambridge, 1733

Postmaster-General, office of, not tenable with seat in House of Commons, 1926

Poulett, Lady Mary, daughter of 4th Earl Powlett, and later, wife of Lord Charles Henry Somerset, 1835

Powell, Sir Gabriel, Sheriff of Carmarthenshire, 2183

Powelson, 2472

Prescott, General Robert (d. 1815), 1818

Preston, Sir Charles, 5th Bart (*c.* 1735–1800), M.P. for the Dysart Burghs (1784–90), 1728 n.

Pretyman-Tomline, Sir George, Bishop of Lincoln (1750–1827), *letters to,* 2173 n., 2329 n.

Primate of Ireland, *see* Stuart, William

Privy Purse, the King's, 1674, 1678

Prussia, Frederica, Queen of, and wife of Frederick William II (1751–1805), 1920

Prussia, Prince Louis Ferdinand of (1772–1806), 1734

Prussia, King of, *see* Frederick William III

Prussia, Queen of, *see* Louisa, Queen of Prussia

Prussia, Princess Louis of, *see* Frederica of Mecklenburg-Strelitz

Pulteney, Sir James (*c.* 1755–1811), 1765, 2136, 2184, 2203–5, 2243, 2246, 2252, 2256, 2367, 2526

Pulteney, Sir William (1729–1805), 2239

Pye, James, Mews Keeper at Kensington (d. 1801), 2335

Quick, John, the actor (1748–1831), 2042

Quigley [O'Coigly], James (*c.* 1762–98), 1691, 1694, 1717, 1742, 1742 n., 1746

Ramsey, Col. William, 2388

Ranby, George II's surgeon, 1754

Randolph, John, Bishop of Oxford (1749–1813), 2038

Recorder of London, *see* Rose, John William

Recorder's Reports, 1793, 1797, 1878, 2204

Reden, Mme de, 1953

Reden, M. de, Envoy from Wurtemberg, 1706, 1953

Reed, David, mutineer, 1834

Reidinger, 2563

Reynolds, Capt. R.N., 1830

Richard, Mr, 1997

Richpanse, General Antoine (1770–1802), nominated (1802) Commandant of Guadeloupe, 224

Ridge, Capt., 2290

Rigby, Richard (1722–88), 2285 n.

Robbins, John, of the *Warrior*, 2349

Robertson, Dr, his house at Greenwich, 2455

Robinson, John (1727–1802), *letter to,* 1932 n.

Robison [*sic*], Lieut., 1811

Robson, Riccard Bateman (d. 1827), 2276, 2276 n.

Rockingham, Marquess of (1730–82), 1678, 2301

Roden, 2nd Earl of (1756–1820), 2315

Rollin, Charles, French historian (1661–1741), 2294

Rome, the British and Irish Colleges in, 1760

Romney, Lord, *see* Marsham, Charles

Rooke, Lieut.-Gen. James (*c.* 1740–1805), 2245, 2250

Rose, George (1744–1818), 2329 n., 2339 n., *letters from,* 2173 n., 2368 n.

Rose, Sir George Henry (1771–1855), 2173 n.

Rose, Sir John William, Recorder of London (until 1803), 1797, 1878, 1927, 2204, 2456

Ross, Major-Gen. Alexander (1742–1827), 2376

Ross, General Sir Charles Lockhart- (1763?–1814), 2575

Rosslyn, Sir James St Clair-Erskine, 2nd Earl of (1762–1837), 1852, 2481, 2486

Rossmore, Robert Cuninghame, Lord (d. 1801), 2022, 2315, 2503, 2510, 2515, 2515 n.

Rostopchin, Count (1765–1826), Russian Foreign Minister, 2123, 2297

Roxburghe, 3rd Duke of (1740–1804), 1812, 2199

letter from, 1806

Royal Military College, the, 2462, 2471

Rumford, Count (1753–1814), 1827

Rush, John, Inspector of Hospitals, 2152

Russell, Lord William (1767–1840), 1729, 1950

Russian Emperor, *see* Paul, Tsar

Russian Empress, *see* Sophia

Rutland, John Henry, 5th Duke of (1778–1857), 1983

Ryan, Nicholas, 1834

Ryder, Dudley, 1st Earl of Harrowby (1762–
1847), 1790, 2140, 2143, 2290
to be Treasurer of the Navy, 2144
resigns office, 2554

St Albans, election (1800), 2315 n.
St Andrew, Order of, 2124
St Clair, Sir James, see Rosslyn
St Cyr, General Laurent Couvion (1764–
1830), 1949
St David's, Bishop of, see Stuart, William;
and Murray, Lord George
St George's Chapel, Windsor, 1927, 2428
St Helens, Lord, see Fitzherbert, Alleyne
St John, Major-Gen. Frederick (1765–1844),
2068, 2074
letter to, 2074 n.
St John-Mildmay, Sir Henry Paulet, 3rd Bart
(1764–1808), 1881
St Patrick, Order of, 1684, 2271
St Paul's, Thanksgiving service at (1798),
1668
St Vincent, Lord, see Jervis
Salisbury, Bishop of, see Douglas, John
Salisbury, 1st Marquess of (1748–1823), 2201,
2202 n., 2269, 2296
letters from, 1754, 2225, 2401
letters to, 1730, 1754, 2035, 2092, 2401
Salm, Rheingrave of, 2050
Sankey, Lieut.-Col., 2519
Sardinia, King of, see Charles Emmanuel
Saumarez, Sir James, Baron De Saumarez
(1757–1836), 2366, 2485, 2496, 2498,
2504, 2518
Saurau, Count, the Imperial Finance Minister,
1848
Saurin, William (?1757–1839), 1904
Saxony, Frederick Augustus, Elector of (1750–
1827), 1848
Schaw, John, a Foreign Office messenger,
2230
Schérer, General Louis Joseph (1745–1804),
1949
Schrader, 1716
Schroeder, M., a Page of the Backstairs,
(d. 1797), 1687, 1708
Schwicheldt, Count Heinrich Ernst von
(1748–1817), 2277
Scott, Brigadier, 2533
Scott, Sir John, Lord Eldon (1751–1838),
1680 n., 1686, 1720, 1726, 1742, 1794,
1800, 1832, 1966, 2023, 2158, 2332, 2336,
2350 n., 2378, 2403, 2427, 2428 n., 2456,
2472, 2520

letters from, 2383, 2392, 2392 n., 2422, 2432,
2448, 2451, 2460, 2543, 2556
appointed Lord Chancellor, 2357, 2357 n.,
2364 n., 2392 n.
Scott, Sir Wm., Lord Stowell (1745–1836),
1859
Secretary at War, see Windham
Seringapatam, capture of (1799), 2041
Sérurier, Jean M. Philibert, French Marshal,
1955
Seymour, Lord George (1763–1848), 2483
letter from, 2483 n.
Seymour, Lord Hugh, see Conway
Shannon, Richard, 2nd Earl of (1728–1807),
2226, 2404
Sharp, William, letter from, 1784
Shaw, Sir James (c. 1764–1843), 2157
Shaw, see Schaw
Shawe, Capt., 2290
Sheffield, Lord (1735–1821), 1724, 1950, 2135,
2163, 2515 n.
letters to, 1678 n., 2278 n.
Shelburne, 2nd Earl of, and 1st Marquess of
Lansdowne (1737–1805), 2357, 2368 n.
Shepherd, Richard, Chargé d'Affaires at
Munich, 1827
Shepherd, Lieut., R.N., 1830
Sheridan, Richard Brimsley (1751–1816),
1664, 1667, 1721–2, 1722 n., 1729,
1757 n., 1911, 1914, 1914 n., 1922, 2092,
2135, 2189, 2265, 2276, 2276 n., 2288,
2288 n., 2339, 2359, 2397 n.
motion for a Call of the House, 2182
Shore, Sir John, Lord Teignmouth (1751–
1834), 1686
Sicily, King and Queen of, see under Naples
Silvester, Sir John (1745–1822), 1878
Simbschen [Simschen], General Joseph Anton
von (1746–1820), 2292
Simcoe, Major-Gen. John Graves (1752–
1806), 1765
Simeon, Sir John (1756–1824), 1724, 1897
Sinclair, Sir John (1754–1835), 1881, 1881 n.,
1885, 1897, 2212
Slade, Sir John (1762–1859), 1857
Sligo, Louisa Catherine, Marchioness of
(1767–1817), 2217
Sligo, 1st Marquess of (1756–1809), 2315
Smith, Mr, 2157
Smith, John Spencer (1769–1845), diploma-
tist, Sir Sidney Smith's brother, 1841,
1843, 1898
Smith, Leonard, letter to, 2158
Smith, Capt. Matthew, 1794

Smith, Ralph, a sadler, 2094

Smith, William (1756–1835), 1897, 1922, 2189, 2288

Smith, Sir Wm. Sidney (1764–1840), 1843, 2120, 2394 n.

annuity for, 2359

Smyth, John (1748–1811), 2144

Sneyd, Nathaniel (1767?–1833), 2301

Solicitor-General, the, *see* Mitford, Sir John and Grant, Sir William

Solicitor-General [I.], the, *see* Toler, John

Solms-Braunfels, Prince Frederick of (1770–1814), 1905

Somerset, Lord Chas. Henry (1767–1831), 1769

letters from, 1829, 1831, 2219

his wife Elizabeth (d. 1815), 1829

refused Government of Jamaica, 2220

Somerton, Lord, *see* Agar, Charles

Somerville, John, 14th Lord (1765–1819), *letters from*, 2212, 2286

Sophia, Princess (1777–1848), 1873, 2042, 2233, 2254, 2461, 2461 n.

Sophia, Tsarina, wife of Paul I (1759–1828), 1948, 1961

Speaker, the, *see* Addington, Henry

Spencer, Col. Sir Brent (1760–1828), *letter from*, 2553 n.

appointed an Equerry, 2424, 2553

Spencer, Lord Charles (1740–1820), 2365, 2365 n.

Spencer, George John, 2nd Earl (1758–1834), 1715, 1760, 1885, 1964, 1983, 2142, 2209, 2235, 2329 n., 2341, 2346, 2349 n., 2350, 2456 n., 2474 n.

letters from, 1665, 1672, 1677, 1683, 1699, 1712, 1732, 1741, 1779, 1781, 1786, 1794, 1805, 1834, 1838, 1844, 1846, 1859, 1862, 1864, 1869, 1892, 1901, 1937, 1963, 1965, 1982, 1991, 2004, 2006, 2016, 2018, 2021, 2024, 2029, 2046, 2055, 2055 n., 2071, 2077, 2086, 2105, 2186, 2190, 2208, 2210, 2213, 2215, 2227, 2234, 2238, 2249, 2280, 2284, 2298, 2310, 2317, 2349, 2353, 2366

letters to, 1672, 1677, 1699, 1741, 1779, 1786, 1805, 1838, 1844, 1846, 1859, 1862, 1869, 1892, 1901, 1924, 1991, 2004, 2006, 2018, 2021 n., 2024, 2029, 2046, 2052, 2055, 2071, 2086, 2105, 2186, 2190, 2208, 2210, 2213, 2215, 2227, 2298, 2310, 2349, 2353, 2366

and the Garter, 1772 n.

letter of resignation (1801), 2349

Spencer, Lord Henry John (1770–95), 2386 A

Spiegel, Mme de, 1728

Spinola, M. de, the Genoese Envoy, 1798

Stafford, 1st Marquess of (1721–1803), 2180, 2192

letter from, 1984

Staffordshire elections, 2180, 2180 n., 2192

Stahremberg [Starhemberg], Comte de, 1704, 1725, 1845, 1850, 1854, 2297

Stair, Lord, *see* Dalrymple, John

Stamfort [Stamford, Stampfort], General de, 1670–1, 1689, 1693, 1719, 1883, 1908, 1959

Stanhope, 3rd Earl (1753–1816), 1691

Stanwix, General Thomas Sloughter (d. 1815), 1752

Staray [Starey], General, 2015, 2025, 2172

State Paper Office, the, 2139, 2141, 2158

Staveley, Major-Gen., Miles (1738–1814), 1769, 2022

Steele, Thomas (1753–1823), 1899, 2087 n., 2144, 2346 n., 2459 n.

Steevens, mutineer, 1779

Steinberg, M. de, the Hanoverian Minister, 1673, 1696, 1698

Stevens, Commander of a packet boat, 1773 n.

Stevens, General Edmond (d. 1825), 1769

Steward, E. J., Mayor of Weymouth, *letter from*, 2477

Steward, Francis, of Weymouth, 1833

Steward, Mrs, 1833, 2376

Stewart, Robert, Viscount Castlereagh (1769–1822), 1759, 1761, 1800, 1802, 1808, 1816, 1820, 1824, 1824 n., 1836, 1861, 1889, 1896, 1927, 1996, 2045, 2146, 2153, 2169, 2211, 2226, 2301, 2315 n., 2327 n., 2331–2, 2338, 2346, 2357, 2405, 2457, 2575

appointed Irish Secretary, *ad. int.* 1701, 1701 n.

resigns office of Privy Seal, [I.], 2405

Steyer, Armistice signed at (Dec. 1800), 2316

Stock, Joseph, Bishop of Killala (1740–1813), 2102

Strachan, Admiral Sir Richard John (1760–1828), 1712, 1712 n.

Strachey, Sir Henry (1737–1810), *letters from*, 2464, 2571

Strafford, Elizabeth, Countess of (d. 1811), 1997, 1999, 2010

Straton, Alexander, diplomatist, 2426

Stuart, Brigadier-Gen., 1852

Stuart, Lieut.-Gen. Sir Chas., Lord Bute's brother (1753–1801), 1852, 2112–13, 2136, 2369 n., 2376, 2426, 2434

Whitworth, Sir Charles, Earl Whitworth (1752–1825), Minister at Petersburg, 1671, 1673, 1783, 1817, 1850, 1854, 1879, 1908, 1908 n., 1959, 2007, 2072, 2082, 2107, 2123, 2209, 2228, 2230, 2235, 2386
letter from, 1888
given Irish peerage, 1987
Whyte, Major-Gen. John, 2526
Wickham, Mrs (d. 1836), 2130, 2134
Wickham, William (1761–1840), Under-Secretary of State, 1682, 1717, 1740, 1742, 1746, 1790, 1800, 1802, 1808, 1816, 1830 n., 1836, 1861, 1904, 1927, 2072, 2080, 2130, 2134, 2151, 2157, 2288, 2516
Wicklow, Viscount (1757–1815), 2315
Wilberforce, William (1759–1833), 1664, 1724, 2137, 2189, 2276
Wilford, Major-Gen. Richard Rich (*c.* 1754–1822), 2524
Wilkes, John (1727–97), 2254
William Frederick, Duke of Gloucester (1776–1834), 2081, 2533, 2567
William Henry, Duke of Clarence (1765–1837), 1895, 2153, 2165, 2428
William Henry, Duke of Gloucester (1743–1805), 1700, 2013, 2507
letters from, 2081, 2567
letter to, 2165 n.
wants peerage for his son, 2567
Willich, Anthony Florian Madinger, 2273
Willis, Dr Francis (1718–1807), 2368 n., 2451
Willis, Dr John (1751–1835), 2368 n., 2372 n., 2451
Willis, Dr Robert Darling (1760–1821), 2368 n., 2451
Willis, Dr Thomas, 2368 n., 2372 n.
Willoughby de Broke, 14th Lord (1738–1816), 1983, 2083
Wilson, Rev. Edward, Canon of Windsor, 1969
Wilson, Lieut., 2318
Wilson, Richard, the Duke of Northumberland's Agent (1759–1834), 1678 n.
Wimpfen, Baron de, 1988, 2139
Winchilsea, 9th Earl of (1752–1826), 2369 n.
Windham, William (1750–1810), 1667, 1686 n., 1760, 1849, 1852, 1922, 1932, 1932 n., 2023, 2033, 2132, 2143, 2189, 2235 n., 2242, 2256, 2288, 2288 n., 2329 n., 2336 n., 2365, 2474 n., 2502 n., 2536 n.
letters from, 2144 n., 2348
letter to, 1908 n.
not anxious to become Treasurer of the Navy, 2144

Windsor, Royal Gardens at, 2464
Winthorp, Capt. Robert, R.N., 1741
Wodehouse, Sir John, Lord Wodehouse (1741–1834), 1983
Wolf, Colonel (of Wurtemberg), 2151
Wolfe, Anne, Baroness Kilwarden (d. 1804), 1746
Wolfe, Arthur, Viscount Kilwarden (1739–1803), 1686, 1746, 2222
Wöllwarth, Baron de, 2125
Wood, Sir Mark (*c.* 1747–1829), 1724, 2140
Woodfall, William (1746–1803), 2108 n., 2199 n.
Worcester, Bishop of, *see* Hurd, Richard
Woronzow, Count, Russian Minister in London (1744–1832), 1845, 1850, 1854, 1908, 1908 n., 2082, 2123, 2142, 2181, 2386, 2484
Wright, John (?1770–1844), bookseller, 2201
Wrottesley, Sir John, 1st Baron Wrottesley (1771–1841), 2276
Wurtemburg, Caroline Alexei, Princess of, *cr.* (1807), Baroness von Rottenburg and (1825), Countess von Urach (1779–1853), 2127
Wurtemberg, Duchess of, *see* Charlotte Augusta Matilda
Wurtemberg, Catherine, Princess of ['Trinette'] (1783–1835), 1697, 1716, 1763, 1778, 1860, 1921, 1988, 2185, 2233, 2387, 2516
Wurtemberg, Charles Eugen, Duke of (1728–93), 1668, 1706, 1747, 1928, 1948
Wurtemberg, Dorothea, Duchess of (1736–98), 1663, 1668, 1697, 1716, 1728
Wurtemberg, Prince Ferdinand of (1763–1834), 1778 n., 1934 n.
Wurtemberg, Princess Ferdinand of (1771–1829), 1778, 1934, 1953, 1970, 2125
Wurtemberg, Princess Frederica of (1732–80), 1928
Wurtemberg, Frederick II, Duke of (1732–97), 1663, 1961, 1970
Wurtemberg, Frederick, Duke of (1754–1816), 1663, 1668, 1673, 1690, 1697, 1706, 1716, 1728, 1731, 1738, 1743, 1747, 1756, 1763, 1780, 1799, 1809, 1835, 1842, 1860, 1873, 1887, 1902, 1906, 1921, 1928, 1934, 1941, 1946, 1948, 1951, 1956, 1961, 1970, 1988, 1993, 2015, 2025, 2050, 2064, 2075, 2088, 2096, 2115, 2121, 2125, 2127, 2130, 2134, 2139, 2147, 2151, 2159, 2161, 2177, 2185, 2188, 2198, 2206, 2214, 2218,